MILITARY RULES OF EVIDENCE MANUAL

Volume 2

Stephen A. Saltzburg
Wallace and Beverley Woodbury University Professor
George Washington University
Law School

Lee D. Schinasi
Associate Professor of Law
Barry University
Dwayne O. Andreas School of Law

David A. Schlueter
Hardy Professor of Law and
Director of Advocacy Programs
St. Mary's University School of Law

QUESTIONS ABOUT THIS PUBLICATION?

For questions about the **Editorial Content** appearing in these volumes or reprint permission, please call:

Ethan A. Shaw, J.D. at .... (617) 248-6706
Email: .... ethan.shaw@lexisnexis.com

For assistance with replacement pages, shipments, billing or other customer service matters, please call:

Customer Services Department at . . . . (800) 833-9844
Outside the United States and Canada, please call . . . . (518) 487-3000
Fax Number . . . . (518) 487-3584
Customer Service Website . . . . http://www.lexisnexis.com/custserv/

For information on other Matthew Bender publications, please call:

Your account manager or . . . . (800) 223-1940
Outside the United States and Canada, please call . . . . (518) 487-3000

Library of Congress Card Number: 97-74883
ISBN: 978-1-4224-8888-1

Cite this publication as:

Stephen A. Salzburg, Lee D. Schinasi & David A. Schlueter, Military Rules of Evidence Manual, § no. at p. no. (7th Ed., Matthew Bender & Co. 2011)

Example:

Stephen A. Salzburg, Lee D. Schinasi & David A. Schlueter, Military Rules of Evidence Manual, § 313.05[1][a] at p. 3-355 (7th Ed., Matthew Bender & Co. 2011)

This publication is designed to provide accurate and authoritative information in regard to the subject matter covered. It is sold with the understanding that the publisher is not engaged in rendering legal, accounting, or other professional services. If legal advice or other expert assistance is required, the services of a competent professional should be sought.

Editorial Offices
121 Chanlon Rd., New Providence, NJ 07974 (908) 464-6800
201 Mission St., San Francisco, CA 94105-1831 (415) 908-3200
www.lexisnexis.com

MATTHEW◆BENDER

(2011–Pub.66911)

Volume 2 Table of Contents

A COMPLETE SYNOPSIS FOR EACH CHAPTER APPEARS AT
THE BEGINNING OF THE CHAPTER

Dedication
Introduction
Forewords

Volume 2 Table of Contents

Volume 2 Table of Contents

Dedication

To our wives, Susan, Bonnie and Linda.

Introduction

I. Our Purposes

Over thirty years ago, we met in Charlottesville, Virginia, and discussed the possibility of preparing a guide to the new Military Rules of Evidence. We believed that the new rules would present many challenges to military judges, military counsel, and those studying the military justice system. We concluded that there was a need for such a book. In the intervening years, we have strived to make the work as useful as possible. With over three decades of experience, military courts have developed a substantial body of case law that explains and interprets the Military Rules. The discussion of those cases has resulted in what began as a modest one volume work in 1981, expanding several years ago to two volumes. We made the judgement that it is important to provide military judges and lawyers with as much authority as possible in this reference work.

As with prior editions of the Manual, one purpose of this book is to offer assistance to military lawyers and judges who use the Military Rules of Evidence in courts-martial. Although many of the Military Rules follow the Federal Rules of Evidence, there are differences. More importantly, the Military Rules contain lengthy material not found in the Federal Rules of Evidence. We attempt to explain what the Rules do, how they work, what problems may be encountered in using them, and sometimes how the problems may be solved. It is our goal to identify the principal areas of concern under these Rules and to provide what help we can.

We have attempted to combine the practical insights that come from working within a special system like the military with the observations, and sometimes the criticisms, of those outside that system who may approach it with a different perspective than many military lawyers share. Our goal has been to provide a balanced view of the Military Rules of Evidence and to identify strengths and weaknesses of many of the Rules that we talk about. But our effort is primarily to explain and to help, not to suggest reforms or to offer lengthy academic discussions about various aspects of evidence. We take the system as it is and want to help those who work in it do the best job possible in order to promote justice and fair play for the military and its members.

Another purpose of our writing is to make available not only to military lawyers, but also to civilian lawyers interested in criminal justice, litigation and evidence, information about military processes. Each of us has developed great respect for the fundamental fairness of the military system and admiration for many of the rules that have been created to protect the interests of those accused of offenses. Contrary to the image that many civilian lawyers have of the military system, often the military system is far more protective of accused persons than its civilian counterpart. Military justice is not perfect any more than civilian justice is, but some military procedures, once they are understood properly, may prove to be attractive to civilian courts. We very much hope that this book will provide a basis for comparing civilian and military evidence and procedural systems in an effort to improve both. As with prior editions, we plan to continue to supplement the book annually so that military lawyers and judges and civilian lawyers interested in

Introduction

military justice can have a convenient and up-to-date reference.

II. Background of the Military Rules of Evidence

Historically, evidentiary rules applicable in court-martial practice have been derived from several sources:

(1.) The Uniform Code of Military Justice, 10 U.S.C. § 801-940;

(2.) The Manual for Courts-Martial;

(3.) Rules of Evidence recognized in the practice of criminal cases in Federal District Courts; and

(4.) Case law from the four service Courts of Criminal Appeals (formerly Courts of Military Review) and the United States Court of Appeals for the Armed Forces (formerly the United States Court of Military Appeals).

The foundation for all of this is the Constitution itself, which directs in Article 1, § 8 that the Congress will regulate the armed forces. The Uniform Code of Military Justice (U.C.M.J.) represents Congressional rulemaking and itself provides some evidentiary rules. *See, e.g.*, Article 31 (right against self-incrimination) and Article 49 (depositions). But the most important provision lies in Article 36, which states:

(a) Pretrial, trial, and post-trial procedures, including modes of proof, for cases arising under this chapter triable in courts-martial, military commissions and other military tribunals, and procedures for courts of inquiry, may be prescribed by the President by regulations which shall, so far as he considers practicable, apply the principles of law and the rules of evidence generally recognized in the trial of criminal cases in the United States district courts, but which may not be contrary to or inconsistent with this chapter.

(b) All rules and regulations made under this article shall be uniform insofar as practicable and shall be reported to Congress.

This provision serves as the underlying authority for specifically promulgating the rules of evidence which have appeared in the Manual for Courts-Martial. Although the evidentiary rules have generally been considered to have the force and effect of statutory law.[1] They must always be tested against the Constitution and the U.C.M.J. Conflict with either or both of those higher sources will fall the *Manual* provision.[2] But if the *Manual* affords greater rights to the accused, then the *Manual* provision, rather than the Constitution or the U.C.M.J., will control. And under the 1969 Manual § 137, federal practice served as a model when an issue was not otherwise covered in the Manual. The common law could be applied if federal practice was not inconsistent with it.

In 1980, the evidentiary rules underwent a dramatic change. Although the basic scheme of military evidentiary law remained intact, all of the former cook-book type discussions of the applicable rules of evidence were replaced by eighty-some tersely

---

[1] This provision serves as the underlying authority for specifically promulgating the rules of evidence which have appeared in the *Manual for Courts–Martial*. Although the evidentiary rules have generally been considered to have the force and effect of statutory law.

[2] *See, e.g.*, United States v. Jacoby, 29 C.M.R. 244 (C.M.A. 1960); United States v. Douglas, 1 M.J. 354 (C.M.A. 1976); United States v. Ware, 1 M.J. 282 (C.M.A. 1976).

worded rules that comprise the Military Rules of Evidence. The Rules remained in Chapter XXVII of the Manual for Courts-Martial (where they had been located since 1951) until 1984 when the Manual was revised; the Rules now appear in Part III.

The formal road to this major change in military practice was relatively short when compared to the lengthy process used to formulate the Federal Rules. This abbreviated process was due in large part to the fact that many of the Military Rules are simply an adoption of the rules adopted by Congress for the federal courts. Although Congress actively participated in drafting of the Federal Rules, it had no part in promulgating the Military Rules. They were initially drafted by a special committee of the Joint Service Committee on Military Justice Working Group. This committee submitted its work to the parent body—the Joint Service Committee on Military Justice. This body has the task of periodically reviewing and submitting proposals for revision of both the U.C.M.J. and the Manual for Courts-Martial. The final product was then reviewed by the Department of Defense and the Office of Management and Budget. The latter in turn circulated it to the Department of Justice. The Rules were finally signed by President Carter on March 12, 1980. Unlike the process used for adopting the Federal Rules, the procedure here did not generally involve widespread public input.

Section III contains rules concerning self-incrimination, search and seizure, and eyewitness identification. Of particular interest are rules governing the procedures to be used for litigating constitutional issues. See, e.g., Rule 304 (confessions and admissions); Rule 312 (an innovative rule governing body views and intrusions); and Rule 302 (a rule creating a limited privilege for communications by an accused to a sanity board).

The Section III Rules provide a combination of both procedural and evidentiary prescriptions. At first blush, there appears to be a question as to whether these Rules are properly within the confines of the President's Article 36 powers. The Drafters' Analysis is silent on this point. It seems safe to conclude that even though these Rules plainly are designed in part to affect out-of-court behavior, they are written so as to focus on evidence, trials and the creation of evidence. Thus, they can be viewed as being sufficiently procedural or evidentiary to withstand challenge. *Cf. United States v. Frederick*, 3 M.J. 230 (C.M.A. 1977) (outside President's authority to promulgate matters affecting substantive law).

The Rules of Section III do not establish defenses nor do they establish the elements of offenses. It also seems safe to conclude that because these Rules carried forward many of the long-standing pre-Rules provisions on the same subject matter, Congress has implicitly approved the President's authority in this area by failing to limit that authority; Article 36 was amended as recently as 1979 and the legislative history on that change reflects no misgivings or reservations on this issue. Rather, the 1979 changes were designed to clarify the President's broad powers in prescribing rules of procedure and evidence. The same view would govern any challenge to privilege rules, discussed next. We note that there is no limitation on the President's power to promulgate procedural rules that is comparable to the Rules Enabling Act, 28 U.S.C. § 2072, which requires some deference to state substantive law in certain contexts.

The early controversy surrounding the Section III Rules centered not so much on the authority of the President to promulgate such rules, but instead about the wisdom of doing so. It seems clear that the drafters envisioned a clear set of stable guidelines for an otherwise fluid area of the law. Yet, several courts have applied less protective constitutional standards with the rationale that the Section III Rules were intended simply to restate constitutional rules as they existed in 1980. Thus, the logic continues, the Rules may now be inapplicable if the constitutional rule has changed. This matter is more fully discussed in our Comment to Section III, infra.

Section V adopted many of the Supreme Court's proposed Federal Rules of Evidence on privileges which were not adopted by the Congress. The drafters chose the route of laying out specific privileges rather than following the development of privileges under common law. There is no treatment of presumptions (found in Article III of the Federal Rules of Evidence) in the Military Rules.

On the whole, the Rules have placed a greater burden on the defense than previously existed to either articulate in timely fashion specific objections or risk waiver. They provide that all relevant evidence should be admitted unless some evidence rule, statute or constitutional principle requires exclusion. Ultimately, they should speed up and simplify the litigation process and probably permit more evidence to be considered at trial. The trial judge is given broad powers to promote fair trial and fair treatment of parties and witnesses. Some of these powers go well beyond existing military authorities.

There can be no doubt that the adoption of the Military Rules of Evidence was a bold, exciting, and innovative step. The title itself, according to the drafters, was intended to make it clear that military evidentiary law should echo the civilian federal law to the extent practicable, but should also reflect the unique and critical reasons behind a separate military justice system. See the Drafters' Analysis for Rule 1103.

Generally speaking, the Military Rules are substantially similar to the Federal Rules of Evidence in Sections I, II, IV, and VI through XI. (The word "section" rather than "article" was used by the drafters to avoid potential confusion with articles of the U.C.M.J.).

III. Amendments to the Military Rules of Evidence

Since the Rules became effective in 1980, they have been amended a number of times by Executive Orders:

- E.O. 12233 (September 1, 1980) (Rules 302, 305(h)(2), 317(c), and 1101(b));
- E.O. 12306 (June 1, 1981) (Rule 410);
- E.O. 12315 (July 29, 1981) (Rule 1101(c));
- E.O. 12473 (April 13, 1984) (Rules 201A, 312, 313, 314, 315, 316, 321);
- E.O. 12550 (February 19, 1986) (Rules 304, 311, 609, 804(a));
- E.O. 12708 (March 23 1990) (Rules 304(b)(1), 506(c));
- E.O. 12767 (June 27, 1991) (Rule 707);
- E.O. 12888 (Rules 311(e)(2), 505(a), (g)(1)(D), (h)(3), (i)(3), (i)(4)(B), (j)(5), 609(a), and 1101(d));

- E.O. 12936 (November 10, 1994) (Rules 305(d)(1)(B), (e), (f), 314(g)(3), and 404(b));

- E.O. 12960 (May 12, 1995) (Rules 311(g)(2), 506(e) and (f), 506(i) and (j));

- E.O. 13086 (May 27, 1998) (Rules 412, 413, 414, and 1102);

- E.O. 13140 (October 6, 1999) (Rules 513 and 611); and

- E.O. 13262 (April 11, 2002) (Rules 415 (no longer applicable) and 615);

- E.O. 13365 (December 3, 2004) (Rules 103(a)(2), 404(a), 701, 702, 703, 803(6), 902 and 1102;

- E.O. 13387 (October 14, 2005) (Rules Rule 317(b));

- E.O. 13447 (September 28, 2007) (Rules 412, 503 and 504);

- E.O. 13468 (July 24, 2008) (Rule 801, Drafters' Analysis);

- Amendments that took effect for courts-martial in 1998—Rules 407, 801(d)(2), 803(24), 804(b)(5) and (6), and Rule 807;

- Amendments that took effect for courts-martial in 2002—Rules 103, 404, 701, 702, 703, 803(6), and 902(11) and (12).

III. Using the Book

A. An Introduction to Military Justice Procedures

Throughout the Rules, the reader will see that various terms, unique to military law, have been substituted in place of those terms found in federal practice. Before discussing the format of this book, it might be helpful for the sake of those not familiar with the military criminal legal system to briefly lay out the procedural process, highlighting terms which the reader will see again in the Rules, our comments, and the Drafters' Analysis. *See generally* D. Schlueter, MILITARY CRIMINAL JUSTICE: PRACTICE AND PROCEDURE §§ 1-7 to 1-8 (7th ed. 2008).

Although anyone subject to the U.C.M.J. may prefer court-martial charges, it is usually the accused's immediate commanding officer who informally investigates the alleged offense (a violation of the punitive articles of the U.C.M.J.) and prepares the sworn charges. The charge sheet (DD Form 458) is forwarded up the chain of command with recommendations as to the type of court-martial which may try the case: summary, special, or general. The summary court-martial, to which the accused must consent, is composed of one officer who generally acts as both the prosecutor and the judge. This officer need not be, but generally is, an armed forces lawyer. The next higher court is the special court-martial, which may be composed of either a military judge alone or a court consisting of not fewer than three officers sitting as court-members. The U.C.M.J. does provide that a special court-martial can be conducted with members but without a military judge, but this is rare. A general court-martial is generally reserved for the more serious offenses and consists of a military judge and at least five officers serving as court-members. The procedural steps leading to the general court-martial are more complex than the other two types of courts. The process includes a thorough, independent Article 32 Investigation by an officer, often a lawyer, who questions witnesses and considers the available evidence in deciding whether probable cause exists to send the case to trial. At this investigation, the accused is represented by counsel and has the opportunity to cross-examine witnesses.

Sending a case to trial consists of a convening authority referring the case to a designated court for trial. This convening authority is a commander authorized by the U.C.M.J. to convene courts. For example, commanding generals of installations are usually general court-martial convening authorities. These individuals also may become involved in acting on pretrial requests for defense witnesses or other discovery. *See, e.g.*, Rules 505, 506.

Preliminary matters, such as arraignment, entering of pleas, and hearing motions to suppress are handled at a pretrial session referred to as the Article 39(a) session. At trial (both merits and sentencing), the accused is represented by a defense counsel (appointed military counsel, individual military counsel, or civilian counsel). The government is represented by the trial counsel. After trial, the results are reviewed by the convening authority and his legal advisor, the staff judge advocate, who reviews it for legal sufficiency. Depending on the type of court and the punishment, the case may be reviewed by the various service appellate courts, the United States Court of Appeals for the Armed Forces and the Supreme Court of the United States.

That foundation having been laid, we turn our attention to the actual mechanics and format of the book. Each Rule receives separate treatment in a four-part format: (A) the official text of each Rule; (B) our editorial comment; (C) the Drafters' Analysis; and (D) annotated cases.

B. Official Text of the Rule

This part contains the exact text of each Rule as prescribed by President Carter in Executive Order 12198, March 12, 1980, and any amendments to date.

C. Editorial Comment

Each Rule is followed by an explanation of the Rule, how it compares with the comparable Federal Rule, and how it applies to military practice. The comments are intended to be brief, making suggestions for the practitioner where appropriate. This section is not so much a "how-to" discussion as it is a starting point for an understanding of what each Rule says and how the Rule has been, or might be, applied by military courts. Because what the federal courts have said about the federal rule counterpart is often helpful to military courts and counsel, we have included selected citations to, and discussions of, federal case law. Where potential problems exist with a Rule, we set those out, not for the purpose of setting forth definitive answers, but rather to better enable counsel and judges to focus on troublesome aspects of the Rules and to enable them to benefit from the experience of the federal courts.

D. Drafters' Analysis

Serving as a legislative history of sorts, the non-binding Drafters' Analysis explains the drafters' intent and should be helpful in discerning what the drafters had in mind in formulating the Rules as they did. The Drafters' Analysis should be especially helpful in understanding rules or provisions not included in the Federal Rules of Evidence. Where there have been amendments to the Analysis, we have included those at the end of the original (1980) Analysis, in order to identify clearly what changes were made to the Rules. We have done so even in those instances when the amendments to the Analysis were intended to delete and replace language in the original 1980 Analysis. We believe it is important for those applying the rules to see what the original Analysis said about the original rule.

E. Annotated Cases

We have made an effort to annotate military decisions reported since the promulgation of the Rules, as well as important Supreme Court decisions. The order in which we present the annotations is as follows: Supreme Court cases are first, Court of Appeals for the Armed Forces cases follow, and these are followed by decisions of the service Courts of Criminal Appeals (Air Force, Army, Coast Guard, and Navy-Marine Corps). Within that scheme, the most recent decision of the court is listed first. With this order, the reader should be able to determine whether a particular court has addressed a Rule.

Foreword to the Sixth Edition (Anniversary Edition)

The following forewords were prepared by Chief Judges of the United States Court of Appeals for the Armed Forces, who have served since the first edition of the Military Rules of Evidence Manual was published in 1981, until the present.

Robinson O. Everett
Chief Judge, United States Court of Appeals for the Armed Forces
1980–1990

When I first went on active duty as a judge advocate, the Uniform Code of Military Justice and the 1951 Manual for Courts-Martial had just taken effect. As directed by Article 36 of the Code, President Truman had prescribed "rules of evidence" to apply uniformly to courts-martial in all the Armed Services. Chapter 11 of the Manual was entitled "Rules of Evidence"; and presumably it was intended to comply with the congressional mandate in Article 36 that, so far as he deemed "practicable" the President "apply the principles of law and the rules of evidence generally recognized in trial of criminal cases in the United States District Courts".

At that time there were no "Federal Rules of Evidence;" and so the Manual provided a guidance for judges and litigators in courts-martial that was not available in federal criminal or civil trials. Some years later, under the direction of the Supreme Court and the Judicial Conference, the Federal Rules of Evidence were promulgated to provide greater certainty in federal trials. In a way, the federal courts were following the precedent established for military justice.

Subsequently, the Manual for Courts-Martial was amended by the President to provide military rules of evidence that with some exceptions follow the federal rules. Thus, with some exceptions, the Military Rules of Evidence lead to the same evidentiary results reached in federal criminal trials. I was serving as Chief Judge of the United States Court of Military Appeals (now Court of Appeals for the Armed Forces) when the change took effect; and so I witnessed some of the beneficial effects of bringing about greater conformity between courts-martial and federal district courts.

However, there still remains a need for further explanation and examination of the current Military Rules of Evidence. Now in the Sixth Edition of their Military Rules of Evidence Manual—a twenty-fifth anniversary edition—Professors Saltzburg, Schinasi, and Schlueter bring us up-to-date on the application of these rules and any current issues. As demonstrated in the earlier editions, these three scholars have extensive and unique experience with this important subject; and for anyone involved or interested in military justice their textbook will be invaluable.

Foreword to the Sixth Edition (Anniversary Edition)

Judge Walter T. Cox III
Chief Judge, United States Court of Appeals for the Armed Forces
1995–1999

It is not surprising that the Military Rule of Evidence Manual is entering its 25th Anniversary with this edition. Professors Stephen Salzburg, Lee Schinasi and David Schlueter are not only master craftsman at compiling and presenting in a user friendly format the growing body of law on the Military Rules of Evidence but they approach the task with scholarship and a deep understanding of the rules and how they function in the real world of military courts-martial. As a result, judges and attorneys alike turn to their fine work for research and ready answers to complex evidentiary issues.

I have had the pleasure of knowing each of these scholars personally as well as professionally and have heard them make many outstanding presentations to military and civilian attorneys on the thorny issues that Rules of Evidence can present. But more important to the introduction of this Edition of the Military Rules of Evidence Manual, over the last 23 years I and my law clerks and attorney advisors have been users of the Manual in the research and preparation of legal opinions and review of claimed trial errors. We have always found the Manual to be well organized and user friendly. I am grateful to have had this Manual for my use.

Susan J. Crawford
Chief Judge, United States Court of Appeals for the Armed Forces
1999–2004

The Military Rules of Evidence Manual is a critical resource for any attorney practicing at the trial or appellate level in the Military Justice System. Any advocate or judge who is not utilizing this book while in the throws of litigation or appellate work is not fully utilizing their available resources. This Manual is a comprehensive source for the Military Rules of Evidence with synopses of the cases interpreting those Rules. There is nothing that attorneys can use or find that can compete with usefulness of this Manual in regards to the Military Rules of Evidence.

It has been my observation as a litigator and appellate judge that advocates who have a command of the Rules of Evidence are much more persuasive and effective in representing their positions. This book can give that command of the Rules to advocates. An attorney or judge who utilizes this Manual and studies the Rules will have an advantage over the practitioners who do not.

Not having a strong grasp or knowledge of the Rules is like going into battle without a sword. The authors of this Manual have endeavored to give advocates a concise, useful and thorough resource of the Military Rules of Evidence. This book is the practitioner's dream. Having this book on your desk in your office and in court can help make your dream of being an outstanding litigator a reality.

Judge H.F. "Sparky" Gierke
Chief Judge, United States Court of Appeals for the Armed Forces
2004–2006

Foreword to the Sixth Edition (Anniversary Edition)

Because our men and women in uniform volunteer to put their lives in harm's way and give their best to preserve our freedom, everyone working in the Military Justice system works hard to make sure they always get the best from all of us. In my view, the charter of the Court of Appeals for the Armed Forces is to afford them a justice system which is second to none. Doing our part as judges, we seek to strike the delicate balance between preserving military discipline and assuring that our men and women in uniform enjoy the freedoms they are defending. Every judge at our court is committed to guaranteeing that the parties at each court-martial receive a fair trial.

Few have made a greater contribution to a fair trial in the military justice system than the authors of the Military Rules of Evidence Manual. The rules of evidence control the information that is presented to the legal decision-maker—both judge and panel member. For 25 years, this treatise has been at the elbow of counsel, judges, academics, and practitioners as they seek to represent clients and solve legal problems. I personally have always considered it an indispensable resource in performing my duties as an appellate judge and as teacher of military law and trial tactics. We have all relied on this extraordinary work as it presents voluminous evidentiary information simply and authoritatively.

It is no surprise that this treatise enjoys the preeminent position as a legal resource in both evidence and military justice. This work is a reflection of the depth and breadth of the knowledge and experience of these three authors. Each of them is a respected scholar, distinguished author, outstanding teacher, skillful practitioner, and caring colleague. I am proud to be a friend of Steve, Lee, and Dave.

In my view, a good book presents well important ideas and information. But a good book becomes a great book when the reader's time with the book is actually an experience in itself. Military Rules of Evidence Manual is a great book that continues to invite us back often to experience the richness and multifaceted dimensions of the rules of evidence. On behalf of many grateful lawyers and judges, I thank Steve, Lee, and Dave for their unique contribution to both the law of evidence and military justice. Congratulations on the milestone of publishing this Twenty-Fifth Anniversary Edition.

Andrew S. Effron
Chief Judge, United States Court of Appeals for the Armed Forces
2006

In 1980, the President adopted the Military Rules of Evidence, incorporating the new Federal Rules of Evidence into the Manual for Courts-Martial with adjustments to accommodate particular aspects of the military justice system. The positive reaction to the rules led the President, in 1984, to adopt a rule-based format in the course of revising the entire Manual for Courts-Martial.

The Uniform Code of Military Justice and the Manual provide the foundation for our military justice system. At trial, counsel and judges build upon that foundation in the course of addressing motions and objections that raise interpretative issues. Further refinement of the structure occurs through the decisions of appellate courts. From time to time, the accumulated experience of trial practice and appellate review produces further changes through the process of legislative amendments and changes to the Manual.

At each stage—whether at trial, on appeal, in drafting committees, or in Congress—the participants rely on the scholarly literature to develop issues, address specific cases, and consider changes to the law. Over the past twenty-five years, participants at all levels have consulted and cited the analysis provided by Military Rules of Evidence Manual in the course of addressing evidentiary issues. We are fortunate that three distinguished scholars—Stephen Saltzburg, Lee Schinasi, and David Schlueter—have devoted their considerable talents to this critical endeavor.

SECTION V

PRIVILEGES

SYNOPSIS

§ 501.01 Official Text

Rule 501.   General Rule.

(a) A person may not claim a privilege with respect to any matter except as required by or provided for in:

(1) The Constitution of the United States as applied to members of the armed forces;

(2) An Act of Congress applicable to trials by courts-martial;

(3) These rules or this Manual; or

(4) The principles of common law generally recognized in the trial of criminal cases in the United States district courts pursuant to Rule 501 of the Federal Rules of Evidence insofar as the application of such principles in trials by courts-martial is practicable and not contrary to or inconsistent with the code, these rules, or this Manual.

(b)   A claim of privilege includes, but is not limited to, the assertion by any person of a privilege to:

(1) Refuse to be a witness;

(2) Refuse to disclose any matter;

(3) Refuse to produce any object or writing; or

(4) Prevent another from being a witness or disclosing any matter or producing any object or writing.

(c) The term "person" includes an appropriate representative of the Federal Government, a State, or political subdivision thereof, or any other entity claiming to be the holder of a privilege.

(d) Notwithstanding any other provision of these rules, information not otherwise privileged does not become privileged on the basis that it was acquired by a medical officer or civilian physician in a professional capacity.

---

§ 501.02   Editorial Comment

[1]   Privileges—In General

Section V addresses the topic of privileges. In applying the rules of the section it is important to remember that privileges are disfavored because they potentially block admission of otherwise reliable, and sometimes, very important evidence. That point was made by the Supreme Court in *Trammel v. United States:*[1]

Testimonial exclusionary rules and privileges contravene the fundamen-

---

[1] Trammel v. United States, 445 U.S. 40, 50 (1980).

tal principle that the public . . . has a right to every man's evidence. As such they must be strictly construed and accepted only to the very limited extent that permitting a refusal to testify or excluding relevant evidence has a public good transcending the normally predominant principles of utilizing all rational means for ascertaining truth (*citations omitted*).

Thus, in reading and applying the rules in Section V, it is important to recognize what public interests are being advanced by the privilege. For example, the public interest may be to protect professional[2] or personal[3] relationships, government secrets,[4] or important sources of confidential information relating to criminal investigations.[5]

Even where the law recognizes a privilege, it may lapse if the holder of the privilege does not maintain the confidentiality of the privileged communication. Dean Wigmore made confidentiality the key element for determining whether a particular privilege should be recognized as he asked four questions:

(1) Did the communication originate in a confidence that it would not be disclosed?

(2) Is the element of confidentiality essential to a full and satisfactory maintenance of the parties' relationship?

(3) Is the relationship one which in the opinion of the community should be fostered?

(4) Will the injury that would inure to the relationship, because of disclosure, be greater than the benefit thereby gained for correct disposal of the litigation?[6]

---

[2] *See* Rules 503 (attorney-client relationship), *below.*

[3] *See* Rule 504 (privilege for marital communications), *below.*

[4] *See* Rules 505 and 506, *below.*

[5] *See* Rule 507 (informer's identity), *below.*

[6] *See* WIGMORE ON EVIDENCE, § 2285 (1961). An emerging alternate basis for adopting privileges is that:

> "[C]ertain privacy interests in the society are deserving of protection by privilege irrespective of whether the existence of such privileges actually operates substantially to affect conduct within the protected relationships." 1 McCormick on Evidence, § 72, at 300 (5th ed. 1999)—citing Black, *The Marital and Physician Privileges—Reprint of a Letter to a Congressman,* 1975 DUKE L.J. 45 (1975).

The Wigmore view is sometimes referred to as the "utilitarian justification" for privileges and emphasizes that the privilege fosters the relationship it is designed to protect. McCormick, on the other hand states that the newer "nonutilitarian" justification recognizes that some interests, such as "privacy," should be protected regardless of whether an evidentiary privilege actually promotes the relationship. McCormick further states that "It is open to doubt whether all of the interests and relationships which have sometimes been urged as sufficiently important to justify the creation of privileges really merit this sort of protection

The *Trammel* decision and the Wigmore criteria represent a delicate balancing of the need for evidence against the need to preserve or promote some public good, usually by preserving confidentiality.

Except for privileges guaranteed by the United States Constitution, such as the privilege against self-incrimination, no jurisdiction is required to adopt any particular privilege. As a result, some jurisdictions, such as the military, have not adopted the doctor-patient privilege at all. Even when a particular privilege has been adopted, there may be great latitude in the application of the privilege, including such issues as who may claim the privilege and what exceptions may exist to it.

[2]   Introduction to Section V

Like Section III, which adds criminal procedure rules to the basic model of the Federal Rules of Evidence, Section V adds substantial material not found in the Federal Rules of Evidence. Article V of the Federal Rules contains only one Rule, Rule 501, as a result of a sometimes bitter struggle over specific rules of privilege. Rather than delay the adoption of the rest of the evidence rules while it debated privilege rules, Congress opted to follow the common law approach previously mandated by Rule 26 of the Federal Rules of Criminal Procedure.

Section V of the Military Rules does follow the Federal Rule to the extent that it recognizes federal common law, but also it provides for nine specific privileges. Additional privileges are located in Rules 301, 302, and 303. Most of the privileges in Section V are "communications" privileges. That is, there is a privilege for any confidential communications between the persons designated in the particular rule. Other rules, however, create privileges for non-communicative information. Rule 504, for example, recognizes a testimonial (or capacity) privilege and Rule 507 recognizes a privilege for a person's identity.

The drafters chose to include specific privileges in order to provide concrete guidance to a world-wide criminal justice system that makes wide use of lay persons in disposing of criminal charges. The specific provisions drew heavily from both prior *Manual* provisions and the proposed Federal Rules on Privilege which were rejected by Congress.[7]

The privileges in Section V apply in virtually all proceedings conducted pursuant to provisions of the Uniform Code of Military Justice. This includes pretrial investigations, hearings on vacations of suspended sen-

---

bought at such a price." 1 McCormick on Evidence § 72, at 341 (6th ed. 2006). This seems consistent with the Supreme Court's observation in *Trammel* that privileges are generally disfavored.

[7] For a more complete discussion of the debate over the rejected federal privileges, see S. Saltzburg, M. Martin, & D. Capra, Federal Rules of Evidence Manual § 501.02, et seq. (9th ed. 2006).

tences, search authorizations, and pretrial confinement determinations. *See* Rule 1101.

Section V covers not only oral testimony, but also situations in which a person claims a privilege not to testify at all or a privilege to decline to produce real evidence. It governs claims by witnesses, potential witnesses, and non-witnesses who wish to prevent disclosure of material.

[3] Regulatory Privileges

Neither the Rule nor the Drafters' Analysis addresses the question of regulatory privileges. As noted in the annotated cases, *below,* several courts have wrestled with the question of whether evidence derived from an accused's participation in a drug rehabilitation program was admissible at his later court-martial. Service regulations generally proscribe use of such evidence. Although Rule 501 does not expressly recognize regulatory privileges, such evidence might be treated as subject to a common law privilege. The same approach used by federal courts in determining whether a state's nondisclosure statute creates a privilege—*see, e.g., In re Hampers,* noted *below*— may be applied by courts-martial in assessing the impact of a service's nondisclosure regulation.

[4] Additional Privileges—The Open Question

The question raised, but not answered, by Rule 501 is whether the military courts must wait for the President or the federal courts to recognize a particular privilege. When a party in a federal court wants the court to adopt a new privilege, the court will usually use the common law (*Wigmore*) template, *above,* in deciding whether the privilege applies. And Rule 501(a)(4) indicates that the "principles of common law" may serve as a source of military privilege. But the Drafters' Analysis indicates that the Rule intends that military courts may adopt federal common law privileges that are generally recognized in federal criminal trials. It should be permissible for military courts to find a trend in federal decisions and to apply the trend so as to find a new privilege or a new application for an established privilege because the common law changes and new principles emerge.[8]

In the case of Rule 513 (psychotherapist-patient privilege), adopted in 1999, the drafters stated that the privilege was adopted to "clarify military law" in light of the Supreme Court's opinion in *Jaffee v. Redmond.*[9] Where the court concluded that Federal Rule of Evidence 501 supported adoption of a federal psychotherapist-patient privilege. But the drafters did not

---

[8] *See, e.g.,* Schimpf, *Talk The Talk; Now Walk The Walk: Giving An Absolute Privilege To Communications Between A Victim And Victim-Advocate In The Military,* 185 MIL. L. REV. 149 (2005).

[9] 518 U.S. 1 (1996).

address the broader question of whether the military courts could apply other privileges.

[5]   Rule 501(a)—General Rule

Rule 501 presents the general rule. Subdivision (a) notes the recognized sources of privileges: the Constitution, statutes, the Military Rules of Evidence, the *Manual,* and the federal common law. Thus, military courts are generally prohibited from applying any privilege that does not come from one of these recognized sources. Although this may seem to unduly restrict the military courts, the limitation promotes uniformity and consistency. And because the federal courts are constantly testing and applying new privileges which may be applicable to military practice, it is not likely that the law of privileges in the military will remain static.[10] For example, the federal courts have addressed the applicability of familial privileges,[11] accountant-client privileges,[12] psychotherapist privileges,[13] and a privilege for "scholars."[14]

[6]   Rule 501(b)—Claim of Privilege

Subdivision (b) is patterned after the Supreme Court's proposed Rule 501 and recognizes that a privilege may be asserted by a person in a number of

---

[10] *Developments in the Law—Privileged Communications,* 98 HARV. L. REV. 1450 (1985) (excellent article on recent developments in law of privileges; in addition to addressing the theories and justifications of privileges, the article discusses the attorney-client, medical and counseling, familial, and institutional privileges, and finally the topic of implied waiver); Woodruff, J., *Privileges Under the Military Rules of Evidence,* 92 MIL. L. REV. 5 (1981) (lengthy article covers Section V of the Military Rules of Evidence; author discusses each of the privilege rules in that Section, compares them with prior military case law, and concludes that the new rules, in some instances, improve military law).

[11] *See, e.g., In re* Grand Jury, 103 F.3d 1140 (3d Cir. 1997) (in case of first impression, rejecting parent-child privilege); *In re* Grand Jury Subpoena, 714 F.2d 223 (2d Cir. 1983) (court declined to recognize "in-law" privilege); *In re* Agosto, 553 F. Supp. 1298 (D. Nev. 1983) (father-son privilege recognized); United States v. Jones, 683 F.2d 817 (4th Cir. 1982) (rejecting child-parent privilege on facts presented, but leaving open question whether such privilege might be recognized on other facts); United States v. Penn, 647 F.2d 876 (9th Cir. 1980) (court declined to create a "family" privilege). *See generally* Schlueter, *The Parent-Child Privilege: A Response to Calls for Adoption,* 19 ST. MARY'S L.J. 35 (1987) (author addresses each of the constitutional, legal, and social arguments for adoption of a parent-child privilege and concludes that there is insufficient reason to add to the list of recognized evidentiary privileges).

[12] *See, e.g.,* Wm. T. Thompson Co. v. General Nutrition Corp., 671 F.2d 100 (3d Cir. 1982) (there is no confidential accountant-client privilege under federal common law); *In re* Enforce Admin. Subpoenas, 98 F.R.D. 414 (S.D. Fla. 1982) (no accountant-client privilege in federal actions).

[13] Jaffee v. Redmond, 518 U.S. 1 (1996) (court applied psychotherapist-patient privilege to communications to licensed social worker).

[14] *In re* Grand Jury Proceedings (Scarce), 5 F.3d 397 (9th Cir. 1993) (court declined to apply "scholar's privilege").

ways—refusing to testify, disclose, or produce the information. And it includes preventing another person from testifying, producing, or disclosing the information.

The Rule does not address the issue of whether the privilege may be claimed to block examination of the material alleged to be privileged. In addressing that point with regard to whether the crime-fraud exception to the attorney-client privilege existed, the Supreme Court, in *United States v. Zolin*,[15] concluded that an *in camera* review of the allegedly privileged material was appropriate. The Court indicated that to obtain *in camera* review, notwithstanding Rule 104(a), the party opposing the privilege must establish, through sufficient evidence not already ruled to be privileged, that there is reason to believe that the crime-fraud exception applies. This is obviously a delicate balance, especially in a bench trial where the privileged information goes to the heart of the case. If the opponent of the privilege can show sufficient evidence to establish grounds for the judge to believe that the matter is probably not privileged, the judge is permitted to examine the material to make a determination as to whether it should be disclosed.

[7]   Rule 501(c)—Definition of Person

Under subdivision (c), patterned after Federal Rule 501, the broad definition of "person" permits representatives of entities to claim the privilege on behalf of the entity. For specific direction on who may claim the privileges, *see* Rules 502(c), 503(c), 504(b)(3), 505(c), 506(c), and 507(b).

[8]   Rule 501(d)—Doctor-Patient Privilege

A specific limitation on the provision in 501(a) is found in subdivision (d) that continues pre-Rules practice by specifically declining to recognize a doctor-patient privilege.[16] According to the Drafters' Analysis subdivision (d) does not affect the limited privilege stated in Rule 302 (Privilege Concerning Mental Examination of an Accused). That privilege is closely related to the privilege against self-incrimination. The strong anti-medical privilege position of the Rule is reflected in the Drafters' Analysis, which states that the military will not look to the law of another jurisdiction in analyzing medical privilege claims.

Although the rules explicitly reject a doctor-patient privilege, in 1999, the drafters added Rule 513, *below*, that recognizes a psychotherapist-patient privilege. And if the physician is working for the defense team, any

---

[15] 491 U.S. 554 (1989). *In re* John Doe, Inc. (United States v. John Doe, Inc.), 13 F.3d 633 (2d Cir. 1994) (trial court may consider ex parte affidavit from party seeking disclosure in deciding whether to conduct in camera hearing under *Zolin*).

[16] *See In re* Grand Jury Subpoena, 460 F. Supp. 150 (W.D. Mo. 1978) (court found no doctor-patient privilege in federal law).

communications by the accused to the physician may be covered under the attorney-client privilege.[17]

§ 501.03 Drafters' Analysis

Section V contains all of the privileges applicable to military criminal law except for those privileges that are found within Rules 301, Privilege Concerning Compulsory Self-Incrimination; Rule 302, Privilege Concerning Mental Examination of an Accused; and Rule 303, Degrading Questions. Privilege rules, unlike other Military Rules of Evidence, apply in "investigative hearings pursuant to Article 32; proceedings for vacation of suspension of sentence under Article 72; proceedings for search authorization; proceedings involving pretrial restraint; and in other proceedings authorized under the Uniform Code of Military Justice or this *Manual* and not listed in rule 1101(a)." Rule 1101(c); *see also* Rule 1101(b).

In contrast to the general acceptance of the proposed Federal Rules of Evidence by Congress, Congress did not accept the proposed privilege rules because a consensus as to the desirability of a number of specific privileges could not be achieved. *See generally* S. Saltzburg & K. Redden, Federal Rules of Evidence Manual 200–201 (2d ed. 1977). In an effort to expedite the Federal Rules generally, Congress adopted a general rule, Rule 501, which basically provides for the continuation of common law in the privilege area. The Committee deemed the approach taken by Congress in the Federal Rules impracticable within the armed forces. Unlike the Article III court system, that is conducted almost entirely by attorneys functioning in conjunction with permanent courts in fixed locations, the military criminal legal system is characterized by its dependence upon large numbers of laymen, temporary courts, and inherent geographical and personnel instability due to the worldwide deployment of military personnel. Consequently, military law requires far more stability than civilian law. This is particularly true because of the significant number of non-lawyers involved in the military criminal legal system. Commanders, convening authorities, non-lawyer investigating officers, summary court-martial officers, or law enforcement personnel need specific guidance as to what material is privileged and what is not.

Section V combines the flexible approach taken by Congress with respect to privileges with that provided in the present *Manual*. Rules 502-509 set forth specific rules of privilege to provide the certainty and stability necessary for military justice. Rule 501, on the other hand, adopts those privileges recognized in common law pursuant to Federal Rule of Evidence 501 with some limitations. Specific privileges are generally taken from those proposed Federal Rules of Evidence which although not adopted by Congress were non-controversial, or from the present Manual.

---

[17] *See* the discussion and Annotated Cases for Rule 502(b)(3), *below.*

Rule 501 is the basic rule of privilege. In addition to recognizing privileges required by or provided for in the Constitution, an applicable Act of Congress, the Military Rules of Evidence, and the *Manual for Courts-Martial,* Rule 501(a) also recognizes privileges "generally recognized in the trial of criminal cases in the United States district courts pursuant to Rule 501 of the Federal Rules of Evidence insofar as the application of such principles in trials by court-martial is practicable and not contrary to or inconsistent with the Uniform Code of Military Justice, these rules, or this Manual." The latter language is taken from present *Manual* paragraph 137. As a result of Rule 501(a)(4), the common law of privileges as recognized in the Article III courts will be applicable to the armed forces except as otherwise provided by the limitation indicated above. Rule 501(d) prevents the application of a doctor-patient privilege. Such a privilege was considered to be totally incompatible with the clear interest of the armed forces in ensuring the health and fitness for duty of personnel. *See* present *Manual* paragraph 151 *c.* The privilege expressed in Rule 302 and its conforming *Manual* change in paragraph 121, is not a doctor-patient privilege and is not affected by Rule 501(d).

It should be noted that the law of the forum determines the application of privilege. Consequently, even if a service member should consult with a doctor in a jurisdiction with a doctor-patient privilege for example, such a privilege is inapplicable should the doctor be called as a witness before a court-martial.

Subdivision (b) is a non-exhaustive list of actions which constitute an invocation of a privilege. The subdivision is derived from Federal Rule of Evidence 501 as originally proposed by the Supreme Court, and the four specific actions listed are also found in the Uniform Rules of Evidence. The list is intentionally non-exclusive as a privilege might be claimed in a fashion distinct from those listed.

Subdivision (c) is derived from Federal Rule of Evidence 501 and makes it clear that an appropriate representative of a political jurisdiction or other organizational entity may claim an applicable privilege. The definition is intentionally non-exhaustive.

§ 501.04   Drafters' Analysis (1999)

The analysis to Mil. R. Evid. 501 is amended—

(1) by striking:

"The privilege expressed in Rule 302 and its conforming Manual change in Para. 121, is not a doctor-patient privilege and is not affected by Rule 501(d)."

(2) by adding at the end:

"1999 Amendment: The privileges expressed in Rule 513 and Rule 302 and the conforming Manual change in R.C.M. 706, are not physician-patient privileges and are not affected by Rule 501(d)."

§ 501.05 Annotated Cases

[1] Rule 501(a)—Sources of Privilege

[a] Sources of Privilege—In General

Supreme Court

Jaffee v. Redmond, 518 U.S. 1 (1996): The administrator of an estate sought the notes of a licensed social worker who had treated respondent-policeman who had killed the decedent while on duty. Citing Federal Rule 501 and the fact that all fifty states and the District of Columbia have codified privileges covering mental health privileges, the Court held that confidential communications between a licensed psychotherapist and his or her patients in the course of providing treatment or diagnosis falls within Rule 501. Noting the key roles played by social workers in providing mental health treatment, the Court extended the privilege to confidential communications made to a licensed social worker in the course of providing psychotherapy.

United States Court of Appeals for the Armed Forces

United States v. Durbin, 68 M.J. 271 (C.A.A.F. 2010): The accused's wife discovered child pornography on his computer and asked him to explain how the images had gotten on his computer. He admitted that it was a one-time thing and volunteered to delete the images. He moved his hands over the touch pad, turned the screen toward his wife and said that he had deleted the images. At trial, the military judge ruled that the accused's wife could waive her marital communications privilege and testify as to what she said to the accused and how the accused acted. The Air Force Court of Criminal Appeals, in an unpublished opinion, held that the judge was correct in permitting the wife to testify as to what she said but that it was harmless error to admit evidence of the accused's actions. The Court of Appeals for the armed forces affirmed. Citing Rule 501(a), the court distinguished federal case law on the subject and noted that the military marital communications privilege is narrower and extends only to the communicating spouse—in this case the accused's wife. Under the rule, the court said, she could waive the privilege. The court acknowledged that a case might arise where the natural consequence of permitting one spouse to testify about a marital conversation would also reveal what the other spouse said, but that was not the situation in this case. The court assumed, but did not decide, that the accused's actions amounted to a privileged communication under Rule 504. Any error in admitting evidence of those actions was deemed harmless.

United States v. Smith, 33 M.J. 114 (C.M.A. 1991): At trial, the accused testified that her husband forced her to commit the crimes charged and that she had been afraid of him. The prosecution introduced a letter written by her to her husband which encouraged him to support her story. The lower court ruled that the letter was not privileged under the crime-fraud exception recognized in the federal courts. (30 M.J. 1022 (A.F.C.M.R. 1990)). The Court of Appeals, however, ruled that the accused had waived the privilege by presenting testimony on the same general subject matter as the letter. In a concurring opinion, Judge Everett rejected the crime-fraud exception, noting that Rule 501 makes no attempt to adopt common-law exceptions to the specifically codified privilege rules in Section V. He also rejected the majority's waiver theory but opined that the letter was not a confidential husband-wife communication because the accused must have known that her letter would be screened by confinement facility personnel.

Navy-Marine Corps Court of Criminal Appeals

United States v. Miller, 32 M.J. 843 (N.M.C.M.R. 1991): The court noted that, although it was not aware of any case applying Rule 501(a)(4) to a privilege arising entirely from a state law, in any event the accused would not have had any standing to claim a California statutory privilege for statements made by his daughter to California officials.

[b]   Sources of Privilege—Judicial Creation of News Reporter Privilege

Navy-Marine Corps Court of Criminal Appeals

United States v. Wuterich, 68 M.J. 511 (N.M.Ct.Crim.App. 2009): After the accused was charged with various offenses arising out of an incident in Iraq, he gave an extensive interview to CBS Sixty Minutes about his version of the events. The government issued a subpoena to CBS to produce to produce the tapes of the entire interview, including the outtakes, but the military judge granted CBS's motion to quash. The government appealed that ruling, and the Court of Criminal Appeals held that the trial judge erred in granting the motion without first examining the tapes in camera. *United States v. Wuterich*, 66 M.J. 685 (N.M.Ct.Crim.App. 2008). The Court of Appeals vacated on other grounds but agreed that an in camera review was necessary. *United States v. Wuterich*, 67 M.J. 63 (C.A.A.F. 2008). On remand, the trial judge conducted the review but concluded that the tapes were protected under the qualified reporter's privilege recognized by the federal courts. The Court of Criminal Appeals vacated that ruling. Noting that this was a case of first impression, and citing *Branzburg v. Hayes*, 408 U.S. 665 (1972), the court concluded that the reporters' privilege was not a constitutionally protected First Amendment privilege within the meaning of Rule 501(a)(1), and the privilege was not one of those federal common law privileges falling within Rule 501(a)(4). The court surveyed the federal case law and concluded that the federal circuit courts are split and that there is "substantial controversy" over whether the privilege exists. Given the disagreement among the federal courts, the court declined to decide with more precision when a privilege rule in the federal courts is "generally recognized" (the language used in Rule 501). Limiting its analysis to the facts of this case, the court found that the reporter's privilege is not commonly recognized in the federal courts and does not apply to the military. Therefore, the trial judge erred in applying that privilege in his rulings.

[c]   Sources of Privilege—Judicial Creation of Physician-Patient Privilege

Air Force Court of Criminal Appeals

United States v. Brown, 38 M.J. 696 (A.F.C.M.R. 1993): The court declined to create a physician-patient privilege to include the accused as an intoxicated, unwilling patient of the military medical system, noting that it lacked the authority to do so. *See* Rule 501(d).

[2]   Rule 501(b)—Claim of Privilege

Supreme Court

University of Pennsylvania v. E.E.O.C., 493 U.S. 182 (1990): Noting that it is not inclined to develop rules of privilege on a case-by-case basis and that balancing the conflicting interests usually associated with privileges is a legislative function, the court rejected a University's argument that it had a common-law privilege not to disclose confidential peer review information on its professors. The court also rejected the argument that that information was protected as a constitutional privilege under the first amendment.

United States v. Zolin, 491 U.S. 554 (1989): The Court concluded that, notwithstanding Rule 104(a) regarding privileges, a court could conduct an *in camera* review of materials allegedly protected by the attorney-client privilege to determine if the crime-fraud exception to that privilege applied. The Court added that in order to obtain an *in camera* review, the party opposing the privilege must present sufficient threshold evidence, which has not already been ruled to be privileged, to support a claim that the exception applies.

United States Court of Appeals for the Armed Forces

United States v. Lewis, 42 M.J. 1 (C.A.A.F. 1995): Rejecting in part the procedures set out in *United States v. Burdine,* 29 M.J. 834 (A.C.M.R. 1989) for determining whether trial defense counsel was ineffective, the court indicated that trial counsel should not be required to justify his actions until after a court of competent jurisdiction reviews the allegations of ineffectiveness and decides that the evidence, if unrebutted, would overcome the presumption of competence. If the defense counsel wishes to challenge the production of privileged information, he may do so under Rule 501(b).

Air Force Court of Criminal Appeals

United States v. Smith, 30 M.J. 1022 (A.F.C.M.R. 1990): Citing federal cases, *United States v. Martel,* 19 M.J. 917 (A.C.M.R. 1985), and Rules 501 and 102, the court concluded that a letter written by the accused to her husband was not privileged under the common law joint participant exception to the marital communications privilege. The court indicated that, although the letter did not explicitly encourage the accused's husband to commit fraud on the court, the letter contained statements inconsistent with the accused's testimony. This case is puzzling. The underlying assumption in the joint participant exception is that the two marital partners have actually engaged in joint criminal activity. Because it was never shown that the letter reached the accused's husband, it is difficult to see how the letter demonstrates joint activity.

United States v. Landes, 17 M.J. 1092 (A.F.C.M.R. 1984): The court declined to create a parent-child privilege because the issue was not preserved for appeal.

United States v. Broady, 12 M.J. 963 (A.F.C.M.R. 1982): During a telephone call to the base hospital in which he requested immediate medical attention for a drug problem, the accused stated that he had used LSD. An Air Force regulation, AFR 30-2, Social Actions Program, ¶ 4-24, provided that evidence of drug use revealed by a service member during requested medical treatment could not be used to support punitive action unless such evidence developed during "emergency" treatment. For varying reasons, the judges concluded that because the accused requested medical assistance he had reached a safe haven. Thus, his statements were inadmissible at his trial on drug charges.

United States v. Lange, 11 M.J. 884 (A.F.C.M.R. 1981): Noting the court's earlier opinions regarding use of evidence relating to an accused's drug rehabilitation, *United States v. Schrock,* 11 M.J. 797 (A.F.C.M.R. 1981), one concurring judge was concerned that such evidence may be used to determine whether jurisdiction exists over the offense. In his view, the evidence is privileged from any use at trial. The majority responded to that concern by noting in footnote 5 that the evidence was offered for a limited purpose, Rule 105, and was not presented to the court members.

United States v. Schmenk, 11 M.J. 803 (A.F.C.M.R. 1981): During the sentencing portion of the trial, the military judge rejected evidence offered by the prosecution to show the accused's participation in an Air Force drug rehabilitation program, which evidence was later included in the staff judge advocate's post-trial review. The court, citing its opinion in *United States v. Cottle, below,* stated that the judge's exclusion of the evidence was correct, but that reviewing authorities could consider it in determining an appropriate post-trial disposition of the case. *See also United States v. Jones,* 11 M.J. 817 (A.F.C.M.R. 1981). A dissent argued that, absent extraordinary circumstances, Rule 501(a) prohibits a claim of any privilege at trial other than those included in Section V and Rules 301–303. *Citing* Rule 102, he noted that Rule 501(a) does not preclude an accused from claiming a privilege regarding matters disclosed prior to the effective date of the Rules (1 Sept. 1980). Matters disclosed after then might also be privileged, notwithstanding

Rule 501(a), if the individual relied upon the "uncontroverted assertions" of Air Force officials and regulations.

United States v. Cottle, 11 M.J. 572 (A.F.C.M.R. 1981): During sentencing, the prosecution offered into evidence material from the accused's Unfavorable Information File (UIF) that two of his urinalysis samples had shown positive for drugs. The court, citing several regulatory provisions governing confidential drug records, stated that only the accused could introduce such evidence unless its admission was permitted by other regulatory provisions. In a footnote the court observed that after 1 September 1980 such broad regulatory privileges might be contrary to Rule 501(a).

Army Court of Criminal Appeals

United States v. Hanks, 29 M.J. 907 (A.C.M.R. 1989): In response to the defense's assertion that the accused could be rehabilitated, the prosecution introduced evidence that the accused had enrolled in a drug rehabilitation program, but had subsequently lapsed back into consuming alcohol. The defense objected only on grounds of relevancy. In this case the defense opened the door to rebuttal evidence. Thus, even if the proper objection had been made, the evidence would have been admissible.

United States v. Martel, 19 M.J. 917 (A.C.M.R. 1985): Noting that Rule 501(a)(4) permits application of federal common law, the court indicated that it would attempt to resolve any "deficiencies or ambiguities" in Rule 504 by interpreting and applying federal common law; in the end the court adopted a joint participant exception to Rule 504.

[3]   Rule 501(d)—Doctor-Patient Privilege

Supreme Court

Jaffee v. Redmond, 518 U.S. 1 (1996): The administrator of an estate sought the notes of a licensed social worker who had treated respondent-policeman who had killed the decedent while on duty. *Citing* Federal Rule 501 and the fact that all fifty states and the District of Columbia have codified privileges covering mental health privileges, the Court held that confidential communications between a licensed psychotherapist and his or her patients in the course of providing treatment or diagnosis falls within Rule 501. Noting the key roles played by social workers in providing mental health treatment, the Court extended the privilege to confidential communications made to a licensed social worker in the course of providing psychotherapy.

Air Force Court of Criminal Appeals

United States v. Brown, 38 M.J. 696 (A.F.C.M.R. 1993): The court declined to create a physician-patient privilege to include the accused as an intoxicated, unwilling patient of the military medical system, noting that it lacked the authority to do so.

§ 502.01   Official Text

Rule 502.   Lawyer-Client Privilege.

(a) *General rule of privilege.* A client has a privilege to refuse to disclose and to prevent any other person from disclosing confidential communications made for the purpose of facilitating the rendition of professional legal services to the client, (1) between the client or the client's representative and the lawyer or the lawyer's representative, (2) between the lawyer and the lawyer's representative, (3) by the client or the client's lawyer to a lawyer representing another in a matter of common interest, (4) between representatives of the client or between the client and a representative of the client, or (5) between lawyers representing the client.

(b) *Definitions.* As used in this rule:

(1) A "client" is a person, public officer, corporation, association, organization, or other entity, either public or private, who receives professional legal services from a lawyer, or who consults a lawyer with a view to obtaining professional legal services from the lawyer.

(2) A "lawyer" is a person authorized, or reasonably believed by the client to be authorized, to practice law; or a member of the armed forces detailed, assigned, or otherwise provided to represent a person in a court-martial case or in any military investigation or proceeding. The term "lawyer" does not include a member of the armed forces serving in a capacity other than as a judge advocate, legal officer, or law specialist as defined in Article 1, unless the member: (a) is detailed, assigned, or otherwise provided to represent a person in a court-martial case or in any military investigation or proceeding; (b) is authorized by the armed forces, or reasonably believed by the client to be authorized, to render professional legal services to members of the armed forces; or (c) is authorized to practice law and renders professional legal services during off-duty employment.

(3) A "representative" of a lawyer is a person employed by or assigned to assist a lawyer in providing professional legal services.

(4) A communication is "confidential" if not intended to be disclosed to third persons other than those to whom disclosure is in furtherance of the rendition of professional legal services to the client or those reasonably necessary for the transmission of the communication.

(c) *Who may claim the privilege.* The privilege may be claimed by the client, the guardian or conservator of the client, the personal representative of a deceased client, or the successor, trustee, or similar representative of a corporation, association, or other organization, whether or not in existence. The lawyer or the lawyer's representative who received the communication may claim the privilege on behalf of the client. The authority of the lawyer to do so is presumed in the absence of evidence to the contrary.

(d) *Exceptions.*   There is no privilege under this rule under the following circumstances:

(1) *Crime or fraud.*   If the communication clearly contemplated the future commission of a fraud or crime or if services of the lawyer were sought or obtained to enable or aid anyone to commit or plan to commit what the client knew or reasonably should have known to be a crime or fraud;

(2) *Claimants through same deceased client.*   As to a communication relevant to an issue between parties who claim through the same deceased client, regardless of whether the claims are by testate or intestate succession or by inter vivos transaction;

(3) *Breach of duty by lawyer or client.*   As to a communication relevant to an issue of breach of duty by the lawyer to the client or by the client to the lawyer;

(4) *Document attested by lawyer.*   As to a communication relevant to an issue concerning an attested document to which the lawyer is an attesting witness; or

(5) *Joint clients.*   As to a communication relevant to a matter of common interest between two or more clients if the communication was made by any of them to a lawyer retained or consulted in common, when offered in an action between any of the clients.

§ 502.02   Editorial Comment

The traditional testimonial privilege protecting the lawyer-client relationship is found in Rule 502. It generally follows the Supreme Court's proposed Federal Rule of Evidence 503.[1]

[1]   Rule 502(a)—General Rule of Privilege

[a]   In General

Subdivision (a) is taken from proposed Federal Rule of Evidence 503(b)

---

[1] The proposed rule and the accompanying Advisory Committee Notes are included in 5 S. Saltzburg, M. Martin, & D. Capra, FEDERAL RULES OF EVIDENCE MANUAL, Part Three, pp 4–30 (9th ed. 2006).

and presents a familiar statement of the general privilege rule. The privilege specifically rests with a client who may refuse to divulge, and who may block disclosure of, confidential communications made to a lawyer for the purpose of obtaining legal services.[2]

[b]   Protected Client-Attorney Communications

Rule 502 protects only confidential client-attorney communications. Although the client holds the privilege, the Rule specifically provides that more than communications from the client to the lawyer are covered. The modern trend seems to be that the privilege is a two-way street.[3] For example, confidential communications from the lawyer to the client[4] or from the lawyer's assistant to a representative of the client could be privileged.[5] Discussions between lawyers working on the client's case and discussions between representatives of the client are also potentially within the general rule. Under (a)(3), communications in a joint conference between clients and their respective lawyers may also be privileged; each client has a privilege not to have his statements divulged.

The rule does not define the term "communication," but the case law makes it clear that writings,[6] oral statements,[7] or communicative conduct[8] are protected. The form of the communication is not as critical as the fact that what was said, written, or done was communicative in nature. Conversely, what the attorney has observed about the client, whether they be the client's actions, demeanor, or possessions—are normally not considered to be a protected communication.[9] The law also seems clear that a client may not immunize pre-existing and otherwise non-privileged documents by

---

[2] *See generally* Gilligan & Imwinkelried, *Waiver Raised to the Second Power: Waivers of Evidentiary Privileges by Lawyers Representing Accused Being Tried In Absentia*, 56 S.C. L. REV. 509 (2005).

[3] *See generally* C. Mueller & L. Kirkpatrick, EVIDENCE § 5.12 at 325 (3d ed. 2003).

[4] *See, e.g.*, United States v. Defazio, 899 F.2d 626 (7th Cir. 1990); Wells v. Rushing, 755 F.2d 376, 379 n.2 (5th Cir. 1985).

[5] Although the rule explicitly refers to communications involving a "representative of a client," that term is not defined in Rule 502. *In re* Bieter Co., 16 F.3d 929 (8th Cir. 1994) (independent contractor was a "representative of the client" for attorney-client privilege purposes in RICO suit).

[6] *See, e.g.*, Moore v. Tri-City Hosp. Auth., 118 F.R.D. 646 (N.D. Ga. 1988) (entries in diary that described communications from attorney).

[7] *See, e.g.*, United States v. Spector, 793 F.2d 932 (8th Cir. 1986) (privilege protected confidential tape recorded statements by client, at direction of attorney).

[8] *See generally* Saltzburg, *Communications Falling Within the Attorney-Client Privilege*, 66 IOWA L. REV. 811 (1981).

[9] *See, e.g.*, *In re* Grand Jury Proceedings (85 Misc. 140), 791 F.2d 663 (8th Cir. 1986) (defendant's signatures and photo not privileged); *In re* Walsh, 623 F.2d 489 (7th Cir. 1980) (appearance, complexion, dress and demeanor not privileged).

simply transferring them to an attorney.[10]

And while an attorney may not receive tangible evidence from the client for purposes of destroying or concealing that evidence,[11] there is authority for the view that, if the client has given the attorney the evidence, the client's identity is privileged.[12] If the attorney has merely observed the evidence without moving it, concealing it, or altering it, then the attorney's observations and how he or she came to locate the evidence through the client's assistance, might be protected.[13]

The topic of the requirement that the communication be "confidential," is discussed, *below*, at Rule 502(b)(4).

[c]   Communications for Purposes of Providing Professional Legal Services

The privilege generally extends to initial discussions or consultations between the parties,[14] even where the attorney or the client later decides not to employ the lawyer or use his services. If the attorney, on the other hand has indicated that he or she may not represent the client the court will probably conclude that the privilege does not exist.[15]

If the communications were made during the existence of the attorney-client relationship, they continue to be privileged even though the relationship does not continue.[16] For example, the Supreme Court has held that the privilege survives the death of the client.[17] Communications not involving legal advice are generally not privileged.[18] For example, the courts have

---

[10] *See* Fisher v. United States, 425 U.S. 391 (1976); United States v. Robinson, 121 F.3d 971 (5th Cir. 1997) (documents in hands of lawyer were discoverable); *In re* Grand Jury, 959 F.2d 1158 (2d Cir. 1992) (pre-existing records not privileged). *See also* Annotated Cases, *below.*

[11] ABA Model Rules of Professional Conduct, Rule 3.4. United States v. Kellington, 139 F.3d 909 (9th Cir. 1998) (attorney convicted for destroying evidence at request of client).

[12] *See, e.g.*, State v. Olwell, 394 P.2d 681 (Wash. 1964).

[13] *See, e.g.*, People v. Meredith, 631 P.2d 46 (Cal. 1981). *See generally* Freedman, *Where the Bodies Are Buried: The Adversary System and the Obligation of Confidentiality*, 10 CRIM. L. BULL. 979 (1974).

[14] *See In re* Auclair, 961 F.2d 65 (5th Cir. 1992).

[15] United States v. Rust, 41 M.J. 472 (1995), annotated, *below. See also* United States v. Dennis, 843 F.2d 652 (2d Cir. 1992) (no privilege where lawyer explicitly declined to represent client).

[16] Levin v. Ripple Twist Mills, Inc., 416 F. Supp. 876 (E.D. Pa. 1976); United States v. Cunningham, 672 F.2d 1064, 1073 n.8 (2d Cir. 1982).

[17] Swidler and Berlin v. United States, 524 U.S. 399 (1998), annotated, *below.*

[18] *See* United States v. Clemons, 676 F.2d 124 (5th Cir. 1982) (attorney's message to client as to time of trial was not privileged).; United States v. Cunningham, 672 F.2d 1064, 1073 n.8 (2d Cir. 1982) (privilege attaches to communication of information, not information itself); United States v. Willis, 565 F. Supp. 1186 (S.D. Iowa 1983). *See also* Coastal States

rejected the privilege where the communication was for purposes of giving business[19] or accounting advice,[20] or for purposes of investment counseling.[21] On the other hand, giving tax advice may be considered privileged.[22]

[d]   Client Identity and Fee Arrangements

As a general rule, the identity of the client is not privileged.[23] In most cases, the client's identity will be public knowledge, especially in a military criminal investigation. There may be cases, however, where the client is not an accused and wishes to remain anonymous. The courts are usually not sympathetic to the argument that the client's intent is dispositive.[24] The courts have, however, recognized several exceptions to the general rule. They may be inclined to find a privilege, for example, where the client's identity constitutes the "last link" in the chain of testimony implicating the client.[25] Similarly, the client's identity may remain privileged in extraordinary circumstances where the identity is considered part of the professional confidential communication.[26]

Gas Corp. v. Department of Energy, 617 F.2d 854 (D.C. Cir. 1980); United States v. Amerada Hess Corp., 619 F.2d 980 (3d Cir. 1980); Thompson & Kastenberg, *The Attorney-Client Privilege: Practical Military Applications of a Professional Core Value,* 49 A.F. L. Rev. 1 (2000).

[19] United States v. Knoll, 16 F.3d 1313 (2d Cir. 1994) (no privilege where documents related only to business transaction with client); United States v. Davis, 636 F.2d 1028 (5th Cir. 1981). *Cf.* In re County of Erie, 473 F.3d 413 (2d Cir. 2007) (lawyer's recommendation to client regarding compliance with legal obligation is legal advice); Rehling v. City of Chicago, 207 F.3d 1009 (7th Cir. 2000) (close question on whether attorney was acting in legal or business capacity; court concluded that advice was legal, because attorney for superintendent for police was not authorized to make business decisions).

[20] *In re* Grand Jury Investigation, 842 F.2d 1223 (11th Cir. 1987).

[21] Liew v. Breen, 640 F.2d 1046 (9th Cir. 1981).

[22] Colton v. United States, 306 F.2d 633 (2d Cir. 1962) (tax advice is prima facie privileged). *Cf.* United States v. Frederick, 182 F.3d 496 (7th Cir. 1999) (taxpayer may not create privilege by simply hiring lawyer to do accountant's work).

[23] *See, e.g.,* In re Shargel, 742 F.2d 61 (2d Cir. 1984) (client's identity not privileged); In re Subpoena to Testify Before Grand Jury (Alexiou v. United States), 39 F.3d 973 (9th Cir. 1994) (lawyer required to disclose identity of client who passed counterfeit bill); In re Grand Jury Subpoena for Attorney for Reyes-Reguena (DeGeurin), 926 F.2d 1423 (5th Cir. 1990) (attorney could be compelled to tell who paid fees for representation of client); Phaksuan v. United States, 722 F.2d 591 (9th Cir. 1983) (identity of client is privileged only where facts demonstrate that client's name is "material only for purpose of showing an acknowledgment of guilt" on part of client of the offense for which he has sought legal advice).

[24] *See* Glanzer & Taskier, *Attorneys Before the Grand Jury; Assertion of the Attorney-Client Privilege to Protect a Client's Identity,* 75 J. Crim. L. & Criminology 1070 (1984).

[25] *In re* Grand Jury Proceedings (GJ90-2), 946 F.2d 746 (11th Cir. 1991) (lawyer could refuse to disclose identity of client where doing so would be last link in the inculpatory chain against the client). *Cf. In re* Grand Jury Matter No. 91-01386, 969 F.2d 995 (11th Cir. 1992) (attorney who received counterfeit money from client could not claim "last link" doctrine).

[26] Ralls v. United States, 52 F.3d 223 (9th Cir. 1995) (lawyer not required to identify

The courts have also generally concluded that fee arrangements are not privileged. Thus, attorneys have been required to disclose who paid their fees,[27] the periods of consultation,[28] and the form of payment.[29]

[e]   Burden of Proof

The burden of demonstrating that an attorney-client relationship exists and that information falls within the privilege rests upon the party asserting the privilege.[30] Whether a privilege exists is for the military judge under Rule 104(a).

[2]   Rule 502(b)—Definitions

Definitions of the key terms used in the general rule are set out in subdivision (b).

[a]   Definitions—Client

Under (b)(1) the term "client" includes more than natural persons. Corporations, organizations, and other legal entities are included. But the Rule provides no specific guidance on who speaks for the entity for purposes of the privilege. The federal courts split on the issue. Prior to 1981, the more limited "control group" test seemed to be the most widely accepted. Under that standard a corporate or "entity" client is entitled to the privilege for communications made by an employee who is in a position to control or to take a substantial role in a decision involving the attorney's advice or is an authorized member of a group that has the authority. In effect, that employee personifies the organization.[31]

The Supreme Court in *Upjohn Co. v. United States*,[32] rejected the "control

---

client, where fee arrangements and identity were inextricably intertwined with confidential communications); Tornay v. United States, 840 F.2d 1424 (9th Cir. 1988) (narrow reading of exception).

[27] Vingelli v. United States Drug Enforcement Agency, 992 F.2d 449 (2d Cir. 1993).

[28] Condon v. Petacque, 90 F.R.D. 53 (N.D. Ill. 1981).

[29] In re Two Grand Jury Subpoenas Duces Tecum Dated August 21, 1985, 793 F.2d 69 (2d cir. 1986).

[30] Weil v. Investment/Indicators, Research & Mgt., Inc., 647 F.2d 18 (9th Cir. 1981) (burden of proving attorney-client relationship rests upon party asserting the privilege).

[31] *See* Mead Data Cent., Inc. v. Department of the Air Force, 566 F.2d 242 (D.C. Cir. 1977); City of Philadelphia v. Westinghouse Elec. Corp., 210 F. Supp. 483 (E.D. Pa. 1962). Broader tests of privilege were found in Harper & Row Publishers, Inc. v. Decker, 423 F.2d 487 (7th Cir. 1970) (scope of employment test), *aff d,* 400 U.S. 348 (1971); Diversified Indus., Inc. v. Meredith, 572 F.2d 596 (8th Cir. 1978) (en banc) (subject matter test); United States v. United Shoe Machinery Corp., 89 F. Supp. 357 (D. Mass. 1950) (all communications by any employee are protected). *See generally Attorney-Client Privilege in Federal Courts: Under What Circumstances Can Corporation Claim Privilege for Communications From Its Employees and Agents to Corporation's Attorney,* 9 A.L.R. FED. 685 (1971).

[32] 449 U.S. 383 (1981).

group" test and opted in favor of greater protection for employees' statements. It identified four factors that may constitute the federal standard. Whether the Court will use the same broad approach in dealing with government agencies claiming a privilege is not yet determined.

Occasionally, a question arises concerning whether a commander is entitled to invoke the lawyer-client privilege in conjunction with confidential discussions with a military lawyer. An analogous situation was addressed in *In re Grand Jury Proceedings,*[33] where the court distinguished between a corporate officer speaking for himself and speaking for the organization:

> If the communicating officer seeks legal advice himself and consults a lawyer about his problems, he may have a privilege. If he makes it clear when he is consulting the company lawyer that he personally is consulting the lawyer and the lawyer sees fit to accept and give communication knowing the possible conflicts that could arise, he may have a privilege. But in the absence of any indication to the company's lawyer that the lawyer is to act in any other capacity than as lawyer for the company in giving and receiving communications from control group personnel, the privilege is and should remain that of the company and not that of the communicating officer.

[b] Definitions—Lawyer

Rule 502(b)(2) addresses the definition of "lawyer." The definition includes not only attorneys authorized to practice law and those individuals reasonably believed by the client to be so authorized,[34] but also military personnel who are representing clients before military criminal or administrative proceedings.[35] The Advisory Committee's Note on proposed Federal Rule of Evidence 503(a)(2), that serves in part as the basis for subdivision (b)(2), states that "authorized . . . to practice law" means that the lawyer must be licensed.

The second sentence of (b)(2) was apparently included to make clear that not all licensed attorneys serving in the armed forces necessarily act as lawyers while serving. The following personnel, including attorneys, who are not serving as judge advocates, legal officers, or law specialists, *see* Article 1, U.C.M.J., fit into one of the three listed categories in (b)(2) and fall within the zone of the privilege:

> (1) those representing individuals before military criminal or administrative proceedings;
>
> (2) those authorized to give professional legal services or reasonably believed by client to be authorized to do so; or

---

[33] 434 F. Supp. 648 (E.D. Mich. 1977), *aff'd,* 570 F.2d 562 (6th Cir. 1978).

[34] *See, e.g.,* United States v. Ostrer, 422 F. Supp. 93 (S.D.N.Y. 1976) (good faith belief).

[35] *See* Article 27, U.C.M.J.

(3) those licensed attorneys authorized to practice and actually practicing law while off-duty.

[c] Definitions—Representative of Lawyer

The definition of "representative" of a lawyer is addressed in Rule 502(b)(3) and is a slight modification of proposed Federal Rule 503(a)(3). Individuals working for, or with, a lawyer may fit within the definition. The Rule, which includes individuals who are assigned or employed to assist a lawyer, probably should not be read so narrowly as to exclude volunteers who are actively assisting lawyers. Application of the privilege should not turn on detailing orders or remuneration but should depend upon whether a person is working for, *i.e.,* under the supervision or control of, a lawyer. The federal courts have applied the privilege to situations involving a client's communications with an accountant,[36] law clerks,[37] stenographers,[38] and engineers.[39]

As the military cases recognize, in some instances a psychiatrist, and perhaps by logical extension, physicians, may be considered a member of the defense team.[40]

[d] Definitions—Confidential Communications

The privilege extends only to "confidential communications." Subdivision (b)(4) defines that term and requires an examination of the communicating party's intent. Whether a communication is confidential will depend on the intent of the person making the communication. Intent, in turn, can usually be determined by the circumstances, timing, and location of the communication.

Statements made in the presence of third persons, who represent neither the client nor the attorney, are suspect, unless the party claiming the privilege can show, for example, that the client and the attorney took steps to protect their conversation by—for example turning aside, or whispering to each other. If the communication was intended to be confidential, interception by a third party (inadvertent or intentional) will not destroy the privilege.

---

[36] United States v. Kovel, 296 F.2d 918 (2d Cir. 1961).

[37] Cold Metal Process Co. v. Aluminum Co. of America, 7 F.R.D. 684 (D. Mass. 1947).

[38] Himmelfarb v. United States, 175 F.2d 924 (9th Cir. 1949).

[39] Lewis v. United Air Lines Transp. Corp., 32 F. Supp. 21 (W.D. Pa. 1940). *Cf.* Dabney v. Inv. Corp. of America, 82 F.R.D. 464 (E.D. Pa. 1979) (law student, not admitted to practice, was not agent of a duly licensed attorney).

[40] *See* Annotated Cases, *below. See also* United States v. Alvarez, 519 F.2d 1036 (3d Cir. 1975). United States v. Layton, 90 F.R.D. 520 (N.D. Cal. 1980) (statements by defendant to psychiatrist, hired by defense counsel, were privileged); United States *ex rel.* Edney v. Smith, 425 F. Supp. 1038 (E.D.N.Y. 1976), *aff'd,* 556 F.2d 556 (2d Cir.), *cert. denied,* 431 U.S. 958 (1977). *See generally* Saltzburg, *Privileges and Professionals; Lawyers and Psychiatrists,* 66 VA. L. REV. 597 (1980).

Although communications in the presence of, or to, third parties[41] may destroy confidentiality,[42] disclosure to third parties who are outside the immediate circle of the lawyer, client, and their representatives, will not always result in a loss of the privilege. If communications are deemed to be "in furtherance of the rendition of professional legal services," the privilege may stand notwithstanding disclosure to third parties. The Advisory Committee Notes on the proposed Federal Rule 503(a)(4) noted that disclosure to spouses, parents, business associates, or joint clients might in some cases be necessary.[43]

Public disclosure, however, will constitute waiver of the privilege.[44] Where the communication involves many individuals, the claimant may have the burden of showing that it remained within privileged channels.[45]

[3] Rule 502(c)—Who May Claim the Privilege

The client, not the lawyer, holds the privilege, although under subdivision (c) the lawyer, his representatives, and specified representatives of the client may claim the privilege on behalf of the client. Subdivision (c) is identical to proposed Federal Rule 503(c) and slightly expanded 1969 *Manual* ¶ 151 *b* (2). Unless contrary evidence is presented, the lawyer's authority to claim the privilege on behalf of the client is presumed. The lawyer may not claim the privilege on his own behalf.

[4] Rule 502(d)—Exceptions

Subdivision (d) contains five "exceptions" to the privilege. Subdivisions (d)(2), claimants through same deceased client, and (d)(4), document attested by lawyer, are not likely to be encountered in military practice.

[a] Exceptions—Crime or Fraud

Under (d)(1), the client's communications concerning involvement in future crimes are not privileged.[46] The Advisory Committee's Note on the

---

[41] *See, e.g., In re* Grand Jury Proceedings, 78 F.3d 251 (6th Cir. 1996) (client's disclosure to agents of attorney's advice waived privilege).

[42] *See, e.g.,* United States v. Landof, 591 F.2d 36 (9th Cir. 1978) (another lawyer, not acting as attorney or agent, was present).

[43] *See, e.g.,* Jenkins v. Bartlett, 487 F.3d 482 (7th Cir. 2007) (president of police officers' association presence during meeting between police officer and his attorney did not defeat privilege; president was present to assist attorney).

[44] *See* Rules 510, 511.

[45] *See* Coastal Corp. v. Duncan, 86 F.R.D. 514 (D. Del. 1980).

[46] United States v. Zolin, annotated *below. See also* United States v. Lentz, 524 F.3d 501 (4th Cir. 2008) (conversation between attorney and defendant regarding reliability of another inmate regarding hiring a hit man was not privileged); *In re* Grand Jury Proceedings (Appeal of the Corporation), 87 F.3d 377 (9th Cir. 1996) (crime-fraud exception can apply even if attorney is unaware of the crime and takes no affirmative steps to further it); United States v. Richard Roe Inc., 68 F.3d 38 (2d Cir. 1995) (party seeking to use crime fraud exception must

proposed Federal Rule states that in applying (d)(1) it would be appropriate to specifically focus, through questions, on what transpired between the lawyer and the client to avoid broad inquiries into lawyer-client communications.

[b]   Exceptions—Breach of Duty

The privilege may also be waived under (d)(3) where a question concerning alleged breaches of duty, by either the client or the lawyer, are raised. In military practice this exception will normally be raised where the accused client is raising post-conviction questions regarding his lawyer's competency.[47] In those cases, the government attorney may use relevant attorney-client conversations to prove that the defense counsel provided adequate representation.

[c]   Exceptions—Joint Clients

Under (d)(5), where a lawyer has initially undertaken to represent several co-accused, communications made by one or more of them are protected in a prosecution against any of them. Only when they sue each other does the privilege disappear. It should also be remembered that under subdivision (a)(3), *above,* clients represented by different lawyers may share information with lawyers representing others with common interests.[48]

[d]   Good Faith Defense

Finally, although not referenced in the rule, if an accused claims good faith reliance on the advice of counsel as a defense this will be deemed to be a waiver of confidentiality, and the privilege will be lost.[49]

§ 502.03   Drafters' Analysis

[1]   General Rule of Privilege

Rule 502(a) continues the substance of the attorney-client privilege now

---

show at least probable cause to believe that crime or fraud has been attempted or committed and that the communications were in furtherance of that crime or fraud); *In re* Grand Jury Proceedings (United States v. Under Seal), 33 F.3d 342 (4th Cir. 1994) (party claiming attorney-client privilege not permitted to rebut prosecutor's prima facie showing of crime fraud exception before grand jury; secrecy of such proceedings justifies ex parte proceeding); *In re* Grand Jury Proceedings, 641 F.2d 199 (5th Cir. 1981) (privilege not available where there is a prima facie showing that relationship was intended to further crime; disclosure of client's name was privileged where identity would, in itself, tend to incriminate the client); *In re* Grand Jury Proceedings, 604 F.2d 798 (3d Cir. 1979) (crime-fraud exception may also be applied to work-product privilege); United States v. Rosenstein, 474 F.2d 705 (2d Cir. 1973); United States v. Shewfelt, 455 F.2d 836 (9th Cir. 1972).

[47] *See* United States v. Allen, 25 C.M.R. 8 (C.M.A. 1957) and cases annotated *below.*

[48] *See* United States v. McPartlin, 595 F.2d 1321 (7th Cir.), *cert. denied,* 444 U.S. 833 (1979).

[49] *See, e.g.,* United States v. Bilzerian, 926 F.2d 1285 (2d Cir. 1991) (privilege may be implicitly waived by asserting good faith defense). *Cf.* United States v. White, 887 F.2d 267 (D.C. Cir. 1989).

found in ¶ 151 *b* (2) of the present *Manual.* The Rule does, however, provide additional detail. Subdivision (a) is taken verbatim from subdivision (a) of Federal Rule of Evidence 503 as proposed by the Supreme Court. The privilege is only applicable when there are "confidential communications made for the purpose of facilitating the rendition of professional legal services to the client." A mere discussion with an attorney does not invoke the privilege when the discussion is not made for the purpose of obtaining professional legal services.

[2]   Definitions

[a]   Client

Rule 502(b)(1) defines a "client" as an individual or entity who receives professional legal services from a lawyer or consults a lawyer with a view to obtaining such services. The definition is taken from proposed Federal Rule 503(a)(1) as ¶ 151 *b* (2) of the present *Manual* lacks any general definition of a client.

[b]   Lawyer

Rule 502(b)(2) defines a "lawyer." The first portion of the paragraph is taken from proposed Federal Rule of Evidence 503(a)(2) and explicitly includes any person "reasonably believed by the client to be authorized" to practice law. The second clause is taken from present *Manual* ¶ 151 *b* (2) and recognizes that a "lawyer" includes "a member of the armed forces detailed, assigned, or otherwise provided to represent a person in a court-martial case or in any military investigation or proceeding" regardless of whether that person is in fact a lawyer. *See* Article 27. Thus an accused is fully protected by the privilege even if defense counsel is not an attorney.

The second sentence of the subdivision recognizes the fact, particularly true during times of mobilization, that attorneys may serve in the armed forces in a nonlegal capacity. In such a case, the individual involved is not treated as an attorney under the Rule unless the individual fits within one of the three specific categories recognized by the subdivision. Subdivision (b)(2)(b) recognizes that a service member who knows that an individual is a lawyer in civilian life may not know that the lawyer is not functioning as such in the armed forces and may seek professional legal assistance. In such a case the privilege will be applicable so long as the individual was "reasonably believed by the client to be authorized to render professional legal services to members of the armed forces."

[c]   Representative of a Lawyer

Rule 502(b)(3) is taken from proposed Federal Rule of Evidence 503(a)(3) but has been modified to recognize that personnel are "assigned" within the armed forces as well as employed. Depending upon the particular situation, a paraprofessional or secretary may be a "representative of a lawyer." *See* ¶ 151 *b* (2) of the present *Manual.*

[d]   Confidential Communication

Rule 502(b)(4) defines a "confidential" communication in terms of the intention of the party making the communication. The Rule is similar to the substance of present *Manual* ¶ 151 *b* (2) that omits certain communications from privileged status. The new Rule is somewhat broader than the present *Manual's* provision in that it protects information that is obtained by a third party through accident or design when the person claiming the privilege was not aware that a third party had access to the communication. Compare Rule ¶ 151 *a* of the present *Manual.* The broader rule has been adopted for the reasons set forth in the Advisory Committee's notes on proposed Federal Rule 504(a)(4). The provision permitting disclosure to persons in further-ance of legal services or reasonably necessary for the transmission of the communication is similar to the provision in the current manual for communications through agents.

Although ¶ 151 *c* of the present *Manual* precludes a claim of the privilege when there is transmission through wire or radio communications, the new Rules protect statements made via telephone, or, "if use of such means of communication is necessary and in furtherance of the communication," by other "electronic means of communication." Rule 511(b).

[3]   Who may Claim the Privilege

Rule 502(c) is taken from proposed Federal Rule 503(b) and expresses who may claim the lawyer-client privilege. The Rule is similar to but slightly broader than ¶ 151 *b* (2) of the present *Manual.* The last sentence of the subdivision states that "the authority of the lawyer to claim the privilege is presumed in the absence of evidence to the contrary."

The lawyer may claim the privilege on behalf of the client unless authority to do so has been withheld from the lawyer or evidence otherwise exists to show that the lawyer lacks the authority to claim the privilege.

[4]   Exceptions

Rule 502(d) sets forth the circumstances in which the lawyer-client privilege will not apply notwithstanding the general application of the privilege.

Subdivision (d)(1) excludes statements contemplating the future commis-sion of crime or fraud and combines the substance of present *Manual* ¶ 151 *b* (2) with proposed Federal Rule of Evidence 503(d). Under the exception a lawyer may disclose information given by a client when it was part of a "communication [which] clearly contemplated the future commission of a crime or fraud," and a lawyer may also disclose information when it can be objectively said that the lawyer's services "were sought or obtained to commit or plan to commit what the client knew or reasonably should have known to be a crime or fraud." The latter portion of the exception is likely to be applicable only after the commission of the offense while the former is applicable when the communication is made.

Subdivisions (d)(2) through (d)(5) provide exceptions with respect to claims through the same deceased client, breach of duty by lawyer of client, documents attested by lawyers, and communications to an attorney in a matter of common interest among joint clients. There are no parallel provisions in the present *Manual* for these rules that are taken from proposed Federal Rule 503(d). The provisions are included in the event that the circumstances described therein arise in military practice.

§ 502.04   Annotated Cases

[1]   Rule 502(a)—General Rule of Privilege

United States Court of Appeals for the Armed Forces

United States v. Romano, 46 M.J. 269 (C.A.A.F. 1997): The court held that a witness' confidential conversations with her lawyer were not waived when she testified in the accused's trial under a grant of immunity. Citing Rule 510(b), the court concluded that testifying under a grant of immunity does not waive any available privileges. The court continued, however, by noting at any retrial of the case the trial judge might consider the issue of whether the privileged information might be disclosed because the accused's constitutional right to present a defense might outweigh the witness' attorney-client privilege.

United States v. Rust, 41 M.J. 472 (C.A.A.F. 1995): The accused's conversations with a JAGC claims officer were not protected under the attorney-client privilege where the attorney had made it clear during their discussions that he represented the United States that he was investigating a possible malpractice claim involving the accused, and his investigation would be reported to others.

United States v. Ankeny, 30 M.J. 10 (C.M.A. 1990): The court held that the accused had entered into an attorney-client relationship before drug charges were preferred against him. Therefore, his confidential communications in which he admitted another offense were privileged.

Air Force Court of Criminal Appeals

United States v. Romano, 43 M.J. 523 (A.F.Ct.Crim.App. 1995): Although a government witness disclosed her confidential communication to her lawyer at an Article 32 investigation, the court concluded that, under the facts, the trial court did not err in permitting her to reclaim the privilege and refuse to again relate the communication. Citing Rule 510, the court noted that, at the time she related the communication, she was a 20-year old, junior grade airman who did not have the benefit of the presence of counsel and revealed the communication under cross-examination.

United States v. Rhea, 29 M.J. 991 (A.F.C.M.R. 1990): In concluding that the trial court properly ordered the defense to turn over incriminating evidence (a calendar annotated by the sexual abuse victim) to the prosecution, the court concluded that the evidence was not privileged. The notations were the victim's, not accused's, and they did not become privileged simply because he had given the calendar to his counsel.

Army Court of Criminal Appeals

United States v. Wallace, 14 M.J. 1019 (A.C.M.R. 1982): While riding with his JAGC officer in charge, the accused (a legal clerk) made statements concerning his involvement with drugs. Those statements were not privileged, because they were not made to the JAGC officer in his capacity as an attorney for the accused.

Navy-Marine Corps Court of Criminal Appeals

United States v. Province, 42 M.J. 821 (N.M.Ct.Crim.App. 1995): The court concluded that pre-existing documents presented by the accused to his attorney were not protected under the attorney-client privilege.

United States v. Richards, 17 M.J. 1016 (N.M.C.M.R. 1984): The court found that an accused had no intention of entering into an attorney-client relationship with the staff judge advocate when he permitted the chaplain to speak with the command about his admission of guilt. Thus, no privilege covered the communications by the chaplain to the command.

United States v. Durnen, 13 M.J. 690 (N.M.C.M.R. 1982): An accused, seeking advice on a possible divorce, visited a Navy legal services office and obtained technical information from Legalman Chief "R." At his later trial on rape charges, evidence of the contemplated divorce was offered by the defense. For the first time on appeal the defense argued that the prosecutor, Lt. *S* (an officer in the legal services office), was disqualified because he had established an attorney-client relationship with the accused. *See* Art. 27(a), UCMJ. The court rejected that argument, holding that the communications between the accused and Legalman "R" were not privileged, and even had they been, Legalman "R" was not an agent for Lt. *S* and there was no attorney-client relationship between the accused and Lt. *S.* Moreover, the court found that the defense waived any right to complain.

[2]   Rule 502(b)(3)—Lawyer's Representative

[a]   Medical Personnel Working for Counsel

United States Court of Appeals for the Armed Forces

United States v. Mansfield, 38 M.J. 415 (C.M.A. 1993): The court noted that communications to physicians or therapists may be protected if they fall within the scope of the attorney-client privilege. Here, the trial court did not err in requiring the defense expert witness to disclose such statements on cross-examination, where they served as a basis for opinion testimony concerning the accused's mental state. The attorney-client relationship, said the court, ends with respect to issues raised by the defense expert's testimony.

United States v. Tharpe, 38 M.J. 8 (C.M.A. 1993): The court reiterated its holding in *United States v. Toledo* that a psychotherapist assisting the defense counsel would probably fit within the definition of lawyer's representative in Rule 502(b)(3).

United States v. Toledo, 25 M.J. 270 (C.M.A. 1987): In dicta, the court noted that the defendant might have been able to protect his volunteered pretrial statements to a government psychologist through the lawyer-client privilege if the defense had paid for those services or if the government had appointed the psychologist to assist the defense. *See also* 26 M.J. 104 (C.M.A. 1988) (on petition for reconsideration, court adhered to earlier decision).

[b]   Other Expert Consultants for Counsel

United States Court of Appeals for the Armed Forces

United States v. Turner, 28 M.J. 487 (C.M.A. 1989): The court held that it was harmless error for the prosecutor to talk with an Army forensic toxicologist who was providing expert assistance to the defense. In this instance, the toxicologist was the defense "lawyer's representative" for purposes of Rule 502 and any information exchanged between the lawyer and the toxicologist was privileged.

Air Force Court of Criminal Appeals

United States v. Langston, 32 M.J. 894 (A.F.C.M.R. 1991): In *dicta* the court distinguished between expert consultants and expert witnesses. The former, the court said, are considered members of the defense team and may receive confidential communications. Unless they are called as witnesses by the defense, they may not be subject to pretrial interviews or to trial questioning by the other party.

[3]   Rule 502(b)(4)—Confidential Communication

United States Court of Appeals for the Armed Forces

United States v. Rhea, 33 M.J. 413 (C.M.A. 1991): When defense counsels learned that they were in possession of a calendar which had been annotated by the sexual abuse victim and which had been given to them by the accused, they sought a ruling from the trial judge on whether they were required to disclose it to the prosecution. The trial court held that they were. On appeal, the service appellate court rejected the accused's argument that his counsels' action had violated the attorney-client privilege. 29 M.J. 991 (A.F.C.M.R. 1990). The Court of Appeals affirmed, noting that the accused's production of the calendar did not amount to a confidential communication. Although the act of producing the evidence constituted a communication as to its source and authenticity, the prosecution did not attempt in any way to use either the accused's or the defense counsel's delivery to authenticate the evidence.

Air Force Court of Criminal Appeals

United States v. Smith, 33 M.J. 527 (A.F.C.M.R. 1991): In an attempt to present exculpatory evidence, the accused presented a false inventory form to his defense counsel, who in turn presented it to the prosecutor. When it was later discovered that the form was false, additional charges of obstruction of justice were preferred and the prosecution indicated that it would call the defense counsel to the stand as a witness. The court concluded that the accused's presentment of the inventory form was not a confidential communication because it was passed on with the knowledge that it would become public.

Army Court of Criminal Appeals

United States v. Nelson, 38 M.J. 710 (A.C.M.R. 1993): In an extensive discussion of the issue, the court concluded that the accused's statements during the initial discussion with his attorney, in the presence of another service member who ultimately was not represented by the same attorney, remained confidential. The court noted that although normally disclosures in the presence of third parties destroy confidentiality, the privilege may apply to joint consultations even if the attorney declines to represent one of the parties after an initial interview.

Navy-Marine Corps Court of Criminal Appeals

United States v. Evans, 35 M.J. 754 (N.M.C.M.R. 1992): The trial judge's inquiry of the accused at sentencing concerning the latter's desire for a punitive discharge impermissibly intruded in privileged attorney-client communications. The judge was attempting to determine what, if any, advice the accused's attorney had given concerning the effects of a punitive discharge.

[4]   Rule 502(c)—Who May Claim the Privilege

[a]   Privilege Survives Client's Death

Supreme Court

Swidler and Berlin v. United States, 524 U.S. 399 (1998): Pursuing an investigation into White House activities regarding "Travelgate," the Office of Independent Counsel sought discovery of statements made by Vince Foster to his lawyer. The Court ruled that the attorney-client privilege survives the death of the client and declined to recognize an "exception" to the privilege where the information was needed for a criminal investigation. In this case, said the Court, the Independent Counsel had not made a sufficient showing that the prevailing case law applying the privilege to deceased clients should be overruled.

[5]   Rule 502(d)(1)—Exceptions—Crime or Fraud

Supreme Court

United States v. Zolin, 491 U.S. 554 (1989): The Court concluded that, notwithstanding Rule 104(a) regarding privileges, a court could conduct an *in camera* review of materials allegedly protected by the attorney-client privilege to determine if the crime-fraud exception to that privilege applied. The Court added that, in order to obtain an *in camera* review, the party opposing the privilege must present sufficient threshold evidence, which has not already been ruled to be privileged, to generate a reasonable belief that the exception applied. On remand from Supreme Court, the circuit court determined that crime-fraud exception applied to conversations between counsel and accused. *United States v. Zolin*, 905 F.2d 1344 (9th Cir. 1990).

Air Force Court of Criminal Appeals

United States v. Smith, 33 M.J. 527 (A.F.C.M.R. 1991): In an attempt to exonerate himself on larceny charges, the accused presented a false inventory form to his defense counsel, who in turn presented it to the prosecutor. When it was later discovered that the form was false, additional charges of obstruction of justice were preferred and the prosecution indicated that it would call the defense counsel to the stand as a witness. Production of this information, the court said, was not privileged because it amounted to an attempt by the accused to use his lawyer to commit fraud.

[6]   Rule 502(d)(3)—Exceptions—Breach of Duty by Lawyer or Client

United States Court of Appeals for the Armed Forces

United States v. Devitt, 20 M.J. 240 (C.M.A. 1985): The accuseds were considered to have waived their attorney-client privilege when they argued on appeal that they were denied effective assistance of counsel because of multiple representation problems.

United States v. Dupas, 14 M.J. 28 (C.M.A. 1982): When a convicted accused claimed ineffective assistance of counsel, trial defense counsel declined to permit appellate defense counsel access to his files. The court noted that a claim of ineffective representation permitted an attorney to disclose only information relevant to the claim. Here it found that the attorney could not invoke the work product rule against his former client.

Army Court of Criminal Appeals

United States v. Lewis, 38 M.J. 501 (A.C.M.R. 1993): Trial defense counsel could not claim the attorney-client privilege on behalf of their client after he argued on appeal that they were ineffective in their representation. The court also held that the defense counsel could not invoke the Rules of Professional Conduct in refusing to divulge confidential communications. Those standards, said the court, permit disclosure when compelled by law, as in this case when the appellate court ordered the defense counsel to provide affidavits in response to the accused's allegations.

United States v. Gates, 36 M.J. 945 (A.C.M.R. 1993): Accused's allegations of ineffectiveness of counsel waived the attorney-client privilege with regard to disclosures which were reasonably necessary to meet the accused's allegations. 36 M.J. at 949, n.2.

United States v. Ridley, 12 M.J. 675 (A.C.M.R. 1981): After the accused wrote a letter to the convening authority complaining of his defense counsel's trial tactics, the counsel, after a number of communications with the accused, terminated their attorney-client relationship and explained his tactics to the convening authority. Citing Rule 502(d)(3), the court concluded that the accused had waived his counsel's obligation not to reveal privileged matters.

United States v. Jackson, 30 M.J. 687 (A.C.M.R. 1990): The accused waived her attorney-client privilege when she elicited the testimony of her lawyer in an attempt to establish a defense based upon advice of counsel.

[7]   Rule 502(d)(5)—Exceptions—Joint Clients

Army Court of Criminal Appeals

United States v. Nelson, 38 M.J. 710 (A.C.M.R. 1993): In an extensive discussion of the issue, the court concluded that the accused's statements during the initial discussion with his attorney, in the presence of another service member who ultimately was not represented by the same attorney, remained confidential. The court also indicated that although the accused and the other service member were "joint clients," the exception in Rule 502(d)(5) did not apply because the communication was not disclosed in an action between them.

§ 503.01   Official Text

Rule 503.   Communications to Clergy.

(a) *General rule of privilege.* A person has a privilege to refuse to disclose and to prevent another from disclosing a confidential communication by the person to a clergyman or to a clergyman's assistant, if such communication is made either as a formal act of religion or as a matter of conscience.

(b) *Definitions.* As used in this rule:

(1) A "clergyman" is a minister, priest, rabbi, chaplain, or other similar functionary of a religious organization, or an individual reasonably believed to be so by the person consulting the clergyman.

(2) A "clergyman's assistant" is a person employed by or assigned to assist a clergyman in his capacity as a spiritual advisor.

(3) A communication is "confidential" if made to a clergyman in the clergyman's capacity as a spiritual advisor or to a clergyman's assistant in the assistant's official capacity and is not intended to be disclosed to third persons other than those to whom disclosure is in furtherance of the purpose of the communication or to those reasonably necessary for the transmission of the communication.

(c) *Who may claim the privilege.* The privilege may be claimed by the person, by the guardian or conservator, or by a personal representative if the person is deceased. The clergyman or clergyman's assistant who received the communication may claim the privilege on behalf of the person. The authority of the clergyman or clergyman's assistant to do so is presumed in the absence of evidence to the contrary.

---

§ 503.02   Editorial Comment

The testimonial privilege protecting communications of a penitent to a clergyman that is now included in Rule 503, is drawn from proposed Federal Rule 506.[1]

[1]   Rule 503(a)—General Rule of Privilege

The general rule, stated in subdivision (a), continues the pre-Rules practice of not extending the privilege to all confidential communications

---

[1] *See* 5 S. Saltzburg, M. Martin, & D. Capra, FEDERAL RULES OF EVIDENCE MANUAL, Part Three, pp 18–19 (9th ed. 2006).

with clergy, but limiting it to those communications made either as a formal act of religion, such as religious confession, or as a matter of conscience. Proposed Federal Rule 506 would have extended the privilege to all confidential communications with a clergyman in his professional capacity. The Military Rule is likely to be as protective.

Subdivision (a) seems consistent with what little military and federal case law exists.[2] The Rule differs from pre-Rules law in that the holder of the privilege may prevent disclosure by a third party eavesdropper. *See also* (b)(2).

[2] Rule 503(b)—Definitions

The definitions of "clergyman," clergyman's assistant," and "confidential" communication are addressed in subdivision (b). The definition of clergyman specifically notes those individuals who may qualify. It is not so broad as to include self-styled or self-determined ministers. In this regard the Advisory Committee Note on the proposed Federal Rule states that:

> A fair construction of the language requires that the person to whom the status is sought to be attached be regularly engaged in activities conforming at least in a general way with those of a Catholic priest, Jewish rabbi, or minister of an established Protestant denomination, though not necessarily on a full time basis. No further specification seems possible in view of the lack of licensing and certification procedures for clergymen.[3]

The communications also qualify if made to a person reasonably believed by the penitent to be a "clergyman"—*see* the comparable "reasonable belief" provision in Rule 502(b)(2)—or if made to a clergyman's assistant.[4]

In 2007, Rule 503(b) was amended to include to a new provision which defines "clergyman's assistant."[5] Under Rule 503(a), confidential communications made by a person to a clergyman's assistant are as protected as though they were made to a clergyman. Thus, the privilege in the military is

---

[2] *See, e.g., In re* Grand Jury Investigation, 918 F.2d 374 (3d Cir. 1990) (statements to Lutheran minister during family counseling). United States v. Kidd, 20 C.M.R. 713 (A.B.R. 1955) (chaplain's stated opinion of accused revealed no confidences relating to matters of faith or conscience); United States v. Wells, 446 F.2d 2 (2d Cir. 1971) (letter given to priest was not privileged); Mullen v. United States, 263 F.2d 275 (D.C. Cir. 1958) (defendant's confession to Lutheran minister was privileged).

[3] *See* 5 S. Saltzburg, M. Martin, & D. Capra, FEDERAL RULES OF EVIDENCE MANUAL, Part Three, p 18 (9th ed. 2006). *See also* Varner v. Stovall, 500 F.3d 491 (6th Cir. 2007) (state did not violate First Amendment by limiting clergy member privilege to ministers in official capacity and not extending privilege to all religious communications).

[4] *See generally* Note, *Catholic Sisters, Irregularly Ordained Women and the Clergy Penitent Privilege,* 9 U.C.D.L. REV. 523 (1976).

[5] E.O. 13447, September 28, 2007. The Drafters renumbered existing 503(b)(2) as (b)(3) and included the definition in new 503(b)(2).

potentially broader than similar privileges recognized in the federal courts and in state practice. The original Drafters' Analysis noted that, as in the 1969 Manual for Courts-Martial, extending the privilege to communications made to chaplain's assistants was "in specific recognition of the nature of the military chaplaincy."[6]

In order to claim the privilege for communications to a clergyman's assistant, the assistant must have been "employed by" or "assigned to" a clergyman. Depending on the religion or religious organization involved, the person holding that position may not actually be called an "assistant." The key here is that in many religious organizations, the roles and duties of the clergy have been extended to other persons, who often have specialized training—short of full ordination or certification—and are authorized by the organization to provide spiritual counseling.

The definition on its face does not appear to cover the volunteer—someone who provides assistance to a clergy member but is not formally employed, or assigned, to the clergy member. Before the amendment, an argument could have been made that a communication to a volunteer clergyman's assistant would be protected. That reading would have been consistent with the policies behind the privilege. If the clergy member demonstrates acceptance of the help of a volunteer, arguably the volunteer then is "employed" by the clergy member. There is nothing in the language of the amendment to require that an assistant be a paid employee.

The definition of confidential communications is found in subdivision (b)(3). It parallels a similar provision in Rule 502(b)(4). As we noted in our discussion of that provision, the definition turns on the penitent's intent and is broad enough to include oral and written statements if made to the clergyman in confidence for the purpose of seeking spiritual counseling. If the statements were made for non-spiritual purposes, the privilege does not exist.[7] Note that the privilege may exist even if third persons are present or later hear the communication—if the disclosure to those persons was in furtherance of the purpose of the communication or was to those persons reasonably necessary for the transmission.[8]

---

[6] *See* Drafters' Analysis, Rule 503, *below.* Although the Drafters' Analysis for the 2007 amendment provides no reason for now including a definition for the term, presumably a question had been raised regarding application of the privilege for communications to those assisting members of the clergy.

[7] *See* United States v. Coleman, 26 M.J. 407 (C.M.A. 1988), annotated *below. See also* United States v. Gordon, 655 F.2d 478 (2d Cir. 1981) (defendant's statements to priest concerning business transaction were not privileged).

[8] *See, e.g., In re* Grand Jury Investigation, 918 F.2d 374 (3d Cir. 1990) (privilege applied in statements made to family counseling sessions conducted by Lutheran minister with others present).

[3]   Rule 503(c)—Who May Claim the Privilege

Under subdivision (c) the privilege may be claimed by the clergyman, not on his own behalf but on behalf of the individual. The Rule recognizes the prima facie authority on the part of a clergyman to so claim the privilege.

The Rule contains no specific exceptions.[9] In particular, the penitent's stated intent to commit a crime does not negate the privilege. The Advisory Committee's Note on 506(b), the counterpart to the general rule in subdivision (a), states that "[t]he nature of what may reasonably be considered spiritual advice makes it unnecessary to include in the rule a specific exception for communications in furtherance of crime or fraud as in [the lawyer-client privilege]." *See* Rule 510 for waiver of privilege through voluntary disclosure.

§ 503.03   Drafters' Analysis

[1]   General Rule of Privilege

Rule 503(a) states the basic rule of privilege for communications to clergy and is taken from proposed Federal Rule of Evidence 506(b) and present *Manual* ¶ 151 *b* (2). Like the present *Manual,* the Rule protects communications to a clergyman's assistant in specific recognition of the nature of the military chaplaincy, and deals only with communications "made either as a formal act of religion or as a matter of conscience."

[2]   Definitions

[a]   Clergyman

Rule 503(b)(1) is taken from proposed Federal Rule of Evidence 506(a)(1) but has been modified to include specific reference to a chaplain. The Rule does not define "a religious organization" and leaves resolution of that question to precedent and the circumstances of the case. "Clergyman" includes individuals of either sex.

[b]   Confidential

Rule 503(b)(2) is taken generally from proposed Federal Rule of Evidence 506(a)(2) but has been expanded to include communications to a clergyman's assistant and to explicitly protect disclosure of a privileged communication when "disclosure is in furtherance of the purpose of the communication or to those reasonably necessary for the transmission of the communication." The Rule is thus consistent with the definition of "confidential" used in the lawyer-client privilege, Rule 502(b)(4), and recognizes that military life often requires transmission of communications through third parties. The proposed Federal Rule's limitation of the privilege to

---

[9] *See* Cooper, *Chaplains Caught In The Middle: The Military's "Absolute" Penitent-Clergy Privilege Meets State "Mandatory" Child Abuse Reporting Laws,* 49 NAVAL L. REV. 128 (2002).

communications made "privately" was deleted in favor of the language used in the actual Military Rule for the reasons indicated. The Rule is somewhat more protective than the present *Manual* because of its application to statements that although intended to be confidential are overheard by others. *See* Rules 502(b)(4) and 510(a) and the Analysis thereto.

[3]   Who may Claim the Privilege

Rule 503(c) is derived from proposed Federal Rule of Evidence 506(c) and includes the substance of the present *Manual* ¶ 151 *b* (2) which provides that the privilege may be claimed by the "penitent." The Rule supplies additional guidance as to who may actually claim the privilege and is consistent with the other Military Rules of Evidence relating to privileges. *See* Rules 502(c); 504(b)(3); 505(c); 506(c).

§ 503.04   Drafters' Analysis (2007 Amendment)

2007 Amendment: The previous subsection (2) of MRE 503(b) was renumbered subsection (3) and the new subsection (2) was inserted to define the term "clergyman's assistant."

§ 503.05   Annotated Cases

United States Court of Appeals for the Armed Forces

United States v. Shelton, 64 M.J. 32 (C.A.A.F. 2006): The accused's wife suspected that the accused had had sexual contact with her 4-year-old daughter and talked to her family minister about the matter. The accused met with the minister and admitted his acts of misconduct; later in a meeting with both the minister and his wife, he repeated his statements. His wife later reported the incriminating statements to the installation's abuse hotline, which in turn reported the matter to the CID. The Court of Criminal Appeals held that the accused's statements were not protected under the clergy member privilege, but the Court of Appeals reversed. The court concluded that the accused's incriminating statements were protected under the clergy penitent privilege because the accused's conversation with the minister was a matter of conscience and were made to the minister in his spiritual capacity. Finally, the court concluded that the accused had intended for his communications to be confidential, even though his wife had been present. She had been present, the court noted, because the minister had concluded that her presence was necessary to further the purpose of the accused's meeting with the minister.

United States v. Napoleon, 46 M.J. 279 (C.M.A. 1997): While in pretrial confinement, the accused was visited by an NCO who also happened to be a lay minister at the air base chapel. The court rejected the argument that statements made by the accused to the NCO were protected under the clergyman privilege. Noting that the definition of "lay minister" is broad, the court concluded that, under the facts, the NCO was not a clergyman as defined in Rule 503. Further, it appeared that during the NCO's visit the accused was seeking emotional assistance rather than religious "guidance and forgiveness."

United States v. Coleman, 26 M.J. 407 (C.M.A. 1988): The accused made incriminating statements to his father-in-law, who was a minister, concerning the state of his marriage and the fact that he had committed indecent sexual acts on his nine-year-old daughter. The court concluded that the accused's statements were neither made as a formal act of religion nor as a matter of conscience. Instead, the accused was seeking consolation and help in his capacity as a son-in-law.

Air Force Court of Criminal Appeals

United States v. Garries, 19 M.J. 845 (A.F.C.M.R. 1985): The court ruled that the NCO to whom the accused had made statements was not a clergyman within the definition of Rule 503 nor did the accused reasonably believe him to be one. The NCO was a deacon in the accused's church and, although he had later become an ordained minister, at the time of the communications he was not authorized to give any spiritual counseling.

Navy-Marine Corps Court of Criminal Appeals

United States v. Isham, 48 M.J. 603 (N.M.Ct.Crim.App. 1998): The accused made incriminating statements to a chaplain as part of a counseling session designed to deal with his stress and depression. When the accused made statements indicating that he might hurt himself or others, the chaplain interrupted him and explained that, if he learned of such threats, he would have to report them to the authorities. Noting the paucity of military cases discussing the clergy-penitent privilege, the court held that the trial court committed reversible error in admitting the accused's statement to the chaplain. Under the circumstances, the accused's statements were confidential and thus protected under the privilege.

United States v. Richards, 17 M.J. 1016 (N.M.C.M.R. 1984): Although an accused's admissions to a chaplain were privileged because they involved a "matter of conscience," the court found that the accused waived the privilege when he agreed that the chaplain should discuss the matter with the legal officer.

§ 504.01   Official Text

Rule 504.   Husband-Wife Privilege.

(a) *Spousal incapacity.*   A person has a privilege to refuse to testify against his or her spouse.

(b) *Confidential communication made during marriage.*

(1) *General rule of privilege.*   A person has a privilege during and after the marital relationship to refuse to disclose, and to prevent another from disclosing, any confidential communication made to the spouse of the person while they were husband and wife and not separated as provided by law.

(2) *Definition.*   A communication is "confidential" if made privately by any person to the spouse of the person and is not intended to be disclosed to third persons other than those reasonably necessary for transmission of the communication.

(3) *Who may claim the privilege.*   The privilege may be claimed by the spouse who made the communication or by the other spouse on his or her behalf. The authority of the latter spouse to do so is presumed in the absence of evidence of a waiver. The privilege will not prevent disclosure of the communication at the request of the spouse to whom the communication was made if that spouse is an accused regardless of whether the spouse who made the communication objects to its disclosure.

(c) *Exceptions.*

(1) *Spousal incapacity only.*   There is no privilege under subdivision (a) when, at the time the testimony of one of the parties to the marriage is to be introduced in evidence against the other party, the parties are divorced or the marriage has been annulled.

(2) *Spousal incapacity and confidential communications.* There is no privilege under subdivisions (a) or (b):

(A) In proceedings in which one spouse is charged with a crime against the person or property of the other spouse or a child of either, or with a crime against the person or property of a third person committed in the course of committing a crime against the other spouse;

(B) When the marital relationship was entered into with no intention of the parties to live together as spouses, but only for the purpose of using the purported marital relationship as a sham, and with respect to the privilege in subdivision (a), the relationship remains a sham at the time the testimony or statement of one of the parties is to be introduced against the other; or with respect to the privilege in subdivision (b), the relationship was a sham at the time of the communication; or

(C) In proceedings in which a spouse is charged, in accordance with Articles 133 and 134, with importing the other spouse as an alien for prostitution or other immoral purpose in violation of 8 U.S.C. § 1328; with transporting the other spouse in interstate commerce for immoral purposes or other offense in violation of 18 U.S.C. §§ 2421–2424; or with violation of such other similar statutes under which such privilege may not be claimed in the trial of criminal cases in the United States district courts.

(d) *Definitions.* As used in this rule:

(1) The term "a child of either" includes not only a biological child, adopted child, or ward of one of the spouses but also includes a child who is under the permanent or temporary physical custody of one of the spouses, regardless of the existence of a legal parent-child relationship. For purposes of this rule only, a child is: (i) an individual under the age of 18; or (ii) an individual with a mental handicap who functions under the age of 18.

(2) The term "temporary physical custody" includes instances where a parent entrusts his or her child with another. There is no minimum amount of time necessary to establish temporary physical custody nor must there be a written agreement. Rather the focus is on the parent's agreement with another for assuming parental responsibility for the child. For example, temporary physical custody may include instances where a parent entrusts another with the care of their child for recurring care or during absences due to temporary duty or deployments.

§ 504.02   Editorial Comment

The military and federal courts have generally recognized two distinct privileges related to marital relationships. One relates to the capacity of one spouse to testify against the other. The second relates to confidential communications made during the marriage. Rule 504 addresses both.[1]

[1]   Rule 504(a)—Spousal Incapacity

The first privilege in Rule 504 is located in subdivision (a)—the capacity

---

[1] *See A Critique Of The Marital Privileges: An Examination of the Marital Privileges in the United States Military Through the State and Federal Approaches to the Marital Privileges*, 36 VAL. U. L. REV. 119 (2001).

of a spouse to testify.[2] It adopts the approach of *Trammel v. United States,*[3] and changes the pre-Rules practice that permitted each spouse to prevent the other from testifying.[4] Under the rule, only the testifying spouse may decide whether or not to testify, and even that choice is denied under 504(c)(1) if at the time of the testimony the parties are divorced or the marriage has been annulled. The privilege is available, however, while the parties are married, even if the testimony in question involves events occurring prior to a *valid* (not a sham) marriage.[5]

Communications are covered by the other marital privilege, in Rule 504(b), which belongs to the communicating spouse. The testifying spouse, therefore, would not necessarily be free to relate confidential communications made by the accused spouse during the marriage. That privilege would belong to the accused.[6]

The rule does not address the issue of whether an accused could ever attempt to block the testifying spouse from taking the stand, if it appears that the government has in any way coerced the spouse to do so—for example through a grant of immunity or other promise of non-prosecution. The argument in that case would be that the testifying spouse had not voluntarily waived the privilege not to testify.[7] One could argue that the underlying assumption of *Trammel,* is that the testifying spouse takes the stand voluntarily. On the other hand, even assuming the testifying spouse is not doing so voluntarily, it is not clear that the accused spouse would have any standing to object; the capacity privilege in Rule 504(a) arguably belongs only to the testifying spouse.

---

[2] Although Rule 504 is titled "Husband-Wife Privilege," some commentators treat the spousal capacity privilege as an issue related to "competency" of a witness to testify. *See* 1 MCCORMICK, § 66 at 317 (6th ed. 2006). And Rule 504(a) itself is titled "Spousal Incapacity." Other similar rules label the provision as a "privilege." *See* Texas Rule of Evidence 504(b) ("Privilege Not to Testify in Criminal Case"). Regardless of the label, the result is the same—a person may decide whether or not to testify against his or her spouse.

[3] 445 U.S. 40 (1980). *See also* United States v. Premises Known as 281 Syosset Woodbury Road, Woodbury, N.Y., 71 F.3d 1067 (2d Cir. 1995) (adverse testimonial privilege generally only applies to criminal proceedings).

[4] *See, e.g.,* United States v. Lovell, 8 M.J. 613 (A.F.C.M.R. 1979); United States v. Gibbs, 4 M.J. 922 (A.F.C.M.R. 1978); United States v. Seiber, 31 C.M.R. 106 (C.M.A. 1961).

[5] *See, e.g., In re* Grand Jury Proceedings (Emo), 777 F.2d 508 (9th Cir. 1985) (marriage of accused and witness two days before trial was not a sham where the couple had lived together for two years and was entered in good faith).

[6] *See* Rule 504(b)(1).

[7] *See generally* Lempert, *A Right to Every Woman's Evidence,* 66 IOWA L. REV. 725 (1981) (arguing that government can pressure spouse into testifying). *Cf.* Texas Rule of Evidence 504(b) (requiring that spousal testimony be voluntary).

[2]   Rule 504(b)—Confidential Communications Made During Marriage

A spouse's privilege to prevent disclosure of confidential communications is provided in subdivision (b), which is comparable to the privileges in Rules 502 and 503. This privilege is distinct from the capacity privilege, although both may arise in the same case.

The general rule for marital communications is stated in subdivision (b)(1). An individual may forever block disclosure of confidential communications made to one's spouse during their marriage, assuming the marriage was valid.[8] The question of whether a valid marriage existed is a threshold question for the judge to decide under Rule 104(a).

The privilege applies even after the marriage has ended.[9] But any communications made when the parties were legally separated are not covered by this provision.[10] If the parties are still married, though separated at the time of trial, a testifying spouse might refuse to testify against the accused spouse under the incapacity privilege, unless it is barred under subdivision (c).

Communications under subdivision (b)(2) are considered confidential only if made in private.[11] This is a variance on comparable provisions in Rules 502(b)(4) and 503(b)(2) that contain no "privacy" requirement; the presence of third parties in those instances will not in itself negate the confidentiality. Here the presence of third parties generally negates any presumption of privacy.[12] Normally, the burden of proving that a privilege exists rests upon the party claiming the privilege. But because the case law

---

[8] United States v. Rivera, 527 F.3d 891 (9th Cir. 2008) (communications between defendant and woman were not protected marital communications; only evidence was that they had children together); United States v. Hamilton, 19 F.3d 350 (7th Cir. 1994) (spousal privilege not invoked until valid marriage is proven).

[9] Pereira v. United States, 347 U.S. 1 (1954).

[10] *See, e.g.,* United States v. Porter, 986 F.2d 1014 (6th Cir. 1993) (court joined Second, Seventh, Eighth, and Ninth Circuits in holding that privilege does not extend to communications after permanent separation but before legal divorce; search for truth outweighs protection of communications between adults found to be permanently separated); United States v. Roberson, 859 F.2d 1376 (9th Cir. 1988) (marital communications privilege not applicable to statements made during period where marriage had become irreconcilable; defendant had filed for divorce and moved out of home); United States v. Witness Before Grand Jury, 791 F.2d 234 (2d Cir. 1986) (marriage must be "viable"; here no privilege where during last 11 years of 23-year marriage couple had been separated).

[11] *See also* United States v. Archer, 733 F.2d 354 (5th Cir. 1984) (marital privilege does not block testimony of third person regarding out-of-court statements made by one spouse about the other).

[12] *See, e.g.,* Pool v. United States, 260 F.2d 57 (9th Cir. 1958). *Cf.* United States v. Thompson, 716 F.2d 248 (4th Cir. 1983) (marital communications privilege presumptively applies to conversations between spouses).

recognizes that private marital communications are presumptively confidential,[13] the burden of proving the lack of confidentiality shifts to the party opposing the privilege.[14]

Disclosures to those third parties who are reasonably required to transmit the intended confidential communications are permitted, however. As in Rules 502 and 503, the communicating spouse may prevent disclosure of any confidential communications (made in private) that were overheard by third parties.[15]

Subdivision (b)(3) makes it clear that the privilege to prevent disclosure by anyone of confidential communications is held by the spouse who made them. The privilege may be claimed either by the communicating spouse or by the other in the former's behalf; the authority to do so is presumed. However, according to (b)(3), the privilege will not prevent an accused from disclosing or requiring his spouse to disclose communications, even if they were made by that spouse to the accused and the communicating spouse objects. Many common law cases give the privilege to both spouses, but this Rule is more limited.

[3] Rule 504(c)—Exceptions

Subdivision (c) lists several situations where either or both the "spousal incapacity" privilege in subdivision (a) and the "confidential communications" privilege in subdivision (b) may not be invoked. Also, as noted earlier, a spouse has no grounds to refuse to testify against an accused spouse where the marriage has ended. *See* (c)(1).

Under (c)(2) both privileges fall where anti-marital acts are involved. The provisions of (c)(2)(A) and (c)(2)(C) are for the most part consistent with 1969 *Manual* ¶ 148 *e,* except that under (c)(2)(A) a crime against the child of either spouse now will also negate both privileges under this Rule.[16] This provision rests in part on *Wyatt v. United States.*[17] Violation of federal statutes similar to those noted in (c)(2)(C) will also negate both privileges.

In an extensive discussion of the issue, the Court of Appeals for the Armed

---

[13] Blau v. United States, 340 U.S. 332 (1951).

[14] *See* United States v. McCollum, 58 M.J. 323 (C.A.A.F. 2003), annotated, *below.*

[15] United States v. Neal, 532 F. Supp. 942 (D. Colo. 1982) (husband did not waive privilege when FBI, with his wife's consent, eavesdropped on phone conversations).

[16] *See, e.g.*, United States v. Banks 556 F.3d 967 (9th Cir. 2009) (under facts, grandchild was not the functional equivalent of child or step-child; therefore, exception did not apply); United States v. White, 974 F.2d. 1135 (9th Cir. 1992) (threat to kill spouse and children was not privileged).

[17] 362 U.S. 525 (1960). *See also* proposed Federal Rule of Evidence 505(c)(1), included in 5 S. Saltzburg, M. Martin, & D. Capra, FEDERAL RULES OF EVIDENCE MANUAL, Part Three, pp 16–18 (9th ed. 2006).

Forces held in *United States v. McCollum*,[18] that the exception in Rule 504(c)(2)(A), regarding children, is to be read literally and therefore did not apply where the minor victim was the wife's sister. The court rejected the argument that the underlying policies supporting the exception should be applied where the crime is against a "de facto" child of either spouse. As noted in the discussion, below, the Rule was amended to expand the definition of child.[19]

The exception stated in subdivision (c)(2)(B) limits application of both privileges where the marriage is a sham. For purposes of the capacity of a spouse to testify under (a), a sham marriage in effect at the time a witness is called to testify negates the privilege.[20] The privilege for confidential communications under (b) does not exist if at the time of the communications the marriage was a sham even if it later ripened into a valid marriage. It is apparent that military judges will have to engage in some preliminary fact-finding under Rule 104(a) as to the validity of the marriage when ruling on claims of both marital privileges.

Although the Rule does not cover the matter, some federal courts have recognized a "joint participant" exception to both the marital communication privilege[21] and the spousal immunity privilege[22] where the spouses are partners in crime. The rationale for the exception generally rests on the proposition that the public's interest in justice and revelation of truth outweigh domestic tranquility and the public's interest in maintaining marriages. Several military courts have adopted the exception.[23] A good

---

[18] 58 M.J. 323 (2003), annotated, *below.*

[19] *See generally* Aldridge, *To Catch a Predator or to Save His Marriage: Advocating for an Expansive Child Abuse Exception to the Marital Privileges in Federal Courts,* 78 FORDHAM L. REV. 1761 (2010); Goodno, *Protecting "Any Child": The Use of the Confidential-Marital-Communications Privilege in Child-Molestation Cases,* 59 U. KAN. L. REV. 1 (2010); Richard, *Expanding The "Child Of Either" Exception To The Husband-Wife Privilege Under The New M.R.E. 504(d),* 60 A.F. L. REV. 155 (2007).

[20] Lutwak v. United States, 344 U.S. 604 (1953).

[21] *See* United States v. Miller, 588 F.3d 897 (5th Cir. 2009) (communications not privileged where conversation related to joint criminal activity); United States v. Evans, 966 F.2d 398 (8th Cir. 1992) (private interspousal statements about ongoing drug conspiracy fell into partner-in-crime exception); United States v. Estes, 793 F.2d 465 (2d Cir. 1986) (holding that the defendant's statement to his wife following a completed theft were within the marital communications privilege, since the wife could not be involved as an accessory after the fact unless she knew that a theft had taken place and the communication of that fact was a necessary prerequisite to her involvement); United States v. Broome, 732 F.2d 363 (4th Cir. 1984); United States v. Ammar, 714 F.2d 238 (3d Cir. 1983).

[22] United States v. Clark, 712 F.2d 299 (7th Cir. 1983). *Cf. In re* Grand Jury Subpoena, 755 F.2d 1022 (2d Cir. 1985); United States v. Ammar, 714 F.2d 238, 258 (3d Cir. 1983); Appeal of Malfitano, 633 F.2d 276 (3d Cir. 1980).

[23] *See* United States v. Smith, 30 M.J. 1022 (A.F.C.M.R. 1990); United States v. Martel, 19 M.J. 917 (A.C.M.R. 1985).

argument can be made, however, that under military due process standards, military courts should choose the more protective rule (in this case the broader privilege under 504 that includes no such exception). This Rule may be a good candidate for revision to reflect the Federal Rule.

[4]   Rule 504(d)—Definitions

In 2007, Rule 504 was amended by adding a new subsection (d), which is intended to clarify terminology in Rule 504(c)(2)(A). That provision creates an exception for both the confidential communications privilege and the spousal incapacity privilege. Under that rule, there is no privilege for marital confidential communications, and a spouse cannot refuse to testify against the accused-spouse, in those cases where "one spouse is charged with a crime against the person or property of the other spouse or a *child of either*." As originally written, the Rule did not further specify what was meant by the term "child of either."

The term was addressed, however, in *United States v. McCollum*.[24] In *McCollum*, the accused was charged with a sexual offense against his wife's 14-year-old sister, who was living temporarily with the accused and his wife. When confronted by his wife, the accused admitted his conduct. The Air Force Court of Criminal Appeals concluded that the accused's statements to his wife were not privileged, in part, because he had consented to the disclosure of his statements. On appeal, the Court of Appeals for the Armed Forces specified the issue of whether there was a "de facto child" exception to the husband-wife privilege, and if so, whether it applied to the accused's case.

In an extensive discussion of the issue, the court concluded that there was no "de facto child" exception in Rule 503(c)(2)(A), thus rejecting the government's argument that the term "child of either" included a child under the care or custody of one of the spouses. The court said that in construing the language of a statute or rule, it should be given its common and approved usage and the language of Rule 504 did not include any relationship other than a legal or biological connection between one of the spouses and the child. The court also noted that the President could have provided a more complete definition to connote not only a legal or biological relationship, but also a custodial relationship.[25]

The President did so in the 2007 amendment. First, Rule 504(d)(1) now

---

[24]   United States v. McCollum, 58 M.J. 323 (C.A.A.F. 2003).

[25]   The court recognized that five states had adopted some form of exception for offenses against children. Only Texas, the court noted, had adopted an exception for a crime against "any child." The others required some sort of protection for foster children. United States v. McCollum, 58 M.J. 323, 341 (C.A.A.F. 2003). *Cf.* United States v. Banks 556 F.3d 967 (9th Cir. 2009) (dissenting opinions notes that "in twenty-six jurisdictions, there is no privilege where the accused has been charged with criminal abuse of *any child,* regardless of whether there is a familial affiliation with the victim-child," emphasis in original).

includes a definition for "child." The definition includes not only a person who is under the age of 18, Rule 504(d)(1)(i), but also an older person with a mental handicap who "functions" as a child, Rule 504(d)(1)(ii). Determining a person's chronological age should normally not present any difficulties. But a party invoking the definition of child in Rule 504(d)(1)(ii), may need expert testimony to demonstrate that the adult victim suffers from a mental impairment and is functioning as someone under the age of 18.

Second, Rule 504(d)(1) expands the definition of "child of either" to include not only children who are legally the children of one of the spouses, but also children who are in the "permanent or temporary physical custody" of one of the spouses, the so-called "de facto child" discussed in *McCollum*. The Drafters' Analysis uses that term and notes that before the amendment the "distinction between legal and 'de facto' children resulted in unwarranted discrimination among child victims and ran counter to the public policy of protecting children by addressing disparate treatment among child victims entrusted to another."

Including the term "temporary physical custody" in Rule 504(d)(1), required yet another subsection to define that term. According to Rule 504(d)(2), in determining whether a spouse had temporary physical custody of a child, the length of the custody is not important. Rather the focus is on the spouse's "agreement" to assume parental responsibility for the child.

As written, the new provisions expand the coverage of the exception and should include foster children, an issue mentioned but not decided by the court in *McCollum*. And while the amendment broadens the coverage of the exception in Rule 504(c)(2)(A), and promotes the policy of protecting children, it still leaves gaps. By limiting the exception to those cases where the accused or the accused's spouse has "custody" of a child, the drafters have not addressed the case where the child victim is merely visiting or playing with children of either spouse—where there may not be an "agreement."[26]

§ 504.03   Drafters' Analysis

[1]   Spousal Incapacity

Rule 504(a) is taken generally from *Trammel v. United States,* 445 U.S. 40

---

[26] As the court in *McCollum* noted, Texas has adopted an exception to the martial privileges that applies to any child victim, regardless of a relationship to either spouse. As originally drafted Texas Rule 504, the victim exception required some connection to the household. An amendment removed that restriction, thus expanding the scope of the exception. *See* Schlueter & Barton, TEXAS RULES OF EVIDENCE MANUAL § 504.02[7][e] (8th ed. 2009) (noting that amendment to Rule, extending exception to "any" minor child, was based on Ludwig v. State, 931 S.W.2d 239 (Tex. Crim. App. 1996), where court could not determine extent of exception from face of rule; court relied on extrajudicial sources and determined that drafters had intended to extend exception to any minor child).

(1980) and significantly changes military law in this area. Under present law, *see* present *Manual* ¶ 148 *e,* each spouse has a privilege to prevent the use of the other spouse as an adverse witness. Under the new rule, the *witness* spouse is the holder of the privilege and may choose to testify or not to testify as the witness spouse sees fit. *But see* Rule 504(c) (exceptions to the privilege). Implicit in the rule is the presumption that when a spouse chooses to testify against the other spouse the marriage no longer needs the protection of the privilege. Rule 504(a) must be distinguished from Rule 504(b), *Confidential communication made during marriage,* which deals with communications rather than the ability to testify generally at trial.

Although the witness spouse ordinarily has a privilege to refuse to testify against the accused spouse, under certain circumstances no privilege may exist, and the spouse may be compelled to testify. *See* Rule 504(c).

[2]   Confidential Communication Made During Marriage

Rule 504(b) deals with communications made during a marriage and is distinct from a spouse's privilege to refuse to testify pursuant to Rule 504(a). *See* present *Manual* ¶ 151 *b* (2).

[a]   General Rule of Privilege

Rule 504(b)(1) sets forth the general rule of privilege for confidential spousal communications and provides that a spouse may prevent disclosure of any confidential spousal communication made during marriage even though the parties are no longer married at the time that disclosure is desired. The accused may always require that the confidential spousal communication be disclosed. Rule 504(b)(3).

No privilege exists under subdivision (b) if the communication was made when the spouses were legally separated.

[b]   Definition

Rule 504(b)(2) defines "confidential" in a fashion similar to the definition utilized in Rules 502(b)(4) and 503(b)(2). The word "privately" has been added to emphasize that the presence of third parties is not consistent with the spousal privilege, and the reference to third parties found in Rules 502 and 503 has been omitted for the same reason. Rule 504(b)(2) extends the definition of "confidential" to statements disclosed to third parties who are "reasonably necessary for transmission of the communication." This recognizes that circumstances may arise, especially in military life where spouses may be separated by great distances or by operational activities, in which transmission of a communication via third parties may be reasonably necessary.

[c]   Who may Claim the Privilege

Rule 504(b)(3) is consistent with present *Manual* ¶ 151 *b* (2) and gives the privilege to the spouse who made the communication. The accused may, however, disclose the communication even though the communication was made to the accused.

[3]   Exceptions

[a]   Spousal Incapacity Only

Rule 504(c)(1) provides exceptions to the spousal incapacity rule of Rule 504(a). The rule is taken from present *Manual* ¶ 148 *e* and declares that a spouse may not refuse to testify against the other spouse when the marriage has been terminated by divorce or annulment. Annulment has been added to the present military rule as being consistent with its purpose. Separation of spouses via legal separation or otherwise does not affect the privilege of a spouse to refuse to testify against the other spouse. For other circumstances in which a spouse may be compelled to testify against the other spouse *see* Rule 504(c)(2).

Confidential communications are not affected by the termination of a marriage.

[b]   Spousal Incapacity and Confidential Communications

Rule 504(c)(2) prohibits application of the spousal privilege, whether in the form of spousal incapacity or in the form of a confidential communication, when the circumstances specified in paragraph (2) are applicable. Subparagraphs (A) and (C) deal with anti-marital acts, *e.g.*, acts that are against the spouse and thus the marriage. The Rule expressly provides that when such an act is involved a spouse may not refuse to testify. This provision is taken from proposed Federal Rule 505(c)(1) and reflects in part the Supreme Court's decision in *Wyatt v. United States*, 362 U.S. 525 (1960). *See also Trammel v. United States*, 445 U.S. 40 (1980). The Rule thus recognizes society's overriding interest in prosecution of anti-marital offenses and the probability that a spouse may exercise sufficient control, psychological or otherwise, to be able to prevent the other spouse from testifying voluntarily. The Rule is similar to present *Manual* ¶ 148 *e* but has deleted the *Manual's* limitation of the exceptions to the privilege to matters occurring after marriage or otherwise unknown to the spouse as being inconsistent with the intent of the exceptions.

Rule 504(c)(2)(B) is derived from paragraphs 148 *e* and 151 *b* (2) of the present *Manual*. The provision prevents application of the privilege as to privileged communications if the marriage was a sham at the time of the communication, and prohibits application of the spousal incapacity privilege if the marriage was begun as a sham and is a sham at the time the testimony of the witness is to be offered. Consequently, the Rule recognizes for purposes of subdivision (a) that a marriage that began as a sham may have ripened into a valid marriage at a later time. The intent of the provision is to prevent individuals from marrying witnesses in order to effectively silence them.

§ 504.04   Drafters' Analysis (2007 Amendment)

2007 Amendment: (d) Definition. Rule 504(d) modifies the rule and is intended to afford additional protection to children. Previously, the term "a child of either," referenced in Rule 504(c)(2)(A), did not include a "de facto" child or a child who is under the physical custody of one of the spouses but lacks a formal legal parent-child relationship with at least one of the spouses. See *United States v. McCollum,* 58 M.J. 323 (C.A.A.F. 2003). Prior to this amendment, an accused could not invoke the spousal privilege to prevent disclosure of communications regarding crimes committed against a child with whom he or his spouse had a formal, legal parent-child relationship; however, the accused could invoke the privilege to prevent disclosure of communications where there was not a formal, legal parent-child relationship. This distinction between legal and "de facto" children resulted in unwarranted discrimination among child victims and ran counter to the public policy of protecting children by addressing disparate treatment among child victims entrusted to another. The "marital communications privilege should not prevent 'a properly outraged spouse with knowledge from testifying against a perpetrator' of child abuse within the home regardless of whether the child is part of that family." *United States v. McCollum,* 58 M.J. 323, 342 n.6 (C.A.A.F. 2003) (citing *United States v. Bahe,* 128 F.3d 1440, 1446 (10th Cir. 1997).

§ 504.05   Annotated Cases

[1]   Rule 504(a)—Spousal Incapacity

United States Court of Appeals for the Armed Forces

United States v. Hughes, 28 M.J. 391 (C.M.A. 1989): Noting that the spousal incapacity privilege in Rule 504 only covers in-court testimony, the court ruled that a nonconfidential out-of-court statement by the accused's wife could be introduced at trial to corroborate his confession.

[2]   Rule 504(b)—Confidential Communications Made During Marriage

United States Court of Appeals for the Armed Forces

United States v. Durbin, 68 M.J. 271 (C.A.A.F. 2010): The accused's wife discovered child pornography on his computer and asked him to explain how the images had gotten on his computer. He admitted that it was a one-time thing and volunteered to delete the images. He moved his hands over the touch pad, turned the screen toward his wife and said that he had deleted the images. At trial, the military judge ruled that the accused's wife could waive her marital communications privilege and testify as to what she said to the accused and how the accused acted. The Air Force Court of Criminal Appeals, in an unpublished opinion, held that the judge was correct in permitting the wife to testify as to what she said but that it was harmless error to admit evidence of the accused's actions. The Court of Appeals for the Armed Forces affirmed. Citing Rule 501(a), the court distinguished federal case law on the subject and noted that the military marital communications privilege is narrower and extends only to the communicating spouse—in this case the accused's wife who could waive the privilege. The court acknowledged that a case might arise where the natural consequence of permitting one spouse to testify about a marital conversation would also reveal what the other spouse said, but that was not the situation in this case. The court assumed, but did not decide, that the accused's actions amounted to a privileged communication under Rule 504. Any error in admitting evidence of those actions was deemed harmless.

United States v. McCollum, 58 M.J. 323 (C.A.A.F. 2003): The accused was charged with various sexual offenses against two minor girls. At trial, the prosecution offered, over defense objection, several statements made by the accused to his wife concerning the offense. In a lengthy discussion of the issue, the Court of Appeals ruled that it was harmless error to admit the statements. The first statement, in which the accused told his wife that he had not ejaculated when having relations with the victim, was presumptively confidential and the government had failed to rebut that presumption. The second statement, in which the accused indicated that he was thinking about telling other family members what he had done, was also a confidential communication. The court rejected the prosecution's argument that the accused had consented to his wife relating his statements to others; in this case, there was no evidence that the accused either expressly or implicitly authorized his wife to disclose his incriminating statements.

United States v. McElhaney, 54 M.J. 120 (C.A.A.F. 2000): At trial, the military judge ruled that the accused's wife could testify about her conversations with the accused regarding his adulterous relationship with his legal ward because they constituted a crime against the wife. The Court of Criminal Appeals concluded that the wife was not a victim but that the accused had validly waived whatever privilege he may have had. The Court of Appeals also found a valid waiver. The accused had revealed a "significant part" of his otherwise protected privileged communication to his wife, when he wrote to his ward that the "cat was out of the bag" and made other successive and voluntary disclosures to his ward and her parents.

United States v. Peterson, 48 M.J. 81 (C.A.A.F. 1998): At trial the prosecution introduced incriminating statements made by the accused to his wife. After a hearing on the issue, the military judge ruled that the husband-wife privilege did not apply to some of the statements because they were made in the presence of the accused's brother. Noting that the credibility of the witnesses at that hearing was an important issue, the court held that the trial court did not abuse its discretion in concluding that the statements were not confidential.

United States v. McCarty, 45 M.J. 334 (C.A.A.F. 1996): The court held that the accused failed to show that his wife's conversation with the victim's mother included any confidential communications between the accused and his spouse.

United States v. Tipton, 23 M.J. 338 (C.M.A. 1987): At trial the prosecution introduced letters written by the accused to his wife, from whom he was separated. Noting the specific guidance in Rule 504(b)(1), the court held that the letters were confidential communications protected by the Rule because the accused and his wife were not legally separated at the time the letters were written. Under federal practice, the letters might have been admissible due to the length or permanency of the separation. *See, e.g., United States v. Byrd,* 750 F.2d 585 (7th Cir. 1984). But, under the military rule, if the spouses were not legally separated at the time the communications were made, the communications are privileged "no matter how disharmonious their marital relationship may have been at the time of the communication." The court also rejected the argument that the letters were nonetheless admissible at sentencing, where the Rules of Evidence are relaxed. *See* Rule 1101(b).

Army Court of Criminal Appeals

United States v. Walker, 54 M.J. 568 (Army Ct.Crim.App. 2000): During an investigation into charges that the accused had committed an indecent act on a child, his wife was interviewed and make a written statement in which she said, "[The accused] did tell me what happened; however, I do not wish to disclose what he said." The trial judge treated the statement as a party admission under Rule 801. On appeal, the court held that the statement was protected by the martial communications privilege and that the government's introduction of the statement constituted an "adverse inference" and thus violated Rule 512(a)(2). Further, there was no finding by the military judge that introduction of evidence of the wife's invocation of the privilege was required by the interests of justice, as recognized in the rule.

United States v. Whitehead, 30 M.J. 1066 (A.C.M.R. 1990): The accused's statements to his wife that she should tell investigators what time he had come home was not a confidential communication because he intended his statement to be disclosed to third persons. The court apparently focused on the fact that the accused had told his wife to relay certain information to third persons.

United States v. Murphy, 30 M.J. 1040 (A.C.M.R. 1990): The court held that the accused's wife could not claim the marital communications privilege with regard to the fact that he had been absent from the house at about the time he allegedly killed his first wife and children. The court indicated that accused's absence in this case was neither a communication nor a communicative act.

United States v. Martel, 19 M.J. 917 (A.C.M.R. 1985): The accused's statements to his wife were not considered to be confidential because he intended that she would in turn convey the information to her brother.

However, his later dramatic act of throwing back the cover of their bed to reveal stolen goods amounted to a confidential "communication" because he intended to convey a message.

Navy-Marine Corps Court of Criminal Appeals

United States v. Vandyke, 56 M.J. 812 (N.M.Ct.Crim.App. 2002): The accused was charged with various offenses arising out of his false claims that his wife was residing with him. At trial, the accused's wife testified against him, without any objection, that she had not lived at the address noted and testified further that she had asked for divorce and returned her wedding ring to the accused and in the process related several conversations that they had had about their marital problems. On appeal, the court rejected the accused's argument that admitting his wife's testimony was plain error because it was protected under the marital communications privilege. The court held first, that the accused's wife was the only one who could claim the privilege for statements she had made. It held, second, that the wife's testimony did not reveal any confidential communications, because some of them were never intended to be confidential and the others were made in the presence of third persons. Finally, the court concluded that some of her testimony related only to mere acts, i.e., the fact that she had returned her ring, and not communications.

[3]   Rule 504(c)—Exceptions

[a]   Rule 504(c)(2)(A)—Child or Spouse Victim

United States Court of Appeals for the Armed Forces

United States v. Taylor, 64 M.J. 416 (C.A.A.F. 2007): When the accused's wife discovered that he had been having an affair with a 15-year-old girl, she confronted him. He admitted the affair, said it was a mistake, and said he wanted to salvage the marriage. At his subsequent special court-martial, the trial judge denied his motion in limine seeking to exclude his statements to his wife as being privileged communications. The judge ruled that the exception in Rule 504(c)(2)(A) applied because the accused had committed adultery, a crime against his wife. The Court of Appeals agreed. Tracing the history of the martial privileges in the military, the court concluded that the exception for "crime against the person or property of the other spouse . . ." included the offense of adultery. In dissent, Judge Ryan wrote that the plain meaning of those words and the common law limited the exception to those cases where there is actually a crime against the person of the spouse. Anti-marital acts, she wrote, are not within the exception.

United States v. McElhaney, 54 M.J. 120 (C.A.A.F. 2000): At trial, the military judge ruled that the accused's wife could testify about her conversations with the accused regarding his adulterous relationship with his legal ward because they constituted a crime against the wife. The Court of Criminal Appeals concluded that the wife was not a victim but that the accused had validly waived whatever privilege he may have had. The Court of Appeals also found a valid waiver. In this case the accused had revealed a "significant part" of his otherwise protected privileged communication to his wife, when he wrote to his ward that the "cat was out of the bag" and made other successive and voluntary disclosures to his ward and her parents.

Army Court of Criminal Appeals

United States v. Murphy, 30 M.J. 1040 (A.C.M.R. 1990): The court concluded that because the accused's spouse had not personally invoked her spousal privilege not to testify at this trial on charges that he murdered his first wife and son, she was not unavailable for purposes of Rule 804. The court did not address the issue of the absence of a privilege under Rule 504(c)(2)(A) because the accused had been charged with murdering his child.

[b] Other Exceptions—Crime-Fraud

United States Court of Appeals for the Armed Forces

United States v. Smith, 33 M.J. 114 (C.M.A. 1991): At trial the accused testified that her husband forced her to commit the crimes charged and that she had been afraid of him. The prosecution introduced a letter written by her to her husband which encouraged him to support her story. The service appellate court ruled that the letter was not privileged under the crime-fraud exception recognized in the federal courts. 30 M.J. 1022 (A.F.C.M.R. 1990). The Court of Appeals ruled however, that the accused had waived the privilege by presenting testimony on the same general subject matter as the letter. In a concurring opinion, Judge Everett opined that the letter was not privileged because the accused must have known that her letter would be screened by confinement facility personnel.

[c] Other Exceptions—Joint-Participant Exception

United States Court of Appeals for the Armed Forces

United States v. Custis, 65 M.J. 366 (C.A.A.F. 2007): The accused was taken to the base hospital for a blood alcohol test. Unbeknownst to the officers, the lab technician who took the blood was the accused's wife. Later that day, the accused and his wife took additional blood samples and substituted them for the samples at the hospital. The trial court and the Court of Criminal Appeals held that there was a common law crime or fraud exception to the privilege. The Court of Appeals reversed, holding that the text of Rule 504 contains no crime or fraud exception and that the military courts may not create an exception. The Court also concluded that the accused's single statement to a co-worker that his wife "had his back" did not waive the marital communications privilege.

Army Court of Criminal Appeals

United States v. Archuleta, 40 M.J. 505 (A.C.M.R. 1994): At trial an incriminating statement made by the accused to his wife was admitted as a criminal joint venture exception to the marital communications privilege. Noting that Rule 504 contains no such exception, the court concluded that the federal common-law exceptions do not apply *per se* to the military's marital communications privilege. The court further concluded that the statement was confidential, and that the statement in question was not part of a joint venture.

United States v. Martel, 19 M.J. 917 (A.C.M.R. 1985): The court held that the marital communications privilege did not apply to any of the communications between the accused and his wife because they were involved in a joint criminal venture. Although the Rule contains no such exception, the court looked to federal cases which have adopted such a common law exception. It seemingly adopted as the test whether both spouses have been "substantial participants in patently illegal activity."

§ 505.01 Official Text

Rule 505. Classified Information.

(a) *General Rule of Privilege.* Classified information is privileged from disclosure if disclosure would be detrimental to the national security. As with other rules of privilege this rule applies to all stages of the proceedings.

(b) *Definitions.* As used in this rule:

(1) *Classified Information.* "Classified information" means any information or material that has been determined by the United States government pursuant to an executive order, statute, or regulation, to require protection against unauthorized disclosure for reasons of national security and any restricted data, as defined in 42 U.S.C. § 2014(y).

(2) *National Security.* "National security" means the national defense and foreign relations of the United States.

(c) *Who may Claim the Privilege.* The privilege may be claimed by the head of the executive or military department or government agency concerned based on a finding that the information is properly classified and that disclosure would be detrimental to the national security. A person who may claim the privilege may authorize a witness or trial counsel to claim the privilege on his or her behalf. The authority of the witness or trial counsel to do so is presumed in the absence of evidence to the contrary.

(d) *Action Prior to Referral of Charges.* Prior to referral of charges, the convening authority shall respond in writing to a request by the accused for classified information if the privilege in this rule is claimed for such information. The convening authority may:

(1) Delete specified items of classified information from documents made available to the accused;

(2) Substitute a portion or summary of the information for such classified documents;

(3) Substitute a statement admitting relevant facts that the classified information would tend to prove;

(4) Provide the document subject to conditions that will guard against the compromise of the information disclosed to the accused; or

(5) Withhold disclosure if actions under (1) through (4) cannot be taken without causing identifiable damage to the national security.

Any objection by the accused to withholding of information or to the conditions of disclosure shall be raised through a motion for appropriate relief at a pretrial session.

(e) *Pretrial Session.* At any time after referral of charges and prior to arraignment, any party may move for a session under Article 39(a) to consider matters relating to classified information that may arise in connection with the trial. Following such motion or sua sponte, the military judge promptly shall hold a session under Article 39(a) to establish the timing of requests for discovery, the provision of notice under subdivision (h), and the initiation of the procedure under subdivision (i). In addition, the military judge may consider any other matters that relate to classified information or that may promote a fair and expeditious trial.

(f) *Action after Referral of Charges.* If a claim of privilege has been made under this rule with respect to classified information that apparently contains evidence that is relevant and necessary to an element of the offense or a legally cognizable defense and is otherwise admissible in evidence in the court-martial proceeding, the matter shall be reported to the convening authority. The convening authority may:

(1) institute action to obtain the classified information for use by the military judge in making a determination under subdivision (i);

(2) dismiss the charges;

(3) dismiss the charges or specifications or both to which the information relates; or

(4) take such other action as may be required in the interests of justice.

If, after a reasonable period of time, the information is not provided to the military judge in circumstances where proceeding with the case without such information would materially prejudice a substantial right of the accused, the military judge shall dismiss the charges or specifications or both to which the classified information relates.

(g) *Disclosure of Classified Information to the Accused.*

(1) *Protective Order.* If the government agrees to disclose classified information to the accused, the military judge, at the request of the government, shall enter an appropriate protective order to guard against the compromise of the information disclosed to the accused. The terms of any such protective order may include provisions:

(A) Prohibiting the disclosure of the information except as authorized by the military judge;

(B) Requiring storage of material in a manner appropriate

for the level of classification assigned to the documents to be disclosed;

(C) Requiring controlled access to the material during normal business hours and at other times upon reasonable notice;

(D) Requiring appropriate security clearances for persons having a need to examine the information in connection with the preparation of the defense; all persons requiring security clearances shall cooperate with investigatory personnel in any investigations which are necessary to obtain a security clearance.

(E) Requiring the maintenance of logs regarding access by all persons authorized by the military judge to have access to the classified information in connection with the preparation of the defense;

(F) Regulating the making and handling of notes taken from material containing classified information; or

(G) Requesting the convening authority to authorize the assignment of government security personnel and the provision of government storage facilities.

(2) *Limited Disclosure.* The military judge, upon motion of the government, shall authorize:

(A) the deletion of specified items of classified information from documents to be made available to the defendant,

(B) the substitution of a portion or summary of the information for such classified documents, or

(C) the substitution of a statement admitting relevant facts that the classified information would tend to prove, unless the military judge determines that disclosure of the classified information itself is necessary to enable the accused to prepare for trial. The government's motion and any materials submitted in support thereof shall, upon request of the government, be considered by the military judge in camera and shall not be disclosed to the accused.

(3) *Disclosure at Trial of Certain Statements Previously Made by a Witness.*

(A) *Scope.* After a witness called by the government has testified on direct examination, the military judge, on motion of the accused, may order production of statements in the possession of the United States under R.C.M. 914. This provision does not preclude discovery or assertion of a privilege otherwise authorized under these rules or this Manual.

(B) *Closed Session.* If the privilege in this rule is invoked during consideration of a motion under R.C.M. 914, the government may deliver such statement for the inspection only by the military judge in camera and may provide the military judge with an affidavit identifying the portions of the statement that are classified and the basis for the classification assigned. If the military judge finds that disclosure of any portion of the statement identified by the government as classified could reasonably be expected to cause damage to the national security in the degree required to warrant classification under the applicable executive order, statute, or regulation and that such portion of the statement is consistent with the witness' testimony, the military judge shall excise the portion from the statement. With such material excised, the military judge shall then direct delivery of such statement to the accused for use by the accused. If the military judge finds that such portion of the statement is inconsistent with the witness' testimony, the government may move for a proceeding under subdivision (i).

(4) *Record of Trial.* If, under this subdivision, any information is withheld from the accused, the accused objects to such withholding, and the trial is continued to an adjudication of guilt of the accused, the entire unaltered text of the relevant documents as well as the government's motion and any materials submitted in support thereof shall be sealed and attached to the record of trial as an appellate exhibit. Such material shall be made available to reviewing authorities in closed proceedings for the purpose of reviewing the determination of the military judge.

(h) *Notice of the Accused's Intention to Disclose Classified Information.*

(1) *Notice by the Accused.* If the accused reasonably expects to disclose or to cause the disclosure of classified information in any manner in connection with a court-martial proceeding, the accused shall notify the trial counsel in writing of such intention and file a copy of such notice with the military judge. Such notice shall be given within the time specified by the military judge under subdivision (e) or, if no time has been specified, prior to arraignment of the accused.

(2) *Continuing Duty to Notify.* Whenever the accused learns of classified information not covered by a notice under (1) that the accused reasonably expects to disclose at any such proceeding, the accused shall notify the trial counsel and the military judge in writing as soon as possible thereafter.

(3) *Content of Notice.* The notice required by this subdivision shall include a brief description of the classified information. The description, to be sufficient, must be more than a mere general

statement of the areas about which evidence may be introduced. The accused must state, with particularity, which items of classified information he reasonably expects will be revealed by his defense.

(4) *Prohibition Against Disclosure.* The accused may not disclose any information known or believed to be classified until notice has been given under this subdivision and until the government has been afforded a reasonable opportunity to seek a determination under subdivision (i).

(5) *Failure to Comply.* If the accused fails to comply with the requirements of this subdivision, the military judge may preclude disclosure of any classified information not made the subject of notification and may prohibit the examination by the accused of any witness with respect to any such information.

(i) *In Camera Proceedings for Cases Involving Classified Information.*

(1) *Definition.* For purposes of this subdivision, an "in camera proceeding" is a session under Article 39(a) from which the public is excluded.

(2) *Motion for In Camera Proceeding.* Within the time specified by the military judge for the filing of a motion under this rule, the government may move for an in camera proceeding concerning the use at any proceeding of any classified information. Thereafter, either prior to or during trial, the military judge for good cause shown or otherwise upon a claim of privilege under this rule may grant the government leave to move for an in camera proceeding concerning the use of additional classified information.

(3) *Demonstration of National Security Nature of the Information.* In order to obtain an in camera proceeding under this rule, the government shall submit the classified information and an affidavit ex parte for examination by the military judge only. The affidavit shall demonstrate that disclosure of the information reasonably could be expected to cause damage to the national security in the degree required to warrant classification under the applicable executive order, statute, or regulation.

(4) *In Camera Proceeding.*

(A) *Procedure.* Upon finding that the government has met the standard set forth in subdivision (i)(3) with respect to some or all of the classified information at issue, the military judge shall conduct an in camera proceeding. Prior to the in camera proceeding, the government shall provide the accused with notice of the information that will be at issue. This notice shall identify the classified information that will be at issue whenever that information previously has been made available to the accused in connection with proceedings in the same case. The government may describe the information by generic category, in such form as the military judge may approve, rather than identifying the classified information when the government has not previously made the information available to the accused in connection with pretrial proceedings. Following briefing and argument by the parties in the in camera proceeding the military judge shall determine whether the information may be disclosed at the court-martial proceeding. Where the government's motion under this subdivision is filed prior to the proceeding at which disclosure is sought, the military judge shall rule prior to the commencement of the relevant proceeding.

(B) *Standard.* Classified information is not subject to disclosure under this subdivision unless the information is relevant and necessary to an element of the offense or a legally cognizable defense and is otherwise admissible in evidence. In presentencing proceedings, relevant and material classified information pertaining to the appropriateness of, or the appropriate degree of, punishment shall be admitted only if no unclassified version of such information is available.

(C) *Ruling.* Unless the military judge makes a written determination that the information meets the standard set forth in (B), the information may not be disclosed or otherwise elicited at a court-martial proceeding. The record of the in camera proceeding shall be sealed and attached to the record of trial as an appellate exhibit. The accused may seek reconsideration of the determination prior to or during trial.

(D) *Alternatives to Full Disclosure.* If the military judge makes a determination under this subdivision that would permit disclosure of the information or if the government elects not to contest the relevance, necessity, and admissibility of any classified information, the government may proffer a statement admitting for purposes of the proceeding any relevant facts such information would tend to prove or may submit a portion or summary to be used in lieu of the information. The military judge shall order that such statement, portion, or summary be used by the accused in place of the classified information unless the military judge finds that use of the classified information itself is necessary to afford the accused a fair trial.

(E) *Sanctions.* If the military judge determines that alternatives to full disclosure may not be used and the government continues to object to disclosure of the information, the military judge shall issue any order that the interests of justice require. Such an order may include an order:

(i) striking or precluding all or part of the testimony of a witness;

(ii) declaring a mistrial;

(iii) finding against the government on any issue as to which the evidence is relevant and necessary to the defense;

(iv) dismissing the charges, with or without prejudice; or

(v) dismissing the charges or specifications or both to which the information relates.

Any such order shall permit the government to avoid the sanction for nondisclosure by permitting the accused to disclose the information at the pertinent court-martial proceeding.

(j) *Introduction of Classified Information.*

(1) *Classification Status.* Writings, recordings, and photographs containing classified information may be admitted into evidence without change in their classification status.

(2) *Precautions by the Military Judge.* In order to prevent unnecessary disclosure of classified information, the military judge may order admission into evidence of only part of a writing, recording, or photograph or may order admission into evidence of the whole writing, recording, or photograph with excision of some or all of the classified information contained therein.

(3) *Contents of Writing, Recording, or Photograph.* The military judge may permit proof of the contents of a writing, recording, or photograph that contains classified information without requiring introduction into evidence of the original or a duplicate.

(4) *Taking of Testimony.* During the examination of a witness, the government may object to any question or line of inquiry that may require the witness to disclose classified information not previously found to be relevant and necessary to the defense. Following such an objection, the military judge shall take such suitable action to determine whether the response is admissible as will safeguard against the compromise of any classified information. Such action may include requiring the government to provide the military judge with a proffer of the witness' response to the question or line of inquiry and requiring the accused to provide the military judge with a proffer of the nature of the information the accused seeks to elicit.

(5) *Closed Session.* The military judge may exclude the public during that portion of the presentation of evidence that discloses

classified information.

(6) *Record of Trial.* The record of trial with respect to any classified matter will be prepared under R.C.M. 1103(h) and 1104(b)(1)(D).

(k) *Security Procedures to Safeguard Against Compromise of Classified Information Disclosed to Courts-Martial.* The Secretary of Defense may prescribe security procedures for protection against the compromise of classified information submitted to courts-martial and appellate authorities.

§ 505.02   Editorial Comment

Rule 505 creates a privilege for classified information that, together with Rule 506, is similar to an "executive privilege" that some civilian courts have recognized.[1] In substance, the Rule generally follows a similar privilege recognized in 1969 *Manual* ¶ 151 *b.* In form, it is closely patterned after H.R. 4743, 96th Cong., 1st Sess. (1979), that addressed in detail the handling of classified information in pretrial, trial, and appellate proceedings. Also evident in the Rule is the impact of the Supreme Court's decisions in *United States v. Reynolds*[2] and *United States v. Nixon.*[3]

Rule 505 in turn serves as a model for Rule 506, which provides a privilege for government information that is not of a classified nature. Although both Rules involve privileges that can be stated rather easily, they are extremely complex Rules because of the procedures that are established in an effort to protect unnecessary exposure of sensitive governmental information without prejudicing an accused's chance for a fair trial. As a practical matter, classified information or evidence is only rarely used, and the fact that there are few reported decisions on these Rules bears this out. When the issue is raised, however, all parties must be attuned to the technical requirements of this Rule—noting in particular special notice and written response and findings requirements not found in most of the other privilege rules.

---

[1] *See generally* Kastenberg, *Analyzing The Constitutional Tensions and Applicability of Military Rule of Evidence 505 In Courts-Martial Over United States Service Members: Secrecy in the Shadow of Lonetree,* 55 A.F. L. REV. 233 (2004).

[2] 345 U.S. 1 (1953). *See also* Maher, *The Right to a Fair Trial in Criminal Cases Involving the Introduction of Classified Information,* 120 MIL. L. REV. 83 (1988) (the article addresses the potential constitutional problems with cases involving classified information, including lack of access by the defense to the information, the notice requirement in Rule 505, use of *ex parte* affidavits, and lack of public access to the trial).

[3] 418 U.S. 683 (1974). *See generally* United States v. North, 910 F.2d 843, 893 (D.C. Cir. 1990) (reversing and vacating convictions on other grounds, but upholding districts court's approach to classified information); United States v. Smith, 780 F.2d 1102 (4th Cir. 1985) (en banc) (courts must apply *Roviaro* balancing test, 353 U.S. 53 (1957), when determining whether classified information is offered).

Subdivisions (a), (b), and (c) of Rule 505 set out the basics of the privilege. The remaining subdivisions, (d) through (k), are primarily concerned with the procedures to be used in applying the privilege.

[1]   Rule 505(a)—General Rule of Privilege

Classified information may be privileged from disclosure only when disclosure would be detrimental to national security, *i.e.*, the national defense or foreign relations of the United States.[4] In 1993, Rule 505(a) was amended by adding one sentence to emphasize that Rule 505, like all other privileges in Section V, applies at all stages of the trial and is not relaxed at the sentencing stage of a court-martial.

[2]   Rule 505(b)—Definitions

Information may be "classified" by an executive order, statute or regulation. In addition, the privilege extends to "restricted data" as defined by 42 U.S.C. § 2014(y):

> (y) The term "Restricted Data" means all data concerning (1) design, manufacture, or utilization of atomic weapons; (2) the production of special nuclear material; or (3) the use of special nuclear material in the production of energy, but shall not include data declassified or removed from the Restricted Data category pursuant to section 2162 of this title.

[3]   Rule 505(c)—Who May Claim the Privilege

Under Rule 505(c), the privilege may be claimed either by the appropriate head of the executive or military department or government agency; a witness or prosecutor may claim it on behalf of that head if so authorized. The authority to do so is presumed; this is not the case in many civilian courts.[5] Before claiming the privilege, the claimant must first determine that the information is properly classified and that disclosure would be detrimental to national security.

[4]   Rule 505(d)—Action Prior to Referral of Charges

The Rule takes into account that the issue of disclosure of classified information may arise at any stage of the proceedings. If the privilege is claimed prior to referral of charges to trial, the defense counsel should first attempt to obtain discovery through the convening authority. Subdivision (d) notes that, if such a request is made, the convening authority must respond in writing. Although no mention is made of a written defense request for the information, that would seem to be the preferred method. The convening authority's options include limited disclosure, either through substitutions or deletions, control over access to the documents, and withholding disclosure.

---

[4] *See* United States v. Reynolds, 345 U.S. 1 (1953).

[5] *See, e.g.,* Coastal Corp. v. Duncan, 86 F.R.D. 514 (D. Del. 1980) (requiring showing that head of agency wished to invoke privilege).

If limited disclosure is made, the accused can ask for greater disclosure later.

In 1994, R.C.M. 405(g)(1)(B) and 405(g)(6) were amended.[6] R.C.M. 405(g)(1)(B) now requires an Article 32 Investigation Officer to inform the Convening Authority of any defense requests for information protected by Rules 505 or 506. The rule thus provides notice to the Convening Authority and others that a protective order under R.C.M 405(g)(6) may be required. That latter provision now specifically provides that a Convening Authority may issue protective orders and impose certain conditions.[7]

[5] Rule 505(e)—Pretrial Session

If the defense is not satisfied with the convening authority's response the issue may be raised through motion at a pretrial session as provided for in subdivision (e). At that Article 39(a) session, to be conducted after referral of charges, any party may raise the discovery issue, even if it has not been first raised with the convening authority. The military judge is apparently given some leeway here to determine the appropriate method of handling the issue, that includes deciding on the timing of discovery requests by the defense, providing for notice by the defense of an intent to disclose classified information, *see* (h), and for necessary in camera hearings, *see* (i). And, if the parties are ready, the military judge may proceed with an in camera proceeding to determine whether a privilege exists. *See* subdivision (i).

[6] Rule 505(f)—Action After Referral of Charges

Although it is not clear from the Rule itself, the drafters apparently intended that subdivision (f) would address the options available to the government following a preliminary determination by the military judge that the confidential material is relevant and apparently could be admissible if it were disclosed. The convening authority may obtain the pertinent information to present to the judge for his or her determination of the privilege claim, or he or she may take one of the other options noted in that subdivision, including dismissal of the charges.[8] Note that subdivision (f) requires that a military judge must, under some circumstances of undue delay, dismiss charges or specifications that cannot fairly be tried without the information sought by the accused.

---

[6] Change 7, *Manual for Courts-Martial*, United States (1984), E.O. 12,936, Nov. 10, 1994, effective Dec. 9, 1994.

[7] *See generally* Borch, *Analysis of Change 7 to the 1984 Manual for Courts-Martial*, ARMY LAW, Jan. 1995, at 22.

[8] *See* 1969 *Manual* ¶ 33 *f* and Article 43(e), U.C.M.J., which address the appropriateness of delay in prosecuting cases involving matters affecting national security. *See also* United States v. Fernandez, 913 F.2d 148 (4th Cir. 1990) (upholding dismissal of indictment where Attorney General refused to permit disclosure of classified information).

[7] Rule 505(g)—Disclosure of Classified Information to the Accused

Subdivision (g) generally addresses those situations in which disclosure of classified information is voluntarily made to the defense. The government, under (g)(1), may request the military judge to issue a protective order that may include any of the suggested provisions noted in that subdivision—*e.g.,* storage, access, security clearance, and record keeping requirements. In 1993, Rule 505(g)(1), was amended in subdivision (g)(1)(D) to emphasize that the judge has the authority to require the necessary security clearance of all personnel involved in the court-martial, at all stages. It also makes clear that those needing the clearance are required to submit to any necessary investigations needed to get the clearance.

Under (g)(2), the government may also request authorization from the military judge to make only a limited disclosure—either through substitutions and/or deletions. The government's motion to do so may include a request that the motion and supporting matters be considered by the military judge alone and not be disclosed to the accused.[9] Subdivision (g)(3) covers those situations where, pursuant to R.C.M. 914, the defense is entitled to see other documents or prior statements of a witness. Where that material is classified, the prosecution may provide the information for inspection by the military judge, in camera, along with an affidavit identifying the classified portions and the reasons for the classification. If the designated portions are classified and could "reasonably be expected" to damage national security and are consistent with the witness' testimony, they may be deleted. If the designated portions are inconsistent with the witness' testimony, however, then the prosecution may request an in camera proceeding under subdivision (i). If information is kept from an accused who objects, a record of the entire document is to be made and kept under seal in the event of an appeal.

[8] Rule 505(h)—Notice of Accused's Intention to Disclose Classified Information

Subdivision (h) provides for defense notice of an intent to disclose classified information in a court-martial. The notice must be written and

---

[9] R.C.M. 914, that is patterned after the Jencks Act (18 U.S.C. § 3500), provides in pertinent part:

Motion for production. After a witness other than the accused has testified on direct examination, the military judge, on motion of a party who did not call the witness, shall order the party who called the witness to produce, for examination and use by the moving party, any statement of the witness that relates to the subject matter concerning which the witness has testified, and that is:

In the case of a witness called by the trial counsel, in the possession of the United States; or

In the case of a witness called by the defense, in the possession of the accused or defense counsel.

copies served on both the prosecution and military judge either within the time specified by the military judge or before arraignment. The Rule includes a continuing duty to give notice and prohibits disclosure prior to giving notice and providing the prosecution with a reasonable opportunity to request an in camera proceeding under subdivision (i). Rule 505(h)(3) was amended in 1993 to require the defense to state with particularity what classified information it intends to offer at trial. Failure to comply with these requirements may result in the court's barring the use of the information.[10] The privilege itself extends, of course, to pretrial proceedings, but it is not entirely clear from the plain language of subdivision (h) whether the defense must give notice to the government prior to disclosing classified information at an Article 32 investigation. The better practice would be to read the requirement broadly and provide some notice to the government.

[9] Rule 505(i)—In Camera Proceedings for Cases Involving Classified Information

Should the prosecution wish to contest the disclosure of classified information, before or after a claim of privilege has formally been made, subdivision (i) provides for an "in camera proceeding," something generally new to military practice. An in camera proceeding according to the Rule is an Article 39(a) session closed to the public. The prosecution triggers the process with a timely motion and presentation of the classified information itself to the military judge alone for his or her consideration. In addition, the prosecution must present an affidavit demonstrating a reasonable expectation of damage to national security. *See* (i)(3).

In 1993, Rule 505(i)(3) was changed to clarify an ambiguity in the rule concerning who was supposed to receive the government's affidavit showing that damage would be caused by disclosure of the classified information. The rule now makes clear that the government is to submit its affidavit only to the military judge for in camera consideration. A provision was also added to provide guidance on the admissibility of classified information at sentencing proceedings. Under the amendment, relevant classified information may be introduced at sentencing, but only if similar unclassified evidence is not otherwise available. The amendment thus requires an element of necessity that is consistent with the spirit of Rule 505.

If the prosecution meets the requirements of (i)(3), an in camera proceeding is held after appropriate notice to the defense concerning the information at issue. *See* (i)(4)(A). The information may be described by generic category when it has not yet been disclosed to the defense and the government wishes to guard against revelation. After hearing from the parties the military judge must make rulings prior to the proceeding during which disclosure is sought.

---

[10] *See* 505(h)(5). *Cf.* 506(h).

Only classified information that is "relevant and necessary[11] to an element of the offense or a legally cognizable defense and is otherwise admissible" is subject to disclosure. *See* (i)(4)(B). The word disclosure has a dual meaning. It means disclosure to the defense if that has not already occurred and also disclosure as evidence at trial. Failure of the judge to make a *written* determination that the information meets this standard will prevent disclosure. *See* (i)(4)(C). The record of the proceedings will be sealed and attached to the record as an appellate exhibit, however. Also, the accused may seek reconsideration of his or her disclosure request.

In lieu of disclosing classified information, the prosecution under (i)(4)(D) may either admit the relevant facts or provide a summary. Unless the classified information itself is necessary for a fair trial, the judge should order the accused to use the alternative forms offered by the prosecutor. *See also* (g)(1), (2). On the other hand, if the offered alternatives are not acceptable to the military judge and the prosecution still objects to disclosure, the judge may impose sanctions, some of which are noted in (i)(4)(E).

[10] Rule 505(j)—Introduction of Classified Information

Subdivision (j) generally addresses the handling of classified information at trial and affords the military judge broad discretion in dealing with such evidence. As under the in camera proceedings noted in (i), the military judge must balance competing interests: the government's claim of damage to national security and the accused's right to disclosure of all relevant facts necessary for a fair trial. Parts of documents may be excluded, for example, and the scope of questioning may be carefully controlled. An interesting option is for the judge to close the proceedings to the public when counsel, the judge and the court members have security clearances. Of particular note is subdivision (j)(3) that apparently provides an exception to the best evidence, or original document Rule. *See* Rules 1002, 1004. *See also* Rule 506(j)(2).

In 1993, an amendment to Rule 505(j)(5) reflects *United States v. Hershey*,[12] and provides that the military judge has the authority to exclude the public from a court-martial when any classified information, regardless of its manner of presentation, is offered at trial.

---

[11] The 1980 version of the Rules used the word "material" in this context. However, in the 1984 version, the word "necessary" was substituted, the drafters apparently considering this a stylistic change to conform the Rules to other provisions in the Manual for Courts-Martial. *See, e.g.,* R.C.M. 703.

[12] 20 M.J. 433 (C.M.A. 1985).

[11]   Rule 505(k)—Security Procedures to Safeguard Against Compromise of Classified Information Disclosed to Courts-Martial

In addition to the procedural precautions noted in subdivision (j), the Secretary of Defense, under subdivision (k), may provide additional security procedures.

§ 505.03   Drafters' Analysis

Rule 505 is based upon H.R. 4745, 96th Cong., 1st Sess. (1979), that was proposed by the Executive Branch as a response to what is known as the "graymail" problem in which the defendant in a criminal case seeks disclosure of sensitive national security information, the release of which may force the government to discontinue the prosecution. The Rule is also based upon the Supreme Court's discussion of executive privilege in *United States v. Reynolds*, 345 U.S. 1 (1953) and *United States v. Nixon*, 418 U.S. 683 (1974). The Rule attempts to balance the interests of an accused who desires classified information for his or her defense and the interests of the government in protecting that information.

[1]   General rule of privilege

Rule 505(a) is derived from *United States v. Reynolds*, 345 U.S. 1 (1953) and present *Manual* ¶ 151. Classified information is only privileged when its "disclosure would be detrimental to the national security."

[2]   Definitions

[a]   Classified information

Rule 505(b)(1) is derived from section 2 of H.R. 4745. The definition of "classified information" is a limited one and includes only that information protected "pursuant to an executive order, statute, or regulation," and that material which constitutes restricted data pursuant to 42 U.S.C. 2014(y) (1976).

[b]   National security

Rule 505(b)(2) is derived from section 2 of H.R. 4745.

[3]   Who may claim the privilege

Rule 505(c) is derived from present ¶ 151 of the *Manual* and is consistent with similar provisions in the other privilege rules. *See, e.g.*, Rule 501(c). The privilege may be claimed *only* "by the head of the executive or military department or government agency concerned" and then only upon "a finding that the information is properly classified and that disclosure would be detrimental to the national security." Although the authority of a witness or trial counsel to claim the privilege is presumed in the absence of evidence to the contrary, neither a witness nor a trial counsel may claim the privilege without prior direction to do so by the appropriate department or agency head. Consequently, expedited coordination with senior headquarters is advised in any situation in which Rule 505 appears to be applicable.

[4] Action prior to referral of charges

Rule 505(d) is taken from section 4(b)(1) of H.R. 4745. The provision has been modified to reflect the fact that pretrial discovery in the armed forces, prior to referral, is officially conducted through the convening authority. The convening authority should disclose the maximum amount of requested information as appears reasonable under the circumstances.

[5] Pretrial session

Rule 505(e) is derived from section 3 of H.R. 4745.

[6] Action after referral of charges

Rule 505(f) provides the basic procedure under which the government should respond to a determination by the military judge that classified information "apparently contains evidence that is relevant and material to an element of the offense or a legally cognizable defense and is otherwise admissible in evidence." *See generally* the *Analysis* to Rule 507(d).

It should be noted that the government may submit information to the military judge for in camera inspection pursuant to subdivision (i). If the defense requests classified information that it alleges is "relevant and material . . .," and the government refuses to disclose the information to the military judge for inspection, the military judge may presume that the information is in fact "relevant and material . . . ."

[7] Disclosure of classified information to the accused

Paragraphs (1) and (2) of Rule 505(g) are derived from section 4 of H.R. 4745. Paragraph (3) is taken from section 10 of H.R. 4745 but has been modified in view of the different application of the Jencks Act, 18 U.S.C. § 3500 (1976) in the armed forces. Paragraph (4) is taken from sections 4(b) (2) and 10 of H.R. 4745. The reference in H.R. 4745 to a recess has been deleted as being unnecessary in view of the military judge's inherent authority to call a recess.

[8] Notice of the accused's intention to disclose classified information

Rule 505(h) is derived from section 5 of H.R. 4745. The intent of the provision is to prevent disclosure of classified information by the defense until the government has had an opportunity to determine what position to take concerning the possible disclosure of that information. Pursuant to Rule 505(h)(5), failure to comply with subdivision (h) may result in a prohibition on the use of the information involved.

[9] In camera proceedings for cases involving classified information

Rule 505(i) is derived generally from section 5 of H.R. 4745. The "in camera" procedure utilized in subdivision (i) is generally new to military law. Neither the accused nor defense counsel may be excluded from the in camera proceeding. However, nothing within the Rule requires that the defense be provided with a copy of the classified material in question when the government submits such information to the military judge pursuant to Rule 505(i)(3) in an effort to obtain an in camera proceeding under this Rule. If such information has not been disclosed previously, the government may describe the information by generic category, rather than by identifying the information. Such description is subject to approval by the military judge, and if not sufficiently specific to enable the defense to proceed during the in camera session, the military judge may order the government to release the information for use during the proceeding or face the sanctions under subdivision (i)(4)(E).

[10] Introduction of classified information

Rule 505(j) is derived from section 8 of H.R. 4745 and *United States v. Grunden,* 2 M.J. 116 (C.M.A. 1977).

[11] Security procedures to safeguard against compromise of classified information disclosed to courts-martial

Rule 505(k) is derived from section 9 of H.R. 4745.

§ 505.04 Drafters' Analysis (1993)

The Analysis accompanying M.R.E. 505(a) is amended by inserting the following at the end thereof:

The second sentence was added to clarify that this rule, like other rules of privilege, applies at all stages of all actions and is not relaxed during the sentencing hearing under M.R.E. 1101(c).

The Analysis accompanying M.R.E. 505(g) is amended by inserting the following at the end thereof:

Subsection (g)(1)(D) was amended to make clear that the military judge's authority to require security clearances extends to persons involved in the conduct of the trial as well as pretrial preparation for it. The amendment requires persons needing security clearances to submit to investigations necessary to obtain the clearance.

The Analysis accompanying M.R.E. 505(h) is amended by inserting the following at the end thereof:

Subsection (h)(3) was amended to require specificity in detailing the items of classified information expected to be introduced. The amendment is based on *United States v. Collins,* 720 F.2d 1195 (11th Cir. 1983).

The Analysis accompanying M.R.E. 505(i) is amended by inserting the following at the end thereof:

Subsection (i)(3) was amended to clarify that the classified material and the government's affidavit are submitted only to the military judge. The word "only" was placed at the end of the sentence to make it clear that it refers to "military judge" rather than to "examination." The military judge is to examine the affidavit and the classified information without disclosing it before determining to hold an in camera proceeding as defined in subsection (i)(1). The second sentence of subsection (i)(4)(B) was added to provide a standard for admission of classified information in sentencing proceedings.

The Analysis accompanying M.R.E. 505(j) is amended by inserting the following at the end thereof:

Subsection (j)(5) was amended to provide that the military judge's authority to exclude the public extends to the presentation of any evidence that discloses classified information, and not merely to the testimony of witnesses. *See generally United States v. Hershey*, 20 M.J. 433 (C.M.A. 1985), *cert. denied*, 474 U.S. 1062 (1986).

§ 505.05 Annotated Cases

United States Court of Appeals for the Armed Forces

United States v. Pruner, 33 M.J. 272 (C.M.A. 1991): The accused, a former intelligence analyst, sought extraordinary relief from the Court of Criminal Appeals that the convening authority declassify certain information and authorize him to discuss top secret information with his civilian and military counsel without them being required to obtain security clearance. In the alternative, he asked that the charges be dismissed. The court ruled that the lower court correctly denied the requested relief. Citing Rule 505, the court noted that the first request was premature because the accused had not first presented his request to the military judge. The court found that the government had reasonably attempted to accommodate counsel by providing for a simplified, expedited process of seeking clearance. It held that dismissal of the charges was not required, and, if counsel seeks to frustrate the trial process, the government may proceed. *See also United States v. Nichols*, 23 C.M.R. 343, 350–51 (C.M.A. 1957).

Air Force Court of Criminal Appeals

United States v. Flannigan, 28 M.J. 988 (A.F.C.M.R. 1989): When the defense counsel attempted to obtain a copy of an Air Force OSI regulation governing undercover operations, the "Commander of the Air Force OSI" invoked the privilege under Rule 505. The court concluded that he was not the appropriate party to waive or claim the privilege on behalf of the United States; the rule requires the head of the military department concerned to make that decision.

United States v. Ott, 26 M.J. 542 (A.F.C.M.R. 1988): The court rejected the accused's argument that the trial judge should have determined the admissibility of certain information derived under the Foreign Intelligence

Surveillance Act, 50 U.S.C. § 1801, rather than referring the matter to a federal district court. The Act places such issues exclusively under federal court jurisdiction if the Attorney General seeks such review. Because the accused did not appeal the federal district court's findings, the trial judge correctly accepted its rulings.

§ 506.01　Official Text

Rule 506.　Government Information Other Than Classified Information.

(a) *General rule of privilege.* Except where disclosure is required by an Act of Congress, government information is privileged from disclosure if disclosure would be detrimental to the public interest.

(b) *Scope.* "government information" includes official communications and documents and other information within the custody or control of the Federal government. This rule does not apply to classified information (Mil. R. Evid. 505) or to the identity of an informant (Mil. R. Evid. 507).

(c) *Who may claim the privilege.* The privilege may be claimed by the head of the executive or military department or government agency concerned. The privilege for records and information of the Inspector General may be claimed by the immediate superior of the inspector general officer responsible for creation of the records or information, the Inspector General, or any other superior authority. A person who may claim the privilege may authorize a witness or the trial counsel to claim the privilege on his or her behalf. The authority of a witness or the trial counsel to do so is presumed in the absence of evidence to the contrary.

(d) *Action prior to referral of charges.* Prior to referral of charges, the government shall respond in writing to a request for government information if the privilege in this rule is claimed for such information. The government shall:

(1) delete specified items of government information claimed to be privileged from documents made available to the accused;

(2) substitute a portion or summary of the information for such documents;

(3) substitute a statement admitting relevant facts that the government information would tend to prove;

(4) the document subject to conditions similar to those set forth in subdivision (g) of this rule; or

(5) withhold disclosure if actions under (1) through (4) cannot be taken without causing identifiable damage to the public interest.

(e) *Action after referral of charges.* After referral of charges, if a claim of privilege has been made under this rule with respect to government information that apparently contains evidence that is relevant and necessary to an element of the offense or a legally cognizable defense and is otherwise admissible in evidence in the court-martial proceeding, the matter shall be reported to the convening authority. The convening authority may:

(1) institute action to obtain the information for use by the military judge in making a determination under subdivision (i);

(2) dismiss the charges;

(3) dismiss the charges or specifications or both to which the information relates; or

(4) take other action as may be required in the interests of justice.

If, after a reasonable period of time, the information is not provided to the military judge, the military judge shall dismiss the charges or specifications or both to which the information relates.

(f) *Pretrial session.* At any time after referral of charges and prior to arraignment any party may move for a session under Article 39(a) to consider matters relating to government information that may arise in connection with the trial. Following such motion, or sua sponte, the military judge promptly shall hold a pretrial session under Article 39(a) to establish the timing of requests for discovery, the provision of notice under subdivision (h), and the initiation of the procedure under subdivision (i). In addition, the military judge may consider any other matters that relate to government information or that may promote a fair and expeditious trial.

(g) *Disclosure of government information to the accused.* If the government agrees to disclose government information to the accused subsequent to a claim of privilege under this rule, the military judge, at the request of the government, shall enter an appropriate protective order to guard against the compromise of the information disclosed to the accused. The terms of any such protective order may include provisions:

(1) Prohibiting the disclosure of the information except as authorized by the military judge;

(2) Requiring storage of the material in a manner appropriate for the nature of the material to be disclosed; upon reasonable notice;

(3) Requiring controlled access to the material during normal business hours and at other times upon reasonable notice;

(4) Requiring the maintenance of logs recording access by persons authorized by the military judge to have access to the government information in connection with the preparation of the defense;

(5) Regulating the making and handling of notes taken from material containing government information; or

(6) Requesting the convening authority to authorize the

assignment of government security personnel and the provision of government storage facilities.

(h) *Prohibition against disclosure.* The accused may not disclose any information known or believed to be subject to a claim of privilege under this rule until the government has been afforded a reasonable opportunity to seek a determination under subdivision (i).

(i) *In camera proceedings.*

(1) *Definition.* For purposes of this subdivision, an "in camera proceeding" is a closed session under Article 39(a).

(2) *Motion for in camera proceeding.* Within the time specified by the military judge for the filing of a motion under this rule, the government may move for an in camera proceeding concerning the use at any proceeding of any government information that may be subject to a claim of privilege. Thereafter, either prior to or during trial, the military judge for good cause shown or otherwise upon a claim of privilege may grant the government leave to move for an in camera proceeding concerning the use of additional government information.

(3) *Demonstration of public interest nature of the information.* In order to obtain an in camera proceeding under this rule, the government shall demonstrate through submission of affidavits and the information for examination only by the military judge that disclosure of the information reasonably could be expected to cause identifiable damage to the public interest.

(4) *In camera proceeding.*

(A) *Procedure.* Upon finding that the disclosure of some or all of the information submitted by the government under subsection (1) reasonably could be expected to cause identifiable damage to the public interest, the military judge shall conduct an in camera proceeding. Prior to the in camera proceeding, the government shall provide the accused with notice of the information that will be at issue. This notice shall identify the information that will be at issue whenever that information previously has been made available to the accused in connection with proceedings in the same case. The government may describe the information by generic category, in such form as the military judge may approve, rather than identifying the specific information of concern to the government when the government has not previously made the information available to the accused in connection with pretrial proceedings. Following briefing and argument by the parties in the in camera proceeding, the military judge shall determine whether the information may be disclosed at the court-martial proceeding.

When the government's motion under this subdivision is filed prior to the proceeding at which disclosure is sought, the military judge shall rule prior to commencement of the relevant proceeding.

(B) *Standard.* government information is subject to a disclosure under this subdivision if the party making the request demonstrates a specific need for information containing evidence that is relevant to the guilt or innocence of the accused and otherwise admissible in the court-martial proceeding.

(C) *Ruling.* Unless the military judge makes a written determination that the information is not subject to disclosure under the standard set forth in (B), the information may be disclosed at the court-martial proceeding. The record of the in camera proceeding shall be sealed and attached to the record of trial as an appellate exhibit. The accused may seek reconsideration of the determination prior to or during trial.

(D) *Sanction.* If the military judge makes a determination under this subdivision that permits disclosure of the information and the government continues to object to disclosure of the information, the military judge shall dismiss the charges or specifications or both to which the information relates.

(j) *Introduction of government information subject to a claim of privilege.*

(1) *Precautions by military judge.* In order to prevent unnecessary disclosure of government information after there has been a claim of privilege under this rule, the military judge may order admission into evidence of any part of a writing, recording, or photograph or may order admission into evidence of the whole writing, recording, or photograph, with excision of some or all of the government information contained therein.

(2) *Contents of writing, recording, or photograph.* The military judge may permit proof of the contents of a writing, recording, or photograph that contains government information that is the subject of a claim of privilege under this rule without requiring introduction into evidence of the original or a duplicate.

(3) *Taking of testimony.* During examination of a witness, the prosecution may object to any question or line of inquiry that may require the witness to disclose government information not previously found relevant and necessary to the defense if such information has been or is reasonably likely to be the subject of a claim of privilege under this rule. Following such an objection, the military judge shall take such suitable action to determine whether the response is admissible as will safeguard against the

compromise of any government information. Such action may include requiring the government to provide the military judge with a proffer of the witness "response to the question or line of inquiry and requiring the accused to provide the military judge with a proffer of the nature of the information the accused seeks to elicit."

(k) *Procedures to safeguard against compromise of government information disclosed to courts-martial.* The Secretary of Defense may prescribe procedures for protection against the compromise of government information submitted to courts-martial and appellate authorities after a claim of privilege.

§ 506.02 Editorial Comment

government information that is not classified within the meaning of Rule 505, *above,* may nonetheless be privileged under Rule 506. This Rule is generally modeled after Rule 505 but contains a number of significant, yet subtle, differences that may trap the unwary litigant.

[1] Rule 506(a)—General Rule of Privilege

As a general rule, government information, that includes, but is not limited to, official communications, documents and other information within the control of the federal government, is privileged if it would be detrimental to the public interest.

[2] Rule 506(b)—Scope

The exception to the general rule arises in those Acts of Congress that may require disclosure. *See, e.g.,* 5 U.S.C. § 552 (Freedom of Information Act) and 18 U.S.C. § 3500 (Jencks Act). Thus the privilege here is narrower than that in Rule 505. Classified government information and the identity of an informant are covered in Rules 505 and 507, respectively.

[3] Rule 506(c)—Who May Claim the Privilege

In addressing the question of who may claim the privilege, subdivision (c) makes a distinction between government information and information derived from Inspector General records. The former may be claimed by the appropriate agency head; the latter may be claimed by the immediate superior of the inspector general officer responsible for creating the records or information, the Inspector General, or "any other superior authority." The claimants in either case may authorize either a witness or trial counsel to claim the privilege on their behalf, and authorization is presumed as under Rule 505.

[4] Rule 506(d)—Action Prior to Referral of Charges

Like their counterparts in Rule 505, subdivisions (d) through (k) lay out some rather technical procedural requirements. Here, too, the defense should first go through pretrial discovery methods if the privilege is claimed prior to referral of charges. Unfortunately, subdivision (d) only indicates that the "government" must provide a written response to a request for information. The Drafters' Analysis is silent on the subject of who actually must respond, but directs the reader to the Drafters Analysis for Rule 505(d), which notes that pretrial requests for evidence often are forwarded to the convening authority. Because the language of 506(d) is open-ended, in an appropriate case someone other than a convening authority—for example, one of the prosecutors—may act for the government. As a practical matter, the defense request for information should be directed through the prosecutor to the convening authority.

[5]   Rule 506(e)—Action After Referral of Charges

After referral of charges, subdivision (e) explicitly requires that the convening authority be advised when the privilege has been claimed and the information requested appears to be otherwise admissible and relevant to an element of an offense or a valid defense. The Rule is silent as to who must determine that the requested information meets those requirements. Again, the Drafters' Analysis to Rule 505(f), the counterpart to (e), assumes that this process will normally take place after a military judge, in a pretrial session, has made that determination. Note that, under (e), if the information has been requested by the military judge for examination and the information is not turned over within a reasonable time, the military judge *must* dismiss the appropriate charges or specifications. The drafters do not provide any reasons for such a potentially harsh rule, that on its face greatly extends the powers of a military judge. An analogous situation has existed for some time in the area of witness production. Although in theory a military judge could dismiss charges for failure of the government to provide a defense witness, many military judges have opted for "abatement" of the proceedings until the government produced the witness or dismissed the charges. Apparently, the Rule intends to bar all unnecessary delays regarding non-classified information that can be screened in camera without the problems presented by classified material.

[6]   Rule 506(f)—Pretrial Session

Subdivision (f) is similar to 505(e) and deals with using Article 39(a) sessions to establish some of the basic ground rules for discovery requests and privilege claims.

[7]   Rule 506(g)—Disclosure of Government Information to the Accused

Subdivision (g) is a streamlined version of 505(g); the government may request a protective order, although limited disclosure is apparently not an option under this Rule. *Cf.* Rule 505(g).

[8]   Rule 506(h)—Prohibition Against Disclosure

Subdivision (h) requires the defense to delay disclosing information that might be claimed under this privilege until the government has an opportunity to move for an in camera proceeding under (i).

[9]   Rule 506(i)—In Camera Proceedings

Rule 506(i), that addresses *in camera* proceedings, has no teeth to it. *Compare* Rule 505(h). The Drafters' Analysis provides no reasons for the absence of a sanction. That does not mean, however, that the disclosed information is admissible. The *in camera* proceedings noted in Rule 505 and used to determine admissibility of classified information are also available here for determining whether the unclassified government information is privileged and inadmissible. To obtain the *in camera* proceeding, the government bears the burden of first demonstrating that the disclosure reasonably could be expected to cause identifiable damage to the public interest. If the standard is satisfied, the accused is given notice of the proposed hearing. Information not previously disclosed to the accused may be referred to by generic category. The standard for disclosure under (i)(4)(B) is much lower than for disclosure of classified information under Rule 505(i)(4)(B). Under this Rule, the defense is entitled to the information if it is relevant to the issue of guilt or innocence and is otherwise admissible. There is no provision in subdivision (i) for alternatives to complete disclosure.[1] Continued government objection to disclosure may trigger dismissal of appropriate charges. No lesser sanctions are specified.

[10]   Rule 506(j)—Introduction of Government Information Subject to a Claim of Privilege

Under subdivision (j) the military judge is given the authority to take precautions to prevent unnecessary disclosure. Specific provision is made in (j)(2) for consideration of other proof of contents of an original document containing privileged information. *See also* Rule 1002 and Rule 505(j)(3). Not surprisingly, there is no provision for closed hearings under this Rule, since no classified information is involved.

[11]   Rule 506(k)—Procedures to Safeguard Against Compromise of Government Information Disclosed to Courts-Martial

Like its counterpart in Rule 505(k), subdivision (k) provides that the Secretary of Defense may provide procedures to safeguard government information that has been disclosed to trial or appellate authorities after the government has unsuccessfully claimed a privilege.

---

[1]   *Compare* Rule 505(i)(4)(D).

§ 506.03   Drafters' Analysis

[1]   General Rule of Privilege

Rule 506(a) states the general rule of privilege for nonclassified government information. The Rule recognizes that in certain extraordinary cases the government should be able to prohibit release of government information that is detrimental to the public interest. The Rule is modeled on Rule 505 but is more limited in its scope in view of the greater limitations applicable to nonclassified information. *Compare United States v. Nixon,* 418 U.S. 683 (1974) *with United States v. Reynolds,* 345 U.S. 1 (1953). Rule 506 addresses those similar matters found in present *Manual* ¶¶ 151 *b* (1) and 151 *b* (3). Under Rule 506(a) information is privileged only if its disclosure would be "detrimental to the public interest." It is important to note that pursuant to Rule 506(c) the privilege may be claimed only "by the head of the executive or military department or government agency concerned" unless investigations of the Inspectors General are concerned.

Under Rule 506(a) there is no privilege if disclosure of the information concerned is required by an Act of Congress such as the Freedom of Information Act, 5 U.S.C. § 552 (1976). Disclosure of information will thus be broader under the Rule than under the present *Manual. See United States v. Nixon,* 418 U.S. 683 (1974).

[2]   Scope

Rule 506(b) defines "government information" in a nonexclusive fashion, and expressly states that classified information and information relating to the identity of informants are solely within the scope of other Rules.

[3]   Who May Claim the Privilege

Rule 506(c) distinguishes between government information in general and investigations of the Inspectors General. While the privilege for the latter may be claimed "by the authority ordering the investigation or any superior authority," the privilege for other government information may be claimed *only* "by the head of the executive or military department or government agency concerned." *See generally* the *Analysis* to Rule 505(c).

[4]   Action Prior to Referral of Charges

Rule 506(d) specifies action to be taken prior to referral of charges in the event of a claim of privilege under the Rule. *See generally* Rule 505(d) and its *Analysis.* Note that disclosure can be withheld *only* if action under paragraphs (1)-(4) of subdivision (d) cannot be made "without causing *identifiable* damage to the public interest." [Emphasis added].

[5]   Action After Referral of Charges

See generally Rule 505(f) and its *Analysis.* Note that unlike Rule 505(f), however, Rule 506(e) does not require a finding that failure to disclose the information in question "would materially prejudice a substantial right of the accused." Dismissal is required when the relevant information is not disclosed in a "reasonable period of time."

[6] Pretrial Session

Rule 506(f) is taken from Rule 505(e). It is the intent of the Committee that if classified information arises during a proceeding under Rule 506, the procedures of Rule 505 will be used.

[7] Disclosure of Government Information to the Accused

Rule 506(g) is taken from Rule 505(g) but deletes references to classified information and clearances due to their inapplicability.

[8] Prohibition Against Disclosure

Rule 506(h) is derived from Rule 505(h) (4). The remainder of Rule 505(h) (4) and Rule 505(h) generally has been omitted as being unnecessary. No sanction for violation of the requirement has been included.

[9] In Camera Proceedings

Rule 506(i) is taken generally from Rule 505(i), but the standard involved reflects present *Manual* ¶ 151 and the Supreme Court's decision in *United States v. Nixon,* 418 U.S. 683 (1974). In line with *Nixon,* the burden is on the party claiming the privilege to demonstrate why the information involved should not be disclosed. References to classified material have been deleted as being inapplicable.

[10] Introduction of Government Information Subject to a Claim of Privilege

Rule 506(j) is derived from Rule 505(j) with appropriate modifications being made to reflect the nonclassified nature of the information involved.

[11] Procedures to Safeguard Against Compromise of Government Information Disclosed to Courts-Martial

Rule 506(k) is derived from Rule 505(k). Such procedures should reflect the fact that material privileged under Rule 506 is not classified.

§ 506.04 Drafters' Analysis (1990)

Subsection (c) was amended by substituting the words "records and information" for "investigations," which is a term of art vis-a-vis Inspector General functions. Inspectors General also conduct "inspections" and "inquiries," and use of the word "records and information" is intended to cover all documents and information generated by or related to the activities of Inspectors General. Records "includes reports of inspection, inquiry, and investigation conducted by an Inspector General and extracts, summaries, exhibits, memorandums, notes, internal correspondence, handwritten working materials, untranscribed shorthand or stenotype notes of unrecorded testimony, tape recordings, and other supportive records such as automated data extracts. In conjunction with this change, the language identifying the official entitled to claim the privilege for Inspector General records was changed to maintain the previous provision which allowed the superiors of Inspector General officers, rather than the officers themselves, to claim the privilege.

§ 506.05   Annotated Cases

[1]   Rule 506(i)—In Camera Proceedings

United States Court of Appeals for the Armed Forces

United States v. Rivers, 49 M.J. 434 (C.A.A.F. 1998): The court held that the trial court and the Court of Criminal Appeals followed the correct procedure in conducting an in camera review of privileged materials (involving a government witness) sought by the defense. Both courts had concluded that the materials were not relevant or material to the case. The court recognized that appellate review of such issues is not equivalent to the assistance of counsel in "ferreting out information," but also noted that the defense is not entitled to unrestricted access to government materials.

Navy-Marine Corps Court of Criminal Appeals

United States v. Taylor, 60 M.J. 720 (N.M.Ct.Crim.App. 2004): At the accused's trial on charges that he had attempted to purchase a female child, the accused requested production of a Cooperating Witness Utilization Record (CWUR) on one of the prosecution's key witnesses. The Director of the NCIS claimed a privilege under Rule 506, arguing that release of the record would be detrimental to public interests and hamper future investigations. Following an in camera review, the military judge concluded that the CWUR contained information about the credibility of the witness and the manner in which the agents had investigated the offense. The judge ordered that if a redacted copy was not released to the defense, the prosecution could not call the witness to testify. On a government appeal of that ruling, the Court of Criminal Appeals rejected the argument that the judge had failed to balance the government's interests, as required by Rule 506. The court stated that the judge's redactions of the CWUR demonstrated that he had balanced the competing interests. It also rejected the argument that the judge's ruling amounted to an abuse of discretion because there was other impeaching evidence available to the defense.

§ 507.01   Official Text

Rule 507.   Identity of Informant.

(a) *Rule of Privilege.* The United States or a State or subdivision thereof has a privilege to refuse to disclose the identity of an informant. An "informant" is a person who has furnished information relating to or assisting in an investigation of a possible violation of law to a person whose official duties include the discovery, investigation, or prosecution of crime. Unless otherwise privileged under these rules, the communications of an informant are not privileged except to the extent necessary to prevent the disclosure of the informant's identity.

(b) *Who May Claim the Privilege.* The privilege may be claimed by an appropriate representative of the United States, regardless of whether the information was furnished to an officer of the United States or of a State or subdivision thereof. The privilege may be claimed by an appropriate representative of a State or subdivision if the information was furnished to an officer thereof, except the privilege shall not be allowed if the prosecution objects.

(c) *Exceptions.*

(1) *Voluntary Disclosures; Informant as Witness.* No privilege exists under this rule: (A) if the identity of the informant has been disclosed to those who would have cause to resent the communication by a holder of the privilege or by the informant's own action; or (B) if the informant appears as a witness for the prosecution.

(2) *Testimony on the Issue of Guilt or Innocence.* If a claim of privilege has been made under this rule, the military judge shall, upon motion by the accused, determine whether disclosure of the identity of the informant is necessary to the accused's defense on the issue of guilt or innocence. Whether such a necessity exists will depend on the particular circumstances of each case, taking into consideration the offense charged, the possible defense, the possible significance of the informant's testimony, and other relevant factors. If it appears from the evidence in the case or from other showing by a party that an informant may be able to give testimony necessary to the accused's defense on the issue of guilt or innocence, the military judge may make any order required by the interests of justice.

(3) *Legality of Obtaining Evidence.* If a claim of privilege has been made under this rule with respect to a motion under Mil. R. Evid. 311, the military judge shall, upon motion of the accused, determine whether disclosure of the identity of the informant is

required by the Constitution of the United States as applied to members of the armed forces. In making this determination, the military judge may make any order required by the interests of justice.

(d) *Procedures.* If a claim of privilege has been made under this rule, the military judge may make any order required by the interests of justice. If the military judge determines that disclosure of the identity of the informant is required under the standards set forth in this rule, and the prosecution elects not to disclose the identity of the informant, the matter shall be reported to the convening authority. The convening authority may institute action to secure disclosure of the identity of the informant, terminate the proceedings, or take such other action as may be appropriate under the circumstances. If, after a reasonable period of time disclosure is not made, the military judge, sua sponte or upon motion of either counsel and after a hearing if requested by either party, may dismiss the charges or specifications or both to which the information regarding the informant would relate if the military judge determines that further proceedings would materially prejudice a substantial right of the accused.

§ 507.02 Editorial Comment

Recognizing the strong policy of preserving the anonymity of informants, in order to protect them from retaliation, Rule 507 adopts the familiar informant privilege.[1] It generally follows the format of proposed Federal Rule 510.[2]

[1] Rule 507(a)—Rule of Privilege

The general rule of privilege is set out in subdivision (a) which states that federal, state, and local authorities may block disclosure of the identity of an informant (although under (b) state and local claims cannot withstand the objection of the prosecution). An informant is defined in broad fashion and includes ordinary citizens who offer information, as well as paid undercover agents. The communications must have been made to a person whose official duties involve discovery, investigation, and prosecution of crime. Thus, statements to public officials not involved in law enforcement would not qualify under the Rule.

The privilege is limited to "identity" and does not block disclosure of any

---

[1] *See* Roviaro v. United States, 353 U.S. 53 (1957).

[2] *See generally* United States v. Ness, 32 C.M.R. 18 (C.M.A. 1962); United States v. Hawkins, 19 C.M.R. 261 (C.M.A. 1955). For the proposed Federal Rule and the accompanying Advisory Committee Note, *see* 5 S. Saltzburg, M. Martin, & D. Capra, FEDERAL RULES OF EVIDENCE MANUAL, Part 3, pp 24–27 (9th ed. 2006).

statements made by the informant unless they too might directly or indirectly identify the informant.[3]

Although Rule 507 does not address the issue, there is federal authority that the government has a privilege not to disclose its surveillance locations.[4]

[2] Rule 507(b)—Who May Claim the Privilege

According to subdivision (b), both federal and state authorities are potential claimants of the privilege—not the informant.[5] Federal authorities may claim it regardless of whether the recipient of the information was a federal or state officer. But authorities of a state or its subdivisions may claim it only if the information was given to one of *its* officers, and only if the prosecution does not object. The Rule specifically notes that an "appropriate representative" of either entity may claim the privilege but does not further define that term. The Drafters' Analysis to this Rule and the Advisory Committee Note to the proposed Federal Rule indicate that the prosecutor will normally be the appropriate claimant. This certainly will not always be the case, however. Under the facts of a particular case, a military investigator might be the proper claimant.[6]

[3] Rule 507(c)—Exceptions

[a] Exceptions—Prior Disclosure

Subdivision (c) covers those situations where the privilege does not apply. First, under (c)(1), the privilege is not available where the informant's identity has already been disclosed to "those who would have cause to resent the communication." *Roviaro v. United States, above.* This would generally not include disclosures to other law enforcement agencies. The disclosure may come from either a holder of the privilege or the informant himself—a

---

[3] *See* Roviaro v. United States, *above,* and Bowman Dairy Co. v. United States, 341 U.S. 214, 221 (1951).

[4] United States v. Foster, 986 F.2d 541 (D.C. Cir. 1993) (under facts, government did not have privilege to refuse to disclose location of observation post used to watch drug buy); United States v. Angiulo, 847 F.2d 956 (1st Cir. 1988) (government entitled to qualified privilege not to disclose location of microphones used to intercept telephone conversations); United States v. Van Horn, 789 F.2d 1492 (11th Cir. 1986) (government has qualified privilege not to reveal types and locations of electronic surveillance equipment absent defense proof that such information irrelevant and helpful to the defense or is essential to a fair trial). *See also* United States v. Aguirre Aguirre, 716 F.2d 293 (5th Cir. 1983) (trial court's refusal to permit disclosure of informant's location upheld, even though identity was known to the defendant).

[5] *See In re* Grand Jury Investigation (Detroit Police Department Special Cash Fund), 922 F.2d 1266 (6th Cir. 1991) (informer's privilege is not available to grand jury target who seeks to avoid inquiry into his own possible criminal conduct).

[6] *See, e.g.,* Bocchicchio v. Curtis Publishing Co., 203 F. Supp. 403 (E.D. Pa. 1962) (civil action in which local policeman successfully claimed the privilege).

twist on other privilege rules where only the holder may waive a privilege.[7]

The Rule implicitly recognizes that, once such disclosure has been made it is no longer possible to conceal the identity of the person who cooperated with enforcement officials. And, if the informant testifies for the prosecution, the defense should be permitted to inquire into the relationship between the government and the witness.[8] The idea here is that the fact that the person is appearing as a government witness, means that the accused has reason to resent the person, and disclosure of the informant is likely to add little to the hostility that the accused already may feel toward the person. The privilege does not fall, however, where the defense calls the witness in an attempt to discover whether he or she is an informant, since the accused remains unsure whether he or she has reason to be hostile to the informant and the Rule does not want to encourage hostility.

[b]   Exceptions—Need for Evidence

Where the defense can show that the informant's identity is necessary to determine guilt or innocence, the privilege gives way under (c)(2) to the defendant's need for evidence. This exception is based in part on compulsory process considerations and the Sixth Amendment right of an accused to present a defense.[9] The Rule here follows pre-Rules law and provides no concrete guidance on when disclosure is required—only that specific facts and circumstances will play a large part in the determination. As a general rule, the defense burden will not be satisfied by mere speculation that an informant might be helpful.[10]

Not specifically noted in (c)(2), but nonetheless important as a "relevant" factor, is the potential harm to an informant. In the balance, mere tipsters will normally not be identified, *cf.* subdivision (c)(3), while those informants who were active participants in, or eyewitnesses to, the crime generally will be.[11]

[c]   Exceptions—Suppression Motions

Rule 507(c)(3) addresses those situations where an informant's identity may be constitutionally required in an inquiry into the validity of a search or seizure under Rule 311.[12] The provision is generally patterned after

---

[7] *See, e.g.,* United States v. Herrero, 893 F.2d 1512 (7th Cir.), *cert. denied,* 496 U.S. 927, 496 U.S. 927 (1990) (prosecution did not waive privilege where judge issued order against disclosure after prosecutor revealed informants identity at side-bar).

[8] *See, e.g.,* Harris v. United States, 371 F.2d 365 (9th Cir. 1967).

[9] *See, e.g.,* United States v. Silva, 580 F.2d 144 (5th Cir. 1978).

[10] United States v. Marshall, 532 F.2d 1279 (9th Cir. 1976).

[11] *See* United States v. Skeens, 449 F.2d 1066 (D.C. Cir. 1971).

[12] *See generally* Franks v. Delaware, 442 U.S. 928 (1978); McCray v. Illinois, 386 U.S. 300 (1967).

proposed Federal Rule of Evidence 510(c)(3), but, unlike that provision, the Military Rule offers no specific guidance. The proposed Federal Rule would have permitted disclosure if the judge was "not satisfied that the information [used to support obtaining the evidence] was received from an informer reasonably believed to be reliable or credible." Although the plain language of the Military Rule does not so provide, the drafters suggest in their Analysis that the military judge should consider the "prevailing case law utilized in the trial of criminal cases in the federal district courts." This law generally holds that the identity of the informant is not revealed when the informant's only relationship to the case is that officers relied upon him or her in making an arrest or obtaining a warrant. In an exceptional case in which the good faith of the officers who acted is in question, the identity may be revealed, perhaps only to the judge at first, and thereafter also to the accused, if necessary.

[d]   Rule 507(d)—Procedures

Some general guidance on handling claims of informant privilege is included in subdivision (d), which requires some decisions by the convening authority if the prosecution decides to withhold disclosure after a military judge has ruled that disclosure of an informant's identity is required. Failure to disclose may result in dismissal of charges.

Noticeably absent from both the Rule and the Drafters' Analysis is any reference to the possibility of holding in camera proceedings to determine whether disclosure is required. Such private consideration by the judge is specifically noted in proposed Federal Rule 510(c), and seems to find some support in pre-Rules military case law.[13] Although not required or even recommended by Rule 507, that practice is commendable.[14] In addressing in camera hearings in this area the Advisory Committee Note on the proposed Federal Rule states that:

> The limited disclosure to the judge avoids any significant impairment of secrecy, while affording the accused a substantial measure of protection against arbitrary police action. The procedure is consistent with [*McCray v. Illinois*, 386 U.S. 300 (1967)] and the decisions there discussed.

That rationale seems equally applicable under the Military Rule.

§ 507.03   Drafters' Analysis

[1]   Rule of Privilege

Rule 507(a) sets forth the basic rule of privilege for informants and contains the substance of present *Manual* ¶ 151 *b* (1). The new Rule,

---

[13] *See, e.g.,* United States v. Bennett, 3 M.J. 903, 906 n.2 (A.C.M.R. 1977).

[14] *See, e.g.,* United States v. Spires, 3 F.3d 1234 (9th Cir. 1993) (once defendant shows that disclosure of informant is relevant and may be helpful, trial court must hold in camera hearing).

however, provides greater detail as to the application of the privilege than does the present *Manual*.

The privilege is that of the United States or political subdivision thereof and applies only to information relevant to the identity of an informant. An informant is simply an individual who has supplied information resulting in an investigation of a possible violation of law to a proper person and thus includes good citizen reports to command or police as well as the traditional confidential informants who may be consistent sources of information.

[2]   Who may Claim the Privilege

Rule 507(b) provides for claiming the privilege and distinguishes between representatives of the United States and representatives of a state or subdivision thereof. Although an appropriate representative of the United States may always claim the privilege when applicable, a representative of a state or subdivision may do so only if the information in question was supplied to an officer of the state or subdivision. The Rule is taken from proposed Federal Rule of Evidence 510(b), with appropriate modifications, and is similar in substance to ¶ 151 *b* (1) of the present *Manual* which permits appropriate governmental authorities to claim the privilege.

The Rule does not specify who an appropriate representative is. Normally, the trial counsel is an appropriate representative of the United States. The Rule leaves the question open, however, for case by case resolution. Regulations could be promulgated which could specify who could be an appropriate representative.

[3]   Exceptions

Rule 507(c) sets forth the circumstances in which the privilege is inapplicable.

[a]   Voluntary Disclosures; Informant as Witness

Rule 507(c)(1) makes it clear that the privilege is inapplicable if circumstances have nullified its justification for existence. Thus, there is no reason for the privilege, and the privilege is consequently inapplicable, if the individual who would have cause to resent the informant has been made aware of the informant's identity by a holder of the privilege or by the informant's own action or when the witness testifies for the prosecution thus allowing that person to ascertain the informant's identity. This is in accord with the intent of the privilege which is to protect informants from reprisals. The Rule is taken from ¶ 151 *b* (1) of the present *Manual*.

[b]   Testimony on the Issue of Guilt or Innocence

Rule 507(c)(2) is taken from present *Manual* ¶ 151 *b* (1) and recognizes that in certain circumstances the accused may have a due process right under the Fifth Amendment, as well as a similar right under the Uniform Code of Military Justice, to call the informant as a witness. The subdivision intentionally does not specify what circumstances would require calling the informant and leaves resolution of the issue to each individual case.

[c]   Legality of Obtaining Evidence

Rule 507(c)(3) is new. The Rule recognizes that circumstances may exist in which the Constitution may require disclosure of the identity of an informant in the context of determining the legality of obtaining evidence under Rule 311; *see, e.g., Franks v. Delaware,* 438 U.S. 154, 167 (1978); *McCray v. Illinois,* 386 U.S. 300 (1967) (both cases indicate that disclosure may be required in certain unspecified circumstances but do not in fact require such disclosure). In view of the highly unsettled nature of the issue, the Rule does not specify whether or when such disclosure is mandated and leaves the determination to the military judge in light of prevailing case law utilized in the trial of criminal cases in the federal district courts.

[4]   Procedures

Rule 507(d) sets forth the procedures to be followed in the event of a claim of privilege under Rule 507. If the prosecution elects not to disclose the identity of an informant when the judge has determined that disclosure is required, that matter shall be reported to the convening authority. Such a report is required so that the convening authority may determine what action, if any, should be taken. Such actions could include disclosure of the informant's identity, withdrawal of charges, or some appropriate appellate action.

§ 507.04   Annotated Cases

United States Court of Appeals for the Armed Forces

United States v. Gray, 51 M.J. 1 (C.A.A.F. 1999): The court held that the trial judge did not err in the accused's murder trial in ruling that the government was not required to produce an anonymous registered informant. Although the accused had argued that the informant could provide helpful information to rebut the government's case, the court concluded that none of the information supposedly possessed by the informant could be considered exculpatory evidence.

Army Court of Criminal Appeals

United States v. Watkins, 32 M.J. 1054 (A.C.M.R. 1991): At trial, the defense unsuccessfully requested the identity of the person who had identified the accused as the perpetrator of the offenses. The court held that the trial judge properly denied the motion because the defense had only shown the possibility that the informant might provide impeaching evidence regarding a key government witness. Mere speculation, the court said, will not require disclosure.

United States v. Coleman, 14 M.J. 1014 (A.C.M.R. 1982): The court affirmed the trial court's decision not to order disclosure of an informant.

Citing Rule 507, the court noted that the confidential informant only supplied information that led the government to the accused and was not involved in any transaction with the accused. Further, the defense did not show that the informant's identity was necessary for its case.

United States v. Adolph, 13 M.J. 775 (A.C.M.R. 1982): At trial the prosecution refused to disclose the identity of a telephone caller who had told Major *G* (the accused's executive officer) that the accused was going to turn in a stolen rifle. The court ruled that, under subsection (a), Major *G* was a proper recipient of the information; the drafters' analysis includes citizen reports to *command* personnel. The court further noted that, under (b) the trial counsel was an appropriate person to invoke the privilege and that disclosure was not required by (c)(2).

§ 508.01   Official Text

> **Rule 508.   Political Vote.**
>
> A person has a privilege to refuse to disclose the tenor of the person's vote at a political election conducted by secret ballot unless the vote was cast illegally.

§ 508.02   Editorial Comment

It is not surprising that there have been no military developments on Rule 508, which is identical to proposed Federal Rule of Evidence 507. Like its counterpart, it recognizes that not only should secrecy in balloting be protected, but also that after a vote is cast secrecy also should be maintained. Such secrecy is an integral part of a democracy and is considered especially important in a military system sensitive to remaining apolitical.[1]

The privilege may not be claimed if the vote was illegally cast. However, the voter would normally be able to claim the privilege against self-incrimination. *See generally* Article 31(a), U.C.M.J. and Rule 301.

§ 508.03   Drafters' Analysis

Rule 508 is taken from proposed Federal Rule of Evidence 507 and expresses the substance of 18 U.S.C. § 596 (1976) that is applicable to the armed forces. The privilege is considered essential for the armed forces because of the unique nature of military life.

---

[1] *See* 18 U.S.C. § 596 (proscribes polling of armed forces regarding balloting).

§ 509.01   Official Text

> **Rule 509.   Deliberations of Courts and Juries.**
>
> Except as provided in Mil. R. Evid. 606, the deliberations of courts and grand and petit juries are privileged to the extent that such matters are privileged in trial of criminal cases in the United States district courts, but the results of the deliberations are not privileged.

§ 509.02   Editorial Comment

[1]   In General

Both military and civilian law endeavor to preserve the sanctity of the deliberative process of the factfinder.[1] Rule 509 follows pre-Rules law in stating that the deliberations of courts and grand and petit juries are privileged. The Rule specifically notes that the results of deliberation are not privileged. No federal evidence rule covers this privilege. A similar privilege is recognized in decided cases, however. The drafters wrote the Rule so that it will track the approach of the federal courts over time.

[2]   Exception

One exception to the privilege is found in Mil. R. Evid. 606(b), which permits intrusion into the deliberative process when there are questions whether (1) extraneous prejudicial information was improperly brought to the court members' attention; (2) any outside interference was improperly brought to bear upon any court-member; or (3) there was unlawful command influence. We further discuss these narrowly drawn exceptions under Rule 606. If the privilege does not apply, then either testimony or affidavits may be considered in assessing whether something so tainted judicial deliberations that the result should be set aside.

Although it is not clear in the Rule itself, if the privilege applies, the members and third parties are precluded from disclosing the deliberations in courts martial.[2]

[3]   Procedural Issues

Unfortunately, the Rule provides no procedural guidance for determining

---

[1] *See generally* Dean, *The Deliberative Privilege Under M.R.E. 509,* ARMY LAW., Nov. 1981, at 1 (this article addresses the extent of Rule 509 and the three exceptions to the privilege provided therein. Of particular interest is a section covering some of the procedural questions raised by the Rule, *i.e.,* the manner and timing of piercing the court-martial's deliberative process).

[2] *See* United States v. Harris, 32 C.M.R. 878 (A.F.B.R. 1962); United States v. Bourchier, 17 C.M.R. 15 (C.M.A. 1954).

who is to claim the privilege. Rule 606(b) also is silent on this point. Generally, the party relying on the result of the deliberations can be expected to object, although the court may raise the issue *sua sponte*.

To determine if the privilege is properly raised, the military judge may have to slightly intrude into the deliberations in order to determine whether an exception exists under 606(b).[3]

[4] Application of Rule to Judges' Deliberations

In a case of first impression, the Court of Appeals for the Armed Forces held in *United States v. Matthews*[4] that Rule 509 applies to military judges and that evidence of the judge's deliberative process is inadmissible, even if the judge is willing to testify.

At a judge-alone trial one of the defense witnesses invoked the privilege against self-incrimination 13 times during cross-examination. Although the military judge refused to strike the witness's direct testimony he relied on Rule 512(a) and permitted the prosecution to comment on the repeated invocations during his closing argument. The Court of Criminal Appeals ordered a *DuBay* hearing, *inter alia*, on the issue of whether the military judge drew any adverse inference from the witness's invocations of the right to remain silent. At the *DuBay* hearing, the trial judge testified at length about his thought processes in reaching his verdict and that he had drawn an adverse inference from the witness's silence. The Court of Criminal Appeals subsequently affirmed the accused's conviction, concluding that Rule 509 was not a bar against the judge's testimony at the *DuBay* hearing, but that both the trial judge and the *DuBay* hearing judge were incorrect in their application of Rule 512. The court held that Rule 301 provides the sole remedy where a witness refuses to answer questions on cross-examination—striking the direct testimony.

The Court of Appeals did not address the Rule 301 and 512 issues, but instead focused on the question of whether the original trial judge should have been permitted to testify about his deliberations during the *DuBay* hearing. The Court first addressed the issue of whether the term "courts" in Rule 509 applied to military judges. Noting that Rule 509 was based upon a provision originally included in the 1951 Manual for Courts-Martial[5] when the position of military judge did not exist, the Court nonetheless concluded that the term now encompasses military judges.

The Court next addressed the question of the meaning of "privilege" in

---

[3] *See* WEINSTEIN'S FEDERAL EVIDENCE, Chapter 104 (2d ed. 1997).

[4] United States v. Matthews, 68 M.J. 29 (C.A.A.F. 2009). *See* Annotated Cases, *below.*

[5] The Manual's provision stated: The deliberations of courts and of grand or petit juries are privileged but the results of their deliberations are not privileged." 1969 MCM Para. 151. The Drafters' Analysis, *infra*, states that Rule 509 was taken from that provision and modified to assure conformity with Rule 606(b).

Rule 509. The Court noted that the term as used in Rule was ambiguous and that the rule might be construed to be either a privilege like the other privileges in Section V (which may be waived or invoked) or as a privilege which bars disclosure. Citing *Fayerweather v. Ritch*,[6] and applying the federal common law, the Court concluded that the latter approach should be applied to Rule 509. The Court cited a number of reasons supporting the general rule of nondisclosure: protecting the integrity of the legal system; protecting the finality of judgments; avoiding the problem of reliability of a judge's memory about his or her deliberations; and avoiding concerns about the perception that the judge's testimony may be irrebuttable. In short, the record of trial itself, not a *DuBay* hearing, is the means for evaluating a judge's decision.[7] The Court rejected the argument that a judge could waive the protections of Rule 509 and concluded that reading Rule 509 as permitting a waiver would be inconsistent with the federal common law which has been incorporated into Rule 509, and the justifications supporting the protections provided by the Rule.

Matthews does not mean that Rule 509 applies in all cases and for all issues. The Court noted that the federal cases apply the deliberative privilege on a case-by-case basis and draw a distinction between, on the one hand, testimony about the historical facts of the case or where the judge is the only person with knowledge of the facts and, on the other hand, testimony about the judge's deliberative process.[8] The Court also noted that the facts before it did not involve a habeas petition, judicial bad faith, or misconduct,[9] thus implying that in those cases the privilege might not apply. For example, Rule 509 might not prohibit a judge's testimony in a case where there has been a plausible showing that unlawful command influence was brought to bear.[10]

When the Drafters adopted specific evidentiary privileges in the Military Rules of Evidence, they cited several important reasons for codifying privileges in military practice. Those same reasons support amendments to Rule 509 to include specific guidance to military courts and lawyers as to how the Rule may or may not apply in variety of predictable settings.[11]

§ 509.03   Drafters' Analysis

Rule 509 is taken from present *Manual* ¶ 151 but has been modified to

---

[6] Fayerweather v. Ritch, 195 U.S. 276 (1904).

[7] United States v. Matthews, 68 M.J. 29, 40–42 (C.A.A.F. 2009).

[8] United States v. Matthews, 68 M.J. 29, 39 (C.A.A.F. 2009).

[9] United States v. Matthews, 68 M.J. 29, 40–41 (C.A.A.F. 2009).

[10] The exceptions listed in Rule 606(b) may help a court in deciding whether to apply the Rule 509 privilege.

[11] The Court in *Matthews* noted that "[i]n fairness to the [Court of Criminal Appeals], the *DuBay* military judge, and the trial military judge, there is no definitive military case law from this Court on this issue, and sparse federal case law." 68 M.J. at 41.

ensure conformity with Rule 606(b) that deals specifically with disclosure of deliberations in certain cases.

§ 509.04   Annotated Cases

United States Court of Appeals for the Armed Forces

United States v. Matthews, 68 M.J. 29 (C.A.A.F. 2009): At the accused's bench trial the military judge relied on Rule 512(a)(2) and permitted the prosecution to comment during its closing argument on a defense witness's invocation of the privilege against self-incrimination. The Court of Criminal Appeals ordered a *DuBay* hearing and that judge, after taking testimony from the original trial judge, held that Rule 512 supported the trial judge's decision. The Court of Criminal Appeals held that Rule 509 did not bar the trial judge from testifying at the *DuBay* hearing and that both the military judge and the judge in the *DuBay* hearing erred in applying Rule 512 instead of the more specific, controlling provision in Rule 301(f). That rule, the court said, provides that the sole remedy for refusing to answer questions on cross-examination is to strike the witness's direct testimony. The court explained that, regardless of whether the direct testimony is stricken, neither the judge nor the court members may draw an adverse inference from the witness's invocation of the privilege. It concluded that trial counsel's argument was harmless error. *United States v. Matthews*, 66 M.J. 645 (Army Ct.Crim.App. 2008). Without addressing the question of the application of Rules 301 or 512, the Court of Appeals ruled that Rule 509 barred the testimony of the trial judge at the subsequent *DuBay* hearing. In a lengthy discussion of the issue, the Court noted that the term "courts" in Rule 509 applies to military judges but that the term "privilege" in the context of Rule 509 was ambiguous. Applying federal common law on evidentiary privileges, the Court concluded that, subject to narrow exceptions not present in this case, Rule 509 prohibits disclosure of a judge's deliberative process—regardless of whether the judge is willing to testify. The Court remanded the case to the Court of Criminal Appeals for further review.

Navy-Marine Corps Court of Criminal Appeals

United States v. Thomas, 39 M.J. 626 (N.M.C.M.R. 1993): Citing Rule 509, the court held that initial affidavits from the court members and their later court-ordered depositions about what transpired during their voting could not be considered.

§ 510.01   Official Text

Rule 510.   Waiver of Privilege by Voluntary Disclosure.

(a) A person upon whom these rules confer a privilege against disclosure of a confidential matter or communication waives the privilege if the person or the person's predecessor while holder of the privilege voluntarily discloses or consents to disclosure of any significant part of the matter or communication under such circumstances that it would be inappropriate to allow the claim of privilege. This rule does not apply if the disclosure is itself a privileged communication.

(b) Unless testifying voluntarily concerning a privileged matter or communication, an accused who testifies on his or her own behalf or a person who testifies under a grant or promise of immunity does not, merely by reason of testifying, waive a privilege to which he or she may be entitled pertaining to the confidential matter or communication.

---

§ 510.02   Editorial Comment

The privileges noted in these Rules are generally justified on the ground that it is important to maintain confidentiality or secrecy in some contexts in order to promote or to preserve the privacy of various relationships or the security of certain sensitive information. Once the holder of the privilege discloses the protected matter under circumstances indicating that the privacy of the relationship or the security of the information apparently is not critical, the privilege evaporates under Rule 510. The holder of a privilege or his predecessor has the right to voluntarily disclose, or consent to disclosure of, confidential matters or communications. Once this occurs, however, the privilege is removed and usually cannot be restored. (Note that involuntary disclosures are covered in Rule 512).

The waiver part of the Rule is drawn from proposed Federal Rule of Evidence 511 and is consistent with pre-Rules law that also permitted waiver of privileges. Waiver occurs only when the confidential matter or communication, *i.e.,* whatever the privilege covers, is disclosed inappropriately. Thus, a client may disclose that he or she has retained a lawyer, which fact usually is considered outside the protection of the privilege, without losing the protection for privileged communications with counsel.[1] If a significant part of the actual privileged communications is disclosed, waiver results.

The Rule plainly contemplates that not all disclosures of privileged

---

[1] *See* United States v. Aronoff, 466 F. Supp. 855 (S.D.N.Y. 1979).

material will constitute a waiver. One type of disclosure that does not result in waiver involves disclosure of some privileged matter in the context of another privileged communication. For example, one spouse may report to the other what he or she said to a lawyer without losing the privilege. Or, one spouse may tell the lawyer what was said to the other spouse and keep the privilege. Even outside privileged relationships, as noted above, waiver will only be found where, under the circumstances, it would not be appropriate to permit the holder to claim the privilege following disclosure of privileged material. The Rule itself does not elaborate on when a disclosure is appropriate, but the Drafters' Analysis uses the example of disclosure of an informant's identity to another law enforcement agency to illustrate what possibly may be an appropriate disclosure.[2]

Although the standard for a voluntary waiver is an intentional relinquishment of a known right,[3] the Rule implicitly recognizes that, once confidentiality is destroyed, a holder's attempts to claim the privilege will not restore it. The waiver here will stand even if the disclosure was made without the holder realizing the impact of the disclosure. Because the holder has destroyed the privacy or security afforded by the privilege by disclosure, repair cannot be made. It might be argued that the Rule is flexible enough to treat some unknowing disclosures as situations in which it would be appropriate to permit the holder subsequently to claim the privilege. For example, if the privileged material is disclosed by mistake following the exercise of due care, some civilian courts will allow the privilege to be retained, especially if privileged material is mistakenly included when massive amounts of documents are made available for discovery.

Subdivision (b) simply provides that by testifying an accused does not waive a privilege relating to confidential matters. *Compare* Rule 301(e) (accused waives privilege against self-incrimination by voluntarily testifying). The same holds true for witnesses testifying under a grant or promise of immunity.

§ 510.03   Drafters' Analysis

Rule 510 is derived from proposed Federal Rule of Evidence 511 and is similar in substance to present *Manual* ¶ 151 *a* which notes that privileges may be waived. Rule 510(a) simply provides that disclosure of any significant part of the matter or communication under such circumstances that it would be inappropriate to claim the privilege will defeat and waive the privilege. Disclosure of privileged matter may be, however, itself privileged; *see* Rules 502(b)(4); 503(b)(2); 504(b)(2). Information disclosed in the form of an otherwise privileged telephone call (*e.g.,* information overheard by an operator) is privileged, Rule 511(b), and information disclosed via transmis-

---

[2] *See also* United States v. Lipshy, 492 F. Supp. 35 (N.D. Tex. 1979).

[3] *See* Johnson v. Zerbst, 304 U.S. 458 (1938).

sion using other forms of communication may be privileged; Rule 511(b). Disclosure under certain circumstances may not be inappropriate and the information will retain its privileged character. Thus, disclosure of an informant's identity by one law enforcement agency to another may well be appropriate and not render Rule 507 inapplicable.

Rule 510(b) is taken from present ¶ 151 *b* (1) of the *Manual* and makes it clear that testimony pursuant to a grant of immunity does not waive the privilege. Similarly, an accused who testifies on his or her own behalf does not waive the privilege unless the accused testifies voluntarily to the privileged matter of communication.

§ 510.04   Annotated Cases

[1]   Rule 510(a)—(General Rule of Waiver)

[a]   In General

United States Court of Appeals for the Armed Forces

United States v. Custis, 65 M.J. 366 (C.A.A.F. 2007): The accused was taken to the base hospital for a blood alcohol test. Unbeknownst to the officers, the lab technician who took the blood was the accused's wife. Later that day, the accused and his wife took additional blood samples and substituted them for the samples at the hospital. The trial court and the Court of Criminal Appeals held that there was a common law crime or fraud exception to the privilege. The Court of Appeals reversed, holding that the text of Rule 504 contains no crime or fraud exception and that the military courts may not create an exception. The Court also concluded that the accused's single statement to a co-worker that his wife "had his back" did not waive the marital communications privilege.

United States v. McElhaney, 54 M.J. 120 (C.A.A.F. 2000): At trial, the military judge ruled that the accused's wife could testify about her conversations with the accused regarding his adulterous relationship with his legal ward because they constituted a crime against the wife. The Court of Criminal Appeals, concluded that, although the wife was not a victim, the accused had waived whatever privilege he may have had. The Court of Appeals also found a valid waiver. In this case, the court said, the accused had revealed a "significant part" of his otherwise protected privileged communication to his wife, when he wrote to his ward that the "cat was out of the bag" and made other successive and voluntary disclosures to his ward and her parents.

United States v. Smith, 33 M.J. 114 (C.M.A. 1991): At trial, the accused testified that her husband forced her to commit the crimes charged and that she had been afraid of him. The prosecution introduced a letter written by her to her husband which encouraged him to support her story. The service appellate court ruled that the letter was not privileged under the crime-fraud-exception recognized in the federal courts. 30 M.J. 1022 (A.F.C.M.R. 1990).

The Court of Appeals, ruled that the accused had waived the privilege by presenting testimony on the same general subject matter as the letter. In a concurring opinion, Judge Everett rejected the waiver argument, but opined that the letter was not privileged because the accused must have known that her letter would be screened by confinement facility personnel.

Air Force Court of Criminal Appeals

United States v. Romano, 43 M.J. 523 (A.F.Ct.Crim.App. 1995): Although a government witness disclosed her confidential communication to her lawyer at an Article 32 investigation, the court concluded that, under the facts, the trial court did not err in permitting her to reclaim the privilege and refuse to again relate the communication. Citing Rule 510, the court noted that, at the time she related the communication, she was a 20-year old, junior grade airman who did not have the benefit of the presence of counsel and revealed the communication under cross-examination.

[b] Waiver—By Testifying

Army Court of Criminal Appeals

United States v. Jackson, 30 M.J. 687 (A.C.M.R. 1990): The accused waived her attorney-client privilege when she elicited the testimony of her lawyer in an attempt to establish a defense based upon advice of counsel.

United States v. Rushatz, 30 M.J. 525 (A.C.M.R. 1990): The accused waived whatever privilege he had with regard to conversations with two lawyers when he mentioned on both direct and cross-examination the fact that he had had such conversations. *Cf.* McCormick, Evidence § 93 at 224 (3d ed. 1984) (questioning propriety of finding waiver of privilege on cross-examination).

United States v. Martel, 19 M.J. 917 (A.C.M.R. 1985): Although the accused referred to communications with his wife during cross-examination, the court ruled that doing so did not constitute waiver where the wife's testimony concerning those same communications should have been excluded, the accused timely challenged that evidence, and he scrupulously avoided testifying about those communications during his direct examination.

[2] Rule 510(b)—(Exception to General Rule of Waiver)

United States Court of Appeals for the Armed Forces

United States v. Romano, 46 M.J. 269 (1997): The court held that a witness' confidential conversations with her lawyer were not waived when she testified in the accused's trial under a grant of immunity. Citing Rule 510(b), the court concluded that testifying under a grant of immunity does not waive any available privileges. The court continued, however, by noting at any retrial of the case the trial judge might consider the issue of whether the privileged information might be disclosed because the accused's constitutional right to present a defense might outweigh the witness' attorney-client privilege.

§ 511.01 Official Text

Rule 511. Privileged Matter Disclosed Under Compulsion or Without Opportunity to Claim Privilege.

(a) Evidence of a statement or other disclosure of privileged matter is not admissible against the holder of the privilege if disclosure was compelled erroneously or was made without an opportunity for the holder of the privilege to claim the privilege.

(b) The telephonic transmission of information otherwise privileged under these rules does not affect its privileged character. Use of electronic means of communication other than the telephone for transmission of information otherwise privileged under these rules does not affect the privileged character of such information if use of such means of communication is necessary and in furtherance of the communication.

---

§ 511.02 Editorial Comment

[1] In General

As a general rule once privileged matter has been disclosed, confidentiality is also gone and may not later be recaptured. See our discussion of Rule 510. Rule 511, however, permits some relief for the holder of the privilege by creating an exclusionary rule of sorts.

The Rule is patterned after proposed Federal Rule of Evidence 512 and effects some changes in military practice. Under prior military practice, evidence of privileged information could be used if it had been obtained by a third party whether that party came upon the information by design or inadvertence. As we have noted in our discussion of the specific privilege rules found in Section V, some of the privileges permit a matter to remain privileged, even though a third person may be told of the matter, since disclosure of the information may further the interests that the privilege is intended to promote. And we have noted that Rule 510 permits disclosure of privileged information as part of another privileged communication and limits the waiver doctrine to disclosures that are inappropriate.

Rule 511 covers the situation in which there is no voluntary disclosure of privileged information; rather, the privileged material is improperly coerced from the holder or someone else, or is obtained under circumstances in which the holder has no opportunity to claim the privilege.

[2] Rule 511(a)—Compelled or Unknowing Disclosure

Subdivision (a) requires exclusion of privileged matters when offered against the privilege holder in two instances.

First, exclusion is called for where the disclosure was compelled erroneously. The Rule draws no fine lines as to who may do the compelling, but practice indicates, and the Rule apparently assumes, that it will most often arise in a judicial setting when a judge erroneously rejects a privilege claim. If erroneous disclosure is ordered by the judge over the objection of the holder and is discovered while the trial is still in progress, the evidence may be stricken unless it is such inflammatory material that only a mistrial will correct the error. If the error is not discovered until after trial, then the appellate court will assess the damage caused to the holder by the erroneous disclosure at trial.

Second, exclusion is required under subdivision (a) where the disclosure was made without the holder being given an opportunity to claim the privilege. Examples here would include discovery by eavesdroppers or persons who fortuitously overhear or see something not intended for their ears and eyes.

[3]   Rule 511(b)—Telephone or Electronic Submission

Subdivision (b) makes a special exception for use of telephones and other electronic means of communication. Privileged communications relayed over the telephone do not lose their privileged status. The Drafters' Analysis explains the breadth of this provision by noting that the privileged status remains even where the parties know that their telephone conversations are being monitored. It is not clear, however, how this section will work. If *A* knows that *B* is listening in on his conversation with a lawyer, then is *A* making confidential communications? If not, there is no privilege to begin with. A sensible rule is one that presumes that parties who use the phone believe that their conversations are not being overheard but that denies a privilege to one who chooses to say things knowing they will be overheard.

Privileged communications through other electronic means, *e.g.,* radio or telegraph, remain privileged only if the means are necessary and in furtherance of the communication. It matters not that the communication itself is unnecessary as long as the actual means used are considered necessary for the communication.

This Rule operates on the principle that the cat may be out of the bag when privileged material is discovered by a third party, but that it is still important that the holder, who has relied on the privilege and not waived it, be able to protect against having the disclosure intrusion compounded by the use of the material in court. Yet, this Rule protects only the holder against the injury associated with the use of the evidence. Once there is no longer a secret, the Rule does not protect others against whom the privileged material might be used. Of course, the hearsay rules of Section VIII might bar the use of the evidence anyway.

§ 511.03   Drafters' Analysis

Rule 511(a) is similar to proposed Federal Rule of Evidence 512. Placed in the context of the definition of confidential utilized in the privilege rules, *see, e.g.,* Rule 502(b)(4), the Rule is substantially different from present military law inasmuch as present law permits utilization of privileged information that has been gained by a third party through accident or design. *See* present *Manual* ¶ 151 *b* (1). Such disclosures are generally safeguarded against via the definition of confidential used in the new Rules. Generally, the Rules are more protective of privileged information than is the present *Manual.*

Rule 511(b) is new and deals with electronic transmission of information. It recognizes that the nature of the armed forces today often requires such information transmission. Like present *Manual* ¶ 151 *b* (1), the new Rule does not make a nonprivileged communication privileged; rather, it simply safeguards already privileged information under certain circumstances.

The first portion of subdivision (b) expressly provides that otherwise privileged information transmitted by telephone remains privileged. This is in recognition of the role played by the telephone in modern life and particularly in the armed forces where geographical separations are common. The Committee was of the opinion that legal business cannot be transacted in the 20th century without customary use of the telephone. Consequently, privileged communications transmitted by telephone are protected even though those telephone conversations are known to be monitored for whatever purpose.

Unlike telephonic communications, Rule 511(b) protects other forms of electronic communication only when such means is necessary and in furtherance of the communication. It is irrelevant under the Rule as to whether the communication in question was in fact necessary. The only relevant question is whether, once the individual decided to communicate, the *means* of communication was necessary and in furtherance of the communication. Transmission of information by radio is a means of communication that must be tested under this standard.

§ 511.04   Annotated Cases

United States Court of Appeals for the Armed Forces

United States v. Ankeny, 30 M.J. 10 (C.M.A. 1990): During informal discussions with an assistant judge advocate, the accused's defense counsel related the accused's confidential statements. This led to further investigation, an additional charge, and government testimony from a third party. Rejecting a narrow reading of Rule 511, and citing Rule 102 and Article 38, U.C.M.J., the court concluded that counsel's disclosure of the accused's statements and the derivative evidence could not be used against him.

§ 512.01   Official Text

Rule 512.   Comment Upon or Inference from Claim of Privilege; Instruction.

(a) *Comment or inference not permitted.*

(1)   The claim of a privilege by the accused whether in the present proceeding or upon a prior occasion is not a proper subject of comment by the military judge or counsel for any party. No inference may be drawn therefrom.

(2)   The claim of a privilege by a person other than the accused whether in the present proceeding or upon a prior occasion normally is not a proper subject of comment by the military judge or counsel for any party. An adverse inference may not be drawn therefrom except when determined by the military judge to be required by the interests of justice.

(b) *Claiming privilege without knowledge of members.*   In a trial before a court-martial with members, proceedings shall be conducted, to the extent practicable, so as to facilitate the making of claims of privilege without the knowledge of the members. This subdivision does not apply to a special court-martial without a military judge.

(c) *Instruction.*   Upon request, any party against whom the members might draw an adverse inference from a claim of privilege is entitled to an instruction that no inference may be drawn therefrom except as provided in subdivision (a)(2).

---

§ 512.02   Editorial Comment

Permitting comment on the invocation of a privilege whittles away at the privilege by placing a price on its assertion.[1] Rule 512 is an attempt to reduce, if not eliminate, the costs of asserting a privilege. It is generally new to military practice, insofar as it affects privileges other than the privilege against self-incrimination, and is patterned after proposed Federal Rule of Evidence 513.

[1]   Rule 512(a)—Comment or Inference Not Permitted

Subdivision (a)(1) bars comments from both the military judge and counsel on an accused's claim of privilege regardless of when the claim was made. In addition, no adverse inference may be drawn from the claim. *See also* Rule 301(f). We assume that the Rule bars comment and adverse inferences only where a claim of privilege by an accused is valid. If for

---

[1] *See* Griffin v. California, 380 U.S. 609, 614 (1965).

example, an accused refuses to answer questions, within the scope of direct examination, comment would be proper and an adverse inference could be drawn. Similarly, if an accused refuses to reveal a communication that the court rules is not privileged, comment and an adverse inference might follow.

Slightly different treatment is afforded to persons other than the accused under (a)(2). Normally, no comment is permitted. An inference may be drawn only where the judge determines that the interests of justice require it. The Rule provides no further guidance on what might trigger a comment or negative inference. Although the Drafters' Analysis uses an example where an inference might be drawn following a government claim of privilege, there is no reason to prohibit an inference to be drawn under (a)(2) against either side if the interests of justice so dictate. However, before an adverse inference can be drawn against, an accused it is likely that the court will have to find that the accused is somehow responsible for the privilege assertion that troubles the court.

[2] Rule 512(b)—Claiming Privilege Without Knowledge of Members

Subdivision (b) is intended to give meaning to (a) and requires the parties, where practicable, to conceal from the court members the fact that a privilege has been claimed. This is consistent with military and civilian case law[2] and the applicable ABA Standards Relating to Administration of Criminal Justice. Standards 3-5.7 and 4-7.6 provide that a lawyer should not call a witness who he or she knows will claim a valid privilege not to testify, for the purpose of impressing upon the jury the fact of the claim of privilege. In some instances, doing so will constitute unprofessional conduct.

To handle the problem of potential claims, the Drafters' Analysis suggests that out-of-court hearings or sidebar conferences should be used to determine whether a privilege will be claimed and its likely impact, if any, on the trial. Sidebar conferences may often be insufficient to protect the privilege, however. The Advisory Committee Note on the proposed Federal Rule counterpart addresses that point:

> The value of a privilege may be greatly depreciated by means other than expressly commenting to a jury upon the fact that it was exercised. Thus, the calling of a witness in the presence of the jury and subsequently excusing him or her after a sidebar conference may effectively convey to the jury the fact that a privilege has been claimed, even though the actual claim has not been made in their hearing. Whether a privilege will be claimed is usually ascertainable in advance and the handling of the entire matter outside the presence of the jury is feasible. Destruction of

---

[2] *See, e.g.,* Namet v. United States, 373 U.S. 179 (1963); United States v. Bricker, 35 C.M.R. 566 (A.B.R. 1965).

the privilege by innuendo can and should be avoided.[3]

Unanticipated situations are, of course, bound to arise, and much must be left to the discretion of the judge and the professional responsibility of counsel.

[3]   Rule 512(c)—Instruction

Much debate has centered on the effectiveness of an instruction by the judge not to draw any inferences from the claim of a privilege.[4] Subdivision (c) does not settle the question but rather simply permits counsel to request such an instruction. There is apparently no *sua sponte* duty on the military judge to give the instruction in the absence of a request. If a request is made, however, the instruction must be given except where the judge determines that justice requires an inference under Rule 512(a)(2).[5]

§ 512.03   Drafters' Analysis

[1]   Comment or inference not permitted

Rule 512(a) is derived from proposed Federal Rule 513. The Rule is new to military law but is generally in accord with the Analysis of Contents of the present *Manual;* United States Department of the Army. Pamphlet No. 27-2, Analysis of Contents, *Manual for Courts-Martial,* 1969, Revised Edition 27–33, 27–38 (1970).

Rule 512(a)(1) prohibits any inference or comment upon the exercise of a privilege by the accused and is taken generally from proposed Federal Rule of Evidence 513(a).

Rule 512(a)(2) creates a qualified prohibition with respect to any inference or comment upon the exercise of a privilege by a person not the accused. The Rule recognizes that in certain circumstances the interests of justice may require such an inference and comment. Such a situation could result, for example, when the government's exercise of privilege has been sustained, and an inference adverse to the government is necessary to preserve the fairness of the proceeding.

[2]   Claiming privilege without knowledge of members

Rule 512(b) is intended to implement subdivision (a). Where possible

---

[3] Courtney v. United States, 390 F.2d 521 (9th Cir. 1968); Tallo v. United States, 344 F.2d 467 (1st Cir. 1965); United States v. Tomaiolo, 249 F.2d 683 (2d Cir. 1957); San Fratello v. United States, 343 F.2d 711 (5th Cir. 1965); 6 WIGMORE § 1808, pp. 275–276; 6 U.C.L.A. L. REV. 455 (1959). This position is in accord with the general agreement of the authorities that an accused cannot be forced to make his election not to testify in the presence of the jury. 8 WIGMORE § 2268, p. 407 (McNaughton Rev. 1961).

[4] *See, e.g.,* United States v. Nunez, 668 F.2d 1116 (10th Cir. 1981) (improper to give instruction permitting jury to consider witness' invocation of fifth amendment). *Cf.* Baxter v. Palmigiano, 425 U.S. 308, 318 (1976).

[5] *See also* Rule 301(g).

claims of privilege should be raised at an Article 39(a) session or, if practicable, at sidebar.

[3] Instruction

Rule 512(c) requires that relevant instructions be given upon request. *Cf.* Rule 105. The military judge does not have a duty to instruct sua sponte.

§ 512.04 Annotated Cases

United States Court of Appeals for the Armed Forces

United States v. Flores, 69 M.J. 366 (C.A.A.F. 2011): The accused was charged with several offenses arising out of her duties as a member of the security forces in Iraq, where she developed an "unprofessional relationship" with one of the detainees. She pleaded guilty to some of the charges. During closing argument on the charges to which she pleaded not guilty, the trial counsel made five references that the accused argued on appeal were improper comments on her right to remain silent. The first, regarding the issue of whether the testimony of a prosecution witness was corroborated referred to statements she had made to the judge during the *Care* providence inquiry. The other four references impliedly referred to the absence of evidence from the accused. The court concluded that only the first comment regarding the statements made by the accused to the military judge during the *Care* inquiry amounted to plain, but harmless, error. The court noted that while the prosecution may rely on an accused's statements during the *Care* inquiry to support a lesser-included offense, they may not be used as evidence to prove separate offenses—as they were in case. Regarding the other four comments, the court concluded that the arguments were either not plain error or were fair comments on the state of the evidence.

United States v. Ashby, 68 M.J. 108 (C.A.A.F. 2009): The accused was tried on charges arising from the death of civilians when the aircraft he was piloting damaged a cable car in the Italian Alps. During her opening statement, the trial counsel commented on the fact that the accused remained silent when being interrogated by Italian police. The trial judge denied a defense motion for a mistrial, but the judge offered the parties an opportunity to voir dire the members and an opportunity to draft a curative instruction. The defense declined to re-voir the members but suggested revisions to the trial counsel's proposed curative instruction, which the judge gave to the members. The judge also polled the members individually, and each member stated that he would not let the trial counsel's comments impact his decision. Finally, the judge repeated the curative instruction at the close of the evidence. The Court of Appeals held that the trial judge did not err in denying the motion for a mistrial. His immediate curative actions cured any error and rendered it harmless beyond a reasonable doubt.

United States v. Matthews, 68 M.J. 29 (C.A.A.F. 2009): At the accused's bench trial the military judge relied on Rule 512(a)(2) and permitted the prosecution to comment during its closing argument on a defense witness's invocation of the privilege against self-incrimination. The Court of Criminal Appeals ordered a *DuBay* hearing and that judge, after taking testimony from the original trial judge, held that Rule 512 supported the trial judge's decision. The Court of Criminal Appeals held that Rule 509 did not bar the trial judge from testifying at the *DuBay* hearing and that both the military judge and the judge in the *DuBay* hearing erred in applying Rule 512 instead of the more specific, controlling provision in Rule 301(f). That rule, the court said, provides that the sole remedy for refusing to answer questions on cross-examination is to strike the witness's direct testimony. The court explained that, regardless of whether the direct testimony is stricken, neither the judge nor the court members may draw an adverse inference from the witness's invocation of the privilege. It concluded that trial counsel's argument was harmless error. *United States v. Matthews*, 66 M.J. 645 (Army Ct.Crim.App. 2008). Without addressing the question of the application of Rules 301 or 512, the Court of Appeals ruled that Rule 509 barred the testimony of the trial judge at the subsequent *DuBay* hearing. In a lengthy discussion of the issue, the Court noted that the term "courts" in Rule 509 applies to military judges but that the term "privilege" in the context of Rule 509 was ambiguous. Applying federal common law on evidentiary privileges, the Court concluded that, subject to narrow exceptions not present in this case, Rule 509 prohibits disclosure of a judge's deliberative process—regardless of whether the judge is willing to testify. The Court remanded the case to the Court of Criminal Appeals for further review.

United States v. Gray, 51 M.J. 1 (C.A.A.F. 1999): During sentencing at the accused's murder trial, the trial counsel alluded to the fact that the accused had not done anything during the trial to indicate any remorse for his actions. The defense objected and moved for mistrial, which was denied. The military judge instructed the court members that the argument might be construed to be an impermissible comment on the accused's right to remain silent and further instructed them not to draw that inference. The court concluded that, given the protective instruction, the judge did not err in denying the motion for a mistrial.

United States v. Cook, 48 M.J. 64 (C.A.A.F. 1998): In closing arguments the prosecution reminded the court members about the accused's act of yawning during his trial for murdering his young daughter. Defense counsel did not object. Without deciding directly whether the prosecutor's argument amounted to an improper comment on the accused's silence, the court held that, although yawning in the courtroom is not relevant to the question of guilt or innocence, the argument did not constitute plain error.

United States v. Riley, 47 M.J. 276 (C.A.A.F. 1997): The prosecution's lead witness recounted his unsuccessful attempts to obtain a statement from the accused and in the process made three references to the fact that the accused had invoked his rights to counsel and to remain silent; there was no defense objection to that testimony. The court held that admitting those statements amounted to plain error. The court observed that the rule forbidding comment on an accused's silence is grounded on the "open-eyed realization" that an accused's silence equates to a conclusion of guilt because the truly innocent person has nothing to hide by asserting his or her rights.

United States v. Webb, 38 M.J. 62 (C.M.A. 1993): The court held that the prosecutor's closing argument that the defense had failed to call the accused's wife to the stand, as promised in the defense's opening statement, was not an impermissible comment of the accused's failure to testify. The court noted that the propriety of commenting on a missing witness falls within the trial court's discretion, although, if the witness is equally available to both sides, it is normally better to preclude the comment.

Army Court of Criminal Appeals

United States v. Andreozzi, 60 M.J. 727 (Army Ct.Crim.App. 2004): Charged with raping his wife, the accused called a friend to testify that on several occasions the accused had told him that he wanted to save his marriage. After two objections to that testimony the judge instructed the members:

> Members of the court, you can't consider that part of the testimony. It is not before you. It is hearsay testimony. The trial counsel has not had an opportunity to cross-examine the person who allegedly made the statement; therefore you may not consider it.

The trial judge later denied a defense motion for a mistrial on the grounds that the instruction was a comment on the accused's right to remain silent. In his final instructions, the judge gave the standard instruction on the right of an accused to not testify at trial. On appeal, the court concluded that the judge's improper statement was extremely brief and isolated and that the follow-up instructions cured any possible prejudice.

United States v. Walker, 54 M.J. 568 (Army Ct.Crim.App. 2000): During an investigation into charges that the accused had committed an indecent act on a child, his wife was interviewed and make a written statement in which she said, "[The accused] did tell me what happened; however, I do not wish to disclose what he said." The trial judge treated the statement as a party admission under Rule 801. On appeal, the court held that the statement was protected by the martial communications privilege and that the government's introduction of the statement constituted an "adverse inference" and thus violated Rule 512(a)(2). Further, there was no finding by the military judge that introduction of evidence of the wife's invocation of the privilege was required by the interests of justice, as recognized in the rule.

Coast Guard Court of Criminal Appeals

United States v. Heath, 39 M.J. 1101 (C.G.C.M.R. 1994): The prosecutor's statements during closing argument about the accused's mendacity during the providency inquiry and his lack of rehabilitative potential did not amount to an improper comment on the accused's silence at trial.

Navy-Marine Corps Court of Criminal Appeals

United States v. Dossey, 66 M.J. 619 (N.M.Ct.Crim.App. 2008): During his trial on charges of involuntary manslaughter and making a false statement, the accused did not testify. During closing arguments the prosecutor said, "[w]e have shown—and there hasn't been any evidence presented to the contrary—that [the accused] shot [the victim]." The military judge sustained the defense objection to the statement and later instructed the members concerning the accused's right to remain silent. On appeal, the court held that in the context of the trial, the prosecutor's comments were nothing more than an argument on the state of the evidence and the strength of the government's case. The statement appeared only once in over 16 pages of transcript for the prosecutor's argument. Further, the defense appeared to concede the point by arguing that there wasn't any real dispute concerning the evidence that was presented against the accused regarding the victim. The court also rejected the argument that the prosecutor's argument constituted prosecutorial misconduct.

United States v. Pimienta, 66 M.J. 610 (N.M.Ct.Crim.App. 2008): The accused, who was charged with making a false official statement and involuntary manslaughter, was tried in absentia. During closing arguments, the trial counsel said: "We have shown—and there hasn't been any evidence presented to the contrary—that [the accused] shot [the victim]." The military judge sustained the defense objection. The Court of Criminal Appeals rejected the defense argument that the trial counsel's statement was an impermissible comment on the fact that the accused did not testify on his own behalf and reasoned that trial counsel's argument was nothing more than a comment on the strength of the prosecution's case. The court also noted that the defense apparently conceded the point that accused shot the victim. Finally, the court observed that the trial judge had instructed the members not to draw any adverse inferences from the fact that the accused had not appeared for his trial.

United States v. Cabrera-Frattini, 65 M.J. 950 (N.M.Ct.Crim.App. 2008): During his closing arguments, the trial counsel argued that the government's case was unrebutted. Although the accused did not object, the military judge interrupted the prosecutor, received assurances that the prosecutor's argument was not a comment on the accused's right to remain silent at trial, and instructed the court members that the accused had a right not to testify and that the burden never shifted to him to prove his innocence. The court reviewed the record and concluded that no plain error had occurred. To the extent that the argument was improper, the court said that, it was harmless beyond a reasonable doubt.

United States v. Toohey, 60 M.J. 703 ((N.M.Ct.Crim.App. 2004): During direct examination of a DPS Special Agent, the trial counsel established that the accused had not mentioned facts that he later used to support his defense at trial. There was no objection but on appeal the accused argued that such questioning amounted to an impermissible comment on his right to remain silent. Finding no plain error, the court stated that while eliciting evidence of pretrial silence to show consciousness of guilt is impermissible, counsel may point out that an accused has tailored his testimony at trial. Further, the prosecutor's questioning would have been entirely appropriate in rebuttal. Finally, the court rejected the accused's argument that the defense counsel's redirect examination about the same omissions by the accused during the interview amounted to ineffective assistance of counsel. The court held that counsel had made a reasonable tactical decision to elaborate on the accused's silence during the interview.

United States v. Wright, 47 M.J. 555 (N.M.Ct.Crim.App. 1997): The court concluded that an arresting officer's testimony that the accused did not seem surprised when he was apprehended did not amount to an impermissible comment on the accused's silence. The testimony, said the court, focused on the accused's demeanor. Even assuming the evidence was inadmissible, it was nonprejudicial.

United States v. Jackson, 40 M.J. 820 (N.M.C.M.R. 1994): The prosecutor's closing argument that the accused's tears at trial were in effect an admission of guilt was an impermissible comment on the accused's decision not to testify at trial. Although on curative instructions were not given, the court concluded that the comment on the accused's nontestimonial behavior was harmless error.

United States v. Dennis, 39 M.J. 623 (N.M.C.M.R. 1993): The prosecutor's comment during closing argument that no evidence had been presented to rebut the prosecution's key witness did not constitute an improper reference to the accused's silence at trial. Even assuming it did, the error was harmless.

United States v. Ray, 15 M.J. 808 (N.M.C.M.R. 1983): *Citing* Rule 512, the court stated that where the accused has voluntarily testified on direct examination, the prosecution may comment on his refusal to respond to cross-examination.

§ 513.01   Official Text

Rule 513.   Psychotherapist-Patient Privilege.

(a) *General Rule of Privilege.*   A patient has a privilege to refuse to disclose and to prevent any other person from disclosing a confidential communication made between the patient and a psychotherapist or an assistant to the psychotherapist, in a case arising under the UCMJ, if such communication was made for the purpose of facilitating diagnosis or treatment of the patient's mental or emotional condition.

(b) *Definitions.*   As used in this rule of evidence:

(1)   A "patient" is a person who consults with or is examined or interviewed by a psychotherapist for purposes of advice, diagnosis, or treatment of a mental or emotional condition.

(2)   A "psychotherapist" is a psychiatrist, clinical psychologist, or clinical social worker who is licensed in any state, territory, possession, the District of Columbia or Puerto Rico to perform professional services as such, or who holds credentials to provide such services from any military health care facility, or is a person reasonably believed by the patient to have such license or credentials.

(3)   An "assistant to a psychotherapist" is a person directed by or assigned to assist a psychotherapist in providing professional services, or is reasonably believed by the patient to be such.

(4)   A communication is "confidential" if not intended to be disclosed to third persons other than those to whom disclosure is in furtherance of the rendition of professional services to the patient or those reasonably necessary for such transmission of the communication.

(5)   "Evidence of a patient's records or communications" is testimony of a psychotherapist, or assistant to the same, or patient records that pertain to communications by a patient to a psychotherapist, or assistant to the same for the purposes of diagnosis or treatment of the patient's mental or emotional condition.

(c) *Who May Claim the Privilege.*   The privilege may be claimed by the patient or the guardian or conservator of the patient. A person who may claim the privilege may authorize trial counsel or defense counsel to claim the privilege on his or her behalf. The psychotherapist or assistant to the psychotherapist who received the communication may claim the privilege on behalf of the patient. The authority of such a psychotherapist, assistant, guardian, or conservator to so assert the privilege is presumed in the absence of evidence to the contrary.

(d) *Exceptions.* There is no privilege under this rule:

(1) when the patient is dead;

(2) when the communication is evidence of spouse abuse, child abuse, or neglect or in a proceeding in which one spouse is charged with a crime against the person of the other spouse or a child of either spouse;

(3) when federal law, state law, or service regulation imposes a duty to report information contained in a communication;

(4) when a psychotherapist or assistant to a psychotherapist believes that a patient's mental or emotional condition makes the patient a danger to any person, including the patient;

(5) if the communication clearly contemplated the future commission of a fraud or crime or if the services of the psychotherapist are sought or obtained to enable or aid anyone to commit or plan to commit what the patient knew or reasonably should have known to be a crime or fraud;

(6) when necessary to ensure the safety and security of military personnel, military dependents, military property, classified information, or the accomplishment of a military mission;

(7) when an accused offers statements or other evidence concerning his mental condition in defense, extenuation, or mitigation, under circumstances not covered by R.C.M. 706 or Mil. R. Evid. 302. In such situations, the military judge may, upon motion, order disclosure of any statement made by the accused to a psychotherapist as may be necessary in the interests of justice; or

(8) when admission or disclosure of a communication is constitutionally required.

(e) *Procedure to Determine Admissibility of Patient Records or Communications.*

(1) In any case in which the production or admission of records or communications of a patient other than the accused is a matter in dispute, a party may seek an interlocutory ruling by the military judge. In order to obtain such a ruling, the party shall:

(A) file a written motion at least 5 days prior to entry of pleas specifically describing the evidence and stating the purpose for which it is sought or offered, or objected to, unless the military judge, for good cause shown, requires a different time for filing or permits filing during trial; and

(B) serve the motion on the opposing party, the military judge and, if practical, notify the patient or the patient's guardian, conservator, or representative that the motion has been filed and that the patient has an opportunity to be heard as set forth in subparagraph (e)(2).

(2) Before ordering the production or admission of evidence of a patient's records or communication, the military judge shall conduct a hearing. Upon the motion of counsel for either party and upon good cause shown, the military judge may order the hearing closed. At the hearing, the parties may call witnesses, including the patient, and offer other relevant evidence. The patient shall be afforded a reasonable opportunity to attend the hearing and be heard at the patient's own expense unless the patient has been otherwise subpoenaed or ordered to appear at the hearing. However, the proceedings shall not be unduly delayed for this purpose. In a case before a court-martial composed of a military judge and members, the military judge shall conduct the hearing outside the presence of the members.

(3) The military judge shall examine the evidence or a proffer thereof in camera, if such examination is necessary to rule on the motion.

(4) To prevent unnecessary disclosure of evidence of a patient's records or communications, the military judge may issue protective orders or may admit only portions of the evidence.

(5) The motion, related papers, and the record of the hearing shall be sealed and shall remain under seal unless the military judge or an appellate court orders otherwise.

§ 513.02   Editorial Comment

Rule 513, which was added in 1999, recognizes a psychotherapist-patient privilege for military criminal justice proceedings.[1] Although the Drafters' Analysis indicates that the rule "clarifies" the privilege for purposes of military law, there was really nothing to clarify. The few cases that had addressed the issue had concluded that no such privilege exists in military practice, notwithstanding the Supreme Court's recognition of a common law privilege in *Jaffee v. Redmond*, 518 U.S. 1 (1996). Thus, the privilege was entirely new to military law. Although it is new to military practitioners, the Drafters' Analysis indicates that the rule is based in part on proposed Federal Rule of Evidence 504 (which was ultimately rejected by Congress) and on several state privileges. Therefore, the military bench and bar will surely find some assistance in how the federal and state courts have applied the counterparts to this rule.

---

[1] See Masterton, *The Military's Psychotherapist-Patient Privilege: Benefit or Bane For Military Accused?* ARMY LAW., Nov. 2001, at 18.

[1] Rule 513(a)—General Rule of Privilege

Rule 513(a) generally follows the model of other privileges in the Military Rules of Evidence, that is, the privilege rests with the communicator of the information. The privilege mirrors Rules 502 and 503 in that it recognizes a privilege for communications where the person is obtaining professional assistance. The privilege extends not only to statements made by the patient, but also to confidential statements made by the psychotherapist (or an assistant) to the patient. It thus generally follows the type of coverage set out in the attorney-client privilege. In contrast, under Rule 503, a statement by a clergy member to a person seeking spiritual assistance would not be protected.

While on its face, the privilege may appear broad, in fact it is not so broad. First, it only applies in cases arising under the Uniform Code of Military Justice. Clearly that would include the court-martial itself and also any of the pretrial and post-trial proceedings, including appellate procedures. But it could also extend to Article 15 nonjudicial punishment proceedings and to proceedings conducted under Article 135 (courts of inquiry) and Article 139 (redress of injuries to property). Although the rule itself indicates that the privilege applies to "a case arising under the UCMJ," the Drafters' Analysis indicates that the privilege is not to be applied "in any proceeding other than those authorized under the UCMJ." Thus, use of the word "case" in Rule 513(a) would imply a broader definition of that term. In contrast, Rule 1101 indicates that the Rules of Evidence, including this rule, are more limited in their application.

The Drafters' Analysis indicates that the privilege does not limit the use of such information "internally to the services, for appropriate purposes." It is not entirely clear what this means. It probably means that a patient may claim the privilege if disclosure is sought for purposes of a court-martial, but not if it is sought for purposes of administratively determining the medical or mental fitness of the patient. Nor would the privilege be available in administrative discharge board proceedings.

Second, the privilege apparently only applies to those communications made to a psychotherapist or an assistant to a psychotherapist. Those terms are defined in Rule 513(b). And third, the privilege only covers communications that were made for the purpose of "facilitating diagnosis or treatment of the patient's mental or emotional condition." Together, these two elements send a clear message that the drafters were clearly concerned that the rule should not extend to communications made to a medical doctor and thus undermine the mandate in Rule 501 that in military law there is no doctor-patient privilege.

That line may be difficult to draw. Apparently, if a service member consults with a medical doctor about a physical condition but mentions that he or she is depressed or even suicidal, the communication is not privileged. What if the doctor, in response to confidential communications made by the patient, prescribes an anti-depressant drug in an attempt to treat the patient? It seems clear in that case that the doctor is attempting to treat a potential mental condition of the patient. But if the doctor is not a psychotherapist, as defined in the rule, the communications will not be protected under Rule 513.

[2]   Rule 513(b)—Definitions

Rule 513(b) contains definitions for the key terms used throughout the rule. Its format is similar to that used in other professional privileges—Rule 502 (lawyer-client privilege) and Rule 503 (communications to clergy). In particular, Rule 513(b)(2) and (b)(3) include a good faith belief provision. That is, a patient will otherwise have the benefit of the privilege if he or she reasonably believed that the person providing mental health or emotional assistance is a licensed or credentialed professional. Rule 513(b)(5) defines the "evidence of a patient's records or communications" as the "testimony" of the psychotherapist or records that pertain to the patient. An argument could be made that the privilege thus covers pre-existing records that contain confidential communications made to other psychotherapists—as long as the statements were originally made for the purposes of the diagnosis or treatment of a mental health or emotional condition.

[3]   Rule 513(c)—Who May Claim the Privilege

As noted *above*, the privilege should cover communications made by either the patient, the psychotherapist, or an assistant to the latter.[2] Nonetheless, only the patient—or someone acting on behalf of the patient—may actually claim the privilege. That could include the trial or defense counsel.

[4]   Rule 513(d)—Exceptions

The eight exceptions in Rule 513(d) virtually swallow the privilege. According to the drafters, the exceptions are intended to emphasize that commanders have access to all information necessary to insure military readiness.

The privilege does not survive the death of the patient. *See* Rule 513(d)(1). This provision seems hard to reconcile with the prevailing view, for example, that the attorney-client privilege survives the death of the client. In particular, mental health information is often sensitive and privacy interests would seem to outbalance any need for disclosure.

Rule 513(d)(2) recognizes the familiar spousal or child abuse exception. *See also* Rule 504(c).

Rule 513(d)(3) and (d)(4) are potentially very broad exceptions. In Rule

---

[2] *See generally* Flippin, *Military Rule Of Evidence (MRE) 513: A Shield To Protect Communications of Victims and Witnesses to Psychotherapists*, ARMY LAW., Sep. 2003, at 1.

513(d)(3), not only may federal or state law require disclosure, but service regulations may also require disclosure. Although this exception certainly furthers the concerns of the drafters that important information not be protected, there is no further guidance on what sort of regulation might require the information.

In Rule 513(d)(4), communications are not privileged if the psychotherapist or the assistant believes that the patient poses a danger to himself or another person.[3]

Rule 513(d)(5) covers the familiar crime-fraud exception. The cases interpreting this exception for the attorney-client privilege are likely to be helpful in interpreting and applying this exception.

The broadest exception rests in Rule 513(d)(6). Under that provision, the communications are not privileged if anyone believes that disclosure is necessary to protect military personnel, readiness, or the mission. The exception provides no guidance on who may make that assessment. And the Drafters' Analysis is silent on examples of when this exception might apply.

Under Rule 513(d)(7), otherwise protected communications by an accused may be disclosed if the accused offers statements or other evidence concerning his mental state or condition, and that evidence would not otherwise be covered by the provisions of R.C.M. 706 or Military Rule of Evidence 302. Unlike the other exceptions, this exception explicitly involves a judicial officer in deciding whether to order disclosure, probably because it involves an accused involved in a court-martial.

Finally, Rule 513(d)(8) provides an exception grounded on constitutional principles. Although the Drafters' Analysis is silent on this point, the exception probably envisions those situations where an accused's right to confrontation would be limited by a witness invoking the privilege under this Rule. *See also* Rule 412(b)(1)(C).

[5]   Rule 513(e)—Procedure to Determine Admissibility of Patient Records or Communications

Rule 513(e) includes an extensive and detailed list of procedural steps that must be taken in deciding whether a privilege will be recognized. The underlying assumption of this provision is that the matter will be raised at a court-martial. But as noted *above*, the rule and the accompanying analysis suggest that the privilege may be invoked at any proceeding authorized under the Uniform Code of Military Justice. If that is the case, then there are no explicit procedural guidelines for addressing the privilege in proceedings other than court-martial proceedings.

---

[3] *See, e.g.*, United States v. Auster, 517 F.3d 312 (5th Cir. 2008) (court did not decide whether "dangerous patient" exception applied because defendant had been told repeatedly by therapist that his statements could be reported to authorities and victims).

§ 513.03   Drafters' Analysis (1999)

Military Rule of Evidence 513 establishes a psychotherapist-patient privilege for investigations or proceedings authorized under the Uniform Code of Military Justice. Rule 513 clarifies military law in light of the Supreme Court decision in *Jaffee v. Redmond*, 518 U.S. 1, 116 S. Ct. 1923, 135 L. Ed. 2d 337 (1996). *Jaffee* interpreted Federal Rule of Evidence 501 to create a federal psychotherapist-patient privilege in civil proceedings and refers federal courts to state laws to determine the extent of privileges. In deciding to adopt this privilege for courts-martial, the committee balanced the policy of following federal law and rules, when practicable and not inconsistent with the UCMJ or MCM, with the needs of commanders for knowledge of certain types of information affecting the military. The exceptions to the rule have been developed to address the specialized society of the military and separate concerns that must be met to ensure military readiness and national security. See *Parker v. Levy*, 417 U.S. 733, 743 (1974); *United States ex rel. Toth v. Quarles*, 350 U.S. 11, 17 (1955); *Department of the Navy v. Egan*, 484 U.S. 518, 530 (1988). There is no intent to apply Rule 513 in any proceeding other than those authorized under the UCMJ. Rule 513 was based in part on proposed Fed. R. Evid. (not adopted) 504 and state rules of evidence.

Rule 513 is not a physician-patient privilege. It is a separate rule based on the social benefit of confidential counseling recognized by *Jaffee*, and similar to the clergy-penitent privilege. In keeping with American military law since its inception, there is still no physician-patient privilege for members of the Armed Forces. See the analyses for Rule 302 and Rule 501.

[1]   General rule of privilege

The words "under the UCMJ" in this rule mean Rule 513 applies only to UCMJ proceedings, and do not limit the availability of such information internally to the services, for appropriate purposes.

[2]   Exceptions

These exceptions are intended to emphasize that military commanders are to have access to all information that is necessary for the safety and security of military personnel, operations, installations, and equipment. Therefore, psychotherapists are to provide such information despite a claim of privilege.

§ 513.04   Annotated Cases

United States Court of Appeals for the Armed Forces

United States v. Jenkins, 63 M.J. 426 (C.A.A.F. 2006): After the accused threatened individuals with a knife, he was sent to a command-ordered mental health evaluation by a clinical psychologist. During sentencing at his court-martial sentencing, the government offered the testimony of the psychologist to relate his observations and conclusions. The military judge overruled the defense objections to the testimony. On appeal, the court rejected the accused's arguments that admitting information from the mental examination were privileged under Rule 513. Without deciding whether the accused's statements to the psychologist were confidential, the court concluded that the testimony was admissible under the exceptions in Rule 513(d)(4) and (d)(6). The court recognized that the language in those exceptions does not state the specific context in which each exception might apply. Thus, the court continued, the military judge must make a fact-specific finding on whether any exception applies. The court held that the judge's decision to apply the exceptions-based at least in part on the opinion testimony of the experienced psychologist-was not an abuse of discretion.

United States v. Paaluhi, 54 M.J. 181 (C.A.A.F. 2000): Citing its decision in *United States v. Rodriguez*, *below*, the court held that statements the accused made to a military clinical psychologist before November 1, 1999 (adoption of Rule 513), were not privileged.

United States v. Rodriguez, 54 M.J. 156 (C.A.A.F. 2000): After he attempted to commit suicide, the accused made statements to federal civilian psychiatrist. In a pre-Rule 513 (but post-*Jaffe*, *above*) case, the court declined to recognize a psychotherapist-patient privilege under Rule 501(a)(4) as a federal common law privilege applicable to military practice. In an extensive discussion of the issue, the court concluded that the privilege was not recognized under Rule 501, as demonstrated by the President's promulgation of Rule 513, which in turn was not an adoption of *Jaffee*, but was rather a more limited privilege. Thus, the accused's statements to the medical doctor were not privileged.

United States v. Flack, 47 M.J. 415 (C.A.A.F. 1998): As a result of confidential statements made by defendant's daughter to a social worker with a Family Advocacy Program, agents began investigation of defendant. In a case preceding the promulgation of Rule 513, the court held that even assuming that the military recognized a psychotherapist-patient privilege, the defendant failed to show that he had standing to invoke the privilege or that it even applied to the case.

Army Court of Criminal Appeals

United States v. Demmings, 46 M.J. 877 (Army Ct.Crim.App. 1997): In a lengthy discussion of the issue, the court concluded that it could hold that confidential communications to a mental health professional in the course of diagnosis and treatment are protected from compelled disclosure. But, the court did not actually decide that issue because the accused had waived the issue at trial by failing to assert the privilege. Given the state of the law at the time of trial, said the court, the defense counsel was not ineffective in failing to raise the issue.

SECTION VI

WITNESSES

SYNOPSIS

§ 601.01   Official Text

> **Rule 601.   General Rule of Competency.**
> Every person is competent to be a witness except as otherwise provided in these rules.

§ 601.02   Editorial Comment

[1]   In General

Like its Federal counterpart, Military Rule of Evidence 601 is the key provision for determining who is competent to be a witness. At common law, and under previous editions of the *Manual for Courts-Martial*, witnesses could be prohibited from testifying if they suffered from certain categorical disabilities. At various times these were: mental infirmities, infamy, extreme youth, senility, bias or interest in the proceedings, spousal incapacity, co-accused or conspiratorial affiliations, religious beliefs, or official connections with the tribunal.[1]

Rule 601 alters these limitations by providing that every person is competent to be a witness[2] with a few exceptions found in other Section VI Rules. These other Rules cover the oath or affirmation requirement (Rule 603), interpreters (Rule 604), the disqualification of military judges (Rule 605) and court members (Rule 606). *See also* Section V on privileges.

The military version of Rule 601 follows the Federal Rule.[3] However, it has been altered to eliminate any reference to state law in civil cases.

[2]   Military Judge's Role in Deciding Competency Issues

In declaring that all persons are competent to testify, the Rule raises a question concerning the trial judge's common law power to voir dire witnesses to insure that their capabilities to observe, understand, recollect and communicate are adequate.[4] Although the policy of the Rule is against

---

[1] *See,* Connally, *"Out Of The Mouth[s] Of Babes": Can Young Children Even Bear Testimony?* ARMY LAW., Mar. 2008, at 1.

[2] *See, e.g.,* United States v. Mills, 597 F.2d 693 (9th Cir. 1979) (rejecting infamy as a reason not to permit a witness to testify); United States v. Lemere, 16 M.J. 682 (A.C.M.R. 1983) (three-and-one-half-year-old sexual assault victim was properly allowed to testify because categorical disabilities such as extreme youth have been rejected by the Military Rules of Evidence).

[3] *See, e.g.,* United States v. Gates, 10 F.3d 765 (11th Cir. 1993) (Rule allows mentally incompetent to testify and assumes jurors will evaluate testimony in light of witness' limitations).

[4] *See* Schlueter, Saltzburg, Schinasi & Imwinkelried, MILITARY EVIDENTIARY FOUNDATIONS § 3-1, et seq., (4th ed. 2010) (sample questioning of witness to determine competency).

exclusion of witnesses because of arbitrary classifications, some voir dire questions may aid the judge in making rulings under Rules 403 and 611(a) concerning a witness's testimony.

For example, there is no reason to permit an intoxicated or drugged witness to testify while under the influence. It is not adequate to say that intoxication affects only weight because the witness's intoxicated state may make cross-examination difficult, if not impossible. Moreover, there is something offensive about a court's acceptance of a drugged or drunk witness in its search for truth.[5] A continuance and a medical examination will assure the appearance of fairness and an adequate opportunity for cross-examination.[6] The witness who is intoxicated at trial must be distinguished from the witness who is sober at trial, but was intoxicated at the time of the events observed. No continuance will aid the latter type of witness, and his testimony probably should be admitted unless its prejudicial effect substantially outweighs its probative value.

United States v. Ramirez,[7] suggests that the trial judge's responsibilities over a witness's testimony encompasses three areas. First, consistent with Rule 403, the bench has an independent responsibility to insure that every witness's testimony is not unfairly prejudicial. Second, based on Rule 603, witnesses who cannot take or comprehend an oath or affirmation are unlikely to present helpful testimony, and as a result, should be excluded. Third, witnesses who are so impaired that their testimony is not the product of personal knowledge, as specified in Rule 602, have no foundation upon which to provide reliable testimony and should also be excluded. Under each of these circumstances, the military judge retains independent authority to hold an Article 39(a) session for the sole purpose of determining witness competence.[8]

[3] Expansive Philosophy of Rule 601

Even before Rule 601 was adopted, the basic tendency in federal and military courts was to allow virtually all witnesses to testify. This tradition, coupled with Rule 601, means that counsel will have to shift their attention from challenging a witness's competency *before* she testifies to litigating the weight her testimony should be given *after* she testifies. The Rule's objective

---

[5] *See generally*, United States v. Meerbeke, 548 F.2d 415 (2d Cir. 1976) (discussing witness's use of drugs).

[6] *See, e.g.*, United States v. Hyson, 721 F.2d 856 (1st Cir. 1983) (witness found to have been under influence while testifying; judge struck prior testimony, arranged for witness to be treated, and had witness recalled; expert testified concerning the examination and treatment of witness).

[7] 871 F.2d 582 (6th Cir. 1989).

[8] *See, e.g.*, United States v. Gutman, 725 F.2d 417 (7th Cir. 1984) (hearing appropriate where witness is potentially incompetent because of insanity).

is to provide court members with the greatest amount of arguably reliable evidence possible, with the expectation that court members can decide the appropriate weight to be given imperfect witnesses. Fact finders should not be denied the benefit of evidence that has some probative value unless there is a good reason to keep the evidence from them.[9]

The trend is to follow the Rule as written and to allow all witnesses to testify. *United States v. Morgan*[10] illustrates the trend. There the accused's conviction for sexually molesting a four-year-old child was affirmed despite his contention that the victim was incompetent to testify because of her age. Affirming the conviction, the court held that civilian and military courts have consistently found very young witnesses to be competent, even though such witnesses often appear hesitant, apprehensive, or afraid. While these limitations are appropriately raised by opposing counsel, they go to weight, not to admissibility.

Similarly, in *United States v. McRary*,[11] the accused was charged with kidnapping. In order to establish his mental responsibility, defense counsel attempted to call the accused's wife as a witness. Even though she had previously been found mentally incompetent to stand trial with respect to her participation in the charged criminal venture, the court said, in the process of reversing the conviction on other grounds, that mental incompetence rarely, if ever, could be a ground for disqualification.[12]

Even where a witness may be excluded for an incompetency, such as when the victim of child sexual abuse is too young to appreciate the responsibilities of testifying or the obligation to tell the truth, her previous out of court hearsay statements may still be admissible. The rationale for this result is that the basis for admitting hearsay evidence is not connected to the child's ability to understand the judicial process or appreciate an oath.

For example, if an otherwise incompetent child witness has made an excited utterance that qualifies under Rule 803(2), or a statement for the purposes of medical diagnosis or treatment under Rule 803(4), the reliability of those statements is linked with the circumstantial guarantees of trustworthiness surrounding the hearsay exceptions, not with the child's qualifications to be a witness. In *Idaho v. Wright*,[13] the Supreme Court rejected a *per se* exclusionary rule that would have prevented finders of fact from hearing

---

[9] *See, e.g.*, United States v. Charles, 561 F. Supp. 694 (S.D. Tex. 1983) (defendants' motion to strike hypnotized witness granted).

[10] 31 M.J. 43 (C.M.A. 1990).

[11] 616 F.2d 181 (5th Cir. 1980).

[12] *See also* United States v. Lightly, 677 F.2d 1027 (4th Cir. 1982) (error to reject defense witness because he had been found criminally insane and incompetent to stand trial and he was subject to hallucinations).

[13] 497 U.S. 805 (1990).

a child victim's hearsay statements simply because the witness herself was incompetent to testify.

§ 601.03 Drafters' Analysis

Rule 601 is taken without change from the first portion of Federal Rule of Evidence 601. The remainder of the Federal Rule was deleted due to its sole application to civil cases.

In declaring that subject to any other Rule, all persons are competent to be witnesses, Rule 601 supersedes ¶ 148 of the present *Manual* that requires, among other factors, that an individual know the difference between truth and falsehood and understand the moral importance of telling the truth in order to testify. Under Rule 601 such matters will go only to the weight of the testimony and not to its competency. The Rule's reference to other rules includes Rules 603 (Oath or Affirmation), 605 (Competency of Military Judge as Witness), 606 (Competency of Court Member as Witness), and the rules of privilege.

The plain meaning of the Rule appears to deprive the trial judge of any discretion whatsoever to exclude testimony on grounds of competency unless the testimony is incompetent under those specific rules already cited *above, see, e.g., United States v. Fowler*, 605 F.2d 181 (5th Cir. 1979), a conclusion bolstered by the Federal Rules of Evidence Advisory Committee's Note. S. SALTZBURG & K. REDDEN, Federal Rules of Evidence Manual; 270 (2d ed. 1977). Whether this conclusion is accurate, especially in the light of Rule 403, is unclear. *Id.* at 269; *see also United States v. Callahan*, 442 F. Supp. 1213 (D. Minn. 1978).

§ 601.04 Annotated Cases

[1] Rule 601—General Rule of Competency

[a] Competency of Witness—Age

United States Court of Appeals for the Armed Forces

United States v. Morgan, 31 M.J. 43 (C.M.A. 1990): The accused's conviction for sexually molesting a four-year-old child was affirmed despite his contention that the victim was incompetent to testify. In the court's opinion, civilian and military courts have consistently found very young witnesses to be competent, even though those witnesses often appear hesitant, apprehensive, or afraid.

United States v. LeMere, 22 M.J. 61 (C.M.A. 1986): The court held that a three-and-one-half-year-old sodomy victim was competent to testify even though "her subsequent confusion of truth, falsity, reality and fantasy suggested that the trial counsel's efforts thereby to impress upon . . . [her] the duty to testify truthfully were not entirely effective." In the court's view, this witness's confusion "only affected the weight to be accorded her testimony, rather than its admissibility."

Air Force Court of Criminal Appeals

United States v. Allen, 13 M.J. 597 (A.F.C.M.R. 1982): Charged with having sexually abused several very young children, the accused unsuccessfully claimed that the victims were incompetent to testify because of their ages. The reviewing court also rejected his claim, finding that Rule 601 "clearly creates more than a mere presumption of competence," and that it "actually redefines the term 'competent witness's so as to include any person" not acting as military judge or court member.

Army Court of Criminal Appeals

United States v. Lemere, 16 M.J. 682 (A.C.M.R. 1983): A three-and-one-half-year-old sexual assault victim was properly allowed to testify because categorical disabilities such as extreme youth have been rejected by the Military Rules of Evidence.

United States v. Urbina, 14 M.J. 962 (A.C.M.R. 1982): Finding that the five-year-old victim of various sexual offenses was competent to testify, the court noted that Rule 601 "eliminates the categorical disabilities, such as extreme youth, which previously existed." The court went on to hold that a witness's ability to distinguish between truth and falsehood as well as an ability to understand the moral importance of telling the truth are matters that more properly affect weight than competence.

[b]   Competency of Witness—Credibility Problems

United States Court of Appeals for the Armed Forces

United States v. Matias, 25 M.J. 356 (C.M.A. 1987): Convicted of drug distribution, the accused unsuccessfully contended that error occurred when the uncorroborated testimony of a "chronic liar" was used against him. The court held that "credibility was a question to be resolved by the members under appropriate instructions [and that] there is no additional legal requirement that the testimony of a competent witness who is also generally regarded as a 'liar' be corroborated."

[c]   Competency of Witness—Foundational Requirements

United States Court of Appeals for the Armed Forces

United States v. Brown, 28 M.J. 470 (C.M.A. 1989): Setting aside the accused's sentence for AWOL, the court held that a government aggravation witness was incompetent to testify about the accused's past extrinsic misconduct because the witness had no personal knowledge of the matters. The court went on to say that learning about such misconduct from police reports is insufficient.

[d]   Competency of Witness—Hypnotized Witnesses

Supreme Court

Rock v. Arkansas, 483 U.S. 44 (1987): Remanding the accused's conviction for shooting her husband, the Court found the Arkansas rule establishing a per se ban against her hypnotically refreshed testimony worked a significant detriment, and violated her rights to Due Process and Compulsory Process. The Court viewed the overly broad limitation on the accused's right to testify as arbitrary and disproportionate.

[e] Competency of Witness—Mental Competency

Air Force Court of Criminal Appeals

United States v. Geiss, 30 M.J. 678 (A.F.C.M.R. 1990): The accused's conviction for sexually abusing his mentally disabled, fourteen-year-old daughter, was affirmed despite his argument that "less than ideal" government pretrial interviews caused the victim's testimony to be "confabulated" and inadmissible. The court reasoned that evidence of suggestive questioning or coercive pretrial interviews goes to the credibility of a witness rather than to admissibility, even where the witness is mentally disabled.

Army Court of Criminal Appeals

United States v. Lyons, 33 M.J. 543 (A.C.M.R. 1991), *aff'd,* 36 M.J. 183 (C.M.A. 1992): In an aggravated rape case, where the victim was a deaf-mute, mentally impaired 18-year-old girl with a mental age of three, the court specifically found that the victim's extremely limited communicative abilities were sufficient, and that she was competent to testify. The court also held that the accused's right of confrontation was not violated by the witness's limited ability to remember underlying events or to be cross-examined on them.

[f] Competency of Witness—Self-contradictory Testimony

United States Court of Appeals for the Armed Forces

United States v. White, 45 M.J. 345 (C.A.A.F. 1996): Affirming the accused's conviction for raping a young woman with the mental ability of an eight-year-old, this court held that no rule of evidence precludes a witness from testifying simply because that witness's testimony is contradictory or is contradicted by the testimony of other witnesses.

[g] Competency of Witness—Sentencing

Army Court of Criminal Appeals

United States v. Taylor, 21 M.J. 840 (A.C.M.R. 1986): The court held that "arbitrariness is not among the grounds for disqualification as a witness." The real issue was whether an extenuation and mitigation witness had relevant testimony to present and whether that testimony's probative value outweighed its prejudicial effect.

§ 602.01   Official Text

Rule 602.   Lack of Personal Knowledge.

A witness may not testify to a matter unless evidence is introduced sufficient to support a finding that the witness has personal knowledge of the matter. Evidence to prove personal knowledge may, but need not, consist of the testimony of the witness. This Rule is subject to the provisions of Military Rule of Evidence 703, relating to opinion testimony by expert witnesses.

---

§ 602.02   Editorial Comment

[1]   Requirement for Personal Knowledge and Relevance

Rule 602 is one of the provisions that highlights the differences in testimonial foundations between expert and lay witnesses. Taken directly from its federal counterpart, Rule 602 provides that a lay witness may not testify unless evidence is introduced establishing that the witness has personal knowledge of what he or she says.[1] The Rule goes on to state that such a foundation may, but need not, be established through the witness himself. A witness's foundation may appropriately include the witness's own inferences and opinions so long as they are based on personal knowledge.[2] Rule 602 is closely related to Rule 701, which provides that laymen may give opinion testimony if that testimony is "rationally based on the perception of the witness."

To a large extent, Rule 602 continues traditional military practice. Counsel is able to initiate testimony without having to first qualify the witness in any formal sense. Only if it becomes apparent during the witness's testimony that a factual foundation is absent, should an inquiry be conducted. If this occurs, evidence must be presented demonstrating what the witness knows and how the witness gained that information. Of course, if opposing counsel has interviewed the witness prior to trial, and has a good faith belief that the witness has no personal knowledge to support all or part of that witness's testimony, counsel may seek a hearing before the witness takes the stand in order to avoid having the court members hear either the objection or testimony that does not satisfy the Rule.

---

[1] *See, e.g.*, United States v. Hernandez, 693 F.2d 996 (10th Cir. 1982), *cert. denied*, 459 U.S. 1222 (1983) (Catholic priests not permitted to give testimony concerning conditions in homeland of defendant charged with illegal entry into United States, where they did not know defendant and did not know about his reentry).

[2] *See, e.g.*, United States v. Lemire, 720 F.2d 1327 (D.C. Cir. 1983) (FBI agent could use charts to testify since he had knowledge of matters referred to therein).

[2] Relationship to Other Rules

The most important function Rule 602 provides is to act as a mechanism for insuring that only reliable evidence reaches the triers-of-fact. In many ways, this goal complements Rule 602 must be considered in conjunction with Section VIII's hearsay provisions and Section X's best evidence requirements.

A witness who testifies that "I only know what Sergeant Jones told me. He said . . . ." has personal knowledge of what he heard Sergeant Jones say, but not of the underlying facts or events. What Jones said raises a hearsay problem. Similarly, a witness who says "I only know what the paper said. It said. . . ." has personal knowledge only of what is on the paper, but there may be a best evidence problem.

Even where a declarant's out of court statement appears to be admissible, as *e.g.*, an excited utterance under Rule 803(2), it still must be shown that the declarant has personal knowledge of the actual events. Hearsay declarants are witnesses. All witnesses must have personal knowledge, although admissions may be admitted against a party without the proponent's showing personal knowledge.

[3] Role of the Judge

The trial judge decides under this Rule not whether the evidence offered actually is believable, but whether, as a matter of law, a reasonable court member could believe that the witness has first hand knowledge of it, so that a reasonable court member could believe it. In other words, there is a difference between improbable evidence, that the trial judge should admit, and completely unbelievable and unsupported evidence that should be excluded.

[4] Relationship of Rule 602 to Admissions

A limited exception to Rule 602 deals with an accused's admissions or confessions. Even if defense counsel can establish that the accused had no basis in fact for a statement, it will still be admitted under the usual approach to personal admissions, covered by Rule 801(d)(2)(A). A party is responsible for his or her statement and can explain the basis for them.

[5] Relationship of Rule 602 to Expert Witnesses

The final sentence of Rule 602 concerns the provision's interaction with expert or opinion testimony under Rule 703. This sentence was inserted to underscore the drafter's intent that the requirement of personal knowledge would not limit an expert's testimony. Expert witnesses will still be permitted to offer their opinions, even though they may be based on information provided by others, and even though the information itself might not be independently admissible as evidence.

[6] Personal Knowledge and Believability

Finally, it is important to note that this provision does not address matters of weight or credibility, that are reserved entirely for the finders of fact. To implement the Rule, the trial bench should not exclude evidence merely because a witness is uncertain or hesitant about his or her testimony.[3] Uncertainty or hesitancy affects only the evidence's weight, and that is an issue for counsel to litigate.

§ 602.03 Drafters' Analysis

Rule 602 is taken without significant change from the Federal Rule and is similar in content to ¶ 138*d* of the present *Manual*. Although the *Manual* expressly allows an individual to testify to his or her own age or date of birth, the Rule is silent on the issue.

Notwithstanding that silence, however, it appears that it is within the meaning of the Rule to allow such testimony. Rule 804(b)(4) [Hearsay Exceptions; Declarant Unavailable—Statement of Personal or Family History] expressly permits a hearsay statement "concerning the declarant's own birth . . . or other similar fact of personal or family history, even though declarant had no means of acquiring personal knowledge of the matter stated." It seems evident that if such a hearsay statement is admissible, in-court testimony by the declarant should be no less admissible. It is probable that the expression "personal knowledge" in Rule 804(b)(4) is being used in the sense of "first hand knowledge" while the expression is being used in Rule 602 in a somewhat broader sense to include those matters which an individual could be considered to reliably know about his or her personal history.

§ 602.04 Annotated Cases

[1] Rule 602—Lack of Personal Knowledge

[a] Personal Knowledge—Extrinsic Offense Evidence

United States Court of Appeals for the Armed Forces

United States v. Brooks, 22 M.J. 441 (C.M.A. 1986): In this drug prosecution, the court suggested that opposing counsel should always consider testing a witness's basis of knowledge when that witness testifies concerning uncharged misconduct. Such an examination can prevent inadmissible and prejudicial evidence from reaching the fact-finders.

[b] Personal Knowledge—Foundation Required

United States Court of Appeals for the Armed Forces

United States v. Avila, 47 M.J. 490 (C.A.A.F. 1998): The accused was convicted of wearing an unauthorized decoration and other offenses. At trial, the Division G-1 testified that the brigade commander would never have

---

[3] *See, e.g.,* M.B.A.F.B. Federal Credit Union v. Cumis Insurance Society, 681 F.2d 930 (4th Cir. 1982) (witness need not be certain to have personal knowledge).

authorized such an award for a soldier with the accused's poor disciplinary record. Finding error but no prejudice in this government evidence, the court held that the G-1's testimony lacked a proper foundation for establishing his ability to gauge whether the brigade commander would have acted in a certain way under these circumstances.

United States v. Williams, 26 M.J. 487 (C.M.A. 1988): During the accused's court-martial for raping his six-year-old daughter, trial counsel cross-examined a Trial Defense Service lawyer's assistant about whether she believed the victim was truthful. Finding error, the court held that this witness did not have "sufficient personal knowledge of the victim to render a reliable opinion on this matter. . . . An hour an[d] a half stint as a disinterested and uninvolved witness to a defense interview fails this test for reliable character assessment."

United States v. Dorsey, 16 M.J. 1 (C.M.A. 1983): The court found that the military judge committed error by rejecting the accused's attempt to introduce "independent evidence" establishing the basis for the defense's assertion that the prosecutrix recently had sex with the accused's roommate.

[c]   Personal Knowledge—Hearsay Applications

United States Court of Appeals for the Armed Forces

United States v. McGill, 15 M.J. 242 (C.M.A. 1983): The court found that "presumably relevant evidence," testimony concerning an Article 15 punishment, should not have been admitted against the accused during the sentencing part of the trial, because the government witness was unable to demonstrate personal knowledge of the underlying events. The court went on to say that no hearsay exception justified the testimony.

Navy-Marine Corps Court of Criminal Appeals

United States v. Littles, 35 M.J. 644 (N.M.C.M.R. 1992): This larceny of government weapons and related offenses case was before the court for reconsideration of its prior decision. During the sentencing portion of the accused's court-martial, trial counsel called an NIS agent who testified that the accused sold the stolen weapons to his father. The agent went on to say he remembered from reading a National Crime Information Center (NCIC) report, that the accused's father had a long criminal record and was currently incarcerated for parole violations. Ostensibly, trial counsel offered this evidence pursuant to R.C.M. 1001(b)(4) (aggravating circumstances directly related to or resulting from the offense of stealing a weapon). Setting aside the accused's sentence, this court held that the agent did not have sufficient personal knowledge of the father's criminal misconduct to testify about it. In the court's opinion, the agent's testimony was an attempt at making inadmissible hearsay evidence appear credible.

[d]   Personal Knowledge—Incomplete Personal Knowledge

United States Court of Appeals for the Armed Forces

United States v. Roberts, 69 M.J.23 (C.A.A.F. 2010): The accused's convictions for raping and assaulting his wife were affirmed despite his contention that evidence was excluded in violation of the Constitution. After the victim testified on direct examination, defense counsel was prohibited from asking her about an alleged improper sexual relationship or from presenting other evidence establishing the relationship. Defense counsel contended the defense had a right to show that the victim had a motive to lie about the alleged rape. The court found that defense counsel failed to establish the relevance of the evidence or that it was anything other than conjecture. Prospective defense witnesses were unable to provide a sufficient basis of knowledge for their testimony. The court specifically indicated that Rule 602 prohibited such proof from being admitted.

[e]   Personal Knowledge—Sentencing Applications

United States Court of Appeals for the Armed Forces

United States v. Brown, 28 M.J. 470 (C.M.A. 1989): In this AWOL prosecution, the court highlighted the military judge's responsibility for ensuring that witnesses have a factual predicate supporting their testimony. It set aside the accused's sentence, because a government witness who testified about extrinsic offenses had no personal knowledge and derived his information from a police report.

§ 603.01   Official Text

Rule 603.   Oath or Affirmation.

Before testifying, every witness shall be required to declare that the witness will testify truthfully, by oath or affirmation administered in a form calculated to awaken the witness's conscience and impress the witness's mind with the duty to do so.

---

§ 603.02   Editorial Comment

[1]   General Requirements

This provision, like its federal counterpart, requires that a witness swear or affirm that he or she will tell the truth before the witness is permitted to testify. The Rule establishes no specific colloquy to be used in carrying out this requirement. Any process that is sufficient to "awaken the witness's conscience . . ." is satisfactory. Although normally the judge determines the form of the oath or affirmation, the trial judge may consider the witness's reasons for wishing to take the oath or affirmation in a different form.[1] The object here is to impress upon prospective witnesses that they have a duty to tell the truth while testifying. To a large extent these requirements codify past military practice.[2]

The oath requirement is part of the Rules' effort to insure that only accurate information reaches fact-finders. Recent commentaries question the oath's continued validity. But no one has demonstrated that it is not an effective symbol for some witnesses of the importance the law places on honesty.

This Rule is written to permit atheists, conscientious objectors, children, and individuals with emotional difficulties to satisfy the basic criterion. The idea is to find a procedure that will establish the witness's willingness to tell the truth and the concomitant acceptance of responsibility for false statements. As a procedural matter, counsel who know that a witness will not swear, but will affirm, should so indicate before the witness takes the stand to avoid embarrassing the witness and confusing the court members if they were to hear a witness refuse to swear to tell the truth.

---

[1] *See, e.g.,* United States v. Ward, 989 F.2d 1015 (9th Cir. 1993) (trial court erred in not permitting witness to substitute words "fully integrated honesty" for the word, "truth." Court concluded that witness's reasons for modifying oath were based on First Amendment principles; court recognized that trial judge could refuse request to modify oath if it appeared that witness was attempting to create safe harbor for perjury).

[2] *See* R.C.M. 807 for applicable oaths.

[2] Excluding Witnesses From Testifying

A witness who refuses to promise to testify truthfully may be excluded.[3] But, absent a valid privilege claim, no witness can refuse to provide testimony when summoned. The contempt power remains available to compel a recalcitrant witness to provide evidence, and it may have to be exercised on behalf of an accused in order to satisfy his compulsory process right.

If the court decides under Rule 104(a) that a witness is incapable of understanding the duty to tell the truth, the Drafters' Analysis to Rule 601 suggests that the witness may be excluded. Given the liberality of Rule 601, a witness should be barred from testifying only as a last resort, after the judge has tried every form of oath or affirmation or substitute that might awaken the witness's conscience. Excluding a witness should be a rare occurrence.

An excellent example of finding ways to qualify a witness is contained in *United States v. Lyons.*[4] In this aggravated rape case, the victim was a deaf-mute, mentally impaired, 18-year-old girl with a mental age of three. Despite defense challenges on competency grounds, the court specifically found that the victim's extremely limited communicative abilities were sufficient, and that she was competent to take an oath and testify. Even under these extreme circumstances, the court held that the accused's right of confrontation was not violated by the witness's limited ability to communicate, remember underlying events, or be cross-examined on them.

[3] Pretrial Hearings and Sentencing Proceedings

The application of Rule 603 will be limited during the sentencing portion of a court-martial. Rule 1101(c) permits an accused to take the stand and make an unsworn statement. Although the government is prohibited from cross-examining the accused with respect to this statement, it may present evidence in rebuttal.

Rule 104(a)'s provision that the military judge is not bound by the rules of evidence in adjudicating preliminary questions does not mean that judges should often allow witnesses to testify without taking an oath or affirmation.

§ 603.03 Drafters' Analysis

Rule 603 is taken from the Federal Rule without change. The oaths found within Chapter XXII of the Manual satisfy the requirements of Rule 603. Pursuant to Rule 1101(c), this Rule is inapplicable to the accused when he or she makes an unsworn statement under ¶ 75c(2) of the *Manual.*

---

[3] *See, e.g.,* United States v. Fowler, 605 F.2d 181 (5th Cir. 1979).

[4] 33 M.J. 543 (A.C.M.R. 1991), *aff'd,* 36 M.J. 183 (C.M.A. 1992).

§ 603.04 Annotated Cases

[1] Requirement of Oath—Child Witnesses

Air Force Court of Criminal Appeals

United States v. Allen, 13 M.J. 597 (A.F.C.M.R. 1982): The accused claimed that four and five-year-old victims of sexual attacks should not have been permitted to testify against him because they were incapable of taking an oath and distinguishing right from wrong. But the court found that Rule 603 was specifically designed to permit such witnesses to testify. The rule requires only that a process be used which awakens the witness's conscience and impresses upon him a duty to tell the truth.

Army Court of Criminal Appeals

United States v. Lemere, 16 M.J. 682 (A.C.M.R. 1983): Finding that a three-and-one-half-year-old sodomy victim generally appreciated her obligation to speak the truth, the court held that the witness's apparent "confusion of truth, falsity, reality and fantasy . . ." only affected the weight and credibility of the testimony.

[2] Requirement of Oath—Failure to Give Oath

Navy-Marine Corps Court of Criminal Appeals

United States v. Washington, 61 M.J. 574 (N.M.Ct.Crim.App. 2005): At the accused's general court-martial for sexually abusing his 10-year-old daughter and related offenses, trial counsel inadvertently neglected to administer the oath to the accused's daughter before she testified. However, before releasing her from the stand, trial counsel did administer an oath. Trial defense counsel posed no objection and requested no relief. Affirming findings and sentence, the court held that no harm or prejudice resulted from trial counsel's actions, they did not amount to plain error, and that in any event the accused waived the issue by failing to make a timely objection.

§ 604.01 Official Text

Rule 604. Interpreters.

An interpreter is subject to the provisions of these rules relating to qualifications as an expert and the administration of an oath or affirmation that the interpreter will make a true translation.

---

§ 604.02 Editorial Comment

Because courts-martial are conducted all over the world, large numbers of non-English speaking witnesses play a role in military justice. A reasonable requirement that their testimony be accurately communicated to those court members and judges who may understand only English is found in Rule 604. The Rule is taken from its federal counterpart and does not substantially alter prior *Manual* practice.

This provision establishes specific procedures for using an interpreter. First, the interpreter must be qualified in the same manner as any expert witness. This includes proof that the interpreter is competent to translate the foreign language into English, and that he or she is able to perform this function during the trial itself. To insure that the translation will be accurate, Rule 604 requires that the interpreter swear or affirm that he or she will "make a true translation." This last requirement means that the interpreter will not analyze the testimony during translation, but will provide an exact English version of it.

Rule 604 does not indicate when an interpreter is required.[1] It is likely that confrontation and compulsory process rights require an interpreter: (1) when it is reasonably possible that without one, a witness may not understand questions or be understood by the tribunal; and (2) when the defendant makes a timely request that an interpreter be appointed.

Although Rule 1101(d) states that the Military Rules of Evidence (other than privilege rules) do not apply to Article 32 hearings and related processes, defense counsel may be unable to adequately prepare a defense without an interpreter—*e.g.*, when some of the government's witnesses are foreign nationals, defense counsel unassisted by an interpreter will be unable to meaningfully discuss the case with these witnesses. Thorough preparation and cross-examination will then be undermined. Appointment of an interpreter in these hearings would be useful. If an interpreter is appointed, then there is no reason why a court would not be able to use this Rule as persuasive authority, even though it is not binding under Rule 1101.

---

[1] *See, e.g.*, United States v. Moon, 718 F.2d 1210 (2d Cir. 1983), *cert. denied*, 466 U.S. 971 (1984) (defendant has no right under federal statute to his own interpreter rather than court-appointed interpreter).

This Rule and the Drafters' Analysis do not discuss how an accurate "transcript" can be assured when an interpreter is used. A court reporter will not be transcribing what he or she hears said to or by a non-English-speaking witness, but will record what is said to or by the interpreter. If an audio recording of the entire proceeding is not kept for appellate review, evidence of possible inaccuracies may be lost. Thus, an English tape recording is extremely valuable whenever an interpreter is used.

§ 604.03   Drafters' Analysis

Rule 604 is taken from the Federal Rule without change and is consistent with ¶ 141 of the present *Manual*. The oath found in *Manual* ¶ 114*e* satisfies the oath requirement of Rule 604.

§ 604.04   Annotated Cases

[1]   Interpreter Qualifications

Coast Guard Court of Criminal Appeals

United States v. Sheehan, 62 M.J. 568 (C.G.Ct.Crim.App. 2005): During the accused's trial for sexually abusing a child, the government used an interpreter to translate the child's testimony from Spanish into English. The military judge neglected to find the interpreter qualified, but trial defense counsel failed to object. The court said that no evidence had been offered to question the accuracy of the interpreter's translations, and as a result no basis for finding plain error existed.

§ 605.01   Official Text

Rule 605.   Competency of Military Judge as Witness.

(a) The military judge presiding at the court-martial may not testify in that court-martial as a witness. No objection need be made to preserve the point.

(b) This rule does not preclude the military judge from placing on the record matters concerning docketing of the case.

---

§ 605.02   Editorial Comment

[1]   General Requirements

Military justice requires that trial judges play a central role in determining how evidence will be presented and how it will be used. But Rule 605 prohibits them from being witnesses in cases they preside over.[1] Subdivision (a) of the Rule is taken from its federal counterpart, and resembles Article 26(d) of the Uniform Code of Military Justice. Subdivision (b) is not found in the Federal Rules, having been added to clarify existing military practice.

Rule 605(a) is a simple statement of judicial incapacity. It categorically prohibits the military judge from serving as a witness while presiding at a court-martial. The drafters felt this provision was so important that they created an exception to Rule 103's general requirement of a timely and specific objection, and provided that counsel need not object to the judge's testimony in order to preserve a claim of error on appeal. The resulting "automatic exception" recognizes the reality that counsel generally will be reluctant to challenge a judge who is so bold as to believe that he or she can be an impartial judge of his or her own testimony, and that judges ought to be aware of the impropriety of assuming the role of evidence-giver and evidence-assessor in the same case.

Applying this Rule in military environments causes particular challenges. It is not uncommon for a single trial judge to preside over all the cases in a circuit or area jurisdiction concept. Under these circumstances, the military judge may hear cases with interrelated facts. An example of this potential issue occurs where several service members are apprehended for drug related conspiracy offenses. If the same military judge hears more than one of these cases he or she must insure that no fact or testimony from one proceeding finds its way directly or indirectly into his or her decision making

---

[1] *See, e.g.,* Washington v. Strickland, 693 F.2d 1243 (5th Cir. 1982) (*en banc*), *rev'd on other grounds*, 466 U.S. 668 (1984) (impermissible for trial judge to testify in habeas proceeding that his sentence would not have been different had the defendant offered mitigation evidence).

processes in another proceeding, particularly if she is sitting in the latter case without members.

[2] Additional Provisions Barring Testimony by Judges

It could be argued that Rule 605 is not needed, as general due process considerations should prohibit the trial judge from testifying, and thus aligning himself or herself with one party or the other.[2] But the Rule avoids any constitutional problem and any need for constitutional decision making.

Article 26(d) of the Code already provides the accused with protection in this area by stating that "no person is eligible to act as military judge in a case if he is . . . a witness for the prosecution. . . ." Rule 605 extends this protection to the government as well.

Although one might argue that, had Congress intended Article 26(d)'s provisions to protect the government, it would have included them in the Code itself, that argument seems weak. Congress apparently wanted to assure that the defendant would never be prejudiced, but in no way indicated that the government should be prejudiced. Probably, Congress thought it more likely that a judge would be inclined to testify for the prosecution and absolutely prohibited that.[3]

[3] Exceptions to the Rule

Two exceptions to Rule 605(a) should be mentioned. First, there is no incapacity with respect to a trial judge testifying during subsequent proceedings that concern a trial he or she presided over. This could occur with respect to limited rehearings ordered pursuant to *United States v. Dubay*,[4] or *United States v. Ray*.[5] Second, a trial judge might avoid subdivision (a)'s prohibitions by taking judicial notice of facts. Judicial notice would not result in either counsel's examining the bench with respect to the accuracy or foundation of such facts. Notice of adjudicative facts would only be taken in accordance with Rule 201.

[4] Unique Military Provision

Rule 605(b) was created in response to military exigencies. Due to the lack of trial court clerks and similar administrative assistants, military judges must often manage their own dockets. This situation could present problems of proof in litigating speedy trial motions.

As a result, subdivision (b) specifically allows the bench to spread

---

[2] *Cf.* Connally v. Georgia, 429 U.S. 245 (1977).

[3] *See, e.g.*, Brown v. Lynaugh, 843 F.2d 849 (5th Cir. 1988) (testimony by trial judge concerning defendant's escape from courtroom on behalf of government violated due process).

[4] 37 C.M.R. 411 (C.M.A. 1967).

[5] 43 C.M.R. 171 (C.M.A. 1971).

documentary and related matters on the record with respect to its docketing of the case. This is similar to Rule 103(b). Unfortunately, the Rule and the Drafters' Analysis fail to define how this should be accomplished. The bench would be well-advised to provide the parties, as well as the reporter, with a statement, in writing if possible, of the matters involved and the facts to be recorded. This should minimize errors and assure that the parties have a chance to be heard on disputed points. It must also be recognized that speedy trial motions will be litigated during Article 39(a) sessions, which means that the Rules of Evidence will be relaxed, allowing testimony that may moot the judge's need to supplement the record. *See* our discussion of Rule 104(a).

[5]   Relationship to Judicial Notice

The rule clearly prevents a judge from testifying at trial. But what if the judge, in taking judicial notice, relates information that he or she obtained in deciding whether to take judicial notice? That issue was addressed in *United States v. Bari*,[6] where the trial judge in a supervised release revocation hearing addressed the question of whether the accused was the person identified as the robber in a bank surveillance tape. In revoking Bari's supervised release the judge considered evidence that a bank's surveillance videotape showed a robber wearing a yellow rain hat and that a yellow rain hat was found in the garage owned by Bari's landlord. He stated on the record:

> In addition, and I think this is the strongest piece of evidence frankly, we have the yellow hat. I am convinced from looking at the surveillance video [from the bank] of September 9 that [the hat found in the garage] is the same type of hat as appears in the video. It may not be precisely the actual hat, but it is the same type of hat. It is just too much of a coincidence that the bank robber would be wearing the same hat that we find in [his landlord's] garage.

To emphasize the similarities between the hat found in the landlord's garage and the hat worn by the robber, the judge stated: "there are clearly lots of yellow hats out there," and that "[o]ne can Google yellow rain hats and find lots of different yellow rain hats." He also stated that "[w]e did a Google search, and you can find yellow hats, yellow rain hats like this. But there are also lots of different rain hats, many different kinds of rain hats that one could buy." Concluding that the Federal Rules of Evidence do not apply with full force at supervised release revocation proceedings, the Court of Appeals rejected the argument that the judge's research and comments violated Federal Rule of Evidence 605. Instead, it agreed with the government argument that the judge had in effect taken judicial notice under Rule 201—"in some relaxed form"—and that it was not unreasonable to conduct an internet search to confirm his intuition of what was a matter of common

---

[6]   599 F.3d 176 (2d Cir. 2010).

knowledge—the availability of yellow rain hats.

To avoid such problems both counsel and judges should make it clear that the court is taking "judicial notice" and not providing testimony about his or her personal knowledge or research. The latter would seem to be a violation of Rule 505.

§ 605.03 Drafters' Analysis

Rule 605(a) restates the Federal Rule without significant change. Although Article 26(d) of the Uniform Code of Military Justice states in relevant part that "no person is eligible to act as a military judge if he or she is a witness for the prosecution. . . ." and is silent on whether a witness for the defense is eligible to sit, the Committee believes that the specific reference in the Code was not intended to create a right and was the result only of an attempt to highlight the more grievous case. In any event, Rule 605, unlike Article 26(d), does not deal with the question of eligibility to sit as a military judge, but deals solely with the military judge's competency as a witness. The rule does not affect voir dire.

Rule 605(b) is new and is not found within the Federal Rules of Evidence. It was added because of the unique nature of the military judiciary in which military judges often control their own dockets without clerical assistance. In view of the military's stringent speedy trial rules, *see, e.g., United States v. Burton*, 21 C.M.A. 112, 44 C.M.R. 166 (1971), it was necessary to preclude expressly any interpretation of Rule 605 that would prohibit the military judge from placing on the record details relating to docketing in order to avoid prejudice to a party. Rule 605(b) is consistent with present military law.

§ 605.04 Annotated Cases

[1] Judge Testimony—Appellate Uses

United States Court of Appeals for the Armed Forces

United States v. Rice, 25 M.J. 35 (C.M.A. 1987): The court held that a military judge's "post trial testimony on [a] different matter" could not be used to impeach his findings. "Such an appellate tactic is no more than an attempt to accomplish the precise inquiry into the trial judge's mind, which is prohibited by Mil. R. Evid. 606."

[2] Judge Testimony—Speedy Trial Issues

United States Court of Appeals for the Armed Forces

United States v. Burris, 21 M.J. 140 (C.M.A. 1985): Relying on Rule 605, this court held that the chief trial judge of the circuit, who was originally scheduled to be the military judge in this case, should not have testified at the trial concerning defense allegations of delay.

§ 606.01   Official Text

Rule 606.   Competency of Court Member as Witness.

(a) *At the court-martial.* A member of the court-martial may not testify as a witness before the other members in the trial of the case in which the member is sitting. If the member is called to testify, the opposing party, except in a special court-martial without a military judge, shall be afforded an opportunity to object out of the presence of the members.

(b) *Inquiry into validity of findings or sentence.* Upon an inquiry into the validity of the findings or sentence, a member may not testify as to any matter or statement occurring during the course of the deliberations of the members of the court-martial or, to the effect of anything upon the member's or any other member's mind or emotions as influencing the member to assent to or dissent from the findings or sentence or concerning the member's mental process in connection therewith, except that a member may testify on the question whether extraneous prejudicial information was improperly brought to the attention of the members of the court-martial, whether any outside influence was improperly brought to bear upon any member, or whether there was unlawful command influence. Nor may the member's affidavit or evidence of any statement by the member concerning a matter about which the member would be precluded from testifying be received for these purposes.

---

§ 606.02   Editorial Comment

[1]   Reason for the Rule

This provision is one of the most crucial Military Rules of Evidence. It is designed to protect the integrity of the courts-martial process. Courts are called upon to determine guilt or innocence, and, if an accused is ultimately convicted, they also assess an appropriate sentence. The drafters recognized that these important responsibilities would be compromised if the members simultaneously served as witnesses or were subjected to improper external forces in arriving at their verdicts or sentences. Subdivisions (a) and (b) of the Rule generally are taken from and consistent with the Federal Rule, and also are consistent with, but somewhat more expansive than, past military practice.[1]

[2]   Rule 606(a)—Testimony of Court Members During Trial

Subdivision (a) states that a court member should not testify as a witness

---

[1] *See generally 1969 Manual ¶¶ 62f and 63.*

when sitting as factfinder. The Rule is not one of strict incompetence, as its second sentence indicates that opposing counsel must object (but outside the hearing of other members) to such conduct in order to preserve any possible error for appeal. This is an interesting contrast with Rule 605(a), which indicates that no objection is necessary when the trial judge testifies as a witness.

By prohibiting the triers of fact from testifying, the drafters recognized that it is not possible for court members to sit as neutral arbiters and to evaluate, without bias, their own testimony. Other pragmatic considerations also support the Rule. Counsel desire to prepare a case well before the trial date. Examining potential witnesses who are also going to sit as jurors would make any pretrial discussions impossible. Similarly, counsel will want to talk with a witness just prior to direct examination. This could not be accomplished if the witness is also a court member. Equally important, how aggressive could opposing counsel be in cross-examining or impeaching a witness if that same witness must later sit in judgment of counsel's case?

While 606(a) mandates that counsel not plan on using court members during their case-in-chief, it does not address what should be done when it is determined *during* trial that a court member may have relevant and very important testimony to offer. This event is more likely to occur in military than in federal practice, because many military communities are small and closely knit organizations.

The problem envisioned here could easily arise as follows: During trial the government learns that an unanticipated witness must be called. In response, defense counsel discovers that a court member is the sole source of valuable impeachment evidence concerning that witness. Rule 606(a), however, will not permit the court member to testify over a timely government objection. This result raises problems of constitutional magnitude, as the accused's ability to present his defense is severely limited.

In this situation, it is doubtful that the trial judge could allow the court member to testify for the very reasons that give rise to Rule 606(a). Hence, trial counsel will insist upon a mistrial as the only appropriate remedy. It is unlikely that the judge can save the case by excusing the testifying court member, even if sufficient members are left to constitute a quorum. government counsel still would feel that any attempt to impeach the court member or to vigorously cross-examine him would prejudice his case in the remaining members' eyes.

Although no single solution will settle all 606(a) problems, a thorough *voir dire* of prospective court members should help to minimize them. In this respect, counsel for both sides should insure that the triers of fact do not have personal knowledge of the case and that they are not too closely associated with any potential witnesses. Care in voir dire may avoid trouble later.

[3]   Rule 606(b)—Inquiry into Validity of Findings or Sentence

[a]   The General Rule of Exclusion

Subdivision (b) addresses the role court members play in post-trial challenges to the proceedings. Initially, it prohibits a member from testifying about his or her or any other member's: (1) actual deliberations, (2) impressions, (3) emotional feelings or (4) mental processes used to resolve an issue at bar.[2] The Rule also states that, if the court members cannot testify, then their affidavits or similar documentary statements will not be admissible.[3]

[b]   The Exceptions

Alternatively, 606(b) allows court members to testify if the possibility exists of: (1) extra-record prejudicial information being brought to their attention,[4] (2) outside influence being exerted upon them,[5] or (3) command control being used to guide the proceedings' outcome. This aspect of subdivision (b) is virtually identical with its federal counterpart, except that the drafters added a specific provision addressing command influence.[6] This additional language is important in courts-martial and is also consistent with Executive and Congressional desires to demonstrate the independence of military criminal trials.

By allowing court members to testify under some circumstances[7] and not others, subdivision (b) represents the military drafters' adoption of a

---

[2] *See, e.g.*, United States v. Davila, 704 F.2d 749 (5th Cir. 1983) (no error for trial judge to deny post trial request by defendants to interview jurors concerning mental processes); United States v. Musto, 540 F. Supp. 318 (D.N.J. 1982) (discussing impeachment of verdicts and concluding that no hearing concerning jury deliberations should be held until a party can make a showing that such a hearing is justified); United States v. Duzac, 622 F.2d 911 (5th Cir. 1980) (no post-indictment inquiry was necessary where the jury sent the trial judge a note indicating "certain prejudices" among the jurors prevented a verdict on one count).

[3] In United States v. Higdon, 2 M.J. 445, 455 (A.C.M.R. 1975), the court used Federal Rule 606(b) to reject a court member's affidavit alleging improper balloting techniques.

[4] *See, e.g.*, United States v. Bassler, 651 F.2d 600 (8th Cir. 1981) (although not prejudicial, the court found that a juror's note-taking violated the trial judge's instructions and that this was an "extrinsic influence"); United States v. Aimone, 715 F.2d 822 (3d Cir. 1983) (trial judge properly gave supplemental charge to jurors when one juror complained of conduct of foreperson; no post-trial inquiry needed).

[5] *See, e.g.*, United States v. Bagnariol, 665 F.2d 877 (9th Cir. 1981), *cert. denied*, 456 U.S. 962 (1982) (juror's misconduct in doing research at library does not require reversal); United States v. Castello, 526 F. Supp. 847 (W.D. Tex. 1981) (new trial granted where juror conducted a ballistics test during weekend recess).

[6] *See* Article 37(a), Uniform Code Of Military Justice for prohibitions in this area. *See also* United States v. Howard, 48 C.M.R. 939 (C.M.A. 1974) (reversing a conviction because it appeared that the convening authority attempted to influence the treatment of soldiers tried before a general court-martial).

[7] *See, e.g.*, Sullivan v. Fogg, 613 F.2d 465 (2d Cir. 1980) (a hearing into juror competence

Congressional compromise. The balance is struck between the necessity for accurately resolving criminal trials in accordance with rules of law, on the one hand, and the desirability of promoting finality in litigation and of protecting members from harassment and second-guessing, on the other hand.

This result permits court members to testify with respect to *objective* manifestations of impropriety—*e.g.*, that inadmissible evidence was placed in their deliberation room, *see United States v. Pinto*,[8]—but prohibits their testimony if the alleged transgression is *subjective* in nature—*e.g.*, allegations that the court members ignored the trial judge's instructions and convicted the accused because he failed to take the stand in his own defense.[9]

Military and federal litigation demonstrates that Rule 606(b) will prevent counsel from examining court members to determine whether they followed the bench's instructions, violated their juror oaths, or were emotionally influenced by some event at trial.[10] In *Tanner v. United States*,[11] the Supreme Court reinforced Rule 606(b)'s prohibitions. There the defendant contended that some jurors had abused alcohol and controlled substances during lunch breaks and at other times. The defendant also alleged that these abuses caused the jurors to be inattentive during the trial, and even occasionally fall asleep. Affirming the conviction, Justice O'Connor held that alcohol and substance abuses are not the types of "extraneous prejudicial information" or "outside influence" anticipated by the Rule, and thus cannot be reached by an impeaching affidavit or juror testimony.

To some extent, Justice O'Connor's opinion depends on the other aspects of trial to protect an accused's rights. A thoroughly conducted voir dire, and constant observation of the jurors by the military judge, counsel, and other jurors should serve to identify those individuals not complying with their oath. In the Court's opinion, invalidating judgments weeks or months after the trial because of such juror allegations would "seriously disrupt the finality of the process." The Court also questioned whether our system of justice could withstand any attempt to perfect the jury system.

The result may be different, however, if during deliberations a court member learns that a fellow court member lied when questioned on voir dire

---

was required one month after trial when the court learned a juror complained of hearing "voices" and "vibrations" in the jury room).

[8] 486 F. Supp. 578 (E.D. Pa. 1980). *See also*, United States v. Robinson, 645 F.2d 616 (8th Cir. 1981) (jurors may testify about publicity and attempted tampering); United States v. Freeman, 634 F.2d 1267 (10th Cir. 1980) (conviction was reversed where an FBI agent, at the court's request, operated a video-tape machine in the jury room).

[9] *See* United States v. Edwards, 486 F. Supp. 673 (S.D.N.Y. 1980).

[10] *See* United States v. Greer, 620 F.2d 1383 (10th Cir. 1980).

[11] 483 U.S. 107 (1987).

in an attempt to sit on the panel. Rule 606(b) applies to court member deliberations, not to pretrial voir dire questioning. Under these circumstances, the matter would properly be the subject of further investigation, and that court member testimony in support would be appropriate.[12]

[c]   Rule 606 Not Applicable to Military Judges

The Court of Appeals for the Armed Forces has held that Rule 606(b) does not apply to a military judge's deliberations.[13] In a lengthy analysis of the issue in *United States v. McNutt*,[14] the court analyzed federal court decisions on the issue, and the fact that the Supreme Court has not addressed the issue, in concluding that the plain meaning of Rule 606 and the underlying policies of the rule, supported a conclusion that the rule does not apply to the military judge's thought processes in reaching a verdict or sentence.

But the Court of Appeals for the Armed Forces held in *United States v. Matthews*[15] that Rule 509, which cross references Rule 606, applies to military judges. The issue was whether the original trial judge should have been permitted to testify about his deliberations during a subsequent *DuBay* hearing. Regarding the relationship of Rules 509 and 606, the court observed:

> M.R.E. 606(b) addresses if and when a court member may testify about the deliberations at the court-martial. The corollary rule regarding the competency of a military judge as a witness, M.R.E. 605, does not address inquiry into a military judge's deliberations.
>
> * * * * *
>
> Nevertheless, the application of M.R.E. 606 to only court members does not preclude M.R.E. 509 from applying to military judges. M.R.E. 606 limits M.R.E. 509 to the extent M.R.E. 509 protects the deliberations of court members; however, this limitation does not prevent or preclude M.R.E. 509 from applying to a military judge's deliberations.[16]

The Court observed that the term "privilege" in Rule 509 was ambiguous and that the rule might be construed to be either a privilege like the other privileges in Section V—which may be waived or invoked—or as a privilege which bars disclosure. Citing *Fayerweather v. Ritch*,[17] and applying the federal common law, the Court concluded that the latter

---

[12] *See, e.g.*, United States v. Colombo, 869 F.2d 149 (2d Cir. 1989) (permissible to accept evidence from an alternate juror that a sitting juror lied in order to be selected for the jury).

[13] United States v. McNutt, 62 M.J. 16 (C.A.A.F. 2005); United States v. Hill, 62 M.J. 271 (C.A.A.F. 2006), annotated, *below*.

[14] United States v. McNutt, 62 M.J. 16 (C.A.A.F. 2005).

[15] United States v. Matthews, 68 M.J. 29 (C.A.A.F. 2009).

[16] 68 M.J, at 36, n.5.

[17] Fayerweather v. Ritch, 195 U.S. 276 (1904).

approach should be applied to Rule 509. Thus, evidence of the judge's deliberative process is privileged and inadmissible—even if the judge is willing to testify.

The Court cited a number of reasons supporting the general rule of nondisclosure—protecting the integrity of the legal system; protecting the finality of judgments; avoiding the problem of reliability of a judge's memory about his or her deliberations; and avoiding concerns about the perception that the judge's testimony may be irrebuttable. The Court concluded that reading Rule 509 as permitting a waiver would be inconsistent with the federal common law which has been incorporated into Rule 509, and the justifications supporting the protections provided by that Rule.

The *Matthews* decision is discussed in greater detail at Rule 509, above.

§ 606.03   Drafters' Analysis

[1]   At the court-martial

Rule 606(a) is taken from the Federal Rule without substantive change. The Rule alters present military law only to the extent that a member of the court could testify as a defense witness under prior precedent. Rule 606(a) deals only with the competency of court members as witnesses and does not affect other *Manual* provisions governing the eligibility of individuals to sit as members due to their potential status as witnesses. *See, e.g.*, ¶¶ 62*f* and 63. The Rule does not affect voir dire.

[2]   Inquiry into validity of findings or sentence

Rule 606(b) is taken from the Federal Rule with only one significant change. The Rule, retitled to reflect the sentencing function of members, recognizes unlawful command influence as a legitimate subject of inquiry and permits testimony by a member on that subject. The addition is required by the need to keep proceedings free from any taint of unlawful command influence and further implements Article 37(a) of the Uniform Code of Military Justice. Use of superior rank or grade by one member of a court to sway other members would constitute unlawful command influence for purposes of this Rule under ¶ 74*d*(1). Rule 606 does not itself prevent otherwise lawful polling of members of the court, *see generally*, *United States v. Hendon*, 6 M.J. 171, 174 (C.M.A. 1979) and does not prohibit attempted lawful clarification of an ambiguous or inconsistent verdict. Rule 606(b) is in general accord with present military law.

§ 606.04   Annotated Cases

[1]   Rule 606(b)—Inquiry into Validity of Findings or Sentence

[a]   Inquiry into Deliberations—Court Member Misconduct

Supreme Court

Tanner v. United States, 483 U.S. 107 (1987): In a motion for new trial, counsel presented information that during the trial a number of jurors had consumed large quantities of alcohol, several ingested cocaine, and one juror sold another juror marijuana. *Citing* Rule 606(b), the Supreme Court concluded that the trial court correctly denied counsel's attempts to introduce juror affidavits on the issue of substance abuse during deliberations. Substance abuse is not considered an outside influence or prejudicial extraneous information. The Court also rejected the defendant's argument that juror testimony was required under his Sixth Amendment right to trial by a competent and unimpaired jury. That right can be adequately protected through voir dire and observation of the jurors during the trial.

United States Court of Appeals for the Armed Forces

United States v. Motsinger, 34 M.J. 255 (C.M.A. 1992): The accused was tried before a court with members for larceny and related offenses. His punishment included a punitive discharge. During sentencing, trial counsel argued that the accused should be separated because of personnel quality control standards. The military judge interrupted counsel and gave an appropriate corrective instruction. Before final action, the court president sent a letter to the convening authority requesting that the punitive discharge be suspended because it was based on draw-down requirements. The letter did not indicate whether this was the president's personal feelings, or those of the panel. Affirming the accused's findings and sentence, this court held that members are prohibited from impeaching their holdings with post-trial affidavits unless they address extraneous prejudicial information, outside influence, or unlawful command control. Because the president's letter did not raise any of these issues, relief was not required.

United States v. Stone, 26 M.J. 401 (C.M.A. 1988): Two weeks after the accused's larceny and wrongful appropriation conviction, he alleged that there had been laughing in the jury deliberation room, and that this conduct created an "insensitive, insincere and festive atmosphere." When the convening authority was informed of these allegations, he ordered an administrative investigation which discovered no misconduct. Findings and sentence were ultimately approved. The accused's similar allegations and appeal were rejected because they were not raised during trial, and, even if the court members had been unduly mirthful, this circumstance would not demonstrate a lack of fairness or impartiality.

United States v. Witherspoon, 16 M.J. 252 (C.M.A. 1983): Affirming the conviction, the court noted that, when evidence of juror misconduct arises, the appropriate procedure for dealing with the matter calls for referral "to the trial judge for judicial assessment of the facts and the prejudicial impact on the accused's rights."

United States v. Bishop, 11 M.J. 7 (C.M.A. 1981): Relying specifically upon Rule 606(b), the court discussed when post-trial affidavits *should* be considered in determining whether the court members were improperly affected by "extraneous prejudicial information." In this case, the initial defense affidavit contended that certain court members had deliberately viewed the crime scene in order to determine which witnesses were testifying truthfully. In response, the government submitted additional affidavits stating that the members in question had not deliberately viewed the area, but were familiar with it "because their homes were nearby and they passed through the neighborhood." In affirming the conviction, the court found that "a fair reading of the affidavits before us does not show that the personal familiarity of the members had any effect whatsoever on their deliberations or decision in this case."

Army Court of Criminal Appeals

United States v. Witherspoon, 12 M.J. 588 (A.C.M.R. 1981): After the accused was convicted for rape, it was determined that one court member, during an overnight recess, drove through the crime scene on his way home. In order to protect the record, statements concerning the issue were obtained from each member of the court and included in the record's allied papers. While the reviewing court noted that jurors are generally not permitted to impeach their verdicts, some exceptions are appropriate. Here the court relied on Rule 606(b) and found that the facts at bar provided such an exception. After considering the members' post-trial affidavits, the court found no prejudice and affirmed the conviction.

[b] Inquiry into Deliberations—Defense Counsel Initiatives

United States Court of Appeals for the Armed Forces

United States v. Ovando-Moran, 48 M.J. 300 (C.A.A.F. 1998): As the result of mixed pleas, the accused was convicted of AWOL, rape, forcible sodomy, and house-breaking. Affirming the accused's convictions, this court held that defense obtained information from post-trial interviews of court-members clearly invaded the deliberative process. The court went on to say that this material could not be considered for any purpose unless it constituted proof of extraneous prejudicial information, outside influence, or unlawful command influence, none of which were present.

[c] Inquiry into Deliberations—Extraneous Influences

United States Court of Appeals for the Armed Forces

United States v. Johnson, 23 M.J. 327 (C.M.A. 1987): Affirming the accused's murder conviction, the court held that a court member's affidavit, indicating that during deliberations on findings he demonstrated how the murder weapon might have been used, did not constitute "extraneous prejudicial information." The affidavit did require an inquiry into the conviction's validity, since the court found that the member's actions were "merely an examination and evaluation of evidence already produced. . . ."

Air Force Court of Criminal Appeals

United States v. Heimer, 34 M.J. 541 (A.F.C.M.R. 1992): The accused was convicted of sodomizing his stepson. After trial, defense counsel sent a questionnaire to the members concerning their subjective evaluations of what occurred in court. Defense counsel then used these documents to argue for a mistrial. Affirming the accused's convictions, this court found the questionnaire's "subjective" basis for determining error to be improper, holding that Rule 606 only permits limited "objective" criteria to be used.

United States v. Wallace, 28 M.J. 640 (A.F.C.M.R. 1989): Setting aside the accused's sentence for drug offenses, the court held that when the trial judge became aware the members had used "extraneous incorrect information regarding the ease of converting an executed punitive discharge to an administrative discharge," he should have sua sponte convened an Article 39(a) session, rather than simply attach an explanatory post-trial affidavit to the record. The court went on to say that, when the trial judge fails to take some curative action, the convening authority must do so.

United States v. Rice, 20 M.J. 764 (A.F.C.M.R. 1985): Using this Rule as a model, the court held that a trial judge cannot impeach a sentence he has adjudged unless it can be established that (a) extraneous information had been brought to the judge's attention, (b) outside influences had been exerted upon him, or (c) he was the target of unlawful command influence.

Army Court of Criminal Appeals

United States v. Knight, 41 M.J. 867 (Army Ct.Crim.App. 1995): After deliberations on findings had begun, defense counsel moved for a mistrial because the court members had discussed several witnesses' testimony with their driver, and had begun evaluating the witness's testimony before the case was presented to them. Reversing the accused's rape conviction, the court held that Rule 606(b) was properly used here to determine which outside influences had reached the members. In the court's opinion these delicts unquestionably influenced the members' decision.

United States v. Ezell, 24 M.J. 690 (A.C.M.R. 1987): Rule 606(b) was not violated when court members were asked to provide post-trial affidavits concerning (1) whether they saw an improperly attached charge sheet "flyer" which contained a dismissed offense, and (2) what, if any, effect it had on their determinations. The court also said that a post-trial hearing is the preferred way to resolve such matters.

United States v. Hance, 10 M.J. 622 (A.C.M.R. 1980): Relying on prior military authority and Rule 606(b), the court affirmed the accused's murder conviction despite post-trial affidavits from various court members indicating that the government's evidence was insufficient to establish the accused's guilt or mental responsibility. The court found that in order to be successful here, the accused would have to show that the member's deliberations were adversely affected by "extraneous influences"; otherwise the "testimony of jurors will not be received to impeach their verdict. . . ."

Navy-Marine Corps Court of Criminal Appeals

United States v. Sennett, 42 M.J. 787 (N.M. Ct.Crim.App. 1995): The accused was convicted of conspiracy to commit an assault, battery, and disrespect. After sentencing, but before the record of trial was authenticated, the military judge reconvened the court to consider allegations that the members had received extraneous information concerning the accused's court-martial. Trial defense counsel reported that the members discussed unadmitted and inadmissible evidence about how other members of the conspiracy had been sentenced. The military judge's voir dire of the members confirmed defense counsel's allegations. This court held that the members' knowledge of extraneous information did not result in prejudice because the accused defended on the ground that he had not been involved with them or been part of a conspiracy.

[d] Inquiry into Deliberations—Instructions by the Military Judge

Navy-Marine Corps Court of Criminal Appeals

United States v. Schnable, 58 M.J. 643 (N.M. Ct.Crim.App. 2003): The accused was convicted of indecent acts upon his daughter. At trial and without objection, the military judge gave the standard instruction cautioning the members against discussing the case outside of certain specified limitations. On appeal for the first time the accused contended that the instruction was error. Affirming the accused's convictions and sentence this court held that no error occurred because the purpose of the instruction is to protect the deliberations process from needless invasion while protecting the members themselves from "annoyance and embarrassment."

[e] Inquiry into Deliberations—Mental Processes

United States Court of Appeals for the Armed Forces

United States v. Gonzalez, 42 M.J. 373 (C.A.A.F. 1995): This is the second time the court has reviewed the accused's case. Originally tried for larceny and leaving his place of duty, the accused's record was returned to the trial jurisdiction for a mental responsibility determination. At that fact-finding hearing, the military judge who also presided over the accused's court-martial, indicated that had he known of the accused's emotional problems, that information would have had an impact on the sentence he adjudged. Both the Court of Review and this court held that the military judge's statements were violative of Rule 606(b)'s prohibition against commenting on the deliberative process. This court affirmed the original sentence adjudged.

United States v. Straight, 42 M.J. 244 (C.A.A.F. 1995): The accused was convicted of attempted murder, rape, wrongful appropriation of an automobile, forcible sodomy, assault and battery, kidnapping, indecent assault, communicating a threat, and violating a lawful general regulation. In a post-trial declaration, trial defense counsel indicated that she spoke with several court members who indicated that they increased the accused's sentence because of parole possibilities. The accused asked this court to reduce his period of confinement to the sentence the members agreed on before the parole comments were made. Affirming both sentence and findings, the court held that neither the military judge nor an appellate court should inquire into the members' statements or discussions, absent a claim of external influence, and no such claim was made in this case.

United States v. Combs, 41 M.J. 400 (C.A.A.F. 1995): During the sentencing portion of the accused's drug distribution trial, the military judge refused to ask a court member propounded question concerning whether the accused had cooperated with law enforcement officials. After trial, the court reporter informed defense counsel that one of the members said that if the accused had cooperated, his sentence would have been less. Defense counsel immediately asked for a post-trial session to consider this matter. Both the convening authority and the military judge failed to grant her request. This court affirmed the accused's convictions and sentence because the possibility that some court members may have drawn an improper inference from the trial proceedings falls squarely within this provision's deliberative process protections.

Air Force Court of Criminal Appeals

United States v. Langer, 41 M.J. 780 (A.F. Ct.Crim.App. 1995): After the accused was convicted and sentenced for using cocaine, defense counsel submitted a post-trial questionnaire to the members asking them about their deliberative processes. On appeal, the accused contended that the questionnaire's answers demonstrated the members had ignored the military judge's instructions on burden of proof. Affirming the accused's conviction and sentence, this court held that Rule 606(b) protects the member's deliberative processes and, unless the accused can demonstrate that some improper outside influence affected them, he is entitled to no relief. The Court also said that the use of such questionnaires to impeach court members' findings is improper.

Army Court of Criminal Appeals

United States v. Douglas, 22 M.J. 891 (A.C.M.R. 1986): Recognizing that the military judge erred by not "prevent[ing] counsel from examining court members concerning whether they followed instructions or were emotionally influenced by some event at trial," the court failed to grant relief because trial defense counsel requested the hearing and the court was "loathe to permit" an accused relief on a self-induced error.

Navy-Marine Corps Court of Criminal Appeals

United States v. Martinez, 17 M.J. 916 (N.M.C.M.R. 1984): When the trial judge discovered, during a hearing in revision, that the court members had not used a secret written ballot in arriving at their findings, he attempted to determine whether prejudicial error resulted by examining each member concerning possible improper influences. He found no improper influence. Reversing conviction, the court held that the judge required the members to disclose matters from within their personal consciousness, an area that is "off-limits" under the Rule.

[f] Inquiry into Deliberations—Application to Military Judges

United States Court of Appeals for the Armed Forces

United States v. Matthews, 68 M.J. 29 (C.A.A.F. 2009): At the accused's bench trial the military judge relied on Rule 512(a)(2) and permitted the prosecution to comment during its closing argument on a defense witness's invocation of the privilege against self-incrimination. The Court of Criminal Appeals ordered a *DuBay* hearing and that judge, after taking testimony from the original trial judge, held that Rule 512 supported the trial judge's decision. The Court of Criminal Appeals held that Rule 509 did not bar the trial judge from testifying at the *DuBay* hearing and that both the military judge and the judge in the *DuBay* hearing erred in applying Rule 512 instead of the more specific, controlling provision in Rule 301(f). That rule, the court said, provides that the sole remedy for refusing to answer questions on cross-examination is to strike the witness's direct testimony. The court explained that, regardless of whether the direct testimony is stricken, neither the judge nor the court members may draw an adverse inference from the witness's invocation of the privilege. It concluded that trial counsel's argument was harmless error. *United States v. Matthews*, 66 M.J. 645 (Army Ct.Crim.App. 2008). Without addressing the question of the application of Rules 301 or 512, the Court of Appeals ruled that Rule 509 barred the testimony of the trial judge at the subsequent *DuBay* hearing. In a lengthy discussion of the issue, the Court noted that while Rule 606 is limited to court members, Rule 509 is not so limited. The Court continued by noting that the term "courts" in Rule 509 applies to military judges but that the term "privilege" in the context of Rule 509 was ambiguous. Applying federal common law on evidentiary privileges, the Court concluded that, subject to narrow exceptions not present in this case, Rule 509 prohibits disclosure of a judge's deliberative process—regardless of whether the judge is willing to testify. The Court remanded the case to the Court of Criminal Appeals for further review.

United States v. Hill, 62 M.J. 271 (C.A.A.F. 2006): Affirming the accused's convictions and sentence, the court cited its decision in *McNutt, below*, and held that statements made by the military judge to counsel during a post-trial informal "bridging the gap" session, were not covered by Rule 606(b), and thus were reviewable on appeal. The court did not grant relief because trial defense counsel failed to establish any impropriety by the trial judge, and because the court presumed that military judges knew and properly applied the rules of evidence.

United States v. McNutt, 62 M.J. 16 (C.A.A.F. 2005): During a post-trial

"Bridge the Gap" session, the military judge discussed with counsel how he reached the sentence in several cases. During this session the judge stated that he considered the effect good-time calculations would have on the ultimate period the accused would serve for his misconduct. In a lengthy decision, the Court addressed precedent applying Rule 606(b) to a trial judge's deliberations. Applying a plain reading analysis, the court concluded that the rule applies only to court members and does not apply to military judge deliberations. Thus, the judge's comments about his thought process in reaching a sentence could be examined. In this case, the court said, the judge's erroneous consideration of good time credits was prejudicial error.

Navy-Marine Corps Court of Criminal Appeals

United States v. Lentz, 54 M.J. 818 (N.M. Ct.Crim.App. 2001): The accused was convicted of making a false official statement, assault with a means likely to produce death or grievous bodily harm, assault consummated by a battery upon a child the age of 16 years, assault consummated by a battery upon his wife, and adultery. Before this court he contended that the military judge's sentence was illegal because of the judge's alleged out-of-court post-trial statements relating directly to her deliberative process in determining the accused's sentence, and from the fact that the military judge deliberated only 30 minutes on the accused's sentence. Affirming the accused's sentence and findings the court held that Rule 606(b) precludes considering evidence of sentencing deliberations, and that no actual unfairness or any appearance of unfairness arose in this case. The Court also noted that, if a military judge believes it is necessary to discuss a case with counsel, the judge should be circumspect and sensitive as to what is stated, and counsel from both sides be present during the meeting. Finally, the court also noted that the trier-of-fact is not required to deliberate for any set length of time, and brief deliberation, by itself, does not necessarily show the trier of fact failed to give full, conscientious, or impartial consideration to the evidence.

[g] Inquiry into Deliberations—Unlawful Command Influence

United States Court of Appeals for the Armed Forces

United States v. Dugan, 58 M.J. 253 (C.A.A.F. 2003): Pursuant to his pleas the accused was convicted of drug and other offenses. A court-martial panel sentenced him to a bad conduct discharge, nine months confinement, and related punishments. After trial a court member submitted a letter to defense counsel for submission to the convening authority. The letter indicated that during deliberations on sentence some members did not consider: (1) certain mitigating evidence, (2) that the accused would be enrolled in a drug abuse program if he was confined, (3) that a BCD was a given for drug offenses, and (4) that as a result of the convening authority's recent "commanders call" where the harmful affects of drug use were discussed, a panel member highlighted that it was important that their sentence be seen as sending "a consistent message," and that their names would be associated with the results of trial. The service court of appeal found that none of these issues called into question the validity of the sentence and that the trial judge acted properly in not conducting a further investigation into the allegations. Reversing and requiring a *Dubay* hearing, this court held that with respect to the first two allegations no error was committed, but with respect to the last two the trial judge should have conducted a hearing "regarding what was said during deliberations about the commander's comments. . . ."

United States v. Carr, 18 M.J. 297 (C.M.A. 1984): The court found that an unsigned letter from a purported court member to the military judge indicating "that the court members had been subjected to undue pressure from the president" was sufficient to justify a post-trial Article 39(a) hearing because: "Although jurors usually cannot impeach their verdict, this principle is not applied in the military context when there is a contention that an 'outside influence was improperly brought to bear upon any member, or that there was unlawful command influence.' "

Air Force Court of Criminal Appeals

United States v. Accordino, 15 M.J. 825 (A.F.C.M.R. 1983): Holding that the accused's conviction should not be reversed because of a juror's affidavit indicating the presence of unlawful command influence during deliberations on findings, the court stated that they would "not effectuate the interpretation of Mil. R. Evid. 606(b) suggested by the drafter's analysis . . . ." The court based its conclusion on the "belief that the expansive definition of the term 'command influence' embraced by this drafters' analysis would significantly impede the [efficiency] of any jury system," and because incidents of unlawful command influence occurring in jury deliberation rooms is "virtually unknown in the United States Air Force."

[h] Inquiry into Deliberations—Voting Improprieties

United States Court of Appeals for the Armed Forces

United States v. Brooks, 42 M.J. 484 (C.A.A.F. 1995): The accused was convicted of assault, battery, and aggravated assault. Before sentencing, he contended that the members voted improperly on findings. When the trial judge voir dired the members they admitted to multiple votes. The military judge then entered a finding of not guilty to a portion of the charges. The government appealed his decision. The Court of Criminal Appeals set aside the trial judge's holding because the members' actions did not amount to extrinsic interference nor command influence, so no justification existed for questioning them nor overturning their verdict. The Court of Appeals for the Armed Forces affirmed that decision.

United States v. Loving, 41 M.J. 213 (1994): The accused was convicted of premeditated murder, felony murder, attempted murder, and five specifications of robbery. He was sentenced to death. Affirming the accused's convictions and sentence, this court held that it could only use the members' post-trial affidavits to determine whether any extraordinary influences or unlawful command influence had contributed to the death penalty. Finding no error, the court refused to adopt a capital case exception and use the affidavits to impeach the member's consultations, deliberations, or voting procedures.

Air Force Court of Criminal Appeals

United States v. Commander, 39 M.J. 972 (A.F.C.M.R. 1994): The accused was convicted of wrongfully possessing anabolic steroids. After findings, defense counsel asked the military judge to question the members about their understanding of the prescription drug defense, and whether they wanted to reconsider their verdict. The trial judge refused. Affirming the accused's conviction, this court held that an inquiry into how the members used the bench's instructions, without more, would violate both this Rule and R.C.M. 923.

Navy-Marine Corps Court of Criminal Appeals

United States v. Thomas, 39 M.J. 626 (N.M.C.M.R. 1994): The accused was convicted of murdering his wife and sentenced to death. After trial, he filed a Motion for Declaratory Judgment, which was subsequently changed to a specified allegation of error pursuant to Article 66(c), Uniform Code of Military Justice. Among other assertions, the accused contended that the military judge erred by refusing to poll the court members concerning how many times they voted during findings. Relying on R.C.M. 922(e), the court found that the military judge acted correctly and thoroughly when he asked each member whether that member concurred in the panel's decision regarding findings, aggravating circumstances, and sentence. The court said that after each member positively responded, there was no basis for expanding the poll.

§ 607.01   Official Text

Rule 607.   Who May Impeach.

The credibility of a witness may be attacked by any party, including the party calling the witness.

---

§ 607.02   Editorial Comment

[1]   In General

Litigators must be intimately familiar with Rule 607. In conjunction with Rule 613, it should be considered both when calling a party's own witnesses and when contemplating cross-examining an opponent's witnesses. It is important, particularly for inexperienced counsel, to recognize that the federal and military application of this Rule and Rule 613 may differ from the procedures learned in law school or used in state courts.

Before the Military Rules of Evidence were promulgated, and at common law, a party was prohibited from impeaching his or her own witness except in special circumstances. Traditionally, those circumstances included confrontations with hostile witnesses, counsel being surprised by a witness's damaging testimony, or counsel being required to call a witness deemed essential to the calling party's case. Rule 607, which is identical to its federal counterpart, rejects the common law idea that a party calling a witness is required to vouch for that witness's testimony.[1] Now counsel, on direct examination, may impeach a witness he or she has called.[2]

Commentators long argued for this change. They perceived that the traditional practice artificially limited counsels' ability to accurately present a case. The common law practice assumed that proponents of testimony had some real choice as to whom they would call as witnesses. In most cases this is unrealistic. Parties must use those witnesses who have knowledge of the case facts. Those who participate in a crime will have knowledge. Those who witness it may have additional knowledge. People to whom confessions are made may have something to add. But these people all must be taken as they are. Counsel cannot substitute for them.

Impeachment of character witnesses may be different. They are often carefully selected, screened, and prepared before trial. As a result, it is less

---

[1] *See, e.g.*, United States v. Perner, 14 M.J. 181 (C.M.A. 1982) (without mentioning Rule 607, the court specifically rejected the "voucher rule," finding that it is a "vestigial 'remnant of primitive English trial practice' and is generally condemned in modern practice").

[2] *See, e.g.*, United States v. Mourad, 729 F.2d 195 (2d Cir. 1984) (not necessary to strike government witness' direct testimony where he failed to return for cross-examination, but the cross-examination was virtually completed).

likely that an impeachment witness will in turn be personally attacked. Similarly, a party will not impeach his or her own expert or character witness. In fact, such witnesses are worth little if they are impeached by either side.

[2]   Impeachment with Prior Statements

Rule 607 is intended to permit impeachment, not to permit the introduction of inconsistent statements where there is no reason for impeachment other than an attempt to bring inadmissible hearsay before the court members. This might occur under the following circumstances. The accused is charged with sexually molesting his stepdaughter. Some time after the offense, the victim made a full statement to the OSI implicating her father. Shortly before trial, the victim and her mother visited the OSI and recanted the original statement. The victim then informed trial counsel that she would not testify against her father. Notwithstanding the victim's position, government counsel still called her as a witness. Once on the stand, the victim immediately denied being sexually assaulted. Trial counsel would then like to impeach the victim with her previous out of court statement implicating her father.

If the victim's prior statement satisfies Rule 801(d), it can be admitted as substantive evidence, that is, for the truth of the matter asserted, as well as for impeachment purposes. Any witness can be called and asked about statements that are non-hearsay and admissible under Rule 801 where they are properly being offered for the truth of the matter asserted.

However, where the statement does not qualify under Rule 801 as non-hearsay, but is offered under Rule 613(a)—as a prior inconsistent statement—its use would be improper.[3] In our example, trial counsel was simply attempting to "smuggle" a prior inconsistent statement that could be used only for impeachment purposes into evidence as what he or she hoped the court members would believe was substantive proof.

Even though the military judge would provide an instruction demonstrating that the testimony could only be used for impeachment purposes, such subtle evidentiary distinctions are easily missed by lay finders of fact. Federal courts have applied the prohibition against using impeachment evidence in this way to both prosecutors[4] and defense counsel.[5]

Alternatively, if the proponent of the witness elicits some helpful material

---

[3] *See, e.g.,* United States v. Fay, 668 F.2d 375 (8th Cir. 1981) (no error to refuse defendant opportunity to call witness solely to impeach with inconsistent statements not admissible as substantive evidence).

[4] *See, e.g.,* United States v. Hogan, 763 F.2d 697 (5th Cir. 1985) (conviction reversed where government called a witness primarily to impeach him with inadmissible hearsay).

[5] *See, e.g.,* United States v. Sebetich, 776 F.2d 412 (3d Cir. 1985) (improper for defense counsel to call a witness as a ruse for avoiding hearsay provisions).

from the witness, but also is damaged by portions of the witness's testimony, impeachment with inconsistent statements directed at the damaging testimony should be allowed.[6] Similarly, if a party is surprised and hurt by a witness's testimony, impeachment is certainly proper.

The reverse situation may also confront counsel. Based on our example above, let's assume the same victim decides to testify against her father at trial. Government counsel is aware that on cross-examination defense counsel will try to impeach the victim with the second statement she made to OSI. In this situation, government counsel may raise the previous inconsistent statement with the witness, thereby impeaching her, but also deflating opposing counsel's potential attack.

[3]   Impeachment with Prior Acts

We believe the proponent of a witness should be permitted to use evidence of "prior bad acts" to impeach his or her own witness under Rule 608(b). The same result should obtain under Rule 609 with respect to evidence of previous convictions. A party should not be forced to await impeachment by an opponent; he or she should be allowed to show that a witness has blemishes. Some courts call this taking the "sting" out of impeachment by an opponent. The legislative history of the Federal Rules displays no Congressional intent to limit their application of Rules 608 and 609 to only "cross-examination."[7] Here, the Drafters' Analysis is much clearer than anything in the legislative history of the Federal Rules of Evidence. It is doubtful, however, that a direct examiner should be permitted to call a witness solely to impeach.

In this area, an interesting question can arise concerning trial counsel's ability to impeach his or her own witness with evidence of that witness's pretrial agreement. Under most circumstances, such an examination would be in anticipation of defense counsel using the pretrial agreement as proof that the witness was biased or influenced by a deal with the government, and as a result is only testifying against the accused to preserve lenient treatment.[8] But where the government witness and the accused were

---

[6] *See, e.g.,* United States v. DeLillo, 620 F.2d 939 (2d Cir. 1980) (the government was allowed to impeach portions of its own witnesses' testimony, even though the witnesses' overall testimony was favorable).

[7] *See* 2 S. Saltzburg, M. Martin & D. Capra, FEDERAL RULES OF EVIDENCE MANUAL § 607.02 (9th ed. 2006) for a more detailed discussion of this area.

[8] *See, e.g.,* United States v. Henderson, 717 F.2d 135 (4th Cir. 1983), *cert. denied*, 104 S. Ct. 1006 (1984) (prosecution could elicit fact that its witness entered plea agreement); United States v. Edwards, 716 F.2d 822 (11th Cir. 1983) (government could rehabilitate witness by showing that he had been convicted and sentenced); United States v. Halbert, 640 F.2d 1000 (9th Cir. 1981) (permissible for the prosecutor to establish that his witness had already pleaded guilty to the crime for which the accused was tried); United States v. Edwards, 631 F.2d 1049 (2d Cir. 1980) (cooperation agreement between the government and its key witness

co-actors, defense counsel may not want this evidence to reach the members because they could use it to reason that the accused is as guilty as his co-accused has just admitted to being.

Under these circumstances, if defense counsel states for the record that he or she will forgo impeachment based on the government witness's pretrial agreement, then a strong case can be made for excluding the evidence. At this point, government counsel does not have an attack to anticipate and minimize.[9] The evidence's relevance becomes questionable because bias or motive to fabricate will not be raised, and as a result, the pretrial agreement's probative value might be substantially outweighed by its prejudicial effect. Members may wonder, however, why the witness is not being prosecuted and the deal could remain important.

When counsel impeaches his or her own witness, a question concerning whether he or she can use direct or cross-examination techniques to accomplish this end may be raised. Read literally, Rule 611(c), provides that only a cross-examiner can use leading questions. Because the Military and Federal Rules of Evidence often interchangeably use the terms "impeachment" and "cross-examination," the better reading of this provision allows the party impeaching his or her own witness to conduct that portion of the examination with leading questions. When counsel returns to favorable or substantive testimony, he or she must then use direct examination techniques.

Rule 607 does not set forth the types of impeachment that are permissible. Subsequent Rules cover many of the most familiar modes of impeachment, and Rule 402 indicates that, as long as the credibility of a witness is pertinent, relevant evidence detracting from it should be admitted unless another Rule stands in the way.[10]

Trial judges should be particularly sensitive when balancing the probative value of impeachment evidence against its potentially prejudicial effects. The concern here is that court members may not be able to properly evaluate how impeachment evidence should be used and, for emotional reasons, may use the testimony substantively. Similarly, much impeachment evidence is

---

was viewed as permissible self-impeachment rather than improper bolstering); United States v. Hedman, 630 F.2d 1184 (7th Cir. 1980) (government may impeach its witnesses by showing they have been granted immunity).

[9] *Compare*, United States v. LeFevour, 798 F.2d 977 (7th Cir. 1986) (no error for government counsel to impeach with an immunity agreement even though there would be no defense attack); *and* United States v. Gambino, 926 F.2d 1355 (3d Cir. 1991) (government permitted to impeach witness with pretrial agreement were jury properly instructed on its use); *with* United States v. Thomas, 998 F.2d 1202 (3d Cir. 1993) (reversible error for judge to admit evidence of plea where defense counsel would not raise it).

[10] *See* United States v. Banker, 15 M.J. 207 (C.M.A. 1983), for a discussion of the interrelationship between Rule 607 and other impeachment rules.

hearsay testimony that it is not being offered for the truth of the matter asserted. Under these circumstances court members might be prone to use the impeaching hearsay testimony for substantive purposes. Rule 105 limiting instructions might prevent some abuses. Other abuses can be avoided by combining Rules 403 and 611(a) to protect witnesses from improper harassment or embarrassment. However, trial judges and counsel must be alert to circumstances where exclusion is the only effective remedy. In close cases, trial judges should also render special findings.

[4] Constitutional Impeachment Issues

Read together, Rules 402 and 607 provide that all relevant impeachment evidence is admissible unless specifically barred by these Rules, the Constitution, the *Manual for Courts-Martial*, or another provision of Congress. While Rule 607 does not specify the various forms impeachment evidence may take, the Supreme Court has repeatedly recognized government and defense counsels' need for a wide range of impeachment tools.

For example, in *United States v. Abel*,[11] the Court held that it was appropriate for government counsel to impeach a defense witness with evidence of that witness's bias even though no Rule of Evidence specifically provided for such an attack.[12] Federal and military courts have continuously recognized and applied counsel's ability to impeach a witness with evidence of that witness's poor powers of observation, inadequate memory, communication limitations, emotional impairments,[13] and previous specific contradictions. When these common law techniques are employed, military judges must be aware of their potential for unfair prejudice, and insure that Rule 403's balancing test is effectively applied and articulated on the record.

In some circumstances, defense counsel's need to impeach his or her own witness is so central to the accused's case that it rises to the level of a constitutional right.[14] For example, in *Chambers v. Mississippi*,[15] the accused was charged with murdering a policeman. As part of its case, the defense called an individual named McDonald in order to establish that McDonald had previously confessed to the crime. During its direct examination the defense introduced one of McDonald's out-of-court statements,

---

[11] 469 U.S. 45 (1984).

[12] The military drafters solved this specific problem by adding Rule 608(c), *Evidence of bias*, a provision not included within the Federal Rules of Evidence.

[13] *But see* United States v. Peters, 732 F.2d 1004 (1st Cir. 1984) (no error in preventing defendant from cross-examining government witness concerning his psychiatric history); United States v. Butt, 955 F.2d 77 (1st Cir. 1992) (no error in trial court's refusal to admit defense evidence of witness' psychiatric history, as federal courts hold that mental instability is relevant to credibility only when present during the time frame of events testified to).

[14] *See, e.g.*, United States v. Havens, 446 U.S. 620 (1980) (Supreme Court recognized that under some circumstances illegally seized evidence may be used to impeach a witness).

[15] 410 U.S. 284 (1973).

but McDonald recanted and sought to explain the reason for giving the statement. When the defense moved to cross-examine McDonald about three other statements, the trial judge denied the motion because of Mississippi's voucher rule. In reversing, the Supreme Court found that the State's use of its voucher rule had denied the accused his right to a fair trial, and his ability to present an adequate defense.[16]

Under other circumstances, the Constitution may bar what would otherwise be appropriate impeachment evidence.[17] For example, can a witness be impeached with his or her out of court statement if that statement was made under circumstances controlled by Article 31?[18] While the Federal Rules of Evidence do not directly address this issue, Military Rules 301, 304, 305 and 306 provide substantive and procedural guidance on these matters.

§ 607.03   Drafters' Analysis

Rule 607 is taken without significant change from the Federal Rule. It supersedes *Manual* ¶ 153*b*(1) that restricts impeachment of one's own witness to those situations in which the witness is indispensable or the testimony of the witness proves to be unexpectedly adverse.

Rule 607 thus allows a party to impeach its own witness. Indeed, when relevant, it permits a party to call a witness for the sole purpose of impeachment. It should be noted, however, that an apparent inconsistency exists when Rule 607 is compared with Rules 608(b) and 609(a). Although Rule 607 allows impeachment on direct examination, Rules 608(b) and 609(a) would by their explicit language restrict the methods of impeachment to cross-examination. The use of the expression "cross-examination" in these rules appears to be accidental and to have been intended to be synonymous with impeachment while on direct examination. *See generally* S. Saltzburg & K. Redden, Federal Rules of Evidence Manual (2d ed. 1977). It is the intent of the Committee that the Rules be so interpreted unless the Article III courts should interpret the Rules in a different fashion.

---

[16] *See also* United States v. Johnson, 3 M.J. 143 (C.M.A. 1977) (adopting the holding for military practice).

[17] *See, e.g.*, United States v. Miller, 676 F.2d 359 (9th Cir. 1982) (on cross-examination government may not raise issues unrelated to direct examination of defendant in order to use statements obtained in violation of *Miranda* to impeach); Nezowy v. United States, 723 F.2d 1120 (3d Cir. 1983), *cert. denied*, 104 S. Ct. 3533 (1984) (government may not ask witness whether she invoked her privilege before grand jury).

[18] *See, e.g.*, Jenkins v. Anderson, 447 U.S. 231 (1980), and Fletcher v. Weir, 455 U.S. 603 (1982), providing that in a non-military setting, absent *Miranda* warning problems, the Constitution does not prohibit the use of prior silence as impeachment evidence).

§ 607.04 Annotated Cases

[1] Who May Impeach—Attacking One's Own Witness

Navy-Marine Corps Court of Criminal Appeals

United States v. Terry, 61 M.J. 721 (N.M.Ct.Crim.App. 2005): The accused was convicted of rape, conspiracy to commit rape, and related offenses. Part of the government's case included calling the accused's co-conspirators who had already reached pretrial agreements with the prosecution and been convicted. In anticipation of defense counsel's cross-examination, and without objection, trial counsel asked each witness about their related convictions. Rejecting the accused's argument of plain error, the court held that the testimony was properly admitted in anticipation of a defense challenge as to each witness's bias. Thus, it was not an attempt to prove the accused's guilt by association, which would have been improper.

[2] Who May Impeach—Credibility Attacks

United States Court of Appeals for the Armed Forces

United States v. Jones, 49 M.J. 85 (C.A.A.F. 1998): The accused was convicted of attempted rape, attempted carnal knowledge, and other acts upon a female under 16 years of age. The issue on appeal concerned whether the military judge erred by prohibiting defense counsel from cross-examining the victim concerning her perceptions, associations, and beliefs in demons, spirits, and the use of Ouija boards. The accused contended these matters would have negatively affected the victim's credibility. Finding error but no prejudice, the court held that the trial judge's mistake was harmless because defense counsel had conducted an extensive cross-examination of the victim, which exposed her credibility limitations. The court went on to say that even had defense counsel pursued this cross-examination it would not have negatively affected the prosecution's case nor perfected the defense's theory.

United States v. White, 45 M.J. 345 (C.A.A.F. 1996): Affirming the accused's conviction for raping a young woman with the mental ability of an eight-year-old, the court highlighted the appropriateness of defense counsel impeaching the victim by demonstrating her limited emotional capabilities, instances of inconsistent and contradictory testimony, and poor character for truthfulness.

Air Force Court of Criminal Appeals

United States v. Nixon, 30 M.J. 501 (A.F.C.M.R. 1989): As part of the government's case-in-chief, trial counsel called the accused's daughter to establish how her mother was killed. When the child answered "Dad picked her . . . up and accidentally dropped her," trial counsel was allowed to ask the girl if she had previously said that "Daddy killed my Mommy." Affirming the conviction, the court held that Rule 607 permits a party to attack its witness's credibility.

[3]   Who May Impeach—Defining Impeachment

United States Court of Appeals for the Armed Forces

United States v. Banker, 15 M.J. 207 (C.A.A.F. C.M.A. 1983): The court recognized that "[i]mpeachment can be defined as an attack on the credibility or believability of a witness . . . . In general, it is a process of explaining away a witness's testimony as to the existence of a fact at issue in a trial." Such evidence was defined as including the following: bad character for truthfulness, Rule 608(a) and (b); prior inconsistent statements, Rule 613; bias, prejudice, or similar motive to misrepresent, Rule 608(c); and contradiction, Rule 607. This case demonstrates the importance of counsel's identifying the theory of impeachment.

[4]   Who May Impeach—Impeaching a Confession

Air Force Court of Criminal Appeals

United States v. Slovacek, 21 M.J. 538 (A.F.C.M.R. 1985): The court held that "the government may impeach a portion of a confession it has offered on the merits." However, the court also warned military judges and counsel that the method of conducting the impeachment and admitting the evidence must be in accord with these rules.

[5]   Who May Impeach—Impeachment by Contradiction

Navy-Marine Corps Court of Criminal Appeals

United States v. Shaner, 46 M.J. 849 (N.M. Ct.Crim.App. 1997): The accused, a 23-year-old sailor, was charged with sodomy and indecent acts upon a 15-year-old boy. In limine, defense counsel moved to suppress Rule 404(b) evidence that the accused and the victim were hugging, kissing, and fondling each other on "dates." During trial, the accused testified that he was totally heterosexual, not sexually active for religious reasons, and had never been physically active with the victim. The trial judge admitted the government's evidence as uncharged misconduct and this court affirmed, adding that the testimony was also admissible as part and parcel proof as well as "powerful impeachment by contradiction evidence." However, the court noted that when extrinsic offense evidence is used for impeachment purposes, it should be offered in rebuttal, not during the government's case in chief.

[6]   Who May Impeach—Motions in Limine

Supreme Court

Ohler v. United States, 529 U.S. 753 (2000): Affirming the accused's convictions for importation of marijuana and possession of marijuana, the Court held that an accused who preemptively introduces evidence of her prior conviction during direct examination may not claim on appeal that the admission of that conviction was error. This result was reached even though the government had made a successful pretrial motion to use the conviction against the accused if she testified.

[7] Who May Impeach—Related Applications

United States Court of Appeals for the Armed Forces

United States v. Newman, 14 M.J. 474 (C.A.A.F. C.M.A. 1983): Relying in large part on the fact that "Mil. R. Evid. 607 explicitly repudiates the notion that a party who calls a witness and offers his testimony vouches for his credibility," the court held that a convening authority who grants testimonial immunity to either a government or defense witness does not, as a result, express his personal view as to the witness's credibility. Consequentially, convening authorities are no longer disqualified from acting in cases where they have granted immunity. This case appears to overrule *United States v. Flowers,* 13 M.J. 571 (A.C.M.R. 1982), where the court reversed the accused's drug related conviction because two key government witnesses testified against the accused *after* receiving clemency from the convening authority. The court specifically held that the convening authority was disqualified from acting because he granted clemency and that Rule 607 did not change that result.

§ 608.01   Official Text

Rule 608.   Evidence of Character, Conduct, and Bias of Witness.

(a) *Opinion and Reputation Evidence of Character.*   The credibility of a witness may be attacked or supported by evidence in the form of opinion or reputation, but subject to these limitations: (1) the evidence may refer only to character for truthfulness or untruthfulness, and (2) evidence of truthful character is admissible only after the character of the witness for truthfulness has been attacked by opinion or reputation evidence or otherwise.

(b) *Specific Instances of Conduct.*   Specific instances of the conduct of a witness, for the purpose of attacking or supporting the witness's character for truthfulness, other than conviction of crime as provided in Rule 609, may not be proved by extrinsic evidence. They may, however, in the discretion of the court, if probative of truthfulness or untruthfulness, be inquired into on cross-examination of the witness (1) concerning the witness's character for truthfulness or untruthfulness, or (2) concerning the character for truthfulness or untruthfulness of another witness as to which character the witness being cross-examined has testified. The giving of testimony, whether by an accused or by any other witness, does not operate as a waiver of the accused's or the witness's privilege against self-incrimination when examined with respect to matters that relate only to character for truthfulness.

(c) *Evidence of Bias.*   Bias, prejudice, or any motive to misrepresent may be shown to impeach the witness either by examination of the witness or by evidence otherwise adduced.

---

§ 608.02   Editorial Comment

[1]   Foundations for Using Rule 608

The essence of litigation is in many ways focused on which party's witnesses the finder of fact will believe. Success in this endeavor depends on both the honesty and the apparent honesty of the trial's participants.[1]

Rule 607 recognizes the importance of witness credibility, and Rule 608 covers several common forms of impeachment that are aimed solely at determining which witness's testimony should carry the most weight or be

---

[1] *See* Schlueter, Saltzburg, Schinasi & Imwinkelried, MILITARY EVIDENTIARY FOUNDA-TIONS § 5-8 (4th ed. 2010) (sample foundation for impeaching witness with character evidence).

believed.[2] Rule 608 is based on the philosophy that witnesses who have a propensity to lie will act in accordance with that propensity while testifying.[3]

This provision is most effective when trial judges assure it is only used to investigate truthfulness, and not general character. In this light it must be distinguished from Rule 404(a), discussed *above*. Military courts appear to have applied this standard correctly and uniformly. For example, in *United States v. Weeks*,[4] the court found that, absent unusual circumstances, incidents of past drug usage or sale do not necessarily demonstrate an adverse character for truthfulness. Federal cases have also consistently taken this position. In *United States v. Robinson*,[5] the court refused to find a correlation between a witness's past abuse of controlled substances and character for truthfulness.[6]

It is important to remember that any witness's prior abuse of drugs or alcohol may be admissible for traditional common law impeachment purposes. Counsel can use such proof to demonstrate that the witness may have been unable to properly observe or remember the events in question.

In *United States v. Duty*,[7] the court held that it would not permit a witness's credibility to be attacked with pornographic photographs because "fornication is no more a barometer of untruthfulness than celibacy is an indicator of truthfulness, and it is probable that at least as many lies have been uttered by persons fully clothed as by those who are nude."

The military version of this Rule is more complete than its federal counterpart. The court-martial provision specifically provides that evidence of bias or prejudice may be used for impeachment purposes. The Rule is also broader than previous *Manual* practice which placed some limitations on character impeachment evidence.[8]

---

[2] *See, e.g.*, United States v. Yarborough, 18 M.J. 452 (C.M.A. 1984) (distinguishing Rule 404(a)(1), the court stated that "character evidence as to truthfulness, unlike other types of character evidence, does not bear directly on guilt or innocence . . . .").

[3] *See, e.g.*, United States v. Watson, 669 F.2d 1374 (11th Cir. 1982) (error to exclude credibility character evidence offered to impeach key government witness).

[4] 17 M.J. 613 (N.M.C.M.R. 1983).

[5] 956 F.2d 1388 (7th Cir. 1992).

[6] *See also* United States v. Fortes, 619 F.2d 108 (1st Cir. 1980) (defense counsel attempted to cross-examine a government witness about his involvement in drug trafficking. The Court of Appeals held that the trial judge properly exercised his discretion to exclude the evidence as not sufficiently probative of truthfulness).

[7] 16 M.J. 855 (N.M.C.M.R. 1983).

[8] *See* Manual for Court-Martial, United States (rev. ed. 1969), ¶ 153*b*, and United States v. Tomchek, 4 M.J. 66 (C.M.A. 1977), for a discussion of pre-rules practice and Federal Rule 608.

[2] Rule 608(a)—Opinion and Reputation Evidence of Character

[a] Timing of Character Evidence to Impeach

Like its federal counterpart, subdivision (a) prescribes how a witness's character for truthfulness may be attacked and rehabilitated. It states that reputation or opinion evidence may be used to demonstrate that the witness's character for truthfulness is bad. Only after some attack[9] on credibility has been made, may the witness's character be rehabilitated with favorable opinion or reputation evidence. Thus, the Rule does not permit counsel to bolster an unattacked witness's testimony.[10]

[b] Techniques for Attacking a Witness's Character

Rule 608 contemplates two techniques for attacking a witness's character. First, a witness may be called to testify about a previous witness's bad character for truthfulness. This traditional technique's effectiveness is limited. The impeaching witness will usually testify long after the original witness has left the stand. As a result, the impeaching witness's impact on the court members often will be minimal or counterproductive because it might remind the members of what the original witness said, thereby reinforcing the impeached witness's testimony. Character witnesses are limited to opinion[11] or reputation[12] testimony which might be too obtuse for effective court member use. More importantly, a character witness's testimony can be tested with favorable specific instances of conduct that allows the original witness's character to be effectively reinforced or explained.[13]

The second and often a more effective way to attack a witness's credibility—as discussed in subdivision (b) below—is to question the witness about specific bad truthfulness acts while he or she is still on the stand. This impeachment technique allows the court members to hear the impeaching testimony contemporaneously with the substantive proof. Using specific instances of conduct evidence also has a greater impact on the court members because it is easier for them to place in context. Finally, while

---

[9] *See, e.g.,* United States v. Terry, 702 F.2d 299 (2d Cir.), *cert. denied,* 461 U.S. 931 (1983) (government permitted to ask defense voice expert whether his testimony in other cases had been criticized as unworthy of belief).

[10] *See, e.g.,* United States v. Mack, 643 F.2d 1119 (5th Cir. 1981) (the prosecutor's remark during voir dire that he "wouldn't be here today" if he couldn't prove the accused's guilt held to be improper bolstering).

[11] *See, e.g.,* United States v. Basic Construction Company, 711 F.2d 570 (4th Cir. 1983), *cert. denied,* 104 S. Ct. 371 (1984) (error, but harmless, to exclude opinion evidence offered by defense to impeach government witness).

[12] *See, e.g.,* United States v. Davis, 639 F.2d 239 (5th Cir. 1981) (the accused's narcotics conviction was reversed because two defense character witnesses were not permitted to demonstrate that the key government witness had a poor reputation for veracity).

[13] *See* our discussion of Rule 405.

negative specific act evidence can be explained or denied by the witness being impeached, opposing counsel cannot refute it with favorable specific instances of conduct evidence. The problem with asking the witness about bad acts is that the examiner cannot offer evidence to contradict a denial.

[c] Rehabilitation of Witness

The attack that triggers an opportunity for rehabilitation under Rule 608(a) need not take the form of negative character testimony or specific bad act testimony. Anything that implies the untruthfulness of the witness, slashing cross-examination for example, may satisfy the "or otherwise" language of the provision.[14] However, a particularly effective cross-examination,[15] or evidence of contradiction or inconsistency[16] will generally not be sufficient to justify rehabilitation. Rule 403 is often used to limit the amount of evidence accepted for impeachment and rehabilitation use.

The United States Court of Appeals for the Armed Forces has interpreted the "or otherwise" language broadly.[17] For example, in *United States v. Allard*,[18] a drug sale case, the accused testified that a key government witness was lying. In rebuttal, trial counsel rehabilitated his witness's veracity, but defense counsel's attempt thereafter to establish his client's truthfulness was prohibited. Reversing the judge alone conviction, the court held that once evidence concerning a key government witness's veracity was introduced, the bench should have recognized that the accused's credibility was also in issue and held rehabilitation appropriate. The court went on to say that "the means by which credibility has been attacked is immaterial because it would be illogical to hold that the right to rehabilitate a witness depends on the manner in which his truthfulness was impugned."

It is rather surprising that the drafters of this Rule failed to provide the same complete treatment of reputation evidence that is provided in connection with Rule 405. Is the definition of "reputation" the same under both Rules? The answer should be "yes" despite Rule 608's silence. The two definitions of reputation traditionally are identical at common law, and it is

---

[14] *See* United States v. Porta, 14 M.J. 622 (A.F.C.M.R. 1982) (vigorous cross-examination was viewed as sufficient to place a witness's credibility in issue). *See generally* Schlueter, Saltzburg, Schinasi & Imwinkelried, MILITARY EVIDENTIARY FOUNDATIONS § 5-15 (4th ed. 2010) (sample foundation for rehabilitating a witness with character witness).

[15] *See, e.g.*, United States v. Angelini, 678 F.2d 380 (1st Cir. 1982) (defendant charged with drug possession had no right to offer character evidence regarding truthfulness where cross-examination was insufficiently "slashing" to warrant impeachment).

[16] *See, e.g.*, United States v. Danehy, 680 F.2d 1311 (11th Cir. 1982) (prosecutor's pointing out inconsistencies in defendant's testimony and arguing that it was not credible did not amount to an attack on character for truthfulness warranting rehabilitation).

[17] *See* United States v. Woods, 19 M.J. 349 (C.M.A. 1985) (the court held that "we have now made clear that this Rule should not be interpreted in a restrictive manner").

[18] 19 M.J. 346 (C.M.A. 1985).

doubtful that the drafters would have used the same word in Rule 608 as in Rule 405 without intending that the user of the Rules should look to Rule 405 for guidance as to what the word means.

[d]   Expert Witnesses on Credibility

Both federal[19] and military[20] cases have dealt with the problems caused by expert witnesses providing opinion testimony on credibility issues. This situation is clearly presented in *United States v. Hill-Dunning*.[21] There the defense desired to use an expert psychiatric witness to state that in the expert's professional opinion, the accused was telling the truth concerning certain aspects of having submitted a false claim. The court held that it is permissible for a psychiatrist to testify that her beliefs about a witness's particular emotional state are "based upon an assumption that what the client has said is the truth." However, the court went on to say that it is impermissible for the expert to extend this testimony and state that in her opinion the client is also truthful, particularly about whether the client did or did not do the specific thing charged. The court has "consistently held that the opinions of one witness concerning the credibility of or believability of another witness are inadmissible . . . because they [are] not relevant and helpful."

Military cases have uniformly held that such testimony is beyond the scope of any witness's training or expertise.[22] Thus, it would be error for an expert witness to say that he believed the victim's or the accused's version of the facts.[23] Other courts have excluded such testimony because they viewed the proponent as attempting to use an expert witness as a "human lie detector."[24] As might be expected, this result specifically applies to polygraphers. Most courts limit their testimony, at best, to an opinion about whether the examinee demonstrated deception or not while being tested.[25] The court in *Hill-Dunning* provided the following guidance:

What the rules of evidence are trying to accomplish is to posture the

---

[19] *See, e.g.*, United States v. Earley, 505 F. Supp. 117 (S.D. Iowa 1981) (a polygrapher was not permitted to offer his opinion on truthfulness because his knowledge was gained on a particular occasion through mechanical examination).

[20] *See, e.g.*, United States v. Arruza, 26 M.J. 234 (C.M.A. 1988) (child sexual abuse conviction affirmed despite expert witness' vouching for the victim's truthfulness).

[21] 26 M.J. 260 (C.M.A. 1988).

[22] 26 M.J. 260 (C.M.A. 1988).

[23] *See, e.g.*, United States v. Petersen, 24 M.J. 283 (C.M.A. 1987) (such testimony viewed as being beyond the intent of both Rule 608 and Rule 704).

[24] For an interesting discussion of this issue, *see* United States v. Cameron, 21 M.J. 59 C.M.A. 1985 (conviction reversed where expert said he believed the victim had been truthful).

[25] *See* our discussion of Rule 707, United States v. Scheffer, 44 M.J. 442 (1996), *cert. granted*, 520 U.S. 1227 (1997), and United States v. Gipson, 24 M.J. 246 (C.M.A. 1987).

expert testimony so that the fact-finders can employ this expertise as a tool to evaluate the total evidence before them. The rules strive to create an environment where rational fact-finders can have as much information available as is reasonably necessary to aid them in making an informed and intelligent decision.

United States v. Thorn[26] demonstrates another permissible use of opinion testimony. There the accused was convicted of drug offenses based largely on the testimony of his accomplices. During the government's case-in-chief, defense counsel vigorously attacked each witness's veracity. On redirect, trial counsel called an OSI agent to testify that the attacked witnesses were among the most credible, trustworthy, and reliable he had worked with. Rejecting the "human lie detector" standard, this court held that the testimony was appropriate "lay opinion" evidence.[27] The significant distinction here is that in *Thorn* the witness was not asked to determine who was telling the truth and who was lying. As discussed, military cases have consistently viewed expert opinion testimony aimed at identifying truth-tellers from truth-fabricators as invading the providence of the court members.[28]

[e] Using Affidavits

Equally troublesome is the question whether the affidavit evidence that is acceptable under Rule 405(c) also is acceptable under Rule 608. Arguably, Rule 405(c) evidence is more central to the merits and warrants special treatment. But, there is a good case to be made that although the intent of the drafters is not evident, affidavits should be as readily admissible under Rule 608 as under Rule 405. The reasons for accepting them are the same under both provisions, and the need to assess credibility often may be paramount in cases turning on the testimony of a small number of witnesses.

[3] Rule 608(b)—Specific Instances of Conduct

[a] The General Rule

Rule 608(b) generally provides that a party may not offer evidence of specific instances of past conduct concerning a witness to attack or to support the witness's veracity.[29] This general prohibition, however, is

---

[26] 36 M.J. 955 (A.F.C.M.R. 1993).36 M.J. 955 (A.F.C.M.R. 1993).

[27] *See* our discussion of Rule 701.

[28] *See, e.g.*, United States v. Brenton, 24 M.J. 562 (A.F.C.M.R. 1987) (government expert allowed to testify that the victim did not appear to have been rehearsed, and that a child's spontaneous statements are almost always true).

[29] *See, e.g.*, United States v. Bosley, 615 F.2d 1274 (9th Cir. 1980) (conviction was reversed where the government used extrinsic evidence to demonstrate that the accused had lied about never having delivered cocaine to anyone else). *See generally* Schlueter, Saltzburg, Schinasi & Imwinkelried, MILITARY EVIDENTIARY FOUNDATIONS § 5-7 (4th ed. 2010) (sample foundation for impeaching witness with specific acts not resulting in conviction).

subject to several exceptions.[30] It is important to keep in mind that only specific act evidence relating to credibility may generally be admitted under this Rule.[31] The most important exception is that a witness may be asked about acts which, if true, might cast doubt on credibility.[32]

[b] Exceptions to General Rule of Exclusion

Rule 608(b) addresses the admissibility of a witness's prior acts to impeach the witness. As originally written, Federal Rule of Evidence 608(b) barred counsel from introducing extrinsic evidence concerning a witness's "credibility." Counsel could ask the witness about his or her prior acts, however, if the acts were probative of truthfulness or untruthfulness. But counsel was "stuck" with the witness's answer. The military rule followed the federal model. Both rules created some confusion as to whether the prohibition against extrinsic evidence extended to all prior acts. Both the federal and the military courts eventually concluded that the rule did not bar all such evidence. Thus, the courts have admitted extrinsic evidence of a witness's prior acts if the witness made a blanket denial of any wrongdoing.[33]

On December 1, 2003, Federal Rule of Evidence 608(b) was amended to clarify that the rule bars extrinsic evidence of a witness's prior acts only if those acts are introduced on the issue of the witness's "character for truthfulness." Under Military Rule 1102(a),[34] the amendment to the federal rule became effective for courts-martial on 1 June 2005. At this point there is no Drafters' Analysis for the change to the Military Rule. But the federal Committee Note on this change is helpful, and states:

---

[30] Rule 608(b)(2) provides that a character witness can be asked questions about specific acts of the person whose credibility has been rehabilitated or attacked as a way of impeaching the character witness. This is identical to the cross-examination that is permitted under Rule 405 and that is discussed there. As a summary, we note that the cross-examination must relate to acts that might reasonably call into question reputation or opinion as to truthfulness, that the examiner is not permitted actually to offer extrinsic evidence to prove the acts, and that there must be a good faith basis for any questions that are asked.

[31] *See generally* 2 S. Saltzburg, M. Martin & D. Capra, FEDERAL RULES OF EVIDENCE MANUAL, § 608.02[4] (9th ed. 2006). The authors suggest that seven criteria be used to determine the admissibility of specific instances of conduct evidence under 608(b): (1) dishonest nature of the act; (2) remoteness of the act; (3) impeachment on other grounds; (4) importance of the witness' credibility; (5) inflammatory nature of the act; (6) similarity of the bad act to the issues in the case; and (7) relationship of the witness to the case.

[32] *See, e.g.,* United States v. Manske, 186 F.3d 770 (7th Cir. 1999) (threats to other witnesses were probative of the likelihood that the witness would seek to give false testimony).

[33] *See* the annotated cases *below* at § 608.04[2][a].

[34] Rule 1102, below, was amended in 2004 by labeling the original rule as subdivision (a) and adding a new subdivision (b), which states that certain Federal Rules of Evidence are not applicable to military rules of evidence.

The Rule has been amended to clarify that the absolute prohibition on extrinsic evidence applies only when the sole reason for proffering that evidence is to attack or support the witness's character for truthfulness. *See United States v. Abel*, 469 U.S. 45 (1984); *United States v. Fusco*, 748 F.2d 996 (5th Cir. 1984) (Rule 608(b) limits the use of evidence "designed to show that the witness has done things, unrelated to the suit being tried, that make him more or less believable per se"); Ohio R. Evid. 608(b). On occasion the Rule's use of the overbroad term "credibility" has been read "to bar extrinsic evidence for bias, competency and contradiction impeachment since they too deal with credibility." American Bar Association Section of Litigation, Emerging Problems Under the Federal Rules of Evidence at 161 (3d ed. 1998). The amendment conforms the language of the Rule to its original intent, which was to impose an absolute bar on extrinsic evidence only if the sole purpose for offering the evidence was to prove the witness's character for veracity. *See* Advisory Committee Note to Rule 608(b) (stating that the Rule is "[i]n conformity with Rule 405, which forecloses use of evidence of specific incidents as proof in chief of character unless character is in issue in the case . . .").

The federal Committee Note also provides that as amended, Rule 608(b) permits introduction of extrinsic evidence of prior acts for other non-character grounds of impeachment, such as bias (which is not otherwise specifically referenced in the Federal Rules of Evidence, but is addressed in Military Rule 608(c)), prior inconsistent statements, contradiction, and capacity. The Committee Note states:

[T]he extrinsic evidence prohibition of Rule 608(b) bars any reference to the consequences that a witness might have suffered as a result of an alleged bad act. For example, Rule 608(b) prohibits counsel from mentioning that a witness was suspended or disciplined for the conduct that is the subject of impeachment, when that conduct is offered only to prove the character of the witness. *See United States v. Davis*, 183 F.3d 231, 257 n.12 (3d Cir. 1999) (emphasizing that in attacking the defendant's character for truthfulness "the government cannot make reference to Davis' 44-day suspension or that Internal Affairs found that he lied about" an incident because "[s]uch evidence would not only be hearsay to the extent it contains assertion of fact, it would be inadmissible extrinsic evidence under Rule 608(b)"). *See also* Stephen A. Saltzburg, Impeaching the Witness: Prior Bad Acts and Extrinsic Evidence, 7 Crim. Just. 28, 31 (Winter 1993) ("counsel should not be permitted to circumvent the no-extrinsic-evidence provision act").

Evidence of specific instances of conduct that have resulted in convictions may be admissible in conjunction with Rule 609. As discussed above, subdivision (b) also allows a witness, including the accused, to be asked about specific instances of conduct that are not criminal and have not been the subject of a court-martial or prior non-judicial punishment, if they are probative of character.[35] But, the Rule does not permit the questioner to introduce extrinsic evidence in support of his inquiry[36] unless opposing counsel opens the door to such use.[37] The drafters were concerned that, under normal circumstances, the introduction of extrinsic evidence would cause confusion and tend to distract the court members.

The military judge must determine whether specific acts are related and credible. Even if they are, Rule 403 balancing may be required.

The general prohibition on extrinsic evidence does not necessarily mean that the questioner "must take the witness's answer," and abandon his inquiry once a "no" is given. Counsel may pursue the investigation by pressing the witness for an admission as long as the questioning is reasonable under Rule 611(a).[38]

Some question exists concerning whether specific instances of conduct may be inquired into on direct as well as cross-examination. Recognizing that the text of the Rule would seem to restrict the use of such evidence to cross-examination, the military drafters have nevertheless suggested that the better approach here is to permit the direct examiner to impeach his or her own witness. It may be that the Federal Rules, from which Rule 608 is taken, frequently use the words "cross-examine," when they mean "impeach." If so, this is a liability the Military Rules now share.

Another direct examination technique for introducing favorable specific acts evidence applies after a character witness has been cross-examined with "do you know," or "have you heard" questions. The direct examiner is traditionally allowed to ask the witness about limited truthfulness acts in

---

[35] *See, e.g.,* United States v. O'Malley, 707 F.2d 1240 (11th Cir. 1983) (defendant could be questioned concerning his failure to report cash contributions to a trust fund); United States v. Leake, 642 F.2d 715 (4th Cir. 1981) (conviction was reversed because the trial judge improperly limited defense counsel's cross-examination of key government witnesses concerning specific instances of conduct relating to truthfulness); United States v. Cole, 617 F.2d 151 (5th Cir. 1981) (the government was permitted to ask an accused charged with willful misapplication of funds whether he had submitted false excusals from work to his employer).

[36] *See, e.g.,* United States v. DiMatteo, 716 F.2d 1361 (11th Cir. 1983) (error to admit extrinsic evidence that defense witness in drug smuggling case was involved in other smuggling); United States v. Reed, 715 F.2d 870 (5th Cir. 1983) (defendant in extortion case could not impeach victim with extrinsic evidence of acts not leading to convictions).

[37] *See, e.g.,* United States v. Lightle, 728 F.2d 468 (10th Cir. 1984) (defendant opened the door to extrinsic evidence of other acts as a result of eliciting certain information on direct examination of defense witnesses).

[38] In United States v. Owens, 21 M.J. 117 (C.M.A. 1985), the court said Rule 608(b)'s prohibition against using extrinsic evidence "does not mean that further cross-examination of the accused is impermissible," rather it allows questions to be rephrased in such a way that the accused will be induced into abandoning his previous denials.

response. The military judge must ensure that, when the credibility related direct and cross-examination becomes this extensive, it will not divert the court members' attention away from their evaluation of the historical proof.

As we discussed in Rule 607, *above*, this provision's ban on using extrinsic evidence for impeachment purposes applies only to testimony aimed at credibility issues. *United States v. Abel*,[39] demonstrates that impeachment based on establishing inconsistent statements and specific contradictions is not a veracity matter and not necessarily controlled by this Rule.

[c]   Other Limits on Asking About the Witness's Acts

Two additional issues may arise with respect to using extrinsic acts. First, counsel must have a "plausible basis" upon which to believe that the acts occurred.[40] Fishing expeditions and factual assumptions should be viewed as insufficient to justify questioning. Opposing counsel should explore the basis for using such extrinsic evidence *in limine*. Second, it is unclear whether a witness can be impeached with a specific act if the witness was previously acquitted of having committed it. Rule 404(b) generally allows such evidence to reach the finders of fact after counsel establishes its factual predicate. Arguably, the result should be different under Rule 608(b), and the balance between probative value and prejudicial effect should be struck in favor of exclusion. Counsel is not permitted to establish a factual predicate, the probative value of an act to which the witness has been acquitted of may be low, and it is clear that a witness who went to trial to contest a charged act will not admit that is occurred when examined about it in a subsequent proceeding.

[d]   Self-Incrimination Privilege

The last sentence of subdivision (b) provides that all witnesses, including the accused, retain their privilege against self-incrimination as to questions asked about specific acts that relate only to credibility.[41] The Rule accommodates Fifth Amendment interests and recognizes that they may predominate over impeachment needs. Its benefits can be seen in the following example. If the accused is charged with robbery, and takes the stand in his own defense, he does not waive his privilege against self-incrimination with respect to any examination about unrelated forgery offenses that might shed light on credibility. The idea here is that a "waiver" rule would place too great a price upon the accused's right to testify in his or her own defense. It

---

[39] 469 U.S. 45 (1984).

[40] *See, e.g.,* United States v. Elizondo, 920 F.2d 1308 (7th Cir. 1990) (error occurred where the prosecutor had no basis upon which to believe the bad act occurred).

[41] *See, e.g.,* United States v. Dalfonso, 707 F.2d 757 (3d Cir. 1983) (no error in trial judge's permitting a government witness to claim the privilege against self-incrimination as to prior acts unrelated to the instant case).

should be noted, however, that the Rule does not prohibit questions with respect to previous convictions governed by Rule 609 or interrogation about other misconduct if it is relevant to an issue other than credibility. For example, under Rule 404(b), the evidence might be used to show plan, design, intent, knowledge, and other issues. Thus, any witness, including the accused, can object to answering incriminating question about acts when the only purpose for the question is to elicit Rule 608(b) impeachment. No witness, including the accused, may decline to answer questions within the scope of direct examination that seek to elicit relevant information on an issue unrelated to Rule 608(b).

[3]   Rule 608(c)—Evidence of Bias

Subdivision (c) of the Military Rule allows a witness to be impeached by evidence of bias, prejudice, or motive to misrepresent.[42] It adopts previous *Manual* practice. No similar provision is found in the Federal Rule. However, commentators agree that its omission is not significant and the federal courts have consistently admitted such evidence.[43] Indeed, when the defense offers evidence of bias,[44] excluding it presents serious confrontation rights issues.[45]

To implement 608(c), the military drafters provide that evidence of bias or prejudice may be introduced through the examination of witnesses, "or by evidence otherwise adduced."[46] Thus, extrinsic evidence plainly is allowed under (c), although not under (b).[47] However, military courts have limited the use of extrinsic evidence when it is collateral to any important trial

---

[42] *See, e.g.*, United States v. Abel, 469 U.S. 45 (1984) and United States v. Leja, 568 F.2d 493 (6th Cir. 1977), both cases specifically recognize bias evidence admissibility even though Federal Rule 608 is silent on the matter.

[43] *See* Schlueter, Saltzburg, Schinasi & Imwinkelried, MILITARY EVIDENTIARY FOUNDATIONS § 5-12 (4th ed. 2010) (sample foundations for impeaching a witness with evidence that the witness is biased).

[44] *See, e.g.*, United States v. Ray, 731 F.2d 1361, 1362 (9th Cir. 1984) (error to prohibit defendant from impeaching government witness about his remaining active in cocaine trafficking after entering a plea agreement with the government; dealing might have been grounds for bias).

[45] While Davis v. Alaska, 415 U.S. 308 (1974) establishes the constitutional requirements for such testimony, *see* United States v. Tracey, 675 F.2d 433 (1st Cir. 1982) for a discussion of the limitations on its use.

[46] *See, e.g.*, United States v. Bishop, 453 F.3d 30 (1st Cir. 2006) (extrinsic evidence of specific acts tending to show bias not excluded by Rule 608(b); (United States v. Rubier, 651 F.2d 628 (9th Cir. 1981) (after defense counsel established that a government witness had been granted immunity for his testimony, the prosecutor could offer the agreement itself to demonstrate no bias).

[47] *See, e.g.*, United States v. Banker, 15 M.J. 207 (C.M.A. 1983) (the court found that specific acts of conduct which cannot be used to attack credibility under Rule 608(b) may be used to demonstrate a witness' bias, prejudice or motive to misrepresent).

issue[48] or the proponent fails to establish the evidence's relevance by means other than his or her own "bare assertions."[49]

§ 608.03   Drafters' Analysis

[1]   Opinion and reputation evidence of character

Rule 608(a) is taken verbatim from the Federal Rule. The Rule, that is consistent with the philosophy behind Rule 404(a), limits use of character evidence in the form of opinion or reputation evidence on the issue of credibility by restricting such evidence to matters relating to the character for truthfulness or untruthfulness of the witness. General good character is not admissible under the Rule. Rule 608(a) prohibits presenting evidence of good character until the character of the witness for truthfulness has been attacked. The Rule is similar to ¶ 153*b* of the present *Manual* except that the Rule, unlike ¶ 153*b*, applies to all witnesses and does not distinguish between the accused and other witnesses.

[2]   Specific instances of conduct

Rule 608(b) is taken from the Federal Rule without significant change. The Rule is somewhat similar in effect to the military practice now found in ¶ 153*b*(2) of the *Manual* in that it allows use of specific instances of conduct of a witness to be brought out on cross-examination but prohibits use of extrinsic evidence. Unlike ¶ 153*b*(2), Rule 608(b) does not distinguish between an accused and other witnesses.

The fact that the accused is subject to impeachment by prior acts of misconduct is a significant factor to be considered by the military judge when he or she is determining whether to exercise the discretion granted by the Rule. Although the Rule expressly limits this form of impeachment to inquiry on cross-examination, it is likely that the intent of the Federal Rule was to permit inquiry on direct as well, *see* Rule 607, and the use of the term "cross-examination" was an accidental substitute for "impeachment." *See* S. Saltzburg & K. Redden, Federal Rules of Evidence Manual 312–13 (2d ed. 1977). It is the intent of the Committee to allow use of this form of evidence on direct-examination to the same extent, if any, it is so permitted in the Article III courts.

The Rule does not prohibit receipt of extrinsic evidence in the form of prior convictions, Rule 609, or to show bias, Rule 608(c). *See also* Rule 613 (Prior statements of witnesses). When the witness has testified as to the character of another witness, the witness may be cross-examined as to the character of that witness. The remainder of Rule 608(b) indicates that

---

[48] United States v. Gonzalez, 16 M.J. 423 (C.M.A. 1983).

[49] *See, e.g.,* United States v. Hunter, 17 M.J. 738 (A.C.M.R. 1984) (evidence of past drug dealing was not admissible because defense counsel failed to establish its relevance or effect upon the witness's credibility).

testimony relating only to credibility does not waive the privilege against self-incrimination. *See generally* Rule 301.

Although Rule 608(b) allows examination into specific acts, counsel should not, as a matter of ethics, attempt to elicit evidence of misconduct unless there is a reasonable basis for the question. *See generally* ABA Projects on Standards for Criminal Justice, Standards Relating to the Prosecution Function and the Defense, Prosecution Function, Prosecution Function 5.7(d); Defense Functions 7.6(d) (Approved draft 1971).

[3]   Evidence of bias

Rule 608(c) is taken from present Manual ¶ 153*d* and is not found within the Federal Rule. Impeachment by bias was apparently accidentally omitted from the Federal Rule, *see, e.g.,* S. SALTZBURG & K. REDDEN, FEDERAL RULES OF EVIDENCE MANUAL 313, 314 (2d ed. 1977), but is acceptable under the Federal Rules; *see, e.g., United States v. Leja,* 568 F.2d 493 (6th Cir. 1977); *United States v. Alvarez-Lopez,* 559 F.2d 1155 (9th Cir. 1977). Because of the critical nature of this form of impeachment and the fact that extrinsic evidence may be used to show it, the Committee believed that its omission would be impracticable.

It should be noted that the Federal Rules are not exhaustive and that a number of different types of techniques of impeachment are not explicitly codified.

The failure to so codify them does not mean that they are no longer permissible. *See, e.g., United States v. Alvarez-Lopez,* 559 F.2d 1155 (9th Cir. 1977) (Rule 412). Thus, impeachment by contradiction, *see also* Rules 304(a)(2); 311(j), and impeachment via prior inconsistent statements, Rule 613, remain appropriate. To the extent that the Military Rules do not acknowledge a particular form of impeachment, it is the intent of the Committee to allow that method to the same extent it is permissible in the Article III courts. *See, e.g.,* Rules 402–403.

Impeachment of an alleged victim of a sexual offense through evidence of the victim's past sexual history and character is dealt with in Rule 412, and evidence of fresh complaint is admissible to the extent permitted by Rules 801 and 803.

§ 608.04   Annotated Cases

[1]   Rule 608(a)—Opinion and Reputation Evidence of Character

[a]   Character Evidence—Bolstering Prohibited

United States Court of Appeals for the Armed Forces

United States v. Watson, 11 M.J. 483 (C.M.A. 1981) (pre-Rules case): The accused was convicted of larceny and drug related offenses. During the government's case in chief, the prosecution used opinion and reputation evidence to bolster the credibility of an undercover informant who had not testified. The court found that, because the informant had not been a witness on the merits, his credibility was never in issue and the trial judge should have excluded the evidence. The court went on to note that under other circumstances an informant's credibility might be placed in issue, even though he does not testify. However, this scenario would probably be limited to pre-trial hearings litigating legal issues. *See* Article 39(a) and Rule 104. Note that a hearsay declarant whose statements are used at trial may be impeached and, if impeached, rehabilitated under Rule 806.

Navy-Marine Corps Court of Criminal Appeals

United States v. Abdirahman, 66 M.J. 668 (N.M.Ct.Crim.App. 2008): The accused's conviction for rape was reversed based on the cumulative effect of trial errors. One involved character testimony. The prosecutrix testified and was cross-examined concerning numerous minor inconsistencies between her trial and Article 32 testimony, whether she was in fact telling the truth, and minor details concerning how the alleged rape had taken place. Following cross-examination, trial counsel called the victim's supervisor who testified to his favorable opinion of the prosecutrix's truthfulness. Defense counsel posed a timely objection but on an incorrect ground—he alleged an inadequate foundation as opposed to inappropriate bolstering. Although a slashing cross-examination that may undermine the members' confidence in a witness's credibility may amount to an attack on the witness, the court concluded that in this case defense counsel's cross-examination did not call the victim's credibility into question and therefore the supervisor's testimony was impermissible bolstering. The court found the error to be harmless and noted that defense counsel had made the wrong objection at trial.

[b] Character Evidence—Credibility Attacked—Rehabilitation Appropriate

United States Court of Appeals for the Armed Forces

United States v. Varela, 25 M.J. 29 (C.M.A. 1987): The accused's entire direct examination concerning his use of cocaine was, "No, I did not." On cross-examination, trial counsel asked the accused if he would have to forfeit his $16,000 submariner's reenlistment bonus if he were convicted. The accused replied, "I believe so." Before redirect examination, trial counsel sought a motion *in limine* to exclude truthful character testimony on the ground that credibility had not been attacked. This court ruled that the exclusion was prejudicial error because the triers of fact, who were also submariners, "would have readily understood the implications of" trial counsel's questions—*i.e.*, as a submariner the accused "had a major financial stake in the outcome of the trial" and "had more to lose by admitting cocaine use than would most sailors."

United States v. Woods, 19 M.J. 349 (C.M.A. 1985): The accused's drug related conviction was reversed because the trial judge excluded defense character witnesses who would have testified to the accused's truthfulness and veracity. In this very short opinion, the court stated "we have now made clear that this rule [608(a)(2)] should not be interpreted in a restrictive manner."

United States v. Allard, 19 M.J. 346 (C.M.A. 1985): In this sale of drugs case, a government agent testified that he sold marijuana to the accused. During his case in chief, the accused testified that the agent was lying. In rebuttal, the trial counsel presented reputation evidence of the informant's veracity. When defense counsel attempted to introduce similar credibility evidence about the accused, the trial judge excluded it, contending that the accused's credibility had not been attacked. Reversing the conviction, in this judge alone case, the court held that, once evidence concerning a key government witness's veracity had been introduced, the military judge should recognize that the accused's credibility had also been placed in issue and permitted defense counsel to rehabilitate the accused if he desires. The court said that "the means by which credibility has been attacked is immaterial, because it would be illogical to hold that the right to rehabilitate a witness depends on the manner in which his truthfulness was impugned."

United States v. Everage, 19 M.J. 189 (C.M.A. 1985): The accused's conviction for drug offenses was reversed because the military judge improperly excluded evidence of the accused's good character for truthfulness. This court interpreted Rule 608(a) as allowing defense counsel to admit such evidence when: (a) his client's reputation for veracity has been directly attacked; (b) evidence of a prior conviction under Rule 609(a) has been admitted "for the purpose of attacking credibility;" (c) specific instances of a witness's misconduct were inquired into pursuant to Rule 608(b); and (d) the tenor of cross-examination can be characterized as an attack on the witness's veracity. The court specifically rejected trial counsel's contention that 608(a) can only be used by the defense if government counsel "sought not only to demonstrate that the accused had lied on the stand but also to establish that she was an habitual liar."

Air Force Court of Criminal Appeals

United States v. Porta, 14 M.J. 622 (A.F.C.M.R. 1982): Affirming a conviction, the court held that a vigorous defense cross-examination amounted to placing a key government witness's credibility in issue, thus permitting trial counsel to call rehabilitation witnesses.

United States v. Harvey, 12 M.J. 501 (A.F.C.M.R. 1981): An accused on trial for drug related offenses attempted to impeach the government's key witness by demonstrating that the witness had previously used marijuana over 100 times. The court determined that defense counsel's cross-examination was an attack on credibility which justified trial counsel's calling the witness's past commander for rehabilitation purposes. The court recognized that "incidents of past wrongful marijuana usage do not necessarily concern character for untruthfulness," but felt that under the circumstances (including trial defense counsel's characterization of his cross-examination of the witness as "total and complete destruction"), credibility had been placed in issue.

Army Court of Criminal Appeals

United States v. Luce, 17 M.J. 754 (A.C.M.R. 1984): The court held that a government witness's credibility for truthfulness had been attacked by a defense contention that the key government witnesses lied in order to enhance their careers.

[c]   Character Evidence—Credibility Not Attacked—Rehabilitation Inappropriate

United States Court of Appeals for the Armed Forces

United States v. Toro, 37 M.J. 313 (C.M.A. 1993): This drug abuse court-martial was a swearing contest between the accused and several government informants who were themselves drug abusers. After the informants testified, and were attacked by defense counsel, the prosecution called an OSI agent who said that in his opinion the informants were reliable, credible, trustworthy, and the very best sources he had worked with. Affirming the conviction, this court said that the OSI agent had overstepped when he said the informants were the very best. The court held that such testimony was inappropriate because it did not involve traditional veracity evidence. However, because the accused had not objected at trial, and because the error did not affect a substantial right, it was waived.

United States v. Cox, 18 M.J. 72 (C.M.A. 1984): The court concluded that a rehabilitation witness may give his opinion concerning general character for truthfulness, but he may not give his opinion concerning the validity of a specific fact, allegation or event about which the impeached witness testified.

United States v. Blanchard, 11 M.J. 268 (C.M.A. 1981) (pre-Rules case): The government's case consisted of one witness, an undercover informant who observed the crime. During its case the defense produced reputation and opinion evidence to show that the informant should not be believed. In rebuttal the government attempted to rehabilitate its witness by calling his squadron commander. This officer testified that, in his opinion, the informant was a truthful person. Not satisfied with this attempt at rehabilitation, trial counsel also introduced the informant's Airman Performance Report. The defense's objection to this offer was overruled. Finding error, but no prejudice, the court said it was "unable to agree that the proper practice allows evidence of good military performance to specifically bolster a reputation impeached on the grounds of lack of truth and veracity." The court found no correlation between credibility and duty performance.

Air Force Court of Criminal Appeals

United States v. Halsing, 11 M.J. 920 (A.F.C.M.R. 1981): The sole issue on appeal was whether defense counsel should have been permitted to rehabilitate his client's credibility by using reputation or opinion evidence after his client had been cross-examined. The trial judge's refusal to permit this testimony was affirmed. The reviewing court found that rehabilitation is permitted only after credibility has been specifically attacked. Trial counsel did aggressively question the accused about his version of the facts and pointed out various inconsistencies. But this examination was not tantamount to holding the accused out as a liar or as unworthy of belief.

Army Court of Criminal Appeals

United States v. Hawley, 30 M.J. 1247 (A.C.M.R. 1990): Trial counsel offered rebuttal evidence that an assault victim was truthful, but that "appellant was not always a truthful person." Finding error, but no prejudice, the court held that even though the victim had been extensively cross-examined, her character for truthfulness had not been attacked. *Citing United States v. Varela,* 25 M.J. 29 (C.M.A. 1987), the court reasoned that the cross-examiner was seeking to establish that the witness was well-intentioned, but his observation of events was faulty. The court also said that trial counsel committed no error in attacking the accused's credibility after he testified.

United States v. Ryan, 21 M.J. 627 (A.C.M.R. 1985): Recognizing that Rule 608(a)(2) "should not be interpreted in a restrictive manner," the court found that the accused's character had not been impeached, and rehabilitation was not permitted, where trial counsel's sole cross-examination of the accused consisted of one question to which a defense objection was sustained.

United States v. Morrissey, 14 M.J. 746 (A.C.M.R. 1982): The Army Court of Criminal Appeals determined that the accused's credibility was not placed in issue despite the judge asking him: "SGT Morrissey, somebody is not telling the truth in this courtroom. Can you think of any reason for [the government's witness] to lie?" As a result, the reviewing court found that defense counsel was correctly prohibited from calling rehabilitation witnesses.

United States v. Foushee, 13 M.J. 833 (A.C.M.R. 1982): The accused unsuccessfully appealed his conviction for being an accessory after the fact to assault. The court reasoned that defense testimony regarding the accused's character for truthfulness was properly excluded, because the accused's veracity had not been attacked. The court found that trial counsel's cross-examination of the accused did not amount to an attack on truthfulness.

[d]   Character Evidence—Expert and Other Opinion Testimony

[i]   Appropriately Used

Air Force Court of Criminal Appeals

United States v. Thorn, 36 M.J. 955 (A.F.C.M.R. 1993): The accused was convicted of various drug offenses, largely on the testimony of his accomplices. During the government's case-in-chief, defense counsel vigorously attacked each witness's veracity. On redirect, trial counsel was permitted to call an OSI agent who stated that these witnesses were among the most credible, reliable, and trustworthy he had ever worked with. Affirming the accused's convictions, this court held that the agent's testimony was not improper "human lie detector" evidence, but appropriate lay opinion.

United States v. Brenton, 24 M.J. 562 (A.F.C.M.R. 1987): The accused contended that he had not sexually abused his stepdaughter and presented expert testimony demonstrating that her conduct after the alleged offense "did not show the normal characteristics of a sexually abused child. . . ." In rebuttal, the government used expert testimony to establish that: (a) the victim did not appear to have rehearsed her story, (b) it was rare for a child to make up a false incest story and carry it to the point of lying at trial, and (c) when a child's story is initially spontaneous, it is almost always true. The court rejected the accused's allegation that the government opinion evidence "improperly invaded the providence of the court [because it] expressed opinions that the victim was telling the truth."

Coast Guard Court of Criminal Appeals

United States v. Calogero, 44 M.J. 697 (C.G. Ct.Crim.App. 1996): A general court-martial composed of officer and enlisted members convicted the accused of numerous sexual offenses. The government's case included evidence from a clinical psychologist concerning her favorable opinion about the victim's veracity. Affirming findings and sentence, the court held that while it is improper for an expert to testify about the victim's truthfulness, no error occurred here because the defense counsel initiated this line of inquiry, and trial counsel was merely being allowed to respond.

[ii]   Expert and Other Opinion Testimony—Inappropriately Used

United States Court of Appeals for the Armed Forces

United States v. Hill-Dunning, 26 M.J. 260 (C.M.A. 1988): Affirming the accused's conviction for larceny and submitting a false claim, the court said that while it is permissible for an expert psychiatric witness to state that his opinion is "based upon a belief in the truthfulness of what another person [often the accused] has told him," it is impermissible for any witness, including an expert, to say that in his opinion "the other person is truthful."

United States v. Arruza, 26 M.J. 234 (C.M.A. 1988): The accused's child sexual abuse conviction was affirmed despite an expert witness's vouching for the victim's truthfulness. The court held that such "testimony goes beyond the scope of the expertise of the witness who is not trained to be an expert with 'specialized knowledge . . . to determine if a child-sexual-abuse victim was telling the truth.' "

United States v. Petersen, 24 M.J. 283 (C.M.A. 1987): Relying on a consistent chain of military and civilian authority, the court held that an expert witness in a child sexual abuse case could not "simply testify that she believed the victim's version of what occurred." In the court's opinion such evidence was beyond the ambit of this provision and Rule 704, and required reversal where the contest was largely a swearing match between the accused and his adolescent daughter.

United States v. Cameron, 21 M.J. 59 (C.M.A. 1985): The accused's conviction for sexually molesting his twelve-year-old stepdaughter was reversed because a government rebuttal witness testified that in her opinion the victim's testimony had been "truthful." Citing numerous authorities, the court held that this witness should have been limited to providing opinion or reputation evidence on the victim's veracity and not been allowed to act as a "human lie detector." This case is also noteworthy for its unique fact pattern and because reversal resulted from an evidentiary error in a judge alone trial.

Army Court of Criminal Appeals

United States v. Williams, 23 M.J. 792 (A.C.M.R. 1987): Distinguishing *United States v. Perner,* 14 M.J. 181 (C.M.A. 1982) (which relied on 1969 *Manual* paragraphs 138*f* and 153(b)(2)(a)), the court held that because "the military judge is vested with the widest possible discretion in deciding whether supportive character evidence should be allowed," a witness who only observed the victim during two prior interviews could express an opinion on that witness's truthful character. Recognizing that the 1969 *Manual*'s requirement for "long acquaintance" is not contained in Rule 608(a), the court held that each witness must still possess a basis of knowledge concerning his opinion testimony. Interview observations totaling less than two hours here apparently satisfied that standard, although the court indicated that an adequate cross-examination would expose this testimony's obvious defects.

[iii]   Expert and Other Opinion Testimony—Child Sexual Abuse Cases

United States Court of Appeals for the Armed Forces

United States v. Robbins, 52 M.J. 455 (C.A.A.F. 2000): Affirming the accused's child sexual abuse convictions, this Court held that even though an expert witness was erroneously used by the prosecution as a human lie detector, that delict did not amount to plain error. However, the Court did emphasize that expert witnesses are not allowed to "opine as to the credibility or believability of victims or other witnesses."

United States v. Birdsall, 47 M.J.404 (C.A.A.F. 1998): The accused's convictions for sexually abusing his two young sons were reversed because a government expert witness was permitted to testify that the victims' allegations were "neither unfounded nor coached," and that the children were "victims of incest." The court said that admission of this testimony clearly prejudiced the accused because his trial was essentially a "credibility contest." The court went on to say, "If anything is established in the area of expert testimony in child abuse cases, it is that the expert in child abuse may not act as a human lie detector for the court-martial."

United States v. Knox, 46 M.J. 688 (N.M. Ct.Crim.App. 1997): Reversing the accused's conviction for raping his five-year-old daughter and sodomizing his four-year-old son, this court held that when a government expert witness/social worker testified that she "believed the child," the military judge should have granted defense counsel's request for a mistrial. Relying upon *Krulewitch v. United States,* 336 U.S. 440, 453 (1949) the court opined that the trial judge's prompt cautionary instructions were insufficient, and that the court would not indulge in the "naive assumption" that such errors can be overcome by telling finders of fact to ignore what they have heard. Quoting from Krulewitch, the court said that all practicing lawyers know such assumptions to be "unmitigated fiction."

[iv] Expert and Other Opinion Testimony—Confession Admissibility

Navy-Marine Corps Court of Criminal Appeals

United States v. Tovar, 63 M.J. 637 (N.M. Ct. Crim. App. 2006): During the accused's trial for indecent assault and related offenses, a criminal investigator was allowed to testify that the acccused's initial version of events was deceptive and that his final version, which was incriminating, was more complete. Finding no plain error and affirming the accused's convictions and sentence, the court said that this case concerns what in the vernacular of the military justice system called "human lie detector" testimony. The court noted that such testimony is generally defined as a witness's opinion concerning whether the declarant was truthful in making a specific, and that Military and Federal cases reject such testimony for several reasons: (1) Opinions as to truthfulness exceed the scope of any witness's expertise. No witness, expert or otherwise, has the specialized knowledge necessary to determine whether a declarant was telling the truth. (2) Such testimony exceeds the limits on character evidence set forth in Rule 608, as it offers an opinion concerning the declarant's truthfulness on a specific occasion, rather than knowledge of the declarant's reputation for truthfulness in the community. (3) Such opinion testimony places a stamp of truthfulness or untruthfulness on a declarant's testimony in a manner that usurps the jury's exclusive function to weigh evidence and determine credibility. The court found that the witness in this case was not offering prohibited opinion testimony, given the fact that the accused did not contest the difference between his initial and final statements, and there was no plain error in admitting the witness's testimony.

United States v. Schlamer, 47 M.J. 670 (N.M. Ct.Crim.App. 1997), *aff'd,*

52 M.J. 80 (1999): Tthe accused was convicted of murdering another Marine. During trial, government counsel asked the NCIS agent who obtained the accused's confession whether the accused appeared to be "making this information up" or whether the agent thought the confession was "false." Trial defense counsel objected and the accused raised it as an issue here. Affirming these convictions, the court held that the questioning did not have a substantial impact on the litigation, did not constitute error, but if there was error, it was harmless.

United States v. Knox, 46 M.J. 688 (N.M. Ct.Crim.App. 1997): Reversing the accused's conviction for raping his five-year-old daughter and sodomizing his four-year-old son, this court held that when a government expert witness/social worker testified that she "believed the child," the military judge should have granted defense counsel's request for a mistrial. Relying upon *Krulewitch v. United States,* 336 U.S. 440, 453 (1949), the court opined that the trial judge's prompt cautionary instructions were insufficient, and the court would not indulge in the "naive assumption" that such errors can be overcome by telling finders of fact to ignore what they have heard. Quoting from *Krulewitch,* the court said that all practicing lawyers know such assumptions to be "unmitigated fiction."

[e]   Character Evidence—Previous Inconsistent Statements Inadmissible

Navy-Marine Corps Court of Criminal Appeals

United States v. Diaz, 61 M.J. 594, 595 (N.M.Ct.Crim.App. 2005): Affirming the accused's convictions for raping his 12-year-old daughter, the court held that contrary to the accused's contentions, defense counsel was properly denied the right to cross-examine his own credibility witness with evidence of her previous inconsistent statement. The court held that, while it was appropriate for defense counsel to ask the witness "if she believed the victim is a truthful person," defense counsel could not ask the witness if she had previously said the victim had a "tendency to lie."

[f]   Character Evidence—Relationship to Other Rules

United States Court of Appeals for the Armed Forces

United States v. Robertson, 39 M.J. 211 (C.M.A. 1994): This case demonstrates the difficulty some courts and lawyers have in applying Rules 404(a), 405, and 608(a). The accused was charged with cocaine abuse. Without the accused testifying, defense counsel called a witness to establish the accused's character for "honesty." Trial counsel's objection was sustained. Affirming the accused's conviction, this court held that there must be an attack on a witness's credibility before the military judge will permit that witness's credibility to be rehabilitated. The court may have wrongly assumed that the purpose of the testimony was to bolster credibility. Usually, "honesty" is not the same as "truthfulness." Honesty is a character trait that may permissibly be established pursuant to Rule 404(a)(1).

Air Force Court of Criminal Appeals

United States v. Pruitt, 43 M.J. 864 (A.F. Ct.Crim.App. 1996): Despite his pleas, a court with members convicted the accused of stealing $1000 and signing false documents to cover his crime. After defense counsel called the accused as a witness, and presented opinion testimony concerning the accused's good military character and truthfulness, trial counsel attacked with specific instances of the accused's misconduct. Unfortunately, the military judge allowed trial counsel to introduce extrinsic evidence of the misconduct as well. In a particularly well written and educational opinion, this court held that trial counsel's use of the extrinsic evidence was error because none of the uncharged acts were relevant to truthfulness. However, the court found no prejudice and affirmed.

[g]   Character Evidence—Sexual Assault Cases

United States Court of Appeals for the Armed Forces

United States v. Toohey, 63 M.J. 353 (C.A.A.F. 2006): The accused was convicted of rape and assault. During trial, the military judge excluded character evidence of peacefulness. The Navy-Marine Court of Criminal Appeals found this ruling to be harmless error. The Court of Appeals agreed and held that the error was non-constitutional and did not have a substantial influence on findings. Citing *United States v. Diaz,* 45 M.J. 494, 496 (C.A.A.F. 1997), the court found that the prosecution met its four part test: (1) the government's case was strong and conclusive; (2) the defense's theory of the case was weak or implausible; (3) the excluded evidence was not significant; and (4) the proffered evidence was low in quality and was cumulative.

Navy-Marine Corps Court of Criminal Appeals

United States v. Terry, 61 M.J. 721 (N.M.Ct.Crim.App. 2005): The accused was convicted of rape, conspiracy to commit rape, and related offenses. After trial counsel's redirect examination of a victim-advocate witness, the military judge, without objection, asked the witness if, based on his experience, he could tell when a female might be covering up a consensual sexual encounter by claiming it was rape. Trial counsel asked a similar follow-on question. Finding harmless error, the court held that it was improper to ask one witness if another witness was telling the truth. Such "human lie detector" attempts are viewed as invading the fact-finder's providence.

Air Force Court of Criminal Appeals

United States v. McElhaney, 50 M.J. 819 (A.F. Ct.Crim.App. 1999): Convicted of sexually assaulting his future wife's underage niece, the accused unsuccessfully contended on appeal that the trial judge erred by failing to require the presence of an out-of-jurisdiction witness who would have testified about the victim's poor character for truthfulness. The reviewing court held that the defense witness did not have a sufficient basis upon which to offer such opinion testimony. Equally important, the court found that the accused's witness request was really based on the defense's desire to have this witness deny the victim's allegations that he also had a sexual relationship with her. In the court's opinion, a child sexual assault victim's previous similar unsubstantiated complaints against another is not probative of the victim's truthfulness or untruthfulness.

[h]   Character Evidence—Timing

Navy-Marine Corps Court of Criminal Appeals

United States v. Midkiff, 15 M.J. 1043 (N.M.C.M.R. 1983): The court observed that reputation and opinion evidence concerning a witness's reputation for truthfulness is to be measured "at the time of trial and during periods not remote thereto . . . ."

[2]   Rule 608(b)—Specific Instances of Conduct

[a]   Specific Instances of Conduct—Accused Lying at Trial

United States Court of Appeals for the Armed Forces

United States v. Trimper, 28 M.J. 460 (C.M.A. 1989): The accused, an Air Force JAG officer, was convicted of drug abuse offenses. During the accused's case in chief, he denied ever using cocaine. In rebuttal, the government was permitted to introduce extrinsic evidence of the accused's positive "private urinalysis" test. Affirming the conviction, the court held this evidence was properly admitted because "if a witness makes a broad collateral assertion on direct examination that he has never engaged in a certain type of misconduct or if he volunteers such broad information in responding to appropriately narrow cross-examination, he may be impeached by extrinsic evidence of the misconduct."

Air Force Court of Criminal Appeals

United States v. Garcia, 25 M.J. 652 (A.F.C.M.R. 1987): Affirming the accused's cocaine use conviction, the court held that: "where the accused makes a sweeping denial of past misconduct he opens the door to permit introduction of extrinsic evidence contradicting that claim. The accused here denied ever using 'any other drugs,' and while [his use of marihuana] was not an issue at trial, a witness who makes a collateral assertion on direct examination may be" attacked with such proof. *See also United States v. Banker,* 15 M.J. 207 (C.M.A. 1983) (an accused's gratuitous allegation that he never used drugs allowed the government to introduce evidence contradicting it).

United States v. Feagans, 15 M.J. 667 (A.F.C.M.R. 1983): When the accused testified that he had led a crime-free life prior to the charged offense, trial counsel was properly permitted to question him about pre-service criminal conduct and related pretrial statements made to an OSI agent.

Army Court of Criminal Appeals

United States v. McSwain, 24 M.J. 754 (A.C.M.R. 1987): On direct examination the accused stated that: "I've never been in this kind of trouble; I'd never been in that situation. . . ." Trial counsel then established that the accused had been in similar trouble, received an Article 15 punishment, and lied about the incident when reporting to his new unit. Rejecting the accused's contention that this evidence violated Rule 608(b), the court reasoned that the Rule limits extrinsic evidence concerning a general character for truthfulness; it does not prohibit such testimony "when offered to impeach the witness through contradiction" of direct examination.

Navy-Marine Corps Court of Criminal Appeals

United States v. Bowling, 16 M.J. 848 (N.M.C.M.R. 1983): The court held that when an the accused voluntarily testifies to sweeping denials of involvement in similar criminal misconduct, it is permissible to impeach his credibility by using extrinsic evidence of those crimes, even though such a result may be an exception to Rule 608(b). However, if this exception is to be used, the military judge should specifically find that the accused's statements were volunteered and not elicited, and that their admission will not violate Rule 403.

[b]   Specific Instances of Conduct—Bolstering

Air Force Court of Criminal Appeals

United States v. Porta, 14 M.J. 622 (A.F.C.M.R. 1982): The court found that counsel may not use Rule 608(b) to bolster a witness's testimony by calling a subsequent witness to say that "ninety-five percent of what [the previous witness said] has been truthful and been verified by other people." Such testimony goes beyond reputation or opinion evidence concerning a general character for truthfulness.

[c]   Specific Instances of Conduct—Defense Requests for Discovery of Credibility Evidence

Army Court of Criminal Appeals

United States v. Jenkins, 18 M.J. 583 (A.C.M.R. 1984): Error occurred when the trial judge refused to provide defense counsel with evidence concerning a key government witness's prior forgery conviction. The court held that defense counsel could have used the evidence in question to cross-examine the government's witness "about specific instances of conduct which are probative of truthfulness or untruthfulness for the purpose of attacking or supporting the credibility of the witness." However, the court refused to "speculate as to whether defense counsel would have had a reasonable basis to ask [the witness] about his forgery offense even though his conviction was disapproved." We believe that reliance on the conviction's disapproval is misplaced here. In order to ask questions an accused need not have proof beyond a reasonable doubt; a reasonable belief that an event occurred is sufficient. As a result, questions concerning a witness's behavior may be permissible even though the events resulted in an acquittal. It is important to note that the conviction itself would not be admissible under this Rule; it is extrinsic evidence. Questions about the events are permissible, but the cross-examiner is bound by the witness's answer.

United States v. Hunter, 17 M.J. 738 (A.C.M.R. 1983): The court found no error in the military judge's refusing to provide defense counsel with CID evidence showing that the government's key witness in a drug case was himself a drug dealer who had improperly diverted government funds for his own use. The court held that this evidence would not have undermined the witness's credibility nor "helped the defense."

[d]   Specific Instances of Conduct—Extrinsic Proof Admissible

Air Force Court of Criminal Appeals

United States v. Matthews, 50 M.J. 584 (A.F. Ct.Crim.App. 1999): The accused was convicted of using marijuana on one occasion. During trial she denied the offense, conceded the accuracy of the laboratory test, implied no knowledge of how the illicit drug may have been in her urine, and presented "good military character" evidence. In rebuttal, trial counsel was permitted to introduce evidence that the accused had failed a subsequent command directed urinalysis. Affirming the accused's conviction and sentence, this court held that evidence of the subsequent command directed urinalysis was admissible to rebut her favorable character testimony. The court went on to say that holding otherwise would have permitted the accused to paint an inaccurate picture of her character and conduct.

United States v. Stroh, 46 M.J. 643 (A.F. Ct.Crim.App. 1997): The accused was convicted of perpetrating the most sordid sexual offenses against his daughter's six-year-old playmate. The accused testified in his own defense, denying all allegations and stating that "it is not my character" to sexually abuse children. On cross-examination, trial counsel questioned the accused about incidents which demonstrated his sexual deviance. During redirect, the accused denied the allegations, particularly that his daughter had made a complaint accusing him of sexually molesting her. In rebuttal, trial counsel called the criminal investigator who testified in support of the government's position. The trial judge's final instructions indicated that the investigator's testimony could only be used for impeachment purposes. Affirming the accused's convictions, this court held that an accused who elected to testify is subject to impeachment just like any other witness. Here it was appropriate for trial counsel to attack the accused's character for truthfulness by cross-examining him concerning specific instances of conduct which were probative of truthfulness.

Navy-Marine Corps Court of Criminal Appeals

United States v. Moore, 55 M.J. 772 (N.M. Ct.Crim.App. 2001): The accused was convicted of three specifications of violating a lawful general order, rape, adultery, and two specifications of indecent assault. On appeal, this Court held that the military judge did not abuse his discretion by denying the accused an opportunity to cross-examine the prosecutrix regarding a statement she made, in which she told the court she had not had sex with any one else for nine months. This Court also held that the military judge did not abuse his discretion by denying the accused the opportunity to present evidence of the victim's sexual relationship with a third party. The Court went on to say that a military judge has the discretion to allow cross-examination regarding specific instances of misconduct when relevant to a witness's veracity under Rule 608(b).

[e] Specific Instances of Conduct—Extrinsic Proof Not Admissible

United States Court of Appeals for the Armed Forces

United States v. McElhaney, 54 M.J. 120 (C.A.A.F. 2000): A general court-martial convicted the accused of numerous child sexual offenses. *In limine,* trial counsel moved to suppress the accused's cross-examination of the victim concerning an alleged previous false rape report she had made. Both before trial and during trial, the military judge prohibited the examination. Agreeing with the Court of Criminal Appeal, Judge Effron wrote for the Court of Appeals for the Armed Forces and found the challenged testimony inadmissible by relying on the Court's previous opinion in *United States v. Velez,* 48 M.J. 220, 227 (C.A.A.F. 1998) "The mere filing of a complaint is not even probative of the truthfulness or untruthfulness of the complaint filed . . . thus, its relevance on the question of credibility of a different complaint in an unrelated case, such as the accused's escapes us." Judge Effron went on to say that, "The record in this case reflects nothing more than a mere complaint of rape made by the victim against Mr. Perez; defense counsel preferred no evidence showing the complaint to be false, other than the unsurprising denial of Mr. Perez."

United States v. Spindle, 28 M.J. 35 (C.M.A. 1989): In this murder case, a crucial but unavailable witness's pretrial testimony was received. The accused unsuccessfully contended that he should have been allowed to impeach the absent witness by showing that the witness had stolen money from a fellow soldier just prior to absenting himself. Affirming the conviction, the court held that this misconduct might have been admissible if the judge believed it was related to the witness's credibility. However, the court observed that extrinsic evidence of a witness's misconduct, short of a conviction, is not received to impeach his credibility except when the extrinsic evidence shows bias, prejudice, or a motive to misrepresent.

United States v. Owens, 21 M.J. 117 (C.M.A. 1985): In this premeditated murder case, the court held it was proper for trial counsel to impeach the accused by eliciting the accused's admissions to prior acts of intentional falsehood. While the court also held that trial counsel could not suggest improper evidence in reaching this result, they recognized that Rule 608(b)'s prohibition against using extrinsic evidence "does not mean that further cross-examination of appellant is impermissible." Within reason, such examination can include rephrased questions which deal in the specific matters the accused has lied about "so as to gradually but dramatically induce the accused to abandon his previous more general denial."

United States v. Cottle, 14 M.J. 260 (C.M.A. 1982): In this pre-Rules case, the court held that, while a witness's credibility may be attacked by asking him about specific instances of conduct, such acts cannot be proved by extrinsic evidence. The court noted that to permit such attacks would only "confuse the finder of fact with an infinite number of collateral issues."

Air Force Court of Criminal Appeals

United States v. Aubin, 13 M.J. 623 (A.F.C.M.R. 1982): The accused unsuccessfully sought a new trial, contending that he should have been permitted to impeach a key government witness's credibility with extrinsic proof of specific instances of conduct. In rejecting this claim the court recognized that while Rule 608(b) permits examination on specific instances of conduct relating to credibility, the Rule does not allow the witness to be contradicted by extrinsic evidence. This reasoning is applicable where the only use of extrinsic evidence would be to prove a "bad act" which, if proved, might impeach credibility. It should not be forgotten, however, that use of extrinsic evidence to impeach a witness on another theory—*e.g.*, to show bias or motive to lie under Rule 608(c), may be permissible.

Army Court of Criminal Appeals

United States v. Wilson, 12 M.J. 652 (A.C.M.R. 1981): The Court of Criminal Appeals held that the military judge committed prejudicial error in ruling that an accused with two Article 15 punishments for making a false official statement and for larceny could be impeached on the basis of the nonjudicial punishments if he chose to testify. Although the government could have asked the accused whether he committed the underlying acts, it could not inquire into the punishments: "To permit such questions would violate the principle of *United States v. Cofield*, 11 M.J. 422 (C.M.A. 1981) [discussed under Rule 609], that records of conviction by summary courts-martial lack sufficient reliability to permit their use for impeachment. Records of Article 15 punishment possess even less reliability . . . ."

Coast Guard Court of Criminal Appeals

United States v. Stellon, 65 M.J. 802 (C.G.Ct.Crim.App. 2007): The accused was convicted of rape. The government's proof included the accused's confession and testimony from the victim. Defense counsel's cross-examination of the victim focused on her 2004 false rape complaint made against a different man. At trial and on appeal, the accused contended that the military judge improperly limited his cross-examination of the victim concerning her false complaint and improperly excluded related police testimony and physical evidence. Relying on *Delaware v. Van Arsdall,* 475 U.S. 673, the court affirmed the accused's conviction and held that trial judges have wide latitude to impose reasonable limits on repetitive or marginally relevant cross-examinations. Here the military judge found that further cross-examination would have resulted in litigating an entirely different case and violated Rule 403 by misleading or confusing the finders of fact.

[f] Specific Instances of Conduct—Misconduct and Truthfulness

Army Court of Criminal Appeals

United States v. Lee, 48 M.J. 756 (Army Ct.Crim.App. 1998): The accused was convicted of numerous fraud and forgery related offenses. In limine, trial counsel successfully moved to prevent the defense from crossing-examining a government witness about that witness's alleged attempted bribery of a military policeman. The defense asserted that the attempted bribery was a crimen falsi act making it relevant to truthfulness. Rejecting the defense's contention, this court held that although Rule 608(b) does not specifically enumerate which acts pertain to truthfulness or untruthfulness, the touchstone of admissibility is the logical connection between the underlying conduct and the witness's veracity. The court went on to say that this is not to be a rigid standard and should be left to the trial judge's discretion. On these facts, the court held that even if the trial judge erred it was harmless.

[g] Specific Instances of Conduct—Rehabilitation Permitted

Air Force Court of Criminal Appeals

United States v. Prince, 24 M.J. 643 (A.F.C.M.R. 1987): The accused was convicted of using cocaine. His offense was discovered through a properly conducted urinalysis. At trial, the accused defended on the theory of innocent use, testifying that "his wife had surreptitiously slipped cocaine powder into his mixed drink. . . ." Mrs. Prince then testified and admitted that she "attempted to find a way to improve her husband's sexual performance" by using cocaine powder in this fashion. Trial counsel attacked her credibility on cross-examination. In rebuttal, defense counsel attempted to rehabilitate Mrs. Prince by calling her sister to explain that she told Mrs. Prince about the cocaine powder aphrodisiac and how to use it. The trial judge excluded this testimony, relying on Rule 608(b). Reversing the conviction, this court held that Rule 608(b) was inapposite. The evidence addressed whether the sister had actually made such a suggestion to Mrs. Prince. In the court's opinion, such testimony would be relevant as part of the "defense theory of innocent ingestion."

[h]   Specific Instances of Conduct—Specific Acts Not Related to Credibility

United States Court of Appeals for the Armed Forces

United States v. Robertson, 39 M.J. 211 (C.M.A. 1994): The accused was convicted of cocaine abuse. At trial, a friend testified that the accused innocently ingested the drug. During cross-examination of the friend, trial counsel impeached her credibility with evidence of previous arrests for fraud and burglary. Finding error but no prejudice, the court held that an arrest is governmental action, not conduct of the witness, and therefore says nothing about that witness's credibility. Trial counsel's error in this case was failing to establish the underlying facts of this witness's arrest, and then establishing how that conduct relates to truthfulness or untruthfulness.

United States v. Branoff, 34 M.J. 612 (A.F.C.M.R. 1992): The central issue in this drug use and introduction case, concerned the accused's discovery rights. During trial, she was denied access to an OSI regulation, and unredacted copies of some witnesses' statements. The accused claimed that had this information been provided, she would have used it to impeach the government's agents. Affirming her convictions, the court held that comparing extrinsic agent conduct with regulatory procedures was an improper method for attacking credibility. The court relied on the military judge's *in camera* review indicating that the evidence did not disclose bias, prejudice, or a motive to misrepresent.

United States v. Corbett, 29 M.J. 253 (C.M.A. 1989): Although it affirmed the accused's drug offense conviction, the court held that an impeached government witness should not have been permitted to testify about his accusations to the OSI with respect to several airmen who were later convicted by a court-martial. The court said such evidence did not establish the truthfulness of the witness's testimony against Corbett.

Air Force Court of Criminal Appeals

United States v. Tyler, 26 M.J. 680 (A.F.C.M.R. 1988): Affirming the accused's drug distribution conviction, this court held that a governmental informant could not be cross-examined concerning his having submitted a previous and unrelated false claim, because this "collateral matter" would have caused confusion and distracted the members.

United States v. Jefferson, 23 M.J. 517 (A.F.C.M.R. 1986): After determining that the accused's previous shoplifting conviction could not be used against him under Rule 404(b) or 608(a), the court held that it was error to admit that evidence under Rule 608(b)(1) because "shoplifting has been held to be an offense that does not involve dishonesty." Thus, the conviction was not helpful in determining truthfulness.

United States v. Pierce, 14 M.J. 738 (A.F.C.M.R. 1982): After pleading guilty to possession of marijuana, the accused testified under oath on sentencing. During cross-examination, trial counsel asked the accused if he had ever used marijuana. Defense counsel's objection was overruled. Finding error but no prejudice, the reviewing court characterized the prosecutor's questions as inadmissible specific instance of conduct evidence that was unrelated to the witness's credibility. Recognizing that the trial bench has substantial discretion in this area, the court noted that "the military judge should decide whether the question puts undue emphasis on an offense for which there is no conviction."

Army Court of Criminal Appeals

United States v. Bender, 30 M.J. 815 (A.C.M.R. 1990): In this bench case, the court found error, but no prejudice, in the judge's considering evidence of the accused's similar improper child sexual offenses as directly bearing on the victim's credibility.

Navy-Marine Corps Court of Criminal Appeals

United States v. Weeks, 17 M.J. 613 (N.M.C.M.R. 1983): The court held, that absent unusual circumstances, incidents of past drug usage or sale do not necessarily demonstrate an adverse character for truthfulness.

United States v. Duty, 16 M.J. 855 (N.M.C.M.R. 1983): The court held that a government informant's credibility could not be attacked with pornographic photographs and reasoned as follows: "[F]ornication is no more a barometer of untruthfulness than celibacy is an indicator of truthfulness, and it is probable that at least as many lies have been uttered by persons fully clothed as by those who are nude. We therefore hold that neither posing nude for photographs nor engaging in an active sex life is an act of corruption that is probative of a propensity for truthfulness or untruthfulness."

[i] Specific Instances of Conduct—Specific Acts Related to Credibility

Supreme Court

United States v. Abel, 469 U.S. 45 (1984): It was not error for government counsel to cross-examine a defense witness with specific characteristics of a prison gang he and the accused were members of in order to establish bias on that witness's part.

United States Court of Appeals for the Armed Forces

United States v. Stavely, 33 M.J. 92 (C.M.A. 1991): Reversing the accused's conviction for submitting a fraudulent insurance claim, the court held that defense counsel was erroneously prohibited from asking the government's key witness about the specifics of her having lied under previous circumstances on other occasions.

United States v. Wind, 28 M.J. 381 (C.M.A. 1989): The court held that in rebuttal to the accused's drug entrapment defense, trial counsel properly offered a statement from another sailor indicating that the accused purchased drugs from him on a regular basis.

Air Force Court of Criminal Appeals

United States v. Boone, 17 M.J. 567 (A.F.C.M.R. 1983): The court found that the military judge should have allowed defense counsel to question a key government witness about his false, pre-service enlistment contract statements that denied marijuana usage. Such testimony would have been directly probative of the witness's truthfulness.

Army Court of Criminal Appeals

United States v. Crumley, 22 M.J. 877 (A.C.M.R. 1986): The court held that specific instances of conduct are admissible under this Rule "if offered solely to impeach the credibility of a witness who voluntarily denies involvement in similar misconduct. . . ." *Citing United States v. Bowling,* 16 M.J. 848 (N.M.C.M.R. 1983) and *United States v. Havens,* 446 U.S. 620 (1980), the court said that it was "immaterial whether denial comes on direct or cross-examination because there is no difference between [an accused's] statement on direct examination and his answers to questions put to him on cross-examination that are plainly within the scope of [his] direct examination."

Navy-Marine Corps Court of Criminal Appeals

United States v. Stafford, 22 M.J. 825 (N.M.C.M.R. 1986): The court found that the trial judge erred in prohibiting defense counsel from cross-examining a government witness about her alleged attempt at altering her urinalysis test results. The court held that such evidence would have been "probative of truthfulness," so its exclusion foreclosed legitimate inquiries into credibility. It stated that Rule 608(b) "permits inquiry into specific instances of conduct which relate to *crimen falsi,* e.g., perjury, subordination of perjury, false statement, fraud, swindling, forgery, bribery, false pretenses and embezzlement." Thus, this government witness's perpetration of a "fraud upon the government by submitting a urine sample which was not her own is highly probative of her character for truthfulness, and proper cross-examination concerning this alleged incident would have fit neatly within the requirements of Mil. R. Evid. 608(b)."

United States v. Braswell, 14 M.J. 885 (N.M.C.M.R. 1983): The court found that the proponent of a character witness may not elicit specific instances of conduct evidence during direct examination, but it reasoned that such evidence may be admissible on redirect examination to rehabilitate the witness.

[j]   Specific Instances of Conduct—Waiver

Air Force Court of Criminal Appeals

United States v. Dicupe, 14 M.J. 915 (A.F.C.M.R. 1982): The court rejected the accused's claim that extrinsic offense evidence had been improperly admitted against him. It found that defense counsel had objected neither to the evidence nor to the military judge's sua sponte limiting instruction; defense counsel had used the evidence during his cross-examination of the government's witness; and the trial judge had discretion to admit the evidence.

[3]   Rule 608(c)—Evidence of Bias

[a]   Evidence of Bias—Coercion Causing Bias

United States Court of Appeals for the Armed Forces

United States v. Welker, 44 M.J. 85 (C.A.A.F. 1996): Consistent with his pleas, the accused was convicted of numerous sexual offenses upon his stepdaughter. During sentencing, the victim testified for her stepfather saying that she did not want him to go to jail, that the family needed therapy, and that the family should stay together. Over defense objection, trial counsel established the threats and inducements the victim's mother had used to procure her daughter's favorable defense testimony. Affirming findings and sentence, this court held that trial counsel's cross-examination was proper because it demonstrated the unrealistic and coerced nature of the victim's testimony.

[b]   Evidence of Bias—Collateral Evidence

United States Court of Appeals for the Armed Forces

United States v. Gonzalez, 16 M.J. 423 (C.M.A. 1983): Where the defense's evidence of bias against a government witness was so tenuous that it seemed collateral to any important issue at trial, its exclusion was appropriate.

Air Force Court of Criminal Appeals

United States v. Jones, 30 M.J. 898 (A.F.C.M.R. 1990): In this drug abuse case, the court found error, but no prejudice, in trial counsel's using a rebuttal witness to establish specific instances of a defense witness's dishonesty. The court said that "although extrinsic evidence of bias may be introduced, the theory of bias that supports introduction of the evidence must not be so tenuous as to be collateral to the trial." Here the incident was "minor . . . and probably more a result of a misunderstanding that a deliberate lie."

[c]   Evidence of Bias—Defense Evidence—Improperly Excluded

United States Court of Appeals for the Armed Forces

United States v. Collier, 67 M.J. 347 (C.A.A.F. 2009): The accused was convicted of stealing military property and obstructing justice. The military judge relied on Rules 403 and 611 to limit the defense counsel's ability to cross-examine the key government witness about her failed homosexual romantic relationship with the accused. Defense counsel's theory of the case was that the breakup produced the fabricated charges. The military judge found sufficient evidence to establish the failed homosexual romantic relationship and concluded that the relationship was relevant, but limited defense counsel to establishing that the accused and the witness had a failed close friendship. Defense counsel contended the judge's ruling violated the accused's Sixth Amendment right to confrontation because the witness's bias and resulting motive to lie could not be effectively established without proving the failed romantic homosexual relationship. Trial counsel contended there was essentially no difference between a failed friendship and a failed romantic relationship for the purposes of showing bias. Finding a Sixth Amendment violation, the court reversed the accused's convictions using the constitutional harmless beyond a reasonable doubt standard. The witness's testimony was central to the defense's case and was not cumulative. The judge's error essentially prohibited the accused from establishing her best defense and as a result may have tipped the credibility balance in the government's favor.

Coast Guard Court of Criminal Appeals

United States v. Olean, 56 M.J. 594 (C.G. Ct.Crim.App. 2001): The accused was convicted of two specifications of maltreatment, making a false official statement, sodomy, adultery, and failure to obey a lawful general order. The accused contended that the judge erred to his substantial prejudice by improperly admitting, over defense counsel's objection, propensity evidence of the accused's alleged domestic violence and his assault on a subordinate. The accused further alleged that the judge erred in excluding vengeful statements made to the accused by the prosecution's principle witness, which were witnesses by two people. Affirming in part and setting aside in part, this Court held that evidence of uncharged misconduct in the form of testimony of victims, who stated they were aware of accused's alleged domestic violence and related assault on a ubordinate, was admissible to prove the element of the maltreatment offense that the victims experienced mental pain or suffering from the accused's comments and behavior, due to the fear of physical assault. Further, the Court held that the military judge erred in excluding evidence of vengeful statements made by the principle government witness that she intended to "take down" the accused if she was going to be "kicked out" of the Coast Guard, as such evidence was admissible proof of bias or prejudice which might have impeached the witness; and the error in excluding the evidence of bias of the witness was prejudicial. The court based its conclusion on the fact that the testimony of the witness as victim and eyewitness was critical for all but one of the alleged offenses of which the accused was convicted, the testimony was not cumulative, and exclusion of the evidence left defense counsel without the ability to offer members an explanation of why witnesses might lie.

[d]   Evidence of Bias—Details of Pretrial Agreement

United States Court of Appeals for the Armed Forces

United States v. Carruthers, 64 M.J. 340 (C.A.A.F. 2007): During the accused's trial for larceny of government property, defense counsel contended that the military judge improperly limited his cross-examination of a key co-conspirator regarding that witness's pretrial agreement sentence limitations. Affirming the accused's sentence and findings, the court relied on *United States v. James,* 61 M.J.132 (C.A.A.F. 2005), and held that, although exposing a witness's motivation for testifying is a proper and important function of the Sixth Amendment, trial judges retain wide latitude to impose limits on defense counsel's inquiry. The court said that latitude was properly exercised here as defense counsel's cross-examination was sufficient.

United States v. James, 61 M.J. 132 (C.A.A.F. 2005): During the sentencing portion of the accused's trial for using and distributing ecstasy, defense counsel was prohibited from cross-examining a key government witness concerning the details of that witness's pretrial agreement with the government to testify against James. Affirming the accused's convictions and sentence, the court held that, while it is permissible to cross-examine a witness concerning his motive to lie and misrepresent, trial judges retain wide latitude insofar as how they may constitutionally limit that cross-examination. Using Rule 403 logic, the court held cross-examinations aimed at harassing a witness, confusing the issues at trial, or producing marginally relevant testimony may be prevented. Surveying other cases with similar issues, the court opined that, while the judge did not abuse his discretion here, because the witness had in fact already been sentenced for his previous offenses, a different result may obtain where the witness is waiting for sentencing.

[e]   Evidence of Bias—Military Judge Responsibilities

United States Court of Appeals for the Armed Forces

United States v. Bins, 43 M.J. 79 (C.A.A.F. 1995): While in Crete, SFC Bins committed numerous forcible sexual offenses on the same victim. At trial he was prevented from showing that the victim had received a monetary civil settlement for his attacks. Finding error, but no prejudice, the court held that the military judge usurped the members' role in determining whether the prosecutrix's testimony was improperly influenced by the settlement. The court highlighted that weight and credibility are matters for the members alone to decide.

[f]   Evidence of Bias—Motives Causing Bias

United States Court of Appeals for the Armed Forces

United States v. Moss, 63 M.J. 233 (C.A.A.F. 2006): The accused was convicted of sexually molesting his 14 year-old niece. During the trial, defense counsel was prohibited from introducing evidence showing that the prosecutrix was constantly in trouble with her family, teachers and others in position of authority; was a liar; and was often out late with boys. The court found that such evidence was crical to the accused's theory that the criminal complaint was lodged to divert attention away from the prosecutrix's behavior and in favor of eliciting sympathy for her.

United States v. Gray, 40 M.J. 77 (C.M.A. 1994): The accused was convicted of sodomy and adultery with a subordinate's wife, and committing indecent acts with the subordinate's nine-year-old daughter. Defense counsel unsuccessfully attempted to introduce evidence showing that the Texas Department of Human Services (DHS) had investigated both the subordinate and his wife for child and spousal abuse. Reversing the accused's convictions, this court held that the testimony should have been admitted because it helped demonstrate that the charges against the accused were a ruse designed to deflect the DHS investigation away from his subordinate's family.

United States v. Bahr, 33 M.J. 228 (C.M.A. 1991): The court reversed the accused's conviction for sexually abusing his daughter because defense counsel was not permitted to cross-examine the prosecutrix about statements in her diary which demonstrated a motive to lie, previous false rape claims, and other attempts at getting friends to allege that they had been sexually abused. In the court's opinion, the accused's inability to fully demonstrate his daughter's numerous motives to misrepresent was an abridgment of the right to confrontation.

United States v. Banker, 15 M.J. 207 (C.M.A. 1983): The court found that specific acts of conduct that cannot be used to attack credibility under Rule 608(b) may be admissible to demonstrate a witness's bias, prejudice or motive to misrepresent.

Air Force Court of Criminal Appeals

United States v. Cerniglia, 31 M.J. 804 (A.F.C.M.R. 1990): Affirming the accused's cocaine-use conviction, the court held that trial counsel properly impeached a defense witness with extrinsic evidence of a lie. In the court's opinion, because the witness himself was under investigation for drug offenses, his false direct testimony was merely an attempt to exonerate himself and demonstrated a substantial motive to misrepresent.

United States v. Joyner, 25 M.J. 730 (A.F.C.M.R. 1987): Testifying at his drug use prosecution, the accused stated that he had never used marihuana, didn't understand why his urinalysis was positive, and in fact volunteered for a second urinalysis which was reported negative. In rebuttal, trial counsel offered the negative results of a different, earlier urinalysis, taken approximately one year before the charged event. This report, trial counsel showed, was actually positive when additional analysis had been done. Relying on this Rule, the court stated that the evidence was properly admitted because it "reflected a possible motive to misrepresent . . . that [the accused] volunteered to submit to a second test because he had reason to believe that the result would be negative even though he knew that he had used marihuana."

United States v. Boone, 17 M.J. 567 (A.F.C.M.R. 1983): Relying on the spirit, if not the letter, of Rule 608(c), the court found no error in trial counsel's asking a key prosecution witness about the witness's motive for testifying.

Army Court of Criminal Appeals

United States v. George, 40 M.J. 540 (A.C.M.R. 1994): The accused was charged with using cocaine on a single occasion. Defense counsel unsuccessfully attempted to impeach the government's forensic expert by showing that the witness had a significant financial interest in the company which tested the drugs. Reversing the accused's conviction, this court held that the military judge improperly curtailed defense counsel's cross-examination. The court said that had counsel been permitted to continue, the members would have become aware of the witness's financial interest in favorably portraying how the drug testing laboratory worked.

United States v. Alexander, 27 M.J. 834 (A.C.M.R. 1989): In this child sexual abuse case, civilian defense counsel attempted to impeach the victim by showing that she had a recent history of juvenile delinquency, frequent absences from school, and a sexual relationship with her boyfriend. The court held that the military judge properly sustained trial counsel's Rule 404(b) objection to the testimony as it was only offered to demonstrate that the victim was a "bad kid." The trial judge properly established that if the accused had extrinsic evidence proving the victim had a motive to lie, or was biased or prejudiced against the accused, then the evidence could be admitted.

Navy-Marine Corps Court of Criminal Appeals

United States v. Hayes, 15 M.J. 650 (N.M.C.M.R. 1983): The accused's larceny conviction was reversed because defense counsel was prohibited from conducting an adequate cross-examination into a government witness's bias and motive to misrepresent.

[g]   Evidence of Bias—Nexus to Credibility Issues Missing

United States Court of Appeals for the Armed Forces

United States v. Saferite, 59 M.J. 270 (C.A.A.F. 2004): Tried in absentia for stealing over $100,000 of computer equipment, the accused was convicted of numerous theft-related offenses. During sentencing, trial defense counsel admitted a statement from the accused's wife praising his value as a father and husband. In rebuttal, trial counsel introduced evidence indicating that the accused's wife was involved in his escape from confinement, and as a result was a highly biased witness. Finding harmless error, this court held that the accused's escape was already before the court as he was being tried in absentia, and thus the court-members were not substantially affected by the error in admitting the evidence.

Army Court of Criminal Appeals

United States v. Hunter, 17 M.J. 738 (A.C.M.R. 1984): Evidence that a key government witness "was engaged in a systematic diversion of drugs and CID funds" was held inadmissible because trial defense counsel failed to establish (beyond his "bare assertions") that the testimony would have any bearing on the witness's credibility.

Navy-Marine Corps Court of Criminal Appeals

United States v. Weeks, 17 M.J. 613 (N.M.C.M.R. 1983): Evidence of past drug dealing was not admissible against the government's key witness under the "motive" or "bias" theory of Rule 608(c) because defense counsel failed to establish its relevance or effect upon the witness's testimony. In substance the court found such evidence to be "mere speculation on the part of defense counsel."

[h]   Evidence of Bias—Plausible Basis for Belief That Witness is Biased

Army Court of Criminal Appeals

United States v. Means, 20 M.J. 522 (A.C.M.R. 1985): The court held that it would have been appropriate for trial defense counsel to cross-examine a consensual sexual offense victim with extrinsic evidence (Article 32 transcripts) concerning her previous rape claims because defense counsel had an adequate basis for believing that the victim was biased.

[i]   Evidence of Bias—Pretrial Agreement Evidence

Navy-Marine Court of Criminal Appeals

United States v. Rojas, 15 M.J. 902 (N.M.C.M.R. 1983): Although it found that the trial judge had not abused his discretion by prohibiting defense counsel from impeaching the government's key witness (and a co-accused) with certain facts concerning the witness's pretrial agreement, the court recognized "that cross-examination into any motive or incentive a witness may have for falsifying his testimony must be permitted."

[j]   Evidence of Bias—Racial Bias

Army Court of Criminal Appeals

United States v. Harris, 34 M.J. 1213 (A.C.M.R. 1992): The accused, a black Army officer and commander of a company-sized detachment, was convicted of sexually harassing and intimidating two white enlisted female soldiers who were members of his unit. During trial, government counsel demonstrated that the accused threatened these soldiers with Article 15 punishment if they did not consent to sex with him. The accused's key witness testified that the two female soldiers framed the accused in order to avoid punishment for their own misconduct. During cross-examination of this defense witness, trial counsel emphasized that the witness was racially biased in favor of blacks. Reversing the accused's convictions, the court held that while Rule 608(c) allows for impeachment based on racial bias, the inquiry here was improper because it focused on the all-white panel's emotional bias, while the military judge did not use Rule 403 to control trial counsel's cross-examination.

[k] Evidence of Bias—Relationships Causing Bias

Supreme Court

Olden v. Kentucky, 488 U.S. 227 (1988) (per curiam): At his trial on rape charges, the defense theory was that the victim had lied about her contact with the defendant in order to protect her illicit relationship with another man. The trial court, however, refused to let counsel impeach the victim with evidence of that illicit relationship. Citing the constitutional right of confrontation and the right to present evidence of motive and bias, the Court concluded that the trial bench had committed reversible error.

United States v. Abel, 469 U.S. 45 (1984): It is proper to cross-examine a defense witness for the purpose of showing that he and the accused were members of the same prison gang that was sworn to perjury and self-protection on each member's behalf. The Court said that a "witness's and a party's common membership in an organization, even without proof that the witness or party had personally adopted its tenets, is certainly probative of bias," and therefore admissible.

United States Court of Appeals for the Armed Forces

United States v. Tippy, 25 M.J. 121 (C.M.A. 1987): Reversing the accused's drug distribution conviction, the court held that the military judge improperly limited cross-examination of an undercover OSI agent which would have demonstrated that the agent was "manipulative" and "would do whatever is necessary for personal gain [including] sexual relationships."

Air Force Court of Criminal Appeals

United States v. Snodgrass, 37 M.J. 844 (A.F.C.M.R. 1993): During the presentencing portion of this guilty plea murder case, the accused unsuccessfully attempted to introduce documentary evidence concerning how leniently his co-actor had been treated in Philippine court. Rejecting the accused's contention that this evidence would have demonstrated a basis for the co-actor to lie about the accused's being the criminal mastermind, this court said that there was no showing of any relationship between how the co-actor had been treated and her testimony against the accused. The court went on to say that under such circumstances, it was not inclined to presume such a relationship existed.

United States v. Fayne, 26 M.J. 528, 531 (A.F.C.M.R. 1988): Referring to this case as "a domestic dispute that escalated into a court-martial," the court held defense counsel should have been permitted to cross-examine the "victim spouse" about her extramarital relationship with another prosecution witness. Such testimony was evidence of bias on her part and a motive to misrepresent.

United States v. Johnson, 20 M.J. 610 (A.F.C.M.R. 1985): The court held that this provision allowed trial counsel to cross-examine a key defense witness concerning that witness's alleged homosexual relationship with the accused. However, the court also said that trial counsel must be able to establish an "independent basis" for his questions should they be challenged by the defense.

[l]   Evidence of Bias—Relationship to Rule 613—Extrinsic Evidence of Inconsistent Statements

Air Force Court of Criminal Appeals

United States v. Vines, 57 M.J.519 (A.F. Ct.Crim.App. 2002): Affirming the accused's convictions for rape, indecent acts and related offenses, this court held that trial defense counsel was competent in presenting evidence used to impeach the victim and show that she had a bias to fabricate the charges against his client. The court indicted that over government objection, defense counsel cross-examined the victim about numerous prior allegations of rape she had made to co-workers concerning her previous boyfriend. When the victim denied making these allegations, defense counsel introduced the co-workers' testimony regarding the prior rape allegations.

[m]   Evidence of Bias—Sentencing

Air Force Court of Criminal Appeals

United States v. Alis, 47 M.J. 817 (A.F.Ct.Crim.App. 1998): The accused was the staff judge advocate at Mountain Home Air Force Base. Pursuant to his pleas, he was convicted of fraternization, sodomy, and conduct unbecoming an officer, and sentenced to dismissal, six months confinement, and ancillary punishments. Affirming the accused's convictions and punishment, the court found that no error occurred when the accused was prohibited from introducing evidence of bias against an aggravation witness. The court held that, even though the aggravation witness had experienced duty performance difficulties wholly apart from any involvement with the accused, that was not a sufficient basis to demonstrate that the witness would lie or otherwise misrepresent the truth to ingratiate himself with the command.

[n]   Evidence of Bias—Specificity Required

United States Court of Appeals for the Armed Forces

United States v. Owen, 24 M.J. 390 (C.M.A. 1987): Affirming the accused's rape and sodomy convictions, the court said in dictum that "to a considerable extent, Mil. R. Evid. 608(c) appears to swallow Mil. R. Evid.

608(b). If the extrinsic evidence of conduct is offered to attack the *credibility* of a witness, it is ostensibly inadmissible under 608(b). However, if the same extrinsic evidence is offered to show that the witness is *biased*, etc., it is admissible under 608(c)." Here defense counsel failed to specify which tactic he intended to use in attacking the prosecutrix, and the court refused to guess.

§ 609.01   Official Text

Rule 609.   Impeachment by Evidence of Conviction of Crime.

(a) *General rule.* For the purpose of attacking the credibility of a witness, (1) evidence that a witness other than the accused has been convicted of a crime shall be admitted, subject to Mil. R. Evid. 403, if the crime was punishable by death, dishonorable discharge, or imprisonment in excess of one year under the law under which the witness was convicted, and evidence that an accused has been convicted of such a crime shall be admitted if the military judge determines that the probative value of admitting this evidence outweighs its prejudicial effect to the accused; and (2) evidence that any witness has been convicted of a crime shall be admitted if it involved dishonesty or false statement, regardless of the punishment. In determining whether a crime tried by court-martial was punishable by death, dishonorable discharge, or imprisonment in excess of one year, the maximum punishment prescribed by the President under Article 56 at the time of the conviction applies without regard to whether the case was tried by general, special, or summary court-martial.

(b) *Time limit.* Evidence of a conviction under this rule is not admissible if a period of more than ten years has elapsed since the date of the conviction or of the release of the witness from the confinement imposed for that conviction, whichever is the later date, unless the court determines, in the interests of justice, that the probative value of the conviction supported by specific facts and circumstances substantially outweighs its prejudicial effect. However, evidence of a conviction more than ten years old as calculated herein, is not admissible unless the proponent gives to the adverse party sufficient advance written notice of intent to use such evidence to provide the adverse party with a fair opportunity to contest the use of such evidence.

(c) *Effect of pardon, annulment, or certificate of rehabilitation.* Evidence of a conviction is not admissible under this rule if (1) the conviction has been the subject of a pardon, annulment, certificate of rehabilitation, or other equivalent procedure based on a finding of the rehabilitation of the person convicted, and that person has not been convicted of a subsequent crime which was punishable by death, dishonorable discharge, or imprisonment in excess of one year, or (2) the conviction has been the subject of a pardon, annulment, or other equivalent procedure based on a finding of innocence.

(d) *Juvenile adjudications.* Evidence of juvenile adjudications is generally not admissible under this rule. The military judge, however, may allow evidence of a juvenile adjudication of a witness other than the accused if conviction of the offense would be admissible to attack the credibility of an adult and the military judge is satisfied that admission in evidence is necessary for a fair determination of the issue of guilt or innocence.

(e) *Pendency of appeal.* The pendency of an appeal therefrom does not render evidence of a conviction inadmissible except that a conviction by summary court-martial or special court-martial without a military judge may not be used for purposes of impeachment until review has been completed pursuant to Article 64 or Article 66 if applicable. Evidence of the pendency of an appeal is admissible.

(f) *Definition.* For purposes of this rule, there is a "conviction" in a court-martial case when a sentence has been adjudged.

§ 609.02   Editorial Comment

[1]   Bases for the Rule

Rule 609, like pre-Military Rules of Evidence practice, the common law, and its Federal Rules of Evidence counterpart—provides that any witness, including an accused, can have his or her credibility challenged with evidence of previous qualifying convictions.[1] The rationale for admitting this proof is that certain convictions enable the finder of fact being able to assess a witness's credibility because such convictions demonstrate that the witness has violated the law, and witnesses who have violated the law are more likely to lie than witnesses who have not.

Although this rationale applies to a testifying accused as much as to other witnesses, it is obvious that a particular danger exists here because court members might convict an impeached accused simply because they perceived him or her to be a bad person, and not pay sufficient attention to whether the charged offense was proved beyond a reasonable doubt. The possibility of prejudice under these circumstances is similar to that which occurs when the government uses proof of other criminal acts under Rules 404(b), 413 or 414. Throughout Congressional debate on Federal Rule 609, a central issue was how to balance the probative value of prior convictions against the danger they would be impermissibly used as propensity evidence, particularly against an accused. Congress searched for a rule that would fairly assist fact-finders in assessing a witness's credibility, but one

---

[1] *See, e.g.,* United States v. Lopez-Medina, 596 F.3d 716 (10th Cir. 2009) (cross-examiner entitled to elicit the nature of conviction offered to impeach but not to inquire about the specific underlying facts and circumstances). *See* Schlueter, Saltzburg, Schinasi & Imwinkelried, MILITARY EVIDENTIARY FOUNDATIONS § 5-11 (4th ed. 2010) (sample foundation for impeaching witness with prior conviction).

that would also protect the accused from unfair prejudice. The original provision was amended by Congress in 1991. In turn, both were adopted by the military.

From a historical point of view, pre-rules practice bears little resemblance to Rule 609. Because the military and federal versions of this Rule are so similar, court-martial practice is now directly linked to all the federal nuances. As one might expect, however, the military drafters have added some wrinkles of their own to Rule 609.

[2]   Rule 609(a)—General Rule

[a]   Implementing the Rule

This subdivision provides that certain, but not all convictions, can be used to attack a witness's credibility.[2] It is important to remember that, if evidence of a previous conviction is not offered for credibility purposes, this provision does not apply. For example, an accused is charged with drug trafficking. On direct he says that he has never used, seen, or handled controlled substances. government counsel on cross-examination could then introduce evidence of the accused's previous drug use conviction. Here the conviction is admitted to contradict the accused's testimony on a relevant issue. Admission would not be based on Rule 609.

However, when a previous conviction is offered for credibility purposes, the Rule provides two general standards controlling admissibility of felony convictions; one applies only to the accused, and one is for all other witnesses. *Crimen falsi* convictions, either felony or misdemeanor, are automatically admissible against a witness, including the accused. Traditionally, convictions that qualify for use can be proved by counsel asking the witness if he or she has ever been convicted of a crime, or counsel can introduce a public record demonstrating the conviction.

The Rule identifies two distinct categories of qualifying convictions.[3] Convictions for offenses punishable by death, dishonorable discharge, or imprisonment in excess of one year under the law of the prosecuting jurisdiction may be admitted.[4] *Crimen falsi* convictions must be admitted.

---

[2] *See, e.g.,* United States v. Bogers, 635 F.2d 749 (8th Cir. 1980) (fact that the impeaching conviction took place six months after the charged crime was no bar to its admission).

[3] Rule 410 discusses *nolo contendere* pleas. For the purposes of admission under this Rule, a judgment entered as a result of a nolo plea possesses the same finality and legal status as a jury conviction. *See* United States v. Williams, 642 F.2d 136 (5th Cir. 1981) (admitting *nolo* convictions clearly within Rule 609's provisions; United States v. Williams, 642 F.2d 136 (5th Cir. 1981) (convictions based upon pleas of *nolo contendere* are admissible because such a plea "admits every essential element of the offense" and because Rule 609 "creates no difference between convictions according to the pleas that preceded them").

[4] *See, e.g.,* United States v. Mansaw, 714 F.2d 785 (8th Cir. 1983) (misdemeanor prostitution conviction not admissible to impeach government witness).

With respect to previous military convictions, subdivision (a)(2) specifically provides that the maximum punishment is to be determined by reference to Article 56 of the Uniform Code of Military Justice. As a result, the level of court-martial that tried the accused is not relevant; only the maximum possible punishment for the charged offense will affect admissibility.[5]

Both military and federal courts have struggled with how much detail about the previous conviction should be admitted.[6] Some allow punishment to be revealed; others do not.[7] In *United States v. Rojas*,[8] the court evaluated existing federal authority and determined that while facts indicating the number, date, and nature of each previous conviction can be admitted, Rule 609 is not authority for admitting details about the adjudged sentence or crime. In that court's view, such evidence is simply too prejudicial. In *Gora v. Costa*,[9] the court held that counsel should be permitted to prove the crime charged, the date of the offense, and the disposition of the charges. It should be noted, however, that additional testimony can be admitted during a Rule 104 hearing conducted to establish the (a)(2), *crimen falsi*, nature of a previous conviction.

[b] Motions *in Limine*

Rule 609 will often require military judges to make difficult balancing determinations.[10] For example, as will be discussed, courts have to decide whether a particular conviction is a dishonesty offense that is automatically admissible, or whether it is a non-crimen falsi conviction requiring the court to strike a difficult balance between prejudicial effect and probative value.

---

[5] Adoption of the Rule also changed former *Manual* practice, which permitted certain non-federal convictions to be used if they were considered to be of comparable gravity to a federal felony; now the law of the convicting jurisdiction and the punishment provided there are looked to exclusively.

[6] *See, e.g.,* United States v. Swanson, 9 F.3d 1354 (8th Cir. 1993) (although government should not delve into specific details surrounding prior convictions, a different situation is presented when an accused, on direct, attempts to explain away his conviction; here, the defendant may be cross-examined on facts relevant to his direct testimony); United States v. Lipscomb, 702 F.2d 1049 (D.C. Cir. 1983) (*en banc*) (trial court has discretion to decide how much background information it needs concerning a conviction in order to balance).

[7] *See, e.g.,* United States v. Tumblin, 551 F.2d 1001 (5th Cir. 1977) (error occurred when the prosecutor cross-examined the accused concerning the length of the accused's confinement, the period of freedom between release and the next arrest, and the accused's unemployment between confinements; impeachment limited to proving the fact, date and nature of the conviction).

[8] 15 M.J. 902 (N.M.C.M.R. 1983).

[9] 971 F.2d 1325 (7th Cir. 1992).

[10] *See, e.g.,* United States v. Del Toro Soto, 676 F.2d 13 (1st Cir. 1982) (upholding *in limine* ruling by trial judge that a defendant in a mail theft case could be impeached with 1971 convictions for drug possession and grand larceny).

We believe that in most cases, motions *in limine*[11] will benefit: (1) both parties by giving them advance notice on how an important trial issue will likely be resolved; (2) the military judge who will need time and counsels' preparation to correctly decide difficult issues; and (3) the appellate court which will need as complete a record as possible to understand what occurred below. While such motions are often resolved before the court-martial begins, even when the bench decides to reserve its decision, all trial participants will be aware of the potential issues and can assure that, until the court rules, potentially excludable evidence is not placed before the members.

Particularly with respect to Rule 609 issues, motions *in limine* are very helpful to both trial and defense counsel. From the accused's point of view, knowing whether potentially devastating evidence of his previous criminal misconduct will be admitted if he or she testifies is crucial to determining trial strategy in a contest, and even more important for conducting meaningful pretrial negotiations with the government, Knowing in advance of trial whether this very important evidence will be admissible makes it possible for both parties to protect their interests in a way that would be impossible otherwise. Trial judges should be sensitive to these realities.[12]

Current military and Supreme Court practice treat Rule 609 and related motion practice essentially the same. In *Luce v. United States*,[13] the Court held that federal defendants who do not testify are prohibited from appealing a trial judge's decision allowing them to be impeached with evidence of previous convictions.[14] This resolution permits the trial bench to make *in limine* resolutions without worrying about defendants who have no intention of testifying and are only creating hypothetical issues for appellate purposes. In the Court's opinion, requiring defendants to testify under these circumstances will enable reviewing courts "to determine the impact erroneous impeachment may have in light of the record as a whole. This tends to discourage counsel from making motions to exclude impeachment evidence solely to 'plant' reversible error in the event of conviction."

The United States Court of Appeals for the Armed Forces followed the *Luce* rationale in *United States v. Sutton*.[15] There the court reversed the

---

[11] *See* our discussion of Rule 103, Rulings on Evidence, and Rule 104, Preliminary Questions.

[12] *See, e.g.,* United States v. Burkhead, 646 F.2d 1283 (8th Cir. 1981) (while the bench generally retains discretion as to whether to rule *in limine,* refusal here led to reversal).

[13] 469 U.S. 38 (1984).

[14] *See, e.g.,* United States v. Hendershot, 614 F.2d 648 (9th Cir. 1980) (to preserve an adverse *in limine* ruling, the accused need state his intention to testify and the nature of his testimony); United States v. Halbert, 668 F.2d 489 (10th Cir. 1982) (that trial judge should assure that defendant will testify if his *in limine* motion to exclude convictions is successful).

[15] 31 M.J. 11 (C.M.A. 1990). *Sutton* reversed existing military practice that adopted an

accused's drug-use conviction, on other grounds, but held that the defense must present evidence on an *in limine* issue in order to preserve any potential error for appeal. The Court said its decision was designed to encourage *in limine* resolutions, and military judges' willingness[16] to resolve complex and important evidentiary issues before trial.

Similarly, counsel and judges should be aware of the Supreme Court's holding in *Ohler v. United States*.[17] There the Court held that an accused who preemptively introduces evidence of her prior conviction during direct examination may not claim on appeal that the admission of that conviction was error. This result was obtained even though Government counsel had made a successful pretrial motion to use the conviction against the accused if she testified.[18]

[3]   Rule 609(a)(1)—Felony Convictions

[a]   In General

In 1993, Change 6,[19] *Manual for Courts-Martial*, amended Military Rule of Evidence 609(a). This change specifically clarified how counsel and military judges could use proof of previous convictions. The Drafter's Analysis indicates that their amendment closely resembles its federal counterpart, which was adopted in December 1991.

The change to Rule 609 did two important things. First, it removed the language prohibiting evidence of a previous conviction from being elicited during direct examination. Second, it better defined the relationship between Rules 403 and 609, as they concern impeachment of witnesses other than the accused.

---

approach at odds with *Luce*. For example, in United States v. Gamble, 27 M.J. 298 (C.M.A. 1988), the court stated that "whatever might be the rule in federal district courts, the evidentiary issue raised by the accused's motion *in limine* was properly preserved for appellate review even though the accused failed to testify."

[16] However, in United States v. Cannon, 33 M.J. 376 (C.M.A. 1991), the court held that nothing requires trial judges to decide *in limine* objections at the time they are made. In the court's opinion, circumstances may auger in favor of waiting until the issue has been more fully developed at trial. *See also* United States v. Jones, 43 M.J. 708 (A.F. Ct.Crim.App. 1995) (judges not required to rule at trial if they feel hearing the witness' actual trial testimony will help more accurately resolve the matter).

[17] 529 U.S. 753 (2000).

[18] *See* our discussion of Rule 607, *supra*. Defense counsel specifically should be aware of the tension which now exists concerning the tactical decision of preemptively removing the sting from harmful impeachment evidence they know the government has and will use against their client, and the possibility of waiving any potential error which may be associated with that evidence's admission. *See, e.g., United States v. El-Alamin,* 574 F.3d 915 (8th Cir. 2009) (because accused introduced his prior convictions, he waived his right to appeal trial court's denial of his motion in limine to exclude evidence of the convictions).

[19] Exec. Order No. 12888, 58 FED. REG. 248 (1993).

[b]   When Impeachment Can Occur

The original Rule's requirement that evidence of previous convictions could only be admitted during cross-examination was found to be inapplicable by military and federal appellate courts.[20] The limitation was inconsistent with Rule 607's specific language allowing the credibility of a witness to be attacked by any party, including the party calling the witness. Similarly, Rule 611 was viewed as providing whatever additional authority might be needed to conduct effective direct and cross-examination.

The Federal Advisory Committee's Note[21] highlights that this amendment was not intended to encourage proving convictions by extensive witness examination. In the Committee's view, that procedure might waste time and mislead the finders of fact.[22] Counsel will more effectively impeach a witness by introducing applicable documentary evidence, particularly when it is contained in the witness's official military personnel file.

[c]   Impeaching the Accused vs. Impeaching Other Witnesses

The second change to Rule 609(a) removed the ambiguity surrounding how the balance between probative value and prejudicial effect should be viewed when convictions are introduced against witnesses other than the accused.[23] The 1993 change left the existing special balancing test for an accused who testifies unaffected—to be excluded, the conviction's probative value need simply be outweighed by its prejudicial effect upon the defendant.[24] This is a higher and more difficult standard for the offering party to overcome Rule 403's provisions, which now specifically apply to all witnesses other than the accused.[25] For nonaccused witnesses, Rule 403 requires that otherwise admissible evidence of a previous conviction be excluded only if its probative value is *substantially* outweighed by the danger of unfair prejudice.[26]

The need for two standards is a reflection of how important and

---

[20] *See, e.g.*, United States v. Bad Cob, 560 F.2d 877 (8th Cir. 1977) (counsel permitted to anticipate and remove the "sting" of impeachment).

[21] *See* 3 S. Saltzburg, M. Martin & D. Capra, FEDERAL RULES OF EVIDENCE MANUAL § 609.02[4] (9th ed. 2006).

[22] *Id.*

[23] *See* Green v. Bock Laundry Mach. Co., 490 U.S. 504 (1989) (no balancing applicable to witnesses other than an accused).

[24] This standard is often referred to as the preponderance or 50/50 balancing test.

[25] Sometimes the standard for applying this evidence requires that it actually be more helpful than harmful to be admitted. In any event, there will be no presumption of admissibility where the accused might be harmed.

[26] In close cases, the drafters intended that the evidence should be admitted rather than excluded. *See* United States v. Teeter, 12 M.J. 716 (A.C.M.R. 1981) (balance should be exercised generally "in favor of admission").

potentially devastating conviction evidence can be on guilt or innocence determinations. Criminal defendants face unique prejudicial risks when Rule 609 evidence is offered against them. Fact-finders may misinterpret conviction evidence as proof of the accused's criminal propensity or disposition to commit criminal offenses. This is so even where the military judge provides tailored limiting instructions.[27] Thus, the amended Rule continues to require that, when offered against the accused, a previous conviction's *impeachment* value must outweigh its criminal character *propensity* prejudicial effect.

Bifurcating Rule 609 has placed defense witnesses in the same position as all other non-accused witnesses. Rule 403 protections apply. The special accused-only balancing test does not. This is because the danger of unfair prejudice diminishes when there is no risk that a conviction will be misused as propensity evidence—which is most likely when the accused is impeached.

Rule 403 adequately addresses the possibility that fact-finders could view the accused's witnesses as criminally predisposed to commit crimes, and that this conclusion might then "spill-over" to the accused, unfairly prejudicing his or her defense. Even in cases where a defense witness is so closely aligned with the accused that it may be difficult for the finders of fact to distinguish between the two, Rule 403's balancing provisions should be sufficient, provided that counsel and the military judge explore the specific circumstances in each case.

The following criteria are among those which can be considered in evaluating the Rule's balancing requirements as they pertain to the accused:

(1) How important is the accused's testimony to the truth-finding process?

(2) Did the prior offense display a conscious disregard for the requirements of the law?

(3) Was the prior crime so similar to the charged offense that it may tend to be misused as evidence of the accused's general bad character?

(4) Is there other better impeachment evidence?

(5) Is it unfair to permit the accused to be unimpeached if other witnesses are impeached?

(6) Will the case turn in large measure on the credibility of the accused?

(7) How old is the prior conviction? and

(8) What has the witness's conduct been following the conviction?

These are not easy factors to apply and judges will differ on how much weight to give each. Many federal appellate courts have pointed out the wisdom of trial judges who state their reasons for Rule 609(a)(1) rulings on

---

[27] *See* our discussion of Rule 105.

the record.[28] The rationale for this practice is the same as that supporting special findings pursuant to Rule 403 determinations.

[d]   Protecting Government Witnesses

The 1993 change also established that the government is entitled to Rule 403 protection for its witnesses.[29] This portion of the change was based, in part, on the Supreme Court's holding in *Green v. Bock Laundry Machine Co.*[30] There the Court addressed whether the balancing test could be used to protect prosecution and civil witnesses as well as criminal defendants under Federal Rule of Evidence 609(a)(1). It held that (a)(1) only protects criminal defendants, and that Rule 403 could not be used to exclude evidence of prior convictions offered to impeach witnesses other than a criminal defendant who decides to testify.

Federal and military drafters believed that both the government and the defense have an equal interest in finders of fact not turning impeachment evidence into criminal propensity character testimony. Such conversions do not serve the interests of justice.[31]

However, existing military and federal practice demonstrate that, under most circumstances, the risk of unfairly prejudicing the government's case by impeaching its witnesses with evidence of their previous convictions is low.[32] A government witness's conduct is not the subject of trial, and the government's interests can be effectively protected by Rule 403. As with defense witnesses, special concern must be provided to government witnesses who occupy an unusually compelling position in the litigation.[33]

[4]   Rule 609(a)(2)—*Crimen Falsi* Convictions

Rule 609(a)(2) addresses the second category of convictions that may be

---

[28] *See, e.g.,* United States v. Key, 717 F.2d 1206 (8th Cir. 1983) and United States v. Fountain, 642 F.2d 1083 (7th Cir. 1981). In both cases the courts expressed a distinct preference for trial judges to explain the factors they considered in exercising this Rule's balancing provisions, but both affirmed convictions even though no explanations were given. *See also* United States v. Key, 717 F.2d 1206 (8th Cir. 1983) (court expresses preference for on-the-record balancing, but presumes in this case the balancing was done); United States v. Fountain, 642 F.2d 1083 (7th Cir. 1981) (although reviewing court favored trial judges using special findings to balance (a)(1) factors, the conviction here was affirmed without them).

[29] *See* United States v. Thorne, 547 F.2d 56 (8th Cir. 1976), and United States v. McCray, 15 M.J. 1086 (A.C.M.R. 1983) (government witnesses entitled to no protection).

[30] 490 U.S. 504 (1989).

[31] *See, e.g.,* United States v. Valencia, 61 F.3d 616 (8th Cir. 1995) (discussing the balance between using previous criminal acts evidence under both 609 and 404(a)).

[32] *See, e.g.,* United States v. Nevitt, 563 F.2d 406 (9th Cir. 1977) (discussing whether government witnesses need protection from evidence of their prior convictions).

[33] As Davis v. Alaska, 415 U.S. 308 (1974), establishes, military judges must ensure that an accused's constitutional right to confrontation is not abridged by limiting his ability to present impeachment evidence.

admitted—the so called, *crimen falsi* convictions.[34] In this provision, however, the balancing test is abandoned.[35] In its place is a standard providing that all convictions involving "dishonesty or false statements" are admissible.[36]

This classification is meant to be more restrictive than (a)(1), allowing admission only if the previous offense, felony or misdemeanor, involved *crimen falsi*,[37] that is the intent to lie or to make a false or misleading statement. Under this provision, crimes that contain a statutory element which requires proof of criminal fraud, perjury, false statement, embezzlement, or false pretenses would be automatically admissible.[38] As a result, prior military convictions for fraud against the government (Article 132); uttering worthless checks (Article 123(a)), and related offenses will be automatically admissible, even though their maximum punishments are below subdivision (a)(1)'s requirements. The drafters felt this result was necessary because *crimen falsi* convictions most clearly demonstrate a witness's credibility.[39] Without (a)(1)'s balancing, all *crimen falsi* convictions may be admissible against either party, absent constitutional problems of military due process and fundamental fairness, or timeliness problems under Rule 609(b).[40] If a conviction qualifies under (a)(2) as well as under (a)(1), then the balancing by (a)(1) is unnecessary.

A substantial gray area exists with respect to offenses that are not crimen

---

[34] *See generally*, Martin, *Narrowing The Doorway: What Constitutes a Crimen Falsi Conviction Under Revised Military Rule of Evidence 609(a)(2)?*, ARMY LAW., Sep. 2010, at 35.

[35] *See, e.g.*, United States v. Toney, 615 F.2d 277 (5th Cir. 1980) (while Rule 403 cannot be used to exclude dishonesty convictions, a persuasive dissent opined that "in cases where the possibility of prejudice is extremely great," trial judge discretion is desirable).

[36] *See, e.g.*, United States v. Gellman, 677 F.2d 65 (11th Cir. 1982) (defense witness in prosecution for failure to file a tax return properly impeached with his own failure to file since this was a dishonesty offense); Zukowski v. Dunton, 650 F.2d 30 (4th Cir. 1981) (misdemeanor conviction for willfully failing to provide income tax information qualifies under (a)(2)); United States v. Mucci, 630 F.2d 737 (10th Cir. 1980) (a misdemeanor conviction for issuing or transferring a check with knowledge that it could be dishonored qualifies as a dishonesty offense).

[37] *See, e.g.*, United States v. Brackeen, 969 F.2d 827 (9th Cir. 1992) (*en banc*) (joining other circuits, this court held that robbery is not a crime of "dishonesty or false statement").

[38] *See, e.g.*, United States v. Coats, 652 F.2d 1002 (D.C. Cir. 1981) ((a)(2) convictions are automatically admissible in evidence).

[39] *See e.g.*, United States v. Harper, 527 F.3d 396 (5th Cir. 2008) (because misdemeanor conviction for theft- by-check has as an element "an act of dishonesty or false statement" it is not subject to balancing under Rule 609(a)(2)).

[40] *Compare* United States v. Dixon, 547 F.2d 1079 (9th Cir. 1976) (characterizing such evidence as automatically admissible) *with* United States v. Toney, 615 F.2d 277 (5th Cir. 1980) (persuasive dissent indicated that in those cases where the possibility of prejudice is "extremely great," trial judge discretion is desirable).

falsi per se, but which may actually have a dishonesty or false statement component.[41] The question in this area concerns whether the proponent is allowed to look behind the conviction and prove its *crimen falsi* character if it was not apparent from or part of the charge itself.[42]

Many federal courts have held that counsel can show the dishonest or deceitful manner in which the crime was committed.[43] *In United States v. Hayes,*[44] the court discussed how a conviction for importing cocaine could come within (a)(2)'s definition, if the government established it was based upon false written or oral statements made to customs officials. However, if the crime was founded on nothing more than secrecy or stealth, then it would have to qualify under Rule 609(a)(1).[45]

In either event, the proponent must affirmatively establish the offense's *crimen falsi* properties if she is to be successful.[46] Other courts refuse to automatically admit offenses that were not charged with a *crimen falsi* component.[47] Those courts look exclusively to the statutory elements of the offense, and find irrelevant the manner with which the crime was committed.[48]

If a military judge concludes that a conviction is inadmissible as *crimen falsi*, the conviction still may be admissible under (a)(1). Moreover, even if the conviction itself is not admitted, counsel may ask about the specific acts under Rule 608(b). Although Rule 403's balancing provisions will apply, the proponent has a strong argument in favor of permitting questions as long as the facts involve some element of deceit.

When Federal Rule of Evidence 609 was amended in 1990, the Advisory

---

[41] *See, e.g.,* United States v. Whitman, 665 F.2d 313 (10th Cir. 1981) (larceny offense is a dishonesty offense if it involved fraudulent or deceitful means).

[42] *See, e.g.,* United States v. Grandmont, 680 F.2d 867 (1st Cir. 1982) (robbery offenses not *per se* dishonesty offenses, but government can show that they involved deceit or false statement; purse snatching not dishonesty offense but properly admitted under (a)(1)).

[43] *See, e.g.,* United States v. Givens, 767 F.2d 574 (9th Cir. 1985) (*crimen falsi* aspect of theft offense allowed to be proven).

[44] 553 F.2d 824, 827 (2d Cir.), *cert. denied,* 434 U.S. 867 (1977).

[45] It should be noted that subdivision (a)(2) covers all witnesses, including an accused, and gives no more protection to an accused than it gives to the government.

[46] *See, e.g.,* United States v. Cameron, 814 F.2d 403 (7th Cir. 1987) (court narrowly constructed 609(a)(2) holding that the statutory basis of the impeaching crime did not include a *crimen falsi* provision).

[47] *See, e.g.,* United States v. Mehrmanesh, 689 F.2d 822 (9th Cir. 1982) (drug smuggling not dishonesty offense absent showing that fraud or deceit was employed); United States v. Slade, 627 F.2d 293 (D.C. Cir. 1980) (unlicensed possession of a pistol is not a dishonesty crime).

[48] *See, e.g.,* United States v. Lewis, 626 F.2d 940 (D.C. Cir. 1980) (in this drug prosecution, court found that charging not the manner of criminal commission was what determined automatic *crimen falsi* admissibility).

Committee declined to amend Rule 609(a)(2) to more clearly indicate what might be admitted as *crimen falsi* offenses. Recently, however, the Advisory Committee on the Federal Rules of Evidence proposed an amendment to Federal Rule 609(a), to resolve the controversy over what sorts of crimes fall into this category. As amended, the rule would read as follows:

Rule 609. Impeachment by Evidence of Conviction of Crime

(a) General rule—For the purpose of attacking the character for truthfulness of a witness,

(2) evidence that any witness has been convicted of a crime shall be admitted regardless of the punishment, if it readily can be determined that establishing the elements of the crime required proof or admission of an act of dishonesty or false statement by the witness.

According to the accompanying Committee Note, the Advisory Committee intended to amend Rule 609(a)(2) to reflect that that provision applies only when a false statement or act of dishonesty was the basis of the conviction. Thus, the rule does not apply in those situations where deceit was involved in committing the offense, but was not actually an element of the charged offense. The Note continues by pointing out that the amendment is intended to give effect to Congress's intent to limit the automatic features of Rule 609(a)(2) to those convictions for "crimes such as perjury, subornation of perjury, false statement, criminal fraud, embezzlement, or false pretense, or any other offense in the nature of crimen falsi, the commission of which involves some element of deceit, untruthfulness, or falsification bearing on the [witness's] propensity to testify truthfully."

The amendment to the Federal Rule is expected to take effect on December 1, 2006.

[5] Problems Not Addressed

As noted *above*, the pending amendment to Federal Rule 609(a)(2) will finally address the debate over what constitutes a *crimen falsi* offense, at least for federal cases. Under the operation of Military Rule of Evidence 1102, that amendment could become applicable to the military in June 2008, absent any changes by Congress to the Federal Rule, or intervening action by the President to amend Rule 609. In the meantime, military courts will no doubt continue to correctly and consistently apply a narrower definition of *crimen falsi*.[49]

Military and federal drafters have also refused to add specific language to the Rule indicating that prior conviction evidence is only admissible for impeachment purposes. They believed that, based on the Rule's title, the content of its first sentence, and its placement among the impeachment rules, further clarification is unnecessary.

---

[49] *See* United States v. Frazier, 14 M.J. 773 (A.C.M.R. 1982) (larceny and housebreaking viewed as not qualifying for admission under *crimen falsi* standards).

[6]   Rule 609(b)—Time Limit

Under Rule 609(b), evidence of a conviction generally will not be admissible if it is more than ten years old.[50] This timeliness requirement is not found in the common law, nor in previous *Manual* provisions.[51] The drafters have provided that the time is measured from the date of conviction or the date the witness was released from confinement,[52] whichever is later in time. Consequently, if the witness was convicted of robbery in 2004 and confined for two years thereafter, he or she could be impeached with the conviction until 2016.[53]

Rule 609(b)'s legislative history indicates that the drafters created a strong presumption against the use of stale convictions, but permitted it to be rebutted by a showing that: (1) the interests of justice require admission of an old conviction; (2) its probative value, supported by *specific* facts and circumstances,[54] substantially outweighs its prejudicial effect; and (3) the proponent of such evidence has provided the adverse party with "sufficient advance written notice" of an intent to use the evidence. In *United States v. Cavender*,[55] the court examined the Rule's balancing requirements and determined that Congress intended that the trial judge make special findings of fact as part of any Rule 609(b) resolution.

Rule 609(b) does not define the prior notice that is required. In the absence of a binding judicial definition we suggest that the following criteria be used:

(1) Opposing counsel should be given written notice, or an oral representation should be made on the record of the proponent's intentions to use such evidence;

(2) Where possible, the notice should be served at least 24 hours before

---

[50] *Compare,* United States v. Pritchard, 973 F.2d 905 (11th Cir. 1992) (no error in admitting defendant's conviction for burglary thirteen years prior to instant trial, because it was probative impeachment evidence of truthfulness), *with* United States v. Reeves, 730 F.2d 1189 (8th Cir. 1984) (no error in exclusion of 18-year-old breaking and entering conviction offered to impeach government witness); and United States v. Toner, 728 F.2d 115 (2d Cir. 1984) (evidence of stale convictions excluded).

[51] *See* United States v. Weaver, 1 M.J. 111 (C.M.A. 1975), for a discussion of pre-Rules practices.

[52] *See, e.g.,* United States v. Rogers, 542 F.3d 197 (7th Cir. 2008) (court held that "confinement" in Rule 609(b) referred to imprisonment and not periods of probation or parole).

[53] *See, e.g.,* United States v. Daniel, 957 F.2d 162 (5th Cir. 1992) (computation of ten-year period from date of conviction or release from confinement does not include probation periods).

[54] *See, e.g.,* United States v. Gilbert, 668 F.2d 94 (2d Cir. 1981) (a more than 10-year-old conviction for mail fraud could be used to impeach the defendant where the court made specific findings).

[55] 578 F.2d 528 (4th Cir. 1978).

the date of trial to permit in limine motions and rulings;[56]

(3) The notice should include a copy of any official, public, or other documentary evidence that will be used to establish the conviction;

(4) If such documentary evidence is not available, opposing counsel should be provided with a statement specifying where the witness was convicted, upon what charges, and based on what plea; and

(5) The statement should also specify what appellate review, if any, has taken place.

The proponent should be asked on the record why the interests of justice require the admission of this evidence. The opponent should be given a chance to be heard. The trial judge should state the ruling and the reasons therefore on the record.

Such a detailed requirement will limit frivolous issues, while providing opposing counsel with sufficient information upon which to prepare a challenge. However, as mentioned in our discussion of Rule 412's notice requirements, failure to comply should not automatically result in prohibiting counsel's use of his evidence. Instead the proceedings should be delayed until adequate notice and preparation can be accomplished.

It should also be noted that this limitation only applies to previous convictions used for impeachment, not for sentencing or other purposes.

[7]   Rule 609(c)—Effect of Pardon, Annulment, or Certificate of Rehabilitation

Rule 609(c) contains two specific limitations upon counsel's ability to use evidence of previous convictions. Subdivision (c)(1) states that, if an otherwise admissible conviction has been the subject of a pardon, annulment, certificate of rehabilitation, or similar process that is predicated upon a finding that the witness has rehabilitated himself, then evidence of that conviction will not be admissible.[57] If a witness has demonstrated conduct inconsistent with his or her criminal past, the drafters concluded that the past should no longer be used for impeachment. However, if after rehabilitation the witness is convicted of a crime punishable by death, dishonorable discharge, or confinement for more than a year, then evidence of the previous conviction will be admissible. Of course the timeliness limitations of Rule 609(b) apply here.

Military cases have considered whether completion of a course similar to those previously conducted by the Army's Retraining Brigade, or at the Air

---

[56] *See, e.g.,* United States v. Cofield, 11 M.J. 422 (C.M.A. 1981) (counsel and trial judges encouraged to use pretrial evidentiary hearings).

[57] *See, e.g.,* United States v. Pagan, 721 F.2d 24 (2d Cir. 1983) (certificate setting aside youthful offender's conviction and discharging him unconditionally is equivalent of finding of rehabilitation).

Force's 3320th Correction and Rehabilitation Squadron, qualify under the Rule's definition of rehabilitation. Notwithstanding the fact that Department of Defense Directives required all military confinement facilities to primarily rehabilitate those service members coming within their jurisdiction, *United States v. Rogers,*[58] held that an accused who satisfactorily completed the Army Retraining Brigade's program and who had been returned to duty had not undergone a sufficiently satisfactory rehabilitation to have his previous court-martial conviction excluded.

This decision is questionable. If an accused completes a service-sponsored rehabilitation program and satisfactorily returns to duty, Rule 609(c)(1)'s requirements would seem to have been met, and if so proof of the previous conviction should be inadmissible. The Drafters' Analysis is in accord with this view.[59]

Subdivision (c)(2) states that if a conviction has been the subject of a pardon, annulment, or related proceeding based on a finding of not guilty, then evidence of the conviction is not admissible. This second aspect of the Rule is more absolute than the first. If the witness is subsequently convicted of another offense of any description, proof of the original conviction still will be excluded, because the accused is deemed innocent and the conviction cannot, therefore, properly support an impeachment attempt.

[8]   Rule 609(d)—Juvenile Adjudications

Rule 609(d) provides that evidence of juvenile adjudications generally is not admissible, and may not be used against an accused. The Rule permits impeachment of witnesses other than the accused if the trial judge believes it is necessary to a fair resolution of the case, and the impeachment evidence would have been admissible had the witness previously been tried as an adult.

The drafters of subdivision (d) were sensitive to the public policy requirements that juveniles should not be stigmatized by their youthful misconduct. But the drafters also were concerned with problems of confrontation and compulsory process. The balance struck in 609(d) is consistent with the Supreme Court's Sixth Amendment decisions.[60]

---

[58] 17 M.J. 990 (A.C.M.R. 1984).

[59] *See generally* Schinasi & Green, *Impeachment by Prior Conviction, Military Rule of Evidence 609,* ARMY LAW. Jan. 1981, at 1.

[60] *Cf.* Davis v. Alaska, 415 U.S. 308 (1974), (society's desire to protect juveniles could not be used to frustrate an accused's constitutional right to a fair trial); Burr v. Sullivan, 618 F.2d 583 (9th Cir. 1980) (the accused's state conviction had to be reversed because the trial judge improperly prevented defense counsel from using evidence of juvenile adjudications against government witnesses who were also co-conspirators); United States v. Bates, 617 F.2d 585 (10th Cir. 1980) (the accused's conviction for being an accessory to murder was reversed because defense counsel seeking impeachment evidence was denied a transcript of

[9]   Rule 609(e) & (f)—Pendency of Appeal; Definition

Taken together, subdivisions (e) and (f) specify when the court-martial proceeding itself becomes a conviction for purposes of admissibility. Prior military authority permitted admission of convictions only after the appellate process was completed. These provisions partially change past practice, and partially adopt the current federal system.

Rule 609(f) states that a conviction occurs when the court-martial adjudges a sentence. Subdivision (e) states that, if the case was tried by a general court-martial, or a special court-martial empowered to adjudge a bad conduct discharge, then evidence of the conviction is admissible at any time after the sentence is adjudged. However, with respect to summary courts-martial and non-bad conduct discharge special courts-martial, the conviction is not admissible until it has been reviewed by a judge advocate or similarly legally-trained officer (*see* Article 64), and has undergone further appellate review where appropriate (*see* Article 66). Evidence that an appeal is pending will be admissible with respect to a general or punitive discharge special court-martial.[61] Such evidence may weaken the force of the impeachment but does not affect the admissibility of the conviction itself.[62]

These changes in military practice pose interesting practical problems. For instance, how will the accused's conviction be viewed if during a trial he or she was impeached with evidence of a prior conviction that was subsequently reversed? What if a key defense witness was impeached with a conviction that is subsequently reversed?

The first case, where the accused is the impeached witness, poses the greater chance of prejudice. But both situations raise the issue of whether a conviction should stand when a key witness is impeached on the basis of a conviction that is held to be invalid. A reviewing court would have to consider the following things: (1) the importance of the impeached witness's credibility; (2) the emphasis placed on the overturned conviction; (3) the other impeachment evidence used against the witness; (4) the likely impact of the evidence that the overturned conviction was on appeal; (5) the nature of the conviction and its likely impeachment effect; and (6) the possibility that the prior case will be retried and the conviction reinstated.

§ 609.03   Drafters' Analysis

[1]   General rules

Rule 609(a) is taken generally from the Federal Rule but has been slightly

---

a previous juvenile proceeding involving a participant in the murder who was a key government witness).

[61] *See, e.g.,* United States v. Klayer, 707 F.2d 892 (6th Cir. 1983) (state conviction may be used pending appeal, even though state courts do not permit such use).

[62] *See e.g.,* United States v. Jackson, 549 F.3d 963 (5th Cir. 2008) (accused had the right to present proof concerning a witness's appeal to ameliorate the impeachment).

modified to adapt it to military law. For example, an offense for which a dishonorable discharge may be adjudged may be used for impeachment. This continues the present rule as found in ¶ 153*b*(2)(b)(1) of the present *Manual*. In determining whether a military offense may be used for purposes of impeachment under Rule 609(a)(1), recourse must be made to the maximum punishment imposable if the offense had been tried by general court-martial. The Table of Maximum Punishments, ¶ 127*c,* and related sentencing provisions should be consulted.

Rule 609(a) differs slightly from the present military rule. Under Rule 609(a)(1), a civilian conviction's availability for impeachment is solely a function of its maximum punishment under "the law in which the witness was convicted." This is different from ¶ 153*b*(2)(b)(3) of the present *Manual* that allows use of a non-federal conviction analogous to a federal felony or characterized by the jurisdiction as a felony or "as an offense of comparable gravity." Under the new rule, comparisons and determinations of relative gravity will be unnecessary and improper.

Convictions that "involve moral turpitude or otherwise affect . . . credibility are admissible for impeachment under ¶ 153*b*(2)(b) of the present *Manual*. The list of potential convictions expressed in ¶ 153*b*(2)(b) is illustrative only and non-exhaustive. Unlike the *Manual* rule, Rule 609(a) is exhaustive.

Although a conviction technically fits within Rule 609(a)(1), its admissibility remains subject to a finding by the military judge that its probative value outweighs its prejudicial effect to the accused.

Rule 609(a)(2) makes admissible convictions involving "dishonesty or false statement, regardless of punishment." This is similar in intent to ¶ 153*b*(2)(b)(4) of the present *Manual* which makes admissible "a conviction of any offense involving fraud, deceit, larceny, wrongful appropriation, or the making of false statement." The exact meaning of "dishonesty" within the meaning of Rule 609 is unclear and has already been the subject of substantial litigation. The Congressional intent appears, however, to have been extremely restrictive with "dishonesty" being used in the sense of untruthfulness. *See generally* S. SALTZBURG & K. REDDEN, FEDERAL RULES OF EVIDENCE MANUAL 336–345 (2d ed. 1977). Thus, a conviction for fraud, perjury, or embezzlement would come within the definition, but a conviction for simple larceny would not. Pending further case development in the Article III courts, caution would suggest close adherence to this highly limited definition.

It should be noted that admissibility of evidence within the scope of Rule 609(a)(2) is not explicitly subject to the discretion of the military judge. The application of Rule 403 is unclear.

While the language of Rule 609(a) refers only to cross-examination, it would appear that the Rule does refer to direct examination as well. *See* the

Analysis to Rules 607 and 608(b). As defined in Rule 609(f), a court-martial conviction occurs when a sentence has been adjudged.

[2]   Time limit

Rule 609(b) is taken verbatim from the Federal Rule. As it has already been made applicable to the armed forces, *United States v. Weaver,* 1 M.J. 111 (C.M.A. 1975), it is consistent with the present military practice.

[3]   Effect of pardon, annulment, or certificate of rehabilitation

Rule 609(c) is taken verbatim from the Federal Rule except that convictions punishable by dishonorable discharge have been added. Rule 609(c) has no equivalent in present military practice and represents a substantial change as it will prohibit use of convictions due to evidence of rehabilitation. In the absence of a certificate of rehabilitation, the extent to which the various Armed Forces post-conviction programs, such as the Air Force's 3320th Correction and Rehabilitation Squadron and the Army's Retraining Brigade, come within Rule 609(c) is unclear, although it is probable that successful completion of such a program is "an equivalent procedure based on the finding of the rehabilitation of the person convicted" within the meaning of the Rule.

[4]   Juvenile adjudications

Rule 609(d) is taken from the Federal Rule without significant change. The general prohibition in the Rule is substantially different from ¶ 153*b*(2)(b) of the present *Manual* that allows use of juvenile adjudications other than those involving an accused. The discretionary authority vested in the military judge to admit such evidence comports with the accused's constitutional right to a fair trial, *Davis v. Alaska,* 415 U.S. 308 (1974).

[5]   Pendency of appeal

The first portion of Rule 609(e) is taken from the Federal Rule and is substantially different from ¶ 153*b*(2)(b) of the present *Manual* that prohibits use of convictions for impeachment purposes while they are undergoing appellate review. Under the Rule, the fact of review may be shown but does not affect admissibility. A different rule applies, however, for convictions by summary court-martial or by special court-martial without a military judge. The Committee believed that because a legally trained presiding officer is not required in these proceedings, a conviction should not be used for impeachment until legal review has been completed.

[6]   Definition

This definition of conviction has been added because of the unique nature of the court-martial. Because of its recognition that a conviction cannot result until at least sentencing, *cf.* Lederer, *Reappraising the Legality of Post-trial Interviews,* THE ARMY LAWYER, July, 1977, at 12, the Rule may modify *United States v. Mathews,* 6 M.J. 357 (C.M.A. 1979).

§ 609.04   Drafters' Analysis (1986)

Reference to "Article 65(c)" was changed to "Article 64" to correct an error in MCM, 1984.

§ 609.05   Drafters' Analysis (1993)

The amendment to Mil. R. Evid. 609(a) is based on the 1990 amendment to Fed. R. Evid. 609(a) The previous version of Mil. R. Evid. 609(a) was based on the now superseded version of the Federal Rule. This amendment removes from the rule the limitation that the conviction may only be elicited during cross-examination. Additionally, the amendment clarifies the relationship between Rules 403 and 609. The amendment clarifies that the special balancing test found in Mil. R. Evid. 609(a)(1) applies to the accused's convictions. The convictions of all other witnesses are only subject to the Mil. R. Evid. 403 balancing test. *See Green v. Bock Laundry Machine Co.*, 490 U.S. 504 (1989).

§ 609.06   Annotated Cases

[1]   Rule 609(a)—General Rule

[a]   Prior Convictions—Balancing Factors—Before 1993 Amendment

Supreme Court

Green v. Bock Laundry Machine Co., 490 U.S. 504 (1989): At trial, the defendant impeached the plaintiff with his prior felony convictions for burglary and a related offense. Noting that Federal Rule of Evidence 609(a)(1) is ambiguous with regard to its applicability in civil cases, the Court concluded that Congress intended that only an accused in a criminal case would have the benefit of the balancing of probative values and dangers. Thus, a trial judge has no discretion to use the Rule 403 balancing test in deciding whether to admit an impeaching conviction against a witness other than an accused in a criminal case.

United States Court of Appeals for the Armed Forces

United States v. Brenizer, 20 M.J. 78 (C.M.A. 1985): The accused unsuccessfully contended that his previous court-martial conviction should have been excluded because the military judge failed to explain, on the record, whether the probative value of the conviction outweighed its prejudicial effect. Without resolving this issue, the court itself conducted a very thorough analysis of the conviction's admissibility and found no error in its use at trial.

Army Court of Criminal Appeals

United States v. Collier, 27 M.J. 806 (A.C.M.R. 1989): Relying on *United States v. Brenizer,* 20 M.J. 78 (C.M.A. 1985), the court held that the accused's previous disrespect conviction was admissible at his court-martial for similar misconduct because its impeachment value was high, it occurred close in time to the charged offense, both the charged and previous offenses were similar in nature, the accused's testimony was crucial to his defense, and the accused's credibility was a central issue in this case. The court went on to say that "when an accused's credibility is on trial, it is preferable that as much information as possible be provided the court to aid it in its decision."

United States v. McCray, 15 M.J. 1086 (A.C.M.R. 1983): Finding error but no prejudice, the court stated that it was improper for the trial judge to balance the probative value of the government witness's prior convictions against the prejudicial effect on the impeached witness. "The balancing test required under Rule 609(a) does not permit consideration of potential prejudice to any witness except the accused."

[b]   Prior Convictions—Balancing Factors—Subsequent to the 1993 Amendment

Air Force Court of Criminal Appeal

United States v. Ross, 44 M.J. 534 (A.F.Ct.Crim.App. 1996): Charged with using marijuana, the accused testified that she was surprised by the positive urinalysis result. Thereafter, trial counsel sought to impeach the accused with evidence of her five-month-old conviction for similar misconduct. Over defense counsel's objection, the trial judge admitted the accused's conviction because (1) the previous offense was identical with the charged offense, (2) the previous offense was close in time to the charged offense, (3) the accused's credibility was a central issue, (4) her testimony was crucial, and (5) the conviction's probative value outweighed its prejudicial effect. The bench also provided appropriate limiting instructions. However, this court found harmless error in the military judge's failure to use Rule 609(a)(1)'s more restrictive accused's special balancing test which provides that the previous conviction's prejudicial effect to the accused "*simply outweigh,*" as opposed to Rule 403's "substantially outweigh," its probative value.

[c]   Prior Convictions—*Crimen Falsi* Convictions

Army Court of Criminal Appeals

United States v. Jenkins, 18 M.J. 583 (A.C.M.R. 1984): In dictum, the court noted that forgery offenses fall within Rule 609(a)(2)'s definition of crimes involving dishonesty or false statement.

United States v. Frazier, 14 M.J. 773 (A.C.M.R. 1982): The court found that, while the accused's previous civilian convictions for housebreaking and grand larceny would not qualify for admission under Rule 609(a)(2)'s *crimen falsi* standard, they were admissible under Rule 609(a)(1). The court also noted that the accused's prior marijuana conviction appeared inadmissible under either standard, but its use at trial did not constitute prejudicial error. Citing substantial federal authority, the court suggested that military judges use special findings when dealing with evidence in this area.

[d]   Prior Convictions—Motions *in Limine*

Supreme Court

Ohler v. United States, 529 U.S. 753 (2000): Affirming the accused's convictions for importation of marijuana and possession of marijuana, the Court held that an accused who preemptively introduces evidence of her prior conviction during direct examination may not claim on appeal that the admission of that conviction was error. This result was reached even though the government had made a successful pretrial motion to use the conviction against the accused if she testified.

Luce v. United States, 469 U.S. 38 (1984): During trial on federal drug charges, the accused's *in limine* motion to preclude the government from impeaching him with a previous conviction was denied. As a result the accused did not testify. Affirming conviction, the court held that to preserve such errors for review, defendants must testify at trial, notwithstanding the trial judge's adverse ruling. Without such testimony the court cannot weigh the conviction's probative value against its prejudicial effect. Any possible harm flowing from the trial court's ruling would be "conjecture" if it could not be measured against the accused's trial testimony. Further, without such testimony the court cannot know if the government would have actually used the conviction or if the accused would have testified. Requiring defendants to testify under these circumstances will enable reviewing courts "to determine the impact erroneous impeachment may have in light of the record as a whole, and tends to discourage making motions to exclude impeachment evidence solely to 'plant' reversible error in the event of conviction."

United States Court of Appeals for the Armed Forces

United States v. Cobia, 53 M.J. 305 (C.A.A.F. 2000): The accused was convicted of child sexual abuse offenses. Both the trial and defense counsel agreed that the accused was being tried at court-martial for the same offenses he pled guilty to in a State court proceeding. In limine, defense counsel unsuccessfully moved to suppress references to the accused's North Carolina convictions as either substantive or impeachment evidence. During the defense case-in-chief, the accused introduced the transcript of his State Court guilty plea hoping to "take the sting out" of his conviction. Relying on the Supreme Court's decision in *Ohler v. United States,* 529 U.S. 753 (2000), the court held that once the accused preemptively uses his previous conviction on direct examination, he may not later claim that its admission was erroneous. The Court went on to say that based on *United States v. Gray,* 51 M.J. 1, 25 (C.A.A.F. 1999) the accused's prior conviction could have been introduced as substantive evidence, not just credibility impeachment proof. Citing *Gray*; the court said, "guilty pleas and accompanying statements in one jurisdiction are generally admissible in other jurisdictions to prove the elements of the other crime. . . . Therefore, the transcript of the accused's North Carolina plea to similar offenses on the same dates is relevant and not collateral. The transcript is also admissible as prior inconsistent statements under Mil. R. Evid. 613, or [as substantive evidence] an admission under Mil. R. Evid. 801(d)(2)."

United States v. Miller, 48 M.J. 49 (C.A.A.F. 1998): The accused was convicted of conspiracy, robbery, and assault with the intent to commit robbery. In limine, defense counsel sought to protect his client from impeachment by a prior special court-martial conviction for assaulting an NCO. The trial judge refused to rule at that time, advising defense counsel to renew his motion during trial. Before the defense rested they renewed their motion. The judge indicated that until he heard the accused testify, he could not make a decision on the previous conviction's admissibility. Defense counsel then refused to place their client on the stand. Because this case was tried before *Luce v. United States*, 469 U.S. 38 (1984), became controlling on courts-martial, this court held that the issue was preserved for appeal despite the accused not testifying. Affirming the accused's convictions, this court held that the accused's previous conviction has some impeachment value because it demonstrated his "lack of respect for established order and would be relevant in determining whether appellant would 'take lightly his obligation to testify truthfully.' "

United States v. Bell, 44 M.J. 403 (C.A.A.F. 1996): During the accused's trial for robbery and robbery related offenses, defense counsel offered transcripts concerning the former testimony of two co-accused. Both transcripts provided an alibi defense. Trial counsel did not object to the statements, but offered evidence that the co-accused had already been convicted of the same offenses the accused was charged with. Defense counsel never offered the statements at trial but contends on appeal he was unfairly deprived of their important testimony. Affirming the accused's convictions, the court first held that no waiver occurred because they would not retroactively apply *Luce v. United States*, 469 U.S. 38 (1984) (evidence must be presented to preserve error for appeal not applied in the military until *United States v. Sutton*, 31 M.J. 11 (C.M.A. 1990), after the date of the charged offenses). The court then held that because it would have been permissible for trial counsel to impeach the two defense witnesses had they testified, it was permissible to impeach their Rule 801(d)(1) former testimony as well.

United States v. Sitton, 39 M.J. 307 (C.M.A. 1994): During his court-martial for absence without leave and larceny, the accused moved, *in limine*, to prevent trial counsel from impeaching a crucial defense witness with evidence of that witness's prior convictions. This court affirmed the military judge's decision to allow impeachment because the witness's credibility was important, the previous convictions were only three months old, and they involved offenses different from those facing the accused, mitigating the chance of guilt-by-association.

United States v. Gamble, 27 M.J. 298 (C.M.A. 1988): Notwithstanding its previous decisions in this area, the United States Court of Appeals for the Armed Forces departed from the Supreme Court's guidance in *Luce v. United States, above.* In *Gamble* the court stated that "whatever might be the rule in federal district courts, the evidentiary issue raised by appellant's motion *in limine* was properly preserved for appellate review" even though the accused failed to testify.

United States v. Cofield, 11 M.J. 422 (C.M.A. 1981): The court recognized that when an accused desires to testify in his own defense, the question whether the probative value of the conviction outweighs its prejudicial effect is extremely important and that defense counsel may seek a pretrial resolution of this issue by using a motion *in limine.* The court generally encouraged *in limine* resolutions but was also sensitive to the problems caused by pre-trial rulings. Without having heard all the evidence in a case, a court may find it more difficult to strike a proper balance between the importance and potential danger of particular evidence. And a judge who decides before trial to suppress specific evidence may be forced by a change in trial circumstances to reverse himself, which might mean a mistrial. We believe that a careful judge can make maximum use of *in limine* proceedings with minimum risk if he considers taking the following steps: (1) Obtain as much information concerning the previous conviction as possible (Rule 103(a)(2) offers of proof should be used here); (2) determine whether the accused actually intends to take the stand or what the probability that he will testify is; (3) if the accused is unsure of his strategy, consider delaying a ruling until the defense begins its case; (4) condition all *in limine* resolutions on the development of the facts indicated at the *in limine* hearing; (5) specify under what circumstances the *in limine* resolution may have to be abandoned; and (6) err on the side of protecting the accused from prejudice. If the court does refuse to rule *in limine,* its reasoning should be spread on the record. *See United States v. Gerard,* 11 M.J. 440 (C.M.A. 1981).

Army Court of Criminal Appeals

United States v. Clarke, 25 M.J. 631 (A.C.M.R. 1987): During the accused's indecent assault and sodomy trial, the government attempted to admit a 1982 rape conviction. Over defense objection, the military judge held that while he would "make a final ruling after we get further into the case . . . the defense should plan on admissibility of that conviction. . . ." In order to "steal the prosecution's thunder," defense counsel asked the accused about the conviction on direct examination. This court reasoned as follows: "appellant's failure to wait and assert his objection constituted waiver. . . . If admission of the prior conviction was erroneous, it was an error resulting from calculated defense strategy. Appellant should not benefit from an error he induced by a tactical decision."

Navy-Marine Corps Court of Criminal Appeals

United States v. Rusinskas, 35 M.J. 808 (N.M.C.M.R. 1992): The accused was convicted of numerous larceny and bad check offenses. *In limine*, defense counsel sought to exclude evidence of the accused's previous state court conviction for burglary. When the military judge overruled defense counsel's objection, the accused chose not to testify on the merits. Appellate defense counsel contended the state court conviction was improperly admitted. Affirming these convictions, the court held that, consistent with military and civilian authority, the accused's decision not to testify waived his right to appeal the military judge's holding.

[e]   Prior Convictions—Sentencing Proceedings—Rules Inapplicability

United States Court of Appeals for the Armed Forces

United States v. Barnes, 33 M.J. 468 (C.M.A. 1992): During the sentencing portion of the accused's trial for uniquely military offenses, drunk driving, and drug distribution, evidence of a previous civilian conviction for drunk driving was admitted. Without citing specific authority for his position, the accused contended that the government's use of this evidence was improper. Affirming both the sentence and findings, the court held that Rule 609(a)'s limitations on proof did not apply in the accused's case because his previous conviction was not used to impeach his credibility.

Navy-Marine Corps Court of Criminal Appeals

United States v. May, 18 M.J. 839 (N.M.C.M.R. 1984): The court held that this Rule does not provide the basis upon which to admit evidence of previous convictions during the sentencing portion of trial. By definition, the Rule applies only to matters affecting a witness's credibility, not to sentence appropriateness.

United States v. Rojas, 15 M.J. 902 (N.M.C.M.R. 1983): The court specifically relied on federal decisions limiting impeachment under this rule to: facts indicating the number of prior convictions, the nature of each crime, and the date of each conviction. It ruled that Rule 609 is not authority for admitting details about the sentence adjudged.

[f]   Prior Convictions—Specificity of Instructions

United States Court of Appeals for the Armed Forces

United States v. Collier, 29 M.J. 365 (C.MA. 1990): This case demonstrates that counsel and military judges must be precise in how they use impeachment evidence. Here the accused's disobedience conviction was reversed because trial counsel and the military judge improperly categorized the accused's previous incidents of misconduct as character evidence. The court also rejected government appellate counsel's argument that the extrinsic offenses were admissible under Rule 609. The military judge's instructions were tailored to Rule 404, and trial counsel had not established a sufficient 609 foundation to allow admission.

Air Force Court of Criminal Appeals

United States v. Huettenrauch, 16 M.J. 638 (A.F.C.M.R. 1983): Reversing a conviction, the court found that the accused's previous conviction for shoplifting was improperly admitted because it did not involve dishonesty or false statements, nor was it punishable by imprisonment for more than one year.

[g]   Prior Convictions—State Court Convictions

Coast Guard Court of Criminal Appeals

United States v. Ballard, 39 M.J. 1028 (C.G.C.M.R. 1994): The accused was convicted of assault with a dangerous weapon and violating a lawful general order. After testifying on the merits, the accused was impeached with two North Carolina misdemeanor larceny convictions which he alleged should not have been admitted. Affirming the accused's conviction, the court held that this evidence was properly used because even though North Carolina categorizes the offenses as misdemeanors, each carries a two-year maximum punishment which satisfies Rule 609(a)(1).

[h]   Prior Convictions—Summary Court-Martial Convictions and Nonjudicial Punishments

United States Court of Appeals for the Armed Forces

United States v. Brown, 23 M.J. 149 (C.M.A. 1987): The accused's conviction for distributing marihuana was reversed, because the military judge admitted evidence of a prior Article 15 involving marihuana. The court rejected the notion that such evidence qualifies as a prior conviction under this Rule, and held that the nonjudicial punishment added very little to the government's case and merely painted the accused as a bad person with a propensity to commit crimes.

Army Court of Criminal Appeals

United States v. Rogers, 17 M.J. 990 (A.C.M.R. 1984): Relying on *Middendorf v. Henry,* 425 U.S. 25 (1976) and *United States v. Cofield,* 11 M.J. 422 (C.M.A. 1981) the court found that "a summary court-martial where the accused was not represented by counsel cannot be used for impeachment purposes under Mil. R. Evid. 609(a)." However, this Rule does not apply to summary court-martials where the accused "affirmatively waives his right to be represented by counsel."

Navy-Marine Corps Court of Criminal Appeals

United States v. Casey, 45 M.J. 623 (N.M. Ct.Crim.App. 1996): The accused, while acting as the Bachelor Enlisted Quarters' desk supervisor, was charged with numerous offenses including larceny, dereliction of duty, and communicating a threat. He contended that error occurred when the military judge prohibited defense counsel from impeaching a government witness's credibility by using evidence of that witness's previous nonjudicial punishment for false swearing as proof of a prior conviction under Rule 609. Affirming the accused's convictions, this court held that nonjudicial punishment does not qualify as a conviction, and thus was inadmissible for that purpose. However, the underlying false statement would have been admissible under Rule 608(b) to prove untruthfulness if defense counsel had made an offer of proof on that basis.

[2] Rule 609(c)—Effect of Pardon, Annulment, or Certificate of Rehabilitation

United States Court of Appeals for the Armed Forces

United States v. Clarke, 27 M.J. 361 (C.M.A. 1989): Rejecting the accused's claim that his previous rape conviction should have been suppressed because he had earned a certificate of training completion at the U.S. Army Retraining Brigade, this court did not equate the Army's program for restoring a soldier to duty with the Rule's requirement for general rehabilitation or equivalent procedure.

Army Court of Criminal Appeals

United States v. Rogers, 17 M.J. 990 (A.C.M.R. 1984): Despite the accused's successful completion of the Retraining Brigade's correction program, the court found as follows:

> The fact that Rogers may have been sufficiently rehabilitated to justify a return to duty is "not equivalent to a finding that he has been so completely rehabilitated that the probative value of his conviction on the issue of his credibility has been diminished." *Williams v. United States,* 421 A.2d 19, 23 (D.C. App. 1980). Thus, we hold that completion of the Retraining Brigade program and return to duty are not an "equivalent procedure based on a finding of the rehabilitation of the person convicted" as required by Mil. R. Evid. 609(c).

United States v. Stevens, 13 M.J. 832 (A.C.M.R. 1982): During the sentencing portion of trial, the government successfully offered evidence of the accused's prior conviction into evidence despite defense counsel's contention that his client had been rehabilitated at the United States Army Retraining Brigade. The Army Court of Review affirmed, holding that Rule 609(c) "applies only to the use of convictions for impeachment purposes and is inapplicable to evidence of previous convictions on sentencing."

[3] Rule 609(d)—Juvenile Adjudications

[a] Use Against Government Witness—Prohibited

United States Court of Appeals for the Armed Forces

United States v. Miller, 48 M.J. 49 (C.A.A.F. 1998): The accused was convicted of conspiracy, robbery, and assault with the intent to commit robbery. In limine, the military judge prohibited the accused from impeaching a key government witness with evidence of that witness's prior juvenile adjudication for larceny. Affirming the accused's convictions, this court held that, because defense counsel's case was not based on this witness's bias or prejudice against the accused, the juvenile adjudication would only have had a "tangential" effect on the proceedings, and as a result its admission was not "necessary for a fair determination of the issues . . ." The court was quick to point out that had this been an adult conviction, the result may well have been different.

[4]   Rule 609(e)—Pendency of Appeal

United States Court of Appeals for the Armed Forces

United States v. Krewson, 12 M.J. 157 (C.M.A. 1981): Pursuant to a pretrial agreement the accused pleaded guilty to assault with the intent to commit rape. On appeal, he challenged the admissibility of his civilian conviction for a similar offense. The accused contended that the civilian's conviction was not admissible because proof of finality was absent and because the conviction post-dated the charge in question. Reversing, the court found that the specific *Manual* provisions requiring appellate review for court-martial convictions apply with equal vigor to civilian convictions.

Air Force Court of Criminal Appeals

United States v. Lachapelle, 10 M.J. 511 (A.F.C.M.R. 1980) (pre-Rules case): After the accused testified in his own defense, the prosecution successfully offered a promulgating order establishing that he had previously been convicted by a special court-martial. Trial defense counsel made no objection. *See* our discussion of Rule 103(a)(1). Appellate defense counsel contended that the conviction was admissible because the promulgating order did not demonstrate final supervisory review as required by then current *Manual* ¶¶ 75b(2) and 153b(2)(b). Although the court side-stepped the issue, finding that a sufficient time had elapsed since conviction to permit an inference of review—*see United States v. Graham,* 1 M.J. 308 (C.M.A. 1976)—it recognized that Rule 609(e) and (f) alter prior practice. Subdivision (f) allows a conviction to be admitted (for impeachment purposes) when a sentence is adjudged; subdivision (e) provides that pending appellate review will not affect admissibility, but may be offered to establish weight. While the court only alluded to the issue, it is important to note that the requirements for admitting prior convictions during the sentencing portion of trial remain substantially unchanged by Rule 609.

[5]   Rule 609(f)—Definition

Army Court of Criminal Appeals

United States v. Jenkins, 18 M.J. 583 (A.C.M.R. 1984): In dictum the court left unresolved whether a conviction could be admitted for impeachment purposes if the convening authority had subsequently disapproved the findings and sentence (*see* Rule 609(e) for summary and special courts-martial without a military judge). Although the Rules do not specifically address this matter, we believe that no single approach should govern all cases. If the convening authority's disapproval was based on his belief that, notwithstanding the trial court's decision, the government had not adequately established the accused's guilt, our view is that the convening authority acted as an appellate authority (*see* Rule 609(c) and (e)) and the conviction should not be admitted. However, we believe that if the disapproval is for another reason—*i.e.*, rehabilitation (*see* Rule 609(c)), clemency or mission requirements—then the trial forum will have to make an ad hoc resolution based in part on the factors discussed in *United States v. Rogers*, 17 M.J. 990 (A.C.M.R. 1984) (burden is upon the witness being impeached to demonstrate that the conviction has no impeachment value) and *United States v. Collins*, 552 F.2d 243 (8th Cir. 1977) (a final conviction with a suspended sentence held admissible for impeachment purposes).

United States v. Stafford, 15 M.J. 866 (A.C.M.R. 1983): Affirming a conviction, the court stated "that it is not necessary that a sentence be imposed for a civilian conviction before it may be used to impeach a witness under Mil. R. Evid. 609."

§ 610.01   Official Text

Rule 610.   Religious Beliefs or Opinions.

Evidence of the beliefs or opinions of a witness on matters of religion is not admissible for the purpose of showing that by reason of their nature the credibility of the witness is impaired or enhanced.

---

§ 610.02   Editorial Comment

Military[1] and federal[2] versions of Rule 610 prohibit any party from impeaching or rehabilitating a witness's character with evidence of religious opinions or beliefs.[3] This provision recognizes that to permit questioning of a witness about religious views is dangerous for several reasons. First, such an examination intrudes upon a private area that receives first amendment protection. Second, experience demonstrates that religious opinions or beliefs are not very probative of any significant issue before the court.[4] Third, religious opinions and beliefs are tremendously emotional issues, and may lead the court members into distorting, ignoring, or blindly accepting a witness's testimony because of antipathy or sympathy for his religious views.[5]

The Rule bars only an inquiry into beliefs and opinions for the purpose of attacking or supporting credibility. It does not prohibit all mention of religion or religious matters. It may be permissible to inquire into the religious activities of a witness if the inquiry would produce relevant evidence. For example, a witness may have observed a criminal act from his or her seat in church. Rule 610 does not prevent counsel from establishing how and why its witness happened to be in a position to view the crime. A limiting instruction on this point would be appropriate.[6]

However, trial participants should be conscious of the Rule's underlying philosophy which is that neither side is permitted to argue that a witness should be believed or disbelieved because of his or her church attendance, failure to attend church, religious affiliation, absence of religious affiliation,

---

[1] *See, e.g.,* United States v. Felton, 31 M.J. 526 (A.C.M.R. 1990) (finding error but no prejudice in the military judge allowing evidence of the accused's and the victim's religious beliefs to reach the jury).

[2] *See, e.g.,* Contemporary Mission, Inc. v. Bonded Mailings, 671 F.2d 81 (2d Cir. 1982) (trial judge properly excluded extensive cross-examination of witness on his affiliation with Catholic church).

[3] No previous *Manual* provision addressed this topic.

[4] *See* our discussion of relevance under Rules 401 and 402.

[5] Such a result would clearly run afoul of Rules 403 and 611(a).

[6] *See* our discussion of Rule 105.

or presence or absence of particular beliefs.

Church affiliation may legitimately be the subject of inquiry though. For example, where a church official is charged with an offense or is the victim of an offense, a witness's membership in the church might be used to show bias towards the accused or even towards the victim.

The line between inadmissible religious evidence and admissible character evidence is not always clear. For example, in *United States v. Brown*,[7] the accused was charged with using cocaine. Trial counsel established his case by relying on urinalysis results. The accused's defense focused on his good military character,[8] and concomitantly, that because of strong religious beliefs he would never use drugs. The trial judge suppressed all mention of religious beliefs or affiliations. Reversing the accused's conviction, the court held that an accused's proof of strong religious beliefs against abusing drugs is part and parcel evidence of his good soldier defense, and is admissible.

Similarly, in *United States v. Thomas*,[9] the court held that the military judge made no error in admitting government evidence demonstrating that the accused said he used drugs as part of his religious beliefs and rituals. The court found this testimony was properly admitted because it was not used to impeach credibility.

Nothing in the Rule covers the evidentiary use of political affiliations, which would raise many of the same concerns that underpin Rule 610. This shortcoming is important in today's military society where political, social, cultural, sexual, and religious beliefs often become intertwined. There is good reason for a court to analogize to Rule 610 in making rulings regarding questions addressed to a witness about political or social beliefs and opinions.

§ 610.03 Drafters' Analysis

Rule 610 is taken without significant change from the Federal Rules and has no present equivalent in the *Manual for Courts-Martial*. The Rule makes religious beliefs or opinions inadmissible for the purpose of impeaching or bolstering credibility. To the extent that such opinions may be critical to the defense of a case, however, there may be a constitutional justification for overcoming the Rule's exclusion. *Cf. Davis v. Alaska*, 415 U.S. 308 (1974).

§ 610.04 Annotated Cases

United States Court of Appeals for the Armed Forces

United States v. Brown, 41 M.J. 1 (C.M.A. 1994): This staff sergeant was convicted of using cocaine. The government's case consisted of a positive

---

[7] 41 M.J. 1 (C.M.A. 1994).

[8] *See* our discussion of Rule 404(a).

[9] 40 M.J. 252 (C.M.A. 1994).

urinalysis. The accused attempted to use the good soldier defense and demonstrate that it was inconsistent with his character and religious beliefs to abuse drugs. The trial judge excluded the religious aspect of this testimony. This court reversed the accused's conviction holding that proof of strong religious beliefs against abusing drugs is part and parcel evidence of Rule 404(a)(1)'s good soldier defense.

United States v. Thomas, 40 M.J. 252 (C.M.A. 1994): The accused was convicted of marijuana abuse. A government witness testified that the accused admitted to using drugs as part of his religious beliefs. For the first time on appeal, the accused contended that this evidence violated Rule 610. Affirming his conviction, the court held that evidence of the accused's religious beliefs was properly admitted because it was not used to impeach his credibility.

Army Court of Criminal Appeals

United States v. Felton, 31 M.J. 526 (A.C.M.R. 1990): The accused's convictions for assault with intent to commit sodomy, and related offenses, were affirmed in part. During trial, the military judge allowed evidence of the victim's and accused's religious beliefs to reach the court members. Finding error but no prejudice, the court held that attempting to establish a witness's veracity, or the accused's lack of criminal intent, by demonstrating that either is a religious person is improper.

§ 611.01   Official Text

Rule 611.   Mode and Order of Interrogation and Presentation.

(a) *Control by the military judge.*   The military judge shall exercise reasonable control over the mode and order of interrogating witnesses and presenting evidence so as to (1) make the interrogation and presentation effective for the ascertainment of the truth, (2) avoid needless consumption of time, and (3) protect witnesses from harassment or undue embarrassment.

(b) *Scope of cross-examination.*   Cross-examination should be limited to the subject matter of the direct examination and matters affecting the credibility of the witness. The military judge may, in the exercise of discretion, permit inquiry into additional matters as if on direct examination.

(c) *Leading questions.*   Leading questions should not be used on the direct examination of a witness except as may be necessary to develop the testimony of the witness. Ordinarily leading questions should be permitted on cross-examination. When a party calls a hostile witness or a witness identified with an adverse party, interrogation may be by leading questions.

(d) *Remote live testimony of a child.*

(1) In a case involving abuse of a child or domestic violence, the military judge shall, subject to the requirements of subsection (3) of this rule, allow a child victim or witness to testify from an area outside the courtroom as prescribed in R.C.M. 914A.[1]

(2) The term "child" means a person who is under the age of 16 at the time of his or her testimony. The term "abuse of a child" means the physical or mental injury, sexual abuse or exploitation, or negligent treatment of a child. The term "exploitation" means child pornography or child prostitution. The term "negligent treatment" means the failure to provide, for reasons other than poverty, adequate food, clothing, shelter, or medical care so as to endanger seriously the physical health of the child. The term "domestic violence" means an offense that has as an element the use, attempted use, or threatened use of physical force against a person and is committed by a current or former spouse, parent, or guardian of the victim; by a person with whom the victim shares a child in common; by a person who is cohabiting with or has cohabited with the victim as a spouse, parent, or guardian; or by a person similarly situated to a spouse, parent, or guardian of the

---

[1] *See,* Hudspeth, *Remote Testimony and Executive Order 13430: A Missed Opportunity,* 57 NAVAL L. REV. 285 (2009).

victim.

(3) Remote live testimony will be used only where the military judge makes a finding on the record that a child is unable to testify in open court in the presence of the accused, for any of the following reasons:

(A) The child is unable to testify because of fear;

(B) There is substantial likelihood, established by expert testimony, that the child would suffer emotional trauma from testifying;

(C) The child suffers from a mental or other infirmity; or

(D) Conduct by an accused or defense counsel causes the child to be unable to continue testifying.

(4) Remote live testimony of a child shall not be utilized where the accused elects to absent himself from the courtroom in accordance with R.C.M. 804(c).

§ 611.02   Editorial Comment

[1]   In General

Rule 611 is a continuation of the trend in court-martial practice initiated by the Uniform Code of Military Justice as amended in 1968, which provided trial judges with broad discretion in controlling the litigation.

Subsection (d), added by the 1999 amendment to Rule 611, provides effective new techniques for dealing with child witnesses while still protecting the individual accused's constitutional rights. The Rule's original provisions restate and codify the bench's tremendous flexibility in running criminal trials. Rule 611 complements Rule 403 and seeks to assure that trials are fair and efficient and that witnesses are fairly treated.

[2]   Rule 611(a)—Control by the Military Judge

[a]   Scope

Subdivision (a) states that the bench shall exercise reasonable control over the interrogation of witnesses and the presentation of evidence. The provision requires that the bench involve itself in three important areas of court-martial litigation.

[b]   Trial Process Issues

First, the military judge must insure that evidence is presented so as to maximize its contribution to the search for truth. This restatement of common law principles allows the bench to control when testimony should be struck,[1] how real or demonstrative evidence will be used, whether

---

[1] *See, e.g.,* United States v. Nunez, 668 F.2d 1116 (10th Cir. 1981) (where prosecution

counsel may ask for narrative testimony or must ask specific questions, when witnesses may be called[2] and recalled,[3] the order in which witnesses testify, and even the internal ordering of a particular witness's testimony.[4] Similarly, it may be used to control the extent to which rebuttal[5] and surrebuttal[6] evidence is admitted, how witnesses will be examined during evidentiary hearings,[7] and whether a party's case can be reopened after that party has rested.[8] Rule 611(a) can also be used as a rule of completeness for oral testimony, much like Rule 106 is used to complete the record for written evidence.[9]

The drafters recognized that military judges play an indispensable role in the administration of justice, and that their experience and common sense can assist in promoting a fair trial for both parties.[10] Viewed in this light, Rule 611 is a primary vehicle for military judges to use in conducting

---

witness refused to answer a defense question, there was no need to strike his testimony since the defense had a full opportunity to examine the witness).

[2] *See, e.g.,* United States v. Butera, 677 F.2d 1376 (11th Cir. 1982) (no error for court to permit sequential testimony of key government witness where cross-examination after each appearance was permitted).

[3] *See, e.g.,* United States v. Ranier, 670 F.2d 702 (7th Cir. 1982) (upholding trial judge's refusal to permit a defendant to recall for further impeachment a government witness who already had been impeached); United States v. Clark, 617 F.2d 180 (9th Cir. 1980) (the trial judge properly exercised his discretion in refusing to allow defense counsel to recall an expert witness where the defense made no offer concerning how the witness would add to the trial).

[4] In United States v. Jackson, 549 F.2d 517 (8th Cir.), *cert. denied,* 430 U.S. 985 (1977), the court praised government counsel's trial tactic of repeatedly calling the same FBI agent throughout his case-in-chief, rather than simply putting that agent on the stand for one very lengthy and complicated examination.

[5] *See, e.g.,* Smith v. Conley, 584 F.2d 844 (8th Cir. 1978) (upholding the trial judge's decision to exclude an expert witness called during rebuttal when that same witness was available during the calling party's case-in-chief). *See generally* Schlueter, Military Criminal Justice, § 15-12 (6th ed. 2004) (*citing* military cases).

[6] *See, e.g.,* United States v. Glass, 709 F.2d 669 (11th Cir. 1983) (no error in prohibiting surrebuttal testimony).

[7] *See, e.g.,* United States v. Green, 670 F.2d 1148 (D.C. Cir. 1981) (defendant has right to cross-examine government witness at a suppression hearing).

[8] *See, e.g.,* United States v. Crawford, 533 F.3d 133 (2d Cir. 2008) (following criteria identified for reopening a case after it has been sent to the jury: timeliness of motion, character of testimony, effect of granting the motion and establishing a reasonable explanation for failure to present the evidence during the party's case-in-chief); United States v. Terry, 729 F.2d 1063 (6th Cir. 1984) (no error in denying defendants' motion to reopen case for further impeachment of government witness).

[9] *See, e.g.,* United States v. McElroy, 587 F.3d 73 (1st Cir. 2009) (no error in admitting testimony and exhibits summarizing the government's case).

[10] *See* United States v. Graves, 1 M.J. 50 (C.M.A. 1975), where the United States Court of Appeals for the Armed Forces said that the trial judge is required to assure that the accused receives a fair trial.

proceedings in a manner that is both fair and conducive to ascertaining the truth.[11]

[c]   Timeliness Issues

Second, Rule 611(a) requires that the military judge shall conduct the proceedings in such a way as to avoid the needless consumption of trial time. Control here is similar to that exercised under Rule 403, which allows the judge to exclude evidence to avoid "undue delay." Examinations into tangential or side issues can be limited under Rule 611 in order to focus attention on the real issues in a case.[12] Cumulative or redundant evidence can and should be controlled under this provision.

[d]   Witness Protection Issues

Third, the trial judge must protect witnesses from harassment or undue embarrassment. This requires the bench to draw a fine distinction between piercing, but effective cross-examination, which is permissible, and interrogation aimed at belittling a witness and subjecting him or her to needless public ridicule, which is not. As a result, impeachment and fair, even slashing cross-examination is permitted, but attempts to confuse a witness, to bring out facts that do not amount to permissible impeachment, and to intimidate a witness should be curtailed. Such attempts serve no legitimate trial purpose, and will not assist the finder of fact in better understanding an issue of consequence to the litigation.

The 1995 Amendment to the Drafter's Analysis highlights an additional area of concern for counsel and military judges. It provides that, when a child witness is unable to testify because of fear of the accused, or attendant mental infirmities, "alternatives to live in-court testimony may be appropriate." Careful witness preparation, often including the assistance of psychologists and other mental health professionals, may facilitate obtaining testimony in this area. Further, the court's consideration of alternatives should include the public policy issues attendant to protecting children from emotional trauma, and the need for effective use of (1) the systemic requirement for an oath; (2) the accused's need to effectively cross-examine the victim; and (3) the court members' requirement to carefully observe the witness's demeanor and sincerity. In 1999, Subsection (d) (see our discussion *below*) was added to Rule 611 for these very purposes. Confrontation and effective assistance of counsel issues are always present in any attempt to shelter a youthful witness from her alleged assailant.[13]

---

[11] *See, e.g,* United States v. Castro, 813 F.2d 571 (2d Cir. 1987) (trial court appropriately used its judgment to redact statements).

[12] *See also* our discussion of Rules 401 and 402 which deal with relevancy.

[13] *Compare* Coy v. Iowa, 487 U.S. 1012 (1988) (confrontation clause violated by allowing child victim to testify behind a screen which prevented her from seeing the accused) and United States v. Daulton, 45 M.J. 212 (1996) (violation of confrontation clause and

Rule 611(a) authorizes the military judge to protect a witness from harassment or undue embarrassment. This means that, when conducting an examination based on Rule 608 or Rule 609, the trial court's attention should also be on protecting the witness from unfair treatment, and even limiting direct or cross-examination when necessary to accomplish that goal.

Rule 611(a)'s focus is slightly different from Rule 403's interests. Rule 611(b) protects witnesses. Rule 403 protects parties. When the accused is a witness, both rules come into play. Constitutional issues arise when protecting a prosecution witness from unfair harassment or embarrassment could conflict with the accused's right to confrontation.[14]

[e] Military Judge Discretion

Military[15] and federal[16] appellate authority have consistently provided great deference to the trial court in exercising its Rule 611 powers.[17] In part this is the result of appellate court sensitivity to the reality of trying criminal cases. Reviewing judges are often asked to resolve very complex legal and factual issues based only on a cold trial record. Determining the courtroom atmosphere, and the other intangibles affecting both how the case was tried by the lawyers, and how it may have been viewed by the military judge, is always difficult when attempted from a distant appellate courtroom. Most reviewing courts recognize that it often will appear easier in hindsight that the military judge should have been more aggressive or more restrained then it appeared to the judge in the heat of trial.

Difficult issues may arise when a claim is made that a military judge

---

reversible error caused by trial court allowing a child witness to testify in court while the accused was excluded and watched on closed-circuit television) *with* Maryland v. Craig, 497 U.S. 836 (1990) (right to confrontation not violated by allowing child to testify over a one-way closed circuit television). *See also* United States v. Longstreath, 45 M.J. 366 (1996) (no abuse of discretion where the military judge refused to strike portions of the accused's daughter's testimony when she would not respond to cross-examination) and our discussion of Rule 301(f)(2).

[14] *See, e.g.,* United States v. Foster, 982 F. 2d 551 (D.C. Cir. 1993) (conviction reversed where trial judge limited cross-examination of key government drug prosecution witness); United States v. Riggi, 951 F.2d 1368 (3d Cir. 1991) (finding error in trial court's decision to restrict defendant's recross of thirteen government witnesses concerning new material they testified to on redirect as violative of Sixth Amendment's Confrontation Clause and traditional application of this Rule); United States v. Andrew, 666 F.2d 915 (5th Cir. 1982) (judge has leeway to restrict cross-examination once confrontation clause is satisfied).

[15] *See, e.g.,* United States v. Pearson, 33 M.J. 913, 915 (A.F.C.M.R. 1991) (military judge has discretionary control over the presentation of evidence, and can adjusted testimony for good reason).

[16] *See, e.g.,* United States v. Young, 745 F.2d 733 (2d Cir. 1984) (trial judge has broad discretion with respect to most trial issues).

[17] *See, e.g.,* United States v. Maddox, 944 F.2d 1223 (6th Cir. 1991) (no error found when trial court allowed witness to say that defendant silently threatened him while he was on the stand—threat demonstrated consciousness of guilt).

showed bias. This was an issue in *United States v. Loving.*[18] There the accused was convicted of premeditated murder, felony murder, attempted murder, and five specifications of robbery. He was ultimately sentenced to death. Both the findings and the sentence were affirmed. However, on review the accused contended that error occurred when the military judge characterized one of defense counsel's contentions as "ridiculous," and threatened to "deal with defense counsel" after counsel had challenged a ruling. Relying on *Liteky v. United States,*[19] the court held that such expressions of impatience, dissatisfaction, annoyance, and anger are not generally sufficient to establish bias or partiality. The court went on to say that even a stern and short-tempered judge's ordinary efforts at courtroom administration do not create an atmosphere of bias or partiality.

However, in *United States v. Thomas,*[20] the opposite result was reached. There the court reversed a conviction because "[t]he appellant was denied a fair hearing in the trial forum as a result of . . . rulings, comments, and actions by the military judge which, *in toto,* materially strengthened the prosecution case before the triers of fact and, at the same time, improperly limited and vitiated that of the defense."

Loving establishes a boundary trial judges should not exceed or even approach. The trial judge's actions placed a very difficult burden upon defense counsel, particularly with respect to making and preserving the record for appeal.[21] No valid purpose is served by military judges taking extreme or unpleasant positions in the court room concerning any trial event. Such conduct demeans the military's criminal justice system, and causes those accused of crime to doubt the fairness of any conviction or sentence produced in such an environment. Military attorney professional standards are appropriately high and rigorously enforced. Remedies for unprofessional lawyer conduct can be more effectively exercised outside of the courtroom where it will not negatively impact a trial.

[3]   Rule 611(b)—Scope of Cross-Examination

[a]   Timing Mechanism

Rule 611(b) is primarily a timing mechanism.[22] Neither the military[23] nor

---

[18] 41 M.J. 213 (C1994).

[19] 510 U.S. 540 (1994).

[20] 18 M.J. 545 (A.C.M.R. 1984).

[21] *See* our discussion of Rule 103.

[22] *See, e.g.,* Hankins v. Civiletti, 614 F.2d 953 (5th Cir. 1980) (when a party testified he opened himself to cross-examination "with regard to matters relevant to his direct testimony").

[23] *See* United States v. Owens, 21 M.J. 117 (C.M.A. 1985), where the court indicated that the extent to which cross-examination should be permitted rests largely in the trial court's sound discretion.

the federal[24] version addresses when and to what extent an accused or any witness may be cross-examined. The Rule continues traditional military practice that generally limits cross-examination to those matters covered on direct,[25] and those affecting impeachment and the credibility of a witness. Credibility issues are always appropriate for cross-examination because counsel places a witness's veracity in issue as a result of calling that witness to testify.[26] However, this Rule also provides a mechanism for allowing cross-examination to extend beyond the bounds of direct testimony when, in the military judge's discretion, such an extension is necessary. Under these circumstances, the Rule requires that counsel proceed as if on direct examination (unless dealing with a hostile witness, an adverse witness identified with an adverse party).

When the Federal Rule was drafted, the Advisory Committee was in favor of, and the Supreme Court actually adopted, a broader rule allowing more latitude in cross-examination. Ultimately, Congress rejected the "wide-open" approach, and the Military Rule also rejects it.

As a result, the military judge controls whether a party may exceed the bounds of direct examination.[27] The discretion afforded trial judges permits more liberal cross-examination when it will assist the fact-finder in understanding other proof, or is necessary to avoid burdening witnesses with several court appearances.

[b]   Unique Military Provisions

The military drafters did attempt to address the constitutional implications of Rule 611(b) in Rule 301, a provision with no federal counterpart. Although we will not repeat our discussion of Rule 301 here, it is important to note that Rule 301(e) states that, when an accused voluntarily testifies, he or she waives his Fifth Amendment privilege only with respect to those

---

[24] In United States v. Wolfson, 573 F.2d 216 (5th Cir. 1978), the court concluded that the scope of direct examination means the "subject matter" of the examination. The Rule also affords the judge discretion to allow additional cross-examination, but itself provides no guidelines for exercising this discretion.

[25] *See, e.g.,* United States v. Gullett, 713 F.2d 1203 (6th Cir. 1983), *cert. denied,* 104 S. Ct. 973 (1984) (witness for government could invoke privilege against self-incrimination and refusal to answer did not impair defense, since the questions were outside the scope of the direct examination).

[26] *See, e.g.,* United States v. Smalley, 754 F.2d 944 (11th Cir. 1985) (credibility always in issue on cross-examination).

[27] For a very interesting discussion of how court room testimony can be more effectively used, *see* Richey, *A Modern Management Technique for Trial Courts to Improve the Quality of Justice: Requiring Direct Testimony to Be Submitted in Written Form Prior to Trial,* 72 GEO L.J. 73 (1983), where the author, a federal judge, proposes that the trial bench require parties to submit, *in limine,* their direct testimony questions. The author argues that this practice would eliminate wasted time while promoting better juror understanding of the facts. The article includes samples of orders that the author has used.

matters contained in his direct examination. government counsel may not expand the testimony into related or foundational areas. Rule 301(e) also provides that when the accused is tried for more than one offense, he or she may testify about only one of those charges and retain the protection against self incrimination with respect to the others. *See also* Rule 608(b).

[4]   Rule 611(c)—Leading Questions

[a]   Common Law Foundation

Rule 611(c) covers leading questions. It largely restates the common law and previous *Manual* provisions which established that leading questions may be used on cross-examination, but generally cannot be used on direct examination. These are generalizations only. Sometimes leading questions are allowed on direct, but barred on cross-examination. The Rule itself recognizes this when it provides that the direct examiner may lead in order to develop a witness's testimony and to deal with hostile or adverse witnesses (discussed below). Leading questions on direct usually are allowed to identify a witness and his or her relationship to the military or offense in question. Witnesses may be led through foundational matters to avoid wasting the court's time. Leading questions also may be allowed on direct examination when a party is examining a witness who requires special attention. Included in this category are children,[28] timid or frightened adults, and witnesses who suffer memory lapses, or possess physical, emotional,[29] or communicative disabilities.[30] Military judges have enormous discretion in permitting or barring counsel from leading. Although the discretion could be abused, when the military judge erroneously permits leading questions, the error will unlikely be sufficient to justify appellate intervention.[31]

[b]   Impeaching Own Witness

Rule 611(c), when read with Rule 607, allows a direct examiner to ask leading questions in order to impeach his or her own witness. For example, leading questions should be allowed to establish that the direct examiner's witness has a prior conviction admissible under Rule 609 or has committed

---

[28] *See, e.g.,* United States v. Rossbach, 701 F.2d 713 (8th Cir. 1983) (prosecutor could properly lead 15- and 17-year-old sexual assault victims).

[29] *See, e.g.,* United States v. Lyons, 36 M.J. 183 (C.M.A. 1992) (trial counsel allowed great latitude in conducting direct examination of deaf-mute, mentally impaired, sexual abuse victim).

[30] *Compare* United States v. Littlewind, 551 F.2d 244 (8th Cir. 1977) (conviction affirmed despite the accused's contention that the trial court improperly permitted government counsel to examine young rape victims by leading questions), *with* State v. Orona, 589 P.2d 1041 (N.M. 1979) (conviction reversed on similar facts because the prosecution's questions were so leading that "every word describing the alleged offense [came] from the prosecuting attorney rather than from the witness").

[31] *See, e.g.,* United States v. DeFirore, 720 F.2d 757 (2d Cir. 1983) (prosecutor could lead government witness; reversals for leading questions will be rare).

"prior bad acts" admissible under Rule 603(b)(1).

The second sentence of Rule 611(c) indicates that on cross-examination leading questions "ordinarily" will be permitted. They may not be allowed when one party questions a witness who is friendly to it and is considered adverse to the direct examiner.

[c] Hostile Witnesses

The third sentence of 611(c) allows leading questions to be asked on direct examination when a party calls a hostile witness, or a witness identified with an adverse party. The drafters left the term "hostile witness" undefined. Under previous *Manual* practice, counsel had to demonstrate a witness's hostility before asking leading questions. This meant something more than showing the witness was unfavorable. Counsel had to establish that the witness would not adequately respond to his or her questions and had been unwilling to cooperate during pretrial discussions.

This situation is particularly likely to occur in a military setting where defense counsel will often have to call witnesses aligned with the command in order to establish its defense. Such witnesses may be unwilling to assist defense counsel. As a result, normal direct examination will prove troublesome, and may in fact produce harmful testimony due to counsel's inability to effectively limit the witness's responses. Even if a witness cannot be shown to be "actually" hostile, it may be that most officers and senior enlisted persons will be "identified" with the government. The "identified with" language of the Rule should make it less necessary in many cases to make a finding about actual hostility.

If the government calls a witness who actually is hostile to the accused or is identified with the government, there is good reason to allow leading questions by a cross-examiner who is permitted to go beyond the scope of the direct examination. If the witness were recalled by the cross-examiner, subdivision (c) would permit leading questions, and the reason for permitting broad cross-examination may be to avoid any recall for the convenience of the witness or the court-martial.

[5] Rule 611(d)—Remote Live Testimony of a Child

Rule 611(d) addresses important constitutional and confrontational issues. It focuses on how counsel and military judges deal with child witnesses, who by necessity must testify under highly stressful and sometimes intimidating courtroom conditions about emotional and very personal events. While Rule 611(d) codifies for the military a significant portion of existing Federal statutory practice and Supreme Court guidance, it still leaves many questions unsettled.

The constitutional foundation for Rule 611(d) has been settled by the

Supreme Court in it *Maryland v. Craig*.[32] *Craig* addressed the conflict between the Sixth Amendment's criminal defendant protections and the government's public policy interests in effectively prosecuting cases.[33] In *Craig*, a one-way closed circuit television system was used to allow a child to testify at a location remote from the accused and the courtroom. Upholding the constitutionality of that process, the Supreme Court said that while "the Confrontation Clause reflects a preference for face-to-face confrontation at trial," it is a preference that "must occasionally give way to considerations of public policy and the necessities of the case."[34] The Court went on to say that "the state interest in protecting child witnesses from the trauma of testifying in a child abuse case is sufficiently important to justify the use of a special procedure that permits a child witness in such cases to testify at trial against a defendant in the absence of face-to-face confrontation with the defendant."[35]

The Supreme Court's opinion was subsequently codified in 18 U.S.C.§ 3509. Military Rule of Evidence 611(d) is generally based on that authority. While the new military rule plows no new ground, it also has not adopted the Federal model in toto.

Unlike 18 U.S.C. § 3509(b)(1)(A), which applies in all "proceedings involving an alleged offense against a child," Rule 611(d)(1) limits its application to only cases involving "abuse of a child or domestic violence." In this way, the Military Rule follows Rules 413 and 414 limitations, confining its requirements to limited categories of criminal misconduct. As a result, child victims or witnesses in courts-martial involving other types of criminal offenses will be unaffected by Rule 611(d). Subdivision (d)(2) provides a list of definitions, that includes the definition of a child as someone "under the age of 16 at the time of his or her testimony," as well as definitions for "abuse of a child," "exploitation," and the other foundational components that fall within its coverage.

Once it is established that the offense(s) in question qualify under Rule 611(d)(1) and (2), the military judge is empowered to permit the child victim or witness to testify from "an area outside the courtroom as prescribed by R.C.M. 914A," which is also new. This amended provision states that the exact procedure to be employed by the bench should be determined "based on the exigencies of the situation," although the *Manual* here recommends two-way closed circuit television, and provides a detailed list of requirements for accomplishing that result.

---

[32] 497 U.S. 836 (1990).

[33] *See* United States v. Gigante, 166 F.3d 75 (2d Cir. 1999) (discussing applicable criteria).

[34] 497 U.S. at 849.

[35] 497 U.S. at 855.

Subparagraph 611(d)(3) defines the requirements for allowing remote live testimony to be used. It provides that the trial judge must make specific findings on the record demonstrating that a child victim or witness is unable to testify in open court and in the presence of the accused, based on four reasons, that have been taken directly from 18 U.S.C. 3509(b)(1)(B). These reasons include: (a) fear, (b) substantial likelihood of emotional trauma, (c) existing mental or related infirmity, or (d) conduct by the accused or defense counsel limiting the ability of the child to continue testifying. The Military drafters chose not to include 18 U.S.C. 3509(b)(1)(C), which states:

> The court shall support a ruling on the child's inability to testify with findings on the record. In determining whether the impact on an individual child of one or more of the factors described in subparagraph (B) is so substantial as to justify an order under subparagraph (A), the court may question the minor in chambers, or at some other comfortable place other than the courtroom, on the record for a reasonable period of time with the child attendant, the prosecutor, the child's attorney, the guardian ad litem, and the defense counsel present.

The omitted language is important because it anticipates at least three issues likely to arise in litigation over Rule 611(d): the standard to be applied in determining what impact is sufficient to bring a youthful witness under its coverage; the trial judge's obligation to make a satisfactory finding on this issue; and the advisability of conducting such hearings "in chambers, or at some other comfortable place other than the courtroom" with the defense counsel present and the accused absent. A related fourth issue not identified in the Federal or military rule is the admissibility of cautionary instructions under Rule 105, or the judge's obligation to provide them sua sponte.

Rule 611(d)(3) provides that remote testimony will be permitted only when the military judge makes a finding that the child is unable to testify in open court. But, the rule provides no standard for the bench to use. What does "unable to testify" mean? If the witness is able to relate most of what (s)he could have testified to without being separated from the accused, is that sufficient? Or, must the witness be totally unable to speak? If the child witness is unable to provide substantially the same testimony with the accused present as (s)he would have without the accused present, a strong vase is made that the remote viewing process should be employed. "Substantially the same" should include both the verbal and demeanor components of a child witness's testimony.

Also largely undefined are Rule 611(d)(3)'s four foundational reasons for determining when remote testimony will be permitted. Three, including fear ((d)(3)(A)), mental or other infirmity ((d)(3)(C)), and counsel or accused conduct ((d)(3)(D)), are undefined, while testimony producing an emotional trauma ((d)(3)(B)) is qualified by a "substantial likelihood" standard. Additionally, the emotional trauma ((d)(3)(B)) basis has an expressed condition precedent for "expert testimony." Suffering from mental or other infirmity ((d)(3)(C)), which is similar in kind, has no such condition precedent.

In *United States v. Garcia,*[36] the court discussed a process for applying 18 U.S.C. 1 § 3501 that appears applicable to Rule 611(d). In *Garcia,* the accused was charged with a sexual offense against a young victim. Finding that the bench's process for conducting a two-way remote examination of the witness was appropriate, the court discussed a "case-specific," three-part test that judges and counsel could follow. In the court's opinion the judge must: first, determine that the remote process is necessary to protect the welfare of the child witness; second, consider the available evidence of record, including expert testimony, to determine whether the applicable conditions have been satisfied; and third, determine whether the alleged "injury" the child might suffer is "more than de minimis."

Another distinction between Military Rule of Evidence 611(d) and its federal precursor is that 18 U.S.C. 1 § 3509(b)(1)(A) states that the party desiring to use the two-way closed circuit video technique "shall apply for such an order at least 5 days before the trial date, unless the court finds on the record that the need for such an order was not reasonably foreseeable." Despite the absence of a notice rule, prudent trial counsel will raise 611(d) issues before trial to avoid unnecessary delay and confusion.

§ 611.03   Drafters' Analysis

[1]   Control by the military judge

Rule 611(a) is taken from the Federal Rule without change. It is a basic source of the military judge's power to control proceedings and replaces *Manual* ¶ 149*a* and that part of ¶ 137 dealing with cumulative evidence. It is within the military judge's discretion to control methods of interrogation of witnesses. The Rule does not change present law. Although a witness may be required to limit an answer to the question asked, it will normally be improper to require that a "yes" or "no" answer be given unless it is clear that such an answer will be a complete response to the question. A witness will ordinarily be entitled to explain his or her testimony at some time before completing that testimony. The *Manual* requirement that questions be asked through the military judge is now found in Rule 614.

Although the military judge has the discretion to alter the sequence of proof to the extent that the burden of proof is not affected, the usual sequence for examination of witnesses is: prosecution witnesses, defense witnesses, prosecution rebuttal witnesses, defense rebuttal witnesses, and witnesses for the court. The usual order of examination of a witness is: direct examination, cross-examination, redirect examination, recross-examination, and examination by the court, ¶ 54*a*.

---

[36] 7 F.3d 885 (9th Cir. 1993).

[2]   Scope of cross-examination

Rule 611(b) is taken from the Federal Rule without change and replaces ¶ 149*b*(1) of the present *Manual* that is similar in scope. Under the Rule the military judge may allow a party to adopt a witness and proceed as if on direct examination. *See* Rule 301(b)(2) (judicial advice as to the privilege against self-incrimination for an apparently uninformed witness); Rule 301(f)(2) (effect of claiming the privilege against self-incrimination on cross-examination); Rule 303 (Degrading Questions); and Rule 608(b) (Evidence of Character, Conduct, and Bias of Witness).

[3]   Leading questions

Rule 611(c) is taken from the Federal Rule without significant change and is similar to ¶ 149*c* of the present *Manual*. The reference in the third sentence of the Federal Rule to an "adverse party" has been deleted as being applicable to civil cases only. A leading question is one that suggests the answer that is desired from the witness. Generally, a question that is susceptible to being answered by "yes" or "no" is a leading question.

The use of leading questions is discretionary with the military judge. Use of leading questions may be appropriate with respect to the following witnesses among others, children, persons with mental or physical disabilities, the extremely elderly, hostile witnesses, and witnesses identified with the adverse party.

It is also appropriate with the military judge's consent to utilize leading questions to direct a witness's attention to a relevant area of inquiry.

§ 611.04   Drafters' Analysis (1995 Amendment)

The 1995 amendment to the *Manual For Courts-Martial* contains the following additional Drafters' Analysis comments for this provision:

> When a child witness is unable to testify due to intimidation by the proceedings, fear of the accused, emotional trauma, or mental or other infirmity, alternatives to live in-court testimony may be appropriate.

§ 611.05   Drafters' Analysis (1999 Amendment)

Military Rule of Evidence 611. The Analysis accompanying Rule 611 is amended by adding the following:

1999 Amendment: Rule 611(d) is new. This amendment to Rule 611 gives substantive guidance to military judges regarding the use of alternative examination methods for child victims and witnesses in light of the U.S. Supreme Court's decision in *Maryland v. Craig*, 497 U.S. 836 (1990) and the change in Federal law in 18 U.S.C. section 3509. Although *Maryland v. Craig* dealt with child witnesses who were themselves the victims of abuse, it should be noted that 18 U.S.C. section 3509, as construed by Federal courts, has been applied to allow non-victim child witnesses to testify remotely. *See United States v. Moses,* 137 F.3d 894 (6th Cir. 1998) (applying section 3509 to a non-victim child witness, but reversing a child sexual assault conviction on other grounds) and *United States v. Quintero,* 21 F.3d 885 (9th Cir. 1994) (affirming conviction based on remote testimony of non-victim child witness, but remanding for re-sentencing). This amendment recognizes that child witnesses may be particularly traumatized, even if they are not themselves the direct victims, in cases involving the abuse of other children or domestic violence. This amendment also gives the accused an election to absent himself from the courtroom to prevent remote testimony. Such a provision gives the accused a greater role in determining how this issue will be resolved.

§ 611.06 Annotated Cases

[1] Rule 611(a)—Control by the Military Judge

[a] Control by the Military Judge—Guilty Pleas

Army Court of Criminal Appeals

United States v. Mullens, 24 M.J. 745 (A.C.M.R. 1987): The accused's guilty pleas to child sexual abuse offenses were sustained on appeal despite his contention that certain portions of the pretrial agreement's required stipulation of facts alleging similar extrinsic offenses were improperly admitted. In the court's opinion, the accused need not agree to any matter contained in the stipulation and is free to withdraw from it. However, such conduct would nullify the pretrial agreement itself. In the court's view, the military judge's proper role in this process "does not involve use of his authority to bind the parties by entering the forbidden field of pretrial agreement negotiations. . . . The military judge's role [is] one of determining whether the stipulation is admissible." In this light, the court recognized that government-required stipulations to previous similar acts, or even potentially inadmissible pretrial statements, are permissible.

Coast Guard Court of Criminal Appeals

United States v. Skidmore, 64 M.J. 655 (C.G.Ct.Crim.App. 2007): Affirming the accused's cocaine use and possession conviction, the court held that during the pre-sentencing portion of trial the military judge did not abuse his discretion by permitting inquiry into the accused's pretrial statements concerning his negative attitude about military justice. The court found defense counsel had "opened the door" to this line of questioning.

[b] Control by the Military Judge—Judge's Use of Authority

United States Court of Appeals for the Armed Forces

United States v. Satterley, 55 M.J. 168 (C.A.A.F. 2001): The accused was convicted of absence without leave, willful destruction of military property, and larceny. As part of his pleas, the accused entered into a stipulation of fact stating that he stole nine computers but that only five were recovered by the government. Prior to sentencing, the accused made a lengthy unsworn statement indirectly referencing the unrecovered computers. Defense counsel asked to reopen his case so the accused could make an additional unsworn statement after a court member raised questions concerning the additional computers. Affirming the accused's convictions, this Court held that the military judge did not abuse his discretion in denying defense counsel's request because the bench exercised reasonable control over the proceedings.

United States v. Stroup, 29 M.J. 224 (C.M.A. 1989): Calling this court-martial of an Air Force Captain an "abomination," and referring to trial counsel's conduct as "unethical," the court pointedly placed "ultimate blame" for this "runaway" proceeding on the military judge who failed to adequately control events and counsel.

Army Court of Criminal Appeals

United States v. Montgomery, 56 M.J. 660 (Army Ct.Crim.App. 2001): The accused was convicted of willfully disobeying a superior commissioned officer, assault consummated by a battery, and adultery. At trial, the military judge's denial of continuances adversely affected a subsequent defense request for two witnesses who would potentially testify about the character of the prosecution's principle witness. Additionally, the military judge refused to permit defense counsel to cross examine the prosecution's principal witness concerning a lie the witness made to the police about her identity after being stopped in an area known for prostitution and narcotics activity, and about checks the witness had forged. This Court held that the military judge's erroneous decisions to preclude cross-examination and extrinsic evidence impeaching a critical government witness had a cumulative effect, and were sufficiently prejudicial to require reversal. The Court noted that an abuse of discretion review standard applies to both a denial of a request for the production of a witness and a military judge's limitations upon cross-examination regarding specific instances of misconduct. The Court concluded that the military judge had, in fact, abused his discretion.

United States v. Wright, 13 M.J. 824 (A.C.M.R. 1982): In the course of affirming a conviction, the court, characterizing its own commentary as *obiter dicta,* elaborated on the trial judge's responsibilities concerning the presentation of evidence. A trial judge, it said, has considerable latitude in controlling the timing and presentation of evidence in order to assure that trials proceed efficiently. It expressed particular concern about needless and avoidable trial interruptions which cause court members to linger in "vacuous idleness" while the military judge rules on legal matters.

[c]   Control by the Military Judge—Mental Responsibility Issues

United States Court of Appeals for the Armed Forces

United States v. Bledsoe, 26 M.J. 97 (C.M.A. 1988): Recognizing that Military Rule of Evidence 302(b)(2) prohibits government counsel from using expert psychiatric testimony until the defense does, the court held that Rule 611(a) allows military judges "some discretion as to the sequence in which expert witnesses testify about an accused's sanity." Therefore, no error necessarily occurs if the judge exercises discretion in a limited, "informed manner." Such was not the case here, where trial counsel presented his evidence first in order to "gain the tactical advantage."

[d]   Control by the Military Judge—Order of Presenting Evidence

United States Court of Appeals for the Armed Forces

United States v. Wingart, 27 M.J. 128 (C.M.A. 1988): In this child sexual abuse case, the court accused both parties of having done a "tactical tap dance" concerning the sentencing admissibility of efficiency reports. The court said that, if neither party desires to admit the APR's, then the military judge has "the authority to obtain the documents as relevant court exhibits. . . ." *See United States v. Smith,* 16 M.J. 694 (A.F.C.M.R. 1983) (APR's should always be introduced as sentencing evidence), and our discussion of this case under Rule 404(b).

Air Force Court of Criminal Appeals

United States v. Grover, 63 M.J. 653 (A.F. Ct. Crim. App. 2006): Pursuant to a motion in limine, defense counsel sought to exclude any evidence of his client's marital problems from being introduced during the sentencing phase of trial. government counsel agreed not to introduce such testimony during her case-in-chief. Beginning with her first witness, trial counsel elicited the testimony she previously agreed not to present. When trial defense counsel objected, the military judge failed to promptly and consistently exclude the challenged evidence. Finding both error and prejudice, the court reassessed the accused's sentence holding that "although a court-martial is not a tea dance, it cannot be permitted to desolve, as this one did, into a no-holds barred trashing of the accused."

United States v. Murphy, 29 M.J. 573 (A.F.C.M.R. 1990): During trial counsel's case-in-chief, he called a defense expert "to interview [him] under oath." At trial and on appeal, defense counsel claimed that this "preemptive strike" was improper. The court held that "though we impute no bad faith to the prosecutor . . . [w]e surmise that a good objection would lie in terms of relevancy and ineffective use of courtroom time."

[e]   Control by the Military Judge—Rebuttal Evidence

United States Court of Appeals for the Armed Forces

United States v. Wirth, 18 M.J. 214 (C.M.A. 1984): The court provided the following analysis of rebuttal evidence at trial: "Its value lies in explaining, repelling, counteracting or disproving evidence introduced by the other party; generally, it is normally restricted to the proponent's presentation of testimony made necessary by the opponent's testimony; and its relevance must be determined in light of the testimony first introduced on the issue in question."

Air Force Court of Criminal Appeals

United States v. Gittens, 36 M.J. 594 (A.F.C.M.R. 1992): Affirming the accused's conviction for attempted rape, the court said that no error occurred when trial counsel was permitted to call a rebuttal witness concerning whether the victim made a prior inconsistent statement. This testimony was not collateral and was within the bench's wide latitude in controlling the presentation of rebuttal evidence.

Army Court of Criminal Appeals

United States v. Luce, 17 M.J. 754 (A.C.M.R. 1984): The court declined to adopt a universal rule regulating the use of inadmissible evidence offered to rebut previously admitted evidence that should have been excluded. Instead, the court allocated broad discretion to the trial judge to rule on admissibility in a manner that will promote fair trials.

[f]   Control by the Military Judge—Reopening

Army Court of Criminal Appeals

United States v. Schwarz, 24 M.J. 823 (A.C.M.R. 1987): Relying on Rule 611, R.C.M. 913(c)(1), and R.C.M. 1001(a)(1), the court held that "it is a matter within the military judge's sound discretion whether to let counsel reopen his case either during the prefindings or presentencing stage of a court-martial."

[g]   Control by the Military Judge—Sentencing

United States Court of Appeals for the Armed Forces

United States v. Strong, 17 M.J. 263 (C.M.A. 1984): The court relied on Rule 611 in fashioning a formula to determine whether it would be appropriate to relax the Military Rules of Evidence during sentencing. *See* Rule 1101(c).

Air Force Court of Criminal Appeals

United States v. Pearson, 33 M.J. 913, 915 (A.F.C.M.R. 1991): The accused was convicted of sexually abusing a six-year-old child. During trial, the military judge expressed a "willingness" to hear trial counsel's sentencing witnesses during the government's proof on findings. Although the witnesses did not testify out of order, eventually the accused contended on appeal that the bench's willingness indicated a lack of impartiality. Affirming, this court held that the military judge has discretionary control over the presentation of evidence, and could have adjusted testimony for good reason. However, because those events never occurred, and the accused failed to preserve his objection at trial, relief was denied.

United States v. Weikel, 24 M.J. 666 (A.F.C.M.R. 1987): The court rejected the accused's contention that aggravation evidence was improperly admitted during the sentencing portion of child sexual abuse court-martial. It stated that "the military judge exercises reasonable control over the proceedings, including the order of interrogating witnesses and presenting evidence so as to make the interrogation and presentation effective for the ascertainment of the truth." *See also* R.C.M. 801(a)(3).

Coast Guard Court of Criminal Appeals

United States v. Anderson, 55 M.J. 588 (C.G. Ct.Crim.App. 2001): Consistent with his pleas, the accused was convicted of wrongfully using marijuana, wrongfully using hallucinogenic mushrooms containing psilocyn, wrongfully distributing hallucinogenic mushroom tea containing psilocyn, wrongfully introducing marijuana onto a military installation, and dereliction of duties. During sentencing the prosecution presented opinion testimony of the accused's character during its case-in-chief. The accused contended the testimony was inadmissible. On appeal, the Court held that, although opinion evidence of the accused's character should not have been admitted during the prosecution's case-in-chief, the accused was not prejudiced because the accused introduced evidence of his military character during his case on sentencing. Consequently, the prosecution's evidence would have been admissible in rebuttal. Moreover, it could be assumed that the military judge, as the sentencing authority, was not inappropriately influenced by the premature admission of the evidence that was admissible on rebuttal.

[h]   Control by the Military Judge—Treatment of Counsel

United States Court of Appeals for the Armed Forces

United States v. Loving, 41 M.J. 213 (C.A.A.F. 1994): The accused was convicted of premeditated murder, felony murder, attempted murder, and five specifications of robbery. He was sentenced to death. Affirming the accused's convictions and punishment, this court held that no error occurred when the military judge characterized one of the accused's contentions as "ridiculous," or when he threatened to "deal with defense counsel" after counsel had challenged a ruling. *Citing Liteky v. United States,* 114 S. Ct. 1147 (1994), the court held that expressions of impatience, dissatisfaction, annoyance, and anger are not generally sufficient to establish bias or partiality. In the court's opinion, even a stern and short-tempered judge's ordinary efforts at courtroom administration do not create an atmosphere of bias or partiality.

[i]   Control by the Military Judge—Trial Delays

United States Court of Appeals for the Armed Forces

United States v. Royster, 42 M.J. 488 (C.A.A.F. 1995): The accused was convicted of conduct unbecoming an officer. A two-month continuance was granted during his court-martial. When trial reconvened, the military judge ordered that redacted copies of the record be provided to all court members so that their memories could be refreshed. Affirming the accused's convictions and sentence, the court held that, the trial judge's resourceful solution to a difficult problem was within his discretion and did not prejudice the accused.

Navy-Marine Corps Court of Criminal Appeals

United States v. Ray, 15 M.J. 808 (N.M.C.M.R. 1983): Relying on Rule 611(b), the court found that, the military judge did not abuse his discretion by granting trial counsel's request to recall the accused after a 20-day trial delay. The court noted, however, that future prosecution requests should be preceded by an "offer of proof which would disclose the scope of the desired examination," and suggested that such requests should be denied if they constitute repetitive questioning or harassment, or if the prosecution seeks to go beyond the scope of direct examination.

[j]   Control by the Military Judge—Witness Embarrassment

Navy-Marine Corps Court of Criminal Appeals

United States v. Hayes, 15 M.J. 650 (N.M.C.M.R. 1983): In discussing the appropriate boundaries of cross-examination, the court noted that military judges must guard against counsel *unduly* embarrassing witnesses. "Questions asked with the intent to belittle the witness or subjecting him or her to public ridicule are clearly prohibited because they are probative of no valid issue before the court."

[2]   Rule 611(b)—Scope of Cross-examination

[a]   Scope of Cross-examination—Attack of the Accused

United States Court of Appeals for the Armed Forces

United States v. Castillo, 29 M.J. 145 (C.M.A. 1989): The court held that, by testifying on direct examination about an offense for which he is being tried, an accused does not waive his privilege against self-incrimination with respect to uncharged misconduct at an entirely different time and place, although the prosecutor is still entitled to admit such evidence when it complies with Rule 404(b). It added that an accused who testifies about a charged offense waives his privilege against self-incrimination as to any facts concerning the particular transaction which gave rise to the charge on which he elected to testify, even though those facts may establish his guilt of other crimes.

United States v. Owens, 21 M.J. 117 (C.M.A. 1985): The court highlighted the importance of using this Rule to determine how far a trial counsel can go in cross-examining a defendant who lied about never knowingly providing incomplete answers on an official government document. This is an area which rests largely in the sound discretion of the trial judge.

Air Force Court of Criminal Appeals

United States v. Barnard, 32 M.J. 530 (A.F.C.M.R. 1990): The accused's conviction for writing bad checks was affirmed. Relying on this Rule, the court held that, an accused who chooses to testify on the merits is subject to the same cross-examination as any other witness. As a result, the prosecutor did not impermissibly comment on the accused's right to counsel by asking him whether he saw a lawyer before making a pretrial statement.

United States v. Pierce, 14 M.J. 738 (A.F.C.M.R. 1982): Rejecting the accused's claim that the military judge abused his discretion by allowing the accused to be impeached with specific instances of misconduct, the court cautioned that although the trial bench's discretion in the conduct of cross-examination is "substantial," it is not "unlimited."

Army Court of Criminal Appeals

United States v. Schuring, 16 M.J. 664 (A.C.M.R. 1983): On cross-examination, trial counsel was permitted to ask the accused if he told his pretrial confinement cell mate that he (the accused) had killed a "crazy girl." The reviewing court found the question proper as it dealt with a purported admission by the accused which contradicted his exculpatory testimony, thus affecting credibility.

[b] Scope of Cross-examination—Attack of a Witnesses

Supreme Court

Olden v. Kentucky, 488 U.S. 227 (1988) (per curiam): At his trial on rape charges, the defense theory was that the victim had lied about her contact with the defendant in order to protect her illicit relationship with another man. The trial court, however, refused to let counsel impeach the victim with evidence of that illicit relationship. Citing the constitutional right of confrontation and the right to present evidence of motive and bias, the Court concluded that the trial court had committed reversible error.

United States Court of Appeals for the Armed Forces

United States v. Collier, 67 M.J. 347 (C.A.A.F. 2009): The accused was convicted of stealing military property and obstructing justice. The military judge relied on Rules 403 and 611 in limiting the ability of the defense counsel to cross-examine the key government witness about her failed homosexual romantic relationship with the accused. Defense counsel's theory of the case was that the breakup produced fabricated charges. The military judge found sufficient evidence to establish the failed homosexual romantic relationship and concluded that the relationship was relevant, but limited defense counsel to establishing that the accused and the witness had a failed close friendship. Defense counsel contended the judge's ruling violated the accused's Sixth Amendment right to confrontation because the witness's bias and resulting motive to lie could not be effectively established without proving the failed romantic homosexual relationship. Trial counsel contended there was essentially no difference between a failed friendship and a failed romantic relationship for the purposes of showing bias. Finding a Sixth Amendment violation, the court reversed the accused's convictions using the constitutional harmless beyond a reasonable doubt standard. The witness's testimony was central to the defense's case and was not cumulative. The judge's error essentially prohibited the accused from establishing her best defense and as a result may have tipped the credibility balance in the government's favor. The court reasoned that, while military judges retain wide latitude in applying reasonable limits to cross-examination, the protections in Rules 403 and 611 are 'marginally relevant' when compared with the right to confrontation. The judge's latitude is given less deference when as here findings of fact and conclusions of law were not made. Evidence of bias by definition is prejudicial to the opposing side's case and causes witnesses to be embarrassed and feel threatened. However, unless the evidence is unfairly prejudicial it does not permit completely shutting the door on otherwise relevant cross-examination. The judge's latitude on limiting cross-examination begins only after there has been sufficient cross-examination.

United States v. Stavely, 33 M.J. 92 (C.M.A. 1991): At the accused's court-martial for submitting a fraudulent insurance claim, his neighbor presented the bulk of incriminating testimony. On cross-examination, defense counsel was prohibited from asking her about related incidents where she had lied. Reversing the conviction, the court held that, because this witness's testimony was so important, and defense counsel's examination focused on credibility, the military judge should have afforded the defense far wider latitude.

Air Force Court of Criminal Appeals

United States v. Moore, 12 M.J. 854 (A.F.C.M.R. 1981): At his trial for submitting a false claim, the accused attempted to cross-examine a key government witness concerning her four-year-old mental health evaluation, which demonstrated that she had various behavioral disorders. Defense counsel claimed this evidence affected the witness's credibility and bias. The trial judge directed defense counsel not to inquire into this area while allowing examination on any "possible witness bias against the accused." On appeal the ruling was held to be a proper exercise of discretion.

Army Court of Criminal Appeals

United States v. Krzcuik, 34 M.J. 1002 (A.C.M.R. 1992): Pursuant to his pleas, the accused was convicted of larceny and related offenses. In response to defense counsel's direct examination, the accused's first sergeant testified that the accused always gave 110% at work. On cross-examination, trial counsel asked this witness to explain the accused's duties. The first sergeant replied that the accused was no longer able to perform them because his security clearance had been revoked due to this court-martial. The accused claimed trial counsel's cross was not limited to the scope of direct. The court disagreed and affirmed, holding that trial counsel's questions properly clarified the witness's testimony.

United States v. Peterson, 26 M.J. 906 (A.C.M.R. 1988): In this multiple drug distribution case, the court held it was particularly appropriate for the prosecutor to examine the defense witness on his attitude towards the rehabilitation of the accused as a repeat drug offender and thereby attack the witness's candor and estimate of character.

Navy-Marine Corps Court of Criminal Appeals

United States v. Hayes, 15 M.J. 650 (N.M.C.M.R. 1983): The court reversed the accused's conviction because the trial judge improperly limited defense counsel's cross-examination of a key government witness. Recognizing that cross-examination is not an "unlimited license to expose for exposure's sake," the court noted that cross-examination properly extends to the "subject of direct examination and matters affecting credibility of the witness."

[c] Scope of Cross-examination—Constitutional Issues

United States Court of Appeals for the Armed Forces

United States v. Collier, 67 M.J. 347 (C.A.A.F. 2009): The accused was convicted of stealing military property and obstructing justice. The military judge relied on Rules 403 and 611 in limiting the ability of the defense counsel to cross-examine the key government witness about her failed homosexual romantic relationship with the accused. Defense counsel's theory of the case was that the breakup produced fabricated charges. The military judge found sufficient evidence to establish the failed homosexual romantic relationship and concluded that the relationship was relevant, but limited defense counsel to establishing that the accused and the witness had a failed close friendship. Defense counsel contended the judge's ruling violated the accused's Sixth Amendment right to confrontation because the witness's bias and resulting motive to lie could not be effectively established without proving the failed romantic homosexual relationship. Trial counsel contended there was essentially no difference between a failed friendship and a failed romantic relationship for the purposes of showing bias. Finding a Sixth Amendment violation, the court reversed the accused's convictions using the constitutional harmless beyond a reasonable doubt standard. The witness's testimony was central to the defense's case and was not cumulative. The judge's error essentially prohibited the accused from establishing her best defense and as a result may have tipped the credibility balance in the government's favor. The court reasoned that, while military judges retain wide latitude in applying reasonable limits to cross-examination, the protections in Rules 403 and 611 are 'marginally relevant' when compared with the right to confrontation. The judge's latitude is given less deference when as here findings of fact and conclusions of law were not made. Evidence of bias by definition is prejudicial to the opposing side's case and causes witnesses to be embarrassed and feel threatened. However, unless the evidence is unfairly prejudicial it does not permit completely shutting the door on otherwise relevant cross-examination. The judge's latitude on limiting cross-examination begins only after there has been sufficient cross-examination.

[d] Scope of Cross-examination—Other Crimes or Acts Evidence

United States Court of Appeals for the Armed Forces

United States v. Castillo, 29 M.J. 145 (C.M.A. 1989): The court held that by testifying on direct examination about an offense for which he is being tried, an accused does not waive his privilege against self-incrimination with respect to uncharged misconduct at an entirely different time and place. It added, however, that the prosecutor is still entitled to admit such evidence when it complies with Rule 404(b). Similarly, an accused who testifies about a charged offense waives his privilege against self-incrimination as to any facts concerning the particular transaction which gave rise to the charge on which he elected to testify, even though those facts may establish his guilt of other crimes.

[e] Scope of Cross-examination—Sentencing Evidence

Air Force Court of Criminal Appeals

United States v. Sawyer, 32 M.J. 917 (A.F.C.M.R. 1991): During sentencing, the accused called his commander who testified that the accused had excellent rehabilitative potential. On cross-examination, trial counsel explored the witness's knowledge of the accused's charged and post-charging sexual offenses. Affirming findings and sentence, the court held that trial counsel's examination properly tested the witness's basis of knowledge.

Army Court of Criminal Appeals

United States v. White, 33 M.J. 555 (A.C.M.R. 1991): During the sentencing portion of the accused's drug abuse court-martial, he called a supervisor who testified to the accused's excellent duty performance. On cross-examination, trial counsel asked the witness if she knew that the accused was still using drugs. Affirming the findings and sentence, the court held that when a lay witness gives an opinion, wide latitude must be given on cross-examination to test the basis or persuasive value of that testimony.

[f] Scope of Cross-examination—Sex Offenses

United States Court of Appeals for the Armed Forces

United States v. Collier, 67 M.J. 347 (C.A.A.F. 2009): The accused was convicted of stealing military property and obstructing justice. The issue at trial and on appeal concerned the military judge relying on Rules 403 and 611 to limit the ability of the defense counsel to cross-examine the key government witness about her failed homosexual romantic relationship with the accused. Defense counsel's theory of the case was that the breakup produced the fabricated charges. The military judge found that sufficient evidence had been presented to establish the failed homosexual romantic relationship and that the relationship was relevant. However, the military judge allowed defense counsel to establish only that the accused and the witness had a failed close friendship. Defense counsel contended the judge's ruling violated the accused's Sixth Amendment right to confrontation. Defense counsel argued that the witness's bias and resulting motive to lie could not be effectively established without proving the failed romantic homosexual relationship. Trial counsel contended there was essentially no difference between a failed friendship and a failed romantic relationship for the purposes of showing bias. Reversing the accused's convictions the court held that, while military judges retain wide latitude in applying reasonable limits to cross-examination, the protections in Rules 403 and 611 are 'marginally relevant' when compared with the right to confrontation. The judge's latitude is given less deference when as here findings of fact and conclusions of law were not made. Evidence of bias by definition is prejudicial to the opposing side's case and causes witnesses to be embarrassed and to feel threatened. However, unless the evidence is unfairly prejudicial it does not permit completely shutting the door on otherwise relevant cross-examination. The judge's latitude on limiting cross-examination begins only after there has been sufficient cross-examination.

United States v. Welker, 44 M.J. 85 (C.A.A.F. 1996): Consistent with his pleas, the accused was convicted of numerous sexual offenses upon his stepdaughter. During sentencing, the victim testified for her stepfather saying that she did not want him to go to jail, that the family needed therapy, and that the family should remain together. Over defense objection, trial counsel established the magnitude of the accused's charged and uncharged crimes against his stepdaughter, as well as the threats and inducements the victim's mother had used to procure her daughter's favorable defense testimony. Affirming findings and sentence, this court held that trial counsel's cross-examination was within the scope of direct, and constituted proper specific contradiction of the victim's previous statements.

[f]   Scope of Cross-examination—Striking Direct Testimony

Navy-Marine Corps Court of Criminal Appeals

United States v. Vandermark, 14 M.J. 690 (N.M.C.M.R. 1982): Finding that the trial judge properly exercised his discretion in striking the direct testimony of a witness who refused to be cross-examined on a certain issue, the court opined that "[a]ccommodating conflicts between an accused's interest in testifying and the need to insure truth through cross-examination is one of the trial judge's most important functions."

[3]   Rule 611(c)—Leading Questions

[a]   Leading Questions—Hostile Witness Bases

United States Court of Appeals for the Armed Forces

United States v. Loving, 41 M.J. 213 (C.A.A.F. 1994): The accused was convicted of premeditated murder, felony murder, attempted murder, and five specifications of robbery. He was sentenced to death. Affirming the accused's convictions and punishment, the court held that no error occurred when the military judge failed to allow defense counsel to treat one of his witnesses as hostile, and take her as if on cross-examination. In the court's opinion, defense counsel failed to establish a justification for his request, particularly because the witness demonstrated such clear affection for the accused.

[b]   Leading Questions—Sex Offenses

United States Court of Appeals for the Armed Forces

United States v. Quick, 26 M.J. 460 (C.M.A. 1988): Affirming the accused's conviction for sexually molesting his four-year-old daughter, the court held that the victim could be called by the defense and cross-examined as a hostile witness.

Army Court of Criminal Appeals

United States v. Boykin, 36 M.J. 655 (A.C.M.R. 1992): Affirming the accused's convictions for indecent acts with a child, the court said no error occurred when trial counsel used extensive leading questions to develop the testimony of a six-year-old witness. In the court's opinion, government counsel's questions were not so leading as to create a situation where it was he and not the witness who was testifying.

[c]   Leading Questions—Foundation for Exclusion

Army Court of Criminal Appeals

United States v. McCollum, 56 M.J. 837 (Army Ct.Crim.App. 2002): During the accused's court-martial for raping and committing indecent acts upon a child, the military judge required the accused's absence from the courtroom while the victim was on the stand. Affirming the accused's convictions and sentence the court held that its review of the military judge's ruling did not extend to constitutional questions; that those had already be settled by previous appellate resolutions. Here the court limited its findings to whether there was an adequate factual and procedural foundation for the accused's exclusion. The government's compliance with this Rule came from a licensed clinical social worker with a master's degree in social work. Qualified as an expert witness, she was able to demonstrate the emotional harm and difficulty the victim would suffer if required to testify in the accused's presence. The military judge made case specific findings indicating that the victim's fear of testifying was more than *de minimis* and not simply a generalized fear of the courtroom, but was directly connected to the accused's presence even though the young victim said she was not afraid of the accused.

[4]

[a]   Rule 611(d)—Remote Live Testimony of a Child

United States Court of Appeals for the Armed Forces

United States v. Pack, 65 M.J. 381 (C.A.A.F. 2007): The accused was convicted of sexually abusing his 8-year-old daughter. Pursuant to *Maryland v. Craig*, 497 U.S. 836 (1990), the trial judge permitted the victim to testify from a remote location via one-way closed-circuit television. The trial judge overruled defense counsel's objection to this process and found that remote testimony was necessary to protect the child's welfare, the child would be traumatized if she testified, and the emotional distress she would suffer would be more than "*de minimis*." The issue on appeal concerned only whether *Crawford v. Washington*, 541 U.S. 36 (2004), had by implication overruled *Craig*. The court affirmed the accused's convictions and held that *Crawford* had not overruled *Craig* by implication. The court reasoned that the Supreme Court does not favor that practice, the victim had in fact been cross-examined during trial, *Crawford* did not require face-to-face cross-examination, and the great weight of authority since *Crawford* has also refused to overrule or limit *Craig*.

[b]   Taking Testimony of Child Victim or Witness

Navy-Marine Corps Court of Criminal Appeals

United States v. Shabazz, 52 M.J. 585 (N.M. Ct.Crim.App. 1999): This case was tried before the effective date of Rule 611(d). While *Shabazz* does not involve a child witness issue, and therefore would not be affected by Rule 611(d), the case is very important because it points out problems that military judges and counsel must be sensitive to when dealing with remote witness testimony and video-teleconferencing. The accused was tried in Okinawa for distributing marijuana and for maiming. A key government witness to the maiming offense was located in the United States but refused to return to Okinawa for trial. Over defense objection, the military judge permitted her testimony to be received by video-teleconference. Unfortunately, the trial judge failed to maintain proper control over the remote site, and the audio portion of the videotape clearly demonstrated that the witness, while testifying, was being coached by someone off-camera. Despite the clear potential impropriety, the trial record failed to adequately identify or deal with this problem. On appeal, the government conceded that it could not be established "from the record before us the full extent of the coaching Mrs. White received during her testimony." Setting aside the accused's maiming conviction, this court held that "the Sixth Amendment right to confront Mrs. White was violated when the military judge failed to ensure the reliability of her testimony. . . ." The court went on to say that the trial judge abused his discretion by accepting inadequate proffers that were intended to demonstrate that no impropriety occurred.

§ 612.01   Official Text

Rule 612.   Writing Used to Refresh Memory.

If a witness uses a writing to refresh his or her memory for the purpose of testifying, either

(1) while testifying, or

(2) before testifying, if the military judge determines it is necessary in the interests of justice, an adverse party is entitled to have the writing produced at the hearing, to inspect it, to cross-examine the witness thereon, and to introduce in evidence those portions which relate to the testimony of the witness. If it is claimed that the writing contains privileged information or matters not related to the subject matter of the testimony, the military judge shall examine the writing in camera, excise any privileged information or portions not so related, and order delivery of the remainder to the party entitled thereto. Any portion withheld over objections shall be attached to the record of trial as an appellate exhibit. If a writing is not produced or delivered pursuant to order under this rule, the military judge shall make any order justice requires, except that when the prosecution elects not to comply, the order shall be one striking the testimony or, if in discretion of the military judge it is determined that the interests of justice so require, declaring a mistrial. This rule does not preclude disclosure of information required to be disclosed under other provisions of these rules or this Manual.

---

§ 612.02   Editorial Comment

[1]   Refreshing Memory Generally

In large part, the military version of Rule 612 mirrors its federal counterpart. However, the drafters viewed the federal language dealing with the Jencks Act, 18 U.S.C. § 3500,[1] as being more restrictive than discovery in military practice. As a result, they omitted any reference to the Act.

Rule 612 provides that a writing may be used to refresh a witness's memory while the witness is on the stand, or before the witness testifies.[2] If the writing is used at trial, it must be made available to the opposing party, who can employ it in an effort to show that the witness is not really

---

[1] *See, e.g.,* United States v. Soto, 711 F.2d 1558 (11th Cir. 1983) (discusses relationship of Jencks Act and Rule, concluding that police officers' destruction of handwritten notes and reports after they were reduced to typed copies violated no rule).

[2] *See* Schlueter, Saltzburg, Schinasi & Imwinkelried, MILITARY EVIDENTIARY FOUNDATIONS § 11-5 (4th ed. 2010) (examples of using writing to refresh witness's memory).

remembering but is being coached. If memory was refreshed before trial, disclosure of the material used to refresh it may, but need not, be required by the trial judge in the interests of justice. However, those portions of the document that do not aid in renewing the witness's memory should be redacted as being irrelevant.

Although the Rule is limited to refreshing memory, there is a decided trend in civilian courts to treat any use of documents to "prepare" a witness as falling under the Rule. For example, in *Berkey Photo, Inc. v. Eastman Kodak Co.,*[3] the court warned that even counsel's work product, that would otherwise be exempt from production (see our discussion *below*), might be admissible under this Rule if it were purposefully used to prepare a witness for trial. In the court's words: "To put the point succinctly, there will be hereafter powerful reason to hold that materials considered work product should be withheld from prospective witnesses if they are to be withheld from opposing parties."

[2] Privileged Information in the Writing

A party's ability to obtain evidence is not absolute even under Rule 612(1). Statements used to refresh recollection may be protected from disclosure if they contain privileged information or matters not related to the content of the witness's testimony. If privilege or relevance claims are made, the trial judge shall order the document produced and examine it in camera. The bench must excise any privileged information or other matter not reasonably related to the witness's testimony. Once this redaction has occurred, the military judge should then order the remainder of the document turned over to opposing counsel.

The Rule also provides that, if any material has been withheld by the bench, it must be appended to the record of trial so that appellate review will be facilitated. Although the Rule and its Drafters' Analysis are silent on this matter, military authority requires a copy of the record of trial to be served on defense counsel and the accused. If the record contains privileged information, Rule 612's provision for keeping it from the accused may be frustrated. Thus, when the record is served, the withheld material should be separately forwarded to the appellate agencies for review and consideration.[4]

If a privilege is waived by disclosure to a witness, then the waiver would allow the previously privileged material to be disclosed. If the trial court's order to produce or disclose evidence is not respected, the bench may order corrective action. Any order that justice requires may be entered against the accused, but if the government withholds evidence, the court must strike the

---

[3] 457 F.Supp. 404 (S.D.N.Y. 1977), *rev'd on other grounds,* 603 F.2d 263 (2d Cir. 1979), *cert. denied,* 444 U.S. 1093 (1980).

[4] *Compare* with Section V of Military Rules of Evidence discussing privileges.

direct testimony, or in the judge's discretion, declare a mistrial when justice requires.

It should be noted that nothing in Rule 612 is intended to preempt the military's already broad discovery rules, that require the prosecution to permit defense counsel to examine any document accompanying the charges, including the report of investigation and papers sent with the charges on a rehearing.

[3] Documents Used at Trial to Refresh Memory

Rule 612 alters past military practices very little. Paragraph 146*a* of the previous *Manual* permitted a witness's recollection to be refreshed with any form of documentary evidence as long as opposing counsel was given the opportunity to examine it and to introduce it if he or she felt it was inconsistent with the proponent's case or it would assist him in some other fashion.[5]

Experience under the Military and Federal Rule indicates that virtually any document may be used to refresh a witness's recollection.[6] This includes statements previously made by the witness or by someone other than the witness; originals, duplicates, and copies of documents; and even statements that may seem inconsistent or contrary to the witness's testimony. Similarly, the refreshing document need not be independently admissible.[7] Often it will have hearsay, best evidence, authentication, or other infirmities that prohibit it from being considered as substantive evidence. As long as the members do not see a document used to refresh recollection, a short limiting instruction that the document itself is not admissible should suffice to assure that the document is not misused.[8]

[4] Relationship to Rule 803(5)

Refreshing memory is only one technique counsel can use to assist a witness who is currently unable to testify because of a memory failure or lapse. The other technique is to use the hearsay exception for recorded recollections.[9] Rule 803(5) allows qualifying supporting documents to be admitted and read to the members as substantive evidence. *United States v.*

---

[5] *See, e.g.,* United States v. Carey, 589 F.3d 187 (5th Cir. 2009) (any writing may be used to refresh recollection regardless of whether the witness being refreshed authored it).

[6] As the court said in 20th Century Wear, Inc. v. Sanmark-Starburst, Inc., 747 F.2d 81 (2d Cir. 1984), even tape recordings and similar medium can be used to refresh a witness' memory.

[7] *See, e.g.,* United States v. Scott, 701 F.2d 1340 (11th Cir. 1983) (government could use documents that were inadmissible because of discovery violation to refresh memory of witness).

[8] *See, e.g.,* United States v. Harris, 908 F.2d 728 (11th Cir. 1990) (proper to tell jury that refreshing documents used on cross-examination were not admissible).

[9] *See* Schlueter, Saltzburg, Schinasi & Imwinkelried, MILITARY EVIDENTIARY FOUNDA-

Riccardi,[10] provides the classic distinction between how recorded recollection and refreshed memory evidence should be viewed:

> The primary difference between the two classifications is the ability of the witness to testify from present knowledge: where the witness's memory is revived, and he presently recollects the facts and swears to them, he is obviously in a different position from the witness who cannot directly state the facts from present memory and who must ask the court to accept a writing for the truth of its contents because he is willing to swear, for one reason or another, that its contents are true.

Practice also demonstrates that counsel need do very little to take advantage of Rule 612. It is generally sufficient if the witness states that his present recollection of the events is now depleted, but if he were permitted to refer to a known document, his or her memory might be refreshed.[11] No further demonstration is necessary.

[5] Memory Refreshed Before Trial

The second aspect of Rule 612 made a change in military practice. It allows opposing counsel to determine whether a witness has used any document or writing in preparation for trial. If this has occurred, counsel may request that the document be produced for possible use during cross-examination. The court has discretion to allow this. Careful counsel will ask opposing witnesses whether they have consulted documents in preparation for trial.

Neither the Drafters' Analysis nor the Rule itself suggest any time restraints on the implementation of 612(2). It is uncertain whether a witness's reference to a document six weeks before trial would be as likely to result in an order to turn over the document as when memory is refreshed on the morning of trial.

To resolve these questions counsel and the military judge may want to use a Rule 403 analysis and consider: (1) the degree to which the witness actually relied upon the document; (2) how similar his or her in-court testimony is to the document's content; (3) what other documents, conversations, or independent events may have contributed to refreshing the witness's memory; (4) how important to the litigation is the refreshing document; and (5) whether it contains privileged or work product doctrine information.

It does appear, however, that the witness must have used the document for

---

TIONS § 11-5 (4th ed. 2010) (discussion of, and sample foundations for, past recollection recorded and present memory refreshed).

[10] 174 F.2d 883, 886 (3d Cir. 1949).

[11] In United States v. Jimenez, 613 F.2d 1373 (5th Cir. 1980), the court warned prosecutors to establish that a witness needs to have his recollection refreshed before a statement is shown to him.

the specific purpose of preparing for trial. Although the time lag between use and testimony need not be outcome-determinative in every case, it may be that fears concerning the "planting" of ideas with a witness increase the more a witness is focusing on the testimony to be given at trial. This is more likely to be the case when memory is refreshed immediately before or during the recess of a trial.

Difficulties in applying the Rule will arise when an otherwise proper request for a document conflicts with the attorney-client privilege or with the work product doctrine. For example, in preparing her client for trial, an attorney may have collected and organized certain information to facilitate a witness's testimony. This might include the accused's personal statement. Under Rule 1101, which makes privileges applicable throughout the proceedings, and under Rule 502, we believe an accused may refer to his or her own statement to refresh memory without waiving any privilege. There is less reason to be protective of work product, and if a witness uses work product to prepare testimony, the trend in federal cases, as illustrated by *Berkey Photo, above*, is to hold that the work product should be subject to disclosure under the Rule.[12]

§ 612.03   Drafters' Analysis

Rule 612 is taken generally from the Federal Rule but a number of modifications have been made to adapt the Rule to military practice. Language in the Federal Rule relating to the Jencks Act, 18 U.S.C. § 3500, which would have shielded material from disclosure to the defense under Rule 612 was discarded. Such shielding was considered to be inappropriate in view of the general military practice and policy that utilizes and encourages broad discovery on behalf of the defense.

The decision of the president of a special court-martial without a military judge under this Rule is an interlocutory ruling not subject to objection by the members, ¶ 57a.

Rule 612 codifies the doctrine of past recollection refreshed and replaces that portion of ¶ 146a of the present *Manual* that now deals with the issue. Although the present *Manual* rule is similar, in that it authorizes inspection by the opposing party of a memorandum used to refresh recollection and permits it to be offered into evidence by that party to show the improbability of it refreshing recollection, the Rule is somewhat more extensive as it also deals with writings used before testifying.

Rule 612 does not affect in any way information required to be disclosed under any other rule or portion of the *Manual. See, e.g.,* Rule 304(c)(1).

---

[12] *See, e.g.,* United States v. Nobles, 422 U.S. 225 (1975), for a discussion of Rule 612's possible application to a very broad category of pretrial statements including those which may not otherwise be discoverable and those which were not used to refresh the witness's recollection.

§ 612.04   Annotated Cases

United States Court of Appeals for the Armed Forces

United States v. Haston, 24 M.J. 313 (C.M.A. 1987): During trial, a German witness was unable to recall the details of her Article 32 testimony and the accused's sexual assault. The military judge, in a side bar conference, "suggested a lunch recess would be appropriate, and then recommended that refreshing [the witness's] memory could take place in the trial counsel's office during the break." Defense counsel concurred in the process. Rejecting appellate defense counsel's contention that the military judge's suggestion violated Rule 612 and the accused's right to confrontation, the court said: (a) Rule 612 is not an "exclusive catalogue of instances under which a witness's recollection may be refreshed," (b) it is "designed to regulate the discovery of documents [and] and accused's only remedy thereunder is production of the document used to refresh recollection . . . ," (c) the accused "had more than adequate opportunity to confront the witness," and (d) defense counsel "was also privileged to point out to the members the fact that [the victim's] memory had been refreshed by the document."

Air Force Court of Criminal Appeals

United States v. Hopwood, 29 M.J. 530 (A.F.C.M.R. 1990): During this forgery and false official statement trial, defense counsel questioned a key government witness about that witness's out of court statement. Although defense counsel never offered the statement, trial counsel did over objection. The reviewing court held that the writing was properly used to establish an accurate basis for refreshed memory.

§ 613.01   Official Text

Rule 613.   Prior Statements of Witnesses.

(a) *Examining Witness Concerning Prior Statement.* In examining a witness concerning a prior statement made by the witness, whether written or not, the statement need not be shown nor its contents disclosed to the witness at that time, but on request the same shall be shown or disclosed to opposing counsel.

(b) *Extrinsic evidence of prior inconsistent statement of witness.* Extrinsic evidence of a prior inconsistent statement by a witness is not admissible unless the witness is afforded an opportunity to explain or deny the same and the opposite party is afforded an opportunity to interrogate the witness thereon, or the interests of justice otherwise require. This provision does not apply to admissions of a party-opponent as defined in Military Rule of Evidence 801(d)(2).

---

§ 613.02   Editorial Comment

[1]   Rule 613(a)—Examining Witness Concerning Prior Statement

[a]   Relationship to Rule 801(d)(1)

This is one of the key Rules litigators use to attack an opposing party's witnesses.[1] It deals with introducing evidence of a witness's previous out-of-court inconsistent statements for impeachment purposes.[2] The military drafters adopted Rule 613 from its federal counterpart without change.[3] Although the Rule's principle effect is with respect to prior inconsistent statements, the word "inconsistent" does not appear in the Rule's title. This is intentional, because subdivision (a) addresses the use of *any* prior statement of a witness, whether offered as substantive or impeachment

---

[1] *See, e.g.,* United States v. Aubin, 13 M.J. 623 (A.F.C.M.R. 1982): After a key government witness testified during the accused's trial, defense counsel was permitted to call its own witness to relate, in detail, the prior inconsistent statements made by the government's witness.

[2] In United States v. Mendoza, 18 M.J. 576 (A.C.M.R. 1984), even though defense counsel failed to object at trial, the reviewing court found error when the military judge sua sponte decided to consider impeachment evidence "in deciding the merits of the case." *See* Schlueter, Saltzburg, Schinasi & Imwinkelried, MILITARY EVIDENTIARY FOUNDATIONS § 5-10, et seq. (4th ed. 2010) (sample foundations for impeaching witness with oral and written statements and testimony).

[3] The original edition of the 1984 Manual for Court Martial incorrectly stated Rule 613 (a), excluding the following language: "the witness at that time, but on request the same shall be shown or disclosed to." In March 1989, a technical amendment to the Rule itself and the Drafters' Analysis corrected this error.

evidence, and whether the statement is inconsistent or consistent with the witness's testimony.[4] The Drafters' Analysis questions this, but we think that the Drafters' Analysis misses the connection between Rules 801(d)(1) and 613.[5] Rule 801(d)(1) controls the *substantive* use of inconsistent statements, consistent statements, and prior identifications as *exemptions* to the hearsay rules.

Subdivision (a) of Rule 613 applies to Rule 801 as well as to statements offered solely for impeachment.[6] Using Rule 613 allows counsel to examine a witness about a prior statement without first showing or disclosing the contents of the statement to the witness, whether the statement is admissible as substantive evidence or only as impeachment evidence.[7]

Subdivision (b) of Rule 613 is also a rule of procedure. It requires that a witness have an opportunity to explain or deny any inconsistent statement. The Rule affects all inconsistent statements used for impeachment. It has no real impact on prior statements admissible as substantive evidence under Rule 801(d)(1)(A). Rule 801(d)(1) itself requires that the witness be subject to cross-examination on the prior statement. As a result, Rule 801(d)(1)(A) imposes an absolute requirement that there be an opportunity for cross-examination if a statement is to be used as substantive evidence.

[b]   Foundation Requirement

This Rule changed the foundation requirements for use of prior statements. At common law, and under pre-Military Rules of Evidence practice, if a witness was to be impeached with a prior inconsistent statement a foundation had to be established first. To accomplish this, counsel had to direct the witness's attention to the time and place of the statement, and the person or persons to whom it was made, and then ask the witness if he or she made the statement. This requirement applied whether the prior statement was oral or written. Like the common law, the military's prior rule operated to protect the witness from unfair surprise by informing the witness of his or her past statement. Some supporters of the old rule believed that, when the witness was faced with his or her alleged prior statement, the witness was more likely to be truthful about it.

But many critics believed that the rule had the opposite effect, and that the

---

[4] *See,* Conn, *A View From the Bench Using a Witness's Prior Statements and Testimony at Trial.* ARMY LAW., Mar. 2007, at 39.

[5] The United States Court of Appeals for the Armed Forces has addressed this issue in United States v. Taylor, 44 M.J. 475, 476 (1996), and United States v. Ureta, 44 M.J. 290 (1996), discussed in our Annotated Cases.

[6] *See, e.g.,* United States v. Harris, 18 M.J. 809 (A.F.C.M.R. 1984) (although it was error to admit a witness's pretrial statements under Rule 803(24), the court recognized that the statements could have been used for impeachment purposes under this provision).

[7] *See* Behan, *The Thrill and Excitement of Impeachment by Contradiction,* ARMY LAW., Oct. 2004, at 10.

process of establishing a foundation prior to using inconsistent statements allowed the dishonest witness to reshape his or her testimony, anticipate questions, and thus frustrate counsel by preventing the witness's cross-examination from being an effective truth-developing mechanism.

Although the literature indicates that federal judges often failed to honor the strict common law foundational requirements,[8] their military counter-parts scrupulously enforced them. Rule 613 abandons past practice and provides that, when counsel is examining a witness based on an inconsistent oral or written pretrial statement, that statement need not be shown to the witness, nor must its contents be disclosed to the witness during cross-examination. If opposing counsel, however, requests the statement, it must be shown or disclosed to him or her.[9]

While the Rule is unclear as to how disclosure should be made, it appears that counsel need do no more than provide the opposing party with the statement in the same form it was received. Thus, if counsel obtained a document displaying the previous inconsistent statement, the document should be shown. If the information was transmitted in oral form, counsel need only disclose the statement, and its accompanying transmittal details. In either event, disclosure is not required until the witness is actually examined about his or her prior statement. It is important to note that no information need be given to opposing counsel unless a specific request is made for it.

[2] Rule 613(b)—Extrinsic Evidence of Prior Inconsistent Statement of Witness

[a] Timing of Witness's Explanation

On its face, Rule 613(b) allows the impeaching party an almost absolute right to delay the witness's opportunity to talk about his prior inconsistent statement and to explain or deny it. The statement may be in evidence for some time before the witness is recalled. In fact, the prior inconsistent statement need not be offered or mentioned during cross-examination, but may be withheld until other witnesses are called. This may be particularly useful if counsel is attempting to demonstrate collusion among witnesses.

Thus the statement may be offered to impeach a witness after the witness has left the stand. The Rule provides that the witness must be afforded an opportunity to explain or deny an inconsistent statement, but does not

---

[8] However, some federal judges now feel that Rule 613 has created an untenable situation for witnesses. Relying on the connection between Rule 613 and 611(a), these judges now require counsel to establish a foundation before using the previous statements. *See* United States v. Devine, 934 F.2d 1325 (5th Cir. 1991) (trial court retained traditional common law foundational requirements).

[9] *See, e.g.,* United States v. Lawson, 683 F.2d 688 (2d Cir. 1982) (opposing counsel has right to see written statement used to impeach witness).

require that the opportunity be afforded before the statement is offered. A subsequent opportunity is acceptable.[10] This may unfairly detract from the witness's ability to put the statement in perspective. Also, any delay associated with keeping the witness on call for the moment when the opportunity to explain is afforded will needlessly keep the witness at the courthouse or nearby. This is particularly troubling in the military, where witnesses for both sides may have substantial command responsibilities. Of course, the trial court retains its discretion to control the presentation of evidence and witnesses under Rule 611(a), and thus may order that any use of prior inconsistent statements proceed as at common law unless the court is shown a bona fide reason for departing from the familiar foundation requirement.

Situations may arise in which the impeached witness may become unavailable after his or her testimony, but before he or she has had an opportunity to explain or deny the inconsistent statement. Under these circumstances, Rule 613(b) clearly gives the military judge authority to admit the inconsistent statement despite the absence of an opportunity to explain or deny if the interests of justice so require.

[b]   Extrinsic Evidence of Statement

Rule 613(b) makes it clear that extrinsic evidence may be admitted before the witness is offered an opportunity to "explain or deny" the statement. The inconsistent statement may be revealed by another witness. The party who called the witness is entitled to explain the circumstances under which the statement was made and the reasons why the statements may have differed from trial testimony.

For example, when the previous statement was made, the witness may have been acting in response to threats, fear, or duress, the statement may have been taken out of context; the witness may have misunderstood questions, or misspoke when the prior statement was made.

[c]   Dispensing with the Foundation

The last sentence of Rule 613(b) provides that the opportunity to explain or deny any inconsistency may be abrogated when the "interests of justice otherwise require." Although neither the Rule itself nor the Drafters' Analysis illustrates when this exception is likely to be invoked, we suggest that this provision might be important when a party discovers that an inconsistent statement exists after a witness is excused and the witness is then outside the trial court's jurisdiction. The provision might also be

---

[10] In United States v. King, 560 F.2d 122 (2d Cir. 1977), the court recognized counsel's ability to introduce a prior inconsistent statement without laying a foundation, but noted such tactics might lead to later exclusion of that evidence if it would take counsel more time to substantiate the statement than was warranted under the circumstances.

important when the witness has been discharged from the service and cannot be located.

[d]   The Burden of Recalling the Witness

Nowhere in the Rule is it indicated which party must afford the impeached witness the opportunity to explain or to deny an inconsistent statement. Is it the responsibility of the party attacking the witness to give the witness a chance to explain? Or is this left to the party who is relying on the witness? In our view, the attacking party should bear the burden, since he or she knows the attack is coming and that the witness might not be available to explain or deny the statement if it is held in reserve rather than used while the witness first testifies. If the attacker does not indicate that the witness may have to be recalled, then the chances increase that the witness will become unavailable at the time the impeachment takes place. Moreover, at common law the attacker had to lay a foundation. Rule 613 appears to authorize a delayed "foundation" or opportunity for the impeached witness to be heard and not to shift the burden of providing the foundation.

[e]   Basis of Knowledge

Rule 613 is silent on the standard counsel is required to meet concerning whether a prior inconsistent statement exists at all before impeachment is allowed. The Rule does not require counsel to establish the inconsistent statement with extrinsic proof. This lack of a foundational requirement means that a witness could be attacked with an alleged inconsistent statement that never existed.

Whether the inconsistent statement was actually made is a matter opposing counsel should explore *in limine* when possible, or after a timely trial objection followed by an Article 39(a) session. The military judge should require the proponent to establish a good faith basis for believing that the statement was made and is accurate.[11] This process would be similar to the requirement imposed on trial counsel pursuant to Rule 404(b), or upon counsel for both sides under Rule 405 when examining a character witness about prior bad acts.

[f]   Party Admissions

Finally, it should be noted that Rule 613 does not govern if Rule 801(d)(2) admissions are introduced. They may be offered and accepted as *substantive* evidence without a foundation having been laid first.

§ 613.03   Drafters' Analysis

[1]   Examining witness concerning prior statement

Rule 613(a) is taken from the Federal Rule without change. It alters

---

[11] *See, e.g.,* United States v. Almonte, 956 F.2d 27 (2d Cir. 1992) (proponent bears the burden of authenticating the inconsistent statement).

military practice inasmuch as it eliminates the foundation requirements found in *Manual* ¶ 153*b*(2)(c) of the present *Manual.* While it will no longer be a condition precedent to admissibility to acquaint a witness with the prior statement and to give the witness an opportunity to either change his or her testimony or to reaffirm it, such a procedure may be appropriate as a matter of trial tactics.

It appears that the drafters of Federal Rule 613 may have inadvertently omitted the word "inconsistent" from both its caption and the text of Rule 613(a). The effect of that omission, if any, is unclear.

[2]   Extrinsic evidence of prior inconsistent statement of witness

Rule 613(b) is taken from the Federal Rule without change. It requires that the witness be given an opportunity to explain or deny a prior inconsistent statement when the party proffers extrinsic evidence of the statement. Although this foundation is not required under Rule 613(a), it is required under Rule 613(b) if a party wishes to utilize more than the witness's own testimony as brought out on cross-examination. The Rule does not specify any particular timing for the opportunity for the witness to explain or deny the statement nor does it specify any particular method. The Rule is inapplicable to introduction of prior inconsistent statements on the merits under Rule 801.

§ 613.04   Drafters' Analysis (1987)

The phrase "to him at that time, but on request the same shall be shown or disclosed" was added to correct its inadvertent omission from MCM, 1984.

§ 613.05   Annotated Cases

[1]   Rule 613(a)—Examining Witness Concerning Prior Statement

[a]   A Witness's Prior Statements—Bias and Rule 608 Relationship

Air Force Court of Criminal Appeals

United States v. Vines, 57 M.J.519 (A.F. Ct.Crim.App. 2002): Affirming the accused's convictions for rape, indecent acts and related offenses, the court held that trial defense counsel was competent in presenting evidence used to impeach the victim and show that she had a bias to fabricate the charges against his client. The court indicted that over government objection, defense counsel cross-examined the victim about numerous prior allegations of rape she had made to co-workers concerning her previous boyfriend. When the victim denied making these allegations, defense counsel introduced the co-workers' testimony regarding the prior rape allegations.

[b]   A Witness's Prior Statements—Collateral Matters

United States Court of Appeals for the Armed Forces

United States v. Banker, 15 M.J. 207 (C.M.A. 1983): In a drug prosecution the trial judge rejected a prior statement of the key government witness who had denied use of drugs while he was working as an informant on the ground that it would impeach on a collateral matter. Although the court affirmed the conviction, it reasoned that the witness's prior statement was not offered simply to show that the witness was inconsistent, but also to negate the witness's claim that he was free of drugs and had only the best motives for cooperating with the government. It found that the evidence was admissible for this purpose, but that its exclusion was not prejudicial.

Air Force Court of Criminal Appeals

United States v. Tyler, 26 M.J. 680 (A.F.C.M.R. 1988): The accused's drug distribution conviction was affirmed despite his contention that the military judge erroneously prohibited him from cross-examining a key government witness about that witness's unrelated false insurance claims. The court viewed the evidence as "collateral," minimally probative of truthfulness, and confusing.

[c]   A Witness's Prior Statements—Distinguished from Hearsay

United States Court of Appeals for the Armed Forces

United States v. Kindle, 45 M.J. 284 (C.A.A.F. 1996): The accused was convicted of manslaughter. At trial, he unsuccessfully attempted to introduce a statement the deceased's wife made after the crime. The accused contended that this statement was admissible under Rule 803(24), and would have helped establish his self-defense claim. Affirming the accused's conviction, the court held that even though the testimony could not be used for substantive purposes under a hearsay exception, it was admissible as a prior inconsistent statement and could be used to impeach the declarant's credibility when she denied making it.

[d]   A Witness's Prior Statements—Offer of Proof Required

United States Court of Appeals for the Armed Forces

United States v. Palmer, 55 M.J. 205 (C.A.A.F. 2001): The accused was convicted of unlawful possession, distribution, and use of marijuana. At trial, three witnesses testified about the accused's possession, distribution, and use of marijuana. During the defense case, a Specialist testified about a conversation he heard between the accused and one of the government's witnesses. The defense argued that the testimony was admissible under Rule 613, to prove that the government witness made a statement prior to trial that was inconsistent to his testimony at trial. The prosecution objected on hearsay grounds. The judge sustained the government's objection. The Army Court of Criminal Appeals affirmed the conviction. This court held that the military judge did not abuse his discretion by excluding evidence of a prior inconsistent statement of a witness, where defense counsel offered the evidence under a hearsay exception as evidence of the witness's state of mind, and where defense counsel never alluded to the inconsistency between the pretrial statement of the witness and his trial testimony as the basis for admission of the statement. The court went on to state that when the basis for admissibility of evidence is not obvious, an offer of proof is required to clearly and specifically identify the evidence sought to be admitted and its significance.

[e]   A Witness's Prior Statements—Relationship to Rule 801(d)

United States Court of Appeals for the Armed Forces

United States v. Taylor, 44 M.J. 475, 476 (C.A.A.F. 1996): During this court-martial for premeditated murder, burglary, and larceny, trial and defense counsel introduced prior inconsistent and consistent statements to impeach or bolster witness. The military judge provided instructions on how the statements could be used. Affirming the accused's convictions and sentence, this court discussed the interplay between substantive hearsay evidence introduced under Rule 801, and impeachment hearsay evidence introduced pursuant to Rule 613. Importantly, the court held that any error which may have occurred in the use of this evidence was waived because defense counsel failed to make a timely objection.

United States v. Ureta, 44 M.J. 290 (C.A.A.F 1996): Affirming the accused's convictions for sexually abusing his daughter, this court held that where the declarant wife is available at trial and testifies that she made a previous statement but now recants it, extrinsic evidence of that statement is not admissible under Rule 613(b). However, when the statement is contained in previous Article 32 testimony, and qualifies for admission under 801(d)(1)(A), the transcript itself may be admissible as substantive evidence.

United States v. Button, 34 M.J. 139 (C.M.A. 1992): The accused's stepdaughter told her mother that the accused was sexually abusing her. Thereafter, the victim made similar complaints to OSI agents and social workers. Her verbatim Article 32 testimony was consistent with these complaints. At trial, the prosecutrix recanted all previous statements, but admitted to having made them. Trial counsel was then permitted to introduce the statements. Reviewing military and federal authority, the court held that it was error to admit the OSI and social worker statements because declarant acknowledged the specific inconsistencies between them and her in-court testimony. However, the conviction was affirmed because the Article 32 testimony had been properly admitted.

United States v. Jackson, 12 M.J. 163 (C.M.A. 1981): This court noted the difference between prior inconsistent statements admitted under Rule 613 for impeachment purposes and those admitted under 801(d)(1) for substantive purposes. Counsel would be wise to heed the Court's warning that prior statements can only be used for the truth of the matter asserted therein when they qualify under Rule 801(d)(1)'s exemption from the hearsay rule.

Air Force Court of Criminal Appeals

United States v. Toro, 34 M.J. 506 (A.F.C.M.R. 1992): In this drug prosecution, trial counsel used five of the accused's cohorts to prove the offenses charged. On cross-examination, defense counsel attacked all witnesses with their prior inconsistent statements. Thereafter, trial counsel was permitted to introduce 19 written statements (which the members were allowed to take with them into deliberations) demonstrating his witnesses' consistency. Affirming all convictions, this court said that the Military Rules of Evidence provide sufficient maneuvering room for trial counsel's tactics. *See* our discussion of this case under Rule 801(d)(1)(B).

Navy-Marine Corps Court of Criminal Appeals

United States v. Tiller, 41 M.J. 823 (N.M. Ct.Crim.App. 1995): In this rape and assault case, the accused's rape conviction was reversed because the trial judge erroneously excluded constitutionally-required evidence demonstrating that the victim had engaged in consensual sexual intercourse with another man thirty minutes before the alleged offense occurred. The court also noted that on cross-examination, and pursuant to Rule 801(d)(1)(A), defense counsel unsuccessfully attempted to impeach the victim with her prior inconsistent statement because he failed to establish that the statement had been adopted at the Article 32 hearing. As a result, instead of being able to use the pretrial statement as substantive evidence under Rule 801(d)(1)(A), the military judge limited its use to impeachment only.

[f]   A Witness's Prior Statements—Silence as an Inconsistent Statement

Army Court of Criminal Appeals

United States v. Langford, 15 M.J. 1090 (A.C.M.R. 1983): A defense witness was properly cross-examined about her previous silence at a civilian hearing which dealt with the same issues she was testifying to at the accused's trial. The court said that the "prior silence of a witness may be used to impeach his or her in-court testimony as an inconsistency if it would have been natural to speak at the previous time."

[g]   A Witness's Prior Statements—Showing Inconsistent Statement to Witness

United States Court of Appeals for the Armed Forces

United States v. Callara, 21 M.J. 259 (C.M.A. 1986): The court emphasized that this Rule does not require a cross-examiner to show the witness his prior statement before asking the witness about it. "Indeed the statement need not be shown or disclosed by the cross-examiner unless the opposing counsel makes a specific request."

[2] Rule 613(b)—Extrinsic Evidence of Prior Inconsistent Statement of Witness

[a] Extrinsic Evidence of Statement—Calling a Witness to Impeach

United States Court Appeals for the Armed Forces

United States v. Gibson, 39 M.J. 319 (C.M.A. 1994): During his last few months at the United States Naval Academy, the accused was charged with the statutory rape of a twelve-year-old family friend. Both the accused and the victim made numerous pretrial admissions concerning their relationship. At an Article 32 investigation, the victim specifically adopted all of her previous statements, but recanted them at trial. Reversing the accused's conviction on other grounds, the court held that the victim was properly impeached with her pretrial statements because of the unique familial circumstances under which they were made.

United States v. Dodson, 21 M.J. 237 (C.M.A. 1986): Reading Rules 607 and 613(b) together, the court held that while it would have been improper for trial counsel to call a witness for the sole purpose of impeaching that witness with his prior inconsistent statement, evaluation of the entire record indicates that the prosecution had other legitimate reasons for using the witness.

[b] Extrinsic Evidence of Statement—Witness Denies Making Statement

Army Court of Criminal Appeals

United States v. Rodko, 34 M.J. 980 (A.C.M.R. 1992): This court characterized the accused's conviction for sodomizing his natural daughter as a classic swearing contest between the assailant-father and the victim-daughter. During cross-examination, the prosecutrix denied making previous inconsistent statements about her father's conduct. The military judge then prevented defense counsel from admitting those statements. Reversing the accused's conviction, this court held that because the victim denied making inconsistent out-of-court statements, they were admissible. In the court's opinion, this evidence may have had an impact on the members' deliberations concerning witness credibility.

[c] Extrinsic Evidence of Statement—Witness Equivocates

Air Force Court of Criminal Appeals

United States v. Harrow, 65 M.J. 190 (C.A.A.F. 2007): The question in this unpremeditated murder case was whether the accused service-member or her husband was responsible for the death of their child. Defense counsel extensively cross-examined the husband, but was prohibited from introducing his pretrial statement because the witness maintained he had no memory of its contents. The trial judge ruled that failure to remember is not an inconsistency. Affirming the accused's convictions, the court held that the husband's equivocal answers properly could be viewed as inconsistent with his pretrial statement, so that the statement should have been admitted. However, the court went on to say that the trial judge's decision to preclude admission of the statement was harmless error because the government's case was very strong, the accused's case was weak, the judge's instructions regarding inconsistent statements reiterated the point that the father's credibility was at issue, and trial defense counsel's cross-examination effectively impeached the witness.

United States v. Harrow, 62 M.J. 649 (A.F.Ct.Crim.App. 2006): The question in this unpremeditated murder case was whether the accused service-member or her husband were responsible for the death of their child. Defense counsel extensively cross-examined the father, but was prohibited from introducing his pretrial statement because the witness maintained he had no memory of its contents. The trial judge ruled that failure to remember is not an inconsistency. Affirming the accused's convictions, the court held that the father's equivocal answers properly could be viewed as inconsistent with his pretrial statement, so that the statement should have been admitted. However, the court went on to say that the trial judge's decision to preclude admission of the statement was not an abuse of discretion because it was properly within the range of choices available on these facts. The court ultimately found harmless error because the government's case was very strong, and trial defense counsel's cross-examination effectively impeached the witness.

[d]   Extrinsic Evidence of Statement—Timing

United States Court Appeals for the Armed Forces

United States v. Callara, 21 M.J. 259 (C.M.A. 1986): In discussing when a witness should be confronted with his inconsistent pretrial statement, the court said that "the Rule does not specify any particular timing for the opportunity for the witness to explain or deny the statement nor does it specify any particular method." As a result, the opportunity to explain or deny may come *after* the alleged inconsistency has been revealed.

§ 614.01   Official Text

Rule 614.   Calling and Interrogation of Witnesses by the Court-Martial.

(a) *Calling by the court-martial.* The military judge may, sua sponte or at the request of the members or the suggestion of a party, call witnesses, and all parties are entitled to cross-examine witnesses thus called. When the members wish to call or recall a witness, the military judge shall determine whether it is appropriate to do so under these rules or this Manual.

(b) *Interrogation by the court-martial.* The military judge or members may interrogate witnesses, whether called by the military judge, the members, or a party. Members shall submit their questions to the military judge in writing so that a ruling may be made on the propriety of the questions or the course of questioning and so that questions may be asked on behalf of the court by the military judge in a form acceptable to the military judge. When a witness who has not testified previously is called by the military judge or the members, the military judge may conduct the direct examination or may assign the responsibility to counsel for any party.

(c) *Objections.* Objections to the calling of witnesses by the military judge or the members or to the interrogation by the military judge or the members may be made at the time or at the next available opportunity when the members are not present.

---

§ 614.02   Editorial Comment

[1]   Rule 614(a)—Calling by the Court-Martial

[a]   Background

Rule 614 is consistent with past court-martial practice and the common law. Although it is generally also consistent with its Federal Rules counterpart, substantial additions were necessary to accommodate military procedures.

Applied with Rule 607, this provision acts to limit the already infrequent incidents of judges or court members calling witnesses. Now that a party may impeach his or her own witness, a barrier to obtaining testimony has been removed, and the need for the court to call a witness to avoid restrictive impeachment has also been removed.

[b]   Techniques for Using the Rule

Subdivision (a) recognizes that even though counsel will generally present all witnesses possessing relevant and important testimony, the trial bench[1] and the court members may sua sponte call or recall witnesses. The bench may also be asked to call witnesses by either party.

Any witness called by the judge or court members may be examined by both sides as if on cross-examination. As a result, leading questions may be used. When the members desire to call or recall a witness, their request must be approved by the bench. Either party may object. The ultimate resolution of any objection naturally resides with the trial judge.[2]

In determining how to exercise its discretion, the court should balance the need to clarify or supplement the evidence presented by the parties against the possibility of interfering with the parties' control of their cases.[3] *United States v. Dandy*,[4] is helpful in this area. There the court found three instances where it might be appropriate for a trial judge to intervene in the proceedings. The first is where the issues and testimony are sufficiently complex that clarification or explanation is required. The second occurs when it is important for the record to reflect that a particular witness is extraordinarily difficult or contentious, and the attorney's efforts at examining the witness will not adequately demonstrate that result. The third instance arises when explaining the reasons why one of the attorneys is not prepared, is acting obstreperously, or is confusing the facts.

In each of these situations, the bench must always keep in mind that it's actions and words have a substantial influence on the members, the witnesses, and the outcome of the court-martial. The military judge must not become so involved with a party or witness that it appears that the judge favors or disfavors that party or witness. Such a result would call into question the bench's impartiality.[5]

In this light, military judges should avoid asking questions or calling witnesses for the sole purpose of attacking or rehabilitating a witness's credibility. Moreover, after asking questions, a military judge should provide a limiting instruction indicating that nothing in the judge's questioning should be interpreted as demonstrating the judge's view of a witness's credibility, or the weight which should be accorded to any testimony.

---

[1] *See, e.g.,* United States v. Bartlett, 633 F.2d 1184 (5th Cir. 1981) (trial judge may conduct limited interrogation as long as it is fairly done and demonstrates no bias).

[2] *See* our discussion of Rule 611(a).

[3] *Compare* United States v. Beaty, 722 F.2d 1090 (3d Cir. 1983) (reversing conviction because court cross-examined three of defendant's four witnesses) *with* United States v. Tilton, 714 F.2d 642 (6th Cir. 1983) (affirming conviction, but expressing concern that trial judge went beyond role of neutral arbitrator in questioning witnesses).

[4] 998 F.2d 1344 (6th Cir. 1993).

[5] *See, e.g.,* United States v. Robinson, 635 F.2d 981 (2d Cir. 1980) (the accused's conviction was affirmed even though "the trial judge's conduct of the trial left much to be desired").

[2] Rule 614(b)—Interrogation by the Court-Martial

[a] Procedures for Asking Questions

Unlike its federal counterpart, Rule 614(b) allows court members, as well as the military judge and counsel, to interrogate witnesses. The Rule applies whether the witness was called by the members, the judge, or the parties. In this respect, the military drafters have continued traditional court-martial practice, but have formalized the procedure so that it is necessary for members' questions to be submitted in writing to the bench before they can be asked. Requiring questions first to be submitted to the bench allows the trial judge and counsel to cure defective questions and to reject improper ones. The traditional practice of attaching all questions to the trial record as appellate exhibits has been continued.

[b] Who Conducts the Trial Examination

The last sentence of 614(b) provides that, if the court members desire a witness's presence, and the trial judge determines the request is proper, the judge may assign the responsibility of initiating examination to either party, or the bench may examine the witness itself. Past practice indicates that this examination usually will be conducted by the party standing to benefit most from such evidence. In any event, as noted above, both parties—even the party who conducts the first examination—may proceed as if on cross-examination and may use leading questions. We believe the drafters' use of the phrase "direct examination" in 614(b) means initial examination as opposed to a restrictive form of questioning. Any other reading would be inconsistent with subdivision (a).

[c] Judicial Neutrality Required

Military judicial authority has closely examined the trial judge's role in obtaining testimony, particularly from the accused.[6] In *United States v. Shackleford*,[7] the court reversed the accused's conviction, finding that he was denied a fair trial due to the bench's examination, which included information obtained from an "improvidenced" guilty plea.[8] Before the trial judge examines a witness or permits the members to examine a witness, the judge should determine whether that witness's testimony needs clarification or completion, and if so, questioning should be conducted with the greatest restraint. The military judge and the members must continue to appear and in fact be neutral; they must not prematurely lean toward any position or favor either party, and they must not impose on the presumption of

---

[6] *See, e.g.,* United States v. Melendez-Rivas, 566 F.3d 41 (1st Cir. 2009) (error for trial judge to: conduct a "cross-examination" of defense witness and exam the accused in such a way as to demonstrate skepticism in his testimony).

[7] 2 M.J. 17 (C.M.A. 1976).

[8] *See* our discussion of Rule 410.

innocence. The judge must take care also not to invade the province of the court members.

[d]   Reasons for Using the Rule

Read together, subdivisions (a) and (b) allow the judge and members to obtain testimony that may be essential to a party's case. The classic situation concerns the prosecution's failure to present evidence on an element of the offense. If, for example, the accused were charged with larceny of personal property valued at more than $100 and the prosecution presented no evidence concerning the property's value, the court members or the bench could require that a witness be called or further examined in order to determine if that element can be proved.

Although previous military authority was unclear on this point, such practices have been permitted because they are essential to a fair and just resolution of the case. However, any appearance of impropriety may be limited if, instead of eliciting the testimony itself, the bench merely suggests to counsel that inquiry into the area is necessary. In fact, the more essential the testimony, the greater is the need for the court and the members to appear neutral.

[e]   Potential Problems

Some courts have taken a very narrow view of this provision and believe that the bench's impartiality falls into question once it calls or interrogates witnesses essential to a party's case. In *United States v. Karnes*,[9] the court indicated that such problems could be minimized if, during a bench trial, the court produced special findings explaining why it called the witnesses in question. Similarly, if the bench calls witnesses during a trial with members, an appropriate instruction should be offered.[10]

The problem is more complex in a court-martial setting where members fully appreciate their ability to call and interrogate witnesses. Officers and noncommissioned officers who traditionally sit on court-martial panels in all services are educated in the Uniform Code of Military Justice, and criminal investigatory techniques. They have often been required to take or participate in disciplinary actions upon their subordinates. As a result, the court members' basis of knowledge about how the system works provides both beneficial and troubling possibilities. For example, when the members themselves call or interrogate witnesses, they bring significant *prosecutorial* investigation and disciplinary experience into play. Their competencies can clarify legitimate trial uncertainties, or focus additional accusatory interest

---

[9]   531 F.2d 214 (4th Cir. 1976).

[10]   *See also* Comment, 89 HARV. L. REV. 1906 (1976), where the author would have trial judges refrain from calling any significant government witness and would draw a line between a fact-finder's calling of witnesses to clarify evidence and calling them to bolster a party's case.

upon the accused in a way that might call the member's neutrality into question. The margin for error is very slim when experienced, educated, talented, and highly placed leaders in the military community are asked to be both investigators and court members.

This reality distinguishes court-martial practice from criminal litigation in any civilian federal or state courthouse. At a minimum, it places additional burdens upon the military judge and reviewing courts to insure that the members' role as neutral and independent fact-finders does not become confused with the members' previous and aspirational command and criminal justice concerns.

Careful counsel and trial judges will closely observe court-member involvement in the proceedings, and watch for any sign that a member is becoming partisan. Once court-member examinations start, military judges must be prepared to remind the members of their role in the proceedings.

[3] Rule 614(c)—Objections

[a] Timing and Procedure

Subdivision (c) provides that, if counsel has an objection to any examination conducted by the members or the judge or to the judge's decision to call or recall a witness, that objection need not be made in the members' presence and may be raised "at the next available opportunity when the members are not present." While this appears to be in conflict with Rule 103's requirement for timely objections, the drafters recognized that a timely objection may either alienate the court members or demonstrate a conflict with the judge.

[b] Military Judge's Role

There is no reason why a military judge who sees a party making an obvious error should refrain from calling the error to the party's attention, and if a party forgets to offer promised evidence, the judge may remind the party of the gap in the proof. Court-members and the court should not have to sit idly by, confused, when a proper question might provide necessary understanding. But the court and the members must understand that the parties are entitled to present their cases in what they believe is the most effective way and to present them to a neutral fact-finder. Thus, too much premature questioning by the court and the members may impair a party's opportunity to present evidence and the appearance of impartiality.

As professor Saltzburg suggests in his article, *The Unnecessarily Expanding Role of the American Trial Judge,* 64 VA. L. REV. 1 (1978), trial judge and court member examinations can often be avoided if the bench will discuss any troubling evidentiary and proof issues with counsel during an out-of-court hearing. This technique will help shield the members from any possible human bias or interest the bench may have, while making the record more complete, thereby assisting the finders of fact in accurately resolving the case before them. Professor Saltzburg's article also posits guidelines for trial judges to consider.

§ 614.03   Drafters' Analysis

[1]   Calling by the court-martial

The first sentence of Rule 614(a) is taken from the Federal Rule but has been modified to recognize the power of the court members to call and examine witnesses. The second sentence of the subdivision is new and reflects the members' power to call or recall witnesses. Although recognizing that power, the Rule makes it clear that the calling of such witnesses is contingent upon compliance with these Rules and this *Manual*. Consequently, the testimony of such witnesses must be relevant and not barred by any Rule or *Manual* provision.

[2]   Interrogation by the court-martial

The first sentence of Rule 614(b) is taken from the Federal Rule but modified to reflect the power under these Rules and *Manual* of the court members to interrogate witnesses. The second sentence of the subdivision is new and modifies ¶ 54*a* and ¶ 149*a* of the present *Manual* by requiring that questions of members be submitted to the military judge in writing. This change in current practice was made in order to improve efficiency and to prevent prejudice to either party. Although the Rule states that its intent is to ensure that the questions will "be in a form acceptable to the military judge," it is not the intent of the Committee to grant carte blanche to the military judge in this matter. It is the Committee's intent that the military judge alter the questions only to the extent necessary to ensure compliance with these Rules and *Manual*. When trial is by special court-martial without a military judge, the president will utilize the same procedure.

[3]   Objections

Rule 614(c) is taken from the Federal Rule but modified to reflect the powers of the members to call and interrogate witnesses. This provision generally restates present law but recognizes counsel's right to request an Article 39(a) session to enter an objection.

§ 614.04   Annotated Cases

[1]   Rule 614(a)—Calling by the Court-Martial

[a]   Court-Member Called Witnesses—In General

United States Court of Appeals for the Armed Forces

United States v. Jones, 26 M.J. 197 (C.M.A. 1988): As a tactical decision, neither side desired to call a social worker who had interviewed the victim of child sexual abuse. Once both sides rested, the members requested and examined the social worker. The reviewing court held that court member's "rights" to call witnesses in their own "search for the truth" is limited by the military judge's determination on relevance, competency, and "criteria of admissibility," and affirmed the conviction.

Air Force Court of Criminal Appeals

United States v. Dubose, 19 M.J. 877 (A.F.C.M.R. 1985): Finding error but no prejudice, the court held that the military judge improperly instructed court members that they were not permitted to call witnesses. The convening authority had cured the error below by disapproving the relevant specifications.

[b]   Court-Member Called Witnesses—Right to Cross-Examine

Navy-Marine Corps Court of Criminal Appeals

United States v. Campbell, 37 M.J. 1049 (N.M.C.M.R. 1993): The accused was convicted of larceny. After both sides rested, the court members asked that several witnesses, including the victim, be recalled. Contrary to this provision, the military judge prohibited defense counsel from conducting a cross-examination of the recalled victim. Finding error but no prejudice, the court held that while an accused's right to cross-examine is constitutionally guaranteed, reversal is not required where defense counsel's examination would have been cumulative, with no effect on the litigation's outcome.

[c]   Court-Member Called Witnesses—Sentencing

Army Court of Criminal Appeals

United States v. Woodard, 39 M.J. 1022 (A.C.M.R. 1994): Pursuant to his pleas, the accused was convicted of rape, sodomy, and indecent acts with his nine-year-old stepdaughter and his nine-year-old natural son. During the sentencing portion of the trial, a defense expert questioned the need to confine the accused because of the accused's emotional condition. Thereafter, a court member inquired about the United States Disciplinary Barracks' mental health treatment capabilities. Over defense objections, the prosecution introduced an affidavit from the Disciplinary Barracks' Director of Mental Health Services explaining their program. Finding a hearsay error, but affirming all convictions and the sentence, this court held that the panel member's inquiry and the military judge's desire to obtain relevant testimony in response were both appropriate.

[2]   Rule 614(b)—Interrogation by the Court-Martial

[a]   Interrogation by Court-Martial—Court Member Questions

United States Court of Appeals for the Armed Forces;

United States v. Hill, 45 M.J. 245 (C.A.A.F. 1996): The court characterized this case as a "comprehensive challenge to the practice of court-martial members asking questions of witnesses during trial. . . ." The accused was convicted, on mixed pleas, of various larceny and related offenses. The trial judge's initial instructions to the members invited them to "feel free to ask questions." The members ultimately asked 125 questions, with the president of the court asking 53. Neither trial level counsel objected to this activity. On appeal, the accused contended that the large number and content of the questions demonstrated a lack of impartiality. Affirming the accused's convictions, this court adopted government counsel's argument that "Court-members need not be inert to be impartial." While the court recognized that under certain circumstances, the sheer number of questions may highlight a bias, they preferred to take a more "holistic" approach to such matters and examine the overall proceeding to determine if error or inappropriate conduct occurred. Based on these factors, the court found that the members' queries demonstrated their attentiveness to the testimony rather than any partiality or impropriety.

[b]   Interrogation by Court-Martial—Judge Questions

United States Court of Appeals for the Armed Forces

United States v. Cooper, 51 M.J. 247 (C.A.A.F. 1999): Affirming the accused's convictions for conduct unbecoming an officer and offenses related to indecent exposure, this court held that because defense counsel failed to pose a timely trial objection, the military judge's (a) questioning of certain witnesses, (b) personal expressions of frustration with defense counsel, and (c) negative comments on the quality of certain defense evidence did not divest the judge of his appearance of impartiality, deny the accused military due process, nor amount to plain error.

United States v. Acosta, 49 M.J. 14 (C.A.A.F. 1998): The accused was convicted of wrongfully distributing drugs. After defense counsel cross-examined the government's key witness, the military judge asked that witness a series of 89 questions that, in the court's words, resulted in "no reasonable member of the panel [having] any question but that the accused was predisposed to distribute illegal drugs." Finding no error, this court held that a "reasonable person" reviewing the entire record would still come away believing in the bench's impartiality.

United States v. Dock, 40 M.J. 112 (C.M.A 1994): During the accused's court-martial for murder, lengthy and complex psychiatric testimony was presented. Before this court, the accused contended that the military judge lost his impartiality because he *sua sponte* asked numerous hypothetical questions which were improper and obviously biased in the government's favor. Citing this Rule, the court affirmed the accused's convictions holding that the judge's examination was necessary to the court members' fair interpretation of complicated and extensive opinion testimony.

[c]   Interrogation by Court-Martial—Sentencing

Air Force Court of Criminal Appeals

United States v. Satterley, 52 M.J. 782 (A.F. Ct.Crim.App. 1999):

Consistent with his pleas, the accused was convicted of willfully destroying government property and other offenses. During the sentencing portion of trial the accused made an unsworn statement. Thereafter a court-member asked a question relevant to missing government property. Affirming the accused's findings and sentence the court held that the military judge did not abuse his discretion by denying defense counsel's request to reopen and present additional unsworn testimony on this matter.

Army Court of Criminal Appeals

United States v. Cephas, 25 M.J. 832 (A.C.M.R. 1988): During the sentencing portion of the accused's drug distribution trial, his first sergeant testified that the accused's duty performance was good, but that he had no rehabilitative potential. Neither trial nor defense counsel asked further questions. Thereafter, the military judge indicated he was concerned about the "dichotomy inherent in the first sergeant's answers and announced that he was going to ask some questions." Both counsel objected, indicating such examination might produce inadmissible hearsay and "other crimes evidence." Undeterred, the judge questioned this witness and learned that the accused had four previous drug related offenses. Relying on R.C.M. 1001(b)(5), the court sustained the military judge's examination because the government could have presented "opinion testimony concerning the accused's previous performance as a service member and potential for rehabilitation. Cross-examination is allowed into relevant and specific instances of conduct." Additionally, it was well within the trial judge's duty "to properly ask questions of any witness to clear up uncertainties in the evidence and to develop further the facts for the better understanding of the fact-finder."

§ 615.01   Official Text

Rule 615.   Exclusion of Witnesses.

At the request of the prosecution or defense the military judge shall order witnesses excluded so that they cannot hear the testimony of other witnesses, and the military judge may make the order *sua sponte*. This rule does not authorize exclusion of (1) the accused, or (2) a member of an armed service or an employee of the United States designated as representative of the United States by the trial counsel, or (3) a person whose presence is shown by a party to be essential to the presentation of the party's case, or (4) a person authorized by statute to be present at courts-martial, or (5) any victim of an offense from the trial of an accused for that offense because such victim may testify or present any information in relation to the sentence or that offense during the pre-sentencing proceedings.

---

§ 615.02   Editorial Comment

[1]   In General

At common law and under previous military practice, prospective witnesses were not permitted to be in the courtroom while other witnesses were testifying.[1] A perceived need for this sequestration was based upon the belief that if witnesses were allowed to hear each other's testimony, the possibility for collusion or the unconscious melding of stories was too great.

Like the Federal Rule on which it is based, Military Rule 615 provides that either party, or the trial judge *sua sponte*, may require all prospective witnesses to be excluded during testimony.[2] The Rule does not apply to arguments, instructions, or ministerial aspects of a proceeding. Although the court may have inherent power to exclude witnesses from all aspects of a

---

[1] For an excellent example of how the Court of Appeals for the Armed Forces has appropriately treated this issue, *see* United States v. Miller, 48 M.J. 49 (C.A.A.F. 1998). In *Miller*, the accused was convicted of conspiracy, robbery, and assault with the intent to commit robbery. Before the introduction of evidence, trial counsel indicated that a law enforcement agent would be seated at his table during trial, and that this agent would be designated as a government representative. Trial counsel went on to say that the agent would also be a witness. Overruling defense counsel's objections, the military judge permitted the agent to sit at counsel table and testify after other witnesses. Affirming the accused's convictions, this court held that "[o]nce trial counsel designated SA Biller as a government representative, the military judge had little discretion to exclude him."

[2] *See, e.g.,* United States v. Guthrie, 557 F.3d 243 (6th Cir. 2009) (rule not violated when prosecutor talks to victim during recess; prohibition is against witnesses talking to other witnesses and prosecutors coaching witnesses during a recess).

trial,[3] no party has a right to sequester witnesses except during testimony.

Rule 615 has been interpreted as elevating sequestration to a right, but a right that is not absolute. The Rule recognizes three exceptions to the sequestration right. The Military and Federal Rules differ in their treatment of these exceptions because the Military Rule is confined to criminal cases.

In 2002, Rule 615 was amended[4] to expand the list of those witnesses who need not be excluded from the courtroom. Specifically addressed are persons who are authorized by statute to remain in the courtroom and any victims affected by the charges against the accused.

[2]   Rule 615(1)—Accused's Presence Required

[a]   Constitutional Protections

Rule 615(1) provides that sequestration does not apply to the accused even if he is to be a witness. If an accused voluntarily absents himself or herself from the courtroom after being arraigned, the *Manual* provides that the accused may be tried *in absentia*.

Defense counsel need do nothing in order to avoid the sequestration rule. An accused's right to be in the courtroom is controlled by the Sixth and Fourteenth Amendments, not the Rules of Evidence. However, as *Perry v. Leeke*,[5] and *Geders v. United States*,[6] demonstrate, the trial judge may make reasonable and very short-term limitations upon the accused's ability to consult with counsel during recesses or similar breaks in the proceedings.[7] Such extraordinary, even short term limitations upon the attorney-client relationship, will rarely be needed in the military.

[3]   Rule 615(2)—Designated Representative of the United States

[a]   Basis for the Rule

Subdivision (2) indicates that if the prosecutor designates a member of the military or an employee of the United States as a representative of the government, that individual, even though he or she may testify, need not be sequestered. This aspect of Rule 615 is like its federal counterpart and the

---

[3] *But see, e.g.,* United States v. Juarez, 573 F.2d 267 (5th Cir. 1977) (defense witness properly excluded from closing arguments because arguments "often restate witness testimony, the trial court could justifiably fear that witnesses present at such arguments might learn the testimony of other witnesses, thus jeopardizing the fairness of a second trial should one be necessary").

[4] Executive Order 13262 (April 11, 2002).

[5] 488 U.S. 272 (1989).

[6] 425 U.S. 80 (1976).

[7] *See, e.g.,* United States v. DiLapi, 651 F.2d 140 (2d Cir. 1981) (although harmless error, it was improper for the trial judge to prohibit the accused from speaking with anyone, including defense counsel, during a five-minute recess in the government's cross-examination).

common law, which permits a government agent familiar with the case to sit at counsel table and assist the prosecutor.[8] Although in past court-martial practice this right has not often been utilized, federal district courts have recognized that an agent's presence, particularly during long and complex trials, or trials which concern specialized subject matters, allows the government to better meet the uncertainties of litigation.

For example, *In re United States,*[9] the court held that a government agent could be the prosecution's representative under Rule 615(2). The court opined, however, that the trial judge, via Rule 611(a), can require the government to present such a designated agent-witness at the beginning of its case, thus limiting the possibility of collusion or undue influence upon his testimony by other witnesses.

While a trial judge can require counsel to present his witness out of order, there is no requirement for this alternative in the Rule or the authority supporting it.[10] If the government can establish that presenting the witness's testimony out of sequence would substantially harm its case, then the judge may permit the witness to testify after remaining in the courtroom. In either event, the government should be able to use the witness during rebuttal should it be necessary. Of course, rebuttal[11] and pretrial evidentiary hearings[12] also can be controlled through the proper use of Rules 611 and 615.

[b]   Unrecognized Assistance for Trial Counsel

While it appears that Rule 615(2) is being interpreted by military courts as it has been by civilian courts, the Rule has not been widely used in courts-martial. Trial counsel particularly fail to take advantage of the Rule by not having the law enforcement agency representative who investigated the case designated to sit at counsel table and assist the prosecution. We are uncertain why military prosecutors have failed to take advantage of this valuable trial tool when their civilian counterparts have consistently used it.[13] As the court said in *United States v. Spina,*[14] "[t]he Government has an

---

[8] *See, e.g.,* United States v. Butera, 677 F.2d 1376 (11th Cir. 1982) (no error in exempting government's principal investigating officer from sequestration).

[9] 584 F.2d 666 (5th Cir. 1978).

[10] *But see* United States v. Mitchell, 733 F.2d 327 (4th Cir. 1984) (better practice if case agent is to be immune from sequestration is to have him testify first).

[11] *See, e.g.,* United States v. Ell, 718 F.2d 291 (9th Cir. 1983) (sequestration order applies to rebuttal witnesses, even those who testified in case-in-chief; prejudice is presumed from violation and prosecution must show it was harmless).

[12] *See, e.g.,* United States v. Brewer, 947 F.2d 404 (9th Cir. 1991) (Rule 615 applies to pretrial evidentiary hearings).

[13] *See, e.g.,* United States v. Payan, 992 F.2d 1387 (6th Cir. 1993) (officer in charge of the criminal investigation permitted to remain at counsel's table).

absolute right to name a representative" and to have him or her sit at counsel table. In *Spina,* the trial judge permitted government counsel to designate more than one exempted representative.[15]

[4]   Rule 615(3)—Essential Persons

[a]   Basis for the Rule

Subdivision (3) contains the final exception to sequestration. It provides that a witness need not be excluded if a party can demonstrate that the witness is essential to its presentation.[16] This determination is made by the trial judge after balancing the party's need for the witness and the type of assistance the witness will provide against the public policy considerations giving rise to the sequestration rule.[17] Rule 615(3) will most commonly be exercised in the military in connection with expert witness testimony, particularly psychiatrists.[18] While the responsibility to establish a witness's "essentiality" is upon counsel, the bench may make such a finding *sua sponte.*

[b]   Practical Considerations

In order for sequestration to be effective, the trial judge should instruct each witness not to discuss his or her testimony with anyone other than counsel for either side.[19] Similarly, the judge should insure that counsel will not discuss what other witnesses have said with witnesses yet to testify. While it may be difficult for counsel to prepare witnesses without suggesting what the prior testimony has been, military judges have the power to take appropriate steps to assure that counsel and witnesses respect the goals of the sequestration rule.[20]

---

[14] 654 F. Supp. 94 (S.D. Fla. 1987).

[15] *See also* United States v. Alvarado, 647 F.2d 537 (5th Cir. 1981) (more than one government witness may be excused from sequestration even though one of the witnesses will testify late in the government's case; decision is within the judge's discretion).

[16] *See, e.g.,* Oliver B. Cannon & Son, Inc. v. Fidelity & Casualty Co., 519 F. Supp. 668, 669 (D. Del. 1981) (setting forth restrictive test for determining when a witness' presence is actually essential).

[17] *See, e.g.,* government of the Virgin Islands v. Edinborough, 625 F.2d 472 (3d Cir. 1980) (suggesting that the mother of minor rape victim may be essential to the prosecutor's case and may be present while her daughter testifies).

[18] *See* our discussion of Rule 703, and United States v. Phillips, 515 F. Supp. 758 (E.D. Ky. 1981) (where the accused's principal defense was lack of mental responsibility, the trial court properly allowed a prosecution psychologist to be present during the defense's case *only*).

[19] *But see* United States v. Scharstein, 531 F. Supp. 460 (E.D. Ky. 1982) (refusing to bar witnesses from talking to each other).

[20] *See, e.g.,* United States v. Arias-Santana, 964 F.2d 1262 (1st Cir. 1992) (trial court may make non-discussion orders where appropriate).

[c]   Lack of Effective Remedy for Violations

Some violations of sequestration may be harmless.[21] Other violations may require a remedy, although military judges probably do not have the power to cite such witnesses for contempt.[22] The bench should permit counsel to bring out and comment on the sequestration violation. Certainly, it relates to witness credibility.[23] The court could add its own comment on the violation. The bench could also prohibit a witness from testifying or strike his or her testimony.[24] This remedy has not been widely used since it deprives a party and the fact-finder of testimony that might be critical to a fair decision.[25]

[5]   Rule 615(4)—Persons Authorized by Statute to be Present

Rule 615(4) parallels language in Federal Rule 615, that was added to the latter rule in 1998 to provide that witnesses could not be barred from the court if their presence was "authorized by statute." According to the Committee Note for the federal rule, the amendment was intended, in part, to cover the Victim of Crime Bill of Rights.[26] But the language in the federal rule is not limited to that particular statute and leaves the door open for permitting other witnesses to remain in the courtroom, if any statute permits it.

On the other hand, the Drafters' Analysis to the military rule indicates that the term "statute" in Rule 615(4) refers to those statutes that are "applicable to courts-martial." That seems consistent with the Court of Appeals decision in *United States v. Spann*,[27] annotated *below*, where the court rejected the

---

[21] *See, e.g.,* United States v. Womack, 654 F.2d 1034 (5th Cir. 1981) (where a prosecution witness violated the court's sequestration rule, no relief was granted; the accused could not show prejudice; the witness's testimony was uncontradicted, consistent with prior statements, and corroborated).

[22] *See* Article 48 of the Uniform Code of Military Justice.

[23] *See, e.g.,* United States v. Arruda, 715 F.2d 671 (1st Cir. 1983) (where two sequestered witnesses met together during trial, the effect was identical to a violation of sequestration order; no error, however, in permitting them to testify and to be impeached with evidence of their meetings).

[24] *See, e.g.,* United States v. Gibson, 675 F.2d 825 (6th Cir. 1982) (upholding exclusion of defense witness who violated order with defendant's knowledge).

[25] In United States v. Oropeza, 564 F.2d 316 (9th Cir. 1977), the court held that "[s]equestration of witnesses and sanctions for violations of a sequestration order are matters within the discretion of the court" and that "[a] witness is not disqualified merely because he remains in the courtroom after a sequestration order." However, in United States v. Avila-Macias, 577 F.2d 1384 (9th Cir. 1978), the court held that the trial judge did not abuse his discretion by excluding a surrebuttal witness who violated his sequestration order. The court emphasized, however, disqualification is not the preferred remedy.

[26] 42 U.S.C. 10606. *See generally* Saltzburg, Martin & Capra, FEDERAL RULES OF EVIDENCE MANUAL; § 615.02[9] (9th ed. 2006).

[27] 51 M.J. 89 (1999).

argument that the federal Victim of Crime Bill of Rights applied to courts-martial.

[6] Rule 615(5)—Victim's Right to be Present

Rule 615(5) reflects the Victim Rights Clarification Act of 1997,[28] which also addresses the question of whether victims may be exempted from exclusion, and to some extent the new statutory definition of victim.[29] As noted in the Drafters' Analysis, the definition of "victim" for persons under the age of 18 may extend to other persons such as another family member. Given the potential issues of who represents the underage or incompetent victim, the military judge will surely be called upon to decide who the "victim" is and then determine whether that person, or persons, will testify. Finally, as noted in the Drafters' Analysis, a victim's right to attend the trial is still subject to other rules of evidence and any court rules concerning conduct in the courtroom.

§ 615.03 Drafters' Analysis

Rule 615 is taken from the Federal Rule with only minor changes of terminology. The first portion of the Rule is in conformity with present practice; *e.g.,* ¶ 53*f.* The second portion, consisting of subdivisions (2) and (3), represents a substantial departure from current practice and will authorize the prosecution to designate another individual to sit with the trial counsel. Rule 615 thus modifies ¶ 53*f.* Under the Rule, the military judge lacks any discretion to exclude potential witnesses who come within the scope of Rule 615(2) and (3) unless the accused's constitutional right to a fair trial would be violated. Developing Article III practice recognizes the defense right, upon request, to have a prosecution witness, not excluded because of Rule 615, testify before other prosecution witnesses.

Rule 615 does not prohibit exclusion of either accused or counsel due to misbehavior when such exclusion is not prohibited by the Constitution of the United States, the Uniform Code of Military Justice, this *Manual* or these Rules.

§ 615.04 Drafters' Analysis (2002 Amendments)

2002 Amendment: These changes are intended to extend to victims at courts-martial the same rights granted to victims by the Victims' Rights and Restitution Act of 1990, 42 U.S.C. 10606(b)(4), giving crime victims "[t]he right to be present at all public court proceedings related to the offense, unless the court determines that testimony by the victim would be materially affected if the victim heard the testimony at trial," and the Victim Rights Clarification Act of 1997, 18 U.S.C. 3510, which is restated in subsection (5). For the purposes of this rule the term "victim" includes all persons

---

[28] U.S.C. 3510.

[29] *See* 42 U.S.C. 10607(e)(2).

defined as victims in 42 U.S.C. 10607(e)(2), which means "a person that has suffered direct physical, emotional, or pecuniary harm as a result of the commission of a crime, including (A) in the case of a victim that is an institutional entity, an authorized representative of the entity; and (B) in the case of a victim who is under 18 years of age, incompetent, incapacitated, or deceased, one of the following (in order of preference): (i) a spouse; (ii) a legal guardian; (iii) a parent; (iv) a child; (v) a sibling; (vi) another family member; or (vii) another person designated by the court." The victim's right to remain in the courtroom remains subject to other rules, such as those regarding classified information, witness deportment, and conduct in the courtroom. Subsection (4) is intended to capture only those statutes applicable to courts-martial.

§ 615.05   Annotated Cases

[1]   Exclusion of Witnesses—Agent at Trial Counsel's Table

Army Court of Criminal Appeals

United States v. Miller, 48 M.J. 49 (C.A.A.F. 1998): The accused was convicted of conspiracy, robbery, and assault with the intent to commit robbery. Before the introduction of evidence, trial counsel indicated that a law enforcement agent would be seated at his table during trial, and that this agent would be designated as a government representative. Trial counsel went on to say that the agent would also be a witness. Overruling defense counsel's objections, the military judge permitted the agent to sit at counsel table and testify after other witnesses. Affirming the accused's convictions, this court held that "[o]nce trial counsel designated SA Biller as a government representative, the military judge had little discretion to exclude him."

United States v. Ayala, 22 M.J. 777 (A.C.M.R. 1986): The court found no error in the military judge's allowing a CID agent to sit at counsel table throughout the trial, even though the agent testified after other government witnesses. The court indicated that it could not generally condone the practice, however, because it might "infringe upon the accused's due process rights and become a source of possible appellate litigation." We would note that the judge has authority under Rule 611(a) to control the order of proof in order to protect an accused from any unfairness in the utilization of exceptions from sequestration.

Navy-Marine Corps Court of Criminal Appeals

United States v. Scott, 13 M.J. 874 (N.M.C.M.R. 1982): Affirming the accused's murder conviction, the court recognized that Rule 615(2) specifically permits military policemen and criminal investigators who might be potential witnesses to be designated as representatives of the United States and to remain in court despite a sequestration order. In the instant case, the witness designated as the representative of the United States heard three other witnesses testify before he took the stand. The reviewing court held that the judge did not abuse his discretion in rejecting the accused's attempts to compel the agent to take the stand before hearing the other witnesses.

[2] Exclusion of Witnesses—Expert Witness at Defense Counsel's Table

United States Court of Appeals for the Armed Forces

United States v. Banks, 36 M.J. 150 (C.M.A. 1992): The court reversed the accused's child sexual abuse conviction due to expert opinion and scientific evidence errors. In resolving these matters, the court noted that, pursuant to a defense request, its expert witness was correctly permitted to sit at counsel table during the presentation of related government expert testimony.

[3] Exclusion of Witnesses—Expert Witness at Trial Counsel's Table

United States Court of Appeals for the Armed Forces

United States v. Barron, 52 M.J. 1 (C.A.A.F. 1999): During the accused's trial for sexually assaulting an eight-year-old girl, the prosecution called an expert witness in pediatric medicine and related medical fields. After the witness testified, the military judge allowed her to remain in the courtroom. During trial counsel's cross-examination of a defense expert witness, the government expert passed several notes to trial counsel in an attempt to aid his cross-examination. Trial counsel apparently used these notes in formulating questions. Defense counsel objected to this process, moved to disqualify the government witness from further participation in the case, and characterized the government's expert as a "de facto prosecutor." In response, the judge ordered the witness to stop passing notes to trial counsel and then informed the members that this witness's conduct was "entirely inappropriate," and that in evaluating her testimony they should consider that she "departed from her role as an expert witness and became a de facto member of the prosecution." The judge went on to instruct, "You should, therefore, in effect consider [that the government witness] has shown herself to be a biased witness in favor of the alleged child victim in this case," and that "in effect [the government's witness] has a mark against her." Relying on Rules 702 and 706, this court held that the trial judge's actions were appropriate, that no prejudicial error occurred, and that the defense was not entitled to a mistrial.

United States v. Croom, 24 M.J. 373 (C.M.A. 1987): Relying on state and federal authority, the court held that it was "patently reasonable" for trial counsel to request that his expert psychiatric witness be allowed to join him at counsel table and to assist the government in evaluating the defense's medical testimony. The court went on to say that as a general rule, there is "little, if any, reason for sequestering a witness who is to testify in an expert capacity and not on the facts of the case."

[4]   Exclusion of Witnesses—Rebuttal Witnesses

Air Force Court of Criminal Appeals

United States v. Gittens, 36 M.J. 594 (A.F.C.M.R. 1992): Affirming the accused's conviction for attempted rape, the court said that no error occurred when trial counsel was permitted to call a rebuttal witness who had been present in the courtroom and had observed the trial proceedings to that point. This court based its opinion on the fact that trial counsel did not know the witness would be necessary, and that defense counsel was unable to demonstrate any prosecutorial bad faith.

[5]   Exclusion of Witnesses—Relationship with Rule 611

Navy-Marine Corps Court of Criminal Appeals

United States v. Rodriguez-Rivera, 60 M.J. 843 (N.M.Ct.Crim.App. 2005): In affirming the accused's sodomy and indecent liberties convictions, this court held that, absent a specific ruling by the military judge sequestering potential witnesses, no error occurred when the victim's parents were allowed to remain in the courtroom during her testimony even if they discussed it with her at trial breaks. Further, the court found that the combination of Rules 615 and 611 provided the military judge with broad discretionary powers in dealing with witnesses and spectators.

[6]   Exclusion of Witnesses—Sanctions for Violating the Rule

United States Court of Appeals for the Armed Force

United States v. Quintanilla, 63 M.J. 29 (C.A.A.F. 2006): The accused was tried for murder and sentenced to death for killing his executive officer and severely wounding his commanding officer. The military judge, over defense objection, allowed the victims' family members to remain in the courtroom even though they would testify during sentencing if the accused were convicted. The government conceded that the judge erred in permitting the members to remain in the courtroom but concluded that it need not decide whether the error was prejudicial since the family members testified only during sentencing and the court remanded for a new sentencing proceeding on other grounds.

United States v. Roth, 52 M.J. 187 (C.A.A.F. 1999): The accused pled guilty to wrongful disposition of night vision goggles and other sensitive military property. Contrary to his plea, the accused was convicted of conspiracy to sell and attempted sale of this same property. During the sentencing portion of trial, defense counsel called a witness who had been seated in the courtroom throughout the proceedings. Trial counsel objected on Rule 615 grounds, and the military judge sustained the objection. This court reversed the accused's sentence even though defense counsel invited the situation by opening the door to the potentially damaging "gang member" evidence this witness would have allegedly rebutted, and by failing to have the witness sequestered. However, in the court's opinion, the military judge abused her discretion by employing the ultimate sanction of preventing the witness from testifying. The court went on to say that, if this witness had been allowed to testify, there would have been no demonstrable harm to the government's case, and preventing the testimony was "fundamentally unfair."

[7]   Exclusion of Witnesses—Sentencing Applicability—Pre-2002 Amendment

United States Court of Appeals for the Armed Forces

United States v. Langston, 53 M.J. 335 (C.A.A.F. 2000): During the accused's providence colloquy, and over defense objection, the three victims of the accused's criminal misconduct were allowed to remain in the courtroom and listen to his admissions of guilt. Subsequently, these victim-witnesses testified during the sentencing portion of trial. Defense counsel failed to mention the problem during his cross-examination of them. Finding error but no prejudice in the trial judge's holding, this court found that Rule 615's exclusionary provisions apply to trial testimony, arguments, instructions, providence inquires, and ministerial aspects of trial. The court went on to say that the presence of these victim-witnesses did not jeopardize the fairness of the proceedings.

Navy-Marine Corps Court of Criminal Appeals

United States v. Evans, 55 M.J. 732 (N.M. Ct.Crim.App. 2001): The accused was convicted of raping a female under the age of sixteen, indecent assault upon another female, and false swearing concerning the offenses. At trial the military judge, over defense objection, allowed the victims to testify during the government's case on sentencing. The accused contended the judge erred in allowing the testimony, and moved to exclude the testimony because the victims had been in the courtroom during closing arguments on findings, and because they had been seen talking to each other prior to the closing arguments and during deliberations. This court held that, even if the military judge had erred, the accused failed to demonstrate how their presence during closing argument or their brief conversations "affected the veracity of the testimony provided by the victims on sentencing." Accordingly, the court found no merit in the assignment of error and went on to say that, even if one witness is present during the testimony of another witness and that witness later testifies, some prejudice must be shown before relief will be granted. In this case, no such prejudice was found.

[8]   Exclusion of Witnesses—Victim Bill of Rights Act—Pre-2002 Amendment

United States Court of Appeals for the Armed Forces

United States v. Spann, 51 M.J. 89 (C.A.A.F. 1999): The accused was convicted of rape. At trial he contended that the victim and her mother should have been sequestered. The trial judge overruled the accused's objection despite the government's intent to use and actual use of them as witnesses. Affirming the accused's conviction, this court held that although Federal Rule of Evidence 615 had been amended to reflect the witness attendance requirements of the "Victim of Crime Bill of Rights,"42 U.S.C. 1 § 10606, the President, as of the date of the accused's trial, had not chosen to amend Military Rule of Evidence 615 in a similar manner. As a result, the court, in a very informative opinion, held that the military judge's determination that the Victim of Crime Bill of Rights superseded Military Rule of Evidence 615 was error, but on these facts harmless.

Navy-Marine Corps Court of Criminal Appeals

United States v. Ducharme, 59 M.J. 816 (N.M.Ct.Crim.App. 2004): As a result of his mixed pleas, the accused was convicted of conduct which led to the death of another Marine. Before trial, defense counsel was given the opportunity to challenge the presence of the victim's mother in the courtroom during litigation on the merits. The government had already informed the accused that it intended on calling the victim's mother during sentencing. Finding waiver and harmless error in the alternative, the court affirmed the accused's conviction and sentence.

[9]   Exclusion of Witnesses—Witness Out-of-Court Conversations

Air Force Court of Criminal Appeals

United States v. Michael, 33 M.J. 900 (A.F.C.M.R. 1991): An amphetamine use conviction was based solely on the testimony of airmen with drug abuse backgrounds. Immediately before trial, the prosecutor sent one of his witnesses to refresh the memory of another witness who was in pretrial confinement. Relying on Rule 615, the court found no legal impropriety with trial counsel's actions. However, based on Article 66, Uniform Code of Military Justice (service courts of appeal must also believe the findings and sentence are correct in fact), this court felt that the prosecutor's actions created a substantial doubt about witness credibility, and as a result, reversed the conviction.

SECTION VII

OPINIONS AND EXPERT TESTIMONY

SYNOPSIS

§ 701.01   Official Text

Rule 701.   Opinion Testimony by Lay Witnesses.

If the witness is not testifying as an expert, the witness' testimony in the form of opinions or inferences is limited to those opinions or inferences which are (a) rationally based on the perception of the witness, and] (b) helpful to a clear understanding of the witness' testimony or the determination of a fact in issue, and (c) not based on scientific, technical or other specialized knowledge within the scope of Rule 702.

---

§ 701.02   Editorial Comment

[1]   Lay vs. Expert Opinion Testimony

Rule 701 governs the testimony of ordinary or "lay" witnesses. Opinion testimony by expert witnesses is covered by Rules 702, 703 and 705. The distinction between lay witness opinion testimony and expert witness opinion testimony resides largely in the basis for each category. Lay witnesses are permitted to offer an opinion or inference in a very limited number of cases and only based on perceptions the average person would be entitled to draw from events they are familiar with and understand. Expert opinion testimony requires the witness to possessing scientific, technical, or other specialized knowledge about the issue in question. Such knowledge exceeds that possessed by the average citizen and the court-members.[1]

Lay witness opinion testimony has traditionally not been preferred by the law. When witnesses summarize or offer shortcuts in the form of conclusions or opinions, it is feared that they invade the province of the factfinder by depriving the factfinder of the opportunity to draw its own inferences and conclusions rather than accepting those of witnesses.

[2]   Lay Opinions Must Be "Helpful" to the Finders of Facts

Most modern evidentiary rules have recognized that it is almost impossible to draw any sharp line between fact and opinion. The 1969 *Manual* ¶ 138 *e* restricted lay opinion testimony to opinions that were commonly drawn and could not be conveyed to a court by "a mere recitation of the observed facts." The restriction was easier to state than to apply.

Rule 701 is much more permissive. It allows lay witnesses to testify in the form of opinions or inferences as long as they are helpful to a clear understanding of the witness's testimony or they are helpful in determining

---

[1] *See, e.g.,* United States v. Gillespie, 852 F.2d 475 (9th Cir. 1988) (error to admit lay opinion testimony by therapist that child had been abused by a man, and not a woman, because use of anatomically correct dolls requires compliance with Rule 702).

a fact in issue. The distinctions between understanding the testimony of a witness and determining a fact in issue is not easy to draw, since it appears that any improvement in the understanding of testimony would also improve the determination of a fact in dispute. Fortunately, it is not important that the distinction be drawn in most cases. What is important is that helpful opinions be admitted.

The Rule requires that the opinion or inference be "rationally based on the perception of the witness." It should be emphasized that there are two requirements here. The first is that the witness has perceived that which the witness testifies about. This may mean that the witness has seen something; it may mean that the witness has heard something; or in some cases it may mean that the witness has felt or touched something. All of these would qualify as perceptions of the witness. The second requirement is that the perceptions be rationally based. Most sensory perception will qualify, but there are limits to what witness can rationally perceive. For example, it is doubtful that ESP would be accepted as a rational perception, at least not at the present time.

Rule 701 has shifted the debate about opinion evidence to where it belongs. Rather than arguing about whether it is *necessary* to have opinion evidence, as the common law required, lawyers now argue about whether it is *helpful* to the lay finders of fact. If such evidence is helpful, courts will welcome the help.[2]

[3] The Amended Rule—Enforcing the Distinction Between Lay and Expert Witnesses

In December 2004, Military Rule 701 was amended by Executive Order 13365, to maintain its commonality with Federal Rule 701. When the drafters amended Rule 701[3] they did so to eliminate the risk that expert witnesses might evade Rule 702's foundational and reliability obligations by simply testifying as lay witnesses. The amended provision requires careful consideration of whether a proffered lay witness's testimony is in reality based on scientific, technical, or other specialized knowledge and thus within the ambit of Rule 702. Amended Rule 701 does not speak in terms of expert or lay *witnesses,* rather discussing expert and lay *testimony.* This is important because experts may be lay witness as to factual observations

---

[2] In United States v. Barrett, 703 F.2d 1076 (9th Cir. 1983) and United States v. Jackson, 688 F.2d 1121 (7th Cir. 1982), the court found that it was helpful for lay witnesses to identify the defendant from surveillance photographs. In Bohannon v. Pegelow, 652 F.2d 729 (7th Cir. 1981), the court held that it was also helpful for a lay witness to testify that an arrest was racially motivated.

[3] Military Rule of Evidence 1102 provides that changes to the Federal Rules of Evidence shall apply to the Military Rules of Evidence 18 months after their effective date unless the President takes contrary action. Federal Rule of Evidence 701 was amended in December 2000.

ordinary people could make. It is clearly possible for a witness to provide both expert and lay testimony in the same case. When a witness testifies in both capacities, the proponent must qualify the expert under Rule 702 for that portion of his or her testimony requiring opinions based on scientific, technical, or other specialized expertise.[4]

Amended Rule 701 does not change traditional military practice as it applies to most lay witness testimony. Lay witnesses will be permitted to testify about the appearance of persons or things, the identity of persons, their manner of conduct, their competency, degrees of light or darkness, sound, size, weight, and distance. Most importantly, lay witnesses will be permitted to offer opinion when necessary to explain what they perceived and their opinions are of a type that ordinary people can reasonably state.[5] The line between permissible lay opinions and those requiring special expertise is thoroughly discussed in *State v. Brown,*[6] where the court evaluated a similar Tennessee Rule of Evidence and explained that lay testimony "results from a process of reasoning familiar in everyday life," while expert testimony "results from a process of reasoning which can be mastered only by specialists in the field." The court applied its logic and reasoned that a lay witness could testify that a liquid appeared to be blood. But a witness would have to be qualified as an expert before she would be permitted to testify that bruising around the eyes was indicative of skull trauma.

Military courts will have to analyze very carefully the precise testimony offered by a witness. For example, in *United States v. Davis,*[7] the accused was convicted of conspiring to escape from confinement. An important part of the government's case included lay opinion testimony comparing shoe print evidence taken at the escape route with the accused's own shoes. On appeal, the defense contended that this testimony should have been excluded

---

[4] In United States v. Figueroa-Lopez, 125 F.3d 1241, 1246 (9th Cir. 1997), law enforcement agents were permitted to testify as laymen concerning the accused's suspicious conduct, but were required to satisfy Rule 702 when their testimony addressed their lengthy experience with the code drug dealers use to consummate illegal transactions.

[5] *E.g.,* laymen will still be permitted to testify about the value of their property or its business circumstances as discussed in Lightning Lube, Inc. v. Witco Corp, 4 F.3d 1153 (3d Cir. 1993). This result is based on the witness's experiences and observations, not on any specialized knowledge an expert would bring to the analysis. This is a common result in courts-martial where an officer is permitted to testify that what he found in the accused's locker appeared to be a controlled substance. But even here the proponent must still lay a foundation demonstrating the lay witnesses familiarity with that particular controlled substance. *See* United States v. Westbrook, 896 F.2d 330 (8th Cir. 1990), where lay witnesses who were heavy amphetamine users were permitted to testify that a substance was amphetamine, but it was held to be error for other witnesses to have similarly testified when they did not have the same familiarity with amphetamines.

[6] 836 S.W.2d 530, 549 (1992).

[7] 44 M.J. 13 (C.A.A.F. 1996).

because it was offered through a lay witness, not a forensic expert. The court affirmed, holding that the evidence was properly admitted because it was used only to demonstrate obvious physical similarities. Under these circumstances, the witness's opinion did not require expert training or experience, was not based on possibly inadmissible information passed to him by outside sources, and was rationally based on criteria the witness personally observed which would be helpful to the finder of fact.

[4] Dangers of Lay Opinions

When using Rule 701, courts will have to be aware of the inherent dangers presented by certain types of lay opinion.[8] For example, when witnesses are called to identify photographs depicting someone involved in a criminal act, courts may prefer witnesses who are not police or parole officers to avoid suggesting to the factfinder an accused's prior criminal record, which might not be admissible under other provisions, such as Rules 404 and 609.[9]

[5] Rehabilitative Potential and Sentencing

Lay opinion testimony plays a particularly significant role during the sentencing phase of a court-martial. Here, in an attempt to influence the punishment adjudged, both parties provide the finder of fact with personal and professional background information about the accused, his or her duty performance, and character.

The difficulties counsel face in satisfactorily accomplishing these goals were discussed in *United States v. Ohrt.*[10] There the court examined both government and defense evidence on "rehabilitative potential." Using standards from *United States v. Horner,*[11] and RCM 1001(b)(5), the court said that rehabilitative potential refers to an assessment of the accused's character and potential which can only properly "be expressed by a witness who has a rational basis for his conclusions, founded upon the accused's service performance and character." Setting aside Ohrt's sentence, the court said that in too many instances, government witness' testimony is predicated upon the seriousness of the offense, and not upon an "opinion envisioned by RCM 1001(b)(5)."

United States v. Pompey,[12] illustrates the difference between good and bad lay opinion sentencing testimony. Defense counsel offered favorable reha-

---

[8] *See e.g.,* United States v. York, 600 F.3d 347 (5th Cir. 2010) (father of defendant permitted to testify to circumstances of his son's birth indicating organic brain damage).

[9] *See, e.g.,* United States v. Farnsworth, 729 F.2d 1158 (8th Cir. 1984) (no error in permitting parole officer, whose status was not revealed, to identify a defendant in bank surveillance film); and United States v. Butcher, 557 F.2d 666 (9th Cir. 1977).

[10] 28 M.J. 301 (C.M.A. 1989).

[11] 22 M.J. 294 (C.M.A. 1989).

[12] 33 M.J. 266 (C.M.A. 1991).

bilitative potential evidence that was rationally based on the accused's duty performance and individual skills. Trial counsel presented much more generalized evidence which centered on the crime's impact. The court found error and prejudice in the government's evidence, because it was not tied to the accused's own situation and capabilities. It held that the need for focused opinion testimony applies to both sides, during their cases-in-chief, or during rebuttal.

Similarly, in *United States v. Kirk*,[13] the court reversed an accused's sentence because her commander's testimony concerning rehabilitative potential evidence was based solely on the severity of the charged offenses. In the court's opinion, this evidence was not helpful to finders of fact partially because it lacked an adequate foundation. In *United States v. Aurich*,[14] the court reached the same result saying that a commander's opinion about whether an accused should be returned to his unit, without a reasoned and knowledgeable opinion concerning the accused's rehabilitative potential, proves nothing and is inadmissible.

The cases discussed above emphasize the importance of viewing lay opinion evidence as only being helpful to factfinders if it is based on valid personal knowledge, and not on speculation, assumptions, or hypothetical testimony. *Ohrt* and its progeny also demonstrate that even when the witness has personal knowledge about the accused, his or her lay opinion is only valuable if it is tied directly to the accused's character and not used as a euphemism for other issues which are beyond the witness' basis of knowledge or capacity to meaningfully address.

[6]   Relationship to Rule 704

Rule 701 must be read in conjunction with Rule 704, which permits opinions on the ultimate issue in the case.[15] Yet, Rule 704 permits opinion testimony only if it fits under Rules 701 or 702. Thus, only *helpful* opinions are admissible.[16] Opinions that attempt to tell court members how to decide a case are neither helpful nor permissible. For example, no witness should

---

[13]   31 M.J. 84 (C.M.A. 1990).

[14]   31 M.J. 95 (C.M.A. 1990).

[15]   *See, e.g.,* United States v. Smith, 550 F.2d 277 (5th Cir. 1977) (witness permitted to testify that defendant knew and understood the requirements of a statute). *Compare with* United States v. Phillips, 600 F.2d 535 (5th Cir. 1979) (court suggests that a social security agent probably should not have been permitted to testify that a defendant understood the meaning of the word "disability").

[16]   For example, in United States v. Ruppel, 666 F.2d 261 (5th Cir. 1982), the court held that it was highly prejudicial to admit testimony concerning the defendant's state of mind, but no error occurred in United States v. Thompson, 708 F.2d 1294 (8th Cir. 1983), admitting opinion testimony indicating that the defendant was involved in criminal activity, or in United States v. Lawson, 653 F.2d 299 (7th Cir. 1981), where lay testimony indicating that the accused was sane at time of offenses was also permitted.

offer an opinion that a defendant is guilty or innocent.[17] This is an easy example. More difficult issues arise and in some cases, the line between permissible and impermissible opinion is fine indeed.[18]

§ 701.03   Drafters' Analysis

Rule 701 is taken from the Federal Rule without change and supersedes that portion of ¶ 138 *e* which deals with opinion evidence by lay witnesses. Unlike the present *Manual* Rule that prohibits lay opinion testimony except when the opinion was of a "kind which is commonly drawn and which cannot, or ordinarily cannot, be conveyed to the court by a mere recitation of the observed facts," the Rule permits opinions or inferences whenever rationally based on the perception of the witness and helpful to either a clear understanding of the testimony or the determination of a fact in issue. Consequently, the Rule is broader in scope than the *Manual* provision it replaces. The specific examples listed in the *Manual,* "the speed of an automobile, whether a voice heard was that of a man, woman or child, and whether or not a person was drunk" are all within the potential scope of Rule 701.

§ 701.04   Drafters' Analysis (2004)

2004 Amendment: Rule 701 was modified based on the amendment to Fed. R. Evid. 701, effective 1 December 2000, and is taken from the Federal Rule without change. It prevents parties from proffering an expert as a lay witness in an attempt to evade the gatekeeper and reliability requirements of Rule 702 by providing that testimony cannot qualify under Rule 701 if it is based on "scientific, technical, or other special knowledge within the scope of Rule 702."

§ 701.05   Annotated Cases

[1]   Lay Opinions—Assault Cases

Navy-Marine Corps Court of Criminal Appeals

United States v. Muirhead, 48 M.J. 527 (N.M.Ct.Crim.App. 1998): The accused was convicted by general court-martial of assaulting his six-year-old stepdaughter with the intent to inflict grievous bodily harm. The accused's theory of the case was that the accused had not harmed his stepdaughter, but that she had accidentally injured herself. The accused contended that the military judge erred by permitting an NCIS Agent to testify that the accused should have been able to hear if his stepdaughter had

---

[17] *Cf.* United States v. Bell, 21 M.J. 662 (A.C.M.R. 1985) (witness allowed to testify concerning whether he "formulated an opinion" about the accused's complicity in the charged offense).

[18] *See, e.g.,* Central R.R. v. Monahan, 11 F.2d 212 (1926) (Judge Learned Hand, *citing Wigmore,* observed that American jurisprudence is much too restrictive in dealing with opinion).

fallen down the stairs. Affirming the accused's conviction, this court held that the NCIS Agent's opinion testimony was admissible because it was rationally related to her perceptions and helpful to the trier-of-fact.

[2] Lay Opinions—Drug Cases

United States Court of Appeals for the Armed Forces

United States v. Tyler, 17 M.J. 381 (C.M.A. 1984): The court concluded that a lay witness may provide opinion testimony concerning the identity of controlled substances, even though that witness is neither a chemist nor trained to identify the substances by chemical analysis. The court required, however, that a witness must demonstrate "proper qualifications" before testifying. These qualifications might arise from drug use. Experience with a drug ordinarily would support lay testimony identifying the physical appearance, odor and psychological effect of the drug.

Air Force Court of Criminal Appeals

United States v. Accordino, 15 M.J. 825 (A.F.C.M.R. 1983): An undercover OSI agent's opinion testimony that the substances given him by the accused were cocaine was properly admitted because the testimony was rationally based on the witness' perceptions, and it helped the jury properly determine the facts in issue.

Coast Guard Court of Criminal Appeals

United States v. Francis, 25 M.J. 614 (C.G.C.M.R. 1987): The court held that, in order for lay opinion testimony concerning the impact of discrediting conduct on a military organization to be of value, it must contain "first hand knowledge" of the underlying facts, and personal information about how those facts affected the units in question. Mere hypotheticals and suppositions from experience are not sufficient. However, because the accused's offenses (distributing drugs, obstructing justice, and sodomy) were service discrediting on their face, any error was harmless.

[3] Lay Opinions—Identification

Army Court of Criminal Appeals

United States v. Bell, 21 M.J. 662 (A.C.M.R. 1985): A witness was allowed to testify concerning whether he "formulated an opinion" concerning the accused's complicity in an aggravated assault because the court felt that the testimony was rationally based on the witness's perceptions and was helpful to the court-member's understanding of what happened.

United States v. Howell, 16 M.J. 1003 (A.C.M.R. 1983): No error was created by the government using the accused's roommate to identify the accused as the person depicted in a photograph, because the testimony was rationally based on the witness's perceptions and was helpful to the finders of fact.

[4]   Lay Opinions—Interpreting Another's Communications

United States Court of Appeals for the Armed Forces

United States v. Roberson, 65 M.J. 43 (C.A.A.F. 2007): The accused was convicted by a special court-martial with members of unauthorized absence, larceny, and forgery. His defense was based on duress. Several witnesses testified that a co-actor threatened to kill the accused if the accused did not steal and forge two of his roommate's checks. The military judge excluded testimony of a defense witness who would have testified about the co-actor's statements indicating an intent to harm the accused, and the witness's opinion that the accused's appeared frightened when he heard about those statements. The court held that the excluded lay opinion testimony was admissible because it supported the accused's contention that he feared his co-actor. The court added that as long as the witness's opinion was based upon his personal observation, was relevant, and did not require a unique ability or specialized training, it should have been admitted to help establish the accused's emotional state. However, the error in excluding the lay testimony was deemed harmless.

United States v. Byrd, 60 M.J. 4 (C.A.A.F. 2004): The accused was tried for forcibly and sexually molesting his daughter. While in pretrial confinement he sent several letters to his wife and daughter hoping to dissuade them from testifying against him. Over defense objection, the accused's wife was permitted to read selected portions of the letters to the members and then provide an explanation of the words. Finding error in how the process was generally conducted, but not sufficient prejudice to justify reversal, this court held that existing Federal practice normally does not permit a lay witness to testify concerning subjective interpretations or conclusions about what another person has said or written. The court went on to hold that such testimony might be admissible if it were offered to explain a coded or code-like conversation. This is a case of first impression for military courts.

[5]   Lay Opinions—Mental Condition

United States Court of Appeals for the Armed Forces

United States v. White, 69 M.J. 236 (C.A.A.F. 2010): The accused's convictions for signing false official documents were affirmed despite her contention that the military judge improperly excluded lay opinion testimony and documentary evidence which would have demonstrated her lack of a motive to lie. The accused entered the Army in 1995 and transferred to the Air Force in 2003. When she entered the Army she indicated on credentialing documents that she had a criminal past. When she transferred to the Air Force she indicated on different documents that she did not have a criminal record. The military judge admitted the Army forms indicating her yes answer to a criminal past, but excluded other Army documents which did not address criminality. The military judge also excluded defense lay opinion testimony from the accused's co-workers. Their testimony would have minimized the importance of the forms. While the court recognized that the relevance standard is very low, the court found that the excluded lay testimony had no nexus to the accused's state of mind or intent to lie at the time she executed the Air Force forms.

United States v. Roberson, 65 M.J. 43 (C.A.A.F. 2007): The accused was convicted by a special court-martial with members of unauthorized absence, larceny, and forgery. His defense was based on duress. Several witnesses testified that a co-actor threatened to kill the accused if the accused did not steal and forge two of his roommate's checks. The military judge excluded testimony of a defense witness who would have testified about the co-actor's statements indicating an intent to harm the accused, and the witness's opinion that the accused appeared frightened when he heard about those statements. The court held that the excluded lay opinion testimony was admissible because it supported the accused's contention that he feared his co-actor. The court added that as long as the witness's opinion was based upon his personal observation, was relevant, and did not require a unique ability or specialized training, it should have been admitted to help establish the accused's emotional state. However, the error in excluding the lay testimony was deemed harmless

Navy-Marine Corps Court of Criminal Appeals

United States v. Schnable, 65 M.J. 566 (N.M.Ct.Crim.App. 2006): The accused was convicted of indecent acts upon his 13-year-old daughter and communicating a threat. At trial, the child's mother testified that the victim had been diagnosed with mild mental retardation and suffered from a speech impediment. The mother had home schooled her child and was very familiar with the child's emotional limitations, which she explained to the court. The accused objected on the grounds that testimony about mental retardation must be presented by a qualified expert under Rule 702. Affirming the accused's conviction, the court held that, based on the mother's observations both as a teacher and a parent, her opinions were rationally based on perception and were helpful to the finder of fact in understanding the victim's mental functioning, credibility, and testimony.

[6]   Lay Opinions—Personal Information

Army Court of Criminal Appeals

United States v. Williams, 23 M.J. 792 (A.C.M.R. 1987): Although the court recognized that a layman "may testify to the general nature of his own physical condition, or the state of his health," it found no error in the exclusion of a witness's testimony about her own blood type. The court viewed this evidence as inconsistent with the *Manual*'s prohibitions against hearsay.

[7]   Lay Opinions—Prejudicial to Good Order and Discipline

United States Court of Appeals for the Armed Forces

United States v. Littlewood, 53 M.J. 349 (C.A.A.F. 2000): Part of the government's evidence establishing that the accused sexually assaulted a child and that this conduct was indecent, prejudicial to good order and discipline, and service discrediting, came from the accused's battalion commander. Trial defense counsel objected contending that the battalion commander was unqualified to provide such testimony, that the evidence was irrelevant and speculative. Finding error but no prejudice, this court held that the battalion commander's opinion was not helpful or beyond the ken of the average military judge or member. More importantly, the court also found that the questioned testimony consisted mainly of "bald assertions, unsupported by reasoning or particular facts showing the manner in which these charged offenses embarrassed the command or undermined moral.

Navy-Marine Corps Court of Criminal Appeals

United States v. Jackson, 54 M.J. 527 (N.M.Ct.Crim.App. 2000): Affirming the accused's rape and adultery convictions, this court held that no error occurred when the accused's commanding officer testified that in his opinion, the accused's conduct was prejudicial to good order and discipline. The court found that the commander based his opinion on personal observations, that his opinion was relevant and more probative that prejudicial.

[8]   Lay Opinions—Rehabilitative Potential and Sentencing

United States Court of Appeals for the Armed Forces

United States v. Pompey, 33 M.J. 266 (C.M.A. 1991): The accused was convicted of drug use, and sentenced to a discharge and one-month confinement. Defense counsel presented favorable rehabilitative potential evidence rationally based on the accused's duty performance and individual skills. Trial counsel presented much more generalized evidence which centered on the crime's impact. The court found error and prejudice in the government's evidence because it was not tied to the accused's own situation and capabilities. It held that the need for focused opinion testimony applies to both sides, during their cases-in-chief, or during rebuttal, and that the "doctrine of curative inadmissibility" would not be recognized here.

United States v. Aurich, 31 M.J. 95 (C.M.A. 1990): Affirming the accused's sentence in this drug case, the court held that a commander's opinion about whether an accused should be returned to his unit, without a reasoned and knowledgeable opinion concerning the accused's rehabilitative potential, proves nothing and is inadmissible.

United States v. Kirk, 31 M.J. 84 (C.M.A. 1990): The court reversed the accused's sentence, in this failure to obey regulations court-martial, because her commander improperly testified that the accused lacked rehabilitative potential. On appeal, government counsel conceded that the record did not establish an adequate foundation for such opinion testimony. The court held that rehabilitative potential evidence which is based solely on the severity of charged offenses is not helpful to finders of fact.

United States v. Ohrt, 28 M.J. 301 (C.M.A. 1989): The court thoroughly examined "rehabilitative potential" testimony. *See also United States v. Horner,* 22 M.J. 294 (C.M.A. 1989) ("rehabilitative potential refers to the accused. It is based upon an assessment of . . . [the accused's] character and potential"). The court set aside the accused's sentence, observing that, in too many instances, a government witness's testimony is predicated upon the seriousness of the offense, not upon an "opinion envisioned by RCM 1001(b)(5) [which] can only be expressed by a witness who has a rational basis for his conclusions, founded upon the accused's service performance and character."

Army Court of Criminal Appeals

United States v. Yerich, 47 M.J. 615 (Army Ct.Crim.App. 1997): During the sentencing portion of the accused's drug distribution and related offenses court-martial, trial counsel called the accused's company commander and four NCOs to provide aggravation testimony. Each knew and worked with the accused; each provided opinions concerning his lack of rehabilitative potential. Trial defense counsel did not challenge the testimony. On appeal the accused contended that admission of this evidence constituted plain error because the witnesses did not have a sufficient basis upon which to provide their opinions. Rejecting the accused's contention that he was entitled to a rehearing on sentence, this court found that the government's sentencing witnesses demonstrated a rational basis for their opinion testimony because each had more than sufficient personal knowledge about the accused to meet the foundational requirements for lay opinion testimony.

United States v. Stimpson, 29 M.J. 768 (A.C.M.R. 1989): The court held that the prosecution witnesses on sentencing had a rational basis for testifying that the accused had no potential for rehabilitation. Each had properly factored into his opinion the severity of the offenses and the accused's duty performance. Although the court noted that counsel had, in effect, improperly used a euphemistic question to elicit from the witnesses their opinion on whether the accused should be punitively discharged, it concluded that the trial judge was not impermissibly influenced.

United States v. Taylor, 21 M.J. 840 (A.C.M.R. 1986): Opinion testimony about what specific sentence a court-martial should adjudge was held to be inadmissible because it provided no real assistance in resolving any fact in issue and amounted to "little more than choosing up sides."

[9] Lay Opinions—Relationship to Expert Testimony

United States Court of Appeals for the Armed Forces

United States v. Hall, 66 M.J. 53 (C.A.A.F. 2008): While on convalescent leave, the accused cared for the nine-month-old son of a friend. The accused was subsequently convicted of maiming the child by placing him in dangerously hot water. Part of the government's proof included testimony from a criminal investigator who had a master's degree in forensic science and experience with child burn cases. This special agent testified that in her opinion the child's injuries were textbook evidence of non-accidental immersion burns. Over defense objection her testimony was received as lay opinion evidence pursuant to Rule 701. On appeal, the government conceded error but not harm. The court affirmed the Navy-Marine Corps Court of Criminal Appeals' finding of harmless error by relying on four factors: (1) the overwhelming strength of the government's case; (2) the weakness and implausibility of the accused's case; (3) the admitted materiality of the questioned evidence; and (4) the fact that the challenged evidence did not have had a substantial impact on the verdict.

United States v. Davis, 44 M.J. 13 (C.A.A.F. 1996): While a prisoner at the United States Disciplinary Barracks, the accused was convicted of conspiring to escape from confinement. Part of the government's case included a comparison of shoe print evidence taken at the escape route with the accused's own shoes. The accused contended that this testimony should have been excluded because it was offered through a lay witness not a forensic expert. This court affirmed findings and sentence holding that the military judge, sitting alone, properly used the evidence to only demonstrate obvious physical similarities.

Army Court of Criminal Appeals

United States v. Jackson, 22 M.J. 604 (A.C.M.R. 1986): This case illustrates how, when a proffered expert witness does not qualify under Rule 702, careful counsel will seek to introduce his testimony under Rule 701. The court noted that Rule 701 deprives [that witness] of the opportunity to testify to opinions based on facts or data . . . perceived or made known to the expert, at or before the hearing," but permits a lay person to testify to "opinions based on her own personal observations."

Navy-Marine Corps Court of Criminal Appeals

United States v. Abdirahman, 66 M.J. 668 (N.M.Ct.Crim.App. 2008): The accused's conviction for rape was reversed based on the cumulative effect of trial errors. One error involved testimony by a nurse practitioner that the victim's physical and emotional conditions were similar to those of other rape victims she had examined. The court held that such opinion testimony was improperly admitted because trial counsel had not informed the defense that an expert would be called, and the witness was never qualified or offered as an expert. The court added that, while it would have been appropriate for this nurse practitioner to testify about the victim's observable conditions, only a properly qualified expert could provide opinion testimony interpreting them.

United States v. Silvis, 31 M.J. 707 (N.M.C.M.R. 1990): Affirming the accused's rape conviction, the court held that testimony establishing the victim's post-offense suicide attempt was properly admitted by lay witnesses. The court relied on civilian cases to hold that the aura of scientific reliability attached to "rape trauma syndrome" evidence was not required here.

[10]   Lay Opinions—Veracity

Air Force Court of Criminal Appeals

United States v. Clark, 12 M.J. 978 (A.F.C.M.R. 1982): At the trial of an accused charged with committing an indecent act upon a female under 16 years of age, the government called an OSI agent who testified that when he asked the accused if he committed the offense, the accused denied it and "looked away from me when he stated it." The OSI agent was then allowed to testify that based on his previous training and experience he believed the accused's body language indicated that the accused had lied. Defense counsel objected to this opinion testimony. The court found that the testimony was improper, but not prejudicial. It identified several problems with the testimony: the OSI agent's training in the area was inadequate; no measurable test was offered for determining veracity; the testimony was uncertain and qualified; it was not founded on scientific principles; the agent had not verified past body language interrogation results; and his conclusions as to truthfulness were, as a result, only conjecture.

§ 702.01 Official Text

Rule 702. Testimony by Experts.

If scientific, technical, or other specialized knowledge will assist the trier of fact to understand the evidence or to determine a fact in issue, a witness qualified as an expert by knowledge, skill, experience, training, or education, may testify thereto in the form of an opinion or otherwise, if (1) the testimony is based upon sufficient facts or data, (2) the testimony is the product of reliable principles and methods, and (3) the witness has applied the principles and methods reliably to the facts of the case.

---

§ 702.02 Editorial Comment

[1] In General

Rule 702 governs the admissibility of expert opinion testimony.[1] In December 2004, the Rule was amended by Executive Order 13365, to maintain its commonality with Federal Rule 702. Military Rule 702, like its Federal counterpart, was amended in response to the Supreme Court's opinions in *Daubert v. Merrell Dow Pharmas. Inc.*,[2] and *Kumho Tire Co. v. Carmichael.*[3] Both cases are important in establishing the standards military judges use in determining the admissibility of expert opinion testimony.[4] They overruled the long standing "general acceptance" standard used since *Frye v. United States*,[5] and established new standards courts must use for admitting expert testimony. The opinions characterized the trial judge's function in this process as that of a "gatekeeper" who must ensure that unreliable expert testimony is excluded. *Kumho* extended *Daubert's* gate-

---

[1] Military Rule of Evidence 1102 provides that changes to the Federal Rules of Evidence shall apply to the Military Rules of Evidence 18 months after their effective date unless the President takes contrary action. Federal Rule of Evidence 702 was amended in December 2000.

[2] 509 U.S. 579 (1993).

[3] 526 U.S. 137 (1999)

[4] The amended Rule, its predecessor, *Daubert*, *Kumho*, and virtually every military, federal, and state court case dealing with opinion testimony focus on the "expert" witness's contribution to the proceedings. Interestingly, current trial practice has moved toward prohibiting the use of the term "expert witness" in the jury's presence out of concern that lay finders of fact will believe the "experts" testimony automatically deserves added value or greater weight. *See,* Hon. Charles Richey, Proposals to Eliminate the Prejudicial Effect of the Use of the Word "Expert" Under the Federal Rules of Evidence in Criminal and Civil Jury Trials, 154 F.R.D. 537, 559 (1994) (providing limiting instructions and a standing order prohibiting the use of the term "expert" in jury trials).

[5] 293 F. 1013 (D.C. Cir. 1923).

keeper requirements to all expert opinion testimony, not just such testimony based on scientific principles.[6]

Amended Rule 702 codifies the gatekeeper role for trial judges, and states, guidelines for military judges to use in assessing the reliability and helpfulness of an expert's opinion testimony. Rule 702 should be read in conjunction with *Bourjaily v. United States*[7] and Rule 104(a). Together they provide that the proponent of Rule 702 evidence has the burden of satisfying the Rule's foundational requirements by a preponderance of the evidence.

[2] Assisting the Trier of Fact

Rule 702 is the standard courts use to measure the admissibility of evidence that is dependent upon scientific, technical, and other specialized skills.[8] This provision states that, if an expert can "assist the trier of fact" because of his or her uncommon knowledge or experience, then the expert may be permitted to testify.[9] Such proof is admitted because experts have the

---

[6] In Kumho Tire Co. v. Carmichael, 526 U.S. 137 (1999) the Court held: "We conclude that *Daubert's* general holding setting forth the trial judge's general 'gatekeeping' obligation applies not only to testimony based on 'scientific' knowledge, but also to testimony based on 'technical' and 'other specialized' knowledge." As a result, opinion testimony from an expert who is not a scientist should receive the same reliability scrutiny as opinion testimony from a "scientific" expert. This was the result in Watkins v. Telsmith, Inc., 121 F.3d 984, 991 (5th Cir. 1997), where the court held: "[I]t seems exactly backwards that experts who purport to rely on general engineering principles and practical experience might escape screening by the district court simply by stating that their conclusions were not reached by any particular method or technique." However the opinion testimony is defined, the military judge must find that it uniformly satisfies the requirements of amended Rule 702 as well as its amplification in *Daubert* and *Kumho. See*, American College of Trial Lawyers, Standards and Procedures for Determining the Admissibility of Expert Testimony after Daubert, 157 F.R.D. 571, 579 (1994) ("Whether the testimony concerns economic principles, accounting standards, property valuation or other nonscientific subjects, it should be evaluated by reference to the 'knowledge and experience' of that particular field.").

[7] 483 U.S. 171 (1987).

[8] *See, e.g.,* United States v. Gillespie, 852 F.2d 475 (9th Cir. 1988) (error to admit lay opinion testimony by therapist that child had been abused by a man, and not a woman, because use of anatomically correct dolls requires compliance with standards for expert opinion testimony).

[9] Federal courts have admitted expert testimony for a wide range of legal issues. Examples include: United States v. Alexander, 849 F.2d 1293 (5th Cir. 1987) (expert testimony on cephalometry, the measurement of dimensions of the head is admissible); United States v. Rose, 731 F.2d 1337 (8th Cir. 1984) (proper for expert to give opinion as to shoe-print comparison); United States v. Schmidt, 711 F.2d 595 (5th Cir. 1983) (upholding exclusion of psycholinguistics expert); United States v. Distler, 671 F.2d 954 (6th Cir. 1981) (upholding "oil matching" by chromatograph analysis); United States v. Rackley, 724 F.2d 1463 (8th Cir. 1984) (permissible for trial judge to permit a demonstration of how narcotics-sniffing dog performed); United States v. Pugliese, 712 F.2d 1574 (2d Cir. 1983) (government agent permitted to testify about characteristics of heroin addicts); United States v. Langford, 802 F.2d 1176 (9th Cir. 1986) (upholding the admission of identification testimony by the

knowledge and training to help factfinders understand other evidence in the case, or understand the way in which evidence relates to attendant legal questions.[10] If it were not for expert witnesses, complex scientific and technical testimony, or ordinary testimony with unusual or unexpected applications, might be misinterpreted by court members or military judges, causing errors in findings and sentences. Unlike the common law, Rule 702 has no requirement that an expert be absolutely necessary or that the subject matter of expert testimony be totally beyond the ken of court members. The test is whether the expert can be helpful.[11]

[3]   Greater Admissibility

Rule 702 has been widely interpreted as permitting greater admissibility of expert testimony than was the case under previous court-martial practice, and the 1969 *Manual.*[12] Rule 702 permits the trial court to admit any expert testimony it finds helpful.[13] However, the Drafters' Analysis indicates that the Rule was not intended to eliminate all previous *Manual* constraints, and should not be interpreted as an indication that previously inadmissible expert or opinion testimony is now automatically admissible.[14] Rule 702 empowers

---

defendant's cousin and his parole officer who viewed bank surveillance films); United States v. Anderson, 851 F.2d 384 (D.C. Cir. 1988) (expert testimony on how pimps operate was admissible in Mann Act prosecution); United States v. Angiulo, 847 F.2d 956 (1st Cir. 1988) (expert opinion testimony by FBI agent admissible on structure and operations of Costa Nostra and relationship of defendants to that organization); United States v. Cruz, 797 F.2d 90 (2d Cir. 1986) (holding that the trial judge properly permitted a government agent to testify regarding the food stamp program and the use of food stamps in narcotics sales); United States v. Gigante, 729 F.2d 78 (2d Cir. 1984) (affirming trial judge's admission of expert opinion as to numbers that a codefendant dialed on a phone).

[10] *See, e.g.,* United States v. Farrell, 563 F.3d 364 (8th Cir. 2009) (expert's testimony concerning strength of government's case erroneously admitted).

[11] *See, e.g.,* United States v. Meeks, 35 M.J. 64 (C.M.A. 1992) (FBI agent allowed to testify about crime scene because "the proper standard is helpfulness, not absolute necessity").

[12] *See, e.g.,* United States v. Kyles, 20 M.J. 571 (N.M.C.M.R. 1985) (court recognized that these rules were designed to broaden the admissibility of expert testimony but only when they will assist the finder of fact in understanding an important trial issue).

[13] In discussing helpfulness, the Advisory Committee's note concerning Rule 702 provides that the test for deciding when experts can be used is "whether the untrained layman would be qualified to determine intelligently and to the best possible degree the particular issue without enlightenment from those having a specialized understanding of the subject. . . ." Experience demonstrates that review of this issue generally is limited to determining whether the military judge had abused her discretion.

[14] The adoption of this Rule also resulted in the deletion of ¶ 142 *e* of the 1969 *Manual.* That paragraph had made inadmissible polygraph test results and the results of procedures involving drugs or hypnosis. This area is now specifically addressed in Rule 707. *See generally* Oeveren, *Admissibility of Polygraph Results Under Military and Federal Rules of Evidence,* 12 The ADVOC. 257 (1980); Williams, *Admissibility of Polygraph Results Under the Military Rules of Evidence,* ARMY LAW., June 1980, at 1.

courts to evaluate expert testimony in light of the scientific principles considered reliable at the time the expert testifies. As a result, some types of expert testimony might be deemed more or less reliable at different times.

[4] Historic Standard for Using Scientific Evidence— *Frye v. United States*

A long standing limitation on the use of scientific and other expert testimony stemmed from the famous case of *Frye v. United States*, 293 F. 1013 (D.C. Cir. 1923). There the court ruled that, to be admissible, expert testimony had to be based on scientific principles that were generally accepted" in the applicable scientific community. Although *Frye's* holding concerned a systolic blood pressure deception test, the precursor to our polygraph machine,[15] the theory had been applied to a wide variety of scientific and related opinion testimony.

After the Federal[16] and Military.[17] Rules of Evidence were adopted, the general acceptance standard remained alive and well in some courts, even though nothing in Rule 702, its federal legislative history, or the Military Drafter's *Analysis* specifically required it.

General acceptance in the applicable scientific community was required by many courts because trials produce a final result between the parties and cannot be adjusted as science improves. In the scientific community, scientists can correct their mistakes and admit past errors. In fact, scientists are encouraged to do so. In criminal litigation, judgments are generally final. Erroneous convictions and sentences to mistaken acquittal will not be undone if it appears that they resulted from bad science. Thus, courts preferred tried and true techniques and were skeptical when confronted with novel scientific evidence. As the Court said in *Frye*:[18]

> Just when a scientific principle or discovery crosses the line between the experiential and demonstrable stage is difficult to define. Somewhere in this twilight zone, the evidential force of the principle must be recognized and while courts will go a long way in admitting expert

---

[15] *See* our Editorial Comment to Military Rule of Evidence 707, which specifically addresses polygraph examinations.

[16] *See, e.g.,* Beech Aircraft Corp. v. Rainey, 488 U.S. 153 (1988) ("The drafting history makes no mention of Frye, and a rigid 'general acceptance' requirement would be at odds with the 'liberal thrust' of the Federal Rules and their 'general approach of relaxing the traditional barriers to opinion testimony.' ").

[17] The Drafters' Analyses to Rules 702 and 703 indicates that when the Military Rules were adopted, the exact standards applicable for using scientific evidence had not yet been well established in civilian courts under the Federal Rules of Evidence. The military drafters were apparently content to wait for civilian judicial guidance. As our subsequent discussion will show, military appellate courts were not willing to wait, and in fact were several years ahead of their civilian counterparts in providing accurate interpretations for using Rule 702.

[18] 293 F. at 1014.

testimony deduced from a well-recognized scientific principle or discovery, the thing from which the deduction is made must be sufficiently established to have gained general acceptance in the particular field in which it belongs.

[5]   Supreme Court Direction on Using Scientific Evidence— *Daubert, Kumho,* and *Joiner*

In *Daubert v. Merrell Dow Pharms., Inc.,*[19] the Supreme Court rejected Frye's 70 year old "general acceptance" requirement for admitting scientific evidence, and in its place established a new standard for Federal trials.[20] The issue in *Daubert* was whether plaintiffs could prove that a link existed between Bendectin, a drug manufactured by Merrel Dow, and birth defects sustained by infants born to mothers who used the drug. The District Court found plaintiff's evidence to be inadmissible because it had not been published or submitted for peer review. The District Court held that expert opinion testimony that is based on a methodology that diverges significantly from the procedures accepted by recognized authorities in the field cannot be shown to be generally accepted as a reliable technique. The Court of Appeals affirmed. But, the Supreme Court remanded, holding that Rule 702 superseded *Frye.* The court noted that the common law may serve as an aid to the Rule's application,[21] but held that the strict *Frye* standard was at odds with the Rules' liberal thrust and general approach of relaxing the traditional barriers to opinion testimony.

In reaching this decision, the Court found that Rule 702 places sufficient limits on the admissibility of scientific evidence, and that trial judges can adequately perform the task of insuring that an expert's testimony rests on reliable grounds, is relevant to the "task at hand," and will assist the trier of fact. To accomplish these tasks, judges must use Rule 104(a) to make a preliminary assessment of whether the testimony's underlying reasoning or methodology is scientifically valid and can be properly applied to the issues at bar.

Among the many factors the Court said bear on how this issue should be resolved are whether the theory or technique the proponent seeks to have her expert testify about: (1) can be and has been tested; (2) has been subjected to peer review and publication; (3) has a known or potential error rate; (4)

---

[19] 509 U.S. 579 (1993).

[20] *See, e.g.,* United States v. Bonds, 12 F.3d 540 (6th Cir. 1993) (Sixth Circuit case of first impression affirming convictions and admissibility of DNA expert testimony viewed as both relevant and reliable as defined by the United States Supreme Court in *Daubert*).

[21] The court relied upon its previous holding in United States v. Abel, 469 U.S. 45 (1984), where it said, "In principle, under the Federal Rules, no common law of evidence remains. 'All relevant evidence is admissible except as otherwise provide. . . .' In reality, of course, the body of common law knowledge continues to exist, though in the somewhat altered form of a source of guidance in the exercise of delegated powers."

benefits from the existence and maintenance of standards controlling its operation; and (5) has attracted widespread acceptance within a relevant scientific community. The inquiry is meant to be flexible, with the focus being on the applicable scientific principles and methodologies.

Litigation under the Rules, as opposed to under *Frye,* will place more of a premium on cross-examination, the presentation of contrary evidence, and careful instructions by the trial bench. In the Court's opinion, these litigation techniques are preferable to *Frye's* wholesale exclusion of scientific evidence. However, the Court warned that the trial judge's responsibility is not to gather "cosmic understanding" about any scientific theory or application, but to be a "gatekeeper" in determining whether the theory or application can assist in resolving the legal dispute at bar.[22] The Court indicated that, while performing the gatekeeping function, it would be unreasonable to require that the subject, applicability, and validity of scientific testimony must be known to a certainty. Nothing else in the litigation process must meet this standard, and it is particularly ill suited to science where arguably there may be no certainties.

Daubert essentially requires a two step analysis, focusing on reliability and relevance. First, the expert proof must be based on a scientific method. Second, there must be an adequate fit between the expert testimony and a contested trial issue.

In order to meet the first step, counsel must demonstrate that there is some valid scientific foundation for the expert's testimony. This should come from an independent and valid source, and not be the product of the expert's own *"ipse dixit."* Courts applying *Daubert* look to see if the expert's research was produced independently from the litigation, or if it was created for the sole purpose of being used in a courtroom. Independent research has a built in reliability component. Research for the purpose of litigation needs support from other established sources.

Kumho Tire Co.v. Patrick Carmichael,[23] significantly expanded upon and clarified the Court's holding in *Daubert. Kumho* was sued for defectively manufacturing a tire that failed in operation causing a fatality and other injuries. The District Court excluded plaintiff's expert witness testimony because it lacked a reliable methodology and was in some parts self-contradictory. The Eleventh Circuit reversed, holding that the *Daubert* factors were limited to scientific evidence, not testimony based on skill or experience.

---

[22] Concerning these responsibilities, Chief Justice Rehnquist said, concurring in part and dissenting in part: "I do not doubt that Rule 702 confides to the judge some gatekeeping responsibility in deciding questions of the admissibility of proffered expert testimony. But I do not think it imposes on them either the obligation or the authority to become amateur scientists in order to perform that role."

[23] 526 U.S. 137 (1999).

The Supreme Court disagreed and found the trial judge's resolution to be correct. The Court went on to say that: (a) the *Daubert* factors apply to the testimony of engineers and other experts who are not scientists; (b) Rules 702 and 703 grant all expert witnesses testimonial latitude unavailable to other witnesses only when that testimony has a reliable basis in the knowledge and experience of the witness's discipline; (c) the *Daubert* factors do not constitute a definitive checklist or test, but should be applied in a flexible manner and only when they assure a reasonable measure of reliability; (d) among the factors a court should consider in determining whether to apply the *Daubert* factors are the nature of the case, the expert's particular expertise, and the subject of his/her testimony; and (e) whether the *Daubert* factors are reasonable measures of reliability in a given case is a matter of law for the trial judge to resolve, and a trial judge has broad latitude in making such determinations. The *Kumho* Court ultimately determined that the problem here was not the reliability of the expert witness' methodology in general, but whether the expert used that methodology in a way that enabled him to reliably determine why the tire failed.

In *General Electric Co. v. Joiner*,[24] a toxic tort case, the Court again examined the process for evaluating novel and uncertain scientific opinion testimony—here whether polychlorinated biphenyls (PCBs) contributed to plaintiff's lung cancer. The Court also addressed the standards that apply to reviewing a trial judge's decision admitting or excluding such evidence, particularly when that evidence is "outcome determinative."

Reversing the circuit court, the Court affirmed the trial judge's decision to exclude plaintiffs' experts' explanative theory testimony because it "did not rise above subjective belief or unsupported speculation." Similarly, the Court affirmed its long standing position that trial court evidentiary rulings are measured on appeal by an "abuse of discretion standard," and emphasized that nothing in *Daubert* changed that.

The Court also reaffirmed its basic *Daubert* precepts: (a) the Federal Rules of Evidence take a more flexible and lenient approach to opinion and expert testimony than the common law allowed; (b) trial judges must perform "gatekeeper" functions on all scientific evidence; (c) trial judges must ensure that the scientific evidence is both relevant and reliable. Although the Court in *Daubert* indicated that trial courts must focus on principles and methodology, not on the conclusions that they generate, *Joiner* indicated that principles and methodologies often cannot be sharply distinguished from conclusions. The Court found that there was simply too great an analytical gap between the plaintiffs' data and their expert witnesses' proffered opinions. The Court concluded that nothing in *Daubert* requires trial judges to admit opinion testimony "connected to existing data only by the *ipse dixit* of the expert."

---

[24] 522 U.S. 136 (1997).

[6]   The Amended Rule

The 2004 amendment to the Rule codifies the approach of *Daubert* and *Kumho* but does not codify the *Daubert* factors. This is intentional because the Court itself does not see the *Daubert* or *Kumho* factors as exclusive or dispositive.[25] However, the amended Rule is drafted broadly enough to deal with the myriad of questions that will arise in litigation.[26] The *Daubert* factors will be more useful in some cases than in others, and no single factor is likely to be dispositive of admissibility or exclusion.[27]

The amended rule should not be read as a statutory or judicial justification for challenging all expert testimony.[28] Nor should it be read to hold that only one party's view of a disputed issue can be based on reliable evidence Federal courts have held that the amendment is expansive enough to allow for competing principles or methods in the same field of expertise to be introduced.[29]

The amendment to Rule 702 does not address what standard military judges should use in deciding whether or not to admit the questioned evidence. A Federal case, *In re Paoli R.R. Yard Pcb Litig.*,[30] is very helpful here. There the court opined that proponents of Rule 702 evidence "do not

---

[25] Federal courts interpreting *Daubert* and *Kumho* quickly recognized this reality. *See* Tyus v. Urban Search Management, 102 F.3d 256 (7th Cir. 1996) (*Daubert* factors do not easily apply to expert testimony from a sociologist), and Kannankeril v. Terminix Int'l, Inc., 128 F.3d 802, 809 (3d Cir. 1997) (lack of peer review or publication not dispositive where the expert's opinion was supported by "widely accepted scientific knowledge").

[26] Interesting conflicts will continue to arise as presented by Claar v. Burlington N.R.R., 29 F.3d 499 (9th Cir. 1994) (testimony excluded where expert failed to consider other obvious causes for the plaintiffs condition) and Ambrosini v. Labarraque, 101 F.3d 129 (D.C. Cir. 1996) (possibility of uneliminated causes presents a question of weight and not admissibility so long as the most obvious causes have been considered and reasonably ruled out by the expert). Other difficult questions are represented in Sheehan v. Daily Racing Form, Inc., 104 F.3d 940, 942 (7th Cir. 1997) (is the expert "being as careful as he would be in his regular professional work outside his paid litigation consulting").

[27] *See, e.g.*, Heller v. Shaw Industries, Inc., 167 F.3d 146, 155 (3d Cir. 1999) (each stage of expert's testimony must be reliable and each stage must be evaluated using both practical and flexible evaluation techniques).

[28] *See* Kumho Tire Co. v. Carmichael, 526 U.S. 137 (1999) (the trial judge has discretion "both to avoid unnecessary 'reliability' proceedings in ordinary cases where the reliability of an expert's methods is properly taken for granted, and to require appropriate proceedings in the less usual or more complex cases where cause for questioning the expert's reliability arises").

[29] *See, e.g.*, Heller v. Shaw Indust., Inc., 167 F.3d 146, 160 (3d Cir. 1999) (permissible for expert testimony on both sides of a contested issue to be admitted as long as each has met the reliable standards of this rule); Ruiz-Troche v. Pepsi Cola, 161 F.3d 77, 85 (1st Cir. 1998) ("Daubert neither requires nor empowers trial courts to determine which of several competing scientific theories has the best provenance.").

[30] 35 F.3d 717, 744 (3d Cir. 1994).

have to demonstrate to the judge by a preponderance of the evidence that the assessments of their experts are correct, they only have to demonstrate by a preponderance of evidence that their opinions are reliable. . . ." Concerning this standard, the Ninth Circuit, on remand, in *Daubert v. Merrell Dow Pharms., Inc.*,[31] highlighted that the "evidentiary requirement of reliability is lower than the merits standard of correctness."

Rule 702's new language provides that military judges must not only scrutinize the principles and methods used by the expert, but they must also determine whether those principles and methods have been properly applied to the facts of the case. *In re Paoli R.R. Yard Pcb Litig.*,[32] addresses this issue by holding that "any step that renders the analysis unreliable renders the expert's testimony inadmissible. This is true whether the step completely changes a reliable methodology or merely misapplies that methodology."

The amendment does not alter established court-martial practice that allows calling expert witnesses to educate factfinders concerning general scientific or similar principles even if those specific principles will not be directly used to resolve the issues at bar. For example, expert witnesses can provide background information on DNA or blood splatter evidence even though that background testimony may not be contentious.

Finally, as a matter of interpretation and application, the amendment helps to clarify the distinction between the issues controlled by Rules 702 and 703. The amendment makes it easier to see that Rule 702 deals with the reliability of an expert's testimony—that is, the sufficiency of or foundation for the basis for that testimony. On the other hand, Rule 703 addresses the types of evidence an expert can reasonably rely upon in establishing that reliability or foundation. The interesting issue here most often concerns situations where an expert has relied on otherwise inadmissible information in reaching his opinion. Rule 703 requires the trial court to determine whether that information is of a type reasonably relied on by other experts in the field, and if so the expert may use it in reaching her opinion. The sufficiency of that information, however, remains a Rule 702 issue.

[7]   Relying on Established Principles

Some scientific evidence and opinion testimony may have such an established scientific, technical, legal, judicial, or evidentiary foundation that further litigation into its reliability would be wasteful of the court's time. Under these circumstances, the Supreme Court said "theories that are so firmly established as to have attained the status of scientific law, such as the laws of thermodynamics, properly are the subject of judicial notice under Fed. Rule Evid. 201." Similarly, pursuant to Rule 611(a), the military judge and counsel could agree on stipulations of fact and expected testimony that

---

[31] 43 F.3d 1311, 1318 (9th Cir. 1995).

[32] 35 F.3d at 745.

would eliminate needless litigation into already settled areas. In this light, it should be remembered that Rule 103(a)(1) requires counsel to challenge the admissibility of scientific and expert testimony, or risk an appellate court viewing the issue as having been waived, absent plain error under 103(d). To the extent no objection is leveled, the proponent may proceed without having to stipulate, obtain judicial notice, or lay a specific foundation.

[8] The Foundational Military Judicial Authority

Six years before the Supreme Court abandoned *Frye* in favor of *Daubert*, the Court of Appeals for the Armed Forces had already taken that step in *United States v. Gipson.*[33] There the court was faced with determining the admissibility of defense polygraph evidence. Instead of reexamining the issue on "general acceptance" standards, the court looked to the Rules of Evidence as the measure for evaluating scientific proof. The court said that: "Taken together, the Rules seem to describe a comprehensive scheme for processing expert testimony . . . .. We therefore agree that *Frye* has been superseded and 'should be rejected as an independent controlling standard for admissibility.'"

In support of its position, the court resolved this case by employing a flexible standard, linking its evaluation to the current state of science and the law, relying upon the military judge to properly measure the testimony's value and connection to the trial issues, and counting upon counsel to properly make a record. The court went on to hold that: "[D]epending on the competence of the examiner, the suitability of the examinee, the nature of the particular testimony process employed, and such other factors as may arise, the results of a particular examination may be as good or better than a good deal of expert and lay evidence that is routinely and uncritically received in criminal trials." The court also reminded counsel that the initiative for admitting scientific testimony rests on the evidence's proponent who "still bears the burden of establishing the foundational predicates" for its use.

Based on these criteria, the court reversed the accused's conviction because the defense's exonerating evidence had been summarily excluded by the military judge. Interestingly, the court did not require the expert testimony, or its underlying scientific basis, to meet an absolute standard of certainty, reliability, or proof. In this respect, the court specifically linked scientific evidence to other nonscientific testimony courts habitually are asked to evaluate.

The tenor of *Gipson's* approach to expert witnesses and scientific evidence testimony has been consistently followed by military authorities.[34] For

---

[33] 24 M.J. 246 (C.M.A. 1987).

[34] An example of where *Gipson's* interpretation of the Rules of Evidence augured against admission can be seen in United States v. Pope, 30 M.J. 1188 (A.F.C.M.R. 1990). There the court affirmed a military judge's refusal to admit defense *ex parte* polygraph examination

example, in *United States v. Meeks*,[35] the accused was charged with particularly gruesome murders. There were no eyewitnesses to the crime, and limited government evidence was available. In support of his case, trial counsel was permitted to use an FBI agent as an expert witness for the purpose of providing analysis of the crime scene. At trial and on appeal, the accused contended that this testimony was speculative, invaded the province of the court members, and was not helpful or necessary.

Affirming findings and sentence, the court relied on its previous decision in *United States v. Stark*.[36] In *Stark*, the court said that "Under Mil. R. Evid. 702, admissibility of expert testimony has been broadened. Anyone who has substantive knowledge in a field beyond the ken of the average court member arguably is an expert within that field."[37] (Emphasis provided.) As a result, the court held that trial counsel had met his burden of demonstrating the FBI agent's expertise, training, and ability to assist court members in understanding complex crime scene evidence. Relying on State[38] and federal[39] authority, the court found that crime scene investigation evidence is generally recognized as a body of specialized knowledge and is admissible under Rule 702.

In *United States v. King*,[40] the court made clear that not all expert testimony is admissible. In this child sexual abuse case, the government's evidence included unobjected-to expert witness testimony that the court viewed as being clearly prejudicial. Although the court affirmed the accused's conviction due to other evidence, it set aside the defendant's sentence because of gratuitous expert witness generalizations that, among other things, described the accused as a regressive pedophile who irreversibly damaged his very young victims.

Recognizing that *Gipson* could be abused by the overly aggressive use of scientific and opinion evidence, the court in *King* offered guidelines military judges and counsel can use when dealing with Rule 702 testimony. The court said that in the future it expected to see: (1) more focused use of expert

---

because the examination procedures and quality control systems were insufficient, the test suffered from the "friendly examiner syndrome," and the defense had not sufficiently established the scientific basis for admitting this evidence.

[35] 35 M.J. 64 (C.M.A. 1992).

[36] 30 M.J. 328 (C.M.A. 1990).

[37] The court's holding here is based on the same position it had taken in United States v. Peel, 29 M.J. 235 (C.M.A. 1989), and United States v. Farrar, 28 M.J. 387 (C.M.A. 1989).

[38] *See, e.g.,* State v. Asherman, 478 A.2d 227 (Conn. 1984) (crime scene investigations concerning bite marks, hair, and blood properly admitted).

[39] *See, e.g.,* United States v. Pearce, 912 F.2d 159 (6th Cir. 1990) (crime scene investigation concerning methods and techniques employed in drug conspiracy properly admitted).

[40] 35 M.J. 337 (C.M.A. 1992).

witnesses; (2) attention to the Rule's foundational requirements for admitting expert opinion testimony; (3) military judges critically reviewing the substance of opinion testimony to insure that it is relevant, reliable, and helpful to finders of fact; and (4) counsel limiting the use of such witnesses to only those who have a rational expert basis for their opinions, or who know something special and germane about the case.

Another example of military appellate courts endeavoring to maintain the thrust of Rule 702, *Daubert*, and *Gipson* is *United States v. Nimmer*.[41] There the accused was convicted of wrongfully using cocaine. The government's case consisted primarily of urinalysis evidence. In rebuttal, defense counsel attempted to introduce expert testimony concerning the negative results of hair sample tests conducted on the accused. After intense pretrial litigation, the military judge excluded the defense's evidence because he believed hair analysis did not rest on a reliable foundation. The Navy-Marine Court of Criminal Appeals affirmed the accused's conviction and the military judge's exercise of his discretion. Reversing, the Court of Appeals for the Armed Forces found that even though Nimmer had been tried two years before the Supreme Court's decision in *Daubert* and the military judge had complied with the court's then current standard in *Gibson*, an even "more enlightened" approach to scientific evidence was necessary. *Nimmer* is an important decision because it demonstrates that the Court of Appeals for The Armed Forces is prepared to remain on the leading edge of scientific evidence litigation.

The Services' Courts of Criminal Appeals have also followed *Daubert's* guidance. In *United States v. Ruth*,[42] the accused was charged with numerous forgery and false pretense offenses. The accused contended that the military judge failed to comply with *Daubert* and *Gipson*, and did not make a thorough preliminary evaluation of the government's questioned documents examiner, and the evidence he produced. Affirming the accused's convictions, the court held that handwriting analysis is not a scientific technique and does not depend on the factors governing the admissibility of expert scientific testimony announced in *Daubert*. Instead, the court relied on *Daubert's* more limited application and Rule 702, to find that in order to admit technical evidence, the proponent must produce a qualified expert whose testimony will be reliable enough to help the trier of fact.

Ruth's outcome is consistent with federal authority. For example, in *United States v. Starzepzel*,[43] the court held that a forensic document examination does not fall within *Daubert's* reliability standards for scientific evidence because it is based on subjective criteria and the examiner's

---

[41] 43 M.J. 252 (1995).

[42] 42 M.J. 730 (Army Ct.Crim.App. 1995).

[43] 880 F. Supp. 1027 (S.D.N.Y. 1995).

practical experience. Nevertheless, the court held that trial judges must still insure that the expert's testimony meets Rule 702's reliability standards. Although the court held that the forensic document examiner could testify, the court limited his proof to matters that would not appear to the jurors to be based on scientific standards, and provided limiting institutions indicating that the expert's testimony was based on practical rather than scientific capabilities.

It is now clear beyond any doubt that all expert testimony is governed by Rule 702 and *Daubert/Gipson*, whether or not it is based on scientific, technical, or subjective and experiential foundations. The trial judge must still insure that there is a "fit" between the expert's testimony and a controverted issue in the case, and there is a sufficient showing of reliability. The more unique, arbitrary, contentious, and subjective the expert's opinions are, the less likely they are to be reliable and helpful, and the more likely they are to be excluded.

[9] Drug Testing by Gas Chromatography/Mass Spectrometry (GC/MS) or Tandem Stage Quadrapole Mass Spectrometer (MS/MS)

In *United States v. Campbell*,[44] the court used the Supreme Court's guidance from *Daubert* to address how drug analysis evidence should be handled at court-martial. Campbell was convicted of using LSD. The government's proof consisted of expert witnesses who testified to the reliability of the gas chromatography tandem mass spectrometry method of evaluating urine samples for the presence of lysergic acid diethylamide. Reversing the accused's conviction, the majority found that, although the law does not specify a particular cut-off level for proving knowing LSD use, the government's case was nevertheless insufficient because it contained no evidence showing it had taken into account what is necessary to eliminate the reasonable possibility of unknowing ingestion or a false positive. Two judges dissented, indicating that the majority position is not consistent with the court's previous decisions in this area, and that it is inconsistent with the weight of the trial evidence.

On reconsideration, the court affirmed its decision and provided additional guidance on how drug cases could be prosecuted in the future. Initially, the court restated the relationship government counsel must establish between their test results and the permissive inference of knowing and wrongful use when proved by expert witnesses. In the court's opinion, trial counsel's proof must show:

(1) that the 'metabolite' is 'not naturally produced by the body' or any substance other than the drug in question;

(2) that the cutoff level and reported concentration are high enough to

---

[44] 50 M.J. 154 supplemented on reconsideration, 52 M.J. 386 (C.A.A.F. 2000).

reasonably discount the possibility of unknowing ingestion and to indicate a reasonable likelihood that the user at some time would have 'experienced the physical and psychological effects of the drug"; and

(3) that the testing methodology reliably detected the presence and reliably quantified the concentration of the drug or metabolite in the sample.

In this case the court said that trial counsel failed to establish the "frequency of error and margin of error in the testing process." The court went on to say that if the government's expert witness proof cannot meet the standards set out above, then "the prosecution must produce other direct or circumstantial evidence of knowing use in order to meet its burden of proof. If the government relies upon test results, it is not precluded from using evidence other than the three-part standard if such evidence can explain, with equivalent persuasiveness, the underlying scientific methodology and the significance of the test results so as to provide a rational basis for inferring knowing, wrongful use."

Relying on *Daubert, Kumho,* and *Joiner,* the court held factors that may be used to establish the reliability and relevance of the scientific evidence include the expert's credentials, the data used to formulate the opinion, a showing that the data is used by other experts in the field, and that whether the methodology can be used by another expert The court opined that the criteria used to satisfy its test need not be "tailored to the specific characteristics of the person whose test results are at issue. It is sufficient if the expert testimony reasonably supports the inference with respect to human beings as a class."

[10]   "Truthfulness" Opinion Evidence

There are boundaries beyond which expert witnesses cannot cross. One boundary prevents counsel from using expert testimony to establish a witness's credibility, or to attack the credibility of an opponent's witness.[45] This generally occurs in the following way. Counsel asks an expert, such as a psychologist or drug counselor, whether the expert, based on his or her training and experience, and his or her involvement with the witness, believes that the witness' statements are true or should be believed.[46]

Military and federal courts have generally excluded such testimony on

---

[45] *See, e.g.,* United States v. Whitted, 11 F.3d 782 (8th Cir. 1993) (opinion on rehearing) (finding plain error in admission of expert medical opinion unequivocally diagnosing sex offense victim as having been sexually abused essentially told jury that victim was telling the truth and her story was believable).

[46] *See, e.g.,* United States v. Scop, 856 F.2d 5 (2d Cir. 1988) (expert may not assess trustworthiness or credibility of other testimony; where witness' credibility is in issue, expert may assume truthfulness and offer opinion based on the substance of that testimony).

Rule 702 grounds. For example, in *United States v. Partyka*,[47] the court reversed a child sexual abuse conviction because the military judge improperly allowed a government psychologist to testify that the accused's unsworn statement was not true. In the court's opinion, this testimony did not assist the finder of fact in understanding the evidence, but caused them to speculate on inadmissible matters. In *United States v. Beasley*,[48] defense psychiatric expert witnesses were correctly prohibited from testifying that key government witnesses were psychopathic liars with no conception of the truth. The court held that such expert medical opinion testimony on truthfulness invades the factfinder's province to decide who they will believe.

A slightly different situation is presented by *United States v. Cacy*,[49] a child sexual abuse prosecution. Part of the government's case there included expert witness testimony indicating that the victim's behavior was consistent with that of a sexually-abused child, and that the victim did not appear to have been rehearsed. The expert also said, over defense objection, that she cautioned the victim to be truthful and ultimately recommended her for further treatment. The court interpreted all testimony about truthfulness and further medical treatment as being erroneously admitted expert opinion testimony on credibility.

Another prohibited variant on using an expert to comment on truthfulness is illustrated by *United States v. Marrie*.[50] There, the accused was convicted of sodomy and indecent acts with males under the age of sixteen. During the government's case-in-chief, trial counsel was allowed to ask a psychiatric expert witness how frequently preteen boys make false homosexual allegations. The witness replied that she had never observed such conduct during her career. Finding error but no prejudice, the court affirmed the accused's convictions, holding that the testimony should have been excluded because it allowed the expert witness to comment on the victims' relative truthfulness.

United States v. King,[51] represents an acceptable way to use expert opinion testimony. Here, trial counsel asked his expert whether she thought five-year-old children were capable of fabricating sexual abuse allegations. Affirming the accused's convictions, the court held that while child abuse expert witnesses are not permitted to testify about the credibility or believability of victims or their individual reports of abuse, they can testify about a child's ability to separate truth from fantasy, and discuss common

---

[47] 30 M.J. 242, 243 (C.M.A. 1990).

[48] 72 F.3d 1518 (11th Cir. 1996).

[49] 43 M.J. 214 (C.A.A.F. 1995).

[50] 39 M.J. 993 (A.F.C.M.R. 1994).

[51] 32 M.J. 709 (A.C.M.R. 1991).

patterns of consistency in such accounts. This result is consistent with the authority mentioned above because it would exclude expert testimony only when the evidence will likely be interpreted by factfinders as placing an impermissible, scientific-evidence-based stamp of truthfulness or untruthfulness on the proof.

Questions concerning how much credibility or weight should be given to a particular item of proof are traditionally viewed as being beyond the capabilities of any witness, expert or lay. In *United States v. Wagner,*[52] the court held that a security policeman's opinion as to whether a confessing suspect's pretrial statement was truthful should not have been admitted because it was used to "assist the members in making their determination on the accused's credibility. The court went on to say that, consistent with Rule 702, it found that no scientific, technical, or other specialized training qualifies an individual "as an expert on 'truthtelling in confessions.' "

The same result was reached in *United States v. Petersen,*[53] a child sexual molestation case. The accused's court-martial was largely a "contest where the members either believed the victim, whose testimony was not free from contradiction, or the accused." Part of the government's case included a child sexual abuse expert witness who stated that she "greatly believed" the victim's testimony. Reversing the conviction, the court held that although the witness may have been an expert "in the general area of child sexual abuse . . . her expertise did not extend to the specific issue of the credibility of such victims . . . [and] we have, thus far, rejected this type of testimony as being without the ambit of" the Military Rules of Evidence."

[11] Who May Testify as an Expert

A person may qualify as an expert as a result of special knowledge, skill, experience, training, or education.[54] In other words, anything that makes someone more knowledgeable, skillful, or experienced than the average person might qualify one as an expert.[55] The general rule is that trial judges have great discretion in controlling expert testimony.[56] Judges should remember, however, that Rule 401 establishes a low threshold of relevance,

---

[52] 20 M.J. 758 (A.F.C.M.R. 1985).

[53] 24 M.J. 283 (C.M.A. 1987).

[54] United States v. Garries, 19 M.J. 845 (A.F.C.M.R. 1985), demonstrates that the standard in this area has been reasonably set.

[55] *See, e.g.,* United States v. Crosby, 713 F.2d 1066 (5th Cir. 1983) (upholding trial judge's ruling that expert witness on post-traumatic stress syndrome must be medical doctor); Dunn v. Sears, Roebuck & Co., 639 F.2d 1171 (5th Cir. 1981) (employee of party may qualify as expert). However, *compare* United States v. Gilliss, 645 F.2d 1269 (8th Cir. 1981) (psychiatrist permitted to testify even though he misstated test of legal responsibility), *with* United States v. 10,031 Acres of Land, 850 F.2d 634 (10th Cir. 1988) (expert's testimony on value of land was inadmissible due to a mathematical error in his calculations).

[56] *See* United States v. Lopez, 543 F.2d 1156 (5th Cir. 1976).

and Rule 402 creates a presumption that relevant evidence should be admissible. Thus, judges should not arbitrarily exclude evidence that might be helpful.[57] The expert who is called to testify need not be "an outstanding practitioner," but need only be a person who can help the jury.[58] The judge retains discretion to exclude expert testimony on extraneous matters, especially where those matters might be highly prejudicial.[59]

[12]   Final Thoughts

The 2002 amendment to Rule 702, plus the Supreme Court's guidance in *Daubert* and *Kumho*, highlight the necessity for military counsel to be precise in formulating their proffers of and objections to expert testimony.[60] Careful case preparation, including a clear and articulable understanding of what aspect or element of the case is in controversy, and how the expert testimony will help the finders of fact resolve that element is necessary.

The proponent of expert testimony must establish that the foundation for its use is based upon sufficient facts or data, is reliable in theory, and was reliably applied to the issue at bar. Opponents of such evidence should focus on both the scientific validity and application of the proponent's testimony, as well as its ability to adequately and positively impact the issue in question. In effect, opponents have two separate avenues of attack. One is they can attempt to show that the proponent's opinion testimony is nothing more than "junk science" and is unreliable. Failing this, even if the opinion testimony passes the reliability standard, opponents may still prevail if they can show that it was unreliably applied.

Finally, evidence that is otherwise scientifically valid and appropriately applied may also be excluded if it is a bad "fit" with the real questions facing the triers of fact, or is simply ineffective in assisting the finders of fact in resolving those questions.

---

[57] *See* United States v. Garvin, 565 F.2d 519 (8th Cir. 1977).

[58] *See* United States v. Barker, 553 F.2d 1013 (6th Cir. 1977).

[59] *See* United States v. Green, 548 F.2d 1261 (6th Cir. 1977).

[60] This position in reinforced in United States v. King, 35 M.J. 337 (C.M.A. 1992). There the accused was convicted of sexually abusing his daughter and another child. A portion of the government's evidence included unobjected-to expert witness testimony which the court viewed as being clearly prejudicial. Although the court affirmed the accused's conviction due to other evidence, it set aside his sentence because of gratuitous expert witness generalizations which, among other things, described the accused as a regressive pedophile who irreversibly damaged his very young victims. The court said that in the future it expects to see: (a) more focused use of expert witnesses; (b) attention to foundational requirements for admitting expert opinion testimony; (c) military judges critically reviewing the substance of opinion testimony to insure that it is relevant, reliable, and helpful to finders of fact; and (d) counsel limiting the use of such witnesses to only those who have a rational expert basis for their opinions, or who know something special and germane about the case.

§ 702.03   Drafters' Analysis

Rule 702 is taken from the Federal Rule verbatim, and replaces that portion of *Manual* ¶ 138 *e* dealing with expert testimony. Although the Rule is similar to the present manual rule, it may be broader and *may* supersede *Frye v. United States,* 293 F. 1013 (D.C. Cir. 1923), an issue now being extensively litigated in the Article III courts. The Rule's sole explicit test is whether the evidence in question "will assist the trier of fact to understand the evidence or to determine a fact in issue." Whether any particular piece of evidence comes within this test is normally a matter within the military judge's discretion.

Under Rule 103(a), any objection to an expert on the basis that the individual is not in fact adequately qualified under the Rule will be waived by a failure to so object.

Paragraph 142 *e* of the present *Manual,* "Polygraph tests and drug-induced or hypnosis-induced interviews," has been deleted as a result of the adoption of Rule 702. Paragraph 142 *e* states: "The conclusions based upon or graphically represented by a polygraph test and the conclusions based upon, and the statements of the person interviewed made during a drug-induced or hypnosis-induced interview are inadmissible in evidence." The deletion of the explicit prohibition on such evidence is not intended to make such evidence per se admissible and is not an express authorization for such procedures. Clearly, such evidence must be approached with great care. Considerations surrounding the nature of such evidence, any possible prejudicial effect on a factfinder, and the degree of acceptance of such evidence in the Article III courts are factors to consider in determining whether it can in fact "assist the trier of fact." As of late 1979, the Committee was unaware of any significant decision by a United States Court of Appeals sustaining the admissibility of polygraph evidence in a criminal case, *see, e.g., United States v. Masri,* 547 F.2d 932 (5th Cir. 1977); *United States v. Cardarella,* 570 F.2d 264 (8th Cir. 1978), although the Seventh Circuit, *see, e.g., United States v. Bursten,* 560 F.2d 779 (7th Cir. 1977) (holding that polygraph admissibility is within the sound discretion of the trial judge), and perhaps the Ninth Circuit, *United States v. Benveniste,* 564 F.2d 335, 339 n.3 (9th Cir. 1977), at least recognize the possible admissibility of such evidence. There is reason to believe that evidence obtained via hypnosis may be treated somewhat more liberally than is polygraph evidence. *See, e.g., Kline v. Ford Motor Co.* 523 F.2d 1067 (9th Cir. 1975).

§ 702.04   Drafters' Analysis (2004)

2004 Amendment: Rule 702 was modified based on the amendment to Fed. R. Evid. 702, effective 1 December 2000, and is taken from the Federal Rule without change. It provides guidance for courts and parties as to the factors to consider in determining whether an expert's testimony is reliable in light of *Daubert v. Merrell Dow Pharms., Inc.,* 509 U.S. 579 (1993), and *Kumho Tire Co. v. Carmichael,* 526 U.S. 137 (1999) (holding that gatekeeper function applies to all expert testimony, not just testimony based on science).

§ 702.05   Annotated Cases

[1]   Rule 702—Expert Testimony—Foundation Requirements

[a]   Foundation Requirements—Helpfulness Standard

Air Force Court of Criminal Appeals

United States v. Anderson, 36 M.J. 963 (A.F.C.M.R. 1993): Affirming the accused's murder conviction, the court said no error occurred when a policeman testified that an injury had been caused by a kick to the neck. In the court's opinion, this evidence was admissible because it was helpful and assisted the trier of fact in understanding how the crime was committed. The court said it would only reverse for an abuse of discretion, and none had been established.

United States v. Sawyer, 32 M.J. 917 (A.F.C.M.R. 1991): During the sentencing portion of this master sergeant's court-martial for carnal knowledge and indecent acts, defense counsel unsuccessfully attempted to qualify a psychologist as an expert in recidivism and child sexual abuse. Affirming findings and sentence, the court held that, because this witness failed to specify his related training and education, there was no showing his testimony would be helpful, and the military judge did not abuse his discretion by excluding it.

United States v. Ryder, 31 M.J. 718 (A.F.C.M.R. 1990): During the accused's court-martial for maiming, a government ophthalmologist presented opinion testimony about the victim's "psychotic state." Affirming the conviction, the court held that, with respect to this aspect of the ophthalmologist's testimony, it was nothing more than a lay observation that the victim was not acting crazy; it was not intended as a psychiatric evaluation.

Army Court of Criminal Appeals

United States v. Dibb, 26 M.J. 830 (A.C.M.R. 1988): In this bad check case, the court held that no error occurred when the military judge prevented a defense expert, and the accused's mother, from testifying about "the psychological effects of a transient mental disturbance caused by sensitivity to urea formaldehyde gas." The court said the accused failed to establish how such expert testimony might be helpful, and how his mother qualified as an expert witness.

Navy-Marine Corps Court of Criminal Appeals

United States v. Kyles, 20 M.J. 571 (N.M.C.M.R. 1985): Affirming the accused's bigamy conviction, the court held that although the Rules of Evidence were designed to broaden the admissibility of expert testimony, the "essential limiting parameter" to using this evidence is whether it assists the factfinder in understanding an important trial issue. Because the accused's proffered expert testimony (concerning service member marriage and divorce problems) could be characterized as general knowledge information, the evidence was properly excluded.

[b]   Foundation Requirements—Technical or Other Specialized Knowledge

Army Court of Criminal Appeals

United States v. Ruth, 42 M.J. 730 (Army Ct.Crim.App. 1995): The accused engaged in a fraudulent scheme to swindle other soldiers. As a result, he was convicted of numerous larceny, forgery, and false pretense offenses. The accused contended that the military judge failed to make a thorough preliminary evaluation of the government's questioned documents examiner, and the evidence he produced. Affirming the accused's convictions, the court held that handwriting analysis is not a scientific technique and does not depend on the factors governing the admissibility of expert scientific testimony. *See Daubert v. Merrell Dow Pharms.*, 509 U.S. 579 (1993) (rejecting *Frye v. United States*, 293 F. 1013 (D.C. Cir. 1923) requirements for general acceptability in the relevant scientific community). Instead, the court held that, to admit technical evidence, the proponent must produce a qualified expert whose testimony will be helpful to the trier of fact.

[c]   Foundation Requirements—Testimony by an Expert

[i]   Who is an Expert—Chaplains

Air Force Court of Criminal Appeals

United States v. Kroop, 34 M.J. 628 (A.F.C.M.R. 1992): The accused, a senior Air Force officer, was convicted of adultery and fraternization. During the sentencing portion of his guilty plea trial, a chaplain's letter describing the causes for the accused's problems was excluded. Although the bench had relaxed the sentencing rules of evidence for both parties (*see* R.C.M. 1001(c)(3)), and had previously admitted similar documents, this one was excluded because trial counsel contended the chaplain was unqualified to present such opinions. Reassessing the accused's sentence on other grounds, the court held that Rule 702 is permissive and designed to encourage the use of opinion testimony. In the court's opinion, trial counsel's arguments went to weight and not admissibility of this letter.

[ii]   Who is an Expert—Criminal Investigators

United States Court of Appeals for the Armed Forces

United States v. Smith, 34 M.J. 200 (C.M.A. 1992): During this contested cocaine abuse trial, the accused contended that his urinalysis test indicated high levels of Benzoylecgonine because of innocent contact with cocaine users. In rebuttal, a CID agent testified that he had extensive exposure to other people smoking crack cocaine, could identify when they were using it, and had never tested positive. Defense counsel failed to object. Affirming the conviction, the court held that criminal drug investigators, under some circumstances, may be permitted to give expert testimony on the physical characteristics and identification of contraband.

United States v. Mustafa, 22 M.J. 165 (C.M.A. 1986): In this murder case, the court rejected the rule of *Frye v. United States*, 293 F. 1013 (D.C. Cir. 1923), under Rule 702. It reasoned that Rule 702 requires a "much lower threshold for determining whether a given person is an expert and requires only that the proffered witness have some specialized knowledge as a result of experience or education. No longer are parties to litigation limited to [the use of] experts in the strictest sense of the word. . . . The witness need not be 'an outstanding practitioner,' but only someone who can help the jury." As a result, a CID agent, who had taken a five-day course in blood spatter evidence and had previously been involved in one case where such testimony was an issue, could be qualified as an expert under this provision.

[iii]   Who is an Expert—Drug and Alcohol Abuse Counselor

United States Court of Appeals for the Armed Forces

United States v. Farrar, 28 M.J. 387 (C.M.A. 1989): Affirming the accused's conviction for wrongful use of cocaine, the court held that a defense witness was properly prohibited from testifying that, as a drug and alcohol abuse counselor, with a masters degree in social work, "his expertise included such knowledge or skill as a human drug-abuse detector." In the court's opinion, this testimony would not have been helpful to the finder of fact as it was totally unsupported by any scientific evidence, in the form of learned treatises or otherwise.

Air Force Court of Criminal Appeals

United States v. Myles, 29 M.J. 589 (A.F.C.M.R. 1989): The court held that a retired Air Force member who worked as a drug counselor at the base and in the community was competent to testify about common drug use customs and how an individual might be affected after abusing various illegal substances.

[iv]   Who is an Expert—Masters Degree in Counseling

United States Court of Appeals for the Armed Forces

United States v. Hammond, 17 M.J. 218 (C.M.A. 1984): The court held that the director of a woman's resource center, who possessed a masters degree in counseling plus additional professional experience and education, was an expert qualified to testify concerning the effects of "rape trauma syndrome." The court specifically held that the witness "was a person who [could] help the jury." It reasoned that the Rule was therefore satisfied.

[v]   Who is an Expert—Nurse's Aides

Army Court of Criminal Appeals

United States v. Jackson, 22 M.J. 604 (A.C.M.R. 1986): The court held that a nurse's aid with 18 years experience in dealing with sexually abused children, but with only a high school education, should have been permitted to testify as an expert in her field. Exclusion of this evidence was clearly erroneous and an abuse of the military judge's discretion. This court warned that special caution must be exercised in dealing with proffered expertise which "is essential to an accused's defense and where the accused may be unable to obtain the services of an expert whose credentials strike the court as impressive when compared with those of a government expert." It added that "[t]he essential question for a trial judge who is determining whether a witness should be accepted as an expert is whether the witness's specialized knowledge will assist the finder of fact in understanding the evidence or in understanding a fact in issue."

[vi]   Who is an Expert—Pharmacists

Air Force Court of Criminal Appeals

United States v. Accordino, 15 M.J. 825 (A.F.C.M.R. 1983): The court found that an Air Force pharmacist's opinion testimony concerning the use of cocaine and related drugs was properly admitted, as it assisted the trier of fact in understanding disputed issues.

[vii]   Who is an Expert—Psychologists

United States Court of Appeals for the Armed Forces

United States v. Banks, 36 M.J. 150 (C.M.A. 1992): The accused's conviction for sexually molesting his stepdaughter was set aside because of numerous expert witness and scientific evidence problems. Here, the court held that the military judge erred as a matter of law, when he refused to allow a defense clinical psychologist to testify about the relevance of specific measurements for a normal prepubertal vagina, solely because the psychologist was not a medical doctor. As the court noted, this rebuttal testimony from a qualified expert, not proffered as a medical doctor, would have assisted the trier of fact in understanding previous related government evidence.

United States v. Moore, 15 M.J. 354 (C.M.A. 1983): A properly trained and experienced psychologist can qualify as an expert witness on matters concerning "the mental or emotional state of an individual and the impact of the particular state on the individual's behavior."

Air Force Court of Criminal Appeals

United States v. Garries, 19 M.J. 845 (A.F.C.M.R. 1985): Relying on Rule 702, the court found a government forensic pathologist qualified as an expert witness due to the witness's knowledge, skill, experience, training and education. As a result the witness was properly permitted to establish the relevance of certain evidence by identifying human blood stains on it.

[viii]   Who is an Expert—Self-taught Forensic Investigator

United States Court of Appeals for the Armed Forces

United States v. Mance, 26 M.J. 244 (C.M.A. 1988): The accused's drug use conviction was affirmed despite his contention that the military judge "erroneously applied the test for acceptance of expert scientific testimony articulated in *Frye v. United States,* 293 F. 1013 (D.C. Cir. 1923), rather than the test of 'logical relevance' found in the Military Rules of Evidence and applied in *United States v. Gipson,* 24 M.J. 246, 251 (C.M.A. 1987)." The court held that testimony from a "self-taught [defense] forensic expert" on passive inhalation and "false positive" results, "would have served only to confuse and to mislead the factfinders, not to help them."

[ix]   Who is an Expert—Social Workers

United States Court of Appeals for the Armed Forces

United States v. Peel, 29 M.J. 235 (C.M.A. 1989): Affirming the accused's rape and assault convictions, the court held that a Ph. D. social worker with expertise in child sexual abuse was competent to testify about an adult rape victim's behavior. The court said that "anyone who has substantive knowledge in a particular field which exceeds that of the average court member arguably is an expert within that field."

[x]   Who is an Expert—Traffic Accident Investigators

United States Court of Appeals for the Armed Forces

United States v. Harris, 46 M.J. 221 (C.A.A.F. 1997): Major Harris was convicted of drunk driving, involuntary manslaughter, and related offenses. A state highway patrolman with extensive specialized training and experience in over 100 fatal traffic accident investigations testified as a government expert witness. He established that the accused was intoxicated and that the accused's vehicle caused the skid marks leading to the deceased's body. This witness also provided opinion testimony on many other aspects of the crime scene. The accused contends it was error to accept the highway patrolman as an expert witness. Affirming the accused's convictions, the court said that anyone with substantive knowledge beyond that possessed by the average court-member may be qualified as an expert. The court also restated its position that crime scene analysis is an area of specialized knowledge. Based on these criteria, the court held that this highway patrolman was qualified as an expert witness and that his opinion testimony was properly accepted.

[d]   Foundation Requirements—Preserving Error

United States Court of Appeals for the Armed Forces

United States v. Latorre, 53 M.J. 179 (C.A.A.F. 2000): During the sentencing portion of the accused's child sexual abuse court-martial, a government expert witness testified concerning general psychiatric testing methods he used in evaluating individuals such as the accused. It appears that the trial record on making and preserving error left a great deal to be desired. In order to determine whether the military judge properly admitted this testimony the court said first that it would assume the accused made a timely objection, and then the court said that even though the accused opened the door to this testimony, they would also assume that the government nevertheless had to lay a proper foundation for its use. Assuming away most of Rule 103(a)(1) requirements, the court ultimately said that trial counsel failed to establish that his expert witness' testimony had been accepted by the relevant scientific community, or had even been reviewed by it. Although the court ultimately found no prejudice in the government's proof, we wonder about imposing an obligation on trial counsel to establish a foundation to testimony that was not specifically and correctly objected to. A reviewing court places all trial participants in a tenuous position when the reviewing court, for the first time and on its own, identifies areas that should have been more fully explored below.

United States v. Ruth, 46 M.J. 1 (C.A.A.F. 1997): The accused was convicted of larceny in pursuing what this court referred to as a "get rich quick" scheme. The government's evidence included expert opinion testimony from a questioned documents examiner. At trial, the accused requested that a specific civilian expert witness be provided to impeach the government's proof. Defense counsel contended, and the court agreed, that limiting the accused to using one government expert to attack another government expert is the functional equivalent of allowing the "fox [to] guard the hen house." The accused also contended that *Daubert v. Merrell Dow Pharms., Inc.,* 509 U.S. 579 (1993), provided the basis for reevaluating the scientific validity and admissibility of "handwriting analysis." Without commenting on *Daubert's* effect, this court affirmed the accused's convictions finding that defense counsel failed to make an adequate trial offer of proof to obtain the civilian expert. However, *citing United States v. Velasquez,* 64 F.3d 844 (3d Cir. 1995), the court also recognized that Rule 702's liberal standard of admissibility augured in favor of admitting evidence like that requested by the defense. *See also* Rule 706(a).

United States v. King, 35 M.J. 337 (C.M.A. 1992): This is an important case for counsel and military judges. The accused was convicted of sexually abusing his daughter and another child. A portion of the government's evidence included unobjected-to expert witness testimony which the court viewed as being clearly prejudicial. Although the court affirmed the accused's conviction due to other evidence, it set aside his sentence because of gratuitous expert witness generalizations which, among other things, described the accused as a regressive pedophile who irreversibly damaged his very young victims. The court said that in the future it expects to see: (a) more focused use of expert witnesses; (b) attention to foundational requirements for admitting expert opinion testimony; (c) military judges critically reviewing the substance of opinion testimony to insure that it is relevant, reliable, and helpful to finders of fact; and (d) counsel limiting the use of such witnesses to only those who have a rational expert basis for their opinions, or who know something special and germane about the case.

[2] Rule 702—Topics Appropriate for Expert Testimony

[a] Expert Opinions—Analytical Model Evidence

United States Court of Appeals for the Armed Forces

United States v. Sanchez, 65 M.J. 145 (C.A.A.F. 2007): The accused was convicted of rape and forcible sodomy of his 8-year-old stepdaughter. In limine, defense counsel challenged the reliability of a government expert witness's findings that the victim had been sexually abused. Defense counsel contended that the expert's opinion was inadmissible because there was no established error rate for her conclusions, and that other experts had reached different results on similar data. Affirming the accused's convictions, the court held that the government expert's methodology and application were reliable. The court noted that *Daubert v. Merrell Dow Pharms.*, 509 U.S. 579 (1993), no longer required general acceptance, that differences of opinion go to weight not admissibility, that some studies do not lend themselves to error rates, and that the expert's testimony was relevant and helpful to the finders of fact. The court went on the say that the trial judge performed her gatekeeper function by ensuring that the expert employed the same level of intellectual rigor emblematic of other experts in her field. Finally, the court noted that the gatekeeping inquiry is a flexible one that must be tied to the facts of a particular case.

United States v. Halford, 50 M.J. 402 (C.A.A.F. 1999): The accused was convicted of rape. At trial he challenged the victim's credibility by noting her inconsistencies, retractions, and refusals to talk about the crime. In response, trial counsel was permitted to call a medical expert who stated that the victim's conduct was the product of an "acute stress disorder." Affirming the accused's conviction and sentence, this court said the challenged evidence was relevant and admissible because it placed trial defense counsel's attack in context and explained to the members why the victim acted as she did. The court went on to say that acute stress disorder, rape trauma syndrome, rape trauma model, or similar analytical model evidence may be admissible when the proponent can satisfy the following requirements: (a) qualifications of the expert (Rule 702); (b) fit of the subject matter (Rule 702); (c) basis for the expert's opinion (Rule 703); (d) relevance of the expert's testimony (Rule 401); (e) reliability of the evidence presented (Rule 703); and (f) lack of unfair prejudice in providing that evidence and the expert's opinion (Rule 403).

[b] Expert Opinions—Child Sexual Abuse Cases

United States Court of Appeals for the Armed Forces

United States v. Quintanilla, 56 M.J. 37 (C.A.A.F. 2001): The accused was convicted of forcible sodomy on a child under the age of sixteen, indecent assault, and indecent acts. The three teenage victims delayed reporting the incidents for time periods ranging from a week to more than a month. At trial, the government offered an expert to testify on the subject of delayed reporting of sexual assaults by victims of abuse. The accused contended that the military judge abused his discretion by qualifying the witness as an expert, and by allowing the witness's testimony. This court held that the military judge did not abuse his discretion in qualifying a witness as an expert, and in admitting his testimony concerning delayed reporting of sexual assaults by victims of abuse. The court based its decision on the fact that witness had a bachelor's degree in psychology and a master's degree in "guidance counseling," he had completed three-fourths of a doctoral degree, and for sixteen years the witness had specialized in the treatment and risk assessment of sex offenders, and in the treatment of victims of sexual abuse. The court went on to say that admission of opinion testimony by an expert in a court-martial is governed by Rule 702, which requires qualification of the expert by "knowledge, skill, experience, training, or education." The rules of evidence provide expert witnesses with testimonial latitude broader than other witnesses on the theory "that the expert's opinion will have a reliable basis in the knowledge and experience of his discipline."

United States v. Rynning, 47 M.J. 420, 421 (C.A.A.F. 1998): Affirming the accused's convictions for sexually abusing his natural daughter, this court held that the expert testimony concerning the child sexual victim's behavioral characteristics or behavioral patterns was properly admitted. In the court's opinion, such evidence is particularly valuable when it is introduced to explain what might otherwise be viewed by the court-members as "counterintuitive behavior."

Air Force Court of Criminal Appeals

United States v. McElhaney, 50 M.J. 819 (A.F.Ct.Crim.App. 1999): Convicted of sexually assaulting his future wife's underage niece, the accused unsuccessfully contended on appeal that the trial judge erred by allowing a government child psychiatrist to testify during sentencing about the accused's future dangerousness and the impact the accused's crimes had on the youthful victim's emotional development. The accused's objection focused on the expert having never examined the accused. Affirming findings and sentence, this court held that the expert had a sufficient basis for his testimony because he had reviewed the report of investigation, the accused's letter to the victim, and similar allegations that the accused's natural daughter had made against him. Relying on the Rule 702 tests established in *United States v. Stinson,* 34 M.J. 233 (C.M.A. 1992), and *United States v. Banks,* 36 M.J. 150 (C.M.A. 1992), this court held that the failure of the expert to personally examine the accused goes only to weight and not to admissibility.

Navy-Marine Corps Court of Criminal Appeals

United States v. Diaz, 61 M.J. 594, 595 (N.M.Ct.Crim.App. 2005): Affirming appellant's convictions for raping his 12-year-old daughter, the court held that contrary to appellant's contentions, a government expert's testimony explaining how the lack of physical evidence of sexual abuse was not inconsistent with the charges was helpful and properly admitted.

[c]   Expert Opinions—Confessions—Voluntariness

United States Court of Appeals for the Armed Forces

United States v. Griffin, 50 M.J. 278 (C.A.A.F. 1999): Contrary to the accused's pleas, a military judge sitting alone convicted him of sexually abusing his young daughter and related offenses. Part of the government's evidence included the accused's confession to which defense counsel posed a timely but unsuccessful objection. In an attempt to demonstrate the confession's involuntariness and falsity, the accused offered expert testimony from a clinical psychologist who had done extensive research in the area of coercion, voluntariness, and confessions. Affirming the trial judge's decision to exclude this evidence, the court held that the expert witness testified he was unable to opine whether the confession was false or coerced, and that the expert admitted to having reservations about the normative standards used in such evaluations. Based on the defense's own expert witness testimony, the court found that the accused failed to meet the *Daubert v. Merrell Dow Pharms., Inc.,* 509 U.S. 579 (1993), test for reliability.

[d]   Expert Opinions— *Daubert* and Scientific Evidence

Supreme Court

Kumho Tire Co. v. Patrick Carmichael, 526 U.S. 137 (1999): *Kumho* significantly expands upon and clarifies the Court's previous holding in *Daubert v. Merrell Dow Pharms., Inc.,* 509 U.S. 579 (1993), which established a four-part test for evaluating the admissibility of scientific evidence. Kumho was sued for defectively manufacturing a tire that failed in operation causing a fatality and other injuries. The District Court excluded plaintiff's expert witness testimony because it lacked a reliable methodology and was in some parts self-contradictory. The Eleventh Circuit reversed, holding that the *Daubert* factors were limited to scientific evidence, not testimony based on skill or experience. The Supreme Court disagreed and found the trial judge's resolution to be correct. The Court went on to say that: (a) the *Daubert* factors apply to the testimony of engineers and other experts who are not scientists; (b) Rule 702 and 703 grant all expert witnesses testimonial latitude unavailable to other witnesses only when that testimony has a reliable basis in the knowledge and experience of the witness' discipline; (c) the *Daubert* factors do not constitute a definitive checklist or test, but should be applied in a flexible manner and only when they constitute a reasonable measure of reliability; (d) among the factors a court should consider in determining whether to apply the *Daubert* factors are the nature of the case, the expert's particular expertise, and the subject of his/her testimony; (e) whether the *Daubert* factors are reasonable measures of reliability in a given case is a matter of law for the trial judge to resolve; and (f) trial judges have broad discretion in making Daubert rulings. The Supreme Court ultimately determined that the problem here was not the reliability of the expert witness's methodology in general, but whether the expert used that methodology in a way that enabled him to reliably determine why the tire failed.

General Electric Co. v. Joiner, 522 U.S. 136 (1997): In this toxic tort case, the Court examined the process for evaluating novel and uncertain scientific opinion testimony—here whether polychlorinated biphenyls (PCBs) contributed to plaintiff's lung cancer. The Court also addressed the standards that apply to reviewing a trial judge's decision admitting or excluding such evidence, particularly when that evidence is "outcome determinative." Reversing the circuit court's holding, the Court affirmed the trial judge's decision to exclude plaintiffs' experts' explanative theory testimony because it "did not rise above subjective belief or unsupported speculation." Similarly, the Court affirmed its long standing position that trial court evidentiary rulings are measured on appeal by an "abuse of discretion standard," and that nothing in *Daubert v. Merrell Dow Pharms., Inc.*, 509 U.S. 579 (1993), changed that. The Court also reaffirmed its basic *Daubert* precepts: (a) the Federal Rules of Evidence take a more flexible and lenient approach to opinion and expert testimony than the common law allowed; (b) trial judges must perform "gatekeeper" functions on all scientific evidence; and (c) trial judges must ensure that the scientific evidence is both relevant and reliable. Despite the suggestion in Daubert trial courts must focus on principles and methodology, not on the conclusions that they generate, the Court indicated that there is no sharp line separating methodology from conclusions. Here the Court found that there was simply too great an analytical gap between the plaintiffs' data and their expert witnesses' proffered opinions. As a result, the Court concluded that nothing in *Daubert* requires trial judges to admit opinion testimony "connected to existing data only by the ipse dixit of the expert."

Daubert v. Merrell Dow Pharmas. Inc., 509 U.S. 579 (1993). In this civil case, the Court reversed and remanded a grant of summary judgment, holding that Rule 702 supersedes the "general acceptance" standard of *Frye v. United States*. The Court went on to say that this provision requires trial judges to ensure that an expert's opinion testimony is based on demonstrated reliability and scientific relevance to the issues at trial. This case is more thoroughly discussed in our Editorial Comment.

United States Court of Appeals for the Armed Forces

United States v. Billings, 61 M.J. 163 (C.A.A.F. 2005): The court found harmless error in the military judge's allowing a government expert to testify that he could distinguish gold from gold plate in a photograph, and affirmed appellant's convictions for robbery-related offenses and organized criminal activity. Although the jeweler qualified as an expert, the court found that his testimony failed to satisfy *Daubert v. Merrell Dow Pharmas. Inc*, 509 U.S. 579 (1993), and amounted to proof by *ipsi dixit* condemned in *General Electric Co. v. Joinder*, 522 U.S. 136 (1997) (the gap between the experts analytical testimony and the available data was too great).

United States v. Schlamer, 52 M.J. 80 (C.A.A.F. 1999): The accused was convicted of murdering another Marine. During trial, government hair-comparison analysis testimony was elicited. The accused contended, for the first time on appeal, that it was error for the trial judge to have considered this expert opinion evidence without a *Daubert* hearing. Affirming the accused's convictions, the court held that most jurisdictions have admitted hair-comparison analysis expert testimony without a hearing when it is established that the examiner followed standard procedures. The court went on to say that, if requested, military judges may conduct *Daubert* hearings to determine reliability and admissibility on such issues. However, in the court's opinion, no error, plain or otherwise, occurred here.

United States v. Nimmer, 43 M.J. 252 (C.A.A.F. 1995): The accused was convicted by a court with members of wrongfully using cocaine. The government's case consisted primarily of urinalysis evidence. In rebuttal, defense counsel attempted to introduce expert testimony concerning the negative results of hair sample tests conducted on the accused. After intense pretrial litigation, the military judge excluded this evidence because he believed hair analysis did not rest on a reliable foundation. The Navy Court of Review affirmed the accused's conviction and the military judge's exercise of his discretion. Reversing, this court found that even though Nimmer had been tried two years before the Supreme Court's decision in *Daubert v. Merrell Dow Pharms., Inc.*, 509 U.S. 579 (1993) (Federal Rules of Evidence superseded the general acceptance standard), and that the military judge had complied with this court's then current standard in *United States v. Gipson*, 24 M.J. 246 (CMA 1987) (Military Rules of Evidence superseded the general acceptance standard), the court nevertheless believed that "a more enlightened litigation is necessary."

United States v. Mustafa, 22 M.J. 165 (C.M.A. 1986): In this murder case, the court rejected the rule of *Frye v. United States*, 293 F. 1013 (D.C. Cir. 1923), under Rule 702. It reasoned that Rule 702 requires a "much lower threshold for determining whether a given person is an expert and requires only that the proffered witness have some specialized knowledge as a result of experience or education. No longer are parties to litigation limited to [the use of] experts in the strictest sense of the word. . . . The witness need not be 'an outstanding practitioner,' but only someone who can help the jury." As a result, a CID agent, who had taken a five-day course in blood spatter evidence and had previously been involved in one case where such testimony was an issue, could be qualified as an expert under this provision.

United States v. Wirth, 18 M.J. 214 (C.M.A. 1984): In a case concerning sexual abuse of young children, the court found that the admission of the accused's past related conduct was improper because the proponent had not offered expert testimony linking those acts with the crimes charged. Scientific evidence could have been used here to make testimony, which was otherwise inadmissible and probably confusing, probative and thus admissible.

Air Force Court of Criminal Appeals

United States v. Blaney, 50 M.J. 533 (A.F.Ct.Crim.App. 1999): The accused was convicted of forcible oral sodomy upon an enlisted man while both "slept" on the floor of the accused's quarters. The accused's defense, in part, was based on various forensic psychiatric theories that would have established that no crime was committed because both the accused and the victim suffered from various sleep related disorders. To support the accused's trial defense he requested expert witness testimony. The convening authority and the trial judge denied these requests. This court viewed the legal issue not as concerning the validity of the science involved nor the qualifications of the proffered witnesses, but as to whether the requested expert psychiatric testimony would have helped the trier of fact. *See* our discussion of Rule 702. In affirming the accused's convictions, this court relied upon *United States v. Houser,* 36 M.J. 392 (C.M.A. 1993), for the legal standard controlling admission of expert testimony. In relevant part the court there held that six foundational issues must be established: (1) the qualifications of the expert (MRE 702); (2) the subject matter of the expert testimony (MRE 702); (3) the basis for the expert testimony (MRE 703); (4) the relevance of the evidence (MRE 401, 402); (5) the reliability of the evidence (MRE 702, 703, 705); and (6) whether the probative value of the requested testimony outweighs any unfairness in its admission (MRE 403). The court here found that items mentioned above had not been satisfactorily established by the proponent.

United States v. Rhea, 29 M.J. 991 (A.F.C.M.R. 1990): At trial, the accused unsuccessfully attempted to prevent a clinical psychologist from testifying about the role parental duress plays in interfamilial sexual abuse cases. Affirming the conviction, this court held that "the witness' testimony assisted that factfinder in understanding an important trial issue" and noted "that the witness gave no opinion as to the victim's truthfulness or credibility," which also supported admission.

Army Court of Criminal Appeals

United States v. Dozier, 28 M.J. 550 (A.C.M.R. 1989): The accused's conviction for telephonically using indecent language to the wife of a fellow soldier was set aside because the trial judge improperly excluded potentially exonerating expert testimony concerning "phonetic transcriptions." Recognizing that Rule 702 was "intended to broaden the admissibility of expert testimony, not limit it," the court said that, even though the evidence alluded to may not have received wide acceptance in the scientific community, "it is the relevance and helpfulness of the evidence which determines its admissibility." *See United States v. Downing*, 753 F.2d 1224 (3d Cir. 1985), for a thorough discussion of "helpfulness."

Navy-Marine Corps Court of Criminal Appeals

United States v. Clark, 61 M.J. 707 (N.M.Ct.Crim.App. 2005): During the accused's trial on arson and related offenses, the military judge admitted a "negative" urinalysis report as part of the government's case concerning the accused's criminal motives. For the first time on appeal, the accused contended this was error because the military judge had not sua sponte conducted a hearing on the admissibility of those reports pursuant to *Daubert v. Merrell Dow Pharaceuticals*, 509 U.S. 579 (1993). Relying on *Kumho Tire Co. v. Carmichael*, 526 U.S. 137 (1999), the court held that because trial defense counsel never challenged the urinalysis test results, there was no need to hold a *Daubert* hearing, and as a result any objection was waived.

[e]   Expert Opinions—Different Perpetrator Defense

Air Force Court of Criminal Appeals

United States v. Dimberio, 52 M.J. 550 (A.F.Ct.Crim.App. 1999): This case discusses the interaction between the "alternate perpetrator defense" and the admissibility of defense medical expert testimony concerning the alternate perpetrator's character. The accused was convicted of assaulting his infant son by violently shaking him. The accused's defense was based largely on the theory that the accused's wife committed the crime. In support of the accused's contention, he offered expert medical testimony that would have demonstrated that the accused's wife suffered from various forms of personality disorders and related "borderline traits." Affirming the trial judge's decision to exclude this testimony, the reviewing court held that "regardless of the party who proffers such evidence, unless the proffered evidence qualifies for one of the three stated exceptions, the prohibition of Mil. R. Evid. 404(a) applies whether the character trait in question is the accused's, a witness', or any other person's, and regardless of whether a witness or other person is alleged to be the perpetrator."

[f]   Expert Opinions—DNA Testing

United States Court of Appeals for the Armed Forces

United States v. Allison, 63 M.J. 365 (C.A.A.F. 2006): At the accused's trial for rape and related offenses, defense counsel challenged expert witness DNA testimony by alleging that government experts were not qualified to interpret the foundational statistical information. Affirming the accused's convictions, the court held that both government experts had received training in DNA statistical analysis and that both had considerable experience in conducting such analysis. The court also held that the method of calculation used by the experts had been widely accepted by other experts in the field.

United States v. Youngberg, 43 M.J. 379 (C.A.A.F. 1995): In this murder and indecent act case, the court examined for the first time whether DNA test results are admissible at a court-martial. Relying on *United States v. Gipson*, 24 M.J. 246 (CMA 1987), and *Daubert v. Merrell Dow Pharms., Inc.*, 509 U.S. 579 (1993), both indicating that the *Frye v. United States*, 293 F. 1013 (D.C. Cir. 1923), general acceptance standard was superseded by the Military and Federal Rules of Evidence, the court held that DNA testing is admissible when a proper foundation is laid. The court affirmed the accused's conviction viewing trial counsel's proffer as satisfying both *Gibson* and *Daubert*.

United States v. Hill, 63 M.J. 718 (A.F.Ct.Crim.App. 2006): Affirming the accused's conviction for sexually molesting the 11-year-old daughter of a friend, the court found no error in a properly qualified expert witness testifying that DNA samples taken from the accused's fingernails not only matched the victim's DNA, but also likely came from either oral or vaginal contact with the victim.

[g] Expert Opinions—Drug Testing—General

United States Court of Appeals for the Armed Forces

United States v. Blazier, 69 M.J. 218 (C.A.A.F. 2010): The accused was convicted of dereliction of duty and wrongful use of controlled substances. Part of the government's proof included laboratory reports used by the supervising chemist when he testified concerning the composition of the possessed drugs. The chemist's testimony interpreting the laboratory reports relied upon machine generated laboratory reports and upon the analyses of other chemists who did not testify. The convictions were affirmed in *United States v. Blazier*, 68 M.J. 544 (A.F.Ct.Crim.App. 2008), which was decided before *Melendez-Diaz v. Massachusetts*, 129 S. Ct. 2527 (2009), held that, "certificates of analysis" used in drug prosecutions to establish the illegality of seized substances fell within the "core-class of testimonial statements" and violated the accused's Sixth Amendment rights). The convictions were reversed and the case remanded in *United States v. Blazier*, 68 M.J. 439 (C.A.A.F. 2010) (applying *Melendez-Diaz v. Massachusetts* but returning the record with specified questions concerning why the military judge did not compel the government to produce the essential laboratory witnesses). In its second look at the case, the court concluded that an expert may rely on machine-generated data because the Rules of Evidence define it as not being hearsay, and also may rely on but not repeat testimonial hearsay that is otherwise appropriate for expert opinion testimony so long as the expert's opinion is his own. The court also held that when testimonial hearsay is admitted, the Confrontation Clause is satisfied only if the declarant of that hearsay is subject to cross-examination at trial, or is unavailable but had been previously subjected to cross-examination and warned that the Confrontation Clause may not be circumvented by having an expert testify at trial to otherwise inadmissible testimonial hearsay. The court found that this occurred in violation of *Melendez-Diaz v. Massachusetts* and returned the record for a harmful error analysis.

United States v. Green, 55. M.J. 76 (C.A.A.F. 2001): Upon returning from a lengthy period of leave, the accused provided a urine sample for a command-directed urinalysis, the results of which were positive for the cocaine metabolite benzoylecgonine. At trial, the accused was convictedof one specification of unauthorized absence and two specifications of wrongful use of cocaine. On appeal, the accused contended the evidence in his case was insufficient to prove wrongful use. This court held that a positive urinalysis, which was accompanied by the testimony of an expert witness interpreting the result, was sufficient to support the permissive inference of knowing, wrongful use of cocaine. This court went on to say that the military judge, as gatekeeper with respect to scientific evidence, may determine in appropriate circumstances that drug test results, as explained by expert testimony, permit consideration of the permissive inference that the presence of a controlled substance demonstrates knowledge and wrongful use.

[h]   Expert Opinions—Drug Testing—by Gas Chromatography/ Mass Spectrometry (GC/MS) or Tandem Stage Quadrapole Mass Spectrometer (MS/MS)

United States Court of Appeals for the Armed Forces

United States v. Campbell, 50 M.J. 154, *supplemented on reconsideration,* 52 M.J. 386 (C.A.A.F. 2000): The accused was convicted of using LSD. The government's proof consisted of expert witnesses who testified to the reliability of the gas chromatography tandem mass spectrometry method of evaluating urine samples for the presence of lysergic acid diethylamide. Reversing the accused's conviction, the court found that, although the law does not specify a particular cut-off level for proving knowing LSD use, the government's case was nevertheless insufficient because it contained no evidence showing it had taken into account what is necessary to eliminate the reasonable possibility of unknowing ingestion or false positive. Two judges dissented, indicating that the majority position is not consistent with the court's previous decisions in this area, and that it is inconsistent with the weight of the trial evidence. On reconsideration, the court affirmed its decision and provided additional guidance on how drug cases could be prosecuted in the future. Initially, the court restated the relationship government counsel must establish between their test results and the permissive inference of knowing and wrongful use when proved by expert witnesses. In the court's opinion, trial counsel's proof must show: "(1) that the 'metabolite' is 'not naturally produced by the body' or any substance other than the drug in question"; (2) "that the cutoff level and reported concentration are high enough to reasonably discount the possibility of unknowing ingestion and to indicate a reasonable likelihood that the user at some time would have 'experienced the physical and psychological effects of the drug' "; and (3) "that the testing methodology reliably detected the presence and reliably quantified the concentration of the drug or metabolite in the sample." In this case the court said that trial counsel failed to establish the "frequency of error and margin of error in the testing process." The court went on to say that if the government's expert witness proof cannot meet the standards set out above, then "the prosecution must produce other direct or circumstantial evidence of knowing use in order to meet its burden of proof. If the government relies upon test results, it is not precluded from using evidence other than the three-part standard if such evidence can explain, with equivalent persuasiveness, the underlying scientific methodology and the significance of the test results so as to provide a rational basis for inferring knowing, wrongful use." Relying on *Daubert v. Merrell Dow Pharms., Inc.*, 509 U.S. 579, 589 (1993) (scientific testimony must be both reliable and relevant); *General Electric Co. v. Joiner*, 522 U.S. 136, 144–145 (1997) (an expert's opinions must be "sufficiently supported" by the "studies on which they purport to rely"); and *Kumho Tire Co., Ltd. v. Carmichael*, 526 U.S. 137, 153–155 (1999) (focusing not simply on the reasonableness in general of an expert's approach but also on the particular matter to which the expert's testimony was directly relevant), the court held "factors that may be used to establish the reliability and relevance of the scientific evidence include the expert's credentials, the data used to formulate the opinion, and a showing that data was used by other experts in the field, and that whether the methodology can be used by another expert. The court opined that the criteria used to satisfy its test need not be "tailored to the specific characteristics of the person whose test results are at issue. It is sufficient if the expert testimony reasonably supports the inference with respect to human beings as a class."

Air Force Court of Criminal Appeals

United States v. Bush, 44 M.J. 646 (A.F.Ct.Crim.App. 1996): In what this court called a case of first impression for federal criminal jurisprudence, the court held that the accused's drug use conviction was properly based upon scientific analysis of his hair which demonstrated recent cocaine use. The court noted that both defense and government experts generally agreed on the scientific validity of the gas chromatography/mass spectrometry (GC/MS) or the tandem stage quadrapole mass spectrometer (MS/MS) techniques for analyzing hair samples to determine drug abuse.

[i] Expert Opinions—Exhibitionism Diagnosis

Air Force Court of Criminal Appeals

United States v. Huberty, 50 M.J. 704 (A.F.Ct.Crim.App. 1999): The accused was convicted of various sexual offenses including sodomy, adultery, committing indecent acts, and fondling his genitals in a public place. At trial defense counsel proffered the testimony of a forensic psychologist for the purpose of demonstrating whether the accused met the criteria for a diagnosis of "exhibitionism." Affirming the bench's decision to exclude this testimony, the court held that the witness himself "candidly conceded the absence of valid scientific support for his theory." The court went on to say that unless the proponent of scientific evidence can establish the relevance, reliability, and helpfulness of the evidence, it should be excluded.

[j]   Expert Opinions—Eyewitness Identification

Air Force Court of Criminal Appeals

United States v. Garcia, 40 M.J. 533 (A.F.C.M.R. 1994): The accused was convicted of taking indecent liberties with a thirteen-year-old female. At trial, defense counsel unsuccessfully attempted to introduce expert testimony attacking the reliability of several witnesses who identified the accused. The trial judge prohibited this expert from testifying because she thought such evidence was generally inadmissible. Finding error but no prejudice, the court held that expert testimony concerning eyewitness identification reliability is appropriate, because it assesses the psychological impact that stress, suggestibility, feedback, and confidence have on the witness.

Army Court of Criminal Appeals

United States v. Brown, 45 M.J. 514 (Army Ct.Crim.App. 1996): The accused was convicted of stealing a utility company truck and of various other offenses. A key trial issue concerned the vehicle driver's eyewitness identification of the accused, both at the scene and at a subsequent photographic line-up. To impeach the government's evidence, defense counsel sought to use an expert witness who specialized in cross-racial identifications. The trial judge prohibited this witness from testifying, indicating that the matter could be adequately addressed in other ways, including cross-examination. Finding error but no prejudice, this court affirmed the accused's convictions holding that while the *pre-Daubert v. Merrell Dow Pharms., Inc.*, 509 U.S. 579 (1993) status of the law generally excluded such testimony, the current trend is to admit it. In the court's opinion, an expert will be able to assist the finders of fact in understanding the role played by stress, anxiety, excitement, suggestibility, cross-racial identification, memory processes, and feedback. Further, much of this testimony will be counter-intuitive, thus requiring expert witness assistance. *Citing United States v. Garcia*, 40 M.J. 533, 538 (A.F.C.M.R. 1994), the court said, "we fail to see how the only defense evidence directly attacking the government's circumstantial identification evidence could ever be a waste of time, too confusing, or cumulative."

[k] Expert Opinions—Handwriting Analysis

Navy-Marine Corps Court of Criminal Appeals

United States v. Elmore, 56 M.J. 533 (N.M.Ct.Crim.App. 2001): The accused was convicted of dereliction of duty, false official statement, larceny, forgery, and larceny of mail. He contended that the military judge erred in admitting the expert testimony of a handwriting examiner because handwriting analysis does not meet the tests for validity and reliability established by the Supreme Court. This court held that expert testimony in the field of handwriting analysis is generally valid and reliable, and may properly be admitted in trials by a court-martial; and that the military judge did not abuse his discretion in admitting this expert testimony in the field of handwriting analysis. The court based its decision on the fact that the military judge heard and considered extensive testimony on the personal qualifications of the expert, and gave an instruction as to how members might consider the testimony in their deliberations. The court went on to say that a military judge must apply a flexible *Daubert* analysis in evaluating the admissibility of proffered expert testimony, whether it be scientific, technical, or other specialized knowledge.

[l] Expert Opinions—Hair Sample Analysis

United States Court of Appeals for the Armed Forces

United States v. Bush, 47 M.J. 305 (C.A.A.F. 1997): In what this court referred to as possibly the first drug-use prosecution by hair analysis, it held that the accused's conviction was properly based upon scientific theories and analysis consistent with *Daubert v. Merrell Dow Pharms., Inc.,* 509 U.S. 579 (1993), and *United States v. Gipson,* 24 M.J. 246 (C.M.A. 1987). While the court noted that there was disagreement among the trial level experts, it held that the military judge properly exercised his gatekeeping function in resolving to admit the expert testimony (see the trial judge's very thorough special findings, attached to the decision). The facts that only limited peer review and publications were offered in support of the government's theory, and that evidence of applicable error rates was also absent, were viewed by the court as not being dispositive.

United States v. Nimmer, 43 M.J. 252 (C.A.A.F. 1995): The accused was convicted by a court with members of wrongfully using cocaine. The government's case consisted primarily of urinalysis evidence. In rebuttal, defense counsel attempted to introduce expert testimony concerning the negative results of hair sample tests conducted on the accused. After intense pretrial litigation, the military judge excluded this evidence because he believed hair analysis did not rest on a reliable foundation. The Navy Court of Review affirmed the accused's conviction and the military judge's exercise of his discretion. Reversing, the court found that even though Nimmer had been tried two years before the Supreme Court's decision in *Daubert v. Merrell Dow Pharms., Inc.,* 509 U.S. 579 (1993) (Federal Rules of Evidence superseded the general acceptance standard), and that the military judge had complied with this court's then current standard in *United States v. Gipson*, 24 M.J. 246 (CMA 1987) (Military Rules of Evidence superseded the general acceptance standard), the court nevertheless believed that "a more enlightened litigation is necessary."

[m]   Expert Opinions—Intent vs. Motive Opinion Evidence

United States Court of Appeals for the Armed Forces

United States v. Gardinier, 67 M.J. 304 (C.A.A.F. 2009): In *United States v. Gardinier*, 65 M.J. 60 (C.A.A.F. 2007), the court reversed his child sexual abuse convictions because a handwritten incriminating statement, a video-taped confession, and incriminating statements made by the prosecutrix had all been erroneously admitted. Subsequently, the Army Court of Criminal Appeals affirmed the accused's convictions and found that the errors were harmless beyond a reasonable doubt. Reversing and remanding on Article 31(b) and Sixth Amendment grounds, the court here noted that the inadmissible four hour videotaped confession contained the administration of a "computer voice stress test" that was explained to the accused as an advanced polygraph which does not create false positives. Defense counsel did not object to this testimony, and the court indicated that the test evidence appeared to violate Rule 707 although it did not rest its decision on this violation.

Army Court of Criminal Appeals

United States v. Tilton, 34 M.J. 1104 (A.C.M.R. 1992): The accused was convicted of conspiracy to rob a bank, and related offenses. At trial, the accused was prohibited from presenting expert testimony concerning his conscious or subconscious motivations for planning the elaborate crimes. Affirming the accused's convictions, this court said the military judge accurately distinguished between defense evidence of the accused's capability to form the intent to commit a crime, which was admissible, and defense evidence offered to establish a motive for why the accused might have committed an offense, which was inadmissible.

[n]   Expert Opinions—Interview Techniques

United States Court of Appeals for the Armed Forces

United States v. Banks, 36 M.J. 150 (C.M.A. 1992): The accused's conviction for sexually molesting his stepdaughter was set aside because of numerous expert witness and scientific evidence problems. Here, error occurred because the trial judge excluded a defense videotape which would have been used in rebuttal to demonstrate inappropriate, government expert witness interview techniques of the victim. In the court's opinion, seeing the actual interview was vital if the members were to accurately evaluate the opinion evidence.

[o] Expert Opinions—Legal Opinion Evidence

United States Court of Appeals for the Armed Forces

United States v. Benedict, 27 M.J. 253 (C.M.A. 1988): The court found reversible error in the trial judge allowing a government psychiatrist to give her opinion on matters of law (legal definition of insanity taken from an article on military justice and trial practice) as opposed to medicine. In the court's opinion, such evidence usurped the military judge's "role in providing legal guidance to the court members."

[p] Expert Opinions—Luminol Testing

United States Court of Appeals for the Armed Forces

United States v. Holt, 46 M.J. 853 (N.M.Ct.Crim.App. 1997), *aff'd,* 52 M.J. 173 (C.A.A.F. 1999): The accused was convicted of premeditated murder and larceny. On appeal for the first time, he contended that luminol testing, which was used to identify blood spatter evidence on his clothing, was improperly admitted because the theory concerns a new or novel, not widely accepted scientific process. Affirming the accused's convictions, the court held that experts for both sides testified that luminol testing is accepted by the relevant scientific community as being a viable, routinely used, and extremely sensitive presumptive test for the presence of blood. The court went on to say that because it was apparently part of the accused's trial strategy to not challenge luminol testing, he has forfeited the right to do so on appeal.

Army Court of Criminal Appeals

United States v. Hill, 41 M.J. 596 (Army Ct.Crim.App. 1994): This case concerns how counsel should properly use evidence of luminal testing. The accused was convicted of attempted unpremeditated murder, housebreaking, and related offenses. Over defense objection, trial counsel proved that the accused's clothing had undergone luminal testing which demonstrated hidden bloodstains. Affirming the accused's convictions, the court held that while luminal testing results may be admissible, nonprejudicial error occurred here because trial counsel failed to establish the test's reliability. *See also United States v. Burks,* 36 M.J. 447 (C.M.A. 1993) (luminal testing may be used to show why a criminal investigation focused on the accused).

[q] Expert Opinions—Mental Responsibility Issues

United States Court of Appeals for the Armed Forces

United States v. Dubose, 47 M.J. 386 (C.A.A.F. 1998): The accused was convicted of numerous bomb manufacturing and possession offenses. At trial, he unsuccessfully relied on a mental responsibility defense. This court set aside the accused's convictions because the Court of Criminal Appeals applied an incorrect standard in reviewing the expert and lay mental responsibility testimony; it opined that "clear and convincing objective evidence, not merely subjective medical opinion" was required. In the Court of Appeals for the Armed Forces' opinion, Article 50a of the Uniform Code of Military Justice does not distinguish between objective or subjective proof, nor does it place a premium on lay or expert witnesses' testimony. Article 50 merely provides that the accused has the burden of proving this affirmative defense by "clear and convincing evidence."

United States v. St. Jean, 45 M.J. 435 (C.A.A.F. 1996): The accused, an Air Force First Lieutenant, was convicted of murdering his wife. The government's case included significant forensic testimony, particularly that provided by a board certified psychiatrist who offered a "psychological autopsy" of the victim in an attempt to rebut the accused's contention that his wife actually took her own life. The trial judge carefully limited the psychiatrist's testimony to include only statements about whether the victim exhibited characteristics consistent with the profile of a suicidal risk. Further, the psychiatrist was not permitted to comment on the accused's veracity or credibility, or to needlessly include evidence gathered from reviewing police reports. Trial defense counsel moved to suppress the psychiatrist's testimony contending that it: (a) amounted to an opinion on the ultimate issue (*see* Rule 704), (b) was impermissible comment on the accused's credibility (*see* Rule 608), (c) did not qualify for admission because it was non-scientific and subjective testimony amounting to nothing more that "a flip of a coin" (*see* Rule 702), and (d) was unfairly prejudicial (*see* Rule 403). Affirming the accused's conviction and the use of this expert's testimony, the court held that the military judge properly limited trial counsel's use of his expert, adequately balanced the evidence's probative value against its potential prejudicial impact, and found that opinion testimony can be used to define the characteristics of persons who possess certain mental conditions.

United States v. Rhea, 33 M.J. 413 (C.M.A. 1991): Returning a portion of the child sexual abuse charges for rehearing, the court held that a clinical psychologist properly testified about parental duress in cases of incest. The court rejected the accused's contention that there is no scientific or technical basis for such expert evidence.

United States v. Jones, 26 M.J. 197 (C.M.A. 1988): Affirming the accused's child sexual abuse conviction, the court held that a social worker who "was not a trained mental-health professional" could testify as an expert witness in explaining how a retarded victim of such crimes might have reacted. The court viewed this testimony as helpful because "[t]he behavior patterns and responses of a severely retarded person are probably not familiar to the average court member."

[r]   Expert Opinions—Polygraph Evidence

United States Court of Appeals for the Armed Forces

United States v. Rodriguez, 37 M.J. 448 (C.M.A. 1993): This drug case was tried shortly before the Military Rules of Evidence's prohibition on admitting polygraph results became effective. *See* Rule 707. After the accused, a master sergeant, testified on direct that he had never used cocaine, government counsel was permitted to introduce polygraph evidence indicating he had. Reversing the conviction, this court said that given the government's failure to establish the reliability of "this weapon of devastation" (polygraph machine), its results were improperly admitted.

United States v. Gipson, 24 M.J. 246 (C.M.A. 1987): Abandoning *Frye v. United States,* 293 F. 1013 (D.C. Cir. 1923), the court held that: "The state of the polygraph technique is such that, depending on the competence of the examiner, the suitability of the examinee, the nature of the particular testimony process employed, and such other factors as may arise, the results of a particular examination may be as good or better than a good deal of expert and lay evidence that is routinely and uncritically received in criminal trials." Recognizing that the scientific principles governing polygraph evidence are still in flux, the court added that its decision established no "immutable principles," and that the proponent of polygraph evidence "still bears the burden of establishing the foundational predicates" for its use. Based on the above, the conviction was reversed because the accused's exonerating examination results were summarily excluded by the military judge.

Air Force Court of Criminal Appeals

United States v. Pope, 30 M.J. 1188 (A.F.C.M.R. 1990): This court found that no error occurred when the trial judge refused to admit a defense *ex parte* polygraph examination because: (a) the parties had not stipulated to the test results; (b) the examination procedures and quality control systems were insufficient; (c) the test suffered from the "friendly examiner syndrome;" and (d) the defense had not sufficiently established the scientific basis for admitting this evidence.

United States v. Tyler, 26 M.J. 680 (A.F.C.M.R. 1988): At the accused's drug distribution trial, he unsuccessfully attempted to attack the credibility of a government informant by establishing that the informant refused a polygraph. Affirming the conviction, the court held that "neither the willingness nor the unwillingness of a witness to take a polygraph test is admissible" because: (a) "it is not probative of the witness's truthfulness"; (b) there are many reasons consistent with honesty for not submitting to a polygraph examination; (c) substantial authority indicates it is improper to bolster the credibility of a witness by showing that he has "passed" a polygraph or that a "prosecution witness had submitted to a lie detector examination but that the accused refused to do so" and (d) such evidence "has the clear potential to divert the factfinders into an area not directly related to the issue of guilt or innocence."

United States v. Helton, 10 M.J. 820 (A.F.C.M.R. 1981): At the accused's trial for possession of marijuana, he requested that a properly certified polygraph operator be permitted to testify that he had been truthful in denying culpability to some, but not all, of the charged offenses. On appeal the Air Force Court of Review affirmed the trial judge's decision to reject this evidence. Relying in part on relevancy criteria, the court held that:

> Until it can be demonstrated that the opinion testimony resulting from polygraph testing is generally more reliable than the court-martial fact finder in determining truthfulness, it cannot be determined that such evidence will aid the court in performance of its function, Mil. R. Evid. 702, and hence that it is relevant. Mil. R. Evid. 401. [10 M.J. at 824.]

The court also found polygraph evidence to be within Rule 403's prohibitions, as the finders of fact would probably be inclined to attach "undue weight" to the examiner's testimony. The court did not want questions of credibility being resolved by expert witnesses. What the Court could have said also is that nothing in Rule 608 permits testimony as to someone's opinion concerning truthfulness on a particular occasion.

Army Court of Criminal Appeals

United States v. McKinnie, 29 M.J. 825 (A.C.M.R. 1989): Affirming the accused's fraternization conviction, the court found no error in the trial judge excluding the accused's exculpatory, *ex parte* polygraph examination, because it was "less reliable than one in which the parties agree beforehand to accept the results. . . ." In this court's opinion, the accused's willingness to take a second government test did not require reaching a different result.

Coast Guard Court of Criminal Appeals

United States v. Howard, 24 M.J. 897 (C.G.C.M.R. 1987): Relying on *United States v. Gipson,* 24 M.J. 246 (C.M.A. 1987), the court affirmed the accused's conviction even though the military judge excluded evidence of the accused's exculpatory polygraph examination. In the court's opinion, the trial judge's special findings clearly demonstrated that he conducted a thorough evidentiary hearing into the evidence's admissibility and decided that it "did not meet threshold tests for admissibility, in that the helpfulness test under MRE 702 had not been met and that the danger of confusion and misleading the members tipped the MRE 403 balance toward exclusion of the evidence."

[s]   Expert Opinions—Phenolphthalein Testing

United States Court of Appeals for the Armed Forces

United States v. Schlamer, 47 M.J. 670 (N.M.Ct.Crim.App. 1997), *aff'd,* 52 M.J. 80 (C.A.A.F. 1999): The accused was convicted of murdering another Marine. The key evidence against the accused came from his confession. During trial, government counsel used an expert witness, a forensic serologist, to testify about a blood-screening test employing phenolphthalein that he ran on a knife seized from the accused's car. Defense counsel objected to the expert's testimony which minimally linked an unidentifiable blood residue found on the accused's knife with the crime scene. The defense argued that a sufficient demonstration of scientific reliability had not been made. Affirming the accused's convictions, the court held that the expert's opinion was properly admitted because: (a) prior decisions of this court and the Court of Appeals for the Armed Forces have held that luminol testing, a process much less reliable than phenolphthalein testing is sufficiently reliable; and (b) the trial judge's very careful limiting instructions insured that the expert opinion would only be used to corroborate the accused's confession.

[t]   Expert Opinions—Profile Evidence

United States Court of Appeals for the Armed Forces

United States v. Harrow, 65 M.J. 190 (C.A.A.F. 2007): The question in this unpremeditated murder case was whether the accused service-member or her husband was responsible for the death of their five-month-old child. A forensic pediatrician provided the following testimony as part of the government's case: (a) biological parents are the most common people to fatally abuse their children; (b) the most significant trigger for a baby shaking incident is "persistent crying;" and (c) medical professionals consider certain behavioral factors to determine if an injury is accidental or "inflicted." The court agreed with the accused that statements (a) and (b) constituted inadmissible profile evidence. The court failed to find prejudice because the testimony applied equally to the accused and to the baby's father. The court also rejected the accused's contention that the testimony was prejudicial because it "lined up" with other government proof in demonstrating that the accused and not the baby's father was responsible for her death. The court said it was not aware of any authority supporting the accused's position, and that proof does not become inadmissible profile evidence simply because it tends to incriminate the accused.

United States v. Hays, 62 M.J. 158 (C.A.A.F. 2005): The accused was convicted of soliciting another to commit carnal knowledge with a child. During the government's case in chief, an FBI witness was qualified as an expert in the behavioral aspects of child sexual victimization. The witness described the typical behavior and fantasies of a generalized group of men who use computers to view child pornography. The defense made no objection to this profile evidence. On appeal the accused argued that the expert witness applied those characteristics to the accused, and opined that the accused solicited the rape of a child so that the accused might view the pictures taken during the crime. Affirming the accused's conviction, the court held that, because trial defense counsel did not object, relief could only be provided on a plain error basis. In the court's opinion, because the case was tried to the military judge alone, and she applied the proper standard for viewing the evidence, relief would be inappropriate.

United States v. Bresnahan, 62 M.J. 137 (C.A.A.F. 2005): The accused was convicted of shaking his three-month-old baby to death. A defense expert witness was called to suggest that the accused's wife was really at fault. On cross-examination, trial counsel asked this witness whether he was aware of two scientific studies indicating that men were much more likely to commit such crimes. The expert admitted he was. Affirming the accused's conviction, the court held that, while profile evidence is generally inadmissible, it may be used to rebut similar defense testimony—here that the accused's wife was more likely the perpetrator.

United States v. Traum, 60 M.J. 226 (C.A.A.F. 2004): Contrary to her pleas, a general court-martial panel convicted the accused of premeditatedly murdering her infant daughter. A central issue at trial and on appeal was whether the following testimony by a forensic pediatrician amounted to impermissible "profile evidence:" (a) "if a child is less than four years of age, the most common cause of trauma death is going to be child maltreatment; (b) eighty percent of children who die, die from a one-time event; and (c) overwhelmingly, the most likely person to kill a child is going to be his or her own biological parent." The court then explained that profile evidence is defined as testimony that presents a "characteristic profile" of an offender, such as a pedophile or child abuser, and then places the accused's personal characteristics within that profile as proof of guilt. Affirming the accused's conviction, this court held that statements (a) and (b) were properly admitted because they focused on the "characteristics of the battered child," not a "child battering profile." However, the court found statement (c) to be impermissible profile evidence, but also found that the weight of evidence against the accused rendered its admission harmless error.

United States v. Huberty, 53 M.J.369 (C.A.A.F. 2000): LTC Huberty was convicted by officer members of sodomy, indecent acts, and adultery. The case on appeal focused on: (a) the exclusion of defense expert witness testimony that would have indicated the accused did not fit the psychological profile of an exhibitionist and thus was unlikely to have committed the charged offenses, and (b) the admissibility of government rebuttal expert testimony indicating that the accused had been "grooming" his 17-year-old victim for sex. Affirming the accused's convictions and sentence, this court held that the defense's proffered testimony was inadmissible because it had not been accepted by the scientific community and was generally unreliable. *See United States v. Houser*, 36 M.J. 392 (1993), and *United States v. Latorre*, 53 M.J. 179 (2000). Conversely, the court held that trial counsel's expert testimony did not constitute inadmissible "profile evidence," and even if it was profile testimony it was admissible to rebut the testimony of the accused's expert witness and to explain that the victim's behavior was consistent with a theory that the accused had "groomed her." The testimony was not admitted for the purpose of showing that the accused fit the profile of a sex abuser. *See United States v. Banks*, 36 M.J. 150 (C.M.A. 1992).

United States v. Pagel, 45 M.J. 64 (C.A.A.F. 1996): The accused was convicted of carnal knowledge, sodomy, and committing indecent acts upon his minor daughter. During trial, government counsel offered dysfunctional family "profile" evidence indicating that the accused's familial relationships were indicative of those which lead to sexual abuse. Affirming the accused's convictions, this court held that on "numerous occasions [it] has recognized that the behavioral characteristics or behavioral patterns of an alleged victim in a sexual abuse case may need to be explained by expert testimony, especially where that behavior would be counter-intuitive." The court also noted that counsel and the military judge were particularly sensitive to the legal parameters embracing such expert testimony.

United States v. Banks, 36 M.J. 150 (C.M.A. 1992): The accused's conviction for sexually molesting his stepdaughter was set aside because of numerous expert witness and scientific evidence problems. Here, the court held that it was reversible error for the prosecution to show that the accused met the character profile of a parent in a family which included a child sexual abuser. The court went on to say that using such character profile evidence to establish guilt or innocence is generally improper. However, this testimony may be used in a limited fashion to help explain sanity issues, as investigative tools for establishing reasonable suspicion, or as rebuttal evidence to clarify potentially misleading testimony introduced by other parties.

Air Force Court of Criminal Appeals

United States v. Harrow, 62 M.J. 649 (A.F.Ct.Crim.App. 2006): The question in this unpremeditated murder case was whether the accused service-member or her husband were responsible for the death of their five-month-old child. Without objection, a forensic pediatrician provided the following testimony as part of the government's case: (a) biological parents are the most common people to fatally abuse their children; (b) the highest level of fatal child abuse is in infants under the age of 12 months; (c) the most significant trigger for a baby shaking incident is "persistent crying"; and (d) medical professionals consider certain behavioral factors to determine if an injury is accidental or "inflicted." The court held that expert testimony indicating a biological parent is the most likely person to kill a child is generally viewed as impermissible profile evidence. As a result, the court held that admission of the testimony was an obvious or clear error, but otherwise harmless.

Navy-Marine Corps Court of Criminal Appeals

United States v. Dorsch, 34 M.J. 1042 (N.M.C.M.R. 1992): During the accused's child molestation court-martial, defense counsel was prohibited from introducing psychiatric testimony indicating the accused did not fit the psychological profile of a typical child sexual abuser. Affirming the accused's conviction, the court said the testimony was inadmissible because defense counsel.

[u]   Expert Opinions—Psychological Stress Evaluations

Army Court of Criminal Appeals

United States v. Bothwell, 17 M.J. 684 (A.C.M.R. 1983): On trial for house-breaking and larceny, the accused unsuccessfully offered expert testimony based on Psychologic Stress Evaluations (PSE) which he stated would have established his truthfulness. Relying on *Frye v. United States*, 293 F. 1013 (D.C. Cir. 1923), and Rule 702, trial counsel urged that PSE had not yet gained general acceptance in the scientific community and thus was not admissible. The accused argued that Rule 702 had expanded *Frye* and that, under Rules 401 and 403 his evidence should have been admitted as relevant, helpful evidence. The reviewing court stated that, absent "any definitive authority to the contrary, we are unwilling to abandon a rule [*Frye*] that has been applied in the military for almost thirty years." However, the court did suggest that in the future, counsel seeking to admit novel scientific evidence should attempt to demonstrate reliability by showing: (1) the validity of the underlying scientific principles, (2) the validity of the technique applying those underlying principles, and (3) the proper application of the technique to the particular facts in question. *See* Giannelli, *The Admissibility of Novel Scientific Evidence: Frye v. United States, a Half-Century Later,* 80 COLUM. L. REV. 1197 (1980).

[v]   Expert Opinions—Recanted Testimony

Army Court of Criminal Appeals

United States v. Suarez, 32 M.J. 767 (A.C.M.R. 1991): The court held that this provision is the primary rule for dealing with scientific evidence in the form of expert testimony. As a result, it affirmed the accused's child sexual abuse convictions, stating that testimony which explains why victims often recant their original statements was admissible and helpful.

[w]   Expert Opinions—Sentencing Evidence

United States Court of Appeals for the Armed Forces

United States v. Ellis, 68 M.J. 341 (C.A.A.F. 2010): The accused was convicted of indecent acts with a 13-year-old child, possession of child pornography, adultery with the child's mother and related offenses. During sentencing the government called a forensic psychology expert with a specialization in sexual offender assessments who testified that the accused's risk of recidivism was moderately high. Defense counsel did not challenge the expert's qualifications but did object to the reliability of the expert's methodology, the factual basis for his testimony, his application of the methodology to the accused's situation and his opinion that risk of recidivism evidence was relevant to rehabilitation potential. At oral argument appellate defense counsel conceded that he was not challenging the appraisal methodology. The court affirmed the accused's sentence and held that defense counsel's arguments went to the weight, not admissibility, of the expert's testimony.

United States v. McElhaney, 54 M.J. 120 (C.A.A.F. 2000): A general court-martial convicted the accused of numerous child sexual abuse offenses. During sentencing, and over defense objection, trial counsel was permitted to call an expert witness (child psychiatrist) who testified that "the accused exhibited characteristics in common with pedophiles and to offer an opinion on the accused's future dangerousness based upon those characteristics." The majority found that because the government's foundation for this testimony was insufficient, its admission constituted error, and they overturned the sentence. An illuminating dissent, tied to RCM 1001, would have admitted the evidence.

United States v. Stinson, 34 M.J. 233 (C.M.A. 1992): During the sentencing portion of the accused's court-martial for sexually abusing his nine-year-old daughter, trial counsel called a psychologist who testified about the accused's rehabilitative potential. Defense counsel objected contending that the witness was not qualified, exceeded the bounds of her expertise, and lacked a sufficient factual predicate to be relevant. Affirming the findings and sentence, this court held that: (a) qualified expert testimony on an accused's rehabilitative potential is admissible; (b) this witness was qualified because she possessed substantive, helpful knowledge exceeding the factfinders' abilities; (c) the military judge properly limited the expert's testimony to relevant issues consistent with her proven training and experiences; and (d) even though the expert never met the accused, her testimony was admissible because the lack of personal contact affects only weight, not admissibility.

Air Force Court of Criminal Appeals

United States v. Williams, 35 M.J. 812 (A.F.C.M.R. 1992): The accused was convicted of rape. During sentencing, and over defense objection, a government expert testified about the accused's "future dangerousness." In the forensic psychiatrist's opinion, the accused's past conduct was an accurate predictor of his future criminal behavior. Although this court affirmed the accused's convictions and sentence, it believed the evidence was erroneously admitted. Relying on R.C.M. 1001(b)(4) & (5), and past military authority, the court held that while a low likelihood of future dangerousness is a mitigating factor, evidence of a high likelihood is not an aggravating factor otherwise courts-martial would be punishing accusers for possible future crimes, instead of for actual crimes. The court went on to note that some statements contained in *United States v. Stinson*, 34 M.J. 233 (C.M.A. 1992), cited above, seem to support admission of such testimony.

Army Court of Criminal Appeals

United States v. Snodgrass, 22 M.J. 866 (A.C.M.R. 1986): The court held that expert opinion testimony concerning the long term effects of incest and sexual child abuse was properly presented during the sentencing portions of the accused's court-martial for having sodomized a child under the age of sixteen.

[x]   Expert Opinions—Simulated Conditions Evidence

United States Court of Appeals for the Armed Forces

United States v. Kaspers, 47 M.J. 176 (C.A.A.F. 1997): During the accused's trial for conspiring to murder his wife, the military judge admitted opinion testimony from a Washington State Police accident-reconstruction expert witness. The testimony was used to demonstrate the feasibility of the competing theories in this case that the victim accidentally slipped to her death, or that the accused pushed her off a cliff. The expert's testimony and supporting video tapes of his tests contributed to the conclusion that in order to fall to her death, the accused's wife must have been pushed. Trial defense counsel thoroughly challenged the evidence's reliability. Affirming the accused's convictions, this court found that the military judge properly exercised his gatekeeping function and evaluated all surrounding circumstances, including reliability, before admitting the specialized evidence. The court went on to say that this case was the "model of advocacy envisioned by both *Gipson* and *Daubert*" (*see* our Rule 702 Editorial Comments on these cases).

[y]   Expert Opinions—Sexual Assault Cases

Air Force Court of Criminal Appeals

United States v. Wright, 48 M.J. 896 (A.F.Ct.Crim.App. 1998): The accused was convicted of indecent assault, housebreaking, and related offenses. Over defense counsel's *in limine* objection, the military judge allowed a government psychologist to present expert testimony concerning how the victims of prolonged child sexual abuse respond to that conduct and other traumatic circumstances in their lives, including the charged rape. Affirming the accused's convictions, this court held that the psychologist's testimony was properly received because it came from a witness who possessed specialized knowledge that would be helpful to the finders of fact in understanding other evidence. The court specifically noted the trial judge's very appropriate actions in excluding expert testifying about victim credibility, or the accused's guilt or innocence.

Navy-Marine Corps Court of Criminal Appeals

United States v. Abdirahman, 66 M.J. 668 (N.M.Ct.Crim.App. 2008): The accused's conviction for rape was reversed based on the cumulative effect of trial errors. One error involved testimony by a nurse practitioner that the victim's physical and emotional conditions were similar to those of other rape victims she had examined. The court held that such opinion testimony was improperly admitted because trial counsel had not informed the defense that an expert would be called, and the witness was never qualified or offered as an expert. The court added that, while it would have been appropriate for this nurse practitioner to testify about the victim's observable conditions, only a properly qualified expert could provide opinion testimony interpreting them.

[z] Expert Opinions—Syndrome Evidence

[i] Syndrome Evidence—Battered Child

Supreme Court

Estelle v. McGuire, 502 U.S. 62 (1991): The accused was convicted of murdering his infant daughter. On a habeas corpus petition, the Ninth Circuit Court of Appeals set aside the accused's conviction because battered child syndrome evidence had been improperly used during trial. In that court's opinion, the testimony was inadmissible, in part, because no evidence linked the accused with the prior crimes. Reversing the Ninth Circuit's holding, the Court said that the evidence was admissible because it was permitted under state law, was used to prove an element of the offense (that the victim had suffered repeated injuries which were not accidentally inflicted), and the prosecution did not have to prove who inflicted those injuries.

United States Court of Criminal Appeals

United States v. Lee, 28 M.J. 52 (C.M.A. 1989): In a child sexual abuse court-martial, defense counsel unsuccessfully challenged the government's use of a clinical psychologist to establish that the "victim's symptoms were consistent with a traumatic, possibly sexual, experience. . . ." Affirming the conviction, the court held that a psychologist was qualified to present such evidence, and that it was helpful and not unfairly prejudicial.

Air Force Court of Criminal Appeals

United States v. Irvin, 13 M.J. 749 (A.F.C.M.R. 1982): The accused unsuccessfully contended that her involuntary manslaughter and assault convictions should be reversed because the government's psychiatric expert was allowed to give his opinion concerning the "battered child syndrome." Relying on Rule 702, the court found that the witness possessed specialized knowledge that assisted the finders of fact in understanding the evidence and determining the issues.

[ii] Syndrome Evidence—Child Sexual Abuse Accommodation Syndrome Evidence

Air Force Court of Criminal Appeals

United States v. Hansen, 36 M.J. 599 (A.F.C.M.R. 1992): The accused was convicted of sexually abusing his natural daughter. During trial, the prosecution offered expert testimony on child sexual abuse accommodation syndrome evidence to aid the finders of fact in evaluating the victim's recantation of her pretrial statements and claimed loss of memory. Affirming the accused's convictions, the court held that the testimony properly focused on traits and consistencies found among sex abuse victims and was not improperly used to vouch for the victim's credibility. The court also mentioned that the trial judge's limiting instructions were crucial to the proper use of this evidence.

[iii]   Syndrome Evidence—Post-Traumatic Stress Disorder

United States Court of Appeals for the Armed Forces

United States v. Johnson, 35 M.J. 17 (C.M.A. 1992): The court affirmed the accused's conviction for sexually abusing his teenage stepdaughter. During trial, the military judge held that a government psychotherapist could testify about the victim's demonstrated characteristics of post-traumatic stress disorder, but nothing more. Notwithstanding this limitation, trial counsel improperly elicited testimony concerning the witness's opinion on sexually abused children and family patterns. Appellate relief was not granted here because defense counsel failed to make a timely objection, on cross-examination the witness impeached her own testimony, the military judge gave prompt and effective limiting instructions, and the expert's testimony played an insignificant role in the trial's outcome.

Army Court of Criminal Appeals

United States v. Bostick, 33 M.J. 849 (A.C.M.R. 1991): The accused was tried by military judge alone for attempted sodomy and indecent assault. During the government's case-in-chief, the trial counsel and military judge questioned prosecution expert witnesses about whether the victim suffered from rape trauma and post-traumatic stress disorders. Reversing the convictions, the court held that, while such evidence may be admissible when it is relevant, helpful, and not unfairly prejudicial, it should have been excluded here because the experts were also asked if they believed that the offenses occurred, and whether the victim was believable or credible.

United States v. Carter, 22 M.J. 771 (A.C.M.R. 1986): After thoroughly analyzing the existing state, federal, and military law concerning the admissibility of post-trauma stress disorder evidence, the court held that "notwithstanding the unsettled nature of the issue, we have determined that it is appropriate to admit such testimony" because: (a) sufficient scientific data is available "to support the existence of rape trauma syndrome," (b) rape trauma syndrome is now "officially recognized by the psychiatric community as valid and is generally accepted as a valid scientific principle," (c) such testimony "assists the triers of fact in determining the issue of consent, particularly where the court members have no personal experience with rape victims" and (d) there were no eyewitnesses to the crime, and no apparent physical injuries existed to help substantiate the victim's allegations. The court went on to say that, based on the Rules' redefinition of scientific evidence principles, it no longer perceives *Frye v. United States*, 293 F. 1013 (D.C. Cir. 1923), as a barrier to admissibility in this area. The court suggested that limiting instructions should be given whenever such evidence is admitted.

Coast Guard Court of Criminal Appeals

United States v. Haire, 44 M.J. 520 (C.G. Ct.Crim.App. 1996): Affirming the accused's rape conviction, the court held that victim post-traumatic stress disorder (PTSD) evidence was properly admitted where consent was the crucial issue. In the court's opinion, PTSD is helpful because it assists the finder of fact in understanding and applying testimony which is not expected and probably beyond a layman's experience.

[iv]   Syndrome Evidence—Rape Trauma

United States Court of Appeals for the Armed Forces

United States v. Houser, 36 M.J. 392 (C.M.A. 1993): Affirming the accused's rape and adultery convictions, the court again stated that rape trauma syndrome evidence can be admitted in a court-martial either during the government's case-in-chief, or in rebuttal. To be admissible, such testimony generally must be relevant (Rule 401), presented by a competent expert witness (Rules 702 and 703), reliable (Rule 402), and not unfairly prejudicial or misleading (Rule 403). As in this case, the court said it is not necessary for the expert to see or interview the victim before testifying. The court went on to say that relief will only be granted for abuses of discretion, which they defined as occurring when a reviewing court possesses a definite and firm belief that a lower court made a clear error in judgment when it weighed the relevant factors.

United States v. Reynolds, 29 M.J. 105 (C.M.A. 1989): Affirming the accused's rape conviction, the court held that "the plain rule of law is that an expert's testimony concerning 'rape-trauma syndrome . . . is probative . . . on the issue of consent by the victim.' This is subject to the limitation, of course, that the expert cannot 'opine as to the credibility or believability of' the victim.' "

United States v. Carter, 26 M.J. 428 (C.M.A. 1988): Building upon its decision in *United States v. Gipson,* 24 M.J. 246 (C.M.A. 1987) (cited *below*), the court held that "the test in *Frye v. United States,* 293 F. 1013 (D.C. Cir. 1923), does not exclusively govern admissibility of rape-trauma-syndrome evidence at a court-martial," and that its admission here was proper.

Air Force Court of Criminal Appeals

United States v. Eastman, 20 M.J. 948 (A.F.C.M.R. 1985): Although the court recognized that under certain circumstances evidence of rape trauma syndrome may be properly admitted, reversible error occurred here because trial counsel failed to establish the expert qualifications of the witness used to present this testimony. The court also noted that Air Force Regulations prohibited the witness in question from ever being "called upon to perform the clinical evaluation" discussed.

Army Court of Criminal Appeals

United States v. Tomlinson, 20 M.J. 897 (A.C.M.R. 1985): The accused's rape conviction was reversed because the trial judge mistakenly allowed unconstrained rape trauma syndrome evidence to reach the factfinder. The court "presumed" that the government's witness was qualified and "could have properly testified that the [victim's] symptoms were consistent with a traumatic experience or even a stressful experience . . . ." However, the court viewed this testimony as unfairly prejudicial because it: (a) appeared to be offered as "human lie detector evidence," (b) was not limited to establishing the symptoms of rape trauma syndrome but extended to designating causes for the symptoms, (c) was used to give "a stamp of scientific legitimacy" to the victim's protestations and (d) gave rise to a "clear danger that the court members would consider [the expert testimony] dispositive on the issue of consent."

[v]   Syndrome Evidence—Therapist-Patient Sex

Army Court of Criminal Appeals

   United States v. Rivera, 26 M.J. 638 (A.C.M.R. 1988): The accused, a psychiatrist, was convicted of engaging in a "sexualizing therapist" relationship with the wife of a junior officer. During sentencing, government counsel introduced "therapist-patient sex syndrome" evidence. Finding error, but no prejudice in its admission, the court held that the theory's "scientific legitimacy" had not yet been established. During trial the theory was barely one-year-old and recognized only by the testifying expert. The *Diagnostic and Statistical Manual of Mental Disorders* did not recognize it, nor would the revised future edition. The court said, even applying *United States v. Gipson,* 24 M.J. 246 (C.M.A. 1987) (rejecting strict pre-Rules standards on scientific evidence), this theory had an "insufficiently valid body of scientific knowledge" to support it and, as a result, it would not be helpful to the finders of fact.

[aa]   Expert Opinions—Truthfulness Opinion Evidence

United States Court of Appeals for the Armed Forces

   United States v. Schlamer, 52 M.J. 80 (C.A.A.F. 1999): At trial, defense counsel extensively cross-examined the agent who interrogated the accused about the possibility of the accused's confession being false. On redirect, the agent testified that he did not believe the accused had made a false confession. This court held that no error occurred. Noting that the defense had raised the issue of false confessions, the court distinguished this case from the typical one where a witness is asked to offer an opinion on whether another witness has told the truth. In those cases, courts have traditionally excluded such testimony indicating that the "jury is the lie detector." Because the members were not present when this accused confessed, the court viewed the agent's opinion testimony as being admissible. However, they went on to say that even if error occurred, it was nonprejudicial.

   United States v. Cacy, 43 M.J. 214 (C.A.A.F. 1995): The accused was convicted of sexually abusing his 6-year-old daughter. Part of the government's case included expert witness testimony indicating that the victim's behavior was consistent with that of a sexually-abused child, and that the victim did not appear to have been rehearsed. The expert also said, over defense objection, that she cautioned the victim to be truthful and ultimately recommended her for further treatment. The court interpreted all testimony about truthfulness and further medical treatment as being erroneously admitted expert opinion testimony on credibility. However, the court found the admissions to be harmless error not requiring appellate relief.

United States v. Harrison, 31 M.J. 330 (C.M.A. 1990): In a child sexual abuse case where credibility was the only significant issue, the court reversed a conviction because the trial judge allowed an expert witness to comment on victim credibility. In the court's opinion, allowing a clinical psychologist to give his opinion about whether the victim was sexually assaulted is impermissible because it demonstrates the witness's view on the child's believability. The court said it would have been permissible for the expert to testify about: (a) specific symptoms found among children who have been sexually abused, and whether the victim exhibited those symptoms; and (b) patterns of consistency in the stories of child sexual abuse victims and how the victim's accounts in this case compare.

United States v. Partyka, 30 M.J. 242, 243 (C.M.A. 1990): This court reversed the accused's child sexual abuse conviction because the military judge improperly allowed a government psychologist to testify that the accused's unsworn statement was not true. In the court's opinion, this testimony did not assist the finder of fact in understanding the evidence, but caused them to speculate on inadmissible matters.

United States v. Arruza, 26 M.J. 234 (C.M.A. 1988): In this child sexual abuse case, the court affirmed a conviction even though an expert witness testified that he believed the victim's protestations. In the court's opinion, such testimony wrongly places "an impressively qualified expert's stamp of truthfulness on a witness' story . . . usurp[ing] the exclusive function of the jury to weigh the evidence and determine credibility."

Air Force Court of Criminal Appeals

United States v. Stroh, 46 M.J. 643 (A.F.Ct.Crim.App. 1997): The accused was convicted of perpetrating the most sordid sexual offenses against his daughter's six-year-old playmate. At trial and on appeal, the accused objected to a government expert witness' testimony that the victim "exhibited common behaviors associated with sexually abused children" in her age group. The government expert then cataloged the described behavior. Rejecting the accused's argument that this witness acted as a human lie detector, the court held that the military judge was keenly alert to the requirement that expert testimony not exceed comparisons between a victim's behavior and that of an identified class of abuse victims, and that the expert witness never specifically testified that she believed the victim or that the accused was guilty. The court also highlighted the bench's effective and measured sua sponte jury instructions on these issues.

United States v. Marrie, 39 M.J. 993 (A.F.C.M.R. 1994): The accused was convicted of sodomy and indecent acts with males under the age of sixteen. During the government's case-in-chief, trial counsel was allowed to ask a psychiatric expert witness how frequently preteen boys make false homosexual allegations. The witness replied that she had never observed such conduct during her career. Finding error but no prejudice, the court affirmed the accused's convictions, holding that the testimony should have been excluded because it allowed the expert witness to comment on the victims' relative truthfulness.

Army Court of Criminal Appeals

United States v. Buenaventura, 40 M.J. 519 (A.C.M.R. 1994): The accused was convicted of rape, indecent acts, and indecent liberties upon an eight-year-old girl. The offenses came to light after the victim visited her school's counselor and other medical experts complaining that the accused and her grandfather had sexually assaulted her. During trial, defense counsel unsuccessfully attempted to introduce evidence of the grandfather's abuse, and expert testimony explaining how the victim may have "integrated a non-abusing person [into] the normalization process." Affirming the accused's convictions, this court held that the expert's testimony was not helpful, superfluous, and a waste of time. In the majority's opinion, the psychologist's testimony would have placed an impermissible stamp of untruthfulness on the victim's story.

United States v. King, 32 M.J. 709 (A.C.M.R. 1991): Over defense objection, trial counsel asked his expert witness whether she thought five-year-old children were capable of fabricating sexual abuse allegations. Affirming a conviction, the court held that, while child abuse expert witnesses are not permitted to opine on the credibility or believability of victims or their individual reports of abuse, they can testify about a child's ability to separate truth from fantasy and discuss common patterns of consistency in such accounts.

[ab]   Expert Opinions—Valuation of Stolen Property

Army Court of Criminal Appeals

United States v. Hood, 12 M.J. 890 (A.C.M.R. 1982): The accused pled guilty to various offenses involving black market activity. During the sentencing proceedings, the government was allowed to introduce a chart indicating the relative value of the stolen property if invested over a period of years. This evidence was largely introduced through a CID agent who was permitted to testify, over defense objection, as an expert. Relying on Rule 702, the court held that the overwhelming weight of civilian and military authority provides that the valuation of property may be proved by a witness with the CID agent's training and experience.

§ 703.01   Official Text

Rule 703.   Basis of Opinion Testimony by Experts.

The facts or data in the particular case upon which an expert bases an opinion or inference may be those perceived by or made known to the expert at or before the hearing. If of a type reasonably relied upon by experts in the particular field in forming opinions or inferences upon the subject, the facts or data need not be admissible in evidence in order for the opinion or inference to be admitted. Facts or data that are otherwise inadmissible shall not be disclosed to the jury by the proponent of the opinion or inference unless the court determines that their probative value in assisting the jury to evaluate the expert's opinion substantially outweighs their prejudicial effect.

---

§ 703.02   Editorial Comment

[1]   Background of the Rule

Rule 703 addresses the question of what information an expert may rely upon in forming opinion testimony. In December 2004, Military Rule 703 was amended by Executive Order 13365, to maintain its commonality with Federal Rule 703.[1] As amended and as originally written, the Rule expands the bases upon which expert opinion testimony may rest. The original Federal Rule's Advisory Committee Notes specifically states that Rule 703 was intended to "broaden the basis for expert opinions beyond that in many jurisdictions and to bring the judicial practice into line with the practice of the experts themselves when not in court." By adopting the Federal Rule, the military drafters have also expressed an intention to make the practice of using expert witness testimony more realistic and effective by allowing experts to rely on the same information in court as they traditionally used out of court, even if this information will not be admissible in evidence.[2]

The traditional common law approach was to restrict expert witness

---

[1] Military Rule of Evidence 1102 provides that changes to the Federal Rules of Evidence shall apply to the Military Rules of Evidence 18 months after their effective date unless the President takes contrary action. Federal Rule of Evidence 703 was amended in December 2000.

[2] *See e.g.,* United States v. Ayala, 601 F.3d 256 (4th Cir. 2010) (noting the role *Crawford v. Washington* plays in expert testimony based on statements from nontestifying declarants, the court found no error in experts offering independent judgments based in part on what otherwise would be inadmissible evidence; however, experts cannot simply be "transmitters" for testimonial hearsay); United States v. Turner, 591 F.3d 928 (7th Cir. 2010) (*Crawford v. Washington* and *Melendez-Diaz v. Massachusetts*, not violated when government chemist testified based on test results from other nontestifying chemists where no statements from

testimony to opinions or inferences based upon facts presented in evidence. Since the expert usually had no personal knowledge of the facts, a hypothetical question, often lengthy and complicated, was put to the expert and the expert was then asked to offer views assuming that the facts stated in the question were correct.[3] Proof supporting the assumed facts was required from other witnesses. This provision adopts a much more flexible approach to expert witness testimony.

Under Rule 703, an expert may base his or her opinion upon facts or data that he or she has perceived, learned from study or experiment, or been told about, either by watching the proceeding in court, or from other sources outside court. However, the facts or data upon which the expert bases his or her testimony must be consistent "reasonably relied upon by experts in the particular field," even though the facts or data would not otherwise be admissible in evidence.[4]

To satisfy this provision, counsel must demonstrate that the expert's opinion is grounded on the type of data a reasonable expert in the particular field would use.[5] Rule 703 does not concern the standard counsel must meet to prove the reliability or acceptance of the expert's methodology. Rule 702, *Daubert v. Merrell Dow Pharms., Inc.*,[6] and its progeny control the helpfulness and reliability standards.[7]

This distinction between Rule 703's narrower focus on basis, and Rule 702's broader focus on methodology, helpfulness, and reliability were clearly explained in *In re Paoli RR Yard Pcb Litig.*,[8] where the court said:

> There will be times when an expert's methodology is generally reliable but some of the underlying data is not of a type reasonably relied upon by experts. In those cases, the expert can testify so long as he or she does

---

nontestifying chemist were admitted and the testifying expert unequivocally established his opinions were exclusively his own).

[3] *See, e.g.,* United States v. Wilson, 798 F.2d 509 (1st Cir. 1986) (finding that the Trial Court properly excluded expert from testifying; the expert was expected to answer hypothetical questions unsupported by facts proved by the defense); United States v. Mann, 712 F.2d 941 (4th Cir. 1983) (firearms expert could give opinion as to make of weapon based on hypothetical question).

[4] *See, e.g.,* American Bearing Co. v. Litton Indus., Inc., 540 F. Supp. 1163 (E.D. Pa. 1982) (new trial granted antitrust defendant where trial judge determined that economic expert improperly relied upon another expert to ascertain product market and could not reasonably rely on data supplied by the president of the corporation that retained him to testify).

[5] *See, e.g.,* American Universal Ins. Co. v. Falzone, 644 F.2d 65 (1st Cir. 1981) (state fire marshal could rely on opinions of other investigators); C.A. May Marine Supply Co. v. Brunswick Corp., 649 F.2d 1049 (5th Cir. 1981) (survey must be conducted in accordance with accepted methods).

[6] 509 U.S. 579 (1993).

[7] *See generally* our discussion of Rule 702.

[8] 35 F.3d 717 (3d Cir. 1994).

not significantly rely on the unreliable data, and so long as his or her testimony survives Rule 702 without any reliance on the excluded data. Moreover, if the judge thinks that the expert would reach a different conclusion if he was not able to rely on this data, a conclusion that would no longer help the [proponent] to prove his or her case, the district court can exclude his opinion as irrelevant.

Military courts are also very sensitive to the substantive and definitional distinctions between Rules 702 and 703. The Court of Appeals for the Armed Forces has applied the law in a manner consistent with *In re Paoli RR Litigation*. In *United States v. Combs*,[9] the accused was convicted of murdering his eighteen-month-old son and battering his three-year-old daughter. Affirming the Court of Criminal Appeals in setting aside the murder conviction, the Court of Appeals for the Armed Forces that the military judge improperly excluded defense expert testimony concerning the accused's intent to commit murder. The court found this evidence to be helpful based on Rule 702, of a type reasonably relied upon by experts in the field under Rule 703, and not objectionable because it concerned one of the central issues at trial pursuant to Rule 704. The court went on to recognize that the Military Rules of Evidence liberally allow for expert testimony that assists the trier of fact.

[2] Problems with Determining Basis

Two principal problems arise under Rule 703. The first is how to decide what experts in the particular field reasonably rely upon. To make this determination, the judge may consider: (1) the testimony of the expert who is called; (2) any literature that is offered in support of, or in opposition to, the testimony; and (3) the testimony of other experts.

When deciding whether to admit or to exclude expert testimony, the judge is actually making a preliminary decision on an evidence question. Rule 104(a) controls and permits the military judge to hold a hearing out of the court members' presence. During this proceeding, the judge is not be bound by the Rules of Evidence, other than the privilege rules. In practice this means that the judge may consider hearsay testimony that will often take the form of books and journals, especially learned treatises. The hearsay exception for learned treatises under Rule 803(18), and the procedure for taking judicial notice of facts under Rule 201, will be helpful in admitting such evidence, but the evidence need not be admissible to be considered under Rule 104(a).

An expert's opinion will be excluded if the expert did not rely on the same or similar information as other experts in the field consider. Using Rules 702 and 703 together, the testimony may also be improperly based and subject to exclusion if the expert relied on inappropriate or invalid information even if

---

[9] 39 M.J. 288 (C.M.A. 1994).

other experts have also relied on such data. An expert's opinion will not be helpful to the finder of fact if it lacks an adequate substantive foundation.[10]

[3]   The Problem of Inadmissible Evidence of Basis

The other problem that arises under this Rule is whether an expert who has relied upon facts or data not otherwise admissible in evidence may report the facts or data to the finders of fact in explaining an opinion or inference.[11] If the expert is denied an opportunity to relate the facts or data that support his or her testimony, it is difficult for the judge or court members to evaluate the legitimacy of his opinion. As a result, it seems imperative that some explanation for the expert's opinion be permitted.

It is also clear that, unless care is taken in utilizing Rule 703, parties can "smuggle" a great deal of hearsay and other inadmissible evidence into a case to establish the basis for the expert's testimony. Although the evidence is not being offered for the truth of the matter asserted, there is a possibility that court members may nevertheless use it that way.[12]

[4]   Dealing with "Inadmissible" Basis Evidence

Rule 703 regulates the disclosure to court members of evidence that would be otherwise inadmissible for substantive purposes but was "reasonably relied" upon by the expert in forming an opinion. The amendment to Rule 703 contains a presumption against disclosing the inadmissible facts and data to the court members. The following sequence describes how the amended Rule was intended to be applied:

(1) When otherwise *inadmissible* facts and data,

(2) Were reasonably *relied* upon by an expert in formulating her expert opinion, and

(3) The inadmissible facts and data are offered for the sole purpose of assisting the jury in *evaluating* an expert's opinion,

(4) The trial court when applying this Rule to determine admissibility of *only* the inadmissible facts and data must then,

(5) Consider the information's probative value in assisting the jury to weigh the expert's opinion against the risk of *prejudice* resulting from the jury's *potential misuse* of the information for substantive purposes.

(6) The otherwise inadmissible facts and data may then be disclosed to

---

[10] The hardest question military judges face in determining which facts or data are reasonably relied upon is how much scientific acceptance is required before certain tests may be deemed to be valid. This problem is discussed in our Editorial Comment to Rule 702.

[11] For a good discussion on the general subject of when information relied upon outside of courts should be deemed to be reliable enough for use in court, *see* McElhaney, *Expert Witnesses and the Federal Rules of Evidence,* 28 Mercer L. Rev. 463 (1977).

[12] *See, e.g.,* United States v. Lawson, 653 F.2d 299 (7th Cir. 1981) (stating in *dictum* that expert's testimony based entirely on hearsay would violate confrontation clause).

the jury only if the trial court finds that the *probative value* of the information in assisting the jury to evaluate the expert's opinion *substantially outweighs* its prejudicial effect.

(7) If the otherwise inadmissible facts and data are admitted under this balancing test, the trial judge must give a *limiting instruction*, upon request, informing the jury that the underlying information must not be used for substantive purposes. *See* Rule 105. In determining the appropriate course, the trial court should consider the probable effectiveness or lack of effectiveness of a limiting instruction under the particular circumstances.

Before Rule 703 was amended, Federal and military courts reached inconsistent results on how to treat inadmissible information reasonably relied upon by an expert in forming an opinion or drawing an inference. For example, in *United States v. Rollins,*[13] the court admitted an FBI agent's foundational hearsay statements about what an informant had told him concerning the meaning of drug code language even though that testimony would otherwise have been inadmissible but for its ability to provide the finders of fact with an understanding of the agent's basis for his opinion. An inconsistent result was reached in *United States v. 0.59 Acres of Land,*[14] where that court found it was error to admit similar hearsay statements offered as the basis of an expert opinion without a limiting instruction. These differences of opinion are shared by some commentators.[15]

In *United States v. Harris,*[16] the accused was convicted of drunk driving, involuntary manslaughter, and related offenses. A state highway patrolman with extensive specialized training and experience testified as a government expert witness. He established that the accused was intoxicated and that the accused's vehicle caused the skid marks leading to the deceased's body. This witness also provided opinion testimony on many other aspects of the crime scene, often based on what witnesses observed. The accused contended it was error to accept the highway patrolman's opinion testimony because it amounted to "smuggling" inadmissible hearsay into the courtroom. The Court of Appeals for the Armed Forces rejected the accused's contentions and affirmed his convictions holding that the facts an expert relies upon can be based on personal knowledge, assumed facts, documents supplied by other experts, or even listening to trial testimony. Virtually anticipating the

---

[13] 862 F.2d 1282 (7th Cir. 1988).

[14] 109 F.3d 1493 (9th Cir. 1997).

[15] *See, e.g.,* Carlson, *Policing the Bases of Modern Expert Testimony,* 39 VAND. L. REV. 577 (1986) (advocating limits on the jury's consideration of otherwise inadmissible evidence used as the basis for an expert opinion); Rice, *Inadmissible Evidence as a Basis for Expert Testimony: A Response to Professor Carlson,* 40 VAND. L. REV. 583 (1987) (advocating unrestricted use of information reasonably relied upon by an expert).

[16] 46 M.J. 221 (C.A.A.F. 1997).

amendment to Rule 703, the court went on to say that, when the foundation for an expert's opinion includes such inadmissible evidence, the trial judge should conduct a Rule 403 balance. Although the record failed to reflect that the bench conducted such a balance there, the court found no prejudice because there was sufficient direct testimony from eyewitnesses concerning each issue.

The Rule does not restrict the adverse party from presenting the inadmissible underlying facts or data the proponent's expert relied upon. See our discussion of Rule 705. If the opposing party does so, the attack itself will often be viewed as opening the door to the proponent's rebuttal which will contain the detailed information relied upon in reaching the challenged result, information which may not have been admissible but for the challenge.

[5]   Demonstrating Reasonable Reliance

In *Zenith Radio Corp. v. Matsushita Elec. Indus. Co.,*[17] a complex civil suit, the court postulated several criteria that trial judges can use in resolving reasonable reliance questions. Although the reviewing court felt that the trial judge exceeded his powers by inappropriately substituting his opinion on reliability for the expert's, the criteria discussed below have been viewed as valuable.[18]

Among those questions the trial judge may consider in determining reliability are the following: (1) Is the opinion based on information a court has already viewed as not relevant or trustworthy? (2) Are the expert's opinions actually speculative, clearly wrong, or baseless? (3) Was the information relied upon similar to other data the expert has previously used and is familiar with? (4) Was the information collected and used solely for litigation purposes? (5) Has the expert considered the possible unreliability of his underlying data? (6) Is there anything inherently unreliable about the manner in which the expert employed otherwise valid criteria?

These questions will help trial courts insure that the data experts rely upon in court is of the same quality and reliability as the data they would have relied upon in the field, laboratory, or hospital. As our discussion of Rule 702 demonstrates, the Supreme Court in *Daubert* expects trial judges to exercise such "gatekeeping" functions as are necessary to insure that the expert's testimony rests upon a sound basis. Read together, Rules 104(a), 702, 703 and *Daubert* mandate that trial courts cannot simply delegate this important function to other expert witness.

---

[17] 505 F. Supp. 1313 (E.D. Pa. 1980), *rev'd,* 723 F.2d 238 (3d Cir. 1983), *rev'd on other grounds,* 475 U.S. 574 (1986).

[18] *See, e.g., In re* Paoli RR Litigation, 35 F.3d 717 (3d Cir. 1994) (trial judge has gatekeeper role with respect to expert testimony, including the obligation to determine the basis for reasonable reliance; under Rule 104(a), judge must make an independent determination and cannot delegate this responsibility to other experts).

[6]   Relationship of Rule 703 to Other Rules

Rule 705 provides that an expert may offer facts or data before or after giving an opinion. But, Rule 705 does not control what facts or data may be disclosed or for what purpose. Rule 703 governs what may be disclosed,[19] and often hearsay rules will dictate how facts or data may be used.

The military judge may allow reliable but inadmissible evidence to reach the court members for the purpose of explaining an expert's bases. However, Rules 702, 703, and 705, on their own are not sufficient to make this evidence admissible for the truth of the matter asserted. If the truth needs to be established, other proof will have to establish it. When evidence is presented for limited reasons, careful military judges and counsel will fashion limiting instructions pursuant to Rule 105.

The ability to formulate an effective limiting instruction may be a consideration in the military judge's decision to admit or exclude the challenged evidence. If it is important that the court members hear the testimony, but the judge believes even with a properly drawn limiting instruction, the members will misuse the evidence, Rule 703's balancing test calls for exclusion.

§ 703.03   Drafters' Analysis

Rule 703 is taken from the Federal Rule without change. The Rule is similar in scope to ¶ 138 *e* of the present *Manual,* but is potentially broader as it allows reliance upon "facts or data" whereas the present *Manual*'s limitation is phrased in terms of the personal observation, personal examination or study, or examination or study "of reports of others of a kind customarily considered in the practice of the expert's specialty." Hypothetical questions of the expert are not required by the Rule.

A limiting instruction may be appropriate if the expert while expressing the basis for an opinion states facts or data that are not themselves admissible. *See* Rule 105.

Whether Rule 703 has modified or superseded the *Frye* test for scientific evidence, *Frye v. United States,* 293 F. 1013 (D.C. Cir. 1923) is unclear and is now being litigated within the Article III courts.

§ 703.04   Drafters' Analysis (2004)

2004 Amendment: Rule 703 was modified based on the amendment to Fed. R. Evid. 703, effective 1 December 2000, and is virtually identical to its Federal Rule counterpart. It limits the disclosure to the members of

---

[19] *See, e.g.,* United States v. McCollum, 732 F.2d 1419 (9th Cir. 1984) (permissible for trial judge to allow defense expert to testify that defendant was under hypnosis when he committed a crime, but to bar videotapes offered to demonstrate the defendant's enhanced memory following hypnosis).

inadmissible information that is used as the basis of an expert's opinion. *Compare* Mil. R. Evid. 705.

§ 703.05   Annotated Cases

[1]   Basis of Expert's Opinion—Child Sexual Abuse Cases

United States Court of Appeals for the Armed Forces

United States v. Stark, 30 M.J. 328 (C.M.A. 1990): Affirming the accused's child sexual abuse conviction, the court held that the basis for an expert witness's testimony was sufficient because he had conducted personal interviews of the two child victims, their father, and examined other videotaped interviews of the children.

Air Force Court of Criminal Appeals

United States v. Nelson, 21 M.J. 711 (A.F.C.M.R. 1985): The court found that an expert's observations of a sexually abused child's interaction with anatomically correct dolls and subsequent interviews with that child were a sufficient basis for opinion testimony. The court said that "any type of opinion base that is reasonably relied upon by experts in the particular field" will generally suffice.

United States v. Benedict, 20 M.J. 939 (A.F.C.M.R. 1985): This court found no error in the government's expert witness using an article from the American Journal of Psychiatry to support her opinion that pedophilia did not amount to a mental disease or defect. The court said this Rule "permits consideration of information that is reasonably relied upon by other experts in arriving at sound opinions on the subject."

[2]   Basis of Expert's Opinion—Defense Request for Expert Witness

United States Court of Appeals for the Armed Forces

United States v. Reveles, 41 M.J. 388 (C.A.A.F. 1995): The accused was court-martialed for reckless driving and involuntary manslaughter. During trial he unsuccessfully requested that a forensic expert witness be made available. Affirming the accused's conviction and the trial court's witness denial, this court held that Rule 703 requires opinion testimony to be based on facts or data made available to the expert. Because defense counsel failed to provide the expert with such information, the court found no basis existed for the expert's testimony.

[3]   Basis of Expert's Opinion—DNA Evidence Basis

Air Force Court of Criminal Appeals

United States v. Thomas, 43 M.J. 626 (A.F.Ct.Crim.App. 1995): Affirming the accused's convictions for murder and desecrating the corpse, this court held that prosecution DNA evidence had been properly admitted because it was based on qualified expert testimony and widely accepted medical and scientific principles which established its reliability and helpfulness. The court also said that government counsel was not required to prove the absolute scientific certainty of these theories.

[4] Basis of Expert's Opinion—Foundation Inadequate

United States Court of Appeals for the Armed Forces

United States v. Dimberio, 56 M.J. 20 (C.A.A.F. 2001): The accused was convicted of assaulting his infant son with a means or force likely to cause death or grievous bodily harm. At trial, the military judge excluded testimony about the mental health of the accused's wife. This court held that the military judge did not abuse his discretion as the "evidentiary gate-keeper" by excluding testimony concerning the mental health diagnosis of the accused's wife, offered in support of the defense suggestion that the accused's wife may have been the perpetrator of the crime. The court based its decision on the fact that the defense did not lay an adequate foundation for the introduction of reputation or opinion evidence with respect to the testimony of a doctor who was going to testify that the accused's wife had a personality disorder. The court stated that the doctor did not know the accused's wife long enough to have formed a traditional opinion as to her character or to have heard about her reputation in the community, nor did the defense offer specific instances of conduct by the wife.

United States v. Armstrong, 53 M.J. 76 (2000): The Army Court of Criminal Appeals found harmless error in a key government expert witness' testimony which in part indicated that the victim exhibited conduct consistent with someone who had been sexually abused. Defense counsel objected on numerous grounds including the expert's one hour interview with the victim was insufficient foundation for her testimony. Reversing the lower court, the Court of Appeals held that the error had a substantial effect on the outcome of this case because the government's expert witness was so strong, and without her the victim's "ambiguous" and "uncertain" testimony created grave doubts as to the validity of these findings.

[5] Basis of Expert's Opinion—Hearsay "Smuggling"

United States Court of Appeals for the Armed Forces

United States v. Blazier, 69 M.J. 218 (C.A.A.F. 2010): The accused was convicted of dereliction of duty and wrongful use of controlled substances. Part of the government's proof included laboratory reports used by the supervising chemist when he testified concerning the composition of the possessed drugs. The chemist's testimony interpreting the laboratory reports relied upon machine generated laboratory reports and upon the analyses of other chemists who did not testify. The convictions were affirmed in *United States v. Blazier,* 68 M.J. 544 (A.F.Ct.Crim.App. 2008), which was decided before *Melendez-Diaz v. Massachusetts,* 129 S. Ct. 2527 (2009), held that, "certificates of analysis" used in drug prosecutions to establish the illegality of seized substances fell within the "core-class of testimonial statements" and violated the accused's Sixth Amendment rights). The convictions were reversed and the case remanded in *United States v. Blazier*, 68 M.J. 439 (C.A.A.F. 2010) (applying *Melendez-Diaz v. Massachusetts* but returning the record with specified questions concerning why the military judge did not compel the government to produce the essential laboratory witnesses). In its second look at the case, the court concluded that an expert may rely on machine-generated data because the Rules of Evidence define it as not being hearsay, and also may rely on but not repeat testimonial hearsay that is otherwise appropriate for expert opinion testimony so long as the expert's opinion is his own. The court also held that when testimonial hearsay is admitted, the Confrontation Clause is satisfied only if the declarant of that hearsay is subject to cross-examination at trial, or is unavailable but had been previously subjected to cross-examination and warned that the Confrontation Clause may not be circumvented by having an expert testify at trial to otherwise inadmissible testimonial hearsay. The court found that this occurred in violation of *Melendez-Diaz v. Massachusetts* and returned the record for a harmful error analysis.

United States v. Schap, 49 M.J. 317 (C.A.A.F. 1998): The accused was convicted of a particularly gruesome murder. He defended in part on mental responsibility grounds. However, trial defense counsel was prohibited from examining their forensic psychiatrist concerning statements the accused made during approximately 15 hours of treatment and interviews. Affirming the conviction, the court held that the accused's out-of-court-statements to his psychiatrist did not qualify for admission under either Rule 803(4)'s medical treatment exception, or this Rule's provisions for admitting the data or facts upon which an expert basis his opinion testimony. Recognizing the evidence as having "conduit problems," the court went on to say that it would not allow defense counsel to "smuggle" before the finders of fact hours of hearsay testimony without subjecting the declarant to "the crucible of cross-examination."

United States v. Harris, 46 M.J. 221 (C.A.A.F. 1997): Major Harris was convicted of drunk driving, involuntary manslaughter, and related offenses. A state highway patrolman with extensive specialized training and experience testified as a government expert witness. He established that the accused was intoxicated and that the accused's vehicle caused the skid marks leading to the deceased's body. This witness also provided opinion testimony on many other aspects of the crime scene, often based on what witnesses observed. The accused contended it was error to accept the highway patrolman's opinion testimony because it amounted to "smuggling" inadmissible hearsay into the courtroom. Rejecting the accused's contentions and affirming his convictions, the court held that the facts an expert relies upon can be based on personal knowledge, assumed facts, documents supplied by other experts, or even listening to trial testimony. When the foundation for an expert's opinion includes such inadmissible evidence, the trial judge should conduct a Rule 403 balance. While the record fails to reflect that the bench conducted such a balance here, the court found no prejudice because there was sufficient direct testimony from eyewitnesses concerning each issue.

United States v. Jackson, 38 M.J. 106 (C.M.A. 1993): The accused was convicted of using marijuana. His defense consisted mainly of attacking the government's forensic expert witness and attempting to impeach him with learned treatises. Affirming the accused's conviction, this court said military judges should give limiting instructions whenever hearsay evidence is used on cross-examination to test an expert's opinion. The instruction was required here to address "smuggling" inadmissible hearsay evidence into trial by referring to it during cross-examination.

United States v. Neeley, 25 M.J. 105 (C.M.A. 1987): Although it affirmed the accused's murder conviction, the court expressed concern over "the problem of smuggling hearsay statements into evidence under the guise of an expert witness relying on the hearsay to form an opinion." Here, a government psychologist said she believed the accused attempted to manipulate his MMPI tests, and that "it was the consensus" among five other psychologists that the test results were inflated. The court said that, if this testimony were admitted for the purpose of showing "appellant intentionally inflated the results of his tests, then the evidence [would be] clearly hearsay and not admissible." If, on the other hand, trial counsel were attempting to establish the "basis" for the expert's testimony, then "although the truth of the matter asserted is smuggled into evidence, the only true evidence that appellant inflated the test results came from the witness stand." In the court's opinion, trial judges should use Rule 403 in "resolving the admissibility of this type of hearsay evidence."

Air Force Court of Criminal Appeals

United States v. Myles, 29 M.J. 589 (A.F.C.M.R. 1989): The court held that a retired Air Force member working as a local drug abuse counselor was competent to give his opinion concerning local drug abuse customs, even though that testimony was based upon the hearsay of unnamed drug abusers.

[6] Basis of Expert's Opinion—Rape Accommodation Syndrome

United States Court of Appeals for the Armed Forces

United States v. Raya, 45 M.J. 251 (C.A.A.F. 1996): At trial, the accused challenged the government's ability to have an expert testify concerning Rape Accommodation Syndrome evidence because the expert had never personally examined the prosecutrix. Affirming the conviction, the court held that personal examinations are not required as a condition precedent to expert testimony if the expert's opinion is based on "personal knowledge, assumed facts, documents supplied by other experts, or even listening to the testimony at trial." *United States v. Houser*, 36 M.J. 392, 396 (C.M.A. 1993).

[7]   Basis of Expert's Opinion—Rape Trauma Syndrome

United States Court of Appeals for the Armed Forces

United States v. Hammond, 17 M.J. 218 (C.M.A. 1984): The court held that an expert witness's opinion about "rape trauma syndrome," which was based on her own experience, on reading the stipulation of facts, and on hearing the victim's in-court testimony, was proper. The fact that the expert did not interview or counsel the victim did not render the expert unqualified to arrive at an opinion.

[8]   Basis of Expert's Opinion—Sentencing Considerations

Army Court of Criminal Appeals

United States v. Mahaney, 33 M.J. 846 (A.C.M.R. 1991): The accused was convicted of numerous assaults upon his wife. During sentencing, and over defense objection, the military judge allowed a government expert to testify that the accused's prognosis for improvement as a result of treatment was poor. Finding no error, the court held that such rehabilitative potential evidence was admissible because it was offered by a qualified expert, and not by lay members of the accused's command.

[9]   Basis of Expert's Opinion—Sequestration

United States Court of Appeals for the Armed Forces

United States v. Croom, 24 M.J. 373 (C.M.A. 1987): Reading this Rule and Rule 615 together, the court held that the military judge properly allowed government and defense expert witnesses to remain in the court-room during the entire trial. In reaching the proper balance between a "party's need for the witness' presence against the public considerations behind the general rule of sequestration," the court said it "perceive[d] little, if any, reason for sequestering a witness who is to testify in an expert capacity only and not to the facts of the case." In these instances "some flexibility in applying the general rule of witness exclusion" will assist the parties, allowing them to develop their opinion evidence more quickly and efficiently.

[10]   Basis of Expert's Opinion—Underlying Basis

Army Court of Criminal Appeals

United States v. George, 40 M.J. 540 (A.C.M.R. 1994): The accused was charged with using cocaine on a single occasion. Defense counsel unsuc-cessfully attempted to have his forensic expert testify that the small amount of drugs present in the accused's urine could have been innocently digested, and that there were studies documenting such results. The military judge excluded this testimony because it relied on unadmitted literature. Reversing the accused's conviction, this court held that the underlying basis for an expert's opinion need not be admitted, and that the military judge's actions here interfered with the accused's right to present a defense.

[11]   Basis of Expert's Opinion—Value of Property Assessments

Army Court of Criminal Appeals

United States v. Hood, 12 M.J. 890 (A.C.M.R. 1982): Over defense objection, the government was permitted to call a CID agent who offered his opinion on the value of stolen black market goods. Affirming both findings and sentence, the court held that Rule 703 "permits an expert to base his opinion upon facts or data that he has reviewed or that he has been told about in order to form his opinion."

[12]   Basis of Expert's Opinion—Weight of Expert's Testimony

Air Force Court of Criminal Appeals

United States v. Staley, 36 M.J. 896 (A.F.C.M.R. 1993): Affirming the accused's indecent assault convictions, the court held that no error occurred when an expert witness was prohibited from saying that his previous testimony before an administrative board, on related issues, led to favorable results for the accused there. Both the trial and appellate courts viewed this evidence as misleading, confusing, and not helpful. The record already contained significant foundational evidence of the accused's personal and medical history. This court held that very little would have been gained had the expert's opinion about related administrative hearings been admitted.

United States v. Langston, 32 M.J. 894 (A.F.C.M.R. 1991): In this bad check case, the court held that trial counsel was properly allowed to demonstrate the limited experience of an expert witness, even though that witness had been provided by the government. The court went on to say that this result might have been different had trial counsel challenged the witness' qualifications as an expert.

§ 704.01 Official Text

Rule 704. Opinion on Ultimate Issue.

Testimony in the form of an opinion or inference otherwise admissible is not objectionable because it embraces an ultimate issue to be decided by the trier of fact.

---

§ 704.02 Editorial Comment

[1] Using the Rule

Military Rule 704 substantially follows Federal Rule of Evidence 704—but only subdivision (a) of that Rule. It provides that testimony in the form of an opinion or inference is not objectionable on the grounds that it embraces an ultimate issue to be decided by the finders of fact.[1]

In common law courts, objections to opinion testimony on an ultimate issue would usually be sustained as invading the factfinder's province. This result produced substantial and confusing litigation concerning what was an ultimate issue, and what kinds of testimony amounted to usurpation of the factfinder's role. Prior to Military Rule 704, courts-martial tended to follow the common law approach, although practice here was often uncertain. Rule 704 clarifies matters.

The military and federal drafters created this provision largely to eliminate expert witness testimony frustrations.[2] Under previous court-martial practice, experts were allowed to provide detailed explanations and interpretations of pivotal trial issues, but they were not permitted to give their opinion on what the testimony meant— *i.e.*, actually resolve an ultimate issue. The expert's conclusion about a contested fact or issue was improper comment. Rule 704 views the expert's ultimate issue comments as helpful because they place the expert's testimony in a context that the court members can understand and apply.

[2] Military Judge Responsibilities

To properly execute this provision, the bench has substantial "gatekeeping" functions to maintain. Many of these functions are similar to those discussed in Rules 702 and 703 pursuant to the Supreme Court's guidance in *Daubert v. Merrell Dow Pharms.*[3] and its progeny. For example, it is the military judge's responsibility to insure that the expert's ultimate issue

---

[1] For a discussion of various ultimate issue problems, *see* Traster, *The Ultimate Issue Rule in State and Federal Courts,* 27 DEFENSE L.J. 307 (1978).

[2] *See, e.g.,* United States v. Setser, 568 F.3d 482 (5th Cir. 2009) (error for expert to testify that defendant's operation was a "Ponzi scheme" or constituted a "security fraud").

[3] 509 U.S. 579 (1993).

opinion testimony is actually helpful. If the expert's testimony is comprised of only conclusory statements, addresses guilt or innocence, attempts to explain and apply the law, tells the factfinders who to believe, or is based on inappropriate or invalid data, then it should be exclude as unhelpful.

Similarly, the trial bench has a responsibility to insure that factfinders will accurately apply ultimate issue opinion testimony. The military judge can accomplish this result by instructing the members that they are the sole arbiters of guilt, innocence, or punishment (when a court-martial reaches that stage), credibility, weight, and inferences that can be drawn from all the evidence. The judge may also want to remind court members that expert witnesses are not entitled to more or greater credibility than other lay witnesses simply because they are experts. Although Rule 105 generally requires counsel to request limiting instructions before the military judge provides them, because expert witness testimony on an ultimate issue might be critical to the outcome and is difficult for court members to properly evaluate unaided, the judge may want to take the initiative and ask counsel whether instructions are requested.

[3] Lay vs. Expert Testimony

It should be noted that Rule 704 does not distinguish between lay and expert witnesses. Any opinion that is otherwise admissible can be used despite the fact that it relates to an ultimate issue in the case. But it is important to keep in mind that the testimony must otherwise qualify for admission. This means that lay witness testimony must satisfy the requirements of Rule 701, and that expert testimony must satisfy the requirements of Rules 702 and 703.

This also means that unhelpful testimony, that is testimony not based on the rational perceptions of a lay witness or expert testimony based on facts or data not reasonably relied upon by similar experts, would not be admissible. However, because an expert's ultimate opinion testimony is likely to be more substantive and authoritative than a layman's opinion and more helpful to the finders of fact, it is also more likely to be admitted.[4]

[4] Opinions on Guilt, Truthfulness, and Legal Conclusions

The Drafters' Analysis plainly states that Rule 704 "does not permit a witness to testify about his or her opinion on the guilt or innocence of an accused, or to state legal opinions."[5] This is because the military judge is

---

[4] *See, e.g.,* Mitroff v. Xomox Corp., 797 F.2d 271 (6th Cir. 1986) (ultimate issue opinion testimony by lay witnesses viewed as unlikely to help factfinders).

[5] *Compare* United States v. Ness, 665 F.2d 248 (8th Cir. 1981) (judge properly rejected testimony by defense witnesses that defendant never intended to defraud or injure a bank), *with* United States v. Lipscomb, 14 F.3d 1236 (7th Cir. 1994) (conclusion of law enforcement experts held qualified to opine that circumstances and behavior indicated intent to distribute drugs was not a legal conclusion as to specific individual intent).

responsible for providing the members with all statements concerning the law.[6] Further, no witness helps the court members by offering a judgment on ultimate guilt and innocence.[7] Such testimony adds nothing to the case information court members need to properly perform their duties.[8]

However, in some instances the line between impermissible and permissible opinion testimony is difficult to draw.[9] For example, federal and military courts have permitted experts to offer opinions about observed conduct being the *modus operandi* of counterfeiting[10] or narcotics dealing,[11] seized drugs being controlled substances,[12] the voice on an incriminating tape being the accused's,[13] and an accused's conduct being participation in an aggravated assault.[14] Similarly, while experts are not permitted to provide testimony about who is telling the truth or lying, expert witnesses can testify that their opinions are based on an assumption that the accused or any other witness whose statements were relevant to the expert's conclusions was being truthful when he or she spoke with the expert.[15]

[5]   The Short-lived Military Rule of Evidence 704(b) Exception

As originally written, Rule 704 contained no exceptions. However, in April 1985, the Rule was amended by the addition of subdivision (b),[16]

---

[6] *See* United States v. Popejoy, 578 F.2d 1346 (10th Cir.), *cert. denied,* 439 U.S. 896 (1978).

[7] *See* our discussion of this issue in Rule 702.

[8] *Compare* United States v. Fogg, 652 F.2d 551 (5th Cir. 1981) (held proper for IRS agent to testify as to the correct tax treatment of certain transactions) *with* United States v. Baskes, 649 F.2d 471 (7th Cir. 1980) (upheld restrictions on questions of witness about legal implications of acts).

[9] *See, e.g.,* United States v. Hearst, 563 F.2d 1331 (9th Cir. 1977), *cert. denied,* 435 U.S. 1000 (1978) (upholding the introduction of expert opinion on human motivation to rob a bank).

[10] *See* United States v. Burchfield, 719 F.2d 356 (11th Cir. 1983). *See also* United States v. Radseck, 718 F.2d 233 (7th Cir. 1983) (IRS agent permitted to give opinion that a defendant would not have had large sums of money at his house in light of the types of financial accounts and arrangements he had established).

[11] *See* United States v. Carson, 702 F.2d 351 (2d Cir. 1983). *See also* United States v. Dunn, 846 F.2d 761 (D.C. Cir. 1988) (opinion testimony to the effect that evidence found indicated a retail drug operation did not violate 704(b) to the extent it addressed defendant's mens rea); United States v. Lipscomb, 14 F.3d 1236 (7th Cir. 1994) (conclusion of law enforcement experts held qualified to opine that circumstances and behavior indicated intent to distribute drugs was not a legal conclusion as to specific individual intent).

[12] *See* United States v. Accordino, 15 M.J. 825 (A.F.C.M.R. 1983).

[13] *See* United States v. Bice-Bey, 701 F.2d 1086 (4th Cir. 1983).

[14] *See* United States v. Bell, 21 M.J. 662 (A.F.C.M.R. 1985).

[15] *See* our discussion of Rules 608 and 702. *See also* United States v. Hill-Dunning, 26 M.J. 260 (C.M.A. 1988).

[16] Under the provision of Rule 1102, the federal version automatically went into effect on

which is patterned after Federal Rule 704. Both the Military and Federal Rule were a product of the Insanity Defense Reform Act of 1984, and read as follows:

(a) General rule. Except as provided in subdivision (b), testimony in the form of an opinion or inference otherwise admissible is not objectionable because it embraces an ultimate issue to be decided by the trier of fact.

(b) Exception. No expert witness testifying with respect to the mental state or condition of an accused may state an opinion or inference as to whether the accused did or did not have the mental state or condition constituting an element of the offense charged or of a defense thereto. Such ultimate issues are matters for the trier of fact alone.

Subdivision (b) prohibited expert testimony that would offer an opinion or inference on the issue of the accused's mental state or condition where such constituted an element or defense to the charged offense. Thus, for example, the expert could not offer an opinion on the accused's mental responsibility at the time of the offense, a predisposition to commit an offense (on the issue of entrapment), or on the issue of intent or meditation.

The purpose of this change, as noted in the report of the Senate Committee on the Judiciary, quoted in part in the Drafter's Analysis, was to return to the factfinder the task of determining the ultimate issue of the accused's mental state. In short, it was designated to quell the battle of the experts in the controversial area of insanity. But, as the Rule itself clearly stated, it covered more than just the issue of sanity.

Particularly telling is the statement of the American Psychiatric Association that was included in the Senate Committee's report. It reads as follows:

[I]t is clear that psychiatrists are experts in medicine, not the law. As such, it is clear that the psychiatrist's first obligation and expertise in the courtroom is to "do psychiatry," i.e., to present medical information and opinion about the defendant's mental state and motivation and to explain in detail the reason for his medical-psychiatric conclusions. When, however, "ultimate issue" questions are formulated by the law and put to the expert witness who must then say "yea" or "nay," then the expert witness is required to make a leap in logic. He no longer addresses himself to medical concepts but instead must infer or intuit what is in fact unspeakable, namely, the probable relationship between medical concepts and legal or moral constructs such as free will. These impermissible leaps in logic made by expert witnesses confuse the jury. [Footnote omitted.] Juries thus find themselves listening to conclusory and seemingly contradictory psychiatric testimony that defendants are either "sane" or "insane" or that they do or do not meet the relevant legal

April 10, 1985. However, the change was never published in the *Manual for Courts-Martial*.

test for insanity. This state of affairs does considerable injustice to psychiatry and, we believe, possibly to criminal defendants. In fact, in many criminal insanity trials both prosecution and defense psychiatrists do agree about the nature and even the extent of mental disorder exhibited by the defendant at the time of the act.

Psychiatrists, of course, must be permitted to testify fully about the defendant's diagnosis, mental state, and motivation (in clinical and common sense terms) at the time of the alleged act so as to permit the jury or judge to reach the ultimate conclusion about which they and only they are expert. Determining whether a criminal defendant was legally insane is a matter for legal fact finders, not for experts.

It is important to note that the exception was limited to barring *expert* opinion. Lay opinions on the issue of the accused's mental state or condition could be given—even when they went to the ultimate issue. Congress, and the military drafters, seemed more concerned with the fact that experts such as psychiatrists and mental health experts were invading the province of the court than with the fact that the issue of mental state is often an ultimate issue.

In February 1986, the President restored the original language of the Military Rule 704. Thus, the current language tracks the 1980 version. As the drafters note in their 1986 Analysis, *below*, the April 1985 change to Rule 704, which was never actually published in the *Manual for Courts-Martial*, was intended to go hand in hand with other changes in the affirmative defense of insanity. Because those changes were not incorporated into the Uniform Code of Military Justice, the drafters recommended that the federal version not be applied to military practice.

[6]   Interplay with the Lack of Mental Responsibility Defense

[a]   Changes in the U.C.M.J

Congress followed the lead of the Comprehensive Crime Control Act of 1984, which redefined the federal insanity defense and shifted the burden of persuasion on that defense to the accused, and enacted, as part of the National Defense Authorization Act for Fiscal Year 1987, Title VIII (Military Justice Amendments of 1986) to accomplish a similar result. The statute amends chapter 47 of title 10, United States Code (the Uniform Code of Military Justice) to add § 850(a), that applies to offenses committed after 14 November 1986, the effective date of the Act. The new provision imposes a burden upon the accused to prove lack of mental responsibility by clear and convincing evidence. Lack of mental responsibility is limited to proof that "as a result of a severe mental disease or defect, [the accused] was unable to appreciate the nature and quality or the wrongfulness of the acts." It reads as follows:

§ 850a. Art. 50a. Defense of lack of mental responsibility

(a) It is an affirmative defense in a trial by court-martial that, at the time of the commission of the acts constituting the offense, the accused, as a result of a severe mental disease or defect, was unable to appreciate the nature and quality or the wrongfulness of the acts. Mental disease or defect does not otherwise constitute a defense.

(b) The accused has the burden of proving the defense of lack of mental responsibility by clear and convincing evidence.

(c) Whenever lack of mental responsibility of the accused with respect to an offense is properly at issue, the military judge, or the president of a court-martial without a military judge, shall instruct the members of the court as to the defense of lack of mental responsibility under this section and charge them to find the accused—

(1) guilty;

(2) not guilty; or

(3) not guilty only by reason of lack of mental responsibility.

(d) Subsection (c) does not apply to a court-martial composed of a military judge only. In the case of a court-martial composed of a military judge only, whenever lack of mental responsibility of the accused with respect to an offense is properly at issue, the military judge shall find the accused—

(1) guilty;

(2) not guilty; or

(3) not guilty only by reason of lack of mental responsibility.

(e) twithstanding the provisions of section 852 of this title (article 52), the accused shall be found not guilty only by reason of lack of mental responsibility I—

(1) a majority of the members of the court-martial present at the time the vote is taken determines that the defense of lack of mental responsibility has been established; or

(2) in the case of a court-martial composed of a military judge only, the military judge determines that the defense of lack of mental responsibility has been established.

[b]   Conforming Changes in the Manual for Courts-Martial

Several important changes to the *Manual for Courts Martial* were made to implement the statute. R.C.M. 706(c) was amended to clarify the questions that are to be addressed in a mental examination of an accused. R.C.M. 916 was amended to conform to the statutory allocation of the burden of persuasion and to limit the scope of the mental responsibility defense as prescribed in the statute. The amendment also plainly states that there is no partial mental responsibility defense and that evidence of lack of mental responsibility short of a complete defense is not admissible to negate the alleged mens rea associated with an offense. R.C.M. 921(c) was amended to set forth the voting order when a mental responsibility defense is raised. The amendment provides that the members shall first determine whether the prosecution has proven the elements of an offense beyond a reasonable doubt. Only thereafter will the members address the mental responsibility defense. Should a majority of the members find that the defendant has satisfied the burden of persuasion, they shall return a verdict of not guilty only by reason of lack of mental responsibility. But, if a majority does not find the burden satisfied, the guilty verdict stands.[17]

Although Congress and the President followed in large measure the civilian approach to the insanity defense as set forth in the 1984 comprehensive revision of the defense, Rule 704(b) was rejected. As the amendment to the Analysis provides, the drafters considered and decided against adding the section to the Rule. They reasoned that the statutory qualifications for military court members reduces the risk that they will be unduly influenced by opinions of experts, even on ultimate issues.

This choice was sound. Military judges and court members can profit from full and complete testimony from experts, and they can benefit from understanding how an expert's basic and intermediate diagnoses and findings relate to the ultimate questions that must be determined under the statutory definition of the affirmative defense of lack of mental responsibility. The addition of subdivision (b) to Federal Rule of Evidence 704 might have the perverse effect of reducing the capacity of jurors in civilian courts to evaluate and use expert's testimony.[18]

Military trial and appellate courts are well versed in the requirements of Rules 702 and 703. The restrictions on expert testimony found in those provisions, and the flexibility provided by Rule 705, should assure that in courts-martial, expert testimony is helpful and soundly based. No need for subdivision (b) appears, and the drafters' decision should spare military courts from the wooden, inflexible approach of the amended Federal Rule.

§ 704.03   Drafters' Analysis

Rule 704 is taken from the Federal Rule verbatim. The *Manual* for Courts-Martial is silent on the issue and current military law is unsettled. The Rule does not permit the witness to testify as to his or her opinion as to the guilt or innocence of the accused or to state legal opinions. Rather it simply allows testimony involving an issue which must be decided by the trier of fact. Although the two may be closely related, they are distinct as a matter of law.

---

[17] *See also* Schlueter, MILITARY CRIMINAL JUSTICE: PRACTICE AND PROCEDURE, § 10-5(A)(2) (7th ed. 2008).

[18] *See, e.g.,* 3 S. Saltzburg, M. Martin & D. Capra, FEDERAL RULES OF EVIDENCE MANUAL § 704.02[5] (9th ed. 2006).

§ 704.04   Drafters' Analysis (1986)

Fed. R. Evid. 704(b), by operation of Mil. R. Evid. 1102, became effective in the military as Mil. R. Evid. 704(b) on 10 April 1985. The Joint-Service Committee considers Fed. R. Evid. 704(b) an integral part of the Insanity Defense Report Act, Ch. IV, Pub. L. No. 98-473, 98 Stat. 2058 (1984), (hereafter, the Act). Because proposed legislation to implement those provisions of the Act relating to insanity as an affirmative defense had not yet been enacted in the UCMJ by the date of this Executive Order, the Committee recommended the President rescind the application of Fed. R. Evid. 704(b) to the military. Even though in effect since 10 April 1985, this change was never published in the Manual.

§ 704.05   Drafters' Analysis (1987)

While writing the Manual provisions to implement the enactment of Article 50a, UCMJ ("Military Justice Amendments of 1986," National Defense Authorization Act for Fiscal Year 1987, Pub. L. No. 99-661, Stat., (1986)), the drafters rejected adoption of Fed. R. Evid. 704(b). The statutory qualifications for military court members reduce the risk that military court members will be unduly influenced by the presentation of ultimate opinion testimony from psychiatric experts.

§ 704.06   Annotated Cases

[1]   Opinion on Ultimate Issue—Child Sexual Abuse

United States Court of Appeals for the Armed Forces

United States v. Hays, 62 M.J. 158 (C.A.A.F. 2005): The accused was convicted of soliciting another to commit carnal knowledge with a child. During the government's case in chief, an FBI witness was qualified as an expert in the behavioral aspects of child sexual victimization. Trial defense counsel objected, contending that much of his testimony was improper opinion on the ultimate issue of whether an actual solicitation occurred. Affirming the conviction, the court held that a qualified expert may testify about the strategies employed by sexual predators to encourage others to commit sexual offenses against children, and that the expert may also offer his opinion as to whether the events proved in court could be seen as part of such a strategy.

United States v. Birdsall, 47 M.J.404 (C.A.A.F. 1998): The accused's convictions for sexually abusing his two young sons were reversed because a government expert witness was permitted to testify that, in his opinion, the charged sexual abuse had "in fact occurred." The court found such testimony to be inadmissible because it was not useful to the jury. Relying on *United States v. Whitted,* 11 F.3d 782, 785 (8th Cir. 1993), the court held that expert witnesses testifying in this area can inform the jury of: (1) the characteristics of sexually abused children; (2) compare those characteristics to the characteristics exhibited by the alleged victim; (3) the victim's statements identifying the abuser as a family member if the victim was properly motivated to ensure the statements' trustworthiness and (4) in summary fashion discuss the medical evidence and express an opinion that this evidence is either consistent or inconsistent with the victim's allegations of sexual abuse.

[2] Opinion on Ultimate Issue—Chemical Analysis

Air Force Court of Criminal Appeals

United States v. Accordino, 15 M.J. 825 (A.F.C.M.R. 1983): An Air Force chemist's opinion testimony describing the chemical nature of certain substances used by the accused was properly admitted even though, in the court's view, "it embrace[d] an ultimate issue to be decided by the trier of fact."

[3] Opinion on Ultimate Issue—Eyewitness Identification

Army Court of Criminal Appeals

United States v. Brown, 45 M.J. 514 (Army Ct.Crim.App. 1996): The accused was convicted of stealing a utility company truck and of various other offenses. A key trial issue concerned the vehicle driver's eyewitness identification of the accused. To impeach the government's evidence, defense counsel sought to use an expert witness who specialized in cross-racial identifications. The trial judge prohibited the witness from testifying. Finding error but no prejudice, the court affirmed the accused's convictions holding that it was improper to exclude the expert's testimony simply because it affected an ultimate issue in the case the identification's accuracy. The court went on to say that "Giving the members information upon which to base a credibility determination is not a valid basis for excluding the testimony."

[4] Opinion on Ultimate Issue—Opinions on Guilt

Army Court of Criminal Appeals

United States v. Bell, 21 M.J. 662 (A.C.M.R. 1985): Recognizing that "opinion testimony on the guilt or innocence of the accused . . . is viewed as unhelpful," and thus should not be admitted, the court nevertheless allowed a government witness to testify concerning the opinion he formed about the accused's complicity in an aggravated assault case.

[5] Opinion on Ultimate Issue—Intent Evidence

United States Court of Appeals for the Armed Forces

United States v. Combs, 39 M.J. 288 (C.M.A. 1994): The accused was convicted of murdering his eighteen-month-old son and battering his three-year-old daughter. Affirming the Service Court of Criminal Appeals in setting aside the murder conviction, this court held that the military judge improperly excluded defense expert testimony concerning the accused's intent to commit murder. The court found this evidence to be helpful (*see* Rule 702), of a type reasonably relied upon by experts in the field (*see* Rule 703), and not objectionable because it concerned one of the central issues at trial. The court went on to recognize that the Rules of Evidence liberally allow for expert testimony which will assist the trier of fact.

[6] Opinion on Ultimate Issue—Mental Illness Definitions

Air Force Court Criminal Appeals

United States v. Benedict, 20 M.J. 939 (A.F.C.M.R. 1985): The accused's conviction for indecent acts with a ten-year-old girl was affirmed despite his contention that it was error for the trial judge to admit expert testimony which indicated that "pedophilia does not meet the definition of mental disease or defect as contemplated in military law." The court went on to say that the testimony was not improper simply because it embraced the legal definition of mental illness, and that the trial court properly exercised its discretion by admitting the evidence.

United States v. Irvin, 13 M.J. 749 (A.F.C.M.R. 1982): Convicted of killing her young adopted child, the accused unsuccessfully contended that "the military judge erred by permitting psychiatrist's testimony amounting to ultimate legal conclusions under the guise of medical diagnosis." The reviewing court found that the challenged evidence did not "in any way usurp the function of the members in ultimately deciding both the cause of the injuries and the accused's criminal responsibility therefor."

[7] Opinion on Ultimate Issue—Prejudicial to Good Order and Discipline

Navy-Marine Corps Court of Criminal Appeals

United States v. Jackson, 54 M.J. 527 (N.M.Ct.Crim.App. 2000): Affirming the accused's rape and adultery convictions, this court held that no error occurred when the accused's commanding officer testified that in his opinion, the accused's conduct was prejudicial to good order and discipline. The court highlighted that opinion testimony on an ultimate issue is admissible as long as the witness does not offer an opinion on guilt or innocence.

[8] Opinion on Ultimate Issue—Truthful Testimony Opinions

United States Court of Appeals for the Armed Forces

United States v. Diaz, 59 M.J. 79 (C.A.A.F. 2003): An officer panel convicted the accused of unpremeditated murder and assault upon his infant daughter. In limine, and at various other times during trial, defense counsel requested and was granted an order prohibiting two government expert witnesses from testifying that it was their opinion the accused murdered his daughter. Irrespective of the court's orders and the trial counsel's assurances that such testimony would not be offered, both witnesses testified in the prohibited manner. Reversing the accused's convictions and sentence, this court held that the questioned testimony created prejudicial error because it had invaded the court members' exclusive function to weigh the evidence.

United States v. Hill-Dunning, 26 M.J. 260 (C.M.A. 1988): The accused was convicted of larceny and submitting a false official statement which erroneously indicated she was still married. During trial, the military judge allowed a defense expert to establish that the accused used "coping mechanisms [to] unconsciously deny and repress" her divorce, but did not permit the expert "to express her opinion as to whether or not the accused actually knew whether she was married or divorced at a certain period." Affirming the conviction, but holding that the judge's ruling was "too broad," the court said that, while this witness could have testified that "her expert opinion was based on her assumption that the accused was being truthful, she was properly prevented from saying that "in her opinion, the accused was being truthful."

United States v. Arruza, 26 M.J. 234 (C.M.A. 1988): This Army Chaplain's child sexual abuse conviction was affirmed, even though a psychiatrist testified that the victim was telling the truth about her "sexual encounter" with the accused. The court said it has "consistently held that child-abuse experts are not permitted to opine as to the credibility or believability of victims or other witnesses."

United States v. White, 25 M.J. 50 (C.M.A. 1987): Although it is permissible for an expert witness on child abuse to relate out-of-court statements received from the victims of such crimes, the court held that the expert may not "express an opinion that he believes [those] statements."

United States v. Petersen, 24 M.J. 283 (C.M.A. 1987): Charged with sexually molesting his adolescent daughter, the accused's court-martial was largely a "contest where the members either believed the victim, whose testimony was not free from contradiction, or appellant." Part of the government's case included a child sexual abuse expert witness who stated that she "greatly believed" the victim's testimony. Reversing the conviction, the court held that although the witness may have been an expert "in the general area of child sexual abuse . . . her expertise did not extend to the specific issue of the credibility of such victims . . . [and] we have, thus far, rejected this type of testimony as being without the ambit of Mil. R. Evid. 704 or 608. . . ."

Air Force Court of Criminal Appeals

United States v. Garcia, 40 M.J. 533 (A.F.C.M.R. 1994): The accused was convicted of taking indecent liberties with a thirteen-year-old female. At trial, defense counsel unsuccessfully attempted to introduce expert testimony attacking the reliability of several witnesses who identified the accused. The trial judge prohibited this expert from testifying because she thought his testimony would invade the court members' providence to determine witness credibility. Finding error but no prejudice, the court held that admitting information which helped the finders of fact make difficult credibility calls was appropriate.

United States v. Farrar, 25 M.J. 856 (A.F.C.M.R. 1988): In this cocaine abuse case, the court held that proffered defense testimony from a drug abuse counselor indicating that his experiences permitted "him to make a judgment whether the accused was truthful when she denied cocaine use" had been properly excluded. Relying on *United States v. Cameron,* 21 M.J. 59 (C.M.A. 1985), the court stated that this Rule's "relaxation on admitting opinions on the ultimate issue did not extend to opinion testimony on the guilt or innocence of the accused, for such opinions were viewed as unhelpful."

United States v. Wynn, 23 M.J. 726 (A.F.C.M.R. 1986): The trial judge's decision to allow a store detective to testify that "in her opinion, the accused was intentionally secreting merchandise with no thought of paying for it" was proper. The court held that this witness did no more than relate her basis for apprehending the accused, and that her testimony was not a comment or opinion concerning the accused's intention to commit the crime charged or "the ultimate question of guilt or innocence."

United States v. Wagner, 20 M.J. 758 (A.F.C.M.R. 1985): The court held that a security policeman's opinion as to whether a confessing suspect's pretrial statement was truthful should not have been admitted because it was used to "assist the members in making their determination on appellant's credibility, which was one of the ultimate issues of the instant case. This is where the trial judge erred, Rule 704 notwithstanding." We would have preferred that the court ground its opinion in Rule 702, finding that no scientific, technical or other specialized training qualifies an individual "as an expert on 'truthtelling in confessions.' "

§ 705.01   Official Text

> ### Rule 705.   Disclosure of Facts or Data Underlying Expert Opinion.
>
> The expert may testify in terms of opinion or inference and give the expert's reasons therefor without prior disclosure of the underlying facts or data, unless the military judge requires otherwise. The expert may in any event be required to disclose the underlying facts or data on cross-examination.

§ 705.02   Editorial Comment

[1]   Using the Rule

This provision is taken from Federal Rule 705. It governs the form and timing of an expert's testimony. Before the Rules were adopted, courts disagreed on whether the data used by experts in formulating their opinions had to be established on direct examination, as a condition precedent to receiving the expert's testimony, or whether it could be assumed as valid subject to cross-examination. Rule 705 answers this question by placing responsibility for disclosing infirmities in an expert's basis of opinion upon opposing counsel.[1]

Rule 705 provides the direct examiner with greater flexibility than the common law allowed. It permits opinion to be offered before, or after, introduction of the underlying facts or data. Thus, counsel may proceed in a manner best calculated to assist the members. Rule 705 does not authorize any disclosure of fact or data not otherwise admissible. The judge decides under Rule 703 whether to permit disclosure. Assuming that the judge permits disclosure, the otherwise inadmissible information may be introduced through the expert during direct examination as a way of bolstering the expert's testimony.

But, the drafters did not require this information or any other to be established during direct examination. They left it to the proponent's discretion, apparently recognizing that there are times when such proof will only confuse the finders of fact and waste the court's time. However, to the extent errors or inconsistencies reside in the expert's testimony, opposing counsel has the motive and opportunity to establish those weaknesses during cross. Opposing counsel may force disclosure of the bases for an expert opinion. Doing so will open the door for the proponents to fully explain the underlying facts and data.

---

[1] *See, e.g.,* Smith v. Ford Motor Company, 626 F.2d 784 (10th Cir. 1980) (burden of establishing weaknesses in expert's opinion and assumptions is upon opposing counsel).

While it appears that the proponent has a great deal of leeway in concluding whether to present the underlying facts or data during direct, this choice may be academic only. Expert testimony is often complex and difficult to understand. Medical and other experts have unique and highly technical vocabularies that often make it difficult for laymen to understand their testimony. Realizing these problems causes experienced counsel to provide as much explicative information as possible early in the expert's testimony.

[2] The Right to Cross-Examine

Under the Rule an expert may give opinions or state inferences on direct examination without disclosing the underlying facts or data. On cross-examination, the Rule states that the expert "may in any event be required to disclose the underlying facts." This is a confusing Rule.

It seems that the drafters intended to assure that the cross-examiner always would be able to probe the basis for an expert opinion. Yet, the second sentence of the Rule seems to suggest that the trial judge *may* permit the cross-examiner to inquire into the underlying facts, but that there is some discretion to deny an opportunity to do so. We can think of few, if any, circumstances in which cross-examination about the basis of expert opinion should be denied. Of course, under Rule 403 this examination may be restricted in length and scope in order to avoid confusion and waste of time. But some cross-examination would seem to be required. Indeed, several courts have suggested that the government has an obligation "not to obstruct a criminal defendant's cross-examination of expert testimony."[2]

[3] Disclosure on Direct Examination

The first sentence of the Rule gives the trial judge authority to require an expert to disclose the facts or data upon which an opinion or inference is based before stating the opinion or inference. In our view, if it is likely that a challenge will be made to the propriety of admitting a particular opinion, it would make sense for the trial judge to assure that the facts or data upon which the opinion is based are first presented in order to prevent any opinion that might not be permissible from actually coming before court members, who might have a difficult time striking it from their minds thereafter.[3]

§ 705.03 Drafters' Analysis

Rule 705 is taken from the Federal Rule without change and is similar in result to the requirement in ¶ 138 *e* of the present *Manual* that the "expert may be required, on direct or cross-examination, to specify the data upon which his opinion was based and to relate the details of his observation,

---

[2] *See* United States v. Mangan, 575 F.2d 32 (2d Cir.), *cert. denied,* 439 U.S. 931 (1978).

[3] *See, e.g.,* United States v. Barton, 731 F.2d 669 (10th Cir. 1984) (government could ask defense expert what a firearm test actually showed as part of cross-examination).

examination, or study." Unlike the present *Manual,* Rule 705 requires disclosure on direct examination only when the military judge so requires.

§ 705.04   Annotated Cases

[1]   Disclosure of Basis—Balancing under Rule 403

Air Force Court of Criminal Appeals

United States v. Cole, 29 M.J. 873 (A.F.C.M.R. 1990): Setting aside the sentence in the accused's child sexual abuse case, the court held that "there is a limit to how far counsel may go in inquiring into the basis for an expert opinion. Military judges should be alert to this issue and apply the balancing test of Mil. R. Evid. 403 . . . ," and discuss limiting instructions with counsel. Unless military judges are vigilant in using this provision, inadmissible extrinsic offense and other improper evidence will find its way into the record of trial.

[2]   Disclosure of Basis—Child Abuse Cases

United States Court of Appeals for the Armed Forces

United States v. Jones, 26 M.J. 197 (C.M.A. 1988): Even though the court members called an expert witness concerning a retarded victim's reaction to child sexual abuse, the court found no error in government counsel's eliciting "the underlying basis for such an opinion."

[3]   Disclosure of Basis—Disclosure, not Hearsay Exception

United States Court of Appeals for the Armed Forces

United States v. Harris, 46 M.J. 221 (C.A.A.F 1997): Major Harris was convicted of drunk driving, involuntary manslaughter, and related offenses. A state highway patrolman with extensive specialized training and experience testified as a government expert witness. He established that the accused was intoxicated and that the accused's vehicle caused the skid marks leading to the deceased's body. This witness also provided opinion testimony on many other aspects of the crime scene, often based on what witnesses observed. The accused contended it was error to accept the highway patrolman's opinion testimony because it amounted to "smuggling" inadmissible hearsay before the court. Affirming the accused's convictions, the court held that an expert's testimony is often based on what would otherwise be inadmissible testimony. However, Rule 705 allows opposing counsel to cross-examine the expert and disclose such weaknesses. The court also noted that Rule 705 should not be viewed as an exception to the hearsay rule, but as a means for disclosing that the expert's testimony may be based on hearsay, admissible or otherwise.

[4]   Disclosure of Basis—Extrinsic Offense Evidence

Air Force Court of Criminal Appeals

United States v. Plott, 35 M.J. 512 (A.F.C.M.R. 1992): A general court-martial convicted the accused of rape, adultery, and child sexual abuse. During findings, a defense expert stated that the accused had a docile and passive character. Trial counsel cross-examined the witness about the accused's previous violent outbursts. Defense counsel contended it was improper to use other crimes evidence in this manner. Affirming the accused's convictions, the court said no error occurred, because trial counsel simply used evidence contained in the same records relied upon by the expert.

[5] Disclosure of Basis—Hearsay Problems Using the Opinions of Other Experts

United States Court of Appeals for the Armed Forces

United States v. Neeley, 25 M.J. 105 (C.M.A. 1987): In a concurring opinion affirming the accused's premeditated murder conviction, the court reasoned that "although an expert should be allowed to testify that he has consulted other experts and considered their opinions in formulating his own conclusions, the specifics of the other experts' opinions cannot be elicited on direct examination, if the hearsay prohibition is to be respected." The court observed, however, that opposing counsel may bring to the factfinder's attention "any details about opinions that were relied upon by an expert."

[6] Disclosure of Basis—Judge's Role

Air Force Court of Criminal Appeals

United States v. Gill, 37 M.J. 501 (A.F.C.M.R. 1993): The accused was convicted of lethal assaults on his 4-month-old daughter. During an Article 39(a) session concerning mental responsibility issues, the trial judge compared the evidence in this case with similar propositions from other cases he had been involved with. Affirming the accused's convictions, this court said it was not improper for the military judge to rely on information gleaned from general experience and common sense. The bench's statements were consistent with the accused's right to confrontation, because they were not the product of any special expertise or training and were made known to both parties so that they might offer relevant testimony on the issue.

[7] Disclosure of Basis—Lay Witnesses

Army Court of Criminal Appeals

United States v. Peterson, 26 M.J. 906 (A.C.M.R. 1988): During the sentencing portion of the accused's drug distribution trial, a defense witness testified about the accused's good character. Without objection, trial counsel subsequently asked the witness if he maintained that opinion in light of the accused's conviction. The witness said he did. Affirming the conviction, the court held that a lay witness who has given an opinion on direct examination may be called upon to give his or her reasons therefor on cross-examination to weaken or destroy the persuasive value of the opinion."

[8]   Disclosure of Basis—Opinions of Other Experts

United States Court of Appeals for the Armed Forces

United States v. Mansfield, 38 M.J. 415 (C.M.A. 1993): The accused's original 1984 murder conviction was the subject of substantial appellate litigation concerning trial defense counsel's competence in dealing with mental responsibility issues. After the findings and sentence were set aside, the accused was retried in 1987, and convicted again. Here he unsuccessfully renewed many of the original issues. In this court's opinion, no error occurred when trial counsel was permitted to cross-examine defense psychotherapists about incriminating statements the accused offered to them. The court said any expert who presents a testimonial opinion is subject to disclose the underlying basis for that opinion.

§ 706.01   Official Text

Rule 706.   Court Appointed Experts.

(a) *Appointment and compensation.*   The trial counsel, the defense counsel, and the court-martial have equal opportunity to obtain expert witnesses under Article 46. The employment and compensation of expert witnesses is governed by R.C.M. 703.

(b) *Disclosure of employment.*   In the exercise of discretion, the military judge may authorize disclosure to the members of the fact that the military judge called an expert witness.

(c) *Accused's experts of own selection.*   Nothing in this rule limits the accused in calling expert witnesses of the accused's own selection and at the accused's own expense.

---

§ 706.02   Editorial Comment

[1]   Rule 706(a)—Appointment and Compensation

[a]   Background of the Rule

Military Rule 706 is very different from its federal counterpart. Under Article 46 of the Uniform Code of Military Justice, trial counsel, defense counsel and the bench have equal opportunities to obtain expert witnesses. R.C.M. 703 covers compensation. Because of the Code and *Manual* provisions, parts of the Federal Rule are unnecessary in the Military Rules of Evidence.

However, the basic justification for this provision is the same under either the military or the federal systems. This Rule is meant to insure that all trial participants recognize their obligation and ability to obtain expert witness testimony when it is required to insure that a complete record is made, and that the finders of fact have sufficient information upon which to perform their mission. The Code and existing military practice place a premium on access to evidence.

[b]   When to Use the Rule

The military judge's need to call expert witnesses undoubtedly contemplates an unusual trial circumstance. Under most situations, the parties will have identified the areas requiring expert testimony, and presented the necessary evidence on their own. Particularly in military practice, if the bench were to suggest that additional areas needed to be illuminated, counsel would normally insure that the testimony was made available.

Rule 706(a) deals with circumstances beyond those mentioned above. The judge may require additional expert testimony because the parties' own experts are so far apart in their proof that an impartial authority is required to assist the factfinder in evaluating it. Or, the parties may have presented so much complex expert opinion testimony that the finders of fact need assistance to sort through the contradictory evidence.

[c] Alternatives to Court-Appointed Experts

If the military judge decides that an expert may be needed, the matter should be discussed with counsel during an Article 39(a) session. Alternatives to calling an additional expert witness should be seriously considered. Counsel have an independent obligation to insure that their proof is understandable and usable by the factfinders. If the evidence presented to that point in the trial is confusing or incomplete under Rule 611(a) the trial judge can suggest to the parties that certain areas need further explanation, clarity, or organization.

When it is not practicable to correct this problem with the parties' own experts, the trial participants should expect that a great deal of time and resources will be necessary to prepare a new expert witness to testify. The problems associated with the court calling an expert witness can be minimized if the bench or counsel anticipate the need for a neutral expert witness and raise the matter *in limine,* allowing the court appointed expert time to prepare and to observe the trial, where appropriate. Resolving the matter *in limine* will also provide counsel with an opportunity to structure their cases around this extraordinary testimony, particularly if the bench decides to inform the members that an expert has been appointed. *See* Rule 706(b).

[d] Minimizing Opposition to Using the Rule

Counsel and military judges may have significant reservations about calling a court appointed expert. Besides the confusion such experts will cause the members by requiring them to sift through a third set of opinions on complex and controversial evidence, the court appointed expert might be no more qualified than the previous experts.

To help insure that the judge's expert is independent, qualified, and acceptable to both parties, when possible the military judge should allow counsel to participate in the witness selection process. The bench should enlist counsels' views on who the court appointed expert should be, and on the scope of the witness's testimony.

[e] The Court-Appointed Expert at Trial

Before the court's expert witness testifies, the expert should provide both parties and the military judge with a deposition or statement concerning proposed findings and conclusions. The court will want to assure itself that the witness is going to be helpful. If the expert cannot assist the triers of fact, no reason exists to clutter the record with additional testimony. However, if the court's expert does have a valuable contribution to make, allowing the parties access to it early on will facilitate their ability to present additional evidence if it becomes necessary. The expert should also be made available to counsel for pretrial preparation and discovery purposes.

At trial, the court appointed expert may be called by either party, or the military judge. Many courts resolve this issue by requiring the party who stands to benefit most from the expert's testimony to call the witness first. However, irrespective of which party initiates the examination, both counsel may take the witness as if on cross. Military judges need to be particularly sensitive about any examination they engage in. Particularly if the members are informed that the judge has appointed the expert, thorough examination by the bench can produce testimony the members will inappropriately elevate in importance.[1]

[2] Rule 706(b)—Disclosure of Employment

[a] Exaggerated Importance of Testimony

An expert witness, like any other witness (*see* Rule 614), may be called to testify by the military judge. Subdivision (b) authorizes the bench to inform court members of the fact that an expert witness has been called by the judge. This can cause the same problem presented when the bench calls any other witness: There is a danger that the court members will associate the witness with the judge and will tend to give the witness special consideration or deference.

[b] Relationship of Rule 706 to Rule 105

If the judge does inform the court members that he or she has called an expert, the judge should be very careful to instruct the members that they are to evaluate the witness' credibility as they would that of any other witness, and that there is no special significance in the fact that the court has called the witness.[2] The bench should be particularly concerned about the instructions provided on this issue, and as a result may wish to consult with both counsel before addressing the members.

[3] Rule 706(c)—Accused's Experts of Own Selection

[a] Defining the Right

Subdivision (c) is included to make it clear that nothing in this Rule limits the accused in calling expert witnesses that the accused has selected and retained. An accused is entitled to obtain the help of a government-provided expert witness under Article 46. But the accused may also obtain independent expert witnesses on his or her own. The only limitation upon the calling of witnesses will be found in the relevance provisions of Rule 402 and Rule 403.

---

[1] *See* our discussion of Rule 611.

[2] For a discussion of the problems that may arise when the judge becomes identified with witnesses, *see* Saltzburg, *The Unnecessarily Expanding Role of the American Trial Judge*, 64 VA. L. REV. 1 (1978).

§ 706.03   Drafters' Analysis

[1]   Appointment and compensation

Rule 706(a) is the result of a complete redraft of subdivision (a) of the Federal Rule that was required to be consistent with Article 46 of the Uniform Code of Military Justice that is implemented in ¶¶ 115 and 116 of the *Manual*. Rule 706(a) states the basic rule that prosecution, defense, military judge, and the court members all have equal opportunity under Article 46 to obtain expert witnesses. The second sentence of the subdivision replaces subdivision (b) of the Federal Rule that is inapplicable to the armed forces in the light of ¶ 116.

[2]   Disclosure of employment

Rule 706(b) is taken from Fed. R. Evid. 706(c) without change. The *Manual* is silent on the issue, but the subdivision should not change military practice.

[3]   Accused's expert of own selection

Rule 706(c) is similar in intent to subdivision (d) of the Federal Rule and adapts that Rule to military practice. The subdivision makes it clear that the defense may call its own expert witnesses at its own expense without the necessity of recourse to ¶ 116.

§ 706.04   Annotated Cases

[1]   Rule 706(a)—Appointment and Compensation

[a]   Appointment of Expert—Denied Requests

Navy-Marine Corps Court of Criminal Appeals

United States v. Pearson, 13 M.J. 922 (N.M.C.M.R. 1982): Relying on Rule 706, the court found that the accused's trial request for expert witnesses was properly denied, as the assistance sought would not have affected the trial's outcome. Further, the accused failed to demonstrate how the court's ruling prejudiced his defense in any manner.

[b]   Appointment of Expert—Offers of Proof

United States Court of Appeals for the Armed Forces

United States v. Ruth, 46 M.J. 1 (C.A.A.F 1997): The accused was convicted of larceny in pursuing what this court referred to as a "get rich quick" scheme. The government's evidence included expert opinion testimony from a questioned documents examiner. At trial, the accused requested that a specific civilian expert witness be provided to impeach the government's proof. Defense counsel contended, and the court agreed, that limiting the accused to using one government expert to attack another government expert is the functional equivalent of allowing the "fox [to] guard the hen house." The accused also contended that *Daubert v. Merrell Dow Pharms.*,

Inc., 509 U.S. 579 (1993), provided the basis for reevaluating the scientific validity and admissibility of "handwriting analysis." Without commenting on *Daubert's* effect, this court affirmed the accused's convictions finding that defense counsel failed to make an adequate trial offer of proof to obtain the civilian expert. However, *citing United States v. Velasquez,* 64 F.3d 844 (3d Cir. 1995), the court also recognized that Rule 702's liberal standard of admissibility augured in favor of admitting evidence like that requested by the defense.

[c] Appointment of Expert—Specific Military or Civilian Expert

Navy-Marine Court of Criminal Appeals

United States v. Dubose, 48 M.J. 942 (N.M.Ct.Crim.App. 1998): The accused was convicted of numerous bomb manufacturing and possession offenses. At trial he unsuccessfully relied on a mental responsibility defense. The case was initially set aside by the United States Court of Appeals for the Armed Forces because this court applied an incorrect standard in reviewing the expert and lay witness mental responsibility testimony. (*See United States v. Dubose,* 47 M.J. 386 (1998), lower court incorrectly opined that "clear and convincing objective evidence, not merely subjective medical opinion" testimony was required to establish the accused's defense.) On further review this court again affirmed the accused's convictions finding that there is no hard and fast rule for determining criminal liability in cases of multiple-personality disorders. The court went on to say that the trial judge did not err in denying the accused's request for a specific expert witness to assist in his defense. In the court's opinion, "While an accused is entitled to expert assistance he is not entitled to any particular [civilian] expert."

[2] Rule 706(c)—Accused's Experts of Own Selection

[a] Accused's Expert—Psychiatric Requests

Navy Marine Court of Criminal Appeals

United States v. Dubose, 44 M.J. 782 (N.M.Ct.Crim.App. 1996): The accused was convicted of possessing an unregistered bomb and related uniquely military offenses. The accused defended, in part, on mental responsibility grounds. To prosecute his defense, the accused requested that a civilian expert be procured at government expense. Affirming the trial judge's refusal to grant the accused's request, this court held that the bench acted properly in providing the accused with a qualified expert from Naval medicine. The court went on to say that if the defense did not accept such assistance, it could use its own resources to obtain expert testimony.

§ 707.01   Official Text

Rule 707.   Polygraph Examinations.

(a) Notwithstanding any other provision of law, the results of a polygraph examination, the opinion of a polygraph examiner, or any reference to an offer to take, failure to take, or taking of a polygraph examination, shall not be admitted into evidence.

(b) Nothing in this section is intended to exclude from evidence statements made during a polygraph examination which are otherwise admissible.

---

§ 707.02   Editorial Comment

[1]   In General

Rule 707 has been the subject of considerable litigation and debate[1] since it was promulgated on June 27, 1991.[2] Two years after the President signed Rule 707 into law, the Supreme Court decided *Daubert v. Merrell Dow Pharms.*,[3] which rejected *Frye v. United States,*[4] its general "acceptance standard," the existing approach to polygraph and scientific evidence, and much of Rule 707's underlying foundation.[5] Three years after *Daubert*, the Court of Appeals for the Armed Forces in *United States v. Scheffer,*[6] relied on the Supreme Court's guidance and found Rule 707 unconstitutional as applied to the accused's case. In 1998, the Supreme Court reversed the Court of Appeals for the Armed Forces' decision in *United States v. Scheffer.*[7] Speaking for the majority, Justice Thomas held that Rule 707 was a reasonable governmental limitation upon the accused's ability to present exculpatory polygraph evidence because the Rule supported other legitimate interests of the criminal justice process: i.e., (1) the obligation to present only relevant and reliable evidence, (2) the need to preserve the jury's credibility determining role, and (3) the desire to avoid needless litigation into collateral issues.

---

[1] *See, e.g.,* Canham, *Military Rule of Evidence 707: A Bright Line That Needs To Be Dimmed,* 140 MIL. L. REV. 65 (1993) (author carefully evaluates polygraph usage, both before and after Rule 707, concluding that this prophylactic rule ignores the accused's rights while excluding potentially relevant and helpful evidence).

[2] *See* Executive Order No. 12767, Section 2, 56 Fed. Reg. 30296.

[3] 509 U.S. 579 (1993).

[4] 293 F. 1013 (D.C. Cir. 1923).

[5] *See* our discussion of Rule 702.

[6] 44 M.J. 442 (1996), *cert. granted,* 520 U.S. 1227 (1997).

[7] 523 U.S. 303 (1998). *See,* Askins, *United States v. Scheffer: An Anomaly In The Military Or A Return To The Per Se Ban Of Polygraph Evidence?* 37 HOUS. L. REV. 175 (2000).

[2]   Basis for the Rule

The Drafters' Analysis indicates that Rule 707 was adopted for "policy" reasons.[8] It has no parallel in the Federal Rules of Evidence, or at common law.[9] The drafters viewed the polygraph machine as an unreliable device, the court-martial use of which impinges upon the integrity of the military justice system. Although the Analysis states that Rule 707 was not intended to accept or reject *United States v. Gipson*,[10] the drafters were clearly dissatisfied with that decision. In their opinion, polygraph evidence poses a real danger of misleading and confusing members, and wasting the court's time. The drafters believed that factfinders will view this evidence as infallible, unimpeachable, or conclusive of trial issues that in turn will cause courts-martial to degenerate into trials about polygraph machines, with court members ignoring the military judge's cautionary instructions.[11] Rule 707's bright-line test also encompasses polygraph results covered by a stipulation.

A prime motivation for the drafters' position appears to be concern about the time, effort, and financial costs potentially involved in litigating issues concerning the reliability of polygraph tests, operator qualifications, and related witness requests. For a worldwide judicial system, this concern is not inconsequential. Without Rule 707's categorical exclusion, parties desiring to admit such evidence would be able to compel witness attendance from beyond the trial court's location, adding expense and delay to the trial process. The drafters viewed this as placing an unjustifiable burden on the administration of justice.

[3]   Scope of the Prohibition

Subdivision (a) categorically excludes all evidence related to the product of polygraph examinations. As a result, military judges cannot entertain any motion, at trial or *in limine*, seeking to admit such testimony. Surprisingly, this provision does not address drug or hypnosis-induced testimony, evidence with a remarkably similar judicial past. Because the Drafters' Analysis is also silent on these points, it is difficult to know whether military judges retain discretion to consider drug and hypnosis evidence. Under the 1969 Manual for Courts-Martial, polygraph, drug, and hypnosis-aided testimony were treated similarly. Paragraph 142 *e* provided that, "The conclusions

---

[8] *See, e.g.,* Barovick, *Rock and a Hard Place: Polygraph Prejudice Persists After Scheffer,* 47 BUFF. L. REV. 1533 (Fall 1999).

[9] *See, e.g.,* Citro, *Playing "Pin the Tail on the Truth" In the Eleventh Circuit: Why Polygraph Evidence Should be Excluded in Federal Courts,* 30 STETSON L. REV. 715 (2000).

[10] 24 M.J. 246 (C.M.A. 1987) (polygraph results may be admissible on a case-by-case basis).

[11] *See* United States v. Alexander, 526 F.2d 161 (8th Cir. 1975) (polygraph evidence was excluded because the court viewed it as "shrouded with an aura of near infallibility, akin to the ancient oracle of Delphi").

based upon or graphically represented by a polygraph test and the conclusions based upon, and the statements of the person interviewed made during a drug-induced or hypnosis-induced interview are inadmissible in evidence."

When Rule 702 was promulgated, the drafters said that "[t]he deletion of the explicit prohibition on such evidence is not intended to make such evidence *per se* admissible and is not an express authorization for such procedures." The drafters went on to note that military practice should observe the degree of acceptance this evidence attains in Article III courts as a method for evaluating whether it actually assists triers of fact. Rule 707 is not on its face a bar against such evidence, and Rules 702 and 703 do not contain *per se* exclusionary rules. But the adoption of Rule 707 may provide persuasive authority to exclude drug and hypnosis-induced evidence.

Subdivision (b) provides that statements obtained during polygraph examinations may be admitted, assuming Article 31 and related provisions have been adhered to.[12] The drafters wanted to ensure that, if a witness makes otherwise admissible statements during the polygraph testing process, those statements, presumably without reference to the polygraph test itself, would be admissible. To that extent, subdivision (b) merely restates existing military and federal law.

[4] The Underlying Prior Federal and Military Judicial Standards

Military and civilian courts have long struggled with polygraph evidence.[13] *Frye v. United States* established a pre-Rules of Evidence standard for viewing it and other scientific evidence requiring expert witness testimony to be based on "generally accepted" scientific principles. The drafters did not address *Frye*'s vitality, particularly in light of the existing and well grounded Court of Appeals' decision in *Gipson, above,* or Rule 707's relation to Rules 702 and 703.[14]

The leading military case on polygraph evidence at the time of Rule 707's promulgation was *United States v. Gipson.* There, the court evaluated past military and federal treatment of polygraph evidence, and categorized scientific evidence into three classes.[15] The highest class concerns principles so well-established that it is unnecessary to prove them in each case. In effect, the court is willing to judicially note the scientific validity of such

---

[12] *See* Rule 305.

[13] *See, e.g.,* United States v. Two Bulls, 918 F.2d 56 (8th Cir. 1990) (under either Rule 702 or *Frye*, polygraph testing still inadmissible until greater scientific reliability established).

[14] *See* United States v. Mustafa, 22 M.J. 165 (C.M.A.) (Federal Rules of Evidence superseded the *Frye* test), *cert. denied*, 479 U.S. 953 (1986) (noted the need to resolve conflicts between Rule 702 and *Frye*).

[15] United States v. Mustafa, 22 M.J. 165, 249.

evidence. Fingerprint, ballistics, and X-ray evidence fall into this category.[16] The bottom class concerns evidence the court calls a "junk pile of contraptions, practices, and techniques which have been universally discredited."[17] Phrenology and astrology fall into this group. The middle category involves scientific and technical endeavors which can neither be summarily accepted nor rejected. Polygraphs had resided there prior to the adoption of Rule 707.[18]

The Military Court of Appeals for the Armed Forces in *Gipson*, like the Supreme Court in *Daubert* six years later, found that *Frye* had been superseded by the Rules of Evidence, and was no longer an independent standard for admissibility of scientific evidence. *Gipson* and *Daubert* held that trial judges have an obligation to determine whether, based on the facts before them, scientific evidence like polygraph examinations should be admitted. Although *Gipson* recognized that polygraph evidence had not yet been widely accepted in criminal courtrooms, it declined to adopt a *per se* rule excluding it.

Gipson also recognized that a constitutional argument could be made that an accused has a right to present polygraph evidence as exculpatory testimony. The court cited *Chambers v. Mississippi*[19] and *Washington v. Texas*[20] and concluded that when scientific testimony is helpful, relevant, and not unfairly prejudicial, it has a role to play in criminal litigation, for both the prosecution and the defense.

The court also noted that in many cases polygraph evidence may be as good as or better than much other expert and lay testimony that routinely and uncritically come before finders of fact. Anticipating the drafters' policy concerns, the court said polygraph evidence is not so collateral, confusing, time-consuming, and prejudicial as to require *per se* exclusion.[21] It recognized that trial judges can effectively instruct members on the appropriate way to use such testimony, and that it is unlikely factfinders will be overwhelmed by the evidence.[22] Despite the *Gipson* decision, polygraph

---

[16] United States v. Mustafa, 22 M.J. 165 (C.M.A.).

[17] United States v. Mustafa, 22 M.J. 165 (C.M.A.).

[18] United States v. Mustafa, 22 M.J. 165 (C.M.A.).

[19] 410 U.S. 284 (1973) (due process violation if accused not permitted to cross-examine witnesses).

[20] 388 U.S. 14 (1967) (Sixth Amendment violation where accused not permitted to call co-participants).

[21] *Gipson*, 24 M.J. at 253.

[22] *See In re* Paoli R.R. Yard PCB Litig., 916 F.2d 829 (3d Cir. 1990) (dismissed 'out of hand' District Court's finding that novel scientific evidence would confuse the jury, which would give it more weight than it deserved because of its scientific nature and the expert's credentials).

evidence was generally excluded in those few post-*Gipson* military cases that addressed the issue.[23]

[5]   The Supreme Court's View

In order for the Supreme Court to reach its decision in *United States v. Sheffer, above,* upholding Rule 707's constitutionality in categorically excluding polygraph evidence, it had to distinguish a significant body of previous holdings concerning an accused's right to a defense and his right to present evidence in support of that defense. Initially the Court characterized its holding in *Chambers v. Mississippi*[24] as not standing "for the proposition that the accused is denied a fair opportunity to defend himself whenever a state or federal rule excludes favorable evidence." Turning to *Rock v. Arkansas,*[25] the majority held that a defendant's right to present evidence must "bow to accommodate other legitimate interests in the criminal trial process." In the Court's opinion, federal and state rule makers have "broad latitude" under the Constitution to establish rules excluding evidence in criminal trials as long as the exclusions are not "arbitrary" or "disproportionate to the purpose they are designed to serve."

This is an interesting result in light of the fact that *Rock* dealt with an issue very similar to Rule 707. There, Arkansas had a *per se* rule that prohibited all witnesses, including the accused, from testifying if their memories had been hypnotically refreshed. Before trial, the accused was treated by a neuropsychologist who hypnotized and refreshed her memory concerning certain events. At trial, the accused was prohibited from testifying about the hypnotically refreshed facts. The State Supreme Court ultimately affirmed the trial court's holding, the accused's conviction, and the statute's *per se* application, finding the dangers of excluding this testimony were not outweighed by its probative value. The state court also found that no constitutional violation occurred because any deprivation the accused suffered was minimal and resulted from her own actions, not those of the court.

The United States Supreme Court held that the Arkansas statute violated the accused's right to present a defense. It said attempts to ensure that only the most trustworthy evidence reaches factfinders operates to the detriment of all defendants who undergo hypnosis, without regard for the circumstances under which the hypnosis took place, or an independent verification of the information produced. The Court said that a state's legitimate interest

---

[23] *See, e.g.,* United States v. Pope, 30 M.J. 1188 (A.F.C.M.R. 1990) (excluded defense *ex parte* polygraph exam); United States v. McKinnie, 29 M.J. 825 (A.C.M.R. 1989); United States v. Tyler, 26 M.J. 680 (A.F.C.M.R. 1988); United States v. Howard, 24 M.J. 897 (C.G.C.M.R. 1987).

[24] 410 U.S. 284 (1973).

[25] 483 U.S. 44, 55 (1987).

in barring unreliable evidence does not extend to *per se* exclusions that may operate to suppress reliable evidence in an individual case. At bottom, it viewed wholesale inadmissibility as an arbitrary and insupportable restriction.

The military drafters did not mention the then four-year-old Supreme Court holding in *Rock*, even though the drafters chose a *per se* rule very similar to that discussed and rejected in *Rock*. The drafters *per se* bar also could be seen as departing from the Military Rules of Evidence: (1) movement away from inflexible interpretations of legal standards, particularly those contained in Section VII and *Frye*; (2) preference for encouraging more evidence to reach the finders of fact; and (3) belief and confidence in properly instructed court members being able to accurately evaluate complex scientific evidence.

The *Scheffer* majority went on to say that the limitations imposed by Rule 707 are appropriate and do not raise constitutional issues because exculpatory polygraph testimony is not sufficiently weighty defense issue. In the Court's opinion, such testimony is not fundamental to an accused's defense particularly in this case where the accused testified and was free to call any witness who possessed relevant "factual" testimony.[26]

While the polarized debate over polygraph reliability was crucial to the Court's decision, the majority went on to say that, even if polygraph technology were universally accepted, there would still be a viable controversy over the now well-known "countermeasures" which can be taken to "fool" polygraph operators. As a result, the Court found Rule 707 to be "a rational and proportional means of advancing the President's legitimate interest in barring unreliable evidence."

Both the concurring and dissenting opinions characterized the majority's position as unwise. Justice Kennedy, concurring, indicated that the majority creates further tension between the Court's previous holding in *Daubert, above,* and the Rules of Evidence's desire to provide trial courts with "considerable discretion" in admitting or excluding scientific evidence.[27]

Dissenting, Justice Stevens initially found that Rule 707 violates Article 36(a) of the Uniform Code of Military Justice.[28] He believed that the blanket exclusion is not consistent with practice in federal courts, and that no special military concern existed to justify the different approach taken in Rule 707. Justice Stevens also disagreed with the majority on constitutional grounds. He stated that their position "barely acknowledges that a person accused of a crime has a constitutional right to present a defense." Quoting *Washington*

---

[26] *See* Washington v. Texas, 388 U.S. 14 (1967).

[27] *See generally,* Military Rules of Evidence 702, 703, 704, 403, 608, and 611.

[28] 10 U.S.C. 36(a).

v. Texas,[29] Justice Stevens said, "a state rule of evidence that excluded 'whole categories' of testimony on the basis of a presumption of unreliability was unconstitutional," and that the same result should occur on these facts.[30]

On a broader plain, Justice Stevens indicated that the modern trend has been to abolish common law limitations on witnesses and permit juries to hear relevant testimony after trial judges have properly instructed them on how to use the evidence. Citing *Hawkins v. United States,*[31] he stated, "[a]ny rule that impedes the discovery of truth in a court of law impedes as well the doing of justice."[32] Further, Justice Stevens opined that nothing in *Daubert, Chambers, Rock,* or *Washington v. Texas* indicates that a state's interest in excluding unreliable evidence "extend[s] to per se exclusions that may be reliable in an individual case."[33]

§ 707.03   Drafters' Analysis

Rule 707 is new and similar to Cal. Evid. Code 351.1 (West 1988 Supp.). The Rule prohibits the use of polygraph evidence in courts-martial and is based on several policy grounds. There is a real danger that court members will be misled by polygraph evidence that "is likely to be shrouded with an aura of near infallibility." *United States v. Alexander,* 526 F.2d 161, 168–169 (8th Cir. 1975). To the extent that the members accept polygraph evidence as unimpeachable or conclusive, despite cautionary instructions from the military judge, the members' "traditional responsibility to collectively ascertain the facts and adjudge guilt or innocence is preempted." *United States v. Alexander,* 526 F.2d 161, 168–169 (8th Cir. 1975). There is also a danger of confusion of the issues, especially when conflicting polygraph evidence diverts the members' attention from a determination of guilt or innocence to a judgment of the validity and limitations of polygraphs. This could result in the court-martial degenerating into a trial of the polygraph machine. *State v. Grier,* 300 S.E.2d 351 (N.C. 1983). Polygraph evidence also can result in a substantial waste of time when collateral issues regarding the reliability of the particular test and qualifications of the specific polygraph examiner must be litigated in every case. Polygraph evidence places a burden on the administration of justice that outweighs the probative value of the evidence. The reliability of polygraph evidence has not been sufficiently established and its use at trial impinges upon the integrity of the judicial system. *See People v. Kegler,* 242 Cal. Rptr. 897 (Cal. Ct. App. 1987). Thus, this amendment adopts a bright-line rule that polygraph evidence is not admissible by any party to a court-martial even if stipulated

---

[29] 388 U.S. 14 (1967).

[30] 523 U.S. at 327.

[31] 358 U.S. 74, 81 (1958).

[32] 523 U.S. at 329.

[33] 523 U.S. at 329.

to by the parties. This amendment is not intended to accept or reject *United States v. Gipson*, 24 M.J. 246 (C.M.A. 1987), concerning the standard for admissibility of other scientific evidence under Mil. R. Evid. 702 or the continued vitality of *Frye v. United States*, 293 F. 1013 (D.C. Cir. 1923). Finally, subsection (b) of the rule ensures that any statements that are otherwise admissible are not rendered inadmissible solely because the statements were made during a polygraph examination.

§ 707.04   Annotated Cases

[1]   Polygraph Examinations—Curative Admissions

United States Court of Appeals for the Armed Forces

United States v. Tyndale, 56 M.J. 209 (C.A.A.F. 2001): The accused was convicted of wrongful use of methamphetamine. Trial counsel moved for a preliminary ruling admitting evidence of the accused's 1994 positive urinalysis and the accused's accompanying explanation regarding innocent ingestion. This court held that evidence of the accused's prior positive urinalysis test for methamphetamine and prior innocent ingestion defense was admissible to show knowledge and intent, and to rebut the current defense of innocent ingestion of methamphetamine. The court also found that the military judge did not commit plain error in admitting evidence of a government polygraph examination to rebut the accused's prior evidence of two polygraph examinations. The Court based its decision on the likelihood that the accused's own erroneously admitted polygraphs negated any potential prejudicial error stemming from the government's polygraph. Since the judge's simultaneous errors in admitting two sets of polygraphs left the panel with conflicting testimony regarding the accused's credibility, there was no "grave doubt" that the claimed error had an unfair prejudicial impact on the members' deliberations.

[2]   Polygraph Examinations—Harmless Error

United States Court of Appeals for the Armed Forces

United States v. Gardinier, 67 M.J. 304 (C.A.A.F. 2009): In *United States v. Gardinier*, 65 M.J. 60 (C.A.A.F. 2007), the court reversed his child sexual abuse convictions because a handwritten incriminating statement, a video-taped confession, and incriminating statements made by the prosecutrix had all been erroneously admitted. Subsequently, the Army Court of Criminal Appeals affirmed the accused's convictions and found that the errors were harmless beyond a reasonable doubt. Reversing and remanding on Article 31(b) and Sixth Amendment grounds, the court here noted that the inadmissible four hour videotaped confession contained the administration of a "computer voice stress test" that was explained to the accused as an advanced polygraph which does not create false positives. Defense counsel did not object to this testimony, and the court indicated that the test evidence appeared to violate Rule 707 although it did not rest its decision on this violation.

United States v. Whitney, 55 M.J. 413 (C.A.A.F. 2001): The accused was convicted of rape, forcible sodomy, assault, assault consummated by battery, and indecent assault. The United States Air Force Court of Criminal Appeals affirmed the decision in part and set it aside in part. This court affirmed holding that, although it was error for polygraph testimony to be admitted, and it was error for the polygraph operator to testify as a human "lie detector" concerning the truthfulness of the accused's statement, both errors were harmless in large part due to the trial judge's curative instruction.

[3] Polygraph Examinations—Human Lie Detector Evidence

United States Court of Appeals for the Armed Forces

United States v. Mullins, 69 M.J.113 (C.A.A.F. 2010): The accused was convicted of sexually abusing his nine and seven year old daughters and possessing child pornography. A government expert opined that the victims' testimony was consistent with that of children who had been sexually abused. The military judge then *sua sponte* instructed the members that they should not view the witness as a human lie detector and that only the members can determine credibility. On redirect the expert testified that children lie about being sexually abused in less than one of every two hundred cases. Thereafter the military judge asked the witness if she had a forensic basis for her testimony. The witness replied that she did not. Defense counsel failed to object. Although the court found the lack of objection to be a plain and obvious error, the court also held the lack of objection did not unduly influence the member's role in determining the ultimate facts and thus was nonprejudicial. The court's decision was based in part on the military judge having just provided an adequate lie detector instruction and on the strength of the government's case which included independent corroborating evidence.

[4] Polygraph Examinations—Pretrial Agreements—Stipulations

United States Court of Appeals for the Armed Forces

United States v. Clark, 53 M.J. 280 (C.A.A.F. 2000): Pursuant to a pretrial agreement, the accused pled guilty to false official statement charges. The stipulation accompanying the pretrial agreement indicated that the accused took and failed a polygraph concerning n these events. The accused did not object to nor raise any error concerning this process. Judge Effron, writing for the majority initially discussed stipulation use holding: "Evidence that otherwise would be inadmissible under the Military Rules of Evidence may sometimes be admitted at trial through a stipulation, if the parties expressly agree, if there is no overreaching on the part of the government in obtaining the agreement, and if the military judge finds no reason to reject the stipulation in the interest of justice." However, relying on this provision and *United States v. Scheffer*, 523 U.S. 303 (1998), Judge Effron found harmless error in using the polygraph stipulation during the guilty plea process. Chief Judge Crawford and Senior Judge Everett filed dissents. Chief Judge

Crawford would have found no error based on *United States v. Mezzanatto*, 513 U.S. 196 (1995), which provides that an accused can waive protections similar to those found in Rule 707 (Mezzanatto waived Rule 410 protections). Chief Judge Crawford opined that polygraph evidence may also be admissible under the "invited-error, curative-admissibility, or opening-the-door doctrine." Similarly, Senior Judge Everett said he had "serious doubts error was committed" and opined that the Court should not accept the majority's "sweeping interpretation of Rule 707 [because] I doubt that the President intended to exclude all references to polygraph testing under these circumstances."

[5] Polygraph Examinations—Retrials

United States Court of Appeals for the Armed Forces

United States v. Lynn, 45 M.J. 403 (C.A.A.F. 1996): The accused was convicted of drug and credit card fraud offenses. Before trial, he passed a polygraph test administered by a private polygrapher. The trial judge refused to allow defense counsel to lay a foundation for admitting the results. The accused's convictions were affirmed by the Court of Criminal Appeals. This court reversed the lower court's holding because of the trial judge's *per se* inadmissibility determination, and returned the record for a hearing on polygraph admissibility.

United States v. Hall, 45 M.J. 255 (C.A.A.F. 1996): The accused was convicted of larceny. Before trial he passed a polygraph test administered by a Department of Defense polygrapher. The trial judge refused to allow defense counsel to lay a foundation for admitting the results. The accused's conviction was affirmed by the Court of Criminal Appeals. This court, consistent with its decision in *United States v. Scheffer*, 44 M.J. 442 (1996), reversed the Service Court's holding, and returned the record for a hearing on polygraph admissibility.

[6] Polygraph Examinations—Sentencing

United States Court of Appeals for the Armed Forces

United States v. Johnson, 62 M.J. 31 (C.A.A.F. 2005): Affirming the accused's conviction for a drug offense, the court held that evidence of a privately administered polygraph examination, which indicated no deception when the accused denied knowing the drugs where in his car, was properly excluded. The court added that the testimony did not qualify for admission under R.C.M. 1001(c) as evidence in extenuation and mitigation.

Air Force Court of Criminal Appeals

United States v. Johnson, 59 M.J. 666 (A.F.Ct.Crim.App. 2003): The accused was convicted by an officer and enlisted panel of possessing 17 pounds of marijuana with the intent to distribute. During sentencing, the accused attempted to introduce evidence indicating that he had previously taken a private polygraph examination and demonstrated no deception when he stated that he did not knowingly possess the contraband. The court affirmed, holding that the only logical purpose such evidence could have been offered for was to impeach the members' findings. Thus, the trial judge's decision to exclude the evidence was proper.

[7]   Polygraph Examinations—Waiver

United States Court of Appeals for the Armed Forces

United States v. Tanksley, 54 M.J. 169 (C.A.A.F. 2000): The accused in this case was a Navy doctor who had attained the rank of Captain. The record indicates that the accused had a long history of sexually abusing his own daughters, and that the instant trial was the result of that misconduct. During the government's case, evidence that the accused failed to take a polygraph examination was initially admitted without defense objection. Affirming findings and sentence, this Court noted that plain error was not present and that in light of the 1300-page record no substantial prejudice was likely.

United States v. Southwick, 53 M.J. 412 (C.A.A.F. 2000): Captain Stefanie Southwick was convicted of distributing ecstasy and cocaine. At trial she attacked OSI's use of the government informant who provided most of the evidence against her. In order to establish that improper procedures were used by the OSI, defense counsel indicated that polygraph results had not been properly employed. Trial counsel argued the contrary during closing argument. On these facts the court found error, waiver by defense counsel, and no harm. As a result, the Court affirmed the accused's convictions and sentence. We note that even though Rule 707's blanket prohibition on polygraph evidence has been upheld by the Supreme Court, it's use here, even if initiated by the government and objected to by the defense, would probably not have been error or improper. The substantive use of polygraph results were never in issue here. At a minimum, the government should be able to show that if its regulations require that service members take a polygraph before undertaking jobs that require this qualification, and the lack of compliance with government regulation is an issue in the case, that the testimony in question here is both relevant and admissible. Further, any concerns defense counsel might have about how this proof would be used could be resolved by a Rule 105 instruction.

[8]   Polygraph Examinations—Pre-Supreme Court Resolution of *United States v. Sheffer*

United States Court of Appeals for the Armed Forces

United States v. Mobley, 44 M.J. 453 (C.A.A.F. 1996): The court set aside the accused's drug convictions and held that when an accused testifies in his own behalf, Rule 707 is an unconstitutional limitation on his right to present a defense and call witnesses. However, because the accused used a privately administered test, the court held that the accused will have to submit to a government polygraph, and indicate if he "shopped" for favorable results with other examiners, as a condition precedent to introducing his results.

United States v. Nash, 44 M.J. 456 (C.A.A.F. 1996): Setting aside the accused's drug convictions, the court held that the military judge erred by applying a *per se* exclusionary rule to the accused's proffer of favorable polygraph evidence. The court also said that the trial judge erred by basing his opinion on the anticipated conflict between two expert witnesses. In this court's opinion, conflicting expert testimony is to be resolved by the triers of fact after receiving proper instructions from the bench. *See also, United States v. Mobley*, and *United States v. Scheffer*, also discussed in this annotation.

United States v. Scheffer, 44 M.J. 442 (C.A.A.F. 1996): In an extraordinary opinion, the court set aside the accused's conviction and held that Rule 707 was unconstitutional as applied to these uttering bad checks, wrongful use of methamphetamine, and absence without leave prosecutions. An OSI administered polygraph indicated no deception when the accused denied using drugs. Relying on Rule 707, the military judge prevented the accused from laying a foundation for its use. The court held that where the accused testifies, a blanket prohibition violates the Sixth Amendment. In the court's opinion, polygraph results could be used to show that an accused's physiological responses to certain questions did not indicate deception. The court went on to say that the foundation for using polygraph evidence must include proof that (a) the examiner is qualified; (b) the equipment worked properly; (c) the equipment was properly used; and (d) the examiner used valid questioning techniques. *See also United States v. Mobley*, and *United States v. Nash*, also discussed in this annotation.

United States v. Berg, 44 M.J. 79 (C.A.A.F. 1996): In this pre-Rule 707 case, the trial court excluded defense offered polygraph evidence because the particular test procedures used were inadequate. However, all five government and defense experts vouched for the general scientific validity and reliability of polygraph examinations.

United States v. Willis, 41 M.J. 435 (C.A.A.F. 1995): A general court-martial convicted the accused of rape and wrongfully purchasing alcohol for a minor. Over defense objection, the military judge admitted evidence of the accused's post-polygraph admissions. Affirming the accused's convictions, the court held that the evidence was not tainted by questions asked during the polygraph examination, and did not create an impermissible inference that the accused failed the test. The court left for another day whether this Rule is unconstitutional because it violates the accused's right to confrontation. On these facts the court found no prejudice.

Army Court of Criminal Appeals

United States v. Williams, 39 M.J. 555 (A.C.M.R. 1994): The accused was convicted of forgery and larceny. During trial, he was prohibited from introducing exculpatory polygraph testimony or the foundation for such evidence. This court remanded the case to the trial jurisdiction for a determination concerning whether the accused's Fifth and Sixth Amendment rights had been violated.

SECTION VIII

HEARSAY

SYNOPSIS

§ 801.01   Official Text

Rule 801.   Definitions.

The following definitions apply under this section:

(a) *Statement.* A "statement" is (1) an oral or written assertion or (2) nonverbal conduct of a person, if it is intended by the person as an assertion.

(b) *Declarant.*   A "declarant" is a person who makes a statement.

(c) *Hearsay.* "Hearsay" is a statement, other than one made by the declarant while testifying at the trial or hearing, offered in evidence to prove the truth of the matter asserted.

(d) *Statements which are not hearsay.*   A statement is not hearsay if:

(1) *Prior statement by witness.* The declarant testifies at the trial or hearing and is subject to cross-examination concerning the statement, and the statement is (A) inconsistent with the declarant's testimony, and was given under oath subject to the penalty of perjury at a trial, hearing, or other proceeding, or in a deposition, or (B) consistent with the declarant's testimony and is offered to rebut an express or implied charge against the declarant of recent fabrication or improper influence or motive, or (C) one of identification of a person made after perceiving the person; or

(2) *Admission by party-opponent.* The statement is offered against a party and is (A) the party's own statement in either the party's individual or representative capacity, or (B) a statement of which the party has manifested the party's adoption or belief in its truth, or (C) a statement by a person authorized by the party to make a statement concerning the subject, or (D) a statement by the party's agent or servant concerning a matter within the scope of the agency or employment of the agency or employment of the agent or servant, made during the existence of the relationship, or (E) a statement by a co-conspirator of a party during the course and in furtherance of the conspiracy. The contents of the statement shall be considered but are not alone sufficient to establish the declarant's authority under subdivision (C), the agency or employment relationship and scope thereof under subdivision (D), or the existence of the conspiracy and the participation therein of the declarant and the party against whom the statement is offered under subdivision

---

(E).

§ 801.02 Editorial Comment

[1] Rule 801(a)—Statement

[a] Scope of the Rule

[i] In General

The Military Rules of Evidence, like their Federal counterpart, have done a great deal to simplify trial practice by locating all evidence rules relating to a single subject in one place. The codification of the evidence rules has, for the most part, led to much greater consistency and predictability.

However, one area of court-martial litigation that causes counsel and military judges much difficulty is recognizing and properly dealing with hearsay evidence.[1] None of the hearsay rules is more complex and confusing than Rule 801. Much of the difficulty and confusion arises because the Rule provides a definition of hearsay in subdivision (c) and then creates *exemptions* from the definition in subdivision (d). These exemptions were known, both at common law and under previous *Manual* practice, as *exceptions* to the hearsay rule. So, for the first time, Rule 801 provides for non-hearsay (*i.e.*, out-of-court statements that are offered for its truth and admitted under an exemption). Despite the semantic change from exceptions to exemptions, there is no real substantive difference between exemptions or exceptions.

[ii] Hearsay and the Confrontation Clause

Hearsay issues in criminal cases must be examined in light of Supreme Court cases dealing with the Confrontation Clause. In *Crawford v. Washington,*[2] the Court interpreted the Confrontation Clause to bar admission of testimonial statements of a declarant who did not appear at trial unless the declarant was unavailable to testify and the defendant had a prior opportunity for cross-examination. Although the Court did not provide a complete definition of "testimonial," its holding means that, whether or not rules of evidence are conditioned on unavailability, testimonial hearsay statements may not be used if the declarant is available. *Crawford* left open whether, when non-testimonial statements are offered, *Ohio v. Roberts,*[3] remains applicable. Under *Roberts*, the Court conditioned the admissibility of

---

[1] *See, e.g.,* United States v. Escobar, 674 F.2d 469 (5th Cir. 1982) (error for government witness to refer to computer information stating that defendant was a suspected marijuana smuggler); United States v. Ocampo, 650 F.2d 421 (2d Cir. 1981) (reversed where witness erroneously testified to what an unidentified informer said).

[2] 541 U.S. 36 (2004).

[3] 448 U.S. 56 (1980).

hearsay evidence on whether it fell under a "firmly rooted hearsay exception" or bore "particularized guarantees of trustworthiness."

The Supreme Court expanded on *Crawford* in the companion cases of *Davis v. Washington* and *Hammon v. Indiana*.[4] Justice Scalia, writing for the Court, elaborated on the meaning of "testimonial" and "interrogation" as they relate to confrontation. Although the Court again declined to offer an exhaustive definition of terms, its 8-1 vote (with Justice Thomas dissenting) offered some clarification to the meaning of both words.

In *Davis*, Michelle McCottry telephoned 911, was cut off, and answered the operator's return call telling the operator that she had been assaulted by her former boyfriend, Davis, who had just fled the scene. Davis was charged with violation of a domestic no-contact order, a felony, but McCottry did not testify at his trial.

In *Hammon*, police responded to a reported domestic disturbance at the home of Amy and Hershel Hammon. They found Amy alone on the front porch, appearing frightened. When the police inquired about the disturbance, Amy told them that nothing was wrong, but also gave them permission to enter. Once inside, one officer kept Hershel in the kitchen. Another officer interviewed Amy in the living room. After hearing Amy's account, the officer asked her to fill out a battery affidavit, and she handwrote the following: "Broke our Furnace & shoved me down on the floor into the broken glass. Hit me in the chest and threw me down. Broke our lamps." Amy did not testify at Hershel's bench trial for domestic battery and violation of probation, but both her affidavit and the testimony of the officer who interviewed her were admitted over Hershel's objection that he had no opportunity to cross-examine and confront Amy.

The Court held that the 911 tape in *Davis* was properly admitted because the primary purpose of the 911 operator's questioning Michelle McCottry was to deal with an emergency, but that the admission of Amy Hershel's battery affidavit violated the Confrontation Clause because the primary purpose was to gather evidence. The Court made clear that a conversation beginning as an interrogation to determine the need for emergency assistance can become an interrogation to obtain testimony. Once the emergency ends, for example, continued interrogation might produce testimonial statements.

Justice Scalia concisely summarized the Court's reasoning in the two cases:

> Without attempting to produce an exhaustive classification of all conceivable statements—or even all conceivable statements in response to police interrogation—as either testimonial or nontestimonial, it

---

[4] 546 U.S. 1213 (2006).

suffices to decide the present cases to hold as follows: Statements are nontestimonial when made in the course of police interrogation under circumstances objectively indicating that the primary purpose of the interrogation is to enable police assistance to meet an ongoing emergency. They are testimonial when the circumstances objectively indicate that there is no such ongoing emergency, and that the primary purpose of the interrogation is to establish or prove past events potentially relevant to later criminal prosecution.

In response to arguments by Washington and Indiana, supported by a number of *amici*, that domestic violence cases require greater flexibility in the use of testimonial evidence because victims are notoriously susceptible to intimidation that prevents them from testifying, Justice Scalia wrote that "when defendants seek to undermine the judicial process by procuring or coercing silence from witnesses and victims, the Sixth Amendment does not require courts to acquiesce." He reiterated his suggestion in *Crawford:* that "the rule of forfeiture by wrongdoing . . . extinguishes confrontation claims on essentially equitable grounds."

More recently, the Supreme Court again addressed the issue of conversations between the police and potential victims in *Michigan v. Bryant.*[5] In that case, which was tried before the Court's decision in *Crawford*, the state court admitted the deceased victim's statements to police identifying Bryant as his assailant, under the *Roberts* reliability standards. The victim had been shot at Bryant's house approximately 25 minutes before the police found him in a store parking lot bleeding to death. At least five policemen asked the victim what happened. Each received similar answers identifying Bryant as the assailant. The Supreme Court held that such statements are testimonial when no ongoing emergency exists and the interrogator's primary purpose was to collect information about past events for use in a subsequent criminal prosecution; statements can be nontestimonial even when made in the course of a police interrogation when the primary purpose for the interrogation objectively appears to be the interrogator's attempt to meet an ongoing emergency and the process used for taking the statements is informal with a focus on current and future events.

Writing for the majority, Justice Sotomayor found that the statements in this case were non-testimonial and explained as follows:

> In addition to the circumstances in which an encounter occurs, the statements and actions of both the declarant and interrogators provide objective evidence of the primary purpose of the interrogation.

* * * * *

The combined approach also ameliorates problems that could arise

---

[5] 131 S. Ct. 1143 (2011).

from looking solely to one participant. Predominant among these is the problem of mixed motives on the part of both interrogators and declarants. Police officers in our society function as both first responders and criminal investigators. Their dual responsibilities may mean that they act with different motives simultaneously or in quick succession.

* * * * *

Victims are also likely to have mixed motives when they make statements to the police. During an ongoing emergency, a victim is most likely to want the threat to her and to other potential victims to end, but that does not necessarily mean that the victim wants or envisions prosecution of the assailant. A victim may want the attacker to be incapacitated temporarily or rehabilitated. Alternatively, a severely injured victim may have no purpose at all in answering questions posed; the answers may be simply reflexive. The victim's injuries could be so debilitating as to prevent her from thinking sufficiently clearly to understand whether her statements are for the purpose of addressing an ongoing emergency or for the purpose of future prosecution. Taking into account a victim's injuries does not transform this objective inquiry into a subjective one. The inquiry is still objective because it focuses on the understanding and purpose of a reasonable victim in the circumstances of the actual victim—circumstances that prominently include the victim's physical state.

The majority focused on the emergency confronting the police in dealing with a shooting a missing shooter and a lack of knowledge as to whether the victim they found was the only target of the shooter, and also noted that the interrogation was informally and haphazardly conducted in a public and exposed location before emergency medical equipment arrived.

Military courts initially stated that if a hearsay statement is nontestimonial, the next step is to apply the *Robert's* reliability test.[6]

However, in *Whorton v. Bockting*,[7] the Supreme Court sent a clear signal that the Confrontation Clause does not apply to nontestimonial hearsay statements. In addressing the question of whether *Crawford* announced a "watershed rule" and should apply retroactively on collateral review, the Court said:

> With respect to *testimonial* out-of-court statements, *Crawford* is more restrictive than was *Roberts,* and this may improve the accuracy of fact-finding in some criminal cases. Specifically, under *Roberts,* there may have been cases in which courts erroneously determined that

---

[6] United States v. Rankin, 64 M.J. 348 (C.A.A.F. 2007) (non-testimonial statements remain subject to Ohio v. Roberts, 448 U.S. 56 (1980)).

[7] 549 U.S. 406 (2007).

testimonial statements were reliable . . . But whatever improvement in reliability *Crawford* produced in this respect must be considered together with *Crawford's* elimination of Confrontation Clause protection against the admission of unreliable out-of-court nontestimonial statements. Under *Roberts*, an out-of-court nontestimonial statement not subject to prior cross-examination could not be admitted without a judicial determination regarding reliability. Under *Crawford*, on the other hand, the Confrontation Clause has no application to such statements and therefore permits their admission even if they lack indicia of reliability.[8]

To date there has been no clear post-*Whorton* holding from the Court of Appeals for the Armed Forces on whether it would continue to apply *Roberts* to nontestimonial statements.[9]

The Supreme Court focused on the definition of testimonial statements in *Melendez-Diaz v. Massachusetts*,[10] a drug distribution and trafficking case. The Court applied *Crawford v. Washington* to the prosecution's use of "certificates of analysis" which identified the seized substance as cocaine. The Supreme Court reversed the accused's convictions and held that the state courts erred in holding that *Crawford* did not apply to the certificates. Justice Scalia wrote for the 5-4 majority that the documents were clearly "affidavits" and fell within the "core class of testimonial statements" excluded by the Sixth Amendment unless the accused had a prior opportunity to cross-examine the unavailable declarant. Although the Court opined that its decision involved little more than a direct application of *Crawford*, its impact on court-martial litigation will be significant. Defense counsel may now challenge "chain of custody documents" by making the same Sixth Amendment arguments the Court found persuasive in *Melendez-Diaz*. In *Bullcoming v. New Mexico*,[11] the Supreme Court followed *Melendez-Diaz v. Massachusetts*, holding that forensic laboratory report are "testimonial" under the Sixth Amendment's Confrontation Clause. The Court's decision requires trial counsel to produce a laboratory report's original author unless the defense had a prior opportunity to cross-examine him. "Surrogates" or other witnesses familiar with the document's creation will not be acceptable particularly when the procecution's witness was not the original author's supervisor or had not participated in the test procedures. The Court rejected prosecution contentions that the document's original author was a "mere

---

[8] *See* United States v. Cuczzella, 66 M.J. 57 (2008) (Stuckey, J. concurring in result) ("In *Bockting*, the Supreme Court explained that nontestimonial hearsay may be admitted even if it lacks indicia of reliability. *Bockting*, 127 S. Ct. at 1183. Of course, such evidence would still be subject to the rules of evidence". Whorton v. Bockting, 549 U.S. 406 (2007)).

[9] 549 U.S. at 419.

[10] 129 S. Ct. 2527 (2009).

[11] 2011 U.S. Lexis 4790 (U.S. June 23, 2011).

scrivener" who simply reported a machine's test results and as a result did not produce "testimonial" evidence, and that the prosecution's witness was sufficiently knowledgeable about the test procedures to satisfy the accused's right to confrontation.

We discuss *Melendez-Diaz* and *Bullcoming* and their impact on military cases, in more detail at Rule 803(6), *below*.

Whether any of the nonhearsay statements falling within Rule 801(d), below, will be considered testimonial is unresolved. Because most of the Confrontation Clause issues are more likely to arise in the context of introducing hearsay statements under one of the exceptions in Rules 803, 804, or 807, we address the Confrontation Clause cases in the Editorial Comments for those rules.[11]

[b] Definition of "Statement"

Subdivision (a) defines a "statement" as an oral or written assertion or other non-verbal conduct that is intended by the person who is acting to be an assertion. The definition of "statement" is important because the word is used in subdivision (c) as part of the actual definition of hearsay. Proffered evidence that does not meet the Rule's definition of a statement is not excludable as hearsay. Usually, it is not difficult to tell whether an oral or written statement is an assertion. Conduct in lieu of a statement may raise a more difficult question. Unless the declarant intended his or her conduct to assert something, the conduct is not a statement and will not fall within the definition of hearsay set forth in (c). The burden of proof here is on the party claiming that the declarant's conduct was intended to be an assertion. As one federal court put it, "[t]he burden of proving that the person performing the nonverbal conduct intended it as an 'assertion' rests upon the party seeking to have it recognized as a 'statement.' "[12]

[c] Nonverbal Conduct

Despite the difficulty that may arise when nonverbal conduct is in issue, both military and federal courts have demonstrated that they can distinguish when conduct is intended as an assertion. For example, in *United States v. Silvis*,[13] a rape prosecution, government counsel established that shortly after the crime occurred, the victim had attempted suicide. Rejecting the accused's contention that this evidence was prohibited hearsay, the court affirmed the accused's conviction and found that the proof was nonverbal conduct that was not intended to be an assertion.

---

[11] 1 Coombs, *United States v. Blazier: So Exactly Who Needs An Invitation To The Dance?*, ARMY LAW., July 2010, at 15.

[12] United States v. Butler, 763 F.2d 11 (1st Cir. 1985).

[13] 31 M.J. 707 (N.M.C.M.R. 1990).

In *United States v. Katsougrakis*,[14] the court reached the opposite result and found that conduct was intended to be an assertion. A government witness testified that he visited a badly burned friend who was recuperating in the hospital. Because the friend was heavily bandaged and unable to speak, the friend communicated with the witness mainly by shaking his head. When the witness asked the friend whether the friend had been paid to start the fire, the friend nodded his head in agreement. On appeal, the court found that the friend's body language was a statement, because it was intended to make an assertion. The statement qualified as properly admitted hearsay evidence because it fell within the exception for declarations against penal interest.[15]

By excluding conduct not intended to be an assertion from the definition of "statement," this Rule is similar to former *Manual* practice. Although a person's out-of-court actions that are not intended to be assertions may be ambiguous, the current trend is to exclude them from definitions of hearsay on the ground that problems of sincerity are considerably reduced when the person is not intending to make an assertion at the time action is taken.[16]

[2]   Rule 801(b)—Declarant

Subdivision (b) defines the word "declarant" as a person who makes a statement. This is a standard definition and is important because it too is used in defining hearsay under subdivision (c). It should be noted that, because of the interrelationship between sections (a) and (b) of this Rule, a declarant includes an actor whose conduct is intended to be an assertion.[17]

[3]   Rule 801(c)—Hearsay

[a]   Statements Offered for Their Truth

Subdivision (c) defines hearsay as a statement offered to prove the truth of the matter asserted unless the statement was made by the declarant while testifying at the trial or hearing in which the statement is offered as evidence.[18] Although the definition of hearsay under subdivision (c) is slightly different from that found at common law and under former military practice, the difference is not very important, and practice under subdivision

---

[14] 715 F.2d 769 (2d Cir. 1983).

[15] *See* our discussion of Rule 804(b)(3), statements against penal interest.

[16] In *United States v. Martinez*, 588 F.3d 301 (6th Cir. 2009), a health care fraud prosecution, the court found harmless error in admitting a video tape containing depictions of a physician's conduct. The court found these depictions to be a statement, inadmissible under any hearsay exception, and clearly intended to be used as a nonverbal assertion.

[17] *See* Connally, *"Out Of The Mouth[s] Of Babes": Can Young Children Even Bear Testimony?* ARMY LAW. March 2008, at 1.

[18] *See, e.g.,* United States v. Thai, 29 F.3d 785 (2d Cir. 1994) (accused, who was responsible for making declarant unavailable by ordering his murder, had waived any hearsay objection to admitting declarant's statements).

(c) resembles former court-martial practice.

There are two parts to this definition. First, statements made at a trial or hearing by a witness that are subject to examination and cross-examination are not hearsay; only statements made outside of a trial or hearing can be hearsay. Second, even out-of-court statements will not be hearsay unless they are offered in evidence at the trial or hearing to prove the truth of what it is that the declarant asserted. Much of the difficulty in hearsay analysis involves determining whether a statement is being offered for its truth.

[b]   Statements Offered for Nonhearsay Purposes

Evidence may play a very important role at trial even though the proponent is not offering it to prove the truth of what a declarant said.[19] Sometimes evidence may be important to simply show that a statement was made. The Drafters' Analysis offers two good examples. First, if a witness hears a person say, "I am going to kill you" to another person (who becomes the accused), and the accused offers testimony of the witness as to what he heard in support of a self-defense claim, the statement that the witness relates is not hearsay. The important thing is not that the statement was true, but that it was made. The fact that it was made may have entitled the accused to respond to the statement with self-protective action.

Second, if a person is being tried for disobeying an order, someone who overheard the order being given may testify to what he heard. The order itself is relevant because the words were uttered. An order is neither true nor false. Either it was issued or it was not. The words that were uttered are important simply because they were said. This is not hearsay.

One way to analyze the question whether a statement is being offered for its truth is to ask whether the proponent of the statement is requesting the trier-of-fact to treat the statement as if it were made by a witness on the stand and to place faith in it as a true representation of some fact. If the answer is no, the statement is not hearsay. If the answer is yes, the statement is hearsay as that term is defined under subdivision (c).

[c]   Statements Offered to Show the Declarant's Belief

Some statements are not for their truth, but to show the belief of the declarant.[20] If, for example, one soldier said to a witness, "There goes General Jones," and later the declarant wanted to offer the testimony of the witness to show that he thought a particular person was General Jones, the statement would not be hearsay. It would not be offered to show that the person indeed was General Jones, but to show the belief of the declarant.

---

[19] *See, e.g.,* United States v. Muscato, 534 F. Supp. 969 (E.D.N.Y. 1982) (out-of-court description of gun admissible to show a match, not for its truth).

[20] *See, e.g.,* United States v. Parry, 649 F.2d 292 (5th Cir. 1981) (defendant's statement that he was working for narcotics agent not hearsay when offered to prove state of mind).

Suppose, however, that the soldier said, "I believe that that is General Jones." Would the witness's testimony be offered to prove only a belief or that the belief was true? Fortunately, no firm answer is required because the statement almost certainly will be admissible under Rule 803(3) to prove state of mind.[21]

[d]   Relationship to Rules 403 and 105

When an out-of-court statement is not offered for the truth of the matter asserted, there is a danger that members might use the statement for its truth. This might require the trial judge to make a Rule 403 ruling as to whether the danger of misuse substantially outweighs the probative value for the purpose offered. If the evidence is admitted, the opponent is entitled to a limiting instruction both at the time the evidence is discussed, and again during final instructions. *See* our discussion of Rule 105.

[4]   Rule 801(d)(1)—Prior Statement by Witness

[a]   Basis for the Rule

This subdivision states that certain statements are not hearsay and goes on to list eight different categories of statements that are treated as non-hearsay. Most, if not all, of these statements are assertions made out of court that are offered for their truth. Thus, each statement meets the definition of hearsay set forth in subdivision (c). However, subdivision (d) provides that, even though these statements qualify as hearsay under subdivision (c), they are defined as non-hearsay. The result is that they are not excluded on hearsay grounds when offered for the truth of the matter asserted. They are treated as though they were exceptions to the hearsay rule, and thus need not also qualify under the exceptions to the hearsay rule that are found in Rules 803 and 804.

[b]   Coverage of the Rule

Subdivision (d)(1) concerns statements by witnesses who are present at a trial or hearing and are subject to cross-examination concerning their prior out-of-court statements. It is important to note that a witness who is present to testify and to be cross-examined does not automatically mean that any former statements by the witness can be admitted without violating the hearsay rule. At common law, statements by anyone, including witnesses present at trial, were hearsay if they were made outside of court at a time when cross-examination was not possible, unless they qualified under the usual hearsay exceptions. Subdivision (d)(1) departs from the common law

---

[21] *See,* United States v, Quinones, 511 F.3d 289 (2d Cir. 2007) (no error admitting informant's statement from the crime scene that his safety was now in question because the defendant was "going to know" he was the informant); United States v. Hansen, 434 F.3d 92 (1st Cir. 2006) (informant's statements not offered for the truth but to provide context for defendant's statements).

and provides that three categories of former statements may be used as long as the person who made the statement is present at trial and is subject to cross-examination.

[5]   Rule 801(d)(1)(A)—Prior Inconsistent Statements

[a]   Foundation for Using the Rule

The first category of prior statements is prior inconsistent statements.[22] They must have been made under oath and subject to the penalty of perjury "at a trial, hearing, or other proceeding, or in a deposition."[23] There is no requirement for an opportunity to cross-examine when the out-of-court statement was made. There is a requirement, however, that the witness whose statements are being offered be available for cross-examination during the in-court testimony.

[b]   Subject to Cross-examination

What if the witness is present and claims to have no memory about the underlying events? Can the "subject to cross-examination" standard be satisfied?[24] This was the issue in *United States v. Owens,*[25] where the court held that a prior identification was admissible from a witness who had no memory of the events in question, or of the circumstances surrounding giving the statement. The Court said that 801(d)(1)(A) is normally satisfied when the witness takes the stand, is placed under oath, and responds to questions. The Court suggested that it would be unusual to allow a witness to avoid being impeached with her previous inconsistent statement by simply declaring that she had no memory of the previous events.

[c]   Made Under Oath

Rule 801(d)(1)(A) requires that the prior inconsistent statement have been given under oath at some kind of formal proceeding. Apparently, the drafters believed that the formal proceeding guarantees an accurate record and suggests to the person who makes the statement the importance of telling the truth, adding another guarantee of trustworthiness to the oath requirement. As the Drafters' Analysis indicates, some federal courts have read this

---

[22] *See, e.g.,* United States v. Butterworth, 511 F.3d 71 (1st Cir. 2007) (testimony need not be diametrically opposed or logically incompatible to be considered inconsistent).

[23] *See, e.g.,* United States v. Odom, 13 F.3d 949 (6th Cir. 1994) (prior grand jury testimony of a witness who recanted his testimony at trial admissible, even though inconsistencies were elicited on cross-examination by the prosecutor).

[24] *See, e.g.,* United States v. Hemmer, 729 F.2d 10 (1st Cir. 1984) (grand jury testimony properly admitted where witness suffered memory lapses and made inconsistent statements); United States v. Russell, 712 F.2d 1256 (8th Cir. 1983) (absence of memory can be inconsistent with prior statement); United States v. Distler, 671 F.2d 954 (6th Cir. 1981) (finding partial or vague recollection to be an inconsistency and rejecting a confrontation attack on (d)(1)(A)).

[25] 484 U.S. 554 (1988).

provision broadly and have allowed in statements that may not have been made under the most reliable circumstances.[26] But, military authority excludes statements made to investigating officials and all "police house interrogations."[27]

Article 32 hearings have consistently been viewed as falling within the Rule's coverage.

[d]   Use as Substantive Evidence

The importance of (d)(1)(A) is clear. It marks a change from prior law.[28] A qualifying statement can be admitted as substantive evidence, not simply for impeachment use.[29] Thus, no limiting instruction is required when a prior inconsistent statement qualifies under Rule 801(d)(1)(A).[30] If a witness is present at trial and has made statements that qualify under this provision, either the prosecution or the defense can call a witness it knows will be unfavorable for the sole purpose of bringing out the prior statements. This is the permissible elicitation of substantive evidence.

This is very different from the situation in which there are prior inconsistent statements that do not qualify under (d)(1)(A). A party may not ethically call a witness it knows will be unfavorable for the sole purpose of eliciting prior statements that are not admissible as substantive evidence. That situation is discussed under Rules 607 and 613.

[6]   Rule 801(d)(1)(B)—Prior Consistent Statements

[a]   Foundation for Using the Rule

Subdivision (d)(1)(B) covers prior consistent statements.[31] Unlike prior inconsistent statements, consistent statements need not have been made under oath, or in a prior proceeding. Any statement made previously to anyone might qualify.[32] However, the Rule covers only those statements that

---

[26] *See, e.g.,* United States v. Castro-Ayon, 537 F.2d 1055 (9th Cir. 1976), *cert. denied,* 429 U.S. 983 (1976) (admitting tape-recorded statements given under oath at a border patrol station).

[27] In United States v. Luke, 13 M.J. 958 (A.F.C.M.R. 1982), and United States v. Powell, 17 M.J. 975 (A.C.M.R. 1984), these Service Courts of Appeals indicated that they will not follow some federal authority which appears to equate police and related interrogations with the "solemnity" of more formal hearings or trials.

[28] *See* 1969 Manual ¶ 39 *a*; United States v. Burge, 1 M.J. 408 (C.M.A. 1976) (Cook, J., concurring).

[29] *Compare* with our discussion of Rule 613. *See* United States v. Taylor, 44 M.J. 475, 476 (C.A.A.F. 1996), and United States v. Ureta, 44 M.J. 290 (C.A.A.F. 1996) for a discussion of these issues.

[30] *See* our discussion of Rules 105, 607 and 613.

[31] *See, e.g.,* United States v. Eagle, 498 F.3d 885 (8th Cir, 2007) (to be admissible there must first be a claim that the witness recently fabricated his testimony).

[32] *See, e.g.,* United States v. Hebeka, 25 F.3d 287 (6th Cir. 1994) (circuit follows majority

are offered to rebut an express or implied charge against the declarant of recent fabrication, improper influence or bad motive.[33] This limitation reflects the common law view that someone who repeats the same story over and over is not necessarily likely to be more truthful than someone who speaks just once. A lie often repeated does not become the truth. The Rule permits a party to show that witnesses has been consistent in what they have been saying, but only after a suggestion is made that they have invented testimony.[34]

[b] The Rule's Timing Requirement

Previous military and federal authorities differed as to whether the prior statement had to have been made before the alleged motive to falsify testimony arose.[35] While some federal courts historically viewed this issue more as a relevance question than a hearsay issue, military courts tended to strictly interpret the Rule. For example, in *United States v. McCaskey,*[36] the court held that consistent pretrial statements are admissible only if they are made before the "alleged recent fabrication or improper influence or motive occurred."[37] Prudent counsel and military judges understand the importance

---

view that Rule 801(d)(1)(B) is applicable when a third party testifies as to someone's prior statement; declarant was subject to cross-examination and recall, so ordinary hearsay dangers were protected against).

[33] In United States v. Browder, 19 M.J. 988 (A.F.C.M.R. 1985), the court reversed conviction because a key government witness's prior consistent statement was not supported by sufficient evidence to demonstrate an express or implied charge of fabrication.

[34] *See, e.g.,* United States v. Sutton, 732 F.2d 1483 (10th Cir. 1984) (cross-examination might suggest fabrication and open door to rehabilitation); United States v. Coleman, 631 F.2d 908 (D.C. Cir. 1980) (suggestion of inaccurate memory permits use of prior consistent statement).

[35] In United States v. Cottriel, 21 M.J. 535 (N.M.C.M.R. 1985), the court rejected the accused's claims and found no error in the trial judge having permitted a four-year-old sodomy victim's father to testify concerning the contents of a prior consistent statement the victim made to him even though "the statement was not made prior to a motive to fabricate or the existence of an improper influence alleged to form the basis of taint." The court said there is no requirement in Rule 801(d)(1) "that the prior consistent statement precede the occurrence of the tainting influence." *See also* United States v. Meyers, 18 M.J. 347 (C.M.A. 1984). The court also held that the use of a prior consistent statement may be proven by the testimony of a third party, even though there is "some meager support" to the contrary.

[36] 30 M.J. 188 (C.M.A. 1990).

[37] However, most federal courts have determined that the common law, which viewed prior consistent statements as generally inadmissible, was adopted by the drafters of Rule 801. The majority of the federal courts have also taken this approach. *See, e.g.,* United States v. Quinto, 582 F.2d 224 (2d Cir. 1978) (court reversed conviction because the statement was made prior to the time that the motive to falsify arose). The court also expressed an intention to follow traditional common law limitations on the admission of prior consistent statements, particularly because they are now admissible as substantive evidence. *See also* United States v. Meyers, 18 M.J. 347 (C.M.A. 1984) (strong dissent would limit such evidence to situations

of timing and follow the court's guidance in *United States v. Hurst*[38] by ensuring that an adequate foundation as to the timing of the pretrial statement is set out on the trial record.[39]

In *Tome v. United States*,[40] the Supreme Court settled the question on timing. It held that a prior consistent statement is not admissible for the truth of the matter asserted under this Rule unless the statement was made *before* the alleged fabrication, improper influence, or motive occurred.[41] In reaching this result Justice Kennedy concluded that the federal drafters had adopted the common law timing rule. He went on to say that had Congress intended a different result, they certainly could have specified it in the Rule.

[c]   Substantive and Other Uses

It should be remembered that Rule 801(d)(1)(B)'s temporal and foundational requirements only apply to using prior consistent statements as substantive evidence.[42] As *Tome* suggests, nothing in the Rule bars the offer of prior consistent statements, which do not meet these standards, from being used to support the credibility of a witness, as opposed to proving the truth of what that witness said. Prior consistent statements are also admissible for non-substantive purposes when they are used to explain inconsistencies in a witness's testimony. When prior consistent statements are admissible for a purpose other than to prove the truth of their contents, most federal courts have required limiting instructions.[43]

It should not be forgotten that the common law distrusted prior consistent statements. Their probative value in many instances is low. A Rule 403 balancing test might well lead to their exclusion when it appears that a witness has been making statements for the purpose of creating a record of consistency.

---

where it specifically contradicts evidence showing a witness has changed her testimony due to some threat, scheme, or bribe).

[38] 29 M.J. 477 (C.M.A. 1990).

[39] *See, e.g.,* United States v. Al-Moayad, 545 F.3d 139 (2d Cir. 2008) (proponent must show that the statements were made before a motive to falsify arose).

[40] 513 U.S. 150 (1995).

[41] *See, e.g.,* United States v. Stuart, 718 F.2d 931 (9th Cir. 1983) (statements made prior to plea agreement could be used for rehabilitation); United States v. Henderson, 717 F.2d 135 (4th Cir. 1983) (prior consistent statements made before bargain was entered with government could be used to rehabilitate government witness).

[42] *See, e.g.,* United States v. Taylor, 41 M.J. 701 (A.F.Ct.Crim.App. 1995) (during the accused's trial for premeditated murder, burglary, and larceny, prior government consistent statements were considered as substantive evidence, but prior defense inconsistent statements were not. On appeal the accused contended that both categories of statements should have been treated the same. Affirming these convictions, the court found that Rule 801 supported the judge's decision).

[43] *See, e.g.,* United States v. Castillo, 14 F.3d 802, 803 (2d Cir. 1994) (limiting instructions required when evidence used for nonsubstantive purposes).

Similarly, prior consistent statements that do not qualify for admission under this Rule may be admissible substantively if they qualify under the residual hearsay exception, Rule 807.

[7]   Rule 801(d)(1)(C)—Prior Identifications

[a]   Foundation for Using the Rule

The third category of prior out-of-court statements by a witness that qualify for admission as substantive evidence is prior identifications.[44] Any identification of a person made "after perceiving the person" identified may be admitted. It is difficult to imagine an identification made *before* perceiving the person; thus, the language that we have quoted from the Rule is unnecessary and results from a deletion of the word "immediately" in an earlier draft of the Rule. Prior identification means at any time prior to the trial or hearing. There is no time constraint on when the identification must have been made. Of course, the identification must comply with the requirements of law. *See* our discussion of Rule 321.

An identification need not have been made under oath or in a proceeding. It can be used whether or not there is any suggestion that the witness is lying. There is no requirement that the witness have any loss of memory as a prerequisite to the use of the statement. Rule 801(d)(1)(C) reflects the modern trend that earlier identifications are more likely to be trustworthy than later identifications, and that due process requirements assure that the identifications will be reliable enough to be used as evidence.

[b]   Subject to Cross-examination

For all of these categories to be applicable, the witness must be subject to cross-examination.[45] It seems evident that a witness who refuses to respond to questions on cross-examination would not satisfy the Rule and any (d)(1) statements of such a witness would have to be stricken. The Supreme Court's decision in *United States v. Owens*, above, has established that memory loss does not render a witness unavailable for cross-examination. The fact that a witness may deny having made a prior statement does not prevent it from being admitted through another witness. As long as the witness is available for cross-examination, the Rule and confrontation concerns are both satisfied.[46]

---

[44] *See, e.g.,* United States v. Baker, 432 F.3d 1189 (11th Cir. 2005) (statements of identification admissible only if declarant is present at trial for cross-examination).

[45] *See, e.g.,* United States v. Elemy, 656 F.2d 507 (9th Cir. 1981) (law enforcement officer may testify to identification if identifying witness is also present).

[46] *See, e.g.,* Nelson v. O'Neil, 402 U.S. 622 (1971) (at joint trial with alibi defense, no error where co-accused testified in own defense, denied making prior statement implicating the accused, and testified in the accused's favor).

[8]   Rule 801(d)(2)—Admission by Party-Opponent

[a]   In General

The remainder of subdivision (d) covers five kinds of statements that previously comprised a familiar exception to the hearsay rule, the admissions exception. Although the five admissions found in subdivision (d)(2) are now deemed to be non-hearsay, the effect of the new Rule is to admit these statements as evidence just as they were admitted when they were hearsay exceptions.[47] As discussed *below*, Rule 801(d)(2) was amended in 1999 to comply with, explain, and in some ways expand upon the Supreme Court's holding in *Bourjaily v. United States*,[48] which specifically addressed the standards for admitting coconspirators statements, but now has been expanded to affect all vicarious admissions.

[b]   Party Admissions and Confrontation Issues

As noted above, the Supreme Court's decisions in *Crawford v. Washington*,[49] *Davis v. Washington*,[50] and *Michigan v. Bryant*,[51] addressed the template for determining whether a hearsay statement satisfies the requirements of the Confrontation Clause. Under *Ohio v. Roberts*,[52] the test had focused on whether the offered hearsay was reliable. Now the test is whether the offered hearsay statement is "testimonial."[53] Under *Roberts*, offering a party's admission generally did not raise confrontation clause concerns. But, under *Crawford*, there may be a question about whether the offered admission is "testimonial." As one commentator has pointed out, it is not likely that for purposes of confrontation, an accused would be entitled to "confront" himself, if the government offers his or her statements into evidence.[54] But for admissions by an agent, it is theoretically possible that an agent's statement to law enforcement officers would be considered testimonial and thus subject to the *Crawford* analysis. *Crawford* strongly suggests that coconspirator statements are not testimonial. And *Boujaily v.*

---

[47] This is not to say that the placement of admissions in Rule 801 may not be significant. Rule 807, the residual exception to the hearsay rule, permits courts to admit evidence that technically does not qualify under a traditional exception, but seems to be reliable enough to be admitted. It is not clear that under the residual exception an analogy can be drawn to admissions, because admissions are not treated as hearsay exceptions.

[48] 483 U.S. 171 (1987).

[49] 541 U.S. 36 (2004).

[50] 547 U.S. 813 (2006).

[51] 131 S.Ct. 1143 (2011).

[52] 448 U.S. 56 (1980).

[53] *See, e.g.,* United States v. Ramirez, 479 F.3d 1229 (10th Cir (2007) (no *Crawford* violation as statements were not testimonial).

[54] *See* 4 S. Saltzburg, M. Martin & D. Capra, FEDERAL RULES OF EVIDENCE MANUAL § 801.02[7] (9th ed. 2006).

United States[55] finds such statements to be firmly rooted. Thus, it is doubtful that coconspirator statements will be excluded by the Confrontation Clause.[56]

[9]   Rule 801(d)(2)(A)—Personal Admissions

[a]   Foundation for Using the Rule

This section of the Rule covers the most familiar of all admissions, the personal admission. It provides that a party's own statements may be useful against him or her, just as they could under previous *Manual* guidance. As in the past, applying the personal exception requires adherence to Article 31's warning requirements and Rules 304 and 305 as well.

Although Rule 602 requires all witnesses, including hearsay declarants, to have personal knowledge concerning the matter about which they are speaking,[57] that requirement does not apply to (d)(2)(A) statements. As a result, counsel cannot keep his or her client's pretrial statements from being admitted by arguing that the client did not know what he or she was talking about. The admissions rule is one of personal responsibility. A person who has made a statement must suffer the use of it by an opponent, who is not burdened with having to show what the admitting party knew and did not know. The party whose admission is offered is free to testify and explain the statement.

Moreover, an admission need not have been intended to admit anything. A self-serving statement, even a boast, may be admitted against the declarant by an opposing party.

[10]   Rule 801(d)(2)(B)—Adoptive Admissions

[a]   Implicit Admissions

This provision covers the common law concept of adoptive admissions.[58] There are two types of adoptive admissions. First, implicit admissions occur when a declarant specifically recognizes and acquiesces in a statement or action. For example, a declarant says: "I agree with you. That is correct." In *United States v. Garrett,*[59] the court provided a three-part test for determining when such evidence may be admitted. The court held that adoptive admissions are admissible if the proponent establishes: "(1) the party against

---

[55] 483 U.S. 171 (1987).

[56] *See generally,* Best, *To Be or Not to Be Testimonial? That is the Question: 2004 Developments in the Sixth Amendment,* ARMY LAW. April 2005, at 65 (very thorough discussion of *Crawford* and the issues counsel and military judges are likely to encounter in applying the Supreme Court's new guidance for hearsay and the Sixth Amendment).

[57] *See* our discussion of Rule 602.

[58] *See, e.g.,* United States v. Shulman, 624 F.2d 384 (2d Cir. 1980) (adopted statement need not incriminate person who made statement).

[59] 16 M.J. 941 (N.M.C.M.R. 1983).

whom it is offered was present during the making of the statement; (2) he understood its content; and (3) his actions or words or both unequivocally acknowledged the statement in adopting it as his own."[60]

[b] Tacit Admissions

Second, tacit admissions occur when a statement is made to a person under circumstances that would cause a reasonable person to deny or indicate some disagreement with the statement but none is made.[61] Rule 801 (d)(2)(B) allows the person's failure to deny or comment on the statement to be viewed as agreement with it.[62]

When contested, the bench's responsibility under Rule 104(a) is to determine whether the person's silence was intended as an agreement, and is otherwise admissible. The trial judge is a factfinder for purposes of the hearsay rule. If the trial judge finds by a preponderance of the evidence that a person's silence represented an agreement, then it and the preceding statement are admissible as substantive proof. Military and federal[63] courts use a reasonable person standard in reaching this result.

For example, in *United States v. Stanley*,[64] the court held that incriminating statements made by another person in the defendant's presence were inadmissible because "while silence may be considered an admission under certain circumstances, it is clear that merely hearing the statements of third persons does not equate to adoption by silence. . . . An inference of assent cannot safely be made . . . unless the circumstances are such that dissent would in ordinary experience have been expressed if the communication had not been correct." Here the defendant's silence could easily have been interpreted as unfamiliarity with the crimes in question. Similarly, in *United States v. Ferris*,[65] the court held that unless the government can establish that a pretrial note to the accused was fully known to him and that he approved of its contents, the document "cannot be deemed to have been adopted or acquiesced in" by the accused.

---

[60] *See, e.g.*, United States v. Paulino, 13 F.3d 20 (1st Cir. 1994) (holding admissible a document bearing defendant's name for rent paid as evidence to rebut defendant's assertion that he had no connection with apartment and its contents).

[61] *Compare* United States v. Basic Constr. Co., 711 F.2d 570 (4th Cir. 1983), *cert. denied*, 464 U.S. 956 (1984) (silence by corporate officer deemed to be an admission) *with* Southern Stone v. Singer, 665 F.2d 698 (5th Cir. 1982) (mere failure to respond to letter does not indicate adoption unless it was reasonable to expect a response).

[62] *See e.g.*, United States v. Duval, 496 F.3d 64 (1st Cir. 2007) (statements made in a small room causes court to find defendant's silence gave rise to a reasonable inference that he adopted them).

[63] *See, e.g.*, United States v. Hoosier, 542 F.2d 687 (6th Cir. 1976) (human behavior most likely would have led the accused to deny his girlfriend's incriminating statement).

[64] 21 M.J. 249 (C.M.A. 1986).

[65] 21 M.J. 702 (A.C.M.R. 1985).

It is important to keep in mind that when a person is under official investigation, or in confinement, arrest, or custody, Military Rule of Evidence 304(h)(3) may prohibit the silence, which otherwise complies with this Rule, from being considered.[66]

[11] Rule 801(d)(2)(C)—Statements by Authorized Persons

[a] Foundation for Using the Rule

The third type of admissions found in 801(d)(2)(C), are statements made by authorized spokespersons.[67] The rationale here is fairly clear. If one person asks someone else to speak for him or her, the requesting party is treated as if he or she had made the statements personally. Although the former *Manual* did not have a specific provision for such statements, the drafters of the Rule indicate that these statements would have qualified under an agency theory previously.

[b] Use by the Prosecution

Authorized statements can be very useful to military prosecutors. Using this provision, a party's books or other records can be introduced even though they were prepared by an agent.[68] Records of drug transactions and similar crimes often result in evidence that might qualify for admission under this subdivision.

[12] Rule 801(d)(2)(D)—Statements by Agents or Servants

[a] Comparison with the Common Law Rule

A fourth type of admissions, covered by subdivision (d)(2)(D), are statements by a party's agent or servant concerning a matter within the scope of the agency or employment while the agency or employment relationship continues.[69] This provision allows in evidence more statements than were admitted at common law where courts required the agent or servant to have been specifically employed for the purpose of making the statement. The Military and Federal Rules depart from this limitation, admitting statements as long as they fall within the agent's scope of authority and are made while

---

[66] *See also* Doyle v. Ohio, 426 U.S. 610 (1976) (post *Miranda* warning statements not admissible).

[67] *See, e.g.,* United States v. Parsons, 646 F.2d 1275 (8th Cir. 1981) (bankruptcy petition prepared by attorney can be used as agent's admission against client).

[68] *See, e.g.,* United States v. Garcia-Duarte, 718 F.2d 42 (2d Cir. 1983) (customer record book of drug transactions was hearsay if used to show that a certain person was engaged in transactions with the book's author).

[69] *See, e.g.,* United States v. Chappell, 698 F.2d 308 (7th Cir. 1983) (testimony before SEC by corporate agent was an admission and could be used to lay foundation for business records); Russell v. United Parcel Serv., 666 F.2d 1188 (8th Cir. 1981) (opinion by agent admissible against principal in diversity action involving alleged employment discrimination).

the agency or employment relationship continued. The rationale for the expanded rule is that agents or employees have an incentive not to make statements that might damage the party who retains them.

[b]   Government Agents

On its face, the Rule would seem to apply to the government as well as to the defense. But, some civilian courts have suggested that statements by government employees do not fall within this provision.[70] It is difficult to see why all government agents should be treated differently from the agents of other entities or individuals.[71] A case could be made that informants ought not to be covered by the rule, since their interests and motivations might not always be the same as the government's. With respect to other agents employed by the Armed Forces, it would seem that statements made by military and civilian members of the force that the government trusts with national security matters ought to qualify for admission under this hearsay exemption.

[c]   Interpreters

Rule 801(d)(2)(D) has an impact on the use of interpreters. Because the Uniform Code of Military Justice has worldwide application, it is common for service-members to be charged with offenses involving foreign nationals and their local police. Accused individuals who are taken into custody under these circumstances are often confronted with language problems, and U.S. government officials must resort to interpreters while communicating with the accused and other witnesses.

Some of the problems that may arise were discussed in *United States v. DaSilva*.[72] There the accused gave DEA agents a false exculpatory statement. At trial, defense counsel objected to the DEA agent referring to the statement because the accused had made it through an interpreter. The trial court admitted the accused's statement in part because the accused expressed an interest in the interpreter helping him communicate with the government officials. The Second Circuit affirmed the accused's conviction, finding a "testimonial identity" between the accused and his translator reliance by the

---

[70] In United States v. Kampiles, 609 F.2d 1233 (7th Cir. 1979), the court held that a government employee's statements do not fall within 801(d)(2)(D) because "in a criminal prosecution, government employees are not considered servants of a party-opponent for the purposes of the admissions rule." We question this reasoning since no corporate defendant in a criminal case wants agents' statements used against it either; but they are so used. Moreover, if agent's statements do not include government agents, the drafters probably could have omitted this exception from the Military Rules.

[71] *See, e.g.,* United States v. Garza, 448 F.3d 294 (5th Cir. 2006) (court noted a split in authority as to whether reports of government agents are admissible against the government, but noted even if they were the statements were inadmissible because they concerned a different case and were never officially adopted).

[72] 725 F.2d 828 (2d Cir. 1983).

accused upon the translator throughout the DEA confrontation. Crucial to the Court's holding was the accused's specific acceptance of the translator's services.

[13]   Rule 801(d)(2)(E)—Statements by Coconspirators

[a]   Defining the Rule

The final category of admissions, Rule 801(d)(2)E), is coconspirators' statements. The Rule provides that statements by one conspirator made during the course[73] and in furtherance of the conspiracy may be admitted against other conspirators.[74] The judge has three separate determinations to make under this Rule. First, the judge must decide whether the declarant conspirator and any accused against whom a statement is offered were members of the same conspiracy. Second, the judge must decide whether the statement was made during the course of the conspiracy, which may require a determination as to when the conspiracy actually ended.[75] Third, the judge must decide whether the statement was in furtherance of the conspiracy. Some courts have not treated this requirement very seriously.[76] Other courts have enforced the requirement with vigor.[77]

Rule 801(d)(2)(E) does not require that a conspiracy be charged, only that it existed during the relevant period.[78] Statements by acquitted conspirators[79] and uncharged (unindicted)[80] conspirators qualify for admission under the Rule.

---

[73] *See, e.g.,* United States v. Astorga-Torres, 671 F.2d 346 (9th Cir. 1982) (error to admit statements made prior to conspiracy).

[74] *See, e.g.,* United States v. Ammar, 714 F.2d 238 (3d Cir. 1983) (finding that statements providing reassurance to conspirators are in furtherance of conspiracy); United States v. Foster, 711 F.2d 871 (9th Cir. 1983) (narrative declarations held not to be in furtherance of conspiracy); United States v. Phillips, 664 F.2d 971 (5th Cir. 1981) (casual retrospective statements not in furtherance of conspiracy); United States v. Pirolli, 673 F.2d 1200 (11th Cir. 1982) (conspirator's statement was relevant to prove the existence of a conspiracy).

[75] *See, e.g.,* United States v. Floyd, 555 F.2d 45 (2d Cir. 1976) (conspiracy ends when "the central criminal purposes of a conspiracy have been attained, a subsidiary conspiracy to conceal [the original crime] may not be implied from circumstantial evidence showing merely that the conspiracy was kept a secret . . .").

[76] *See, e.g.,* United States v. Harris, 546 F.2d 234 (8th Cir. 1976) (statements made by a conspirator after his arrest were admissible because the conspirator did not disassociate himself from the conspiracy after he was arrested).

[77] *See, e.g.,* United States v. Castillo, 615 F.2d 878 (9th Cir. 1980) ("merely narrative declarations" which do not further the conspiracy fall outside 801(d)(2)(D), but statements made in furtherance of the conspiracy by the conspirators fall within the Rule).

[78] *See, e.g.,* United States v. DeVillio, 983 F.2d 1185 (2nd Cir. 1993) (no requirement that defendant actually be charged with conspiracy).

[79] *See, e.g.,* United States v. Barksdale-Contreras, 972 F.2d 111 (5th Cir. 1992) (statements admissible where defendant acquitted of conspiracy).

[80] *See, e.g.,* United States v. Smith, 550 F.2d 277 (5th Cir. 1977) (statement of unindicted

[b] Independent Evidence of the Conspiracy

[i] In General

Before a conspirator's statement can be admitted the military judge needs to resolve two questions: (1) How much evidence must be presented to establish the foundational elements of the conspiracy?[81] (2) Can the hearsay statement itself be used in making this determination? Civilian and military courts had a difficult time resolving these questions.[82] When first adopted, Rule 801(d)(2)(E) did not have an independent evidence requirement as part of the text, but the Rule required the trial judge to find that there was a conspiracy. There was some confusion as to how the judge should make the determination, especially in light of Rule 104(a) which permits a judge to consider any evidence, whether or not admissible (other than privileged information), in making an evidence ruling. A number of different approaches to the independent evidence problem existed before the Federal and Military Rules of Evidence were adopted.[83] Courts disagreed on how the trial judge should assess independent evidence.[84]

[ii] *Bourjaily v. United States*

Bourjaily v. United States[85] resolved the disagreements. The Supreme

---

co-conspirator admissible where it can be shown he played an active role in the conduct of the conspiracy).

[81] *See, e.g.,* United States v. Stipe, 653 F.2d 446 (10th Cir. 1981) (suggesting that conspirators' statements should not be admitted until the requisite foundation is laid); United States v. Alvarez-Porras, 643 F.2d 54 (2d Cir. 1981) (proponent of conspirator's statements must prove conspiracy by preponderance of independent evidence); United States v. Jackson, 627 F.2d 1198 (D.C. Cir. 1980) (substantial independent evidence of conspiracy needed to admit conspirators' statements).

[82] In United States v. Ludlum, 20 M.J. 954 (A.F.C.M.R. 1985), conviction was reversed because the government did not establish "the existence of a conspiratorial agreement" before it admitted a co-conspirator's statement. Similarly, in United States v. Ludlum, 20 M.J. 954 (A.F.C.M.R. 1985), the court reversed the accused's drug related convictions because it found that the government had not established "the existence of a conspiratorial agreement" before it admitted a co-conspirator's statement alleged to be the product of that agreement. In the court's view, "the existence of a conspiratorial agreement could not [have been] established by the language of the statement sought to be admitted. To allow this would be 'boot strapping,' and would permit the questioned evidence itself to furnish the predicate for its own admission."

[83] *See, e.g.,* United States v. Martorano, 557 F.2d 1 (1st Cir. 1977) ("new rules permit a trial judge to base his determination on hearsay and other inadmissible evidence, including perhaps the very statement seeking admission").

[84] *See, e.g.,* United States v. James, 590 F.2d 575 (5th Cir.) (en banc), *cert. denied,* 442 U.S. 917 (1979) (conspirator's statements are not admissible until an evidentiary hearing is conducted demonstrating, with "substantial independent evidence," that a conspiracy existed); United States v. Ludlum, 20 M.J. 954 (A.F.C.M.R. 1985) (court did not allow "the questioned evidence itself to furnish the predicate for its own admission").

[85] 479 U.S. 881 (1987).

Court held that conspirator statements may be admitted only when it is established, by a preponderance of the evidence, that a conspiracy existed and that the declarant and the defendant were participants in it. The Court held that trial judges can consider the proffered hearsay statements themselves in making this determination, although it reserved decision on whether the proffered statements alone would be enough to satisfy the preponderance standard. Most courts have looked for corroborating evidence.[86]

The fact that the trial judge may consider the challenged statements as part of the foundation under the Rule makes meeting the preponderance standard much easier for government counsel to satisfy as long as the independent evidence is sufficiently incriminating on its own. Testimony which is "wholly innocuous" or demonstrative of only innocent conduct will generally be insufficient to meet the standard.[87] One authority has suggested that courts:

> [I]n evaluating the independent evidence presented, use a standard analogous to the reasonable suspicion test that is used to determine the legality of a *Terry* stop under the Fourth Amendment. That test, as applied to coconspirator hearsay, would be: whether the independent evidence, standing alone, presents a fair possibility of illegal activity. The government need not overcome every possible innocent explanation of the facts presented. But, on the other hand, facts that are not at all suggestive of criminal association . . . should not suffice.[88] (footnotes omitted)

[iii]   *Bourjaily* and the 1999 Amendment to Rule 801(d)(2)

Both the military and federal drafters amended Rule 801(d)(2) to build upon the Supreme Court's holding in *Bourjaily v. United States*. Their intention was to accomplish three goals. First, the amendment codifies the Court's holding in *Bourjaily* by expressly providing that the military judge shall consider the contents of a coconspirator's statement in determining "the existence of the conspiracy and the participation therein of the declarant and the party against whom the statement is offered." According to *Bourjaily*, Rule 104(a) requires these preliminary questions to be established by a preponderance of the evidence.

Second, as discussed above, the amendment resolves the issue concerning what evidence in addition to the declarant's statement is required to be

---

[86] *See, e.g.,* United States v. Langlois, 15 F.3d 1216 (1st Cir. 1993) (independent evidence required before conspirator statements deemed sufficient).

[87] *See, e.g.,* United States v. Silverman, 861 F.2d 571 (9th Cir. 1988) (conduct which was consistent with defendant's awareness of the conspiracy was required).

[88] 4 S. Saltzburg, M. Martin & D. Capra, FEDERAL RULES OF EVIDENCE MANUAL § 801.02[6][g] (9th ed. 2006).

admitted in order to establish that a conspiracy existed involving both the declarant and the defendant. Rule 801(d)(2) is now in accord with every court of appeals that has resolved this issue by requiring some evidence in addition to the contents of the statement.[89]

Third, the amendment takes the same approach to authority under subdivision (C) and agency or employment and scope thereof under subdivision (D). Thus, whenever a statement by a declarant is offered as a vicarious admission, a trial judge may consider the contents of the statement in determining whether Rule 801(d) is satisfied, but the judge must also find some independent evidence.

[iv] Confrontation and *Crawford*

The Supreme Court discussed the admissibility of co-conspirator statements in *Crawford v. Washington*.[90] *[SS1]* The Court held that a defendant's right to confrontation was not violated when such statements were admitted pursuant to this Rule, and were made during the course of and in furtherance of the conspiracy. The Court reasoned that such statements by there nature are "non-testimonial." Lower federal courts have consistently taken this approach.[91] See our previous discussion of *Crawford* and its progeny.

[c] Nature of the Pretrial Hearing

A number of courts have struggled with the question of what kind of hearing should be held when ruling on the admissibility of conspirators' statements. With respect to many hearsay questions, and many other questions of evidence law that the judge decides, Rule 104 makes it possible to have a hearing outside the presence of the jury in which the judge listens to all relevant testimony in order to make the preliminary determination on admissibility.

However, when conspirators' statements are offered, this procedure is often unrealistic. It may be that the independent evidence the government relies on amounts to most of the government's case. To make trial counsel

---

[89] *See, e.g.*, United States v. Beckham, 968 F.2d 47, 51 (D.C. Cir. 1992); United States v. Sepulveda, 15 F.3d 1161, 1181–1182 (1st Cir. 1993); United States v. Daly, 842 F.2d 1380, 1386 (2d Cir.), *cert. denied*, 488 U.S. 821 (1988); United States v. Clark, 18 F.3d 1337, 1341–1342 (6th Cir.); United States v. Zambrana, 841 F.2d 1320, 1344–1345 (7th Cir. 1988); United States v. Silverman, 861 F.2d 571, 577 (9th Cir. 1988); United States v. Gordon, 844 F.2d 1397, 1402 (9th Cir. 1988); United States v. Hernandez, 829 F.2d 988, 993 (10th Cir. 1987), *cert. denied*, 485 U.S. 1013 (1988); United States v. Byrom, 910 F.2d 725, 736 (11th Cir. 1990).

[90] 541 U.S. 36 (2004).

[91] *See, e.g.*, United States v. Stover, 474 F.3d 904 (6th Cir. 2007) (defendant's right to confrontation not violated when statements are properly admitted under this rule); *see also*, United States v. Lopez-Medina, 461 F.3d 724 (6th Cir. 2006) (slips of paper characterized as a drug ledger are admissible against the accused as evidence of a drug trafficking conspiracy).

put on that evidence in a preliminary hearing is to try the case twice.[92] Thus, a trial judge in federal court often will allow the government to introduce conspirators' statements with the promise that sufficient independent evidence will be offered to convince the judge to make a ruling, using the preponderance of the evidence standard, that Rule 801(d)(2)(E) is satisfied. If the government fails to keep its promise, any conspirators' statements that were conditionally admitted will be stricken, or a mistrial will be declared when that is necessary to protect the accused.

Some courts have suggested that the government should try to offer its independent evidence first, before offering conspirators' statements. This is a suggestion that may work in a simple conspiracy case, but it may cause problems in a complex and lengthy case by disrupting the order of proof and making it more difficult for the court members to keep up with and understand the testimony.

Another technique used by some courts requires government counsel to demonstrate, orally or in writing, the independent evidence upon which it intends to rely. This gives the judge a chance to make an initial judgment and decide to have a preliminary hearing when: (1) the independent evidence is weak; (2) the conspirators' statements are critical to the government's case; and (3) it might appear unfair to the bench to make the accused stand trial before a decision is made on the admissibility of the conspirators' statements.

There probably is no escape from the proposition that, unless courts are willing to take the time to have hearings similar to full scale trials, they often will have to rely on representations by government counsel concerning the sufficiency of independent evidence.

[d]   Substance and Timing of the Trial Court's Ruling

Courts agree that the trial judge must ultimately find, by a preponderance of the evidence that the: (1) conspiracy exists; (2) person who made the statement was a member of the conspiracy; (3) person against whom it is offered also is a member of the conspiracy; (4) conspiracy was ongoing at the time the statement was made and (5) statement was in furtherance of the conspiracy.[93] Similarly, in all the Federal Circuits trial judges must rule at the conclusion of the government's case concerning the admissibility of conspirators' statements.[94]

However, even if the government has satisfied the preponderance standard

---

[92] *See, e.g.,* United States v. Whitley, 670 F.2d 617 (5th Cir. 1982) (separate hearing on admissibility is not always possible).

[93] *See, e.g.,* United States v. Winship, 724 F.2d 1116 (5th Cir. 1984) (trial judge made correct ruling, although he did not articulate it for the record).

[94] *See, e.g.,* United States v. Jefferson, 714 F.2d 689 (7th Cir. 1983) (proper for judge to make preponderance ruling at end of government's case).

at this time, the matter is still not finally resolved because the accused has yet to present his evidence.[95] In any ordinary hearing on an evidence question, both sides have a chance to be heard, and this is of course applicable to the conspirators' hearsay rule. Thus, the military judge should reconsider the preponderance of the evidence ruling at the close of all the evidence. In some civilian courts this occurs at the time the judge makes a formal ruling admitting the evidence. In other courts the judge simply reconsiders a prior formal ruling.[96] The difference is not significant.

Finally, civilian courts have consistently ruled that lay finders of fact should not be informed of a trial judge's decision that sufficient evidence exists to find a conspiracy for the purposes of Rule 801(d)(2)(E).[97] Passing such information to the court members would, at the very least confuse them, and would more likely influence them to think that the military judge believes the charged crimes actually occurred.[98]

[e]   Some Miscellaneous Considerations

Just as trial judges have to decide whether a conspiracy exists before admitting statements under (d)(2)(E), the judge must make a similar determination under subdivision (d)(2)(C) and (D). Under these subdivisions the judge must decide that someone is indeed authorized or actually an agent before admitting statements.[99]

The fact that a statement qualifies for admission under Rule 801 does not necessarily mean that a confrontation challenge cannot be made.[100] But,

---

[95] *See, e.g.,* United States v. Dean, 666 F.2d 174 (5th Cir. 1982) (in ruling on admissibility court must consider evidence offered by both sides).

[96] *See, e.g.,* United States v. DeRoche, 726 F.2d 1025 (5th Cir. 1984) (remanded to trial judge for further findings where it was not clear that ruling on admissibility was reconsidered at close of evidence).

[97] *See, e.g.,* United States v. Mastropieri, 685 F.2d 776 (2d Cir. 1982) (judge should rule on admissibility of conspirator statements and should not resubmit or discuss admissibility issue with jury); United States v. Bulman, 667 F.2d 1374 (11th Cir. 1982) (error to resubmit admissibility question to jury once judge found no preponderant proof of conspiracy).

[98] *See, e.g.,* United States v. Hartley, 678 F.2d 961 (11th Cir. 1982) (statements of conspirators should be admitted without special instructions like any other evidence).

[99] *See, e.g.,* United States v. Gessa, 971 F.2d 1257 (6th Cir. 1992) (*en banc*) (district court evidentiary rulings are typically subject to "abuse of discretion standard," Rule 801(d)(2)(E)'s requirement of specific factual determinations and legal conclusions warrants review under a "clearly erroneous standard of review").

[100] *See generally* Lilly, *Notes on the Confrontation Clause* and Ohio v. Roberts, 36 U. FLA. L. REV. 207 (1984) (this article explores the inherent conflict between the hearsay rule and the constitutional right to confrontation. Professor Lilly examines the repercussions of the Supreme Court case of *Ohio v. Roberts* in terms of the preference-reliability approach to the use of prior testimony and the historical background of both the hearsay rule and the confrontation clause). *See also* United States v. Ordonez, 737 F.2d 793 (9th Cir. 1983) (to

after *Dutton v. Evans*,[101] it is not likely that a challenge will succeed. This is also evident from *United States v. Inadi*,[102] where the Court held that Confrontation Clause witness unavailability requirements do not apply to conspirators' statements because they possess independent evidentiary significance that is unaffected by whether the declarant testifies, and from *Bourjaily* where the Court held that a firmly established hearsay exception (including a Rule 801(d) exemption) satisfies the Confrontation Clause.

One familiar class of admissions, statements by predecessors in interest, is not included within Rule 801(d). It is doubtful that the residual exception found in Rule 807 can be expanded to cover this testimony, since admissions are not treated as exceptions by the Military Rules of Evidence; they are just non-hearsay. Thus, statements by predecessors in interest will be excluded when offered for their truth unless they qualify under some exception to the hearsay rule— *e.g.,* they are declarations against interest. This should serve as a reminder that, although there is little difference between hearsay exceptions and hearsay exemptions in terms of general admissibility of evidence, when the residual hearsay rule is invoked it refers only to exceptions and thus to Rules 803 and 804, not Rule 801.

§ 801.03   Drafters' Analysis

[1]   Statement

Rule 801(a) is taken from the Federal Rule without change and is similar to ¶ 139 *a* of the present *Manual*.

[2]   Declarant

Rule 801(b) is taken from the Federal Rule verbatim and is the same definition used in present military practice.

[3]   Hearsay

Rule 801(c) is taken from the Federal Rule verbatim. It is similar to the present *Manual* definition, found in ¶ 139 *a,* which states: "A statement which is offered in evidence to prove the truth of the matters stated therein, but which was not made by the author when a witness before the court at a hearing in which it is so offered, is hearsay." Although the two definitions are basically identical, they actually differ sharply as a result of the Rule's exceptions which are discussed *below*.

[4]   Statements which are not hearsay

Rule 801(d) is taken from the Federal Rule without change and removes certain categories of evidence from the definition of hearsay. In all cases,

---

admit conspirator statements found in ledgers made by unidentified person might violate confrontation rights).

[101]   400 U.S. 74 (1970).

[102]   475 U.S. 387 (1986).

those categories represent hearsay within the meaning of the present *Manual* definition.

[a]   Prior statement by witness

Rule 801(d)(1) is taken from the Federal Rule without change and removes certain prior statements by the witness from the definition of hearsay. Under the present *Manual* rule, an out-of-court statement not within an exception to the hearsay rule and unadopted by the testifying witness, is inadmissible hearsay notwithstanding the fact that the declarant is now on the stand and able to be cross-examined, *United States v. Burge*, 1 M.J. 408 (C.M.A. 1976), (Cook, J., concurring). The justification for the present *Manual* rule is presumably the traditional view that out of court statements cannot be adequately tested by cross-examination because of the time differential between the making of the statement and the giving of the in-court testimony. The Federal Rules of Evidence Advisory Committee rejected this view in part believing both that later cross-examination is sufficient to ensure reliability and that earlier statements are usually preferable to later ones because of the possibility of memory loss. *See generally,* 4 J. Weinstein & M. Berger Weinstein's Evidence ¶ 801(d)(1)[01] (1978). Rule 801(d)(1) thus not only makes an important shift in the military theory of hearsay, but also makes an important change in law by making admissible a number of types of statements that are either inadmissible or likely to be inadmissible under present military law.

Rule 801(d)(1)(A) makes admissible on the merits a statement inconsistent with the in-court testimony of the witness when the prior statement "was given under oath subject to the penalty of perjury at a trial, hearing, or other proceeding, or in a deposition." The Rule does not require that the witness has been subject to cross-examination at the earlier proceeding, but requires that the witness must have been under oath and subject to penalty of perjury. Although the definition of "trial, hearing, or other proceeding" is uncertain, it is apparent that the Rule was intended to include grand jury testimony and may be extremely broad in scope. *See, e.g., United States v. Castro-Ayon,* 537 F.2d 1055 (9th Cir.), *cert. denied,* 429 U.S. 983 (1976) (tape recorded statements given under oath at a Border Patrol station found to be within the Rule). It should clearly apply to Article 32 hearings. The Rule does require as a prerequisite, a statement "given under oath subject to the penalty of perjury." The mere fact that a statement was given under oath may not be sufficient. No foundation other than that indicated as a condition precedent in the Rule is apparently necessary to admit the statement under the Rule. *But see* Weinstein's Evidence 801-874 (1978).

Rule 801(d)(1)(B) makes admissible on the merits a statement consistent with the in-court testimony of the witness and "offered to rebut an express or implied charge against the declarant of recent fabrication or improper influence or motive." Unlike Rule 801(d)(1)(A), the earlier consistent statement need not have been made under oath or at any type of proceeding.

On its face, the Rule does not require that the consistent statement offered has been made prior to the time the improper influence or motive arose or prior to the alleged recent fabrication. Notwithstanding this, at least two circuits have read such a requirement into the rule, *United States v. Quinto,* 582 F.2d 224 (2d Cir. 1978); *United States v. Scholle,* 553 F.2d 1109 (8th Cir. 1977). *See also United States v. Dominguez,* 604 F.2d 304 (4th Cir. 1979).

The propriety of this limitation is clearly open to question. *See generally United States v. Rubin,* 609 F.2d 51 (2d Cir. 1979). The limitation does not, however, prevent admission of consistent statements made after the inconsistent statement but before the improper influence or motive arose. *United States v. Scholle, above.* Rule 801(d)(1)(B) provides a possible means to admit evidence of fresh complaint in prosecutions of sexual offenses. Although limited to circumstances in which there is a charge, for example, of recent fabrication, the Rule, when applicable, would permit not only the fact of fresh complaint, as is presently possible, but also the entire portion of the consistent statement.

Under Rule 801(d)(1)(C) a statement of identification is not hearsay. The content of the statement as well as the fact of identification is admissible. This Rule must be read in conjunction with Rule 321 which governs the admissibility of statements of pretrial identification.

[b]   Admission by party opponent

Rule 801(d)(2) eliminates a number of categories of statements from the scope of the hearsay rule. Unlike those statements within the purview of Rule 802(d)(1), these statements would have come within the exceptions to the hearsay rule as recognized in the *Manual.* Consequently, their "reclassification" is a matter of academic interest only. No practical difference results. The reclassification results from a belief that the adversary system impels admissibility and that reliability is not a significant factor.

Rule 801(d)(2)(A) makes admissible against a party a statement made in either the party's individual or representative capacity. This is treated as an admission or confession under ¶ 140 *a* of the present *Manual,* and is an exception to the present hearsay rule.

Rule 801(d)(2)(B) makes admissible "a statement of which the party has manifested the party's adoption or belief in its truth." This is an adoptive admission and is an exception to the present hearsay rule. *Cf.* ¶ 140(*a*)(4) of the present *Manual.* While silence may be treated as an admission on the facts of a given case, *see, e.g.,* Rule 304(h)(3) and the analysis thereto, under Rule 801(a)(2) that silence must have been intended by the declarant to have been an assertion. Otherwise, the statement will not be hearsay within the meaning of Rule 801(a)(2) and will presumably be admissible, if at all, as circumstantial evidence.

Rule 801(d)(2)(C) makes admissible "a statement by a person authorized by the party to make a statement concerning the subject." While this is not expressly dealt with by the *Manual,* it would be admissible under present law as an admission; *cf.* ¶ 140 *b,* utilizing agency theory.

Rule 801(d)(2)(D) makes admissible "a statement by the party's agent or servant concerning a matter within the scope of the agency or employment of the agent or servant, made during the existence of the relationship." These statements would appear to be admissible under present law. Statements made by interpreters, as by an individual serving as a translator for a service member in a foreign nation who is, for example, attempting to consummate a drug transaction with a non-English speaking person, should be admissible under Rule 801(d)(2)(D) or Rule 801(d)(2)(C).

Rule 801(d)(2)(E) makes admissible "a statement by a co-conspirator of a party during the course and in furtherance of the conspiracy." This is similar to the military hearsay exception found in ¶ 140 *b* of the present *Manual.* Whether a conspiracy existed for purposes of this Rule is solely a matter for the military judge. Although this is the prevailing Article III rule, it is also the consequence of the Military Rules' modification to Federal Rule of Evidence 104(b). Rule 801(d)(2)(E) does not address many critical procedural matters associated with the use of co-conspirator evidence. *See generally* Comment, *Restructuring the Independent Evidence Requirement of the Coconspirator Hearsay Exception,* 127 U. Pa. L. Rev. 1439 (1979). For example, the burden of proof placed on the proponent is unclear although a preponderance appears to be the developing Article III trend. Similarly, there is substantial confusion surrounding the question of whether statements of an alleged co-conspirator may themselves be considered by the military judge when determining whether the declarant was in fact a co-conspirator. This process, known as bootstrapping, is not permitted under present military law. *See, e.g., United States v. Duffy,* 49 C.M.R. 208, 210 (A.F.C.M.R. 1974); *United States v. LaBossiere,* 13 C.M.A. 337, 339, 32 C.M.R. 337, 339 (1962). A number of circuits have suggested that Rule 104(a) allows the use of such statements, but at least two circuits have held that other factors prohibit bootstrapping. *United States v. James,* 590 F.2d 575 (5th Cir.) (en banc), *cert. denied,* 442 U.S. 917 (1979); *United States v. Cambindo Valencia,* 609 F.2d 603 (2d Cir. 1979). Until such time as the Article III practice is settled, discretion would dictate that present military law be followed and that bootstrapping not be allowed. Other procedural factors may also prove troublesome although not to the same extent as bootstrapping. For example, it appears to be appropriate for the military judge to determine the co-conspirator question in a preliminary Article 39(a) session. Although receipt of evidence "subject to later connection" or proof is legally possible, the probability of serious error, likely requiring a mistrial, is apparent.

Rule 801(d)(2)(E) does not appear to change what may be termed the "substantive law" relating to statements made by co-conspirators. Thus, whether a statement was made by a co-conspirator in furtherance of a conspiracy is a question for the military judge, and a statement made by an individual after he or she has withdrawn from a conspiracy is not made "in furtherance of the conspiracy."

Official statements made by an officer— as by the commanding officer of a battalion, squadron, or ship, or by a staff officer, in an endorsement or other communication—are not excepted from the operation of the hearsay rule merely by reason of the official character of the communication or the rank or position of the officer making it.

The following examples of admissibility under this Rule may be helpful:

(1) A is being tried for assaulting B. The defense presents the testimony of C that just before the assault C heard B say to A that B was about to kill A with B's knife. The testimony of C is not hearsay, for it is offered to show that A acted in self-defense because B made the statement and not to prove the truth of B's statement.

(2) A is being tried for the rape of B. If B testifies at trial, the testimony of B that she had previously identified A as her attacker at an identification lineup would be admissible under Rule 801(d)(1)(C) to prove that it was A who raped B.

(3) Private A is being tried for disobedience of a certain order given him orally by Lieutenant B. C is able to testify that he heard Lieutenant B give the order to A. This testimony, including testimony of C as to the terms of the order, would not be hearsay.

(4) The accused is being tried for the larceny of clothes from a locker. A is able to testify that B told A that B saw the accused leave the quarters in which the locker was located with a bundle resembling clothes about the same time the clothes were stolen. This testimony from A would not be admissible to prove the facts stated by B.

(5) The accused is being tried for wrongfully selling government clothing. A policeman is able to testify that while on duty he saw the accused go into a shop with a bundle under his arm; that he entered the shop and the accused ran away; that he was unable to catch the accused; and that thereafter the policeman asked the proprietor of the shop what the accused was doing there; and that the proprietor replied that the accused sold him some uniforms for which he paid the accused $30. Testimony by the policeman as to the reply of the proprietor would be hearsay if it was offered to prove the facts stated by the proprietor. The fact that the policeman was acting in the line of his duty at the time the proprietor made the statement would not render the evidence admissible to prove the truth of the statement.

(6) A defense witness in an assault case testifies on direct examination that the accused did not strike the alleged victim. On cross-examination by the prosecution, the witness admits that at a preliminary investigation

he stated that the accused had struck the alleged victim. The testimony of the witness as to this statement will be admissible if he was under oath at that time and subject to a prosecution for perjury.

§ 801.04 Drafters' Analysis (2008)

2008 Amendment: Amend the Analysis accompanying Mil. R. Evid. 801(d)(1)(B) to read as follows:

"Rule 801(d)(1)(B) makes admissible as substantive evidence on the merits a statement consistent with the in-court testimony of the witness "offered to rebut an express or implied charge against the declarant of recent fabrication or improper influence or motive." Unlike Rule 801(d)(1)(A), the earlier consistent statement need not have been made under oath or at any type of proceeding. On its face, the Rule does not require that the consistent statement offered have been made prior to the time the improper influence or motive arose or prior to the alleged recent fabrication. Notwithstanding this, the Supreme Court has read such a requirement into the rule. Tome v. United States, 513 U.S. 150 (1995); see also United States v. Allison, 49 M.J. 54 (C.A.A.F. 1998). The limitation does not, however, prevent admission of a consistent statement made after an inconsistent statement but before the improper influence or motive arose. United States v. Scholle, 553 F.2d 1109 (8th Cir. 1977). Rule 801(d)(1)(B) provides a possible means to admit evidence of fresh complaint in prosecution of sexual offenses. Although limited to the circumstances in which there is a charge, for example, of fabrication, the Rule, when applicable, would permit not only fact of fresh complaint, as is presently possible, but also the entire portion of the consistent statement."

§ 801.05 Annotated Cases

[1] Rule 801(a)—Statement

[a] Constitutional Standards

United States Supreme Court

The annotation:

Bullcoming v. New Mexico, 2011 U.S Lexis 4790 (U.S June 23, 2011): Donald Bullcoming was involved in traffic accident. The other driver noted that Bullcoming appeared to be intoxicated. Thereafter, Bullcoming left the scene of the accident but was later apprehended. After failing a flied sobriety test he was arrested. A warrant was obtained and a blood-alcohol test conducted by the New Mexico Department of Health, Scientific Laboratory Division. The laboratory issued its standard "Report of Blood Alcohol Analysis" Which indicted Bullcoming's blood-alcohol level was 0.21. Based on this evidence Bullcoming Was convicted of aggravated DWI. The laboratory report's original author did not testify at trial. Reversing the accused's conviction the Supreme Court followed *Melendez-Diaz v. Massa-*

chusetts, holding the forensic laboratory reports are "testimonial" under the Sixth Amendment's Confrontation Clause and require the prosecution to produce the laboratory report's original author's unless the defense had a prior opportunity to cross-examine him. The court went on the find that "surrogates" or other witnesses familiar with the document's creation will not be acceptable, particularly when the procecution's witness was not the original author's supervisor or had not participated in the test procedures. The Court rejected prosecution contentions that the document's original author was a "Mere scrivener" who simply reported a machine's test results and thus did not produce "testimonial" evidence, and that the prosecution's witness was sufficiently knowledgeable about the test procedures to satisfy the accused's right to confrontation.

Michigan v. Bryant, 131 S.Ct. 1143 (2011): In this state murder case tried before *Crawford v. Washington*, 541 U.S. 36 (2004), and *Davis v. Washington*, 547 U.S. 813 (2006), the deceased victim's statements to police identifying Bryant as his assailant were admitted based on the *Ohio v. Roberts*, 448 U.S. 56 (1980) "reliability" standard. The victim had been shot at Bryant's house approximately 25 minutes before the police found him in a store parking lot bleeding to death. At least five policemen asked the victim what happened. Each received similar answers identifying Bryant as the assailant. The Washington Supreme Court heard the case after *Crawford* and *Davis* were decided and reversed the accused's conviction. The Supreme Court found that reversal was based on an improperly applied testimonial determination and remanded the case for further proceedings. The majority held that statements are testimonial and inadmissible when no ongoing emergency exists and the interrogator's primary purpose was to collect information about past events for use in a subsequent criminal prosecution. Statements can be nontestimonial and admissible even when made in the course of a police interrogation when the primary purpose for the interrogation objectively appears to be the interrogator's attempt to meet an ongoing emergency and the process used for taking the statements is informal with a focus on current and future events.

Melendez-Diaz v. Massachusetts, 129 S. Ct. 2527 (2009): The defendant was convicted in state court of distributing and trafficking in cocaine. Over his *Crawford v. Washington* objection, the trial judge admitted three "certificates of analysis" showing the results of the forensic analysis performed on substances seized in connection with the defendant's arrest. The certificates were sworn before a notary public by analysts at the State Laboratory Institute of the Massachusetts Department of Public Health, as required under state law. The Appeals Court of Massachusetts affirmed the convictions and relied upon a Massachusetts Supreme Judicial Court ruling that the authors of certificates of forensic analysis are not subject to confrontation under the Sixth Amendment. The United States Supreme Court reversed. Justice Scalia wrote for the majority in a 5-4 decision and concluded that "[t]here is little doubt that the documents in this case fall within the 'core class of testimonial statements' " described in *Crawford*. The Court reasoned that "[t]he documents at issue here, while denominated by Massachusetts law 'certificates,' are quite plainly affidavits," and *Crawford*'s description of the core class of testimonial statements "mentions affidavits twice." The Court rejected the argument that the analysts were not "accusatory" witnesses and thus were not subject to confrontation and concluded that the text of the Sixth Amendment "contemplates two classes of witnesses—those against the defendant and those in his favor." It also rejected the arguments that the analysts were not "conventional" or "typical" witnesses and did not offer testimony prone to distortion or manipulation and therefore were not subject to confrontation. The Court was not persuaded that the Confrontation Clause was satisfied so long as the defendant could call the analysts as witnesses: "[T]he Confrontation Clause imposes a burden on the prosecution to present its witnesses, not on the defendant to bring those adverse witnesses into court." But the Court indicated that state statutes that require the prosecution to give notice of the intent to rely on analysts and the defendant to demand production of the analysts at trial were consistent with the Confrontation Clause: It is common to require a defendant to exercise his rights under the Compulsory Process Clause in advance of trial, announcing his intent to present certain witnesses. . . . There is no conceivable reason why he cannot similarly be compelled to exercise his Confrontation Clause rights before trial. Justice Kennedy wrote for the dissenters and argued that the Court ignored 90 years of precedent in which scientific analysis could be introduced without testimony from the analyst who produced it, raised serious questions about which analysts must be produced, and imposed unnecessary and costly burdens on both state and federal criminal justice systems.

Whorton v. Bockting, 549 U.S. 406 (2007): The accused was tried for sexually assaulting his 6-year-old stepdaughter. Over defense objection, the trial judge determined that the child was too emotionally upset to testify, and allowed the accused's wife and a police detective to recount the child's out-of-court statements about the assaults. A Nevada statute permits out-of-court statements made by a sexually abused or assaulted child under 10 years of age to be admitted if: (1) the statements describe the acts of sexual assault or physical abuse, (2) the court finds that the child is unavailable or unable to testify, and (3) that the time, content, and circumstances of the statements provide sufficient circumstantial guarantees of trustworthiness. The Nevada Supreme Court affirmed the accused's conviction based on *Ohio v. Roberts*, 448 U.S. (1980). The accused subsequently pursued a federal *habeas corpus* petition, which was pending in the Ninth Circuit Court of Appeals when *Crawford v. Washington*, 541 U.S. 36 (2004) was decided. The Ninth Circuit reversed the accused's conviction and held that, under *Teague v. Lane*, 489 U.S. 288 (1989), *Crawford* applied in collateral attack cases. The Supreme

Court reversed the Ninth Circuit and held that *Crawford* does not implicate the fundamental fairness and accuracy of criminal proceedings and did not make profound and sweeping change in the law justifying retroactive application. The Court went on to say that, whatever reliability improvements *Crawford* created, it is important to note that it also eliminated Confrontation Clause protection against the admission of unreliable out-of-court nontestimonial statements. The Court said that, under *Roberts*, out-of-court nontestimonial statements not subject to prior cross-examination were inadmissible without a judicial determination on reliability. The Court said that, under *Crawford*, the Confrontation Clause has no application to such statements and therefore permits their admission even if they lack indicia of reliability.

   Davis v. Washington, 547 U.S. 813 (2006): The Supreme Court elaborated on the meaning of *Crawford v. Washington*, 541 U.S. 36, 53–54 (2004), when it decided the companion cases of *Davis v. Washington* and *Hammon v. Indiana*. In an opinion by Justice Scalia (also the author of *Crawford*), the Court elaborated on the meaning of "testimonial" and "interrogation" as it relates to confrontation. Once again, the Court declined to offer an exhaustive definition of terms, but its 8-1 vote (with Justice Thomas dissenting) offered some clarification of the meaning of both words. In *Davis*, Michelle McCottry telephoned 911, was cut off, and answered the operator's return call and told the operator that she had been assaulted by her former boyfriend, Davis, who had just fled the scene. Davis was charged with violation of a domestic no-contact order, a felony, but McCottry did not testify at his trial. In *Hammon*, police responded to a reported domestic disturbance at the home of Amy and Hershel Hammon. They found Amy alone on the front porch, appearing frightened. When the police inquired about the disturbance, Amy told them that nothing was wrong, but also gave them permission to enter. Once inside, one officer kept Hershel in the kitchen. Another officer interviewed Amy elsewhere in the living room. After hearing Amy's account, the officer asked her to fill out a battery affidavit, and she handwrote the following: "Broke our Furnace & shoved me down on the floor into the broken glass. Hit me in the chest and threw me down. Broke our lamps." Amy did not testify at Hershel's bench trial for domestic battery and violation of probation, but both her affidavit and the testimony of the officer who interviewed her were admitted over Hershel's objection that he had no opportunity to cross-examine and confront Amy. Justice Scalia concisely summarized the Court's reasoning in the two cases:

> Without attempting to produce an exhaustive classification of all conceivable statements—or even all conceivable statements in response to police interrogation—as either testimonial or nontestimonial, it suffices to decide the present cases to hold as follows: Statements are nontestimonial when made in the course of police interrogation under circumstances objectively indicating that the primary purpose of the

interrogation is to enable police assistance to meet an ongoing emergency. They are testimonial when the circumstances objectively indicate that there is no such ongoing emergency, and that the primary purpose of the interrogation is to establish or prove past events potentially relevant to later criminal prosecution.

The Court held that the 911 tape in *Davis* was properly admitted since the primary purpose of the 911 operator's questioning Michelle McCottry was to deal with an emergency, but that the admission of Amy Hershel's battery affidavit violated the Confrontation Clause because the primary purpose was to gather evidence. The Court makes clear that a conversation that begins as an interrogation to determine the need for emergency assistance can become an interrogation to obtain testimony. Once the emergency ends, for example, continued interrogation might produce testimonial statements. In response to arguments by Washington and Indiana, supported by a number of amici, that domestic violence cases require greater flexibility in the use of testimonial evidence because victims are notoriously susceptible to intimidation that prevents them from testifying, Justice Scalia wrote that "when defendants seek to undermine the judicial process by procuring or coercing silence from witnesses and victims, the Sixth Amendment does not require courts to acquiesce." He reiterated his suggestion in *Crawford:* that "the rule of forfeiture by wrongdoing . . . extinguishes confrontation claims on essentially equitable grounds."

Crawford v. Washington, 541 U.S. 36 (2004): A Washington state jury convicted the accused of first-degree assault while armed with a deadly weapon. An important part of the State's case against the accused consisted of his wife's out-of-court statements to police officers describing the charged offense and further implicating her husband. Reversing the accused's conviction and writing for the majority, Justice Scalia stated that because such out-of-court statements are "testimonial" they are barred by the Constitution's Confrontation Clause unless the declarant testifies, or if the declarant is unavailable at trial, the accused must have had a prior opportunity to cross-examine that declarant regarding her statement. Most importantly, the Court went on to say this outcome is required irrespective of whether the statement is seen as being "reliable," thus abrogating *Ohio v. Roberts*, 448 U.S. 56 (1980).

United States Court of Appeals for the Armed Forces

United States v. Blazier, 69 M.J. 218 (C.A.A.F. 2010): The accused was convicted of dereliction of duty and wrongful use of controlled substances. Part of the government's proof included laboratory reports used by the supervising chemist when he testified concerning the composition of the possessed drugs. The chemist's testimony interpreting the laboratory reports relied upon machine generated laboratory reports and upon the analyses of other chemists who did not testify. The convictions were affirmed in *United States v.* Blazier, 68 M.J. 544 (A.F.Ct.Crim.App. 2008), which was decided before *Melendez-Diaz v. Massachusetts*, 129 S. Ct. 2527 (2009), held that, "certificates of analysis" used in drug prosecutions to establish the illegality of seized substances fell within the "core-class of testimonial statements" and violated the accused's Sixth Amendment rights). The convictions were reversed and the case remanded in *United States v. Blazier*, 68 M.J. 439 (C.A.A.F. 2010) (applying *Melendez-Diaz v. Massachusetts* but returning the record with specified questions concerning why the military judge did not compel the government to produce the essential laboratory witnesses). In its second look at the case, the court concluded that an expert may rely on machine-generated data because the Rules of Evidence define it as not being hearsay, and also may rely on but not repeat testimonial hearsay that is otherwise appropriate for expert opinion testimony so long as the expert's opinion is his own. The court also held that when testimonial hearsay is admitted, the Confrontation Clause is satisfied only if the declarant of that hearsay is subject to cross-examination at trial, or is unavailable but had been previously subjected to cross-examination and warned that the Confrontation Clause may not be circumvented by having an expert testify at trial to otherwise inadmissible testimonial hearsay. The court found that this occurred in violation of *Melendez-Diaz v. Massachusetts* and returned the record for a harmful error analysis.

[b]   Constitutional Standards—Harmless Error

United States Court of Appeals for the Armed Forces

United States v. Crudup, 67 M.J. 92 (C.A.A.F. 2008): The accused was convicted of assault and battery upon his wife, resisting apprehension, and making a false official statement. When the wife refused to testify, her pretrial statement implicating the accused was admitted. The remainder of the government's case consisted of witnesses who observed the crimes and the accused's pretrial admissions. Although the court affirmed, it held that admitting the wife's pretrial statement violated the accused's Sixth Amendment confrontation rights. The court found that the error was harmless beyond a reasonable doubt because the statement was relatively unimportant and cumulative and the government's case was overwhelming. The court added that, although the wife could not have been cross-examined, her credibility was effectively impeached by proof of a previous fraud conviction.

[c]   Statement—Nonverbal Assertions—Conduct

Navy-Marine Corps Court of Criminal Appeals

United States v. Silvis, 31 M.J. 707 (N.M.C.M.R. 1990): During the accused's rape trial, government counsel established that, shortly after the crime occurred, the victim had attempted suicide. The court rejected the accused's contention that this evidence was prohibited hearsay, affirmed the conviction and found that the evidence was nonverbal conduct that was admissible to demonstrate a nonconsenting state of mind.

[d]   Statement—Nonverbal Assertions—Drawings

Navy-Marine Corps Court of Criminal Appeals

United States v. Knox, 46 M.J. 688 (N.M.Ct.Crim.App. 1997): The accused was convicted of raping his five-year-old daughter and sodomizing his four-year-old son. Part of the government's evidence against the accused included various drawings his children had made, and an expert witness/ social worker's interpretation of them. Some of the drawings had been made while the children were with the expert, others were made while the children were with law enforcement officials, and still others were made while the children were at home. Reversing the accused's convictions, the court held it was prejudicial error to admit all of the drawings except those made to the social worker. See our discussion of this case under Rule 803(4). In the court's opinion, each drawing was an out-of-court statement, offered and admitted for the truth of the matter asserted. The court went on to say that an effective technique for eliminating the hearsay problems associated with out-of-court drawings is to have the witnesses recreate the drawings in court while they are testifying.

[2]   Rule 801(b)—Declarant

[a]   Computer Stored/Generated Data

Air Force Court of Criminal Appeals

United States v. Greska, 65 M.J. 835 (A.F.Ct.Crim.App. 2007): The accused was convicted of stealing another service-member's digital camera. When trial counsel asked the camera's owner whether there were any photos on the camera's memory chip that were not familiar to him, the owner indicated that there were two and one had a time/date stamp notation on it. Defense counsel's hearsay objection to the time/date stamp notation was overruled. Affirming the accused's burglary and larceny-related convictions, the court held that because Rule 801(b) defines a declarant as a *person,* evidence of the camera's automatic time/date notation was correctly admitted. Although the issue was not raised at trial or on appeal, the court noted that the time/date evidence was properly authenticated by the accused's coconspirators who placed the camera in the accused's hands at the relevant time.

[3]   Rule 801(c)—Hearsay

[a]   Examples of Hearsay

[i]   Examples of Hearsay—Accused's Exculpatory Statements

Air Force Court of Criminal Appeals

United States v. Booker 62 M.J. 703 (A.F.Ct.Crim.App. 2006): During the accused's trial on drug offenses, the military judge refused to admit exculpatory out-of-court statements made by the accused's brother after conducting a careful analysis of their reliability. The judge found reasons why the brother might lie for the accused. The Court of Criminal Appeals affirmed the findings of the military judge.

Navy-Marine Corps Court of Criminal Appeals

United States v. Schnable, 58 M.J. 643 (N.M.Ct.Crim.App. 2003): The accused was convicted of indecent acts upon his daughter. At trial the military judge prohibited the defense from introducing exculpatory statements the accused made to his pastor. Affirming the accused's findings and sentence, the court said this is precisely the type of evidence hearsay prohibitions are designed to exclude, those allowing the accused to testify without ever having to take the stand.

[ii]   Examples of Hearsay—Basis for Investigations

United States Court of Appeals for the Armed Forces

United States v. Gaeta, 14 M.J. 383 (C.M.A. 1983): Relying on both Rule 801(c) and previous *Manual* ¶ 139 *a,* the court noted that a policeman's reasons for initiating an investigation are objectionable at trial not only because they are inadmissible hearsay, but also because they are irrelevant. The court noted the possible prejudicial impact of such testimony: "as a police officer becomes increasingly specific in testifying about his reasons for initiating an investigation, the trier-of-fact is more likely to consider the reports received by the officer for purposes other than merely to understand why the investigation was initiated."

[iv]   Examples of Hearsay—Documentary Evidence

Army Court of Criminal Appeals

United States v. Woodard, 39 M.J. 1022 (A.C.M.R. 1994): Pursuant to his pleas, the accused was convicted of rape, sodomy, and indecent acts with his nine-year-old stepdaughter and his nine-year-old natural son. During the sentencing portion of trial, a court member inquired about the mental health capabilities at the United States Disciplinary Barracks, Fort Leavenworth, Kansas. In response, trial counsel introduced an affidavit from the Disciplinary Barracks' Director of Mental Health Services. Finding error but affirming all convictions and the sentence, the court held that the document was inadmissible hearsay because it was offered for the truth of the matter asserted, addressed an important issue at trial, and was made by a person who did not testify.

[v]   Examples of Hearsay—Specific Contradiction

United States Court of Appeals for the Armed Forces

United States v. Hall, 58 M.J. 90 (C.A.A.F. 2003): The accused was convicted of using cocaine. During trial she testified that her positive urinalysis was due to ingesting tea provided by her mother. In rebuttal, and over defense objection, trial counsel called a CID agent who testified that the accused's mother told him she never provided the accused with any tea. The trial judge admitted this testimony as a specific contradiction and instructed the members it could not be used for the truth of the matter asserted. On appeal, government Appellate counsel conceded it was error to admit the testimony for any purpose but that the error was harmless. Reversing the accused's conviction, the court held that it was unable to see how the testimony could have been used for any purpose other than to establish a factual basis for undermining the accused's innocent ingestion defense. The court went on to say that the trial judge's instructions were not helpful in avoiding the harm.

[b] Examples of Nonhearsay

[i] Examples of Nonhearsay—Credibility Uses

Navy-Marine Corps Court of Criminal Appeals

United States v. Dodson, 16 M.J. 921 (N.M.C.M.R. 1983): Out-of-court statements offered solely to impeach a witness's credibility, and not to establish the truth of the matters asserted, are not excluded by the hearsay rule.

[ii] Examples of Nonhearsay—First-Hand Knowledge

Army Court of Criminal Appeals

United States v. Hood, 12 M.J. 890 (A.C.M.R. 1982): The accused contended that a CID agent's testimony concerning the value of certain contraband was inadmissible hearsay, *citing* Rule 801(c). The Army Court of Criminal Appeals affirmed the conviction, finding there was no hearsay where a witness testified to facts of which he had firsthand knowledge.

Navy-Marine Corps Court of Criminal Appeals

United States v. Tebsherany, 30 M.J. 608 (N.M.C.M.R. 1990): Distinguishing *United States v. Williams,* 26 M.J. 487 (C.M.A. 1988) (error for a witness to testify about her blood type based solely upon information provided by a doctor), the court affirmed a larceny conviction even though a government witness testified that he recalled certain detailed financial information as the result of a pretrial conversation. The court found this witness's testimony admissible because it was not based solely on what someone else told him, but was the result of "understanding matters by reading about them, talking to others about them, or experiencing them."

[iii] Examples of Nonhearsay—Operational Facts

United States Court of Appeals for the Armed Forces

United States v. LeMere, 22 M.J. 61 (C.M.A 1986): The court held that a three-and-one-half-year-old witness's prior out-of-court statement to her mother identifying the accused as the man who sexually assaulted her was not admissible as nonhearsay, *i.e.,* as an operative fact, because it was irrelevant how the victim's mother learned of the offense and why she did any related subsequent act, including notifying the police.

Air Force Court of Criminal Appeals

United States v. Reed, 11 M.J. 649 (A.F.C.M.R. 1981): The accused was charged with a single specification of wrongful solicitation to commit robbery. The government's case included testimony by a witness to the offense. In rebuttal, defense counsel attempted to present another witness who would testify to certain statements made by the government's witness and the accused—all showing the accused's innocence. Trial counsel objected to each statement on hearsay grounds and was sustained by the military judge. In reversing the conviction, the appellate court found the evidence to be admissible under several theories. First, Rule 801(c) allows the declarations to be admitted because they were not offered to prove the truth of the matters asserted. Similarly, the court found the statements were "offered as operative facts and circumstances of the solicitation offense," and admissible for this reason. Finally, the court noted that the statements may have been admissible as "existing mental or emotional conditions" under Rule 803(3).

[iv]   Examples of Nonhearsay—Rebuttal Evidence

United States Court of Appeals for the Armed Forces

United States v. Rynning, 47 M.J. 420, 421 (C.A.A.F. 1998): Affirming the accused's convictions for sexually abusing his natural daughter, the court held that a social worker's testimony regarding the victim's disclosure of abuse was not hearsay and properly admitted. In the court's opinion, this evidence was properly offered to rebut issues raised by defense counsel during his cross-examination of the victim. The accused attempted to impeach his daughter's testimony by highlighting the fact that she initially delayed reporting the crimes, and when she finally did report them she made incomplete complaints.

[v]   Examples of Nonhearsay—Rehabilitating a Witness's Credibility

Navy-Marine Corps Court of Criminal Appeals

United States v. Vanderbilt, 58 M.J. 725 (N.M.Ct.Crim.App. 2003): The accused was convicted of wrongfully selling or disposing of military handguns. She was sentenced to 21 months confinement, a dishonorable discharge, and related punishments. Affirming her convictions and sentence, the court found no error in the admission of a key government witness's statements that another participant in the criminal adventure told him that the accused was involved in their nefarious acts. On cross-examination, defense counsel repeatedly challenged the witness's assertions by alleging that the witness had told something different to an NCIS Agent. In response to this attack, trial counsel called the agent and over defense objection testified to the substance of the declarant's statements. The court found that the NCIS's testimony about what the government witness had told him was admissible not for the truth of the matter asserted, but to rehabilitate the declarant's credibility after defense counsel's attack. In effect, the statements were admitted simply to show they were made to the NCIS agent, not for the purpose of proving the content of those statements.

[vi]   Examples of Nonhearsay—Uncharged Misconduct

United States Court of Appeals for the Armed Forces

United States v. Brown, 28 M.J. 470 (C.M.A. 1989): During sentencing in an AWOL case, trial counsel attempted to rehabilitate an aggravation witness with evidence that the accused had been involved in other misconduct. The witness had learned of the extrinsic events from a police report. Although the court set aside the accused's sentence on different grounds, it said, "it could be argued that the challenged testimony was not offered to show this other misconduct occurred but that a report made available to [the witness] stated such misconduct had occurred."

[4]   Rule 801(d)(1)—Prior Statement by Witness

[a]   Rule 801(d)(1)(A)—Prior Inconsistent Statements

[i]   Prior Inconsistent Statements—Calling a Witness Solely to Impeach

United States Court of Appeals for the Armed Forces

United States v. Ureta, 44 M.J. 290 (C.A.A.F. 1996): The accused's convictions for sexually abusing his daughter were affirmed. On appeal and for the first time, the accused contended that it was error for trial counsel to call a witness solely to impeaching her. The court held that no error occurred because neither trial counsel nor the military judge knew what the witness would say once on the stand.

United States v. Pollard, 38 M.J. 41 (C.M.A. 1993): The accused was convicted of child sexual abuse. The victim made a series of pretrial statements implicating the accused. She recanted them both before and during the court-martial. Reversing this conviction, the court held it was prejudicial error for government counsel to call the victim for the primary purpose of impeaching her with her own out-of-court statements.

[ii]   Prior Inconsistent Statements—Documentary Evidence—Proper Use

United States Court of Appeals for the Armed Forces

United States v. Austin, 35 M.J. 271 (C.M.A. 1992): During this child sexual abuse case, the victim recanted her pretrial statements which incriminated the accused. She then refused to further testify. Over defense objection, the military judge allowed trial counsel to admit her Article 32 testimony, read it to the members, and have the panel take it with them into deliberations. Reversing the accused's conviction, the court held that its prior decisions, the ABA *Standards for Criminal Justice, Trial by Jury* (2d ed. 1982 Supp.), and R.C.M. 702(a), provide that depositions should not be given to court members. While the court recognized that this evidence was also admissible under Rule 804(b)(1), as substantive proof of guilt, and technically not a deposition, it believed the greater weight of authority augured in favor of excluding such evidence from the jury room.

Air Force Court of Criminal Appeals

United States v. Button, 31 M.J. 897 (A.F.C.M.R. 1990): Affirming the accused's child sexual abuse conviction, the court held that when the victim recanted her previous statements, verbatim transcripts of her Article 32 testimony were properly admitted as substantive evidence.

Army Court of Criminal Appeals

United States v. Rudolph, 35 M.J. 622 (A.C.M.R. 1992): The accused was convicted of sexually abusing his stepdaughter. Before trial, the victim testified at an Article 32 investigation where she adopted statements previously given to local police. All of her pretrial statements incriminated the accused. Affirming the accused's conviction, the court held that the victim's verbatim Article 32 testimony, with incorporations, was admissible.

[iii]   Prior Inconsistent Statements—Foundation Absent

United States Court of Appeals for the Armed Forces

United States v. LeMere, 22 M.J. 61 (C.M.A. 1986): The pretrial statements of a three-and-one-half-year-old sodomy victim who testified at the accused's court-martial were held to be inadmissible because they were not: (a) inconsistent with her in court testimony, (b) made under oath or (c) made at a "proceeding" or deposition.

Air Force Court of Criminal Appeals

United States v. Luke, 13 M.J. 958 (A.F.C.M.R. 1982): Convicted of assaulting his wife, the accused successfully challenged the government's use of the wife's prior inconsistent statement as substantive rather than impeachment evidence. The court found that because the statement was not taken under oath, subject to the penalty of perjury, it did not meet Rule 801(d)(1)(A)'s requirements. Citing substantial federal authority, the court noted that while statements made before a grand jury, Article 32 investigation, court of inquiry, or similar formal legal proceeding may qualify, those made to investigating officials (as here) are not sufficiently worthy of belief to satisfy the Rule.

[iv]   Prior Inconsistent Statements—Police House Interrogations

Army Court of Criminal Appeals

United States v. Powell, 17 M.J. 975 (A.C.M.R. 1984): Refusing to follow

United States v. Castro-Ayon, 537 F.2d 1055 (9th Cir.), *cert. denied,* 429 U.S. 983 (1976), the court held that "police house interrogations cannot be compared with the solemnity of a trial" and thus a government witness's previous sworn inconsistent statement given to the CID and admitted as substantive evidence during trial constituted error. *Compare* Rule 613.

[v]   Prior Inconsistent Statements—Previous Court-Martial Testimony

Army Court of Criminal Appeals

United States v. Armstrong, 33 M.J. 1011 (A.C.M.R. 1991): At the accused's first trial for sodomizing his six-year-old daughter, the child's mother testified that the offenses never happened. During retrial, the victim's mother testified that she was present for each offense. The military judge thereafter instructed the members not to consider her first statement as evidence of the truth of the matter asserted therein. In the court's opinion, this instruction was erroneous. But the conviction was affirmed because defense counsel failed to object.

[b]   Rule 801(d)(1)(B)—Prior Consistent Statements

[i]   Prior Consistent Statements—Contradiction Insufficient

Air Force Court of Criminal Appeals

United States v. Adams, 63 M.J. 691 (A.F. Ct. Crim. App. 2006): During the accused's trial for sexually molesting a female under the age of sixteen, the victim testified about how she had been molested and about her prior consistent statements about these offenses to her father and friends. The court found that the statements to her father were inadmissible because they constituted mere repetition of her allegations, but the statements to her friends were properly admitted because they rebutted defense allegations that the victim was lying as a means of excusing poor work performance. Affirming the accused's convictions and sentence, the court recognized that at least four reasons have justified the use of prior consistent statements to rehabilitate a witness's credibility: (1) placing a purported inconsistent statement in context to show it was not really inconsistent with a witness's trial testimony, (2) supporting the denial of making an inconsistent statement, (3) refuting the suggestion that the witness's memory is flawed due to the passage of time, and (4) refuting an allegation of recent fabrication, improper influence, or motive. The court opined that in each instance something in addition to the content of the statement supports the witness's credibility-whether it is timing, context, or some other factor. The court found that the trial judge properly admitted some statements while excluding others. It noted that evidence that the witness said the same thing on other occasions by itself does not have much probative force, because mere repetition does not imply veracity. *United States v. Browder,* 19 M.J. 988 (A.F.C.M.R. 1985): Reversing the accused's drug related convictions, the court held that the trial judge improperly admitted a key government witness's prior consistent statement without first assuring that there was sufficient evidence of record to demonstrate an implied or expressed charge of recent fabrication, improper influence or bad motives. The court held that "evidence of a prior statement by a witness consistent with his or her testimony in court is not admissible solely because the in-court testimony has been contradicted by that of another witness."

[ii]   Prior Consistent Statements—Contradiction Sufficient

Air Force Court of Criminal Appeals

United States v. Hall, 54 M.J. 788 (A.F.Ct.Crim.App. 2001): The accused's assault and drug convictions were affirmed even though the military judge erroneously excluded the accused previous consistent statement. The Court found error because while the accused was on the stand, trial counsel impeached him with evidence of a strong motive to lie. The excluded testimony would have been consistent with his direct testimony.

United States v. Hughes, 48 M.J. 700 (A.F.Ct.Crim.App. 1998), *aff'd on other grounds,* 52 M.J. 278 (C.A.A.F. 2000): The accused was convicted of indecent assault upon two females under 16 years of age. The victims' mother was permitted to testify regarding what one of the victims said to her about the accused's sexual molestation. Affirming the accused's convictions, the court held that the mother's testimony was admissible because it was consistent with the declarant's overall testimony, and it served to dispel any inference that the declarant was improperly influenced or untruthful.

[iii]   Prior Consistent Statements—Defense Counsel Opening the Door

United States Court of Appeals for the Armed Forces

United States v. Lovett, 59 M.J. 230 (C.A.A.F. 2004): The accused was convicted of rape and attendant offenses. During the court-martial, defense counsel originally marked and used on cross-examination a document containing hearsay evidence. On redirect, and over a defense Rule 801(d)(1)(B) hearsay objection, trial counsel offered the written statement as a prosecution exhibit. Similar statements were contained in other government exhibits that had been admitted and not objected to by the defense. In the alternative, the questioned exhibit was also offered pursuant Rule 807, this time without a defense objection. Affirming the trial court's resolution, the Court of Appeals held that the accused suffered no prejudice from the admission of these hearsay statements because they were admitted without objection, and were consistent with and cumulative of the various declarant's own in-court testimony.

United States v. Stroh, 46 M.J. 643 (A.F.Ct.Crim.App. 1997): The accused was convicted of perpetrating the most sordid sexual offenses against his daughter's six-year-old playmate. Without having raised the issue at trial, the accused contended that the military judge committed error by allowing trial counsel to cross-examine a defense witness concerning the victim's prior consistent statements. Substantively, the court rejected the accused's claim holding that irrespective of whether the challenged evidence technically complies with the requirements of this provision, "Defense counsel may not plant a weed in the government's evidence garden and then prevent the prosecutor from pulling it out." Procedurally, the court held that the accused waived the error by failing to object.

[iv] Prior Consistent Statements—Documentary Evidence

United States Court of Appeals for the Armed Forces

United States v. Rhea, 33 M.J. 413 (C.M.A. 1991): Setting aside part of the child sexual abuse charges against the accused, the court held that it was proper for government counsel to support the victim's testimony concerning when she was assaulted by introducing her calendar, which listed each event.

[v] Prior Consistent Statements—Expert Witness Uses

United States Court of Appeals for the Armed Forces

United States v. Ryder, 39 M.J. 454 (C.M.A. 1994): The accused was convicted of numerous drug-related offenses. During trial, a government expert testified that she used certain witnesses' out-of-court statements in analyzing a drug sample. Affirming the accused's convictions, the court stated that it was permissible for the expert to have relied on these hearsay statements for whatever "face value" they may have possessed. The court went on to say that any error which occurred was cured by the witnesses' in-court testimony.

Air Force Court of Criminal Appeals

United States v. Pagel, 40 M.J. 771 (A.F.C.M.R. 1994): The accused was convicted of carnal knowledge, sodomy, and committing indecent acts upon his minor daughter. During the government's case, a psychologist testified to statements the victim had made to him. Defense counsel cross-examined, attempting to demonstrate that the psychologist used suggestive interview techniques. In rebuttal, trial counsel introduced the entire transcript of the interviews. Affirming the accused's convictions, the court held that the rebuttal evidence was properly admitted to rebut defense counsel's contentions.

[vi] Prior Consistent Statements—Foundation Required

Navy-Marine Corps Court of Criminal Appeals

United States v. Waldrup, 30 M.J. 1126 (N.M.C.M.R. 1989): In this drug prosecution, the court held it was error for the trial judge to admit evidence of a prior consistent statement without first determining whether it was made at a time before the motive to fabricate existed. The court went on to say that unless counsel established an adequate basis for admitting the evidence, it would not admit it or engage in speculation concerning this issue.

[vii]   Prior Consistent Statements—Preserving Error

Air Force Court of Criminal Appeals

United States v. Toro, 34 M.J. 506 (A.F.C.M.R. 1992): The accused was convicted of drug offenses. During trial, the prosecution called several witnesses who had used drugs with the accused. On direct, each was asked about his previous criminal record before evidence on the charged offenses was obtained. During cross-examination, defense counsel challenged the witnesses' with previous inconsistent statements, allowing trial counsel to introduce their previous consistent and inculpatory statements. *See* Rule 613. Affirming these convictions, the court held that trial counsel's tactics were proper even though the statements had been obtained after each witness formed a motive to fabricate. In the court's opinion, because *United States v. McCaskey,* 30 M.J. 188 (C.M.A. 1990) (creating the requirement for such statements to be made before the motive to fabricate arises) was decided one month after the accused's trial, and was never intended to be retroactive, absent a trial objection, relief was not required.

[viii]   Prior Consistent Statements—Rebuttal Testimony

United States Court of Appeals for the Armed Forces

United States v. Lee, 28 M.J. 52 (C.M.A. 1989): Affirming the accused's child sexual abuse conviction, the court held it was proper for the government to rehabilitate the prosecutrix with previous consistent statements made to her mother shortly after the offense. The court viewed this testimony as particularly helpful to the finders of fact because it independently and directly corroborated the victim's credibility.

Air Force Court of Criminal Appeals

United States v. Hopwood, 29 M.J. 530 (A.F.C.M.R. 1989): During trial on forgery charges, defense counsel questioned a government witness about a statement the witness previously made to police investigators, but was never offered into evidence. In affirming the conviction, the court held that trial counsel properly introduced the witness's out of court statement as a prior consistent statement during rebuttal.

United States v. Allen, 13 M.J. 597 (A.F.C.M.R. 1982): During the accused's trial for having taken indecent sexual liberties with very young children, the government elicited testimony from the victims about how they first reported the crimes. Affirming the conviction, the court recognized that while the statements may not have been admissible under the theory offered at trial (Rule 803(2)), they were admissible as "legitimate rebuttal refuting . . . the defense's express and implied charges that the children's in-court testimony had been recently fabricated."

Navy-Marine Corps Court of Criminal Appeals

United States v. Helms, 39 M.J. 908 (N.M.C.M.R. 1994): The accused was convicted of committing indecent acts upon his four-year-old natural daughter. At trial, the victim's unresponsive testimony was presented via closed-circuit television. The offenses were established by other witnesses, including the victim's baby-sitter. Although the court affirmed the accused's conviction, it held that Rule 801(d)(1)(B) should not have been used to admit the baby-sitter's testimony. In the court's opinion, because the victim added almost nothing to the proof, there was little to rebut or rehabilitate. *See* our discussion of this case under Rule 807.

[ix]   Prior Consistent Statements—Recent Fabrication

United States Court of Appeals for the Armed Forces

United States v. Jones, 26 M.J. 197 (C.M.A. 1988): The retarded victim of child sexual abuse was extensively cross-examined on her alleged lack of memory and misidentification of the accused. Affirming the conviction, the court held that the victim's previous consistent statement to a social worker was properly admitted as substantive evidence and a rebuttal to the charge of fabrication.

United States v. LeMere, 22 M.J. 61 (C.M.A. 1986): In dictum, the court stated that a three-and-one-half-year-old witness's previous out-of-court statement could have been admitted to rebut the express or implied defense allegations of fabrication and improper motive.

United States v. Meyers, 18 M.J. 347 (C.M.A. 1984): The court found that a "sufficient impeachment foundation existed to justify admission of a [key government witness's] prior consistent statement" because trial defense counsel attempted to demonstrate that the government witness: (a) fabricated his testimony when the witness "did not speak of the matter before, at a time when it would have been natural to speak"; (b) was involved in numerous cases at this time, was overworked and thus confused the accused with someone else; and (c) had "an improper interest in presenting testimony against the accused"— *i.e.,* the witness hoped to obtain an Army recommendation for civilian employment after his enlistment expired. A well-reasoned dissent opined that since the rules permit the use of prior consistent statements, not only as corroborative evidence, but also as "substantive proof," more must be shown to admit the testimony than "the witness said the same thing on other occasions when his motive was the same . . . 'for the simple reason that mere repetition does not imply veracity.' " The dissent would limit this evidence to situations where it specifically "contradicts a suggestion that the witness changed his story in response to some threat or scheme or bribe by showing that his story was the same prior to the external pressure."

[x]   Prior Consistent Statements—Before Motive to Fabricate Arose

United States Court of Appeals for the Armed Forces

United States v. Faison, 49 M.J. 59 (C.A.A.F. 1998): The accused was convicted of sexually abusing his stepdaughter and drug use. The victim's pretrial statements were admitted to rehabilitate her after cross-examination demonstrated a motive to lie. Affirming the accused's convictions, the court held that the military judge properly determined that the challenged consistent statement had been made prior to the motive to misrepresent because the point in time to be measured is the fair implication of the charge of fabrication or improper motive, not the arguable underlying event that may be impossible to determine.

United States v. Allison, 49 M.J. 54 (C.A.A.F. 1998): The accused was convicted of various offenses including sodomizing his stepson. Prior to trial the victim made numerous statements to school and law enforcement officials. Trial counsel used one of those statements to rehabilitate the victim after defense counsel's cross-examination attempted to demonstrate the witness's motive to lie. Affirming the accused's convictions, the court held that "where multiple motives to fabricate or multiple improper influences are asserted, the statement need not precede all such motives or influences, but only the one it is offered to rebut."

United States v. Hurst, 29 M.J. 477 (C.M.A. 1990): In this child sexual abuse case, the court held that a prior consistent statement was admissible because trial counsel established it was made on "a date which clearly preceded the date of the purported tainting."

Air Force Court of Criminal Appeals

United States v. Robles, 53 M.J. 783 (A.F.Ct.Crim.App. 2000): The accused was convicted of sexual offenses against his daughter and his step daughter. During the defense's opening statement counsel indicated that the victim's story had "grown over time;" a theory they pressed during trial. To overcome the defense's allegation of recent fabrication, the prosecution used the victim's prior hand written note and other statements which confirmed her in court testimony. The court found that the note and other statements had been written before the victim's alleged motive to fabricate had arisen, although the court noted that, because defense counsel made such a "broadside attack" on the victim, it wasn't possible to differentiate between the multiple defense allegations.

Army Court of Criminal Appeals

United States v. Hood, 48 M.J. 928 (Army Ct.Crim.App. 1998): Before a court with office and enlisted members, the accused pled not guilty to drug, theft, and solicitation to commit theft offenses. The accused's coconspirator was a key government witness. On cross-examination, the witness was impeached by references to his motive to lie, which was linked to a pretrial agreement the witness had reached with the convening authority. Trial counsel rehabilitated the witness by introducing the witness's consistent pretrial statement. Granting findings and sentencing relief on other grounds, the court held that the witness's consistent pretrial statement was properly admitted because it was made before the witness entered into the pretrial agreement. The court rejected appellate defense counsel's contention (not raised at trial but characterized by the court as a "blanket disqualification" theory) that the statement should have been suppressed because the accused's motive to fabricate really dated from the moment of his apprehension.

Navy-Marine Corps Court of Criminal Appeals

United States v. Vanderbilt, 58 M.J. 725 (N.M.Ct.Crim.App. 2003): The accused was convicted of wrongfully selling or disposing of military handguns. She was sentenced to 21 months confinement, a dishonorable discharge, and related punishments. Affirming her convictions and sentence, the court found no error in the admission of a key government witness's prior consistent statement which he made *before* the defense alleged motive to lie arose. Here the government used the witness's previous statement to rehabilitate his credibility when defense counsel alleged that the witness was only testifying against the accused to preserve his own favorable pretrial agreement. The government was able to show that the statement was made before the pretrial agreement was signed.

[xi] Prior Consistent Statements—After Motive to Fabricate Arose

Supreme Court

Tome v. United States, 513 U.S. 150 (1995): Petitioner was convicted of sexually abusing his four-year-old daughter. During trial, the victim was aggressively cross-examined about having fabricated her allegations. In rebuttal, prosecutors were allowed to introduce the victim's out-of-court consistent statements. Reversing the accused's conviction, the Supreme Court held that because these consistent statements had been made after the alleged motive to fabricate arose, they were inadmissible under this provision.

United States Court of Appeals for the Armed Forces

United States v. McCaskey, 30 M.J. 188 (C.M.A. 1990): Although the court affirmed the accused's conviction for sexually molesting a thirteen-year-old child, the court found error in the admission of the victim's consistent pretrial statements. They had been made *after* the alleged recent fabrication or improper influence or motive occurred. This particularly thorough opinion traces past federal and military authorities governing prior consistent statements.

Navy-Marine Corps Court of Criminal Appeals

United States v. Knox, 46 M.J. 688 (N.M.Ct.Crim.App. 1997): The accused was convicted of raping his five-year-old daughter and sodomizing his four-year-old son. Part of the government's evidence against the accused included various incriminating drawings his children had made, and an expert witness/social worker's interpretation of the drawings. Finding most of the art work to be inadmissible and reversing the accused's convictions, the court said the drawings did not qualify as prior consistent statements because they were not made before the alleged motive to fabricate arose. Here the accused demonstrated that the statements followed an acrimonious separation from his wife, and, as a result, may have been motivated by her hostility for the accused.

[xii]   Prior Consistent Statements—Videotaped Statements

United States Court of Appeals for the Armed Forces

United States v. Morgan, 31 M.J. 43 (C.M.A. 1990): Affirming the accused's conviction for sexually molesting a four-year-old child, the court held that the victim's pretrial videotaped interview with a child psychologist had been properly admitted. In the court's opinion, the evidence was correctly used to rebut allegations of recent fabrication. The court also held, that because the victim testified at trial, the accused's right to effective cross-examination had not been violated.

[c]   Rule 801(d)(1)(C)—Prior Identifications

[i]   Prior Identifications—Memory Problems

Supreme Court

United States v. Owens, 484 U.S. 554 (1988): At trial, the victim recalled his pretrial identification of the defendant but on cross-examination admitted that he could not remember seeing his attacker. The Court rejected the defendant's argument that the witness's lack of memory had violated his rights of confrontation and also rejected the alternative argument that under Federal Rule of Evidence 801(d)(1)(C) the prior identification was inadmissible because the witness's memory loss meant that he was not available for cross-examination as required by that rule. The Court also noted the potential inconsistencies between the memory loss provision in 804(a) and the cross-examination requirement in 801(d), but concluded that "[q]uite obviously, the two characterizations are made for two entirely different purposes and there is no requirement or expectation that they should coincide."

[ii]   Prior Identifications—Procedures Required

Navy-Marine Corps Court of Criminal Appeals

United States v. Thomas, 41 M.J. 732 (N.M.Ct.Crim.App. 1995): The accused was convicted of maiming a fellow Marine by hitting him in the head with a tire jack. While receiving medical attention, and in response to repeated questions, the victim ultimately identified the accused as his assailant. The victim testified to those facts at trial. Finding error but no prejudice, the court held that Rule 801(d)(1)(C)'s provisions apply only to lineups, show-ups, or photographic identifications, not to other prior consistent statements introduced simply to bolster the witness's in-court testimony.

[5]   Rule 801(d)(2)—Admission by Party-opponent

[a]   Rule 801(d)(2)(A)—Personal Admissions

[i]   Personal Admissions—Accused's Own Statement

Navy-Marine Corps Court of Criminal Appeals

United States v. Giles, 58 M.J. 634 (N.M.Ct.Crim.App. 2003): The accused's original conviction for drug related offenses was reversed by the United States Court of Appeals for the Armed Forces. On retrial a charge of perjury was added. The main evidence for the perjury charge came from the accused's own first trial testimony which trial defense counsel objected to as inadmissible hearsay. Although the military judge admitted this evidence as a business record or as an official document, the court held it was not hearsay and properly admitted as her "own statement."

[ii]   Personal Admissions—Confrontation Clause

Supreme Court

Cruz v. New York, 481 U.S. 186 (1987): Rejecting the existing "interlocking confession rule," the High Court held that "where a nontestifying codefendant's confession incriminating the defendant is not directly admissible against the defendant . . . the Confrontation Clause bars its admission at their joint trial, even if the jury is instructed not to consider it against the defendant, and even if the defendant's own confession is admitted against him."

Richardson v. Marsh, 481 U.S. 200 (1987): In a joint murder case, the Court held that "the Confrontation Clause is not violated by the admission of a nontestifying codefendant's confession with a proper limiting instruction, when, as here, the confession is redacted to eliminate not only the defendant's name, but any reference to her existence."

[iii]   Personal Admissions—Constitutional Issues; Rights Warnings

Army Court of Criminal Appeals

United States v. Hill, 13 M.J. 882 (A.C.M.R. 1982): The accused's conviction for inflicting grievous bodily harm on his four-year-old son was reversed because the only evidence linking him with the crime was inadmissible hearsay. The accused's statements to a social worker, which were part of the evidence, were not admissible because the social worker did not testify, and because the statements had not been preceded by Article 31 warnings.

[iv] Personal Admissions—Documentary Evidence

United States Court of Appeals for the Armed Forces

United States v. Barnes, 33 M.J. 468 (C.M.A. 1992): The accused was convicted of drunk driving, drug distribution, and other offenses. During sentencing and on appeal, he contended that the government's evidence used to establish his previous civilian conviction for drunk driving was insufficient. Affirming the sentence and conviction, the court held that because the document in question had been written by the accused during his induction process, it was admissible under this Rule.

United States v. Rivera, 23 M.J. 89 (C.M.A 1986): A highly inculpatory note written by the accused to his stepdaughter discussing their illicit sexual relationship was admissible against the accused because: (1) he "was a party to the proceedings," (2) the note was relevant to the charged offenses, and (3) the note was not unfairly prejudicial.

Army Court of Criminal Appeals

United States v. Antonitis, 26 M.J. 856 (A.C.M.R. 1988): Affirming the accused's conviction for possession with intent to distribute methamphetamine, the court found error in the admission of a typed, but unsigned and "unadopted" pretrial statement allegedly made by the accused. The court said that, although the CID agent who took the statement was properly allowed to testify about the accused's admissions, the DA Form 2823 he used to record them was inadmissible because there was no evidence in the record that the accused adopted what was recorded.

[v] Personal Admissions—Expert Witnesses

United States Court of Appeals for the Armed Forces

United States v. Mansfield, 38 M.J. 415 (C.M.A. 1993): The accused's original 1984 murder conviction was the subject of substantial appellate litigation concerning trial defense counsel's competence in dealing with mental responsibility issues. After the findings and sentence were set aside, the accused was retried in 1987, and convicted again. This time he unsuccessfully renewed many of the original issues. In the court's opinion, no error occurred when trial counsel was permitted to cross-examine defense psychotherapists about damaging statements the accused offered to them. The court said these incriminating statements were the admissions of a party-opponent, which meant that their relevance and authenticity were established beyond cavil.

[vi] Personal Admissions—Privileged Communications

Army Court of Criminal Appeals

United States v. Walker, 54 M.J. 568 (Army Ct.Crim.App. 2000): The accused was convicted of sexually molesting his step-daughter. During trial, the military judge allowed a CID agent to testify that the accused's wife had made an out-of-court statement about the charges against her husband: "[The accused] did tell me what happened; however, I do not wish to disclose what he said." Finding error but no harm in this admission, the court held that the contested statement was innocuous and therefore not able to meet Rule 401's very low standard for relevance, and violative of Rule 504(b)'s spousal communications privilege.

[vii]   Personal Admissions—Providence Inquiry Statements

United States Court of Appeals for the Armed Forces

United States v. Irwin, 42 M.J. 479 (C.A.A.F. 1995): Pursuant to his pleas, the accused was convicted of rape, forcible sodomy, kidnapping, and related offenses. During providence, the accused willingly discussed his misconduct. Over defense objection, trial counsel played the taped recording of the accused's admissions to the members. The accused contended that his statements were inadmissible hearsay. Affirming the accused's convictions and sentence, the court found the providence inquiry statements to be judicial admissions and clearly admissible.

[viii]   Personal Admissions—Substantive Use

United States Court of Appeals for the Armed Forces

United States v. Callara, 21 M.J. 259 (C.M.A. 1986): Distinguishing this provision from Rule 613(a), the court emphasized that admissions by a party opponent are not admitted for impeachment purposes alone; they can also be used as "substantive evidence" of guilt. However, the court recognized that the fine technical distinctions between impeachment and substantive evidence are often lost on court members. As a result, careful counsel and military judges should treat evidence admissible only for impeachment with special attention, and should carefully inform the members concerning its proper use. See our discussion of Rule 105.

Air Force Court of Criminal Appeals

United States v. Garries, 19 M.J. 845 (A.F.C.M.R. 1985): The court found that the accused's pretrial statement to a testifying friend: "I swear, if you don't come and get me I'll kill her," was properly admitted because: (1) it was the accused's own utterance; (2) it was relevant to establishing that the accused murdered his wife; and (3) it was not barred by another rule of evidence.

[b]   Rule 801(d)(2)(B)—Adoptive Admissions

[i]   Adoptive Admissions—Foundational Requirements

Navy-Marine Corps Court of Criminal Appeals

United States v. Garrett, 16 M.J. 941 (N.M.C.M.R. 1983): In order for post-conspiratorial statements to be admitted as adoptive admissions the proponent must establish: "(1) the party against whom it is offered was present during the making of the statement; (2) he understood its content; and (3) his actions or words or both unequivocally acknowledged the statement in adopting it as his own."

[ii] Adoptive Admissions—Adoptions by Use

Navy-Marine Corps Court of Criminal Appeals

United States v. Potter, 14 M.J. 979 (N.M.C.M.R. 1982): Because the accused had introduced the unsworn but written statement of his alleged co-conspirator at a previous magistrate's hearing, the court found that the statement could be used by the government at trial against the accused as an adoptive admission.

[iii] Adoptive Admissions—Tacit Admissions

United States Court of Appeals for the Armed Forces

United States v. Datz, 61 M.J. 37 (C.A.A.F. 2005): At a general court-martial with officer and enlisted members, the accused was convicted of numerous offenses including rape and sexual harassment. The central issue at trial and on appeal was whether the accused's alleged affirmative "head nodding" to interrogators' questions indicating the accused's complicity were improperly admitted. Reversing the accused's convictions and sentence, the court held that proof of the head nodding, when used as adoptive admissions, should have been suppressed because trial counsel did not present a sufficient basis to justify finding that the accused "heard, understood, and acquiesced in the statements."

United States v. Stanley, 21 M.J. 249 (C.M.A. 1986): The court held that incriminating statements made by another person in the defendant's presence were inadmissible because, "while silence may be considered an admission under certain circumstances, it is clear that merely hearing the statements of third persons does not equate to adoption by silence. . . . An inference of assent cannot safely be made . . . unless the circumstances are such that dissent would in ordinary experience have been expressed if the communication had not been correct." Here the defendant's silence could easily have been interpreted as unfamiliarity with the crimes in question.

Army Court of Criminal Appeals

United States v. Farris, 21 M.J. 702 (A.C.M.R. 1985): The court held that, unless the government can establish that a pretrial note to the accused was fully known to him and that he approved of its contents, the document "cannot be deemed to have been adopted or acquiesced in" by the accused.

[iv] Adoptive Admissions—Written Statements

Navy-Marine Corps Court of Criminal Appeals

United States v. Hood, 52 M.J. 582, 583 (N.M.Ct.Crim.App. 1999): Following mixed pleas, a military judge sitting alone found the accused guilty of wrongfully obtaining telephone services. During trial, a copy of the accused's phone bill was admitted against him, not as a business record, but as an adoptive admission. Trial counsel established that when confronted with the phone bill by the victim, the accused admitted complicity. The court held that while Rule 801(d)(2)(B) normally deals with oral statements, nothing in the Rule prevents written statements from also qualifying.

[c] Rule 801(d)(2)(E)—Statements of Co-conspirators

[i] Statements of Co-conspirators—Availability of Declarant

Supreme Court

United States v. Inadi, 475 U.S. 387 (1986): The Court held that no showing of unavailability need be made with respect to conspirators' statements, because they possess independent evidentiary significance which is not affected by the declarant's failure to testify.

[ii] Statements of Co-conspirators—Confrontation Concerns

Supreme Court

Bourjaily v. United States, 483 U.S. 171 (1987): The Court held that, before admitting a co-conspirator's statement, the trial judge must be satisfied by a preponderance of the evidence that a conspiracy existed. In reaching that decision, he may consider any nonprivileged evidence whatsoever, including the proffered hearsay statements themselves. The Court rejected the argument that the Confrontation Clause requires that there be "independent indicia of reliability" for admission of the statements.

Air Force Court of Criminal Appeals

United States v. Marshall, 31 M.J. 712 (A.F.C.M.R. 1990): The accused and two other airmen were apprehended for drug offenses. government counsel chose to grant immunity to one of the other two co-conspirators. At trial, over defense constitutional objections, the immunized witness related incriminating statements made by all accused. Affirming the convictions, the court found that the Military Rules and recent Supreme Court decisions (*see* Borch, *The Use of Co-Conspirator Statements Under the Rules of Evidence; A Revolutionary Change in Admissibility,* 124 MIL. L. REV. 163 (1989)) have dramatically expanded the law here, specifically permitting this testimony.

[iii] Statements of Co-conspirators—Proving the Conspiracy

United States Court of Appeals for the Armed Forces

United States v. Ward, 16 M.J. 341 (C.M.A. 1983): If out-of-court statements made by a co-conspirator are to be used, the proponent must establish the "illicit association between the declarant and the defendant," as well as the scope and magnitude of the conspiracy. The court here could not sustain admission of the statement because these matters were not demonstrated with "sufficient particularity."

Air Force Court of Criminal Appeals

United States v. Ward, 13 M.J. 626 (A.F.C.M.R. 1982): After determining that an extrajudicial statement should not have been admitted against the accused pursuant to Rule 804(b)(3), the court found the statement admissible under the co-conspirators' rule. Although the statements were made after the criminal act, the court found that they were made to conceal the accused's complicity in the charged offenses. The court also noted that the proponent of Rule 801(d)(2)(E) evidence should demonstrate the likelihood of an "illicit association" between the accused and the declarant before offering the declarant's statements.

Navy-Marine Corps Court of Criminal Appeals

United States v. Vanderbilt, 58 M.J. 725 (N.M.Ct.Crim.App. 2003): The accused was convicted of wrongfully selling or disposing of military handguns. Affirming her convictions and sentence, the court found no error in the admission of a key government witness's statements that another participant in the criminal adventure told him that the accused was involved in their nefarious acts.

United States v. Scott, 24 M.J. 578 (N.M.C.M.R. 1987): Pursuant to Article 62, the government successfully challenged a trial judge's decision dismissing all charges due to a lack of subject matter jurisdiction and a lack of sufficient independent evidence to admit a co-conspirator's statement. Adopting *Means v. United States,* 469 U.S. 1058 (1984), the court held that the challenged hearsay statements should have been admitted because the underlying conspiracy "may be established by a preponderance of evidence consisting of independent evidence 'viewed in conjunction with the hearsay statements made by the conspirator concerning [the accused's] participation.' "

United States v. Kellett, 18 M.J. 782 (N.M.C.M.R. 1984): The court found that statements of a coconspirator were properly admitted through an NIS agent because: (1) the co-conspirator had just undergone surgery and would be unavailable for at least two to three weeks; (2) the government was able to show, using independent evidence, that a conspiracy existed; and (3) the statements were made in furtherance of the conspiracy.

[iv]   Statements of Co-conspirators—In Furtherance of Conspiracy

Air Force Court of Criminal Appeals

United States v. Dillon, 12 M.J. 641 (A.F.C.M.R. 1981): Although the court found that an accused's wife's statements were not declarations against her interest when they implicated him in narcotics activity, the statements were admissible as conspirator's statements made during and in furtherance of a conspiracy.

Army Court of Criminal Appeals

United States v. Diamond, 65 M.J. 876 (Army Ct.Crim.App. 2007): The accused was convicted of adultery, gun offenses, conspiracy to commit premeditated murder, premeditated murder, and obstruction of justice. The conspiracy concerned a plan the accused and his paramour created to kill the paramour's husband and cover their acts by lying to the police and ultimately leaving the country. Part of the government's case included incriminating statements the paramour made to the police and others. The paramour did not testify in reliance on her Fifth Amendment privilege and was determined to be unavailable. At trial and on appeal the accused objected to the admission of his paramour's statements and contended that they were testimonial and that their use violated *Crawford v. Washington*, 541 U.S. 36 (2004). The court affirmed the accused's convictions and held that the paramour's statements were properly admitted as non-hearsay co-conspirator statements, and were not testimonial because they were intended to conceal the accused's criminal activity, not prove it at his trial.

United States v. Blacks, 37 M.J. 662 (A.C.M.R. 1993): In this assault and wrongful appropriation case, the accused contended that trial defense counsel had been ineffective for failing to challenge hearsay evidence. Affirming, the court held that a co-conspirator's out-of-court statements had been properly admitted and were in furtherance of the conspiracy, and thus not hearsay, even though they were uttered to a third party.

United States v. Evans, 31 M.J. 927 (A.C.M.R. 1990): The accused's convictions for conspiracy to commit larceny and larceny were achieved by using co-conspirator testimony. Affirming, the court held that statements made by a conspirator to a non-conspirator, which were designed to secure cooperation, allay fears, insure possible future dealings, and obtain assistance were made in furtherance of the conspiracy and were admissible.

Navy-Marine Corps Court of Criminal Appeals

United States v. Clark, 61 M.J. 707 (N.M.Ct.Crim.App. 2005): The accused was convicted of arson and related offenses. After the arson was completed, various members of the conspiracy made statements to friends and family about what they had done. The military judge admitted those statements and indicated on the record that termination of the conspiracy was not a basis for excluding the evidence. Finding harmless error, the court held that once the object of the conspiracy had been accomplished, the conspiracy was terminated and any further statements made by the co-conspirators were not admissible under Rule 801(d)(2)(E).

United States v. Swan, 45 M.J. 672 (N.M.Ct.Crim.App. 1996): The accused was convicted of numerous drug related offenses, including conspiracy. During the government's case in chief, over defense counsel's objections, statements of a co-conspirator were admitted against the accused. Finding error but no prejudice, the court held that the out-of-court statements were not admissible because the purpose for the conspiracy had ended by the time the admitted statements were originally made.

United States v. Ratliff, 42 M.J. 797 (N.M.Ct.Crim.App. 1995): The accused was convicted of conspiracy to commit robbery, robbery by force and violence, assault with intent to commit robbery, and false swearing. Part of the government's case against the accused included statements made by co-conspirators. The accused contended that the admission of these statements was error. Affirming the accused's convictions, the court held that the co-conspirators' statements were a criminal status report of on-going crimes, and an indication that the central purpose for the misconduct had not yet been achieved. As a result, they were uttered in furtherance of the conspiracy and were admissible.

United States v. Garrett, 16 M.J. 941 (N.M.C.M.R. 1983): The court held that, in order for government counsel to use co-conspirators' statements, it must be established that the statements were uttered during the course and in furtherance of the conspiracy. Coconspirator's statements will not be admissible if they are based upon the theory of "an implied continuing conspiracy to conceal guilt. . . ." However, such statements may be admissible if the government alleges and proves the separate conspiracy to obstruct justice.

[v]   Statements of Co-conspirators—Sexual Assault Cases

Navy-Marine Corps Court of Criminal Appeals

United States v. Terry, 61 M.J. 721 (N.M.Ct.Crim.App. 2005): The accused was convicted of rape, conspiracy to commit rape, and related offenses. Over defense counsel's objection, a witness was allowed to testify to a co-conspirator's prior statement: "Oh it was rape all right." The accused contended it was reversible error for the military judge to admit the statement without first conducting a Rule 801(d)(2) hearing to determine whether a conspiracy in fact existed. Rejecting that argument, the court held that the military judge is presumed to know the law, and that the court's own *de novo* review supported the conclusion that no error occurred. The court went on to say that even if there had been error, it was harmless.

§ 802.01   Official Text

Rule 802.   Hearsay Rule.

Hearsay is not admissible except as provided by these rules or by any Act of Congress applicable in trials by court-martial.

---

§ 802.02   Editorial Comment

[1]   Rule 802—Hearsay Rule

[a]   Inadmissible Evidence—Not Incompetent Evidence

When court-martial practice adopted Rule 802 from the Federal Rules of Evidence, it redefined hearsay practice. Rule 802 provides that hearsay is not admissible unless these Rules of Evidence or an act of Congress made specifically applicable to court-martial practice provide otherwise. The federal version of this Rule is similar, but also recognizes the Supreme Court's power to promulgate hearsay provisions.

Under previous court-martial practice, hearsay evidence not covered by an exception was *incompetent,* not merely inadmissible. The distinction was important. For example, if an accused was charged with larceny and the only evidence establishing lawful ownership in someone other than the accused was proved through inadmissible hearsay evidence, an appellate court would have reversed the conviction, even though the defense made no objection to this evidence.[1]

Rule 802, in conjunction with Rules 103(a) and (d), now alters the treatment such evidence will receive on appeal. Since Rule 802 makes hearsay evidence only inadmissible, counsel's failure to object waives any delict, unless plain error is found.

[b]   Limited Exceptions

The drafters of Rule 802 intended it to eliminate judicial power to create new hearsay exceptions. The Rule states that only Congress may create such Rules. Congress, acting through the President and Article 36(a) of the Uniform Code of Military Justice, has provided all the available exceptions as well as Rule 801(d) exemptions from the ban on hearsay evidence.

Although the judiciary may not establish new exceptions, Rule 807 allows for hearsay evidence to be admitted on a case-by-case basis, even though it would not be admissible under any specific exemption or exception. In order to meet that Rule's requirements, a party must satisfy criteria aimed at

---

[1] *See, e.g.,* ¶ 139 *a*, Manual for Courts-Martial, United States (rev. ed. 1969) and United States v. Zone, 7 M.J. 21 (C.M.A. 1979), for a largely historic discussion of incompetent hearsay evidence and appellate remedies when it is improperly admitted against an accused.

assuring the evidence's truthful character and the trial court's need for the evidence, as well as provide opposing counsel with advance notice of its intended use. Congress intended that Rule 807 not be used so as an escape mechanism from Rule 802.[2] If the evidence is admissible under the residual exception it must be because of the particular circumstances at bar. Federal decisions appear in accord, emphasizing as they do a narrow construction of the residual exception.[3]

§ 802.03 Drafters' Analysis

Rule 802 is taken generally from the Federal Rule but has been modified to recognize the application of any applicable Act of Congress.

Although the basic rule of inadmissibility for hearsay is identical with that found in ¶ 39 *a* of the present *Manual,* there is a substantial change in military practice as a result of Rule 103(a). Under the present *Manual,* hearsay is incompetent evidence and does not require an objection to be inadmissible. Under the new Rules, however, admission of hearsay will not be error unless there is an objection to the hearsay. *See* Rule 103(a).

§ 802.04 Annotated Cases

[1] Rule 802—Hearsay Rule

[a] Judge's Discretion Limited

Air Force Court of Criminal Appeals

United States v. Mendoza, 18 M.J. 576 (A.F.C.M.R. 1984): The court found error in a trial judge's *sua sponte* decision to admit hearsay testimony as substantive evidence when its only proper use was for impeachment purposes.

United States v. Parmar, 12 M.J. 976 (A.F.C.M.R. 1982): During the pre-sentencing portion of the accused's trial, defense counsel presented evidence stressing the accused's general good duty performance and desire to be retained in the Air Force. Despite strenuous defense objections, trial counsel was then permitted to call the accused's squadron commander who not only expressed a different view, but also "recited specific undocumented instances of the accused's off-base misconduct." Relying on Rules 802 and 803, the court found that the evidence failed to demonstrate trustworthiness or reliability and held that the trial judge abused his discretion by admitting it. The court considered and rejected the government's argument that no

---

[2] ABA Litigation Section, EMERGING PROBLEMS UNDER THE FEDERAL RULES OF EVIDENCE, 279–80 (1983) indicates that courts are applying the residual exceptions more broadly than Congress apparently intended.

[3] *See, e.g.,* United States v. White, 611 F.2d 531 (5th Cir. 1980) (residual hearsay exception should be used "sparingly" and only when there are sufficient independent guarantees of reliability to justify admission).

error occurred because ¶ 75 *c* (1) of the 1969 Manual for Courts-Martial, relaxed the rules of evidence during sentencing.

[b] Objections Required to Preserve Error

United States Court of Appeals for the Armed Forces

United States v. Reynoso, 66 M.J. 208 (C.A.A.F. 2008): The accused was tried for marijuana use, making false official statements, and presenting false claims concerning his housing allowance. At trial the government called an expert witness to explain the differences between what the accused should have received and what he did receive. The expert presented a chart illuminating these disparities. Defense counsel objected but stated only "foundation" as his ground. After a short voir dire of the expert witness, the exhibit was admitted. On appeal, the accused contended that the exhibit violated Rule 1006 as improperly compiled summary evidence and Rule 802 as inadmissible hearsay. The court noted that, each of these issues may have been appropriate grounds for challenge at trial, but because the record was silent as to either objection waiver had resulted.

Army Court of Criminal Appeals

United States v. Trisler, 25 M.J. 611 (A.C.M.R. 1987): Affirming the accused's larceny conviction, the court held that unobjected to hearsay evidence establishing the value of stolen property is admissible, and the "finder of fact may give the hearsay its natural probative value" in establishing guilt or innocence.

§ 803.01   Official Text

Rule 803.   Hearsay Exceptions; Availability of Declarant Immaterial.

The following are not excluded by the hearsay rule, even though the declarant is available as a witness:

(1) *Present sense impression.* A statement describing or explaining an event or condition made while the declarant was perceiving the event or condition or immediately thereafter.

(2) *Excited utterance.* A statement relating to a startling event or condition made while the declarant was under the stress of excitement caused by the event or condition.

(3) *Then existing mental, emotional, or physical condition.* A statement of the declarant's then existing state of mind, emotion, sensation, or physical condition (such as intent, plan, motive, design, mental feeling, pain, and bodily health), but not including a statement of memory or belief to prove the fact remembered or believed unless it relates to the execution, revocation, identification, or terms of declarant's will.

(4) *Statements for purposes of medical diagnosis or treatment.* Statements made for purposes of medical diagnosis or treatment and describing medical history, or past or present symptoms, pain, or sensations, or the inception or general character of the cause or external source thereof insofar as reasonably pertinent to diagnosis or treatment.

(5) *Recorded recollection.* A memorandum or record concerning a matter about which a witness once had knowledge but now has insufficient recollection to enable the witness to testify fully and accurately, shown to have been made or adopted by the witness when the matter was fresh in the witness's memory and to reflect that knowledge correctly. If admitted, the memorandum or record may be read into evidence, but may not itself be received as an exhibit unless offered by an adverse party.

(6) *Records of regularly conducted activity.* A memorandum, report, record, or data compilation, in any form, of acts, events, conditions, opinions, or diagnoses, made at or near the time by, or from information transmitted by, a person with knowledge, if kept in the course of a regularly conducted business activity, and if it was the regular practice of that business activity to make the memorandum, report, record, or data compilation, all as shown by the testimony of the custodian or other qualified witness, or by certification that complies with Mil. R. Evid. 902(11) or any other

statute permitting certification in a criminal proceeding in a court of the United States, unless the source of the information or the method or circumstances of preparation indicate a lack of trustworthiness. The term 'business' as used in this paragraph includes the armed forces, a business, institution, association, profession, occupation, and calling of every kind, whether or not conducted for profit. Among those memoranda, reports, records, or data compilations normally admissible pursuant to this paragraph are enlistment papers, physical examination papers, outline-figure and fingerprint cards, forensic laboratory reports, chain of custody documents, morning reports and other personnel accountability documents, service records, officer and enlisted qualification records, logs, unit personnel diaries, individual equipment records, daily strength records of prisoners, and rosters of prisoners.

(7) *Absence of entry in records kept in accordance with the provisions of paragraph (6).* Evidence that a matter is not included in the memoranda, reports, records, or data compilations, in any form, kept in accordance with the provisions of paragraph (6), to prove the nonoccurrence or nonexistence of the matter, if the matter was of a kind of which a memorandum, report, record, or data compilation was regularly made and preserved, unless the sources of information or other circumstances indicate lack of trustworthiness.

(8) *Public records and reports.* Records, reports, statements, or data compilations, in any form, of public office or agencies, setting forth (A) the activities of the office or agency, or (B) matters observed pursuant to duty imposed by law as to which matters there was a duty to report, excluding, however, matters observed by police officers and other personnel acting in a law enforcement capacity, or (C) against the government, factual findings resulting from an investigation made pursuant to authority granted by law, unless the sources of information or other circumstances indicate lack of trustworthiness. Notwithstanding (B), the following are admissible under this paragraph as a record of a fact or event if made by a person within the scope of the person's official duties and those duties included a duty to know or to ascertain through appropriate and trustworthy channels of information the truth of the fact or event and to record such fact or event: enlistment papers, physical examination papers, outline-figure and fingerprint cards, forensic laboratory reports, chain of custody documents, morning reports and other personnel accountability documents, service records, officer and enlisted qualification records, records of court-martial convictions, logs, unit

personnel diaries, individual equipment records, guard reports, daily strength records of prisoners, and rosters of prisoners.

(9) *Records of vital statistics.* Records or data compilations, in any form, of births, fetal deaths, deaths, or marriages, if the report thereof was made to a public office pursuant to requirements of law.

(10) *Absence of public record or entry.* To prove the absence of a record, report, statement, or data compilation in any form, or the nonoccurrence or nonexistence of a matter of which a record, report, statement, or data compilation, in any form, was regularly made and preserved by a public office or agency, evidence in the form of a certification in accordance with Mil. R. Evid. 902, or testimony, that diligent search failed to disclose the record, report, statement, or data compilation, or entry.

(11) *Records of religious organizations.* Statements of births, marriages, divorces, deaths, legitimacy, ancestry, relationship by blood or marriage, or other similar facts of personal or family history contained in a regularly kept record of a religious organization.

(12) *Marriage, baptismal, and similar certificates.* Statements of fact contained in a certificate that the maker performed a marriage or other ceremony or administered a sacrament, made by a clergyman, public official, or other person authorized by the rules or practices of a religious organization or by law to perform the act certified, and purporting to have been issued at the time of the act or within a reasonable time thereafter.

(13) *Family records.* Statements of fact concerning personal or family history contained in family Bibles, genealogies, charts, engravings on rings, inscriptions on family portraits, engravings on urns, crypts, or tombstones, or the like.

(14) *Records of documents affecting an interest in property.* The record of a document purporting to establish or affect an interest in property, as proof of the content of the original recorded document and its execution and delivery by each person by whom it purports to have been executed, if the record is a record of a public office and an applicable statute authorizes the recording of documents of that kind in that office.

(15) *Statements in documents affecting an interest in property.* A statement contained in a document purporting to establish or affect an interest in property if the matter stated was relevant to the purpose of the document, unless dealings with the property since the document was made have been inconsistent with the truth of the statement or the purport of the document.

(16) *Statements in ancient documents.* Statements in a document in existence twenty years or more the authenticity of which is established.

(17) *Market reports, commercial publications.* Market quotations, tabulations, directories, lists (including government price lists), or other published compilations, generally used and relied upon by the public or by persons in particular occupations.

(18) *Learned treatises.* To the extent called to the attention of an expert witness upon cross-examination or relied upon by the expert in direct examination, statements contained in published treatises, periodicals, or pamphlets on a subject of history, medicine or other science or art, established as a reliable authority by the testimony or admission of the witness or by other expert testimony or by judicial notice. If admitted, the statements may be read into evidence but may not be received as exhibits.

(19) *Reputation concerning personal or family history.* Reputation among members of the person's family by blood, adoption, or marriage, or among the person's associates, or in the community, concerning the person's birth, adoption, marriage, divorce, death, legitimacy, relationship by blood, adoption, or marriage, ancestry, or other similar fact of the person's personal or family history.

(20) *Reputation concerning boundaries or general history.* Reputation in a community, arising before the controversy, as to boundaries of or customs affecting lands in the community, and reputation as to events of general history important to the community or State or nation in which located.

(21) *Reputation as to character.* Reputation of a person's character among the person's associates or in the community.

(22) *Judgment of previous conviction.* Evidence of a final judgment, entered after a trial or upon a plea of guilty (but not upon a plea of nolo contendere), adjudging a person guilty of a crime punishable by death, dishonorable discharge, or imprisonment in excess of one year, to prove any fact essential to sustain the judgment, but not including, when offered by the government for purposes other than impeachment, judgments against persons other than the accused. The pendency of an appeal may be shown but does not affect admissibility. In determining whether a crime tried by court-martial was punishable by death, dishonorable discharge, or imprisonment in excess of one year, the maximum punishment prescribed by the President under Article 56 at the time of the conviction applies without regard to whether the case was tried by general, special, or summary court-martial.

(23) *Judgment as to personal, family, or general history, or*

boundaries. Judgments as proof of matters of personal, family, or general history, or boundaries essential to the judgment, if the same would be provable by evidence of reputation.

(24) *Other exceptions.* Pursuant to the 1 June 1999 Amendments to the Military Rules of Evidence, this provision has been transferred to Rule 807.

§ 803.02   Editorial Comment

[1]   Rule 803—Hearsay Exceptions—Availability of Declarant Immaterial

[a]   Foundation for the Rule

Read together, Rules 801(d), 803, 804, and 807 present an organized codification of legal authority justifying the admission of proof that would otherwise be excluded because of the prohibition against hearsay evidence. Rule 801(d) excludes from the basic definition of hearsay (801(c)) much of what the military and common law traditionally labeled as hearsay; 804 provides hearsay exceptions applicable when the declarant is unavailable; 803 lists hearsay exceptions applicable whether or not the declarant is available; and Rule 807 contains a single residual exception that provides for the admission of proof, under very limited circumstances, that would otherwise be excluded on hearsay grounds because it failed to meet the foundational or other requirements of an enumerated exception.

The 23 exceptions to the hearsay prohibition contained in Rule 803 are not dependent upon witness unavailability because these exceptions have long common law histories demonstrating reliability that the law recognizes as the functional equivalent of a declarant's in-court testimony. The common law's experience with hearsay demonstrates that in many cases it may actually be more reliable than live witness testimony.

[b]   Hearsay Exceptions and the Confrontation Clause

Hearsay issues in criminal cases must be examined in light of Supreme Court cases dealing with the Confrontation Clause of the Sixth Amendment. The Confrontation Clause requires that in criminal cases the accused have the right to be confronted with the witnesses against him or her. Military and federal practice indicate that "confronted" has had two meanings. The first meaning is the obvious one—to actually cross-examine the witness during the trial in question, thus allowing the court-members to see how the witness deals with both supportive direct examination and challenging cross-examination. The second situation, and the one in question here, concerns under what circumstances "testimonial" hearsay can be considered by a finder of fact for substantive purposes when the witness does not testify during the trial in question, and that witness's statement is admitted pursuant to a hearsay exception or exclusion. This second situation raises the long standing conflict between the Federal and Military Rules of Evidence lengthy lists of "exceptions" or "exclusions" to the hearsay prohibition, and the Confrontation Clause's requirement for "confrontation."

For almost twenty-five years, *Ohio v. Roberts*,[1] was the controlling authority on this question. Along with *United States. v. Inadi*,[2] courts have long examined hearsay statements offered for "substantive purposes," that is to prove the truth of the matter asserted, based on a "reliability" standard. If the hearsay statement qualified under a "firmly rooted" hearsay exception, courts generally found the statement in accord with the confrontation clause. However, where the statement was not among the firmly rooted exceptions, the government had to establish a particularized showing of trustworthiness or fit the statement under a hearsay exception that possessed an independent evidentiary basis.

The Supreme Court's decisions in *Crawford v. Washington*,[3] *Davis v. Washington* and *Hammon v. Indiana*[4] changed a great deal of this logic. They require that all "testimonial" hearsay statements be subjected to cross-examination either during the trial at bar, or previously at another qualifying proceeding. More recently, in *Michigan v. Bryant* 131 S.Ct. 1143 (2011), a state murder case tried before *Crawford v. Washington* and *Davis v. Washington*, the deceased victim's statements to police identifying Bryant as his assailant were admitted based on the *Ohio v. Roberts* "reliability" standard. The victim had been shot at Bryant's house approximately 25 minutes before the police found him in a store parking lot bleeding to death. At least five policemen asked the victim what happened. Each received similar answers identifying Bryant as the assailant. The Washington Supreme Court heard the case after *Crawford* and *Davis* were decided and reversed the accused's conviction. The Supreme Court found that reversal was based on an improperly applied testimonial standard and remanded the case for further proceedings. The Court explained that it granted certiorari because neither *Crawford* nor *Davis* comprehensively defined "testimonial."

The majority held that statements are testimonial and inadmissible when no ongoing emergency exists and the interrogator's primary purpose was to collect information about past events for use in a subsequent criminal prosecution and that statements can be nontestimonial and admissible even when made in the course of a police interrogation when the primary purpose for the interrogation objectively appears to be the interrogator's attempt to meet an ongoing emergency and the process used for taking the statements is informal with a focus on current and future events.

---

[1] 448 U.S. 56 (1980).

[2] 475 U.S. 387 (1986).

[3] 541 U.S. 36 (2004).

[4] 547 U.S. 813 (2006).

Writing for the majority, Justice Sotomayor found that the statements made were non-testimonial. The majority focused on the emergency confronting the police in dealing with a shooting a missing shooter and a lack of knowledge as to whether the victim they found was the only target of the shooter, and also noted that the interrogation was informally and haphazardly conducted in a public and exposed location before emergency medical equipment arrived.

Justice Thomas concurred in the result, finding the evidence admissible because the police interrogation lacked sufficient "formality and solemnity" to create a testimonial statement. Justice Thomas explained that the primary purpose test created by the Court is an "exercise in fiction," "disconnected from history" and "yields no predictable results."

Justice Scalia dissented. Unlike the majority, he believed it is the declarant's intent that matters as trial testimony is not just a narrative of what happened in the past, but a solemn declaration that may invoke the criminal process. Justice Scalia further explained that the interrogator is nonetheless relevant to this process. The identity of the interrogator and the content of his questions affect whether the declarant's intent is to make a solemn statement. Justice Scalia harshly criticized the majority's reasoning and its conclusion:

> Today's tale—a story of five officers conducting successive examinations of a dying man with the primary purpose, not of obtaining and preserving his testimony regarding his killer, but of protecting him, them, and others from a murderer somewhere on the loose—is so transparently false that professing to believe it demeans this institution. But reaching a patently incorrect conclusion on the facts is a relatively benign judicial mischief; it affects, after all, only the case at hand. In its vain attempt to make the incredible plausible, however—or perhaps as an intended second goal—today's opinion distorts our Confrontation Clause jurisprudence and leaves it in a shambles. Instead of clarifying the law, the Court makes itself the obfuscator of last resort. * * *

> * * * *

> Worse still for the repute of today's opinion, this is an absurdly easy case even if one (erroneously) takes the interrogating officers' purpose into account. The five officers interrogated Covington primarily to investigate past criminal events. None—absolutely none—of their actions indicated that they perceived an imminent threat. They did not draw their weapons, and indeed did not immediately search the gas station for potential shooters. To the contrary, all five testified that they questioned Covington [the victim] *before conducting any investigation at the scene*. Would this have made any sense if they feared the presence of a shooter? Most tellingly, none of the officers started his interrogation by asking what would have been the obvious first question if any hint of such a fear existed: Where is the shooter?

In *Melendez-Diaz v. Massachusetts*, 129 S. Ct. 2527 (2009), a drug distribution and trafficking case, the Supreme Court applied *Crawford v. Washington* to the prosecution's use of "certificates of analysis" which identified the seized substance as cocaine. The Supreme Court reversed the accused's convictions and held that the state courts erred in holding that *Crawford* did not apply to the certificates. Justice Scalia wrote for the 5-4 majority that the documents were clearly "affidavits" and fell within the "core class of testimonial statements" excluded by the Sixth Amendment unless the accused had a prior opportunity to cross-examine the unavailable declarant. Although the Court opined that its decision involved little more than a direct application of *Crawford*, its impact on court-martial litigation will be significant. Defense counsel may now challenge "chain of custody documents" by making the same Sixth Amendment arguments the Court found persuasive in *Melendez-Diaz*.

The majority rejected six arguments raised by the dissenters. (1) Notarized certificates of analysis are not accusatory and therefore not testimonial. The majority held that there is no requirement for a declarant's statement to be accusatory in order to be covered by the Sixth Amendment. (2) The Confrontation Clause does not apply to certificates of analysis because they were not compiled by "conventional" witnesses. The majority rejected the distinction between witnesses to events and witnesses whose statements are remote in time and location from an event. (3) Certificates of analysis are different and admissible because they are reliable scientific evidence. The Court viewed this as nothing more than a rationale for returning to the now-rejected logic of *Ohio v. Roberts*. (4) Notarized laboratory reports are admissible as Rule 803(6) Records of Regularly Conducted Activity or Rule 803(8) Public Records and Reports. The majority held that the analyses were made primarily for purposes of prosecution and not to assist in the operation of a business or similar organization's affairs and constituted matters observed pursuant to law enforcement activities.

In *Bullcoming v. New Mexico*, 2011 U.S. Lexis 4790 (U.S. June 23, 2011), the Supreme Court followed *Melendez-Diaz v. Massachusetts*, holding that forensic laboratory report are "testimonial" under the Sixth Amendment's Confrontation Clause. The Court's decision requires trial counsel to produce a laboratory report's original author unless the defense had a prior opportunity to cross-examine him. "Surrogates" or other witnesses familiar with the document's creation will not be acceptable particularly when the procecution's witness was not the original author's supervisor or had not participated in the test procedures. The Court rejected prosecution contentions that the document's original author was a "mere scrivener" who simply reported a machine's test results and as a result did not produce "testimonial" evidence, and that the prosecution's witness was sufficiently knowledgeable about the test procedures to satisfy the accused's right to confrontation.

It should be noted that the Federal and Military versions of Rule 803(6) and Rule 803(8)(B) significantly differ on this precise issue. The military rules specifically provide that "forensic laboratory reports, chain of custody documents," and other similar documents are admissible. To the extent both military rules are inconsistent with *Melendez-Diaz* and *bullcoming*, their provisions are now inconsistent with the Sixth Amendment and will have to be amended. (5) Certificates of analysis are admissible because the accused possessed the power to subpoena the "analyst" through the Compulsory Process Clause or similar state statute. The majority found that this argument was inconsistent with the prosecution's burden of proof. (6) The decision will work a great hardship on the criminal justice system as the guilty may be acquitted of charges *"nol prossed"* on a technicality—that the required analyst did not testify at trial because of increased administrative burdens created by the decision. The majority observed that by its nature the Confrontation Clause makes criminal prosecutions more burdensome, but the Court is without authority to ignore its mandates. The majority in *Melendez-Diaz* also cited studies indicating that jurisdictions that have already adopted a position similar to *Melendez-Diaz* have not experienced the parade of horrors suggested by the dissent.

The Court of Appeals for the Armed Forces anticipated *Melendez-Diaz* and *Bullcoming* in *United States v. Clayton*, 67 M.J. 283 (C.A.A.F. 2009). The court reversed the accused's conviction for drug use, possession, and trafficking offenses because the government used Rule 803(8) to introduce a German Police Report establishing how the drugs were discovered and collected. The Court held that admission of the German Police Report violated *Crawford*'s and the Sixth Amendment prohibition against admitting testimonial hearsay evidence because the report was: (1) made by a law enforcement agency; (2) more than a routine and objective cataloging of unambiguous factual matters; and (3) created with an eye towards prosecution.

Similarly, in *United States v. Williamson*, 65 M.J. 706 (Army Ct.Crim.App. 2007), the accused was tried for possessing marijuana with the intent to distribute. Relying on the Sixth Amendment, defense counsel objected to the government's laboratory report. The case was tried before the effective date of *Crawford*, and the objection was overruled. Although the court held on appeal that the laboratory report was testimonial hearsay and not admissible as a business record, it also held that the error was harmless because sufficient independent proof established the contraband nature of the seized evidence.

However, not all the Service Courts of Criminal Appeals previously agreed. In *United States v. Harris*, 66 M.J. 781 (N.M.Ct.Crim.App. 2008), the accused contended that the Navy Drug Screening Lab Report used to established his complicity should have been excluded based on *Crawford*. On appeal, the court held that the lab report did not violate the Sixth Amendment's right to confrontation or *Crawford* because the lab technicians who prepared the document were not engaged in a law enforcement function or in a search for evidence in anticipation of trial. As a result, the court said the lab report was not "testimonial" in the context prohibited by *Crawford*, and was admissible under the firmly rooted hearsay exception for business records.

In analyzing Confrontation Clause issues, counsel and military judges should first decide whether the statement is being offered for the truth of the matter asserted. If it is not, for example, because it is being offered pursuant to Rule 613 to impeach a witness's credibility by showing that the witness made a prior inconsistent statement, then confrontational concerns are not present. This is because, at least in theory, "proof" on a substantive issue is not being offered, and as a result cannot be considered by the court-members for that purpose.[5]

However, when a statement is being offered for the truth of the matter asserted, counsel and military judges must then decide whether the statement falls within a hearsay exception, and then determine whether the confrontation clause's requirement for cross-examination have been or will be satisfied. If the statement does not fall within a hearsay exception then it is excluded.

When it does fall under an exception or exclusion, the next step is to determine whether the statement is "testimonial." If the statement is being offered for a "testimonial" purpose, then the prosecution must either call the declarant to the stand or establish the declarant's unavailability and then prove that defendant at a previous time had an opportunity to cross-examine that declarant on his or her out-of-court statement.[6]

Evidence will likely be admissible when the statement is the accused's own words,[7] a statement of a coconspirator made during, and in furtherance of, the conspiracy,[8] any other applicable admission,[9] and virtually by definition, any statement made at a previous proceeding.[10] Extending this logic would result in military courts viewing any statement not intended to be used as proof against the accused, at the time it was made, to fall outside of the "testimonial" definition.

The logical and most important issue in this process concerns defining which statements are "testimonial," and therefore require actual confronta-

---

[5] *See* Rule 105's discussion concerning limiting instructions on evidence that can be used for more than one purpose.

[6] Rule 804(b)(6) provides that the witness need not be produced in situations where the defendant caused the declarant to be unavailable.

[7] *See* Rule 801(d)(2)(A).

[8] *See* Rule 801(d)(2)(E).

[9] *See* Rule 801(d)(2).

[10] *See* Rule 801(d)(1).

tion before they can be admitted. Clearly, statements given at any formal proceeding such as an Article 32 hearing or prior judicial or administrative proceeding qualify. The same result applies to statements made during criminal investigations and "interrogations," although the court has not yet clearly defined interrogation.

Most likely, several other types of evidence will also be considered "testimonial." All forensic laboratory reports could come under the "testimonial" label, although the court specifically indicated that business records are not testimonial. This issue is likely to be quickly challenged in courts-martial due to the number of drug cases tried each year. Other early testimonial questions military courts will face include statements made by sexual assault victims, particularly children, when such statements are offered as excited utterances,[11] statements made for purposes of medical diagnosis,[12] and statements being offered under the residual exception.[13]

United States v. Coulter,[14] a child sexual abuse prosecution, deals with many of these issues. There the two-year-old victim was held incompetent to testify because of her age. Using Rule 807, the victim's incriminating statements were admitted through her parents' testimony. Finding no error, the court used a two-step process to determine both hearsay admissibility and constitutionality. First, the court examined the statements under traditional Rule 807 logic, evaluating the following factors: (1) the declarant's mental state and age, (2) she had not been subjected to suggestive questioning, (3) her statements were spontaneous, (4) she did not have a motive to fabricate, and (5) her statements were corroborated by the government's expert medical witness. Secondly, the court analyzed the statements using *Crawford,* finding them to be non-testimonial and therefore admissible because the victim/declarant had not: (1) been questioned by the police or other government officials but by her parents who had a natural concern for their child's well-being; (2) been capable of envisioning her statements someday being used in a criminal proceeding; and (3) been capable of understanding the solemn nature of her declarations or that they could be used to prove some fact or event in the future. Conversely, in *United States v. Taylor.*[15] The court found error in the military judge admitting the accused's wife's pretrial statement through another witness after she claimed spousal privilege. The court found such proof to be testimonial and therefore prohibited by *Crawford.*

Crawford, left open whether, when non-testimonial statements are offered,

---

[11] *See* Rule 803(2). Statements made to social works and others outside of the traditional criminal framework pose difficult questions.

[12] *See* Rule 803(4).

[13] 9. See Rule 807.

[14] 62 M.J. 520 (N.M.Ct.Crim.App. 2005).

[15] 62 M.J. 615 (A.F.Ct.Crim.App. 2005).

Ohio v. Roberts, 448 U.S. 56 (1980), remains applicable. Initially, the military courts took the position that *Roberts* would continue to apply to nontestimonial hearsay statements. However, in *Bockting v, Whorton*, the Supreme Court made it clear that *Crawford* overruled *Roberts* and that otherwise unreliable hearsay statements could be admissible under the *Crawford* test.

[c] Relationship to Other Provisions

Rules 801(d), 803, 804, and 807 exclusively provide that evidence falling within their exceptions are not rendered inadmissible on hearsay grounds. Nothing in any of these Rules requires such evidence to be admitted, however. In order to reach the finder of fact, the evidence still needs to satisfy all other applicable evidentiary requirements such as competency,[16] authentication,[17] best evidence,[18] and relevancy criteria.[19] Even then, witness military judge may exclude the admissible hearsay testimony under Rule 403 as being unfairly prejudicial. Defense counsel can also object that such evidence violates the sixth amendment's Confrontation Clause.

[d] Categories of the Established Exceptions

Rule 803 lists twenty-three exceptions to the general hearsay prohibition found in Rule 802. Each of these address well known specific categories of exceptions. The numbered paragraphs of the Rule will be referred to either as exception (1), etc., or paragraph (1), etc., in the rest of this comment. The first category of exceptions, paragraphs (1) through (4), concerns the admissibility of evidence dealing with the declarant's state of mind, emotional or physical condition.

CATEGORY I. Declarant's state of mind, emotional or physical condition

[2] Rule 803(1)—Present Sense Impression

[a] Basis for the Exception

Exception (1) is taken from the Federal Rules without change. It is similar to the *Manual's* past treatment of spontaneous exclamations. Under paragraph (1), the present sense impression of a declarant is admissible if it describes or explains an event or condition and was made while in the act of perceiving an event or condition or immediately thereafter.[20]

---

[16] See our discussion of Rule 601.

[17] See our discussion of Section IX.

[18] See our discussion of Section X.

[19] See our Discussion of Rules 401 and 402.

[20] *See, e.g.,* United States v. Danford, 435 F.3d 682 (7th Cir. 2005) (accused's casual statement to store manager about how to turn off the alarm well before a fake robbery was staged viewed as non-testimonial).

At common law, this evidence was often referred to as *"res gestae"* (a term also used by various courts to describe exceptions (2), (3), and (4)). Commentators have thoroughly discredited the term as being virtually meaningless and it is not used in this Rule. *Wigmore*, for example, described *res gestae* as being so ambiguous and potentially harmful that it "ought therefore wholly to be repudiated as a vicious element in our legal phraseology."[21]

[b]   Requirement for an Exciting Event

The common law generally limited spontaneous utterances to those generated by an exciting event. This type of spontaneous statement is codified as an excited utterance in exception (2). Although exception 1 broadens the admissibility of spontaneous statements, like its predecessor the exception still seeks to avoid calculated or planned statements, because the opportunity for calculation makes the statements less trustworthy. Thus, Rule 803(1) applies only to statements made at the time of the event or immediately thereafter. The term "immediately thereafter" is not defined in the Rule or its Drafters' Analysis. However, the contemporaneousness of the statement is crucial to its admission, and should be the proponent's main foundational concern. Courts will usually evaluate admissibility on a case-by-case basis, focusing on whether the declarant had an opportunity to reflect on his thoughts and make a calculated, as opposed to a spontaneous, utterance. Generally, a statement must be made as soon as the opportunity to speak arises or immediately thereafter.[22] The burden is on the person who claims the benefit of this or another exception to show entitlement to it.[23]

[c]   Corroboration Needed

Although this provision does not on its face specifically contain a corroboration requirement, many federal courts have read one into the Rule. This is an appropriate interpretation because statements that are admissible under paragraph (1) require a showing of contemporaniety, and counsel's foundation would logically have to demonstrate a nexus between when the statement was made and what event stimulated the statement to qualify. Assuming the witness has personal knowledge of the events, and can be cross-examined on them, such independent testimony will generally be sufficient to support the corroboration requirement. For example, in *United*

---

[21] *See* 6 Wigmore EVIDENCE § 1767 at 182 (3d ed. 1940) for a discussion of the problems associated with using *res gestae* to describe hearsay exceptions.

[22] *See* Wolfson v. Mutual Life Ins. Co. of New York, 455 F. Supp. 82 (M.D. Pa.), *aff'd*, 588 F.2d 825 (3d Cir. 1978) (one hour is too long a time gap). *But see* United States v. Blakey, 607 F.2d 779 (7th Cir. 1979) (23 minutes is acceptable).

[23] In United States v. Cain, 587 F.2d 678 (5th Cir. 1978), the court held that government evidence was improperly admitted because the prosecution's proof failed to demonstrate "whether the declaration . . . was made immediately following the observation or not."

States v. Hawkins,[24] the court held that a 911 phone call was properly admitted where the proponent was able to demonstrate that the call was made only moments after the events occurred, and there was sufficient circumstantial evidence available to show that the statements were reliable. However, in *Bemis v. Edwards*,[25] another 911 case, the court found no abuse of discretion in excluding evidence of the call because the party on the telephone was not personally witnessing the events, but merely relaying someone else's description of them.

[3] Rule 803(2)—Excited Utterance

[a] Basis for the Exception

Identical to the Federal Rule, exception (2) permits a declarant's excited utterances to be admitted.[26] The Rule, like its federal counterpart, recognizes that statements made during a startling event or while under the stress of excitement, possess inherent reliability.[27] The excitement and associated spontaneity remove any opportunity for calculation. However, commentators have noted that such circumstances may also cause error in perception and interpretation leading to inaccurate statements. The admissibility of excited utterances is an indication that courts prefer statements that appear to be sincere, even though the conditions in which a declarant made a statement raise other questions about its accuracy.

One way to distinguish this exception from present sense impressions is to recognize that excited utterances rely on the declarant's startled state of mind for reliability, while present sense impressions depend upon the close timing between the event and the statement.

In distinguishing between paragraphs (1) and (2) of the Rule, it should also be noted that while (1) allows statements explaining or describing the event to be admitted, statements falling under (2) must only "relate" to the

---

[24] 59 F.3d 723 (8th Cir. 1995), *vacated on other grounds*, 516 U.S. 1168 (1996).

[25] 45 F.3d 1369 (9th Cir. 1995).

[26] This exception's linkage to previous military practice was discussed in United States v. Sandoval, 18 M.J. 55 (C.M.A. 1984). There, the court drew an analogy between the 1969 *Manual*'s use of spontaneous exclamations and this provision's use of excited utterances. The court said that such testimony is an "exception to the hearsay prohibition and may be proved either by the person who made the utterance or by someone who heard it." Rule 803(2) has the additional feature of not expressly requiring "independent evidence that the startling event occurred." Similarly, in United States v. Smith, 14 M.J. 845 (A.C.M.R. 1982), the reviewing court noted that although the Military Rules of Evidence have not adopted ¶ 142 *c*'s description or definition of "fresh complaint" evidence, the concept is covered by various Rules, such as Rule 803(2). In this case, the court found that the trial judge properly instructed the members concerning the evidence.

[27] *See, e.g.*, United States v. Golden, 671 F.2d 369 (10th Cir. 1982) (assault victim's statement to his grandmother after he rushed to her house 15 minutes after assault held admissible).

startling event itself.[28] The drafters properly note that on its face the Rule does not require independent proof of the startling event, but the trial judge under Rule 104(a) must find that the exception is satisfied before admitting evidence. Usually this will involve independent evidence, since somehow the judge must find excitement.

[b]   Admissibility Linked to Time

There is little agreement concerning how much time may elapse between the startling event and the excited utterance.[29] While courts are likely to make this determination on a case-by-case basis, experience demonstrates that there is an inverse correlation between the amount of time that expires and the statement's admissibility.[30] The more time goes by, the less likely courts are to find the statement to have been the product of the exciting event.[31] The ultimate determination here will often depend upon the nature or severity of the event[32] and the declarant's age and sophistication.[33]

For example, in *United States v. Chandler*,[34] the accused's wife caught him in bed with a paramour. When his wife attempted to call the military police, the accused attacked, bound, and gagged her. He was ultimately charged with numerous assault and adultery related offenses. The accused pled guilty to all charges except aggravated assault for pointing a loaded

---

[28] *See, e.g.,* United States v. Napier, 518 F.2d 316 (9th Cir.), *cert. denied,* 423 U.S. 895 (1975) (statements made by an assault victim identifying the accused after seeing his photograph in a newspaper days after the crime were held to be properly admitted even though the court failed to explain how the statement related to the startling event).

[29] *See, e.g.,* United States v. Sowa, 34 F.3d 447 (7th Cir. 1994) (finding admissible evidence of a crying three-year-old's identification of defendant as time element was not controlling, particularly with respect to a child declarant).

[30] *See, e.g.,* United States v. Davis, 577 F.3d 660 (6th Cir. 2009) (testimony questioned whether five minutes or 30 seconds had elapsed between the time declarant saw the event and the time she made the 911 call; held goes to weight only).

[31] In United States v. Allen, 13 M.J. 597 (A.F.C.M.R. 1982), the accused was tried for having sexually abused several very young children. At trial he unsuccessfully contended that the 57-day-old statements about the crime made by the victims to their mothers were improperly admitted. Partially agreeing with the accused, the court opined:

> Clearly, defense counsel's contention that Mil. R. Evid. 803(2) requires a reasonable proximity in time between a startling event occasioning an excited utterance and the utterance itself, was correct. Unquestionably, a period of 57 days would not, in this case, have constituted a reasonable proximity of time. Therefore, Mrs. *P*'s testimony and that of Mrs. *D*, if hearsay, did not qualify for admission under the hearsay exception provided by this rule.

[32] *See, e.g.,* United States v. Hartmann, 958 F.2d 774 (7th Cir. 1992) (hearing wife planning to murder husband declarant clearly extends the period).

[33] *See, e.g.,* Morgan v. Foretich, 846 F.2d 941 (4th Cir. 1988) (statements of child declarant made one day after the event and three hours after first opportunity to tell mother held to be admissible).

[34] 39 M.J. 119 (C.M.A. 1994).

firearm at his wife's head. During trial, the military judge allowed a friend to testify concerning what the victim told her about the assault. Affirming all convictions, the court held that the friend's testimony was admissible because the victim made her complaint approximately thirty minutes after she had been assaulted, and based on the nature and severity of what had happened to her, it was reasonable to assume that she was still clearly upset.

In *United States v. Arnold*,[35] the court examined the role time plays in child sexual abuse cases. Here the victim's report of an attack occurred early the morning after, while the victim was apparently still in a highly agitated emotional condition. The court found her statements admissible because they were: (1) "spontaneous, excited [and] impulsive rather than the product of reflection and deliberation," (2) the result of a startling event, and (3) made "under the stress of excitement caused by the event."

However, in *United States v. Grant*,[36] the court came to a different result. There, thirty-six to forty-eight hours passed between the time a six-year-old victim was sexually assaulted by her father and the time she first reported the crime. Although the court affirmed the accused's conviction on other grounds, it held that, because of the time delay, the victim's statements did not possess the excitement or hysteria necessary to qualify them as excited utterances. The court went on to say that the victim's teary eyes and sadness were not enough to demonstrate the absence of contrivance or the presence of excitement.

[c]   Foundational Requirements

Proponents of excited utterances should be particularly concerned with thoroughly exploring the declarant's actual emotional condition at the time a statement is made,[37] as opposed to focusing on ambiguous demonstrations of sadness or anger.[38] A military judge will be interested in an explanation for any delay and why the declarant ultimately chose to speak. Foundational

---

[35]   25 M.J. 129 (C.M.A. 1987).

[36]   42 M.J. 340 (C.A.A.F. 1995).

[37]   *See, e.g.*, United States v. Moses, 15 F.3d 774 (8th Cir. 1994) (affirming conviction and admissibility of declarant's statement made to a policeman as declarant ran toward the officer for help, blurting out defendant's name as his assailant in a prison attack).

[38]   In United States v. Hill, 13 M.J. 882 (A.C.M.R. 1982), the accused's conviction for inflicting grievous bodily harm on his four-year-old son was reversed because of the admission of hearsay evidence identifying him as the culprit. Most of this testimony came from a treating physician who related the mother's story of how her husband had harmed the child. The government offered the mother's statements as excited utterances, but the reviewing court found that there was time for reflection and deliberation, and thus the statements were not the product of spontaneity, excitement or impulsiveness. The court looked to the length of time between the startling event and the utterance, as well as the circumstances surrounding the event itself. It implied that the evidence might have been admissible had trial counsel been able to demonstrate that the child's mother was upset or suffering severe stress or traumatic shock when she talked to the doctor.

testimony concerning youthful declarants and declarants with emotional handicaps, by expert witnesses, who can help a judge understand the reasons for delay may be helpful. Experts may explain why a delay by an adult or more sophisticated witness that might argue against spontaneity does not indicate a lack of spontaneity in a child or limited capability witness. If the judge admits statements, the members may also benefit from hearing expert testimony in order to determine the appropriate weight to give the statements.

There may be reason for skepticism about spontaneity when a declarant's statements are in response to questioning. Although this is not a per se excluding factor, a declarant's response to questions may suggest that the declarant has had time to think about answers and that the answers are the product of questioning rather than excitement.[39]

[4]   Rule 803(3)—Then Existing Mental, Emotional, or Physical Condition

[a]   Basis for the Exception

Rule 803(3) excludes from the hearsay ban statements of a declarant's then existing state of mind, emotional, or physical condition.[40] The exception includes statements of intent, motive, design or plan as well as statements concerning physical or mental ailments.[41] It generally does not permit evidence of present memory or belief to prove the existence of a past condition or fact. It thus follows the traditional distinction between statements of present status, including forward-looking statements that do not

---

[39] In United States v. Roberts, 10 M.J. 308 (C.M.A. 1981), immediately after an assault victim was knifed and "in a condition of shock, very cold and clammy, scared and worried about her kids," she stated that her husband had done it. *Citing* United States v. Burge, 1 M.J. 408 (C.M.A. 1976), the court concluded that the victim's statement was instinctive and impulsive notwithstanding that it was in response to a question by an uninvolved bystander.

[40] *See, e.g.,* United States v. Fontenot, 14 F.3d 1364 (9th Cir. 1994) (state of mind exception does not permit witness to relate declarant's statements as to why he held a particular state of mind, or what he believed might have induced the state of mind; Rule must be limited to declarations of conditions—"I'm scared"—and not belief—"I'm scared because someone threatened me"); United States v. DiMaria, 727 F.2d 265 (2d Cir. 1984) (defendant's statement concerning his state of mind should have been admitted); United States v. Kelly, 722 F.2d 873 (1st Cir. 1983) (victim's statement of fear admissible in extortion case); United States v. Williams, 704 F.2d 315 (6th Cir. 1983) (defendant's statement of intent qualifies under exception, but not relevant and therefore was properly excluded); United States v. Lawrence, 699 F.2d 697 (5th Cir. 1983) (officer who arrested defendant could testify that victim complained that defendant had threatened him). *See also* United States v. Liu, 960 F.2d 449 (5th Cir. 1992).

[41] *See, e.g.,* United States v. Veltmann, 6 F.3d 1483 (11th Cir. 1993) (reversible error to exclude video deposition of witness who had been involved in affair and blackmailed by victim, because it tended to corroborate defendant's presentation of arson, murder victim's suicidal tendencies, and her desperate state of mind on date of death, when she learned that he would no longer send her extortion money).

present memory problems, and backwards-looking statements that do.[42]

An exception to the memory prohibition is created for memory relating to the execution, revocation, identification, or tenor of the declarant's will. The legislative history of this "exception to the exception" indicates the drafters of the Federal Rule felt that such evidence was especially necessary in will contests and that a person could be trusted to recall accurately his actions in connection with disposition of his property.

[b] Military Use

The following examples help demonstrate the military's implementation of the Rule. Assume the declarant said, "I'm going to miss tomorrow's morning formation," and he subsequently failed to appear. This statement may be introduced against the declarant to show his intention to be away. However, if the declarant stated, "I missed yesterday's formation," that statement is inadmissible under exception (3) to show that he was not present. A memory problem arises with the second statement.

The same logic applies to statements of existing physical conditions. The declarant's protestation, "my arm hurts" falls within the exception, while his statement, "my arm hurt yesterday" is excluded when both are offered for their truth.

[c] Declarant and Others State of Mind

The federal drafters may have intended that Rule 803(3) statements be used only to show the declarant's state of mind.[43] If so, then a declaration that the declarant and another individual intended to miss a formation would not be admissible to show what the other individual did. The military Drafters' Analysis appears to have adopted this view of the Rule. The Report of the House Judiciary Committee stated that it construed 803(3) "so as to render statements of intent by a declarant admissible only to prove his future conduct, not the future conduct of another person." It is unclear what the drafters of the federal rule actually intended, but the military drafters may have provided more guidance. To date, there is little uniformity in how military and federal courts resolve this issue.[44]

---

[42] *Compare* Mutual Life Ins. Co. v. Hillmon, 145 U.S. 285 (1892) *with* Shepard v. United States, 290 U.S. 96 (1933).

[43] *See, e.g.,* United States v. Barraza, 576 F3d 798 (8th Cir. 2009) (no error in admitting statements indicating the victim was taking her son on a drug buying trip to Mexico with defendant).

[44] In United States v. Stanley, 21 M.J. 249 (C.M.A. 1986), the court held that it was error to admit the declarant's statements to demonstrate the accused's state of mind. However, in United States v. Pheaster, 544 F.2d 353 (9th Cir. 1975), and United States v. Moore, 571 F.2d 76 (2d Cir. 1978), convictions were affirmed even though the declarant's statements were used to show both the declarant's and another individual's future conduct.

[d]   Accused's Self-serving Statements

Finally, self-serving statements made by defendants can be interpreted as not falling within the expectation because they are untrustworthy and subject to manipulation.[45] For example, if during a lawful search of the accused's car he exclaims, after drugs are found under his seat, "I had no idea they were there," an argument can be made that his statement is unreliable if offered to prove state of mind— *i.e.*, the accused had no knowledge that the drugs were present. Even if a court were to conclude that the Rule permits self-serving statements, Rule 403 could come into play. There is nothing in the text of Rule 803(3) that purports to require a showing of reliability or to authorize exclusion of statements simply because they are self-serving or made under untrustworthy conditions.[46] In many cases, the best course will be to admit the statements and permit the parties to litigate the weight they should receive. This position enforces the Rule as written, provides the members with the available testimony, and permits them to determine whether the self-serving nature of the statement is reason to discount it.

[5]   Rule 803(4)—Statements for Purposes of Medical Diagnosis or Treatment

[a]   Basis for the Exception

The common law basis for this Rule recognizes that people seeking medical advice or help are likely to be telling the truth for selfish reasons.[47] In *White v. Illinois*,[48] the Supreme Court affirmed the accused's conviction for sexually abusing a four-year-old child, and found that the declarant-victim's statements when made in the course of securing medical treatment, were admissible, without the government producing the declarant or

---

[45] In United States v. Ferguson, 15 M.J. 12 (C.M.A. 1983) (a pre-Rules case), the court affirmed the accused's conviction even though his exonerating statements made to a friend five days after the crime, while the accused was still incarcerated, did not qualify for admission under previous *Manual* provisions, because the record failed to demonstrate their "probable sincerity." *See* previous ¶ 142 *b*, spontaneous exclamations, or ¶ 142 *d*, evidence of the accused's state of mind or consciousness of guilt. A concurring opinion noted that these statements would be inadmissible under Rule 803. They would not qualify as present sense impressions (statements were five days old), excited utterances (required emotional stimulation was absent), or as statements of then existing mental, emotional, or physical condition (evidence was improperly offered to prove the existence of a past condition or fact).

[46] *See, e.g.,* United States v. DiMaria, 727 F.2d 265 (2d Cir. 1984) (Rule 803(3) not violated by exculpatory statements made under questionable circumstances).

[47] *See, e.g.,* United States v. Williams, 26 M.J. 487 (C.M.A. 1988) (witness correctly prevented from testifying she had A positive blood, because the defense did not establish that this information was passed to the witness as part of medical treatment "grounded in the self-interest of the patient in seeking medical assistance;" United States v. Iron Thunder, 714 F.2d 765 (8th Cir. 1983) (victim's statement to doctor that she had been raped was admissible).

[48] 502 U.S. 346 (1992).

establishing the declarant's unavailability, because such testimony has sufficient guarantees of reliability to come within this firmly rooted exception, thus satisfying the Confrontation Clause. In *United States v. Santos*,[49] [SS4] a post *Crawford v. Washington* case, the court found that the victim of an assault's statement to a prison nurse concerning the intensity of his wounds was admissible because it was reasonably necessary to diagnosis or treatment. The court also found the statement to be non-testimonial because the nurse was engaged in treatment and was not interrogating the victim in an attempt to gather evidence for trial or for a prison disciplinary proceeding.

Military courts have traditionally required proponents of such testimony to accomplish two things before it will be admissible. First, the declarant has to have a motive for obtaining medical care or diagnosis and thus a reason to tell the truth. Second, the communication must be of a type that experts could rely upon in providing treatment or reaching a diagnosis.[50]

Rule 803(4) incorporates both of these requirements. It allows statements made for the purpose of receiving medical diagnosis or treatment to be admitted when they describe the declarant's medical history, past or present symptoms, or sensations. The effect of the Rule is to require the proponent to show that medical diagnosis or treatment was really sought and to admit the types of declarations that are consistent with seeking such treatment or diagnosis. While 803(4) is identical with the Federal Rule, it is broader than its military precursor in that it admits evidence that describes the inception, general character or external cause of the injury, as long as this evidence is reasonably pertinent to diagnosis or treatment.

[b]   Statements Made for Litigation or Consultation

Rule 803(4) is not limited to statements made to doctors for treatment purposes. It includes doctors who diagnose or are consulted for litigation purposes, as well as those who treat. The Drafters' Analysis appears to miss this point. Any doubt that the Rule is meant to cover diagnosing physicians is removed if one looks to the Advisory Committee's Note accompanying Federal Rule 803(4), from which the Military Rule is taken. The federal drafters indicated that the common law did not allow such statements to be used for substantive purposes because they did not come within the

---

[49]   589 F.3d 759 (5th Cir. 2009).

[50]   In United States v. Ureta, 44 M.J. 290 (C.A.A.F. 1996), a child sexual abuse case, the court held that the victim-declarants statements were admissible because the victim made them for the purpose of medical diagnosis or treatment, and that the victim had some expectation of receiving a medical benefit as a result. Importantly, the court dismissed the accused's contentions that the statements were inadmissible because the medical witnesses who related them also appreciated the legal and investigative implications of obtaining the declarant's statements and making them replete. It was more significant that the statements were those traditionally relied upon by medical experts.

traditional guarantee of truthfulness. They could be admitted, for example, only to establish the basis of an expert's opinion. The drafters concluded that this distinction was one juries would have trouble making and rejected it.

[c]   Source and Use of Statements

Under the Rule, statements need not be made directly to a physician; they need only be made for the purpose of diagnosis or treatment. Thus, statements to nurses, hospital staff, or ambulance personnel would qualify under the Rule. For example, in *United States v. Austin*,[51] the court affirmed the accused's conviction for sexually abusing his daughter, holding that the victim's pretrial statements to a family counselor were made for the purpose of receiving medical treatment and were thus admissible. The court also said that testimony from social workers, clinical psychologists, and psychotherapists, about statements made to them also qualifies.[52]

Similarly, the statements need not have come from the patient. Statements of family members and friends may qualify as well. This occurred in *United States v. Yazzie*.[53] In a child sexual abuse case, statements identifying the accused as the perpetrator were provided by the victim's mother. Affirming the accused's conviction the court held that under these circumstances, the mother's protestations were also used for medical purposes.

[d]   Child Declarants and a Relaxed Standard

In recent years, there has been a significant growth in the number of child sexual molestation cases tried in civilian and military courts.[54] When the victim-declarant is very young, prosecutors often have difficulty establishing that the declarant really understood she was seeing a medical care professional for the purpose of receiving helpful treatment. Thus, the government's ability to comply with Rule 803 (4)'s foundational requirements can be frustrated simply because the victim is too young to articulate the standard.

---

[51] 32 M.J. 757 (A.C.M.R. 1991).

[52] *But see* United States v. Oldham, 24 M.J. 662 (A.F.C.M.R. 1987). Here the court held that a family advocacy officer (a social worker) should not have been permitted to recount what the ten-year-old victim of sexual abuse told him concerning the offenses, because the social worker was "more oriented toward developing trial evidence than medical diagnosis or treatment." The court said that the witness "was not competent to make medical diagnosis" and only talked to the victim out of an interest in gathering information for some future, nonmedical use. The court's decision is consistent with its previous holding in United States v. Williamson, 23 M.J. 706 (A.F.C.M.R. 1986), where the use of similar testimony was affirmed because "the contacts with social workers were initiated by concerned family members . . . seeking . . . assistance with the emotional manifestations of the alleged abuse. . . ."

[53] 59 F.3d 807 (9th Cir. 1995).

[54] In United States v. Lingle, 27 M.J. 704 (A.F.C.M.R. 1989), the court discussed the increasing number of child sexual abuse prosecutions in both military and civilian jurisdictions.

Because familial pressures frequently combine to prevent the victim from testifying, the need for testimony under this exception is increased.

Military courts acknowledge that these cases may require traditional adult standards to be relaxed when applied to very young victims.[55] For example, in *United States v. Quigley*,[56] the court recognized that youthful declarants probably do not have the same understanding or incentive for making statements to medical care professionals as adults do, but that it is possible for counsel to demonstrate that the declarant realized she was in a hospital, doctor's office, or similar location for the purpose of being helped. In *Quigley*, the court also pointed out that witnesses other than the declarant may be able to provide the medical purposes foundation for meeting the Rule's requirements.

The complexity of these issues was discussed in *United States v. Dean*.[57] There the court affirmed the accused's convictions for sexually molesting his daughter. The court clearly understood the difficult balance that military judges must strike in using medical statements made by youthful declarants. On one hand, the court acknowledged how often child witnesses recant their original incriminating statements because of severe family pressures, making the out-of-court evidence that much more important. On the other hand, the court considered Justice Scalia's concerns in *Maryland v. Craig*[58] that there have been many tragic instances of false sexual molestation claims by impressionable and vulnerable child witnesses. Balancing these competing interests, the court held that statements made to the coordinator of a hospital's child protection team and to one of its staff psychologists, on these facts, were made for the purpose of medical treatment and that the child understood the need to be truthful.

[e] Military Application

Military experience with Rule 803(4) indicates that: (1) statements made to physicians may be admissible even though they extend to accusations of criminal fault;[59] (2) this provision applies to psychiatrists and other

---

[55] In United States v. Edens, 31 M.J. 267 (C.M.A. 1990), the court affirmed the accused's child sexual abuse conviction and held that the quantum of proof necessary to satisfy this Rule may be relaxed where the victim is very young.

[56] 40 M.J. 64 (C.M.A. 1994).

[57] 31 M.J. 196 (C.M.A. 1990).

[58] 497 U.S. 836 (1990).

[59] United States v. Arruza, 26 M.J. 234 (C.M.A. 1988), represents current military authority on this point. There the court held that in a child sexual abuse case, admissible medical history evidence includes psychiatrist's statements "regarding what the accused the accused had allegedly done to" the victim. Previous cases, such as United States v. Hill, 13 M.J. 882 (A.C.M.R. 1982), reversed conviction on similar facts because they felt "the trustworthiness rationale did not extend to "accusations of criminal fault," which were generally perceived as not pertinent to medical treatment.

non-physician[60] mental health professionals who treat mental ailments, as well as to physicians who treat physical ailments;[61] (3) the patient's motivation for seeking medical help need only be consistent with promoting diagnosis or treatment;[62] (4) the proponent of this evidence need not establish that the patient understood the nature of his ailment or how it would be treated;[63] and (5) the Rule will be relaxed in cases involving child witnesses, particularly those who are victims of sexual abuse.[64]

Although there is overlap between (3) and (4), Rule 803(4) extends exception (3) in two important aspects. First, it allows evidence of the individual's medical history (*i.e.,* backwards-looking statements) to be admitted as an exception to the hearsay rule. Second, statements relating to the cause of an injury, pain, or sensation may be admitted if reasonably necessary to the doctor's treatment or diagnosis. This means that statements concerning *who* caused the injury may be admissible in describing *how* and *when* the injury occurred.[65] The Rule depends on the expertise of doctors to ferret out false statements.

---

[60] *See e.g.,* United States v. Cottriel, 21 M.J. 535 (N.M.C.M.R. 1985) (statements to social workers also admissible under this Rule).

[61] In United States v. Deland, 16 M.J. 889 (A.C.M.R. 1983), *aff'd,* 22 M.J. 70 (1986), the accused's conviction for sexually molesting his seven-year-old daughter was based, in part, on expert medical and psychiatric testimony describing the victim's post assault emotional state. All medical care was obtained by the victim's mother in an attempt to determine why her daughter was acting strangely and if the child's father had, in fact, sexually assaulted her. The appellate court ruled that this evidence was properly admitted, as Rule 803(4) "(a) applies to psychiatrists treating mental ailments as well as physicians treating physical ailments"; (b) that the patient's motivation for seeking medical help need only be consistent with promoting diagnosis or treatment; and (c) that the proponent of such evidence need not establish that the patient understood the nature of the ailment or how it would be treated.

[62] *See, e.g.,* United States v. Arnold, 18 M.J. 559 (A.C.M.R. 1984) (court found that statements made by a young female student to a school nurse concerning the student's recent sexual abuse could have been admitted as statements made for the purpose of obtaining medical treatment).

[63] *See, e.g.,* United States v. Miller, 32 M.J. 843 (N.M.C.M.R. 1991) (affirming the accused's convictions, the court held that the 12-year-old victim's inability to articulate precisely what treatment was sought was not dispositive).

[64] In United States v. Armstrong, 30 M.J. 769 (A.C.M.R. 1990), a child sexual abuse case, the accused contended that his daughter's statements to a physician should not have been admitted because "there is no substantial showing in the record that her sessions with the doctor promoted her well-being or that she anticipated any medical benefits." Affirming the conviction, the court substantially relied on the trial judge's special findings indicating "that [the victim] understood as much as a five- or six-year-old child does, that she was seeing a doctor, that it was promoting her well-being and that there was an incentive to be truthful." *See also* our Annotated Cases, *below.*

[65] *See, e.g.,* United States v. George, 960 F.2d 97 (9th Cir. 1992) (physician's testimony concerning victim's identification of defendant as assailant was admissible as necessary for attending to victim's emotional and psychological needs).

[f] Linkage to "Fresh Complaint" Testimony

Before leaving this first category of exceptions, it is important to note that the drafters have not included a provision admitting evidence of "fresh complaint" here. Paragraph 142 *c* of the prior *Manual* allowed such evidence to be admitted in sexual offense prosecutions. Its use was limited to proving that the victim complained and identified the offender. The evidence was admissible only for "corroborating the testimony of the victim." Even though no specific mention has been made of fresh complaint in the new Rules, the drafters indicate that paragraphs (1) through (4) may be used to prove many of the same things that fell within the former fresh complaint Rule.[66]

CATEGORY II. Writings and documents

Exceptions (5) through (18) concern the admissibility of writings or documents or of evidence concerning the absence of a recording. These exceptions are particularly important in court-martial practice due to the world-wide nature of military jurisdiction, the unavailability of witnesses resulting from lack of subpoena power outside the United States, discharged and unlocatable witnesses within the United States, and the impracticability of transporting obtainable witnesses thousands of miles between their present duty station and the situs of trial. Many of these Rules are copied directly from the Federal Rules. Two exceptions, (6) and (8), are substantially different and deserve special attention.

[6] Rule 803(5)—Recorded Recollection

[a] Basis for the Exception

Paragraph (5) is identical to the Federal Rule and similar to previous court-martial practice. It provides that when a witness has no present recollection concerning matters he once knew, a memorandum or record displaying his past knowledge can be used to prove that knowledge. The document or memorandum must have been adopted by the witness when the information was fresh in the witness's mind. It must also accurately reflect what the knowledge once was. If the trial judge admits the memorandum or record, it may be read into evidence. This procedure is different from prior *Manual* practice that allowed the proponent to admit the document. The federal drafters felt that permitting the jurors to obtain the document and take it to the deliberation room with them unfairly emphasized the evidence. Although military proponent cannot present the document to the members, the opponent may do so, if he wishes, in order to establish some inconsistency or inaccuracy.

---

[66] In United States v. Sandoval, 18 M.J. 55 (C.M.A. 1984), the court said that Rule 801(d)(1)(B) also provides a possible means for introducing evidence of fresh complaint in sexual offense prosecutions.

This evidence's guarantee of reliability is found in the timing require-ments of the Rule and the opportunity to examine the declarant about the circumstances in which the statement was made. Note that oral statements that were not recorded when made, do not qualify under the Rule.

[b]   Foundation Required

In order to use 803(5) counsel must first establish that the witness's memory is impaired.[67] Once this is accomplished, counsel should attempt to refresh the witness's recollection with the document. *See* Rule 612. If memory cannot be refreshed, then the document's contents will be admis-sible.[68] This sequence of events is recommended because it places a premium upon the witness's ability to testify, and not on the recordation of that testimony. If recollection can be refreshed with the document, then the witness may testify and be fully cross-examined.

It is crucial that the record have been made when the information was fresh in the witness's mind.[69] It is of no consequence that the witness himself did not make the recording; what is important is that the witness, at some time prior to the court-martial, adopted the information contained in the document.

[c]   Multiple Persons Involved

This Rule can also be satisfied if the witness made an oral statement and someone else accurately recorded it. At least, this appears to be the Drafter's intent. However, Congress changed the wording of the Rule so that on its face it appears to require that the witness has made or adopted the statement. At common law it was enough if the witness made the statement and someone else wrote it down as long as both were present to testify. It may be that Congress did not intend to be more restrictive than the common law, but the language of exception (5) is not consistent with the common law. It also is possible that Congress deliberately sought to change the common law, because it did not require the declarant to affirm that the recording was accurate, and it is the declarant's statement that matters. At trial, the declarant cannot confirm the accuracy of the recording because of memory problems. If there were no memory problems, the written statement would not be needed.

---

[67] *See, e.g.,* United States v. Felix-Jerez, 667 F.2d 1297 (9th Cir. 1982) (error to admit Marshal's testimony based on notes he took of what the defendant said without first laying a proper foundation).

[68] *See, e.g.,* United States v. Jones, 601 F.3d 1247 (11th Cir. 2010) (when witness could not remember events, was unable to have her memory refreshed and testified that a video of what occurred accurately recounted the events, court found no error in showing the video to the jury).

[69] *But see* United States v. Lewis, 954 F.2d 1386 (7th Cir. 1992) (affirming conviction and holding that statements reduced to writing six months and three months after being made by declarant are admissible as recorded recollections).

[d]   Military Interpretation

Military courts have taken an expansive approach to this provision, particularly with respect to how it is applied with Rule 612. In *United States v. Gans*,[70] the court discussed counsel's use of writings to refresh memory under Rule 612, and writings used to establish past recollection recorded under paragraph (5). After two lengthy AWOL periods, the accused was tried for sexually molesting his daughter. During the intervening years, the victim apparently changed her mind about testifying. At trial, she demonstrated no real memory of the events. Over defense objection, the military judge admitted a redacted copy of her previous sworn out-of-court statement.

Affirming the accused's conviction, the court held that: (1) the victim's contradictory testimony about her current memory went only to weight; (2) the trial judge need make no finding about the memorandum's truth or accuracy; (3) evidence that the facts were once fresh in the witness's mind can be established by another witness, the victim's mother in this case; and (4) the victim's admission that she intended her out-of-court statement to be truthful demonstrated that it accurately reflected her knowledge at the time.

[7]   Rule 803(6)—Records of Regularly Conducted Activity

[a]   Basis for the Exception

Rule 803(6) is one of the most important and often used Rules of Evidence because it provides techniques for admitting proof that would otherwise be excluded by the rule against hearsay. It was last amended in December 2004, and along with the amendments to Rules 902(11) and 902(12) concerning self-authentication of business records discussed *below*, facilitates the admission of such documents. These amendments also allow the military rule, and its federal model, to develop similarly.

Once a proper foundation is laid, Rule 803(6) permits records of regularly conducted activities to be admitted as an exception to the hearsay rule. The Advisory Committee Notes to the Federal Rule that were adopted by the military drafters state that the exception's reliability is "supplied by systemic checking, by regularity and continuity that produce habits of precision, by actual experience of business in relying upon them, or by a duty to make an accurate record as part of a continuing job or occupation."

The amended military version of this Rule is based on the same assumptions and is taken from Federal Rule 803(6), which describes a business entry as:

(1) Any memorandum, report, or data compilation;

(2) Concerning acts, events, opinions, or diagnosis;

(3) When made at or near the time of the event;

---

[70] 32 M.J. 412 (C.M.A. 1991).

(4) From information transmitted by a person with knowledge of the information;

(5) If the information was recorded in the regular course of business;

(6) And it was the regular practice of the business to record such information;

(7) So long as nothing in the business record process indicates a "lack of trustworthiness."

[b]   Expansive Application Intended

The drafters intended that this exception should be broadly interpreted. For example, the word "memorandum" has been construed so that virtually any document will satisfy its mandate.[71] Similarly, the military drafters have defined the word "business" in its broadest sense to specifically include the Armed Forces.

This exception also allows opinions and diagnosis to be admitted as business entries.[72] The common law generally excluded opinion testimony in favor of purely factual evidence. Prior military practice required live testimony for such evidence to be admitted. However, the Military and Federal Rules specifically include the terms "opinions or diagnoses," contemplating medical diagnosis, prognoses, test results, and similar records as being admissible.

[c]   Foundation Required

Amended Rule 803(6) has significantly reduced the foundational burden on business record proponents.[73] Past military practice allowed evidence custodians and unit personnel clerks to lay the foundation. That has not been changed. In fact, amended paragraph (6) expressly states that foundations can be established by "the testimony of the custodian or other qualified witness. . . ." Importantly, the amended Rule also adds that the foundation can be established by certificate if it complies with Rules 902(11) and (12) or similar statute.

To satisfy the business knowledge aspect of this provision, a proponent need only demonstrate that the witness gained sufficient knowledge about

---

[71] *See, e.g.,* United States v. Young Bros., 728 F.2d 682 (5th Cir. 1984) (computer-generated business records may be used); United States v. Vela, 673 F.2d 86 (5th Cir. 1982) (computerized telephone records admissible even without showing that computers were in proper working order).

[72] *See, e.g.,* United States v. Vandelinder, 20 M.J. 41 (C.M.A. 1985) (opinions contained in the accused's service records held admissible under this Rule).

[73] *See* United States v. Farris, 21 M.J. 702 (A.C.M.R. 1985) and United States v. Hudson, 20 M.J. 607 (A.F.C.M.R. 1985), for a good discussion of foundational requirements. *See also* United States v. Garcia-Duarte, 718 F.2d 42 (2d Cir. 1983) (insufficient foundation to warrant admission of customer record book of drug transaction).

how the business records are maintained and can testify that they are kept in the ordinary course of business activities.[74] While it is important for this witness to know how the records are maintained, the witness need have no personal knowledge about any individual recording or how it was made.

[d]   Business Duty Obligation

Rule 803(6)'s definition of a business record as one "made at or near the time by, or from information transmitted by, a person with knowledge, if kept in the course of a regularly conducted business activity . . ." appears to abandon the business duty requirement for the person making the report. The federal version has the same appearance.

Most commentators agree, however, that, when Congress drafted the Federal Rules, it did not intend to abandon this requirement. There is no reason to believe that the military drafters intended to eliminate it either. Thus, although the person making a business entry need not be specifically identified in the document, the proponent must establish that person had an independent business obligation to make the entry. Business duty is what makes reports reliable. The best explanation of the omission of business duty language is that Congress changed some of the wording of the exception in an unfortunate manner, but without any apparent desire to eliminate the business duty concept. Most federal courts continue to recognize the business duty requirement.[75]

[e]   Potential Trial Attacks

Opposing counsel may attack the offer of a business document on the ground that its "lack of trustworthiness" requires exclusion. This could mean that: (1) the document's author was not being provided with accurate or reliable information; (2) there was no regular practice of recording the event in question; (3) the event did not occur within the regular course of business, or (4) it was not the business of this organization to record the event in question.[76] It could also mean that, because the document was prepared with

---

[74] *See, e.g.,* United States v. Lemire, 720 F.2d 1327 (D.C. Cir. 1983) (memorandum from one defendant to a superior officer was inadmissible where not made in ordinary course of business).

[75] *See, e.g.,* United States v. Plum, 558 F.2d 568 (10th Cir. 1977) (conviction was sustained even though the reviewing court found that a document was improperly admitted as a business record because the person compiling the form was under no duty to perform the mission).

[76] In United States v. Wetherbee, 10 M.J. 304 (C.M.A. 1981) (pre-Rules case), the Court held that a military base's records of receipts at its dining facility could be introduced as a business record even though the base did not comply with the Air Force Manual. The "determinative factor was the procedure employed by a particular enterprise rather than a more general industry standard." *See also* Keough v. Commissioner, 713 F.2d 496 (9th Cir. 1983) (diary kept by casino employee could be admitted as a business record against another employee; gaps in diary went to weight rather than admissibility); United States v. Foster, 711

a view toward prosecution, the author, as well as those feeding him information, had a motive to lie. Military practice has prohibited statements from qualifying as business records if made principally with a view toward prosecution. It is unlikely that much will change since documents made with an eye to use at trial are not likely to be viewed as ordinary business records in any event.

[f]   Application to Drug Prosecutions—Constitutional Issues

As noted in our discussion of the Confrontation Clause issues, *above*, the Supreme Court in *Crawford v. Washington* held that admission of testimonial hearsay statements would violate the Confrontation Clause unless the prosecution showed that the hearsay declarant was unavailable at trial and that the defendant had been provided an opportunity to cross-examine the declarant at the time the statement was made.

A question left open in *Crawford* was whether the Confrontation Clause would apply to business records. There is language in *Crawford* to the effect that business records would not be affected. And the federal courts have not applied *Crawford* where the records were not prepared for the purpose of litigation. As noted, below, in the past the military courts have typically treated laboratory reports as business records, thus raising the question of whether they would be considered testimonial hearsay.

In *Melendez-Diaz v. Massachusetts*,[77] the Court considered how *Crawford* would apply to laboratory reports in criminal drug prosecutions. The accused had been convicted in state court of distributing and trafficking in cocaine. Over defense counsel's *Crawford* objection, the trial judge admitted three "certificates of analysis" showing the results of the forensic analysis performed on substances seized in connection with the accused's arrest. The certificates were sworn before a notary public by analysts at the State Laboratory Institute of the Massachusetts Department of Public Health, as required under state law.

The Appeals Court of Massachusetts affirmed the convictions and relied upon a Massachusetts Supreme Judicial Court ruling that the authors of certificates of forensic analysis are not subject to confrontation under the Sixth Amendment. The United States Supreme Court reversed. Justice Scalia wrote for the majority in a 5-4 decision and concluded that "[t]here is little doubt that the documents in this case fall within the 'core class of testimonial statements' " described in *Crawford*. The Court reasoned that "[t]he documents at issue here, while denominated by Massachusetts law 'certificates,'

F.2d 871 (9th Cir. 1983) (incomplete ledger of drug transactions admissible); United States v. Lieberman, 637 F.2d 95 (2d Cir. 1980) (hotel registration card filled out by guests rather than hotel employees could qualify as business record but could not be used to prove who stayed in the hotel).

[77] 129 S. Ct. 2527 (2009).

are quite plainly affidavits," and *Crawford*'s description of the core class of testimonial statements "mentions affidavits twice."

The Court rejected the argument that the analysts were not "accusatory" witnesses and thus were not subject to confrontation and concluded that the text of the Sixth Amendment "contemplates two classes of witnesses—those against the defendant and those in his favor." It also rejected the arguments that the analysts were not "conventional" or "typical" witnesses and did not offer testimony prone to distortion or manipulation and therefore were not subject to confrontation. The Court was not persuaded that the Confrontation Clause was satisfied so long as the defendant could call the analysts as witnesses: "[T]he Confrontation Clause imposes a burden on the prosecution to present its witnesses, not on the defendant to bring those adverse witnesses into court."

However, the Court indicated that state statutes that require the prosecution to give notice of the intent to rely on analysts and the defendant to demand production of the analysts at trial were consistent with the Confrontation Clause: "It is common to require a defendant to exercise his rights under the Compulsory Process Clause in advance of trial, announcing his intent to present certain witnesses . . . . There is no conceivable reason why he cannot similarly be compelled to exercise his Confrontation Clause rights before trial."

Justice Kennedy wrote for the dissenters and argued that the Court ignored 90 years of precedent in which scientific analysis could be introduced without testimony from the analyst who produced it, raised serious questions about which analysts must be produced, and imposed unnecessary and costly burdens on both state and federal criminal justice systems.

In *Bullcoming v. New Mexico*,[78] the Supreme Court followed *Melendez-Diaz v. Massachusetts*, holding that forensic laboratory report are "testimonial" under the Sixth Amendment's Confrontation Clause. The Court's decision requires trial counsel to produce a laboratory report's original author unless the defense had a prior opportunity to cross-examine him. "Surrogates" or other witnesses familiar with the document's creation will not be acceptable particularly when the procecution's witness was not the original author's supervisor or had not participated in the test procedures. The Court rejected prosecution contentions that the document's original author was a "mere scrivener" who simply reported a machine's test results and as a result did not produce "testimonial" evidence, and that the prosecution's witness was sufficiently knowledgeable about the test procedures to satisfy the accused's right to confrontation.

---

[78] 2011 U.S. Lexis 4790 (U.S. June 23, 2011).

[79] Reserved.

The Supreme Court's decisions in *Melendez-Diaz v. Massachusetts* and *Bullcoming v. New Mexico* requires military courts to rethink how laboratory reports and their supporting chains of custody documents will be used.[80]

Military courts have been careful to look closely at records prepared with an eye to trial. In *United States v. Gardinier*,[81] the accused was convicted of taking indecent liberties with and committing indecent acts upon his underage daughter. Part of the government's evidence included a "Forensic Medical Examination Form" which was completed by a "sexual assault nurse examiner" at the request of civilian police authorities. The nurse testified at trial concerning the patient's history, including an identification of the accused as her assailant, specifics of the forensic examination, and recommendations for follow-on medical treatment. Relying on *Crawford v. Washington* and *United States v. Rankin*,[82] [SS5] the court reversed the accused's convictions and found that both the medical form and the nurse's testimony were testimonial in nature as they: (1) were elicited by or made in response to law enforcement or prosecutorial inquiries, (2) involved more than a routine and objective cataloging of factual matters, and (3) were primarily created with an eye toward prosecution.

---

[80] Pre-*Melendez-Diaz* and *bullcoming* drug prosecutions relied on well established military authority allowing both the laboratory report and chain of custody documents to be admitted as exceptions to the hearsay rule. In United States v. Evans, 45 C.M.R. 353 (C.M.A. 1972) and United States v. Miller, 49 C.M.R. 380 (C.M.A. 1974), the Court held that laboratory reports were admissible as business entry exception to the hearsay rule. Thus, the chemist who analyzed the contraband did not have to be produced even over defense objections. However, defense counsel could obtain the witness if she wanted to test the chemist's competency or the techniques used in evaluating the evidence. In United States v. Vietor, 10 M.J. 69 (C.M.A. 1980), the court held that to obtain the chemist defense counsel had to demonstrate that competency or examination techniques were really in question. Thus, there was no absolute right to the chemist's presence. In United States v. Strangstalien, 7 M.J. 225 (C.M.A. 1979), and United States v. Herrington, 8 M.J. 194 (C.M.A. 1980), the court reaffirmed its view that laboratory reports are made by neutral and detached chemists who are not part of the prosecution team, and thus the chemists could be trusted to portray accurately their analyses in the reports. The court chose to find that laboratory reports were not made principally for the purposes of prosecution. In United States v. Porter, 12 M.J. 129 (C.M.A. 1981), the court rejected defense counsel's contention that government witnesses would have to establish what the laboratory's normal business is and how the lab report accurately reflected that business before the report itself would be admissible In United States v. Cordero, 21 M.J. 714 (A.F.C.M.R.1985) the court held that laboratory reports produced at both military and civilian facilities were admissible and that the witness offering such evidence need not have compiled the data nor need even be "certain of who recorded" it. Such witnesses were only required to identify the record as authentic and state that it was made in the regular course of business.

[81] 65 M.J. 60 (C.A.A.F. 2007).

[82] 64 M.J. 348 (C.A.A.F. 2007) (court found no *Crawford* violation in using documentary evidence to establish the accused's unauthorized absence).

In *United States v. Blazier*,[83] the accused was convicted of dereliction of duty and wrongful use of controlled substances. In its second look at the case, the court concluded that an expert may rely on machine-generated data because the Rules of Evidence define it as not being hearsay, and also may rely on but not repeat testimonial hearsay that is otherwise appropriate for expert opinion testimony so long as the expert's opinion is his own. The court also held that when testimonial hearsay is admitted, the Confrontation Clause is satisfied only if the declarant of that hearsay is subject to cross-examination at trial, or is unavailable but had been previously subjected to cross-examination and warned that the Confrontation Clause may not be circumvented by having an expert testify at trial to otherwise inadmissible testimonial hearsay. The court found that this occurred in violation of *Melendez-Diaz v. Massachusetts* and returned the record for a harmful error analysis.

Similarly, in *United States v. Magyari*,[84] laboratory test results were introduced using a chain of custody documents and the evidence custodian's live testimony. No one from the lab testified. Sustaining the accused's conviction, the court held that *Crawford v. Washington* had not been violated because admission of the lab report was non-testimonial proof. The court went on to say that lab technicians do not equate specific samples of potential contraband with particular individuals, and under these circumstances testing is not in furtherance of any particular law enforcement investigation. The court limited its opinion to the facts of the case and, in the course of doing so rejected "[t]he Government's contention that lab reports are inherently not testimonial because they are business and public records." The court stated that this argument "goes too far."

Military courts have had a more difficult time resolving whether chain of custody forms should be admissible under this Rule. These government documents are used to trace the handling of evidence. They do not warrant that the individuals controlling the substance have failed to alter or tamper with it; they merely determine who handled the evidence. Initially, when the government attempted to use chain of custody documents to demonstrate that fungible contraband seized from the accused was the same contraband analyzed by the forensic chemist, the Court of Appeals reversed the convictions, finding that these documents were prepared by law enforcement personnel who, by definition, were concerned with obtaining convictions. The documents were thus viewed as prosecutorial in nature and inadmissible.[85] In *United States v. McKinney*,[86] the court affirmed this view, but in

---

[83] 69 M.J. 218 (C.A.A.F. 2010).

[84] 63 M.J. 123 (C.A.A.F. 2006).

[85] *See* United States v. Nault, 4 M.J. 318 (C.M.A. 1978); United States v. Porter, 7 M.J. 32 (C.M.A. 1979); and United States v. Neutze, 7 M.J. 30 (C.M.A. 1979).

[86] 9 M.J. 86 (C.M.A. 1980).

a footnote implied that the Military Rules of Evidence might change things. The court was indeed prescient. It withdrew from its original position requiring strict tracing of contraband, as explained in *Nault, above.*[87] In *United States v. Jessen,*[88] the court held that Rule 803(6) and (8) "overturned *Porter* and *Nuetze.*" In *United States v. Tyler,*[89] the court added that "unrebutted evidence" identifying drugs is sufficient to reach the fact-finder.[90] Plainly, Confrontation Clause challenges will continue to be raised when this Rule is used.[91]

In *United States v. Grant,*[92] a case the United States Court of Appeals for the Armed Forces identified as one of first impression, the accused was convicted of using marijuana. The government's evidence included the accused's own confession and a positive urinalysis report that was offered and admitted for the sole purpose of corroborating the accused's confession. Both at trial and on appeal, the accused contended that the urinalysis report did not qualify as a business record because the document was made by the private laboratory that conducted the tests and not by the Air Force hospital where the sample was collected and where the witnesses laying the business entry foundation worked. The government called no witnesses from the laboratory or the hospital to establish a chain of custody, nor did they call any witnesses to describe the laboratory testing procedure. The government's foundation was established by the medical doctor and corpsman responsible for conducting the test at the Air Force Hospital. Based on these facts, the court affirmed the accused's conviction and stated that a business record prepared by a third party (the laboratory here) not a party to the litigation "is properly admitted as part of a second business entity's [the government here] records if the second business integrated the document into its records and relied upon it in the ordinary course of its business."[93] Crucial to the government's proof, the hospital personal testified that they relied on documents of this nature in providing medical assistance, thus

---

[87] *See* United States v. Fowler, 9 M.J. 149 (C.M.A. 1980); and United States v. Courts, 9 M.J. 285 (C.M.A. 1980), which cited United States v. Lane, 591 F.2d 961, 962 (D.C. Cir. 1979), among other federal authorities. *See also* discussion of Rule 901.

[88] 12 M.J. 122 (C.M.A. 1981).

[89] 17 M.J. 381 (C.M.A. 1984).

[90] *See* Raezer, *Introducing Documentary Evidence,* ARMY LAW, Aug. 1985, for an interesting discussion of how laboratory reports and chain of custody documents should be handled.

[91] *See* United States v. Oates, 560 F.2d 45 (2d Cir. 1977), for a particularly enlightening discussion of the confrontation issue. *Compare* Imwinkelried, *The Constitutionality of Introducing Laboratory Report Against Criminal Defendants,* 30 HASTINGS L.J. 621 (1979), *with* Weinstein, *Three Years of the Federal Rules of Evidence,* N.Y.L.J., Feb. 7, 1978, at 1, col. 2.

[92] 56 M.J. 410 (C.A.A.F. 2002).

[93] 56 M.J. at 414.

demonstrating indicia of trustworthiness. Interestingly, the Court went on to say that a chain of custody was not necessary because the report was only being offered to corroborate the accused's confession and it was the confession itself which established the wrongfulness charged.

[8] Absence of Entry in Records Covered by Rule 803(6)

[a] Basis for the Exception

This exception is taken verbatim from the Federal Rules, and is similar to prior court-martial authority. It provides that, if a specific matter is not noted in a record of regularly conducted activity as described in (6) above, that fact may be shown to prove the nonoccurrence or nonexistence of the matter. The information in question must be the type which would normally have been made in the regular course of activity, and the records consulted must qualify under paragraph (6).

[b] Confrontation Issues

Evidence concerning the absence of a business record faces the same Sixth Amendment right to confrontation standards for admissibility as does the business record itself. The Supreme Court has established new standards for admitting such documentary evidence. In *Melendez-Diaz v. Massachusetts*,[94] the defendant was convicted in state court of distributing and trafficking in cocaine. Over his *Crawford v. Washington*[95] objection, the trial judge admitted three "certificates of analysis" showing the results of the forensic analysis performed on substances seized in connection with the defendant's arrest. The certificates were sworn before a notary public by analysts at the State Laboratory Institute of the Massachusetts Department of Public Health, as required under state law. The Appeals Court of Massachusetts affirmed the convictions and relied upon a Massachusetts Supreme Judicial Court ruling that the authors of certificates of forensic analysis are not subject to confrontation under the Sixth Amendment. The United States Supreme Court reversed. Justice Scalia wrote for the majority in a 5-4 decision and concluded that "[t]here is little doubt that the documents in this case fall within the 'core class of testimonial statements' " described in Crawford. The Court reasoned that "[t]he documents at issue here, while denominated by Massachusetts law 'certificates,' are quite plainly affidavits," and Crawford's description of the core class of testimonial statements "mentions affidavits twice." See *Melendez-Diaz* discussed above in § 803.02[7][f].

In *Bullcoming v. New Mexico*, the Supreme Court followed *Melendez-Diaz v. Massachusetts*, holding that forensic laboratory report are "testimonial" under the Sixth Amendment's Confrontation Clause. The Court's

---

[94] 129 S. Ct.2527 (2009).

[95] 541 U.S. 36 (2004).

decision requires trial counsel to produce a laboratory report's original author unless the defense had a prior opportunity to cross-examine him. "Surrogates" or other witnesses familiar with the document's creation will not be acceptable particularly when the procecution's witness was not the original author's supervisor or had not participated in the test procedures. The Court rejected prosecution contentions that the document's original author was a "mere scrivener" who simply reported a machine's test results and as a result did not produce "testimonial" evidence, and that the prosecution's witness was sufficiently knowledgeable about the test procedures to satisfy the accused's right to confrontation.

In *United States v. Orozco-Acosta*,[96] an illegal reentry case, the court held that the admission of a certificate of non-existence of permission to reenter the United States was error because it violated the *Melendez-Diaz v. Massachusetts* prohibition against testimonial documentary records. The court went on to say that the Sixth Amendment bar's such evidence without confrontation because the documents are clearly prepared for purposes of litigation.

[c]   Is it Hearsay?

Many commentators believe paragraph (7) is not required because the existence or nonexistence of a record is not hearsay evidence. Legislative history indicates Congress merely wanted to assure that the evidence would be admissible and that it provided an exception just in case one is needed.

United States v. Rich,[97] presents a good example of how this Rule can be used. There, a bank robbery defendant claimed that a certain person borrowed his car the day the bank was robbed. In rebuttal, an FBI agent established that he had examined all police, credit and city directories without finding a trace of the person mentioned by the accused. Affirming the conviction, the court noted that, had defense counsel made an appropriate objection, the prosecution would have been required to establish the necessary business record foundation for the directories in question before the FBI agent would have been allowed to testify about their content. However, because defense counsel failed to object, the matter was waived.[98]

[9]   Rule 803(8)—Public Records and Reports

[a]   Basis for the Exception

This is one of the most complex and controversial provisions in Rule 803. It is a combination of previous court-martial practice, the Federal Rule, and the military drafters' additions to the Federal Rule. Subparagraph (8) is broader than its federal counterpart, admitting a wider scope of otherwise

---

[96] 607 F.3d 1156 (9th Cir. 2010), 2011 U.S. Lexis 4790 (U.S. June 23, 2011).

[97] 580 F.2d 929 (9th Cir.), *cert. denied*, 439 U.S. 935 (1978).

[98] *See* our discussion of Rule 103.

inadmissible government documents. Like the last sentence of exception (6), the last sentence of this Rule is not consistent with prior federal and military judicial authority, and raises Sixth Amendment confrontation issues. Our comments on exception (6) should be consulted when using the final sentence of this Rule.

The public records exception has a long common law pedigree. The federal and military versions do not distinguish between records kept or made by federal or military organizations and those produced by state or local government entities.[99] Like the common law, this provision is based on the assumption that public officials will properly perform their duty, and because of the complexity and repetitiveness of their responsibilities, it is unlikely they would have an independent memory of what occurred, which would greatly limit their ability to provide meaningful court-martial testimony. Moreover, requiring government officials to constantly testify would detract from their public service obligations.

[b]   Three Separate Provisions

Public records, reports, statements or data compilations, no matter what their form, may be admissible if they are made by or in a public office or agency and if they satisfy subsection (A), (B) or (C) of the Rule.[100] Each part of the Rule has its own coverage.

Records and reports of an agency's activities satisfy (A). The Drafters' Analysis suggests a useful limitation on the concept of an "activity."

Matters observed by someone who had a duty to observe such matters and report them are admissible if contained in public records and reports under subsection (B), except that matters observed by police officers and persons acting in a law enforcement capacity are excluded. On the face of (B), it would appear that such law enforcement observations are unavailable to both sides in a criminal case. However, civilian courts have read (B) as though it were drafted to be parallel to (C). The civilian cases persuasively reason that there is no reason to exclude reports prepared by law enforcement officers who have no reason to favor defendants, when those reports are offered by the defendants. There are confrontation and reliability concerns with permitting the same reports to be offered by the government.

Under (C), factual findings are admissible on behalf of a defendant but not

---

[99] Some federal cases also permit non-governmental forms to be used. *See, e.g.,* United States v. Torres, 733 F.2d 449 (7th Cir. 1984) (tribal roll could be used to show Indian status); United States v. Johnson, 722 F.2d 407 (8th Cir. 1983) (Bureau of Alcohol, Tobacco and Firearms form prepared by manufacturer and kept by Bureau could be used to show that gun had moved in interstate commerce).

[100] The result may be different for foreign government's records. *See, e.g.,* United States v. Pinto-Mejia, 720 F.2d 248 (2d Cir. 1983) (Venezuelan agency's statement concerning history of a ship inadmissible). *See also* United States v. Jones, 29 F.3d 1549 (11th Cir. 1994) (judicial findings of fact in prior federal case not under hearsay exception).

for the government. The Rule recognizes that such findings may be reliable but would raise serious confrontation issues if offered for the government.

[c]   Government Factual Findings Used Against the Prosecution

Subsection (C) of the Rule allows factual findings made pursuant to government authorized investigations to be admitted against the prosecution unless the information is untrustworthy.[101] As drafted, it is not clear whether the "untrustworthy clause" modifies only (C) or all subsections. The better reading of the Rule is that any public record should be excluded if the opponent demonstrates a lack of trustworthiness. This reading makes the public records exception consistent with the business records exception set forth in Rule 803(6). It should be noted that subsection (C) is limited to factual findings, but a finding can involve an evaluation of data or evidence.[102]

[d]   Evaluative Reports

One of the provision's most controversial aspects concerns whether it authorizes the use of "evaluative reports." Many common law jurisdictions prohibited opinion testimony from being considered as part of official documents. However, in *Beech Aircraft Corp. v. Rainey,*[103] the Supreme Court settled the conflict among federal courts on the meaning of "factual findings" in Federal Rule of Evidence 803(8)(C), and held that the term encompasses more than just "facts" and includes evaluative conclusions and opinions. The Court held it was appropriate for the trial court to have considered the conclusions in a Navy report concerning the cause of an airplane crash. While refusing to distinguish between fact and opinion for purposes of the Rule, the Court specifically declined to address the admissibility of legal conclusions contained in official reports.

The Federal Advisory Committee's Note on this Rule may be helpful in applying *Rainey*, and the provision generally. The Committee indicates that the following factors should be considered in determining the admissibility of evaluative reports: (1) how close in time to the issue at bar was the investigation conducted; (2) how current or valuable is the report produced by the time it is used at trial; (3) what special skill or experience did the investigating and reporting officials have which would make their conclu-

---

[101] In United States v. Smith, 521 F.2d 957 (D.C. Cir. 1975), the court found that reading Rules 803(8)(B) and 803(8)(C) together "authorizes the admission of the reports of police officers and other law enforcement personnel at the request of the defendant in a criminal case." The court went on to say that they "do not believe such records may be employed by the prosecution" because of confrontation and bias problems.

[102] For a good discussion of valuative reports, *see* Melville v. American Home Assurance Co., 443 F. Supp. 1064 (E.D. Pa. 1977), *rev'd on other grounds*, 584 F.2d 1306 (3d Cir. 1978).

[103] 488 U.S. 153 (1988).

sions or opinions of value to factfinders; (4) are the evaluative reports the product of an open or publicly reported hearing concerning the issue in question; and (5) did the agency or the individuals conducting the investigation and writing the reports have any inconsistent or conflicting motives?

[e] Expanding the Rule—Linkage to 803(6)

The last sentence of paragraph (8) provides that, notwithstanding (B) and (C), a great many government and police-related documents are admissible against the accused or the prosecution if they record a fact or event, were made by a person who was acting within his official duties, those duties including the obligation to know or ascertain the information's accuracy and trustworthiness, and the individual had the duty to record such factors or events. Once these criteria are established, forensic laboratory reports, chain of custody documents, all officer and enlisted records, finger-print cards, and related documents become admissible public records. These records are also discussed in connection with exception (6).

Laboratory reports require special mention here because they are a crucial part of every controlled substances prosecution.[104] In our Editorial Comments to subparagraph 803(6), we discuss both the Supreme Court's and the military courts' current treatment of laboratory reports. The *Crawford*, *Melendez-Diaz* and *Bullcoming* line of cases make clear that these documents may be inadmissible as violative of the accused's Sixth Amendment right to confrontation.[105]

The Drafters' Analysis opines that evidence excluded under Rule 803(8)(B) should probably be excluded also under Rule 803(6), or the former Rule would be meaningless. In our view, this is incorrect. An activity must be regularly conducted under exception (6); it need not be under exception (8). If it is regularly conducted it may be reliable enough to be admitted. If not, then the case for exclusion is strengthened. Many

---

[104] *See*, United States v. Oates, 560 F.2d 45 (2nd Cir 1979) (laboratory reports and chain of custody documents clearly included in that category of government documents prohibited by the accused's right to confrontation and Congress's intended ban under 803(6) and (8)).

[105] *Compare* United States v. Dowdell, 595 F.3d 50 (1st Cir. 2010) (public record of accused's booking sheet admissible as routine, non-adversarial document); United States v. DeWater, 846 F.2d 528 (9th Cir. 1988) (breathalyzer report admitted under 803(8)(B) because its preparation was routine and non-adversarial); United States v. Rosa, 11 F.3d 315 (2nd Cir. 1993) (medical examiner's report admissible under this Rule because the medical examiner is not part of law enforcement personnel); *with* United States v. Pintado-Isioedia, 448 F.3d 1155 (9th Cir. 2006) (Mexican birth record inadmissible because no showing it fell within the pubic records exception); United States v. Enterline, 894 F.2d 287 (8th Cir. 1990) (rule intended to ban police crime scene investigation reports); United States v. Bohrer, 807 F.2d 159 (10th Cir. 1986) (IRS "contact card" excluded because it was prepared under adversarial circumstances); United States v. Broadnax, 23 M.J. 389 (C.M.A. 1987) (forensic laboratory report containing an opinion from government documents examiner that the accused authored a forged check inadmissible without testimony from document's preparer).

observations that are not part of regularly conducted activities will be excluded under 803(8)(B), even if some observations occurring during regularly conducted activities are admissible.[106]

[10]   Rule 803(9)—Records of Vital Statistics

[a]   Basis for the Exception

This provision is similar to many existing state rules or code provisions. It is based on the California Rule. Exception (9) concerns the admissibility of records or data compilations made in any form which concern birth, death, marriage, and related vital public statistics. The report must have been made to a public office charged by law with collecting such information in order to be admissible as an exception to the hearsay rule.

[b]   Collateral Facts

Some federal courts which have evaluated this Rule question whether it applies only to factual material contained in vital statistics, or whether the Rule is broad enough to encompass collateral facts, such as the cause of death. There are not many federal decisions, and there are arguments for both inclusion and exclusion of collateral facts. Data about births, deaths and similar events are likely to be noncontroversial, whereas opinions as to cause of death might be quite controversial. It is not always clear what courts regard as collateral as opposed to vital statistics.[107]

[11]   Rule 803(10)—Absence of Public Record or Entry

[a]   Confrontation Issues

Evidence concerning the absence of a public record faces the same Sixth Amendment right to confrontation standards for admissibility as does the public record itself. Writing primarily on Rule 803(6), the Supreme Court established new standards for admitting documentary evidence. In *Melendez-Diaz v. Massachusetts*[108] the defendant was convicted in state court of distributing and trafficking in cocaine. Over his *Crawford v. Washington*[109] objection, the trial judge admitted three "certificates of analysis" showing the results of the forensic analysis performed on substances seized in connection with the defendant's arrest. The certificates were sworn before a notary public by analysts at the State Laboratory

---

[106] *See, e.g.,* United States v. King, 613 F.2d 670 (7th Cir. 1980) (conviction for making false official statements was affirmed where the court held that certain governmental forms could be admitted under Rule 803(6) and that Rule 803(8) was not the exclusive provision for admitting such evidence).

[107] *See, e.g.,* Vaughn v. United States, 536 F. Supp. 498 (W.D. Va. 1982) (time of death could be shown in death certificate).

[108] 129 S. Ct. 2527 (2009).

[109] 541 U.S. 36 (2004).

Institute of the Massachusetts Department of Public Health, as required under state law. The Appeals Court of Massachusetts affirmed the convictions and relied upon a Massachusetts Supreme Judicial Court ruling that the authors of certificates of forensic analysis are not subject to confrontation under the Sixth Amendment. The United States Supreme Court reversed. Justice Scalia wrote for the majority in a 5-4 decision and concluded that "[t]here is little doubt that the documents in this case fall within the 'core class of testimonial statements' " described in Crawford. The Court reasoned that "[t]he documents at issue here, while denominated by Massachusetts law 'certificates,' are quite plainly affidavits," and *Crawford'* s description of the core class of testimonial statements "mentions affidavits twice." *Melendez-Diaz* is discussed above at § 803.02[7][f].

In *Bullcoming v. New Mexico*, the Supreme Court followed *Melendez-Diaz v. Massachusetts*, holding that forensic laboratory report are "testimonial" under the Sixth Amendment's Confrontation Clause. The Court's decision requires trial counsel to produce a laboratory report's original author unless the defense had a prior opportunity to cross-examine him. "Surrogates" or other witnesses familiar with the document's creation will not be acceptable particularly when the procecution's witness was not the original author's supervisor or had not participated in the test procedures. The Court rejected prosecution contentions that the document's original author was a "mere scrivener" who simply reported a machine's test results and as a result did not produce "testimonial" evidence, and that the prosecution's witness was sufficiently knowledgeable about the test procedures to satisfy the accused's right to confrontation.

In *United States v. Orozco-Acosta*,[110] an illegal reentry case, the court held that the admission of a certificate of non-existence of permission to reenter the United States was error because it violated the *Melendez-Diaz v. Massachusetts* prohibition against testimonial documentary records. The court went on to say that the Sixth Amendment bar's such evidence without confrontation because the documents are clearly prepared for purposes of litigation.

[b]   Basis for the Exception

Exception (10) performs the same function as Rule 803(7).[111] It provides that, if a diligent search of public records[112] is made, a document certified

---

[110] 607 F.3d 1156 (9th Cir. 2010), 2011 U.S. Lexis 4790 (U.S. June 23, 2011).

[111] *But see* United States v. Stout, 667 F.2d 1347 (11th Cir. 1982) (erroneous use of records to prove more than they really showed).

[112] Federal decisions indicate that this exception can also be applied to international and foreign organizations. *See, e.g.*, United States v. Martinez, 700 F.2d 1358 (11th Cir. 1983) (certificate from Honduras concerning absence of records of ship registration admissible); United States v. M'Biye, 655 F.2d 1240 (D.C. Cir. 1981) (certificate showing absence of

in accordance with Rule 902, or a witness's testimony, may be admitted to show the absence of a record or the nonoccurrence or nonexistence of a matter which otherwise would have been recorded.[113] There was no corollary to this provision in previous military practice.

[c]   Ministerial Event vs. Valuative Function

Pursuant to current military practice, 803(10) could be used against an accused who failed to register his firearm in accordance with unit or other regulations. Absence of registration could be proved by a report indicating that a search has been made of the applicable file and that it contained no reference to the accused.[114] Defense counsel could challenge the reliability of the government's proof if there were evidence indicating that diligence was not used in the search, or if the records were improperly recorded or maintained.[115]

Federal Courts applying this exception have not excluded evidence because of Rule 803(8)(B) or (C)'s prohibitions concerning the government using official documents against an accused. Most courts view subparagraph (10) evidence as having no evaluative component because it only represents a ministerial event. However, a search for the document would generally not have been undertaken but for a pending court-martial. The "in anticipation of trial" aspect to this evidence provides defense counsel with an avenue for attack. Trial counsel can minimize this liability by calling the individual who actually made the search and subjecting that person to cross-examination.[116] Trial counsel may choose to do the same when a search involves complex filling systems that span more than one agency or organization, and/or requires sophistication and independent judgment to complete.[117]

[12]   Rule 803(11)—Records of Religious Organizations

[a]   Basis for the Exception

In many ways, exception (11) is a combination of Rules 803(6) and

---

United Nations' record that defendant worked there is admissible).

[113] *See, e.g.,* United States v. Johnson, 577 F.2d 1304 (5th Cir. 1978) (an IRS employee's testimony that a file search revealed no information concerning the accused's tax liability for the years in question was properly admitted to show the absence of such files, an otherwise very difficult thing to prove); United States v. Wilson, 732 F.2d 404 (5th Cir. 1984) (CIA's statement that it could find no evidence of defendant's association with agency admissible).

[114] *See, e.g.,* United States v. Combs, 762 F.2d 1343 (9th Cir. 1985) (unregistered firearm proved by report after searching applicable records).

[115] *See, e.g.,* United States v. Yakobov, 712 F.2d 20 (2d Cir. 1983) (search among government records for license was inadequate where government had misspelled defendant's name).

[116] *See, e.g.,* United States v. Yakobov, 712 F.2d 20 (2d Cir. 1983) (absence of public record evidence admissible even though court would have excluded same under 803(8)).

[117] *See, e.g.,* United States v. Nicely, 922 F.2d 850 (D.C. Cir. 1991) (far ranging Treasury Department searches considered to be beyond this provision).

803(10). However, it is broader than both Rules. It allows admission of religious records which establish birth, death, marriage, and similar events, even though the transmitting agent does not have a duty to transmit, and even though he has no formal relationship with the religious organization involved. As long as the information in question is kept in the organization's regular course of activity, it will be admissible.

[b] Reliability

Reliability is based on the religious organization's self-interest in knowing about the important events that concern the organization and its members. Like 803(6), a demonstration of orderly record keeping practices is required by the proponent.

[13] Rule 803(12)—Marriage, Baptismal, and Similar Certificates

[a] Basis for the Exception

Exception (12) allows statements of fact contained in marriage, baptism, and similar events to be proved by documentary evidence if such documents were executed by the clergyman, public official, or other person authorized to conduct the ceremony in question at the time the ceremony was held or within a reasonable time thereafter. The Rule provides that practices of the religious organization or a public law be consulted in order to determine whether the maker of the document was authorized to so act.

[b] Reliability

Reliability here is connected to the assumption that an organization would not issue a certificate or other document memorializing an event unless the event actually occurred. It is also important to note that, when the person executing the document or certificate is not a public official, Rule 902's self-authenticating provisions are not satisfied, and the proponent will have to prove that the person was authorized to, and did in fact, make the certificate.

[14] Rule 803(13)—Family Records

[a] Basis for the Exception

This exception is well recognized at common law and stems from the practice of families keeping their important records in bibles. Both federal and military courts have little experience applying it to criminal law cases. It permits facts concerning family or personal history to be proved through genealogies, family portraits, family Bibles, inscriptions in rings, engravings on tombstones, publicly displayed pedigrees, "or the like" (to use the Rule's own words). At common law this exception would be consulted when public or religious records were inadequate or absent.

[b] First-Hand Knowledge Not Required

Application of this exception is potentially very broad as it does not require that the record have been made by someone with first hand knowledge of the facts recorded. Trustworthiness is based on the assumption that family members would not keep inaccurate records concerning their own activities.

[15]   Rule 803(14)—Records of Documents Affecting an Interest in Property

[a]   Basis for the Exception

Modern state property recording statutes are based on this exception that covers documents which purport to establish or affect an interest in property. Were such records inadmissible, the purpose underlying recording statutes would be undermined. The Rule requires that the document used to prove this issue be one that is authorized to be recorded and that it actually be recorded in a public office. The document may be used to prove the contents of the original recorded document and its execution by each person whom purports to have executed it.

[b]   State Statutes Control

State statutes provide both the bases for trustworthiness and the specific procedures which must be used to execute and deliver the recording documents. Those statutes eliminate problems that might stem from persons involved in the filing process not having first hand knowledge about certain events.

[16]   Rule 803(15)—Statements in Documents Affecting an Interest in Property

[a]   Basis for the Exception

Deeds purporting to dispose of property often contain recitals of fact indicating, for example, that the grantors are all heirs of the last recorded owner, or that a power of attorney applies. Exception (15) establishes that these statements are exempt from the hearsay rule.

[b]   Establishing Trustworthiness

Trustworthiness is established by the circumstances under which dispositive documents are executed, and the requirement that each statement pertain to the purpose for the document. Similar guarantees of trustworthiness stem from the fact that dealings which are inconsistent with the document's provisions are inadmissible under this exception.

[17]   Rule 803(16)—Statements in Ancient Documents

[a]   Basis for the Exception

At common law, many jurisdictions required manuscripts and other records to be more than 30 years old before they qualified for admission under the ancient documents exception to the hearsay rule. Exception (16) recognizes that such papers may be admitted if they have been in existence twenty years or more. In many cases, a major problem with ancient is authentication. Rule 901(8) now eases authentication requirements.

[b]　Establishing Trustworthiness

The rational for this exception is that age is some guarantee that a document is not created to obtain an advantage in litigation. Newspaper accounts, letters, records, contracts, maps, certificates, and title documents all commonly fall within this provision.

[18]　Rule 803(17)—Market Reports, Commercial Publications

[a]　Basis for the Exception

The military version of exception (17) has been taken from the Federal Rule and previous editions of the *Manual*. It allows market quotations, directories, government pricing lists and any other published compilations to be admitted for the purpose of establishing value or price. The Rule encompasses virtually any published compilation relied upon by the public or persons in a particular occupation. It does not refer, as did the previous *Manual,* to an absence of entries in reports or publications. *Compare* exceptions (7) and (10).

[19]　Rule 803(18)—Learned Treatises

[a]　Basis for the Exception

Learned treatises have long been favored by the common law, but were generally limited to impeachment uses. Pursuant to 803(18), they are now admitted as an exception to the hearsay rule and thus as substantive evidence.[118] While Rule 703 permits an expert to rely on inadmissible data in formulating his testimony, 803(18) provides that the contents of learned treatises which the expert relied upon can be used for their truth as long as the expert is testifying, available to explain its contents, and subject to cross-examination. Thus, learned treatises are admissible, even though they must be read to the members as opposed to being marked as exhibits and made available during deliberations. Learned treatises—defined in the Rule as published documents, periodicals, or pamphlets concerning medical, scientific, historic, or artistic information—may be used in connection with direct or cross-examination of an expert. However, the exception may only be used when an expert is examined. The Rule assumes that an expert can explain the treatise or answer questions about it, and that, without the expert's presence, members would be unable to use the treatise properly.

Trustworthiness here is based on the assumption that the market place requires learned treaties to be authoritative and particularly accurate or else

---

[118] *See* Imwinkelried, *The Use of Learned Scientific Treatises Under Federal Rule of Evidence 803(18),* 14 ADVOC. 169 (1982). The author concisely explains Rule 803(18), providing guidance on how to lay a foundation for introducing learned treatises at trial.

they will be of little value. Similarly, such publications are generally written by scholars and similar professionals who know that their work will be subjected to critical peer review and scrutiny, and who place their professional reputations in jeopardy with publication. Both this exception and exception (17) rely on "practices" to guarantee trustworthiness; courts will use what is relied upon outside of court to govern important decisions made in court.

[b] Use at Trial

This exception expands the admissibility of reliable authorities, allowing them to be used for more than impeachment or background information.[119] When 803(18) is read in conjunction with Rules 702 and 703, it allows an expert, while testifying on direct, to state that: (1) he used a certain treatise; (2) the treatise is recognized as a reliable reference in the field; and (3) he relied upon it in formulating his expert opinion or conclusions.

However, to be admissible, the learned treatises must be established as reliable. Reliability can be proved through the witness's testimony, through subsequent expert testimony, or by judicial notice. If reliable, the treatise can be used on direct examination if relied upon by the expert, and on cross-examination if called to the attention of the opposing expert. The cross-examiner may use the treatise whether or not the expert agrees that it is reliable and whether or not the expert ever has seen the treatise before. Importantly, when an expert is cross-examined with a learned treatise under this Rule, its contents are admitted as substantive evidence and for their truth. Whether used on direct examination or cross-examination, a treatise may be read to the finders of fact, but may not be given to them as an exhibit, unless it is not feasible to read the treatise into the record.[120] Learned treatises are inadmissible if they have been prepared primarily for litigation purposes and not primarily for other professionals' use. This requirement ensures that the author's reputation will be at stake and thus the substance will be accurate and reliable.[121]

CATEGORY III. Reputation evidence and prior judgments

Paragraphs (19), (20) and (21) cover reputation evidence. Paragraphs (19) and (20) have no counterpart in previous military authority. Paragraph (21)

---

[119] *See, e.g.,* United States v. Jones, 712 F.2d 115 (5th Cir. 1983) (impermissible to cross-examine expert about another expert's testimony, since testimony is not a learned treatise).

[120] *See, e.g.,* United States v. Mangan, 575 F.2d 32 (2d Cir. 1977) (where learned treatise information consisted of detailed charts rather than textual material, the court suggested that notwithstanding the last sentence of this exception, it was difficult to see how a chart could be read into evidence and that "good sense would seem to favor its admission").

[121] *See, e.g.,* United States v. Martinez, 588 F.3d 301 (6th Cir. 2009) (in health care fraud case a video tape prepared exclusively for trial was inadmissible).

can be traced to ¶ 138 *f* of the 1969 *Manual.* Trustworthiness for this category of exceptions is based upon certain types of information about individuals, their families, regions, or historical events being available in the community, and the community being sufficiently interested in that information to have inquired about and discussed it to the extent that a community conclusion has been formed.

[20] Rule 803(19)—Reputation Concerning Personal or Family History

[a] Basis for the Exception

This exception greatly expands the common law and paragraphs (11), (12) and (13) with respect to establishing marriage, divorce, death, legitimacy, and related family and personal history matters. Rule 803(19) now allows such information to be proved by family reputation testimony, or by reputation testimony from personal associates, community members, or related organizations. Pursuant to Rule 405(d), military organizations and installations of virtually any size or composition qualify as communities.

[21] Rule 803(20)—Reputation Concerning Boundaries or General History

[a] Basis for the Exception—Land Use

The first part of exception (20) is an enlargement of paragraphs (14) and (15). It permits reputation evidence to be used for the purpose of determining boundaries or community land usage. The Rule provides that such evidence must have existed prior to the court-martial's formation. It also allows for reputation evidence dealing with private boundaries and private customs.

[b] Historical Events

The second part of this Rule is designed to facilitate proving certain historical events, typically when the requirements for judicial notice cannot be satisfied. The long standing nature of this information and the community's belief in it are generally viewed as satisfying trustworthiness concerns.

[22] Rule 803(21)—Reputation as to Character

[a] Basis for the Exception

Paragraph (21) concerns the type of reputation evidence admitted in Rules 405 and 608. It allows reputation evidence of a person's character among his associates or community members to be admitted as an exception to the hearsay rule. By definition, reputation evidence amounts to what the witness has heard other people say about an individual. These community statements are used and relied upon for their truthfulness.

CATEGORY IV. Judgments

Rules 803(22) and (23) allow evidence of previous judgments concerning convictions, family history or borders to be admitted as exceptions to the hearsay rule.

[23]   Rule 803(22)—Judgment of Previous Conviction

[a]   Basis for the Exception

Exception (22) admits evidence of a final judgment entered after trial, or a plea of not guilty (not *nolo contendere*) to be admitted as proof of any fact essential to the judgment.[122] To be admissible for the truth of the matter asserted, the conviction must be for a crime punishable by death, imprisonment for more than one year, or dishonorable discharge.[123]

[b]   Reliability

Reliability here comes from the "against interest" aspect of a guilty plea and the proof beyond a reasonable doubt standard in litigated cases. A party may establish that an appeal from the conviction is pending, but such appeal will not prohibit the fact of conviction from being used. As in Rule 609, the felony characteristics of military offenses are to be measured by Article 56 of the Uniform Code of Military Justice, and are based on the date of conviction. Rule 803(22) focuses on felony as opposed to misdemeanor convictions, because the incentive defendants have not to plead to felony offenses and to defend strenuously against felony charges provides reason to trust pleas or judgments of conviction for these offenses.

[c]   Using Foreign Convictions

This exception allows convictions from any jurisdiction to be used in evidence.[124] The Drafters' Analysis suggests that foreign convictions were not contemplated by the authors of the Federal Rules, from which the Military Rule is taken. But civilian courts have recognized the legitimate use of foreign convictions.[125] A judge could exclude a foreign conviction under Rule 403 if the probative value were called into question as a result of the

---

[122] *See, e.g.,* United States v. Breitkreutz, 977 F.2d 214 (6th Cir. 1992) (Rule's prohibition against government using judgment of previous conviction for nonimpeachment purposes applies only where evidence offered to prove truth of underlying facts, such as witness actually committed acts charged; use of such evidence to show date and length of sentence is admissible as a public record under Rule 803(8)).

[123] *See, e.g.,* United States v. Bordelon, 43 M.J. 531 (Army Ct.Crim.App. 1995) (Rule used to admit evidence of the accused's previous state court conviction for the same offense he was being court-martialed for).

[124] *See, e.g.,* United States v. $125,938.62, 537 F.3d 1287 (11th Cir. 2008) (judgment of a Nicaraguan court properly admitted to prove the fact of a conviction and sentence but would be inadmissible under Rule 803(8) to prove the facts found by that court).

[125] In Lloyd v. American Export Lines, 580 F.2d 1179 (3d Cir. 1977), a civil proceeding, the court reversed a judgment for the plaintiff because evidence of his prior Japanese conviction for relevant misconduct was not admitted. The court said that the "test of acceptance . . . of foreign judgments for which domestic recognition is sought . . . is

absence of basic due process protections for an accused.

[d]   Confrontation and Use Issues

While prior convictions are admissible on an issue, they are not conclusive under the Rule. However, this evidence is particularly damaging because court members are generally left without a trial record and therefore have no means to question or evaluate the accuracy of the judgments. As a result, evidence of prior convictions may be challenged as unfairly prejudicial under Rule 403.[126]

It is important to remember that a judgment of conviction under this Rule may not be admitted unless a fact essential to that judgment is relevant in the subsequent case.[127] Evidence here is used for substantive purposes, to prove the truth of some issue pending in the subsequent case, not simply to impeach a witness's credibility as Rule 609(a) permits.

[24]   Rule 803(23)—Judgment as to Personal, Family, or General History or Boundaries

[a]   Basis for the Exception

Exception (23) is linked with paragraphs (19) and (20) described above. This Rule includes evidence of judgments concerning personal, family or property boundaries within the exception. The Rule's legislative history indicates that judgments are sufficiently reliable to support their admission as substantive evidence.

§ 803.03   Drafters' Analysis

Rule 803 is taken generally from the Federal Rule with modifications as needed for adaptation to military practice. Overall, the Rule is similar to practice under *Manual* ¶¶ 142 and 144 of the present *Manual*. The Rule is, however, substantially more detailed and broader in scope than the present *Manual*.

[1]   Present sense impression

Rule 803(1) is taken from the Federal Rule verbatim. The exception it establishes is not now recognized in the Manual for Courts-Martial. It is somewhat similar to a spontaneous exclamation, but does not require a startling event. A fresh complaint by a victim of a sexual offense may come

---

whether the foreign proceedings accord with civilized jurisprudence, and are stated in a clear and formal record."

[126] *See* our Rule 403 discussion of Old Chief v. United States, 519 U.S. 172 (1997).

[127] In United States v. May, 18 M.J. 839 (N.M.C.M.R. 1984), the court held that Rule 803(22) did not provide an independent basis for establishing a prior conviction. In that case the court "failed to see where 'any fact essential to sustain the judgment' of the civilian criminal proceeding is even remotely relevant to—and thus necessitates admitting the so-called 'judgment' as proof of—any issue in the present case."

within this exception depending upon the circumstances.

[2] Excited utterance

Rule 803(2) is taken from the Federal Rule verbatim. Although similar to ¶ 142 *b*, of the present *Manual* with respect to spontaneous exclamations, the Rule would appear to be more lenient as it does not seem to require independent evidence that the startling event occurred. An examination of the Federal Rules of Evidence Advisory Committee Note indicates some uncertainty, however. S. Saltzburg & K. Redden, Federal Rules of Evidence Manual 540 (2d ed. 1977). A fresh complaint of a sexual offense may come within this exception depending on the circumstances.

[3] Then existing mental, emotional, or physical condition

Rule 803(3) is taken from the Federal Rule verbatim. The Rule is similar to that found in present *Manual* ¶ 142 *d* but may be slightly more limited in that it may not permit statements by an individual to be offered to disclose the intent of another person. Fresh complaint by a victim of a sexual offense may come within this exception.

[4] Statements for purposes of medical diagnosis or treatment

Rule 803(4) is taken from the Federal Rule verbatim. It is substantially broader than the state of mind or body exception found in ¶ 142 *d* of the present *Manual*. It allows, among other matters, statements as to the cause of the medical problem presented for diagnosis or treatment. Potentially, the Rule is extremely broad and will permit statements made even to non-medical personnel (*e.g.*, members of one's family) and on behalf of others so long as the statements are made for the purpose of diagnosis or treatment. The basis for the exception is the presumption that an individual seeking relief from a medical problem has incentive to make accurate statements. *See generally,* 4 J. Weinstein's & M. Berger, Weinsteins Evidence ¶ 804(4)[01] (1978). The admissibility under this exception of those portions of a statement not relevant to diagnosis or treatment is uncertain. Although statements made to a physician, for example, merely to enable the physician to testify, do not appear to come within the Rule, statements solicited in good faith by others in order to ensure the health of the declarant would appear to come within the Rule. Rule 803(4) may be used in an appropriate case to present evidence of fresh complaint in a sexual case.

[5] Recorded recollection

Rule 803(5) is taken from the Federal Rule without change, and is similar to the present exception for past recollection recorded found in ¶¶ 146 *a* and 149 *c* (1)(b) of the present *Manual* except that under the Rule the memorandum may be read but not presented to the factfinder unless offered by the adverse party.

[6] Record of regularly conducted activity

Rule 803(6) is taken generally from the Federal Rule. Two modifications have been made, however, to adapt the rule to military practice. The definition of "business" has been expanded to explicitly include the armed forces to ensure the continued application of this hearsay exception, and a descriptive list of documents, taken generally from present *Manual* ¶ 144 *d,* has been included. Although the activities of the armed forces do not constitute a profit making business, they do constitute a business within the meaning of the hearsay exception, *see* ¶ 144 *c,* of the present *Manual,* as well as a "regularly conducted activity."

The specific types of records included within the Rule are those which are normally records of regularly conducted activity within the armed forces. They are included because of their importance and because their omission from the Rule would be impracticable. The fact that a record is of a type described within the subdivision does not eliminate the need for its proponent to show that the *particular* record comes within the Rule when the record is challenged; the Rule does establish that the *types* of records listed are normally business records.

Chain of custody receipts or documents have been included to emphasize their administrative nature. Such documents perform the critical function of accounting for property obtained by the United States government. Although they may be used as prosecution evidence, their primary purpose is simply one of property accountability. In view of the primary administrative purpose of these matters, it was necessary to provide expressly for their admissibility as an exception to the hearsay rule in order to clearly reject the interpretation of ¶ 144 *d* of the present *Manual* with respect to chain of custody forms as set forth in *United States v. Porter,* 7 M.J. 32 (C.M.A. 1979), and *United States v. Nault,* 4 M.J. 318 (C.M.A. 1978), insofar as they concerned chain of custody forms.

Laboratory reports have been included in recognition of the function of forensic laboratories as impartial examining centers. The report is simply a record of "regularly conducted" activity of the laboratory. *See, e.g., United States v. Strangstalien,* 7 M.J. 225 (C.M.A. 1979); *United States v. Evans,* 21 C.M.A. 579, 45 C.M.R. 353 (1972).

Paragraph 144 *d* prevented a record "made principally with a view to prosecution, or other disciplinary or legal action . . ." from being admitted as a business record. This limitation has been deleted, *but see* Rule 803(8)(B) and its *Analysis.* It should be noted that a record of "regularly conducted activity" is unlikely to have a prosecutorial intent in any event.

The fact that a record may fit within another exception, *e.g.,* Rule 803(8), does not generally prevent it from being admissible under this subdivision although it would appear that the exclusion found in Rule 803(8)(B) for "matters observed by police officers and other personnel acting in a law enforcement capacity" prevents any such record from being admissible as a record of regularly conducted activity. Otherwise the limitation in subdivision (8) would serve no useful purpose. *See also Analysis* to Rule 803(8)(B).

Rule 803(6) is generally similar to the present *Manual* rule but is potentially broader because of its use of the expression "regularly conducted" activity in addition to "business." It also permits records of opinion which are prohibited by ¶ 144 *d* of the present *Manual*. Offsetting these factors is the fact that the Rule requires that the memorandum was "made at or near the time by, or from information transmitted by a person with knowledge . . . ," but ¶ 144 *c* of the present *Manual* rule expressly does not require such knowledge as a condition of admissibility.

[7] Absence of entry in records kept in accordance with the provisions of paragraph (6)

Rule 803(7) is taken verbatim from the Federal Rule. The Rule is similar to ¶¶ 143 *a* (2)(h) and 143 *b* (3) of the present *Manual*.

[8] Public records and reports

Rule 803(8) has been taken generally from the Federal Rule but has been slightly modified to adapt it to the military environment. Rule 803(8)(B) has been redrafted to apply to "police officers and other personnel acting in a law enforcement capacity" rather than the Federal Rule's "police officers and other law enforcement personnel." The change was necessitated by the fact that all military personnel may act in a disciplinary capacity. Any officer, for example, regardless of assignment, may potentially act as a military policeman. The capacity within which a member of the armed forces acts may be critical.

The Federal Rule was also modified to include a list of records that, when made pursuant to a duty required by law, will be admissible notwithstanding the fact that they may have been made as "matters observed by police officers and other personnel acting in a law enforcement capacity." Their inclusion is a direct result of the fact, discussed above, that military personnel may all function within a law enforcement capacity. The committee determined it would be impracticable and contrary to the intent of the Rule to allow the admissibility of records which are truly administrative in nature and unrelated to the problems inherent in records prepared only for purposes of prosecution to depend upon whether the maker was at that given instant acting in a law enforcement capacity. The language involved is taken generally from ¶ 144 *b* of the present *Manual*. Admissibility depends upon whether the record is "a record of a fact or event if made by a person within the scope of his official duties and those duties included a duty to know or ascertain through appropriate and trustworthy channels of information the truth of the fact or event. . . ." Whether any given record was obtained in such a trustworthy fashion is a question for the military judge. The explicit limitation on admissibility of records made "principally with a view to prosecution" now found in ¶ 144 *d* has been deleted.

The fact that a document may be admissible under another exception to the hearsay rule, *e.g.*, Rule 803(6), does not make it inadmissible under this subdivision.

Military Rule of Evidence 803(8) raises numerous significant questions. Rule 803(8)(A) extends to "records, reports, statements, or data complications" of "public offices or agencies, setting forth (A) the activities of the office or agency." The term "public office or agency" within this subdivision is defined to include any government office or agency including those of the armed forces. Within the civilian context, the definition of "public offices or agencies" is fairly clear and the line of demarcation between governmental and private action can be clearly drawn in most cases. The same may not be true within the armed forces. It is unlikely that every action taken by a service member is an "activity" of the department of which he or she is a member. Presumably, Rule 803(8) should be restricted to activities of formally sanctioned instrumentalities roughly similar to civilian entities. For example, the activities of a squadron headquarters or a staff section would come within the definition of "office or agency." Pursuant to this rationale, there is no need to have a military regulation or directive to make a statement of a "public office or agency" under Rule 803(8)(A). However, such regulations or directives might well be highly useful in establishing that a given administrative mechanism was indeed an "office or agency" within the meaning of the Rule.

Rule 803(8)(B) encompasses "matters observed pursuant to duty imposed by law as to which matters there was a duty to report . . . ." This portion of Rule 803(8) is broader than subdivision (8)(A) as it extends to far more than just the normal procedures of an office or agency. Perhaps because of this extent, it requires that there be a specific duty to observe and report. This duty could take the form of a statement, general order, regulation or any competent order.

The exclusion in the Federal Rule for "matters observed by police officers" was intended to prevent use of the exception for valuative reports as the House Committee believed them to be unreliable. Because of the explicit language of the exclusion, normal statutory construction leads to the conclusion that reports which would be within Federal or Military Rule 803(8) but for the exclusion in (8)(B) are not otherwise admissible under Rule 803(6). Otherwise the inclusion of the limitation would serve virtually no purpose whatsoever. There is no contradiction between the exclusion in Rule 803(8)(B) and the specific documents made admissible in Rule 803(8) (and Rule 803(6)) because those documents are not matters "observed by police officers and other personnel acting in a law enforcement capacity." To the extent that they might be so considered, the specific language included by the committee is expressly intended to reject the subdivision (8)(B) limitation. Note, however, that all forms of evidence not within the specific item listing of the Rule but within the (8)(B) exclusion will be inadmissible insofar as Rule 803(8) is concerned, whether the evidence is military or civilian in origin.

A question not answered by Rule 803(8) is the extent to which a regulation or directive may circumscribe Rule 803(8). Thus, if a regulation establishes a given format or procedure for a report which is not followed, is an otherwise admissible piece of evidence inadmissible for lack of conformity with the regulation or directive? The committee did not address this issue in the context of adopting the Rule. However, it would be at least logical to argue that a record not made in substantial conformity with an implementing directive is not sufficiently reliable to be admissible. *See, e.g.,* Rule 403. Certainly, military case law predating the Military Rules may resolve this matter to the extent to which it is not based purely on now obsolete *Manual* provisions. As the modification to subdivision (8) dealing with specific records retains the present *Manual* language, it is particularly likely that present case law will survive in this area.

Rule 803(8)(C) makes admissible, but only against the government, "factual findings resulting from an investigation made pursuant to authority granted by law, unless the sources of information or other circumstances indicate lack of trustworthiness." This provision will make factual findings made, for example, by an Article 32 Investigating Officer or by a Court of Inquiry admissible on behalf of an accused. Because the provision applies only to "factual findings," great care must be taken to distinguish such factual determinations from opinions, recommendations and incidental inferences.

[9]   Records of vital statistics

Rule 803(9) is taken verbatim from the Federal Rule and has no express equivalent in the present *Manual*.

[10]   Absence of public record or entry

Rule 803(10) is taken verbatim from the Federal Rule and is similar to present *Manual* ¶ 143 *a* (2)(g).

[11]   Records of religious organizations; marriage, baptismal, and similar certificates; family records

Rule 802(11)-(13) are all taken verbatim from the Federal Rule and have no express equivalents in the present *Manual*.

[12]   Records of documents affecting an interest in property; statements in documents affecting an interest in property; statements in ancient documents

Rules 803(14)-(16) are taken verbatim from the Federal Rule and have no express equivalent in the present *Manual*. Although intended primarily for civil cases, they all have potential importance to courts-martial.

[13] Market reports, commercial publications

Rule 803(17) is taken generally from the Federal Rule. Government price lists have been added because of the degree of reliance placed upon them in military life. Although included within the general Rule, the committee believed it inappropriate and impracticable not to clarify the matter by specific reference. The Rule is similar in scope and effect to *Manual* ¶ 144 *f* except that it lacks the *Manual's* specific reference to an absence of entries. The effect, if any, of the difference is unclear.

[14] Learned treatises

Rule 803(18) is taken from the Federal Rule without change. Unlike ¶ 138 *e* of the present *Manual,* which allowed use of such statements only for impeachment, this Rule allows substantive use on the merits of statements within treatises if relied upon in direct testimony or called to the expert's attention on cross-examination. Such statements may not, however, be given to the factfinder as exhibits.

[15] Reputation concerning personal or family history; reputation concerning boundaries or general history

Rules 803(19)-(20) are taken without change from the Federal Rule and have no express equivalents in the present *Manual.*

[16] Reputation as to character

Rule 803(21) is taken from the Federal Rule without change. It is similar to ¶ 138 *f* of the present *Manual* in that it creates an exception to the hearsay rule for reputation evidence. "Reputation" and "community" are defined in Rule 405(d) and "community" includes a "military organization regardless of size". Affidavits and other written statements are admissible to show character under Rule 405(c), and, when offered pursuant to that Rule, are an exception to the hearsay rule.

[17] Judgment of previous conviction

Rule 803(22) is taken from the Federal Rule but has been modified to recognize convictions of a crime punishable by a dishonorable discharge, a unique punishment not present in civilian life. *See also* Rule 609 and its *Analysis.*

There is no equivalent to this Rule in military law. Although the Federal Rule is clearly applicable to criminal cases, its original intent was to allow use of a prior criminal conviction in a subsequent civil action. To the extent that it is used for criminal cases, significant constitutional issues are raised, especially if the prior conviction is a foreign one, a question almost certainly not anticipated by the Federal Rules Advisory Committee.

[18] Judgment as to personal, family or general history, or boundaries

Rule 803(23) is taken verbatim from the Federal Rule, and has no express equivalent in the present *Manual*. Although intended primarily for civil cases, it clearly has potential use in courts-martial for such matters as proof of jurisdiction.

[19] Other exceptions

[NOTE: Rule 803(24) has been deleted and incorporated into Rule 807. The Drafter's original Rule 803(24) analysis remains applicable to Rule 807.] Rule 803(24) is taken from the Federal Rule without change. It has no express equivalent in the present *Manual* as it establishes a general exception to the hearsay rule. The Rule implements the general policy behind the Rules of permitting admission of probative and reliable evidence. Not only must the evidence in question satisfy the three conditions listed in the Rule (materiality, more probative on the point than any other evidence which can be reasonably obtained, and admission would be in the interest of justice) but the procedural requirements of notice must be complied with. The extent to which this exception may be employed is unclear. The Article III courts have divided as to whether the exception may be used only in extraordinary cases or whether it may have more general application. It is the intent of the committee that the Rule be employed in the same manner as it is generally applied in the Article III courts. Because the general exception found in Rule 803(24) is basically one intended to apply to highly reliable and necessary evidence, recourse to the theory behind the hearsay Rule itself may be helpful. In any given case, both trial and defense counsel may wish to examine the hearsay evidence in question to determine how well it relates to the four traditional considerations usually invoked to exclude hearsay testimony: How truthful was the original declarant? To what extent were his or her powers of observation adequate? Was the declaration truthful? Was the original declarant able to adequately communicate the statement? Measuring evidence against this framework should assist in determining the reliability of the evidence. Rule 803(24) itself requires the necessity which is the other usual justification for hearsay exceptions.

§ 803.04 Drafters' Analysis (2004)

2004 Amendment: Rule 803(6) was modified based on the amendment to Fed. R. Evid. 803(6), effective 1 December 2000. It permits a foundation for business records to be made through certification to save the parties the expense and inconvenience of producing live witnesses for what is often perfunctory testimony. The Rule incorporates federal statutes that allow certification in a criminal proceeding in a court of the United States. (See, e.g., 18 U.S.C. § 3505, Foreign records of regularly conducted activity.) The Rule does not include foreign records of regularly conducted business activity in civil cases as provided in its Federal Rule counterpart. This Rule works together with Mil. R. Evid. 902(11).

§ 803.05   Annotated Cases

[1]   Constitutional Requirements

United States Supreme Court

Bullcoming v. New Mexico, 2011 U.S. Lexis 4790 (U.S. June 23, 2011); *Michigan v. Bryant*, 131 S.Ct. 1143 (2011); *Melendez-Diaz v. Massachusetts*, 129 S. Ct. 2527 (2009); *Whorton v. Bockting*, 549 U.S. 406 (2007); *Davis v. Washington*, 547 U.S. 813 (2006); and *Crawford v. Washington*, 541 U.S. 36, 53–54 (2004) are annotated above at section 801.05[1][a].

United States Court of Appeals for the Armed Forces

United States v. Crudup, 67 M.J. 92 (C.A.A.F. 2008): The accused was convicted of assault and battery upon his wife, resisting apprehension, and making a false official statement. When the wife refused to testify, her pretrial statement implicating the accused was admitted. The remainder of the government's case consisted of witnesses who observed the crimes and the accused's pretrial admissions. Although the court affirmed, it held that admitting the wife's pretrial statement violated the accused's Sixth Amendment confrontation rights. The court found that the error was harmless beyond a reasonable doubt because the statement was relatively unimportant and cumulative and the government's case was overwhelming. The court added that, although the wife could not have been cross-examined, her credibility was effectively impeached by proof of a previous fraud conviction. *See Delaware v. Van Arsdall*, 475 U.S. 673, 106 S. Ct. 1431, 89 L. Ed. 2d 674 (1986), discussing constitutional error tested for harmlessness.

[2]   Rule 803(1)—Present Sense Impression

[a]   Present Sense Impression—Co-conspirators

Navy-Marine Corps Court of Criminal Appeals

United States v. Clark, 61 M.J. 707 (N.M.Ct.Crim.App. 2005): The accused was convicted of arson and related offenses. After the arson was completed, one of the coconspirators showed a neighbor the glove used to start the fire. The neighbor responded by saying it smelled like lighter fluid, to which the co-conspirator replied, "no sh____." The court found no error in admitting the neighbor's statement as a present sense impression.

[b]   Present Sense Impression—Law Enforcement Interrogations

Army Court of Criminal Appeals

United States v. Brown, 48 M.J. 578 (Army Ct.Crim.App. 1998): Affirming the accused's convictions for being AWOL, adultery, indecent acts with another, and rape, the court held that the trial judge committed non-prejudicial error by admitting the hearsay statements that one CID agent made to another CID agent concerning the accused's pretrial assertions.

Because the record failed to establish the timeliness or immediacy between these events, the evidence should have been excluded.

[c]   Present Sense Impression—Reflection Negates Admission

Army Court of Criminal Appeals

United States v. Green, 50 M.J. 835 (Army Ct.Crim.App. 1999): The court reversed the accused's rape conviction because the trial judge erroneously admitted government evidence including a hearsay statement the victim made after she had lain in bed and contemplated her own misconduct and how reporting the alleged crime might affect her career. Under these circumstances, the reviewing court found that declarant's actions defeated the guarantees of trustworthiness contemplated by this exception.

[3]   Rule 803(2)—Excited Utterance

[a]   Excited Utterance—Statements to Law Enforcement Officials

United States Court of Appeals for the Armed Forces

United States v. Haner, 49 M.J. 72 (C.A.A.F. 1998): The accused was convicted of two counts of assault consummated by battery, and committing an indecent act with his wife. Without objection, trial counsel used statements made by the accused's wife to police officers as excited utterances. Affirming the accused's convictions, the court held that the statements were properly admitted because they were made less than an hour after her ordeal, while she was still in a state of obvious distress.

[b]   Excited Utterance—Constitutional Standards

Supreme Court

White v. Illinois, 502 U.S. 346 (C.A.A.F. 1992): Affirming the accused's conviction for sexually abusing a four-year-old child, the Court held that spontaneous declarations made by the victim shortly after she was assaulted were admissible without the government producing the declarants or establishing the declarants' unavailability. In the Court's opinion, such testimony has sufficient guarantees of reliability to come within a firmly rooted exception to the hearsay rule, thus satisfying the Confrontation Clause.

[c]   Excited Utterance—Nonverbal Conduct as Timely Complaint

Navy-Marine Corps Court of Criminal Appeals

United States v. Reggio, 40 M.J. 694 (N.M.C.M.R. 1994): The accused was convicted of battering his girlfriend's nineteen-month-old child. The government's key witness was a baby-sitter, who described the victim's grotesque injuries and the nonverbal conduct the victim used to indicate that he had been repeatedly punched. The accused contended that this evidence was inadmissible hearsay and should have been suppressed. Affirming the accused's conviction, the court held that, even though the nonverbal statements were made within either hours or days of the assault, it was clear that they were the product of impulse, not reflection or fabrication, and thus admissible.

[d]   Excited Utterance—Relationship to the Residual Exception

United States Court of Appeals for the Armed Forces

United States v. Cox, 45 M.J. 153 (C.A.A.F. 1996): The accused was convicted of sexually abusing his young daughters. Without objection, the installation's chief of military justice and the child's mother testified that, during a pretrial interview, when one of the children was confronted with physical evidence related to the crimes, she became very upset and made statements which incriminated the accused. Affirming the accused's convictions, the court held that the child's emotional and spontaneous reactions strongly suggested trustworthiness, and that the statements were admissible even if they did not strictly qualify as excited utterances.

[e]   Excited Utterance—Time for Reflection—Admitted Statements

United States Court of Appeals for the Armed Forces

United States v. Donaldson, 58 M.J. 477 (C.A.A.F. 2003): The accused was charged with numerous offenses ranging from failure to report to child sexual abuse. In a trial before a military judge alone, the accused entered a mixed plea-pleading guilty to the minor offenses and not guilty to the child sexual abuse offense. Although the victim testified she was unable to relate the specific details of her assault, in order to perfect it's case, the government, over defense objection, was permitted to introduce statements the victim made to her mother approximately 12 hours after the assault. Both at trial and on appeal the accused contended that these statements did not qualify for admission because they were not made under the stress of the startling event, but were the product of trauma caused by having to retell the events to her mother. Affirming the accused's sentence and conviction, the court methodically evaluated the arguments in favor of and against the accused's position, ultimately finding that the distinction raised the accused was not born out by the evidence and the trial judge's resolution of it. In short, the court agreed with the military judge in finding that the victim's statements to her mother qualify under this Rule because they were not reflective and were made under the stress of excitement caused by the event. The court added that in reaching this result it is proper to consider: (1) the lapse of time between the startling event and the statement, (2) whether the statement was made in response to questions, (3) the age of the declarant, (4) the declarant's mental and physical condition at the time the statement was made, (5) the circumstances and characteristics surrounding the event, and (6) the details and subject matter of the statement itself. Crucial to the court's resolution is its opinion, that because of the child's age, the time lag involved in making the statement when coupled with the fact that the accused threatened to kill her and he mother if she told anyone about what happened, is not dispositive of the issue.

United States v. Feltham, 58 M.J. 470 (C.A.A.F. 2003): A military judge sitting alone convicted the accused of forcible sodomy upon another service member. The victim testified in detail concerning the accused's attack which occurred while the victim was sleeping. The accused did not testify and presented no evidence. Part of the government's case included an excited utterance the victim made to his roommate shortly after the offense. Affirming the accused's conviction and sentence, this court held that even though the victim did not make the excited utterance until he drove home from the accused's apartment, the statement was admissible because it met the long established three-part test from *United States v. Arnold*, 25 M.J. 129 (C.M.A. 1987): (1) the statement was spontaneous and not reflective, (2) the event prompting the utterance was startling, and (3) the declarant was under stress caused by the event when he made the statement.

Army Court of Criminal Appeals

United States v. Green, 50 M.J. 835 (Army Ct.Crim.App. 1999): The court reversed the accused's rape conviction because the trial judge erroneously admitted government evidence including a hearsay statement the victim made after she had lain in bed, calmed down, contemplated how the alleged event would affect her career, and then went to sleep. Based on these circumstances, the reviewing court found declarant's actions clearly demonstrated that her utterances were not made while she was still in a state of nervous excitement caused by a startling event.

Navy-Marine Corps Court of Criminal Appeals

United States v. Muirhead, 48 M.J. 527 (N.M.Ct.Crim.App. 1998): The accused was convicted of assaulting his six-year-old stepdaughter with the intent to inflict grievous bodily harm. Eight days after the incident, the child told her day care provider about the assault. The military judge admitted the child care provider's rendition of what the victim said to her, finding that the child made the statement while still "excited by the stress from that event," and under conditions of spontaneity. The court affirmed the accused's conviction, holding that the time passage between an event and a youthful victim's declaration about the event is not necessarily dispositive of whether the hearsay statement should be admitted. Relying on *United States v. Grant*, 38 M.J. 684, 691 (A.F.C.M.R. 1993), the court said that "as the age of the declarant decreases, the more elastic the elapsed time factor [is], within reason."

[f] Excited Utterance—Time for Reflection—Excluded Statements

United States Court of Appeals for the Armed Forces

United States v. Moolick, 53 M.J. 174 (C.A.A.F. 2000): The accused's conviction for rape was reversed because the military judge improperly excluded the accused's excited utterance, "you grabbed me," which was integral to his defense. Using an abuse of discretion standard, the Court found that the error materially prejudiced the accused's substantial rights mainly because the government and defense cases were so even, and the quality of the excluded evidence was high.

United States v. Grant, 42 M.J. 340 (C.A.A.F. 1995): Thirty-six to forty-eight hours passed between the time this six-year-old victim was sexually assaulted by her father and the time she first reported the crimes. Affirming the accused's sodomy convictions, the court held that, because of the interlude, this victim's statements did not possess the excitement or hysteria necessary to qualify them as excited utterances. In the court's opinion, teary eyes and being sad were not enough. However, the court found the evidence trustworthy enough to be admissible under the residual exception.

Air Force Court of Criminal Appeals

United States v. Barrick, 41 M.J. 696 (A.F.Ct.Crim.App. 1995): After she was raped by the accused, the prosecutrix immediately told a friend what had happened. Eighteen hours thereafter, she also told her boyfriend. The court found error, but no prejudice, in the admission of the friends' statements. In the court's opinion, the statements were the product of remorse and regret, not stress from having just been raped.

United States v. Fling, 40 M.J. 847 (A.F.C.M.R. 1994): This is an interlocutory appeal pursuant to Article 62, UCMJ. The accused was charged with sexually abusing his seven-year-old stepdaughter. Before those allegations arose, the victim indicated that she did not want to be reassigned to Germany with her mother and stepfather, but wanted to stay in the U.S. and frequently visit her biological father. Notwithstanding these protestations, the victim moved to Germany. Shortly thereafter, she complained to her teacher that the accused was sexually abusing her. The child was then referred to other school officials. At trial, the victim failed to testify. The military judge excluded the teacher's testimony because he found it was not produced under stress or excitement. The court affirmed the trial judge's decision, but reversed him on several other grounds, and remanded the case for further proceedings.

Army Court of Criminal Appeals

United States v. Armstrong, 30 M.J. 769 (A.C.M.R. 1990): The court set aside a portion of the accused's child sexual abuse conviction because trial counsel failed to establish that the victim's statements were made under the stress of the alleged startling event. Here, the child's revelations occurred four to five days after the alleged offense.

United States v. Ansley, 24 M.J. 926 (A.C.M.R. 1987): The accused's conviction for sexually assaulting his three-year-old daughter was set aside because the events leading up to her out-of-court statements "did not seem to startle or excite the declarant," which left the court questioning whether the victim "was 'bereft of the reflective capacity' to fabricate." The court said in these circumstances "it does not matter whether the event is in fact startling but only that it is perceived to be such by the declarant." Here the victim spoke in unexcited, calm terms when she told her mother about the alleged sexual assault. This lack of stress and indication of having been startled was important to the court, because "the entire family was aware of [the victim's] sexual curiosity and her attempts to view the bodies of the other members of the family." As a result, the court believed "it was possible that [the victim] may have fabricated a portion of her story."

United States v. Lemere, 16 M.J. 682 (A.C.M.R. 1983): Finding error but no prejudice, the court noted that a three-and-a-half-year-old victim's statements of sexual abuse were improperly admitted into evidence because they were not the product of exciting circumstances that would have temporarily stilled the witness's capacity for reflection and fabrication. The utterances here did not occur until the morning after the assault, approximately sixteen hours later.

Navy-Marine Corps Court of Criminal Appeals

United States v. Muirhead, 48 M.J. 527 (N.M.Ct.Crim.App. 1998): The accused was convicted of assaulting his six-year-old stepdaughter with the intent to inflict grievous bodily harm. Eight days after the incident, the child told her day care provider about the assault. The military judge admitted the child care provider's rendition of what the victim said to her, finding that the child made the statement while still "excited by the stress from that event," and under conditions of spontaneity. The court affirmed the accused's conviction, holding that the time passage between an event and a youthful victim's declaration about the event is not necessarily dispositive of whether the hearsay statement should be admitted. Relying on *United States v. Grant,* 38 M.J. 684, 691 (A.F.C.M.R. 1993), the court said that "as the age of the declarant decreases, the more elastic the elapsed time factor [is], within reason."

United States v. Knox, 46 M.J. 688 (N.M.Ct.Crim.App. 1997): The accused was convicted of raping his five-year-old daughter and sodomizing his four-year-old son. The government's evidence included out-of-court statements the victim made to her mother. The statements were offered and accepted as excited utterances even though they concerned sexual abuse events which occurred more than one year before. Reversing the accused's convictions, the court rejected the government's argument that the victims statements were excited utterances because they were the product of a heated and emotional conversation. In the court's opinion, this testimony should have been recognized as "delayed reporting" statements, and excluded because it left too much room for reflection.

United States v. Thomas, 41 M.J. 732 (N.M.Ct.Crim.App. 1995): The accused was convicted of maiming a fellow Marine by hitting him in the head with a tire jack. While receiving medical attention, and in response to repeated questions, the victim ultimately identified the accused as his assailant. The victim testified to those facts at trial. Finding error but no prejudice, the court held that because the victim's statements were not made under the stress of a startling event or condition, but were actually made in response to repeated questioning, they should have been excluded.

United States v. Spychala, 40 M.J. 647 (N.M.C.M.R. 1994): The accused was convicted of sodomy and indecent assault upon his three-year-old step-grandson. Evidence of the crime was discovered more than thirty days after the event, when the victim mentioned it to his uncle. Only the victim's uncle testified concerning this charge. Reversing the accused's convictions, the court held that, to be admissible as an excited utterance, the victim's statements must have been made contemporaneously with the excitement- or stress-causing event. In the court's opinion, because so much time expired, the victim's statements were more reflective than spontaneous, and thus inadmissible.

[g] Excited Utterance—Timely Complaints—Admitted Statements

United States Court of Appeals for the Armed Forces

United States v. Chandler, 39 M.J. 119 (C.M.A. 1994): The accused's wife caught him in bed with a paramour. When his wife attempted to call the military police, the accused attacked, bound, and gagged her. He was ultimately charged with numerous assault and adultery related offenses. The accused pled guilty to all charges except aggravated assault by pointing a loaded firearm at his wife's head. During trial, the military judge allowed a friend to testify concerning what the victim told her about the assault. Affirming all convictions, the court held that the friend's testimony was admissible because the victim uttered the words in question only thirty minutes after she had been assaulted, and she was still clearly upset by what had occurred.

United States v. Lee, 28 M.J. 52 (C.M.A. 1989): After a child sexual abuse victim testified, the government called her mother to establish that, shortly following the crime, her daughter complained about the accused's actions. Affirming the conviction, the court held that the child's protestations were properly admitted and used as corroborative evidence of the victim's trial testimony and as substantive evidence that the reported offenses actually occurred.

United States v. Arnold, 25 M.J. 129 (C.M.A. 1987): Recognizing the "real world" importance of excited utterances in child sexual abuse cases, the court held that a victim's report of an attack "the first thing in the morning after it has happened, in a highly agitated emotional condition" was admissible, because the statement was: (1) "spontaneous, excited [and] impulsive rather than the product of reflection and deliberation," (2) the result of a startling event, (3) made "under the stress of excitement caused by the event," and (4) remarkably similar to the accused's properly warned confession. But the court also indicated that it would not read the hearsay rule so broadly that confrontation rights are denied.

Air Force Court of Criminal Appeals

United States v. Ortiz, 34 M.J. 831 (A.F.C.M.R. 1992): The victim of spouse abuse appeared at a friend's house, nude and hysterical. The friends immediately called the local MP's. After they arrived, the victim identified the accused as her assailant. However, the victim refused to testify at trial. Affirming the accused's conviction, the court held that because of the spouse's obvious physical and emotional condition she had clearly experienced a startling event, and the statements she made thirty minutes thereafter qualified as excited utterances.

United States v. Pearson, 33 M.J. 913, 915 (A.F.C.M.R. 1991): Approximately three hours after the accused baby-sat for a friend's child, the six-year-old indicated to his mother that he had been sexually abused. The accused objected to the parent's trial testimony, claiming that it was not the product of an excited utterance because it lacked spontaneity. Affirming the conviction, the court held that the lapse of time between the startling event and the out-of-court statement was not dispositive, particularly in a child sexual abuse case. The court believed three hours was reasonable because it constituted the first real opportunity complainant had to privately talk with his mother. The court also rejected the accused's contention that the mother's questioning was a barrier to admission, saying that the key issue was trustworthiness, which had been established.

United States v. Kimble, 30 M.J. 892 (A.F.C.M.R. 1990): In this child sexual abuse case, the court held that the victim's late night phone call and statements to a close family friend about what her father had just done to her were properly admitted as excited utterances.

Army Court of Criminal Appeals

United States v. Urbina, 14 M.J. 962 (A.C.M.R. 1982): The court found that a sexual assault victim's statements to her mother about the crime were excited utterances and admissible because they were made a short time after the event and were motivated by the event. The court went on to say that it did not believe the victim's "degree of excitation" was the key to admissibility and that each case ultimately would be decided on its own facts.

Navy-Marine Corps Court of Criminal Appeals

United States v. Miller, 32 M.J. 843 (N.M.C.M.R. 1991): Eighteen hours after being sexually assaulted by her father, and while at school, obviously emotionally upset, the victim told a friend and her guidance counselor about the crimes. Affirming a conviction, the court held that lapses of time are not the primary focus of this rule. In its opinion, because the 12-year-old victim was clearly under stress caused by her father's misconduct, the statements were not reflective or deliberate.

[h] Excited Utterance—Questions to the Declarant

United States Court of Appeals for the Armed Forces

United States v. Pollard, 38 M.J. 41 (C.M.A. 1993): A general court-martial convicted the accused of child sexual abuse. The victim told a friend what happened approximately 30 minutes after the offense. During trial, defense counsel contended that the friend's testimony should have been excluded because it was not the product of spontaneous exclamations, and was made only in response to questions. Reversing the accused's conviction on other grounds, the court affirmed the Court of Military Review's decision (34 M.J.1008) that asking a child what is wrong does not preclude the child's answers from being admissible. Similarly, the victim's tearful outburst that the accused had been sexually assaulting her sufficiently demonstrated spontaneous, excited, and impulsive conduct, justifying admission.

United States v. Jones, 30 M.J. 127 (C.M.A. 1990): At this retrial, the accused pleaded guilty to involuntarily murdering his son. Thereafter, the government unsuccessfully attempted to prove murder. On appeal, the court held that it was error for a government witness to testify about incriminating statements the accused's wife made concerning her husband's conduct because her utterances were in response to the witness's questions, occurred more than twelve hours after the crucial event, were not shown to be directly related to any startling event or condition, and presented her opinion as to an attitude which had gradually developed.

United States v. LeMere, 22 M.J. 61 (C.M.A. 1986): The court held that Rule 803(2) "cannot readily be applied to a situation where a child calmly answers questions asked by her mother, instead of emotionally volunteering information." It specifically rejected the government's contention that "for a small child excitement can continue much longer than for an adult."

Army Court of Criminal Appeals

United States v. Arnold, 18 M.J. 559 (A.C.M.R. 1984): The court upheld admission of a thirteen-year-old girl's out-of-court statements, made hours after she was sexually abused by her father, even though the girl did not testify because: (1) they were made to a school counselor at the girl's request, (2) the counselor did not question the girl but merely listened to her statement, and (3) the girl's "emotional reaction and appearance" during her pretrial statement were "distinctly abnormal demonstrating she was still under the stress of excitement caused by that event."

[4]   Rule 803(3)—Then Existing Mental, Emotional, or Physical Condition

[a]   Existing Conditions—Accused Statements

United States Court of Appeals for the Armed Forces

United States v. Holt, 58 M.J. 227 (C.A.A.F. 2003): After pleading guilty to numerous bad check offenses, the accused was sentenced by a panel of officers to a bad conduct discharge, confinement, and related punishments. During sentencing, the court admitted government documentary evidence including checks with bank markings demonstrating that the accused's account had been closed, debt collection documents, and a pawn ticket. The Court of Criminal Appeals found this evidence to have been properly admitted because it showed the declarant's then existing state of mind. Before the Court of Appeals, government appellate counsel conceded that Rule 803(3) did not properly apply to these exhibits because the markings on the checks and the other exhibits had been created by third parties, not by the accused. The court remanded the case for further review.

United States Air Force Court of Criminal Appeal

United States v. Benson, 48 M.J. 734 (A.F.Ct.Crim.App. 1998): The accused was convicted by a panel of officer and enlisted members of using a loaded firearm to assault a civilian. Government evidence indicated that the accused stated that he wanted to "bust a cap in [the victim's] ass." After making this statement, the accused recanted it and said he was only kidding and had really shot in self defense. Trial counsel moved *in limine* to prevent the defense from using the accused's subsequent statement, and the trial judge excluded the evidence as inadmissible hearsay. Setting aside findings and sentence, the court held that the accused's second statement should have been admitted as evidence of his then-existing state of mind.

[b]   Existing Conditions—Child Sexual Victim Statements

Air Force Court of Criminal Appeals

United States v. Robles, 53 M.J. 783 (A.F.Ct.Crim.App. 2000): The accused was convicted of sexual offenses against his daughter and his step daughter. During the government's case, over defense objection, the victim's mother was allowed to testify about what the victim told her concerning the last sexual assault which had occurred two weeks previously. Affirming the accused's convictions and sentence, the court found that the challenged statements were erroneously but harmlessly admitted because this Rule "does not permit a statement of memory or belief to prove the fact remembered or believed." The court went on to say that had the statements indicated that the victim was afraid to be alone with the accused or that her genitals hurt, the statements would have qualified for admission under this provision.

[c] Existing Conditions—Declarations Connected to Another Person

United States Court of Appeals for the Armed Forces

United States v. Williams, 26 M.J. 487 (C.M.A. 1988): The court held that a defense witness was correctly prohibited from testifying that her blood type was A positive, because the witness learned this fact from her doctor. Out-of-court statements as to someone else's existing condition do not fit within the letter or rationale of this rule.

United States v. Stanley, 21 M.J. 249 (C.M.A. 1986): Although it affirmed a drug distribution conviction, the court said that statements made by another indicating an intention to cover-up the charged offenses should not have been admitted against the accused. Because the declarant was not present during the accused's drug deals, "there was no evidence to indicate what connection, if any, [the declarant] had with the accused on the same or any conspiracy concerning the sale." The court could not say that the declarant's state of mind was indicative of the accused's state of mind.

[d] Existing Conditions—Memory Statements

United States Court of Appeals for the Armed Forces

United States v. Shepard, 38 M.J. 408 (C.M.A. 1993): Part of the government's evidence, in this premeditated murder prosecution, was pre-offense statements the victim/wife made to friends concerning how afraid she was of the accused, and how he had threatened and assaulted her. Trial defense counsel contended that the evidence was really inadmissible extrinsic offense testimony, and unfairly prejudicial. Affirming an unpremeditated murder conviction, the court said that, even though aspects of this evidence should have been excluded as statements of memory or belief, the challenged testimony was cumulative and therefore harmless.

[e] Existing Conditions—State of Mind—Accused

United States Court of Appeals for the Armed Forces

United States v. Roberson, 65 M.J. 43 (C.A.A.F. 2007): The accused was convicted by a special court-martial with members of unauthorized absence, larceny, and forgery. His defense was based on duress. Several witnesses testified that a co-actor threaten to kill the accused if the accused did not steal and forge two of his roommate's checks. The military judge later excluded the testimony of a single defense witness who would have testified about the co-actor's statements to him indicating an intent to harm the accused. The court held that the excluded hearsay statements were admissible under Rule 803(3) because they demonstrated the co-actor's intent to take such steps as were necessary to collect a debt from the accused, including killing him. Thus, the statements would have indicated a basis for the accused's fear and duress defense. However, the error in excluding the statements was deemed harmless.

United States v. Elliott, 23 M.J. 1 (C.M.A. 1986): The court held that hearsay statements may be admitted under Rule 803(3) to demonstrate the accused's "existing state of mind at the time he made the statements—which might then be used to imply that the same innocent state of mind continued" throughout the charged criminal adventure.

Navy-Marine Corps Court of Criminal Appeals

United States v. Clark, 61 M.J. 707 (N.M.Ct.Crim.App. 2005): The accused was convicted of arson and related offenses. After the arson was completed, one of the co-conspirators showed a neighbor the glove used to start the fire, and the neighbor responded by saying it smelled like lighter fluid, to which the co-conspirator replied, "no sh__." Although the trial court admitted the statement as a co-conspirator's statement under Rule 801, the appellate court held that the hearsay exemption did not apply because the conspiracy had ended. Nonetheless, the court held that the statement was admissible under Rule 803(3) as evidence of complicity.

[f]   Existing Conditions—State of Mind—Victim

United States Court of Appeals for the Armed Forces

United States v. Elmore, 33 M.J. 387 (C.M.A. 1991): The accused's conviction for murdering his wife was affirmed. During trial, government counsel introduced three categories of pretrial statements made by the deceased: (1) she was afraid the accused was going to kill her; (2) the accused had threatened to kill her; and (3) the accused had tried to kill her. The court held that only those statements in which the victim recited her fear of the accused, and not those in which she indicated his intent, could be admitted under this provision.

Air Force Court of Criminal Appeals

United States v. Fling, 40 M.J. 847 (A.F.C.M.R. 1994): This is an interlocutory appeal pursuant to Article 62, UCMJ. The accused was charged with sexually abusing his seven-year-old stepdaughter. Before those allegations arose, the victim indicated that she did not want to be reassigned to Germany with her mother and stepfather, but wanted to stay in the United States and frequently visit her biological father. Notwithstanding these protestations, the victim moved to Germany. Shortly thereafter, she complained to her teacher that the accused was sexually abusing her. The child was then referred to the school psychologist and the school nurse, where she retold her story. At trial, the victim failed to testify. The military judge excluded hearsay testimony from the nurse and the psychologist because he found it had not been the product of an existing state of mind, or emotional or physical condition. Affirming part of the trial judge's decision and returning the accused's case for further proceedings, the court held that those hearsay statements concerning the victim's fear of her father should have been admitted.

United States v. Ortiz, 34 M.J. 831 (A.F.C.M.R. 1992): After she was assaulted by her husband, the victim of spousal abuse went to a friend's house naked and hysterical. Shortly thereafter, the MP's arrived. When they took the victim home, she saw her husband and stated, "You are going to kill me." The victim refused to testify at trial, but an MP recounted her statements. Affirming this conviction, the court held that the victim's spontaneous exclamation was a product of her then-existing emotional condition, and was therefore admissible.

Navy-Marine Corps Court of Criminal Appeals

United States v. Reggio, 40 M.J. 694 (N.M.C.M.R. 1994): The accused was convicted of battering his girlfriend's nineteen-month-old child. The government's key witness was a baby-sitter who described the victim's grotesque injuries and the nonverbal conduct the victim used to indicate that he had been repeatedly punched. The accused contended that this evidence was inadmissible hearsay and should have been suppressed. Affirming the accused's conviction, the court held that the victim's nonverbal statements were clearly related to his then-existing physical and emotional pain, and were thus admissible.

[g] Existing Conditions—Victim's Intent and Subsequent Action

Air Force Court of Criminal Appeals

United States v. Garries, 19 M.J. 845 (A.F.C.M.R. 1985): Convicted of premeditated murder, the accused unsuccessfully contended that various government witnesses should not have been permitted to testify as to his wife's intent to leave the service and the accused at a future date. The reviewing court found this evidence admissible for its truth and held that it could be used to help establish the accused's motive to kill his wife.

Navy-Marine Corps Court of Criminal Appeals

United States v. Dodson, 16 M.J. 921 (N.M.C.M.R. 1983): Although the deceased victim's statements concerning his assailant's actions were admitted as excited utterances under Rule 803(2), the reviewing court held "it would have been better to admit such evidence under Mil. R. Evid. 803(3) to prove that [the victim] acted in conformity with his stated intent."

[h] Existing Conditions—Youthful Declarants

Air Force of Military Review

United States v. Lingle, 27 M.J. 704 (A.F.C.M.R. 1989): The accused's conviction for severely and repeatedly beating a three-year-old child was affirmed, despite his contention that the victim's statements to young friends and baby-sitters about the accused's abuse were improperly admitted. The court recognized that evidence of "fresh complaint" falls within this Rule and should be applied to child abuse victims. They went on to say that constitutional guarantees of confrontation are not violated by this "well-rooted and long-established exception to the hearsay rule. . . ." The fact that a child victim did not immediately come forward and report the incident or reported it only after being questioned by other children or day-care providers, was viewed as consistent with the declarant's young age. The court here viewed the child's age as a "positive factor supporting admissibility and assuring trustworthiness as it lessens the degree of skepticism with which we might view [the victim's] motives."

[5]   Rule 803(4)—Statements for Purposes of Medical Diagnosis or Treatment

[a]   Medical Statements—Adult Victim—Purpose for Statements

United States Court of Appeals for the Armed Forces

United States v. Cucuzzella, 66 M.J. 57 (C.A.A.F. 2008): The accused's wife went to see Ms. Linda Moultrie, a registered nurse and the Family Advocacy Nurse at Charleston Air Force Base Family Advocacy Office. Several weeks after the initial contact, the accused's wife called Ms. Moultrie to make an immediate appointment to see her. During that appointment, the accused's wife initially complained about financial problems, but then, without questioning from Ms. Moultrie, began a four hour conversation about the accused sexually abusing her. The accused's wife testified at her husband's subsequent court-martial. Over defense objection, Ms. Moultrie also testified concerning the wife's protestations to her. Affirming the accused's conviction, the court held that Ms. Moultrie qualified as a health care provider because her responsibilities included receiving statements for the purpose of medical diagnosis, treatment, and referral. The court went on to find that the accused's wife made the statements for the purpose of obtaining medical care or diagnosis and had the expectation medical treatment would be provided, and Ms. Moultrie did not play a law enforcement agent role.

United States v. Haner, 49 M.J. 72 (C.A.A.F. 1998): The accused was convicted of assault and battery upon his wife and committing an indecent act with his wife. During trial, defense counsel did not object to incriminating statements the accused's wife made to medical doctors. On appeal, defense counsel contended that this evidence should have been excluded because the accused's wife did not voluntarily seek medical attention from the doctors. Affirming the accused's convictions, the court held that because the medical examination was conducted both to document injuries and to find injuries that might require further treatment, admission of the wife's statements under this Rule was proper.

[b]   Medical Statements—Constitutional Standards

Supreme Court

White v. Illinois, 502 U.S. 346 (1992): Affirming the accused's conviction for sexually abusing a four-year-old child, the Court held that statements made in the course of securing medical treatment were admissible without the government producing the declarants or establishing the declarants' unavailability. In the Court's opinion, such testimony has sufficient guarantees of reliability to come within a firmly rooted exception to the hearsay rule, thus satisfying the Confrontation Clause.

[c]   Medical Statements—Child Victim Cases—Standards Absent

United States Court of Appeals for the Armed Forces

United States v. Siroky, 44 M.J. 394 (C.A.A.F. 1996): Despite his pleas, members convicted the accused of raping, sodomizing, and assaulting his daughter, and assaulting his wife and stepson. The Air Force Court of Criminal Appeals reversed the accused's rape and sodomy convictions because they found that the two-year-old victim's statements to a child therapist did not qualify for admission under this provision. On certification, the court affirmed the decision below and found that the victim's statements had not been made for the purpose of promoting her well-being, or receiving medical treatment. The court relied on the informal and non-medical appearing environment used by the therapist to obtain the victim's statements.

United States v. Armstrong, 36 M.J. 311 (C.M.A. 1993): The victim of child sexual abuse was not present at the accused's retrial. Most of the damaging testimony came from a psychologist who had treated the victim. Reversing one specification, the court held that because the victim's statements were initially made to the prosecutor for trial preparation purposes, they did not fit this exception merely because the psychologist heard them simultaneously.

United States v. Avila, 27 M.J. 62 (C.M.A. 1988): In this child sexual abuse case, statements made by the victim to a psychologist were improperly admitted because the child was intentionally led to believe that the expert witness was not "associated with the social worker or trial counsel—people that her mother had warned her not to talk to because they were bad and trying to take away her daddy." Finding error, the court held that "unless it appears that the child knows at least that the person is rendering care and needs the information in order to help, the rationale for [this hearsay] exception disappears entirely."

Air Force Court of Criminal Appeals

United States v. Hughes, 48 M.J. 700 (A.F.Ct.Crim.App. 1998), *aff'd on other grounds*, 52 M.J. 278 (C.A.A.F. 2000): The accused was convicted of indecent assault upon two females under 16 years of age. After the four-year-old victim was determined to be unavailable for trial, hearsay evidence of her statements to a medical doctor at a hospital was admitted. The court found error but no prejudice in their admission despite the trial court's extensive findings of fact. In the reviewing court's opinion, these medical exception hearsay statements should have been excluded because there was insufficient evidence of record to establish that the declarant knew she was in the hospital for any purpose other than a "regular examination, check-up thing."

Army Court of Criminal Appeals

United States v. Russell, 66 M.J. 597 (Army Ct.Crim.App. 2008): The accused was convicted of raping his 5-year-old daughter. The government's case consisted of the accused's two confessions and statements the victim made to a friend's mother and to a clinical psychologist. The military judge held that the victim was unavailable after she took the stand and stated she was too afraid to testify. The court held that the psychologist's testimony should have been excluded because there was insufficient proof that the victim's statements were made for the purposes of medical diagnosis or treatment and that the victim had some expectation of receiving a medical benefit from that diagnosis or treatment. In reaching this result, the court looked to the following factors: the psychologist had no background information about the victim before seeing her; the consultation occurred in the psychologist's "homey" office play therapy area; the psychologist was dressed in casual civilian attire; he did not explain the medical purpose for their meeting or what the possible medical benefits the victim might receive as a result; and no medical testing occurred. The court found that the error was harmless.

United States v. Henry, 42 M.J. 593 (Army Ct.Crim.App. 1995): In this case the government appealed a military judge's decision excluding the child sexual abuse victim's statements to medical treatment personnel. The court held that the trial judge properly exercised his discretion because the victim's statements were not made with the expectation of receiving medical benefits, but were collected for the purpose of facilitating a criminal investigation.

United States v. Dunlap, 39 M.J. 835 (A.C.M.R. 1994): After seeing a school puppet show designed to identify children who had been sexually abused, a six-year-old victim told the school nurse about her father's misconduct. When the victim recanted her statements, the nurse testified to what the victim had told her. Reversing the accused's conviction, the court held that the victim's statements were not made for the purpose of receiving medical attention, but for the purpose of reporting a crime, and were thus inadmissible.

United States v. Armstrong, 33 M.J. 1011 (A.C.M.R. 1991): On retrial, the accused was convicted of sodomizing his six-year-old daughter. A significant portion of the government's evidence included two statements from a psychologist. The first was made in the doctor's office, but with trial counsel present. Concerning this evidence, the psychologist indicated he was in charge of the session and that it was for the victim's benefit. The second statement, containing almost the same information, was made by the victim to the psychologist during their following session, without anyone else present. Affirming the conviction, the court said it was reluctant to conclude that statements made in trial counsel's presence were primarily for the purpose of medical treatment, and that they should have been suppressed. However, the second statement was admissible because there was sufficient evidence to establish that the victim knew she was talking with a doctor, and that he was there to help her.

Navy-Marine Corps Court of Criminal Appeals

United States v. Quarles, 25 M.J. 761 (N.M.C.M.R. 1987): Reversing the accused's child sexual abuse conviction, the court held that a clinical psychologist's recantation of the victim's incriminating statements was improperly admitted. The Court went on to say that:

> Military judge did find that [the Department of Social Services] had a valid medical purpose for seeking treatment, his ruling admitting the statements overlooked the requirement that the point of focus in a Mil. R. Evid. 803(4) analysis is the subjective view of the declarant. This record fails to demonstrate that the children [ages four, five and six] knew why they were talking to [the psychologist] or that their truthful answers to his questions were necessary for their treatment.

The court also said that, even if the children were seeing a doctor, their statements would still be inadmissible because of their "contradictory nature." The court recognized that the existing law does not require children to " 'fully' understand the nature of their visit to the doctor. . . ."

[d]   Medical Statements—Child Victim Cases—Standards Met

United States Court of Appeals for the Armed Forces

United States v. Rodriguez-Rivera, 63 M.J. 372 (C.A.A.F. 2006): At trial, the defense objected to the child victim's hearsay statements to a pediatrician. The statements, implicating the accused, were made during an interview by a doctor specializing in child abuse cases. The doctor had been recommended to the parents by the trial counsel. In affirming the conviction, the court held that trial counsel's actions were not a critical factor in deciding whether the medical exception applied. Instead, the court found the critical question to be whether the victim had some expectation of treatment when she talked to the care-givers. The court held that the record here clearly supported a finding that she did.

United States v. Donaldson, 58 M.J. 477 (C.A.A.F. 2003): The accused was charged with numerous offenses ranging from failure to report to child sexual abuse. In a trial before a military judge alone, the accused entered a mixed plea-pleading guilty to the minor offenses and not guilty to the child sexual abuse offense. Although the victim testified she was unable to relate the specific details of her assault, in order to perfect its case the government, over defense objection, was permitted to introduce statements the victim made to a child clinical psychologist. Both at trial and on appeal the accused claimed those statements should have been excluded because there was insufficient evidence to establish that the victim had some expectation of treatment when she talked to the psychologist. Affirming the accused's convictions and sentence, the court agreed that although there was little evidence indicating that the victim understood she would receive some medical benefit from talking with the psychologist, her youth coupled with both her mother's explanations and those of the psychologist herself were sufficient to support the military judge's determination.

United States v. Hollis, 57 M.J. 74 (C.A.A.F. 2002): The accused was convicted of rape, forcible sodomy and indecent acts upon his five-year-old daughter. The key evidence against the accused came from a medical doctor and members of her staff who took statements from the victim, which indicated that a crime had been committed and that the accused had committed the crime. At trial and on appeal, the accused contended this testimony should have been excluded because there was no proof the victim understood she was being treated for sexual abuse or that she would receive any medical benefit for her ailments as a result of the medical staff's questioning. Rejecting the accused's position that the medical interviews were conducted for the purpose of collecting incriminating evidence against him, the court held that, consistent with the military judge's special findings, the evidence clearly demonstrated that the victim was aware of the circumstance for which she was at the doctor's office, she recognized the doctor and the doctor's staff as medical providers, and understood they were there to provide treatment. In resolving this issues the court highlighted that these are preliminary questions of fact which should be initially resolved pursuant to Rule 104(a), and that the court reviews the military judge's decision for abuse of discretion using a clearly erroneous stand and that all conclusions of law are reviewed *de novo.*

United States v. Robbins, 52 M.J. 455 (C.A.A.F. 2000): Affirming the accused's child sexual abuse convictions, the court held that statements the victim and her mother made to a clinical social worker who was part of a "child sexual abuse team," about the accused's criminal acts, were admissible in evidence because the team's primary purpose for collecting the statements was to make referrals for further counseling.

United States v. Kelley, 45 M.J. 275 (C.A.A.F. 1996): Tried before a military judge sitting alone, the accused was convicted of committing indecent acts upon his six-year-old daughter. Part of the government's evidence included testimony from a licensed family counselor who related the victim's statements about how the accused sexually abused her. On appeal, defense counsel contended that this evidence should have been excluded because the record did not establish that the victim suffered from any disorder or that she understood talking to the psychologist would alleviate any malady. Affirming the accused's conviction, the court found that the victim believed if she talked with the psychologist the information she provided would help him "heal" her. The court went on to say that whether the patient had the requisite state of mind and expectation for receiving a medical benefit is a preliminary question of fact for the trial judge to resolve under Rule 104(a).

United States v. Cox, 45 M.J. 153 (C.A.A.F. 1996): The accused's conviction for sexually abusing his young daughters was affirmed. Over defense counsel's trial objection, the government called a therapist who testified about incriminating statements the victims made concerning their father's conduct. Finding that the therapist's statements were properly admitted, the court held that there was a medical purpose for the children's visits, and that the victims expected to be helped by visiting the therapist. The court went on to say that the basis for these findings need not rest solely on the children's testimony, but could also be supported by the mother or therapist.

United States v. Ureta, 44 M.J. 290 (C.A.A.F. 1996): After being sexually abused by her father, the victim reported all offenses to military authorities, a medical doctor, and a social worker. Thereafter, the victim refused to cooperate or testify. At trial, both the medical doctor and the social worker were permitted to explain what the victim had told them. Affirming the accused's rape and carnal knowledge convictions, the court said that both witness's statements were admissible because the victim spoke to them for the purpose of medical diagnosis or treatment, and that the victim had some expectation of receiving a medical benefit as a result. The court dismissed the accused's contentions that the statements were inadmissible because each witness appreciated the legal and investigative implications of obtaining them and making them replete.

United States v. Clark, 35 M.J. 98 (C.M.A. 1992): The accused was convicted of sexually abusing his 5-year-old daughter. He contended that her hearsay statements to a medical doctor should have been excluded because, among other things, they were not made for medical assistance purposes. Affirming these convictions, the court held that the record of trial clearly demonstrated the victim knew she was speaking with a doctor, and was in the hospital to receive treatment for a problem. The court went on to say there was no indication the witness's statements were prompted by any other motivation.

United States v. White, 25 M.J. 50 (C.M.A. 1987): The government's child psychology expert was permitted to relate what his sexually abused juvenile patients told him because: (1) the extrajudicial statements were "clearly" made with the "expectation of receiving medical benefit from the medical diagnosis or treatment that [was] being sought," (2) the psychologist's examination of the victims was not "more oriented to his testimony at trial than to medical diagnosis or treatment," and (3) the victims' motive in talking to the psychologist was "that if [they gave] truthful information, it would help [them] to be healed." In the court's opinion, "such medical history is inherently reliable."

Air Force Court of Criminal Appeals

United States v. Cox, 42 M.J. 647 (A.F.Ct.Crim.App. 1995): A general court-martial convicted the accused of sexually abusing his two young daughters. Both girls spoke with a social worker who was allowed to relate their account of the accused's criminal conduct. Affirming the accused's convictions, the court held that each victim expected some medical benefit from speaking with the social worker, and that the social worker's interviews were medically-related. The fact that the social worker was not a medical doctor, and that her office had none of the trappings of a medical doctor's office, were considered irrelevant.

United States v. Lingle, 27 M.J. 704 (A.F.C.M.R. 1989): Affirming the accused's conviction, the court held that a three-year-old victim of child abuse: (1) possessed the "cognitive ability to reason in abstract terms, *i.e.*, if I tell the doctor what hurts, then I'll get medical treatment . . ." and (2) would be allowed to identify the accused as her assailant. The court viewed its decision as consistent with the "trend" in civilian and military decisions.

Army Court of Criminal Appeals

United States v. Marchesano, 67 M.J. 535 (Army Ct.Crim.App. 2008): The accused was convicted of sexually abusing his daughter's 7-year-old friend. Part of the government's proof consisted of statements the daughter made to a medical doctor about the accused sexually assaulting her. The statements were used by the government for Rule 414 purposes. The court held that, because the doctor very carefully explained who he was and what his medical role would be, the child's subsequent statements were admissible as they were made for the purpose of medical diagnosis or treatment, and there was an expectation that medical treatment would be provided. The court went on to say that sexual abuse cases with very young victims are particularly challenging because, while there is a recognition that some relaxation of the rules is required, that recognition does not eliminate the need to satisfy the test for admissibility.

United States v. Fink, 32 M.J. 987 (A.C.M.R. 1991): Finding that pretrial statements made by a child victim with limited cognitive abilities did not qualify as excited utterances under Rule 803(2), the court held that they were admissible under Rule 803 (4), because they were made to a school nurse after the victim was told to see her for sex problems. In the court's opinion, these events demonstrated that the 12-year-old's decision was motivated by a desire to obtain help for her emotional distress.

United States v. Edens, 29 M.J. 755 (A.C.M.R. 1989): The court held that statements made by two child abuse victims to a board-certified pediatrician were admissible under Rule 803(4). The victims were aware that their statements were part of their medical care, the questions by the doctor were pertinent to his diagnosis and treatment, and there was no indication that the statements were made for any purpose other than to answer those questions.

Navy-Marine Corps Court of Criminal Appeals

United States v. Schnable, 58 M.J. 643 (N.M.Ct.Crim.App. 2003): The accused was convicted of indecent acts upon his daughter. At trial, the military judge permitted a nurse to testify about what the victim told her during a sexual assault examination. Affirming the accused's findings and sentence, the court held that the statements were made for the purposes of medical diagnosis and that the victim had an expectation of receiving a medical benefit as a result of the diagnosis. The court went on to say that when the declarant is a child the traditional adult standards should be relaxed. Statements made for medical purposes find reliability in the state of mind of the declarant, and are premised on the assumption that a patient will tell the truth to a health care provider in order to receive the best possible treatment. As a result, proving the declarant's state of mind is the crucial foundational element. On these facts the court found that because the nurse identified herself to the declarant and took a medical history in a hospital treatment room the record supports finding that the victim's intent was to promote her own well-being.

United States v. Paaluhi, 50 M.J. 782 (N.M.Ct.Crim.App. 1999): The accused was convicted of sexually abusing his 15-year-old daughter. Part of the government's evidence included statements the victim made to a "psychotherapist" whom the court identified as having a bachelor's degree in psychology and a master's degree in clinical social work. Applying the standards established in *United States v. Faciane,* 40 M.J. 399 (C.M.A. 1994), the court found that the victim's statements were made for the purposes of medical diagnosis or treatment and that the victim had an expectation of receiving medical benefit from the treatment or diagnosis being sought. The court went on to say that Rule 803(4) is not limited to statements made only to licensed physicians, but applies to most other health care professionals as well.

United States v. Kelley, 42 M.J. 769 (N.M.Ct.Crim.App. 1995): This accused was convicted of rape, sodomy, indecent liberties, and indecent acts with his 6-year-old daughter. Although the victim was available and testified, statements she made to a state-licensed child counselor explaining the accused's conduct were admitted over defense objection. Affirming the accused's convictions, the court held that this victim's request to "help her with taking out anger on others," was convincing proof she understood the medical process and was there to obtain help.

[e]   Medical Statements—Child Victim Cases—Standards Relaxed

United States Court of Appeals for the Armed Forces

United States v. Quigley, 40 M.J. 64 (C.M.A. 1994): Affirming the accused's child sexual abuse conviction, the court held that, even though very young children may not have the same understanding or incentive as adults for making statements to persons providing medical benefits, it was clear on the record that this five-year-old victim understood she was seeing a doctor for help. The court went on to say that, as occurred here, it is permissible for witnesses other than the patient to provide the requisite foundational information.

United States v. Edens, 31 M.J. 267 (C.M.A. 1990): In affirming the accused's convictions for sexually abusing his five-year-old daughter and her four-year-old friend, the court recognized that, while the quantum of proof necessary to satisfy this Rule may be relaxed, evidence cannot be admitted unless the proponent establishes that the child was aware she was being treated for sexual abuse. In the court's opinion, without this foundation, the entire premise of reliability is dissipated.

United States v. Williamson, 26 M.J. 115 (C.M.A. 1988): Reversing the accused's conviction for sexually molesting his daughter, the court held that, when Rule 803(4) is used, counsel must demonstrate that offered hearsay statements were made while the victim was obtaining treatment and that the victim had some expectation of receiving medical benefit from the diagnosis or treatment. The court also stated it would relax the proof required when a child was being treated.

Air Force Court of Criminal Appeals

United States v. Fling, 40 M.J. 847 (A.F.C.M.R. 1994): This is an interlocutory appeal pursuant to Article 62, UCMJ. The accused was charged with sexually abusing his seven-year-old stepdaughter. Before those allegations arose, the victim indicated that she did not want to be reassigned to Germany with her mother and stepfather, but wanted to stay in the United States and frequently visit her biological father. Notwithstanding these protestations, the victim moved to Germany. Shortly thereafter, she complained to her teacher that the accused was sexually abusing her. The child was eventually taken to the local military hospital's chief of pediatrics, where she retold her story. At trial, the victim failed to testify. The military judge excluded hearsay statements from the pediatrician because he found that the child had not presented herself for medical treatment. Finding error and returning the accused's case for further proceedings, the court held that it was "absurd" to suggest that a seven-year-old would be able to present herself for medical treatment without the assistance of her parents or an adult. Under these circumstances, the court found no evidence suggesting that this doctor was not primarily interested in diagnosing and treating his patient.

United States v. Dean, 28 M.J. 741 (A.F.C.M.R. 1989): In this child sexual abuse case, the court held that the quantum of proof necessary to admit a six-year-old victim's statement to health care professionals may be "relaxed." The court said that "[w]hen the offense to which medical hearsay relates is abuse of a young child, an inflexible application of a test . . . may result in unnecessary suppression of admissible evidence—not because the evidence should not be heard, but because the test is not capable of handling all the situations to which it is applied."

Army Court of Criminal Appeals

United States v. O'Rourke, 57 M.J. 636 (Army Ct.Crim.App. 2002): A military judge convicted the accused of indecent acts with a child and false swearing. Over defense objections, statements the victim made to a social worker and medical doctor were admitted under this exception. Affirming the accused's convictions and sentence, the court held that:

> Under proper circumstances, "statements made to psychologists, social workers, and other health care professionals" may be included under Mil. R. Evid. 803(4). *United States v. Morgan,* 40 M.J. 405, 408 (C.M.A. 1994). Although there may be some relaxation of the quantum of proof required in situations where a child is being treated, the facts still must support a finding that both prongs of the test are met. *See United States v. Williamson,* 26 M.J. 115 (C.M.A. 1988).

Here the court said the victim's statements were admissible because she understood that the social worker provided services similar to those of other health care professionals, she desired to seek help from the social worker, and her responses were voluntary and to open-ended questions.

[f] Medical Statements—Expert Witness Defined

United States Court of Appeals for the Armed Forces

United States v. Nelson, 25 M.J. 110 (C.M.A. 1987): In this child sexual abuse court-martial, the government's case consisted of evidence from the six-year-old victim, a pediatrician, and a psychologist. Both expert witnesses supported the victim's testimony. Affirming the conviction, the court held that Rule 803(4)'s "applicability is not limited to statements made to medical doctors and may include statements to psychologists."

United States v. Welch, 25 M.J. 23 (C.M.A. 1987): The accused unsuccessfully contended that a 12-year-old sexual assault victim's pretrial statements to a Ph.D. psychologist should have been suppressed because: (1) a clinical psychologist is not a medical doctor, and (2) "the victim's motive in making the statements was not to seek medical attention but to perfect a complaint of sexual abuse. . . ." The court held that Rule 803(4) "specifically envisions" that statements need not be made to physicians alone and that statements made to family members, to hospital attendants, and during ambulance drives may also qualify. The court relied on the military judge's special findings of a diagnostic and treatment purpose for the statement.

Air Force Court of Criminal Appeals

United States v. Tornowski, 29 M.J. 578 (A.F.C.M.R. 1989): Affirming this child sexual abuse conviction, the court held that it was proper for a psychiatric social worker to testify that counseling helped the victim "feel better," even though the victim did not address the matter during her testimony. The court went on to say that once the expert witness had established the required foundation, she could then testify about "statements concerning the offenses made by . . . the victim in the course of therapeutic sessions."

United States v. Williamson, 23 M.J. 706 (A.F.C.M.R. 1986): Affirming the accused's sexual child abuse conviction, the court held that an expert witness (social worker) could testify concerning how the crimes were committed and that the accused committed them. *See also United States v. Deland,* 22 M.J. 70 (C.M.A. 1986) (statements made in a therapeutic environment are admissible under this Rule). This expert witness was particularly helpful because counsel effectively used her to explain how she knew the victim's statements were not the product of coaching and that the child "comprehended the sexuality of her experience."

Army Court of Criminal Appeals

United States v. Austin, 32 M.J. 757 (A.C.M.R. 1991): Affirming the accused's conviction for sexually abusing his daughter, the court held that the victim's pretrial statements to a family counselor were made for the purpose of receiving medical treatment, and were thus admissible. The court also said that testimony from social workers, clinical psychologists, and psychotherapists, qualify for admission.

Navy-Marine Corps Court of Criminal Appeals

United States v. Cottriel, 21 M.J. 535 (N.M.C.M.R. 1985): The court held that because this Rule and its "federal counterpart contain no language which strictly limits its applicability to physicians," a social worker's "otherwise hearsay testimony, made for the purpose of medical diagnosis" may be admitted.

[g] Medical Statements—Identifying the Accused

United States Court of Appeals for the Armed Forces

United States v. Arruza, 26 M.J. 234 (C.M.A. 1988): In this child sexual abuse case, the court said that admissible medical history evidence includes a psychiatrist's statements "regarding what the accused had allegedly done to" the victim.

Air Force Court of Criminal Appeals

United States v. Ortiz, 34 M.J. 831 (A.F.C.M.R. 1992): In this spousal abuse case, the issue was whether a treating physician could testify that the victim identified the accused as her assailant. Affirming the accused's conviction, the court held that, even though the victim was unavailable, perpetrator identification testimony was admissible because it addressed two important medical concerns: (1) whether the spouse could recuperate at home, or must be sent to a safe facility; and (2) whether psychiatric assistance was necessary because a family member committed the assault.

Army Court of Criminal Appeals

United States v. Rudolph, 35 M.J. 622 (A.C.M.R. 1992): After the accused sexually abused his stepdaughter, the child was taken to a local hospital where she provided skin and hair samples, and then spoke with a doctor and his nurse. The accused contended that the victim's statements identifying him as her attacker should have been excluded because they were made to the nurse, and were not uttered in anticipation of receiving medical help. Affirming the accused's conviction, the court held that: (1) the victim's statements were made to her doctor; (2) he properly asked the accused's daughter who committed the offenses, and how often they occurred, in order to treat the victim's mental and physical problems; (3) such questions and answers are admissible because they are customary in patient care; and (4) the victim understood she was speaking with a doctor for her own medical help.

United States v. Edens, 29 M.J. 755 (A.C.M.R. 1989): Affirming the accused's conviction for sexually molesting his daughters, the court found it was proper for a pediatrician to testify about the victims' pretrial statements identifying the accused as their assailant. In the court's opinion, even though Dr. Parker interviewed the girls "to determine if sexual abuse had occurred, and if so, to design and administer a treatment plan for the victims and their families," his testimony was admissible because the victims were "sufficiently aware that their statements were part of their medical diagnosis and treatment." The court indicated it might have ruled the other way if "the children's motives were other than to respond to the doctor's questions."

United States v. Brown, 25 M.J. 867 (A.C.M.R. 1988): Stating that it was "concerned" about the military judge's refusal to admit expert medical diagnosis and treatment evidence establishing the accused's responsibility for assaults on his children, the court thoroughly documented the need for and admissibility of such evidence. The court wrote that:

> [I]nnumerable case histories in the medical profession conclude that an abused child becomes an abusing parent. . . . When a child is abused by a parent or other primary care provider, it is obvious that the injury is not merely physical in nature. . . . Failure to determine the identity of the perpetrator of an apparent child abuse injury prevents the diagnosis of potentially serious psychological and emotional injury, thereby hindering proper medical treatment and allowing recurrence of abuse.

Navy-Marine Corps Court of Criminal Appeals

United States v. Salinas, 65 M.J. 927 (N.M.Ct.Crim.App. 2008): The accused was convicted of raping and sodomizing his 6-year-old step daughter. The victim and her Ph.D. psychologist testified at trial. Affirming the accused's convictions, the court held that the victim's statements to her psychologist identifying the accused as her assailant were made for the purpose of medical treatment or diagnosis and that she had some expectation of receiving a medical benefit from making them. The court went on to say that because the accused lived in the same house with the victim, the psychologist needed to explore identity in order to properly structure the victim's treatment.

[h]   Medical Statements—Mental or Physical Ailments

United States Court of Appeals for the Armed Forces

United States v. Deland, 22 M.J. 70 (C.M.A. 1986): A psychiatrist was permitted to testify about what a sexually abused child told him, because the statements were made as part of an effort to obtain medical treatment. The court emphasized that it is the patient's motive for talking to the doctor, not the mother's motive for bringing the child to the doctor, that is important for determining whether an incentive to tell the truth existed. The court specifically refused to distinguish psychiatrists from other doctors in applying this provision and went on to hold that the doctor's identification of the assailant here was vital to diagnosis and was therefore admissible.

[i]   Medical Statements—Relation to Rule 404(b)

Air Force Court of Criminal Appeals

United States v. Hancock, 38 M.J. 672 (A.F.C.M.R. 1993): Affirming the accused's conviction for assaulting his wife, the court held that no error occurred when the military judge allowed a treating physician to testify about the victim's charged and uncharged wounds. In the court's opinion, such testimony was harmless because neither counsel commented on it, and the record justifies believing that the members gave it no consideration.

[j]   Medical Statements—Smuggling Hearsay

United States Court of Appeals for the Armed Forces

United States v. Schap, 49 M.J. 317 (C.A.A.F. 1998): The accused was convicted of a particularly gruesome murder. He defended, in part, on mental responsibility grounds. However, trial defense counsel was prohibited from examining their forensic psychiatrist concerning statements the accused made during approximately 15 hours of treatment and interviews. Affirming the conviction, the court held that the accused's out-of-court-statements to his psychiatrist did not qualify for admission under either this Rule, or Rule 703's provisions for admitting the data or facts upon which an expert bases his opinion testimony. Recognizing the evidence as having "conduit problems," the court went on to say that it would not allow defense counsel to "smuggle" before the finders of fact hours of hearsay testimony without subjecting the declarant to "the crucible of cross-examination."

[6] Rule 803(5)—Recorded Recollection

United States Court of Appeals for the Armed Forces

United States v. Gans, 32 M.J. 412 (C.M.A. 1991): The court explained how counsel can use writings to refresh memory under Rule 612, and admit past recorded recollection under this exception. *See* our discussion of this case in the Editorial Comments, *above.*

Air Force Court of Criminal Appeals

United States v. Turner, 30 M.J. 1183 (A.F.C.M.R. 1990): Affirming the accused's larceny conviction, the court held that a police investigator was properly allowed to use his notes in testifying about the accused's pretrial statements. The witness lacked independent memory, and the court said that "even after referring to the [notes, this witness] could not remember a statement attributed to the accused."

[7] Rule 803(6)—Records of Regularly Conducted Activity (Business Records)

[a] Business Records—Absence Without Leave Proof

Navy-Marine Corps Court of Criminal Appeals

United States v. Jones, 46 M.J. 535 (N.M.Ct.Crim.App. 1997): Lieutenant Jones was convicted of numerous absence without leave, bad check, and cocaine offenses. NAVPERS 1070/606's were the government's main evidence to prove the absences without leave. Reversing the Article 86 violations, the court held that the "page 6" entries should not have been admitted because applicable regulations prohibited using them for officers, they were not timely recorded, and they were made at the staff judge advocate's request resulting in the court finding a lack of indicia demonstrating reliability.

[b] Business Records—Bank Records

United States Court of Appeals for the Armed Forces

United States v. Foerster, 65 M.J. 120 (C.A.A.F. 2007): This case was tried before the Supreme Court's decision in *Crawford v. Washington*, 541 U.S. 36 (2004). However, the court noted that *Crawford* applies to all cases pending on direct review. At the accused's court-martial on larceny and check forgery charges, the victim was unable to testify because he was deployed to Kuwait pending redeployment to Iraq. Part of the government's case included a Fort Sill National Bank "Affidavit of Unauthorized Signature (Forgery Affidavit)" completed by the victim at the bank's request when the victim first reported the crimes and requested reimbursement. Bank officials testified that the form was maintained by the bank and used by them primarily to prevent future crimes. It was released to military authorities as part of the military's criminal investigation. Defense counsel objected *in limine* to the form as a violation of his Sixth Amendment rights, arguing that it was made primarily for the purpose of prosecution and was inadmissible under any hearsay exception. Affirming the Criminal Court of Appeal's decision, the court held that the forgery affidavit was not testimonial and that it was made in compliance with Rule 803(6). The court relied on three factors in distinguishing between testimonial and nontestimonial hearsay: (1) whether the statement was elicited by or made in response to law enforcement or prosecutorial inquiry; (2) whether the statement involved more than a routine and objective cataloging of unambiguous factual matters; and (3) whether the primary purpose for making or eliciting the statement was the production of evidence with an eye toward trial. Here the statement was made at the request of bank officials and in compliance with their own standard operating procedures. The document listed only objective facts and events. And, a contextual analysis indicated that the document was made primarily for the bank's own crime prevention purposes. The court went on to say that while "affidavits" are viewed as presumptively testimonial, the fact that this document was not made by or to law enforcement or government officials or to private individuals acting in concert with or at the behest of law enforcement or government officials removed it from the suspect category. Finally, the court held that a record made by a third party (the victim) that is adopted by a business (the bank) may be admitted under Rule 803(6) when the record is prepared by the second entity in the normal course of business, the second entity shows that it relied on the record, and there are attendant circumstances indicating the document's trustworthiness. Here, bank officials testified to the fraud prevention purpose for the record and its preparation and use in the normal course of their business.

United States v. Harris, 55 M.J. 433 (C.A.A.F. 2001): The accused was convicted of larceny of checks, and forging the stolen checks. At trial, the government was successful in admitting the bank's logbook. The accused argued that the logbook was improperly authenticated, therefore inadmissible. The Navy-Marine Corps Court of Criminal Appeals affirmed the conviction. The court held that a logbook used to record the handling of security videotapes at a bank was admissible under the business record exception to the hearsay rule. The Court went on to say that the logbook was admissible based on the testimony of both the bank fraud investigator and the bank teller, who testified that the logbook was routinely kept in the course of business, and because the entries in the logbook were made as part of a regular procedure. The court also noted that a military judge's decision to admit evidence is reviewed for abuse of discretion, and there was no abuse of discretion in this case.

United States v. Brandell, 35 M.J. 369 (C.M.A. 1992): The court reversed the accused's convictions for writing bad checks because trial counsel failed to lay an adequate foundation for admitting them, and other documentary evidence. In the court's opinion, bank records are not admissible under this provision unless a custodian or other qualified witness testifies.

United States v. Garces, 32 M.J. 345 (C.M.A. 1991): Affirming the accused's conviction for fraudulently using another's credit card, the court held that business entries establishing the crime were properly validated by bank and merchant witnesses, even though in some cases those witnesses were not the custodians of the documents or the ones who made the entries.

Air Force Court of Criminal Appeals

United States v. Dean, 13 M.J. 676 (A.F.C.M.R. 1982): Charged with multiple worthless check offenses, the accused unsuccessfully objected to the introduction of the checks. Relying on Rule 803(6), the reviewing court found that banks are business activities within the Rule's definition, and that the checks in question were properly created records of that organization. In our view, checks are not hearsay under Rule 801(c). They are not admitted for their truth; rather they are admitted because they were made and cashed. Authenticating them may be a problem under Rule 901, but they need not satisfy a hearsay exception to be admitted. On the other hand, if a bank no longer has the checks but has some record of them, this may qualify as a business record.

Navy-Marine Corps Court of Criminal Appeals

United States v. Duncan, 30 M.J. 1284 (N.M.C.M.R. 1990): During his court-martial for larcenies from an automatic teller machine, the accused contended that the victim's testimony and use of computer-generated bank statements to establish the exact amount of each theft was improper. Modifying and affirming the conviction, the court held that admitting entirely computer-generated printouts of transactions in which the keystrokes themselves are the issue does not raise hearsay issues. The court said that, under these circumstances, the proponent need only authenticate the process by which the document was prepared to show that it accurately reflects the input data. *See* our discussion of Rule 901.

[c] Business Records—Computer Records

Navy-Marine Corps Court of Criminal Appeals

United States v. Casey, 45 M.J. 623 (N.M.Ct.Crim.App. 1996): The accused was charged with numerous offenses including larceny from the Bachelor Enlisted Quarters' receipts. The government established these thefts by using the BEQ's computer records. Trial counsel's foundation demonstrated that the records had been made by a person with knowledge, at or near the time of the incident recorded, and in the course of regularly conducted business. Defense counsel responded by showing that the computer system was unreliable, subject to tampering, and often produced inaccurate records. Affirming the accused's convictions, the court held that the computer records were properly admitted because the accused's proof did not demonstrate that the source of the information or the circumstances used to prepare it demonstrated a lack of trustworthiness. The court went on to say that "A computer system does not have to be foolproof, or even the best available, to produce records of adequate reliability."

[d]   Business Records—Constitutional Requirements

United States Supreme Court

Bullcoming v. New Mexico, 2011 U.S. Lexis 4790 (U.S. June 23, 2011); *Michigan v. Bryant*, 131 S.Ct. 1143 (2011); *Melendez-Diaz v. Massachusetts*, 129 S. Ct. 2527 (2009); *Whorton v. Bockting*, 549 U.S. 406 (2007); *Davis v. Washington*, 547 U.S. 813 (2006); and *Crawford v. Washington*, 541 U.S. 36, 53–54 (2004) are annotated above at section 801.05[1][a].

United States Court of Appeals for the Armed Forces

United States v. Gardinier, 65 M.J. 60 (C.A.A.F. 2007): A military judge convicted the accused of taking indecent liberties with and committing indecent acts upon his underage daughter. Part of the government's evidence included a "Forensic Medical Examination Form" which was completed by a "sexual assault nurse examiner" at the request of civilian police authorities. The nurse testified at trial concerning the patient's history, including an identification of the accused as her assailant, specifics of the forensic examination, and recommendations for follow-on medical treatment. Relying on *Crawford v. Washington* (2004) and *United States v. Rankin*, 64 M.J. 348 (C.A.A.F. 2007), the court reversed the accused's convictions and found that both the medical form and the nurse's testimony were testimonial in nature as they: (1) were elicited by or made in response to law enforcement or prosecutorial inquiries, (2) involved more than a routine and objective cataloging of factual matters, and (3) were primarily created with an eye toward prosecution.

United States v. Rankin, 64 M.J. 348 (C.A.A.F. 2007): The accused's unauthorized absence conviction was affirmed, even though no declarant testified concerning the following admitted documentary evidence: a letter from the 1st Marine Expeditionary Brigade personnel officer to appellant's mother, a computer generated "Page 6" of appellant's service record book, a message from Navy Absentee Collection Information Center indicating appellant was apprehended, and a DD-553-Deserter/Absentee Wanted By Armed Forces message. Trial defense made timely hearsay and *Crawford v. Washington*, 541 U.S. 36, (2004) objections. The court held that neither Rule 803(6) nor *Crawford* were apposite despite its reservations about DD Form 553, which was apparently created for the purposes of prosecution and was testimonial in nature. The court found any error in the admission of the Form to be harmless.

Navy-Marine Corps Court of Criminal Appeals

United States v. Rankin, 63 M.J. 552 (N.M.Ct.Crim.App. 2006): The accused was convicted of unauthorized absence. The government's case consisted of two Personnel Support Activity Detachment witnesses who laid the foundation for admitting the accused's service records under Rules 803(6) and (8). On appeal, the accused contended that the documentary evidence should have been excluded under *Crawford v. Washington,* 541 U.S. 36 (2004), as being testimonial. Affirming the accused's conviction and sentence, the court held that the service record entries are not testimonial statements and were properly admitted for three reasons: (1) none of the documents were prepared by law enforcement or prosecution personnel; (2) although the documents are frequently used in court-martial proceedings, that is not the primary purpose for their creation; and (3) the information contained in the documents is largely objective, specifying dates, times, places, and identifying data.

[e] Business Records—Foundation Established

Army Court of Criminal Appeals

United States v. Gans, 23 M.J. 540 (A.C.M.R. 1986): The court held that a photostatic copy of the accused's request for variable housing allowance was properly admitted under this Rule. Its foundation was established by a witness who was intimately familiar with Army finance records and who could establish how and why the document was created.

Navy-Marine Corps Court of Criminal Appeals

United States v. Tebsherany, 30 M.J. 608, 613 (N.M.C.M.R. 1990): During the court-martial for larceny and related offenses, the government established the accused's elaborate life style by using evidence of credit applications he had made to Atlantic City casinos. Rejecting defense counsel's contention that the hotel record custodian was not competent to authenticate the documents, the court held that the witness had sufficient familiarity with the activity to provide the military judge with a rational basis for concluding by a preponderance of the evidence that the elements of the business record exception were met.

United States v. McKinley, 15 M.J. 731 (N.M.C.M.R. 1982): The court found no error in the military judge's admission of certain telephone call verification slips made by RCA Global Communications employees, when the slips were used only to establish who received the long distance calls.

United States v. Robinson, 12 M.J. 872 (N.M.C.M.R. 1982): At trial the accused contended that Prosecution Exhibit 1, a NAVPERS 1070/606 (Rev. 1-77), Record of Unauthorized Absence, should not be admitted against him because it had not been properly signed. The United States Navy-Marine Corps Court of Review rejected the argument:

A mere irregularity or omission in an official record does not of itself place the record outside the exception to the hearsay rule and make it incompetent. Only those irregularities or omissions material to the execution of the document would have that effect. . . . An irregular entry on an official record may be inadmissible but the irregularity does not necessarily render the record itself and other proper entries contained therein inadmissible.

[f]   Business Records—Foundation Requirements not Established

Army Court of Criminal Appeals

United States v. Farris, 21 M.J. 702 (A.C.M.R. 1985): A pretrial written statement damaging to the accused could not be admitted under this Rule because it was (1) handwritten, (2) undated, (3) partially signed, (4) not executed under oath, (5) not made in accordance with regularly conducted business practices, (6) dealt in "prospective nefarious activity" and (7) not supported by the custodian's testimony.

Navy-Marine Corps Court of Criminal Appeals

United States v. Wooton, 25 M.J. 917 (N.M.C.M.R. 1988): The accused's drug related conviction was reversed because trial counsel failed to establish the necessary foundation for chain of custody documents. Recognizing that the Military Rules of Evidence have simplified this process, the court emphasized that Rule 803(6) still "plainly requires that an adequate foundation be laid prior to admitting such reports," and that this foundation must include a witness who could "testify about the circumstances surrounding the document's preparation . . . ."

[g]   Business Records—Laboratory Reports

United States Supreme Court

Bullcoming v. New Mexico, 2011 U.S. Lexis 4790 (U.S. June 23, 2011); *Michigan v. Bryant*, 131 S. Ct. 1143 (2011); *Melendez-Diaz v. Massachusetts*, 129 S. Ct. 2527 (2009); *Whorton v. Bockting*, 549 U.S. 406 (2007); *Davis v. Washington*, 547 U.S. 813 (2006); and *Crawford v. Washington*, 541 U.S. 36, 53–54 (2004) are annotated above at section 801.05[1][a].

United States Court of Appeals for the Armed Forces

United States v. Blazier, 69 M.J. 218 (C.A.A.F. 2010): The accused was convicted of dereliction of duty and wrongful use of controlled substances. Part of the government's proof included laboratory reports used by the supervising chemist when he testified concerning the composition of the possessed drugs. The chemist's testimony interpreting the laboratory reports relied upon machine generated laboratory reports and upon the analyses of other chemists who did not testify. The convictions were affirmed in *United States v. Blazier*, 68 M.J. 544 (A.F.Ct.Crim.App. 2008), which was decided before *Melendez-Diaz v. Massachusetts*, 129 S. Ct. 2527 (2009), held that, "certificates of analysis" used in drug prosecutions to establish the illegality of seized substances fell within the "core-class of testimonial statements" and violated the accused's Sixth Amendment rights). The convictions were reversed and the case remanded in *United States v. Blazier*, 68 M.J. 439 (C.A.A.F. 2010) (applying *Melendez-Diaz v. Massachusetts* but returning the record with specified questions concerning why the military judge did not compel the government to produce the essential laboratory witnesses). In its second look at the case, the court concluded that an expert may rely on machine-generated data because the Rules of Evidence define it as not being hearsay, and also may rely on but not repeat testimonial hearsay that is otherwise appropriate for expert opinion testimony so long as the expert's opinion is his own. The court also held that when testimonial hearsay is admitted, the Confrontation Clause is satisfied only if the declarant of that hearsay is subject to cross-examination at trial, or is unavailable but had been previously subjected to cross-examination and warned that the Confrontation Clause may not be circumvented by having an expert testify at trial to otherwise inadmissible testimonial hearsay. The court found that this occurred in violation of *Melendez-Diaz v. Massachusetts* and returned the record for a harmful error analysis.

United States v. Magyari, 63 M.J. 123 (C.A.A.F. 2006): The accused's drug abuse was discovered during a routine unit inspection. Laboratory test results were introduced using a chain of custody documents and the evidence custodian's live testimony. No one from the lab testified. Sustaining the accused's conviction, the court held that *Crawford v. Washington*, 541 U.S. 36 (2004) has not been violated because admission of the lab report was non-testimonial proof. The court went on to say that lab technicians do not equate specific samples of potential contraband with particular individuals, and under these circumstances testing is not in furtherance of any particular law enforcement investigation. The court suggested, however, that if a laboratory analysis was conducted as part of an in-progress criminal investigation, the results might be testimonial and, if so, *Crawford* would require either live testimony or a previous opportunity to cross-examine. The court limited its opinion to the facts of the case and, in the course of doing so rejected "[t]he Government's contention that lab reports are inherently not testimonial because they are business and public records." The court stated that this argument "goes to far."

United States v. Grant, 56 M.J. 410 (C.A.A.F. 2002): The accused was convicted of using marijuana. The government's evidence against him included the accused's own confession and a positive urinalysis report which was offered and admitted for the sole purpose of corroborating the accused's confession. Both at trial and on appeal, the accused contended that the urinalysis report did not qualify as a business record because the document was made by the private laboratory that conducted the tests and not by the Air Force hospital where the sample was collected and where the witnesses laying the business entry foundation worked. The government called no witnesses from the laboratory or the hospital to establish a chain of custody, nor did they call any witnesses to describe the laboratory testing procedure. The government's foundation was established by the medical doctor and corpsman responsible for conducting the test at the Air Force Hospital. In a case of first impression for the military, the court held, affirming the accused's conviction, that a business record prepared by a third party (the laboratory here) not a party to the litigation is properly admitted as part of a second business entity's (the government here) records if the second business integrated the document into its records and relied upon it in the ordinary course of its business, the facts at bar. Crucial to the government's proof, the hospital personal testified that they relied on documents of this nature in providing medical assistance, thus demonstrating indicia of trustworthiness. Interestingly, the court went on to say that a chain of custody was not necessary because the report was only being offered to corroborate the accused's confession and it was the confession itself which established the wrongfulness charged.

United States v. Cordero, 21 M.J. 714 (A.F.C.M.R. 1985): Rejecting the accused's contention that his rights to due process and confrontation were violated by the admission of lab reports and chain of custody documents as business entries, the court held that Rule 803(6) specifically permits the admission of such forensic evidence when a proper foundation has been established. This foundation will be sufficient if it includes testimony from a witness who can "identify the record as authentic and state that it was made in the regular course of business."

United States v. Porter, 12 M.J. 129 (C.M.A. 1981): Affirming a conviction for possession and sale of marijuana, the court rejected a claim that the laboratory analysis of the substance identified as marijuana was inadmissible because no government witness testified as to the normal business of the laboratory. The court said that since the suspected contraband had been sent by registered mail to the criminal investigation laboratory for chemical analysis, judicial notice could be taken that a crime laboratory is a place in which scientific methods and principles are applied in the testing and analysis of various items in connection with the detection and prosecution of crimes. *See also United States v. Jessen,* 12 M.J. 122 (C.M.A. 1981) (pre-Rules case) (suggests that chain of custody documents previously inadmissible, are admissible under Rule 803(6), (8)).

Air Force Court of Criminal Appeals

United States v. Walker, 38 M.J. 678 (A.F.C.M.R. 1994): The accused was convicted of using and distributing marijuana. Both at trial and on appeal, he contended that the laboratory report used to establish cannabis was improperly admitted because trial counsel failed to provide any evidence about the crime lab's business procedures. Affirming the convictions, the court held that the local OSI agent's testimony satisfied Rule 803(6)'s requirements.

The court added that it is not necessary for government counsel to call the individual who actually prepared the document or conducted the test.

United States v. Hudson, 20 M.J. 607 (A.F.C.M.R. 1985): The accused contended that the "presumption which normally attends the record of a regularly conducted business activity should not be available to the government" in this drug case because sloppy paperwork destroyed its validity. Sustaining conviction the court held that: (1) such matters are traditionally left to the trial court's broad discretion which was not abused in this case; (2) "the argument that opportunities existed to permit tampering with the evidence is not persuasive as the government need not exclude all possible ways the evidence could be changed or interfered with," (3) the trial judge must simply be "reasonably certain" that the evidence has not been altered in any important way; and (4) any irregularities in the chain of custody documents or laboratory reports "relate only to weight and not admissibility."

Army Court of Criminal Appeals

United States v. Williamson, 65 M.J. 706 (Army.Ct.Crim.App. 2007): The accused was tried for possessing marijuana with the intent to distribute. Relying on the Sixth Amendment, defense counsel objected to the government's laboratory report. The case was tried before the effective date of *Crawford v. Washington,* 541 U.S. 36 (2004), and the objection was overruled. Affirming the accused's convictions, the court found that the laboratory report was testimonial hearsay and therefore improperly admitted as a business record. However, the court held that the error was harmless because sufficient independent proof established the contraband nature of the seized evidence. The government's case included testimony from experienced CID and DEA agents who identified the packaging and its contents as being consistent with marijuana trafficking, testimony that a drug detector dog had alerted on the seized evidence, and the accused's own words at the time he was apprehended.

United States v. Schoolfield, 36 M.J. 545 (A.C.M.R. 1992): The accused is HIV- positive. He was convicted of numerous sex-related offenses, including having unprotected and unwarned intercourse with five women. At trial and on appeal, the accused contended that documentary evidence establishing his illness was improperly admitted. Affirming all convictions, the court held that the medical director at Walter Reed Army Medical Center was qualified to establish an adequate foundation for admitting records which demonstrated the accused's condition.

United States v. Harper, 32 M.J. 620 (A.C.M.R. 1991): Reversing the accused's drug use conviction, the court held that the admissibility of a laboratory report as a business record does not bar an accused from attacking the accuracy of the report by calling laboratory technicians. The court said government counsel cannot avoid this result by including, with the laboratory report, affidavits attesting to the quality control procedures used.

Urinalysis results without expert testimony interpreting them will not sustain conviction in the court's opinion.

United States v. Pinkston, 32 M.J. 555 (A.C.M.R. 1991): Affirming the accused's drug distribution conviction, the court held that a laboratory report was properly admitted as a business record because the local evidence custodian testified about: (1) mailing procedures; (2) the chain of custody document; (3) how the laboratory report was received in the mail; and (4) his responsibility for maintaining these documents in the ordinary course of business and for identifying authenticating signatures. The court went on to say that defense counsel can always challenge the report and request the chemist's production.

United States v. Holmes, 23 M.J. 565 (A.C.M.R. 1986): The court found that it was "well settled military law that a laboratory analysis conducted in the regular course of business by a qualified chemist of a private or governmental agency qualifies and is admissible as a business record." The court reasoned that a laboratory report of handwriting analysis was similarly admissible since all "forensic laboratory reports" are covered by the rule.

Navy-Marine Corps Court of Criminal Appeals

United States v. Harris, 66 M.J. 781 (N.M.Ct.Crim.App. 2008): A court with enlisted members convicted the accused of wrongfully using methamphetamine. For the first time on appeal, he contended that the Navy Drug Screening Lab report used to established his complicity should have been excluded as testimonial hearsay under *Crawford v. Washington*, 541 U.S. 36, (2004). The court affirmed the accused's conviction and held that the lab report did not violate the Sixth Amendment right of confrontation because the lab technicians who prepared the document were not engaged in a law enforcement function or in a search for evidence in anticipation of trial. As a result, the court said the lab report was not "testimonial" in the context prohibited by *Crawford*, and was admissible under the firmly rooted hearsay exception for business records.

United States v. Harris, 65 M.J. 594 (N.M.Ct.Crim.App. 2007): A neighbor called the local police when he saw the accused digging in the neighbor's yard. After being apprehended, the accused was turned over to his unit for medical attention. At the hospital, he was treated and tested for drug abuse. Subsequent Navy laboratory analysis indicated the accused had been using methamphetamines. At the accused's trial for substance abuse, defense counsel challenged the government's lab report as violating the accused's Sixth Amendment rights under *Crawford v. Washington*, 541 U.S. 36 (2004). On appeal, the accused argued that even though *United States v. Magyari*, 63 M.J. 123 (C.A.A.F. 2006), held that drug laboratory reports caused by a positive random urinalysis test are not testimonial and do not violate *Crawford* or the Confrontation Clause, and that case is not dispositive because it did not concern a probable cause urinalysis. Here, the government requested the test and results for prosecution purposes. Affirming the accused's conviction the court held that, even though the accused's command sent in a single urine sample taken under a probable cause premise, the Navy laboratory's procedures insured that personnel conducting the test and completing the challenged lab report had no way of knowing the testing premise or the donor's identity.

[h] Business Records—Letters of Reprimand

Army Court of Criminal Appeals

United States v. Williams, 28 M.J. 911 (A.C.M.R. 1989): In a child sexual abuse case, the court found error in the pre-sentencing admission of a United States Army Criminal Investigation Command message indicating that the accused had previously received a letter of reprimand for similar offenses. The court indicated that the accused's misconduct could have been properly established if the letter of reprimand itself, or similar documentary evidence, had been offered pursuant to this Rule.

United States v. Williams, 26 M.J. 644 (A.C.M.R. 1988): During the sentencing portion of the accused's indecent assault court-martial, trial counsel attacked the accused's unsworn testimony ("I've always managed to keep very tight control over myself") with a CID electronic message indicating that the accused had previously received a letter of reprimand for similar misconduct. No other information about the extrinsic event was admitted. Affirming the conviction, the court found that this type of message is routinely used to describe previously substantiated investigations and is sufficiently reliable.

[i] Business Records—Medical Records

United States Court of Appeals for the Armed Forces

United States v. Benedict, 27 M.J. 253 (C.M.A. 1988): Although opinions and diagnoses recorded in a patient's hospital record are admissible under Rule 803(6), "a report of a sanity board convened in conjunction with possible criminal prosecution [is] not." Its admission in this child sexual abuse case contributed to the accused's conviction being overturned.

Army Court of Criminal Appeals

United States v. Morris, 30 M.J. 1221 (A.C.M.R. 1990): Having previously tested positive for HIV, the accused was convicted of consensual sodomy and wanton disregard for human life. At trial, he unsuccessfully contended that the government failed to establish that the contaminated blood was his. Affirming conviction, the court held that the accused's medical records satisfactorily proved the link because, under the circumstances of this case, the trial judge had not abused his discretion in holding that a chain of custody document was unnecessary.

[j] Business Records—Opinion Evidence

United States Court of Appeals for the Armed Forces

United States v. Vandelinder, 20 M.J. 41 (C.M.A. 1985): The court held that an accused's "service records" are admissible under this Rule when offered as good military character evidence because 803(6) specifically "authorizes the reception in evidence of 'opinion' contained in 'records of regularly conducted activity,' such as 'service records.' "

Air Force Court of Criminal Appeals

United States v. Benedict, 20 M.J. 939 (A.F.C.M.R. 1985): A written psychiatric report concerning the accused's mental health was properly admitted against him even though two of its authors did not testify. The court found the document's opinion and diagnostic evidence to be properly admitted as regularly conducted business activity records which do not affront the accused's confrontation rights.

[k]   Business Records—Relationship with Rule 803(8)

United States v. Harris, 55 M.J. 433 (C.A.A.F. 2001): The accused was convicted of larceny of checks, and forging the stolen checks. At trial, the government was successful in admitting the bank's logbook. The accused argued that the logbook was improperly authenticated, therefore inadmissible. The Navy-Marine Corps Court of Criminal Appeals affirmed the conviction. The court held that a logbook used to record the handling of security videotapes at a bank was admissible under the business record exception to the hearsay rule. The Court went on to say that the logbook was admissible based on the testimony of both the bank fraud investigator and the bank teller, who testified that the logbook was routinely kept in the course of business, and because the entries in the logbook were made as part of a regular procedure. The Court also noted that a military judge's decision to admit evidence is reviewed for abuse of discretion, and there was no abuse of discretion in this case.

Army Court of Criminal Appeals

United States v. Williams, 12 M.J. 894 (A.C.M.R. 1982): In analyzing proof of an absence without leave offense, the Army Court of Criminal Appeals highlighted the pragmatic distinctions between using official documents under Rule 803(8) and business entries under Rule 803(6). Here the government initially attempted to admit morning reports as official records. However, the defense objected, alleging that the evidence had not been prepared by someone within the scope of that person's official duties. When the military judge sustained the objection, trial counsel properly sought to introduce the documents as business records. Relying on *United States v. Mullins,* 47 C.M.R. 828 (N.C.M.R. 1973), the court held that:

> [T]he deficiency which prevented the document from qualifying as an official record, *i.e.,* the verifying official's lack of authority due to his military grade, does not preclude it from being admitted as a business entry so long as the prerequisites for a business entry are met.

The court found an adequate foundation for admitting the document had been established by a witness who was "intimately familiar with the internal workings of [the] enterprise." *See United States v. Wilson,* 1 M.J. 325, 328 (C.M.A. 1976).

[l]   Business Records—Relevancy Issues

United States Court of Appeals for the Armed Forces

United States v. Grant, 56 M.J. 410 (C.A.A.F. 2002): The accused was convicted of using marijuana. The government's evidence against him included the accused's own confession and a positive urinalysis report which was offered and admitted for the sole purpose of corroborating the accused's confession. Both at trial and on appeal, the accused contended that the urinalysis report did not qualify as a business record because the document was made by the private laboratory that conducted the tests and not by the Air Force hospital where the sample was collected and where the witnesses laying the business entry foundation worked. The government called no witnesses from the laboratory or the hospital to establish a chain of custody, nor did they call any witnesses to describe the laboratory testing procedure. The government's hearsay foundation was established by the medical doctor and corpsman responsible for conducting the test at the Air Force Hospital. In a case of first impression for the military, the court held, affirming the accused's conviction, that a business record prepared by a third party (the laboratory here) not a party to the litigation is properly admitted as part of a second business entity's (the government here) records if the second business integrated the document into its records and relied upon it in the ordinary course of its business, the facts at bar. However, the accused's further allegation of error was that, unless there was expert testimony interpreting the scientific tests, there is no rational basis upon which fact-finders can draw an inference that marijuana was used. Rejecting this additional contention, the Court held that such determinations depend on relevancy and that relevance determinations have two components: materiality and probative value. The court went on to say that materiality looks to the relation between the propositions that the evidence is offered to prove and the issues in the case. Probative value the court said describes the tendency of evidenced to establish the proposition that is it offered to prove. Here the Court said the evidence was only offered to corroborate the accused's confession and not to independently prove the wrongful use. In the court's words, "the implicit proposition sought to be proved was that the accused had not mistakenly or otherwise admitted to an offense which either had not occurred or that he had not committed."

[m]   Business Records—Video Camera Log

Navy-Marine Corps Court of Criminal Appeals

United States v. Harris, 53 M.J. 514 (N.M.Ct.Crim.App. 2000): A military judge convicted the accused of larceny and forgery. Part of the government's evidence included incriminating surveillance video tapes and photographs of the accused. To establish a foundation for admitting this evidence, the government relied on the "silent witness" theory of authentication, and used the fraud examiner's testimony to establish that a video camera log authenticating the questioned evidence had been kept in the regular course of business. Finding no error in this process, the court held that the log was properly admitted because it had been completed "at the time the tape was being changed, that the individual recording the information was to have personal knowledge of it, and that everyone learned the procedures."

[n]   Business Records—Worthless Checks

Navy-Marine Corps Court of Criminal Appeals

United States v. Dababneh, 28 M.J. 929 (N.M.C.M.R. 1989): In this bad check case, the accused unsuccessfully contended that the questioned documents were inadmissible as they contained stamp-marking and similar notations. The court held that a bank official with knowledge of how checks are processed was able to testify to the extent of the routine reliance of his business upon accurate recordings of account balance information and insufficiency of funds. The court said that an "offering witness [need not] be the recorder or even certain of who recorded the information." The witness must simply "be able to identify the record as authentic and state that it was made and preserved in the regular course of business."

[o]   Business Records—Police Report

United States Court of Appeals for the Armed Forces

United States v. Clayton, 67 M.J. 283 (C.A.A.F. 2009): While assigned in Germany, the accused was convicted of numerous drug-related use, possession, and trafficking offenses. The government introduced a German Police Report to establish on one charge how the drugs were discovered and collected. The court found that this was prejudicial error requiring reversal of the accused's conviction on the affected charge and returned the record for sentencing purposes. The court concluded that the German Police Report violated *Crawford v. Washington,* 541 U.S. 36 (2004), and the Sixth Amendment's prohibition against admitting testimonial hearsay evidence because the report was: (1) made by a law enforcement agency; (2) more than a routine and objective cataloging of unambiguous factual matters; and (3) created with an eye towards prosecution.

[8]   Rule 803(8)—Public Records and Reports

[a]   Public Records—Auditor's Reports

Army Court of Criminal Appeals

United States v. Myers, 22 M.J. 649 (A.C.M.R. 1986): The court held that an audit report, UP AR 230-60 (The Management and Administration of the United States Army Club System (1 March 1981)), was properly admitted under subdivision (8)(B) because its findings were "based upon the facts observed in the scope of the auditor's official duties. . . ." The court also stated that the auditor was not acting in a law enforcement capacity at the time because his mission was to "correct deficiencies cited in reports of club audits and inspections and to correct the underlying reasons for such deficiencies."

[b] Public Records—Constitutional Requirements

Navy-Marine Corps Court of Criminal Appeals

United States v. Rankin, 63 M.J. 552 (N.M.Ct.Crim.App. 2006): The accused was convicted of unauthorized absence. The prosecution's case consisted of two Personnel Support Activity Detachment witnesses who laid the foundation for admitting the accused's service records under Rules 803 (6) and (8). On appeal, the accused contended that the documentary evidence should have been excluded under *Crawford v. Washington,* 541 U.S. 36 (2004), as being testimonial. Affirming the accused's conviction and sentence, the court held that the service record entries are not testimonial statements and were properly admitted for three reasons: (1) none of the documents were prepared by law enforcement or prosecution personnel; (2) although the documents are frequently used in court-martial proceedings, that is not the primary purpose for their creation; and (3) the information contained in the documents is largely objective, specifying dates, times, places, and identifying data.

[c] Public Records—Convictions

Air Force Court of Criminal Appeals

United States v. Frazier, 32 M.J. 651 (A.F.C.M.R. 1991): During the pre-sentencing portion of the accused's court-martial for larceny, trial counsel introduced stipulations of fact from accomplices' trials. In response to defense objections, the prosecution contended that Rule 803(8) permitted the entire record of trial to be admitted. Finding error but no prejudice, the court held that only evidence of the conviction itself was admissible under this Rule.

United States v. Pitts, 18 M.J. 522 (A.F.C.M.R. 1984): The court held that "a redacted copy of a letter, signed by the county magistrate" was insufficient proof of the accused's previous civilian conviction and was not admissible under this Rule.

Army Court of Criminal Appeals

United States v. Charley, 28 M.J. 903 (A.C.M.R. 1989): Reversing the accused's conviction for writing worthless checks, the court held that, although it would have been proper to admit evidence of the accused's previous summary court-martial conviction (DD Form 493, Extract of Military Records of Previous Convictions), admitting the record of proceedings which resulted in the conviction without a specific demonstration of relevancy was prejudicial error.

United States v. Williams, 26 M.J. 644 (A.C.M.R. 1988): The court held that it was improper to attack the accused's unsworn sentencing testimony with a CID report stating that he had previously committed similar indecent assaults. The court said that Rule 803(8) excludes public records and reports that set forth matters observed in a law enforcement capacity. *See* our discussion of this case under Rule 803(6).

United States v. Wright, 20 M.J. 518 (A.C.M.R. 1985): The court held that the accused's record of trial from a previous court-martial conviction was admissible under this Rule. The record was used during the aggravation portion of the government's case to demonstrate the accused's limited rehabilitation potential.

Navy-Marine Corps Court of Criminal Appeals

United States v. May, 18 M.J. 839 (N.M.C.M.R. 1984): Finding that this Rule was not an independent basis upon which to admit the accused's civilian conviction during the sentencing portion of his court-martial, the court noted that "the rules of evidence . . . merely provide for the forum in which evidence of conviction meeting the criteria of paragraph 75 *b* (3)(a) and (b) may be proven."

[d]   Public Records—Error in Record

United States Court of Appeals for the Armed Forces

United States v. Datz, 61 M.J. 37 (C.A.A.F. 2005): The accused was convicted of numerous offenses including rape and sexual harassment. The central issue at trial and on appeal was whether the accused's alleged affirmative "head nodding" to interrogators' questions indicating the accused's complicity were improperly admitted. Reversing the accused's convictions and sentence, the court held that proof of the head nodding, when used as adoptive admissions, should have been suppressed because trial counsel did not present a sufficient basis to justify finding that the accused "heard, understood, and acquiesced in the statements."

Navy-Marine Corps Court of Criminal Appeals

United States v. Arispe, 12 M.J. 516 (N.M.C.M.R. 1981): Upholding convictions for unauthorized absence, the court approved the admission of memoranda entries from the accused's service record even though an entry concerning nonjudicial punishment did not reveal the regulation violated. The court reasoned as follows: "[A] mere irregularity or omission in the entry of a fact required to be rendered in an official record does not of itself place the record outside the exception and make it incompetent. Only those irregularities or omissions material to the execution of the document would have that effect." For an example of an omission which was material to the execution of the document, *see United States v. Anderson,* 12 M.J. 527 (N.M.C.M.R. 1981), where the court found that because neither an accused's signature nor an explanation for its omission appeared on an Enlisted

Performance Evaluation as required by the Bureau of Naval Personnel Manual, the evaluation should not have been admitted at the pre-sentence stage.

[e] Public Records—Laboratory Reports

United States Court of Appeals for the Armed Forces

United States v. Broadnax, 23 M.J. 389 (C.M.A. 1987): Reversing the accused's forgery conviction, the court held that a "forensic laboratory report containing an opinion from a government documents examiner that the accused authored a forged check" could not be admitted over trial defense counsel's objection unless that document's preparer was made available. The court distinguished this holding from *United States v. Strangstalien,* 7 M.J. 225 (C.M.A. 1979), which permits forensic "clinical" laboratory reports (drug analysis) to be admitted without such foundational witnesses. It stated that whenever opinion testimony concerning such "subjective" matters as handwriting exemplars is used, "the government must notify the defense prior to trial of its intent to introduce such evidence so that the government can secure the presence of the expert at trial if requested by the defense."

[f] Public Records—"Police" Reports Excluded

Army Court of Criminal Appeals

United States v. Williams, 28 M.J. 911 (A.C.M.R. 1989): During the pre-sentencing portion of this child sexual abuse case, the court found that a United States Army Criminal Investigation Command message indicating the accused's previous involvement in similar conduct had been improperly admitted. The court noted that "the conclusion of the CID report itself, expressing the opinion that the accused committed an indecent assault, was not admissible. [Rule 803(8)] excludes from admission public records and reports that set forth 'matters observed by police officers and other personnel acting in a law enforcement capacity.' "

United States v. Williams, 26 M.J. 644 (A.C.M.R. 1988): The court held that it was improper to attack the accused's unsworn sentencing testimony with a CID report stating that he had previously committed similar indecent assaults. The court said that Rule 803(8) excludes public records and reports that set forth matters observed in a law enforcement capacity. *See* our discussion of this case under Rule 803(6).

[g] Public Records—Staff Judge Advocate as Law Enforcement Agency

Army Court of Criminal Appeals

United States v. Thornton, 16 M.J. 1011 (A.C.M.R. 1983): Statements made to the assistant staff judge advocate were viewed as having been made to "a person acting in a law enforcement capacity," and thus inadmissible under the public records hearsay exception.

[h]   Public Records—Valuative Conclusions

Supreme Court

Beech Aircraft Corp. v. Rainey, 488 U.S. 153 (1988): The Court settled a conflict among the federal courts on the meaning of "factual findings" in Federal Rule of Evidence 803(8)(C), holding that the term encompasses more than just "facts" and includes valuative conclusions and opinions. *See* our discussion of this case in the Editorial Comments, *above.*

United States Court of Appeals for the Armed Forces

United States v. Wales, 31 M.J. 301 (C.M.A. 1990): The court reversed the accused's fraternization and adultery convictions partially because trial counsel attempted to prove a "custom of the service" by having the trial judge take judicial notice of a nonpunitive Air Force Regulation. In the court's opinion, to obtain a conviction under these circumstances the government must offer a knowledgeable witness who can testify about military customs.

[9]   Rule 803(18)—Learned Treatises

[a]   Learned Treatises—Expert Witness Impeachment

United States Court of Appeals for the Armed Forces

United States v. Schlamer, 52 M.J. 80 (C.A.A.F. 1999): The accused was convicted of murdering another Marine. During trial, defense counsel was not permitted to ask a government forensic serologist about a colleague's professional opinion testimony from another trial concerning hair-comparison analysis' lack of reliability. The accused contended this was prejudicial error. Affirming the convictions, the court held that no authority exists for impeaching an expert witness with out-of-court statements from competing experts' testimony in other trials; such testimony is inadmissible hearsay. Instead, the court held that the appropriate technique for challenging an expert's opinion, on cross-examination, is by introducing the competing view through a learned treatise or scientific article.

[b]   Learned Treatises—Cause of Death Proved

Air Force Court of Criminal Appeals

United States v. Irvin, 13 M.J. 749 (A.F.C.M.R. 1982): Affirming the accused's conviction for manslaughter and assault, the court found that it was not improper for government experts to rely on various learned and scholarly articles when they testified as to the cause of death.

[c]   Learned Treatises—Cross-Examination Uses

United States Court of Appeals for the Armed Forces

United States v. Jackson, 38 M.J. 106 (C.M.A. 1993): The accused was convicted of using marijuana. His defense consisted mainly of attacking the government's forensic expert witness, and attempting to impeach him with learned treatises. Affirming the accused's conviction, the court said the military judge erred when he instructed the court members that learned treatises used during defense counsel's cross-examination of the government's expert, and then relied upon by that witness, were excludable as hearsay evidence. The court went on to find this error harmless.

[d] Learned Treatises—Expert Witness Connection

United States Court of Appeals for the Armed Forces

United States v. King, 35 M.J. 337 (C.M.A. 1992): The accused was convicted of sexually abusing his daughter and another child. A portion of the government's evidence included expert witness testimony that the court saw as being clearly prejudicial. Although the court affirmed the accused's conviction due to other evidence, it set aside his sentence because of gratuitous and prejudicial expert witness testimony. The court seemed to confuse Rule 803 (18) with Rule 702. For example, the court said that just because an expert witness is permitted to testify about his opinions, knowledge, or observations, the witness is not given a license to recount unlimited amounts of hearsay from professional journals. While the court recognized that what occurred here may simply have been counsel's "clumsy attempts" at soliciting expert testimony, it also permitted improper and dangerous evidence to be admitted.

[e] Learned Treatises—Reliability Questions

Air Force Court of Criminal Appeals

United States v. Robinson, 43 M.J. 501 (A.F.Ct.Crim.App. 1995): During the sentencing portion of the accused's court-martial for using marijuana and sexually abusing his stepdaughter, the accused was prevented from introducing a newspaper article which dealt with treatment for sexual offenders. The military judge ruled that it was hearsay. On appeal, the accused claimed that the judge erred because the article was self-authenticating. Affirming the accused's convictions, the court said that, while the document may have been self-authenticating, it was still hearsay and required a witness to demonstrate its reliability.

United States v. Benedict, 20 M.J. 939 (A.F.C.M.R. 1985): Affirming the accused's conviction for indecent acts with a ten-year-old girl, the court held that the American Journal of Psychiatry was in "that category of learned periodicals to be called to the attention of an expert witness during cross-examination and relied upon by an expert witness during direct examination." As a result it was properly admitted as an exception to the hearsay rule.

[10]   Rule 803(22)—Judgment of Previous Convictions

[a]   Judgment of Convictions—Foundational Requirements

Navy-Marine Corps Court of Criminal Appeals

United States v. May, 18 M.J. 839 (N.M.C.M.R. 1984): The court held that this Rule does not provide an independent basis for establishing a prior conviction during the government's sentencing case. The court stated that it "failed to see where 'any fact essential to sustain the judgment' of the civilian criminal proceeding is even remotely relevant to—and thus necessitates admitting the so-called 'judgment' as proof of—any issue in the present case."

[b]   Judgment of Convictions—State Court Convictions

Army Court of Criminal Appeals

United States v. Bordelon, 43 M.J. 531 (Army Ct.Crim.App. 1995): At his court-martial, the accused was convicted of drunk driving and drunk driving-related uniquely military offenses. He had been previously convicted of the same drunk driving offenses in state court. Finding no double jeopardy violation, and affirming the drunk driving convictions, the court said that documentary evidence of the accused's previous state court convictions was admissible under this rule, but "probably" should have been excluded because it was more prejudicial than probative.

§ 804.01   Official Text

Rule 804.   Hearsay Exceptions; Declarant Unavailable.

(a) *Definitions of unavailability.* "Unavailability as a witness" includes situations in which the declarant—

(1) is exempted by ruling of the military judge on the ground of privilege from testifying concerning the subject matter of the declarant's statement; or

(2) persists in refusing to testify concerning the subject matter of the declarant's statement despite an order of the military judge to do so; or

(3) testifies to a lack of memory of the subject matter of the declarant's statement; or

(4) is unable to be present or to testify at the hearing because of death or then existing physical or mental illness or infirmity; or

(5) is absent from the hearing and the proponent of the declarant's statement has been unable to procure the declarant's attendance (or in the case of a hearsay exception under subdivision (b)(2), (3), or (4), the declarant's attendance or testimony) by process or other reasonable means; or

(6) is unavailable within the meaning of Article 49(d)(2).

A declarant is not unavailable as a witness if the declarant's exemption, refusal, claim of lack of memory, inability, or absence is due to the procurement or wrongdoing of the proponent of the declarant's statement for the purpose of preventing the witness from attending or testifying.

(b) *Hearsay exceptions.* The following are not excluded by the hearsay rule if the declarant is unavailable as a witness:

(1) *Former testimony.* Testimony given as a witness at another hearing of the same or different proceeding, or in a deposition taken in compliance with law in the course of the same or another proceeding, if the party against whom the testimony is now offered had an opportunity and similar motive to develop the testimony by direct, cross, or redirect examination. A record of testimony given before courts-martial, courts of inquiry, military commissions, other military tribunals, and before proceedings pursuant to or equivalent to those required by Article 32 is admissible under this subdivision if such a record is a verbatim record. This paragraph is subject to the limitations set forth in Articles 49 and 50.

(2) *Statement under belief of impending death.* In a prosecution for homicide or for any offense resulting in the death of the

alleged victim, a statement made by a declarant while believing that the declarant's death was imminent, concerning the cause or circumstances of what the declarant believed to be the declarant's impending death.

(3) *Statement against interest.* A statement which was at the time of its making so far contrary to the declarant's pecuniary or proprietary interest, or so far tended to subject the declarant to civil or criminal liability, or to render invalid a claim by the declarant against another, that a reasonable person in the position of the declarant would not have made the statement unless the person believed it to be true. A statement tending to expose the declarant to criminal liability and offered to exculpate the accused is not admissible unless corroborating circumstances clearly indicate the trustworthiness of the statement.

(4) *Statement of personal or family history.*

(A) A statement concerning the declarant's own birth, adoption, marriage, divorce, legitimacy, relationship by blood, adoption, or marriage, ancestry, or other similar fact of personal or family history, even though declarant had no means of acquiring personal knowledge of the matter stated; or (B) a statement concerning the foregoing matters, and death also, of another person, if the declarant was related to the other by blood, adoption, or marriage or was so intimately associated with the other's family as to be likely to have accurate information concerning the matter declared.

(5) *Other exceptions.* This provision has been transferred to Rule 807.

(6) *Forfeiture by wrongdoing.* A statement offered against a party that has engaged or acquiesced in wrongdoing that was intended to, and did, procure the unavailability of the declarant as a witness.

§ 804.02   Editorial Comment

[1]   Rule 804—Hearsay Exceptions—Declarant Unavailable

[a]   Using Rule 804

Rule 804 provides the second major set of exceptions to the ban on hearsay evidence found in Rule 802. It was amended in 1999 to add subparagraph 804(b)(6), which provides for the admission of hearsay statements when a witness's unavailability is the result of wrongdoing, *see* our discussion *below*, and transferred the residual exception contained in subparagraph 804(b)(5), along with the residual exception in Rule 803(24), to new Rule 807, also discussed *below*.

While Rule 803 furnishes exceptions that do not depend on a showing that the hearsay declarant is unavailable at trial, Rule 804 conditions the use of hearsay exceptions on counsel's demonstration of declarant unavailability.[1] [SS8] It certainly is arguable that a number of the exceptions found in Rule 804 are every bit as reliable as those found in Rule 803. Former testimony, for example, could be viewed as one of the most reliable of all the hearsay exceptions. The fact remains, however, that the requirement for the declarant to be unavailable suggests that courts are especially hesitant in using the Rule 804 exceptions.

When subdivision (a) is compared to its federal counterpart, it is apparent that the two Rules are quite similar, except for the addition of the sixth definition of unavailability, which is unique to the military. The subdivision is similar to former *Manual* practice. However, 804(a)(3) is somewhat broader than the prior *Manual* provisions, and Rule 804 does not distinguish between capital and non-capital cases as did the prior *Manual*.

[b] Rule 804 and Constitutional Issues

The Supreme Court's rejection of *Ohio v. Roberts*[2] and adoption of the *Crawford v. Washington*[3] standard is discussed at section 801.02 [1][a][i].

In analyzing Confrontation Clause issues, counsel and military judges should first decide whether the statement is being offered for the truth of the matter asserted. If it is not then confrontational concerns are not present. This is because, at least in theory, "proof" on a substantive issue is not being offered, and as a result cannot be considered by the court-members for that purpose.[4]

When a statement is being offered for the truth of the matter asserted, however, counsel and military judges must then decide whether the statement falls within a hearsay exception, and then determine whether the Confrontation Clause's requirement for cross-examination have been or will be satisfied. This is apparently true, regardless of whether the exception falls within Rule 803 or 804. If the statement does not fall within a hearsay exception then it is excluded. When it does fall under an exception or exclusion, the next step is to determine whether the statement is "testimonial." If the statement is being offered for a "testimonial" purpose, then the prosecution must either call the declarant to the stand or establish the declarant's unavailability and then prove that defendant at a previous time

---

[1] *See, e.g.,* United States v. Gabriel, 715 F.2d 1447 (10th Cir. 1983) (where codefendant was available at trial, defendant could not rely upon statements made at a hearing on the codefendant's guilty plea).

[2] 448 U.S. 56 (1980).

[3] 541 U.S. 36 (2004).

[4] *See* Rule 105's discussion concerning limiting instructions on evidence that can be used for more than one purpose.

had an opportunity to cross-examine that declarant on his or her out-of-court statement.[5]

Evidence will likely be admissible when the statement is the accused's own words,[6] a statement of a coconspirator made during, and in furtherance of, the conspiracy,[7] any other applicable admission,[8] and virtually by definition, any statement made at a previous proceeding.[9] Extending this logic would result in military courts viewing any statement not intended to be used as proof against the accused, at the time it was made, to fall outside of the "testimonial" definition.

The logical and most important issue in this process concerns defining which statements are "testimonial," and therefore require actual confrontation before they can be admitted. Clearly, statements given at any formal proceeding such as an Article 32 hearing or prior judicial or administrative proceeding qualify. The same result applies to statements made during criminal investigations and "interrogations," although the court has not yet clearly defined interrogation.

Most likely, several other types of evidence will also be considered "testimonial." For example, forensic laboratory reports could come under the "testimonial" label, although the Supreme Court in *Crawford* indicated that business records are not testimonial. This issue is likely to be quickly challenged in courts-martial due to the number of drug cases tried each year. Other early testimonial questions military courts will face include statements made by sexual assault victims, particularly children, when such statements are offered as excited utterances,[10] statements made for purposes of medical diagnosis,[11] and statements being offered under the residual exception.[12]

Although it is not a Rule 804 case, *United States v. Coulter*, is instructive. In that case the child abuse was held incompetent to testify because of her age. Using Rule 807, the victim's incriminating statements were admitted through her parents' testimony. Finding no error, the court used a two-step process to determine both hearsay admissibility and constitutionality. First, the court examined the statements under traditional Rule 807 logic. Next, the court analyzed the statements using *Crawford,* finding them to be non-

---

[5] Rule 804(b)(6) provides that the witness need not be produced in situations where the defendant caused the declarant to be unavailable.

[6] *See* Rule 801(d)(2)(A).

[7] *See* Rule 801(d)(2)(E).

[8] *See* Rule 801(d)(2).

[9] *See* Rule 801(d)(1).

[10] *See* Rule 803(2). Statements made to social works and others outside of the traditional criminal framework pose difficult questions.

[11] *See* Rule 803(4).

[12] See Rule 807.

testimonial and therefore admissible. The court noted that the declarant had not: (1) been questioned by the police or other government officials but by her parents who had a natural concern for their child's well-being; (2) been capable of envisioning her statements someday being used in a criminal proceeding; and (3) been capable of understanding the solemn nature of her declarations or that they could be used to prove some fact or event in the future. Conversely, in *United States v. Taylor*[13] the court found error in the military judge admitting the accused's wife's pretrial statement through another witness after she claimed spousal privilege. The court found such proof to be testimonial and therefore prohibited by *Crawford*.

For purposes of the exceptions in Rule 804, those provisions require a threshold showing of unavailability, regardless of whether they are testimonial or not. Presumably, "former testimony" statements falling within Rule 804(b)(1) would be considered to be testimonial, but that exception requires that the defendant had an opportunity to cross-examine the declarant. Thus, *Crawford* does not seem to change much for that particular exception. Statements falling into the exceptions in Rule 804(b)(3) (statements against interest), 804(b)(4) (statement of personal family history), and 804(b)(6) (forfeiture exception) would require the *Crawford* analysis, again depending on whether the court found the statements to be testimonial.

Statements offered as "dying declarations" under Rule 804(b)(2) raise some questions, however. Although applying *Crawford* to such statements would normally trigger Confrontation Clause analysis, the Court in *Crawford* recognized that it had held in the 1800's that dying declarations did not violate the defendant's Confrontation Clause rights. But the Court did not further elaborate on whether that case would stand, following *Crawford*.

[c] Constitutional Issues—Determining Unavailability

Before counsel and military judges determine compliance with the new confrontation clause standards in *Crawford* (discussed *above*), statements offered under Rule 804 will still have to comply with its requirements for admission. Among the most troublesome is the obligation to determine a witness's "unavailability." *Crawford* left open whether, when non-testimonial statements are offered, *Ohio v. Roberts*,[14] remained applicable. Under *Roberts*, the Court conditioned the admissibility of hearsay evidence on whether it fell under a "firmly rooted hearsay exception" or bore "particularized guarantees of trustworthiness." However, in *Whorton v. Bockting*,[15] the Supreme Court wrote that *Crawford* was "flatly inconsistent with *Roberts*, which it overruled." The Court continued by noting that the Confrontation Clause has no application to nontestimonial hearsay state-

---

[13] 62 M.J. 615 (A.F.Ct.Crim.App. 2005).

[14] 448 U.S. 56 (1980).

[15] 549 U.S. 406 (2007).

ments and that they may be admitted even if they lack the indicia of reliability. *Crawford* makes availability of a declarant an important factor for all testimonial hearsay, including the exceptions in Rule 803. Because Rule 804 already requires a showing of unavailability, it should be little affected by the decision.

The Supreme Court has indicated that the government must make a "good faith" effort to produce witnesses at trial in order to satisfy the Confrontation Clause of the Sixth Amendment. The seminal case in this area is *Barber v. Page*.[16] There the Court held that Constitutional requirements for using former testimony were not satisfied when the state failed to obtain a witness who was incarcerated in another state, particularly because existing interstate procedures facilitated obtaining the witness. The Court said that "a witness is not 'unavailable' for purposes of the forgoing exception to the confrontation requirement unless the prosecutorial authorities have made a good faith effort to obtain his presence at trial."

After *Barber*, the Supreme Court moved away from its stringent interpretation concerning good faith. In *Mancusi v. Stubbs*,[17] the Court refused to apply the same standards to foreign witnesses, in part finding that procedural advancements that applied to securing the attendance of state witnesses did not apply in the international arena.[18]

In *Ohio v. Roberts*,[19] the Court again indicated that the government's efforts to show unavailability before offering former testimony may not have to be as strenuous as was thought after *Barber*. Relying upon *California v. Green*,[20] the Court held that the lengths to which the prosecution must go to produce a witness are centered upon reasonableness. The Court recognized that the law does not require the doing of a futile act. thus, if there is no possibility of procuring a witness, good faith will demand nothing of the prosecution. However, if a possibility exists that the witness may be procured, then the government must take affirmative measures aimed at producing the declarant before offering former testimony.[21]

Based on the above, it is clear that, when offering former testimony, the government is going to have to do something significantly more than offer evidence that would allow the judge to speculate on a witness's unavailabil-

---

[16] 390 U.S. 719 (1968).

[17] 408 U.S. 204 (1972).

[18] *See, e.g.*, United States v. Kehm, 799 F.2d 354 (7th Cir. 1986) (not necessary to request extradition unless there is an enabling treaty).

[19] 448 U.S. 56 (1980).

[20] 399 U.S. 149 (1970).

[21] *See, e.g.*, United States v. Losada, 674 F.2d 167 (2d Cir. 1982) (government made good faith effort to produce witness).

ity.[22] Similarly, depending upon the circumstances, prosecutors will have to show that the government played no role in contributing to the witnesses absence.[23]

United States v. Inadi contains an excellent model for trial counsel in measuring their efforts at securing a witness's attendance.[24] Discussing what actions prosecutors should have taken when a witness failed to appear because of alleged car trouble, the court said:

> Government counsel did not request a bench warrant, nor does it appear that they made any additional efforts to compel his attendance at trial. We can safely assume that counsel's conduct would have been considerably more aggressive had counsel felt it was necessary in order to 'win.' Under such circumstances, counsel would have sought a bench warrant and refused to assume that the judicial process is so impotent that a witness's hostility is a basis for making no effort under *Barber*.

Military cases have viewed the standard similarly. For example, in *United States v. Hubbard*,[25] the accused contended that a key government witness's Article 32 testimony should have been excluded because the witness was not really unavailable. The reviewing court rejected the accused's arguments based on the following evidence: (1) the witness had gone AWOL two weeks before trial; (2) the CID was notified of his absence and instituted a search of all known area "hangouts"; (3) local airlines were checked for the witness's departure; (4) the witness's parents were contacted; and (5) local police at the parents' location also searched for the witness. The court went on to say that these efforts exceeded those made in *Ohio v. Roberts*,[26] and demonstrated that the "government made a good faith and reasonable effort to secure the [witness'] presence at the trial, and their failure to find him rendered him an unavailable witness within the meaning of Military Rule of Evidence 804(a)(5)."

[d] Military Judge Responsibilities

As *United States v. Dieter*[27] demonstrates, the military judge also has

---

[22] *See, e.g.*, Gov't of the Canal Zone v. Pinto, 590 F.2d 1344 (5th Cir. 1979) (the government failed to show unavailability by simply indicating that witnesses to the crime were tourists scheduled to depart the Canal Zone the day after the crime, rather than showing where the witnesses actually were on the day of trial).

[23] In United States v. Mann, 590 F.2d 361 (1st Cir. 1978), conviction was reversed because the government's efforts to produce a witness were inadequate. In the court's words: "Implicit" in the duty to use reasonable means to procure the presence of an absent witness is the duty to use reasonable means to keep a present witness from becoming absent."

[24] 475 U.S. 387 (1986), *rev'g* 748 F.2d 812, 820 (3d Cir. 1984).

[25] 18 M.J. 678 (A.C.M.R. 1984).

[26] 448 U.S. 56 (1980).

[27] 42 M.J. 697 (Army Ct.Crim.App. 1995).

independent and significant responsibilities for resolving witness unavailability issues. In some circumstances, this responsibility also includes orchestrating the trial proceedings to facilitate an absent declarant's testimony.[28]

In *Dieter*, while the accused was going from Amsterdam to his post at Vilseck, Germany, he was apprehended by German authorities and charged with possessing marijuana. The accused immediately confessed. Prior to trial, government counsel deposed the CID agent who took the accused's oral confession. Both the accused and his counsel were present. Relying on R.C.M. 702, the military judge admitted the deposition. Finding error, but no prejudice, the court said that the military judge abused his discretion by finding the CID agent unavailable because: (1) government counsel had been willing to postpone the trial until all witnesses were present; (2) only a one-day delay would have been necessary; (3) the trial judge did not establish why he would have been unavailable at the future date; (4) having to reschedule the remaining German witnesses was a routine matter; and (5) the military judge did not sufficiently articulate the reasons for his ruling.

[2]   Rule 804(a)—Definition of Unavailability

At common law, each hearsay exception that was conditioned on unavailability had its own requirement for the type of unavailability that would satisfy the exception. Instead of distinguishing among hearsay exceptions, Rule 804(a) provides a definition of unavailability that governs the use of all the exceptions contained in the Rule.[29]

[a]   Rule 804(a)(1)—Privilege from Testifying

The first situation in which a hearsay declarant is unavailable occurs when the declarant claims a privilege at trial and the claim is sustained by the military judge. For example, a declarant may have made a declaration against interest that can be used at trial, but if called to testify, the declarant would assert the privilege against self-incrimination. Assuming that the declarant faces some potential criminal liability, a trial judge would have to sustain the claim, and the declaration against interest could be offered under subdivision (b). The declarant would be unavailable under subdivision (a)(1).

Military decisions indicate that the prosecution may have to do more than simply assert that its witness has a valid privilege against self-incrimination and therefore is unavailable. For example, in *United States v. Vega-Cancel*,[30] the court held that a purported statement against penal interest (Rule

---

[28] *See* our discussion of Rule 611(a).

[29] *See, e.g.,* United States v. US Infrastructure, Inc., 576 F.3d 1195 (11th Cir. 2009) (codefendant unavailable within meaning of the Rule).

[30] 19 M.J. 899 (A.C.M.R. 1985).

804(b)(3)) was improperly admitted against the accused because the trial judge had done no more than ask the witness whether he desired to exercise his right against self-incrimination. While 804(a)(1) allows the military judge to find unavailability based on this privilege, the exception must be based on the judge's "effort to verify whether, and to what extent, a valid Fifth Amendment claim exists." In the court's opinion this will ordinarily require the witness to establish his privilege as a result of a "question by question" examination, and only in those instances where the court finds the witness could "legitimately refuse to answer essentially all relevant questions" could the witness be totally excused. The court concluded by saying:

> We caution military judges that a particularized inquiry into a witness's invocation of his Fifth Amendment rights is necessary to properly apply Mil. R. Evid. 804(a)(1). The military judge must insure that the assertion of the privilege does not extend beyond areas protected by the Fifth Amendment.

Similarly, in *United States v. Valente*,[31] the court said "a prosecution witness is not 'unavailable' under Mil. R. Evid. 804(a)(1), even though he asserts his privilege against self-incrimination, if he can be made available through the granting of immunity." This situation should not be confused with the one discussed in *United States v. Villines*,[32] where defense requests to immunize witnesses it would call during its case in chief were rejected.

[b]   Rule 804(a)(2)—Refusing to Testify

The second situation in which a declarant is unavailable is when the declarant refuses to testify concerning the subject matter of a prior statement even though the trial judge has ordered him to give testimony.[33] A witness who will not talk is no better than a witness who is not present. It is important that the trial judge attempt to get the witness to answer questions that are asked, rather than to assume that the initial reluctance of the witness to speak must immediately be respected. If the trial judge is unable to hold the witness in contempt, as may be the case, then there may be little the trial judge can practically do to force the witness to comply with the order of the court.

[c]   Rule 804(a)(3)—Lack of Memory

A third example of unavailability is a forgetful witness who claims lack of memory concerning the subject matter of a prior statement. This category can prove to be troublesome. If a witness testifies to a lack of memory with respect to the subject matter of the statement, there is no problem if the trial

---

[31]   17 M.J. 1087 (A.F.C.M.R. 1984).

[32]   13 M.J. 46 (C.M.A. 1982).

[33]   *See, e.g.,* United States v. Zappola, 646 F.2d 48 (2d Cir. 1981) (court must attempt to order uncooperative witness to answer before witness is unavailable).

judge believes that the witness truly has a loss of memory. But, if the trial judge decides that the witness is faking a memory loss in order to avoid providing testimony, the judge should attempt to convince the witness that it is important to provide the testimony that is needed in the case. Where the witness persists in refusing to testify, even if the witness is feigning a memory loss, the witness is unavailable for all practical purposes and the hearsay exception may be relied upon.

[d]   Rule 804(a)(4)—Death; Physical or Mental Infirmity

The fourth example is perhaps the most familiar of all. A witness who is dead or who is unable to be present because of a physical or mental illness or infirmity is unavailable within the meaning of the Rule.[34] This is a familiar example at common law.[35]

[e]   Rule 804(a)(5)—Absent from Trial

A fifth situation in which the declarant is unavailable occurs when the declarant is absent from the trial and the party offering a prior statement of the declarant has been unable to procure the attendance of the declarant.[36] With respect to dying declarations, declarations against interest, and statements of personal history, the party offering the statement must have been unable to get any testimony from the declarant in the form of a deposition or any other testimony that an opponent would have a chance to cross-examine. The preference is for cross-examination, if possible, except when the declarant has no need for it, as under Rule 801(d)(2)(A) and (B).

[f]   Rule 804(a)(6)—Military Necessity—Article 49(d)(2)

Finally, subdivision (a) states that a witness is unavailable if the witness is deemed to be unable to be present at trial under Article 49(d)(2) of the Uniform Code of Military Justice. The Drafters' Analysis indicates that the meaning of "military necessity" associated with the Article "must be determined by reference to the cases construing Article 49." For example, *United States v. Obligacion*,[37] required an actual showing of unavailability based upon government counsel's investigation and attempt to obtain the witness. In *United States v. Chavez-Rey*,[38] witness unavailability was based

---

[34] *See, e.g.,* United States v. McGowan, 590 F.3d 446 (7th Cir. 2009) (witness with severe and chronic medical problems and unable to endure the rigors of travel from South Carolina to Chicago properly found to be unavailable).

[35] See Nicolas, *I'm Dying To Tell You What Happened': The Admissibility of Testimonial Dying Declarations Post-Crawford,* 37 HASTINGS CONST. L.Q. 487 Spring 2010.

[36] *See, e.g.,* United States v. Rothbart, 653 F.2d 462 (10th Cir. 1981) (government must avoid encouraging a witness to be absent).

[37] 37 C.M.R. 861 (A.F.B.R. 1967).

[38] 49 C.M.R. (A.F.C.M.R. 1974).

on "consideration[s] of time, expense, and personal safety of the two witnesses."[39]

[3]   Rule 804(b)—Hearsay Exceptions

Only after a declarant is found to be unavailable may the five exceptions found in subdivision (b) be considered.

[a]   Rule 804(b)(1)—Former Testimony

[i]   Basis for the Exception

The first exception in (b)(1) governs testimony that someone gave as a witness at another hearing, whether of the same or a different case, or during the taking of a deposition, as long as the person *against whom* the former testimony is now offered had an opportunity and similar motive to develop the testimony of the missing witness.[40] The opportunity need not have been on cross-examination. It could have come on direct examination or on redirect examination. Additionally, it does not matter whether in the case in which the former testimony is offered, the posture of the party against whom it is offered has changed.[41] What a court must do is examine the prior case in order to see what motive the person had to examine the witness.[42] If the motive is similar to the motive in the case in which the former testimony is offered, and if there was an opportunity for examination, whether the opportunity was taken advantage of or not, then the former testimony rule is satisfied.

It is important to know that the Rule does not require that the issues in the two cases be identical, or that the parties be identical. The Rule focuses on the fair opportunity for a prior examination of a witness at a time when the party against whom former testimony is offered had an incentive to fully examine the witness. It may be easier for a court to find similar motive when the issues are identical or similar, but in some cases the issues may be different and yet a motive to examine the witness fully may be found.

[ii]   Common Law Nexus

The former testimony exception to the hearsay rule has a very strong foundation. The person against whom the testimony is offered had a chance

---

[39] *See also* United States v. Ledbetter, 2 M.J. 37 (C.M.A. 1976).

[40] *See, e.g.*, United States v. King, 713 F.2d 627 (11th Cir. 1983) (reversing use of Rule 403 to exclude government offer of prior testimony qualifying as former testimony).

[41] *But see* United States v. Taplin, 954 F.2d 1256 (6th Cir. 1992) (finding error in trial court's admission of testimony from cohort's suppression hearing despite fact that defendant's attorney was present, because counsel did not have a similar motive or incentive to thoroughly cross-examine at that time).

[42] *See, e.g.*, United States v. Atkins, 618 F.2d 366 (5th Cir. 1980) (government did not have same motive to examine witness at hearing on admissibility of conspirators' statements as at trial).

to examine the witness, the witness had been under oath, and a record was made of the proceedings. In fact, unlike the Federal Rule, Military Rule 804(b)(1) explicitly states that a record of testimony before various military tribunals is admissible "if such record is a verbatim record." This is to emphasize the importance of accuracy in the use of former testimony. As long as former testimony is accurate, the fact that it has been given under oath when a party had a chance to examine a witness means that the only thing missing is the members' ability to observe the declarant's demeanor. Few exceptions have such a strong basis.

This may raise the question of why former testimony is included under Rule 804, rather than under Rule 803. The answer is that live testimony generally is preferred to a record of testimony, precisely because demeanor and an opportunity for first-hand observation of the witness are important. Only when the witness is unavailable may former testimony to be used.

[iii] Deposition Testimony

An example of how testimony taken at a pretrial deposition can be used in a court-martial is found in *United States v. Crockett*.[43] There the court held that videotaped depositions[44] were properly admitted against a defendant because: (1) both he and his counsel were present when they were taken, (2) the videotaped depositions were taken in connection with this particular court-martial, (3) defense counsel had the "opportunity to object to testimony offered on direct examination and to cross-examine the two witnesses" and (4) "unlike a preliminary hearing, when defense counsel may lack any motive to cross-examine prosecution witnesses extensively or even cross-examine at all" this deposition was taken in preparation for a pending trial. Thus, defense counsel knew the relevant issues and possessed the same motive for cross-examination "he would have had if [the witnesses] had testified in person at trial."

[iv] Article 32 Testimony

The most controversial aspect of former testimony arises in connection with Article 32 proceedings. Much of the Drafters' Analysis concerns this issue. While the Federal Rules of Criminal Procedure now make clear that a preliminary hearing is not a discovery device, Article 32 hearings serve the function of a preliminary hearing and the function of a discovery device. Thus, a defense counsel who wants to engage in discovery runs the risk that questions prematurely put to witnesses will be viewed as creating former testimony should the witness become unavailable at trial.

The drafters state that former testimony arising from an Article 32

---

[43] 21 M.J. 423 (C.M.A. 1986).

[44] *See, e.g.*, United States v. Tunnell, 667 F.2d 1182 (5th Cir. 1982) (videotape deposition of witness incapacitated by stroke admitted).

proceeding is admissible only if the motive for the Article 32 examination is the same as at trial. This, of course, is what (b)(1) states. The Supreme Court discussed the need for a similar motive in *United States v. Salerno*,[45] a case in which defense counsel sought to present the previous grand jury testimony of government witnesses who were unwilling to testify at trial. Although grand jury proceedings are *ex parte* by definition, while Article 32 hearings are much like preliminary hearings and permit the accused and defense counsel to participate in all witness examination and present testimony of their own, the Court's guidance is important for military judges and counsel to consider.[46]

In *Salerno*, the defendants were convicted of fraud and racketeering. During their grand jury investigation, unindicted suspects testified that they were not involved in the charged offenses. These suspects invoked their Fifth Amendment privileges at trial, and refused to testify for the defendants. The District Court subsequently denied the defendants' request to admit transcripts of the suspects' grand jury testimony because the prosecutors' motives to develop that testimony at trial were not similar to their motives at the grand jury hearings. The Circuit Court reversed, holding that "adversarial fairness" required the similar motive requirement to "evaporate" under these circumstances.

The Supreme Court disagreed and said that former testimony could not be introduced without a demonstration of congressionally mandated similar motives. Justice Thomas, writing for the eight justice majority, stated that there was no authority for the Court going beyond the plain meaning of this Rule and adopting an "adversarial fairness" standard. In the end, the Court held that, even if the prosecution has acted "unfairly" in developing the evidence only for its own purposes, 804(b)(1) did not provide a basis for admitting the testimony unless the defendants could show that the requirements of the Rule were satisfied. The Court then remanded the case for a determination of the government's motives in developing these witnesses' testimony.

In *United States v. DiNapoli*,[47] (Salerno passed away before the rehearing), the court held that motive similarity before a grand jury and at trial will generally be difficult to establish. To make this evaluation, the court said that first there must be a legitimate question about whether an indictment will issue. The closeness of this question affects the "intensity"

---

[45] 505 U.S. 317 (1992).

[46] *See, e.g.*, United States v. Harenberg, 732 F.2d 1507 (10th Cir. 1984) (court sustained exclusion of grand jury testimony of unavailable witness that was offered by defense); United States v. Young Bros., 728 F.2d 682 (5th Cir. 1984) (trial court erred in finding witnesses who testified before grand jury but refused to testify at trial to be available; court does not decide whether grand jury testimony is former testimony).

[47] 8 F.3d 909 (2d Cir. 1993).

government counsel will use in pursuing any grand jury witness. Second, the degree of credibility grand jurors may ascribe to a witness's testimony also affects how trial-like prosecutors may be in conducting grand jury examinations. The more concerned about believability government counsel are, the more likely their grand jury motives will be similar to their petit jury motives. Finally, the trial court must evaluate whether the prosecution's general grand jury approach is sufficiently similar to the trial approach to justify finding similar motives.

Using this case-by-case evaluation in *DiNapoli*, the court found that prosecutors were not engaged in the same type of all out attack during the grand jury proceedings as they would have pursued at trial. Thus, the court held that the government's motives were different enough to deny the defendant's request to use the grand jury testimony.

[v]   Court-Martial Application

In a court-martial setting, the value of *Salerno* and *DiNapoli* is that they suggest it as important to focus carefully on defense counsel's motives for questioning or not questioning Article 32 hearing witnesses as it is to focus on prosecutors' motives in questioning witnesses before civilian grand juries. Although military[48] and federal cases (preliminary hearings)[49] generally find defense similarity of motive and admit the out-of-court testimony under these circumstances, there is no reason why case-by-case consideration of specific motivation should not be required when the government attempts to offer Article 32 testimony against an accused.

[vi]   Liberal Military Standard

As noted above, and in our Annotated Cases, the United States Court of Appeals for the Armed Forces and the Service Courts of Criminal Appeals have consistently taken a liberal approach in this area. In *United States v. Arruza*,[50] the court held that Article 32 statements from the victim of child sexual abuse were properly admitted against the accused because: (1) "a combination of trial maneuvers and apparent intimidation [by] civilian defense counsel succeeded in silencing the victim," making her unavailable; (2) "the accused's opportunity to cross-examine the witness during the

---

[48] In United States v. Hubbard, 18 M.J. 678 (A.C.M.R. 1984), the accused contended that a key government witness's Article 32 statement should not have been admitted against him because defense counsel did not have the same motive to develop the witness's testimony at the Article 32 hearing as he did at trial. The court held that "[t]he motive of an opponent to the admission of former testimony may be determined by an objective examination of his conduct in light of the circumstances at the time of the former testimony." The facts in this case demonstrated the motive was the same.

[49] *See, e.g.*, Virgin Islands v. Aquino, 378 F.2d 540 (3d Cir. 1967) (finding the testimony admissible but questioning the underlying legal basis).

[50] 26 M.J. 234 (C.M.A. 1988).

Article 32 hearing was available and used by him"; and (3) the government produced a "substantially verbatim" record of the victim's statements. In *United States v. Connor*,[51] the court added that "as long as it can be concluded that the motive for cross-examination at the pretrial hearing was 'similar' to that which would have existed if the witness appeared at trial," the evidence will be admissible.

On occassion defense might offer Article 32 testimony against the government. Under these circumstances it is likely that trial counsel's motive at the Article 32 proceeding will be similar to his motive to prove the case at trial. In some instances, the prosecution will be fully prepared to examine a witness, while defense counsel is less well prepared. It is possible that a military judge could find that the government had a similar motive at the Article 32 proceeding as at trial, but defense counsel did not. If so, there may be a different result if former testimony is offered against the government than if former testimony is offered against the defendant.[52]

[vii]   Tactical Considerations

In this light, the drafters suggest that defense counsel sometimes should assert that they plan not to examine witnesses fully, but only for purposes of discovery, because this will alert the judge in subsequent trials to the fact that defense counsel did not wish to create former testimony. The problem with this suggestion is that it will probably produce automatic statements by diligent defense counsel as to their intent to limit the examination of a witness. There is reason to be skeptical about any disclaimer by defense counsel that is not bolstered with a specific explanation of why the examination is being limited— *e.g.*, investigation is not complete, certain witnesses have not been found, etc. If this is stated on the record during the Article 32 proceeding, and counsel act in accordance with the statement, the case for treating the Article 32 examination as falling outside the hearsay exception is strengthened.

Inevitably, a careful trial judge is going to have to examine the record of the Article 32 proceeding if the government claims that it is entitled to use the former testimony exception. The military judge will examine the completeness of counsel's previous examination, whether defense counsel sought to attack the witness, and whether there were gaps in the questioning that were consistent with the protestations by defense counsel as to the examination's being a limited one.

The actual record of a proceeding will be offered to satisfy the former testimony rule. But, it appears that only the verbatim record of military

---

[51]   27 M.J. 378 (C.M.A. 1989).

[52]   *Cf.* United States v. Klauber, 611 F.2d 512 (4th Cir. 1979) (indicating that the court might follow United States v. Driscoll, 445 F. Supp. 864 (D.N.J. 1978), and treat grand jury testimony as admissible against the government).

proceedings is required by the exception. As at common law, witnesses who have heard testimony in other proceedings outside the military sphere apparently are still free to testify under the exception.

[b]   Rule 804(b)(2)—Statements Under Belief of Impending Death

[i]   Basis for the Exception

The second exception for unavailable declarants is the traditional dying declaration.[53] Although the Rule is similar to its federal counterpart, it eliminates any reference to civil cases, and applies in any case in which an offense results in the victim's death. The exception covers statements made by a declarant who believes that death is imminent, as long as the statement concerns the cause or circumstances of the perceived impending death. Testimony about past events or memories are not admissible. Dying declarations are admissible in prosecutions for homicide, but they are not limited to homicide cases. They may be used in a prosecution for any offense that results in the death of the alleged victim. Thus, if a lesser included offense is charged, but death has resulted from the offense, the statement may be admissible.

[ii]   No Requirement for Death

There is no requirement that the declarant have died as a result of the offense. As long as the declarant is unavailable, the hearsay exception may be used. Of course, there must be a showing that the declarant believed death was imminent when the statement was made. Often, death will follow. But the fact that the declarant misperceived the situation and did not die does not mean that the declaration fails to qualify under the exception. It qualifies as long as the declarant later becomes unavailable, and is offered to prove a homicide or other crime resulting in the victim's death. The exception expands somewhat on previous military practice, but is based on the familiar rationale that people do not lie as they contemplate death and the possibility of "meeting their Maker."

[c]   Rule 804(b)(3)—Statement Against Interest

[i]   Basis for the Exception—Supreme Court Interpretation

The third exception is the familiar one concerning statements against interest. Statements against interest are often confused with admissions, which are covered by Rule 801(d)(2).

A declaration against interest is a statement that was against the interest of the declarant when made; an admission is a statement that is offered against

---

[53] *See, e.g.,* United States v. Two Shields, 497 F.3d 789 (8th Cir. 2007) (statement properly excluded because although declarant's injuries were serious there was no proof he believed he would die from them).

a party by an opponent, even though the admission may have been self-serving to the declarant when made. A declaration against interest may be made by anyone; an admission is a statement by a party or someone associated with the party. The prior *Manual* had no provision for declarations against interest, although they were recognized in court-martial practice.[54]

This exception recently came before the Supreme Court in *Lilly v. Virginia*,[55] where the Court reversed the accused's convictions and held that declarations against the penal interests of an unavailable declarant who testifies against the accused were not "firmly rooted." As a result, the Court used a Confrontation Clause analysis to determine whether the questioned evidence contained "particularized guarantees of trustworthiness." The Court found that such guarantees were not present and the statement was thus not sufficiently reliable because, at the time the declarant (accomplice) made the statement, he was in custody and responding to the police's leading questions. The Court rejected using other evidence to corroborate the confession and stated that reliability must be connected to the statement's inherent trustworthiness. The Court also rejected arguments claiming reliability based on the fact that the declarant had been read his "Miranda" rights, and the statement partially subjected declarant to criminal liability. However, the Court did say that its holding did not apply to statements against penal interest that are offered as admissions against a declarant-defendant, or statements against penal interest which are offered by the accused as exculpatory evidence— *e.g.*, claiming that the declarant, not the defendant, committed the charged offense.

[ii] Expands Common Law to Include Penal Interests

The Military Rule follows the Federal Rule. It expands the class of statements qualifying as declarations against interest beyond those recognized at common law.[56] The Rule provides that statements may be against pecuniary or proprietary interests, which was the situation at common law, or against penal interests. The penal interest part of the Rule is the expansion that many commentators have advocated for some time. The Rule indicates that statements qualify as being against interest if they would have subjected someone to civil or criminal liability at the time that they were made.

[iii] Trustworthiness Requirement

The test under this Rule is whether "a reasonable person in the position of the declarant would not have made the statement unless the person believed

---

[54] *See* United States v. Johnson, 3 M.J. 143 (C.M.A. 1977), for an excellent discussion of the pre-Rules situation.

[55] 527 U.S. 116 (1999).

[56] *See, e.g.*, United States v. Watson, 525 F.3d 583 (7th Cir. 2008) (statement of insider knowledge properly admitted because it exposed the declarant to conspiracy charges).

it to be true."[57] This rationale is based on the assumption that people are reluctant to say things against their self-interest unless those things are the truth. Thus, it is important to determine whether a person would have thought the statement was against his or her interest when made, because, if it was not, there is no guarantee of trustworthiness.[58]

[iv]   Disserving Nature of Declarant's Statements

An issue of concern to military and federal courts is how disserving does the declarant's statement have to be in order to be admitted under this exception. Some courts have required the statement to be categorically in opposition to the declarant's interests.[59] Yet such a high standard possibly conflicts with the Rule's expansive language which makes admissible statements that "tended to subject the declarant to civil or criminal liability." Other courts that have viewed the Rule less strictly have admitted evidence that may be only implicitly disserving.[60]

Federal courts have also looked to the circumstances surrounding how and when a statement was made to determine if it is really disserving. For example, if a friend of the accused is already serving one life sentence for murder, that friend's confession to a serious crime for which the accused is on trial may pose no significant threat to the friend.[61] Or, if at the time of sentencing, one co-accused accepts total responsibility for the crime as a means of demonstrating responsibility and remorse, his statement at the other co-accused's trial will likely be viewed as more self-serving than disserving and excluded.[62]

[v]   Portions of Statements Not Disserving May be Inadmissible

One of the most perplexing questions counsel and military judges face

---

[57] *See, e.g.*, United States v. Bobo, 994 F.2d 524 (8th Cir. 1993) (affirming firearm possession conviction, court said trustworthiness of statements against interest measured by (1) any apparent motive for out of court declarant to misrepresent; (2) general character of the speaker; (3) whether third parties heard the out-of-court statement; (4) whether the declarant made the statement spontaneously; (5) timing of the declaration; and (6) relationship between the speaker and the witness).

[58] *See, e.g.*, United States v. Palumbo, 639 F.2d 123 (3d Cir. 1981) (statement by unindicted conspirator not necessarily against interest).

[59] *See, e.g.*, United States v. Harwood, 998 F.2d 91 (2d Cir. 1993) (where statement only suggests criminal liability it will not be admissible).

[60] *See, e.g.*, United States v. Thomas, 571 F.2d 285 (5th Cir. 1978) (statements are sufficiently disserving if they would have probative value in the declarant's own trial).

[61] *See, e.g.*, United States v. Silverstein, 732 F.2d 1338 (7th Cir. 1984) (statement from friend confessing to crimes held not disserving because friend was already serving three life sentences).

[62] *See, e.g.*, United States v. Albert, 773 F.2d 386 (1st Cir. 1985) (codefendant's statement made during sentencing held to be inadmissible at coactor's trial).

when using 804(b)(3) is whether the declarant's entire statement be used if it contains disserving, self-serving, and neutral portions. In *Williamson v. United States*,[63] the Supreme Court examined this question. There the accused and a co-actor were involved in a drug offense. When the co-actor was arrested, he confessed, implicating the accused and attempting to partially exonerate himself. At the accused's trial the co-actor refused to testify. Over defense objection, the DEA agent who took the co-actor's confession was allowed to testify about the co-actor's inculpatory and exculpatory statements. Although the circuit court affirmed the accused's conviction, the Supreme Court vacated and remanded, holding that this exception to the hearsay rule applies to only self-inculpatory statements. Neutral or self-serving portions of inculpatory statements should not be admitted. The Court also held that collateral statements are inadmissible under this rule. In adopting this narrow definition of (b)(3), the Court said that a declarant's statements must be truly self-inculpatory and not an attempt to shift blame or curry favor with government counsel or police investigators.[64]

To make the self-inculpatory determination, the Court recommended that trial judges and counsel view a declarant's protestations within the setting and context they were made. Statements that appear neutral on their face may be directly against the declarant's penal interests under certain circumstances Rule 803(b)(3) requires counsel and military judges to ask whether the declarant's statement is sufficiently against his penal interests so that a reasonable person would not have uttered it unless it was true.

In *United States v. Jacobs*,[65] the United States Court of Appeals for the Armed Forces had an opportunity to interpret *Williamson*. There the accused had been convicted of several specifications of introducing controlled substances onto military aircraft with the intent to distribute. Concerning one of the specifications, the individual who received the drug shipment was in a Japanese jail and unavailable for trial. As a result, the government was permitted to use that declarant's previous incriminating statements to an undercover OSI agent pursuant to 804(b)(3). The accused first contended that statements against penal interest are not firmly rooted exceptions and that the government failed to meet the standard in *Ohio v. Roberts*,[66] of establishing their sufficient "particularized guarantees of trustworthiness" to satisfy the Confrontation Clause. The court rejected the accused's conten-

---

[63] 512 U.S. 594 (1994).

[64] In the military setting, this logic should be extended to statements the declarant may make in an effort to gain favorable treatment from the convening authority, any subordinate commander, or noncommissioned officer perceived by the declarant as potentially helpful in her attempt to minimize unfavorable action.

[65] 44 M.J. 301 (C.A.A.F. 1996).

[66] 448 U.S. 56 (1980).

tion, holding that its decision in *United States v. Wind*,[67] followed the weight of authority viewing statements against penal interest as firmly rooted.

Next, the court recognized that the real difficulty with admitting most declarations against penal interests is that they are "made by co-actors who frequently have motives to shift or minimize guilt or to gain legal advantage by agreeing to assist the prosecution." Following *Williamson*, the United States Court of Appeals for the Armed Forces held that, because the Supreme Court's decision had been rendered after Jacobs' trial and was not considered by the Air Force Court of Criminal Appeals, the case would have to be remanded to determine whether the declarant's statements were "truly self-inculpatory." The court went on to say that, in order to accomplish this goal, declarant's statement "must be analyzed line by line and sentence by sentence and only those portions of the declaration that are 'truly self-inculpatory' may be admitted." Relying on *Williamson*, the court recognized that this process "can be a fact-intensive inquiry, which would require careful examination of all the circumstances surrounding the criminal activity involved."

Williamson and *Jacobs* are particularly applicable to situations where the declarant is in custody or confinement.[68] Many courts that have evaluated statements made in custody find them to be more self-serving than against the declarant's penal interests. In *Lee v. Illinois*,[69] the Supreme Court viewed post-custodial confessions by accomplices as being particularly unreliable and reversed a conviction because it could find nothing in the record which overcame the existing presumption of unreliability such evidence creates. In the Court's words, "[A]ccusatory statements of co-actors have traditionally been viewed with special suspicion. . . ."

[vi]   Corroborating Evidence Needed to Exculpate an Accused

The last sentence of the exception states that a declaration against interest that tends to expose a declarant to criminal liability and is offered to exculpate an accused is not admissible unless corroborating circumstances clearly indicate the trustworthiness of the statement. However, neither the Rule itself nor the Drafter's Analysis provides a standard for determining the level of corroboration needed. Federal courts exploring this issue have taken opposing views. Some indicate that the quantum of proof for admission must be significant,[70] while others rely more heavily upon the accused's Consti-

---

[67] 24 M.J. 386 (C.M.A. 1987).

[68] *See, e.g.*, United States v. Riley, 657 F.2d 1377 (8th Cir. 1991) (confession obtained while the declarant was in custody held violative of 804(b)(3)).

[69] 476 U.S. 530 (1986).

[70] *See, e.g.*, United States v. Bumpass, 60 F.3d 1099 (4th Cir. 1995) (conviction affirmed as court found no error in excluding a friend's confession because the accused failed to clearly establish corroborating circumstances).

tutional rights to due process and to an effective defense by making the standard only rigorous enough to ensure trustworthiness.[71]

The Drafters believed that, when several people were involved in criminal activity, once one is convicted, that person has no reason to refrain from taking the blame for the offense in an effort to help his confederates. Similarly, the drafters feared that someone imprisoned for a long period of time has little to lose by confessing to a crime that may have been committed by someone else. Thus, the Rule requires corroboration and federal and military courts, even when they disagree on the exact amount of evidence that is required, seem to take the requirement quite seriously.[72]

In *United States v. Alvarez*,[73] the court held that when the government offers statements against interest by a declarant other than a defendant, corroborating circumstances also are required. *Alvarez* represents a judgment that the government should be no better off than the defendant. Arguably it is an unnecessary decision. Most courts have indicated skepticism when a statement by a declarant is a declaration against his or her own interest but it also includes references to third parties. It is common practice to redact the statements to avoid the references to the third parties.[74]

[vii]   The Military Drafter's Position

The Drafters' Analysis seems to take less seriously the arguments against admitting statements by one person implicating another than the Supreme Court accepted in *Williamson*. Unlike the Supreme Court, the drafters apparently accept the theory that any declaration against interest is reliable.

As mentioned above, most military and federal courts which have interpreted 804(b)(3) have been skeptical of statements by one person that implicate another.[75] The courts understand that reasonable people do not usually make statements against their *own* interest; yet, reasonable people

---

[71] *See, e.g.*, United States v. Barrett, 539 F.2d 244 (1st Cir. 1976) (standard of proof cannot be so high as to be "utterly unrealistic").

[72] In United States v. Guillette, 547 F.2d 743 (2d Cir. 1976), the court said the following factors should be considered in judging trustworthiness: (a) the time the declaration was made, (b) the party the declaration was made to, (c) the available corroborating evidence, (d) the extent to which the declaration is really against the declarant's interest, and (e) the declarant's availability. *See also* United States v. Perner, 14 M.J. 181 (C.M.A. 1982) (uncorroborated statements were not admitted where (a) they possessed no indication of reliability, (b) were not made under oath, and (c) were largely ambiguous).

[73] 584 F.2d 694 (5th Cir. 1978).

[74] *See, e.g.*, United States v. White, 553 F.2d 310 (2d Cir. 1977) (statements of a prostitute offered by the government were properly redacted so that references to other criminal misconduct would not reach the finder of fact).

[75] *See, e.g.*, United States v. Dillion, 18 M.J. 340 (C.M.A. 1984) (statements "did not meet the most basic requirements of the penal-interest hearsay exception."); United States v. Perner, 14 M.J. 181 (C.M.A. 1982) (statements possessed no indication of reliability and thus

are more likely to make statements implicating others.

Although statements that tend to exculpate the accused need corroboration, it is clear that, if corroborated, statements need not *necessarily* subject a declarant to liability. The Rule requires only that the statement "tend" to subject the declarant to civil or criminal liability.[76]

[d]   Rule 804(b)(4)—Statement of Personal or Family History

The fourth hearsay exception covers statements of personal or family history. It is divided into two parts. Part (A) provides that a person's statements concerning his or her own birth, adoption, marriage, and family relations are admissible even though the person had no means of acquiring personal knowledge of the matter stated. Part (B) covers statements by a declarant about another's family history. A declarant's statements about another's history are admissible if the declarant is related to the other by blood, adoption, or marriage, or if the declarant was so intimately associated with the family of the other person as to be likely to have accurate information concerning the matter declared.

This Rule is very broad. It allows statements to be admitted even though they were made after a dispute arose and even though the declarant had no personal knowledge about the matter stated. This Rule has had very little military application. It had no counterpart in the prior *Manual*.

An argument can be made that the reliability of many statements covered by this Rule is suspect. At common law, statements seeking to qualify under the exception had to have been made before a dispute arose— *i.e.*, at a time when a person would have had no reason to lie about the matters covered by the exception. But 804(b)(4) eliminates this requirement. Apparently, the drafters believed that a person generally does not tell lies about these matters. It also may be that such lies are likely to be noticed by people who are familiar with the person, his or her family, and his or her background. The Rule may rest on a genuine need for evidence. Family history might not be easily proved by other means. Courts may find that statements made by a friend of the family or relative are more reliable than ones made by a person about himself or herself, since the person's own statements might be self-serving. Of course, statements that are very suspect because of the circumstances in which they were made could conceivably be excluded under Rule 403.

[e]   Rule 804(b)(5)—Other Exceptions

This provision has been moved to Rule 807, discussed *below*.

---

were not admissible; court indicated it will impose a strict standard on the admissibility of such evidence).

[76] *See, e.g.*, United States v. Thomas, 571 F.2d 285 (5th Cir. 1978) ("by referring to statements that 'tend' to subject the declarant to criminal liability, the Rule encompasses disserving statements by a declarant that would have probative value in a trial against the declarant").

[f] Rule 804(b)(6)—Forfeiture by Wrongdoing

When a party participates in or acquiesces in making a declarant unavailable to testify at trial, that party's conduct makes irrelevant the traditional hearsay focus on reliability. Even in a criminal context, such misconduct forfeits the accused's constitutional right to object to hearsay and to insist upon confrontation.[77] Rule 804(b)(6) is written to protect witnesses and to disadvantage parties who engage in misconduct "which strikes at the heart of the system of justice itself."[78]

It is important to note here that the wrongdoing in question need not amount to criminal misconduct, and the Rule's provisions apply to all parties, including the government. Federal courts have not been uniform in their approach to determining whether there is wrongdoing.[79] The overwhelming majority of cases apply a preponderance of the evidence standard.[80]

In *Giles v. California*,[81] the Supreme Court held that an accused's right to confrontation can be forfeited if the prosecution establishes that he took actions that were intended to and did prevent a witness from testifying at trial. The requirement is a specific one. The accused's intent must have been to render the witness unavailable for trial. Simply proving that the accused had the specific intent to murder, assault, or in any other way harm the unavailable witness is insufficient. The Court said this result is mandated by *Crawford v. Washington*, and the common law founding-era forfeiture by wrongdoing exception to the Confrontation Clause.

Dwayne Giles's relationship with his girlfriend had been marked by abuse. She had previously reported his assaults and threats to the police as part of a domestic violence investigation. At trial, the State alleged that the accused killed his girl friend to prevent her from seeing other men. When the prosecution offered the victim's statements into evidence, the accused contended that their admission violated his Sixth Amendment right to

---

[77] *See, e.g.,* United States v. Johnson, 495 F.3d 951 (8th Cir. 2007) (statements of murdered witnesses defendant killed to cover-up his drug offenses properly admitted because defendant's acts forfeited his confrontation rights).

[78] *See* United States v. Mastrangelo, 693 F.2d 269, 273 (2d Cir. 1982), *cert. denied*, 467 U.S. 1204 (1984).

[79] *See, e.g.,* United States v. Aguiar, 975 F.2d 45, 47 (2d Cir. 1992); United States v. Potamitis, 739 F.2d 784, 789 (2d Cir.), *cert. denied*, 469 U.S. 918 (1984); Steele v. Taylor, 684 F.2d 1193, 1199 (6th Cir. 1982), *cert. denied*, 460 U.S. 1053 (1983); United States v. Balano, 618 F.2d 624, 629 (10th Cir. 1979), *cert. denied*, 449 U.S. 840 (1980); United States v. Carlson, 547 F.2d 1346, 1358, 1359 (8th Cir.), *cert. denied*, 431 U.S. 914 (1977).

[80] *See,* United States v. Zlatogur, 271 F.3d 1025 (11th Cir. 2002) (preponderance of the evidence standard held appropriate). *Contra*, United States v. Thevis, 665 F.2d 616, 631 (5th Cir.) (clear and convincing standard), *cert. denied*, 459 U.S. 825 (1982).

[81] 554 U.S. 353 (2008).

confront her. The State argued that the victim's absence was a direct consequence of the accused's murdering her, the murder resulted in forfeiture of his confrontation rights, and his motive in killing her was irrelevant.

The Supreme Court did not agree. Justice Scalia wrote that the original common law basis for the forfeiture by wrongdoing exception permitted use of an unavailable witness's statements only if the witness had been "detained" or "kept away" by the "means or procurement" of the accused. The accused's intent to prevent the witness from testifying is therefore crucial and must be established before the statements can be admitted. The Court went on to indicate that the common law rationale for the specific intent requirement was based on providing a disincentive to an accused who might otherwise intimidate, bribe, or kill witnesses to prevent their testimony.

By vacating the judgment and remanding the case, the Court gave the prosecution a second bite at the apple. The Court indicated that the State is now free to probe Giles's intent in killing his former girlfriend. If there is evidence that an abusive relationship ending in murder existed, that evidence might support a finding that the charged crimes represented an intent by the accused to isolate the victim and prevent her from reporting the crimes or cooperating with a criminal investigation into the accused's abusive behavior. The Court suggested that proving such conduct might satisfy the intent to detain or keep away standard.

§ 804.03   Drafters' Analysis

[1]   Definition of Unavailability

Subdivisions (a)(1)-(a)(5) of Rule 804 are taken from the Federal Rule without change and are generally similar to the relevant portions of ¶¶ 145 *a* and 145 *b* of the present *Manual*, except that Rule 804(a)(3) provides that a witness who "testifies as to a lack of memory of the subject matter of the declarant's statement" is unavailable. The Rule also does not distinguish between capital and non-capital cases.

Rule 804(a)(6) is new and has been added in recognition of certain problems, such as combat operations, that are unique to the armed forces. Thus, Rule 804(a)(6) will make unavailable a witness who is unable to appear and testify in person for reason of military necessity within the meaning of Article 49(d)(2). The meaning of "military necessity" must be determined by reference to the cases construing Article 49. The expression is not intended to be a general escape clause, but must be restricted to the limited circumstances that would permit use of a deposition.

[2]   Hearsay Exceptions

[a]   Former Testimony

The first portion of Rule 804(b)(1) is taken from the Federal Rule with omission of the language relating to civil cases. The second portion is new and has been included to clarify the extent to which those military tribunals in which a verbatim record normally is not kept come within the Rule.

The first portion of Rule 804(b)(1) makes admissible former testimony when "the party against whom the testimony is now offered had an opportunity and similar motive to develop the testimony by direct, cross, or redirect examination." Unlike ¶ 145 *b* of the present *Manual*, the Rule does not explicitly require that the accused, when the evidence is offered against him or her, have been "afforded at the former trial an opportunity to be adequately represented by counsel." Such a requirement should be read into the Rule's condition that the party had "opportunity and similar motive." In contrast to the present *Manual*, the Rule does not distinguish between capital and non-capital cases.

The second portion of Rule 804(b)(1) has been included to ensure that testimony from military tribunals, many of which ordinarily do not have verbatim records, will not be admissible unless such testimony is presented in the form of a verbatim record. The committee believed substantive use of former testimony to be too important to be presented in the form of an incomplete statement.

Investigations under Article 32 of the Uniform Code of Military Justice present a special problem. Rule 804(b)(1) requires that "the party against whom the testimony is now offered had an opportunity and similar motive to develop the testimony" at the first hearing. The "similar motive" requirement was intended primarily to ensure sufficient identity of issues between the two proceedings and thus to ensure an adequate interest in examination of the witness.[1] Because Article 32 hearings represent a unique hybrid of preliminary hearings and grand juries with features dissimilar to both, it was particularly difficult for the committee to determine exactly how subdivision (b)(1) of the Federal Rule would apply to Article 32 hearings. The specific difficulty stems from the fact that Article 32 hearings were intended by Congress to function as discovery devices for the defense as well as to recommend an appropriate disposition of charges to the convening authority.[2] It is thus permissible, for example, for a defense counsel to limit cross-examination of an adverse witness at an Article 32 hearing using the opportunity for discovery, alone, for example, rather than impeachment. In such a case, the defense would not have the requisite "similar motive" found within Rule 804(b)(1).

---

[1] *See, e.g.,* United States v. Salerno, 505 U.S. 317 (1992) (former testimony cannot be introduced without a demonstration of similar motives).

[2] Hutson v. United States, 19 C.M.A. 437 (1970); United States v. Samuels, 10 C.M.A. 206 (1959) (discussing the tactical components of discovery and Article 32 hearings). *See generally Hearing on H.R. 2498 Before a Subcomm. of the House Comm. on Armed Services*, 81st Cong., 1st Sess., 997 (1949).

Notwithstanding the inherent difficulty of determining the defense coun-sel's motive at an Article 32 hearing, the Rule is explicitly intended to prohibit use of testimony given at an Article 32 hearing unless the requisite "similar motive" was present during that hearing. It is clear that some Article 32 testimony is admissible under the Rule notwithstanding the congression-ally sanctioned discovery purpose of the Article 32 hearing. Consequently, one is left with the question of the extent to which the Rule actually does apply to Article 32 testimony. The only apparent practical solution to what is otherwise an irresolvable dilemma is to read the Rule as permitting only Article 32 testimony preserved via a verbatim record that is not objected to as having been obtained without the requisite "similar motive." While defense counsel's assertion of his or her intent in not examining one or more witnesses or in not fully examining a specific witness is not binding upon the military judge, clearly the burden of establishing admissibility under the Rule is on the prosecution and the burden so placed may be impossible to meet should the defense counsel adequately raise the issue. As a matter of good trial practice, a defense counsel who is limiting cross-examination at the Article 32 hearing because of discovery should announce that intent sometime during the Article 32 hearing so that the announcement may provide early notice to all concerned and hopefully avoid the necessity for counsel to testify at the later trial.

The Federal Rule was modified by the committee to require that testimony offered under Rule 804(b)(1) which was originally "given before courts-martial, courts of inquiry, military commissions, other military tribunals, and before proceedings pursuant to or equivalent to those required by Article 32" and which is otherwise admissible under the Rule be offered in the form of a verbatim record. The modification was intended to ensure accuracy in view of the fact that only summarized or minimal records are required of some types of military proceedings.

An Article 32 hearing is a "military tribunal." The Rule distinguishes between Article 32 hearings and other military tribunals in order to recognize that there are other proceedings which are considered the equivalent of Article 32 hearings for purposes of former testimony under Rule 804(b)(1).

[b]   Statement Under Belief of Impending Death

Rule 804(b)(2) is taken from the Federal Rule except that the language, "for any offense resulting in the death of the alleged victim," has been added and reference to civil proceedings has been omitted. The new language has been added because there is no justification for limiting the exception only to those cases in which a homicide charge has actually been preferred. Due to the violent nature of military operations, it may be appropriate to charge a lesser included offense rather than homicide. The same justifications for the exception are applicable to lesser included offenses which are also, of course, of lesser severity. The additional language, taken from ¶ 142 *a*, thus retains the present *Manual* rule, modification of which was viewed as being impracticable.

Rule 804(b)(2) is similar to the dying declaration exception found in ¶ 142 *a* of the present *Manual*, except that the Military Rule does not require that the declarant be dead. So long as the declarant is unavailable and the offense is one for homicide or other offense resulting in the death of the alleged victim, the hearsay exception may be applicable. This could, for example, result from a situation in which the accused, intending to shoot *A, shoots both A* and *B; A* utters the hearsay statement, under a belief of impending death, *B* dies, and although *A* recovers, *A* is unavailable to testify at trial. In a trial of the accused for killing *B, A*'s statement will be admissible.

There is no requirement that death immediately follow the declaration, but the declaration is not admissible under this exception if the declarant had a hope of recovery. The declaration may be made by spoken words or intelligible signs or may be in writing. It may be spontaneous or in response to solicitation, including leading questions. The utmost care should be exercised in weighing statements offered under this exception since they are often made under circumstances of mental and physical debility and are not subject to the usual tests of veracity. The military judge may exclude those declarations which are viewed as being unreliable. *See, e.g.,* Rule 403.

A dying declaration and its maker may be contradicted and impeached in the same manner as other testimony and witnesses. Under the present law, the fact that the deceased did not believe in a deity or in future rewards or punishments may be offered to affect the weight of a declaration offered under this Rule but does not defeat admissibility. Whether such evidence is now admissible in the light of Rule 610 is unclear.

[c] Statement Against Interest

Rule 804(b) is taken from the Federal Rule without change, and has no express equivalent in the *Manual.* It has, however, been made applicable by case law.[3] It makes admissible statements against a declarant's interests, whether pecuniary, proprietary, or penal when a reasonable person in the position of the declarant would not have made the statement unless such a person would have believed it to be true.

The Rule expressly recognizes the penal interest exception and permits a statement tending to expose the declarant to criminal liability. The penal interest exception is qualified, however, when the declaration is offered to exculpate the accused by requiring the "corroborating circumstances clearly indicate the trustworthiness of the statement." This requirement is applicable, for example, when a third party confesses to the offense the accused is being tried for and the accused offers the third party's statement in

---

[3] United States v. Johnson, 3 M.J. 143 (C.M.A. 1977).

evidence to exculpate the accused. The basic penal interest exception is established as a matter of constitutional law by the Supreme Court's decision in *Chambers v. Mississippi*,[4] which may be broader than the Rule as the case may not require either corroborating evidence or an unavailable declarant.

In its present form, the Rule fails to address a particularly vexing problem—that of the declaration against penal interest which implicates the accused as well as the declarant. On the face of the Rule, such a statement should be admissible, subject to the effects, if any, of *Bruton v. United States*,[5] and Rule 306. Notwithstanding this, there is considerable doubt as to the applicability of the Rule to such a situation.[6] Although the legislative history reflects an early desire on the part of the Federal Rules of Evidence Advisory Committee to prohibit such testimony, a provision doing so was not included in the material reviewed by Congress. Although the House included such a provision, it did so apparently in large part based upon a view that Bruton, above, prohibited such statements—arguably an erroneous view of *Bruton, above, see, e.g., Bruton v. United States*, 391 U.S. 123, 128, n.3 (1968); *Dutton v. Evans*, 400 U.S. 74 (1970). The Conference Committee deleted the House provision, following the Senate's desires, because it believed it inappropriate to "codify constitutional evidentiary principles" Weinstein's Evidence at 804-16 (1978) citing Cong. Res. H 11931–32 (daily ed. Dec. 14, 1974). Thus, applicability of the hearsay exception to individuals implicating the accused may well rest only on the extent to which *Bruton, above*, governs such statement. The committee intends that the Rule extend to such statements to the same extent that subdivision 804(b)(4) is held by the Article III courts to apply to such statements.

[d]   Statement of Personal or Family History

Rule 804(b)(4) of the Federal Rule is taken verbatim from the Federal Rule, and has no express equivalent in the present *Manual*. The primary feature of Rule 803(b)(4)(A) is its application, even though the "declarant had no means of acquiring personal knowledge of the matter stated."

[e]   Other Exceptions

[NOTE: Rule 805(b)(5) has been deleted and incorporated into Rule 807. The Drafter's original Rule 804(b)(5) analysis remains applicable to Rule 807.] Rule 804(b)(5) is taken without change from the Federal Rule and is identical to Rule 803(24). As Rule 803 applies to hearsay statements regardless of the declarant's availability or lack thereof, this vision is actually superfluous. As to its effect, *see* the *Analysis* to Rule 803(24).

---

[4]   410 U.S. 284 (1973).

[5]   391 U.S. 123 (1968) (concerning use and admissibility of one codefendant's statements against another).

[6]   *See generally*, 4 J. Weinstein & M. Berger, WEINSTEIN'S EVIDENCE 804-93, 804-16 (1978).

§ 804.04   Drafters' Analysis (1986)

The phrase "claim or lack of memory" was changed to "claim of lack of memory" to correct an error in MCM, 1984.

§ 804.05   Annotated Cases

[1]   Rule 804(a)—Definitions of Unavailability

[a]   Constitutional Standards

Supreme Court

Bullcoming v. New Mexico, 2011 U.S. Lexis 4790 (U.S. June 23, 2011); *Michigan v. Bryant*, 131 S.Ct. 1143 (2011); *Melendez-Diaz v. Massachusetts*, 129 S. Ct. 2527 (2009); *Whorton v. Bockting*, 549 U.S. 406 (2007); *Davis v. Washington*, 547 U.S. 813 (2006); and *Crawford v. Washington*, 541 U.S. 36, 53–54 (2004) are annotated above at section 801.04[1][a].

United States Court of Appeals for the Armed Forces

United States v. Crudup, 67 M.J. 92 (C.A.A.F. 2008): The accused was convicted of assault and battery upon his wife, resisting apprehension, and making a false official statement. When the wife refused to testify, her pretrial statement implicating the accused was admitted. The remainder of the government's case consisted of witnesses who observed the crimes and the accused's pretrial admissions. Although the court affirmed, it held that admitting the wife's pretrial statement violated the accused's Sixth Amendment confrontation rights. The court found that the error was harmless beyond a reasonable doubt because the statement was relatively unimportant and cumulative and the government's case was overwhelming. The court added that, although the wife could not have been cross-examined, her credibility was effectively impeached by proof of a previous fraud conviction. *See Delaware v. Van Arsdall*, 475 U.S. 673 (1986), discussing constitutional error tested for harmlessness.

Army Court of Criminal Appeals

United States v. Gardinier, 63 M.J. 531 (Army Ct. Crim. App. 2006): The accused was convicted of several child sexual molestation offenses. At trial he objected to admitting the victim's incriminating videotaped, statements which were made to a civilian police officer during the criminal investigation. Before admitting the videotape, the military judge conducted a pretrial hearing to determine whether the victim was available to testify. At the hearing, the victim's mother testified that the victim was reluctant to testify, would not provide useful information, and, in any event, she did not want her daughter to testify. Upon further questioning by the military judge, the mother indicated she would not allow her daughter to testify. Thereafter, the military judge admitted the videotaped statements based on unavailability under Rule 804(a), and trustworthiness under Rule 807. The military judge stated that his unavailability decision was based on his belief that it would not be right to compel the child to testify against the mother's wishes, and that he viewed his decision as a "matter of personal conscience." Relying on *Crawford,* the court held that the victim's statements were testimonial, the military judge had erroneously determined that the victim was unavailable, and there had not been the requisite opportunity for the accused to examine the victim either before or during trial. Applying a constitutional error standard, the court held that the inadmissible testimony added little to the government's case, and that the untainted evidence was sufficiently strong to justify affirmance.

[b] Rule 804(a)(1)—Privilege from Testifying

[i] Privilege from Testifying—Counsel's Obligation to Make a Record

Army Court of Criminal Appeals

United States v. Meyer, 14 M.J. 935 (A.C.M.R. 1983): The court found error in a military judge's blanket determination that a witness was unavailable, permitting his previous written statement to be used at trial. The judge did not assure that the witness would claim, and be entitled to claim, the privilege against self-incrimination in response to every question that might be asked. "The test is whether the witness is asked a question the answer to which would forge a link in a chain either tending to incriminate him or leading to evidence that would tend to incriminate him." The proponent of hearsay evidence must establish unavailability as to all aspects of testimony before being permitted to use a statement as a complete substitute for live testimony.

[ii] Privilege from Testifying—Fifth Amendment Claims

Army Court of Criminal Appeals

United States v. Robinson, 16 M.J. 766 (A.C.M.R. 1983): A witness was properly held to be unavailable when trial counsel established that, had the witness been called, the witness would have invoked his right against self-incrimination.

Navy-Marine Corps Court of Criminal Appeals

United States v. Swan, 45 M.J. 672 (N.M.Ct.Crim.App. 1996): The accused was convicted of numerous drug-related offenses, including conspiracy. A key participant in the criminal adventure originally made a statement incriminating the accused, then totally recanted it. At the accused's trial, the participant exercised his Fifth Amendment right not to testify as a result of having been charged with perjury. Although the government provided this witness with testimonial immunity concerning his involvement in the drug transactions, immunity was not provided concerning the perjury charge. Affirming the accused's convictions and the government's refusal to grant immunity for the perjury charge, the court held that the trial judge properly found the witness to be unavailable.

[iii]   Privilege from Testifying—Judge's Obligation to Protect the Record

Army Court of Criminal Appeals

United States v. Vega-Cancel, 19 M.J. 899 (A.C.M.R. 1985): In this case the proper procedure for excluding a witness who desires to claim his fifth amendment privilege was discussed. The court particularly highlighted the military judge's responsibility for insuring that the trial record adequately supports the witness's claim and the bench's resolution.

[iv]   Privilege from Testifying—Requirement for Grants of Immunity

Air Force Court of Criminal Appeals

United States v. Valente, 17 M.J. 1087 (A.F.C.M.R. 1984): The court rendered an important opinion on the use of hearsay evidence by trial counsel as it reasoned that "[f]airness dictates that where the prosecution seeks to introduce the hearsay statement of an absent witness, claiming him to be unavailable, the witness should be made available if it is within the power of the prosecutorial authority." As a result, "a prosecution witness is not 'unavailable' under Mil. R. Evid. 804(a)(1) even though he asserts his privilege against self-incrimination if he can be made available through the granting of immunity." However, this situation should not be confused with defense requests to immunize witnesses it will call during its case-in-chief. *See United States v. Villines,* 13 M.J. 46 (C.M.A. 1982).

[c]   Rule 804(a)(2)—Refusing to Testify

[i]   Refusing to Testify—Emotionally Unable to Testify

Army Court of Criminal Appeals

United States v. Arruza, 21 M.J. 621 (A.C.M.R. 1985): The victim of indecent liberties was found to be unavailable when, after she took the stand at trial, she became "emotionally distraught," and, despite extensive efforts by the trial judge and prosecutor encouraging her to testify, was unable to do so.

[d]   Rule 804(a)(4)—Death; Physical or Mental Infirmity

[i]   Infirmity—Current Status Required

Navy-Marine Corps Court of Criminal Appeals

United States v. Cabrera-Frattini, 65 M.J. 950 (N.M.Ct.Crim.App. 2008): This case was tried before the Supreme Court's decision in *Crawford v. Washington,* 541 U.S. 36 (2004). The accused was convicted of carnal knowledge and related offenses. A prior panel of the court reversed the accused's convictions and found that the trial judge improperly determined that the victim was unavailable before admitting her deposition. The Court of Appeals for the Armed Forces reversed the lower court and affirmed the accused's convictions. *United States v. Cabrera-Frattini*, 65 M.J. 241 (C.A.A.F. 2007). In his second presentation to the Court of Criminal Appeals, the accused contended that the victim's deposition should not have been admitted because at the time it was taken defense counsel was unable to effectively cross-examine her. Affirming the accused's convictions, the court held that the primary purpose of military depositions is to preserve testimony, particularly when as here the witness was not available at the Article 32 hearing. *See* R.C.M. 702(a). The court specifically declined to assess the effectiveness of defense counsel's pretrial questioning and rejected any contention that trial defense counsel was misled concerning how the deposition might ultimately be used.

United States v. Harjak, 33 M.J. 577 (N.M.C.M.R. 1991): The victim in this child sexual abuse case had allegedly been abused by her biological father, the accused, and her stepfather. At trial, the military judge admitted unauthenticated medical reports detailing the victim's six-month-old physical and psychological condition to demonstrate that she was currently unavailable. Reversing the conviction, the court held that, notwithstanding the military judge's empathetic concerns for the victim, the evidence was irrelevant as it did not discuss her current mental and physical condition.

[e]   Rule 804(a)(5)—Absent From Trial

[i]   Absent From Trial—Good Faith Effort to Locate—Declarant Absent

United States Court of Appeals for the Armed Forces

United States v. Burns, 27 M.J. 92 (C.M.A. 1988): A rape victim's Article 32 testimony was held to be inadmissible because no government official attempted to personally subpoena the victim and present her with "the fees and mileage required." The court said that "having failed to use properly the means at its disposal to compel appearance, the government was not free to claim at trial that [the victim] was 'unavailable.' "

Air Force Court of Criminal Appeals

United States v. Baker, 33 M.J. 788 (A.F.C.M.R. 1991): The accused was convicted of drug abuse offenses largely based on his confession and the videotaped statements of his paramour. Setting aside the findings and sentence, the court held that, because trial counsel relied on the absent paramour's husband's statements that she would not return to the States for trial, the government had not sufficiently demonstrated unavailability. In the court's opinion, good faith efforts, however bumbled and fruitless, to obtain a crucial witness were not enough to protect the accused's rights to confrontation. The conviction would probably have been affirmed had trial counsel obtained the paramour's own refusal to attend.

United States v. Griffin, 21 M.J. 501 (A.F.C.M.R. 1985): Where trial counsel's efforts at locating a missing witness appeared to the court to include only "one unsuccessful telephone call," they found that the government had not made a "reasonable effort" to secure the witness's presence and thus her pretrial testimony did not qualify for admission. The court punctuated its opinion by saying that "inconvenience in obtaining a witness is not an acceptable substitute for that person's availability."

United States v. Hogan, 16 M.J. 549 (A.F.C.M.R. 1983): The court found that a prosecutrix's pretrial statement was improperly admitted because "the trial judge made only a perfunctory effort to obtain the testimony of the witness."

Army Court of Criminal Appeals

United States v. Dorgan, 39 M.J. 827 (A.C.M.R. 1994): In this drug distribution case, a key registered source was considered unavailable at trial because the government had lost contact with her. Reversing the conviction, the court held that after defense counsel established the witness's materiality, proceedings should have been delayed long enough for trial counsel to make a diligent attempt at locating and serving the witness.

United States v. Ortiz, 33 M.J. 549 (A.C.M.R. 1991): Affirming the accused's conviction for indecently assaulting his daughter, the court held that the victim's verbatim Article 32 testimony was properly admitted because: (1) all reasonable efforts to obtain her attendance proved unsuccessful; (2) her former testimony demonstrated no inconsistencies or motives to lie; and (3) the accused's right of confrontation was preserved at the Article 32 hearing.

[ii] Absent From Trial—Good Faith Effort to Locate—Established

United States Court of Appeals for the Armed Forces

United States v. Davis, 29 M.J. 357 (C.M.A. 1990): In this drug and larceny prosecution, a relevant and necessary defense alibi witness refused to be served with a subpoena. Trial defense counsel did not request a continuance or abatement in order to secure the witness's presence, and conceded on the record that government counsel's efforts had been reasonable and diligent in attempting to produce the witness. The court held that a trial may proceed in the absence of a relevant and necessary witness if that witness is not amenable to process. *See also Ohio v. Roberts,* 448 U.S. 56 (1980) ("The lengths to which the prosecution must go to produce a witness—is a question of reasonableness").

Air Force Court of Criminal Appeals

United States v. Minaya, 30 M.J. 1179 (A.F.C.M.R. 1990): The accused was tried in Florida for offenses arising out of a sham marriage to a Philippine citizen. Defense counsel requested the production of a civilian witness from the Philippines to establish that his first marriage had been annulled. The government provided a plane ticket and was prepared to expedite the witness's visa request. Shortly before trial, the witness refused to answer phone calls or travel to the U.S. Affirming the conviction, the court held that the military judge properly determined that the witness was unavailable through no fault of the prosecution.

Army Court of Criminal Appeals

United States v. Murphy, 30 M.J. 1040 (A.C.M.R. 1990): Affirming the accused's murder conviction, the court held that, where both parties stipulate that the accused's spouse would not testify against her husband, "there was no need to formally call her into court for the sole purpose of invoking the privilege. We find that the military judge properly excused her from testifying."

United States v. Hubbard, 18 M.J. 678 (A.C.M.R. 1984): The court rejected the accused's contention that a key government witness was not really unavailable because they believed trial counsel had made "a good faith and reasonable effort to secure the [witness's] presence at the trial." *See* the discussion of this case in our Editorial Comments to Rule 804.

United States v. Thornton, 16 M.J. 1011 (A.C.M.R. 1983): In order to establish a witness's unavailability "prosecutorial authorities [must] have made a good faith effort to obtain his presence at trial." This good faith effort can include the use of process or other reasonable means. The court here emphasized that because "the law only requires a good faith effort to obtain the presence of the declarant, the proponent need not pursue a futile act." While hindsight may demonstrate that more could have been done, the court was satisfied that "an active search for the declarant concomitant with the issuance of a subpoena" was sufficient and reasonable.

[iii]   Absent From Trial—Judge's Responsibilities

Army Court of Criminal Appeals

United States v. Dieter, 42 M.J. 697 (Army Ct.Crim.App. 1995): In this case the court held that the military judge abused his discretion by finding a CID agent who had obtained the accused's confession unavailable, because the judge could have made some modifications in the presentation of evidence which would have ensured the declarant's presence. *See* the discussion of this case in our Editorial Comments to Rule 804.

[iv]   Absent From Trial—Overseas Trials

United States Court of Appeals for the Armed Forces

United States v. Hampton, 33 M.J. 21 (C.M.A. 1991): The victim of the accused's assault with intent to commit rape offenses lived in the United States. She rejected all government attempts to obtain her presence for trial in Germany. As a result, the convening authority ordered a videotaped deposition of the victim to be held in the States. The accused's military defense counsel attended this proceeding and questioned the victim. The deposition was introduced at trial. Affirming a conviction, the court held that all reasonable steps to obtain the witness had been taken, making the disposition admissible.

United States v. Crockett, 21 M.J. 423 (C.M.A. 1986): The court held that videotaped depositions were properly admitted against the accused because key government witnesses were "nonamenable to subpoena," and could not be persuaded to accept invitational travel orders from their homes in Florida to the trial forum in Germany. In reaching this result, the court specifically rejected the accused's contention that the witnesses were in fact available because "the court-martial could move to the witnesses' residence in order to hear [their] testimony first hand." The court said moving the trial forum would be unreasonable because military personnel (court members, witnesses, attorneys, etc.) would then "not have been available in Germany for any emergencies," and this negative impact on the Army's mission was unacceptable.

Air Force Court of Criminal Appeals

United States v. Amerine, 17 M.J. 947 (A.F.C.M.R. 1984): The court found that a witness is unavailable when he lives in the United States and cannot be subpoenaed to testify at a general court-martial held outside the United States.

[v]   Absent From Trial—Peripheral Matters

United States Court of Appeals for the Armed Forces

United States v. Wind, 28 M.J. 381 (C.M.A. 1989): The accused unsuccessfully contended that an out-of-court statement by an AWOL sailor indicating that the accused purchased drugs from him should not have been admitted in rebuttal to the accused's entrapment defense, because unavailability had not been satisfactorily established. The court held that the government did not rely solely on the AWOL to prove unavailability; instead, it checked local hospitals, police stations and the coroner's office. The court added that, where an unavailable witness's testimony is "vital," it must be "clearly proved," but where a statement by a missing witness relates to a peripheral matter or has many indicia of reliability, more leeway may be granted the government in proving that it has made a good faith effort to locate the witness.

[vi]   Absent From Trial—Witness's Failure to Answer
Subpoena or Travel Order

Air Force Court of Criminal Appeals

United States v. Henderson, 18 M.J. 745 (A.F.C.M.R. 1984): The court found a witness to be unavailable when that witness failed to answer a properly served subpoena ordering appearance in court.

Navy-Marine Corps Court of Criminal Appeals

United States v. Eiland, 39 M.J. 566 (N.M.C.M.R. 1994): This case is an interlocutory government appeal from a trial judge's decision to abate all proceedings until two witnesses could be procured. The accused was charged with raping a woman in Mallorca, Spain. The court-martial was conducted in Jacksonville, Florida. After defense counsel established the witnesses' materiality, government counsel attempted to obtain their presence. Both witnesses refused invitational travel orders. Defense counsel failed to stipulate to either witness's testimony, and the military judge refused to require such stipulations. Relying on R.C.M. 703, the court affirmed the military judge's decision, holding that live witnesses were essential to a fair trial here.

[f]   Rule 804(a)(6)—Unavailability Under Article 49

[i]   Unavailability Under Article 49—Military Necessity

United States Court of Appeals for the Armed Forces

United States v. Hughes, 52 M.J. 278 (C.A.A.F. 2000), *affirming,* 48 M.J. 700 (A.F.Ct.Crim.App. 1998): The accused was convicted of indecent assault upon two females under 16 years of age. Expert testimony indicated that the four-year-old victim would have been emotionally harmed if required to testify. The child's mother stated that under these circumstances she would not allow her daughter to take the stand and did not believe her daughter would tell the truth if she did testify. Affirming the accused's convictions, the court held the military judge properly determined the victim was unavailable.

United States v. Vanderwier, 25 M.J. 263 (C.M.A. 1987): The accused, a Navy Commander, was convicted of sodomy. Important, though not crucial, evidence of guilt was offered by videotape deposition over defense counsel's objection. Without making special findings, the military judge admitted the evidence upon trial counsel's assertion that there was "a fair inference [the witness] continued to be unavailable" because he was still at sea participating in required Naval training. Finding error but no prejudice, the court held that government counsel should have done more to establish the witness's actual unavailability. Evidence concerning the witness's current duty, location, and next availability date were not addressed. This particularly frustrated the court when it appeared that trial on the merits concluded two days before the claimed unavailability period ended.

Air Force Court of Criminal Appeals

United States v. Marsh, 35 M.J. 505 (A.F.C.M.R. 1992): The accused was convicted of wrongfully using cocaine. Because of Operation Desert Shield, a crucial government witness's testimony was presented by deposition. Trial defense counsel objected contending: (1) they had not received adequate written notice of the deposition hearing; (2) the accused's individually requested military counsel (IMC) was unable to attend; and (3) the witness in question was not actually unavailable. Finding error but no prejudice, the court held that, although timely written notice was not provided, the accused's detailed military counsel was present at the hearing, knowledgeable about the case, and conducted a professional examination of the witness. While the court would have preferred reasonable written notice and the presence of the accused's IMC, military operations necessitated the deposition. Any errors were viewed as nonprejudicial.

[2] Rule 804(b)—Hearsay Exceptions

[a] Rule 804(b)(1)—Former Testimony

[i] Former Testimony—Counsel Changes

Army Court of Criminal Appeals

United States v. Kelly, 15 M.J. 1024 (A.C.M.R. 1983): The court held that a key government witness's prior recorded testimony was properly admitted. The government had demonstrated that the witness was, in fact, unavailable, and the previous recorded statement had been given at a pretrial hearing where defense counsel conducted a vigorous cross-examination of the witness on the same issues raised at trial. The fact that the accused changed counsel before trial was immaterial. *See United States v. Amaya,* 533 F.2d 188 (5th Cir. 1976).

[ii] Former Testimony—Use During Deliberations

United States Court of Appeals for the Armed Forces

United States v. Austin, 35 M.J. 271 (C.M.A. 1992): During this child sexual abuse case, the victim recanted her pretrial statements which incriminated the accused. She then refused to further testify. Over defense objection, the military judge allowed trial counsel to admit her Article 32 testimony, read it to the members, and have the panel take it with them into deliberations. Reversing the accused's conviction, the court held that its prior decisions, the ABA *Standards for Criminal Justice, Trial by Jury* (2d ed. 1982 Supp.), and R.C.M. 702(a), provide that depositions should not be given to court members. While the court recognized that Article 32 testimony is technically not a deposition, they believed the greater weight of authority augured in favor of excluding it from the deliberation room.

[iii] Former Testimony—Defense Counsel's Tactical Decisions

United States Court of Appeals for the Armed Forces

United States v. Arruza, 26 M.J. 234 (C.M.A. 1988): The court held that Article 32 statements from the victim of child sexual abuse were properly admitted against the accused. *See* a discussion of this case in our Editorial Comments accompanying Rule 804.

[iv] Former Testimony—Factual Reliability

United States Court of Appeals for the Armed Forces

United States v. Hubbard, 28 M.J. 27 (C.M.A. 1989): Affirming the accused's murder and sodomy convictions, the court held that an AWOL witness's Article 32 testimony was properly admitted, even though it had been established that the absent witness made previous inconsistent statements and had prior convictions and a poor reputation for trustworthiness. The court said "that factual reliability does not have to be established as a prerequisite for admitting hearsay evidence pursuant to a well-recognized hearsay exception."

[v]   Former Testimony—Similar Motive Requirement

Supreme Court

United States v. Salerno, 505 U.S. 317 (1992): The Court held that former testimony cannot be introduced without a demonstration of similar motive. The case was remanded for appropriate evidentiary hearings. *See* a discussion of this case in our Editorial Comments accompanying Rule 804.

United States Court of Appeals for the Armed Forces

United States v. Crockett, 21 M.J. 423 (C.M.A. 1986): The court held that videotaped depositions were properly admitted against a defendant. *See* a discussion of this case in our Editorial Comments accompanying Rule 804.

[vi]   Former Testimony—Subsequently-Acquired Knowledge

United States Court of Appeals for the Armed Forces

United States v. Spindle, 28 M.J. 35 (C.M.A. 1989): Affirming the accused's murder conviction, the court held that because the record "leaves no doubt that prosecutorial authorities made the requisite 'good-faith effort to obtain [an absent witness'] presence at trial,' " the finders of fact were entitled to consider his verbatim Article 32 testimony. The court said that such testimony was "unaffected by the circumstance that, during the investigation, defense counsel lacked information that would have been useful in cross-examining [the witness] if he had testified at trial."

[b]   Rule 804(b)(3)—Statement Against Interest

[i]   Statements Against Interest—Constitutional Considerations

Supreme Court

Bullcoming v. New Mexico, 2011 U.S. Lexis 4790 (U.S. June 23, 2011); *Michigan v. Bryant,* 131 S.Ct. 1143 (2011); *Melendez-Diaz v. Massachusetts,* 129 S. Ct. 2527 (2009); *Whorton v. Bockting,* 549 U.S. 406 (2007); *Davis v. Washington,* 547 U.S. 813 (2006); and *Crawford v. Washington,* 541 U.S. 36, 53–54 (2004) are annotated above at section 801.05[1][a].

United States Court of Appeals for the Armed Forces

United States v. Othuru, 65 M.J. 375 (C.A.A.F. 2007): The accused, a native Nigerian who immigrated to the United States before joining the

Navy, was convicted of making a false official statement and theft of his basic allowance for housing. In support of his application for a housing allowance, the accused submitted forms indicating he was married. Subsequent investigation revealed that the alleged wife was actually the accused's sister. At trial, incriminating statements made by the accused's mother and alleged wife were admitted as either Rule 804(b)(3) statements against interest, or as Rule 804(b)(4) statements of personal or family history. Relying on *Crawford v. Washington*, 541 U.S. 36 (2004), the court held that the trial judge erred but that the error was constitutionally harmless and affirmed. In the court's opinion, the challenged evidence was not a necessary component of the government's case, and the government had introduced overwhelming admissible evidence that clearly established guilt.

United States v. Rhodes, 61 M.J. 445 (C.A.A.F. 2005): At the accused's trial for drug offenses, the military judge admitted an out of court statement from another service-member implicating both the service-member and the accused in the charges. The service-member testified at the trial and was cross-examined by defense counsel specifically concerning an affidavit the service-member had signed five months after making the original statement indicating he had no memory of those events. Finding no error in the admission of the out of court statement, the court held that its use did not violate the accused's sixth amendment rights, or Rule 804(b)(3). Relying on *Crawford v. Washington*, 541 U.S. 36 (2004), the court held that when a declarant testifies at trial the Confrontation Clause places no additional constraints on the use of his prior testimony. The court went on to say that the service-member's lack of current memory satisfied the unavailability aspect of Rule 804, and that the statement itself was sufficiently self-inculpatory and against the service-member's penal interests to justify admission.

Army Court of Criminal Appeals

United States v. Triplett, 56 M.J. 875 (Army Ct.Crim.App. 2002): Before a court with members, the accused was convicted of conspiracy to commit rape and rape, false statements, larceny, and forcible sodomy. Based on the trial judge's error admitting a co-conspirator's pretrial statement, the court affirmed findings in part and set aside other findings. Part of the government's evidence consisted of a statement made by a co-accused which partially inculpated the accused. In reviewing the trial court's decision to admit this testimony, the court said it would make a *de novo* review of whether the bench abused its discretion and thereby violated the Confrontation Clause. Relying on *Lilly v. Virginia*, 527 U.S. 116 (1999), and *United States v. Egan*, 53 M.J. 570, 574 (Army Ct.Crim.App. 2000), the court adopted the following four part test to determine admissibility: (1) whether the statements were made against penal interest; (2) whether the statements needed to be and were trustworthy; (3) whether the individual [redacted] statements within the larger statements were admissible; and (4) whether any improperly admitted statements harmed the accused. Based on this matrix, the court held that accomplice testimony which inculpates the accused is inherently unreliable because of the declarant's strong motivation to exonerate himself. Further such statements do not fall within a firmly rooted hearsay exception, and as a result are presumptively unreliable and are unlikely to be admitted in any event if the government was involved in procuring them. The court went on to say that unreliability can generally only be rebutted by particularized guarantees of trustworthiness from the surrounding circumstances which allow the court to feel confident of declarant's truthfulness to the degree that cross-examination would be of only marginal utility. Here, the declarant's statements were contradictory and thus not trustworthy, the government participated in their production, and the surrounding circumstances failed to present particularized guarantees of trustworthiness. As a result, the government was unable to rebut the presumption of unreliability and the evidence should have been excluded. Using a constitutional standard for determining whether this error may have reasonably affected the trier of fact's decision, the court found no prejudice in part because the declarant's statements were merely cumulative.

United States v. Vazquez, 18 M.J. 668 (A.C.M.R. 1984): Distinguishing its contrary decision in *United States v. Robinson,* 16 M.J. 766 (A.C.M.R. 1983), the court found that an unavailable declarant's statement against penal interest, which inculpated the accused, was properly admitted even though its "intrinsic indicia of trustworthiness" was suspect because there was substantial independent evidence corroborating each event and assuring that the statement was reliable and trustworthy.

United States v. Robinson, 16 M.J. 766 (A.C.M.R. 1983): Although Rule 804(b)(3) does not require inculpatory statements against interest to be corroborated, the court imposed this obligation based on its evaluation of Federal Rule 804(b)(3)'s legislative history, judicial implementation, and the sixth amendment's confrontation clause.

Navy-Marine Corps Court of Criminal Appeals

United States v. Garrett, 16 M.J. 941 (N.M.C.M.R. 1983): The court interpreted Rule 804(b)(3) to include both exculpatory and inculpatory statements against penal interest. Discussing inculpatory statements, the court found they require "corroborating circumstances that clearly indicate the trustworthiness of the statement." Corroboration here should be "construed in such a manner as to effectuate its purpose of circumventing fabrication." Trustworthiness should be viewed as a measure of the statement itself, and not its declarant.

[ii]   Statements Against Interest—Corroboration—Statements Offered by the Accused

United States Court of Appeals for the Armed Forces

United States v. Benton, 57 M.J.24 (C.A.A.F. 2002): The accused was convicted by a court-martial panel composed of officers and enlisted men of kidnapping and forcible sodomy. Affirming the accused's convictions and sentence, the court held that the trial judge properly excluded certain hearsay evidence favorable to the accused because trial defense counsel failed to establish that the testimony was actually against the declarant's penal interest. In support of its position the court held that the witness's testimony was evasive on its face and fell far short of an unambiguous admission. The court also found the evidence to be inadmissible because there were insufficient corroborating circumstances clearly indicating trustworthiness. Relying on *United States v. Rasmussen*, 790 F.2d 55, 56 (8th Cir. 1986), the court indicated the appropriate standard here should be:

> The trustworthiness of a statement against the declarant's penal interest is determined by analysis of two elements: "the probable veracity of the in-court witness, and the reliability of the out-of-court declarant." *Alvarez, above* 584 F.2d at 701. Factors to be considered in such an analysis include: (1) whether there is any apparent motive for the out-of-court declarant to misrepresent the matter, (2) the general character of the speaker, (3) whether other people heard the out-of-court statement, (4) whether the statement was made spontaneously, (5) the timing of the declaration and the relationship between the speaker and the witness.

United States v. Perner, 14 M.J. 181 (C.M.A. 1982): The accused's conviction for sexually abusing a neighbor's child was affirmed despite the accused's contention that a co-actor's statements against penal interest (allegedly exculpating the accused) should have been admitted. Although the case was tried before the effective date of the Rules, the court applied Rule 804(b)(3) and found the statements inadmissible. They were uncorroborated, possessed no indication of reliability, were not made under oath, were not clearly inculpatory to the declarant, and were largely ambiguous.

Air Force Court of Criminal Appeals

United States v. Warner, 25 M.J. 738 (A.F.C.M.R. 1987): During the accused's trial for cocaine use, he unsuccessfully attempted to introduce an affidavit from a friend which stated that the friend "surreptitiously placed cocaine in the daiquiris he served" the accused shortly before the accused's positive urinalysis tests. Affirming the conviction, the court said that "statements tending to expose the declarant to criminal liability and offered to exculpate the accused [are] not admissible unless corroborating circumstances clearly indicate the trustworthiness of the statement." No evidence in support of this affidavit was offered. In dictum, the court noted that "contrary to what has been suggested as prudent trial practice, the military judge did not state on the record with particularity 'the special facts and circumstances' which convinced him the statement lacked sufficient guarantees of trustworthiness for admission."

[iii]   Statements Against Interest—Firmly Rooted Exception

United States Court of Appeals for the Armed Forces

United States v. Wind, 28 M.J. 381 (C.M.A. 1989): In a drug distribution court-martial, trial counsel used an AWOL sailor's declarations against penal interest to rebut the accused's entrapment defense. The court recognized that statements against penal interest are "well established" and may be admitted in evidence without the government's offering corroboration or independent evidence as to the reliability of the declaration. The court indicated that the proponent of these statements must demonstrate that, when the declarant made a statement, he perceived it was against his penal interest. The court held that such a showing may not be possible if the declarant "will be able to obtain dismissal of the charge, a favorable plea bargain, or some other benefit" from making a statement.

[iv]   Statements Against Interest—Mixed Exculpatory and Inculpatory Statements

Supreme Court

Williamson v. United States, 512 U.S. 594 (1994): The accused and a co-actor were involved in a drug offense. When the co-actor was arrested, he confessed, implicating the accused and attempting to partially exonerate himself. At the accused's trial the co-actor refused to testify. Over defense objection, the DEA agent who took the co-actor's confession was allowed to testify about the co-actor's inculpatory and exculpatory statements. Although the circuit court affirmed the accused's conviction, the Supreme Court vacated and remanded, holding that this exception to the hearsay rule applies to only self-inculpatory statements. Neutral or self-serving portions of inculpatory statements should not be admitted. *See* our discussion of this case in Rule 804's Editorial Comments.

United States Court of Appeals for the Armed Forces

United States v. Jacobs, 44 M.J. 301 (C.A.A.F. 1996): In this drug prosecution, the court held that statements against penal interest are firmly rooted hearsay exceptions not requiring additional proof of reliability. However, because the case was tried before *Williamson v. United States,* 512 U.S. 594 (1994), discussed above, it was returned to the trial jurisdiction for a factual determination concerning which parts of the unavailable declarant's pretrial statements were truly self-incriminatory and which were collateral or exculpatory. *See* our discussion of this case in Rule 804's Editorial Comments.

[v]   Statements Against Interest—Reliability Absent

Supreme Court

Lilly v. Virginia, 527 U.S. 116 (1999): Reversing the accused's convictions, the Court held that declarations against penal interests of an unavailable declarant used against the accused were not "firmly rooted," and as a result the Court used a Confrontation Clause analysis to determine whether the questioned evidence contained "particularized guarantees of trustworthiness." In the Court's opinion, such guarantees were not present and the statement was thus not sufficiently reliable because, at the time the declarant (accomplice) made the statement, he was in custody and responding to leading questions from the police. The Court rejected using other evidence to corroborate the confession, stating that reliability must be connected to the statement's inherent trustworthiness The Court rejected claims of reliability based on the fact that the declarant had been read his "Miranda" rights, and the statement partially subjected declarant to criminal liability. However, the Court did say that its holding did not apply to statements against penal interest which are offered as admissions against the declarant-defendant, or statements against penal interest which are offered by the accused as exculpatory evidence— *e.g.*, claiming that the declarant committed the charged offense.

United States Court Appeals for the Armed Forces

United States v. Stroup, 29 M.J. 224 (C.M.A. 1989): An Air Force captain's conviction for conspiring to steal over one million dollars was reversed because an alleged coconspirator's statements against interest were improperly admitted. The statements had little to do with the accused, referring mainly to other deals or transactions. In the court's opinion "nothing in this transcript or elsewhere establishes reliability, satisfies confrontational values, or adequately compensates for the lack of cross-examination."

Air Force of Criminal Appeals

United States v. Booker, 62 M.J. 703 (A.F.Ct.Crim. App. 2006): During the accused's trial on drug offenses, the military judge refused to admit exculpatory out-of-court statements made by the accused's brother after conducting a careful analysis of their reliability. The judges found reasons why the brother might lie for the accused. The Court of Criminal Appeals affirmed the findings of the military judge.

Army Court of Criminal Appeals

United States v. Egan, 53 M.J. 570 (Army Ct.Crim.App. 2000): The court traces the development of hearsay evidence generally, and statements against penal interest specifically, through recent Supreme Court decisions. It found that pretrial statements given by the accused's two accomplices to local military authorities for the purposes of this prosecution were not sufficiently reliable to be admitted and thus their consideration by the court-martial was reversible error. In dictum, relying on *Williamson v. United States*, 512 U.S. 594 (1994), the court also reminded trial judges that the Supreme Court has created a "fact intensive inquiry" process for determining when statements against penal interests are "truly self-inculpatory." As a result, she suggested that "to aid in appellate review, we encourage [military judges] to outline on the record their detailed justification for every portion of a statement they consider under Mil. R. Evid. 804(b)(3)."

[vi] Statements Against Interest—Self-incriminating Statements—Admissible

Air Force Court of Criminal Appeals

United States v. Baran, 19 M.J. 595 (A.F.C.M.R. 1984): Affirming the accused's rape conviction, the court found that statements made by an unavailable witness were admissible under this rule because: (1) they were "so self-incriminatory that, although a reasonable person might carelessly but truthfully admit such matters, the danger of accusation and prosecution would discourage such a person both from fabricating a false statement to the same effect and from communicating it to another;" (2) the declarant "was aware of the wrongful nature of his acts and believed his statements to be true;" (3) a reasonable person would not have made the statements unless he believed them to be true; and (4) although the statements were important to the prosecution's case, they did not have a "devastating" effect on the accused's case. The dissent would have excluded the statements because it believed (1) the declarant was unaware that his words subjected him to criminal liability, (2) trial counsel failed to affirmatively demonstrate the declarant's unavailability, (3) the statements were "crucial" to the government's case and (4) based on the total circumstances at trial, admitting these statements called into "question whether the accused received due process of law."

[vii] Statements Against Interest—Self-serving Statements—Inadmissible

United States Court of Appeals for the Armed Forces

United States v. Greer, 33 M.J. 426 (C.M.A. 1991): The accused's conviction for stealing and selling airplane parts was reversed because a conspirator's pretrial statement was improperly admitted against him. In the court's opinion, when the conspirator confessed, he was doing it for selfish reasons, believing it would forestall his own prosecution, and not that it would work against his penal interests.

United States v. Dillion, 18 M.J. 340 (C.M.A. 1984): The court held that a statement offered by the accused was properly excluded because it "did not meet the most basic requirements of the penal-interest hearsay exception—namely, that declarant perceive that his statement is against his penal interest." The court reasoned that boasts by a declarant, who dealt in drugs, that he had them for sale were "self-serving" and that the declarant never perceived these statements as "damaging, disserving" or of such a character that he would not have made [them] unless [they were] true."

Air Force Court of Criminal Appeals

United States v. Fisher, 28 M.J. 544 (A.F.C.M.R. 1989): The court reversed the accused's drug abuse conviction because a declaration against interest was improperly used to corroborate a confession. The supporting "non-inculpatory" hearsay statements were inadmissible. The court reasoned that: two years between the event and the declaration were too long; animosity existed between the declarant and the accused, so that a possible motive for the declarant to lie or seek revenge existed; Article 31 warnings were not given before the first declaration statement; and the declarant was unreliable and committed suicide.

Air Force Court of Criminal Appeals

United States v. Garrett, 17 M.J. 907 (A.F.C.M.R. 1984): The court found error in the admission of an immunized co-accused's pretrial statement which minimized the maker's criminal involvement and simultaneously sought to inculpate the accused. *See Bruton v. United States,* 391 U.S. 123 (1968).

United States Coast Guard Court of Criminal Appeals

United States v. Sanchez, 26 M.J. 564 (C.G.C.M.R. 1988): Reversing one of many specifications against the accused, the court held that a co-conspirator's statement was improperly admitted because it minimized the declarant's involvement and portrayed the accused as the more culpable party. Under these circumstances, the court felt the evidence was neither contrary to the declarant's interest, nor supported by other circumstances that would indicate its trustworthiness.

[viii]   Statements Against Interest—Special Findings

Air Force Court of Criminal Appeals

United States v. Pacheco, 36 M.J. 530 (A.F.C.M.R. 1992): The accused was charged with numerous assaults against his wife and children. When the trial judge suppressed several pretrial statements, the government took an interlocutory evidentiary appeal. *See* Article 62, UCMJ. Affirming the trial judge's decision that the statements in question were not against the victim/wife's interests, the court noted that its decision was made more difficult because the bench had not provided competent essential findings of fact. The court said that the trial judge had incorrectly interspersed his findings of fact with his legal conclusions. The court went on to say that military judges should first state the facts, then explain the legal standards and analysis applied to those facts, and finally announce the legal conclusion and attendant decision.

Army Court of Criminal Appeals

United States v. Evans, 31 M.J. 927 (A.C.M.R. 1990): Shortly before he left Germany, a co-conspirator to the accused's conspiracy and larceny charges, made a sworn statement to the CID inculpating the accused. Affirming the conviction, the court used the military judge's detailed special findings to demonstrate that the evidence was admissible under this Rule.

United States v. Belfield, 24 M.J. 619 (A.C.M.R. 1987): After finding that a witness who refused to testify was unavailable within the meaning of Rule 804(a)(1), the court held that his pretrial statement was properly admitted because it "possessed 'intrinsic indicia of trustworthiness' in that it was written, sworn and voluntary." The court added that establishing traditional voluntariness alone was not enough to demonstrate trustworthiness, and that a "particularized" proffer would be required. In this case, the military judge's special findings were so detailed and accurate that the court did not have to "speculate" on the statement's admissibility.

[ix]   Statements Against Interest—Unavailability Established

United States Court of Appeals for the Armed Forces

United States v. Koistinen, 27 M.J. 279 (C.M.A. 1988): Affirming the accused's drug related conviction, the court held that the trial judge properly admitted an unavailable co-actor's out of court statement because: (1) that witness had refused to testify; (2) as a civilian he was beyond the military's jurisdiction to grant immunity; and (3) civilian authorities refused to grant immunity. The court believed the co-actor's pretrial statements were "trustworthy" because they "interlocked" with the accused's confession.

[x]   Statements Against Interest—Unavailability Not Established

United States Court of Appeals for the Armed Forces

United States v. Bruce, 14 M.J. 254 (C.M.A. 1982): The court found that certain statements against penal interest were improperly admitted against the accused because the government had failed to show that the out-of-court declarant was unavailable.

Air Force Court of Criminal Appeals

United States v. Harris, 18 M.J. 809 (A.F.C.M.R. 1984): The court found that although a stipulation of fact offered in support of a witness's guilty plea at that witness's court-martial qualified as a statement against penal interest, it was not admissible at the accused's trial because the witness was available and actually testified.

United States v. Ward, 13 M.J. 626 (A.F.C.M.R. 1982): The accused was convicted of multiple larceny and fraud-related offenses. At trial a government witness testified to statements made by the accused's wife. On review, the government failed to convince the court that the witness's statements were admissible as being against her penal or pecuniary interests. The court found no showing of unavailability and was not inclined to assume unavailability because the witness had actually testified during the defense case.

[c]   Rule 804(b)(4)—Statement of Personal or Family History

[i]   Statements Against Interest—Constitutional Considerations

United States v. Othuru, 65 M.J. 375 (C.A.A.F. 2007): The accused, a native Nigerian who immigrated to the United States before joining the Navy, was convicted of making a false official statement and theft of his basic allowance for housing. In support of his application for a housing allowance, the accused submitted forms indicating he was married. Subsequent investigation revealed that the alleged wife was actually the accused's sister. At trial, incriminating statements made by the accused's mother and alleged wife were admitted as either Rule 804(b)(3) statements against interest, or as Rule 804(b)(4) statements of personal or family history. Relying on *Crawford v. Washington*, 541 U.S. 36 (2004), the court held that the trial judge erred but that the error was constitutionally harmless and affirmed. In the court's opinion, the challenged evidence was not a necessary component of the government's case, and the government had introduced overwhelming admissible evidence that clearly established guilt.

United States v. Groves, 23 M.J. 374 (C.M.A. 1987): The court found reversible error in the admission of the pretrial statement of a larceny defendant's putative wife concerning their marital status. The court viewed this evidence as being inherently suspect because it significantly served the declarant's self-interest, was false in one respect, and was devoid of foundational support. There was no trial court analysis of factors indicating reliability, and this "recant modification" of hearsay rule was not in the "presumptively reliable category of firmly rooted hearsay exceptions."

Army Court of Criminal Appeals

United States v. Groves, 19 M.J. 804 (A.C.M.R. 1985): The accused, an unmarried Army doctor, submitted a claim for dependent travel pay and dislocation allowance when he made a permanent change of station from Fort Bliss, Texas to Fort Hood, Texas. On the form he claimed his wife Nanely and two daughters made the move with him. The accused received $443.40 as a result. At his court-martial for larceny and making a false claim, the accused contended he made a mistake of law or fact in believing he had entered into a common law marriage. To rebut this defense the government attempted to call Nanely as a witness, but the judge sustained her Fifth Amendment objection. As a result, trial counsel, over defense objection, presented Nanely's prior out-of-court statement which indicated that she had never accepted a proposal of marriage from the accused, had filed federal income tax returns as a single unmarried person during all relevant times, and in general did not conduct herself as being married to the accused. Both the accused's trial and defense counsel contend Nanely's statement should not have been admitted because it was untrustworthy and violated the accused's right to confrontation. The court rejected both defense contentions and found that Nanely's statements of personal and family history were reliable as "firmly-rooted" exceptions to the hearsay rule.

[d]   Rule 804(b)(6)—Forfeiture by Wrongdoing

[i]   Constitutional Standard

United States Supreme Court

Giles v. California, 554 U.S. 353 (2008): The accused was charged with murdering his girlfriend. He claimed self-defense at trial. The prosecution offered statements the deceased victim had previously given to police as part of a domestic violence investigation. The statements alleged that the accused assaulted and threatened to kill her. The trial court admitted the statements and the California Supreme Court affirmed. The court held that by murdering his girlfriend the accused made her unavailable for trial and thus forfeited his right to confrontation. Justice Scalia's opinion for the Court held that the accused's right to confrontation can only be forfeited by his wrongdoing if the prosecution proves that the accused's acts were intended to keep the witness from testifying at trial. Unless the prosecution can establish the accused's specific intent to render the witness unavailable for trial, admission of that witness's statements violates *Crawford v. Washington*, 541 U.S. 36 (2004), and the common law founding-era forfeiture by wrongdoing exception to the Confrontation Clause. The Court vacated the judgment and remanded the case to the California courts.

[ii]   Wrongdoing Intended to Procure Unavailability

Army Court of Criminal Appeals

United States v. Marchesano, 67 M.J. 535 (Army Ct.Crim.App. 2008): The accused was convicted of sexually abusing his daughter's 7-year-old friend. After the assault, the daughter made statements to her friend about the accused sexually assaulting her. The accused's daughter did not testify and refused to comply with a subpoena. Her statements were admitted through the victim and used by the government for Rule 414 purposes. The trial judge admitted these statements based in part on a finding that the accused wrongfully participated in making his daughter unavailable. Finding harmless error, the court affirmed the conviction and held that the statements should have been excluded because the government never established that the accused participated in or had a "design" to make the declarant unavailable. The court said that, while the military judge could have imputed to the accused the wrongful motives of his wife in keeping their daughter off the stand, a preponderance of evidence establishing that the accused intended to or acquiesced in that result was required and was absent. The court proposed a four-part test for making this determination in the future: (1) was the witness unavailable through the actions of another; (2) was the act of another wrongful in procuring the witness's unavailability; (3) did the accused expressly or tacitly accept the wrongful acts of another; and (4) did the accused do so with the intent that the witness be unavailable.

§ 805.01   Official Text

Rule 805. Hearsay Within Hearsay.

Hearsay included within hearsay is not excluded under the hearsay rule if each part of the combined statements conforms with an exception to the hearsay rule provided in these rules.

---

§ 805.02   Editorial Comment

[1]   Rule 805—Hearsay Within Hearsay

[a]   Basis for the Rule

This one sentence provision states that double or multiple hearsay is not excluded under Rule 802, if an exception to the hearsay rule satisfies each hearsay problem associated with the statement.[1] Previous editions of the *Manual for Courts-Martial* did not specifically address this issue. Military Rule 805 is identical to the federal version.

[b]   Relationship to Rule 801(c)

The first step in utilizing Rule 805 is to decide whether more than one level of hearsay (as defined by Rule 801(c)) is involved in a particular case. Consider, for example, a case in which an accused is charged with assault and claims self-defense. An investigating officer called to the scene of the dispute talked to a witness who said that he saw someone hand the accused a piece of paper with the words on it "Jones (the alleged victim of the assault) has a gun and is going to kill you." The witness is unavailable at trial and the officer wishes to relate the witness's statement. This example does not present a double hearsay problem. The only hearsay issue involves the witness's statement to the officer about what he saw. The witness's statement would be offered for its truth and would be hearsay under the definition of Rule 801(c). What was written on the note would not be offered for its truth, because whether or not the words on the statement were "true," the fact that the note was relayed to the accused helps to explain the accused's action. The note might raise a best evidence problem under Section X, but its unavailability might well be excused under Rule 1004.

[c]   Relationship to Rule 801(d)

Because of the definitions in Rule 801(d) of various categories of statements as nonhearsay, there are cases in which two statements defined as hearsay by Rule 801(c) must both be accounted for if the evidence is to be

---

[1] *See, e.g.,* United States v. Vosburgh, 602 F.3d 512 (3d Cir. 2010) (statements attempting to prove the age of a girl involved in child pornography improperly admitted because each level of hearsay was not adequately satisfied).

admitted. Consider, for example, a case in which, after an automobile accident, an investigator goes to the scene and talks to the accused. The accused admits fault and is subsequently charged with vehicular or negligent homicide. The officer recorded the statement of the accused in a report of the investigation, but the officer is not present to testify at trial. The officer's report might qualify as a business record or an official record (although it probably would not qualify as a public record if the officer were acting in a law enforcement capacity). If the officer had a memory problem at trial, the report might qualify under Rule 803(5) as prior recollection recorded. Assuming that the report itself qualified under some hearsay exception, it could be used to show what it was that the officer heard. As for what the accused said, it would be an admission and admissible as non-hearsay under Rule 801(d)(2)(A). Because of the way Rule 801 defines hearsay and exempts admissions from the definition, this again technically is a problem of one level of hearsay and one level of "nonhearsay hearsay." The analysis is the same, however, as it is when two hearsay exceptions are relied upon in a case.[2]

[d] Single Versus Double Hearsay

As discussed above, experience demonstrates that it is easy to mistake double hearsay for an ordinary hearsay situation. An example is *United States v. Ruffin*.[3] The Court of Appeals was reviewing the testimony of an expert who testified about a public record that he had examined. The court found that the public record came within Rule 803(14), but said that the trial judge had erred in permitting the expert to relate what he had observed because there was no hearsay exception to cover this. In saying this, the court erred, since a person present to testify about what he saw is not relating hearsay information at all. He is giving first-hand testimony about personal observations and can be cross-examined about them.

[e] Using Double Hearsay

In *United States v. Calogero*,[4] a general court-martial convicted the accused of numerous sexual offenses. The government's case included testimony from an expert in clinical psychology. The witness testified, over defense objection, about information the victim related to the psychologist from the victim's own knowledge, and from what the victim had been told by other patients who had observed the victim in the hospital. Affirming findings and sentence, the court said the expert's testimony constituted hearsay within hearsay but was admissible because the victim's statements to the doctor qualified under Rule 803(4), while the other patient's statements to the victim were admissible under Rule 703. The court's

---

[2] *See* United States v. Dotson, 821 F.2d 1034 (5th Cir. 1987).

[3] 575 F.2d 346 (2d Cir. 1978).

[4] 44 M.J. 697 (C.G.Ct.Crim.App. 1996).

holding is somewhat in error, however. Rule 703 is not a hearsay exception and does not permit facts or data not independently admissible to be offered as substantive evidence.

One of the most common examples of hearsay within hearsay arises when an officer conducts an investigation and comes upon a person who makes a statement in an excited state. The officer records the statement as part of his report. Assuming that the report qualifies as an admissible document under either Rule 803(6) or 803(8) (or as a document that can be read to the jury pursuant to Rule 803 (5)), the excited utterance also could qualify under Rule 803(2). The report would be offered to prove what the officer heard—*i.e.*, the truth of what the officer stated in his report that he heard. The excited utterance would also be used to prove the truth of its contents. Two hearsay exceptions would cover both levels of hearsay, and the evidence would be admissible.

[f]   Relationship to Rule 403

Although Rule 805 admits hearsay within hearsay, as long as there are exceptions that satisfy each hearsay problem, it probably is the case that the more levels of hearsay pyramided together the more likely it is that the court will exclude evidence under Rule 403. It also is likely that confrontation arguments will be taken more seriously when one piece of evidence presents more than one hearsay problem.

§ 805.03   Drafters' Analysis

Rule 805 is taken verbatim from the Federal Rule. Although the *Manual* does not explicitly address the issue, the Military Rule is identical with the new Rule.

§ 805.04   Annotated Cases

[1]   Rule 805—Hearsay Within Hearsay

[a]   Hearsay Within Hearsay—Basis for Admission not Established at Trial

United States Court of Appeals for the Armed Forces

United States v. Gober, 43 M.J. 52 (C.A.A.F. 1995): The accused was convicted of raping and sexually abusing his stepdaughters. At trial, he contended that the victims' natural father was responsible for the offenses, and that the children merely transferred their hostilities to him. In support of his defense, the accused attempted to introduce statements originally made by the victims to their mother, and subsequently by the mother to doctors. During trial, the accused contended that these statements were not being offered for the truth of the matters asserted but, on appeal, he contended that they were admissible under the double hearsay exception. The court affirmed the accused's convictions because it said the accused never offered the evidence under Rule 805.

Navy-Marine Corps Court of Criminal Appeals

United States v. Littles, 35 M.J. 644 (N.M.C.M.R. 1992): This larceny of government weapons and related offenses case was before the court for reconsideration of a prior decision. During the sentencing portion of the accused's court-martial, trial counsel called an NIS agent who testified that the accused sold the stolen weapons to his father. The agent went on to say he remembered from reading a National Crime Information Center (NCIC) report, that the accused's father had a long criminal record and was currently incarcerated for parole violations. Ostensibly, trial counsel offered this evidence pursuant to R.C.M. 1001(b)(4) (aggravating circumstances directly related to or resulting from the offense of stealing a weapon). Setting aside the accused's sentence, the court held that, because nothing in the record established the NCIC report's accuracy and admissibility or the NIS agent's legal basis for testifying about it, the evidence should have been suppressed as it contained two levels of hearsay.

[b]   Hearsay Within Hearsay—Clinical Psychologists' Reports

United States Coast Guard Court of Criminal Appeals

United States v. Calogero, 44 M.J. 697 (C.G.Ct.Crim.App. 1996): A general court-martial convicted the accused of numerous sexual offenses. The government's case included testimony from an expert in clinical psychology. Affirming findings and sentence, the court said the expert's testimony constituted hearsay within hearsay but was admissible. *See* the discussion of this case in our Editorial Comments to Rule 805.

[c]   Hearsay Within Hearsay—Confession Statements

United States Court of Appeals for the Armed Forces

United States v. Taylor, 53 M.J. 195 (C.A.A.F. 2000): Affirming the accused's conviction for attempted murder, the court held that the accused's pretrial confession was properly admitted and that this Rule, in conjunction with Rule 801(d)(2)(A) and 803(6), are generally sufficient to sustain admissibility.

[d]   Hearsay Within Hearsay—Police Reports

United States Court of Appeals for the Armed Forces

United States v. Taylor, 61 M.J. 157 (C.A.A.F. 2005): The accused was convicted of a lengthy desertion. For reasons not specified in the record, trial counsel failed to introduce a muster report or page 6 from the accused's personnel records. Both documents are normally used to prove such offenses. Instead, trial counsel introduced information from two electronic naval messages establishing the beginning and ending dates of the accused's absence. Setting aside the accused's conviction and sentence, the court said that the questioned documents were inadmissible under Rule 803(8) and Rule 805, because the supporting arrest warrant and other police forms were similarly inadmissible hearsay.

Air Force Court of Criminal Appeals

United States v. Slovacek, 21 M.J. 538 (A.F.C.M.R. 1985): The accused was convicted of abducting and sodomizing a three-year-old child. In support of its case, the government offered and the trial judge allowed "a police investigator to testify that the victim's mother told him that her daughter told her that 'six months prior the accused had her perform oral sex on him.' " The court held that such multiple hearsay is permitted by the rules as long as "an exception to the hearsay rule satisfies each hearsay problem associated with the statement."

Army Court of Criminal Appeals

United States v. Cyrus, 46 M.J. 722 (Army Ct.Crim.App. 1997): The accused, a military policeman, was convicted of adultery and associating with known drug dealers. In order to prove that the accused was married, trial counsel used statements the accused's paramour made to investigating military policemen. Reversing the convictions, the court found that the admitted hearsay statements were inadmissible double hearsay. Here, the testifying military policeman relayed what the accused's paramour had said about what the accused had earlier told her. While the court recognized that this Rule allows double hearsay, it also recognized that the proponent must otherwise establish each level of hearsay's admissibility, something that was not accomplished at trial. The accused's statement would be an admission, but the paramour's statement did not fit within any available exemption or exception.

[e]   Hearsay Within Hearsay—Post-Conspiracy Statements

Navy-Marine Corps Court of Criminal Appeals

United States v. Clark, 61 M.J. 707 (N.M.Ct.Crim.App. 2005): The accused was convicted of arson and related offenses. When the accused and his coconspirators returned from the arson they made various statements to friends and spouses about what they had done. The military judge allowed the wife of one of the coconspirators to testify about what the wife of another coconspirator said about the arson. Finding harmless error, the court described this as classic hearsay within hearsay, and found the testimony inadmissible because the wives' statements did not qualify for admission as conspirators' statements.

§ 806.01 Official Text

> **Rule 806. Attacking and Supporting Credibility of Declarant.**
> When a hearsay statement, or a statement defined in Mil. R. Evid. 801(d)(2)(C), (D), or (E), has been admitted in evidence, the credibility of the declarant may be attacked, and if attacked may be supported, by any evidence which would be admissible for those purposes if declarant had testified as a witness. Evidence of a statement or conduct by the declarant at any time, inconsistent with the declarant's hearsay statement, is not subject to any requirement that the declarant may have been afforded an opportunity to deny or explain. If the party against whom a hearsay statement has been admitted calls the declarant as a witness, the party is entitled to examine the declarant on the statement as if under cross-examination.

§ 806.02 Editorial Comment

[1] Attacking and Supporting Credibility of Declarant

[a] Basis for the Rule

This provision is taken without change from the Federal Rule. It is similar to past court-martial practice. Rule 806 indicates that a hearsay statement or a statement introduced as a vicarious admission against a party gives rise to a right on the part of the party against whom the evidence is offered to impeach the credibility of the hearsay declarant.[1]

The Rule states that the credibility of the declarant may be attacked by any evidence which would be admissible to attack the declarant if the declarant had testified as a witness.[2] Thus, the declarant may be shown to be biased. An attack through character evidence may be made. The declarant's veracity may be attacked with proof of previous convictions.[3] An effort may also be

---

[1] It is important to note that the Rule is inapplicable in the following situations: United States v. Price, 792 F.2d 994 (11th Cir. 1986) (where various tape recordings were admitted as personal admissions by the defendant and statements by third parties were only admitted to put the defendant's statements in context, the third parties were not subject to impeachment under Rule 806); United States v. Kabbaby, 672 F.2d 857 (11th Cir. 1982) (no error in excluding prior conviction of informant who did not testify and who made no "statement" against the defendant).

[2] *See, e.g.,* United States v. Katsougrakis, 715 F.2d 769 (2d Cir. 1983), *cert. denied,* 464 U.S. 1040 (1984) (error to prohibit defense from asking defense witness about the reputation of a hearsay declarant).

[3] *See, e.g.,* United States v. Greenidge, 495 F.3d 85 (3d Cir. 2007) (proof of a prior conviction that would have been admissible against the defendant had he testified was

made to show that the declarant was incapable of observing events, hearing statements, or accurately remembering past events. It is likely that specific act impeachment of a declarant under Rule 608(b) probably cannot be accomplished unless the declarant is called to testify, because the Rule bars extrinsic evidence.[4]

Once a declarant is attacked, the declarant may be supported.[5] This is consistent with the rule that rehabilitation of any witness, including a hearsay declarant, is not permitted until an attack takes place. *Accord*, Rule 608(a).

Rule 806 can only be used to attack a nontestifying declarant when that person's out-of-court statements are being offered for the truth of the matters asserted. Once these statements qualify for admission under a hearsay rule, the statements are used for substantive purposes, which places the declarant's credibility in issue. Alternatively, where the declarant's statements are not being offered for their truth, they are not hearsay and will not be considered as substantive proof, and they do not place the declarant's credibility in issue. In this instance, Rule 806 does not permit the declarant to be impeached.[6]

[b]   Use at Trial

An example of how this Rule can be effectively used *in limine* to keep an opposing party from presenting evidence that might support its case is *United States v. Bell*.[7] During the accused's trial for robbery and robbery related offenses, defense counsel had transcripts concerning the former testimony of two co-accuseds. Both transcripts would have provided an alibi defense for the accused. Trial counsel did not object to the statements being admitted, but offered evidence that the co-accused had already been convicted of the same offenses with which the accused was charged. As a result of trial counsel's proffer, defense counsel never offered the statements at trial. On appeal the accused contended he was unfairly deprived of his co-accused's important testimony. Affirming the accused's convictions, the court first held that no waiver occurred here because the Court would not retroactively apply *Luce v. United States*,[8] (conditional rulings are not

---

properly used to impeach his admissible hearsay statement).

  [4] *See generally*, Behan, *The Art of Trial Advocacy: The Thrill and Excitement of Impeachment by Contradiction*, ARMY LAW., Oct. 2004, at 10 (good discussion of Rule 608(b)).

  [5] *See, e.g.*, United States v. Bernal, 719 F.2d 1475 (9th Cir. 1983) (a conspirator's prior consistent statement could be used to rehabilitate a conspirator whom the defendant impeached with a prior inconsistent statement).

  [6] *See, e.g.*, United States v. McClain, 934 F.2d 822 (7th Cir. 1991) (no impeachment allowed where accomplice testimony offered only to show its impact on others).

  [7] 44 M.J. 403 (C.A.A.F. 1996).

  [8] 469 U.S. 38 (1984).

appealable where party's does not offer evidence that is impeached), since *Luce* was not applied in the military until *United States v. Sutton*,[9] which was decided after the date of the charged offenses. The court reasoned on the merits that, since it would have been permissible for trial counsel to impeach the two defense witnesses had they testified, it was permissible to impeach their Rule 801(d)(1) former testimony under Rule 806. Thus, there was no error.

[c]   Prior Inconsistent Statements

One of the traditional forms of impeachment, showing that the witness or declarant has made a prior inconsistent statement, is explicitly permitted by the second sentence of Rule 806.[10] This sentence indicates that when a hearsay declarant, unlike the usual witness, is impeached with an inconsistent statement, there is no requirement that the declarant be afforded an opportunity to deny or explain the statement. Thus, the prior inconsistent statement is automatically admissible to impeach a hearsay declarant or a person whose vicarious admissions have been offered against a party.[11]

[d]   Calling the Declarant for Impeachment

The third sentence of the Rule covers a situation in which a party is not satisfied simply with impeaching the declarant; the party wants to call the declarant to testify as a witness. A party who does so is entitled to examine the declarant on the statement as if under cross-examination. Thus, the party who calls the witness may ask leading questions about the statement that has been offered against him. If the party goes beyond asking questions about the statement, then it would seem that the party must proceed as if on direct examination, unless the court orders otherwise under Rule 611.

§ 806.03   Drafters' Analysis

Rule 806 is taken from the Federal Rule without change. It restates the present military rule that a hearsay declarant or statement may always be contradicted or impeached. The Rule eliminates any requirement that the declarant be given "an opportunity to deny or explain" an inconsistent statement or inconsistent conduct when such statement or conduct is offered to attack the hearsay statement. As a result, Rule 806 supersedes Rule 613(b) which would require such an opportunity for a statement inconsistent within court testimony.

---

[9]   31 M.J. 11 (C.A.A.F. 1990).

[10]   *See, e.g.*, United States v. Wuagneux, 683 F.2d 1343 (11th Cir. 1982) (government permitted to impeach declarant whose declaration against interest was admitted with evidence of prior inconsistent statement).

[11]   *See, e.g.*, United States v. Wali, 860 F.2d 588 (3d Cir. 1988) (defendant allowed to impeach hearsay statements made by co-conspirator against the defendant without regard to whether the co-conspirator was cross-examined).

§ 806.04 Annotated Cases

[1] Attacking and Supporting Credibility of Declarant

[a] Credibility of Declarant—Accused Attacked

United States Court of Appeals for the Armed Forces

United States v. Hart, 55 M.J. 395 (C.A.A.F. 2001): Before going on temporary duty to Saudi Arabia, Senior Airman Davis gave the accused a special power of attorney to take care of his car. When Davis returned, he noticed several items were missing from his car. Affirming the accused's larceny convictions the court held that, where defense counsel's cross-examination of government witnesses sought to introduce the accused's exculpatory statements via a hearsay exception, it was appropriate for government counsel to attack the accused's credibility by using reputation and opinion testimony demonstrating the accused's untruthfulness. Such impeachment of the accused's character for veracity was appropriate here even though the accused did not take the stand.

United States v. Goldwire, 55 M.J. 139 (C.A.A.F. 2001): The accused was convicted of rape and wrongfully possessing alcohol. After defense counsel was permitted to prove the remainder of the accused's allegedly incomplete government offered statement, the prosecution was properly allowed to impeach the accused's credibility just as if the accused had testified at trial. In support of its ruling, the court went on to say that the military judge correctly precluded specific instances of misconduct to be introduced in support of the government's evidence.

Air Force Court of Criminal Appeals

United States v. Goldwire, 52 M.J. 731 (A.F.Ct.Crim.App. 2000): During the accused's rape prosecution, he attempted to demonstrate that his pretrial statements were more worthy of belief than the victim's. Thereafter, trial counsel was permitted to introduce opinion testimony which negatively characterized the accused's truthfulness. Affirming the accused's convictions, the court held that the credibility evidence was properly admitted because, even though Rule 806 does not specifically allude to admissions under Rule 801(d)(2)(A) and (B), such statements were intended to be included in the Rule as the credibility of the party-opponent is always subject to an attack on credibility.

[b] Credibility of Declarant—Calling the Declarant for Impeachment

Air Force Court of Criminal Appeals

United States v. Marshall, 31 M.J. 712 (A.F.C.M.R. 1990): At trial, the accused challenged on confrontation grounds a coconspirator's testimony about what an absent accused said. Affirming the conviction and the finding that Rule 801(d)(2)(E) was not violated, the court "reminded" counsel that the defense could have called the absent witness and attacked him.

[c]   Credibility of Declarant—Prior Convictions

United States Court of Appeals for the Armed Forces

United States v. Crudup, 67 M.J. 92 (C.A.A.F. 2008): The accused was convicted of assault and battery upon his wife, resisting apprehension, and making a false official statement. When the wife refused to testify, her pretrial statement implicating the accused was admitted. The remainder of the government's case consisted of witnesses who observed the crimes and the accused's pretrial admissions. Although the court affirmed, it held that admitting the wife's pretrial statement violated the accused's Sixth Amendment confrontation rights. The court found that the error was harmless beyond a reasonable doubt because the statement was relatively unimportant and cumulative and the government's case was overwhelming. The court added that, although the wife could not have been cross-examined, her credibility was effectively impeached by proof of a previous fraud conviction.

United States v. Bell, 44 M.J. 403 (C.A.A.F. 1996): During the accused's trial for robbery and robbery related offenses, defense counsel offered transcripts concerning the former testimony of two co-accused. Both transcripts provided an alibi defense. In response, trial counsel offered evidence that the co-accused had already been convicted of the same offenses the accused was charged with. Defense counsel never offered the statements at trial. Affirming the accused's convictions, the court held that, because it would have been permissible for trial counsel to impeach the two defense witnesses had they testified, it was permissible to impeach their Rule 801(d)(1) former testimony pursuant to Rule 806.

§ 807.01   Official Text

Rule 807.   Residual Exception.

A statement not specifically covered by Rule 803 or 804 but having equivalent circumstantial guarantees of trustworthiness, is not excluded by the hearsay rule, if the court determines that (A) the statement is offered as evidence of a material fact; (B) the statement is more probative on the point for which it is offered than any other evidence which the proponent can procure through reasonable efforts; and (C) the general purposes of these rules and the interests of justice will best be served by admission of the statement into evidence. However, a statement may not be admitted under this exception unless the proponent of it makes known to the adverse party sufficiently in advance of the trial or hearing to provide the adverse party with a fair opportunity to prepare to meet it, the proponent's intention to offer the statement and the particulars of it, including the name and address of the declarant.

---

§ 807.02   Editorial Comment

[1]   Background of the Rule

Rule 807 is the consolidated product of former Rules 803(24) and 804(b)(5).[1] This change was made to facilitate uniform application and development of the residual hearsay exception. No significant substantive changes were anticipated by this largely form-based change to the Military Rules of Evidence.

The legislative history of the original federal residual exceptions indicates that Congress had substantial doubts about their wisdom. At one point, the House deleted the provisions from the Rules. However, the Senate was able to resurrect them after including important restrictions on their use. Many commentators and courts have agreed that the residual hearsay exception's history and construction indicates that it should be narrowly construed.[2] Because the military drafters did not alter the original federal format or its modification, it appears that they also intended a restrictive interpretation of the Rule, although their Analysis suggests that if civilian courts become more liberal in using the Rule, military courts may follow suit.

---

[1] Pursuant to the 1 June 1999 Amendments to the Military Rules of Evidence, this provision has been added to replace Rules 803(24) and 804(b) (5).

[2] *See, e.g.*, United States v. White, 611 F.2d 531 (5th Cir. 1980) (residual exception should only be used sparingly but sufficient guarantees of reliability are present here to justify admission).

[2] Basis for the Exception

Previous court-martial practice did not recognize a hearsay exception that permitted military judges to develop new rules tailored to fit a particular case or circumstance. Rule 807,[3] known as the "catch-all" or residual exception, is designed for just this purpose.[4] The Rule allows hearsay evidence to be admitted even though it does not fall within any specific or enumerated exception.

Congress created the residual exception to permit growth and development in the law of hearsay. In many ways the provision is a link to the common law. The Advisory Committee wrote that it would be "presumptuous to assume that all possible desirable exceptions to the hearsay rule have been catalogued." As a result, Rule 807 provides trial judges with the ability to develop the law in consonance with legal and scientific advancements.[5] However, Congress also said, "It is intended that the residual hearsay exceptions will be used very rarely, and only in exceptional circumstances."[6]

[3] A Necessary Record

Because the residual exception contains so many variables, without special findings, an appellate court might have great difficulty in determining whether the trial judge properly evaluated the competing issues. Evidence that may be admissible under this provision is by definition unusual. It does not fit within established hearsay exceptions or exemptions. As a result, a decision admitting or rejecting the evidence should be accompanied by a reasoned explanation, particularly because the trial judge must simultaneously consider not only the various requirements of the Rule, but also the "interests of justice" and the "general purposes of these rules."

[4] Trustworthiness Requirement

The Rule provides that statements not specifically covered in Rules 803 or 804 may be admissible here if they possess circumstantial guarantees of trustworthiness equivalent to the enumerated exceptions.[7] The proponent's

---

[3] Rule 803(24) was similar to Rule 804(b)(5). Our comments are applicable to 807. The primary difference between the original two provisions was that 804(b)(5) required a showing of the declarant's unavailability before it could be used. Unavailability was not required in 803(24) nor in 807, although, as our Comments suggest, it is sometimes a factor courts may consider.

[4] In Holmes, *The Residual Hearsay Exceptions: A Primer For Military Use*, 94 MIL. L. REV. 15 (1981), the author thoroughly discusses the federal development and use of Rules 803(24) and 804(b)(5) and provides suggestions for military implementation.

[5] *See* our discussion of Section VII, particularly Rules 702 and 703.

[6] *See* S. Rep. No. 93-1277, 93d Cong. 2d Sess. 19–20 (1974).

[7] *See, e.g.*, United States v. Banks, 514 F.3d 769 (8th Cir. 2008) (ATF purchase form used to prove the name of a gun purchaser not admissible under Rule 803(6) because government failed to lay an adequate foundation but admissible under Rule 807 because record keeping

obligation to establish trustworthiness is the Rule's most important foundational requirement. The cases demonstrate that trustworthiness does not lend
itself to a fixed definition or list of criteria.[8] A review of military decisions
indicates that otherwise inadmissible hearsay statements have been admitted
pursuant to this provision when they:

    (1) Were not made to "police" investigators or other persons seeking
information in an official capacity;[9]

    (2) Bore a close resemblance to one of the enumerated exceptions;[10]

    (3) Were sufficiently detailed, spontaneous, and accurate;[11]

    (4) Were consistent, given under oath, and unrecanted;[12]

    (5) Were volunteered in a neutral environment, without an authority
figure present, and were in the words such a declarant (particularly a
child) would normally use.[13]

Similarly, military decisions indicate that otherwise inadmissible hearsay
statements should not be admitted when they:

    (1) Would have misled or confused the finders of fact;[14]

    (2) Were the suspicious product of a rebellious (particularly youthful)

---

practices were required by law and equivalent to the business record trustworthiness).

  8 *Compare* United States v. Cowley, 720 F.2d 1037 (9th Cir. 1983) (permissible to use
postmark to show that letter passed through a post office on a certain day); Karme v.
Commissioner, 673 F.2d 1062 (9th Cir. 1982) (admitting bank records of Netherlands
Antilles bank without custodian's testimony), *with* United States v. Ruppel, 666 F.2d 261 (5th
Cir. 1982) (post-arrest taped telephone call between conspirators should not have been
admitted).

  9 *See, e.g.*, United States v. Grant, 42 M.J. 340 (C.A.A.F. 1995) (sexual abuse conviction
affirmed and victim's statements held to be admissible, even though they were uttered 36 to
48 hours after the crime, because they were not made as part of an official or police
investigation).

  10 *See, e.g.*, United States v. Quick, 22 M.J. 722 (A.C.M.R. 1986) (sodomy victim's
pretrial statements to babysitter admissible because they resembled evidence admissible
under Rules 803(2) (excited utterances) or 803(4) (statements made for the purpose of
medical diagnosis or treatment)).

  11 *See, e.g.*, United States v. Pollard, 38 M.J. 41 (C.M.A. 1993) (child abuse prosecution
where victim's tearful outburst was specific and impulsive).

  12 *See, e.g.*, United States v. Brown, 25 M.J. 867 (A.C.M.R. 1988) (out of court statements
made by wife and children establishing the accused's guilt for assaulting them held properly
admitted).

  13 *See, e.g.*, United States v. Helms, 39 M.J. 908 (N.M.C.M.R. 1994) (committing
indecent acts prosecution affirmed where the victim's babysitter, relying upon what the victim
had previously told her, provided the key testimony about the crimes).

  14 *See, e.g.*, United States v. Burks, 36 M.J. 447 (C.M.A. 1993) (convicted of bludgeoning
another airman to death, court held an exculpatory, anonymous letter defendant wanted
admitted was fundamentally untrustworthy).

prosecutrix's manipulative scheme;[15]

(3) Mainly exhibited a "blame-spreading content;"[16]

(4) Were the product of an *ex parte* interview under circumstances which failed to satisfy confrontation values or demonstrate the "candor of the declarant and the truth of the statement;"[17]

(5) Stimulated by the prosecutrix's apparent motive to lie;[18]

(6) Relied upon independent evidence to corroborate the declarant's statement;[19]

(7) Were contradictory and not helpful because when given, the victim said she made them for vengeful purposes;[20]

(8) Were from a witness who possessed a demonstrable conflict of interest with the accused;[21]

(9) Were specifically recanted by the declarant whose mother testified that the declarant was a constant liar and could not be trusted, and the victim testified that she lied to get even with her overly strict stepfather;[22]

---

[15] *See, e.g.*, United States v. Quarles, 25 M.J. 761 (N.M.C.M.R. 1987) (victim's out of court statements were improperly admitted even though prosecutors argued that the "young age of the children coupled with their precocious knowledge of the sexual process lends to their statements sufficient reliability to justify admission").

[16] *See, e.g.*, United States v. Yeauger, 27 M.J. 199 (C.M.A. 1988) (co-actor's pretrial statements would "almost certainly" have failed the equivalent circumstantial guarantees of trustworthiness standard"). *See also* United States v. Hinkson, 632 F.2d 382 (4th Cir. 1980) (third party's confession not admissible).

[17] *See, e.g.*, United States v. Giambra, 38 M.J. 240 (C.M.A. 1993) (hearsay statements made by the victim's mother were erroneously admitted).

[18] *See, e.g.*, United States v. King, 16 M.J. 990 (A.C.M.R. 1983) (error to admit the prosecutrix's pretrial statements through CID investigators).

[19] In Idaho v. Wright, 497 U.S. 805 (1990), the Supreme Court held that the relevant circumstances for establishing that a declarant's out of court statements possess sufficient indicia of reliability to make them particularly worthy of belief must come from their inherent trustworthiness and cannot be established by references to other evidence presented at trial. *See* our discussion of this issue *below*.

[20] *See, e.g.*, United States v. Miller, 32 M.J. 843 (N.M.C.M.R. 1991) (child sexual abuse case, trial counsel failed to establish reliability of victim's pretrial statements to NIS agents).

[21] *See, e.g.*, United States v. Williamson, 26 M.J. 115 (C.M.A. 1988) (child sexual abuse conviction was reversed because the victim's grandfather, who was involved in a separate lawsuit to take custody of the child away from her natural father, testified that his granddaughter told him "Daddy had sexually molested" her).

[22] *See, e.g.*, United States v. Lockwood, 23 M.J. 770 (A.F.C.M.R. 1987) (child sexual abuse conviction reversed where out-of-court statements had a plausible basis for being false).

(10) Were not sufficiently similar to an enumerated exception.[23]

Of the many issues contained in these lists, similarity to an enumerated provision has been viewed as one of the most important criteria by military courts interpreting the residual exception. For example, in *United States v. Grant*,[24] the accused was tried for sexually abusing his six-year-old daughter. Relying on both Rule 803(2) and the residual exception, government counsel offered the victim's pretrial complaints which had been made 36 to 48 hours after the crimes. Affirming the accused's convictions, the court held that the statements were admissible under the residual exception because they were not made to investigators or other persons seeking information, and because they bore a close resemblance to excited utterances which enhanced their trustworthiness and admissibility. Similarly, in *United States v. Quick*,[25] a sodomy victim's pretrial statements to her babysitter were held admissible under the residual provision because they closely resembled statements which would have been admissible under Rules 803(2) (excited utterances) or 803(4) (statements made for the purpose of medical diagnosis or treatment).

Criminal defendants generally do not agree with this interpretation of the Rule, and argue that had the drafters intended such evidence to be admissible, they would have crafted broader hearsay definitions. Most federal courts evaluating this defense argument have rejected it. These courts see Congress's use of the term "equivalent circumstantial guarantees of trustworthiness" as providing authority to admit closely related evidence when the interests of justice will be furthered by admission.[26] However, other federal courts have taken principled positions on the other side.[27] Their holdings indicate that the residual exception cannot be used to admit closely related evidence because the Rule applies only to testimony not covered by other Rules. This "unanticipated" use theory supports Congress's direction that the Rule "be used very rarely, and only in exceptional circumstances."

As the Advisory Committee's Note to Rule 803(24) indicated, this Rule does "not contemplate an unfettered exercise of judicial discretion, but [it does] provide for treating new and presently unanticipated situations which demonstrate a trustworthiness within the spirit of the specifically stated exceptions." The Advisory Committee's Note goes on to say that counsel

---

[23] *See, e.g.*, United States v. Spychala, 40 M.J. 647 (N.M.C.M.R. 1994) (declarant's statements were similar to 803(2) but were made so long after the exciting event as to be more reflective than spontaneous).

[24] 42 M.J. 340 (C.A.A.F. 1995).

[25] 22 M.J. 722 (A.C.M.R. 1986).

[26] *See, e.g.*, United States v. Clarke, 2 F.3d 81 (4th Cir. 1993) ("near miss" hearsay evidence admissible under this provision).

[27] *See, e.g.*, United States v. Dent, 984 F.2d 1453 (7th Cir. 1993) (Judge Easterbrook refused to extend the exception to grand jury testimony).

and judges should "take full advantage of the accumulated wisdom and experience of the past in dealing with hearsay" when applying the residual exception.

[5]   Confrontation Clause Requirement.[28]

Along with satisfying hearsay rule requirements, residual exception statements must also satisfy the Confrontation Clause. At one time, the Supreme Court found that firmly rooted exceptions satisfied the Confrontation Clause.[29] Obviously the residual exception is not firmly rooted. As a result the Court had adopted *Idaho v. Wright*[30] to assess non-firmly rooted hearsay and required circumstances that establish the indicia of reliability based on the evidence's inherent trustworthiness.

Today, post-*Crawford*, the question is whether a statement is testimonial. If so, it may not be admitted unless the declarant is present for cross-examination or there has been a prior opportunity for cross-examination about the statement. If not, its admission will violate the Confrontation Clause.[31]

As the annotated cases indicate, civilian and military courts have continued to struggle with the definition of "testimonial hearsay."

For example, *United States v. Coulter*,[32] a child sexual abuse prosecution, deals with some of these issues. The two-year-old victim was held incompetent to testify because of her age but, using Rule 807, the court admitted her statements through her parents' testimony. Finding no error, the court used a two-step process to determine both hearsay admissibility and constitutionality. First, the court examined the statements under traditional Rule 807 logic, evaluating the following factors: (1) the declarant's mental state and age; (2) she had not been subjected to suggestive questioning; (3) her statements were spontaneous; (4) she did not have a motive to fabricate; and (5) her statements were corroborated by the government's expert medical witness. Secondly, the court analyzed the statements using *Crawford,* finding them to be non-testimonial and therefore admissible because the victim/declarant had not: (1) been questioned by the police or other government officials but by her parents who had a natural concern for their child's well-being; (2) been capable of envisioning her statements someday

---

[28] *See, infra,* our discussion in Section [11], Constitutional Considerations.

[29] *See, e.g.,* Bourjaily v. United States, 483 U.S. 171 (1987).

[30] *See* Bullcoming v. New Mexico, 2011 U.S. Lexis 4790 (U.S. June 23, 2011), Michigan v. Bryant, 131 S.Ct. 1143 (2011), Melendez-Diaz v. Massachusetts, 129 S. Ct. 2527 (2009), Whorton v. Bockting, 549 U.S. 406 (2007), Davis v. Washington, 547 U.S. 813 (2006), and Crawford v. Washington, 541 U.S. 36, 53–54 (2004), which are annotated above at section 801.04[1][a].

[31] 497 U.S. 805 (1990).

[32] 62 M.J. 520 (N.M.Ct.Crim.App. 2005).

being used in a criminal proceeding; and (3) been capable of understanding the solemn nature of her declarations or that they could be used to prove some fact or event in the future.

While *White v. Illinois*,[33] indicates that the declarant need not be produced to satisfy Constitutional standards, if the declarant's statement has probative value "that could not be duplicated simply by the declarant later testifying in court," the continuing validity of that case and its applicability to future cases will depend on whether or not a statement is testimonial.

If a statement is not testimonial, to admit it as residual hearsay, a court almost certainly will have to find that the *Wright* standard is satisfied.

Military and federal courts that have evaluated the standards set forth in the residual exception agree that they satisfy *Roberts* and *Wright*.[34] However, because of the complexities military judges face in complying with both the Constitutional and evidentiary requirements associated with residual hearsay, the United States Court of Appeals for the Armed Forces has recommended that trial judges use special findings in ruling on these hearsay issues.[35]

[6] "Materiality" Requirement

Rule 807(A) provides that statements not otherwise admissible can only be "offered as evidence of a material fact." The military and federal drafters use of the word material is interesting here since they obviously avoided it when writing Rule 401. This could be because the term "material" is subject to many and varied definitions. The most likely meaning of the term in this context is "important." Such meaning is consistent with Congress's overall intent that the exception be rarely used. Additionally, it would be inconsistent with the extraordinary nature of residual hearsay evidence to admit it for marginal or inconsequential purposes.

[7] "More Probative" Requirement

Rule 807(B) requires that a statement admitted under this Rule be "more probative on the point for which it is offered than any other evidence which the proponent can procure thorough reasonable efforts." This language signals that the declarant's unavailability, while not specifically required by this provision, is still a consideration in determining its use. If the declarant

---

[33] 502 U.S. 346 (1992).

[34] For a more thorough discussion of these issues, *see* 4 S. Saltzburg, M. Martin & D. Capra, FEDERAL RULES OF EVIDENCE MANUAL § 802[8] (9th ed. 2006).

[35] *See, e.g.,* United States v. Hines, 23 M.J. 125 (C.M.A. 1986) (in dealing with "the interrelationship between the Confrontation Clause" and the evidentiary rules regarding the admissibility of hearsay statements," the court specifically advised trial judges to "state on-the-record the special facts and circumstances which they think indicate that the statements have a sufficiently high degree of trustworthiness and necessity to justify their admission").

is available and can testify, then recourse to Rule 807 would rarely be appropriate because the hearsay would likely be less probative than the declarant's live testimony.[36] However, if the declarant is available, but not reasonably so, then resort to this provision might still be possible. For a world-wide criminal justice system, declarant availability is a relative concept.[37] The drafter's use of the term "reasonable efforts" to procure attendance indicates that herculean or unjustifiably expensive alternatives to procuring a witness's testimony may still be outside the definition.

[8]   "The Interests of Justice" Requirement

Rule 807(C) states that hearsay testimony not otherwise admissible may be used if "the general purpose of these rules and the interests of justice will best be served by admission of the statement into evidence." This foundational requirement is a variant of Rule 102's guidance concerning the purpose and construction of these Rules. As a result, it is of little independent or substantive value to counsel or military judges. Evidence will not be admissible solely because it supports the general purpose of the Military Rules of Evidence or the interests of justice. It must still be connected to and supported by the principles discussed above.

[9]   Notice Requirement

The last sentence of Rule 803(C) contains a notice requirement. Compliance is crucial. Although the Rule does not specify how far in advance notice must be given, it does state that notice must provide the opponent with a fair opportunity to meet the evidence. Thus, timing may depend on how much preparation an opponent needs to fairly respond to the hearsay. The Rule provides that the notice include "the particulars" of the proffered evidence including the declarant's name and address.

Federal courts have split on determining how strictly the timing requirement will be enforced.[38] Some courts have excluded the evidence if notice was inadequate.[39] Other courts have flexibly applied the standard, looking

---

[36] In United States v. Azure, 801 F.2d 336 (8th Cir. 1986), the court held that where the witness was available for trial they would not allow her previous out-of-court statements to be admitted pursuant to this Rule.

[37] An interesting civil law variant to the international aspect of court-martial litigation is contained in FTC v. Amy Travel Service, 875 F.2d 564 (7th Cir. 1989). There the court allowed thousands of consumer affidavits to be admitted as more probative than other evidence reasonably available because the defendant operated a nation-wide business and it would have been "cumbersome and unnecessarily expensive to bring all the consumers in for live testimony."

[38] *Compare* United States v. Evans, 572 F.2d 455 (5th Cir. 1978) (taking a flexible approach) *with* United States v. Oates, 560 F.2d 45 (2d Cir. 1977) (taking a restrictive approach).

[39] *See, e.g.*, United States v. Furst, 886 F.2d 558 (3d Cir. 1989) (evidence excluded when notice given on the same day as trial).

carefully to see what prejudice an opponent might suffer from receiving late, inadequate, or no notice at all.[40] In appropriate cases, in the interests of justice may be best served if the trial court provides opposing counsel with a continuance and enough time to meet the residual exception evidence, rather than simply excluding it. In this way, the court members will benefit from the additional relevant testimony, and opposing counsel will have had an opportunity to fully explore and counter it.

[10]   The Need for Extraordinary Circumstances

Military and civilian courts closely scrutinize statements admitted under the residual exception, particularly if the statements are admitted against an accused.[41] Military courts have consistently held that the Rule is to be strictly construed and used only in exceptional circumstances.[42] The courts also agree that these circumstances most often occur when other witnesses or evidence is simply not available. This sometimes arises in the prosecution of intrafamily criminal offenses and child sexual abuse cases where the assailant is not a family member.[43] An example is *United States v. Lyons.*[44] The accused was convicted of aggravated rape. The victim was a deaf-mute, mentally impaired, 18-year-old girl, with the communicative skills of a three-year-old. Because her direct examination was limited and largely

---

[40] In United States v. Doe, 860 F.2d 488 (1st Cir. 1988), the court cataloged cases interpreting the notice requirement and found that a majority of jurisdictions allowed admission even when notice had been faulty, unless the opponent could demonstrate prejudice.

[41] In United States v. Ruffin, 12 M.J. 952 (A.F.C.M.R. 1982), the court demonstrated the thorough analysis it would use in evaluating 804(b)(5) evidence used against an accused. The accused was convicted of sodomizing his stepdaughters. After both victims refused to testify, the court admitted the girls' pretrial statements detailing the crimes. Rejecting the accused's constitutional challenges, the court found 804(b)(5) had been properly implemented because: (a) defense counsel had been informed that the government would attempt to use the evidence and exactly what the evidence was; (b) the girls had actually made the statements in question; (c) each statement concerned a material fact or issue in the case; (d) each statement was probative of those facts or issues; and (e) the interests of justice would be served by admitting the evidence. The court concluded that the Rule's requirement for "guarantees of trustworthiness" had been met and that no procedural or constitutional right of the accused had been violated.

[42] *See, e.g.,* United States v. White, 17 M.J. 953 (A.F.C.M.R. 1984) (unwilling to participate in what it considered a "crap shoot," the court reversed a conviction because an unavailable government witness's pretrial statement was admitted without a sufficient demonstration of that witness's reliability. Evaluating numerous military and federal authorities, the court characterized the residual hearsay exception as narrowly focused and of limited scope, and indicated it may only be used in truly exceptional circumstances with "rare and even strange factual situations."

[43] *See, e.g.,* United States v. Arnold, 18 M.J. 559 (A.C.M.R. 1984) (court held that Rule 804(b)(5) "appears specifically designed to address the problems of family members who are witnesses to an intra-family criminal offense").

[44] 36 M.J. 183 (C.M.A. 1992).

unintelligible, the government was permitted to use the victim's videotaped reenactment of the crime. The accused contended that this hearsay evidence denied his right of confrontation because the victim was unavailable for cross-examination. Affirming the conviction, the court held that the evidence was properly admitted because it contained equivalent circumstantial guarantees of trustworthiness, and was material, more probative than any other evidence reasonably available, and used in an exceptional circumstance.

§ 807.03   Drafters' Analysis (1999)

[The Drafters have not provided an Analysis for this provision. As a result, we have included the Drafters' original and still applicable Analysis from Rule 803(24), the predecessor to Rule 807.]

Rule 803(24) is taken from the Federal Rule without change. It has no express equivalent in the present *Manual* as it establishes a general exception to the hearsay rule. The Rule implements the general policy behind the Rules of permitting admission of probative and reliable evidence. Not only must the evidence in question satisfy the three conditions listed in the Rule (materiality, more probative on the point than any other evidence which can be reasonably obtained, and admission would be in the interest of justice) but the procedural requirements of notice must be complied with. The extent to which this exception may be employed is unclear. The Article III courts have divided as to whether the exception may be used only in extraordinary cases or whether it may have more general application. It is the intent of the committee that the Rule be employed in the same manner as it is generally applied in the Article III courts. Because the general exception found in Rule 803(24) is basically one intended to apply to highly reliable and necessary evidence, recourse to the theory behind the hearsay Rule itself may be helpful. In any given case, both trial and defense counsel may wish to examine the hearsay evidence in question to determine how well it relates to the four traditional considerations usually invoked to exclude hearsay testimony: How truthful was the original declarant? To what extent were his or her powers of observation adequate? Was the declaration truthful? Was the original declarant able to adequately communicate the statement? Measuring evidence against this framework should assist in determining the reliability of the evidence. Rule 803(24) itself requires the necessity which is the other usual justification for hearsay exceptions.

§ 807.04   Annotated Cases

[1]   Rule 807—Residual Exception

[a]   Residual Exception—Constitutional Standards

United States Supreme Court

Bullcoming v. New Mexico, 2011 U.S. Lexis 4790 (U.S. June 23, 2011); *Michigan v. Bryant*, 131 S.Ct. 1143 (2011); *Melendez-Diaz v. Massachusetts*, 129 S. Ct. 2527 (2009); *Whorton v. Bockting*, 549 U.S. 406 (2007); *Davis v.*

Washington, 547 U.S. 813 (2006); and *Crawford v. Washington,* 541 U.S. 36, 53–54 (2004) are annotated above at section 801.04[1][a].

United States Court of Appeals for the Armed Forces

United States v. Crudup, 67 M.J. 92 (C.A.A.F. 2008): The accused was convicted of assault and battery upon his wife, resisting apprehension, and making a false official statement. When the wife refused to testify, her pretrial statement implicating the accused was admitted. The remainder of the government's case consisted of witnesses who observed the crimes and the accused's pretrial admissions. Although the court affirmed, it held that admitting the wife's pretrial statement violated the accused's Sixth Amendment confrontation rights. The court found that the error was harmless beyond a reasonable doubt because the statement was relatively unimportant and cumulative and the government's case was overwhelming. The court added that, although the wife could not have been cross-examined, her credibility was effectively impeached by proof of a previous fraud conviction. *See Delaware v. Van Arsdall,* 475 U.S. 673 (1986), discussing constitutional error tested for harmlessness.

Air Force Court of Criminal Appeals

United States v. Johnston, 63 M.J. 666 (A.F. Ct. Crim. App. 2006): The accused was convicted of larceny and child pornography offenses before *Crawford v. Washington,* 541 U.S. 36 (2004) was decided. When his wife refused to her incriminating pretrial statements were admitted over defense objection. The court held that, *Crawford* would apply to all courts-martial which were not final (see Article 76, U.C.M.J.) by the date of the Supreme Court's decision. The court found constitutional error in admitting Mrs. Johnson's pretrial statements and reversed the accused's convictions.

Army Court of Criminal Appeals

United States v. Gardinier, 63 M.J. 531 (Army Ct. Crim. App. 2006): The accused was convicted of several child sexual molestation offenses. At trial he objected to admitting the victim's incriminating videotaped, statements which were made to a civilian police officer during the criminal investigation. Before admitting the videotape, the military judge conducted a pretrial hearing to determine whether the victim was available to testify. At the hearing, the victim's mother testified that the victim was reluctant to testify, would not provide useful information, and, in any event, she did not want her daughter to testify. Upon further questioning by the military judge, the mother indicated she would not allow her daughter to testify. Thereafter, the military judge admitted the videotaped statements based on unavailability under Rule 804(a), and trustworthiness under Rule 807. The military judge stated that his unavailability decision was based on his belief that it would not be right to compel the child to testify against the mother's wishes, and that he viewed his decision as a "matter of personal conscience." Relying on *Crawford,* the court held that the victim's statements were testimonial, the military judge had erroneously determined that the victim was unavailable, and there had not been the requisite opportunity for the accused to examine the victim either before or during trial. Applying a constitutional error standard, the court held that the inadmissible testimony added little to the government's case, and that the untainted evidence was sufficiently strong to justify affirmance.

[b]   Residual Exception—Abused Family Members—Generally

Air Force Court of Criminal Appeals

United States v. Ortiz, 34 M.J. 831 (A.F.C.M.R. 1992): The victim of spousal abuse went to her neighbor's house beaten, naked, and hysterical. MP's eventually took her to the hospital where she made statements to them, doctors, and later criminal investigators. When she was released, the victim gave CID agents a handwritten account of what occurred. She followed that by signing a typed account. When the victim refused to testify for the government, her sworn statement was admitted. Affirming the accused's conviction, the court held that the victim's pretrial statement demonstrated particularized guarantees of trustworthiness and was admissible because: (1) it was a reaffirmation of other statements she made which were within firmly rooted hearsay exceptions; (2) it was the product of her own previous handwritten statement; (3) police officials never really "interrogated" the victim; and (4) it was in the interests of justice to admit evidence which was so clearly reliable that cross-examination would have been of only marginal value. The court also noted that this case did not present confrontation issues because, even though the victim failed to testify for the government, she took the stand for her husband during sentencing.

United States v. Griffin, 21 M.J. 501 (A.F.C.M.R. 1985): Although the court found error but no prejudice in the use of the residual hearsay exception, it provided the following guidance on future applications of the Rule: (1) its proper use does not violate the accused's sixth amendment confrontation rights, (2) the Rule's focus is narrow and meant to be "invoked sparingly and in rare circumstances," (3) its greatest application resides in trials where children or other family members are victims, particularly sexual abuse cases, and (4) the provision's requirements are to be strictly construed.

Army Court of Criminal Appeals

United States v. Rousseau, 21 M.J. 960 (A.C.M.R. 1986): In an important decision, the Army Court of Criminal Appeals established that out-of-court statements made by abused spouses, abused children, and parents of abused children may properly be admitted under this Rule. The court stated that "military society has a compelling interest in protecting the welfare of a soldier's family. For that reason, the residual exceptions are particularly well suited to the type of hearsay problems which arise when one family member falls victim to the aggressions of another family member."

[c] Residual Exception—Availability of Other Evidence

United States Court of Appeals for the Armed Forces

United States v. Czachorowski, 66 M.J. 432 (C.A.A.F. 2008): The accused was convicted of sexually molesting his daughter based largely on the hearsay testimony of the child's mother and grandparents. The family members simultaneously heard the victim explain how the crime had been committed. Before trial, trial counsel alleged that the victim refused to testify and had "forgotten" that the molestation even occurred, but presented no proof supporting his allegations. Reversing the accused's conviction, the court held that the out-of-court statements were erroneously admitted because trial counsel did not offer probative evidence establishing the victim's unavailability.

United States v. Grooters, 39 M.J. 269 (C.M.A. 1994): The accused was convicted of attempting to murder someone who had tried to sodomize him. Before trial, the victim made a sworn statement identifying the accused as his assailant. The victim then left Germany for Saudi Arabia, and refused to return. Reversing the lower court's determination that admitting this testimony was harmless error, the United States Court of Appeals for the Armed Forces held that government counsel failed to establish that the error did not contribute to the accused's conviction.

Air Force Court of Criminal Appeals

United States v. Fling, 40 M.J. 847 (A.F.C.M.R. 1994): This is an interlocutory appeal pursuant to Article 62, UCMJ. The accused was charged with sexually abusing his seven-year-old stepdaughter. Before those allegations arose, the victim indicated she did not want to be reassigned to Germany with her mother and stepfather, but wanted to stay in the United States and frequently visit her biological father. Notwithstanding these protestations, the victim moved to Germany. Shortly thereafter, she complained to her teacher that the accused was sexually abusing her. The child was then referred to various school and medical authorities, where she retold her story. When the victim failed to appear, the military judge held that all hearsay testimony was inadmissible under this Rule because trial counsel failed to establish the victim's unavailability. Affirming the military judge's decision, but returning the accused's case for further proceedings, the court held that government counsel may have had sufficient evidence to demonstrate unavailability, but failed to present it. In the court's opinion, counsel inappropriately relied on Rule 104 and presented averments or offers of proof instead of calling witnesses.

United States v. Fisher, 28 M.J. 544 (A.F.C.M.R. 1989): The court held that a deceased witness's out-of-court statement was improperly admitted to corroborate the accused's drug abuse confession. Reversing the conviction, it stated that "one of the necessary predicates for admitting a proposed statement is that it is more probative on the point than any other evidence which the government can procure through reasonable efforts." Here, not only did the government fail to meet this standard, the record demonstrated that other competent evidence actually existed and could have been presented.

United States v. Henderson, 18 M.J. 745 (A.F.C.M.R. 1984): Relying on the residual hearsay exception the court found that a sodomy victim's original pretrial statement indicating her father's complicity was properly admitted because (1) the victim was unavailable as she failed to answer a subpoena; (2) the pretrial statement was clearly made by the victim, as her signature was on it, and testimony by the individual taking the statement verified and (3) based on the entire record of trial sufficient "circumstantial guarantees of trustworthiness" existed. Using *United States v. Crayton,* 17 M.J. 932 (A.F.C.M.R. 1984), the court also found that the same victim's later pretrial statement impeaching her first statement and offered by the accused was not admissible under this Rule because there was no verification of the statement's authenticity.

Army Court of Criminal Appeals

United States v. Pacheco, 36 M.J. 530 (A.F.C.M.R. 1992): The accused was charged with numerous assaults against his wife and children. When the military judge suppressed the wife's out-of-court statements which implicated the accused, trial counsel appealed. *See* Article 62, UCMJ. Affirming the military judge's decision, the court held that the evidence was properly excluded because the government failed to demonstrate that it exhausted every reasonable means of securing the preferable live testimony of other witnesses before attempting to use the victim's out-of-court declaration.

United States v. Arnold, 18 M.J. 559 (A.C.M.R. 1984): The court found that the residual exception was designated to address the problems of family members who are witnesses to intra-family criminal offenses." If, however, as in this case, the government fails to demonstrate its witness's unavailability, the pretrial statement will not be admissible.

United States v. Meyer, 14 M.J. 935 (A.C.M.R. 1983): The court not only found that the government failed to show that a key witness was unavailable, but it also found that the testimony could not be admitted under the residual exception as it was self-serving, admitted little more than was readily apparent, assigned all criminal liability to the accused and generally lacked necessary independent guarantees of trustworthiness.

[d] Residual Exception—Child Abuse Cases—Manipulative Victims

United States Court of Appeals for the Armed Forces

United States v. Giambra, 38 M.J. 240 (C.M.A. 1993): This is the second time the accused's case was before the court (*see* 33 M.J. 331 (C.M.A. 1991), requiring a limited rehearing). Here, the court reversed the accused's conviction for sexually abusing his daughter because hearsay statements made by the victim's mother were erroneously admitted. In the court's opinion, the mother's statements were the untrustworthy product of a rebellious 17-year-old prosecutrix's manipulative scheme and were crucial in the court members voting for conviction.

[e]   Residual Exception—Child Abuse Cases—Judge Responsibilities

United States Court of Appeals for the Armed Forces

United States v. Hughes, 52 M.J. 278 (C.A.A.F. 2000), *affirming,* 48 M.J. 700 (A.F.Ct.Crim.App. 1998): The accused was convicted of indecent assault upon two females under 16 years of age. After the four-year-old victim was determined to be unavailable for trial, hearsay evidence of her verbal and non-verbal conduct was admitted over a defense objection that there had been no showing of the child's ability to understand the significance of telling the truth. Affirming the accused's convictions, the court held that based on the circumstances surrounding the making of the hearsay statements, sufficient evidence existed to demonstrate adequate indicia of reliability; and that the youthful declarant was capable of receiving just impressions of the facts and faithfully relating them. Both the court and the Court of Criminal Appeals would have preferred that the trial judge more fully explore the declarant's ability to distinguish truth from falsity and enter more extensive findings of fact.

[f]   Residual Exception—Child Abuse Cases—Not "More Probative Evidence"

Navy-Marine Corps Court of Criminal Appeals

United States v. Knox, 46 M.J. 688 (N.M.Ct.Crim.App. 1997): The accused was convicted of raping his five-year-old daughter and sodomizing his four-year-old son. Part of the government's evidence against the accused included various incriminating drawings his children had made, and an expert witness/social worker's interpretation of the drawings. Finding most of the art work to be inadmissible and reversing the accused's convictions, the court said the drawings did not qualify for admission under the residual exception because they were not more probative than other evidence reasonably available. Here, the children testified at trial and in the court's opinion their testimony was the most probative evidence available.

[g]   Residual Exception—Child Abuse Cases—Psychologist-Obtained Statements

Army Court of Criminal Appeals

United States v. Stivers, 33 M.J. 715 (A.C.M.R. 1991): The accused was charged with sexually molesting his seven-year-old daughter. At trial, the child was only able to testify concerning a portion of the offenses. The remainder of proof came from a social worker who examined the victim shortly after the offense was reported, and related her more detailed accounts of what occurred. Affirming a conviction, the court found this testimony to be admissible because: (1) the social worker indicated no animosity towards the accused, and had no motive to lie; (2) it was improbable that she had coached the victim prior to their interview; (3) the social worker made sure the child understood that she was there to help and that telling the truth was vital; (4) her questioning was not suggestive or leading; and (e) the victim did not recant her accusations when given the opportunity.

United States v. Fink, 32 M.J. 987 (A.C.M.R. 1991): In this child sexual abuse case, a Ph.D. psychologist treated the daughter/victim and her mother. During trial, the mother recanted her previous damaging out-of-court statements to the psychologist, and indicated that she had not seen him for medical help. Affirming a conviction, the court held that, although the statements might not be admissible under Rule 803(4), they would be under the residual exception because each was: (a) against the mother's pecuniary interests; (b) substantiated by the victim and other witnesses; (c) made while the psychologist was creating a family help plan; and (d) made without an apparent reason to lie.

[h] Residual Exception—Child Abuse Cases—Victim Testifies
United States Court of Appeals for the Armed Forces

United States v. Donaldson, 58 M.J. 477 (C.A.A.F. 2003): The accused was charged with numerous offenses ranging from failure to report, to child sexual abuse. Before a military judge alone, the accused entered a mixed plea, pleading guilty to the minor offenses and not guilty to the child sexual abuse offense. Although the victim testified, she was unable to relate the specific details of her assault. In order to perfect it's case the government was permitted to introduce statements the victim made to a female police officer. Both at trial and on appeal the accused contended that these statements should have been excluded because they were unreliable as not being accompanied by circumstantial guarantees of trustworthiness comparable to those supporting other hearsay exceptions. Affirming the accused's convictions and sentence, this court indicated that in resolving such issues they consider the following circumstances: (1) mental state of the declarant; (2) the spontaneity of the statement; (3) whether suggestive questioning was employed; (4) whether the statements are corroborated; (5) the declarant's age; and (6) the circumstances surrounding how the statement was obtained. Although the court found that the totality of circumstances present in this case supported the military judge's decision, it was troubled by the fact the victim's statements were made to a police officer, during private conversations, and in response to some questioning. The court ultimately overcame their concerns by focusing on the "uniqueness" of the victim's verbal and demonstrative responses which they viewed as "supporting a finding of reliability."

United States v. Johnson, 49 M.J. 467 (C.A.A.F. 1998): As the Army

Court of Criminal Appeals stated in its opinion below (45 M.J. 666), this case involved the somewhat common scenario of a child victim who first accuses her father of sexual abuse and then recants those statements both before and during trial. In response to these events, trial counsel introduced the victim's previous sworn, written statements. To establish trustworthiness, the government's offer included reliance upon circumstances contemporaneous with the statement's creation. Defense counsel proffered non-contemporaneous events to demonstrate a lack of trustworthiness. Affirming the accused's convictions, the court held that when the declarant testifies, the military judge may consider corroborating events beyond the circumstances of the declaration in determining trustworthiness. Relying on *Ohio v. Roberts*, 448 U.S. 56 (1980), the court provided a convenient logic for evaluating hearsay statements: (1) reliability is present when the hearsay statement falls within a firmly rooted exception or when it possesses "particularized guarantees of trustworthiness, (2) corroborating circumstances cannot be used as guarantees of trustworthiness when the declarant is unavailable to testify, (3) corroborating evidence may be used for this purpose when the declarant is available to testify, (4) when corroborating evidence is considered trial judges should examine "both those indicia that add to and detract from a statement's reliability, . . ." and (5) the judge may limit consideration of corroborating circumstances to only "those surrounding the making of the statement."

United States v. Casteel, 45 M.J. 379 (C.A.A.F. 1996): A court-martial convicted the accused of numerous child sexual abuse offenses. During trial, one victim, who was then six years old, testified for the government but in a very abbreviated fashion. She did not mention any sexual offense, and defense counsel conducted no cross-examination. Over defense objection, trial counsel then called a police detective who introduced an audio tape she had made of the victim's previous out-of-court statements, which thoroughly described the accused's conduct. The accused contended this government evidence lacked adequate indicia of reliability and should have been excluded. Affirming the accused's convictions, the court said that the victim's pretrial statements were sufficiently reliable and properly admitted because they were similar to statements against interest, were not the product of suggestive examination techniques, and appeared to be the result of a clear memory rather than a desire to please the investigator.

United States v. Clark, 35 M.J. 98 (C.M.A. 1992): The accused was convicted of sexually abusing his five-year-old daughter. The victim was not available for trial due to the accused's own misconduct. He nevertheless contended that her damaging hearsay statements to a friend, who had also been sexually abused by the accused, should have been excluded. Affirming these convictions, the court said the circumstances surrounding how the victim's statements were obtained rendered them particularly trustworthy because they were voluntary, uncontroverted, unconstrained, and spontaneous; made without a motive to lie; not within the realm of knowledge commonly held by five-year-olds; and similar to statements admissible as excited utterances under Rule 803(2).

Air Force Court of Criminal Appeals

United States v. Robles, 53 M.J. 783 (A.F.Ct.Crim.App. 2000): The accused was convicted of sexual offenses against his daughter and his step daughter. During the government's case, over defense objection, the victim's mother was allowed to testify about what the victim told her concerning the last sexual assault which had occurred two weeks previously. Affirming the accused's convictions and sentence, the court found that the challenged statements were erroneously but harmlessly admitted because the victim's mother testified before the victim herself took the stand or before she had been found unavailable.

Army Court of Criminal Appeals

United States v. O'Rourke, 57 M.J. 636 (Army Ct.Crim.App. 2002): A military judge sitting alone convicted the accused of indecent acts with a child and false swearing. Over defense objections, the victim's first grade teacher was permitted to testify about incriminating statements the victim made to her after the victim watched a school play about protecting children from sexual predators. The court affirmed the accused's convictions, finding the victim's statements to be reliable as they were spontaneous, consistent, without improper motive, and they contained unexpected terminology for a child of her years. The court also found the victim's out of court statements to be necessary because her trial testimony demonstrated an inability or unwillingness to share the details of what occurred and because her prior statements clearly identified the accused as her assailant.

United States v. Johnson, 45 M.J. 666 (Army Ct.Crim.App. 1997): As the court stated, this case involves the somewhat common scenario of a child victim who first accuses her father of sexual abuse, and then recants those statements both before and during trial. In response to these events, trial counsel introduced the victim's previous sworn, written statements. To establish trustworthiness, the government's offer included reliance upon circumstances contemporaneous with the statement's creation. Defense counsel proffered non-contemporaneous events to demonstrate a lack of trustworthiness. Affirming the accused's convictions, the court relied upon *United States v. McGrath,* 39 M.J. 158 (C.A.A.F. 1994), for the proposition that when the declarant testifies the military judge may consider corroborating events "beyond the circumstances of the declaration" in determining trustworthiness. However, when the declarant does not testify, the bench is limited to considering those circumstances dealing only with the statement's creation to establish trustworthiness. The court went on to say, "[W]e are satisfied that the *McGrath* rationale may be extended to permit consideration of any relevant non-contemporaneous evidence, including impeachment evidence." Based on this extension of *McGrath*, the court found that the military judge abused his discretion by failing to consider the non-contemporaneous events, but his failure to do so was viewed as not being prejudicial.

[i]   Residual Exception—Child Abuse Cases—Victim Unavailable

United States Court of Appeals for the Armed Forces

United States v. Dunlap, 25 M.J. 89, 90 (C.M.A. 1987): The court held that pretrial statements made by an 11-year-old victim of sexual abuse to her babysitter were properly admitted against the accused. They bore sufficient indicia of reliability on their "face to be closely related to the evidentiary requirement that the evidence have equivalent circumstantial guarantees of trustworthiness," were corroborated by the victim's prior excited utterances, and were supported by the military judge's special findings as to the "facts and circumstances" justifying admission.

Air Force Court of Criminal Appeals

United States v. Slovacek, 21 M.J. 538 (A.F.C.M.R. 1985): Finding error and an abuse of the trial judge's discretion, the court held that the pretrial statements of a four-year-old sodomy victim were improperly admitted because the government failed to establish that (1) the victim was unavailable at the time of trial; (2) the child's statement possessed the required guarantees of trustworthiness and (3) the defense was notified in advance of trial that the victim's statements would be used.

United States v. Barror, 20 M.J. 501 (A.F.C.M.R. 1985): Because the accused's 14-year-old stepson did not desire "to aid in the prosecution of his father," and thus refused to testify, the government used the witness's pretrial statement which clearly demonstrated the accused's guilt. Rejecting the accused's Sixth Amendment attack on the document, the court found it to be in compliance with this Rule because it had never been repudiated and was made (1) moments after the incident took place, (2) without apparent or implied incentive to lie, (3) under oath and (4) in clear detail. The court also said the residual exception was specifically designed to address problems of family members who are witnesses to or victims of an intrafamily criminal offense."

Army Court of Criminal Appeals

United States v. Marchesano, 67 M.J. 535 (Army Ct.Crim.App. 2008): The accused was convicted of sexually abusing his daughter's 7-year-old friend. After the assault the daughter made statements to her friend about the accused sexually assaulting her. The accused's daughter did not testify and refused to comply with a subpoena. Her statements were admitted through the victim and used by the government for Rule 414 purposes. The court found the trial judge abused her discretion in admitting these statements, although the error was held to be harmless and the accused's conviction was affirmed. The court reasoned that the admitted statements should have been excluded because they were too vague to satisfy the equivalent guarantees of trust worthiness standard, and as the fact that they were the product of questioning detracted from their reliability.

United States v. Russell, 66 M.J. 597 (Army Ct.Crim.App. 2008): The accused was convicted of raping his 5-year-old daughter. The government's case consisted of the accused's two confessions and statements the victim made to a friend's mother and to a clinical psychologist. The military judge held that the victim was unavailable after she took the stand and stated she was too afraid to testify. The court affirmed the accused's convictions and found that the mother's testimony was properly admitted under *Crawford v. Washington,* 541 U.S. 36 (2004), *Davis v. Washington,* 547 U.S. 813 (2006), and Rule 807. The court stated that when the victim complained to her friend's mother, the mother was acting in a situation analogous to someone in *loco parentis.* As a result, the victim's statements were nontestimonial and satisfied Sixth Amendment concerns. Similarly, the statements met Rule 807's standards as they contained sufficient particularized guarantees of trustworthiness to be considered reliable.

Navy-Marine Corps Court of Criminal Appeals

United States v. Muirhead, 48 M.J. 527 (N.M.Ct.Crim.App. 1998): The accused was convicted of assaulting his six-year-old stepdaughter with intent to inflict grievous bodily harm. The victim made statements about the assault to numerous people, including a representative from the local Child Protective Services. Trial defense counsel sought to exclude these statements in limine, but the military judge found them to be admissible because of the stepdaughter's unavailability and "the heavy weight of the medical evidence to support it." Affirming the accused's conviction, the court held that the military judge properly utilized the two-prong test established in *Idaho v. Wright,* 497 U.S. 805 (1990).

[j]   Residual Exception—Co-actor's Statements

United States Court of Appeals for the Armed Forces

United States v. Yeauger, 27 M.J. 199 (C.M.A. 1988): Affirming the accused's conviction for larceny and conspiracy, the court held that a co-actor's pretrial statements would "almost certainly . . . have failed the equivalent circumstantial guarantees of trustworthiness standard" and been suppressed, had the co-actor not been a defense witness. The court said this evidence's value was questionable because of its "blame-spreading content."

Navy-Marine Corps Court of Criminal Appeals

United States v. Yeauger, 24 M.J. 835 (N.M.C.M.R. 1987): On remand from the Court of Military Appeals, the court was asked to reconsider whether the accused's conviction should be upheld in light of *Lee v. Illinois,*

476 U.S. 530 (1986) (codefendant's confession during a joint trial held not reliable enough to warrant its untested admission), and *United States v. Cordero*, 22 M.J. 216 (C.M.A. 1986) (inculpatory hearsay statement made by the accused's wife to a criminal investigator held not reliable enough to satisfy constitutional requirements). The accused was convicted of stealing government funds. His co-actor had previously confessed to the crime, implicating the accused. When the co-actor recanted his confession at the accused's trial, the government was allowed to introduce it through the interviewing NIS agent. Affirming the conviction, the court stated that the co-actor's presence in court "satisfies the main concern of both the Confrontation Clause and the hearsay rule, which is the lack of any opportunity to cross-examine the absent declarant." Thus, neither *Lee* nor *Cordero* was controlling here.

United States v. Yeauger, 20 M.J. 797 (N.M.C.M.R. 1985): Pretrial statements of a co-actor concerning the accused's criminal misconduct were properly admitted against the accused even though the co-actor recanted his statements during the accused's trial. In reaching this result the court thoroughly applied 803(24)'s prerequisites for admission and followed the guidance contained in *United States v. Whalen*, 15 M.J. 872 (A.C.M.R. 1983), which established a four part test for admissibility.

[k]   Residual Exception—Constitutional Considerations

Supreme Court

Davis v. Washington, 126 S. Ct. 2266 (2006): The Supreme Court elaborated on the meaning of *Crawford v. Washington*, 541 U.S. 36, 53–54 (2004), when it decided the companion cases of *Davis v. Washington* and *Hammon v. Indiana*. In an opinion by Justice Scalia (also the author of *Crawford*), the Court elaborated on the meaning of "testimonial" and "interrogation" as it relates to confrontation. Once again, the Court declined to offer an exhaustive definition of terms, but its 8-1 vote (with Justice Thomas dissenting) offered some clarification of the meaning of both words. In *Davis*, Michelle McCottry telephoned 911, was cut off, and answered the operator's return call and told the operator that she had been assaulted by her former boyfriend, Davis, who had just fled the scene. Davis was charged with violation of a domestic no-contact order, a felony, but McCottry did not testify at his trial. In *Hammon*, police responded to a reported domestic disturbance at the home of Amy and Hershel Hammon. They found Amy alone on the front porch, appearing frightened. When the police inquired about the disturbance, Amy told them that nothing was wrong, but also gave them permission to enter. Once inside, one officer kept Hershel in the kitchen. Another officer interviewed Amy elsewhere in the living room. After hearing Amy's account, the officer asked her to fill out a battery affidavit, and she handwrote the following: "Broke our Furnace & shoved me down on the floor into the broken glass. Hit me in the chest and threw me down. Broke our lamps." Amy did not testify at Hershel's bench trial for domestic battery and violation of probation, but both her affidavit and the testimony of the officer who interviewed her were admitted over Hershel's objection that he had no opportunity to cross-examine and confront Amy. Justice Scalia concisely summarized the Court's reasoning in the two cases:

> Without attempting to produce an exhaustive classification of all conceivable statements—or even all conceivable statements in response to police interrogation—as either testimonial or nontestimonial, it suffices to decide the present cases to hold as follows: Statements are nontestimonial when made in the course of police interrogation under circumstances objectively indicating that the primary purpose of the interrogation is to enable police assistance to meet an ongoing emergency. They are testimonial when the circumstances objectively indicate that there is no such ongoing emergency, and that the primary purpose of the interrogation is to establish or prove past events potentially relevant to later criminal prosecution.

The Court held that the 911 tape in *Davis* was properly admitted since the primary purpose of the 911 operator's questioning Michelle McCottry was to deal with an emergency, but that the admission of Amy Hershel's battery affidavit violated the Confrontation Clause because the primary purpose was to gather evidence. The Court makes clear that a conversation that begins as an interrogation to determine the need for emergency assistance can become an interrogation to obtain testimony. Once the emergency ends, for example, continued interrogation might produce testimonial statements. In response to arguments by Washington and Indiana, supported by a number of amici, that domestic violence cases require greater flexibility in the use of testimonial evidence because victims are notoriously susceptible to intimidation that prevents them from testifying, Justice Scalia wrote that when defendants seek to undermine the judicial process by procuring or coercing silence from witnesses and victims, the Sixth Amendment does not require courts to acquiesce." He reiterated his suggestion in *Crawford:* that "the rule of forfeiture by wrongdoing . . . extinguishes confrontation claims on essentially equitable grounds."

Crawford v. Washington, 541 U.S. 36 (2004): A Washington state jury convicted the accused of first-degree assault while armed with a deadly weapon. An important part of the State's case against the accused consisted of his wife's out-of-court statements to police officers describing the charged offense and further implicating her husband. Reversing the accused's conviction and writing for the majority, Justice Scalia stated that because such out-of-court statements are "testimonial" they are barred by the Constitution's Confrontation Clause unless the declarant testifies, or if the declarant is unavailable at trial, defendant must have had a prior opportunity to cross-examine that declarant regarding her statement. Most importantly, the Court went on to say this outcome is required irrespective of whether the statement is seen as being "reliable."

Idaho v. Wright, 497 U.S. 805 (1990): A child sexual abuse victim's statements to a doctor were improperly admitted in this state prosecution because they did not satisfy the Confrontation Clause's requirements for particularized guarantees of trustworthiness. The Court said that these guarantees can only be met when they are present in the process used to obtain the statement. Independent evidence corroborating the statement's truthfulness will not satisfy these requirements.

United States Court of Appeals for the Armed Forces

United States v. Bridges, 55 M.J. 60 (C.A.A.F. 2001): The accused was convicted of assaulting his 22-month-old daughter and 9-month-old son. During trial, the accused's wife told the judge it didn't matter whether she is ordered to testify. She said she would refuse to testify. Subsequently, the judge determined that the accused's wife was "unavailable" to testify and admitted her prior statement under the residual hearsay exception of Rule 804(b)(5). The Court of Criminal Appeals affirmed the findings and sentence. The court held that the accused's Sixth Amendment right to confront the witnesses against him was not violated where the prosecution called the accused's wife as a witness, she refused to testify, and the defense waived cross examination. The Court stated that, once the Confrontation Clause was satisfied, it was appropriate for the military judge to consider factors outside the making of the statement to establish its reliability and to admit it during the prosecution's case-in-chief.

United States v. Hines, 23 M.J. 125 (C.M.A. 1986): In a particularly comprehensive opinion concerning relationship between the Confrontation Clause and the evidentiary rules regarding the admissibility of hearsay statements in a child sexual abuse case, the court affirmed the accused's conviction and use of the residual exception to admit the victims' out-of-court statements when those victims refused to testify after being called to the stand. Relying on extensive Supreme Court authority, the court indicated that admissibility in each case was dependent upon "whether the statements bore sufficient indicia of reliability to permit their introduction in the absence of cross-examination." The accused's confession matched each pretrial statement and was crucial to the court's reliability analysis. The court specifically advised trial judges to "state on-the-record the special facts and circumstances which they think indicate that the statements have a sufficiently high degree of trustworthiness and necessity to justify their admission."

Air Force Court of Criminal Appeals

United States v. Taylor, 62 M.J. 615 (A.F.Ct.Crim.App. 2005): The accused's wife made pretrial statements to AFOSI agents implicating the accused. When she claimed the spousal testimonial privilege and refused to testify, government counsel introduced her hearsay statement through another witness. On appeal, the court concluded that the wife's out-of-court statement was a testimonial statement. Finding constitutional error, the court evaluated the testimony using the harmless beyond a reasonable doubt standard and determined that the inadmissible evidence was not essential to the accused's conviction. As a result, the court failed to grant relief.

United States v. Bridges, 52 M.J.795 (A.F.Ct.Crim.App. 2000): This case presents the common prosecutorial concern of how to admit a prior written statement from a spouse who refuses to testify at her husband's child abuse trial. Here the spouse made a criminal complaint and a sworn statement in support. She was called as a government witness and refused to answer any questions from the trial counsel or the military judge. Thereafter the bench found the accused's wife unavailable, and pursuant to this provision admitted her pretrial statement. The accused's challenge is that the military judge's decision violated his confrontation clause rights. Relying on *Roberts v. Ohio,* 448 U.S. 56 (1980), the court affirmed the accused's convictions and found that the declarant was unavailable and that there were adequate indicia of reliability to support admitting the complaining spouse's out of court statement. The court went on to say that, although this proffer did not fit within the firmly rooted hearsay exception, and thus reliability could not be inferred, the evidence did possess particularized guarantees of trustworthiness which independently justified admission. However, the court found those guarantees from the totality of the circumstances, not just those circumstances surrounding the making of the statement. In *Idaho v. Wright,* 497 U.S. 805 (1990), the Supreme rejected such an analysis, holding that while "we agree that 'particularized guarantees of trustworthiness' must be shown from the totality of the circumstances; we think the relevant circumstances include only those that surround the making of the statement and that render the declarant particularly worthy of belief. To be admissible under the Confrontation Clause, hearsay evidence used to convict a defendant must possess indicia of reliability by virtue of its inherent trustworthiness, not by reference to other evidence at trial." In this case, the court held that, because the spouse took the stand, the confrontation clause was satisfied and that defense counsel's opportunity for cross-examination was similarly satisfied.

United States v. Hansen, 36 M.J. 599 (A.F.C.M.R. 1992): This case interprets *Idaho v. Wright,* 497 U.S. 805 (1990) (only the circumstances surrounding how a hearsay statement was obtained will be evaluated to determine its trustworthiness). The accused was convicted of numerous child sexual abuse offenses. During trial, the victim recanted her previous statements, and claimed a loss of memory. Using the residual exception, trial counsel introduced the victim's incriminating out-of-court statements. Affirming the accused's convictions, the court said that the military judge properly evaluated the statements based on their circumstantial guarantees of trustworthiness and necessity. However, the court went on to say that the trial judge's use of corroborating evidence, as prohibited by *Wright*, was harmless error.

United States v. Hines, 18 M.J. 729 (A.F.C.M.R. 1984): In a very lengthy decision the court conducted its own "*de novo* analysis" of the residual exception, finding three key principles which must be satisfied before residual hearsay testimony can be admitted: (1) "under certain circumstances hearsay statements that would be admissible if pertaining to peripheral evidence, are not admissible, when pertaining to evidence that is 'crucial' or 'devastating;' " (2) "the residual hearsay exceptions will be used rarely, and only in exceptional circumstances" and (3) the residual hearsay exception's application must not be violative of the Constitution's confrontation clause.

Army Court of Criminal Appeals

United States v. Valdez, 35 M.J. 555 (A.C.M.R. 1992): The accused was convicted of abusing, neglecting, and murdering his eight-year-old daughter. Part of the government's case included a statement made by the deceased child to her sister indicating that the accused's kick had caused the injuries which led to death. Defense counsel objected based on surprise. Affirming and modifying the accused's convictions (on other grounds), the court held that the evidence should have been suppressed because the military judge improperly used corroborative facts instead of the circumstances surrounding how the statement was made in determining admissibility. However, because the testimony was cumulative of the accused's own admissions, the court viewed this error as harmless.

Navy-Marine Corps Court of Criminal Appeals

United States v. Coulter, 62 M.J. 520 (N.M.Ct.Crim.App. 2005): During a bench trial for indecent acts with a child, the military judge admitted the parents' testimony detailing the two-year-old child's statements as to the accused's sexual assault upon her. The military judge had previously ruled the child incompetent to testify because of her age. In determining the admissibility of this hearsay evidence, the court conducted a two-part analysis. First, the court examined the testimony under traditional Rule 807 guidelines and found it to be admissible because it possessed equivalent circumstantial guarantees of trustworthiness. The court relied upon the following factors: (1) the declarant's mental state and age, (2) she had not been subjected to suggestive questioning, (3) her statements were spontaneous, (4) she did not have a motive to fabricate, and (5) her statements were corroborated by the government's expert medical witness. Part two of the court's analysis determined that the statements did not violate *Crawford v. Washington*, 541 U.S. 36 (2004). Affirming the accused's convictions, the court held that the victim's statements to her parents were non-testimonial and thus not prohibited by *Crawford*. The court based its decision on the declarant not: (1) having been questioned by the police or other government officials but by her parents who had a natural concern for their child's well-being; (2) being able to envision that her statements might someday be used in a criminal proceeding; and (3) being able to understand the solemn nature of her declarations or that they could be used to prove some fact or event in the future.

United States v. Martindale, 36 M.J. 870 (N.M.C.M.R. 1993): Holding that the victim's pretrial statements to NIS agents were admissible, the court affirmed the accused's conviction for sexually abusing his retarded 12-year-old son. Balancing both constitutional and hearsay standards, the court said that if the confrontation clause is otherwise satisfied, military judges have the discretion to consider all circumstances, including corroborating evidence, in deciding whether residual hearsay testimony possesses the requisite circumstantial guarantees of trustworthiness to justify its admission. We note that *Idaho v. Wright,* decided three years before this case and discussed above, prohibits using independent corroborating factors to establish reliability and trustworthiness.

United States v. Quarles, 25 M.J. 761 (N.M.C.M.R. 1987): Reversing the accused's conviction for numerous child sexual abuse offenses, the court held that the victim's out of court statements were improperly admitted because they "are not sufficiently trustworthy to warrant admission under either residual hearsay rule." The court found that each statement was the product of an *ex parte* interview under circumstances which failed to satisfy confrontation values and to demonstrate the "candor of the declarant and the truth of the statement to such a degree that the need for confrontation is made unnecessary." The court also rejected the government's contention that the "young age of the children coupled with their precocious knowledge of the sexual process lends to their statements sufficient reliability to justify admission."

[l]   Residual Exception—Declarant Present to Testify

United States Court of Appeals for the Armed Forces

United States v. Guaglione, 27 M.J. 268 (C.M.A. 1988): The accused's convictions for fraternization and drug related offenses were reversed because the pretrial statements of two government witnesses were admitted as substantive evidence after those witnesses recanted their earlier incriminating testimony and attempted to exonerate the accused. Citing federal authority, the court said when "a party who proposes to introduce a pretrial statement under the 'residual exception' has a witness who will testify in court to the facts sought to be proved, the trial judge should not admit the statements" under the residual exception.

United States v. Powell, 22 M.J. 141 (C.M.A. 1986): The court held that a military judge properly exercised his discretion under the residual exception to admit "an inconsistent extra-judicial statement as substantive evidence" because: (1) the declarant was available and testified in court, (2) she admitted making the prior statement, (3) her out of court protestations were substantiated by other witnesses, (4) her trial testimony was internally inconsistent, (5) the reasons she gave for changing her testimony were improbable, and (6) she intentionally misled trial counsel. However, the court warned counsel and trial judges to avoid "overly mechanistic applications of" the exception, and not to limit themselves to the factors considered here.

Air Force Court of Criminal Appeals

United States v. Cucuzzella, 64 M.J. 580 (A.F.Ct.Crim.App. 2007): The accused was convicted of assaulting and raping his wife. The victim recanted pretrial statements made to local police and military authorities implicating the accused, and the military judge excluded the statements at trial. The government's evidence consisted mainly of the accused's confession and statements the victim made to a registered nurse who administered the local parent support program at Charleston, Air Force Base. Although the court used Rule 803(4) to sustain admitting the victim's statements, the court went on to hold that those statements were also admissible under the residual exception. In the court's opinion, the victim's statements were evidence of a material fact, were more strongly corroborative of the accused's confession than any other evidence available to the prosecution, and were reliable. Finally, the court found that the interests of justice would not be served by excluding such reliable and probative evidence.

Army Court of Criminal Appeals

United States v. Whalen, 15 M.J. 872 (A.C.M.R. 1983): Relying on the residual hearsay exception, the court found no error in the government's calling a witness solely to elicit a prior statement inconsistent with the witness's trial testimony denying knowledge of the defendant's possession of drugs. The court said that the prior statement met all the requirements of the residual exception.

United States v. Powell, 17 M.J. 975 (A.C.M.R. 1984): Because a key government witness totally changed her testimony at trial, the court held it was proper for the prosecution to have introduced, as substantive evidence, the witness's prior sworn and inconsistent statement. In reaching this result the court relied on the fact that (1) the statement appeared trustworthy, (2) the witness was available to be cross-examined about it, and (3) its use furthered the interests of justice. *See* Rule 102.

Navy-Marine Corps Court of Criminal Appeals

United States v. Kelley, 42 M.J. 769 (N.M.Ct.Crim.App. 1995): The accused was convicted of rape, sodomy, indecent liberties, and indecent acts with his 6-year-old daughter. Although the child was available and testified, statements she made to her babysitter were admitted over the accused's objection. Affirming the accused's convictions, the court held that the residual exception did not require the government to choose between evidence admitted under other exceptions and that available pursuant to the residual exception.

United States v. Barnes, 12 M.J. 614 (N.M.C.M.R. 1981): An assault victim was permitted to testify that, while in the hospital he remembered certain facts, although he did not remember the assault at trial. The court found that the testimony was not past recollection recorded since there was no testimony that the recollection was correct (and we note that there was no recording). The court also said that the hospital recollection did not amount to reliable hearsay under the residual exception. We would note that there was no hearsay involved at all in this case. No out-of-court statements were admitted. The victim testified on the stand concerning what he had remembered in the hospital and what he could remember at trial. The problem was one of personal knowledge and fair cross-examination, not hearsay.

[m]   Residual Exception—The "More Probative" Element

Air Force Court of Criminal Appeals

United States v. Wiley, 36 M.J. 825 (A.C.M.R. 1993): The accused was convicted of sexually abusing his daughter. Both the victim and her mother testified concerning each of many offenses. The accused's son recanted statements made to military authorities and a state social worker about witnessing the crimes. His pretrial statements were admitted under this exception. Finding error but affirming the accused's convictions, the court held that the son's pretrial statements should have been suppressed because they were not more probative than other evidence already admitted.

[n]   Residual Exception—Necessity Element

United States Court of Appeals for the Armed Forces

United States v. Pablo, 53 M.J. 356 (C.A.A.F. 2000): At trial the accused was acquitted of sodomy but convicted of indecent acts with a seven-year-old child. The government's evidence included hearsay statements made by the victim-declarant that were admitted pursuant the "necessary" provision of this Rule. Although the Army Court of Criminal Appeals found error but no harm in the trial judge's determination, the court reversed and held that the victim's testimony should have been excluded. The court went on to say that because the victim testified at trial the error was not constitutional, but reversal was nevertheless required as the government failed to meet it burden of persuasion that the "error did not have a substantial influence on the findings." Chief Judge Crawford and Judge Sullivan filed separate dissents.

United States v. Kelley, 45 M.J. 275 (C.A.A.F. 1996): Tried before a military judge sitting alone, the accused was convicted of committing indecent acts upon his six-year-old daughter. Part of the government's evidence included testimony from a baby-sitter who related the victim's statements about how the accused sexually abused her. Defense counsel contended that this evidence should not have been admitted because the trial judge did not consider extrinsic facts tending to undermine the witness's reliability. Affirming the accused's conviction, the court found the baby-sitter's testimony admissible under the residual exception because it was material, necessary, and reliable. The court went on to say that such proof is particularly necessary in child abuse cases because it is often the only evidence available to support and corroborate the victim's allegations. Although the court indicated that trial judges have the discretion to consider extrinsic circumstances in evaluating admissibility, no abuse occurred here when the judge limited himself to those circumstances surrounding the declarations.

[o]   Residual Exception—Notice Element

United States Court of Appeals for the Armed Forces

United States v. Czachorowski, 66 M.J. 432 (C.A.A.F. 2008): The accused was convicted of sexually molesting his daughter based largely on the hearsay testimony of the child's mother and grandparents. The family members simultaneously heard the victim explain how the crime had been committed. After the military judge granted an *in limine* motion to exclude the statements under Rule 803(2) as being too remote, trial counsel offered them under Rule 807. Although defense counsel stated that he was aware trial counsel intended to offer the evidence, he had not received formal notice of that intention. The court reversed the accused's conviction on other grounds, recognized that there is a split among the federal circuits on the nature of notice required under the Rule, adopted a flexible approach in which formal oral or written notification is not required, and found that adequate notice had been provided.

United States v. Holt, 58 M.J. 227 (C.A.A.F. 2003): After pleading guilty to dishonorable failure to maintain sufficient funds for the payment of his checks, the accused was sentenced by a panel of officers to a bad conduct discharge and confinement. During sentencing a victim's letter was introduced against the accused. The Court of Criminal Appeals found that it was properly admitted because it contained sufficient circumstantial guarantees of trustworthiness. However, the court found error and remanded the case for further review holding the letter should have been excluded because the record was silent as to whether there was other available admissible evidence, and because the accused had not been given the required notice either at trial or on appeal that the document would be used.

Army Court of Criminal Appeals

United States v. Williams, 23 M.J. 792 (A.C.M.R. 1987): The court indicated that evidence of a witness's own blood type might have been admitted under this Rule if the moving party had provided adequate notice to opposing counsel. The court's opinion is significant because it warns counsel not to rely on the residual exceptions as a catch-all for last minute proffers. Counsel who intend to rely upon the residual exception should prepare to do so well before trial. Such preparation should include notifying opposing counsel and the military judge of potential issues.

[p]   Residual Exception—Questioned Documents

Navy-Marine Corps Court of Criminal Appeals

United States v. Dababneh, 28 M.J. 929 (N.M.C.M.R. 1989): In *dictum,* the court held that questioned documents (worthless checks) might be admissible under the residual exception.

[q]   Residual Exception—Resemblance to Other Hearsay Exceptions

United States Court of Appeals for the Armed Forces

United States v. Grant, 42 M.J. 340 (C.A.A.F. 1995): The accused was tried for sexually abusing his six-year-old daughter. Relying on both Rule 803(2) and the residual exception, government counsel offered the victim's pretrial complaints which had been made 36 to 48 hours after the crimes. Affirming the accused's convictions, the court held that the statements were admissible under the residual exception because they were not made to investigators or other persons seeking information, and because they bore a close resemblance to excited utterances which enhanced their trustworthiness and admissibility.

Army Court of Criminal Appeals

United States v. Quick, 22 M.J. 722 (A.C.M.R. 1986): A sodomy victim's pretrial statements to her babysitter were held admissible under the residual provision because they closely resembled statements which would have been admissible under Rules 803(2) (excited utterances) or 803(4) (statements made for the purpose of medical diagnosis or treatment). Further guarantees of trustworthiness were provided by corroborating physical evidence. As discussed in our Editorial Comments, *Idaho v. Wright,* now prohibits using independent corroborating factors to establish reliability and trustworthiness.

[r]   Residual Exception—Sentencing

Navy-Marine Corps Court of Criminal Appeals

United States v. May, 18 M.J. 839 (N.M.C.M.R. 1984): The court stated that the residual hearsay exception could not be used to "preempt" other Manual provisions concerning the admissibility of civilian convictions during the sentencing portion of trial.

[s]   Residual Exception—Statements Linked to the Accused's Confession

United States Court of Appeals for the Armed Forces

United States v. Martindale, 30 M.J. 172 (C.M.A. 1990): The government's evidence at this child sexual abuse trial consisted of the accused's confession and a pretrial statement made by the victim. The emotionally disturbed victim's out-of-court statement was admitted only after the child recanted it during the government's case-in-chief. Affirming the conviction, the court held that "based on the entire record presented to the military judge, *including the accused's confession*, we are satisfied that the hearsay testimony offered to corroborate the accused's admissions was reliable and admissible." (Emphasis added.) Judge Everett dissented.

Air Force Court of Criminal Appeals

United States v. Minaya, 30 M.J. 1179 (A.F.C.M.R. 1990): Affirming the accused's conviction for offenses involving his sham marriage to a Philippine national, the court held that the putative wife's pretrial statements were properly admitted under the residual hearsay exception because the accused previously conceded, in writing, that they were true. The court relied on the bench's detailed special findings in reaching this result.

[t]   Residual Exception—Statements to Law Enforcement Officials

United States Court of Appeals for the Armed Forces

United States v. Hyder, 47 M.J. 46 (C.A.A.F. 1997): In a complex factual scenario, two airmen who were married shortly before trial, were involved in using marijuana and LSD in their dormitory. Before they were married, the accused confessed to drug offenses solely because her soon-to-be-husband identified her to the OSI the day before when he confessed to similar misconduct. At the accused's trial, the only evidence supporting her confession were the statements her husband made to the OSI. Evaluating the hearsay rules, the court determined that the husband's testimony was admissible under the residual exception. Affirming the accused's convictions, the court held that the husband's statements were properly admitted because they were similar to 804(b)(3) and otherwise satisfied the residual exception. A dissent opined, "I am sure police officers all over the world will be extremely interested in the unique path the majority has chosen to break ground.

United States v. Moreno, 36 M.J. 107 (C.M.A. 1992): The accused was convicted of sexually abusing his son. Part of the government's evidence against the accused included videotaped recordings of the son's statements to a social worker, and statements the victim and his mother made to law enforcement officers. The military judge held that this evidence was admissible because it had been corroborated by other testimony. Even though the court affirmed the accused's convictions, it said the statements should have been suppressed because the record failed to establish that the process used to obtain the evidence satisfied the Confrontation Clause's requirements for particularized guarantees of trustworthiness.

United States v. Martindale, 30 M.J. 172 (C.M.A. 1990): Affirming the accused's conviction for sexually molesting his adopted son, the court held that the child's pretrial oral statements to police investigators had been properly admitted because, when combined with the accused's confession, they corroborated the accused's admissions and demonstrated reliability and trustworthiness.

United States v. Barror, 23 M.J. 370 (C.M.A. 1987): Distinguishing this case from *United States v. Hines,* 23 M.J. 125 (C.M.A. 1986), the court reversed the accused's sodomy conviction and held that an unavailable victim's pretrial statement did not bear sufficient indicia of reliability to justify its admission. Unlike *Hines,* the accused here had not confessed to the charge and the prosecution presented "relatively meager facts" supporting the statement's production. The court said that "if this statement is so reliable that confrontation may be excused, then virtually every statement to police will be admissible where the declarant is unavailable."

Army Court of Criminal Appeals

United States v. Cyrus, 46 M.J. 722 (Army Ct.Crim.App. 1997): The accused, a military policeman, was convicted of adultery and associating with known drug dealers. In order to prove that the accused had intercourse with someone other than his wife and that he was married, trial counsel used statements the accused's paramour made to investigating military policemen. Reversing these convictions, the court found that the admitted hearsay statements were not trustworthy nor were they more probative than other evidence reasonably available on these points. The court said it was unable to distinguish the proffered statements from those made to police in the course of most criminal investigations.

United States v. Rudolph, 35 M.J. 622 (A.C.M.R. 1992): Convicted of sexually abusing his stepdaughter, the accused contended that the victim's statements to civilian police investigators identifying him as the perpetrator should not have been admitted under this Rule. Finding error but no prejudice, the court would have excluded the statements because they were unsworn, neither the accused nor his counsel were present when they were taken, and as a result, they were not sufficiently reliable to pass the stringent equivalent circumstantial guarantees of trustworthiness test.

United States v. Murphy, 30 M.J. 1040 (A.C.M.R. 1990): Finding that an important defense witness was unavailable, the court held that, in order for her *ex parte* statements to be admitted "as substitutes for the right of confrontation, they must be shown to have been taken under such circumstances as to effectively assure that confrontation values have been satisfied." These statements were found to be inadequate and to "affirmatively detract from trustworthiness" because they were made to law enforcement officials, and were not under oath. The court went on to say that out-of-court declarations given to criminal investigators are particularly suspect because "they may be the product of the investigator's input," and should be viewed with judicial suspicion.

United States v. Arnold, 18 M.J. 559 (A.C.M.R. 1984): The court rejected the government's contention that out-of-court statements made to the CID by a carnal knowledge victim were "automatically more probative and trustworthy than in-court testimony would be." For such evidence to be admissible, the residual exception "requires either the in-court testimony of the declarant to provide a basis for admissibility, peculiar circumstances that guarantee trustworthiness, or the unavailability of the witness."

United States v. King, 16 M.J. 990 (A.C.M.R. 1983): Holding it was error to admit the prosecutrix's pretrial statements through CID investigators, the court found that this evidence did not contain "the circumstantial guarantees of trustworthiness required by" the residual exception. In part this result was caused by the prosecutrix's apparent motive to lie.

Navy-Marine Corps Court of Criminal Appeals

United States v. Harjak, 33 M.J. 577 (N.M.C.M.R. 1991): The victim in this child sexual abuse case had allegedly been abused by her father, the accused, and her stepfather. During trial, the military judge admitted a pretrial statement she had given to the CID. Reversing the conviction, the court found this evidence inadmissible because the circumstances under which it was obtained did not eliminate the possibility of fabrication, coaching, or confabulation.

United States v. Miller, 32 M.J. 843 (N.M.C.M.R. 1991): Finding error but no prejudice, the court held that, in this child sexual abuse case, trial counsel failed to establish that the victim's pretrial statements to NIS agents were sufficiently trustworthy to be admitted. In the court's opinion, the statements were contradictory and not helpful because, when given, the victim said she made them for vengeful purposes.

[u]   Residual Exception—Strictly Construed

Air Force Court of Criminal Appeals

United States v. White, 17 M.J. 953 (A.F.C.M.R. 1984): Unwilling to participate in what it considered a "crap shoot," the court reversed a conviction because an unavailable government witness's pretrial statement was admitted without a sufficient demonstration of that witness's reliability. Evaluating numerous military and federal authorities, the court characterized the residual hearsay exception as narrowly focused and of limited scope, and indicated it may only be used in truly exceptional circumstances with "rare and even strange factual situations."

Army Court of Criminal Appeals

United States v. Thornton, 16 M.J. 1011 (A.C.M.R. 1983): Finding that the residual exception was erroneously used to admit an assault victim's out-of-court statements, the court noted that this provision was intended to be used "very rarely and only in exceptional circumstances." As a result, they noted it must be strictly construed, and should have barred testimony that lacked any indicia of trustworthiness.

Navy-Marine Corps Court of Criminal Appeals

United States v. Abdirahman, 66 M.J. 668 (N.M.Ct.Crim.App. 2008): The accused's conviction for rape was reversed based on the cumulative effect of trial errors. One error involved testimony by the victim's friends who heard her rape allegations more than 30 minutes after the incident and repeatedly questioned her about what had happened. After holding that the trial judge abused his discretion in admitting the friends' testimony under Rule 803(2), the court also held the statements were inadmissible under the residual exception because: (1) they were not the most probative evidence available; (2) trustworthiness had not been established; and (3) their admission would not satisfy Congress's legislative intent that Rule 807 be used only in exceptional circumstances offering assurances of reliability which were absent here.

[v] Residual Exception—Suggestive Formats Stimulating Child's Statements

Army Court of Criminal Appeals

United States v. Dunlap, 39 M.J. 835 (A.C.M.R. 1994): After seeing a school puppet show designed to identify children who had been sexually abused, a six-year-old victim told the school nurse about her father's misconduct. When the victim recanted her statements, the nurse testified to what the victim had told her. Reversing the accused's conviction, the court found the victim's statements to be inadmissible, even though there were no signs of coaching, because there was a "hint" that an outside source could have affected them. The court went on to say that the puppet show itself was a suggestive format.

[w] Residual Exception—Trustworthiness Element Absent

United States Court of Appeals for the Armed Forces

United States v. Burks, 36 M.J. 447 (C.M.A. 1993): The accused was convicted of bludgeoning another airman to death. At trial, he unsuccessfully offered an exculpatory, anonymous letter authorities found in a military van the accused had been a passenger in. Both at trial and on appeal, the accused contended that the letter was admissible pursuant to the residual hearsay exception, and constitutional due process requirements. Rejecting each defense position, the court held that the letter was fundamentally untrustworthy, and would have misled or confused the finders of fact.

United States v. Williamson, 26 M.J. 115 (C.M.A. 1988): The accused's child sexual abuse conviction was reversed because the victim's grandfather (who was involved in a separate lawsuit to take custody of the child away from her natural father) testified that his granddaughter told him "Daddy had sexually molested" her. The court viewed this evidence as having "circumstantial guarantees of *untrustworthiness*, [and] asked the bench and bar to turn their attention once again to 'indicia of reliability' " which might cloak hearsay statements with equivalent circumstantial guarantees of trustworthiness. The court said that while it "wholeheartedly agree[s] that the goal of detecting and prosecuting child molesters is worthwhile, the end does not justify the means employed here."

Air Force Court of Criminal Appeals

United States v. Lockwood, 23 M.J. 770 (A.F.C.M.R. 1987): The accused's child sexual abuse conviction was based on his daughter's out-of-court statements which were admitted under the residual exception. However, at trial the victim specifically recanted each statement, her mother testified that the child was a constant liar and could not be trusted, and the victim testified that she lied to get even with her overly strict stepfather. Reversing the conviction, the court held that the "military judge abused his discretion by admitting an out-of-court statement and gave a plausible explanation in court why it was false." Such extrajudicial statements lacked the required circumstantial guarantees of trustworthiness.

Navy-Marine Corps Court of Criminal Appeals

United States v. Spychala, 40 M.J. 647 (N.M.C.M.R. 1994): The accused was convicted of sodomy and indecent assault upon his three-year-old step-grandson. Evidence of the crime was discovered more than thirty days after the event when the victim mentioned it to his uncle, who had also been a victim of the accused's sexual abuse. Only the uncle testified. Reversing the accused's convictions, the court held that the uncle's experiences with the accused prohibited it from finding any equivalent circumstantial guarantees of trustworthiness to his testimony.

[x]   Residual Exception—Trustworthiness Element Present

United States Court of Appeals for the Armed Forces

United States v. Pollard, 38 M.J. 41 (C.M.A. 1993): A general court-martial convicted the accused of child sexual abuse. Immediately after the offenses were discovered, the victim, her brother and sister, all made statements implicating the accused. Before trial, each child recanted. Over timely defense objections that the out-of-court evidence lacked trustworthiness and reliability, the military judge admitted the brother's and sister's statements. Reversing on other grounds, the court held that the children's original statements were sufficiently detailed, spontaneous, and accurate to establish truthfulness and trustworthiness. The court and the lower court relied on the military judge's detailed findings to reach its result.

United States v. Smith, 26 M.J. 152 (C.M.A. 1988): The court found no error in the military judge admitting an extract of the testimony of a government witness given during the trial of the accused's co-accused. This statement was held admissible because: the accused had requested a lengthy trial delay, during which time the civilian witness left Europe and would not return; government counsel made a reasonable and good faith effort to obtain the witness; the out-of-court statements possessed circumstantial guarantees of trustworthiness because they were given under oath, in a judicial setting, and recorded verbatim; and the statements had indicia of reliability because declarant possessed firsthand knowledge of the material facts, and these facts were consistent with the accused's own statements.

Air Force Court of Criminal Appeals

United States v. Bridges, 24 M.J. 915 (A.F.C.M.R. 1987): The accused's conviction for assaulting his brother-in-law in his wife's presence was affirmed despite defense counsel's contention that both witnesses' out-of-court statements were improperly admitted. At trial, the accused's wife testified but denied her husband's complicity. The accused's brother-in-law could not be located, despite substantial efforts by the government. In the court's opinion, both witnesses' previous statements detailing the accused's crime possessed the necessary "indicia of reliability" and "circumstantial guarantees of trustworthiness" to justify their admission. The court went on to say that, even though the evidence was obtained by military police officers, the statements were not "influenced by the setting of the interview [hospital rooms, or the accused's house] and the questioning methods used [police simply asked each witness to tell what happened]."

Army Court of Criminal Appeals

United States v. Brown, 25 M.J. 867 (A.C.M.R. 1988): The court rejected the accused's confrontation and hearsay objections to out-of-court statements made by his wife and children which helped establish his guilt for assaulting them. The court based its holding on the fact that all statements were "consistent, given under oath, corroborated by other evidence, unrecanted, "material, probative and in the interests of justice. As discussed in our Editorial Comments, *Idaho v. Wright,* now prohibits using independent corroborating factors to establish reliability and trustworthiness.

Navy-Marine Corps Court of Criminal Appeals

United States v. Bygrave, 40 M.J. 839 (N.M.C.M.R. 1994): The accused was convicted of engaging in unprotected sexual intercourse with two different women after he had been diagnosed as HIV-positive. At trial, one of the victims refused to testify, as she had left the Navy and married the accused. Over defense objection, government counsel was then allowed to introduce her prior out-of-court written statement to the NIS. Returning the record for further action on other grounds, the court held that the victim's statements possessed sufficient indicia of trustworthiness because, when she made them, no reason existed to mislead the NIS agents about whether the accused had used condoms during sex.

United States v. Helms, 39 M.J. 908 (N.M.C.M.R. 1994): The accused was convicted of committing indecent acts upon his four-year-old natural daughter. At trial, the victim's testimony was largely unresponsive. The offenses were established by other witnesses, including the victim's baby-sitter, who testified about what the victim told her concerning the crimes. Affirming the accused's conviction, the court held that the baby-sitter's testimony was admissible because it dealt with material facts, was the only available evidence on certain aspects of the charges, and possessed circumstantial guarantees of trustworthiness because it had been volunteered in the victim's home, without an authority figure present, and in the words a four-year-old would use.

[y] Residual Exception—Videotaped Evidence

United States Court of Appeals for the Armed Forces

United States v. Ureta, 44 M.J. 290 (C.A.A.F. 1996): After being sexually abused by her father, the victim reported all offenses to military authorities, a medical doctor, and a social worker. Thereafter, the victim refused to cooperate or testify. At trial, over defense objection, AFOSI agents were permitted to play a videotape they made of the victim's original complaint. Affirming the accused's rape and carnal knowledge convictions, the court said that, because the victim was unavailable, the evidence demonstrated sufficient particularized guarantees of trustworthiness, and clearly satisfied the foundational requirements of this provision, the trial judge did not abuse his discretion by admitting it. In reaching their result, the court specifically and heavily relied on this trial judge's special findings and the professionalism demonstrated by the OSI agents.

United States v. Palacios, 37 M.J. 366 (C.M.A. 1993): The accused was convicted of sodomizing and committing indecent acts upon his stepdaughter. Because the victim was unavailable, a videotaped conversation of her pretrial testimony was admitted on both charges. Finding numerous procedural and confrontational errors in the admission of this tape, ACMR reversed the accused's sodomy conviction, but affirmed the indecent acts conviction because of independent corroborating evidence. The court set aside the remaining charge, saying that there was a reasonable possibility that the challenged evidence might have contributed to the accused's conviction, and under those circumstances, corroborating testimony could not save the remaining charge.

United States v. Lyons, 36 M.J. 183 (C.M.A. 1992): The accused was convicted of aggravated rape. The victim was a deaf-mute, mentally impaired 18-year-old girl, with the communicative skills of a three-year-old. Because her direct examination was limited and largely unintelligible, the government was permitted to use the victim's videotaped reenactment of the crime.

Air Force Court of Criminal Appeals

United States v. Cabral, 43 M.J. 808 (A.F.Ct.Crim.App. 1996): The accused's conviction for sexually abusing a four-year-old girl was affirmed. At trial and on appeal he contended that a video-taped interview between the victim and an OSI agent had been improperly admitted. Finding that the residual exception's requirements were complied with, the court noted that the agent's initial "rapport building" session with the victim had not been recorded, and that such selective video-taping in the future might auger in favor of exclusion.

SECTION IX

AUTHENTICATION AND IDENTIFICATION

SYNOPSIS

§ 901.01   Official Text

Rule 901.   Requirement of Authentication or Identification.

(a) *General provision.*   The requirement of authentication or identification as a condition precedent to admissibility is satisfied by evidence sufficient to support a finding that the matter in question is what its proponent claims.

(b) *Illustrations.* By way of illustration only, and not by way of limitation, the following are examples of authentication or identification conforming with the requirements of this rule:

(1) *Testimony of witness with knowledge.*   Testimony that a matter is what it is claimed to be.

(2) *Nonexpert opinion on handwriting.*   Nonexpert opinion as to the genuineness of handwriting, based upon familiarity not acquired for purposes of the litigation.

(3) *Comparison by trier or expert witness.*   Comparison by the trier of fact or by expert witnesses with specimens which have been authenticated.

(4) *Distinctive characteristics and the like.*   Appearance, contents, substance, internal patterns, or other distinctive characteristics, taken in conjunction with circumstances.

(5) *Voice identification.*   Identification of a voice, whether heard firsthand or through mechanical or electronic transmission or recording, by opinion based upon hearing the voice at any time under circumstances connecting it with the alleged speaker.

(6) *Telephone conversations.*   Telephone conversations, by evidence that a call was made to the number assigned at the time by the telephone company to a particular person or business, if (A) in the case of a person, circumstances, including self-identification, show the person answering to be the one called, or (B) in the case of a business, the call was made to a place of business and the conversation related to business reasonably transacted over the telephone.

(7) *Public records or reports.*   Evidence that a writing authorized by law to be recorded or filed and in fact recorded or filed in a public office, or a purported public record, report, statement, or data compilation, in any form, is from the public office where items of this nature are kept.

(8) *Ancient documents or data compilation.*   Evidence that a document or data compilation, in any form, (A) is in such condition as to create no suspicion concerning its authenticity, (B) was in place where it, if authentic, would likely be, and (C) has

been in existence 20 years or more at the time it is offered.

(9) *Process or system.* Evidence describing a process or system used to produce a result and showing that the process or system produces an accurate result.

(10) *Methods provided by statute or rule.* Any method of authentication or identification provided by Act of Congress, by rules prescribed by the Supreme Court pursuant to statutory authority, or by applicable regulations prescribed pursuant to statutory authority.

§ 901.02   Editorial Comment

In introducing evidence a proponent must be prepared to show that the evidence is what the proponent says it is and that it satisfies minimum evidentiary standards. With ordinary witnesses, the foundation is relevance, personal knowledge and competence. (Rules 401, 601 and 602). With experts, the foundation is relevance, expertise and a reasonable basis for testimony. (Rules 401, 702 and 703). Other evidence may require more of a foundation. The process of laying this foundation is generally labeled "authentication"—a generic term employed to describe identification of physical or voice evidence, or verification of charts, diagrams, documents, and other physical evidence. Rule 901 prescribes a general requirement for authentication or identification and also provides illustrations of proper ways to satisfy the requirement. With only a minor change in paragraph (b)(10), the Rule follows its federal counterpart. The Rule made it easier for the proponent to authenticate evidence than under pre-Rules law.

[1]   Rule 901(a)—General Provision

[a]   In General

Rule 901(a) addresses the general requirement for authentication or identification: Before admitting a piece of evidence, the military judge must be satisfied that the court members could find by preponderance of the evidence that the evidence is what it purports to be. This subdivision, identical in approach to Rule 104(b), treats authentication as a matter of conditional relevancy. The proffered evidence must, of course, be admissible under other Rules, such as Section IV (relevancy); Section VIII (hearsay); and Section X (best evidence). Authentication is therefore only one of several hurdles a proponent must leap.[1]

The Rule apparently only requires a prima facie showing of authenticity

---

[1] For a discussion of the interplay between the concepts of authentication, best evidence, and hearsay, see Greenberg, *Introduction of Documentary Evidence in Civil Cases under the New Federal Rules of Evidence,* 9 CLEARING HOUSE REV. 1 (1975).

through either direct or circumstantial evidence.[2] The opponent may offer rebuttal or contradictory proof, but as long as court members reasonably could find the evidence to be what its proponent claims it is, the decision whether to believe the evidence is for the court members.

On its face, Rule 901(a) portended abandonment of many step-by-step authentication techniques recognized in pre-Rules practice. Arguably, such abandonment could be viewed as consistent with the Rules' overall approach, which generally is to prefer admission of evidence. But neither the legislative history of the Federal Rules nor federal case law precisely defines the relationship of Rule 901(a) to common law authentication rules.

The Drafters' Analysis to this Rule recognizes a "substantial question" as to its impact on pre-Rules authentication requirements. Despite the apparent minimal authentication requirement of subdivision (a), the Drafters' Analysis suggests that the Rule requires more to authenticate evidence than one might think. For example, a chain of custody is still required. This is generally consistent with the federal cases that have continued to apply traditional techniques in a flexible fashion. In *United States v. Fuentes,*[3] for instance, the court rejected any rigid formula for authenticating tape recordings, but noted that the government must produce clear and convincing evidence of authenticity and accuracy as a foundation for admission. The court stated that common law techniques of authentication could serve as a valuable formulation of factors to be considered by the trial judge in determining admissibility.

There is a strong case to be made for careful screening by the military judge where evidence is not unique and stable and might change in form or quality between the time it is gathered and the time it is offered at trial. The Drafters' Analysis recognizes this and in harmony with existing case law requiring minimal guarantees of reliability as a condition to admission of evidence in criminal trials.

One thing is clear: the evidence that is used to authenticate or identify an item must itself be admissible. Because the members can only make an assessment whether an item is genuine on the basis of the evidence before them, only admissible evidence may be considered by the judge in deciding whether a sufficient foundation has been laid.

[b] Relationship to Other Rules of Evidence

The fact that a piece of evidence is authenticated does not ensure its admissibility. For example, an authenticated letter may contain privileged

---

[2] *See, e.g.,* United States v. Gagliardi, 506 F.3d 140 (2d Cir. 2007) (not error to admit e-mails and transcripts of instant messages which had been cut and pasted into word processing files; court noted that standard of authentication is minimal; witnesses testified that files were accurate, even though they were capable of being edited).

[3] 563 F.2d 527 (2d Cir. 1977).

information under one of the rules in Section V, which would require either some careful masking or even exclusion. And Rule 403 may provide a basis for the trial judge to exclude relevant, authenticated evidence. For example, an autopsy photograph might be presented as an authentic description of the massive wounds to the victim, but be excluded on grounds of undue prejudice or because it unduly appeals to the emotions of the court members.[4]

One of the most common points of confusion arises from the belief that authenticated business documents or records automatically satisfy the exceptions to the hearsay rule and vice versa. That confusion is no doubt fueled by the fact that there is a specific hearsay exception for such documents, Rule 803(6), that lists specific foundation requirements. Although authentication and hearsay issues do present some points of commonality and the bench and the bar often confuse them, these issues should be analyzed separately. The hearsay rule is designed to protect against the introduction of statements made by a declarant who is not subject to confrontation and cross-examination. The requirement of authentication, which is really a relevancy requirement,[5] is designed to ensure that the court considers only evidence which is actually what it purports to be.[6]

[c]   Proving Authenticity—The Mechanics

Rule 901 does not spell out the procedures for actually proving that an item of evidence, whether it is a video or document, is authentic. If the proponent is relying upon any of the illustrations listed in Rule 901, then he or she will almost always have to call a foundation or sponsoring witness, unless there is a stipulation of authenticity.

The Rules of Evidence and Rules of Court-Martial are silent on the actual mechanics of laying the requisite foundation and introducing the item into evidence, and there is no controlling case law that governs the techniques counsel may use. We recommend, however, a four-step process: First, counsel should have the item of evidence marked for identification (if it has

---

[4] *See, e.g.,* United States v. Mobley, 28 M.J. 1024 (A.F.C.M.R. 1989) (admission of photographs of murder victim was harmless error).

[5] Some commentators treat authentication as "underlying logical relevancy," which is distinguished from "facial logical relevancy." *See* E. Imwinkelried & D. Schlueter, FEDERAL EVIDENCE TACTICS, § 9.01[3][a][ii] (Matthew Bender). The latter requires that the evidence, on its face, have a logical connection with an issue in the case. *See* Rule 401. The former focuses on the question of whether the evidence is in fact the item that its proponent claims. Thus, the fact the proponent can show that the letter is really a letter from the accused, as required by Rule 901, does not necessarily mean that it is relevant to any issue in the case as required by Rules 401 and 402.

[6] *See* United States v. Duncan, 30 M.J. 1284 (N.M.C.M.R. 1990) (case contains good discussion of the differences in the rules and noted that it objected to the language, to authenticate a document as a business record).

not been marked before trial), show the item to opposing counsel (and perhaps the military judge), and finally show it to the foundation witness. Second, counsel should elicit testimony from the foundation witness that establishes the foundational elements for the item of evidence. Third, counsel should formally offer (or tender) the item into evidence. Finally, if the judge admits the exhibit, counsel should "publish" the exhibit to the court members by, for example, handing it to them or reading the contents of the document.[7] The item need not be published until such time as counsel wants the members to view it or counsel wishes to reveal the contents to the members. In some instances, counsel may wait until the conclusion of a witness's examination to publish the exhibits authenticated by the witness. If counsel and the judge wish to use courtroom technology for introducing exhibits,[8] the step by step process is modified.[9]

[2]   Rule 901(b)—Illustrations

Subdivision (b) provides ten non-exhaustive illustrations of authentication or identification. On the whole, these examples broaden the proponent's horizons for authenticating evidence in military practice. The Rule recognizes that there are many ways, often overlapping, to authenticate evidence.

[3]   Rule 901(b)(1)—Testimony of Witness with Knowledge

[a]   In General

A time-honored method of authenticating or identifying evidence is to elicit testimony from a witness who is sufficiently familiar with the proffered evidence, *see* Rule 602, that the item is what it purports to be. For example, a witness can authenticate a letter or document he personally wrote or saw another write.[10] A witness familiar with the handwriting or signature in a

---

[7] *See* D. Schlueter, S. Saltzburg, L. Schinasi & E. Imwinkelried, MILITARY EVIDENTIARY FOUNDATIONS, § 1-7 (4th ed. 2010) (discussion of four-step method for "walking and talking" an exhibit into evidence).

[8] *See, e.g.,* Bocchino, Ten Touchstones for Trial Advocacy—2000, 74 TEMP. L. REV. 1 (2001); Heintz, The Digital Divide and Courtroom Technology: Can David Keep Up With Goliath?, 54 FED. COMM. L. J. 567 (2002); Kenny & Jordan, Trial Presentation Technology: A Practical Perspective, 67 TENN. L. REV. 587 (2000); Lederer, Trial Advocacy: The Road to the Virtual Courtroom? A Consideration of Today's—and Tomorrow's—High-Technology Courtrooms, 50 S.C. L. REV. 799 (1999); Lederer, Courtroom Technology in the New Millennium, the Virtual Courtroom is Upon Us, ALI-ABA COURSE OF STUDY MATERIALS: Conference on Life and Health Insurance Litigation (May 2000); Ponder, But Look Over Here: How The Use Of Technology At Trial Mesmerizes Jurors And Secures Verdicts, 29 LAW & PSYCHOL. REV. 289 (2005); Webster, High-Tech Courtroom Visual Presentation System, 80 MI BAR JOUR. 41 (2001); Weibel, Primer on Advanced Courtroom Technology, 21-6 ABIJ 16 (2002).

[9] D. Schlueter, S. Saltzburg, L. Schinasi & E. Imwinkelried, MILITARY EVIDENTIARY FOUNDATIONS § 1-8 (4th ed. 2010) (using courtroom technology for exhibits).

[10] *See, e.g.,* United States v. Hadley, 671 F.2d 1112 (8th Cir. 1982) (certificate of

document or with markings on a piece of physical evidence can authenticate that evidence.[11] Courts have continued to follow the non-limiting language of Rule 901 and recognize that personal knowledge of an authenticating witness will authenticate evidence in a variety of contexts.

[b] Demonstrative Versus Real Evidence

The broad term "Demonstrative Evidence" is sometimes used to refer to any tangible evidence presented at trial, without regard to whether it has any actual historical connection with the case.[12] Depending upon its intended use, it must be authenticated or identified. If it is to be used purely for demonstration or illustration, *i.e.,* in the nature of a courtroom prop, the proponent must still be prepared to show what the item is and how it relates to the case, *e.g.,* it is substantially similar to the gun used in a robbery.[13] If it is used merely as a prop or for illustrative purposes, it normally will not be admitted into evidence, although courts may admit the illustrative exhibit and instruct the court-members on its proper use.[14] The terms "Real," "Physical," and "Original" evidence are normally used to describe tangible evidence which has an historical connection with the case, *e.g.,* the actual assault weapon or the actual drugs seized from the defendant.[15] Because the relevancy of the evidence depends upon the actual historical connection to the case, the proponent must be prepared to show that it is the "real thing,"

---

insurance and canceled check were properly authenticated by witness with personal knowledge); United States v. Mauchlin, 670 F.2d 746 (7th Cir. 1982) (prison official, who had known defendant for sixteen months and had seen him write on six occasions, sufficiently identified file documents). *See generally* D. Schlueter, S. Saltzburg, L. Schinasi, & E. Imwinkelried, MILITARY EVIDENTIARY FOUNDATIONS, § 4-2(B) (4th ed. 2010) (sample foundation).

[11] United States v. Barlow, 568 F.3d 215 (5th Cir. 2009) (testimony by witness that exhibits fairly and fully related chats that she had with defendant was sufficient authentication).

[12] *See generally* 2 McCormick, EVIDENCE § 212 at 3 (6th ed. 2006) (noting that "demonstrative" evidence is a generic term encompassing not only props but also actual or original physical evidence). *See also* E. Imwinkelried & D. Schlueter, FEDERAL EVIDENCE TACTICS, § 9.01[3][b][ii] (Matthew Bender) (noting distinction); Imwinkelried, *The Identification of Original, Real Evidence,* 61 MIL. L. REV. 145 (1973).

[13] *See, e.g.,* Miskis v. State, 756 S.W.2d 350 (Tex. App. Houston [14th Dist.] 1988, pet. ref'd) where the court set out a five-pronged test for admitting duplicate physical evidence: (1) the original is not available, (2) if available, the original would be admissible, (3) the item is relevant, (4) its probative weight outweighs any inflammatory effect, and (5) the jury is instructed that the evidence is not the original.

This method of introducing physical evidence may serve as an alternative if the proponent's witness is not certain that the item is indeed the real article or if the real article is not available for trial.

[14] *See* R.C.M. 921(b) ("any exhibits admitted into evidence . . ." may be taken into deliberation room).

[15] *See* 2 McCormick, EVIDENCE § 212 at 8 (6th ed. 2006).

not just a prop. It will be marked as an exhibit and if a sufficient foundation is laid it will be admitted and examined by the court members during their deliberations.[16] Trial judges may exclude some illustrative evidence under Rule 403; they are less likely to exclude real evidence.

[c]   Physical Evidence—Readily Identifiable

A common method of identifying physical evidence as genuine is through the testimony of a witness who can readily identify the item by distinctive markings or characteristics. The markings may be intrinsic, such as coloring or a manufacturer's serial number, or extrinsic, such as notches or marks made by the witness or another person. The greater the number of such unique characteristics, the greater the likelihood that the item is "readily identifiable" and thus genuine.[17] A common example of using this form of authentication is the identification of a bag of marijuana taken from the accused. The military cases have generally permitted such identifications where the officer who seized the bag has put his initials on it so that he can distinguish the accused's bag from other marijuana that might have similar texture, smell, and physical characteristics.[18]

[d]   Physical Evidence—Chain of Custody

If the item is subject to alteration or change, the proponent may be required to rely upon a chain of custody to show that the item's condition has not been altered[19] or tampered with.[20] The "links" in the chain are normally composed of those individuals who had a substantial opportunity to handle the evidence. Normally, laboratory and postal employees are exempted because of the obvious problem of accounting for each and every person who may have handled a particular item while it was in transit.[21] Mere breaks or gaps in the chain affect only the weight of the evidence, and not its admissibility.[22] Each person in the chain should be prepared to testify as

---

[16] *See* R.C.M. 921(b).

[17] *See, e.g.,* United States v. Parker, 10 M.J. 415 (C.M.A. 1981) (combination of unique physical characteristics was unusual enough to make it more probable than not that they existed in a single object). *See generally* 2 WIGMORE ON EVIDENCE § 411–412 (3d ed. 1940); D. Schlueter, S. Saltzburg, L. Schinasi, & E. Imwinkelried, MILITARY EVIDENTIARY FOUNDATIONS, § 4-8(B) (4th ed. 2010) (sample foundation for readily identifiable object).

[18] *See* Annotated Cases *below*.

[19] United States v. Ettleson, 13 M.J. 348 (C.M.A. 1982); United States v. Fowler, 9 M.J. 149 (C.M.A. 1980); United States v. Nault, 4 M.J. 318, 319 (C.M.A. 1978); United States v. Hudson, 20 M.J. 607 (A.F.C.M.R. 1985). *See generally* Giannelli, *Chain of Custody and the Handling of Real Evidence,* 20 AM. CRIM. L. REV. 527 (1983).

[20] *See, e.g.,* United States v. Howard-Arias, 679 F.2d 363 (4th Cir. 1982) (chain of custody for marijuana should negate reasonable possibility of replacement or tampering).

[21] *See* United States v. Porter, 12 M.J. 129 (C.M.A. 1981). *Cf.* United States v. Carrott, 25 M.J. 823 (A.F.C.M.R. 1988) (four-month gap was fatal to chain of custody).

[22] *See, e.g.,* United States v. Courts, 9 M.J. 285 (C.M.A. 1980); United States v. Jefferson,

to how the item was received, its condition, what he or she did with it, and the process of passing it along to the next person in the chain. In this manner, the proponent can establish, through the personal knowledge of each person in the chain, the unlikelihood that the item has been tampered with.[23]

The length of the chain of custody depends upon the proponent's intended use. If the proponent intends to rely primarily upon a laboratory test of the evidence, there is authority for the proposition that the chain need only run until the time of the testing.[24] What happens after the testing has been completed is usually not relevant to the case.[25] If the proponent wishes to show the historical relevancy of the evidence, it is usually necessary for the chain to run until the evidence is presented at trial. The chain may, but need not, be reflected in an official chain of custody document. *See* discussion of Rules 803(6) and (8), *below*.

[e] Charts, Maps, and Diagrams

Some confusion typically surrounds the verification and evidentiary status of charts, maps, and diagrams.[26] These may be used as mere pedagogical devices at trial to illustrate a witness' testimony,[27] or may be formally offered and admitted into evidence as exhibits. In both instances the proponent must "verify" through the testimony of a witness that the chart or diagram is an accurate depiction of whatever it purports to represent.

---

714 F.2d 689 (7th Cir. 1983) (chain of custody problem goes to weight, not admissibility); United States v. Bizzard, 674 F.2d 1382 (11th Cir. 1982) (unexplained four-week gap in custody of fingerprints went to weight); United States v. Lampson, 627 F.2d 62 (7th Cir. 1980) (problems with chain of custody go to weight, not admissibility, although more concern exists when the issue is the identity of evidence rather than a change in condition). There is federal case law for the proposition that absent any evidence of tampering or bad faith there is a presumption of integrity for the physical evidence. *See, e.g.*, United States v. Wilson, 565 F.3d 1059 (8th Cir. 2009) (cell phone containing child porn was admissible; defendant failed to rebut "presumption of integrity;" United States v. Cannon, 88 F.3d 1495 (8th Cir. 1996) (noting presumption of integrity of physical evidence).

[23] *See generally* D. Schlueter, S. Saltzburg, L. Schinasi & E. Imwinkelried, MILITARY EVIDENTIARY FOUNDATIONS, § 4-8(C) (4th ed. 2010) (sample foundation for chain of custody).

[24] *See generally* Jones v. Commonwealth, 228 Va. 427, 323 S.E.2d 554 (1984) (strict chain of custody required only where the exhibit is offered to support basis of chemical testing or expert testimony).

[25] *Cf.* R.C.M. 703(f) (defense has equal right to evidence which is relevant and necessary). *See generally* Chute, *Due Process and Unavailable Evidence,* 118 MIL. L. REV. 93 (1987).

[26] *See generally* 2 McCormick, EVIDENCE § 213 at 15–16 (6th ed. 2006) (noting varying practices).

[27] *See* Pierce v. Ramsey Winch Co., 753 F.2d 416 (5th Cir. 1985) (charts and summaries used for illustration are not evidence and should not be taken into deliberation room unless all parties consent). *Cf.* R.C.M. 921(b) which indicates that exhibits which have been admitted into evidence may be taken into the deliberation room.

Although the representation need not be to scale, the court should be notified when it is not.

There is no practical difference between laying a foundation for items to be used as mere props and for laying a foundation for items to be admitted into evidence. If a trial judge admits illustrative exhibits into evidence, they may, in the judge's discretion, be taken into the deliberation room along with other exhibits.

Where the witness prepares or marks the chart or diagram during the trial itself, counsel should be careful to clearly incorporate the demonstrative evidence and testimony. This can usually be accomplished by asking the witness to mark the chart or diagram with a certain symbol and then indicating for the "record" that the witness has so marked the item. If an oversized chart is actually introduced into evidence, a copy or photograph of the chart can then be placed in the record of trial for the appellate court to see.[28]

[f] Computer Records and Printouts

Computer printouts and records are now so commonplace that it is usually not difficult to authenticate these types of evidence. The proponent should be prepared to show that the system is reliable and that it is based on valid principles.[29] In the case of computerized business records, a sponsoring witness with personal knowledge about the preparation of the printouts should be able to authenticate the records even if he or she is not familiar with the detailed workings of the computer itself.[30] If the readouts or data are not readily readable by a layperson, an expert may be called to explain what the terms and data represent. And, as noted *above*, the readouts or records may implicate the hearsay rule.[31]

[g] Proving Authenticity of Documents

If the offered document cannot be authenticated under one of the

---

[28] *See, e.g.,* D. Schlueter, S. Saltzburg, L. Schinasi, & E. Imwinkelried MILITARY EVIDENTIARY FOUNDATIONS, § 4-7(B) (4th ed. 2010) (sample foundations); E. Imwinkelried & D. Schlueter, FEDERAL EVIDENCE TACTICS, § 9.01[3][a][V] (Matthew Bender) (discussing effective use of charts and graphs).

[29] *See, e.g.,* United States v. Tank, 200 F.3d 627 (9th Cir. 2000) (computer files and printouts shown to be accurate; deleted materials went only to the weight of evidence). *See generally* D. Schlueter, S. Saltzburg, L. Schinasi & E. Imwinkelried, MILITARY EVIDENTIARY FOUNDATIONS, § 4-3(D) (4th ed. 2010).

[30] *See, e.g.,* United States v. Linn, 880 F.2d 209 (9th Cir. 1989) (records authenticated even though witness was not familiar with differences between data bases," menus, and computer codes); United States v. Miller, 771 F.2d 1219 (9th Cir. 1985) (billing supervisor permitted to authenticate records even though he did not have knowledge about maintenance and operation of computer).

[31] If the computer printouts are business records, then Rule 803(6) is applicable. And if the records are government or public records, Rule 803(8) is applicable.

illustrations in Rule 901(b), a sponsoring witness may nonetheless authenticate the document by showing, through personal knowledge, that the document is what it purports to be. For example, the witness saw the accused sign the false pay voucher or recognizes the handwriting in the letter as that of the victim. As noted in our discussion at Rule 902, *below*, some types of documents may be self-authenticating.

[h] Photographs, Video, and X-rays

Photographs may be authenticated, or verified, in one of two ways. First, the military courts have recognized the "silent witness" view of authenticating photographs.[32] That is, the photograph speaks for itself if it is shown to be the result of a reliable process or system.[33] This is the sort of approach normally taken with x-rays where it is clear that no witness has actually seen what the x-ray purports to display. The same approach may be used to lay a foundation for surveillance films.

The second method of verifying the authenticity of a photograph is to establish through a witness's testimony, not necessarily the photographer,[34] that the photo accurately depicts a scene or event. This theory of admissibility is sometimes referred to as "pictorial testimony" and requires that the foundation witness be familiar with the contents of the photo.

Videotapes may generally be authenticated in the same manner as photographs. One court, in dicta, recognized that a videotape (which it considered to be the equivalent of a photograph) could be authenticated through another method—circumstantial evidence of the contents of the photo and measures taken to ensure that accurate pictures were taken.[35]

[i] Proving Authenticity of Audio Recordings

The contents of an audio recording may also be authenticated through the use of lay witness testimony that establishes the witness is familiar with the recording itself, or with the person's voice heard on the tape.[36] As noted, *below*, Rule 901(b)(5) specifically addresses the use of lay or expert opinion testimony to identify a person's voice. While some federal courts require the

---

[32] United States v. Harris, 55 M.J. 433 (C.A.A.F. 2001) (video camera photographs from bank's drive-up window), annotated, *below*; United States v. Howell, 16 M.J. 1003 (A.C.M.R. 1983) (photos taken at automatic teller machine).

[33] *See* Rule 901(b)(9). *See also* United States v. Rembert, 863 F.2d 1023 (D.C. Cir. 1988) (photographs taken by ATM machine were circumstantially authenticated by their contents along with testimony by bank official concerning operation of machine and camera).

[34] *See* United States v. Richendollar, 22 M.J. 231 (C.M.A. 1986) and United States v. Reichart, 31 M.J. 521 (A.C.M.R. 1950), annotated *below*.

[35] United States v. Reichart, 31 M.J. 521 (A.C.M.R. 1990).

[36] *See, e.g.,* United States v. Powell, 55 M.J. 633 (A.F.Ct.Crim.App. 2001), annotated, *below*: *See generally* D. Schlueter, S. Saltzburg, L. Schinasi & E. Imwinkelried, MILITARY EVIDENTIARY FOUNDATIONS, § 4-5 (4th ed. 2010) (authenticating oral statements).

proponent to establish a seven-pronged predicate for audio recordings, the Court of Appeals has indicated that the Military Rules of Evidence permit, but do not require, the proponent to do so.[37] It should be noted, however, that a witness who knows a person's voice can identify the voice, but cannot testify that the recording is a fair and accurate rendition of a conversation unless the witness actually heard the conversation.

[j]   Other Foundations

Over the years, the courts and commentators have addressed methods for authenticating a variety of other pieces of evidence such as e-mail transmissions,[38] caller-identification,[39] web sites,[40] chat-room discussions,[41] computer animations,[42] and facsimile transmissions.[43] For each of those pieces of evidence, the requisite foundations may derive from one of the listed illustrations in Rule 901(b), or in a combination of those illustrations. At the core, however, is the requirement that some person have personal knowledge about how a particular system or process works.

[4]   Rule 901(b)(2)—Nonexpert Opinion on Handwriting

Any lay witness familiar with the handwriting in question may identify it as long as the familiarity was not acquired solely for purposes of the court-martial.[44] This example of authentication, distinguishable from expert testimony governed by Rule 702 and Rule 901(b)(3), follows pre-Rules law.[45] Although the Rule draws a line between witnesses who have

---

[37] *See* United States v. Blanchard, 48 M.J. 306 (C.A.A.F. 1998), annotated *below*.

[38] *See, e.g.*, United States v. Siddiqui, 235 F.3d 1318 (11th Cir. 2000); D. Schlueter S. Saltzburg, L. Schinasi and E. Imwinkelried, MILITARY EVIDENTIARY FOUNDATIONS, § 4-3(F) (4th ed. 2010) (sample foundation for e-mail transmissions); Note, *When the Postman Rings Twice: The Admissibility of Electronic Mail Under the Business Records Exception to the Federal Rules of Evidence*, 64 FORDH. L. REV. 2285 (1996).

[39] *See generally* D. Schlueter S. Saltzburg, L. Schinasi and E. Imwinkelried, MILITARY EVIDENTIARY FOUNDATIONS, § 4-3(F) (4th ed. 2010) (sample foundation for caller-ID).

[40] *See, e.g.*, United States v. Jackson, 208 F.3d 633 (7th Cir. 2000) (insufficient authentication of website postings).

[41] *See, e.g.*, United States v. Tank, 200 F.3d 627 (9th Cir. 2000); (United States v. Simpson, 152 F.3d 1241 (10th Cir. 1998) (printout of chat-room discussions).

[42] *See generally* D. Schlueter, S. Saltzburg, L. Schinasi and E. Imwinkelried, MILITARY EVIDENTIARY FOUNDATIONS, § (4th ed. 2010) (noting that computer animations or simulations may be used for illustrative or substantive purposes in trial).

[43] *See, e.g.*, Tyson v. State, 873 S.W.2d 53 (Tex. App.—Tyler 1993, pet. ref'd) (noting that fax transmission is a form of telephone transmission); D. Schlueter, S. Saltzburg, L. Schinasi and E. Imwinkelried, MILITARY EVIDENTIARY FOUNDATIONS, § 4-3(E) (4th ed. 2010) (sample foundation for facsimile transmission).

[44] *See* United States v. Pitts, 569 F.2d 343 (5th Cir.), *cert. denied,* 436 U.S. 959 (1978) (lay opinion rejected where familiarity acquired for purposes of the trial).

[45] *See, e.g.,* United States v. Ocamb, C.M.R. 78 (C.M.A. 1961) (witness competent to

familiarity before the court-martial and those who gain it for the court-martial, it purports to be an illustration. Whether an illustration of a binding principle is unclear.

[5] Rule 901(b)(3)—Comparison by Trier or Expert Witness

Rule 901(b)(3) addresses authentication of a wide variety of evidence such as blood, ballistics, fingerprints, and handwriting. Proffered evidence may be authenticated by allowing court members or an expert witness to compare it with an authenticated specimen. The specimen may be used if the court members could find it to be genuine. Where the comparison involves specialized or scientific principles, the proponent should normally employ expert testimony. *See generally* our discussion at Rule 702. This provision apparently expands pre-Rules law that limited comparison of fingerprints to persons skilled in that craft.

[6] Rule 901(b)(4)—Distinctive Characteristics and the Like

Evidence may in some instances be authenticated by simply showing the characteristics of the item itself.[46] For example, in *United States v. Stearns*,[47] the contents of a photograph, in conjunction with other circumstantial or indirect evidence, could serve as authentication in the absence of testimony to establish what the pictures represented. Circumstantial evidence can be as powerful a form of proof for authentication purposes as it can be when guilt is litigated. A common example would be the application of the familiar reply-letter doctrine.[48]

[7] Rule 901(b)(5)—Voice Identification

A voice may be identified by a witness who has either directly or indirectly heard the voice; the witness need not testify as an expert unless the identification process entails analysis of voiceprints.[49]

---

identify signature if he has previously seen him sign his name).

[46] *See, e.g.,* United States v. Cook, 794 F.2d 561 (10th Cir. 1986) (sustaining two defendants' convictions for cocaine offenses, finding that taped conversations were properly admitted where voices were identified by witnesses and circumstantial evidence such as name references and pen register records connected the tapes to the defendants); United States v. Bagaric, 706 F.2d 42 (2d Cir. 1983) (letter authenticated by circumstantial evidence); United States v. Bruner, 657 F.2d 1278 (D.C. Cir. 1981) (circumstantial authentication of prescriptions); United States v. Gordon, 634 F.2d 639 (1st Cir. 1980) (example of authentication by appearance of documents).

[47] 550 F.2d 1167 (9th Cir. 1977).

[48] United States v. Thomas, 33 M.J. 1067 (A.C.M.R. 1991), annotated *below*. See also D. Schlueter, S. Saltzburg, L. Schinasi and E. Imwinkelried, Military Evidentiary Foundations, § 4-2(D) (4th ed. 2010).

[49] *See, e.g.,* United States v. Wright, 37 C.M.R. 447 (C.M.A. 1967) (expert interpreted voiceprint). For a general discussion of use of voice spectrographs *see* Gorecki, *Evidentiary Use of Voice Spectrograph in Criminal Proceedings,* 77 Mil. L. Rev. 167 (1977).

[8]   Rule 901(b)(6)—Telephone Conversations

If counsel cannot establish the identity of a voice on the telephone through a witness's familiarity under Rule 901(b)(5), other circumstantial proof may suffice.[50] This illustration is grounded upon the common everyday assumptions and assurances of reliability associated with telephonic communications. For example, if the proponent can show that the witness determined the phone number of Sergeant X, dialed that number and talked to a person identifying himself as Sergeant X, the ensuing conversation will have been authenticated.[51] Likewise, a telephone conversation with a business may be authenticated if the witness dialed the number assigned to the business and the conversation involved business reasonably transacted over the telephone.[52] Radio transmissions could be authenticated in similar fashion. As with all evidence, the members will decide whether the conversation actually involved the person or business claimed by the proponent.

[9]   Rule 901(b)(7)—Public Records or Reports

Public records, including computer data, may be authenticated, as under pre-Rules practice, by showing custody either through live testimony or the commonly used authenticating or attesting certificates. Accompanying hearsay and secondary evidence (best evidence) principles are covered in Sections VIII and X, respectively. *See also* Rule 902 for records which may be self-authenticating.

[10]   Rule 901(b)(8)—Ancient Documents or Data Compilation

Under subdivision (b)(8), a proponent may authenticate a document or data compilations by showing that it has been in existence for 20 or more years, that its condition raises no questions about its authenticity, and that it was located in a place where one would expect such documents to be stored.[53] This provision generally parallels the hearsay exception in Rule 803(16) for ancient documents.[54] Thus, proving the elements in Rule 901(b)(8) should satisfy the foundation for the hearsay exception. Although

---

[50] *See, e.g.,* United States v. Robinson, 707 F.2d 811 (4th Cir. 1983) (voice identification made by witness who heard the same voice on the phone several times).

[51] *See, e.g.,* United States v. Sawyer, 607 F.2d 1190 (7th Cir. 1979) (telephone conversation authenticated by showing defendant's telephone number and that conversation centered on IRS matters personal to the defendant). *See generally* Shumkler, *Voice Identification in Criminal Cases Under Article IX of the Federal Rules of Evidence,* 49 TEMP. L.Q. 867 (1976).

[52] *See, e.g.,* D. Schlueter, S. Saltzburg, L. Schinasi and E. Imwinkelried, MILITARY EVIDENTIARY FOUNDATIONS, § 4-5(C) (4th ed. 2010) (sample foundation).

[53] *See, e.g.,* United States v. Demjanjuk, 367 F.3d 623 (6th Cir. 2004) (German identification card identifying the defendant as prison guard). *See also* D. Schlueter, S. Saltzburg, L. Schinasi and E. Imwinkelried, MILITARY EVIDENTIARY FOUNDATIONS, § 4-2(F) (4th ed. 2010) (sample foundation for ancient document).

[54] See Rule 803(16) (hearsay exception for statements in ancient documents).

the mere fact that a letter or computer printout is "old" does not in itself establish that it is authentic, if it was not accurate, then inferentially one would expect that someone would have pointed that out during the intervening years.[55]

The "ancient documents" method of authentication was not officially recognized in the 1969 *Manual* and has not found much use in contemporary military practice. Note that the Rule reduced the common law requirement of thirty years to twenty and shifted the emphasis from the document's appearance of authenticity to custody or location of the document.

[11]   Rule 901(b)(9)—Process or System

Where the proffered evidence is the result of a process or system, the proponent may authenticate the evidence by establishing that the process or system produces accurate results. Authentication of x-rays, computer print-outs, and tape recordings would be examples of evidence included in this illustration. The reliability of the system may be judicially noticed. *See* Rule 201. Depending on the complexity of the system or process involved, counsel may have to call an expert witness to establish this method of authentication.

[12]   Rule 901(b)(10)—Methods Provided by Statute or Rule

This provision was included in the Federal Rule to specifically recognize the continued viability of a variety of authentication methods prescribed in the Bankruptcy Act and the Federal Civil and Criminal Rules of Procedure. The Military Rule has been modified to permit future promulgation of methods of authentication or identification. Examples here would include a variety of federal statutes that address authentication of various documents by seals and certificates.[56]

§ 901.03   Drafters' Analysis

[1]   General Provision

Rule 901(a) is taken verbatim from the Federal Rule, and is similar to ¶ 143 *b* of the 1969 *Manual,* which stated in pertinent part that: "A writing may be authenticated by any competent proof that it is genuine is in fact what it purports or is claimed to be." Unlike the 1969 *Manual* provision, however, Rule 901(a) is not limited to writings and consequently is broader in scope. The Rule supports the requirement for logical relevance. *See* Rule 401.

There is substantial question as to the proper interpretation of the Federal Rule equivalent of Rule 901(a). The Rule requires only "evidence sufficient

---

[55] E. Imwinkelried & D. Schlueter, FEDERAL EVIDENCE TACTICS, § 9.01[4][i] (Matthew Bender) (discussing authentication of ancient document).

[56] *See* WEINSTEIN'S FEDERAL EVIDENCE § 901.12[3] (Matthew Bender) (listing statutes).

to support a finding that the matter in question is what its proponent claims." It is possible that this phrasing supersedes any formulaic approach to authentication and that rigid rules such as those that have been devised to authenticate taped recordings, for example, are no longer valid. On the other hand, it appears fully appropriate for a trial judge to require such evidence as is needed "to support a finding that the matter in question is what its proponent claims," which evidence may echo in some cases the common law formulations. There appears to be no reason to believe that the Rule will change the present law as it affects chains of custody for real evidence—especially if fungible. Present case law would appear to be consistent with the new Rule because the chain of custody requirement has not been applied in a rigid fashion. A chain of custody will still be required when it is necessary to show that the evidence is what it is claimed to be and, when appropriate, that its condition is unchanged. Rule 901(a) may make authentication somewhat easier, but is unlikely to make a substantial change in most areas of military practice.

As is generally the case, failure to object to evidence on the grounds of lack of authentication will waive the objection, *see* Rule 103(a).

[2] Illustrations

Rule 901(b) is taken verbatim from the Federal Rule with the exception of a modification to Rule 901(b)(10). Rule 901(b)(10) has been modified by the addition of or by applicable regulations prescribed pursuant to statutory authority. The new language was added because it was viewed as impracticable in military practice to require statutory or Supreme Court action to add authentication methods. The world wide disposition of the armed forces with their frequent redeployments may require rapid adjustments in authentication procedures to preclude substantial interference with personnel practices needed to ensure operational efficiency. The new language does not require new statutory authority. Rather, the present authority that exists for the various Service and Departmental Secretaries to issue those regulations necessary for the day-to-day operations of their departments is sufficient.

Rule 901(b) is a non-exhaustive list of illustrative examples of authentication techniques. None of the examples are inconsistent with present military law and many are found within the present *Manual, see, e.g.,* ¶ 143 *b.* Self-authentication is governed by Rule 902.

§ 901.04   Annotated Cases

[1]   Rule 901(a)—General Provision

Air Force Court of Criminal Appeals

United States v. Deserano, 41 M.J. 678 (A.F.Ct.Crim.App. 1995): Concluding that the prosecution had failed to prove beyond a reasonable doubt that what the accused had inhaled was nitrous oxide, the court noted that the accused's statements in themselves, as to the identity of the substance, were not sufficient to prove the identity of the substance. The court stated, however, that it was not implying that the prosecution must rely on scientific or expert testimony to identify an abused substance.

United States v. Bell, 34 M.J. 937 (A.F.C.M.R. 1992): The accused's pleas of guilty to drug charges relieved the prosecution of proving the chain of custody on the drugs; any objection he might have had was waived by the failure to raise the issue at trial.

Navy-Marine Corps Court of Criminal Appeals

United States v. Brandell, 33 M.J. 723 (N.M.C.M.R. 1991): In considering the accused's argument that the prosecution had failed to "lay the foundation" for various checks and bank records, the court emphasized that the hearsay and authentication rules should be analyzed separately. Although the court concluded that the checks and bank statements relating to the accused's account were authenticated under Rules 901(b)(4) and 902(9), there was no indication that the defense had lodged any specific hearsay objections to the notations on the checks. Thus, that issue was waived.

United States v. Allen, 31 M.J. 572 (N.M.C.M.R. 1990): The court concluded that the prosecution had sufficiently established, by a preponderance of the evidence, the authenticity of a letter from the defendant through the testimony of an NIS agent who testified that he had received it from Philippine authorities. The court apparently derived the preponderance of the evidence standard from *United States v. Lewis*, 19 M.J. 869 (A.F.C.M.R. 1985), a case which dealt with a chain of custody.

[2]   Rule 901(b)(1)—Testimony of Witness with Knowledge

[a]   Witness With Knowledge—Audio Tapes

United States Court of Appeals for the Armed Forces

United States v. Craig, 60 M.J. 156 (C.A.A.F. 2004): During trial, the court admitted into evidence a written transcript of an audio recording of a telephone conversation in which the accused made incriminating statements to one of his co-conspirators. The defense objected on the grounds that portions of the recording itself were inaudible. The Court of Appeals concluded that under the facts, the tape itself was admissible and that it was appropriate for the military judge to provide a substantially accurate written transcript to the members. In reaching that decision, the court cited *United States v. Brandon*, 363 F.3d 341, 344 (4th Cir. 2004), where the court set out four procedures for trial courts to consider: First, the trial court should review the transcript for accuracy. Second, the opposing counsel should be permitted to highlight inaccuracies and provide alternative versions. Third, the jury should be instructed that the tape itself, rather than the transcript, is the evidence in the case. And fourth, the jury should be allowed to compare the tape and transcript and hear counsels' arguments on the meanings of the contents.

United States v. Blanchard, 48 M.J. 306 (C.A.A.F. 1998): At trial, the government introduced an audio recording of a telephone conversation during which the accused had made incriminating statements. The defense unsuccessfully objected that the prosecution had failed to prove the seven-pronged foundation required in several federal circuits. Noting that federal case law on the point might be helpful, the court observed that not all circuits adopt the more rigid seven-prong test for authenticating audio recordings. Further, Rule 901(b)(5) specifically addresses the ability to authenticate another person's voice. The court concluded that the Military Rules of Evidence permit, but do not require, consideration of the seven-pronged test. Applying the more general standards for proving authentication under Rule 901, the court concluded that it was not error to admit the audio recordings; any gaps or other deficiencies would go to the weight of the evidence. On a related point, the court indicated that the judge's listening to the tape before making a preliminary decision on admissibility is not the preferred method of fulfilling the judge's obligation under Rule 104(b).

[b]   Witness With Knowledge—Chain of Custody

United States Court of Appeals for the Armed Forces

United States v. Maxwell, 38 M.J. 148 (C.M.A. 1993): The court held that the government established a sufficient chain of custody for the results of a blood-alcohol test run on the accused by hospital personnel. Although one of the witnesses could not recollect the exact procedures used to handle the samples, circumstantial evidence demonstrated that they belonged to the accused and had not been substantially changed. The court noted that the trial judge need only be satisfied that there is a "reasonable probability" that the sample has remained unchanged in its important respects.

United States v. Gonzales, 37 M.J. 456 (C.M.A. 1993): The court held that the prosecution had established a sufficient chain of custody for a urine sample taken from the accused. The fact that the prosecution witness responsible for securing the sample could not recall how the sample got from a large-mouth jar to a small-mouth jar for transport and testing went to weight, not admissibility. Her testimony that the sample never left her sight until it was in the smaller jar left no missing links in the chain.

United States v. Day, 20 M.J. 213 (C.M.A. 1985): It is not essential that the identity of a drug be established by chemical analysis. Here a lay witness familiar and experienced with controlled substances identified the drugs in question.

United States v. Ettleson, 13 M.J. 348 (C.M.A. 1982): The court found an adequate chain of custody for cocaine seized from the accused where: (1) there was strong uncontroverted evidence that the agent who seized the cocaine passed it directly to the evidence custodian, (2) the agent's field test matched the results reached at the laboratory, and (3) there was no real suggestion of tampering.

United States v. Porter, 12 M.J. 129 (C.M.A. 1981): Affirming a conviction for possession and sale of marijuana, the court said that it "has never required personnel from the criminal investigation laboratory to testify in order to establish a sufficient chain of custody over the evidence." It added that if appellant had affirmatively requested that the analyst who prepared the laboratory report be called in order to examine him as to the competency and the regularity of the procedure employed, a different question would have been presented.

United States v. Lewis, 11 M.J. 188 (C.M.A. 1981): At the accused's trial for possession of heroin, the prosecution identified the contraband through the testimony of a Sergeant *B* who stated that he could identify the evidence with absolute certainty because of his markings on the packet. He had given the evidence to Sergeant *M,* the evidence custodian, who did not testify. But Staff Sergeant *K,* the assistant evidence custodian, testified that he had processed the evidence for shipment to the laboratory and also identified the evidence by markings on the package. The court concluded that although there were breaks in the chain of custody, the package was "readily identifiable" and there was no evidence that the contents had been tampered with.

United States v. Parker, 10 M.J. 415 (C.M.A. 1981) (pre-Rules case): At trial the prosecution introduced two exhibits seized from the accused's car: a knapsack and a plastic bag containing hashish, tin foil, and an empty cigarette package. In concluding that the government had met its burden of showing that the items were seized from the accused and their condition was substantially unchanged at the time of trial, the court found that the knapsack was readily identifiable and that the hashish seized from the accused possessed unique characteristics sufficient to support identification. The combination of these noted physical characteristics was unusual enough to show that it was more probable than not that they existed in a single object. It is not entirely clear from the opinion just how much evidence was presented at trial on the chain of custody. The prosecution did apparently rely on a chain of custody document, the testimony of the MP who seized the evidence, and the CID evidence custodian. The court was apparently not satisfied that the chain was "continuous." But as we note in our Comment, *above,* minor breaches in the chain generally go only to weight and should not always require resort to examination for unique characteristics. Under the Rules the evidence presented here would probably be sufficient to show a continuous chain, *i.e.,* the chain of custody document would be admissible under Rule 803(6) and would demonstrate who had handled it. *But see United States v. Ortiz,* 12 M.J. 136 (C.M.A. 1981) (pre-Rules case) (finding error in admission of evidence where government failed to link envelope seized from suspect to laboratory report). *See also United States v. Jessen,* 12 M.J. 122 (C.M.A. 1981) (noting that "chain of custody" documents that were not previously admissible are now allowed as evidence under Rule 803(6), (8)).

Air Force Court of Criminal Appeals

United States v. Baker, 43 M.J. 736 (A.F.Ct.Crim.App. 1995): Despite numerous administrative glitches in handling of drugs being processed for laboratory testing, the prosecution apparently convinced the judge through a "tortuous process" that the lab reports were actually linked with the drugs seized from the accused.

United States v. Thomas, 38 M.J. 614 (A.F.C.M.R. 1993): Drug paraphernalia found in a paper bag in the accused's room—plastic baggies containing cocaine residue, plastic straws, used condom, and lot number matching other condoms in the accused's room—were unique in appearance and in their association with each other in the bag. Thus, no chain of custody was required.

United States v. Carrott, 25 M.J. 823 (A.F.C.M.R. 1988): The court concluded that the prosecution failed to establish a satisfactory chain of custody of a urine sample where there was an unexplained four-month gap at the laboratory. The court stated that no credible inference that a urine substance has been tested in its unaltered state can be based on a gap in chain of custody documents of the magnitude presented in this case.

United States v. Hudson, 20 M.J. 607 (A.F.C.M.R. 1985): The court noted that the trial judge has broad discretion in ruling on chain of custody matters and all that is required is that it be reasonably certain that the "exhibit has not been changed in any important aspect."

United States v. Lewis, 19 M.J. 869 (A.F.C.M.R. 1985): In ruling that the military judge did not err in admitting the results of a urinalysis test the court indicated that the prosecution bears the burden of showing a chain of custody by a preponderance of the evidence, *i.e.*, that the urine sample which was received at the laboratory was the one taken from the accused and that it had arrived unchanged and unaltered in any important aspects.

Army Court of Criminal Appeals

United States v. Pinkston, 32 M.J. 555 (A.C.M.R. 1991): The court noted that the prosecution had laid a proper foundation for the admission of a laboratory report through the testimony of the local evidence custodian who authenticated the chain of custody form which had been mailed to, and received from, the laboratory. He also testified that he recognized the signature of the authenticating individual at the laboratory and that he had filed the laboratory report in the ordinary course of business.

United States v. Rivera-Cintron, 29 M.J. 757 (A.C.M.R. 1989): At trial, defense counsel conceded that the prosecution had established a chain of custody but attempted to challenge the admissibility of cocaine obtained from the accused by arguing that it had been misidentified. On appeal, the defense argued that the government had failed to preserve the evidence in an unaltered state. In finding that the defense had waived the issue, the court noted, *inter alia,* that it had failed to challenge the chain of custody and had failed to call for any other witnesses who might have shed light on the handling of the contraband.

United States v. Wallace, 14 M.J. 1019 (A.C.M.R. 1982): When the contraband seized from the accused arrived at the laboratory for testing, the examiner discovered inside the packet two items not listed on the chain of custody document. He thereafter prepared a new document noting the two additional items. The court said that a continuous chain of custody had been established. All persons who handled the contraband testified at trial and identified the contraband and minor administrative discrepancies did not create a break.

Navy-Marine Corps Court of Criminal Appeals

United States v. Harvey, 60 M.J. 611 (N.M.Ct.Crim.App. 2004): The accused was convicted on various drug charges, and for the first time on appeal objected to the admission of two pieces of a straw that were apparently used in committing one of the charged offenses. The court noted that the accused had not objected at trial, and had presented no evidence to show that the exhibits had been altered or mishandled. The court noted that, in proving a chain of custody, the prosecution is only required to show with a reasonable probability that the sample tested in the lab is from the alleged source and has not been altered. The prosecution is not required to prove a negative. The court added that any gaps in the chain of custody go to the weight of the evidence and not its admissibility.

[c] Witness With Knowledge—Charts, Maps, and Diagrams

United States Court of Appeals for the Armed Forces

United States v. Stephenson, 33 M.J. 79 (C.M.A. 1991): The court rejected as highly specious the accused's argument in his petition for a new trial that unspecified fraud on the court occurred in the preparation of a diagram of the crime scene. Apparently, the alleged fraud rested in the argument that the diagram, which was introduced by the defense, had been prepared by police investigators on the basis of a government witness's pretrial statements, but that it did not actually represent what took place.

[d] Witness With Knowledge—Documents

United States Court of Appeals for the Armed Forces

United States v. Tebsherany, 32 M.J. 351 (C.M.A. 1991): Computer-generated documents in the forms of hotel receipts, credit application, and records of the accused's wagers in casino were properly authenticated by the supervisor of microfilm and records retention, and records custodian of the casino. The court noted that a foundation witness need only be generally familiar with the records-keeping system. Thus, the fact that the custodian in this case could not describe all of the entries was not determinative.

United States v. Wetherbee, 10 M.J. 304 (C.M.A. 1981) (pre-Rules case): The accused's larceny conviction was based in part upon Air Force forms used to record meal purchases. They were, according to the court, properly authenticated by a witness assigned to the food service staff office *after* the forms were prepared. He was familiar with the procedures used before and after his assignment. The court also noted that a witness involved in the misconduct would not be disqualified from establishing the operations of that same office, although the misconduct would affect his credibility.

Navy-Marine Corps Court of Criminal Appeals

United States v. Dababneh, 28 M.J. 929 (N.M.C.M.R. 1989): Checks written by the accused were held to have been sufficiently authenticated by the live testimony of three witnesses who established that they were written by the accused, cashed by the financial institutions for which they worked, and returned for lack of sufficient funds. The court added that the "insufficient funds" stamp was authenticated when the trial judge took judicial notice of Section 3-510 of the Uniform Commercial Code, which addresses the admissibility of such notations on commercial documents.

[e] Witness With Knowledge—Drugs

Air Force Court of Criminal Appeals

United States v. Evans, 16 M.J. 951 (A.F.C.M.R. 1983): Although the witness had never used marijuana and could not see what substance the accused was smoking, he had smelled burning marijuana before and was therefore able to identify the substance as marijuana.

United States v. Walker, 12 M.J. 983 (A.F.C.M.R. 1982): In a trial on drug charges, two policemen identified the substance used by the accused as marijuana. They were familiar with the odor of burning marijuana, the physical appearance of marijuana cigarettes, and the usual manner in which they are inhaled. *See also United States v. Morris,* 13 M.J. 666 (A.F.C.M.R. 1982).

United States v. Helton, 10 M.J. 820 (A.F.C.M.R. 1981): At trial, the OSI agent who had seized marijuana from the accused testified that he identified the contraband through its odor and appearance. He further testified that his opinion was confirmed by performing a "field test." Citing its earlier opinion in *United States v. Sanchez,* 50 C.M.R. 450 (A.F.C.M.R. 1975), the court noted that results of such a test are admissible in support of testimony identifying marijuana.

[f] Witness With Knowledge—Physical Evidence—Readily Identifiable

Air Force Court of Criminal Appeals

United States v. Thomas, 38 M.J. 614 (A.F.C.M.R. 1993): Drug paraphernalia found in a paper bag in the accused's room—plastic baggies containing cocaine residue, plastic straws, used condom, and lot number matching other condoms in the accused's room—were unique in appearance and in their association with each other in the bag. Thus, the court held that the items were properly authenticated.

[g] Witness With Knowledge—Photographs and X-rays

United States Court of Appeals for the Armed Forces

United States v. Richendollar, 22 M.J. 231 (C.M.A. 1986): The trial judge committed harmless error in not permitting a defense legal clerk to authenticate photographs taken by the defense counsel. The court reminded trial judges that testimony by the photographer is not required to authenticate a photograph.

Air Force Court of Criminal Appeals

United States v. Greska, 65 M.J. 835 (A.F.Ct.Crim.App. 2007): The accused was convicted of stealing another servicemember's digital camera. When trial counsel asked the camera's owner whether there were any photos on the camera's memory chip that were not familiar to him, the owner indicated that there were two and one had a time/date stamp notation on it. Defense counsel's hearsay objection to the time/date stamp notation was overruled. Affirming the accused's burglary and larceny-related convictions, the court held that because Rule 801(b) defines a declarant as a *person*, evidence of the camera's automatic time/date notation was correctly admitted. Although the issue was not raised at trial or on appeal, the court noted that the time/date evidence was properly authenticated by the accused's coconspirators who placed the camera in the accused's hands at the relevant time.

[h] Witness With Knowledge—Videotapes

Air Force Court of Criminal Appeals

United States v. Baker, 43 M.J. 736 (A.F.Ct.Crim.App. 1995): AFOSI agents ran two videos of accused's drug activities. One video had both good audio and picture but did not show the accused; the other had poor audio and poor picture but showed two people dividing drugs. The agents unsuccessfully attempted to dub the two originals into two better tapes. Noting that such attempts create an appearance of wrongdoing, the court ruled that it was not an abuse of discretion to play both tapes separately in front of the members for their consideration. They were not, however, permitted to take the tapes into the deliberation room.

Army Court of Criminal Appeals

United States v. Reichart, 31 M.J. 521 (A.C.M.R. 1990): Noting the differences in authenticating photographs (pictorial testimony, silent witness, and circumstantial evidence) and that videotapes may be treated the same as photographs for purposes of authentication, the court concluded that videotape of the defendant stealing items from the Base Exchange had been authenticated by store employee who testified that the video accurately depicted what she had seen through a television monitor.

Navy-Marine Corps Court of Criminal Appeals

United States v. Schnable, 65 M.J. 566 (N.M.Ct.Crim.App. 2006): The accused was charged with molesting his adopted daughter at various locations while in his vehicle. At trial, the defense unsuccessfully offered into evidence a videotape created with the assistance of the accused, who had directed the videographer what to record. Although the videographer testified in an attempt to lay the foundation for the tape, the court held that only two people knew the actual route taken and could verify the tapes' accuracy—the accused who did not testify and his daughter, who could not remember the specific routes or locations. Thus, the court said, it was not error to exclude the videotape.

[3]   Rule 901(b)(4)—Distinctive Characteristics and the Like

[a]   In General

Navy-Marine Corps Court of Criminal Appeals

United States v. Brandell, 33 M.J. 723 (N.M.C.M.R. 1991): Canceled checks in the accused's case were considered authenticated in accordance with the Hawaii Uniform Commercial Code. Bank statements relating to the accused's account, however, were not considered commercial paper. Instead, they were authenticated by distinctive characteristics, such as letterhead, the account holder's name and address, and the fact that the account numbers matched those on the checks.

[b]   Reply-Letter Doctrine

Army Court of Criminal Appeals

United States v. Thomas, 33 M.J. 1067 (A.C.M.R. 1991): Records of three nonjudicial punishments were sufficiently authenticated under the reply letter doctrine. Although an attached authenticating certificate was defective, the trial court was permitted to consider an attached electrical message requesting production of the records to lay the foundation for the reply letter doctrine; the three records of nonjudicial punishment were sent to the prosecutor in reply to the message. The court reminded that the rules of evidence do not normally apply in deciding the admissibility of evidence and that in this case the electrical message could be considered even though it was not itself authenticated.

[4]   Rule 901(b)(5)—Voice Identification

United States Court of Appeals for the Armed Forces

United States v. Blanchard, 48 M.J. 306 (C.A.A.F. 1998): At trial the government introduced an audio recording of a telephone conversation during which the accused had made incriminating statements. The defense unsuccessfully objected that the prosecution had failed to prove the seven-pronged foundation required in several federal circuits. Noting that federal case law on the point might be helpful, the court observed that not all circuits adopt the more rigid seven-prong test for authenticating audio recordings. Further, Rule 901(b)(5) specifically addresses the ability to authenticate another person's voice. The court concluded that the Military Rules of Evidence permit, but do not require, consideration of the seven-pronged test. Applying the more general standards for proving authentication under Rule 901, the court concluded that it was not error to admit the audio recordings; any gaps or other deficiencies would go the weight of the evidence. On a related point, the court indicated that the judge's listening to the tape before making a preliminary decision on admissibility is not the preferred method of fulfilling the judge's obligation under Rule 104(b).

Air Force Court of Criminal Appeals

United States v. Powell, 55 M.J. 633 (A.F.Ct.Crim.App. 2001): After engaging in non-consensual sexual intercourse with a high school student, the accused continued to communicate with the victim via e-mail and over the telephone. The victim recorded a telephone conversation in which the accused instructed the victim to lie about the encounter. *Citing United States v. Blanchard*, 48 M.J. 306 (1998), the court recognized the flexible approach to the authentication of audiotapes under Rule 901(b)(5). Despite the fact that there was scientific and corroborating verification in *Blanchard*, no such evidence was necessary in this case. Rather, the victim's authentication provided sufficient foundation.

[5]   Rule 901(b)(9)—Process or System

United States Court of Appeals for the Armed Forces

United States v. Harris, 55 M.J. 433 (C.A.A.F. 2001): In a trial on charges of larceny and forgery of checks, the prosecution introduced video camera photographs of the accused at the bank's drive-up windows. In a lengthy discussion of the issue, the court recognized the "silent witness" method of authenticating photographs taken by automated systems. In this case the photographs created from the videotape revealed defendant had been at the drive up windows when both of the checks were allegedly forged. The court concluded that the video system's reliability, the fact that it was in working order when the photo was taken, and the proper safeguarding of the film after its removal established sufficient foundation for authenticating the photos. Additionally, the court noted that testimony of the bank investigator was sufficient to authenticate the photos and that expert witness testimony is not required to establish the reliability of an automated system. *See generally* Schlueter, Saltzburg, Schinasi & Imwinkelried, MILITARY EVIDENTIARY FOUNDATIONS, § 4-9(C) (4th ed. 2010) (sample foundation).

Army Court of Criminal Appeals

United States v. Howell, 16 M.J. 1003 (A.C.M.R. 1983): The court adopted the "silent witness" view of authenticating photographs; the proponent only need establish the reliability of the process or system which produces the photograph.

§ 902.01   Official Text

Rule 902.   Self-Authentication.

Extrinsic evidence of authenticity as a condition precedent to admissibility is not required with respect to the following:

(1) *Domestic public documents under seal.*   A document bearing a seal purporting to be that of the United States, or any State, district, Commonwealth, territory, or insular possession thereof, or the Panama Canal Zone, or the Trust Territory of the Pacific Islands, or of a political subdivision, department, officer, or agency thereof, and a signature purporting to be an attestation or execution.

(2) *Domestic public documents not under seal.*   A document purporting to bear the signature in the official capacity of an officer or employee of any entity included in paragraph (1) hereof, having no seal, if a public officer having a seal and having official duties in the district or political subdivision of the officer or employee certifies under seal that the signer has the official capacity and that the signature is genuine.

(3) *Foreign public documents.*   A document purporting to be executed or attested in an official capacity by a person authorized by the laws of a foreign country to make the execution or attestation, and accompanied by a final certification as to the genuineness of the signature and official position (A) of the executing or attesting person, or (B) of any foreign official whose certificate of genuineness of signature and official position relates to the execution or attestation or is in a chain of certificates of genuineness of signature and official position relating to the execution or attestation. A final certification may be made by a secretary of embassy or legation, consul general, consul, vice consul, or consular agent of the United States, or a diplomatic or consular official of the foreign country assigned or accredited to the United States. If reasonable opportunity has been given to all parties to investigate the authenticity and accuracy of official documents, the court may, for good cause shown, order that they to be treated as presumptively authentic without final certification or permit them to be evidenced by an attested summary with or without final certification.

(4) *Certified copies of public records.*   A copy of an official record or report or entry therein, or of a document authorized by law to be recorded or filed and actually recorded or filed in a public office, including data compilations in any form, certified as correct by the custodian or other person authorized to make the

certification, by certificate complying with paragraphs (1), (2), or (3) of this rule or complying with any Act of Congress, rule prescribed by the Supreme Court pursuant to statutory authority, or an applicable regulation prescribed pursuant to statutory authority.

(4a) *Documents or records of the United States accompanied by attesting certificates.* Documents or records kept under the authority of the United States by any department, bureau, agency, office, or court thereof when attached to or accompanied by an attesting certificate of the custodian of the document or record without further authentication.

(5) *Official publications.* Books, pamphlets, or other publications purporting to be issued by public authority.

(6) *Newspapers and periodicals.* Printed materials purporting to be newspapers or periodicals.

(7) *Trade inscriptions and the like.* Inscriptions, signs, tags, or labels purporting to have been affixed in the course of business and indicating ownership, control, or origin.

(8) *Acknowledged documents.* Documents accompanied by a certificate of acknowledgment executed in the manner provided by law by a notary public or other officer authorized by law to take acknowledgments.

(9) *Commercial paper and related documents.* Commercial paper, signatures thereon, and documents relating thereto to the extent provided by general commercial law.

(10) *Presumptions under Acts of Congress and regulations.* Any signature, document, or other matter declared by Act of Congress or by applicable regulation prescribed pursuant to statutory authority to be presumptively or prima facie genuine or authentic.

(11) *Certified domestic records of regularly conducted activity.* The original or a duplicate of a domestic record of regularly conducted activity that would be admissible under Military Rules of Evidence 803(6), if accompanied by a written declaration of its custodian or other qualified person, in a manner complying with any Act of Congress or rule prescribed by the Supreme Court pursuant to statutory authority, certifying that the record:

(A) was made at or near the time of the occurrence of the matters set forth by, or from information transmitted by, a person with knowledge of those matters;

(B) was kept in the course of the regularly conducted activity; and

(C) was made by the regularly conducted activity as a regular practice.

A party intending to offer a record into evidence under this paragraph must provide written notice of that intention to all adverse parties, and must make the record and declaration available for inspection sufficiently in advance of their offer into evidence to provide an adverse party with a fair opportunity to challenge them.

§ 902.02 Editorial Comment

[1] In General

The traditional burden of authenticating certain familiar evidence has been considerably eased by Rule 902, which relieves the proponent from offering extrinsic evidence to establish that the evidence is what it purports to be. The Rule, which deals only with the question of authenticity of evidence, takes the view that some evidence is so likely to be genuine that its proponent should not be compelled to lay a formal foundation. Instead, the evidence authenticates itself. (Rule 901(b)(4) may reach similar results in some cases.)

Underlying the Rule is the philosophy that extrinsic evidence should only be required when reasonable people might question the genuineness of evidence. Technical and time-consuming foundation requirements are reserved for cases in which they serve a valid purpose. It should be emphasized that nothing in the Rule prevents an opponent of evidence from contesting its authenticity. The Rule assumes that evidence falling into one of the specified classes is so likely to be what it purports to be that no extrinsic evidence is required of the proponent. But nothing inhibits the opponent from offering evidence to prove to the court that an exhibit that has been admitted is not authentic.

The Rule is almost identical to its federal counterpart; paragraph (4a) is added, however, and minor changes are made in paragraph (10).

Each category of evidence covered by the Rule is addressed below.

[2] Confrontation Clause Issues

Serious confrontation issues could arise under this Rule in the wake of the United States Supreme Court's decisions in *Crawford v. Washington*, 541 U.S. 36 (2004) and *Melendez-Diaz v. Massachusetts*, 129 S. Ct. 2527 (2009). Certificates purporting to show a chain of custody or to lay a foundation for other evidence will substitute for testimony, and thus may be deemed "testimonial" for purposes of the Sixth Amendment Confrontation Clause. It is highly likely that the government will claim that such certificates do not address the kind of evidence to which the Confrontation Clause was directed, while defendants will claim that evidence purporting to show that an item is genuine or that it is unchanged and free from tampering is sufficiently important to require live testimony. For additional discussion on the Confrontation Clause issues see our discussion at Section VIII.

[3]   Rule 902(1)—Domestic Public Documents Under Seal

If a public document bears one of the designated official seals and is accompanied by a signature, it is self-authenticating. The signature may be on the document itself or a copy thereof, or on an accompanying attestation certificate. This paragraph is identical to the Federal Rule. The Drafters' Analysis states that judicial notice of seals and signatures is not required.

[4]   Rule 902(2)—Domestic Public Documents Not Under Seal

A public document not bearing a seal may be self-authenticating if it bears an appropriate signature and if a public officer having a seal certifies under seal that (1) the document's signer has the official capacity and (2) the signature on the document is genuine. The paragraph, identical to the Federal Rule, seems to cover only those situations where the officer or employee signing the document has no seal. What of the situation where the individual has a seal but has not used it? Neither the legislative history of the Federal Rule nor the Drafters' Analysis address this point. There would seem to be no reason to distinguish between that situation and one where the signing official does not have a seal. In both cases, it is the certification of the official, under seal, that provides self-authentication.

[5]   Rule 902(3)—Foreign Public Documents

A foreign document may be self-authenticating under this paragraph if it is executed or attested to by an individual authorized to do so by the foreign country's laws and is accompanied by a "final certification."[1] The final certification relates to the genuineness of (1) the signature and (2) the official position of the individual executing or attesting the document. The Rule also provides for chains of certificates of genuineness. That is, the signature and official position of the original signer may in some instances be accompanied by a chain of certificates until an authorized final certification is made. For example, *A* executes a foreign document; *B* (not authorized under the Rule to provide a final certification) attests to *A*'s signature and official position, and *C*, a counsel general, provides a final certification to *B*'s signature and official position.[2]

This paragraph, identical to the Federal Rule, is patterned after Federal

---

[1] United States v. Montemayor, 712 F.2d 104, 105 (5th Cir. 1983) (Mexican birth certificate admitted).

[2] *See, e.g.,* United States v. Rodriguez Serrate, 534 F.2d 7 (1st Cir. 1976) (copy of foreign birth certificate was authenticated using a chain of certifications). *See generally* Annot., 41 A.L.R. Fed. (1979), Proof of Foreign Official Record Under Rule 44(a)(2) of Federal Rules of Civil Procedure.

Rule of Civil Procedure 44(a)(2) and generally follows pre-Rules practice with two exceptions. First, this paragraph now restricts the authority to issue final certification to civilian authorities.[3] Second, the Rule does not permit self-authentication if the authentication process is based solely on the foreign country's laws.

In any event, the paragraph permits relaxation of the requirement of final certification if all parties have had a reasonable opportunity to examine the documents and good cause is shown.[4]

Rule 902 (3) covers foreign public documents. Copies of foreign public records also may be self-authenticating under Rule 903 (4). Moreover, on November 28, 1979, the Senate gave its consent to the ratification by the United States of an international Convention making it easier for parties than it is under Rule 902 to authenticate foreign public documents. Under the Convention, each country designates public officials by title who may stamp what is called an "apostille," a form of certification, on the document itself or affix it to an accompanying paper. The apostille states that the document was signed by an individual acting in his official capacity and that the official's stamp or seal is genuine.

Rule 902(12) now covers self-authentication of foreign business records.

[6] Rule 902(4)—Certified Copies of Public Records

Copies of official records, reports, and data compilations properly on file may be self-authenticating if they are accompanied by a certificate from a custodian or other authorized person and conform with paragraphs (1), (2), or (3). They are also self-authenticating if the certificates conform to Acts of Congress, rules prescribed by the Supreme Court, or to applicable regulations. This paragraph differs from the Federal Rule in that provision is made here for regulatory prescription of the certification process. The certificate is itself a public document. It permits any official public record or report and any document filed in accordance with applicable law to be self-authenticating. This can be an expansive category.

Occasionally, counsel will want to show that a report or record does not exist. Either this paragraph or paragraphs (1), (2), and (3), in conjunction with Rule 803(10), permit counsel to do so by using a certified affidavit of the official who conducted the search.[5] If some public record accompanies

---

[3] In the 1969 *Manual*, ¶ 143 *b* (2)(e) had permitted United States military personnel to do so.

[4] *See, e.g., In re* Sterling Navigation Co., 444 F. Supp. 1043 (S.D.N.Y. 1977) (trial judge relied on Rule 902(3)).

[5] *See, e.g.,* United States v. Stout, 667 F.2d 1347 (11th Cir. 1982) (prosecution relied on Rule 902(4) to authenticate documents from Treasury Department regarding registration of firearms; documents did not meet requirements of 803(10)); Robbins v. United States, 476 F.2d 26 (10th Cir. 1973) (absence of firearm registration); United States v. City of McAlester,

the certificate, this paragraph probably governs. Otherwise, paragraphs (1), (2), and (3) probably govern.

The contents of the authenticating certificate are not prescribed. Any format that certifies correctness should suffice.[6]

[7] Rule 902(4a)—Documents or Records of the United States Accompanied by Attesting Certificates

Spawned by military necessity, this new paragraph provides for self-authentication of both United States documents and records that are kept in accordance with applicable laws or regulations and are accompanied by an attesting certificate. The paragraph applies to both originals and copies and requires that the "custodian" execute the attesting certificate. The Drafters' Analysis causes some confusion by defining an attesting certificate as "a certificate or statement, signed by the custodian of the record *or the deputy or assistant of the custodian . . .*" [emphasis added]. The drafters' definition was taken from 1969 *Manual* ¶ 143 *b* (2)(a) and apparently does not make allowance for the plain language of the Rule which limits self-authentication to evidence attested to by the custodian. This provision will allow for continuation of the common pre-Rules practice of authenticating evidence such as laboratory reports, personnel records and accountability reports with certificates.

Particular attention should be paid to the self-authentication of chain of custody forms and laboratory reports. This paragraph does not really change the common pre-Rules practice of authenticating lab reports, but it may ease the proponent's burden of showing a chain of custody. In the past, the chain was normally proved by live testimony. Chain of custody forms were held to be inadmissible hearsay.[7] Applied broadly, this paragraph, operating in conjunction with Rule 901(a) and Rule 803(6) and (8), could revolutionize prosecution of drug cases. *See* our more detailed discussion of Rule 803(6) and (8), indicating that chain of custody forms and lab reports may be admissible without live witness foundations.

Evidence offered under this paragraph must still qualify under best evidence and hearsay principles, and the proponent may, in limited circumstances, be required to show that the proffered document or record is kept under authority of the United States or a subordinate entity. Should the authority be questioned, the proponent will normally be able to satisfy this paragraph by presenting the applicable statute or regulation. Alternatively the military judge could take judicial notice of the authority. *See* Rule 201A.

---

410 F. Supp. 848 (E.D. Okla. 1976) (search revealed no reference in records to litigation involving city).

6 *But see* United States v. Stone, 604 F.2d 922 (5th Cir. 1979) (authenticating affidavit by the custodian contained inadmissible hearsay).

7 *See* United States v. Porter, 7 M.J. 32 (C.M.A. 1979).

There is a rebuttable presumption that the custodian's signature, which must be legible,[8] is genuine.

[8] Rule 902(5)—Official Publications

Official publications or copies thereof may be self-authenticating if they are purportedly issued by public authority. This provision clearly applies to United States publications. But does the Rule include a regulation published by order of the commanding general of an installation, or a regulation published by a ship's captain? No specific guidance on this point can be found in the Rule, the legislative history, or the Drafters' Analysis. The Rule assumes that few people will fraudulently hold out a publication as a government publication. A good argument can be made that this holds true for regulations as well. Moreover, the Rule's preference for admissibility would seem to support self-authentication of local official publications or their equivalent. The issue might prove to be of academic interest only in light of the fact that a judge might take judicial notice of regulations under Rule 201 or 201A and render Rule 902 (5) irrelevant.

[9] Rule 902(6)—Newspapers and Periodicals

Periodicals and newspapers are self-authenticating.[9] The unlikelihood that someone is issuing bogus copies of these documents supports self-authentication. A question arises, however, as to whether Rule 902 (6), which is identical to the Federal Rule, applies if counsel merely offers a newspaper clipping or excerpt from a periodical? The case for self-authentication is much weaker, since the possibility exists that an excerpt is incomplete, has been altered, or its source has mistakenly been identified. An excerpt could be authenticated under Rule 901. A microfilm, microfiche, or other similar copy of a newspaper or periodical probably would be self-authenticating. Duplicates are admissible under Rule 1003. Although Rule 1003 does not address authentication issues, the rationale for the rule supports treating complete copies of a periodical or newspaper the same as the original absent a genuine question regarding the copies.

It should be emphasized that nothing in Rule 902(6) or any other part of Rule 902 provides an exception to the hearsay rule. The Rule is limited to authentication.

[10] Rule 902(7)—Trade Inscriptions and the Like

This paragraph, which is identical to its federal counterpart, treats tags, labels, inscriptions, and the like as self-authenticating if they appear to have

---

[8] *See, e.g.,* United States v. Lawson, 42 C.M.R. 847 (A.C.M.R. 1970).

[9] *See, e.g.,* Price v. Rochford, 947 F.2d 829 (7th Cir. 1991) (newspaper articles were self-authenticating).

been affixed in a course of business.[10] This provision will find little use in military criminal trials. It might be helpful, however, in establishing government ownership in a case involving, for example, larceny of government property which clearly bears a U.S. stamp.[11]

[11]   Rule 902(8)—Acknowledged Documents

Documents accompanied by a certificate of acknowledgment by either a notary or other properly authorized officer are self-authenticating. Under the federal counterpart, the acknowledgment will normally be executed by a notary. Article 136, U.C.M.J., however, confers upon a large category of military personnel the "general powers of a notary public." Under this Rule, documents properly acknowledged by those personnel would probably be self-authenticating. The certificate need not be affixed with a seal.[12]

[12]   Rule 902(9)—Commercial Paper and Related Documents

Certain commercial paper may be self-authenticating under the provisions of "general commercial law," *i.e.,* the Uniform Commercial Code. For example, under 3-307 of the Code, signatures on negotiable instruments are presumed genuine.[13] This paragraph apparently eases the pre-Rules practice requiring a three-step foundation for returned checks.[14] Other banking records could be self-authenticating under paragraph (4), provided that they are government records.

[13]   Rule 902(10)—Presumptions Under Acts of Congress and Regulations

This final paragraph is a modification of the Federal Rule. Language was added to permit designation of additional matters worthy of self-authentication. For example, 26 U.S.C. § 6063 states that a signature on a tax return is presumptively authentic.

[14]   Rule 902(11)—Certified Domestic Records of Regularly Conducted Activity

In 2000, the Supreme Court added two new provisions to Federal Rule

---

[10] *See, e.g.,* United States v. Alvarez, 972 F.2d 1000 (9th Cir. 1992) (inscription on gun was self-authenticating).

[11] *Cf.* United States v. Gibson, 13 C.M.R. 825 (A.F.B.R. 1953) (lay witnesses, identification at time of larceny of stolen blankets bearing markings of *U.S. Army* and *U.S. Navy* held insufficient to establish ownership).

[12] *See generally* Annot., *Sufficiency of Certificate of Acknowledgment,* 25 A.L.R.2d 1124, 1129 (1952).

[13] *See, e.g.,* United States v. Carriger, 592 F.2d 312 (6th Cir. 1979) (mere production of promissory note is prima facie evidence of validity); United States v. Little, 567 F.2d 346, 349 n.1 (8th Cir. 1977), *cert. denied,* 435 U.S. 969 (1978) (corporate checks admissible under Rule 902(a)). *See also* Uniform Commercial Code §§ 1-202 (third-party documents), 3-510 (evidence of dishonor and notice of dishonor), 8-105(2) (signature on negotiable instrument).

[14] *See, e.g.,* United States v. Baugh, 33 C.M.R. 913 (A.F.B.R. 1963).

902 that now permit counsel in federal cases to take advantage of authenticating certificates for both domestic and foreign records of a regularly conducted activity, e.g., the familiar business records. The amendments reflected what already existed in Rule 902(1) to (4) for other records and in some state rules of evidence.[15] Under Rule 1102, those amendments to the Federal Rules of Evidence went into effect for military cases in June 2002.

However, Rule 902 was amended in December 2004 by EO 13365, to conform the Rule to the Federal model. But the 2004 Executive Order adopts only the Federal amendment to Rule 902(11) and apparently makes the change to Rule 902(11) official. As noted at Rule 1102, *below,* the President has decided that Federal Rule 902(12) does not apply to the military.

Under Rule 902(11), the proponent may authenticate a domestic record (either the original or a copy) by first, showing that the documents would be otherwise admissible under the business record exception, Rule 803(6); second, obtaining a written statement from the custodian or other qualified person that the record meets the requirements of Rule 803(6); third, providing written notice to the opponent of the intention to rely on this rule; and fourth, provides the opponent with an opportunity to inspect the records and the opponent has a fair opportunity to challenge the evidence.

There is no requirement that the authenticating document accompanying the records be under oath, but the Rule limits certificates to those complying with any Act of Congress or rule prescribed by the Supreme Court pursuant to statutory authority. It is not immediately clear which Acts or Rules govern and whether they subject the person who signs the certificate to criminal punishment for a false statement. However, the Advisory Committee Note to the 2000 Amendment adding Rule 902 (11) to the Federal Rules of Evidence states that "[a] declaration that satisfies 28 U.S.C. § 1746 would satisfy the declaration requirement of Rule 902(11), as would any comparable certification under oath."

If for some reason, the military judge decides that the records are not self-authenticating under Rule 902(11), the proponent should be free to rely on the live testimony of the custodian or some other qualified witness—the procedure followed before Rule 902 was amended.

The amendment adding Rule 902(11) occurred prior to the Supreme Court's decision in *Crawford v. Washington,* 541 U.S. 36 (2004). As suggested above, certificates that are used as a substitute for live testimony may raise questions under the Sixth Amendment Confrontation Clause as interpreted in *Crawford.*

---

[15] *See. e.g.,* Texas Rule of Evidence 902(10) (rule includes a sample affidavit for purposes of authenticating business records).

§ 902.03 Drafters' Analysis

Rule 902 has been taken from the Federal Rule without significant change except that a new subdivision, 4a, has been added and subdivisions (4) and (10) have been modified. The Rule prescribes forms of self-authentication.

[1] Domestic Public Documents Under Seal

Rule 901(1) is taken verbatim from the Federal Rule, and is similar to aspects of ¶¶ 143 *b* (2)(c) and (d) of the present *Manual.* The Rule does not distinguish between original documents and copies. A seal is self-authenticating and, in the absence of evidence to the contrary, is presumed genuine. Judicial notice is not required.

[2] Domestic Public Documents not Under Seal

Rule 902(2) is taken from the Federal Rule without change. It is similar in scope to aspects of ¶¶ 143 *b* (2)(c) and (d) of the present *Manual* in that it authorizes use of a certification under seal to authenticate a public document not itself under seal. This provision is not the only means of authenticating a domestic public record under this Rule. *Compare* Rule 902(4); 902(4a).

[3] Foreign Public Documents

Rule 902(3) is taken without change from the Federal Rule. Although the Rule is similar to ¶¶ 143 *b* (2)(e) and (f) of the present Manual, the Rule is potentially narrower than the present military one as the Rule does not permit "final certification" to be made by military personnel as does the *Manual* rule nor does it permit authentication made solely pursuant to the laws of the foreign nation. On the other hand, the Rule expressly permits the military judge to order foreign documents to "be treated as presumptively authentic without final certification or permit them to be evidenced by an attested summary with or without final certification."

[4] Certified Copies of Public Records

Rule 902(4) is taken verbatim from the Federal Rule except that it has been modified by adding "or applicable regulation prescribed pursuant to statutory authority." The additional language is required by military necessity and includes the now existing statutory powers of the President and various Secretaries to promulgate regulations. *See generally* Analysis to Rule 901(b).

Rule 902(4) expands upon prior forms of self-authentication to acknowledge the propriety of certified public records or reports and related materials domestic or foreign, the certification of which complies with subdivisions (1), (2), or (3) of the Rule.

[5] Documents or Records of the United States Accompanied by Attesting Certificates

This provision is new and is taken from the third subparagraph of ¶ 143 *b* (2)(c) of the present *Manual*. It has been inserted due to the necessity to facilitate records of the United States in general and military records in particular. Military personnel do not have seals and it would not be practicable to either issue them or require submission of documents to those officials with them. In many cases, such a requirement would be impossible to comply with due to geographical isolation or the unwarranted time such a requirement could demand.

An "attesting certificate" is a certificate or statement, signed by the custodian of the record or the deputy or assistant of the custodian, which in any form indicates that the writing to which the certificate or statement refers is a true copy of the record or an accurate "translation" of a machine, electronic, or coded record, and that the signer of the certificate or statement is acting in an official capacity as the person having custody of the record or as the deputy or assistant thereof.

Paragraph 143(2)(a) of the present *Manual*. An attesting certificate does not require further authentication and, absent proof to the contrary, the signature of the custodian or deputy or assistant thereof on the certificate is presumed to be genuine.

[6] Official Publications; Newspapers and Periodicals; Trade Inscriptions and the Like; Acknowledged Documents; Commercial Paper and Related Documents

Rules 902(5)-(9) are taken verbatim from the Federal Rule and have no equivalents in the *Manual* or in military law.

[7] Presumptions Under Acts of Congress and Regulations

Rule 902(10) was taken from the Federal Rule but was modified by adding "and Regulations" in the caption and "or by applicable regulation prescribed pursuant to statutory authority." *See generally* the Analysis to Rule 901(10) for the reasons for the additional language. The statutory authority referred to includes the presently existing authority for the President and various Secretaries to prescribe regulations.

§ 902.04 Drafters' Analysis (1987)

The word "exception" was changed to "execution" to correct an error in MCM, 1984.

§ 902.05 Drafters' Analysis (2004)

2004 Amendment: Rule 902(11) was modified based on the amendment to Fed. R. Evid. 902(11), effective 1 December 2000, and is taken from the Federal Rule without change. It provides for self-authentication of domestic business records and sets forth procedures for preparing a declaration of a custodian or other qualified witness that will establish a sufficient foundation for the admissibility of domestic business records. This Rule works together with Mil. R. Evid. 803(6).

§ 902.06 Annotated Cases

[1] Rule 902(4)—Certified Copies of Public Records

United States Supreme Court

Melendez-Diaz v. Massachusetts, 129 S. Ct. 2527 (2009): The defendant was convicted in state court of distributing and trafficking in cocaine. Over his *Crawford v. Washington* objection, the trial judge admitted three "certificates of analysis" showing the results of the forensic analysis performed on substances seized in connection with the defendant's arrest. The certificates were sworn before a notary public by analysts at the State Laboratory Institute of the Massachusetts Department of Public Health, as required under state law. The Appeals Court of Massachusetts affirmed the convictions and relied upon a Massachusetts Supreme Judicial Court ruling that the authors of certificates of forensic analysis are not subject to confrontation under the Sixth Amendment. The United States Supreme Court reversed. Justice Scalia wrote for the plurality and concluded that "[t]here is little doubt that the documents in this case fall within the 'core class of testimonial statements' " described in *Crawford*. The Court reasoned that "[t]he documents at issue here, while denominated by Massachusetts law 'certificates,' are quite plainly affidavits," and *Crawford*'s description of the core class of testimonial statements "mentions affidavits twice." The Court rejected the argument that the analysts were not "accusatory" witnesses and thus were not subject to confrontation and concluded that the text of the Sixth Amendment "contemplates two classes of witnesses—those against the defendant and those in his favor." It also rejected the arguments that the analysts were not "conventional" or "typical" witnesses and did not offer testimony prone to distortion or manipulation and therefore were not subject to confrontation. The Court was not persuaded that the Confrontation Clause was satisfied so long as the defendant could call the analysts as witnesses: "[T]he Confrontation Clause imposes a burden on the prosecution to present its witnesses, not on the defendant to bring those adverse witnesses into court." But the Court indicated that state statutes that require the prosecution to give notice of the intent to rely on analysts and the defendant to demand production of the analysts at trial were consistent with the Confrontation Clause: It is common to require a defendant to exercise his rights under the Compulsory Process Clause in advance of trial, announcing his intent to present certain witnesses. . . . There is no conceivable reason why he cannot similarly be compelled to exercise his Confrontation Clause rights before trial. Justice Thomas provided the fifth vote, noting briefly in his concurring opinion that the sworn certificates were in effect affidavits and as such fell within the core definition of testimonial hearsay. Justice Kennedy wrote for the dissenters and argued that the Court ignored 90 years of precedent in which scientific analysis could be introduced without testimony from the analyst who produced it, raised serious questions about which analysts must be produced, and imposed unnecessary and costly burdens on both state and federal criminal justice systems. Citing Rules 902(4) and 902(11), the dissent also said that the majority's opinion could be read to require the testimony of custodians and record keepers rather than using a certificate.

[2] Rule 902(4a)—Documents or Records of the United States Accompanied by Attesting Certificates

Army Court of Criminal Appeals

United States v. Thomas, 33 M.J. 1067 (A.C.M.R. 1991): An authenticating certificate attached to various documents was sufficient to satisfy the self-authentication requirements of Rule 902(4)(a), although the certificate did not specifically list the attached documents. The court noted that the defendant could have disputed the authenticity of the documents but did not do so.

United States v. Barrios, 31 M.J. 750 (A.C.M.R. 1990): Although the court did not encourage use of photocopied authentication certificates, in this case the laboratory report was sufficiently authenticated where both the report and the attached certificate were photocopies.

United States v. Jaramillio, 13 M.J. 782 (A.C.M.R. 1982): The prosecution introduced, over defense objection, the accused's DA Form 2-1 (Personnel Qualification Record Part II). On appeal, the court held that the document was inadmissible because the authenticating certificate was signed by a warrant officer whose duty, position and relationship to the document was not indicated.

[3] Rule 902(6)—Newspapers and Periodicals

Air Force Court of Criminal Appeals

United States v. Vilorio, 63 M.J. 610 (A.F.Ct.Crim.App. 2006): During sentencing, the military judge admitted a prosecution exhibit consisting of a printout of an online version of a newspaper, which detailed the accused's arrest in the victim's hometown. The prosecution did not call any sponsoring witness for the exhibit, arguing that it was self-authenticating under Rule 902(6). The Court of Criminal Appeals held that it was error to admit the exhibit without some additional foundation. Online versions of newspapers, the court said, are not sufficiently reliable to be self-authenticating. The court reassessed the accused's sentence.

[4] Rule 902(8)—Acknowledged Documents

Army Court of Criminal Appeals

United States v. Woodard, 39 M.J. 1022 (A.C.M.R. 1994): An affidavit sworn to before a state notary public satisfied the self-authentication requirement of Rule 902(8).

[5]   Rule 902(9)—Commercial Paper and Related Documents

Air Force Court of Criminal Appeals

United States v. Dean, 13 M.J. 676 (A.F.C.M.R. 1982): When documents such as checks are offered as self-authenticating under Rule 902(9), the court recommended that the offeror ask the military judge to take judicial notice of the appropriate UCC section.

Navy-Marine Corps Court of Criminal Appeals

United States v. Brandell, 33 M.J. 723 (N.M.C.M.R. 1991): Canceled checks in the accused's case were considered authenticated in accordance with the Hawaii Uniform Commercial Code. Bank statements relating to the accused's account, however, were not considered commercial paper. Instead, they were authenticated by distinctive characteristics, such as letterhead, the account holder's name and address, and the fact that the account numbers matched those on the checks. The court noted that a certifying statement attached to the bank records did not make them self-authenticating, but it could be considered in assessing the admissibility of the records under Rule 104(a).

United States v. Dababneh, 28 M.J. 929 (N.M.C.M.R. 1989): Checks written by the accused were held to have been sufficiently authenticated by the live testimony of three witnesses who established that they were written by the accused, cashed by the financial institutions for which they worked, and returned for lack of sufficient funds. The court added that the "insufficient funds" stamp was authenticated when the trial judge took judicial notice of Section 3-510 of the Uniform Commercial Code, which addresses the admissibility of such notations on commercial documents.

United States v. Matthews, 15 M.J. 622 (N.M.C.M.R. 1982): The court ruled that Rule 902(9) could not be used to authenticate a statement on the back of a money order to the effect that payment had been refused because the check was stolen. The court stated that Rule 902(9) is only applicable insofar as the UCC applies and § 3-510, which governs evidence of dishonor, does not cover this situation.

[6]   Rule 902(11)—Certified Domestic Records of Regularly Conducted Activity

United States Supreme Court

Melendez-Diaz v. Massachusetts, 129 S. Ct. 2527 (2009): The defendant was convicted in state court of distributing and trafficking in cocaine. Over his *Crawford v. Washington* objection, the trial judge admitted three "certificates of analysis" showing the results of the forensic analysis performed on substances seized in connection with the defendant's arrest. The certificates were sworn before a notary public by analysts at the State Laboratory Institute of the Massachusetts Department of Public Health, as required under state law. The Appeals Court of Massachusetts affirmed the convictions and relied upon a Massachusetts Supreme Judicial Court ruling that the authors of certificates of forensic analysis are not subject to confrontation under the Sixth Amendment. The United States Supreme Court reversed. Justice Scalia wrote for the pluarlity and concluded that "[t]here is little doubt that the documents in this case fall within the 'core class of testimonial statements' " described in *Crawford*. The Court reasoned that "[t]he documents at issue here, while denominated by Massachusetts law 'certificates,' are quite plainly affidavits," and *Crawford*'s description of the core class of testimonial statements "mentions affidavits twice." The Court rejected the argument that the analysts were not "accusatory" witnesses and thus were not subject to confrontation and concluded that the text of the Sixth Amendment "contemplates two classes of witnesses—those against the defendant and those in his favor." It also rejected the arguments that the analysts were not "conventional" or "typical" witnesses and did not offer testimony prone to distortion or manipulation and therefore were not subject to confrontation. The Court was not persuaded that the Confrontation Clause was satisfied so long as the defendant could call the analysts as witnesses: "[T]he Confrontation Clause imposes a burden on the prosecution to present its witnesses, not on the defendant to bring those adverse witnesses into court." But the Court indicated that state statutes that require the prosecution to give notice of the intent to rely on analysts and the defendant to demand production of the analysts at trial were consistent with the Confrontation Clause: It is common to require a defendant to exercise his rights under the Compulsory Process Clause in advance of trial, announcing his intent to present certain witnesses. . . . There is no conceivable reason why he cannot similarly be compelled to exercise his Confrontation Clause rights before trial. Justice Thomas provided the fifth vote, noting briefly that in this case the sworn certificates were in effect affidavits and as such fell clearly within the core definition of testimonial hearsay. Justice Kennedy wrote for the dissenters and argued that the Court ignored 90 years of precedent in which scientific analysis could be introduced without testimony from the analyst who produced it, raised serious questions about which analysts must be produced, and imposed unnecessary and costly burdens on both state and federal criminal justice systems. Citing Rules 902(4) and 902(11), the dissent also said that the majority's opinion could be read to require the testimony of custodians and record keepers rather than using a certificate.

§ 903.01   Official Text

Rule 903.   Subscribing Witness' Testimony Unnecessary.

The testimony of a subscribing witness is not necessary to authenticate a writing unless required by the laws of the jurisdiction whose laws govern the validity of the writing.

---

§ 903.02   Editorial Comment

Normally, writings may be authenticated under either Rule 901 or 902. However, if a statute (almost always a state statute) requires the testimony of a subscribing or attesting witness to authenticate a document, then under Rule 903 that state requirement controls.

The common law recognized a preference for the live testimony of the individual who signed the proffered document as either a subscribing or attesting witness. Only after producing the witness, or sufficiently explaining his or her absence, could the proponent resort to other methods of authentication. The subscribing witnesses' testimony was not binding, however, and could be explained or contradicted by other evidence. Most states have abolished the requirement of authentication through subscribing witnesses' testimony; those remaining statutes would normally require it in authenticating wills or marriage contracts.[1]

This Rule, which is identical to the Federal Rule, comes into play only when the state statute requires both document be witnessed and that subscribing witness authenticate it. Rule 903 could have an impact on the government and defense in military cases. For example, a marriage contract might be offered in defense to a charge of violation of Article 132, U.C.M.J. (*e.g.,* false claim for dependent travel). Or, a properly executed marriage contract may be relied upon by the prosecution where the accused is charged with bigamy. In either instance, the state statutes controlling the execution and authentication of the offered marriage contract should be consulted. If they do not require a subscribing witness's testimony, counsel may authenticate the evidence under Rule 901 or 902.

Congress could, of course, require subscribing witnesses to be called to authenticate federal writings, but it has shown no inclination to embrace the common law requirement that most states have repudiated.

§ 903.03   Drafters' Analysis

Rule 903 is taken verbatim from the Federal Rule and has no express equivalent in the present *Manual*.

---

[1] *See generally* WEINSTEINS'S FEDERAL EVIDENCE, Chapter 903 (2d ed. 1997).

SECTION X

CONTENTS OF WRITINGS, RECORDINGS, AND PHOTOGRAPHS

SYNOPSIS

§ 1001.01 Official Text

Rule 1001. Definitions

For purposes of this section, the following definitions are applicable:

(1) *Writings and recordings.* "Writings" and "recordings" consist of letters, words, or numbers, or their equivalent, set down by handwriting, typewriting, printing, photostating, photographing, magnetic impulse, mechanical or electronic recording, or other form of data compilation.

(2) *Photographs.* "Photographs" include still photographs, X-ray films, video tapes, and motion pictures.

(3) *Original.* An "original" of a writing or recording is the writing or recording itself or any counterpart intended to have the same effect by a person executing or issuing it. An "original" of a photograph includes the negative or any print therefrom. If data are stored in a computer or similar device, any printout or other output readable by sight, shown to reflect the data accurately, is an "original."

(4) *Duplicate.* A "duplicate" is a counterpart produced by the same impression as the original, or from the same matrix, or by means of photography, including enlargements and miniatures, or by mechanical or electronic re-recording, or by chemical reproduction, or by other equivalent techniques which accurately reproduce the original.

---

§ 1001.02 Editorial Comment

Section X covers what is usually referred to as the "best evidence rule." The expression "best evidence," however, is a misnomer and does not even appear in the rules themselves. Indeed, the use of the popular phrase "best evidence" might mislead one into believing that the rule is broader than it actually is. While counsel will almost always want to present the "best" or most persuasive evidence available, there is no rule of evidence requiring counsel to do so.[1] The rule is narrow and only requires the proponent to produce the original of a writing, recording, or photograph when the content of one of those items is in issue in the case. Sometimes the rule is referred

---

[1] *See* Nance, *The Best Evidence Principle*, 73 IOWA L. REV. 227 (1988) (author notes that there is a best evidence principle which applies to all evidence; if the proponent fails to present the most persuasive evidence, the opponent can ask the jury to draw an adverse inference from that failure). *See generally* E. Imwinkelried & D. Schlueter, FEDERAL EVIDENCE TACTICS, § 10.01[3][a] (Matthew Bender); D. Schlueter, S. Saltzburg, L. Schinasi & E. Imwinkelried, MILITARY EVIDENTIARY FOUNDATIONS, § 8-1 *et seq.* (4th ed. 2010).

to as the "original writings" rule. But that term is also too narrow because the rule covers more than traditional writings.

The "best evidence" or "original writing" rule developed at a time when there were good reasons to worry about the accuracy of copies, many of which were made by hand. With the development of modern, mechanical forms of copying, concerns about the accuracy of copies has greatly diminished. As a result, Section X of the Military Rules of Evidence provides that, where the proponent wishes to prove the contents of a writing, recording, or photograph, the proponent generally must produce either the original writing or a duplicate. If neither is available, other forms of proof may be admitted. Each of the Section X rules is examined below.

The heart of the best evidence rule is Rule 1002. It makes clear that Section X (except for Rule 1006) does not come into play unless the proponent is offering a writing, recording, or photograph to prove its content.

[1]   Rule 1001(1)—Writings and Recordings

Paragraph (1) defines "writings" and "recordings" in broad fashion as "letters, words, or numbers, or their equivalent" produced through a variety of methods. As written, the definition should be flexible enough to cover virtually every conceivable, yet undeveloped, method of producing letters, words or numbers. The Rule is also probably broad enough to include "symbols" that have verbal qualities to them. For example, the "peace" sign of the 1960's, an arrow, or depiction of a familiar obscene gesture could be considered as the "equivalent" of letters, or words.

Sometimes the writing will be on a bulky or immovable object such as the inscription on a monument or the inspection sticker on an automobile. In that case although the words or numbers constitute the original writing, a photograph of the writing would serve as an admissible "duplicate." Moreover, the common law distinguished between writings and chattels that contain words or numbers. A chattel containing word or numbers was not deemed to be a writing, and any form of proof as to the description of the chattel was permissible. Federal authorities continue to adhere to this view.[2]

[2]   Rule 1001(2)—Photographs

Where the contents of a photograph are in issue, such as a libelous or obscene picture, a best evidence problem is presented. *See* our comments at Rule 1002. For purposes of this Rule, it is important to note that paragraph (2) defines photographs to include still photographs, x-rays, video tapes, and motion pictures.[3] Most of the time when photographs are used at trial, they

---

[2] *See, e.g.,* United States v. Duffy, 454 F.2d 809 (5th Cir. 1972).

[3] *See, e.g.,* United States v. Davenport, 14 M.J. 547 (A.C.M.R. 1982) (videotape is a photograph).

are not offered to prove their contents; they are offered to illustrate or to be incorporated within the testimony of a witness. For example, when a witness states that a photograph is a fair and accurate depiction of the scene of an event, the proponent of the photograph is not proving the contents thereof; the proponent is having the witness adopt the contents of the photograph as part of the testimony. In all such cases, the proponent must authenticate the photograph pursuant to Section IX, but Section X is not implicated.

[3] Rule 1001(3)—Original

Section (3) defines an "original" writing, recording, and photograph. The writing or recording itself is an original, as is any counterpart intended to be treated as an original. 1969 *Manual* ¶ 143a(1) treated complete carbon copies as duplicate originals. Identical photostatic copies were also considered as duplicate originals if they were intended to serve as originals. Under Paragraph (3), carbon copies are now considered as originals only if they were intended to serve as such. Otherwise they are "duplicates" within the definition of Paragraph (4).

An original photograph under Section (3) includes both the negative and any prints made from the negative. Computer printouts are also treated as originals.

[4] Rule 1001(4)—Duplicate

Paragraph (4) defines the term "duplicate" as a counterpart produced by the same impression as the original or by other accurate means of reproduction. The means or process used to create the duplicate is not crucial as long as it represents a technique insuring accuracy. A duplicate may be created simultaneously with the original or at a later time. Not within this definition are those copies subsequently produced manually, *i.e.,* handwritten or typed.

Paragraph (4), in conjunction with Rule 1003, changed former military practice and relaxed the Best Evidence Rule. Photostatic copies of original documents were normally considered under pre-Rules practice to be secondary evidence if they were not intended to serve as originals.[4] Now, although they remain duplicates and are not treated as originals, they are presumptively as admissible as an original under Rule 1003. But Section X no longer favors carbon copies. It no longer treats complete carbon copies as duplicate originals unless they were intended to serve as originals.[5] Now, absent that intent, they are treated as duplicates and not originals. They remain presumptively admissible, however, under Rule 1003.

In discussing pre-Rules practice, the Drafters' Analysis makes nothing of the distinction between the two categories of duplicate originals. The

---

[4] 1969 *Manual* ¶ 143a(1).

[5] 1969 *Manual* ¶ 143a(1).

Drafters' Analysis may be misleading insofar as it suggests that all documents formerly labeled as "duplicate originals" are now governed by Paragraph (4) and are duplicates. Duplicate originals that are intended to be originals, whether carbon copies or otherwise, were treated as originals before and are still originals under Paragraph (3). Only when there is no intent that a duplicate be treated as an original is Paragraph (4) used, and this is where the Rule, as applied to carbons, differs from pre-Rules practice.

§ 1001.03   Drafters' Analysis

[1]   Writings and Recordings

Rule 1001(1) is taken verbatim from the Federal Rule and is similar in scope to *Manual* ¶ 143*d* of the present *Manual*. Although the present *Manual* is somewhat more detailed, the *Manual* was clearly intended to be expansive. The Rule adequately accomplishes the identical purpose through a more general reference.

[2]   Photographs

Rule 1001(2) is taken verbatim from the Federal Rule and has no express equivalent in the present *Manual*. It does, however, reflect current military law.

[3]   Original

Rule 1001(3) is taken verbatim from the Federal Rule and is similar to ¶ 143*a*(1) of the present *Manual*. The present *Manual*, however, treats "duplicate originals," *i.e.,* carbon and photographic copies made for use as an original, as an "original" while Rule 1001(4) treats such a document as a "duplicate."

[4]   Duplicate

Rule 1001(4) is taken from the Federal Rule verbatim and includes those documents ¶ 143*a*(1) of the present *Manual* defines as "duplicate originals." In view of Rule 1003's rule of admissibility for "duplicates," no appreciable negative result stems from the reclassification.

§ 1001.04   Annotated Cases

[1]   Rule 1001(2)—Photographs

Army Court of Criminal Appeals

United States v. Davenport, 14 M.J. 547 (A.C.M.R. 1982): The court stated that a videotape is a "photograph" under Rule 1001(2) and its qualities as real evidence require treatment as a marked exhibit.

[2]   Rule 1001(3)—Original

Air Force Court of Criminal Appeals

United States v. Maxwell, 42 M.J. 568 (A.F.Ct.Crim.App. 1995): The court held that hard-copy versions of explicit images seized from the accused's computer were considered originals for purposes of the best evidence rule.

United States v. Gonzalez, 14 M.J. 501 (A.F.C.M.R. 1982): The judge refused to admit affidavits by defense witnesses during sentencing. On appeal, the court noted that they were admissible under Rule 1002 and ¶ 75*c*(3) of the 1969 Manual for Courts-Martial, even though they were in electrical message format and therefore were not originals under Rule 1001(3).

§ 1002.01 Official Text

Rule 1002. Requirement of an Original.

To prove the content of a writing, recording, or photograph, the original writing, recording, or photograph is required, except as otherwise provided in these rules, this Manual, or by Act of Congress.

---

§ 1002.02 Editorial Comment

The traditional Best Evidence Rule, now captured in Rule 1002, requires a party wanting to prove the contents of a writing, recording, or photograph to produce the *original* unless otherwise exempted.[1] This Rule is substantially similar to the Federal Rule, although a minor textual change recognizes that the *Manual* itself might provide an exception to the requirement of an original.

The Rule generally follows pre-Rules practice, but changed military practice insofar as most of the pre-Rules *Manual* exceptions to the requirement of an original are not specifically recognized in Section X.[2] However, as the Drafters' Analysis notes, this was offset by other Rules that will normally allow admission of the same evidence. For example, Rules 1003 to 1007 provide exceptions to Rule 1002, and a substantial number of federal statutes relieve the proponent from presenting the original.[3]

Defining what constitutes the original should normally not present a problem.[4] One of the most commonly encountered problems, however, is to determine whether the proponent of evidence is attempting to prove the contents of the writing, recording, or photograph. There seems to be a universal urge to object on "best evidence" grounds whenever testimony draws attention to a document. That an event or statement has been reduced to writing or recorded on videotape does not in itself trigger the Rule and prevent a witness from testifying as to the event or statement.[5] The Rule does not apply, for instance, when a writing is used to support a witness's opinion or when it is used in court to refresh recollection. And in *United States v. Rose*,[6] a witness's testimony concerning a tape-recorded conversa-

---

[1] *See, e.g.*, Los Angeles News Service v. C.B.S. Broadcasting, Inc., 305 F.3d 924 (9th Cir. 2002) (plaintiff was required to produce original label or explain why it could not produce it).

[2] *See, e.g.*, 1969 *Manual* ¶ 143a(f) (fingerprints comparison).

[3] For a listing of examples, *see generally* WEINSTEIN'S FEDERAL EVIDENCE, Chapter 1002 (2d ed. 1997).

[4] *See* our discussion of Rule 1001(3).

[5] United States v. Jewson, 5 C.M.R. 80 (C.M.A. 1952).

[6] 590 F.2d 232 (7th Cir. 1978), *cert. denied*, 442 U.S. 929 (1979).

tion did not violate the Best Evidence Rule, because the testimony concerned the contents of the conversation not the contents of the tape recording. Usually, a picture or film is offered as a representation of what a witness saw, or a tape recording is offered to illustrate what a witness heard. In these instances, the picture, film, or tape is not offered to prove its contents, but to illustrate or to complete testimony, and the Best Evidence Rule is inapplicable. If, however, the film or picture is allegedly obscene or libelous, the contents are being proved when it is offered, and Rule 1002 is applicable.

The mere fact that a laboratory report has been prepared on a drug sample does not require its production under this Rule to establish the sample's identity; the identity may be independently established through testimony of the chemist.[7] The identity of the drug is in issue, not the contents of the lab report, unless, of course, the proponent offers the report into evidence. The point here is that the proponent may often avoid potential Best Evidence Rule problems by simply relying upon testimony that relates the personal knowledge of the witness rather than the contents of a writing or other recording that reflects that knowledge.

Some of the confusion among counsel in application of the Best Evidence Rule centers on misapplication of what might be loosely termed a "best" or most persuasive evidence notion.[8] In a drug case, the laboratory report is normally the most persuasive evidence of the drug's identity, and in proving a confession, the most persuasive evidence of what the accused said usually lies in his signed written statement or a video tape recording of his confession. But the fact that more persuasive evidence exists in the form of a writing, recording, or photograph does not trigger Rule 1002 when oral testimony is offered. The Rule only operates when someone is trying to prove the *contents* of an item.[9] Note, however, that the existence of better evidence may result in exclusion of evidence to save time under Military Rules 403 or 611, or to vindicate the reliability concerns of particular provisions like Military Rules 803(6) or 807.

Rule 1002 is only one of several interrelated hurdles to admissibility.

---

[7] *See, e.g.,* United States v. Smith, 566 F.3d 410 (4th Cir. 2009) (ATF agent offered expert testimony regarding location of manufacture of weapons; court rejected argument that agent's testimony about written sources that he had consulted violated the Best Evidence Rule; court said that he was not relating the contents of the materials but was instead relying on information normally relied upon by experts to form an opinion).

[8] *See* Nance, *The Best Evidence Principle,* 73 Iowa L. Rev. 227 (1988) (author notes that there is a best evidence *principle,* which applies to all evidence).

[9] *See, e.g.,* Jackson v. Crews, 873 F.2d 1105 (8th Cir. 1989) (best evidence rule did not prevent counsel from questioning witness about a flyer used to solicit potential witnesses where the questions were designed to show how the witness was contacted instead of the contents of the flyer).

Offered writings, recordings, and photographs are subject to the limitations of Section VIII (hearsay) and Section IX (authentication).[10]

§ 1002.03 Drafters' Analysis

Rule 1002 is taken verbatim from the Federal Rule except that "this Manual" has been added in recognition of the efficacy of other *Manual* provisions. The Rule is similar in scope to the best evidence rule found in ¶ 143*a*(19) of the 1969 *Manual* except that specific reference is made in the rule to recordings and photographs. Unlike the 1969 *Manual.* the Rule does not contain the misleading reference to "best evidence" and is plainly applicable only to writings, recordings, or photographs.

It should be noted that the various exceptions to Rule 1002 are similar to but not identical with those found in the 1969 *Manual. Compare* Rules 1005–1007 *with* ¶ 143*a*(2)(f) of the 1969 *Manual.* For example, ¶¶ 143*a*(2)(e) and 144*c Manual* exempted banking records and business records from the rule as categories while the Rule does not. The actual difference in practice, however, is not likely to be substantial as Rule 1003 allows admission of duplicates unless, for example, "a genuine question is raised as to the authenticity of the original." This is similar in result to the 1969 *Manual*'s treatment of business records in ¶ 144*c*. Omission of other *Manual* exceptions, *e.g.,* certificates of fingerprint comparison and identity, *see* Rules 703, 803; evidence of absence of official or business entries, and copies of telegrams and radiograms, do not appear substantial when viewed against the entirety of the Military Rules which are likely to allow admissibility in a number of ways.

The Rule's reference to "Act of Congress" will now incorporate those statutes that specifically direct that the best evidence rule be inapplicable in one form or another. *See, e.g.,* 1 U.S.C. § 209 (copies of District of Columbia Code of Laws). As a rule, such statutes permit a form of authentication as an adequate substitute for the original document.

§ 1002.04 Annotated Cases

Air Force Court of Criminal Appeals

United States v. Perez, 36 M.J. 583 (A.F.C.M.R. 1992): OSI agents' testimony concerning what they had observed on video surveillance monitors did not violate best evidence rule where a "duplicate original" of the videotape was introduced and played in court. The court noted that watching the video monitor was analogous to watching an event through binoculars or monitoring an X-ray machine at security check points. It also indicated that there is no general rule which requires that only the "best" evidence be admitted.

---

[10] For discussions of applicability of this Rule, *see generally* Berger, *Article X, Contents of Writings, Recordings, and Photographs,* 33 FED. B.J. 87 (1974); Note, *Contents of Writings, Recordings and Photographs,* 27 ARK. L. REV. 357 (1973).

United States v. Gonzalez, 14 M.J. 501 (A.F.C.M.R. 1982): The judge refused to admit affidavits by defense witnesses during sentencing. On appeal, the court noted that they were admissible under Rule 1002 even though they were in electrical message format and therefore were not originals under Rule 1001(3).

§ 1003.01   Official Text

Rule 1003.   Admissibility of Duplicates.

A duplicate is admissible to the same extent as an original unless (1) a genuine question is raised as to the authenticity of the original or (2) in the circumstances it would be unfair to admit the duplicate in lieu of the original.

---

§ 1003.02   Editorial Comment

A "duplicate," as defined in Rule 1001(4), is as readily admissible as an original unless there is a genuine question about the original's authenticity or fairness dictates that under the circumstances the duplicate should not be admitted. In short, duplicates are admissible unless the opponent can show good reason for requiring production of the original.[1] The rationale for this liberal rule, which presumes reliability, rests in large part on technology capable of producing virtually identical duplicates, thereby insuring a high degree of accuracy and precision.

Identical to its federal counterpart, this Rule changed pre-Rules practice, which permitted only "duplicate originals" to be treated as originals. Identical carbon copies were considered duplicate originals regardless of any intent to treat them as originals. Photocopies, however, were duplicate originals only if they were intended to be treated, or were in fact treated, as originals. Thus, under pre-Rules practice if counsel subsequently made a photocopy of the document solely for purposes of trial, it was not considered a duplicate original, but was treated as secondary evidence.

Now, the term "duplicate original" is gone, carbon copies receive no special status, and photocopies made solely for purposes of trial will normally be admissible under this Rule. But duplicates *intended* to have the same effect as originals are still treated as originals. *See* our discussion of Rules 1001(3) and 1002.

Probably the most important issue at trial with respect to 1003 will center on when a duplicate will not be treated as an original. The Rule states that a duplicate should not receive favored treatment if a "genuine" question of the authenticity of the original is raised. This clearly places a burden on the opponent to present information, or at least a particularized claim, that indicates specifically what is wrong with the duplicate.[2] The authenticity

---

[1] *See, e.g.,* United States v. Westmoreland, 312 F.3d 302 (7th Cir. 2002) (four tape recordings were first generation copies and were admissible as duplicates; defendant had not presented any evidence to challenge authenticity); United States v. Morgan, 555 F.2d 238 (9th Cir. 1977) (applying Rule 1003, court held photocopy to be presumptively admissible).

[2] *See, e.g.,* United States v. Chang An-Lo, 851 F.2d 547 (2d Cir. 1988) (defendant failed

question may be raised on the face of the offered duplicate where, for example, a number of handwritten annotations have been made, or where portions of the document are blurred. Extrinsic evidence, such as another conflicting duplicate that is supposedly also an accurate copy of the original may raise a serious question of authenticity.[3]

The Rule also will not admit a duplicate where it would be unfair to do so. Fairness might dictate exclusion where, for instance, the duplicate represents only an extract of the original and the missing portions would be useful for cross-examination.

Rule 1003 is intended to do away with purely technical objections, but not to claims that a duplicate is incomplete, altered, or otherwise misleading or incorrect. Judges faced with an objection to admissibility must decide whether there is a good reason to require the original to be produced or to have its absence explained. The nature of the objection, the quality of the duplicate, its role in the trial, and lastly, the equities of the specific trial setting should be considered.[4] If a duplicate is not admissible under this Rule, it may be admissible under Rule 1004, as long as the absence of an original is properly explained.

§ 1003.03   Drafters' Analysis

Rule 1003 is taken verbatim from the Federal Rule. It is both similar to and distinct from the present *Manual.* To the extent that the Rule deals with those copies which were intended at the time of their creation to be used as originals, it is similar to the present *Manual's* treatment of "duplicate originals." ¶ 143*a* (1), except that under the present *Manual* there is no distinction to be made between originals and "duplicate originals." Accordingly, in this case the Rule would be narrower than the present *Manual.* To the extent that the Rule deals with copies not intended at their time of creation to serve as originals, however, *e.g.,* when copies are made of preexisting documents for the purpose of litigation, the Rule is broader than the present *Manual* because the present *Manual* would prohibit such

---

to show a genuine question of authenticity of duplicates of Brazilian hotel telephone records); United States v. DiMatteo, 716 F.2d 1361 (11th Cir. 1983) (re-recorded tape admissible absent claim of lack of genuineness); United States v. Hausmann, 711 F.2d 615 (5th Cir. 1983) (duplication of receipt properly admitted when there was no genuine issue as to authenticity); United States v. Balzano, 687 F.2d 6 (1st Cir. 1982) (copy of tape admissible even though the government erased the original while making the copy); Amoco Prod. Co. v. United States, 619 F.2d 1383 (10th Cir. 1980) (copy of deed excluded because most critical part was not completely reproduced).

[3] *See* United States v. Enstam, 622 F.2d 857 (5th Cir. 1980) (genuine question not raised where prosecution could not explain original's disappearance and duplicate did not show original's colorations).

[4] *See, e.g.,* Amoco Production Co. v. United States, 619 F.2d 1383 (10th Cir. 1980) (duplicate file copy excluded because critical part was not completely reproduced).

evidence unless an adequate justification for the non-production of the original existed.

§ 1003.04   Annotated Cases

Air Force Court of Criminal Appeals

United States v. Perez, 36 M.J. 583 (A.F.C.M.R. 1992): OSI agents' testimony concerning what they had observed on video surveillance monitors did not violate best evidence rule where a "duplicate original" of the videotape was introduced and played in court.

United States v. Christman, 11 M.J. 570 (A.F.C.M.R. 1981): The court permitted the government appellate counsel to file its copy of a properly admitted trial exhibit. After examining the record transcript and the authenticating certificate of the record custodian, the court concluded that under Rule 1003 the document was a duplicate of the one used at trial.

Army Court of Criminal Appeals

United States v. Woodard, 39 M.J. 1022 (A.C.M.R. 1994): A facsimile copy of an affidavit was a duplicate within the meaning of Rule 1003. The court noted that there was no objection at trial that the facsimile was not an accurate reproduction, nor did counsel give any reason for requiring production of the original.

§ 1004.01   Official Text

Rule 1004.   Admissibility of Other Evidence of Contents.

The original is not required, and other evidence of the contents of a writing, recording, or photograph is admissible if:

(1) *Originals lost or destroyed.*   All originals are lost or have been destroyed, unless the proponent lost or destroyed them in bad faith; or

(2) *Original not obtainable.*   No original can be obtained by any available judicial process or procedure; or

(3) *Original in possession of opponent.*   At a time when an original was under the control of the party against whom offered, the party was put on notice, by the pleadings or otherwise, that the contents would be a subject of proof at the hearing, and the party does not produce the original at the hearing; or

(4) *Collateral matters.*   The writing, recording, or photograph is not closely related to a controlling issue.

---

§ 1004.02   Editorial Comment

A proponent may offer secondary evidence in lieu of an original writing, recording, or photograph if he or she does so through a recognized exception to the Best Evidence Rule. Rule 1004, identical to the Federal Rule, notes four commonly recognized exceptions. Others are presented in Rules 1005 (Public Records), 1006 (Summaries), and 1007 (Testimony or Written Admission of Party). Once an exception is shown, and Rule 1002 is overcome, the proponent is free to rely upon any form of secondary evidence. In theory, once the door is opened there are no technical degrees of secondary evidence. As a practical matter, however, counsel will normally want to present the most persuasive evidence available.[1] Rule 1004 provided no major changes in military practice, although minor changes are apparent as we note in the following discussions on the four exceptions.

[1]   Rule 1004(1)—Originals Lost or Destroyed

Section (1) is consistent with pre-Rules law and excuses production of an original that has been lost or destroyed, other than in bad faith.[2] Tradition-

---

[1] *See* United States v. Gerhart, 538 F.2d 807 (8th Cir. 1976) (secondary evidence subject to opponent's attack on question of weight). *See also* E. Imwinkelried & D. Schlueter, FEDERAL EVIDENCE TACTICS, § 10-4 (Matthew Bender).

[2] *See, e.g.,* United States v. Rhodes, 11 C.M.R. 73 (C.M.A. 1953) (copies could be used after destruction of letters by co-conspirator); Medical Lab. Mgmt. Consultants v. American Broadcasting Cos., 306 F.3d 806 (9th Cir. 2002) (if proponent can show loss of original

ally, the proponent bears the burden of showing that the original has been destroyed or that a reasonable search has failed to locate the original. In determining the sufficiency of the proponent's search, one commentator has suggested consideration of four factors: (1) suspicion of fraud, (2) importance of the instrument, (3) age of the instrument, and (4) lapse of time since the instrument was last seen.[3]

A lost or destroyed original must still be authenticated under Section IX. This normally requires the proponent to establish that the original existed, was executed, and was later lost or destroyed. The particular order of proof here is not crucial. The military judge, however, may prescribe the order under Rule 611(a). Questions of whether the original ever existed are for the court members, *see* Rule 1008, but whether an original has been lost or destroyed is a question for the military judge. *See also* Rule 104.

[2] Rule 1004(2)—Original Not Obtainable

Section (2) permits a proponent to offer secondary evidence if the original cannot be secured through available judicial process or procedure. This provision arguably narrows similar pre-Rules practice that permitted secondary evidence where production of the original was not feasible. If production is possible, yet costly in time or money, it is unclear whether the proponent may employ this exception to escape the requirement of producing the original. One commentator has suggested that the absolute terms of this provision should implicitly include the phrase "to the extent practicable and reasonable" and permit judges to fully exercise their discretion.[4] The Drafters' Analysis is silent on this point. But the Advisory Committee's Note that accompanied the identical Federal Rule indicates that the drafters of that rule contemplated making a party utilize a subpoena *duces tecum* accompanying a deposition in another jurisdiction, which suggests that some expense is contemplated. Thus, in federal courts, it seems that the plain wording of Rule 1004(2) might well control.

[3] Rule 1004(3)—Original in Possession of Opponent

Under Section (3), a proponent may use secondary evidence if the original

---

through inadvertence, secondary evidence may be used); United States v. Bueno-Risquet, 799 F.2d 804 (2d Cir. 1986) (finding that various forms were properly admitted to prove the contents of bags that had been stolen during the trial); Wright v. Farmers Co-op, 681 F.2d 549 (8th Cir. 1982) (court suggests that specific testimony should be adduced concerning the ground upon which a finding that an original has been lost is to be based); Schiavone-Chase Corp. v. United States, 553 F.2d 658 (Ct. Cl. 1977) (copies could be used when standard government procedure resulted in destruction of documents).

[3] Weinstein's Federal Evidence, Chapter 1004 (Matthew Bender). *See also* Burt Rigid Box, Inc. v. Travelers Property Cas. Corp., 302 F.3d 83 (2d Cir. 2002) (court cited "diligence" requirement in Rule and stated that that is question for court, not the factfinder).

[4] Weinstein's Federal Evidence, Chapter 1004 (Matthew Bender). *See also* Burt Rigid Box, Inc. v. Travelers Property Cas. Corp., 302 F.3d 83 (2d Cir. 2002) (court cited "diligence" requirement in Rule and stated that that is question for court, not the factfinder).

is in the hands of the opponent who fails to produce it at trial after receiving notice to do so. This section is similar to pre-Rules law except that now notice must first be given to the opponent. No special format is required for the notice as long as it is reasonable. If the accused needs the original, because it is better evidence for some reason, the prosecution cannot validly refuse an order to turn it over to the defense. Because of potential self-incrimination problems, the prosecution should not demand in open court production of an original in possession of the accused.[5]

[4]   Rule 1001(4)—Collateral Matters

Section (4) generally follows pre-Rules case law and excuses production of the original if it is relevant only to collateral matters.[6] This provision is grounded on expediency and inserts a needed degree of flexibility into a potentially technical Best Evidence Rule. When faced with matters that are potentially collateral, military judges should consider the importance of the offered evidence and its role in the trial. In many cases close examination of the evidence will reveal that the Best Evidence Rule should not even come into play because the contents of the original are not in question although a witness had made a passing reference to it.

§ 1004.03   Drafters' Analysis

Rule 1004 is taken from the Federal Rule without change, and is similar in scope to the present *Manual*. Once evidence comes within the scope of Rule 1004, secondary evidence is admissible without regard to whether "better" forms of that evidence can be obtained. Thus, no priority is established once Rule 1002 is escaped. Although the present *Manual* states in ¶ 143a(2) that "the contents may be proved by an authenticated copy or by the testimony of a witness who has seen and can remember the substance of the writing" when the original need not be produced, that phrasing appears illustrative only and not exclusive. Accordingly, the Rule, the present *Manual,* and common law are in agreement in not requiring categories of secondary evidence.

[1]   Originals Lost or Destroyed

Rule 1004(1) is similar to the present *Manual* except that the Rule explicitly exempts originals destroyed in "bad faith." Such an exemption is implicit in the present *Manual.*

[2]   Original not Obtained

Rule 1004(2) is similar to the justification for nonproduction in ¶ 143a(2)

---

[5] McKnight v. United States, 115 F. 972 (6th Cir. 1902) (reversible error to require prosecutor in open court to demand defendant to produce); United States v. DeBell, 28 C.M.R. 269 (C.M.A. 1959) (dissenting opinion noted that prosecutor's tactic of demanding production in open court was a deliberate invasion of privilege against self-incrimination).

[6] *See, e.g.,* United States v. Jewson, 5 C.M.R. 80 (C.M.A. 1952) (secondary evidence admissible to impeach accused).

of the present *Manual*, "an admissible writing . . . cannot feasibly be produced."

[3] Original in Possession of Opponent

Rule 1004(3) is similar to the present *Manual* provision in ¶ 143*a*(2) that when a document is in the possession of the accused, the original need not be produced except that the present *Manual* explicitly does not require notice to the accused, and the Rule may require such notice. Under the Rule, the accused must be "put on notice, by the pleadings or otherwise, that the contents would be a subject of proof at the hearing." Thus, under certain circumstances, a formal notice to the accused may be required. Under no circumstances should such a request or notice be made in the presence of the court members. The only purpose of such notice is to justify use of secondary evidence and does not serve to compel the surrender of evidence from the accused. It should be noted that Rule 1004(3) acts in favor of the accused as well as the prosecution and allows notice to the prosecution to justify defense use of secondary evidence.

[4] Collateral Matters

Rule 1004 is not found within the present *Manual* but restates military law. The intent behind the Rule is to avoid unnecessary delays and expense. It is important to note that important matters which may appear collateral may not be so in fact due to their weight. *See, e.g., United States v. Parker,* 13 C.M.A. 579, 33 C.M.R. 111 (1963). (Validity of divorce decree of critical prosecution witness not collateral when witness would be prevented from testifying due to spousal privilege if the divorce were not valid). The Rule incorporates this via its use of the expression "related to a controlling issue."

§ 1004.04 Annotated Cases

[1] Rule 1004(1)—Originals Lost or Destroyed

Air Force Court of Criminal Appeals

United States v. Gill, 40 M.J. 835 (A.F.C.M.R. 1994): The recipient of an indecent letter handed to her by the accused was permitted to relate the contents of the letter because her testimony established that the original letter had been destroyed.

§ 1005.01 Official Text

Rule 1005. Public Records.

The contents of an official record, or of a document authorized to be recorded or filed and actually recorded or filed, including data compilations in any form, if otherwise admissible, may be proved by copy, certified as correct or attested to in accordance with Mil. R. Evid. 902 or testified to be correct by a witness who has compared it with the original. If a copy which complies with the foregoing cannot be obtained by the exercise of reasonable diligence, then other evidence of the contents may be given.

---

§ 1005.02 Editorial Comment

Rule 1005 presents an exception to the requirement of Rule 1002 that an original writing or recording must be used to prove the contents thereof. This Rule provides that copies of official records or documents authorized and actually to be recorded or filed may be presented instead of the original. It is a rule of preference. Although duplicates generally benefit from a presumption of reliability, *see* Rule 1003, Rule 1005 indicates two preferred methods of dealing with copies of public documents. This Rule was intended to preempt Rule 1003 insofar as the contents of public documents are in question.

The legislative history of the almost identical Federal Rule indicates that the special treatment for public documents represented a judgment that it should never be necessary to disrupt public offices by having original documents produced, but that there should be some guarantee that a substitute evidence is reliable. In lieu of even requiring production of an original, the drafters favored two forms of secondary evidence. If these cannot be submitted, other evidence may be offered.

To satisfy the Rule, a proponent may either have the copy certified as correct under Rule 902(4), (4a) *or* compared with the original by a witness who can testify that the offered copy is a correct reproduction. Only if reasonable diligence does not produce a certified, attested, or a compared copy, may the proponent rely upon other forms of secondary evidence. It should be obvious that, as long as the original public record is available, it should be possible to use the forms of proof preferred by this Rule.

The Rule is substantially similar to the Federal Rule; the words "or attested to" were added in recognition of Rule 902(4a). The 1969 *Manual* ¶ 143a(2)(c) exempted "official records" from the Best Evidence Rule and ¶ 143a(2)(e) exempted banking entries. Rule 1005 is clearly broad enough to cover both provisions. Apparently not covered, however, is a related 1969 *Manual* provision that formerly permitted the head of an executive or military department or agency to certify that release of certain records would be contrary to public interest.[1] This may be covered by the privilege rules, however.[2]

§ 1005.03   Drafters' Analysis

Rule 1005 is taken verbatim from the Federal Rule except that "or attested to" has been added to conform the Rule to the new Rule 902(4a). The Rule is generally similar to *Manual* ¶ 143a(2)(c) of the present *Manual* although some differences do exist, however. The Rule is somewhat broader in that it applies to more than just "official records." Further, although the present *Manual* permits "a properly authenticated" copy in lieu of the official record, the Rule allows secondary evidence of contents when a certified or attested copy "cannot be obtained by the exercise of reasonable diligence." The Rule does, however, have a preference for a certified or attested copy.

§ 1005.04   Annotated Cases

United States Court of Appeals for the Armed Forces

United States v. Taylor, 61 M.J. 157 (C.A.A.F. 2005): At the accused's special court-martial on desertion charges, the prosecution offered, over numerous defense objections, a copy of a document entitled "declaration of desertion message" with testimony of a foundation witness. He testified that the document is created when a service member fails to report for duty. After concluding that the document was not admissible under a hearsay exception, the court added that even if an exception applied, the document did not qualify as an admissible copy under Rule 1005. There was no evidence, the court said, that a witness had compared the copy to the original and was not attested to or certified. Nor was there any evidence that the prosecution, using reasonable diligence, was unable to obtain a certified or attested copy or a copy that had been compared to the original. The court concluded that it was reversible error to admit the exhibit.

---

[1] *See 1969 Manual* ¶ 143 *a*(2)(d).

[2] *See* Rules 505(a), 505(c), 506(a), 505(d).

§ 1006.01   Official Text

Rule 1006.   Summaries.

The contents of voluminous writings, recordings, or photographs which cannot conveniently be examined in court may be presented in the form of a chart, summary, or calculation. The originals, or duplicates, shall be made available for examination or copying, or both, by other parties at reasonable time and place. The military judge may order that they be produced in court.

---

§ 1006.02   Editorial Comment

Numerous or bulky originals often represent an inconvenient form of evidence. Rule 1006 represents a time-honored exception to the Best Evidence Rule and permits admission of evidence in the form of summaries, charts, or calculations when the originals cannot be conveniently examined in court.[1]

As a precondition to admissibility of this secondary evidence, the proponent must provide a reasonable opportunity for the opponent to examine or copy the originals that serve as the foundation for the summary.[2] What constitutes a reasonable opportunity will depend on the circumstances of the case, although the military judge should be satisfied that the opponent has had ample time to prepare for cross-examination or to gather rebuttal evidence. Presentation of bulky or numerous originals for the first time at trial will normally call for a continuance. In any event, the judge may require

---

[1] *See, e.g.,* United States v. Drougas, 748 F.2d 8 (1st Cir. 1984) (seven telephone charts used to summarize conspirators calls); United States v. Radseck, 718 F.2d 233 (7th Cir. 1983) (summary charts of trial evidence may be admissible and sent to jury room if judge permits); United States v. Kaatz, 705 F.2d 1237 (10th Cir. 1983) (summary of 2300 exhibits); Donovan v. Janitorial Services, Inc., 672 F.2d 528 (5th Cir. 1982) (trial court properly admitted summary of payroll records); United States v. Seelig, 622 F.2d 207 (6th Cir. 1980) (chart summarized 161 underlying exhibits involving 1,409 transactions); Nichols v. Upjohn, 610 F.2d 293 (5th Cir. 1980) (94,000 page document summarized by testimony); United States v. Denton, 556 F.2d 811 (6th Cir.), *cert. denied,* 434 U.S. 892 (1977) (composite tape recording). *Cf.* United States v. Baker, 10 F.3d 1374 (9th Cir. 1993) (lengthy computer printout summarizing details of FBI agent's testimony on drug deals not admissible under Rule 1006; Rule does not encompass summaries of previously admitted oral testimony); United States v. Catabran, 836 F.2d 453 (9th Cir. 1988) (computer printout of business ledger was the actual record, not a summary even though it was stored in a computer).

[2] United States v. Modena, 302 F.3d 626 (6th Cir. 2002) (error to admit summaries where government had placed condition on defense examination of materials); United States v. Seelig, 622 F.2d 207 (6th Cir. 1980) (error to admit summaries where underlying records were not made available to defendants).

production of the originals in court to examine them for himself or herself.[3]

The Rule expands pre-Rules practice which required that the summarization had to be prepared by a person trained or qualified to do so. This individual was then to be called as the foundation witness.[4] Rule 1006 contains no such limitation, although in highly technical matters the proponent will normally wish to rely upon the testimony of a qualified witness. Furthermore, the Rule does not limit the type of secondary evidence to summaries; charts and calculations are also covered by Rule 1006.

Before authenticating the secondary evidence the proponent must establish that the underlying originals are otherwise admissible;[5] a summary, chart, or calculation based on inadmissible evidence will itself be inadmissible.

Use of charts and summaries under Rule 1006 should be distinguished from use of summaries prepared before, or during, the trial itself as demonstrative evidence.[6] Charts and summaries used merely as pedagogical aids during the trial may, but need not, be admitted as exhibits.[7] If they are, the court should give a limiting instruction under Rule 105 that informs the court members that those summaries are not evidence, but are instead only aids in understanding other evidence.[8] No instruction need be given if the chart or summary was admitted under Rule 1006.[9]

§ 1006.03 Drafters' Analysis

Rule 1006 is taken from the Federal Rule without change, and is similar

---

[3] *See* United States v. Soulard, 730 F.2d 1292 (9th Cir. 1984) (trial judge should examine summary charts out of the presence of the jury).

[4] United States v. Calhoun, 7 M.J. 905 (A.F.C.M.R. 1979), *petition denied,* 8 M.J. 176 (C.M.A. 1979) (witness not qualified).

[5] United States v. Samaniego, 187 F.3d 1222 (10th Cir. 1999) (conviction reversed where government failed to establish foundation for underlying records); United States v. Sutherland, 656 F.2d 1181 (5th Cir. 1981) (testimony must establish that transcripts accurately summarize tape recordings).

[6] *See, e.g.*, United States v. Milkiewicz, 470 F.3d 390 (1st Cir. 2006) (extensive discussion about using charts under Rule 1006 and as pedagogical aids under Rule 611(a); court suggested that the latter charts may be admissible as exhibits); United States v. Williams, 264 F.3d 561 (5th Cir. 2001) (noting distinction). *See also* Saltzburg, *Summaries: Two Types*, 10 Crim. Just. 33–36 (Winter 1996).

[7] United States v. Wood, 943 F.2d 1048 (9th Cir. 1991) (summaries uses as pedagogical aids should not be used by jury during its deliberations); Pierce v. Ramsey Winch Co., 753 F.2d 416 (D.C. Cir. 1985) (trial judge has discretion whether to permit use of charts during trial; if used, they should not be sent to jury room).

[8] *See* Rule 105, *above. See* United States v. Solis, 299 F.3d 420 (5th Cir. 2002) (no abuse of discretion in admitting summary of trial evidence and jury received limiting instructions); United States v. DeBoer, 966 F.2d 1066 (6th Cir. 1992) (instruction required).

[9] United States v. Bray, 26 M.J. 661 (1998) (no limiting instruction required for summary admitted under Rule 1006).

to the exception to the best evidence rule now found in ¶ 143*a*(2)(b) of the present *Manual*. Some difference between the Rule and the present *Manual* exists, however, because the Rule permits use of "a chart, summary, or calculation" while the *Manual* permits only "a summarization." Additionally, the Rule does not include the present *Manual* requirement that the summarization be made by a "qualified person or group of qualified persons," nor does the Rule require, as the present *Manual* appears to, that the preparer of the chart, summary or calculation testify in order to authenticate the document. The nature of the authentication required is not clear although some form of authentication is required under Rule 901(a).

It is possible for a summary that is admissible under Rule 1006 to include information that would not itself be admissible if that information is reasonably relied upon by an expert preparing the summary. *See generally* Rule 703.

§ 1006.04   Annotated Cases

United States Court of Appeals for the Armed Forces

United States v. Reynoso, 66 M.J. 208 (C.A.A.F. 2008): During the testimony of a prosecution's expert witness on personnel administration matters, the prosecution offered a summary of the difference in BAH rates and COLA for both San Francisco and Virginia. During defense counsel's voir dire, the witness admitted that he had not personally verified the underlying information. The defense's objection to lack of a foundation was overruled and the exhibit was admitted. For the first time on appeal, the accused argued that the exhibit was not admissible as a summary under Rule 1006. The Court of Appeals ruled that the accused had forfeited his objection. Citing federal case law and the Drafters' Analysis, the court held that there is an exception to the requirement that the summary be based on admissible evidence—when an expert has reasonably relied upon the information in formulating the summary. Thus, there was no plain error in admitting the exhibit.

§ 1007.01   Official Text

Rule 1007.   Testimony or Written Admission of Party.

Contents of writings, recordings, or photographs may be proved by the testimony or deposition of the party against whom offered or by the party's written admission, without accounting for the non-production of the original.

---

§ 1007.02   Editorial Comment

In lieu of presenting or accounting for an original, a proponent may offer an opponent's admission of the contents of the original. After all, if the opponent does not challenge the accuracy of an exhibit, there is no point in requiring the proponent to expend time and resources in laying an elaborate foundation. Rule 1007 intends, however, to assure that a proponent really does concede accuracy. Thus, the Rule requires that the admissions must be either in the form of testimony or depositions given under oath or written admissions. This rule of convenience is identical to Federal Rule 1007, but had no equivalent in either the 1969 *Manual* or military case law.

Although the Rule will probably not find much use, its relationship to other Rules should be recognized. For example, Rule 1007 does not bar a proponent from using an opponent's oral unsworn admissions to prove the contents of an original; the original will have to first be accounted for, however.[1] Application of this Rule should not be confused with a situation where primary evidence is offered to establish an event that may have been memorialized in a writing, recording, or photograph. In that case the Best Evidence Rule and its exceptions are inapplicable.[2]

The Hearsay Rule is also potentially involved here. Rule 801(d)(2) treats admissions of an opponent as nonhearsay. It would also seem to permit admissions by authorized speakers, employees, or co-conspirators to be used under Rule 1007 against an opponent to establish the contents. Rule 1007, however, acts as a limitation on Rule 801(d)(2) insofar as only written or sworn admissions could be used to prove the contents of an original without accounting for nonproduction of the original.

An illustration may help explain the potential interplay of these principles. Assume a case in which the accused has confessed both orally and in writing to sending a written threat. His confessions describe in detail the contents of the written threat that has since been lost. How may the prosecution establish the contents of the written threat? The prosecution may account for the lost

---

[1] *See, e.g.,* Rule 1004 (originals lost or destroyed, etc.).

[2] *See* the discussion at Rule 1002.

original under Rule 1004(1) and proceed to offer either the oral or written confessions of the accused as secondary evidence. Alternatively, the prosecution may employ Rule 1007 and offer the accused's written confession without accounting for the lost original. The oral statements could be used to prove that a threat, otherwise proved, was mailed, because the statements would be used for a purpose other than to prove the contents of a writing.

§ 1007.03   Drafters' Analysis

Rule 1007 is taken from the Federal Rule without change and has no express equivalent in the present *Manual*. The Rule establishes an exception to Rule 1002 by allowing the contents of a writing, recording, or photograph to be proven "by the testimony or deposition of the party against whom offered or by the party's written admission."   .

§ 1008.01   Official Text

Rule 1008.   Functions of Military Judge and Members.

When the admissibility of other evidence of contents of writings, recordings, or photographs under these rules depends upon the fulfillment of a condition of fact, the question whether the condition has been fulfilled is ordinarily for the military judge to determine in accordance with the provisions of Mil. R. Evid. 104. However, when an issue is raised (a) whether the asserted writing ever existed, or (b) whether another writing, recording, or photograph produced at trial is the original, or (c) whether other evidence of contents correctly reflects the contents, the issue is for the trier of fact to determine as in the case of other issues of fact.

---

§ 1008.02   Editorial Comment

Rule 1008 is one of several Military Rules addressing the respective functions of the military judge and the court members. *See* our discussions of Rules 104(b), 401, 402, 602, and 901(a). The Rule is identical to the Federal Rule and differentiates between questions which go to the competency (*i.e.*, the technical rules of evidence) of the evidence and those which go to conditional relevance (*i.e.*, whether to believe admitted evidence). As a general rule, competency questions are decided only by the military judge. Included within this realm are application of rules of exclusion, privileges, relevance, and hearsay.

The first sentence of Rule 1008 addresses a basic competency question that arises under Section X: The judge must determine whether the requirements of the exceptions to the Best Evidence Rule have been met before permitting use of secondary evidence. For example, under Rule 1003, the judge must first determine whether:

    (1) the offered evidence constitutes a "duplicate"; and

    (2) a genuine question has been raised about the original's authenticity; or

    (3) it would be unfair to admit the duplicate.

Under Rule 1004, the military judge must decide whether:

    (1) the original is lost or destroyed;

    (2) the proponent destroyed or lost the original in bad faith;

    (3) the original is obtainable through judicial process;

    (4) notice was given to the opponent who has control of the original;

    (5) the offered evidence goes to a collateral matter.

And under Rule 1005, the judge must decide whether the proponent exercised reasonable diligence in attempting to obtain a properly certified or compared copy.

The second sentence of Rule 1008 places in the hands of the court members the responsibility to decide, when the issue is raised, (1) whether the asserted writing ever existed, (2) whether another writing, recording, or photograph produced at trial is the original, and (3) whether the secondary evidence accurately reflects the original's contents. This provision requires the judge not to engage in fact-finding, but to decide only whether there is enough evidence on the issue to persuade a reasonable court member.[1] These three questions are reserved for the court members because they go to the heart of a dispute, and the drafters concluded that no legal knowledge is needed to decide these questions.

§ 1008.03 Drafters' Analysis

Rule 1008 is taken from the Federal Rule without change, and has no formal equivalent in current military practice. The Rule specifies three situations in which the members must determine issues which have been conditionally determined by the military judge. The members have been given this responsibility in this narrow range of issues because the issues that are involved go to the very heart of a case and may prove totally dispositive. Perhaps the best example stems from civil practice. Should the trial judge in a contract action determine that an exhibit is in fact the original of a contested contract, that admissibility decision could determine the ultimate result of trial if the jury were not given the opportunity to be the final arbiter of the issue. A similar situation could result in a criminal case for example in which the substance of a contested written confession is determinative (this would be rare because in most cases the fact that a written confession was made is unimportant, and the only relevant matter is the content of the oral statement that was later transcribed) or in a case in which the accused is charged with communication of a written threat. A decision by the military judge that a given version is authentic could easily determine the trial. Rule 1008 would give the members the final decision as to accuracy. Although Rule 1008 will rarely be relevant to the usual court-martial, it will adequately protect the accused from having the case against him or her depend upon a single best evidence determination by the military judge.

---

[1] *See also* the discussion of Rules 104(b) and 901(a).

SECTION XI

MISCELLANEOUS RULES

SYNOPSIS

§ 1101.01   Official Text

Rule 1101.   Applicability of Rules.

(a) *Rules applicable.*   Except as otherwise provided in this Manual, these rules apply generally to all courts-martial, including summary courts-martial; to proceedings pursuant to Article 39(a); to limited factfinding proceedings ordered on review; to proceedings in revision; and to contempt proceedings except those in which the judge may act summarily.

(b) *Rules of privilege.*   The rules with respect to privileges in Sections III and V apply at all stages of all actions, cases, and proceedings.

(c) *Rules relaxed.*   The application of these rules may be relaxed in sentencing proceedings as provided under R.C.M. 1001 and otherwise as provided in this Manual.

(d) *Rules inapplicable.*   These rules (other than with respect to privileges and Mil. R. Evid. 412) do not apply in investigative hearings pursuant to Article 32; proceedings for vacation of suspension of sentence pursuant to Article 72; proceedings for search authorizations; proceedings involving pretrial restraint; and in other proceedings authorized under the code or this Manual and not listed in subdivision (a).

---

§ 1101.02   Editorial Comment

[1]   Rule 1101(a)—Rules Applicable

Military Rule 1101 is modeled after its federal counterpart, but because of procedural and jurisdictional differences between the two systems, alterations in the Military Rule were required. Subdivision (a) states that unless the *Manual* provides otherwise, these Rules are applicable to all courts-martial, including summary courts, Article 39(a) sessions, limited factfinding proceedings ordered by reviewing agencies, proceedings in revision, and non-summary contempt proceedings.

[2]   Rule 1101(b)—Rules of Privilege

We have extensively discussed these matters in Rule 104, and therefore will not repeat our discussion here. It is important to note, however, that the Rules of Evidence generally will be applicable during those portions of the court-martial aimed at resolving the ultimate issues at bar. Most of the Rules will not apply when litigating pretrial evidentiary or constitutional matters, but subdivision (b) requires that the privileges of Section V "apply at all stages of all actions, cases and proceedings."

[3]   Rule 1101(c)—Rules Relaxed

Unlike federal criminal trials, courts-martial extend litigation through sentencing. Rule 1101(c) continues traditional military practice by allowing the evidentiary rules to be relaxed here. This provision also recognizes that other *Manual* paragraphs may impact on the Rule, and have allowed for their application.

[4]   Rule 1101(d)—Rules Inapplicable

Rule 1101(d) provides that except with respect to privileges, the Military Rules of Evidence also do not apply to Article 32 investigations; proceedings to vacate suspensions of sentences under Article 72; proceedings involving search authorizations; and proceedings regarding restraints or confinements.

Although Rules 104, 1101(a), (c), and (d) specify that evidentiary limitations are not applicable to a wide range of proceedings, this does not mean that all evidentiary constraints are gone. Federal experience indicates that judges and magistrates will still heavily borrow from the Rules to facilitate hearings and to ensure that their determinations are founded on evidence of a type usually relied upon by tribunals. Trial courts will still find indispensable the requirement that witnesses who do not understand English and their interpreters both take an oath. It seems that many of the exceptions for various proceedings in Rule 1101 serve principally to avoid cumbersome hearsay and authentication problems.

Note that the 1993 amendment to Rule 1101 specifically makes the exclusionary rule in Rule 412 applicable at pretrial investigations. The change parallels references to the same effect in amendments to the Drafters' Analysis for Rules 303 and 412.

§ 1101.03   Drafters' Analysis

The Federal Rule has been revised extensively to adapt it to the military criminal legal system. Subdivision (a) of the Federal Rule specifies the types of courts to which the Federal Rules are applicable, and subdivision (b) of the Federal Rule specifies the types of proceedings to be governed by the Federal Rules. These sections are inapplicable to the military criminal legal system and consequently were deleted. Similarly, most of Federal Rule of Evidence 1101(d) is inapplicable to military law due to the vastly different jurisdiction involved.

[1]   Rules Applicable

Rule 1101(a) specifies that the Military Rules are applicable to all courts-martial, including summary courts-martial, to Article 39(a) proceedings, limited factfinding proceedings ordered on review, revision proceedings, and contempt proceedings. This limited application is a direct result of the limited jurisdiction available to courts-martial.

[2]   Rules of Privilege

Rule 1101(b) is taken from subdivision (c) of the Federal Rule and is similar to present military law. Unlike the Federal Rules, the Military Rules contain detailed privileges rather than a general reference to common law. *Compare* Federal Rule of Evidence 501 with Military Rule of Evidence 501-512.

[3] Rules Relaxed

Rule 1101(c) conforms the rules of evidence to military sentencing procedures as set forth in *Manual* ¶ 75 *c.* Courts-martial are bifurcated proceedings with sentencing being an adversarial proceeding. Partial application of the rules of evidence is thus appropriate. The Rule also recognizes the possibility that other *Manual* provisions may now or later affect the application of the rules of evidence.

[4] Rules Inapplicable

Rule 1101(d) is taken in concept from subdivision (d) of the Federal Rule. As the content of the Federal Rule is, however, generally inapplicable to military law, the equivalents of the Article III proceedings listed in the Federal Rule have been listed here. They include Article 32 investigative hearings, the partial analog to grand jury proceedings, proceedings for search authorizations, and proceedings for pretrial release.

§ 1101.03a   Drafters' Analysis (1993)

Mil. R. Evid. 1101(d) was amended to make the provisions of Mil. R. Evid. 412 applicable at pretrial investigations.

§ 1101.04   Annotated Cases

[1]   Rule 1101(c)—Rules Relaxed

United States Court of Appeals for the Armed Forces

United States v. Boone, 49 M.J. 187 (C.A.A.F. 1998): The court had held earlier that the accused had been denied the effective assistance of counsel during sentencing and had remanded the case to the Court of Criminal Appeals for a possible rehearing on the sentence. That court, however, decided to reassess the sentence itself. 44 M.J. 742 (Army Ct.Crim.App. 1996). In concluding that the lower court had erred in not ordering a rehearing, the court noted in a footnote that although the Rules of Evidence do not apply to sentencing, otherwise inadmissible evidence is not admissible at sentencing.

United States v. Henderson, 29 M.J. 221 (C.M.A. 1989): Reversing judgment as to whether an actuarial expert can present relevant evidence concerning an accused's anticipated retirement benefits, the court held that such testimony was "so uncertain and remote as to substantially risk confusing the sentencing authority," and was thus inadmissible even under relaxed sentencing rules.

United States v. Glazier, 26 M.J. 268 (C.M.A. 1988): Pursuant to his plea, appellant was convicted of wrongfully using marijuana and stealing a government vehicle. Because of insufficient evidence, involuntary manslaughter charges had been dismissed. During presentencing, defense counsel unsuccessfully moved to redact a stipulation of fact with respect to the dismissed charges. Affirming the conviction, the court held that it saw "no reason why evidence, even though otherwise inadmissible under the Military Rules of Evidence, cannot come into the trial by way of stipulation . . . This is particularly true in a negotiated guilty plea where the accused is willing to stipulate to otherwise inadmissible testimony in return for a concession favorable to him . . ."

United States v. Martin, 20 M.J. 227 (C.M.A. 1985): The court used Rule 1101(c) to hold that extrinsic offense evidence could be used against an accused during the presentencing portion of his trial as long as that evidence was not unfairly prejudicial. The court viewed its interpretation of 1101(c) as necessary to facilitate the relative "goodness/badness" sentencing determinations that factfinders must make.

United States v. Strong, 17 M.J. 263 (C.M.A. 1984): Although the court recognized that the Military Rules of Evidence may be relaxed during sentencing, it evaluated the government's proffer in this case as if it had been admitted before findings.

United States v. Gonzalez, 16 M.J. 58 (C.M.A. 1983): The court found error in the military judge's exclusion of certain defense extenuation and mitigation affidavits, despite the "formal rules of evidence" being relaxed during the sentencing portion of trial.

United States v. McGill, 15 M.J. 242 (C.M.A. 1983): The court found error in the admission of appellant's Article 15 punishment despite Rule 1101(c)'s guidance that the Military Rules of Evidence are relaxed during the sentencing portion of trial. The court observed that this provision does not relieve the government of its responsibility to "demonstrate that its evidence is in some way reliable."

Air Force Court of Criminal Appeals

United States v. Evans, 25 M.J. 859 (A.F.C.M.R. 1988): During the sentencing portion of appellant's drug possession trial he stated: "One stupid act now threatens my whole future." Trial counsel, over defense objection, then admitted a German Customs Office report indicating that "appellant and one of his cohorts had been to Amsterdam before where they had used hashish and marijuana." Finding error and prejudice in the admission of this evidence, the court held that although the Rules of Evidence are relaxed during sentencing, the statements in question were "hearsay for which we find no recognized exception [and] decline to extend the rule to unsworn statements contained in reports by law enforcement agents . . ." The court went on to note that this testimony would have been admissible without the hearsay objection.

United States v. Elrod, 18 M.J. 692 (A.F.C.M.R. 1984): After finding that there was no authority to relax the evidence rules as to presentencing matters initially offered by the prosecution, the court went on to state that Rule 1101(c) is not authority for relaxing the Rules beyond the parameters set out in ¶ 75 *c* of the *Manual for Courts-Martial.*

United States v. Gudel, 17 M.J. 1075 (A.F.C.M.R. 1984): Recognizing that the Military Rules of Evidence may be relaxed during sentencing, the court nevertheless found error in the admission of unreliable hearsay evidence.

Army Court of Criminal Appeals

United States v. Charley, 28 M.J. 903 (A.C.M.R. 1989): A worthless check conviction was reversed because during sentencing the military judge improperly admitted evidence from the accused's Official Military Personnel File. The court held that sentencing proceedings are adversarial and the Military Rules of Evidence remain in effect. The court stated that the rules may be relaxed for the defense but, with the exception of rebuttal, not for the government.

United States v. Matthews, 13 M.J. 501 (A.C.M.R. 1982): Sentenced to death for murder and rape, appellant contended that the current military system for imposing capital punishment is inadequate and unconstitutional. Affirming both findings and sentence (except for some forfeitures), the court relied on Rule 1101(c) to demonstrate the validity of the current system, highlighting the accused's ability to thoroughly present extenuation and mitigation without being limited by the strict rules of evidence.

United States v. Hancock, 12 M.J. 685 (A.C.M.R. 1981): Because counsel defending an accused charged with escape from custody and unauthorized absence waived any objection to two exhibits (a record of conviction and the promulgating order relating thereto, neither of which reflected that supervisory review had been completed) the court held that the accused could not complain on appeal that they were defective. The court indicated in a footnote that it did not want to provide stricter evidence rules during sentencing than on findings. Thus, the same waiver standard would be applied to both.

Navy-Marine Corps Court of Criminal Appeals

United States v. Arispe, 12 M.J. 516 (N.M.C.M.R. 1981): Although 1101(c) allows the Rules of Evidence to be "relaxed" during sentencing procedures, other *Manual* provisions must still be adhered to. As the court stated: "Matters presented in aggravation or extenuation and mitigation for purposes of sentencing must comply with the rules of evidence as noted in paragraphs 76 *a* (2) and 75 *c* [1969] MCM." Rule 1101(c)'s mandate is general in nature; it is not intended to override other specific Manual requirements.

[2]   Rule 1101(d)—Rules Inapplicable

Army Court of Criminal Appeals

United States v. Martel, 19 M.J. 917 (A.C.M.R. 1985): Relying on Rules 504(b) and 1101(d), the court found error in an Article 32 hearing officer's consideration of statements which should have been excluded under the spousal privilege. The court also stated that while the Military Rules of Evidence are not generally applicable during Article 32 hearings, they should be used as a guide for ensuring that "the proceedings are conducted in a fundamentally fair manner."

Navy-Marine Corps Court of Criminal Appeals

United States v. Matthews, 15 M.J. 622 (N.M.C.M.R. 1982): Because the Rules of Evidence do not apply at Article 32 hearings, appellant was not prejudiced by the investigating officer's consideration of certain hearsay statements offered against the defense.

§ 1102.01   Official Text

Rule 1102.   Amendments.

(a) Amendments to the Federal Rules of Evidence shall apply to the Military Rules of Evidence 18 months after the effective date of such amendments, unless action to the contrary is taken by the President.

(b) Rules Determined Not To Apply. The President has determined that the following Federal Rules of Evidence do not apply to the Military Rules of Evidence: Rules 301, 302, 415, and 902(12).

---

§ 1102.02   Editorial Comment

[1]   In General

Rule 1102 addresses the application of any amendments to the Federal Rules of Evidence to the Military Rules of Evidence and the fact that the President has decided that certain Federal Rules do not apply to the Military Rules of Evidence.

[2]   Rule 1102(a)—Application of Federal Rules Amendments to the Military Rules

One criticism of prior *Manual* practice was that it could not easily assimilate improvements developed in federal, state, or military courts. In order to change a *Manual* provision, the President had to authorize the alteration and then promulgate it by Executive Order. The realities of this process inhibited amendments. What resulted was a series of ad hoc judicial actions that sought to keep military practice in line with federal developments.[1]

Rule 1102 was intended to remove these liabilities. As promulgated in 1980, the rule provided that any federal amendment would apply 180 days after the effective date of the amendment. But in 1997, the time was extended to 18 months.

Rule 1102(a) states that such changes to military practice will automatically occur unless the President takes action to the contrary. This period will begin to run from the effective date of the federal amendment's implementation, not from the date the amendment is proposed by the Supreme Court. According to the Drafters' Analysis, extending the time to 18 months was designed to make it possible to consider any Presidential changes to the federal rule through the military's annual review process of the Manual for Courts-Martial.

---

[1] *See, e.g.,* Article 36; and United States v. Weaver, 1 M.J. 111 (C.M.A. 1975), where the Court of Appeals for the Armed Forces adopted Federal Rule 609(b).

Under the Rules Enabling Act,[2] amendments to the Federal Rules of Evidence are normally generated in the Federal Rules of Evidence Advisory Committee and ultimately approved by the Judicial Conference and the Supreme Court, which is required to forward the amendments to Congress by May 1st. Congress, in turn, has an opportunity to reject or change the amendment by December 1st. If Congress fails to act, the Supreme Court's amendment to the rule goes into effect on December 1st, unless otherwise provided by law.[3] Under the operation of Military Rule of Evidence 1102, those amendments would be applicable—absent any intervening action by the President—18 months later. Despite the intended effect of the 1997 amendment to extend the effective date of federal rules to 18 months, it is often difficult for military practitioners and the bench to know exactly how, and when, a particular federal amendment affects military practice. And despite the hope that extending the time to 18 months would permit timely consideration of changes to the military rule, based upon the federal amendments, even that time frame has proven to be too short.

[3] Rule 1102(b)—Certain Federal Rules Not Applicable to the Military Rules

Rule 1102 was amended in 2004 by making the existing rule, subdivision (a), and by adding a new subdivision (b).[4] Rule 1102(b) now explicitly provides that Federal Rules 301 (Presumptions in General in Civil Actions and Proceedings), 302 (Applicability of State Law in Civil Actions and Proceedings), 415 (Evidence of Similar Acts in Civil Cases Concerning Sexual Assault or Child Molestatation), and 902(12) (Certified Foreign Records) do not apply to the Military Rules of Evidence. According to the Drafters' Analysis, those Federal Rules were not adopted because they apply only to civil cases.

§ 1102.03 Drafters' Analysis

Rule 1102 has been substantially revised from the original Federal Rule that sets forth a procedure by which the Supreme Court promulgates amendments to the Federal Rules subject to Congressional objection. Although it is the Committee's intent that the Federal Rules of Evidence apply to the armed forces to the extent practicable, see Article 36(a), the Federal Rules are often in need of modification to adapt them to the military criminal legal system. Further, some rules may be impracticable. As Congress may make changes during the initial period following Supreme Court publication, some period of time after an amendment's effective date was considered essential for the armed forces to review the final form of amendments and to propose any necessary modifications to the President.

---

[2] 28 U.S.C. §§ 2070, *et seq.*

[3] 28 U.S.C. § 2074 (prescribing effective date).

[4] *See* Executive Order 13365, dated 3 December 2004.

Six months was considered the minimally appropriate time period.

Amendments to the Federal Rules are not applicable to the Armed Forces until 180 days after the effective date of such amendment, unless the President directs earlier application. In the absence of any Presidential action, however, an amendment to the Federal Rules of Evidence will be automatically applicable on the 180th day after its effective date. The President may, however, affirmatively direct that any such amendment not apply, in whole or part, to the armed forces and that direction shall be binding upon courts-martial.

§ 1102.04   Drafters' Analysis (1997)

1997 Amendment. The Rule is amended to increase to 18 months the time period between changes to the Federal Rules of Evidence and automatic amendment of the Military Rules of Evidence. The extension allows for the timely submission of changes through the annual review process.

§ 1102.05   Drafters' Analysis (2004)

2004 Amendment. See Executive Order 13365, dated 3 December 2004. The amendment to the Federal Rules of Evidence, effective in United States District Courts, 1 December 2000, creating Rule 902(12) is not adopted. Federal Rules 301, 302, and 415, were not adopted because they were applicable only to civil proceedings.

§ 1103.01   Official Text

Rule 1103.   Title.

These rules may be known and cited as the Military Rules of Evidence.

---

§ 1103.02   Editorial Comment

The Drafters' Analysis indicates that they adopted the title "Military Rules of Evidence" to highlight the commonality of these Rules and the Federal Rules of Evidence.

§ 1103.03   Drafters' Analysis

In choosing the title, Military Rules of Evidence, the Committee intends that it be clear that military evidentiary law should echo the civilian federal law to the extent practicable, but should also ensure that the unique and critical reasons behind the separate military criminal legal system be adequately served.

TABLE OF CASES

[References are to sections and footnotes]

TABLE OF CASES

TABLE OF CASES

TABLE OF CASES

TABLE OF CASES

TABLE OF CASES

TABLE OF CASES

TABLE OF CASES

[References are to sections and footnotes]

E

G

TABLE OF CASES

H

I

TABLE OF CASES

TABLE OF CASES

TABLE OF CASES

TABLE OF CASES

TABLE OF CASES

N

TABLE OF CASES

TABLE OF CASES

TABLE OF CASES

T

TABLE OF CASES

[References are to sections and footnotes]

TABLE OF CASES

INDEX

[References are to Rules.]

[References are to Rules.]

[References are to Rules.]

I

[References are to Rules.]

·INVOLUNTARY STATEMENTS
Confessions and admissions distinguished
  . . . Rule 304(c)
Impeachment of witnesses . . . Rule 304(b)(1)
Motion to suppress . . . Rule 304(a); Rule
  304(d)
Privilege against admissibility of . . . Rule
  511(a); Rule 511(b)
Suppress, motion to . . . Rule 304(a); Rule
  304(d)
Warning about rights is involuntary, statement
  without first being given . . . Rule 305(a)

J

JUDICIAL NOTICE
Adjudicative facts . . . Rule 201
Domestic and foreign laws . . . Rule 201A

JURY (See COURT MEMBERS)

JURY DELIBERATION PRIVILEGE
Generally . . . Rule 509

L

LAWYER-CLIENT PRIVILEGE
Generally . . . Rule 502

LAY WITNESS OPINION
Generally . . . Rule 701

LEARNED TREATISES
Hearsay exception . . . Rule 803(18)

LIABILITY
Insurance inadmissible to prove negligence
  . . . Rule 411
Payment of medical and similar expenses
  . . . Rule 409
Product liability and subsequent remedial mea-
  sures . . . Rule 407

LIE DETECTOR TESTS
Generally . . . Rule 707

LIMITED ADMISSIBILITY RULE
Generally . . . Rule 105

LINEUPS
Generally . . . Rule 321

LOCKERS
Reasonable expectation of privacy . . . Rule
  314(d)

M

MARKET REPORTS
Hearsay exception . . . Rule 803(17)

MARRIAGE CERTIFICATES
Hearsay exception . . . Rule 803(12)

MEDICAL DIAGNOSIS OR TREATMENT
Hearsay exception as to statement for purposes
  of . . . Rule 803(4)

MEDICAL EXPENSES
Admissibility for proving liability . . . Rule 409

MENTAL CONDITION, THEN EXISTING
Hearsay exception . . . Rule 803(3)

MENTAL EXAMINATIONS
Exclusion of medical testimony of accused refusing to cooperate in examination . . . Rule
  302(d)
Privilege of accused against disclosure of statement made at . . . Rule 302

***MIRANDA*-STYLE WARNINGS**
Generally . . . Rule 301; Rule 305

MISLEADING EVIDENCE
Relevant evidence excluded if . . . Rule 403

MOLESTATION
Children as victims of . . . Rule 414

MOTIONS
Strike . . . Rule 103(a)(1)
Suppress (See SUPPRESS, MOTION TO)

MOTOR VEHICLE SEARCHES
Generally . . . Rule 314(f)(3)-(g); Rule
  315(g)(3)-(4)

MULTIPLE HEARSAY
Generally . . . Rule 805

N

NEWSPAPERS
Self-authenticating documents . . . Rule 902(6)

NONVERBAL ASSERTIONS
Hearsay rule . . . Rule 801(a)

NOTICE, JUDICIAL
Adjudicative facts . . . Rule 201
Domestic and foreign laws . . . Rule 201A

O

OATHS
Interpreters' requirements . . . Rule 604
Prerequisite to testimony . . . Rule 603

OBJECTIONS
Preservation of error . . . Rule 103(a)(1)

OFFERS OF PROOF
Generally . . . Rule 103(a)(2)

OFFERS TO COMPROMISE
Generally . . . Rule 408

OFFICIAL RECORDS OR REPORTS
Self-authenticating documents . . . Rule 902(4)-
  (5)

OPINION TESTIMONY
Experts (See EXPERT TESTIMONY)
Lay witnesses . . . Rule 701
Reputation (See REPUTATION EVIDENCE)

ORAL COMMUNICATIONS
Interception of . . . Rule 317
Voluntary oral confession . . . Rule 304(h)

ORIGINALS
Admissibility (See ADMISSIBILITY, subhead: Originals)
Content, when necessary to produce original to prove
    Photographs (See PHOTOGRAPHS, subhead: Contents, originals proving)
    Recordings (See RECORDINGS, subhead: Contents, originals proving)
    Writings (See WRITINGS, subhead: Contents)
Defined . . . Rule 1001
Duplicates (See DUPLICATES)
Lost, destroyed, or otherwise unavailable . . . Rule 1004
Photographs (See PHOTOGRAPHS)
Recordings (See RECORDINGS)
Summaries . . . Rule 1006
Writings (See WRITINGS)

OTHER CRIMES, WRONGS, OR ACTS
Admissibility . . . Rule 404(b)
Sexual offenses
    Child molestation cases . . . Rule 414
    Sexual assault . . . Rule 413

P

PATIENT RECORDS
Generally . . . Rule 513

PAYMENT OF MEDICAL EXPENSES
Admissibility for proving liability . . . Rule 409

PERIODICALS
Self-authenticating documents . . . Rule 902(6)

PERSONAL HISTORY
Charts under hearsay exception . . . Rule 803(13)
Hearsay exception for statement of . . . Rule 804(b)(4)
Reputation evidence . . . Rule 803(19)

PHOTOGRAPHS
Contents, originals proving
    Other evidence . . . Rule 1004
    Party admission . . . Rule 1007
    Requirement . . . Rule 1002
Defined . . . Rule 1001(2)
Duplicates . . . Rule 1001(4)
Originals . . . Rule 1001(3)

PHYSICAL CONDITION, THEN EXISTING
Hearsay exception . . . Rule 803(3)

PHYSICIAN-PATIENT PRIVILEGE
Generally . . . Rule 501(d)

PLAIN ERROR RULE
Generally . . . Rule 103(d)

PLEAS, PLEA DISCUSSIONS, AND RELATED STATEMENTS
Admissibility . . . Rule 410

POLITICAL VOTE
Privileged . . . Rule 508

POLYGRAPH EXAMINATIONS
Generally . . . Rule 707

PREJUDICIAL EVIDENCE
Compromise and offers to compromise . . . Rule 408
Relevant evidence excluded if . . . Rule 403
Witness prejudice . . . Rule 608(c)

PRELIMINARY QUESTIONS
Generally . . . Rule 104

PRESENT SENSE IMPRESSIONS
Hearsay exception . . . Rule 803(1)

PRESERVATION OF ERRORS
Generally . . . Rule 103(a)(1)

PRINTOUTS
Originals if reflecting data accurately . . . Rule 1001(3)

PRIOR INCONSISTENT STATEMENT
Generally . . . Rule 613
Hearsay . . . Rule 801(d)(1)

PRIVILEGES
Generally . . . Rule 501
Attorney-client . . . Rule 502
Classified information . . . Rule 505
Clergy communications . . . Rule 503
Client-lawyer . . . Rule 502
Comment upon claim . . . Rule 512
Confidential communication
    Generally . . . Rule 510
    Marriage, made during . . . Rule 504
    Psychotherapist and patient, between . . . Rule 513
Counselor-patient . . . Rule 513
Court deliberations . . . Rule 509
Degrading questions . . . Rule 303
Disclosure and (See DISCLOSURE)
Electronic transmission of privileged communication . . . Rule 511(b)
Government information
    Classified . . . Rule 505
    Unclassified . . . Rule 506
Husband-wife . . . Rule 504
Inferences from claim . . . Rule 512
Informant
    Communications not privileged . . . Rule 507(a)
    Identity . . . Rule 507

[References are to Rules.]

WARRANTS, SEARCH (See SEARCH AU-
THORIZATIONS)

WASTE OF TIME
Relevant evidence excluded if . . . Rule 403

**WEIGHT AND CREDIBILITY OF EVI-
DENCE**
Generally . . . Rule 104(e)

WIFE-HUSBAND PRIVILEGE
Generally . . . Rule 504

WIRETAPPING
Generally . . . Rule 317

WITNESSES
Accused, testimony by . . . Rule 104(d)
Availability to be determined by military judge
 . . . Rule 104(a)
Bias of . . . Rule 408; Rule 608(c)
Calling and interrogation by court-martial
 . . . Rule 611; Rule 614
Character evidence of . . . Rule 404(a)(3); Rule
608
Child's remote live testimony . . . Rule 611(d)
Co-conspirators' statements under hearsay rule
 . . . Rule 801(d)(2)
Co-defendants' statements . . . Rule 306
Competency (See COMPETENCY OF WIT-
NESSES)
Conduct of witness, evidence of . . . Rule 608
Copy of public record, testifying to authenticity
of . . . Rule 1005
Court member as witness . . . Rule 606
Exclusion . . . Rule 615
Expert testimony (See EXPERT TESTIMONY)
Eyewitness identification, out-of-court . . . Rule
321
Impeachment of (See IMPEACHMENT OF
WITNESSES)
Informants . . . Rule 507
Interpreter of witness testimony . . . Rule 604
Judge as witness, military . . . Rule 605
Lay witness opinion . . . Rule 701

WITNESSES—Cont.
Lineups . . . Rule 321
Military judge as witness . . . Rule 605
Motion to suppress eyewitness identification
 . . . Rule 321(c)
Oath or affirmation
 Interpreters' requirements . . . Rule 604
 Prerequisite to testimony . . . Rule 603
Opinion testimony . . . Rule 701
Out-of-court eyewitness identification . . . Rule
321(a)
Personal knowledge requirement . . . Rule 602
Prior inconsistent statement . . . Rule 613; Rule
801(d)(1)
Qualifications to be determined by military judge
 . . . Rule 104(a)
Religious beliefs, practices, or opinions
 . . . Rule 610
Sequestration . . . Rule 615
Subscribing witness' testimony for authentication
of evidence . . . Rule 903
Suppress eyewitness identification, motion to
 . . . Rule 321(c)
Unavailable (See HEARSAY EXCEPTIONS,
subhead: Unavailable declarant)
Writing used to refresh memory . . . Rule 612

WRITINGS
Complete writing requirement . . . Rule 106
Contents
 Admission of opponent, proven by
 . . . Rule 1007
 Originals proving
 Other evidence . . . Rule 1004
 Party admission . . . Rule 1007
 Requirement . . . Rule 1002
Witness' memory, used to refresh . . . Rule 612

X

X-RAY FILMS
Generally . . . Rule 1001(2)